Contemporary Authors®

NEW REVISION SERIES

Explore your options!

Gale databases are offered in a variety of formats

GALE

The information in this Gale publication is also available in some or all of the formats described here. Your Gale Representative will be happy to fill you in. Call toll-free 1-800-877-GALE.

GaleNet

A number of Gale databases are now available on GaleNet, our new online information resource accessible through the Internet. GaleNet features an easy-to-use end-user interface, the powerful search capabilities of BRS/SEARCH retrieval software and ease of access through the World Wide Web.

Diskette/Magnetic Tape

Many Gale databases are available on diskette or magnetic tape, allowing systemwide access to your most-used information sources through existing computer systems. Data can be delivered on a variety of mediums (DOS-formatted diskettes, 9-track tape, 8mm data tape) and in industry-standard formats (comma-delimited, tagged, fixed-field).

CD-ROM

A variety of Gale titles are available on CD-ROM, offering maximum flexibility and powerful search software.

Online

For your convenience, many Gale databases are available through popular online services, including DIALOG, NEXIS, DataStar, ORBIT, OCLC, Thomson Financial Network's I/Plus Direct, HRIN, Prodigy, Sandpoint's HOOVER, the Library Corporation's NLightN and Telebase Systems.

Contemporary Authors®

A Bio-Bibliographical Guide to
Current Writers in Fiction, General Nonfiction,
Poetry, Journalism, Drama, Motion Pictures,
Television, and Other Fields

**JEFF CHAPMAN
PAMELA S. DEAR
JOHN D. JORGENSON**
Editors

NEW REVISION SERIES *volume* 53

GALE

DETROIT • NEW YORK • TORONTO • LONDON

STAFF

♾™ This book is printed on acid-free paper that meets the minimum requirements
of American National Standard for Information Sciences-
Permanence Paper for Printed Library Materials, ANSI Z39.48-1984.

Library of Congress Catalog Card Number 81-640179

ISBN 0-7876-0124-1
ISSN 0275-7176

Printed in the United States of America.

Gale Research, an International Thomson Publishing Company.
ITP logo is a trademark under license.
10 9 8 7 6 5 4 3 2 1

Contents

Preface vii

CA Numbering System and
Volume Update Charts xi

Authors and Media People
Featured in This Volume xiii

Author Listings 1

Indexing note: All *Contemporary Authors New Revision Series* entries are indexed in the *Contemporary Authors* cumulative index, which is published separately and distributed with even-numbered *Contemporary Authors* original volumes and odd-numbered *Contemporary Authors New Revision Series* volumes.

As always, the most recent *Contemporary Authors* cumulative index continues to be the user's guide to the location of an individual author's listing.

Contemporary Authors
was named an
"Outstanding
Reference Source" *by*
the American Library
Association Reference
and Adult Services
Division after its 1962
inception.
In 1985 it was listed by
the same organization
as one of the
twenty-five most
distinguished reference
titles published in the
past twenty-five years.

Preface

The *Contemporary Authors New Revision Series* (*CANR*) provides completely updated information on authors listed in earlier volumes of *Contemporary Authors* (*CA*). Entries for individual authors from *any* volume of *CA* may be included in a volume of the *New Revision Series*. *CANR* updates only those sketches requiring significant change.

Authors are included on the basis of specific criteria that indicate the need for significant revision. These criteria include bibliographical additions, changes in addresses or career, major awards, and personal information such as name changes or death dates. All listings in this volume have been revised or augmented in various ways. Some sketches have been extensively rewritten, and many include informative new sidelights. As always, a *CANR* listing entails no charge or obligation.

How to Get the Most out of *CA*: Use the Index

The key to locating an author's most recent entry is the *CA* cumulative index, which is published separately and distributed with even-numbered original volumes and odd-numbered revision volumes. It provides access to *all* entries in *CA* and *CANR*. Always consult the latest index to find an author's most recent entry.

For the convenience of users, the *CA* cumulative index also includes references to all entries in these Gale literary series: *Authors and Artists for Young Adults, Authors in the News, Bestsellers, Black Literature Criticism, Black Writers, Children's Literature Review, Concise Dictionary of American Literary Biography, Concise Dictionary of British Literary Biography, Contemporary Authors Autobiography Series, Contemporary Authors Bibliographical Series, Contemporary Literary Criticism, Dictionary of Literary Biography, Dictionary of Literary Biography Documentary Series, Dictionary of Literary Biography Yearbook, DISCovering Authors, DISCovering Authors: British, DISCovering Authors: Canadian, DISCovering Authors: Modules, Drama Criticism, Hispanic Literature Criticism, Hispanic Writers, Junior DISCovering Authors, Major Authors and Illustrators for Children and Young Adults, Major 20th-Century Writers, Native North American Literature, Poetry Criticism, Short Story Criticism, Something about the Author, Something about the Author Autobiography Series, Twentieth-Century Literary Criticism, World Literature Criticism,* and *Yesterday's Authors of Books for Children.*

A Sample Index Entry:

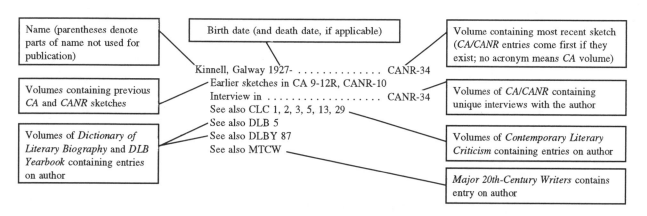

For the most recent *CA* information on Kinnell, users should refer to Volume 34 of the *New Revision Series,* as designated by "CANR-34"; if that volume is unavailable, refer to CANR-10. And if CANR-1 is unavailable, refer to CA 9-12R, published in 1974, for Kinnell's First Revision entry.

How Are Entries Compiled?

The editors make every effort to secure new information directly from the authors. Copies of all sketches in selected *CA* and *CANR* volumes previously published are routinely sent to listees at their last-known addresses, and returns from these authors are then assessed. For deceased writers, or those who fail to reply to requests for data, we consult other reliable biographical sources, such as those indexed in Gale's *Biography and Genealogy Master Index,* and bibliographical sources, such as *National Union Catalog, LC MARC,* and *British National Bibliography.* Further details come from published interviews, feature stories, and book reviews, and often the authors' publishers supply material.

* Indicates that a listing has been compiled from secondary sources believed to be reliable but has not been personally verified for this edition by the author sketched.

What Kinds of Information Does an Entry Provide?

Sketches in *CANR* contain the following biographical and bibliographical information:

- **Entry heading:** the most complete form of author's name, plus any pseudonyms or name variations used for writing

- **Personal information:** author's date and place of birth, family data, educational background, political and religious affiliations, and hobbies and leisure interests

- **Addresses:** author's home, office, or agent's addresses as available

- **Career summary:** name of employer, position, and dates held for each career post; resume of other vocational achievements; military service

- **Membership information:** professional, civic, and other association memberships and any official posts held

- **Awards and honors:** military and civic citations, major prizes and nominations, fellowships, grants, and honorary degrees

- **Writings:** a comprehensive, chronological list of titles, publishers, dates of original publication and revised editions, and production information for plays, television scripts, and screenplays

- **Adaptations:** a list of films, plays, and other media which have been adapted from the author's work

- **Work in progress:** current or planned projects, with dates of completion and/or publication, and expected publisher, when known

- **Sidelights:** a biographical portrait of the author's development; information about the critical reception of the author's works; revealing comments, often by the author, on personal interests, aspirations, motivations, and thoughts on writing

- **Biographical and critical sources:** a list of books and periodicals in which additional information on an author's life and/or writings appears

Related Titles in the *CA* Series

Contemporary Authors Autobiography Series complements *CA* original and revised volumes with specially commissioned autobiographical essays by important current authors, illustrated with personal photographs they provide. Common topics include their motivations for writing, the people and experiences that shaped their careers, the rewards they derive from their work, and their impressions of the current literary scene.

Contemporary Authors Bibliographical Series surveys writings by and about important American authors since World War II. Each volume concentrates on a specific genre and features approximately ten writers; entries list works written by and about the author and contain a bibliographical essay discussing the merits and deficiencies of major critical and scholarly studies in detail.

Available in Electronic Formats

CD-ROM. Full-text bio-bibliographic entries from the entire *CA* series, covering approximately 100,000 writers, are available on CD-ROM through lease and purchase plans. The disc combines entries from the *CA, CANR,* and *Contemporary Authors Permanent Series* (*CAP*) print series to provide the most recent author listing. It can be searched by name, title, subject/genre, and personal data, and by using boolean logic. The disc will be updated every six months. For more information, call 1-800-877-GALE.

Magnetic Tape. *CA* is available for licensing on magnetic tape in a fielded format. Either the complete database or a custom selection of entries may be ordered. The database is available for internal data processing and nonpublishing purposes only. For more information, call 1-800-877-GALE.

Online. The *Contemporary Authors* database is made available online to libraries and their patrons through online public access catalog (OPAC) vendors. Currently, *CA* is offered through Ameritech Library Services' Vista Online (formerly Dynix), and is expected to become available through CARL Systems. More OPAC vendor offerings will follow soon.

GaleNet. *CA* is available on a subscription basis through GaleNet, a new online information resource that features an easy-to-use end-user interface, the powerful search capabilities of the BRS/Search retrieval software, and ease of access through the World-Wide Web. For more information, call Melissa Kolehmainen at 1-800-877-GALE, ext. 1598.

Suggestions Are Welcome

The editors welcome comments and suggestions from users on any aspects of the *CA* series. If readers would like to recommend authors whose entries should appear in future volumes of the series, they are cordially invited to write: The Editors, *Contemporary Authors,* 835 Penobscot Bldg., Detroit, MI 48226-4094; call toll-free at 1-800-347-GALE; fax to 1-313-961-6599; or e-mail at conauth@gale.com.

CA Numbering System and Volume Update Chart

Occasionally questions arise about the *CA* numbering system and which volumes, if any, can be discarded. Despite numbers like "29-32R," "97-100" and "150," the entire *CA* series consists of only 132 physical volumes with the publication of *CA New Revision Series* Volume 53. The following charts note changes in the numbering system and cover design, and indicate which volumes are essential for the most complete, up-to-date coverage.

CA **First Revision**

- 1-4R through 41-44R (11 books)
  Cover: Brown with black and gold trim.
  There will be no further First Revision volumes because revised entries are now being handled exclusively through the more efficient *New Revision Series* mentioned below.

CA **Original Volumes**

- 45-48 through 97-100 (14 books)
  Cover: Brown with black and gold trim.
- 101 through 152 (52 books)
  Cover: Blue and black with orange bands.
  The same as previous *CA* original volumes but with a new, simplified numbering system and new cover design.

CA **Permanent Series**

- *CAP*-1 and *CAP*-2 (2 books)
  Cover: Brown with red and gold trim.
  There will be no further *Permanent Series* volumes because revised entries are now being handled exclusively through the more efficient *New Revision Series* mentioned below.

CA **New Revision Series**

- *CANR*-1 through *CANR*-53 (53 books)
  Cover: Blue and black with green bands.
  Includes only sketches requiring extensive changes; **sketches are taken from any previously published *CA*, *CAP*, or *CANR* volume.**

If You Have: You May Discard:

If You Have:	You May Discard:
CA First Revision Volumes 1-4R through 41-44R **and** *CA Permanent Series* Volumes 1 and 2	*CA* Original Volumes 1, 2, 3, 4 and Volumes 5-6 through 41-44
CA Original Volumes 45-48 through 97-100 **and** 101 through 152	**NONE:** These volumes will not be superseded by corresponding revised volumes. Individual entries from these and all other volumes appearing in the left column of this chart may be revised and included in the various volumes of the *New Revision Series*.
CA New Revision Series Volumes *CANR*-1 through *CANR*-53	**NONE:** The *New Revision Series* does not replace any single volume of *CA*. Instead, volumes of *CANR* include entries from many previous *CA* series volumes. All *New Revision Series* volumes must be retained for full coverage.

A Sampling of Authors and Media People
Featured in This Volume

Diane Ackerman

In poetry and prose works including *Jaguar of Sweet Laughter: New and Selected Poems, A Natural History of Love,* and *The Rarest of the Rare,* Ackerman explores science and history with a poetic sensibility, often, for example, incorporating the subjects of chemistry and biology into her verse. She received the Peter I. B. Lavan Younger Poet Award from the Academy of American Poets in 1985.

Alice Adams

An American novelist and short-story writer, Adams is known for works in which female characters struggle to establish and maintain an identity within their romantic relationships, careers, and families. She received a National Book Critics Circle Award nomination in 1975 for *Families and Survivors,* and has received multiple O. Henry Awards for her short fiction.

Sandy Asher

Asher is known primarily for her young adult novels, including *Just Like Jenny, Things Are Seldom What They Seem,* and *Everything Is Not Enough,* which explore the many difficult issues faced by young adults, particularly those related to family, school, and love. In addition to juvenile fiction, Asher is also a prolific playwright and author of instructional creative writing books.

Russell Atkins

Since the publication of *Phenomena* in 1961, avant-garde poet and composer Atkins has been considered among America's most experimental artists. Hailed by some critics as an innovative voice in poetry, Atkins often tackles controversial topics like drug addiction and sexual aberration. His works include *Objects, Presentations,* and *Here in The.*

Ann Beattie

Beattie is an American novelist and short-story writer known for her fiction about the generation that came of age in the late 1960s and early 1970s. In such works as *Distortions, Secrets and Surprises, Where You'll Find Me, and Other Stories,* and *Love Always,* Beattie writes in a journalistic style as she explores the lives of characters who become disillusioned with the world around them.

Saul Bellow

Winner of the Nobel Prize for Literature, a Pulitzer Prize, and three National Book Awards, Bellow is one of the preeminent figures in contemporary American literature. His works, including *The Adventures of Augie March, Herzog, Mr. Sammler's Planet,* and *Humboldt's Gift,* explore the human condition against the backdrop of a mechanistic, impersonal world.

Brigid Brophy

A British novelist, essayist, and outspoken social critic, Brophy came to prominence in the 1960s. Her works, including *Fifty Works of English and American Literature We Could Do Without* and *Reads: A Collection of Essays,* polarized critics, some praising Brophy's wit and social criticism, others describing selections of her writing as "sneering" and "vulgar."

William F. Buckley, Jr.

After coming to public attention with the publication of *God and Man at Yale,* Buckley became one of the most visible of American conservative commentators. Championing right-wing political values, Buckley's works include political essays, newspaper columns, espionage novels, and editorials. He founded the *National Review* in 1955.

Humphrey Carpenter

Carpenter is a respected editor and literary biographer whose works include the critically acclaimed *The Inklings: C. S. Lewis, J. R. R. Tolkien, Charles Williams, and Their Friends,* and *W. H. Auden: A Biography.* In addition to biographies, Carpenter's works also include literary criticism and children's literature.

Andrei Codrescu

Codrescu is a Rumanian-born, American novelist, poet, editor, translator, journalist, and regular commentator on National Public Radio's *All Things Considered.* Known for his wry wit and humorous criticism, Codrescu is also a respected poet described by one critic as someone who offers his audience "a clear penetration into the soul of America." His works include the acclaimed documentary film and book *Road Scholar* and the autobiography *The Life and Times of an Involuntary Genius.*

Pat Conroy

Conroy is a bestselling novelist who tells bitter yet humorous stories of the contemporary American South. Known for their expressions of love as well as brutality, Conroy's works include *The Water Is Wide, The Great Santini, The Lords of Discipline,* and *The Prince of Tides.*

Ossie Davis

Best known as an actor, Davis is also an American playwright, screenwriter, and director. A prominent figure in the civil rights movement of the 1960s, Davis gave the eulogies at the funerals of both Malcolm X and Dr. Martin Luther King, Jr. His works include *The Big Deal in New York, Today Is Ours, Escape to Freedom,* and the Tony Award-nominated *Purlie.*

Anita Desai

Typically involving female Indian characters coping with the difficulties of contemporary life in a repressive Indian society, Desai's novels include *Voices in the City, Baumgartner's Bombay* and *Bye-Bye, Blackbird.* Critics laud Desai for her descriptive abilities and for her ability to illustrate both eastern and western cultures.

Colin Dexter

Dexter is an English novelist known primarily for his "Inspector Morse" mysteries. Critics laud Dexter's talent for revealing relevant clues while maintaining the reader's mystification until after Morse has unmasked the murderer. Dexter received Gold Dagger Awards for *The Wench Is Dead* and *The Way through the Woods,* and the Lotus Club Medal of Merit in 1996.

Stephen Dunn

Largely considered America's foremost poet of the middle-class, Dunn is praised for his personal, intelligent verse which explores marriage, family, careers, and suburbia. He received an Academy of American Poets Award in 1970, the Theodore Roethke Prize in 1977, and the Levinson Prize in 1987. His works include *Full of Lust and Good Usage, Work and Love,* and *New and Selected Poems: 1974-1994.*

Ralph Ellison

Ellison was an African-American author whose reputation was established with his only novel, the National Book Award-winning *Invisible Man.* Known for its complex and experimental narrative and acclaimed by critics, *Invisible Man* is considered one of the most influential works of the twentieth century.

Robert A. Heinlein

Heinlein was an American novelist, juvenile-fiction writer, and short-story writer who is considered one of the defining voices of contemporary science fiction. A controversial as well as prolific author, Heinlein's works include *Have Space Suit—Will Travel, The Number of the Beast* and the Hugo Award-winning *Stranger in a Strange Land.*

Adrienne Kennedy

An acclaimed African-American playwright, Kennedy is known for complicated, introspective, often violent works which explore the struggle for African-American identity in a white society. Her works include *Sun: A Poem for Malcolm X Inspired by His Murder* and the Obie Award-winning *Funnyhouse of a Negro.*

Elmore Leonard

Leonard is an American novelist and screenwriter whose works include *Stick, Glitz, Desperado, Rum Punch, Get Shorty,* and the Edgar Award-winning *LaBrava.* A short-story writer and western novelist since the 1950s, Leonard attracted critical attention and a substantial audience during the 1980s.

David Lodge

Lodge is an English novelist, playwright, and critic known for works satirizing religious and academic practices. His novels, including *Changing Places, How Far Can You Go?,* and the Whitbread Award-winning *Small World: An Academic Romance,* are based in part on his own experiences as a child, soldier, student, and professor.

Thomas Merton

Merton was a prolific writer whose works include poetry, essays, biographies, autobiographies, and translations. Critics view Merton as a complex and paradoxical man, having taken a vow of silence during his time as a Trappist monk while simultaneously writing for a wide audience. His works include *The Monastic Journey, Elected Silence,* and *The Tower of Babel.*

Alice Munro

One of Canada's most successful and acclaimed writers, Munro has received three Governor General's Literary Awards. Primarily a short-story writer, Munro is known for works, including *Dance of the Happy Shades, The Beggar Maid,* and *The Progress of Love,* which explore the lives of ordinary poor or lower-middle-class Canadians.

Howard Nemerov

A former poet laureate of the United States, Nemerov was an acclaimed American critic, novelist, short-story writer, dramatist, and poet. Encompassing a broad range of forms and styles, his verse is noted for its wit and technical excellence. *The Collected Poems of Howard Nemerov* won the Pulitzer Prize, the National Book Award, and the Bollingen Prize.

Anais Nin

Nin is best known for her erotica, and for the seven volumes of her diary, which she began writing at the age of eleven and continued until her death in 1977. Also a novelist, critic, and short-story writer, Nin's works include *The House of Incest, Cities of the Interior, In Favor of the Sensitive Man and Other Essays,* and *Under a Glass Bell.*

Anne Rice

Rice is a bestselling American novelist and critic best known for her works focusing on isolated characters, including vampires and castrati, and their search for identity. Some critics praise Rice's attention to detail and her ornate prose style. Her works include *Interview with the Vampire, The Tale of the Body Thief, The Queen of the Damned,* and *Memnoch the Devil.*

Adrienne Rich

After receiving the Yale Series of Younger Poets Award in 1951 for her first collection, *A Change of World,* Rich evolved into one of America's leading feminist poets. Known for addressing social issues, Rich's works include the National Book Award-winning *Diving into the Wreck* and the National Book Critics Circle Award-nominated *The Dream of a Common Language.*

Anne Rivers Siddons

Described by one critic as "Atlanta's best-known writer," Siddons is an American novelist whose works typically focus on the lives of southern women in a humorous and insightful style. Praised for their depth of character, Siddons' works include *Heartbreak Hotel, Go Straight on Peach-tree, Colony,* and *Downtown.*

Dan Simmons

A lauded science-fiction and horror writer, Simmons' *Song of Kali* received the World Fantasy Award for best first novel in 1985. Known for graphic description and thematic complexity, Simmons' other works include the Hugo Award-winning *Hyperion* and the Bram Stoker Award-winning *Carrion Comfort.*

R. L. Stine

One of the most prolific authors of all time, Stine is an American young-adult and children's-horror writer who produces more than one new book a month. Though largely dismissed by critics, his works, including the bestselling "Fear Street" and "Goosebumps" series, are credited with turning many young people into avid readers.

Anne Tyler

A bestselling American novelist, Tyler gained prominence in the mid-1970s with *Celestial Navigation* and *Searching for Caleb.* Often compared to Eudora Welty, Tyler garnered two Pulitzer Prize nominations before finally winning the award in 1988 for *Breathing Lessons.*

Wendy Wasserstein

Wasserstein is an American dramatist and screenwriter whose works explore the many issues facing contemporary women attempting to achieve both professional and personal fulfillment. Known for their comic edge, her works include *Uncommon Women and Others, Isn't It Romantic, The Man in a Case,* and the Pulitzer Prize- and Tony Award-winning *The Heidi Chronicles.*

Paul West

A highly acclaimed and respected novelist, West is also praised for his poetry, essays, and criticism. Known for the energy, inventiveness, and intelligence of his prose, West first received high critical praise with the *Alley Jaggers* trilogy. A prolific writer, West's other works include *Tenement of Clay, Rat Man of Paris, Lord Byron's Doctor, Words for a Deaf Daughter, The Very Rich Hours of Count von Stauffenberg,* and the Lannan Prize-winning *Love's Mansion.*

Contemporary Authors®

NEW REVISION SERIES

*Indicates that a listing has been compiled from secondary sources believed to be reliable but has not been personally verified for this edition by the author sketched.

ACKERMAN, Diane 1948-

PERSONAL: Born October 7, 1948, in Waukegan, IL; daughter of Sam (a restaurant owner) and Marcia (Tischler) Fink. *Education:* Attended Boston University, 1966-67; Pennsylvania State University, B.A., 1970; Cornell University, M.F.A., 1973, M.A., 1976, Ph.D., 1978. *Avocational interests:* Astronomy, skin diving, horseback riding, flying planes.

ADDRESSES: *Home*—126 Texas Lane, Ithaca, NY 14850. *Agent*—Janklow and Nesbitt, 598 Madison Ave., New York, NY 10022.

CAREER: Writer. Social worker in New York City, 1967; government researcher at Pennsylvania State University, 1968; Cornell University, Ithaca, NY, teaching assistant, 1971-78, lecturer, 1978-79; University of Pittsburgh, Pittsburgh, PA, assistant professor of English, 1980-83; Washington University, St. Louis, MO, director of writers' program and writer in residence, 1984-86; *New Yorker,* New York City, staff writer, 1988—. Writer in residence, William and Mary College, 1983, Ohio University, 1983; visiting writer, Columbia University, 1986, New York University, 1986, Cornell University, 1987. Member of literature panels, including New York State Council on the Arts, 1980-83; member of advisory board, Planetary Society, 1980—. Has participated in readings, residencies, and workshops.

AWARDS, HONORS: Academy of American Poets Poetry prize, Cornell University, 1972; Corson Bishop French Prize, Cornell University, 1972; Abbie Copps Prize, Olivet College, 1974; Rockefeller graduate fellowship, 1974-76; Heermans-McCalmon Playwriting Prize, Cornell University, 1976; creative writing fellowships, National Endowment for the Arts, 1976 and 1986, and Creative Artists Public Service Program, 1980; Corson Bishop Poetry Prize, Cornell University, 1977; poetry prize, *Black Warrior Review,* 1981; Pushcart Prize VIII, 1984; Peter I. B. Lavan Younger Poet Award, Academy of American Poets, 1985; semi-finalist, Journalist-in-Space Project.

WRITINGS:

POETRY

(With Jody Bolz and Nancy Steele) *Poems: Ackerman, Bolz, and Steele* (chapbook), Stone Marrow Press (Cincinnati), 1973.
The Planets: A Cosmic Pastoral, Morrow (New York City), 1976.
Wife of Light, Morrow, 1978.
Lady Faustus, Morrow, 1985.
Jaguar of Sweet Laughter: New and Selected Poems, Random House (New York City), 1991.

NONFICTION

Ideas into the Universe (series of nine radio programs), Canadian Broadcasting Corp. (Toronto), 1975.
(Contributor) Carl Sagan, *Other Worlds,* Bantam (New York City), 1975.
Twilight of the Tenderfoot: A Western Memoir, Morrow, 1980.
On Extended Wings: An Adventure in Flight (memoir), Atheneum (New York City), 1985.
A Natural History of the Senses, Random House, 1990.

The Moon by Whale Light, and Other Adventures among Bats, Penguins, Crocodilians, and Whales, Random House, 1991.

A Natural History of Love, Random House, 1994.

The Rarest of the Rare: Vanishing Animals, Timeless World, Random House, 1995.

Monk Seal Hideaway (juvenile; photographs by Bill Curtsinger), Crown (New York City), 1995.

A Bat in the Banquet Hall (juvenile), Crown, 1997.

OTHER

Reverse Thunder (play), Lumen, 1988.

Diane Ackerman and Maxine Kumin Reading from Their Poetry (sound recording), Library of Congress (Washington, DC), 1994.

Contributor to anthologies, including *The Morrow Anthology of Younger Poets,* edited by Dave Smith and David Bottoms, Morrow, 1985; *Norton Introduction to Literature,* edited by Jerome Beaty and J. Paul Hunter, 4th edition, Norton, 1986; *Norton Introduction to Poetry,* edited by Hunter, 3rd edition, Norton, 1986; *The Paris Review Anthology,* edited by George Plimpton, Norton, 1989; and numerous other poetry and prose anthologies. Contributor of poems and nonfiction to literary journals, periodicals, and newspapers, including *New Yorker, Poetry, Life, Omni, Kenyon Review, American Poetry Review, Parnassus: Poetry in Review, Michigan Quarterly Review, Paris Review,* and *New York Times;* contributor of reviews to *New York Times Book Review.*

ADAPTATIONS: On Extended Wings: An Adventure in Flight was adapted for the stage in 1987 by Norma Jean Griffin.

SIDELIGHTS: Diane Ackerman has been hailed by several critics for her poetry and for her prose explorations into the world of science and natural history. Although the two genres are seemingly very different from each other, Ackerman's sensibility blends the two, bringing a poetic touch to her nonfiction work and incorporating the subjects of chemistry and biology into her verse. She once said in *Contemporary Poets:* "People sometimes ask me about all of the Science in my poetry, thinking it odd that I should wish to combine Science and Art, and assuming that I must have some inner pledge or outer maxim I follow. But the hardest job for me is trying to keep Science out of my poetry. We live in a world where amino acids, viruses, airfoils, and such are common ingredients in our daily sense of Nature. Not to write

about Nature in its widest sense, because quasars or corpuscles are not 'the proper realm of poetry,' as a critic once said to me, is not only irresponsible and philistine, it bankrupts the experience of living, it ignores much of life's fascination and variety."

Ackerman's voracious appetite for knowledge and her eager appreciation of the natural world are evident in *Jaguar of Sweet Laughter: New and Selected Poems,* according to *New York Times Book Review* contributor David Kirby. He asserted: "Diane Ackerman's poems not only operate in the present but press toward the future. . . . Just about everything Ms. Ackerman writes, prose or poetry, is exploratory. . . . [Her] speakers push ahead; they probe, open, take off lids, peel back covers, inspect, taste, sniff." Her constant sense of wonder is the key to the appeal of her work, concluded Kirby: "Ms. Ackerman trains her telescope on the bend in the river, all but pitching over the rail as she strains towards the next surprise."

Ackerman explored the world of animals in *The Moon by Whale Light, and Other Adventures among Bats, Penguins, Crocodilians, and Whales,* a collection of four essays expanded from articles previously published in the *New Yorker.* Allying herself with experts on each species, Ackerman went into the field to gain first-hand experience with the animals. She recorded her observations in detail, along with thoughts on the folklore of each animal. Fraser Harrison noted in *New Statesman and Society,* "Ackerman is at her best when describing the animals in her own eloquent words. She is a hands-on journalist in a very literal sense, for, as befits the author of *A Natural History of the Senses,* she always insists on touching her subjects, even the whales. Especially vivid is her account of sitting astride an alligator, its mouth bound with tape, and feeling her way round its 'beautiful, undulating skin.'" Harrison found Ackerman's portrayal of penguins "shamelessly anthropomorphic" yet justifiable; her depiction of their habitat, he added, has a poetic quality. "And it is this quality," he concluded, "that makes her a considerable nature writer as well as an intrepid, sharp-eyed journalist, for she has the imaginative gift to identify with the character of her animals and the intelligence to keep them in their ecological place."

Michiko Kakutani of the *New York Times* offered similar praise, writing that Ackerman "has a gift for sparkling, resonant language, and her descriptions of various animals and their habitats are alive with verbal energy and delight. She describes bats as delicately assembled packages of 'fur and appetite' and characterizes their high-pitched cries as 'vocal Braille.'" Kakutani further praised the author for providing a great deal of "fascinating" information about the lives of each species. She took exception, however, to the philosophical discourses that Ackerman wove into her essays. Her "speculations about animals and what they represent tend to become silly and mawkish," criticized Kakutani. "Such passages distract and irritate the reader, even if they do not entirely destroy the pleasures of *The Moon by Whale Light*. They also suggest that Ms. Ackerman should stick to writing about the world of nature and not venture into the more abstract realm of metaphysical rumination."

Franklin Burroughs offered another perspective on Ackerman's philosphical musings. Writing in *Southern Review,* he enthusiastically endorsed Ackerman's "fine eye for detail, her adventurousness, and her humor" and noted: "When these essays first appeared in the familiar milieu of *The New Yorker,* they seemed to fall within its civilized, flexible conception of an American middle voice: informative, engaging, modest, witty, and thoroughly *professional,* not subject to the enthusiasms, large claims, and idiosyncrasies of the writer for whom writing itself remains the central, animating adventure." In their longer form in the book, however, the essays "assume the large religious themes that descend from Emerson," Burroughs asserted. He conceded that at times, Ackerman was unable to do justice to the lofty ideas she presented. "When the book reaches out toward the grander, more or less unitarian-universalist themes that have been so recurrent in American writing of this sort . . . it seems to me to lose credibility and distinction," he explained, yet he concluded that Ackerman's accounts of her field trips were stimulating and thoroughly conveyed the emotions humans feel when interacting with other species. Ackerman used a more straightforward, journalistic approach in her 1995 book *The Rarest of the Rare: Vanishing Animals, Timeless World,* documenting her journeys to observe near-extinct creatures.

Ackerman shifted her focus from the animal world to the human province of romantic love with her 1994 collection of essays, *A Natural History of Love. Washington Post Book World* contributor Barbara Raskin characterized this volume as "an audaciously brilliant romp. . . . Using an evolutionary history as her launchpad, Ackerman takes off on a space flight in which she describes, defines, theorizes, analyzes, analogizes, apologizes, generalizes, explains, phi-

losophizes, embellishes, codifies, classifies, confesses, compares, contrasts, speculates, hypothesizes and generally carries on like a hooligan about amatory love. It's a blast." Beginning with a quick survey of 2,000 years of love, Ackerman proceeds with an analysis of famous literary passages on romance, the chemistry of love, the effects of lovelessness on children and cultures, and many more subjects. Some critics believed too many topics were included and too many different writing styles used. Chris Goodrich, writing in the *Los Angeles Times,* praised *A Natural History of Love* as an enjoyable read, but found it "surprisingly shapeless," with contents "that vary between the arresting and the superficial, the illuminating and the irksome. Reading the book, you spend half your time wishing it were better, and the other half captivated by those passages in which Ackerman . . . has found a particularly good lens through which to view her subject." Still, he allowed that the book was "a pleasure," and described Ackerman as "a beguiling, even seductive writer." Raskin also emphasized the author's power with words, stating: "Of all the loves Ackerman describes, none is greater than her own love of language. . . . She produces hard-hitting metaphors and sweet constellations of similes that are like confectionery recipes for fresh insights."

BIOGRAPHICAL/CRITICAL SOURCES:

BOOKS

Contemporary Poets, St. James (Chicago and London), 1985.
Dictionary of Literary Biography, Volume 120: *American Poets since World War II, Third Series,* Gale (Detroit), 1992.

PERIODICALS

Boston Globe, July 3, 1994, p. A16; June 12, 1995, p. 26.
Chicago Tribune, September 6, 1994, section 5, p. 2.
Los Angeles Times, October 20, 1985; July 8, 1994, p. E8; February 18, 1995, p. F14.
Los Angeles Times Book Review, November 29, 1992, p. 10; October 29, 1995.
Mirabella, September, 1991, pp. 76-78.
New Republic, November 20, 1976.
New Statesman and Society, May 21, 1993, pp. 35-36.
Newsweek, September 22, 1986.
New York Times, November 29, 1991, p. C27.

New York Times Book Review, June 29, 1980; December 22, 1985; November 3, 1991, p. 14; December 29, 1991, p. 7; June 26, 1994, p. 12.
Publishers Weekly, September 11, 1995, p. 71.
Southern Review, October, 1992, pp. 928-36.
Vogue, September, 1991, pp. 384-88.
Wall Street Journal, November 26, 1991, p. A12.
Washington Post, June 10, 1980; November 28, 1991, p. C3.
Washington Post Book World, June 19, 1994, p. 2.*

*   *   *

ADAMS, Alice (Boyd)   1926-

PERSONAL: Born in Fredericksburg, VA, August 14, 1926; daughter of Nicholson (a professor) and Agatha (a writer; maiden name, Boyd); married Mark Linenthal, Jr. (a professor), 1946 (divorced, 1958); children: Peter. *Education:* Radcliffe College, B.A., 1946.

ADDRESSES: Home—2661 Clay St., San Francisco, CA 94115. *Agent*—Amanda Urban, International Creative Management, 40 West 57th St., New York, NY 10019.

CAREER: Writer. Has held various office jobs, including secretary, clerk, and bookkeeper. Instructor at the University of California at Davis, 1980, University of California at Berkeley, and at Stanford University.

AWARDS, HONORS: O. Henry Awards, Doubleday & Co., 1971-82 and 1984-96, for short stories; National Book Critics Circle Award nomination, 1975, for *Families and Survivors;* National Endowment for the Arts fiction grant, 1976; Guggenheim fellowship, 1978; O. Henry Special Award for Continuing Achievement, 1982; Best American Short Stories awards, 1992, 1996.

WRITINGS:

Careless Love, New American Library (New York City), 1966, published in England as *The Fall of Daisy Duke,* Constable (London), 1967.
Families and Survivors (novel), Knopf (New York City), 1975.
Listening to Billie (novel), Knopf, 1978.
Beautiful Girl (short stories), Knopf, 1979.
Rich Rewards (novel), Knopf, 1980.

To See You Again (short stories), Knopf, 1982.
Molly's Dog (short stories), Ewert, 1983.
Superior Women (novel), Knopf, 1984.
Return Trips (short stories), Knopf, 1985.
Second Chances (novel), Knopf, 1988.
After You've Gone (short stories), Knopf, 1989.
Mexico: Some Travels and Some Travelers There, introduction by Jan Morris, Prentice Hall (New York City), 1990.
Caroline's Daughters (novel), Knopf, 1991.
Almost Perfect (novel), Knopf, 1993.
A Southern Exposure (novel), Knopf, 1995.

Contributor of short stories to anthologies, including *Best American Short Stories,* 1976, *Prize Stories: The O. Henry Awards,* 1971-82, and 1984-88. Contributor to periodicals, including *New Yorker, Atlantic, Shenandoah, Crosscurrents, Grand Street, Mademoiselle, Virginia Quarterly Review, New York Times Book Review, Vogue, Redbook, McCall's,* and *Paris Review.*

SIDELIGHTS: In many of her short stories and novels, Alice Adams writes about women struggling to find their place in the world. Adams challenges her female characters, whether they live alone or with a man, to establish meaningful lives and to work creatively both with life's blessings and its disappointments. Robert Phillips writes in *Commonweal:* "The usual Adams character does not give in to his or her fate, but attempts to shape it, however misguidedly . . . . Women become aware not only of missed opportunities, but also of life's endless possibilities." While men occupy important positions in the female characters' lives, Adams's books tend to focus on the women's own struggles with identity. "The conflict—not the outward conflict between men and women, but the private and inward conflict of individual women—runs through all Adams' work," notes Stephen Goodwin in the *Washington Post Book World.* "Her women value men, but prize their own independence." Adams's women generally find true contentment in work and the freedom to make their own choices. According to William L. Stull in the *Dictionary of Literary Biography Yearbook,* "each of her novels concerns a woman's search for satisfying work as a means to economic, artistic, and finally political independence."

And yet the experience of romantic love constantly recurs in Adams's work. Beverly Lowry maintains in the *New York Times Book Review* that "nobody writes better about falling in love than Alice Adams. The protagonists of her stories . . . fall with eyes open, knowing full well that the man in question might be inappropriate. . . . Such women think they should know better. They do know better. That is the glory of an Adams heroine, she is that smart and still goes on. 'Ah,' she says to herself, sighing, 'this again: love.' And plunges in." While the romantic pairings may or may not work out, "Adams' women often learn, in the course of her novels, that the stereotyped 'happy ending' is not feasible and that they must focus on work and on developing a healthy respect for themselves," writes Larry T. Blades in *Critique.* "These are perhaps the ultimate rich rewards."

Adams established herself as a novelist with her books *Families and Survivors* and *Listening to Billie.* The first follows the ups and downs of two sisters during three decades of their lives. The second details a character buffeted by the suicides of her husband and her father, and her struggle to deal with their deaths. It was in these novels, notes Sheila Weller in *Ms.* magazine, that Adams first revealed herself as "a wonderfully old-fashioned writer." She revealed, continues Weller, the qualities that underlie her fiction: "the Dickensian coincidence, the solemn omniscience, the sense of lives destined to intertwine." In addition to laying the foundation for her fiction, Adams also honed a style to serve her thematic concerns in these early novels. "In a prose style that was somehow both grave (even ominous) and unlabored almost to the point of being dashed off," observes Weller, "she showed how time burnishes character, how we come to accrue what we refer to as the 'lessons' of life." Adams succeeded, in Weller's words, in creating a "powerful wistfulness."

In *Rich Rewards,* Adams focuses on a middle-aged woman who has spent her life in a series of disappointing and often addictive relationships with men. At the novel's beginning the heroine, Daphne, having recently broken off a relationship with an abusive lover, intends to immerse herself in her work as an interior decorator, she becomes embroiled in a friend's troubled marriage and eventually finds herself reunited with a lover from her youth. According to Blades, "*Rich Rewards* chronicles the maturation of Daphne from a woman who devotes her life to punishing and humiliating sexual encounters into a woman who can establish a productive love relationship because she has first learned to respect herself." In the *New York Times Book Review,* Anne Tyler calls it "a marvelously readable book. It's mysterious

in the best sense—not a setup, artificial mystery but a real one, in which we wonder along with the heroine just what all the chaotic events are leading up to." *Chicago Tribune Book World* contributor Lynne Sharon Schwartz calls *Rich Rewards* "a stringent story elegantly told, and enhanced by a keen moral judgment. . . . As in her earlier novels,. . . Alice Adams is concerned with the shards of broken families and with the quickly severed ties that spring up in place of families. But in *Rich Rewards* the harshness latent in such tenuous relations is more overt than before. . . . It takes a sort of magician to render hope from the brew of pain, muddle, and anomie that Alice Adams has managed charmingly to concoct. Once again she brings it off with panache."

However, critics have also faulted the author's "reward" for Daphne, and have called the ending unrealistic compared to the rest of the book. Blades admits that "the novelistic contrivances used to bring the lovers back together also suggest the unrealistic nature of the resolution. There is the sense of enchantment, of a fairy godmother waving her wand and saying, 'Let Daphne and Jean-Paul fall in love again, and let the plot be twisted to accomplish this.'" However, he defends Adams's choice: "Readers who complain about Adams' use of coincidence in *Rich Rewards* have recognized an element conspicuously present in the author's overall purpose. 'This is a novel,' Alice Adams seems to say, 'and since I'm writing it, I can create a happy ending. Real life might end differently.'" Considering Daphne's growth as a character, Tyler writes that the ending fits the story: "If the conclusion seems a bit sudden and easy, lacking the texture of the rest of the story, it is also the 'rich reward' that Daphne deserves. Draw a moral, if you like: Daphne is one of the most admirable female characters in recent fiction."

Superior Women concerns the relationship among four young women during their years at Radcliffe and afterwards. The novel has frequently been compared to Mary McCarthy's *The Group,* which describes the lives of eight women who attended Vassar in the thirties. As in *The Group, Superior Women* takes its characters through graduation and into the outside world, showing how political and social events affect their lives. This technique has met with some criticism. "The effects of viewing a whole age through gauze in this fashion is pretty deadening," claims Michael Wood in the *London Review of Books.* Jonathan Yardley, a *Washington Post Book*

World contributor, states: "What we . . . have is a shopping list of public events, causes and fads. As the women leave Radcliffe and enter the world, Adams dutifully trots them through everything from civil rights to Watergate." And yet other critics find Adams's usual style, allied with a swifter pace, produces a highly satisfactory work. John Updike in the *New Yorker* writes, "The novel . . . reads easily, even breathlessly; one looks forward, in the chain of coincidences, to the next encounter, knowing that this author always comes to the point from an unexpected angle, without fuss." And Barbara Koenig Quart remarks in *Ms.* that Adams's talent holds the reader through any weak points: "Not at all systematically, to be sure, and with fairly thin references to the extraordinary events of those turbulent decades, still, Adams holds us firmly with a lively narrative pace. She creates an almost gossipy interest in what happens to her characters; and she can't write a bad sentence, though hers is the kind of fine unobtrusive style that you notice only if you're looking for it."

Some reviewers have questioned the "superiority" of the young students. Their experiences are similar to other young coeds of the time, and their discussions usually revolve around sex. *West Coast Review of Books* contributor Dorothy Sinclair doubts their credibility: "There is so little that is believable about these young women that one suspects the usually deep and honest Adams of running amuck. Certainly there seems to be nothing 'superior' or original about their endless chatter of 'necking.' (Do they, or don't they 'do it'? They never tell.)" Annabel Edwards in *Books and Bookmen* objects to "the very use of the title *Superior Women* with apparently no ironic overtones at all." Wood, however, feels that the women display an above average concern for each other: "Her characters are genuinely kind and easy, anxious about each other. . . . Certainly Adams's characters, men and women, are nicer than most folks in fiction, or in fact."

Adams's novel *Second Chances* portrays the lives of men and women who face the onset of their sixties and the stigma of "old age." Like Adams's other characters, they worry about relationships and suffer losses, but in this book a marriage dissolving through death forces them to evaluate their own lives. Adams told Mervyn Rothstein in an interview for the *New York Times:* "The novel grew out of the fact I was getting toward being 60 myself. It struck me that 60 is not middle-age. I do not know a lot of people who are 120. . . . I began looking at people who are 10

to 15 years older. The book is for me a kind of exploration." *Second Chances* also gave Adams a chance to speak truthfully about aging. In an interview with Kim Heron for the *New York Times Book Review,* Adams says, "I have the perception that people talk about old age in two ways. One is to focus on the horrors of it, not that they should be underestimated, and the other is to romanticize it."

The book starts with a group of long-term friends, all of them examining changes in their relationships. The scene soon changes to memory, and the reader is filled in on the characters' sometimes highly intricate lives. Barbara Williamson relates in the *Washington Post Book World* that "the backward and forward motion of time in the novel happily captures the way old people tell wistful, probably falsified tales of when they were young and beautiful. And the stories of their youth are the liveliest parts of the novel." But Williamson also finds that the characters' very gracefulness inhibits Adams's attempts to portray old age truthfully: "The picture presented in this novel seems too kind, too pretty. Old age, we suspect, is not a gentle stroll on the beach at twilight with kind and caring friends. Where, we ask, is the 'rage against the dying of the light'?" But *Los Angeles Times Book Review* contributor Joanna Barnes praises the depiction of the pain that exists in all relationships, whether among the young or the old. Barnes writes: "In a larger sense, it is the nature of friendship under Adams' delicate examination here. She recreates, too, the haunting undertone of the loneliness present in all human intercourse, that separateness which, despite the presence of kindly acquaintances and lovers, can never be bridged nor breached."

Second Chances "is both the richest and the most satisfying novel that Adams . . . has produced," writes Diane Cole in Chicago *Tribune Books.* She adds, "Throughout, Adams demonstrates her gift for capturing the telling detail—the apartment decor, conversation topics, or fears left unsaid—that defines a particular era, setting or social milieu. . . . She has succeeded in painting a moving group portrait of friendship through the ages." *New York Times Book Review* contributor DeMott also feels that *Second Chances* is Adams's strongest work. DeMott believes "the strength flows partly from Ms. Adams's capacity to evoke fellow feeling, kindness and devotion as entirely natural inclinations of the heart. Her people care intensely for one another, and, although not beyond rage, seem beyond meanness. Equally important to the book's success is her grasp of conditions of feeling that are special to the middle classes just now entering their 60's and 70's. . . . [*Second Chances*] is a touching, subtle, truth-filled book."

In *Almost Perfect,* Adams creates "an oddly affecting morality tale that tastes like good medicine with no more than the requisite spoonful of darkly humorous sugar," in the words of *World Literature Today* contributor B. A. St. Andrews. In her tale, the author sets familiar characters and issues in a familiar setting; as Anita Shreve writes in the *Washington Post Book World,* "Once again we are on familiar Adams territory: atop the hills of San Francisco, inside the well-appointed interiors of the successful and near-successful, and enmeshed in a constellation of interconnecting and constantly observed relationships." The central relationship observed here is that of Stella Blake, a journalist, and Richard Fallon, a commercial artist. At first, Richard seems almost perfect, as does Stella's relationship with him. Soon, however, Stella's condition in life and work improves, while Richard's gets worse. Their relationship soon suffers strains and other relationships around them grow more complicated. Through these relationships, observes Shreve, "Adams explores the consequences of hate, love and just plain bitchiness in a universe in which everyone seems to be connected to everyone else." Moreover, Lawrence Thornton notes in the *New York Times Book Review,* "Ms. Adams's chronicle of Richard's descent into psychotic depression is minutely recorded. And it is the double trajectory—Stella's rise to success and self-esteem against Richard's self-destruction—that gives the novel its compelling signature."

Reviews of *Almost Perfect* find much to praise in its author's use of character and setting. "A lot goes on in the two-year span of the novel," writes Victoria Jenkins in *Tribune Books,* "and it's all marvelously well told—full of revealing detail, smart dialogue and astute observation. Adams' characters are drawn with such precision and complexity that it's easy to imagine forgetting that they are characters in fiction and to mistakenly remember them as real people." Jenkins also lauds Adams's style. "*Almost Perfect* has a breathless, gossipy tone. The story is told in the present tense from the points of view of many different characters with many parenthetical asides. We're drawn in as though we're part of the circle of friends, confided in and gossiped to." And as Thornton writes, "Ms. Adams explores the tension of [Stella's and Richard's] deteriorating relationship with something approaching the novelist's equivalent of perfect pitch. She paces the story by means of

highly concentrated episodes and uses the present tense effectively to increase the sense of urgency."

Shreve finds that like the relationship between Adams's two main characters, the novel turns out to be not quite perfect. "One wishes Adams had shifted her emphasis from the banal soap opera of beautiful people to the pathos of the vacuum, about which she writes with more authenticity," the reviewer recommends. Thornton offers a different view. He maintains that "*Almost Perfect* is a moving novel about important subjects. It is abundant with what Henry James called 'felt life.'" And Josephine Humphries concludes in the *Los Angeles Times Book Review,* "*Almost Perfect* is an unflinching novel, the work of a wise and uncompromising mind. It resists easy resolutions, offers neither redemption nor revelation but leaves open the possibility of both at some point in the future."

In *Caroline's Daughters,* the title character and her third husband return to San Francisco from a long stay in Europe. Upon her arrival home, Caroline finds each of her five daughters in some degree of crisis. Caroline's daughters range in age from twenty-five to forty-one. Caroline's first husband died in World War II, leaving her to take care of their daughter, Sage, by herself. The three middle daughters were fathered by her second husband, a doctor. Liza is married with children and hopes to write a book. Fiona is a restaurateur and Jill, a lawyer and high-class call girl. The youngest girl's father is Caroline's current husband. Portia is struggling to find her place. Adams weaves together the lives of this mother and her daughters and suggests that the daughters need their mother more than she needs them. As Christopher Lehmann-Haupt comments in the *New York Times,* "What Ms. Adams's witty scenes add up to is any number of things: a portrait of San Francisco, a profile of the 1980's, a still life of women after liberation." In fact, in the opinion of *Women's Review of Books* contributor Barbara Rich, "One of the delights of the book is the way in which it illuminates the superficial sheen of the Reagan years, and how it reflects back upon the principals' lives." Even so, notes Hilma Wolitzer in the *Los Angeles Times Book Review,* "Despite its contemporary style, and its current setting and concerns, *Caroline's Daughters* is a roomy and tantalizing old-fashioned read."

Ellen Pall believes that this book has much to offer its readers. "*Caroline's Daughters* is crammed with plot," she writes. "Careers rise and fall, affairs begin and end, people fall in and out of love and fortunes are won and lost as the lives of the sisters intertwine in gratifyingly shocking ways." And, adds Wolitzer, "There is enough intrigue here to keep things animated and suspenseful, and enough sensual detail—more often related to food and clothing than to sex—to create a lush atmosphere." Dispelling the fear that a novel with so many characters and so much happening would become far too complex for the reader, Barbara Rich counters, "If the cast of characters and their convoluted scripts sound overwhelming, they may well have been in the hands of a less skillful writer. Alice Adams knows exactly where she is going, and why. She delivers a fluid, meaty, sexy and rewarding novel." Pall's praise for Adams's craftsmanship is more tempered. "Fluent though the prose is, it is otherwise unremarkable," she writes, "and a few of the characters seem to have sprung more from the pages of glossy magazines than the depths of the author's imagination or experience. And the very end of the novel feels artificial and arbitrary. Nevertheless," she believes, "this is an immensely satisfying book."

In *A Southern Exposure,* Adams departs from her San Francisco of recent decades for the sandhills of North Carolina just prior to World War II, when the Depression still dominates American life. A New England couple, Harry and Cynthia Baird, leave their home for a new life in the South and settle in a small community peopled by a famous poet, his depressed wife, her psychiatrist, a wealthy gossip, among others. In following the town's many social encounters, Adams crafts a portrait of people and place. The novel's "melodramas feel witty, given Adam's intelligent characterization, and are at equal pitch with her descriptions of Pinehill's flush, distracting beauty," comments a *Publishers Weekly* reviewer. *Booklist* contributor Nancy Pearl adds, "Adams' perfect pitch for dialogue has never been put to better use."

Beautiful Girl was Adams's first published collection of short stories. Although half of the stories had won the O. Henry Prize, the tales did not fully satisfy *New York Times Book Review* critic Katha Pollitt. While praising Adams's gifts as a storyteller, Pollitt laments the ubiquitous presence of one "recognizable type" of heroine in the collection: "I kept waiting for Miss Adams to flash an ironic smile toward these supremely sheltered, idle, unexamined people. . . . She never does." *Hudson Review* contributor Dean Flowers believes that in *Beautiful Girl,* Adams portrays difficult problems with too much ease: "At

their best these stories explore complex relationships in a quick, deceptively offhand manner. They tend to begin with a tense problem (a wife dying, a divorce impending, a moment of wrath, an anxious move to a new place) and unravel gradually, without much climax except a muted sense of recovered balance and diminished expectation.. . . One feels neither gladness nor sorrow in such conclusions, but rather an implicit appeal of stylish melancholy." Still, the intensity of her characters' feelings can belie the author's seemingly neat appraisals of their lives. Susan Schindehette comments in her *Saturday Review* appraisal of the stories collected in *Return Trips:* "It is Adams' gift to reveal the tremendous inner workings beneath the apparent tranquility and make characters come to life in her spare, elegant style."

Reviewers frequently praise Adams's concise, understated use of language. "Some writers have such lovely voices they always make you want to hum along. Alice Adams is like that; she is fond of the word 'perfect,' and it suits her," writes Lois Gould in the *New York Times Book Review.* She continues, "For Miss Adams, applying her elegant, rhythmic style to the form, the challenge lies in making it new, fitting it to her own literary place and our time." Adams conveys the rough sides of life as well as the tender. Douglas Hill observes in the *Globe and Mail,* "Adams writes decidedly grown-up fiction, though it's by no means X-rated. She uses language almost surgically, and can be quite candid and direct about matters sexual and vulgar. Her characteristic tone is light, even at times airy. But there's always a hint of darkness underneath; for Adams the course of adult affection and love is always at greatest risk when it seems safest and most placid." Critics also like the compactness of Adams's writing and the careful use of detail. "The typical Alice Adams short story announces itself in the very first sentence as a thing of edgy wit and compressed narrative power," says Pollitt. And Phillips in *Commonweal* notes that Adams "suppresses and condenses, allowing the reader to make vital connections between situation and character."

Adams moved to California in the fifties, and the state and its residents figure prominently in her work. *To See You Again* is a "collection of 19 short stories [that] may surprise readers who have been led to think that all fictional California women are angst-ridden, sex-crazed or mellowed-out," writes Paul Gray in *Time.* Some reviewers have taken issue with the book's even tone. While Benjamin DeMott admires the irony and understatement in the collection, he notes in the *New York Times Book Review:* "Life in this book is indeed lived,. . . in easygoing obedience to the key emotional imperative of the age (Change Your Life). None of Miss Adams's people ever tears a passion to tatters. . . . But these stories do suffer from a lack of tonal variety." Mary Morris, in a *Chicago Tribune Book World* article, says that "[Adams] has spared us the fights, she has spared us the asking of the unaskable, the struggle to love. And in the end she has also spared us what we want most, the drama." Morris claims "the protagonists' inability to achieve involvement" frustrates the reader. Adams's characters in *To See You Again* "don't reach out, they don't fight back. What they do is leave, remember or fantasize." But the strength of the book, Linda Pastan writes in the *American Book Review,* lies in "the cumulative effect" that makes "the reader feel as though he knows the San Francisco of Alice Adams in the special way one knows a place inhabited by friends."

Adams earned ample praise with her third collection of stories, *Return Trips,* which "shows a master writer at the height of her powers," says Stull. He relates: "The title is apt in every way, from the dedication [to Adams's son, Peter Adams Linenthal] to the travel motifs that link these fifteen accounts of women recalling or revisiting people and places that shaped their lives." All the stories in the collection depict women struggling along on a physical or spiritual journey. According to Isabel Raphael in the London *Times:* "To make a return trip, [Adams] seems to be saying, you must leave where you are, and there is no guarantee that things will be the same when you come back, or that you yourself will be unaffected by the journey. But with a solid experience of love in your life on which to base a sense of identity, you will not lose your way." And Elaine Kendall concludes in the *Los Angeles Times* that in *Return Trips,* "unburdened by complex rigging, her imagination sails swiftly and gracefully over a sea of contemporary emotional experience, sounding unexpected depths."

Adams's next collection of short stories appeared in 1989 in *After You've Gone.* As Ron Carlson explains in the *New York Times Book Review,* "The 14 short romances in Alice Adams's new collection are—with two exceptions—about women. These women are professionals . . . who live in the upscale world of gracious houses in cities from California to Maryland." The stories are also about the aftermath of lost relationships. Catherine Petroski details the themes of these stories in *Tribune Books,* "Several stories of uneasy co-existence . . . deal pointedly with the difficulties people have in sustaining relationships and why, given the difficulties, they persist in them." She adds, "The other major strain running through the collection is the theme of old friendships." Carlson expresses disappointment with these works. "Reading the stories becomes like reading about people in stories and not—as in the best realistic fiction—about people we know." Yet, in Petroski's opinion, "Alice Adams' new collection of short stories, her fourth, is the work of a writer at the height of her powers—lucid, confident, refined, adept, provocative, perspicacious, startling and satisfying."

As Elizabeth Ward observes in the *Washington Post Book World,* "Alice Adams' reputation is as a connoisseur of contemporary American relationships, a specialist in the affairs of white, middle-or upper middle-class, well-educated, well-traveled women." *Washington Post Book World* contributor Goodwin sees in Adams a "worldliness," which is "more than an attitude, a matter of style or sophistication; it amounts to a metaphysics, the wisdom of the world. Adams casts a cold eye on romance, nostalgia, anything that smacks of sentiment. She is staunchly on the side of those who believe that happiness, if it lies anywhere, lies in reality." Adams's future as a writer remains bright, writes Hill in the *Globe and Mail,* since she "is one of a number of productive American writers . . . whose fictional accomplishments are substantial now and will likely loom even larger in years to come."

BIOGRAPHICAL/CRITICAL SOURCES:

BOOKS

Contemporary Literary Criticism, Gale (Detroit), Volume 6, 1976, Volume 13, 1980, Volume 46, 1988.
Dictionary of Literary Biography Yearbook: 1986, Gale, 1987.

PERIODICALS

American Book Review, July, 1983.
Atlanta Journal Constitution, January 2, 1990, p. B3; November 17, 1991, p. K6; August 1, 1993, p. N10.
Belles Lettres, winter, 1989, p. 7; winter, 1993, p. 37.
Booklist, December 15, 1978; January 15, 1982; June 15, 1984; July, 1985; August, 1995, p. 1907.

Books and Bookmen, March, 1985; February, 1986.

Boston Globe, April 7, 1991, p. A18; October 30, 1991, p. 60; July 28, 1993, p. 23.

Chicago Tribune, September 1, 1985.

Chicago Tribune Books, September 14, 1980; May 2, 1982; September 3, 1989, p. 3; March 10, 1991, p. 1; July 18, 1993, p. 3.

Christian Science Monitor, February 20, 1975; October 16, 1985, p. 22; June 17, 1988, p. 20.

Commonweal, March 25, 1983, p. 188.

Critique, summer, 1986.

Globe and Mail (Toronto), November 10, 1984.

Harvard Magazine, February, 1975.

Hudson Review, summer, 1979; spring, 1985.

Listener, January 29, 1976.

London Review of Books, February 21, 1985.

Los Angeles Times, April 13, 1982; August 19, 1985; October 10, 1989, p. V3.

Los Angeles Times Book Review, November 16, 1980; September 14, 1986, p. 14; May 8, 1988, p. 13; October 14, 1990, p. 14; March 10, 1991, p. 3; July 11, 1993, p. 3.

Ms., September, 1980, p. 18; September, 1984, p. 28.

New England Review, autumn, 1986.

New Leader, March 27, 1978.

New Republic, February 4, 1978.

New Statesman, January 16, 1976.

Newsweek, February 3, 1975.

New Yorker, February 10, 1975; November 5, 1984, p. 160; August 2, 1993, p. 83.

New York Times, January 30, 1975; January 10, 1978; April 11, 1982, p. 7; August 21, 1985, p. C17; May 19, 1988; March 21, 1991, p. C21.

New York Times Book Review, March 16, 1975; February 26, 1978; January 14, 1979; September 14, 1980, p. 13; April 11, 1982; September 23, 1984, p. 9; September 1, 1985; September 21, 1986, p. 42; May 1, 1988, p. 11; October 8, 1989, p. 27; April 7, 1991, p. 12; December 1, 1991, p. 20; July 11, 1993, p. 7; December 4, 1994, p. 88.

Observer (London), January 18, 1976; August 14, 1988, p. 41.

People, April 3, 1978.

Publishers Weekly, January 16, 1978; July 31, 1995, p. 65.

Rapport, Number 3, 1992, p. 24.

Rolling Stone, April 20, 1978.

San Francisco Review of Books, spring, 1985, p. 19; Number 1, 1988, p. 35.

Saturday Review, November-December, 1985, p. 73.

Spectator, December 3, 1988, p. 35.

Story Quarterly, Number 11, 1980.

Time, December 26, 1977; April 19, 1982.

Times (London), January 9, 1986.

Times Literary Supplement, January 16, 1976; January 31, 1986, p. 112; July 28, 1988, p. 840.

Tribune Books (Chicago), May 1, 1988, p. 7; September 3, 1989, p. 4; March 10, 1991, p. 1; July 18, 1993, p 3; August 15, 1993, p. 8.

Village Voice, January 9, 1978.

Washington Post, October 24, 1989, p. C3; November 21, 1991, p. D3.

Washington Post Book World, February 23, 1975; January 13, 1978; January 21, 1979; October 12, 1980, p. 9; May 9, 1982; September 2, 1984, p. 3; September 15, 1985, p. 5; May 6, 1988; March 10, 1991, p. 1; June 27, 1993, p. 1.

West Coast Review of Books, March, 1978; November, 1984, p. 26.

Women's Review of Books, February, 1985, p. 14; July, 1991, p. 41; December, 1993, p. 23.

World Literature Today, spring, 1994, p. 369.

*   *   *

AFFABEE, Eric
  See STINE, R(obert) L(awrence)

*   *   *

AGOSIN, Marjorie   1955-

PERSONAL: Born in 1955 in Bethesda, MD; daughter of M. and Frida Agosin; married John Wiggins, 1977; children: Joseph Daniel, Sonia Helene. *Education:* Indiana University—Bloomington, Ph.D., 1982. *Religion:* Jewish.

ADDRESSES: Home—27 Paine St., Wellesley, MA 02181. *Office*—Department of Spanish, Wellesley College, Wellesley, MA 02181.

CAREER: Writer. Professor of Spanish at Wellesley College.

AWARDS, HONORS: Fulbright fellow in Argentina; Good Neighbor Award from the National Association of Christians and Jews; Latino Literature Prize,

University of Miami North South Center, 1995; Letras de Oro Prize in Poetry.

WRITINGS:

POETRY

Conchali, illustrations by Della Collins Cook, Senda Nueva, 1980.

Brujas y algo mas, Latin American Literary Review Press (Pittsburgh, PA), 1984, translation by Cola Franzen published in dual-language edition as *Witches and Other Things,* 1985.

Hogueras, Universitaria, 1986.

Zones of Pain, translated by Franzen, White Pine (Fredonia, NY), 1988.

Bonfires, Bilingual Review Press, 1990.

Generous Journey: A Celebration of Foods from the World, Black Rock Press/University of Nevada Press, 1991.

Circles of Madness: Mothers of the Plaza de Mayo, translation from the Spanish text, *Circulos de locura: Madres de la Plaza de Mayo,* by Celeste Kostopulos-Cooperman, White Pine, 1992.

Sargazo = Sargasso: Poems, translated by Franzen, White Pine, 1993.

Towards the Splendid City, translated by Richard Schaaf, Bilingual Press/Editorial Bilingue (Tempe, AZ), 1994.

Dear Anne Frank, Azul Edition (Washington, DC), 1994.

Noche estrellada, University of Miami North South Center (Miami), 1996.

EDITOR

(And contributor with Elena Gascon-Vera and Joy Renjilian-Burgy) *Maria Luisa Bombal: Apreciaciones criticas,* Bilingue, 1987.

Landscapes of a New Land: Fiction by Latin American Women, White Pine, 1989.

Secret Weavers: Stories of the Fantastic by Women Writers of Argentina and Chile, White Pine, 1992.

Surviving beyond Fear, White Pine, 1993.

These Are Not Sweet Girls: Latin American Women Poets, White Pine, 1994.

The Alchemy of the Palate: A Collection of Kitchen Stories, White Pine, 1995.

What Is Secret: An Anthology of Chilean Women Writers, White Pine, 1995.

A Dream of Light and Shadow: Portraits of Latin American Women Writers, University of New Mexico Press (Albuquerque), Volume 1, 1995, Volume 2, 1996.

OTHER

Las desterradas del paraiso: Protagonistas en la narrativa de Maria Luisa Bombal, Senda Nueva, 1983.

Pablo Neruda, translated by Lorraine Ross, Twayne (Boston), 1986.

Silencio e imaginacion: Metaforas de la escritura femenina, Katun, 1986.

Scraps of Life, the Chilean Arpilleras: Chilean Women and the Pinochet Dictatorship, translated by Franzen, Red Sea Press, 1987.

Women of Smoke: Latin American Women in Literature and Life, translated by Naomi Lindstrom, edited by Yvette E. Miller, Latin American Literary Review Press, 1988, published as *Mujeres de humo,* 1989.

(With Ines Doz Blackburn) *Violeta Parra, santa de pura greda: Un estudio de su obra poetica,* Planeta, 1988.

Landscapes of a New Land, White Pine, 1990.

La felicidad, Editorial Cuarto Propio (Santiago, Chile), 1991, translation by Elizabeth Horan published as *Happiness: Stories,* White Pine, 1993.

Literatura fantastica del cono sur: Las mujeres, EDUCA, 1992.

Las hacedoras: Mujer, imagen, escritura (criticism), Editorial Cuarto Propio, 1993.

Sagrada memoria: Reminiscencias de una nina judia en Chile, Editorial Cuarto Propio, 1994, translation by Kostopulos-Cooperman published as *A Cross and a Star: Memoirs of a Jewish Girl in Chile,* University of New Mexico Press, 1995.

Furniture Dreams, Black Rock Press/University of Nevada Press, 1995.

(With Emma Sepulveda) *Hay Otra Voz: Essays on Hispanic Women Poets,* Ediciones Maerona (Puerto Rico), 1995.

Memory of Cloth: The History of the Chilean Arpillera, University of New Mexico Press, 1996.

Ashes of Revolt: Essays on Human Rights, White Pine, 1996.

SIDELIGHTS: Marjorie Agosin's writing demonstrates a unique marriage of cultures. The author grew up in Chile, and her work has drawn many comparisons to the "magic realist" style of other South American writers. She is also Jewish and often writes about the Holocaust and anti-Semitism in her native land. In *A Cross and a Star: Memoirs of a Jewish Girl in Chile,* Agosin wrote about her family from the perspective of her mother's life as a young girl in Osorno, a town in southern Chile inhabited primarily by German immigrants. Because of her faith, Agosin's mother was barred from attending the German school, the Catholic school, and the English school; the only school that would accept her was an institution for orphans and Indians. "There she was accepted and loved, for Indians, like her own people, were poor, excluded, persecuted, spat on," related *Women's Review of Books* contributor Mary Lowenthal Felstiner. "She learned silence and resignation, being unable to imagine a place—not Europe, not the forests of Chile—where people wouldn't condemn Jews. The family's suppression is captured in an image: the long gloves always worn by the narrator's grandmother to conceal a concentration camp tattoo." The narrator describes a journey back to Osorno during the 1990s; her initial feeling of homecoming was tainted when she saw that portraits of Hitler were still a popular item, displayed and sold everywhere. Felstiner added: "Agosin shows anti-Semitism echoing through the Chilean population. . . . The distinctive 'foreigners' in Chile, by the way they spoke, ate and kept to themselves, were not the Spanish-speaking Jews but the many German Christians. Chileans respected them—and despised the Jews."

Agosin's preoccupation with human rights manifests itself again in *Happiness: Stories,* a collection of short fiction. Many of the stories deal with imprisonment and torture. Often, the characters are women on the fringe of society: beggars, prostitutes, and others who are shunned by society. Their stories are full of strange and fantastic events: flowers blooming amid a frozen landscape; cannibalism. Naomi Lindstrom, a reviewer for *World Literature Today,* called Agosin's prose "lyrical," and declared: "Agosin excels at evoking painful scenes, not only of such physical miseries as hunger, cold, and torture but also of extreme feelings of estrangement."

Agosin's other works include *Scraps of Life, the Chilean Arpilleras: Chilean Women and the Pinochet Dictatorship,* and *Toward the Splendid City. Scraps of Life* examines the lives of the Chilean *arpillersitas*—the women who make the wall hangings known as *arpilleras* that depict the hardships of their daily lives under the Pinochet dictatorship. Writing in the *Women's Review of Books,* Linda Rennie Forcey stated that Agosin "shows how [the women] learn to surmount fear, to survive economically and to create a collective voice." In the poems from *Toward the Splendid City,* Agosin writes about

a number of cities around the world, including Jerusalem, Rome, and Santiago.

BIOGRAPHICAL/CRITICAL SOURCES:

PERIODICALS

Americas, January/February, 1993, pp. 44-49.
Booklist, October 1, 1994, p. 230.
Boston Review, June, 1989, pp. 12-14, 22-23.
Chicago Tribune, November 15, 1992, section 6, p. 1.
Choice, September, 1991, p. 46.
Hispania, March, 1987; September, 1987.
Library Journal, January, 1992, pp. 180-81; March 15, 1995, p. 74.
Los Angeles Times Book Review, December 24, 1989.
New York Times Book Review, April 29, 1990, p. 19; March 20, 1994, section 7, p. 18.
Publishers Weekly, December 6, 1991, p. 66.
Times Literary Supplement, July 14-20, 1989, p. 782.
Women's Review of Books, May, 1988, p. 8; February, 1996, pp. 1, 3.
World Literature Today, winter, 1982; summer, 1994, p. 542.

*   *   *

ALDRIDGE, Sarah
See MARCHANT, Anyda

*   *   *

ALLEN, Oliver E.   1922-

PERSONAL: Born June 29, 1922, in Cambridge, MA; son of Frederick Lewis and Dorothy (a homemaker; maiden name, Cobb) Allen; married Deborah Hutchison (a college administrator), May 8, 1948; children: Stephen, Frederick, Henry, Letitia, Jennie. *Education:* Harvard University, A.B., 1943. *Politics:* Democrat.

ADDRESSES: Home and office—42 Hudson St., New York, NY 10013. *Agent*—Emilie Jacobson, Curtis Brown Ltd., 10 Astor Pl., New York, NY 10003.

CAREER: Life, New York City, correspondent, writer, and editor, 1947-60; Time-Life Books, New York City, editor and planning director, 1960-76; freelance writer, 1976—. *Military service—* U.S. Army, 1943-46; became first lieutenant.

WRITINGS:

NONFICTION; PUBLISHED BY TIME-LIFE (ALEXANDRIA, VA)

(With James Underwood Crockett) *Wildflower Gardening,* 1977.
(With Crockett) *Decorating with Plants,* 1978.
Pruning and Grafting, 1978.
The Windjammers, 1978.
Shade Gardens, 1979.
Winter Gardens, 1979.
The Pacific Navigators, 1980.
Building Sound Bones and Muscles, 1981.
The Airline Builders, 1981.
Secrets of a Good Digestion, 1982.
The Atmosphere, 1983.

NONFICTION

The Vegetable Gardener's Journal, Stewart, Tabori & Chang (New York City), 1985.
Gardening With the New, Small Plants: The Complete Guide to Growing Dwarf and Miniature Shrubs, Flowers, Trees, and Vegetables, Houghton (Boston), 1987.
New York, New York: A History of the World's Most Exhilarating and Challenging City, Atheneum (New York City), 1990.
The Tiger: The Rise and Fall of Tammany Hall, Addison-Wesley (Reading, MA), 1993.

*   *   *

ALLEN, Pamela   1934-

PERSONAL: Born April 3, 1934, in Devonport, Auckland, New Zealand; daughter of William Ewart (a surveyor) and Esma (a homemaker; maiden name, Griffith) Griffiths; married William Robert Allen (head of an art school), December 12, 1964; children: Ben, Ruth. *Education:* Elam School of Art (now Auckland University), diploma of fine art, 1954; attended Auckland Teachers Training College, 1955-56.

ADDRESSES: Home and office—P.O. Box 215, Milsons Point, Sydney, New South Wales 2061, Australia. *Agent*—Curtis Brown Ltd., 27 Union St., Paddington, Sydney, New South Wales 2021, Australia.

CAREER: Pio Pio District High School, New Zealand, art teacher, 1956; Rangitoto College, Auckland, New Zealand, art teacher, 1957-58, 1960-64; writer and illustrator, 1979—.

MEMBER: Australian Society of Authors, Children's Book Council of Australia.

AWARDS, HONORS: Picture Book of the Year commendation from Children's Book Council of Australia, and New South Wales Premier's Literary Award in children's book category, both 1980, and Book Design Award commendation from Australian Book Publishers Association, 1980-81, all for *Mr. Archimedes' Bath;* Australian Picture Book of the Year Award from Children's Book Council of Australia, and New South Wales Premier's Literary Award in children's book category, both 1983, and honor diploma for illustration from International Board on Books for Young People, 1984, all for *Who Sank the Boat?;* Children's Book of the Year Award from Children's Book Council of Australia, 1984, for *Bertie and the Bear;* Russell Clark Award for Illustration from New Zealand Library Association, 1986, for *A Lion in the Night,* and represented in the Bologna International Illustrator's Exhibition, 1987, for same; Australian Children's Book of the Year Award, 1986, for *Watch Me;* winner of Helen Paul Encouragement Award, 1989, for *Fancy That;* Australian Picture Book of the Year Award commendation, and shortlisted for AIM New Zealand Children's Book Award, both 1990, for *I Wish I had a Pirate Suit;* winner of AIM Children's Book Award and New Zealand Picture Book of the Year, and shortlisted for Picture Book of the Year Award from Children's Book Council of Australia, all 1991, for *My Cat Maisie;* shortlisted for Picture Book of the Year Award from Children's Book Council of Australia, 1993, for *Belinda;* shortlisted for Russell Clark Award for Illustration from New Zealand Library Association, 1993.

WRITINGS:

SELF-ILLUSTRATED CHILDREN'S BOOKS

Mr. Archimedes' Bath, Collins (Australia and New Zealand), 1980.

Who Sank the Boat?, Thomas Nelson (Australia), 1982, Coward McCann (U. S. A.), 1983.

Bertie and the Bear (Junior Literary Guild selection), Thomas Nelson, 1983, Coward McCann, 1984.

A Lion in the Night, Thomas Nelson, 1985, Orchard Books, 1986.

Simon Said, Thomas Nelson, Orchard Books, 1985.

Watch Me, Thomas Nelson, Orchard Books, 1985.

Herbert and Harry, Thomas Nelson, 1986.

Mr. McGee, Thomas Nelson, 1987.

Hidden Treasure, Putnam (New York City), 1987.

Fancy That!, Thomas Nelson, Orchard Books, 1988.

I Wish I had a Pirate Suit, Viking/Penguin (Australia and New York City), 1989.

Simon Did, Thomas Nelson, Orchard Books, 1988.

Watch Me Now, Thomas Nelson, Orchard Books, 1989.

My Cat Maisie, Viking/Penguin (Australia and NY), 1990.

Black Dog, Viking/Penguin (Australia), 1991.

Belinda, Viking/Penguin, 1992.

Mr. McGee Goes to Sea, Viking/Penguin, 1992.

Alexander's Outing, Viking/Penguin, 1993.

Mr. McGee and the Blackberry Jam, Viking/Penguin, 1993.

Clippity-Clop, Viking/Penguin, 1994.

ILLUSTRATOR

Jan Farr, *Mummy, Do Monsters Clean Their Teeth?* Heinemann (New Zealand), 1975.

Farr, *Mummy, How Cold Is a Witch's Nose?* Heinemann, 1976.

T. E. Wilson, *Three Cheers for McGinty,* Heinemann, 1976.

Wilson, *McGinty Goes to School,* Heinemann, 1976.

Wilson, *McGinty the Ghost,* Heinemann, 1976.

Wilson, *McGinty in Space,* Heinemann, 1976.

Farr, *Big Sloppy Dinosaur Socks,* Heinemann, 1977.

Farr, *Mummy, Are Monsters Too Big for Their Boots?* Heinemann, 1977.

N. L. Ray, *The Pow Toe,* Collins (Australia), 1979.

Sally Fitzpatrick, *A Tall Story,* Angus & Robertson (Australia), 1981.

OTHER

Contributor to *School* magazine (New South Wales).

WORK IN PROGRESS: Waddle Giggle Gargle.

SIDELIGHTS: Pamela Allen told *CA:* "One does not go to school to learn to make a picture book. When I made the conscious decision to write and illustrate a picture book, I spent some time thinking about the order of my priorities. I put as my first priority the child. The child I had in mind was young and not yet able to read—a preschool child. Through my picture books I wanted to communicate with this young child.

"Young children gather meaning from many clues, language being only one possibility. I use pictures, sound, drama, and language. All of this only comes alive when it is shared. There is the adult, the child, and the book: the fun they have together is what it is all about."

Allen's books have been translated into Danish, French, Japanese, and Swedish.

BIOGRAPHICAL/CRITICAL SOURCES:

PERIODICALS

Reading Time, Number 5, 1983.
Review, December, 1984.

        *   *   *

AMBRUS, Gyozo Laszlo   **1935-**
    (Victor G. Ambrus)

PERSONAL: Born August 19, 1935, in Budapest, Hungary; son of Gyozo (a chemical scientist) and Iren (Toth) Ambrus; married Glenys R. Chapman (an illustrator), 1958; children: Mark, Sandor John. *Education:* Received early education in Hungary and attended Hungarian Academy of Fine Art for three years; Royal College of Art, London, England, Diploma A.R.C.A., 1959. *Politics:* Democrat. *Religion:* Roman Catholic. *Avocational interests:* Military history (especially the Napoleonic wars); collecting arms, armor, and antique weapons; travel; old architecture; paintings.

ADDRESSES: Home—52 Crooksbury Rd., Farnham, Surrey, England.

CAREER: Author, artist, designer, and illustrator of books for children. Lecturer on illustration, West Surrey College of Art, Surrey, England, 1964-80, and other universities. Member of Council for National Academic Awards of Great Britain. Has exhibited work at the Royal Academy, Biennale of Bratislava, in Bologna, Italy, in Tokyo, Japan, and in

Belgium. Works included in permanent collections at University of Southern Mississippi, Library of Congress, and Oxford University Press, London, England.

MEMBER: Royal College of Art (associate member), Royal Society of Arts (fellow), Royal Society of Painters, Etchers, and Engravers (fellow), Pastel Society (London).

AWARDS, HONORS: Kate Greenaway Gold Medal for most distinguished work in illustration of a children's book, Library Association of Great Britain, 1964, for *The Three Poor Tailors,* and 1975, for *Horses in Battle* and *Mishka;* first prize from Daler-Ronney/Pastel Society, 1994, and World Wildlife Fund, 1995; granted diplomas from Royal Engravers and from Royal Society of Arts.

WRITINGS:

SELF-ILLUSTRATED; UNDER NAME VICTOR G. AMBRUS

The Three Poor Tailors, Oxford University Press (Oxford, England and New York City), 1965, Harcourt (New York City), 1966.
Brave Soldier Janosh, Oxford University Press, 1967.
The Little Cockerell, Oxford University Press, 1968.
The Seven Skinny Goats, Oxford University Press, 1969, Harcourt, 1970.
(Reteller) *The Sultan's Bath,* Harcourt, 1972.
Hot Water for Boris, Oxford University Press, 1972.
A Country Wedding, Oxford University Press, 1973.
Horses in Battle, Oxford University Press, 1975.
Mishka, Oxford University Press, 1975.
(Adaptor) Brothers Grimm, *The Valiant Little Tailor,* Oxford University Press, 1980.
Dracula: Everything You Always Wanted to Know but Were Too Afraid to Ask, Oxford University Press, 1981.
(With D. Lindsay) *Under the Double Eagle: Three Centuries of History in Austria and Hungary,* Oxford University Press, 1981.
Blackbeard, Oxford University Press, 1981.
Dracula's Bedtime Storybook: Tales to Keep You Awake at Night, Oxford University Press, 1982.
Grandma, Felix and Mustapha Biscuit, Morrow (New York City), 1982.
Son of Dracula, Oxford University Press, 1985.
Dracula's Late-night TV Show, Oxford University Press, 1990.
Count, Dracula, Oxford University Press, 1991, Crown (New York City), 1992.

What's the Time, Dracula?, Oxford University Press, 1991, new edition published as *What Time Is it, Dracula?,* Crown, 1992.
Never Laugh at Bears: A Transylvanian Folk Tale, Bedrick/Blackie (New York City), 1992.

ILLUSTRATOR; UNDER NAME VICTOR G. AMBRUS

Ian Serraillier, *The Challenge of the Green Knight,* Oxford University Press, 1966.
Helen Kay, *Henri's Hands for Pablo Picasso,* Abelard-Schuman (London), 1966.
William Cowper, *The Diverting History of John Gilpin,* Abelard-Schuman, 1969.
Robert J. Unstead, *Living in a Crusader Land,* A. & C. Black (London), 1971.
Bonnie Highsmith, *Kodi's Mare,* Abelard-Schuman, 1973.
Winifred Finlay, *Cap o' Rushes and Other Folk Tales,* Kaye & Ward (London), 1973.
Alexander Cordell, *The Traitor Within,* Globe Books (Basingstoke, Hants, England), 1975.
Helen Griffiths, *Just a Dog,* Holiday House (New York City), 1975.
The Story of Britain, A. & C. Black, 1976.
Sir Bernard Miles, *Favorite Tales from Shakespeare,* Hamlyn (London), 1976.
Miles, adaptor, *Robin Hood,* Rand McNally (Chicago), 1978.
Unstead, *The Life of Jesus,* Hamlyn, 1981.
James Riordan, *Tales of King Arthur,* Rand McNally, 1982.
Riordan, *Tales from the Arabian Nights,* Rand McNally, 1983.
Riordan, *Peter and the Wolf,* Oxford University Press, 1987.
Rudyard Kipling, *How the First Letter Was Written,* Peter Bedrick Books (New York City), 1987.
Riordan, *Myths and Legends,* Hamlyn, 1988.
Riordan, *Pinocchio,* Oxford University Press, 1988.
Riordan, *Gulliver's Travels,* Oxford University Press, 1992.
A Treasury of Stories from Around the World, Kingfisher Books (New York City), 1993.
Anna Sewell, *Black Beauty: The Autobiography of a Horse,* Holt (New York City), 1993.
Joan Aiken, *The Shoemaker's Boy,* Simon & Schuster (New York City), 1994.
Horse Stories, Kingfisher Books, 1994.
Virginia Haviland, *Favorite Fairy Tales Told in France,* Beech Tree Books (New York City), 1994.
(With Tony Karpinski) *Shakespeare and Macbeth: The Story Behind the Play,* Viking (New York City), 1994.

Lucille Recht Penner, *Knights and Castles,* Random House (New York City), 1995.
Thundering Hooves, Kingfisher Books, 1996.

Illustrator of over one hundred and fifty additional books, including *Canterbury Tales,* Oxford University Press, 1990; *The Odyssey,* Oxford University Press, 1993; and *Don Quixote,* Oxford University Press, 1995.

SIDELIGHTS: Gyozo Laszlo Ambrus told *CA:* "Being an illustrator/author, story and pictures always go together when I am working on an idea for a book. And I am never too sure which comes first! I am also something of a split personality. When other authors stick to a certain line of books, I switch between subjects as far apart as the history of the Habsburg Empire and the comic strip frolics of Count Dracula.

"In many ways this is the most enjoyable thing about working on books—you never know what's going to occupy your drawing board next. In my days I have seen dinosaurs, sailing ships, romantic heroines, horses by the dozen, nursery rhyme characters, knights of King Arthur, Father Christmas—come and go in quick succession. Never a dull moment!

"To me the most rewarding experience as an author is to see a well-worn, dog-eared book of mine on the school library shelves—or to have a small child come up and say—'I know you—you are Dracula.'"

BIOGRAPHICAL/CRITICAL SOURCES:

BOOKS

Martin, Douglas, *The Telling Line,* Julia Macrae Books/Walker Books, 1989.
Something about the Author Autobiography Series, Volume 4, Gale, 1987.

PERIODICALS

Books for Keeps, September, 1990, p. 11; January, 1994, p. 9.
Books for Your Children, autumn, 1990, p. 2; summer, 1994, p. 9.
Junior Bookshelf, December, 1990, p. 264; April, 1991, p. 54.
Times Educational Supplement, December 7, 1990, p. 31.

ANKERSON, Dudley (Charles)   1948-

PERSONAL: Born September 4, 1948, in Hereford, England; son of Richard and Norah Madeleine Ankerson; married Silvia Galicia (a teacher), December 8, 1973; children: Catherine, Richard. *Education:* Sidney Sussex College, Cambridge, M.A., 1971, D.Phil., 1981. *Politics:* Social Democrat. *Religion:* Roman Catholic.

ADDRESSES: Office—Foreign and Commonwealth Office (Madrid), 1 Charles St., London SW1A 1AH, England.

CAREER: British Foreign and Commonwealth Office, London, England, 1976-84, held posts such as second secretary of embassy in Buenos Aires, Argentina, 1978-81, first secretary of embassy in Mexico City, Mexico, 1985-88, and counsellor at embassy in Madrid, 1993—.

MEMBER: Marylebone Cricket Club.

WRITINGS:

(Contributor) D. A. Brading, editor, *Caudillo and Peasant in the Mexican Revolution,* Cambridge University Press (Cambridge, England), 1980.
Agrarian Warlord: Saturnino Cedillo and the Mexican Revolution in San Luis Potosi, Northern Illinois University Press (De Kalb), 1985, published in Mexico as *El caudillo agrarista: Saturnino Cedillo y la revolucion Mexicana en San Luis Potosi,* translated by Leonor Corral Camou, Instituto Nacional de Estudios Historicos de la Revolucion Mexicana (Mexico City), 1994.

WORK IN PROGRESS: Research on the politics of Central America since 1960.

SIDELIGHTS: "Following a period of studying the history of Latin America at university," Dudley Ankerson wrote, "I was drawn to look at the first major revolutionary upheaval of the twentieth century: the Mexican revolution. I decided to conduct a study of this movement on a regional basis, and selected as my field of study the state of San Luis Potosi. I was particularly interested in the career of the regional strongman who dominated local politics there for two decades—Saturnino Cedillo, a man whom the author Graham Greene had called upon when he visited Mexico in 1938 and who features in Greene's account of his journey, *The Lawless Roads.*

I discussed with Greene his meeting with Cedillo and refer to it in my book.

"It seemed to me that Cedillo's career marked the passing of the old, rural-based system of Mexican politics and the transition to the new machine politics, which are a feature of contemporary Mexico. Like his better known counterpart, Emiliano Zapata, Cedillo was a small landholder, who joined the revolution in protest at the abuses of neighboring large landowners (*hacendados*). He later came to control the state and established a traditional form of *caudillo* rule there. This proved to be out of step with the more structured political system that emerged in Mexico in the 1930s. This fact led to Cedillo's overthrow by the central government in 1938, when he launched an abortive military uprising, the last such upheaval in Mexican history."

Ankerson added: "I have retained my interest in Latin America and have served with the British Foreign Office in both Argentina and Mexico, where I have been involved in reporting upon events in Central America. At some time in the future I would like to write a book about the history and contemporary politics of this last-mentioned region.

"Outside my work, I am interested in international affairs, classical music, sport, and religion. The first part of my undergraduate degree was in classical studies, and I retain an interest in Greek and Roman history and Greek and Latin literature. I speak fluent Spanish and can converse in French, Italian and Portuguese."

*   *   *

ANVIC, Frank
   See SHERMAN, Jory (Tecumseh)

*   *   *

APPIAH, Peggy   1921-

PERSONAL: Born May 21, 1921, in England; daughter of Stafford (a British cabinet minister) and Isobel (Swithenbank) Cripps; married Joe E. Appiah (a barrister and Ghanaian government official), July 18, 1953 (died, 1990); children: Anthony, Isobel, Adwoa, Abena. *Education:* Attended Maltman's

Green School and Whitehall Secretarial College. *Religion:* Christian. *Avocational interests:* Arts, crafts, handwork, history, social welfare, studying Ashanti culture and history, collecting Ashanti gold weights, gardening.

ADDRESSES: Home—P.O. Box 829, Kumasi, Ashanti, Ghana. *Agent*—David Higham Associates, 5-8 Lower John St., London W1R 4HA, England.

CAREER: Novelist and freelance writer, 1965—. British Ministry of Information, London, England, research assistant, 1943-45; Racial Unity, London, secretary, 1951-53. Kumasi Children's Home, Kumasi, Ashanti, Ghana, chair of advisory committee, 1968-93.

MEMBER: Society for the Aid of Mentally Retarded Children.

WRITINGS:

CHILDREN'S BOOKS

Ananse the Spider: Tales from an Ashanti Village, illustrated by Peggy Wilson, Pantheon (New York City), 1966.
Tales of an Ashanti Father, illustrated by Mora Dickson, Deutsch (London), 1967, Beacon Press (Boston), 1989.
The Children of Ananse, illustrated by Dickson, M. Evans (London), 1968.
The Pineapple Child and Other Tales from Ashanti, illustrated by Dickson, M. Evans, 1969, Beacon Press, 1989.
The Lost Earring (reader), illustrated by J. Jarvis, M. Evans, 1971.
Yao and the Python (reader), illustrated by Jarvis, M. Evans, 1971.
Gift of the Mmoatia, illustrated by Nii O. Quao, Ghana Publishing, 1972.
Why There Are So Many Roads (folktales), illustrated by A. A. Teye, African University Press, 1972.
Ring of Gold, illustrated by Laszlo Acs, Deutsch, 1976.
Why the Hyena Does Not Care for Fish and Other Tales from the Ashanti Gold Weights, illustrated by Joanna Stubbs, Deutsch, 1977, Ghana Publishing, 1996.
Abena and the Python, Quick Service Books, 1991.
Afua and the Mouse, Quick Service Books, 1991.
Kofi and the Crow, Quick Service Books, 1991.
The Twins, Quick Service Books, 1991.

Kyekyekulee, Grandmother's Tales, Quick Service Books, 1993.
Busybody, Asempa, 1995.
The Rubbish Heap, Asempa, 1995.

ADULT BOOKS

A Smell of Onions (novel), Longman (London), 1971.
A Dirge Too Soon (novel), Ghana Publishing, 1976.
Poems of Three Generations, University of Science and Technology, 1978.

WORK IN PROGRESS: Translating Ashanti proverbs and providing explanations, for a book to be edited by her son, Anthony Appiah; *Ratteltat,* a children's book; a book on the history of Asante place names; three books to be published in Nigeria.

SIDELIGHTS: English-born Peggy Appiah had always wanted to write children's books. Raising a family in Ghana—where children's books and even toys were relatively scarce—encouraged her to do so. Blending a love of Ashanti myth and fable with memories of her own favorite children's tales, she began to collect tales from the west coast of Africa that would teach many of the same lessons learned in Aesop. The result was a first volume of folktales, *Ananse the Spider: Tales from an Ashanti Village,* which *Kirkus Reviews* lauds for its authentic rendering: "Her versions sound as good as they read." Appiah had hit on a motif and theme that resonated for her and her readers. "All the books I have so far published have been about Ashanti, where I live," she states in *Twentieth-Century Children's Writers.* "The country is full of stories."

In the early 1950s, Appiah began work with a British organization known as Racial Unity, whose purpose was to create harmony between the races. By 1952 she had become secretary of Racial Unity. In that same year she met her future husband, Joe E. Appiah, a law student from Ghana. One year later the couple married, causing shock in some corners.

Once Joe Appiah had finished his studies in England, the couple set up home in Kumasi, Ghana, in the ancient west coast region of Ashanti, rich in culture and tradition. Appiah began collecting Ashanti stories, both fables and those that were associated with the antique gold weights which she collected. The weights were made of brass, "in every possible shape from animals to guns, birds to insects, peanuts to

people, sieves to spades," she once explained. "[They] were used for weighing the gold which was the main form of currency until the introduction of money. I started going to the villages to ask questions about them." The villagers obliged her by telling her the stories and fables that the figures represented.

Appiah put these tales together into stories for her own children. She noticed their similarity to the fables of Aesop. The stories talk about village and forest life, both themes close to her heart. Some of the characters were reminiscent of those of Appiah's childhood; for example, the trickster spider, Kwaku Ananse, committed antics similar to those of Brer Rabbit. From telling the stories to her own children, Appiah was soon writing them down. "It was undoubtedly the [lack of] children's books and reading aloud that started me on my own career as a writer of books for children," she recalls in her *Something about the Author Autobiography Series* (*SAAS*) essay. "I realised early that there were few books for children with a local background, and not many children were lucky enough in town to have elders in the family who told them the folktales."

While Appiah gathered her tales together, her husband faced the uncertain political turmoil in Ghana. He went to prison for the first time in 1961, and was released a year later. Over the next eighteen years, he would be in and out of custody as well as in and out of governmental positions several times as new power brokers took over the government. Appiah's children were educated mainly in England, and she spent much of her time at a house they had purchased in Brighton.

Appiah's first published book was *Ananse the Spider: Tales from an Ashanti Village,* which contains tales the local villagers had told her about the clever spider of their tradition who is either successful in his tricks or outwitted by other, more clever animals. A *Kirkus Reviews* critic finds that Ananse is "caught in a home-spun web" in Appiah's book. Appiah continued her folktales with *Tales of an Ashanti Father,* a compilation of twenty-two stories featuring animals. Kwaku Ananse returns, but also such characters as lizards and tortoises. Several of the tales are reminiscent of Western stories: "The Tortoise and the Hare" is similar to the Aesop tale of the same title and "Why the Lizard Stretches His Neck" reminds a reviewer in *Publishers Weekly* of a Rudyard Kipling story. "The tales move quickly in this sparkling, varied collection," the reviewer comments. The story is "admirably spare in the telling yet also colorful," a *Horn Book* critic concludes.

Appiah continued her series of Ashanti folktales with *The Children of Ananse* and *The Pineapple Child and Other Tales from Ashanti,* the latter of which is "justifiably labelled a 'Children's Classic,'" according to a reviewer in *Growing Point*. In this collection, Appiah retells animal fables which give explanations for a multitude of natural phenomena, and simple stories of village folk which illuminate the complexity of human beings. Greed, death, and the reason for rain are among the topics found in Appiah's folktales, "richly suggesting the atmosphere of community life in Ghana," according to the critic for *Growing Point*. A further installment in Appiah's Ashanti tales is *Why the Hyena Does Not Care for Fish and Other Tales from the Ashanti Gold Weights.* With these stories, Appiah uses the figures represented in her collection of brass gold weights to tell traditional fables. "This is a book to intrigue scholars and the general reader alike," notes a *Growing Point* contributor. "Her style is simple and uncluttered, always lively and reads well aloud," comments a reviewer in the *Times Literary Supplement*.

"To write stories for children," Appiah explains in *SAAS*, "one has to be very conscious of one's surroundings. The folktales really bring the animals alive and you learn the different characteristics and what they stand for. The little royal antelope is king of the beasts. The tortoise is the wise man, the dog rather a fool. The cat is unlucky to some areas as is the owl. The elephant is a big fool."

Appiah's *Ring of Gold* is a departure from the folktale theme. "A good, old-fashioned children's book," Rosemary Stones in the *Times Literary Supplement* calls the work. The story of two town cousins, Abena and Kwame, visiting their country cousins, Adwoa and Kabwena, *Ring of Gold* tells about the difficult task of setting up a library in a small town. The discovery of a gold ring helps the children in their money-making schemes, as do the efforts of a couple in England, and in the end the little village gets not only a library, but also a museum. Appiah contrasts city and country throughout her book and interweaves local lore in the story. "Much background knowledge about the country can be acquired" from the work, notes a *Junior Bookshelf* writer. A *Growing Point* contributor finds it to be "a leisurely, good-hearted story of an Ashanti village."

"I find writing stories something like life in a village," Appiah once explained. "There are not too many people at a time and one can keep track of their movements. I usually start my story with some incident which strikes me; then the people take over, as they do in real life. Sometimes they don't do at all what I expect. I find it difficult to cut down on the incidents and in deciding which to keep. Just as in real life one's characters are doing things all the time and you have to pick out the relevant actions. I'm always being told 'keep to the story.' But stories in life don't have a beginning and an end!"

"Ghana is good for writing because one never knows what is going to happen from day to day," she once stated. "The unexpected is always turning up and life sometimes takes on the quality of a grown-up fairy story. I have always loved fairy stories and folk tales, so I'm never surprised by events. One learns to laugh with people over all sorts of things, even if one should not, and to enjoy even what is sad because it is shared with other people. The main pleasure in life is sharing things with people and that is why I enjoy writing."

BIOGRAPHICAL/CRITICAL SOURCES:

BOOKS

Something about the Author Autobiography Series, Volume 19, Gale (Detroit), 1995, pp. 53-112.
Twentieth-Century Children's Writers, 4th edition, St. James Press (Detroit), 1995.

PERIODICALS

Booklist, June 1, 1981, p. 1296.
Books, April, 1989, p. 12.
Growing Point, March, 1977, p. 3059; November, 1977, p. 3204; July, 1989, pp. 5178-5182.
Horn Book, August, 1981, p. 441.
Junior Bookshelf, October, 1977, p. 295; April, 1978, p. 84.
Kirkus Reviews, October, 1, 1966, p. 1050.
New York Times Book Review, November 6, 1966, p. 48.
Publishers Weekly, January 13, 1989, p. 91.
School Library Journal, January, 1982, p. 58.
Times Educational Supplement, November 18, 1977, p. 31; July 15, 1983, p. 18; March 27, 1987, p. 26; July 24, 1987, p. 23.
Times Literary Supplement, October 16, 1969, p. 1193; December 10, 1976, p. 1554; December 2, 1977, p. 1410.*

ARNOLD, Guy 1932-

PERSONAL: Born May 6, 1932, in Birkenhead, England; son of George Croft and Margaret Arnold. *Education:* Oxford University, M.A. (with honors), 1955. *Politics:* Radical. *Religion:* Agnostic.

ADDRESSES: Home—163 Seymour Pl., London W1H 5TP, England. *Agent*—Michael Shaw, Curtis Brown Ltd., 162-168 Regent St., London W1R 5TB, England.

CAREER: Freelance writer, lecturer, and traveler, 1955-58, 1960-61; teacher of English in Newmarket, Ontario, 1958-60; Ryerson Institute, Toronto, Ontario, lecturer in political geography, 1961-63; Government of Northern Rhodesia, consultant in youth services, 1963-64; Overseas Development Institute, London, England, researcher, 1965-66; writer and lecturer, 1966—. Director, Africa Bureau (London), 1968-72. *Military service:* British Army, 1951-52; became lieutenant.

WRITINGS:

Longhouse and Jungle, Chatto & Windus (London), 1959.

Towards Peace and a Multiracial Commonwealth, Chapman & Hall (London), 1964.

Economic Co-operation in the Commonwealth, Pergamon (Oxford, England), 1967.

Kenyatta and the Politics of Kenya, Dent (London), 1974.

The Last Bunker, Quartet (London), 1976.

(With Ruth Weiss) *Strategic Highways of Africa,* Friedman, 1977.

Modern Nigeria, Longman (London), 1977.

Britain's Oil, Hamish Hamilton (London), 1978.

Aid in Africa, Kogan Page (London), 1979.

Held Fast for England, Hamish Hamilton, 1980.

The Unions, Hamish Hamilton, 1981.

Modern Kenya, Longman, 1981.

Aid and the Third World, Robert Royce (London), 1985.

Third World Handbook, Cassell (London), 1989.

The Black Forest to the Black Sea (travel), Cassell, 1989.

Britain since 1945, Cassell, 1989.

Journey 'Round Turkey (travel), Cassell, 1989.

Wars in the Third World since 1945, Cassell, 1991.

South Africa: Crossing the Rubicon, Macmillan (London), 1992.

Brain Wash: The Cover-up Society, Virgin (London), 1992.

The End of the Third World, Macmillan, 1993.

Political and Economic Encyclopaedia of Africa, Longman, 1993.

Historical Dictionary of Aid and Development Organizations, Scarecrow Press (Folkestone, Kent, England), 1996.

Contributor to journals.

WORK IN PROGRESS: The Maverick State; Resources of the Third World; The United Nations: World Government by Stealth.

SIDELIGHTS: Guy Arnold led a scientific expedition to the interior of Borneo, 1955-56, collected folklore in Guiana among the Wapisiana Indiana, and assisted in the establishment of the Canadian University Service Overseas.

*   *   *

ASHER, Sandra Fenichel 1942-
(Sandy Asher)

PERSONAL: Born October 16, 1942, in Philadelphia, PA; daughter of Benjamin (a physician) and Fanny (Weiner) Fenichel; married Harvey Asher (a professor), January 31, 1965; children: Benjamin, Emily. *Education:*Attended University of Pennsylvania, 1960-62; Indiana University, B.A., 1964; graduate study in child development at University of Connecticut, 1973; Drury College, elementary education certificate, 1974. *Religion:* Jewish.

ADDRESSES: Home—721 South Weller Ave., Springfield, MO 65802. *Office*—Department of Literature, Drury College, 900 North Benston, Springfield, MO 65802. *Agent*—Harold Ober Associates, Inc., 425 Madison Ave., New York, NY 10017.

CAREER: WFIU-Radio, Bloomington, IN, scriptwriter, 1963-64; Ball Associates (advertising agency), Philadelphia, PA, copywriter, 1964; *Spectator,* Bloomington, drama critic, 1966-67; Drury College, Springfield, MO, instructor in creative writing, 1978-85, writer in residence, 1985—. Instructor in creative writing for children's summer programs, Summerscape, 1981-82, and Artworks, 1982; instructor, Institute of Children's Literature, 1986—. Guest Speaker at conferences, workshops, and schools.

MEMBER: International Association of Theatre for Children and Young People (member of board of directors, 1989—), Dramatists Guild, Authors League of America, National Council of Teachers of English Assembly on Literature for Adolescents, Society of Children's Book Writers and Illustrators (Missouri advisor, 1986-89; member of board of directors, 1989—), Children's Reading Round Table of Chicago, Phi Beta Kappa.

AWARDS, HONORS: Honorable mention from *Envoi* magazine, 1970, for poem, "Emancipation"; award of excellence from Festival of Missouri Women in the Arts, 1974, for *Come Join the Circus;* honorable mention, Unitarian Universalist Religious Arts Guild, 1975, for play *Afterthoughts in Eden;* poetry award from *Bitterroot* magazine, 1975; creative writing fellowship in playwriting from National Endowment for the Arts, 1978, for *God and a Woman;* first prize in one-act play contest from Little Theatre of Alexandria, 1983, and Street Players Theatre, 1989, for *The Grand Canyon;* first prize from Children's Musical Theater of Mobile contest and Dubuque Fine Arts Players contest, both 1984, for *East of the Sun/West of the Moon;* Mark Twain Award nomination, 1984, for *Just Like Jenny;* University of Iowa Outstanding Books for Young Adults Award and Child Study Association Best Books Award, both 1985, for *Missing Pieces; Little Old Ladies in Tennis Shoes* was named best new play of the season by the Maxwell Anderson Playwriting Series, 1985-86, and was a finalist for the 1988 Ellis Memorial Award, Theatre Americana.

God and a Woman won the Center Stage New Horizons contest, 1986, Mercyhurst College National Playwrights Showcase, 1986-87, and the Unpublished Play Project of the American Alliance for Theatre in Education, 1987-88; *Things Are Seldom What They Seem* was nominated for Iowa Teen Award and Young Hoosier Award, both 1986-87; Children's Theatre Indianapolis Children's Theatre Symposium playwriting awards, from Indiana University/Purdue University, 1987, for *Prince Alexis and the Silver Saucer,* and 1989, for *A Woman Called Truth;* Joseph Campbell Memorial Fund Award from the Open Eye, 1991-92, for *A Woman Called Truth; Dancing with Strangers* won playwriting contests sponsored by TADA!, 1991, and Choate Rosemary Hall, 1993; New Play Festival Award from the Actors' Guild of Lexington, Inc., 1992, for *Sunday, Sunday; Once, in the Time of Trolls* won a playwriting contest sponsored by East Central College in Union, MO, 1993; *A Woman Called Truth*

was voted an Outstanding Play for Young Audiences by the U.S. Center of the International Association of Theatres for Children and Young People, 1993; *Just Like Jenny, Things Are Seldom What They Seem,* and *Everything Is Not Enough* were all Junior Library Guild selections.

WRITINGS:

PLAYS

(Under name Sandy Asher) *Come Join the Circus* (one-act), first produced in Springfield, MO, at Springfield Little Theatre, December, 1973.

(Under name Sandy Asher) *Afterthoughts in Eden* (one-act), first produced in Los Angeles, CA, at Los Angeles Feminist Theatre, February, 1975.

A Song of Sixpence (one-act), Encore Performance Publishing, 1976.

The Ballad of Two Who Flew (one-act), published in *Plays,* March, 1976.

(Under name Sandy Asher) *How I Nearly Changed the World, but Didn't* (one-act), first produced in Springfield, at National Organization for Women Herstory Women's Fair, November, 1977.

Witling and the Stone Princess, published in *Plays,* 1979.

(Under name Sandy Asher) *Food Is Love* (one-act), first produced in Springfield at Drury College, January, 1979.

(Under name Sandy Asher) *The Insulting Princess* (one-act; first produced in Interlochen, MI, at Interlochen Arts Academy, May, 1979), Encore Performance Publishing (Orem, UT), 1988.

The Mermaid's Tale (one-act; first produced in Interlochen at Interlochen Arts Academy, May, 1979), Encore Performance Publishing (Vacaville, CA), 1988.

Dover's Domain, Pioneer Drama Service (Denver, CO), 1980.

The Golden Cow of Chelm (one-act; first produced in Springfield at United Hebrew Congregation, December, 1980), published in *Plays,* 1980.

(Under name Sandy Asher) *Sunday, Sunday* (two-act), first produced in Lafayette, IN, at Purdue University, March, 1981.

(Under name Sandy Asher) *The Grand Canyon* (one-act), first produced in the Little Theatre of Alexandria, Virginia, 1983.

(Under name Sandy Asher) *Little Old Ladies in Tennis Shoes* (two-act; first produced in Philadelphia, PA, at the Society Hill Playhouse, 1985), Dramatic Publishing Co. (Woodstock, IL), 1989.

East of the Sun/West of the Moon (one-act), first produced in the Children's Musical Theatre of Mobile, AL, 1985.

(Under name Sandy Asher) *God and a Woman* (two-act), first produced in Erie, PA, at the National Playwrights Showcase, 1987, produced in a one-act version entitled *A Woman Called Truth* (first produced in Houston, TX, at the Main Street Theatre, 1989), Dramatic Publishing Co., 1989.

Prince Alexis and the Silver Saucer (one-act), first produced in Springfield at Drury College, 1987.

The Wise Men of Chelm (one-act; first produced in Louisville, KY, at the Jewish Community Center, 1991), Dramatic Publishing Co., 1992.

All on a Saturday Morning (one-act), first produced in Columbia, MO, 1992.

Blind Dating (one-act), first produced in New York City at TADA!, 1992.

Perfect (one-act), first produced in New York City at The Open Eye: New Stagings for Youth, 1992.

Where Do You Get Your Ideas? (adapted for the stage from the author's book of the same title), first produced in New York City at The Open Eye: New Stagings for Youth, 1992.

Dancing with Strangers (three one-acts), first produced in Wallingford, CT, 1993.

Also author of the play, *Once, in the Time of Trolls.* Contributor of plays to anthologies, including *Center Stage,* Harper (New York City), 1990.

NONFICTION

The Great American Peanut Book, illustrated by Jo Anne Metsch Bonnell, Tempo, 1977.

Where Do You Get Your Ideas?: Helping Young Writers Begin, illustrated by Susan Hellard, Walker & Co. (New York City), 1989.

Wild Words!: How to Train Them to Tell Stories, illustrated by Dennis Kendrick, Walker & Co., 1989.

UNDER NAME SANDY ASHER; JUVENILE NOVELS

Summer Begins, Elsevier-Nelson (New York City), 1980, published as *Summer Smith Begins,* Bantam (New York City), 1986.

Daughters of the Law, Beaufort Books (New York City), 1980, published in England as *Friends and Sisters,* Gollancz (London), 1982.

Just Like Jenny, Delacorte (New York City), 1982.

Things Are Seldom What They Seem, Delacorte, 1983.

Missing Pieces, Delacorte, 1984.

Everything Is Not Enough, Delacorte, 1987.

Out of Here: A Senior Class Yearbook (short story collection), Dutton/Lodestar (New York City), 1993.

UNDER NAME SANDY ASHER; FOR CHILDREN

Teddy Teabury's Fabulous Fact, Dell (New York City), 1985.

Teddy Teabury's Peanutty Problems, Dell, 1987.

Princess Bee and the Royal Good-night Story (picture book), illustrated by Cat Bowman Smith, A. Whitman (St. Niles, IL), 1990.

UNDER NAME SANDY ASHER; "BALLET ONE" SERIES; FOR CHILDREN

Best Friends Get Better, Scholastic (New York City), 1989.

Mary-in-the-Middle, Scholastic, 1990.

Pat's Promise, Scholastic, 1990.

Can David Do It?, Scholastic, 1991.

OTHER

Contributor of stories and articles to periodicals, including *Highlights for Children, Humpty Dumpty's Magazine, Parents Magazine, ALAN Review, Journal of Reading, Spark!, Theater for Young Audiences Today,* and *Writer's Digest.*

SIDELIGHTS: Sandra Fenichel Asher, known primarily for her young adult novels under the name Sandy Asher, feels keenly responsible for what she says and how she says it, and these "dual concerns . . . are clearly manifested" in her work, to quote Judith S. Baughman in the *Dictionary of Literary Biography Yearbook: 1983.* Baughman emphasizes that Asher's books "treat serious problems facing most teenagers—strains in parent-child or sibling relationships; confusions about sexuality; uncertainties about one's own place in the home, the school, or the community at large; emerging perceptions of change and loss." In general, Baughman commends Asher for the "creation of fully realized characters confronting believable and compelling problems," adding that the author "proves that young adult fiction can achieve the same high standards as the best of adult literature."

Asher is known for her realistic novels featuring teens overcoming the ordinary—though often traumatic—problems of growing up. Her characters, as she once described them, are typically "nice kids" who behave well in school and at home but who nevertheless must confront such issues as grief, loneliness, fear, anger, frustration, and the dawning of romantic love. She gleans most of her material from events she experienced and people she knew in her own childhood.

Asher bases many of her fictional characters on people she has known in real life. In her first young adult novel, *Summer Begins,* Summer Smith's school principal, Dr. Kyle, is based on the stern man who held that job in Asher's own elementary school for a time, and the author combined three of her favorite junior and senior high school teachers into Summer's English teacher, Mrs. Morton. The central conflict of the book, as well as in several books that followed, is also grounded in Asher's own personal feelings in trying to become an individual, independent of her parents.

The relationship between mothers and daughters is a special part of the theme of children becoming individuals. It is an important feature in *Summer Begins,* as well as *Daughters of the Law* and *Missing Pieces.* As Asher states in *Something about the Author Autobiography Series* (*SAAS*), however, these "mother/daughter relationships [are] not really like my mother's and mine, but [are] related to our struggle to understand one another, a struggle that ended too soon when she died." Asher actually began writing *Daughters of the Law* years before *Summer Begins,* though it was published a few months later.

Daughters of the Law tackles another personal issue for Asher who is Jewish: the Holocaust and its continuing effects on Jewish families even decades after the end of World War II. The story is set during the early 1970s when Ruthie Morgenthau is trying to come to terms with the horrors her mother Hannah endured in Europe at the hands of the Nazis. Unable to communicate with her mother, who is also mourning the recent death of Ruthie's father, Ruthie finds some escape by making drawings and in her friendship with Denise Riley, an idealistic girl who likes to crusade for just causes. Through Denise, Ruthie learns that the world is not all misery, and Denise discovers that the world is not as simple as she'd like it to be.

Asher's background in dancing served her well in *Just Like Jenny,* in which thirteen-year-old Stephanie Nordland envies Jenny Gianino's dancing ability. Still drawing on people she once knew, Asher turned her second-grade teacher Mrs. Lomozoff into Stephanie and Jenny's dynamic music teacher Mrs.

Deveraux, and the author also transferred her desire to become a professional dancer into her young characters in this story. In her *SAAS* essay, Asher says she gave Jenny and Stephanie the dancing abilities she felt she did not possess herself, "so they could live out that dream for me." The story centers on Stephanie's difficulty in believing in herself and her feeling that her friend is a better dancer. "The remainder of [the] novel," explains Baughman, "dramatizes the young protagonist's confused efforts to define more clearly both the nature of her friendship with Jenny and her own identity and goals."

Things Are Seldom What They Seem touches upon a more delicate issue: sexual abuse. Asher admits she based the story upon a teacher she had in the fourth grade. "I don't remember the music teacher's name. I know he was energetic and funny and we liked him. Except that he hugged and tickled us too much, and we didn't care for that. One day he just wasn't there anymore, and nobody would tell us why," she recalls in *SAAS*. Asher later realized that the teacher had been discovered to be a child molester and lost his job. She felt it was important to write a story about this. *Things Are Seldom What They Seem* is a warning to young people, and it also points out that molesters are not so easy to identify. "They aren't aliens," Asher observes. "They're human beings, just like the rest of us."

Even though Asher's novel concentrates on the reactions and emotions the young characters feel about their drama teacher, rather than trying to sensationalize the problem, parents and teachers censored *Things Are Seldom What They Seem.* It was taken off library shelves around the country. In her *SAAS* essay, Asher doubts that such actions serve to protect children: "I suppose those adults think the world is a safer place for their children without my book and others like it. They're in for some cruel surprises. Unfortunately, so are their kids."

Although Asher has some personal experience with the topic addressed in *Things Are Seldom What They Seem,* a much closer subject to her heart is the loss of a family member, which is the theme of *Missing Pieces.* When she was in her twenties, she endured the loss of both of her parents, her grandmother, and her grandfather in the space of only a few years. "*Missing Pieces,*" she reveals in *SAAS*, ". . . deals with my feelings after my father's death." The novel is about a high school student named Heather Connelly and the enormous losses she suffers during one horrible year. Similarly, the semi-autobiographical setting for *Everything Is Not Enough* comes from Asher's yearly summer trips to Atlantic City, where she used to love going to the beach and strolling along the boardwalk. She turned this place into Braden's Port for her sixth young adult novel.

After *Everything Is Not Enough,* Asher moved away from young adult novels and concentrated more on stories for younger children, as well as continuing to write plays. Her most notable play of this period is probably *God and a Woman,* which she later retitled *A Woman Called Truth,* her award-winning drama about Sojourner Truth. Asher also worked on the "Ballet One" series, which draws from her childhood experiences in dance class, and two humorous books for grade school children featuring her character Teddy Teabury.

It was not until 1993 that Asher returned to fiction for teenagers, publishing the short story collection, *Out of Here: A Senior Class Yearbook.* Though it is not a novel, the nine stories in this book have a unifying theme. As Asher explains in *SAAS, Out of Here* reflects the problems she had trying to fit in at Leeds Junior High and Germantown High in Philadelphia. Admitting that she never figured out most of the unwritten social rules the popular girls followed in school, she writes: "I've tried to write about that confusion in . . . *Out of Here."* Set in a 1990s high school, each story in *Out of Here* centers on different senior class students who must face a particular coming-of-age problem. Calling the collection "an accurate portrayal of high school," a *School Library Journal* contributor says that young adults "will recognize themselves and their classmates in these teenagers."

Asher considers her role as a writer of fiction for young people a responsibility not to be taken lightly. In a speech quoted by Baughman, Asher declares: "The biggest difference, it seems to me, between writing for adults and writing for young teenagers is that when you write for young teenagers, there's a very good chance some of your readers will take you seriously." Drawing upon her own experiences, Asher has become the writer she always wanted to be. "Slowly but surely," she concludes in *SAAS,* "I've repaired broken bridges to my past and laid old sorrows to rest. I hope I also show readers that this does happen."

Asher told *CA:* "I credit my teachers, from elementary school through college and beyond, with instilling in me the confidence needed to write. I write for young people because I know the characters in books are often the only trustworthy friends they have. Peter Pan, Jo March, and the Scarecrow of Oz stuck with me through some hard times."

BIOGRAPHICAL/CRITICAL SOURCES:

BOOKS

Dictionary of Literary Biography Yearbook: 1983, Gale (Detroit), 1984.
Something about the Author Autobiography Series, Volume 13, Gale, 1992.

PERIODICALS

Booklist, September 15, 1987, p. 140; November, 1989, p. 42; June 1, 1993, p. 1806.
Bulletin of the Center for Children's Books, December, 1987, p. 61.
Horn Book Guide, July, 1989, pp. 95, 144; spring, 1994, p. 85.
Junior Bookshelf, December, 1988, p. 312.
Kirkus Reviews, June 15, 1987, p. 921; December 15, 1989, p. 1832; July 1, 1993, p. 856.
Publishers Weekly, February 13, 1987, p. 94; June 14, 1993, p. 72.
School Library Journal, August, 1987, p. 88; September, 1987, p. 184; December, 1989, p. 98; January, 1990, p. 110; March, 1990, p. 184; July, 1993, p. 98.
Voice of Youth Advocates, June, 1987, p. 74; February, 1990, p. 350; December, 1993, p. 286.

*   *   *

ASHER, Sandy
   See ASHER, Sandra Fenichel

*   *   *

ASTIN, Alexander W(illiam)   1932-

PERSONAL: Born May 30, 1932, in Washington, DC; son of Allen Varley (director of National Bureau of Standards) and Margaret L. (Mackenzie) Astin; married Helen Stavridou (a professor of education), February 11, 1956; children: John Alexander, Paul Allen. *Education:* Gettysburg College, A.B. (music),

1953; University of Maryland, M.A., 1954, Ph.D., 1957. *Politics:* Independent. *Religion:* None.

ADDRESSES: Home—2681 Cordelia Rd., Los Angeles, CA 90049. *Office*—Department of Education, 3005 Moore Hall, University of California, 405 Hilgard Ave., Los Angeles, CA 90024.

CAREER: U.S. Veterans Administration, Washington, DC, counseling psychologist in Perry Point, MD, 1954-57, assistant chief of psychology research unit at Veterans Administration Hospital in Baltimore, MD, 1959-60; National Merit Scholarship Corp., Evanston, IL, 1960-65, began as research associate, became director of research; American Council on Education, Washington, DC, director of research, 1965-73; University of California, Los Angeles, professor of education, 1973-94, Allan M. Cartter professor of higher education, 1994—; Higher Education Research Institute, Los Angeles, president, 1974-83, director, 1983—. Trustee, Gettysburg College, 1983-86, Eckerd College, 1986—, St. Xavier College, Chicago, and Marjorie Webster Junior College, Washington, DC. Consultant to U.S. Surgeon General's Advisory Committee on Smoking and Health. *Military service:* U.S. Public Health Service, 1957-59; served as department chief of psychology research, USPHS Hospital in Lexington, KY; became lieutenant commander.

MEMBER: American Association for the Advancement of Science (fellow), American Association for Higher Education (director), American College Personnel Association (senior scholar), American Educational Research Association, American Personnel and Guidance Association, American Psychological Association (fellow), Center for Advanced Study of Behavioral Science (fellow), Psychometric Society, Phi Sigma Kappa.

AWARDS, HONORS: Award for outstanding research, American Personnel and Guidance Association, 1965, for studies of college characteristics and college effects; Institute for Advanced Study in the Behavioral Sciences fellow, 1967-68; award for distinguished contribution to research and literature, National Association of Student Personnel Administrators, 1976; Outstanding Contribution to Knowledge Award, American College Personnel Association, 1978; E. F. Lindquist Award, American Educational Research Association/American College Testing Program, 1983, for outstanding research

dealing with college student growth and development; Distinguished Alumnus, Phi Sigma Kappa Fraternity, 1984; "Most admired for creative, insightful thinking," *Change* magazine poll, 1985; Excellence in Education Award, National Association of College Admissions Counselors, 1985; Outstanding Service award, Council of Independent Colleges, 1986; Outstanding Research award, Association for the Study of Higher Education, 1987; honoree, Roll of Service, National Association of Student Financial Aid Administrators, 1991; Career Research Award, California Association for Institutional Research, 1992; Extended Research Award, American Association for Counseling and Development, 1992; Sidney Suslow Award, Association for Institutional Research, 1992; recipient of ten honorary degrees from various universities.

WRITINGS:

Who Goes Where to College?, Science Research Associates (Palo Alto, CA), 1965.

The College Environment, American Council on Education (Washington, DC), 1968.

(With Robert J. Panos) *The Educational and Vocational Development of College Students,* American Council on Education, 1969.

Predicting Academic Performance in College, Free Press (New York City), 1971.

(With C. B. T. Lee) *The Invisible Colleges,* McGraw (New York City), 1972.

(With wife, Helen S. Astin) *Open Admissions at City University of New York,* Prentice-Hall (Englewood Cliffs, NJ), 1974.

Preventing Students from Dropping Out: A Longitudinal, Multi-Institutional Study of College Dropouts, Jossey-Bass (San Francisco, CA), 1975.

(With others) *The Power of Protest: A National Study of Student and Faculty Disruptions with Implications for the Future,* Jossey-Bass, 1975.

Academic Gamesmanship: Student-Oriented Change in Higher Education, Praeger (New York City), 1976.

Four Critical Years: Effects of College on Beliefs, Attitudes, and Knowledge, Jossey-Bass, 1977.

Maximizing Leadership Effectiveness, Jossey-Bass, 1981.

Minorities in American Higher Education: Recent Trends, Current Prospects, and Recommendations, Jossey-Bass, 1982.

Achieving Educational Excellence: A Critical Assessment of Priorities and Practices in Higher Education, Jossey-Bass, 1985.

Assessment for Excellence: The Philosophy and Practice of Assessment and Evaluation in Higher Education, Oryx/Macmillan (New York City), 1991.

What Matters in College? Four Critical Years Revisited, Jossey-Bass, 1993.

Contributor of over 200 articles to more than forty professional journals.

*   *   *

ATKINS, Russell   1926-

PERSONAL: Born February 25, 1926, in Cleveland, OH; son of Perry Kelly and Mamie Atkins. *Education:* Attended Cleveland School of Art (now Cleveland Institute of Art), 1943-44, and Cleveland Institute of Music, 1944-45; private music study, 1950-54. *Politics:* "Nothing particular." *Religion:* None.

ADDRESSES: Home—6005 Grand Ave., Cleveland, OH 44104.

CAREER: Editor, writer and composer; cofounder and editor of *Free Lance* magazine, 1950-1979. Publicity manager and assistant to director, Sutphen School of Music (of National Guild of Community Music Schools), Cleveland, OH, 1957-60; lecturer, Poets and Lecturers Alliance, 1963-65; writing instructor, Karamu House, 1972-86; writer in residence, Cuyahoga Community College, summer, 1973; instructor, Ohio Program in the Humanities, 1978. Affiliated with Iowa Workshop, University of Iowa, 1953-54. Member, Artists-in-Schools Program of Ohio Arts Council and National Endowment for the Arts, 1973—. Participant, Bread Loaf Writers' Conference, 1956; member of literary advisory panel, Ohio Arts Council, 1973-76; member, Cleveland State University Poetry Forum; member, Coordinating Council of Literary Magazines of National Endowment for the Arts. Consultant to WVIZ-TV, 1969-72, Karamu Writers Conference, 1971, and to Cleveland Board of Education, 1972-73.

MEMBER: Committee of Small Magazine Editors and Publishers, Poets League of Greater Cleveland (member of board of trustees).

AWARDS, HONORS: Honorary Ph.D., Cleveland State University, 1976; individual artist grant, Ohio Arts Council, 1978.

WRITINGS:

POETRY

A Podium Presentation, Poetry Seminar Press, 1960.
Phenomena, Free Lance Poets and Prose Workshop, Wilberforce University, 1961.
Objects, Hearse Press, 1963.
Objects 2, Renegade Press, 1963.
Heretofore, Paul Breman (London), 1968.
Presentations, Podium Press, 1969.
Sounds and Silences: Poetry for Now, edited by Richard E. Peck, Delacorte (New York City), 1969.
Here in The, Cleveland State University Poetry Center (Cleveland, OH), 1976.
Celebrations, edited by Arnold Adoff, Follett, 1977.
Whichever, Free Lance Press, 1978.
Juxtapositions: A Manifesto, privately printed, 1991.

MUSICAL COMPOSITIONS

(With Langston Hughes and Hale Smith) *Elegy* (poetry set to music), Highgate Press, 1968.
Objects (for piano), Free Lance Press, 1969.

Also composer of unpublished musical works.

OTHER

Psychovisual Perspective for 'Musical' Composition (chapbook; musical theory), Free Lance Press, 1958.
Two by Atkins: The Abortionist and The Corpse: Two Poetic Dramas to Be Set to Music, Free Lance Press, 1963.
The Nail, to Be Set to Music (poetic libretto), Free Lance Press, 1970.
Maleficium (short stories), Free Lance Press, 1971.
Poetry: An Introduction through Writing, edited by Lewis Turco, Reston Prentice-Hall (Reston, VA), 1972.
"By Yearning and by Beautiful" (poem set to music by Hale Smith), first performed at Lincoln Center for the Performing Arts, New York City, 1986.
Letters to America, edited by Jim Daniels, Wayne State University Press (Detroit), 1995.

Contributor to anthologies, including *Silver Cesspool,* edited by Adelaide Simon, Renegade Press, 1964; *Penguin Book of Verse,* edited by Willemien Vroom, Penguin (England), 1973; *Poems, 1978-1983,* edited by Robert Fox, Ohio Arts Council,

1983; *80 on the 80s: A Decade's History in Verse,* edited by Robert McGovern and Joan Baranow, Ashland Poetry Press (Ashland, OH), 1990; *An Ear to the Ground: An Anthology of Contemporary American Poetry,* edited by Marie Harris and Kathleen Aguero, University of Georgia Press (Athens), 1991; *Beyond the Reef* (children's reader), Houghton (Boston), 1991; *Anthology of Western Reserve Literature,* edited by David R. Anderson and Gladys Haddad, Kent State University Press (Kent, OH), 1992; *Scarecrow Poetry: The Muse in Post-Middle Age,* edited by Robert McGovern and Stephen Haven, Ashland Poetry Press, 1994.

Contributor of poems and articles to *New York Times Book Review, Beloit Poetry Journal, Western Review, Minnesota Quarterly, Hearse, Poetry Now, The Gamut,* and numerous other journals.

WORK IN PROGRESS: Revising and adding to "Spyrytuals," for piano; a volume of poetry delineating stylistic development in technique as "meaning."

SIDELIGHTS: Russell Atkins' writing, says Ronald Henry High in the *Dictionary of Literary Biography,* distinguishes him as "one of the leading experimental figures of the past three decades." His works in music and poetic drama, according to High, place him firmly in the avant-garde. An early exponent of concrete poetry—in which the arrangement or design of the words takes precedence over the words themselves—Atkins' "starkly dramatic handling of such subjects in poetry as dope addiction, sexual aberration, necrophilia, and abortion went beyond the academic reserve of the early 1950s," High continues. His theory of psychovisualism, the critic states, is based on Gestalt hypotheses which study the formation of patterns, and "explains how we perceive the nonverbal 'high and low' in music," by recognizing the function of the brain in understanding music.

Atkins's education in the arts—from his parents' and teachers' encouragement in music, painting, drawing, poetry, and play writing in elementary school through his own extracurricular study of literary classics and poetry in high school—led to the publication of his early work in the late 1940s and early 1950s in journals including *Experiment, View,* and the *Beloit Poetry Journal.* At age twenty-six he co-founded *Free Lance,* which High describes as "probably the oldest black-owned literary magazine, although white writers were included in its pages." Contributors included Langston Hughes, Rose Greene, Beatrice Augustus, Helen Collins, and Vera

Steckler, and the journal found audiences in the United States, England, Scotland, Ireland, France, Denmark, Sweden, and Australia. High notes that *Free Lance* "was established as Cleveland's avant-garde periodical" and was "significant in that it played a major part in the development of ideas and techniques of the New American poetry."

Atkins published two plays in 1963: *The Abortionist* and *The Corpse. The Abortionist* concerns a doctor who seeks revenge against a colleague by performing a violent abortion on the colleague's daughter; in *The Corpse* a widow visits her husband's tomb each year to watch his body decay. High comments: "Until the 'theatre of the absurd,' which was imported from Europe, established itself in the 1960s, Atkins' little poem-plays were avant-garde and unique on the American scene. A nude woman being given an abortion on the stage was not commonplace in the 1950s; neither was a widow kneeling in a mausoleum fondling her husband's bones and skull ordinary American playfare."

Atkins' poetry collection *Phenomena* was published in 1961. "The works had all been written in the middle '50s," Atkins wrote in an essay for *Contemporary Authors Autobiography Series* (*CAAS*). "When the book was published. . ., it went (as expected) unnoticed by the establishment." "*Phenomena* and especially [the poem] 'Of Angela' struck some readers as 'explicitly crude,'" High observes. "The entire book has an unsettling mood which overtakes the reader, even when the meaning escapes one. Strangely enough, the book was a remarkable forecast of the 1960s' themes: nudity, four-letter words, police brutality, and sexual aberration."

Atkins published several more collections of poetry in the 1960s, and began the next decade with *The Nail* and *Maleficium,* both published in *Free Lance* in 1970 and 1971 respectively. *The Nail,* a poetic libretto adapted from the short story by Pedro Antonio de Alarcon, tells of a judge who is unaware that the fugitive murderess he is hunting is his lover. *Maleficium,* according to High, "is a series of twenty short stories, many of which portray their characters as having an underlying viciousness." An example is "Story No. 2," in which a young man writes to his mother to tell her of his crimes, including murder and rape. Two more poetry collections appeared in the 1970s: *Here in The* in 1976 and *Whichever* in 1978. High comments, "Unfortunately, there has been no critical review of [*Here in The*]; however, the poems are written in a refined, mellower style, yet within the experimental framework which so characteristically flavors Atkins's writing." Of *Whichever,* High observes, "The poems in this volume are on a wide range of subjects . . . but seem to be less complex than poems in previous collections; however, there is no doubt that the works flow from Atkins's pen. There is freshness and excitement in each one of them."

"Unfortunately, there has been little critical comment on Atkins's works, which could be due in part to their daring nature," High concludes. "Also, his works are disparate and perhaps need to be collected in order for readers to recognize him as one of the most innovative forces in poetry of the past thirty years. . . . As more people get familiar with Atkins, his approach to literary expression will be better appreciated and more fully understood. As his work is more performed and more read, as it garners more critical attention and documentation, his genius will come to be recognized in the United States as it is in Europe."

BIOGRAPHICAL/CRITICAL SOURCES:

BOOKS

Breman, Paul, *You Better Believe It,* Penguin, 1973.
Contemporary Authors, Autobiography Series, Volume 16, Gale (Detroit), 1992, pp. 1-19.
Dictionary of Literary Biography, Volume 41: *Afro-American Poets since 1955,* Gale, 1985, pp. 24-32.
Redmond, Eugene B., *Drum Voices,* Doubleday, 1976.
Stuckenschmidt, H. H., *20th Century Music,* McGraw, 1969.

PERIODICALS

Free Lance (special Russell Atkins issue), number 14, 1970-71.*

*   *   *

AXINN, Donald E(verett)   1929-

PERSONAL: Born July 13, 1929, in New York, NY; son of Michael and Ann (Schneider) Axinn; married Joan Fingold; children: four. *Education:* Middlebury College, B.A., 1951; Hofstra University, M.A. (with distinction), 1975.

ADDRESSES: Home—Sands Point, NY. *Office*—Donald E. Axinn Companies, 131 Jericho Turnpike, Jericho, NY 11753.

CAREER: Vice-president of Axinn & Sons Lumber Co., 1951-58; Donald E. Axinn Companies (developers of office and industrial parks), Jericho, NY, founder and chairman, 1958—. Creator of Axinn-Levine Associates, 1959-65; partner of stock investment firm, Alexander Associates, 1960—, and art investment firm, William Pall Associates, 1972-78; director and partner of publishing company, Farrar, Straus & Giroux, 1971—. Hofstra University, associate dean of College of Liberal Arts an Sciences, 1973, 1974, director of Institute of the Arts, 1973, 1974, advisor, Bakers Scholars, Hofstra School of Business, 1975, 1976, advisor of planning and development, Bread Loaf Writers' Conference, 1984-83, and board of trustees, trustee and trustee emeritus, 1970—, secretary, 1973-74, vice-chairman, 1974-75, 1988-89. Chairman of Nassau County Fine Arts Commission, 1970-73; trustee of Waldemar Cancer Research Institute, 1966-68, Pro-Arte Symphony Orchestra, 1967-70, New York Ocean Sciences Laboratories, 1969-71, New York State Nature and Historical Preserve Trust, trustee, 1978-83, and Friends for Long Island's Heritage, 1980-86; director of New York Quarterly Poetry Review Foundation, 1969-76.

Member of advisory board of Outward Bound, Inc., 1974-78; member of Governor's Task Force on Cultural Life and Arts, 1975—; treasurer and member of advisory council, Interfaith Nutrition Network, 1983—; member of Long Island Regional Economic Development Council, 1985-88; North Shore-Cornell University Hospital, member of finance committee and associate trustee, 1985-91, sponsor of Michael M. Axinn Annual Memorial Conferences, 1986-90; Hofstra University, sponsor of annual Axinn Library Lecture, 1990—; Port Washington Public Library Association, trustee, 1990-93; The Nature Conservancy, trustee and vice chairman, 1990—; Taproot, trustee, 1992-94; Marine Sciences Research Center, member of visiting committee, 1992—. *Military service:* U.S. Army Reserve, Strategic Intelligence, 1951-58. Civil Air Patrol, 1953-59; became first lieutenant.

MEMBER: International PEN, Academy of American Poets (director, 1995—), Authors Guild, Long Island Poetry Collective, Poets and Writers (member of board of directors and of executive committee,

1980—), Poetry Society of America (member of board of governors, 1987-95), Poets House, Walt Whitman Birthplace Association, Aircraft Owners and Pilots Association, Antique Airplane Club, Bayport Aerodrome Society, Bonanza Pilots Association, Long Island Early Fliers Club, Super Cub Pilots Association, Middlebury College Alumni Association (vice-president, 1978), Long Island Association, Delta Upsilon, Racquet Club of Old Westbury, Players Club (New York City).

AWARDS, HONORS: Awards for architectural design and community enhancement; Brotherhood Award from National Conference of Christians and Jews, 1977; honor award from Beta Gamma Sigma, 1978; Long Island Humanitarian Award from American Jewish Committee, 1978; Tennessee Williams fellow at Bread Loaf Writer's Conference, 1979; Citizen's Award from Mental Health Association of Nassau County, 1984; Hofstra University, recipient of George M. Estabrook Distinguished Service Award, and Hofstra University Library renamed Joan and Donald E. Axinn Library, both 1987; Interfaith Nutrition Network, humanitarian award, 1989; honorary Doctor of Letters, Middlebury College, 1989; honorary Doctor of Law, Southern Vermont College, 1991; honorary Doctor of Humane Letters, Hofstra University, 1991, and State University of New York, 1996.

WRITINGS:

Sliding Down the Wind (poems), Swallow Press (Athens, OH), 1978.
The Hawk's Dream and Other Poems, Grove (New York City), 1982.
Against Gravity (poems), Grove, 1986.
The Colors of Infinity (poetry), Blue Moon Books (Tucson, AZ), 1990.
Spin (fiction), Station Hill Press (Barrytown, NY), 1991, Arcade/Little, Brown (Boston, MA), 1994.
Dawn Patrol (poetry), Cooperative Editrice Antigruppo Siciliano with Cross-Cultural Communications Station Hill Press, 1992.
The Latest Illusion (poetry), Arcade/Little, Brown, 1995.

Contributor of numerous articles and approximately ninety poems to various magazines, journals and other periodicals, including *Antaeus, Bread Loaf Quarterly, Confrontation, Maine Times, Newsday, New England Review, New York Quarterly, New York Times, Poetry Miscellany, Poetry Now, SunStorm, Trapani Nuovo,* and *Writers' Forum.*

WORK IN PROGRESS: The Ego Makers, a novel.

B

BARKER, A(udrey) L(ilian) 1918-

PERSONAL: Born April 13, 1918, in England; daughter of Harry (an engineer) and Elsie A. (Dutton) Barker. *Education:* Attended county secondary schools in England.

ADDRESSES: Home—103 Harrow Rd., Carshalton, Surrey SM5 3QF, England.

CAREER: British Broadcasting Corp. (BBC), London, secretary and sub-editor, 1949-78; freelance writer. Member of panel of judges, Katherine Mansfield Prize, 1984, Macmillan Silver Pen Award, 1986, and Arts Council Bursaries, 1989.

MEMBER: Royal Society of Literature (fellow), English PEN (member of executive committee, 1981-85).

AWARDS, HONORS: Atlantic Award in Literature, 1946; Somerset Maugham Award, 1947, for *Innocents: Variations on a Theme;* Cheltenham Festival Literary Award, 1962; South East Arts Creative Book Award, 1981; Macmillan Silver Pen Award, 1988; Society of Authors Traveling Scholarship, 1988.

WRITINGS:

Innocents: Variations on a Theme (short stories), Hogarth Press (Honolulu, HI), 1947, Scribner (New York City), 1948.
Apology for a Hero, Scribner, 1950.
Novelette, with Other Stories, Scribner, 1951.
"Pringle" (television script), broadcast on BBC-TV, 1958.
The Joy-Ride and After, Hogarth Press, 1963.

Lost upon the Roundabouts (short stories), Hogarth Press, 1964.
A Case Examined (novel; also see below), Hogarth Press, 1965.
The Middling: Chapters in the Life of Ellie Toms, Hogarth Press, 1967.
John Brown's Body (also see below), Hogarth Press, 1969.
Femina Real (short stories), Hogarth Press, 1971.
A Source of Embarrassment (novel), Hogarth Press, 1974.
A Heavy Feather (novel), Hogarth Press, 1978.
Life Stories (autobiography and fiction), Hogarth Press, 1981.
Relative Successes (novel), Hogarth Press, 1984.
No Word of Love (short stories), Hogarth Press, 1985.
The Gooseboy (novel; also see below), Hutchinson (London), 1987.
The Woman Who Talked to Herself (novel), Hutchinson, 1989.
(Author of introduction) Elizabeth Taylor, *Hester Lilly,* Virago, 1990.
Element of Doubt (ghost stories), Vintage (New York City), 1992.
A. L. Barker Omnibus (contains *John Brown's Body, A Case Examined,* and *The Gooseboy*), Vintage, 1992.
Zeph (novel), Hutchinson, 1992.

Also author of *The Haunt,* 1995. Contributor to *Wave Me Goodbye: Stories of World War II,* edited by Anne Boston, Virago (New York City), 1988, *Dark Fantasies,* edited by Chris Morgan, Hutchinson, 1989. Also contributor of short stories to various publications in England, France, Germany, Holland, South Africa, and the United States.

SIDELIGHTS: A. L. Barker has often been called a "writer's writer"—a title that reflects her ability if not her popularity. Her work tends to be complex, and she concentrates on the short story; even some of her novels take on an episodic form reminiscent of the short story. *The Middling,* for example, is subtitled *Chapters in the Life of Ellie Toms;* a later work, *A Heavy Feather,* "has the sense that what one is reading is not a novel, . . . but rather a collection of short stories," comments Francis King in *Spectator.* In addition, her anthology *Life Stories* "eschew[s] the traditional forms of autobiography," writes *Times Literary Supplement* contributor David Profumo. The critic elaborates, noting that "much of [Barker's] best work has drawn strength from avoiding the artificial neatness that narrative shapelessness imposes on the representation of life." King also sees a distinctive approach in the author's "memoir": "She set about linking together these fables or . . . extended metaphors for her experiences, instead of directly relating the experiences themselves."

Many themes appear throughout Barker's work, including "the isolation of human personality, the impossibility of communication, and the ambivalence of love," lists Kim D. Heine in a *Dictionary of Literary Biography* essay. "Throughout her fiction, Barker explores the world of social and psychological outcasts: the ill, the poor, the lonely." But while her subjects may seem ordinary or common, Barker uses her skill to explore the private nature beyond their surfaces. For example, *John Brown's Body* "carries us characteristically into the private exotic world behind the drab, commonplace exterior," describes a *Times Literary Supplement* reviewer. "Like life itself," writes King of *Relative Successes,* "Miss Barker constantly provides tricks, surprises and sudden, disconcerting illuminations of what previously was dark." Concludes the critic: "The freshness of vision that she brings to the often humiliating circumstances in which her characters entrap themselves is matched by the freshness of her style."

Because of the extreme situations in which her characters exist, King believes that "many of Miss Barker's stories are concerned—as she herself has recognized—with the jarring impact caused by a collision between innocence and experience." But this collision is relieved, notes Heine, by an "ironic detachment [that] renders her work not oppressive but strangely comic. Through caricature and understatement," adds the critic, "Barker infuses her work with humor. She has a penchant for horror and the macabre, which ironically lightens the tone by lifting the weight of unrelieved realism." In her *Spectator* review of *The Gooseboy,* Anita Brookner makes a similar observation: "Not insistent enough to be labelled 'stoical,' [Barker] catches perfectly the downside of events, their very lack of emphasis giving her the tone she needs. She is a quietly excellent and very English writer, who believes in fatalism as others believe in action."

Whatever her theme or subject, Barker is frequently praised for the consistent quality of the several aspects of her writing. In *John Brown's Body,* for instance, a *Times Literary Supplement* critic finds that "without ever sounding pretentiously 'poetic,' Miss Barker succeeds in using startling memorable imagery." Barker also possesses a talent for conciseness that allows her to integrate several elements so that an episode "leaves in the reader's mind an illuminating, utterly recognizable picture of human sadness and absurd resilience," writes Anne Duchene in the *Times Literary Supplement.* Profumo similarly comments on Barker's ability to bring out various images and themes: "Her art is not concerned to juggle histrionically with a plot, to strive for technical developments which cause gasps of astonished admiration, but rather to work quietly and with understatement: she can make loneliness interesting, and invest suburban greyness and domestic trivia with a sense of menace or exoticism—a much more difficult feat." And Philip Howard sees in *The Gooseboy,* "a pleasure in eccentricity, and class and character cattily observed," he notes in the London *Times.* "A. L. Barker has a strong idiosyncrasy, and a sharp eye for detail. She has original and entertaining notions. . . . Dialogue and plot work through indirections and obliquities." As with much of Barker's work, Howard notes that in this novel "you never guess what is going to happen next."

Barker told *CA:* "I am by choice and capacity a short story writer. I believe the short story to be one of the two most challenging literary forms: the other—which I am not qualified to attempt—is poetry. Some poets can create a word-perfect, completely integrated short story in a dozen lines.

"The possibilities for the short story have always been enough to occupy me. It is a lifetime's engagement, and as life time dwindles, tantalisingly the scope increases. Technically a form, it now seems to be blessedly formless. A thousand words, or twenty thousand, in Austen's English, or Joyce's, the moment is all, is what I want to catch, with a turn of phrase, a hint, an implication, a repetition. Ideally, the moment should persist, like a flavour, so that the reader after reading, or days or years later, finds the moment complete, for better for worse, and beyond reproach or censure."

BIOGRAPHICAL/CRITICAL SOURCES:

BOOKS

Barker, A. L., *Life Stories,* Hogarth Press, 1981.
Dictionary of Literary Biography, Volume 14: *British Novelists since 1960,* Gale (Detroit), 1982.

PERIODICALS

New Statesman, July 28, 1978; October 2, 1981; August 10, 1984; May 31, 1985.
New Yorker, February 26, 1979.
Saturday Review, April 28, 1979.
Spectator, July 29, 1978; September 26, 1981; August 4, 1984; October 3, 1987.
Times (London), October 1, 1987.
Times Literary Supplement, November 2, 1967; November 13, 1969; August 27, 1971; March 22, 1974; July 21, 1978; September 25, 1981; August 3, 1984; June 21, 1985; October 30, 1987.

*   *   *

BARRANGER, M(illy) S(later)   1937-

PERSONAL: Born February 12, 1937, in Birmingham, AL; daughter of Clem C. (an engineer) and Mildred (Hilliard) Slater; married Garic Kenneth Barranger (an attorney), August 26, 1961 (divorced 1984); children: Heather D. *Education:* Alabama College (now University of Montevallo), B.A., 1958; Tulane University, M.A., 1959, Ph.D., 1964. *Avocational interests:* Music, films, travel.

ADDRESSES: Home—10 Banbury Lane, Chapel Hill, NC 27514. *Office*—Dramatic Art Department, University of North Carolina, CB #3230, Graham Memorial, Chapel Hill, NC 27599.

CAREER: Louisiana State University in New Orleans (now University of New Orleans), special lecturer in English, 1964-69; Tulane University, New Orleans, LA, assistant professor, 1969-73, associate professor

of theatre and speech, 1973-82, chair of department, 1971-82; Visiting Young Professor of Humanities, University of Tennessee, 1981-82; University of North Carolina at Chapel Hill, professor of dramatic art and chair of department, 1982—. Executive director of Tulane Center Stage Theatre, 1973-78; executive producer of Playmakers Repertory Company, 1982—. Scholar-in-residence, Yale Drama School, 1982. Member of board of trustees, Paul Green Foundation, 1982—.

MEMBER: American Theatre Association (vice president of administration, 1975-77; president, 1978-79), Association for Theatre in Higher Education College of Fellows, National Theatre Conference (president, 1988, 1989), League of Professional Theatre Women (member of New York branch), Southeastern Theatre Conference.

AWARDS, HONORS: New Orleans Bicentennial Award for Achievement in the Arts, 1976; Southwest Theatre Conference Award for Professional Achievement, 1978; President's Award for Outstanding Achievement in the Performing Arts, University of Montevallo, 1979.

WRITINGS:

(Editor with Daniel Dodson) *Generations: A Thematic Introduction to Drama,* Harcourt (New York City), 1971.
(Contributor) *Dictionary of Church History,* Westminster (Louisville, KY), 1971.
Theatre: A Way of Seeing, Wadsworth (Belmont, CA), 1980.
Theatre: Past and Present, Wadsworth, 1984.
(Coeditor) *Notable Women in the American Theatre,* CIS Press, 1989.
Understanding Plays, Allyn & Bacon (Newton, MA), 1989.
Jessica Tandy: A Bio-Bibliography, CIS Press, 1991.
Margaret Webster: A Bio-Bibliography, CIS Press, 1994.

Contributor of articles to books and periodicals, including *College Language Association Journal, Modern Drama, Theatre Journal, Theatre News, Southern Quarterly, Southern Theatre, New Orleans Review, Oxford Guide to Women's Writing in the United States, Text and Performance Quarterly, Dramatics Magazine, Journal of American Theatre and Drama, Tennessee Williams Literary Journal, St. James Guide to Biography,* and *Quarterly Journal of Speech.*

BARRETT, Lois (Yvonne)   1947-

PERSONAL: Born November 9, 1947, in Enid, OK; daughter of H. Preston (a minister) and Audrey (a homemaker; maiden name, Wilson) Barrett; married Thomas B. Mierau (a teacher), June 26, 1977; children: Barbara, Susanna, John. *Education:* University of Oklahoma, B.A. (with highest honors), 1969; Mennonite Biblical Seminary, Elkhart, IN, M.Div., 1983; Union Institute, Cincinnati, Ph.D., 1992. *Avocational interests:* Music (performance and composition).

ADDRESSES: Home—1508 Fairview, Wichita, KS 67203.

CAREER: Wichita Eagle, Wichita, KS, reporter, 1969-70; *Mennonite,* Newton, KS, associate editor, 1971-77; freelance writer, 1977-79; Bethel College, North Newton, KS, instructor in communications, 1979-80; Mennonite Church of the Servant, Wichita, minister, 1983-92; ordained Mennonite minister, 1985; Mennonite Church, General Conference, Commission on Home Ministries, Newton, executive, 1992—. Member of executive council of Institute of Mennonite Studies, 1983—. Member, central planning committee of New Call to Peacemaking, 1977-80, U.S. Peace Section of Mennonite Central Committee, 1980-83, steering committee of Wichita's Churches United for Peacemaking, 1984-92, and Inter-Mennonite Confession of Faith Committee, 1988-95. President of Wichita's Midtown Citizens Association, 1978-79.

AWARDS, HONORS: Award from American Bible Society, 1983.

WRITINGS:

The Vision and the Reality, Faith & Life (Newton, KS), 1983.
Building the House Church, Herald Press (Scottdale, PA), 1986.
The Way God Fights, Herald Press, 1987.
Doing What Is Right, Herald Press, 1989.
(With John Stoner) *Letters to American Christians,* Herald Press, 1989.

Contributor to periodicals, including *Gospel Herald, Builder, Sojourners, Other Side,* and *Friends Journal.*

WORK IN PROGRESS: Research on mission and the nature of the church and on spirituality and ethics.

BIOGRAPHICAL/CRITICAL SOURCES:

BOOKS

Wolseley, Roland E., *Careers in Religious Communications,* Herald Press, 1977.

*   *   *

BASS, Rick   1958-

PERSONAL: Born March 7, 1958, in Fort Worth, TX; son of C. R. (a geologist) and Lucy (a homemaker; maiden name, Robson) Bass. *Education:* Utah State University, B.S., 1979.

ADDRESSES: Home—c/o Fix Ranch, Route 1, Troy, MT 59935. *Agent*—Timothy Schaffner, Schaffner Agency, 264 Fifth St., New York, NY 10001.

CAREER: Writer. Has also worked as a petroleum geologist.

MEMBER: Outdoor Writers of America, Sierra Club.

AWARDS, HONORS: PEN/Nelson Algren Award special citation, 1988, for *The Watch.*

WRITINGS:

The Deer Pasture (natural history essays), Texas A&M University Press (College Station, TX), 1985.
Wild to the Heart (wilderness essays), Stackpole (Harrisburg, PA), 1987.
Oil Notes (essays), Seymour Lawrence (New York City), 1988.
The Watch (stories), Norton (New York City), 1988.
Oil Notes (nonfiction), Houghton (Boston), 1989, reprinted, Southern Methodist University Press (Dallas), 1995.
Winter: Notes from Montana (nonfiction), Houghton, 1991.
The Ninemile Wolves: An Essay, Clark City Press (Livingston, MT), 1992.
Platte River (stories), Houghton, 1994.
In the Loyal Mountains (stories), Houghton, 1995.
The Lost Grizzlies: A Search for Survivors (nonfiction), Houghton, 1995.

Work represented in anthologies, including *Tales from Gray's,* Gray's Sporting Journal Press, *Best*

Stories from the South, 1988, Algonquin Books, *Best American Short Stories,* and *The Pushcart Prize XIII.* Contributor to periodicals, including *Paris Review, Esquire, GQ,* and *Quarterly.*

SIDELIGHTS: Rick Bass writes about the essence of wildness, the vanishing wilderness and its species, and other environmental issues in his fiction and nonfiction collections. A native of Texas who lives on an isolated Montana ranch, Bass has reaped critical praise for works that combine observations of the natural world with personal reflections. "Although Mr. Bass is essentially a romantic, he balances humor against pathos and relieves the lyricism in his prose with an occasional gritty touch," writes Susan Lowell in the *New York Times Book Review.* "When Mr. Bass gets to what he's looking for, he goes past technical excellence to his best work, which is fresh and strange." *Bloomsbury Review* contributor John Murray calls Bass "one of the most gifted young writers to appear in quite a few years," adding that a "truly significant writer is emerging here."

At one time or another, Rick Bass has lived in Texas, Mississippi, Vermont, Utah, Arkansas, and Montana. He was born in south Texas and grew up there, absorbing stories and family lore from his grandfather during deer-hunting trips. These early forays into Texas hill country form the basis of the author's first book, *The Deer Pasture,* published when he was twenty-seven years old. As Murray notes in another *Bloomsbury Review* piece, the many physical relocations Bass has undergone have not changed his essential spirit. "Bass is characteristically southwestern in his independence, his restlessness, his humor, his vitality, his sunny outlook, his distrust of unchallenged authority, and his disdain for affectation and pretense," the critic writes. "All of Rick Bass's subsequent books . . . have steadily built upon the promise of *The Deer Pasture* and have borne witness to the persistent influence of his home region."

Bass received a degree in geology from Utah State University in 1979 and went to work as a petroleum geologist in the South, prospecting for new oil wells. This experience informed one of his best-known nonfiction books, *Oil Notes.* Written in journal form, *Oil Notes* offers meditations on the art and science of finding energy in the ground, as well as reflections on the author's personal life and his outdoor adventures. According to Rhoda Koenig in *New York* magazine, *Oil Notes* is "a portrait of the industry and

the ideal driller" that "gives a picture of Bass as a very gentle, indeed mild-mannered knight, someone whom homeless and repulsive dogs know as a soft touch, and someone who is rather worryingly accident-prone for a man whose occupation is dealing with flammable substances." *Times Literary Supplement* reviewer Ronald Wright observes that in *Oil Notes* Bass "has accomplished the remarkable feat of doing for oil exploration what Isaak Walton did for fishing. With quirky charm and a chunky style, he conveys the fascination of the black, oozy life-essence waiting in the cracks and folds of the earth."

Bass is a passionate environmentalist whose nonfiction in particular celebrates efforts to reclaim a wilder America. Books such as *The Ninemile Wolves* and *The Lost Grizzlies: A Search for Survivors* demonstrate his conviction that America's larger predators should be allowed to survive and thrive. In an essay for *Western American Literature,* Terrell Dixon maintains that Bass is deeply engaged "with the landscapes of the West, the creatures who inhabit, try to inhabit, or once inhabited them, and the need to protect both the animals and the land." The reviewer further notes that with Bass's move to Montana, his nonfiction "began to feature a tough-minded environmentalism that has made his voice one of the most important of those contemporary western writers who work to conserve the land. His recent nonfiction urges us to cherish and protect what remains of our western wilderness landscapes."

Critical praise has also attended the publication of Bass's fiction, much of which is in short story form. In a Chicago *Tribune Books* review of the author's first collection, *The Watch,* Joseph Coates declares that Bass's protagonists "are the last cowboys, Huck Finns who lit out for what's left of the Territory only to find it full of Tom Sawyers selling quiche or playing some other stupid game that mortgages their own freedom and threatens to destroy ours." Perhaps not surprisingly, the masculine sports of hunting, fishing, and drinking are central to many of Bass's stories, but according to Mark Kamine in the *New Leader,* Bass "does not glamorize these American male pastimes, he realizes how easy it is to hide behind them, to use them to avoid confronting the more substantial challenges presented to us in living with ourselves and among others." Dixon feels that Bass's fiction serves as another vehicle to present the author's deepest concerns. "Bass's interest in depicting and protecting the wilderness of the Rocky Mountain West is paralleled by the way his imagination works with places in other parts of the West and South," Dixon writes. "The result is a significant contribution to the growing body of ecofiction."

In an interview with the *Bloomsbury Review*, Bass spoke lovingly of his Montana ranch and suggested he would like to stay there for quite some time. "I'm fond of pretty much every place in the country, but Yaak is the best place for me to live, just to hole up," he noted. "So as long as it stays unspoiled and kind of hidden, I'll stay up here. If it changes, then I'll have to find some other place. That's all there is to it." Bass once told *CA* that a certain amount of isolation is essential to his writing, so his current location is ideal, especially in the wintertime. As John Murray concludes in the *Bloomsbury Review:* "One has the sense . . . that [Bass] means to stay in Montana for good. The place has seeped into his blood, and, despite the bitter-cold temperatures of January and the various perils of living in an isolated mountain valley, Bass seems to be—like so many other major writers of our time who have settled in the northern Rockies—hopelessly in love with the place and willing to accept its challenges in order to savor its beauties."

BIOGRAPHICAL/CRITICAL SOURCES:

BOOKS

Contemporary Literary Criticism, Volume 79, Gale (Detroit), 1993.

PERIODICALS

Bloomsbury Review, April-May, 1991, pp. 9-10, 14.
Los Angeles Times Book Review, March 13, 1994, pp. 3, 11.
New Leader, February 6, 1989, pp. 19-20.
Newsweek, January 9, 1989, p. 57.
New York, July 17, 1989, pp. 49-50.
New York Times, July 24, 1989, p. C16; July 30, 1992, p. C17.
New York Times Book Review, March 5, 1989, p. 11; November 26, 1995, p. 10.
North American Review, September, 1989, pp. 69-72.
Time, July 17, 1989, p. 84.
Times Literary Supplement, November 24, 1989, p. 1297.
Tribune Books (Chicago), December 11, 1988, pp. 1, 12; February 17, 1991, p. 6; March 20, 1994, pp. 3, 11.
Western American Literature, May, 1995, pp. 97-103.

Wilderness, summer, 1991, pp. 34, 36.*

—*Sketch by Anne Janette Johnson*

* * *

BASSETT, Lisa 1958-

PERSONAL: Born January 26, 1958, in Winter Park, FL; daughter of Samuel Taylor III and Barbara (an art teacher; maiden name, Crisler) Bassett; married to J. William Johnston. *Education:* Rollins College, B.A. (with honors), 1984; University of Texas at Austin, M.A., 1986, Ph.D., 1992. *Religion:* Christian.

ADDRESSES: Home—Dallas, TX. *Agent*—Dilys Evans, P.O. Box 400, Norfolk, CT 06058.

CAREER: University of Texas at Austin, assistant instructor in English, 1986-89, Department of Electrical and Computer Engineering, lecturer in technical communications, 1992-95.

MEMBER: Lewis Carroll Society of North America, Modern Language Association of America.

WRITINGS:

JUVENILE

A Clock for Beany (Junior Literary Guild selection), Dodd (New York City), 1985.
Beany and Scamp (Junior Literary Guild selection), Dodd, 1987.
Very Truly Yours, Charles L. Dodgson, Alias Lewis Carroll, Lothrop (New York City), 1987.
Beany Wakes Up for Christmas, G. P. Putnam's Sons (New York City), 1988.
Koala Christmas, E. P. Dutton (New York City), 1991.
The Bunnies' Alphabet Eggs, Outlet Books (New York City), 1993.
Ten Little Bunnies, Outlet Books, 1993.

WORK IN PROGRESS: Research on Shakespeare and Renaissance literature.

SIDELIGHTS: Lisa Bassett told *CA:* "I hope that in writing for children I can create the kind of world I always found in books. As a child I could enter the fantasy world of a book wholeheartedly, particularly the world of magical animals. My children's books are about animals, Beany bear and Scamp squirrel, and they are inspired by the whimsical drawings of my sister, Jeni Bassett. The friendship between Beany and Scamp is beautifully embodied in the warmth and charm of Jeni's illustrations. I write the stories with Jeni's pictures in mind.

"My biography of Lewis Carroll, *Very Truly Yours, Charles L. Dodgson, Alias Lewis Carroll,* is also about friendship. I wanted to introduce children to the Carroll who befriended hundreds of children in his lifetime. I want my readers to meet the man as he revealed himself to the actual children who knew him. Biographies for juvenile readers that are written like novels never appealed to me. I always had the feeling I was reading a fictional account rather than a realistic portrayal of the biographical subject. In my book, I want to let children meet Carroll and form their opinions about the man by reading his own words (in letters to children) and the words of the children who wrote about their relationships with him.

"My interest in Carroll began long ago when I read the Alice books to my sister. She had been ill for quite a while and to entertain her, I read about Alice's adventures. We laughed together, especially over Humpty Dumpty. Later as a college student, I read Carroll's letters and found the same hilarious nonsense in his epistles to children. I also found a man whom I thought children would like to know. I hope young people and adults finish my book about Carroll with a special sense of the man's love of childhood and children."

*   *   *

BATTISCOMBE, E(sther) Georgina (Harwood) 1905-
(Gina Harwood)

PERSONAL: Born November 21, 1905, in London, England; daughter of George (a master cotton spinner, and member of Parliament) and Ellen (Hopkinson) Harwood; married Christopher Francis Battiscombe (a lieutenant colonel, Grenadier Guards), October 1, 1932 (died, 1964); children: Aurea (Mrs. George Lawrence Morshead). *Education:* Lady Margaret Hall, Oxford, B.A. (with honors), 1927. *Religion:* Anglican. *Avocational interests:* "Architecture, in particular Victorian stained glass windows."

ADDRESSES: Home—40 Phyllis Court Dr., Henley-on-Thames, Oxfordshire RG9 2HU, England. *Agent*—A. M. Heath & Co., Ltd., 40-42 William IV St., London WC2N 4DD, England.

CAREER: Writer. County organizer, St. John and Red Cross Hospital libraries, 1948-53.

MEMBER: Royal Society for Literature (fellow), Society of Authors, Cavalry and Guards.

AWARDS, HONORS: James Tait Black Prize for Biography, 1963, for *John Keble: A Study in Limitations.*

WRITINGS:

(Under name Gina Harwood, with A. W. Hopkinson) *The Mantle of Prayer,* Mowbray (London), 1931.

(Under name Gina Harwood) *Haphazard,* Mathews & Marrot (London), 1932.

Charlotte Mary Yonge: The Story of an Uneventful Life, Constable (London), 1943.

Two on Safari, Muller (London), 1946.

English Picnics, Harville (London), 1949.

Mrs. Gladstone: The Portrait of a Marriage, Constable, 1956, Houghton (Boston), 1957.

John Keble: A Study in Limitations, Constable, 1963, Knopf (New York City), 1964.

Christina Rossetti (pamphlet), Longmans, Green for British Council and National Book League (London), 1965.

(Editor, with Marghanita Laski, and contributor) *A Chaplet for Charlotte Yonge,* Cresset (London), 1965.

Queen Alexandra, Houghton, 1969.

Shaftesbury: A Biography of the Seventh Earl, 1801-1885, Constable, 1974, published as *Shaftesbury: The Great Reformer, 1801-1885,* Houghton, 1975.

Reluctant Pioneer: The Life of Elizabeth Wordsworth, Constable, 1978.

Christina Rossetti: A Divided Life, Constable, 1981.

The Spencers of Althorp, Constable, 1984.

(Editor and author of introduction) *Queen Alexandra's Christmas Gift Book,* National Trust (London), 1984.

(Compiler and author of introduction) *Winter Song* (poetry), Constable, 1992.

Contributor of articles and reviews to *Times Literary Supplement, Country Life, Time and Tide, Economist,* and other newspapers.

SIDELIGHTS: In her biographies of nineteenth-century English figures, "Georgina Battiscombe is marvellously immersed in the niceties of Victorian daily life and this gives pleasure in itself," writes Michael Ratcliffe in a London *Times* review. Battiscombe's subjects have included English clergyman and poet John Keble, the British reformer Lord Shaftesbury, Queen Alexandra, and poet Christina Rossetti.

Published in 1943, Battiscombe's first biography, *Charlotte Mary Yonge: The Story of an Uneventful Life,* profiles a Victorian novelist whose stories of England's family life and religion were popular before World War II. "For the modern reader the attractions of Battiscombe's biography lie first in its vivid picture of a style of life that has nothing in common with the present," comments David Hopkinson in the *Dictionary of Literary Biography.* As Hopkinson points out, the important aspects of this biography are its portrayal of Yonge's study with John Keble (a clergyman and poet and one of the founders of the Oxford Movement, which sought to reintroduce some Catholic practices to the Anglican Church) and Yonge's efforts to improve women through education and religion.

Battiscombe examined the life of Keble in her 1963 biography, *John Keble: A Study in Limitations.* The book strives to give an accurate perspective on Keble's popularity as a poet and his influence on English religious life through his involvement in the Oxford Movement. Battiscombe lauds Keble as the initiator and one of the leading figures of this movement, "but she describes his limitations in full detail and shows how they, as much as his flowing virtues, have subsequently affected the nature of Anglicanism," observes Hopkinson. This biography reveals, adds Hopkinson, that "Keble's judgment was fallible, and for all his saintliness and the love and devotion he attracted and inspired, he was without the power to look ahead."

In the biography *Queen Alexandra,* a *Times Literary Supplement* reviewer finds that Battiscombe "has done wonders with her subject." Adds the reviewer, "So much of modern biography rests for its success on revelation . . . that we sometimes forget that there is another path to success: a sympathetic understanding of the human character described. Along that difficult path Mrs. Battiscombe moves in triumph." Hopkinson calls Battiscombe's book *Shaftesbury: A Biography of the Seventh Earl, 1801-1885* "a work of careful scholarship, valuable to the student but

enjoyable to the general reader." She captures a figure who, as a member of Parliament and as a philanthropist, fought to restrict child labor and other excesses of industrialization. "Her virtuosity in achieving command of so recondite a figure makes this perhaps the finest of her biographical works," comments Hopkinson.

Christina Rossetti: A Divided Life is a biography of another woman of letters influenced by John Keble. Christina Rossetti was the sister of the painter and poet Dante Gabriel Rossetti. A poet herself, her work reflects her Italian and English background, her strongly held religious beliefs, and a certain sadness. Michael Ratcliffe observes: "[Battiscombe] brings to her . . . subject gifts of urbanity and commonsense that particularly suit Christina Rossetti's asperity and caustic wit." In the Rossetti biography, writes W. W. Robson in the *Times Literary Supplement,* Battiscombe "sets out the external, historical facts, such as they are, in a sensible and orderly way; and she handles the poetry with perception and tact. This beautifully produced book is a pleasure to read, from the point of view of presentation, and style, and in every other way."

Battiscombe has also written a history of Princess Diana's family, *The Spencers of Althorp,* and edited a collection of poetry about old age, *Winter Song,* which includes the work of William Wordsworth, W. B. Yeats, and T. S. Eliot. "Similar to her creative impulse as a biographer," writes Hopkinson, "the anthology is characterized by the creation of a firm historical background to her subjects' lives and achievements."

BIOGRAPHICAL/CRITICAL SOURCES:

BOOKS

Dictionary of Literary Biography, Volume 155: *Twentieth-Century British Literary Biographers,* Gale (Detroit), 1995.

PERIODICALS

British Book News, November, 1985, p. 642.
New York Times Book Review, November 30, 1969.
Times (London), May 21, 1981.
Times Educational Supplement, November 11, 1988, p. 27.
Times Literary Supplement, September 10, 1969; September 4, 1981.
Washington Post Book World, January 17, 1982.

BEATON, M. C.
  See CHESNEY, Marion

*   *   *

BEATTIE, Ann   1947-

PERSONAL: Born September 8, 1947, in Washington, DC; daughter of James A. and Charlotte (Crosby) Beattie; married David Gates (a psychiatrist), 1972 (divorced, 1980); married Lincoln Perry (an artist). *Education:* American University, B.A., 1969; University of Connecticut, M.A., 1970, further graduate study, 1970-72.

*ADDRESSES: Home—*Charlottesville, VA. *Agent—*Lynn Nesbit, International Creative Management, 40 West 57th St., New York, NY 10019.

CAREER: Writer. University of Virginia, Charlottesville, visiting writer and lecturer, 1975-77, 1980; Harvard University, Cambridge, MA, Briggs-Copeland Lecturer in English, 1977-78; Northwestern University, Evanston, IL, writer in residence at Center for the Writing Arts, 1994.

AWARDS, HONORS: Guggenheim fellowship, 1978.

WRITINGS:

Distortions (short stories), Doubleday (New York City), 1976, reprinted, Vintage Books (New York City), 1991.
Chilly Scenes of Winter (novel), Doubleday, 1976, reprinted, Vintage Books, 1991.
Secrets and Surprises (short stories), Random House (New York City), 1979, reprinted, Vintage Books, 1991.
Falling in Place (novel), Random House, 1980, reprinted, Vintage Books, 1991.
The Burning House (short stories), Random House, 1982.
Love Always (novel), Random House, 1985.
Spectacles, Workman Publishing (New York City), 1985.
Where You'll Find Me, and Other Stories, Linden Press/Simon & Schuster (New York City), 1986.
Alex Katz (art criticism), Abrams (New York City), 1987.
Picturing Will (novel), Random House, 1989.
What Was Mine (short stories), Random House, 1991.

Another You, Knopf (New York City), 1995.

Contributor of numerous short stories to periodicals, including *Esquire, GQ,* and *New Yorker.*

ADAPTATIONS: Beattie's short story "A Vintage Thunderbird" was adapted by Robert Clem into a short film with the same title in 1983.

SIDELIGHTS: Novelist and short story writer Ann Beattie "has become perhaps our most authoritative translator-transcriber of the speech-patterns, nonverbal communications, rituals, and tribal customs of those members (white, largely middle-class) of a generation who came of age around 1970—who attended or dropped out of college, smoked dope, missed connections, lived communally, and drifted in and out of relationships with a minimum of self-recognized affect or commitment," comments Robert Towers in the *New York Review of Books.* Beattie portrays these people who feel "that their lives are entirely out of control, that they lack power and cannot be expected to take responsibility for the consequences of their actions," Margaret Atwood observes in the *Washington Post Book World.* She adds, "Adrift in a world of seemingly pointless events . . . these characters cry out for meaning and coherence, but their world hands them nothing more resonant than popular song titles and T-shirt slogans." In exploring these lives in suburban angst, Beattie has been compared to such contemporary American authors as John Cheever, John Updike, Joseph Heller, and J. D. Salinger, chroniclers of the previous generation.

Beattie's prose style and plotting match her subject matter. As Pico Iyer points out in a *London Magazine* article, "Numbness pervades the parched, exhausted mood of her stories. Utterly toneless, she reads them herself into a plain, flat voice that suggests deadened feelings or, on occasion, a determined attempt to fight back tears." The reviewer finds that "her wan sentences and neutral cadences follow one upon another with sharp, chill clarity." Others have likened Beattie's style to that of a photographer or documentarist; she conveys the image of a detached recorder. In the words of Richard Locke, writing in the *New York Times Book Review,* Beattie's "tepid nihilism or defeated shopping-mall consumerism is depicted in a deadpan, super-realistic style: I am not a camera but a videotape machine." Through this approach, Beattie's fiction turns the focus away from words and toward actions. Her "best writing is concerned with wordlessness," suggests Patricia Storace in the *New York Review of Books.* "She is a marvelous witness of how behavior, rather than words, carries coded messages of love and hate."

Beattie first honed her craft writing short stories for the *New Yorker.* These and other short stories were gathered into five collections published between 1976 and 1991: *Distortions, Secrets and Surprises, The Burning House, Where You'll Find Me, and Other Stories,* and *What Was Mine.* These collections reflect not only the characteristic concerns and style of their author, but also an evolution in Beattie's writing. Reviewers tend to hold up *Distortions, The Burning House,* and *What Was Mine* as milestones in Beattie's development as a short story writer.

Reviewers, such as Kristin Hunter, frequently mention that the stories in *Distortions* are comprised of "humorless still-lifes of people who do not have any meaningful connections to humanity and who do not move, feel or grow." Hunter continues, "The stylistic excellence of her writing is undeniable, but Beattie is unable to make us feel any empathy for most of the characters in *Distortions*—perhaps because they are too self-absorbed to feel anything for each other." *New York Times* reviewer Anatole Broyard notes: "You never know what her people are going to say or do, surprise follows surprise. But, in the end, inscrutability proves to be boring." Yet, Broyard adds, "I am convinced that Ann Beattie is, potentially, a good writer. In spite of a style that virtually eliminates personality, she still manages to haunt the reader with her work. The things her characters say and do are rather like the inexplicable noises very old houses make in the middle of the night. You wake up in alarm when you hear them— what can *that* be?—then reason asserts itself and you go uneasily back to sleep."

Other reviewers have found Beattie's style praiseworthy. John Romano writes in *Commentary:* "Her sentences are often plain, flat, their grammar exposed like the lighting fixtures in avant-garde furniture boutiques, and the effect is at first wearying. Only later does the sympathetic center of her work betray itself. We may feel misled by the outward reserve, but, again, her willingness to distort when necessary, her passion for the particular, is ultimately an index of her concern for the integrity of things and people in themselves." Author John Updike is another admirer of Beattie's style. "Her details—which include the lyrics of the songs her characters overhear on the radio and the recipes of

the rather junky food they eat—calmly accrue," he writes in the *New Yorker.* "Her dialogue trails down the pages with an uncanny fidelity to the low-level heartbreaks behind the banal; her resolutely unmetaphorical style builds around us a maze of familiar truths that nevertheless has something airy, eerie, and in the end lovely about it." Updike finds that Beattie's "America is like the America one pieces together from the *National Enquirer*s that her characters read—a land of pathetic monstrosities, of pain clothed in cliches, of extraterrestrial trivia. Things happen 'out there,' and their vibes haunt the dreary 'here' we all inhabit."

Novelist Margaret Atwood hails *The Burning House,* Beattie's third story collection, in the *New York Times Book Review.* She explains that "a new Beattie is almost like a fresh bulletin from the front: We snatch it up, eager to know what's happening out there on the edge of that shifting and dubious no man's land known as interpersonal relations." In following the relationships in these stories, Beattie shows that "there are no longer any ties that bind, not securely, not definitively: jobs, marriages, the commitments of love, even the status of parent or child—are all in a state of flux," Atwood discovers. She adds that "freedom, that catchword of sixties America, has translated into free fall, or a condition of weightlessness, and the most repeated motifs in the book are variants of this."

At the heart of much of the critical discussion of these works is Beattie's evolution as a short story writer. Broyard comments in another *New York Times* review that the author's characters and themes seem to have come alive. "Miss Beattie seems to be changing—in my opinion, for the better," he writes. "Most of her characters now have recognizable desires, color in their cheeks, energy in their movements. Sometimes they even cry." Carolyn Porter sees new developments in the author's style. "If . . . Beattie's narrative method works by a metonymic unraveling, a movement from one detail to the next," Porter suggests in *Contemporary American Women Writers: Narrative Strategies,* "her advances in *The Burning House* derive from a new focus on and control of that method." Porter recognizes that Beattie's "more frequent use of the first person, her willingness to let metaphors grow from and give resonance to the train of associations on which her stories ride, her use of the past tense—all these are marks of an author still experimenting, but with tools now refined and proven." *London Magazine* contributor Pico Iyer offers a dissenting view on the subject of Beattie's development. He maintains, "because her theme so rarely varies or evolves . . . her tales seem almost mass-produced. All the off-beat tunes she plays are in the same (minor) key; after reading a few, one feels that one could write a few."

The overall merit of the stories is another issue in the critical debate. In Iyer's opinion, "These stories may be best regarded as a collection of photos in an album: each records a situation, revives a memory and redeems nothing. . . . Privy to anomie, her stories become party to it; faithful to the details of the world, they seem treacherous to the energy and heroic idealism that are America's saving grace." *Washington Post Book World* reviewer Jonathan Yardley finds much more of value here. He writes, "Ann Beattie is a writer of formidable, scary talents, and she is in rare form in several of the 16 stories collected in *The Burning House*. . . . She sees with a clarity that admits compassion but not sentimentality. Her eye for detail is penetrating and selective." He continues, "Her work affords me enormous pleasure and, from time to time, a welcome sense of unexpected discovery."

According to Ron Hansen in the *New York Times Book Review*, Beattie's "earlier [short story] collections were praised for their inventiveness, their humor and eccentricities, their almost photojournalistic chronicling of our worldly disconnections." However, in a later collection, *What Was Mine*, observes Hansen, "Ms. Beattie has forsaken irony for honest introspection, and her famous detachment has given away to greater sympathy and tenderness." He finds that "she seems truly interested in and mystified by the people she writes about. And she's wonderful at finding the telling image." Donna Rifkind offers a different evaluation of *What Was Mine* in a *Washington Post Book World* review. "These facts, presented shallowly and indiscriminately, add up to nothing more than bits and pieces of the way we live now." Concludes Rifkind, "While several stories in Beattie's uneven new book manage to dig below the surface, most of them show her to be an archeologist of modern-day America whose random shards and remnants do not even begin to recreate a city."

Patricia Storace admits that there is unevenness in Beattie's writing, but she also sees growth. "Like her most interesting characters," maintains Storace, "her work is a mixture of weaknesses and strengths. She is in the exceptional position of a writer whose powers may guide her into unknown territory, and whose weaknesses are marked by an easy glamour and ap-

peal than can undermine the reality of her gifts." *New York Times* reviewer Michiko Kakutani offers stronger praise. "In the best of these fictions, the reader can watch Ms. Beattie put her natural gifts—for dialogue, for social detail, for describing the incongruous effluvia of contemporary life—at the service of an evolving authorial vision." Kakutani ends by writing that "these stories are not simply Polaroid pictures of the passing parade of life, but finely orchestrated paintings created by an artist, who has continued to grow and mature over the years."

Some reviewers such as Jonathan Yardley have characterized Ann Beattie as a "miniaturist . . . whose strength is brevity and who seems most sure of herself when loose ends are left untied; as a result," contends Yardley, "she is more suited to the form of the story than that of the novel." Others have seen promise and further development of Beattie's talents in her novels, *Chilly Scenes of Winter, Falling in Place, Love Always,* and *Picturing Will. Chilly Scenes of Winter* offers Beattie's first extended look at the 1960s generation who find themselves lost and disillusioned in the 1970s. In an interview with Bob Miner, Beattie said: "I *was* going out of my way in the novel to say something about the '60s having passed. It just seems to me to be an attitude that most of my friends and most of the people I know have. They all feel sort of let down, either by not having involved themselves more in the '60s now that the '70s are so dreadful, or else by having involved themselves to no avail. Most of the people I know are let down—they feel cheated—and these are the people I am writing about."

Critic Sheila Weller writes that she had been waiting for a fictional account of the "turn-of-the-decade hero," and applauds Beattie's depiction of the novel's protagonist, Charles, which was accomplished with "sublime wit and humanity." Weller continues: "Beattie has written a very sophisticated valentine to those young men who happened upon adulthood at a time when Love was all over postage stamps and placards and rock stations but was just about to be withdrawn by the culture, the economy, and the women they had innocently come to take for granted." David Thorburn also compliments Beattie on her portrait of Charles. He comments: "The hero himself is wonderfully alive: a gentle bewildered man, extravagantly loyal to old friends and to the songs of the sixties, drifting through a final nostalgia for the mythologies of adversary selfhood he absorbed in college and toward an embarrassed recognition of his hunger for such ordinary adventures as marriage and fatherhood. The unillusioned tenderness that informs Beattie's portrait of her central character is a rare act of intelligence and mimetic art."

But Beattie does not allow her characters to wallow in the decade's faded glory, as many of her contemporaries have done. As John Romano writes: "She conveys adroitly the sensibility of After-the-Fall, without making fictive claims for the heights from which we fell. The Golden Age mythology and its attendant rhetoric will inevitably attach, for a while, to talk about the 60's. This represents, of course, a historical distortion, matched in its badness of fit only by the myth that the New Left was the Antichrist." He adds, "Beattie's presentation of Charles's nostalgia for the 60's suggests that such longing has the limits of an elegy to lost innocence, and the advantages, too. It distorts, but it also provides, however disingenuously, the idea that things can be better than they are, because they have been better before now. As usual, the prospects for hope seem to depend upon some degree of mystification."

Beattie's second novel, *Falling in Place,* was published in 1980. At the center of the work is a suburban family descending into chaos. As John Clavin Batchelor explains in the *Village Voice,* the novel "weaves a trap from which [the central] family cannot escape; their home is destroyed in the end by their own sloth, envy, selfishness, and lack of grace." Although, like Beattie's earlier fiction, the novel is peopled by characters adrift from the 1960s and it treats some of the same concerns, Locke argues that *Falling in Place* "is stronger, more accomplished, larger in every way than anything [Beattie has] done." He comments that "there's a new urgency to the characters' feelings and a much greater range and number of characters and points of view." Moreover, Locke points out, "These characters are not just quickly sketched-in; no fewer than five have distinct points of view: we learn and come to feel a lot about them and about the way they see the world."

As with her previous works, *Falling in Place* has drawn critical attention for its almost journalistic depiction of Beattie's world. *New York Review of Books* contributor Robert Towers remarks on how Beattie's realistic style reminds him of other media. He writes, "On a page-by-page basis the novel held my interest as an exceptionally good documentary film or television program might." Jack Beatty finds

fault with Beattie's characteristic view of the world. He maintains in a *New Republic* review, "My own view is that Ann Beattie's sociological realism is superficial, a reflective realism of accurate detail—what songs are in, what clothes, what expressions—rather than the kind of critical realism whose exemplar is *Buddenbrooks*." Pearl K. Bell, a reviewer for *Commentary,* is especially critical of Beattie's style. "Making no comic gestures, taking everything in with her customary neutrality and giving it all back," comments Bell, "Miss Beattie seems oblivious to her readers, unperturbed by their inevitable irritation and boredom." At the same time, reviewers such as Whitney Balliett offer praise for *Falling in Place.* Balliett feels that "Ann Beattie is a natural writer. Her prose never preens or tires or obstructs. At its coolest, it holds heat." And, Locke contends, "*Falling in Place* is certainly . . . the most impressive American novel this season and establishes Ann Beattie not merely as the object of a cult or as an 'interesting' young novelist, but as a prodigiously gifted and developing writer who has started to come of age."

In her next novel, *Love Always,* Beattie's "theme is a somber one, the failure of love between parents and children, between husbands and wives, between couples of every sexual persuasion," observes *New York Times* reviewer Christopher Lehmann-Haupt. The novel tells the story of Nicole Nelson, the fourteen-year-old star of the soap opera *Passionate Intensity.* She takes a vacation from the Hollywood sets to visit her aunt Lucy Spencer, who writes a pseudo-advice column for an offbeat magazine in Vermont. These two and the other characters, including Nicole's agent and Lucy's friends and colleagues, all become intertwined in a chaotic free-for-all that ricochets toward the moment when Nicole's mother dies offstage in an accident. In the end, concludes John Updike in the *New Yorker,* "This novel is sadder than satire, for it is about the emptiness not of these lives but of our lives."

The fact that *Love Always* leaves its readers with a somber, sad feeling in the end is interesting given the humorous elements of the book. "*Love Always* is clearly Beattie; as intelligent as ever about contemporary pain and oddness, but less composed and quite a bit funnier," notes Richard Eder in the *Los Angeles Times Book Review.* He adds that "Beattie's use of comedy is exuberant, sometimes uncontrolled, occasionally precious." Lehmann-Haupt offers a similar view, suggesting that "Miss Beattie's narrative technique is essentially Keystone comedy, with sudden jump-cuts from one character's point of view to another and outrageous collisions among the various subplots of the comedy." However, in the opinion of Elizabeth Rosner in the *San Francisco Review of Books,* Beattie's humor is not enough. "Instead of the tightly woven display of wit and satire Beattie seems to have intended," Rosner writes, "the book is a loose collection of plotlines going nowhere." She concludes, "This novel is missing both intensity and passion, and the weak humor it contains is inadequate to take their place."

Rosner also faults Beattie for the sketchiness of her characters. She charges Beattie with writing "a script with too many characters and not enough characterization, all stuff and no substance." John Updike, too, questions the author's characterization. He explains in the *New Yorker,* "The characters are oddly transparent—jellyfish through which one keeps seeing the same salt water." *New Republic* contributor Frank Rich maintains that the characters are not only sketchy but they also offer nothing new to Beattie's world. "As a spokesperson for a generation, Ann Beattie is beginning to sound like a broken record," he writes. "And the needle is stuck in a narrow groove that emits only the muffled sounds of the wealthy, Waspy, childless, and most narcissistic baby boomers." Richard Eder admits that "the men in Beattie's novels, and particularly this one, are shadowy. They loom in and out like woolly mammoths, damaging and elusive and just possibly extinct." But, he adds, "The women hold things together or fail to; they till a contaminated soil. The children are damaged flowers registering the contamination." And, one child, in particular, elicits praise from Eder. "Nicole is a sustained tour de force," comments the reviewer. "Nobody has managed to portray so sharply the entertainment world's dehumanization of the child star."

Picturing Will, Beattie's fourth novel, "is a bittersweet story that captures the psychological terrain of parenthood with the sure hand and accuracy of a photographer," observes Tim Falconer in *Quill and Quire.* "In fact, photography is a central image in the book." The book follows Jody, a small-town portrait photographer with artistic aspirations, her young son, Will, her lover, Mel, and her ex-husband, Wayne. As the novel progresses, Will's mother becomes captivated by her emerging career as an artist and his father drops out of the picture; only his "stepfather" comes forward to give him the love and affection expected of a parent. As it pictures Will and his family, Merle Rubin comments in the *Christian Sci-*

ence Monitor, the novel "focuses on the peculiarities of the parent-child relationship in a world of splintered families and parents whose attitudes run the gamut from intense empathy to outright refusal of responsibility." The events of the novel make clear, in Rubin's words, "that adults . . . cannot always calculate the effect they have on children; that a child's unfathomable mixture of imagination and ignorance, vulnerability and resilience, exposes him to danger and hurt while protecting him in unexpected ways."

"The novel states clearly the evil of our lightness," Richard Eder writes in the *Los Angeles Times Book Review.* "But as a novel, it is not very successful. Jody, Mel and Wayne are hollow, to be sure, but hollowness prolonged becomes tedium." Rand Richards Cooper offers a similar view in *Commonweal.* The reviewer finds the story "is both fragmentary and tedious. Its events are desultory in the extreme." He adds, "*Picturing Will* is a novel of pointless, annoying digressions. . . . The digressive mode weakens the larger elements of the novel as well." Falconer admits that "the book doesn't have much of a plot. Almost everything that happens is just a way for Beattie to explore the doubts, fears, and occasional joys of parenthood." Yet, in the opinion of this reviewer, "There's an understated perceptiveness to all of Beattie's writing, and *Picturing Will* is certainly no exception."

T. Coraghessan Boyle presents his evaluation of this novel in the *New York Times Book Review.* "In *Picturing Will,* Ann Beattie has created a surprising, lyrical and deeply affecting work that is both radical in its movement and perfectly attuned to its telling," he maintains. "Her style has never been better suited to a longer work, and she writes out of a wisdom and maturity that are timeless. But look to the details, the small things. They are everything here." Boyle characterizes "*Picturing Will* [as Beattie's] best novel since *Chilly Scenes of Winter* in 1976, and its depth and movement are a revelation."

In her short stories and novels, Ann Beattie has continued to chronicle the lives of those people in her world, people who came of age in the 1960s, but who have had to live in the 1970s, 1980s, and now the 1990s. "Miss Beattie's power and influence . . . arise from her seemingly resistless immersion in the stoic bewilderment of a generation without a cause," explains John Updike in the *New Yorker,* "a generation for whom love as well as politics is a consumer item too long on the shelves and whose deflationary mood is but dimly brightened by the background chirping of nostalgia-inducing pop tunes and the faithful attendance of personable pet dogs." Beattie's characters, themes, and style, as well as the widely differing evaluations of her work have, at times, threatened to marginalize her writing, to make her a cult figure. But as Richard Locke suggests in the *New York Times Book Review,* "Her fiction has none of the usual gimmicks and attractions that create a cult. . . . It's sometimes hard to imagine readers staying with it." Yet, many are attracted to this character of her writing. "Ann Beattie is a master of indirection," Boyle maintains. "Her stories are propelled not so much by event as by the accumulation of the details that build a life as surely as the tumble and drift of sediment builds shale or sandstone. Pay attention to the small things, she tells us. All the rest will fall in place."

BIOGRAPHICAL/CRITICAL SOURCES:

BOOKS

Contemporary Literary Criticism, Gale (Detroit), Volume 8, 1978, Volume 13, 1980, Volume 18, 1981, Volume 40, 1986, Volume 63, 1991.

Montresor, Jaye Berman, *The Critical Response to Ann Beattie,* Greenwood Press (Westport, CT), 1993.

Murphy, Christina, *Ann Beattie,* Twayne (Boston), 1986.

Rainwater, Catherine, and William J. Scheick, editors, *Contemporary American Women Writers: Narrative Strategies,* University Press of Kentucky (Lexington), 1985, pp. 9-25.

Short Story Criticism, Volume 11, Gale, 1992.

PERIODICALS

America, May 12, 1990, p. 469; October 12, 1991, p. 253.

American Spectator, April, 1990, p. 45.

Atlantic Monthly, December, 1976, p. 114; June, 1980, p. 93.

Boston Globe, April 20, 1987, p. 23; January 21, 1990, p. B49; February 3, 1990, p. 9; May 26, 1991, p. A13.

Christian Science Monitor, September 29, 1976, p. 19; January 31, 1979, p. 19; June 4, 1980, p. 17; February 9, 1983, p. 15; August 26, 1985, p. 21; November 10, 1986, p. 30; February 5, 1990, p. 12.

Commentary, February, 1977, p. 62; February, 1979, p. 71; July, 1980, pp. 59-61; March, 1983, p. 55.

Commonweal, September 6, 1985, p. 474; May 18, 1990, p. 322.

Hudson Review, spring, 1977, p. 150; autumn, 1977, p. 447; summer, 1983, p. 359.

London Magazine, March, 1983, p. 87.

London Review of Books, December 5, 1985, p. 22.

Los Angeles Times, January 18, 1990, p. E1; May 2, 1991, p. E7.

Los Angeles Times Book Review, June 9, 1985, p. 3; October 12, 1986, p. 2; July 19, 1987, p. 6; January 21, 1990, p. 3.

Maclean's, June 23, 1980, p. 52; July 1, 1985, p. 65; February 26, 1990, p. 54; August 19, 1991, p. 43.

Ms., December, 1976, p. 45; January, 1979, p. 42; July, 1980, p. 28; July, 1985, p. 16.

Nation, October 30, 1982, p. 441.

New Republic, June 7, 1980, p. 34; July 15, 1985, p. 42.

Newsweek, August 23, 1976, p. 76; January 22, 1979, p. 76; May 5, 1980, p. 86; June 17, 1985, p. 81; January 22, 1990, p. 62.

New York, January 22, 1990, p. 30.

New Yorker, November 29, 1976, p. 164; June 9, 1980, p. 148; August 5, 1985, p. 80.

New York Review of Books, May 15, 1980, p. 32; July 18, 1985, p. 40; May 31, 1990, p. 33; August 15, 1991, pp. 9-11.

New York Times, August 24, 1976, p. 33; January 3, 1979; September 25, 1982, p. 16; May 27, 1985, p. 13; October 1, 1986, p. C23; January 4, 1990, p. C20; April 23, 1991, p. C16.

New York Times Book Review, August 15, 1976, p. 14; January 14, 1979, p. 14; May 11, 1980, p. 1; September 26, 1982, p. 1; June 2, 1985, p. 7; October 12, 1986, p. 10; June 28, 1987, p. 24; January 7, 1990, p. 1; May 31, 1990, p. 33; May 26, 1991, p. 3.

People, February 5, 1990, pp. 89-95.

Quill and Quire, February, 1990, p. 27; May, 1991, p. 30.

San Francisco Review of Books, summer, 1985, p. 18.

Saturday Review, August 7, 1976, p. 37.

Southern Review, winter, 1992, p. 145.

Time, May 12, 1980, p. 79; July 1, 1985, p. 60; January 22, 1990, p. 68.

Times Literary Supplement, March 27, 1981, p. 333; October 25, 1985, p. 1203; August 14, 1987, p. 873.

Tribune Books, October 5, 1986, p. 3; May 24, 1987, p. 4; January 31, 1988, p. 7; January 28, 1990, p. 3; May 5, 1991, p. 5; July 19, 1992, p. 8.

Village Voice, August 9, 1976, p. 33; March 26, 1979, p. 86; June 2, 1980, p. 38.
Vogue, January, 1990, p. 106.
Voice Literary Supplement, November, 1982, p. 6.
Washington Post, February 4, 1990, p. F1.
Washington Post Book World, October 3, 1976, p. F5; January 7, 1979, p. E1; May 25, 1980, p. 1; September 19, 1982, p. 3; May 26, 1985, p. 3; January 28, 1990, p. 5; May 12, 1991, p. 8.
Women's Review of Books, April, 1984, p. 5.
Yale Review, summer, 1977, p. 584.*

—*Sketch by Bryan Ryan*

*   *   *

BEDARD, Michelle
See FINNIGAN, Joan

*   *   *

BELLOW, Saul 1915-

PERSONAL: Born June 10, 1915 (some sources say July 10, 1915), in Lachine, Quebec, Canada; came to Chicago at the age of nine; son of Abraham (a Russian emigre and businessman) and Liza (Gordon) Bellow; married Anita Goshkin (a social worker), December 31, 1937 (divorced); married Alexandra Tschacbasov, February 1, 1956 (divorced); married Susan Glassman (a teacher), 1961 (divorced); married Alexandra Ionesco Tuleca (a mathematician), 1974 (divorced); married Janis Freedman (a professor), 1989; children: (first marriage) Gregory, (second marriage) Adam, (third marriage) Daniel. *Education:* Attended University of Chicago, 1933-35; Northwestern University, B.S. (with honors in sociology and anthropology), 1937; graduate study in anthropology at University of Wisconsin, 1937 (abandoned his studies because "every time I worked on my thesis, it turned out to be a story").

ADDRESSES: Agent—Harriet Wasserman Literary Agency, 137 East 36th St., New York, NY 10016.

CAREER: Worked for a time on WPA Writers' Project, writing biographies of authors; Pestalozzi-Froebel Teachers College, Chicago, IL, instructor, 1938-42; Encyclopaedia Britannica, Inc., Chicago, member of editorial department of "Great Books" project, 1943-46; University of Minnesota, Minne-apolis, member of English department, 1946, assistant professor, 1948-49, associate professor of English, 1954-59; Boston University, Boston, MA, professor of English, 1993—. New York University, New York City, visiting lecturer, 1950-52; Princeton University, Princeton, NJ, creative writing fellow, 1952-53; Bard College, Annandale-on-Hudson, NY, faculty member, 1953-54; University of Puerto Rico, Rio Piedras, visiting professor of English, 1961; University of Chicago, Chicago, celebrity in residence, 1962, became Grunier Distinguished Services Professor, member of Committee on Social Thought, 1962-93, chair, 1970-76. Presented Jefferson Lecture for National Endowment for the Humanities in 1977; has presented Tanner Lectures at Oxford University. Fellow, Academy for Policy Study, 1966; fellow, Brandford College of Yale University. *Military service:* Merchant Marine, 1944-45.

MEMBER: Authors League, American Academy of Arts and Letters, PEN, Yaddo Corporation.

AWARDS, HONORS: Short stories included in *Best American Short Stories,* 1944, "Notes of a Dangling Man," and 1950, "Sermon by Doctor Pep"; Guggenheim fellowship in Paris and Rome, 1948; National Institute of Arts and Letters grant, 1952; National Book Award, 1954, for *The Adventures of Augie March,* 1965, for *Herzog,* and 1971, for *Mr. Sammler's Planet;* O. Henry Award, 1956, for "The Gonzaga Manuscripts," and 1980, for "A Silver Dish"; Ford grant, 1959, 1960; Friends of Literature Fiction Award, 1960; James L. Dow Award, 1964; Prix International de Litterature (France), 1965, for *Herzog;* Jewish Heritage Award, B'nai B'rith, 1968; Croix de Chevalier (France), 1968; Formentor Prize, 1970; Pulitzer Prize, 1976, for *Humboldt's Gift;* Nobel Prize for Literature, 1976; Gold Medal, American Academy of Arts and Letters, 1977; Emerson-Thoreau Medal, American Academy of Arts and Sciences, 1977; Neil Gunn International fellowship, 1977; Brandeis University Creative Arts Award, 1978; Commander, Legion of Honour (France), 1983; Malaparte Prize for Literature (Italy), 1984; Commander, Order of Arts and Letters (France), 1985; National Medal of Arts, 1988, for "outstanding contributions to the excellence, growth, support and availability of the arts in the United States." D.Litt. from Northwestern University, 1962, and Bard College, 1963; Litt.D. from New York University, 1970, Harvard University, 1972, Yale University, 1972, McGill University, 1973, Brandeis University, 1974, Hebrew Union College, 1976, and Trinity College (Dublin), 1976.

WRITINGS:

NOVELS

Dangling Man, Vanguard (New York City), 1944.

The Victim, Vanguard, 1947.

The Adventures of Augie March (also see below), Viking (New York City), 1953, published with introduction by Lionel Trilling, Modern Library (New York City), 1965.

Henderson the Rain King (also see below), Viking, 1959.

Herzog (early drafts published in *Esquire,* July, 1961, and July, 1963, in *Commentary,* July, 1964, and in *Saturday Evening Post,* August 8, 1964; also see below), Viking, 1964, published with criticism, edited by Irving Howe, 1976.

Mr. Sammler's Planet (originally appeared in a different form in *Atlantic;* also see below), Viking, 1970.

Humboldt's Gift, Viking, 1975.

The Dean's December, Harper (New York City), 1982, published in limited edition with illustrations by Robert Heindel, Franklin Library, 1982.

More Die of Heartbreak, Morrow (New York City), 1987.

SHORT STORIES

Mosby's Memoirs, and Other Stories (contains "Leaving the Yellow House," "The Old System," "Looking for Mr. Green," "The Gonzaga Manuscripts," "A Father-to-Be," and "Mosby's Memoirs"; also see below), Viking, 1968.

Him with His Foot in His Mouth, and Other Stories (contains "Cousins," "A Silver Dish," "What Kind of Day Did You Have?," "Zetland: By a Character Witness," and "Him with His Foot in His Mouth"), Harper, 1984.

Short stories reprinted in numerous anthologies.

UNCOLLECTED SHORT STORIES

William Phillips and Philip Rahv, editors, *Partisan Reader: Ten Years of Partisan Review, 1934-1944* (contains "Two Morning Monologues"), introduction by Lionel Trilling, Dial (New York City), 1946.

Nelson Algren, editor, *Nelson Algren's Own Book of Lonesome Monsters* (contains "Address by Gooley MacDowell to the Hasbeens Club of Chicago"), Geis, 1963.

Penny Chapin Hills and L. Rust Hills, editors, *How We Live: Contemporary Life in Contemporary Fiction* (contains "Herzog Visits Chicago"), Macmillan (New York City), 1968.

PLAYS

Under the Weather (three one-act comedies: *Orange Souffle,* published in *Esquire,* January, 1965, *A Wen,* published in *Esquire,* October, 1965, and *Out from Under*), first produced in London, June 7, 1966; produced in Spoleto, Italy, at Festival of Two Worlds, July 14, 1966; produced on Broadway at the Cort Theatre, October 27, 1966.

The Last Analysis, a Play (full-length; first produced on Broadway at the Belasco Theatre, October 1, 1964; acting edition of first version of play printed under original title *Bummidge*), rewritten version published by Viking, 1965.

Also author of play *The Wrecker,* published in *New World Writing 6* (also see below), 1954.

OTHER

(Author of foreword) Feodor Dostoevsky, *Winter Notes on Summer Impressions,* Criterion Books, 1955.

Seize the Day; With Three Short Stories and a One-Act Play (novella; also contains stories "Father-to-Be," "The Gonzaga Manuscripts," and "Looking for Mr. Green," and play, *The Wrecker*), Viking, 1956, published singly as *Seize the Day,* 1961, published with introduction by Alfred Kazin, Fawcett (New York City), 1968.

(Translator of title story) Isaac Bashevis Singer, *Gimpel the Fool, and Other Stories,* Noonday, 1957.

(Author of text with C. Zervos) Jesse Reichek, *Dessins,* Editions Cahiers d'Art (Paris), 1960.

(Editor with Keith Botsford [first three volumes also with Jack Ludwig] *The Noble Savage,* five volumes, Meridian, 1961-62.

Recent American Fiction; A Lecture Presented under the Auspices of the Gertrude Clarke Whitall Poetry and Literature Fund, Library of Congress (Washington, DC), 1963.

(Editor and author of introduction) *Great Jewish Short Stories,* Dell (New York City), 1963, reprinted, 1985.

Acceptance Speech by Saul Bellow, Author of "Herzog," Fiction Winner National Book Awards, March 9, 1965, privately printed, c. 1965.

The Portable Saul Bellow (contains *Henderson the Rain King* and *Seize the Day,* plus selections from *The Adventures of Augie March, Herzog,* and *Mr. Sammler's Planet,* and "Leaving the Yellow House," "The Old System," and "Mosby's Memoirs" from *Mosby's Memoirs, and Other Stories*), critical introduction by Gabriel Josipovici, Viking, 1974.

To Jerusalem and Back: A Personal Account (memoirs), Viking, 1976.

The Nobel Lecture (first published in *American Scholar,* 1977), Targ Editions, 1979.

Herzog (sound recording of Bellow reading excerpts from novel), Caedmon (New York City), 1978.

A Theft (novella; Quality Paperback Book Club dual main selection; also see below), Penguin (New York City), 1989.

The Bellarosa Connection (novella; also see below), Penguin, 1989.

Something to Remember Me By: Three Tales (novellas; contains *Something to Remember Me By, A Theft,* and *The Bellarosa Connection*), Viking, 1991.

It All Adds Up: From the Dim Past to the Uncertain Future (essays), Viking, 1994.

Conversations with Saul Bellow, edited by Gloria L. Cronin and Ben Siegel, University Press of Mississippi (Jackson), 1994.

Also author of "Deep Readers of the World, Beware!," 1959; *Oedipus Schmoedipus, the Story That Started It All,* 1966; *Keynote Address before the Inaugural Session of the XXXIV International PEN Congress, June 13, 1966, at Loeb Student Center, New York University,* 1966; *The Future of the Moon,* 1970; and the Carolyn Benton Cockefair Lecture, "The Novel in a Technological Age," 1973. Contributor to books, including *The Open Form: Essays for Our Time,* edited by Alfred Kazin, Harcourt (New York City), 1961; *The Great Ideas Today,* six volumes, edited by Robert M. Hutchins and Mortimer J. Adler, Atheneum (New York City), 1961-66; *To the Young Writer,* edited by A. L. Bader, University of Michigan Press (Ann Arbor), 1963; *First Person Singular: Essays for the Sixties,* edited by Herbert Gold, Dial, 1963; *Saul Bellow and the Critics* (contains "Where Do We Go from Here: The Future of Fiction"), edited by Irving Malin, New York University Press, 1967; *The Art & the Public* (essays), edited by James E. Miller Jr., and Paul D. Herring, University of Chicago Press, 1967; and *Technology and the Frontiers of Knowledge* (contains "Literature in the Age of Technology"), Doubleday (New York City), 1975. Also contributor

to numerous periodicals, including *Partisan Review, Hudson Review, Sewanee Review, New Yorker, New Republic, Nation, New Leader, Saturday Review, Holiday, Reporter, Horizon, Esquire, Commentary,* and *New York Times Book Review.* Founder and co-editor of *Noble Savage,* 1960-62.

An extensive collection of Bellow's manuscripts, including most of the novels, correspondence, and memorabilia, is housed at the Regenstein Library of the University of Chicago. The Humanities Research Center at the University of Texas at Austin holds several manuscripts of *Seize the Day.*

ADAPTATIONS: The Wrecker was televised in 1964; a sound recording of the Chicago Radio Theatre presentation of the plays *Orange Souffle* and *The Wrecker* was produced by All-Media Dramatic Workshop, 1978; a television adaptation of *Seize the Day,* featuring Robin Williams and a cameo appearance by Bellow, was broadcast by Public Broadcasting Service, May 1, 1987.

WORK IN PROGRESS: Working on "many things at once."

SIDELIGHTS: Pulitzer Prize and Nobel Prize-winning novelist Saul Bellow has taken a place among the leading figures in twentieth-century American literature. In his writing and teaching, Bellow champions human and moral possibilities in the face of personal and social struggle. He also takes to task intellectuals, artists, and social commentators who focus on value-free function, technique, practice, and experimentation. In a *Times Literary Supplement* article, Julian Symons compared Bellow to two British "other-sayers," George Orwell and Wyndham Lewis. "In the United States," writes Symons, "Saul Bellow has, for the past twenty years and more, been saying unpopular things about American culture in general, and about the relationship between the society and its literature in particular." Continues Symons: "When he says American intellectuals are becoming more and more alike, and 'often as philistine as the masses from which they have emerged' he has to be listened to."

Bellow has pursued his career as a writer with a steady commitment to the art of fiction as an indispensable form of knowledge. His canon stands as a testament to the vital life of the human mind and spirit and to the power of art. "I feel," Bellow explained to Gordon L. Harper in an interview for the *Paris Review,* "that art has something to do with the achievement of stillness in the midst of chaos. A stillness which characterizes prayer, too, and the eye of the storm. I think art has something to do with an arrest of attention in the midst of distraction." Tommy Wilhelm of *Seize the Day* and Sammler of *Mr. Sammler's Planet* offer prayers out of such still centers amid turbulent emotional storms, and Eugene Henderson exclaims in *Henderson the Rain King* that "this is not a sick and hasty ride, helpless, through a dream into oblivion. No, sir! It can be arrested by a thing or two. By art, for instance. The speed is checked, the time is redivided. Measure! That great thought. Mystery."

Bellow challenged Lionel Trilling and Arthur C. Clarke in *Harper's* for claiming that scientific truth, a manifestation of man's "maturity," will redeem society through technology "from the childish need for art," including the telling of stories to one another. "Science and technology," Bellow argued "are not likely to remove this narrative and spellbinding oddity from the soul." But Bellow acknowledged that technology can be distracting to the artist and threatening to his art: "The present age has a certain rationalizing restlessness or cognitive irritability: a participatory delirium that makes the arresting powers of any work intolerable. . . . Technology has weakened certain points of spiritual rest. Wedding guests and ancient mariners both are deafened by the terrific blaring of the technological band."

In his Nobel Prize for Literature acceptance speech, delivered in Stockholm on December 12, 1976, Bellow reaffirmed his conviction that art is more important than science in exploring significant values in twentieth-century human experience. Following Marcel Proust, Bellow explained, "Only art penetrates what pride, passion, intelligence and habit erect on all sides—the seeming realities of this world. There is another reality, the genuine one, which we lose sight of. This other reality is always sending us hints, which, without art, we can't receive. Proust calls these hints our 'true impressions'. . . . The value of literature lies in these intermittent true impressions. . . . What [Joseph] Conrad said was true: art attempts to find in the universe, in matter as well as in the facts of life, what is fundamental, enduring, essential." To Bellow, the novel is "a sort of latter-day lean-to, a hovel in which the spirit takes shelter"; as such, the novel performs the same function that Robert Frost claimed for poetry; it provides "a momentary stay against confusion," and in a world where confusion has become king, momentary stillnesses and humble sanctuaries for the spirit are not insignificant contributions.

The three National Book Awards, the Pulitzer and Nobel Prizes, and the many other honors he has received attest to the quality of Bellow's works. In his essay "Where Do We Go from Here: The Future of Fiction," Bellow has supplied a central standard for the evaluation of the novel: "It becomes art when the views most opposite to the author's own are allowed to exist in full strength. Without this a novel of ideas is mere self-indulgence, and didacticism is simply axe-grinding. The opposites must be free to range themselves against each other, and they must be passionately expressed on both sides. It is for this reason that I say it doesn't matter much what the writer's personal position is, what he wishes to affirm. He may affirm principles we all approve of and write very bad novels." Or as Philip Bummidge says in Bellow's play *The Last Analysis:* "I am convinced that lies are bad art." Giving fair play to the opposition, working through murkiness to clarity, a novel earns its vision. For half a century, Bellow has striven in his work—his art—to give shape and substance to the abstractions by which human beings live. Although individual works have not always risen to his own highest standard, each contributes to a whole that demonstrates a writer deeply engaged with the complexity of human existence and fully committed to his art as a form of understanding. His versatility and willingness to take risks have led Bellow to extend his efforts to the short story (*Mosby's Memoirs, and Other Stories* and *Him with His Foot in His Mouth, and Other Stories*), the familiar essay, literary criticism, the drama, and the philosophical-political travelogue (*To Jerusalem and Back: A Personal Account*), but at the core of his art stand the novels.

Joseph, the Kafkaesque protagonist and Dostoevskian underground figure of *Dangling Man,* Bellow's first novel, exists between the military nightmare of World War II and civilian economic opportunism, between the material world of action and the ideal world of thought, between detachment and involvement, life and death. A compulsive diarist and a man condemned to an existential freedom without moral precedent, Joseph is, as Tony Tanner describes him in *Saul Bellow,* "a man up to his neck in modern history. Joseph oscillates between corrosive inertia and compulsive self-inquiry, wrestling with irresolvable paradoxes of world and spirit which have a drastically deleterious effect on his character and bring him to the point of futility and exhaustion." As Joseph mismanages his freedom and perceives ever more vividly the disparity between his "ideal constructions" and the "craters of the spirit" that the real world places daily in his path, he grows less confident of his ability to understand the universe or to discern his proper identity in it. Finally, in quasi-optimistic desperation, Joseph decides that he will find no answers in his detached state; thus he insists that his draft board subject him immediately to the same fate his countrymen are enduring. Marcus Klein has seen this movement toward community as part of a pattern in the contemporary American novel, a "strategy of accommodation." In *After Alienation: American Novels in Mid-Century* he observes, "Joseph must give himself to idiopathic freedom, and that way is madness, or submit to the community's ordinary, violent reality. He hurries his draft call. He surrenders."

Asa Leventhal of *The Victim* is a good man, a middle-aged, happily married Jew who has unknowingly caused the gentile Kirby Allbee to lose his job. In his subsequent decline, Allbee becomes a drunk, loses his wife in an auto accident, and blames Leventhal—and by extension all Jews—for his wretchedness. Because he has always felt very tentative about his place in the scheme of things, Leventhal is susceptible to Allbee's unwarranted accusations and subsequent persecutions. Determining what he owes to himself and what he owes to others—that is, how he should live as a good man—becomes Leventhal's primary concern and the integrating principle in the novel.

The Victim develops on two levels, the realistic and the symbolic. At the realistic levels, its themes are guilt, fear of failure, anti-Semitism, and existential responsibility; and these themes are embodied in the characterizations, the dialogue, and patterns of metaphor, especially those involving tickets and acting. These matters expand, however, to become questions of Death and Evil at the symbolic level, where Bellow draws heavily on classical mythology for the encounters of Levanthal with death, and on the American myth of guilt and redemption, Nathaniel Hawthorne's *The Scarlet Letter,* for his confrontation with guilt in the person of Allbee.

In *Fiction of the Forties* Chester E. Eisinger sees the main thematic concerns of *The Victim* as anti-Semitism and existential responsibility: Asa is "a man who falls short of love and understanding and humanity. . . . His plight is a function of the anti-Semitism, real and imagined that he feels engulfs him. Loaded with these disabilities [self-interest and fear of victimization] . . . Asa is asked to consider the nature and extent of one human being's responsibility to another." In *Saul Bellow's Fiction,* Irving Malin interprets *The Victim* as "a novel of fathers and sons." Leventhal rejects his natural father, is tyrannized by business fathers, disturbed by a kind of paternal conscience in Allbee, and becomes, first, a surrogate father to his nephews Mickey and Philip and to his brother Max and, finally, with his wife's pregnancy, a real father, thus achieving a natural and psychological resolution to his ambivalence toward fatherhood. According to Jonathan Baumbach's *The Landscape of Nightmare: Studies in the Contemporary Novel,* Allbee functions as Leventhal's psychological and symbolic double; he "is not the cause but the occasion of Leventhal's victimization—the objectification of his free-floating guilt. . . . Allbee is . . . the personification of his evil possibilities, . . . the grotesque exaggeration of his counterpart. He represents Leventhal's failings carried to their logical insanity." Only by acknowledging that he has such a counterpart can Leventhal come to terms with the evil in himself and thus become fully human. Keith Opdahl reaches a similar conclusion in *The Novels of Saul Bellow: An Introduction:* "Bellow subordinates the theme of man's feat of imaginary evil to that of man's denial of the real evil in the world and himself. Each of the characters, Bellows shows, views the other as a symbol of evil he would deny. The moral issue between the two men becomes an issue concerning the nature of the world and man's ability to face it." John J. Clayton claims in *Saul Bellow: In Defense of Man* that the theme of the book lies in Leventhal's "casting off of his self-imposed burdens by learning to accept himself and others rather than to judge and blame, by learning to have an open heart." Both Opdahl and Clayton mention in their discussions of plot the many parallels between Bellow's novel and Feodor Dostoevsky's *The Eternal Husband,* but James Hall, in *The Lunatic Giant in the Drawing Room,* sees Franz Kafka's *The Trial* and James Joyce's *Ulysses* as the two books "that obviously stand behind *The Victim.*"

The differences in focus and emphasis of these critical views are indicative of the scope of meanings in the multi-layered complexity of Bellow's blending of realism and symbolism, a strategy that Bellow employed in both of his first two novels as, in part, a way of paying dues to the literary establishment and the tradition of the well-made novel. With Harper in the *Paris Review* interview, Bellow was explicit about his intent as a novelistic newcomer: "I think when I wrote those early books I was timid. I still felt the incredible effrontery of announcing myself to the world (in part I mean the WASP world) as a writer and an artist. I had to touch a great many bases, demonstrate my abilities, pay my respects to formal requirements. In short, I was afraid to let myself go." During the composition of *The Adventures of Augie March,* however, Bellow experienced a kind of artistic liberation: "When I began *Augie March,* I took off many of these restraints. I think I took off too many, and went too far, but I was feeling the excitement of discovery." In fact, as Bellow explained to Harvey Breit in *The Writer Observed,* "The great pleasure of the book was that it came easily. All I had to do was to be there with buckets to catch it."

A *Bildungsroman,* or novel of education, and a quest novel, *The Adventures of Augie March* traces Augie's erratic pursuit of a worthwhile fate. Telling his own story "free style," Augie relives his experiences for the reader from his boyhood in Chicago to his wanderings in Michigan, Mexico, and the African Sea to his maturity as a husband and import businessman in Paris. Augie encounters a Chaucerian pilgrimage of Bellovian characters, and from each Augie learns something about "bitterness in his chosen thing" and thus something about his search for a worthwhile fate. He does not find the fate he imagined, but he does affirm the validity of the search: "Columbus too," says Augie, "thought he was a flop, probably, when they sent him back in chains. Which didn't prove there was no America."

Despite Bellow's admission that he went "too far" and violated formal unity, *Augie March* does have a firm organizing principle, the tension of opposites. Refusing to lead a disappointed life, Augie seeks a worthwhile fate in accordance with what he calls the "axial lines of life," which lead one to "Truth, love, peace, bounty, usefulness, harmony." Augie is a free and optimistic spirit, but Bellow exposes him to characters, ideas, and situations inimical to his freedom and his optimism. The figure Kayo Obermark supplies a name for the negative factors, *moha,* the limitations imposed by the finite and imperfect, "the Bronx cheer of the conditioning forces." Einhorn's and Georgie's handicaps, Simon's monomania and loveless marriage, the superficiality of the Magnuses, the varied victimizations of Jimmy Klein and Mim Villars, the limited love of Stella, the lost children everywhere—all testify to the power of *moha* and assail the fortress of Augie's dream of happiness on the axial lines of life. But Augie stands firm in his optimism, earning the book's affirmative vision through his awareness of life's dark side and his resilience in the face of it. "It is important to keep

in mind," observes Brigitte Scheer-Schaezler in her study *Saul Bellow,* "that Augie's desire for life in the sun is not motivated by a shunning of action or a rejection of consciousness but arises from his knowledge of darkness, the darkness which he says has widened his outlook." "Indeed," says Sarah Blacher Cohen in the *Saul Bellow Journal,* "Augie is the picaresque apostle who, meeting up with errant humanity, eagerly listens to their confessions and generously pardons their sins, even blessing them for their anti-trespasses."

Whereas Augie defines his humanity through his charm, striving, and compassion, Tommy Wilhelm in *Seize the Day* defines his humanity through his slovenliness, selfishness, and suffering—and, most important, through his desire to be better than he is. "The shrill quality of the marriage relationship between Tommy and his wife," writes Robert Detweiler in *Saul Bellow: A Critical Essay,* "may echo Bellow's own situation at the time. He worked on the story while living in a desert shack in Nevada and waiting out the residency requirements for a divorce."

An anti-hero, Wilhelm has messed up his life. By changing his name (Saul Bellow was born Solomon Bellows), dropping out of school, and failing in business, Tommy has embarrassed and alienated his father, Dr. Adler, a selfish retired physician. Out of his foolish pride, Wilhelm has quit a good job and now can find no other. His mismanagement of his life has led to estrangement from his wife and painful separation from his two boys. In loneliness and desperation, Wilhelm has turned for companionship and advice to a kind of surrogate father, Dr. Tamkin, a quack psychologist, aspiring poet, slick operator in the stock market, and mainline Bellovian reality-instructor. On the titular day depicted in *Seize the Day,* Wilhelm's lifelong miscalculations and bad judgments bring him to his knees. His father and wife turn deaf ears to his appeals for help, Tamkin abandons him after misguiding him into losing his last savings in the stock market, and Tommy ends the day crying unceasingly in a funeral home over the body of a stranger.

"Wilhelm's drowning," notes Opdahl, "is first of all the climax of his day of failure. The water in which he drowns is both the world and his masochistic self which have murdered him." The masochistic self here is what Tamkin termed the "pretender soul"; its death at least opens the way for the emergence of Wilhelm's "true soul," but that redemptive possibility is not realized within the pages of the novel. Clinton W. Trowbridge observes in *Critique: Studies in Modern Fiction* that "the image of the drowning Wilhelm is the controlling one, but because of the book's ironic structure it is an image that functions in two ways. On a first reading, and on each rereading on the surface of our experience, it intensifies sympathy for Wilhelm's condition. Even when Wilhelm is being depicted least sympathetically, when he is most in the wrong, most a slob, we are continually made aware that we are witnessing the strugglings of a drowning man and we want to see him rescued." Writing in Earl Rovit's *Saul Bellow: A Collection of Critical Essays,* M. Gilbert Porter observes that "the unity of effect achieved in *Seize the Day* results from the skillful blending of all the elements of fiction in tightly constructed scenic units functioning very much like poetic images built around a controlling metaphor. Each scene extends the central image of Wilhelm's drowning by embodying a particular aspect of his life that has contributed to the pressure that finally overwhelms him in literal failure and symbolic death and rebirth. Unity is enhanced further by cross references between scenes." In its compactness, unity, and intensity, *Seize the Day* approaches the configuration of poetry.

At age fifty-five, the manic gentile Henderson, in Bellow's *Henderson the Rain King,* stands six feet four, weighs two hundred and thirty pounds, has an M.A. from a prestigious eastern university, a second wife, seven children, a three-million-dollar estate, and a voice within him crying, "I want, I want, I want," testifying to both his unhappiness and his aspiration. Although he has most of the things that Madison Avenue equates with human happiness, Henderson feels that a central element is missing from his life. His vigorous but bumbling quest to discover that element leads him through whimsical pig-farming, gratuitous violence, and antisocial behavior to Africa, where through exotic experiences with African tribes he determines that he can "burst the spirit's sleep" and still the voice within him by serving others as a physician in emulation of his hero Sir Wilfred Grenfill. In the final scene, his dance around the New York-bound plane with the lion cub and the Persian orphan during the refueling stop in symbolic Newfoundland is a rhapsodic celebration of his movement toward community and his confirmed new vision of the possibilities of life over death: "God does not shoot dice with our souls," cries the joyful Henderson, "and therefore grun-tu-molani. . . . I believe there is justice, and that much is promised." According to Walter Clemons and Jack Kroll

in a *Newsweek* interview with the author, "Of all his characters, Bellow has said, Henderson, the quixotic seeker of higher truth, is most like himself."

The theme of the novel is a recurrent one in Bellow's fiction: that the world is tough and mysterious, that man is subject to great errors and subsequent pain, but that he yearns for nobility and joy and feels in his deepest soul that such things are possible. "*Henderson the Rain King* is clearly Bellow's most full-blown comic novel," writes Cohen in *Saul Bellow's Enigmatic Laughter.* "The dreaded nightmare experiences of the earlier realistic novels are transformed into the playful and dreamlike episodes of romance. The comic flaws which the early heroes were often too obtuse to notice are magnified in Henderson, who both flamboyantly exhibits them and exorcises them through his own jocose language."

The comic development of Henderson assumes many forms. Opdahl argues that the novel is in part a good-natured satire on Ernest Hemingway. At least three critics have explored waste land motifs, vegetation myths, and related anthropological matters appropriate for a novelist who holds a bachelor's degree in anthropology: Elsie Leach in *Western Humanities Review,* Detweiler in *Modern Fiction Studies,* and Howard Harper in *Desperate Faith.* Klein, in *After Alienation,* finds Henderson's growth complemented by a pattern of animal imagery involving cats, camels, frogs, octopuses, cows, and bears as Henderson is transformed from pig farmer to lionlike kingly spirit. His development is also supported by an elaborate matrix of music and musical allusion as Henderson, singer and violinist manque, moves from native drums and flutes to Mozart and Handel. Preceding the publication of the novel, Bellow published "Deep Readers of the World, Beware!," in the *New York Times Book Review:* "Novels are being published today which consist entirely of abstractions, meanings, and while our need for meanings is certainly great our need for concreteness, for particulars, is even greater. . . . We must leave it to inspiration to redeem the concrete and the particular and to recover the value of flesh and bone."

One man's frantic attempts to formulate a synthesis to shore up his disintegrating life is the substance of Bellow's 1964 novel *Herzog.* Herzog seeks clarity and justice as a professor of history with a Ph.D. and an impressive professional bibliography. But with the discovery that his wife, Madeleine, and his good friend Gersbach have made him a cuckold and abandoned him to his isolated personal fate, Herzog finds himself lost in the modernist waste land of cynical "reality instructors" and existential nothingness, "down in the mire of post-Renaissance, post-humanistic, post-Cartesian dissolution, next door to the void." Such hostile territory is particularly hard on a sensitive intellectual whose sensibilities are at war with his intellect. With his feelings, he resists the negations of the reality instructors, but the chaotic evidence of his personal life makes an intellectual assent to their conclusions almost irresistible. His final transcendence of their teachings and his own anguish in the pastoral setting of Ludeyville testifies to the power Herzog discovers in simple being and the "law of the heart"; at peace at last, he says, "*I am pretty well satisfied to be, to be just as it is willed, and for as long as I may remain in occupancy.*"

Some critics argue that the stress and resolution in *Herzog* is typical of the Bellow canon. "It is this problem," Alfred Kazin says in *Contemporaries,* "first of representing all that a man intends and plans and then of getting him not merely to recognize the countervailing strength of life but to humble himself before it, that is the real situation in all Bellow's novels." Where Kazin sees acceptance and submission, Ihab Hassan, in *Radical Innocence: Studies in the Contemporary American Novel,* sees affirmation in the protagonist as the sequel to his conflict between self and the world: "the movement is from acid defeat to acceptance, and from acceptance to celebration. The querulous and ill-natured hero becomes prodigal and quixotic. In this process something of the dignity that the fictional hero has lost to history is restored to him."

A majority of critics agree, as Harold Bloom observes in the Modern Critical Views collection *Saul Bellow,* that *Herzog* "seems to be Bellow's best and most representative novel." In *Time to Murder and Create,* however, John W. Aldridge sees the novel "as the Waste Land cliche irrigated and transformed in the Promised Land while the platitude of Alienation is converted into the even hoarier platitude of Accommodation and Togetherness. For what he finally holds up for our inspection is a new hopeful doctrine of potato love not uncolored by righteous disdain." Richard Poirier, in Earl Rovit's *Saul Bellow: A Collection of Critical Essays,* dismisses the novel as empty rhetoric and its author as intellectually dishonest: "What I call the gap in his novels between their intellectual and historical pretensions, on one side, and the stuff of life as he renders it, on the other, prevents me from believing that he is himself convinced by his snappy contempt for 'the commonplaces of the Waste Land outlook, the cheap mental stimulants of Alienation.'"

Bellow's seventh novel, *Mr. Sammler's Planet,* is an indignant depiction of contemporary America from the perspective of one of Bellow's most formidable "men thinking," Sammler, a Cracow-born Anglophile in his seventies and a Jewish survivor of a Nazi pogrom in Poland. His war injuries have left him with a tempered detachment and vision in only one eye. Thus Sammler sees outward and inward. His good right eye records characters, actions and events in the world around him. His blind left eye subjects current events to introspective analysis, the historical and philosophical perspective. "The damaged eye seemed to turn in another direction, to be preoccupied separately with different matters." The novel oscillates from action to reflection as Sammler tries to make sense of a planet that seems to be coming unglued. Within that general strategy there are complementary movements from past to present, from public to private, from life to death. Three obliquely related plots provide the structural matrix of the narrative: 1) a pickpocket who plies his trade on the Forty-second Street Bus and exposes himself to Sammler to warn him not to interfere; 2) a book manuscript on space travel and inhabitation of the moon stolen from its author, Dr. Govinda Lal, by Sammler's daughter, Shula; and 3) the slow dying of Dr. Gruner from an aneurysm in his brain.

Bellow told Jane Howard in an interview for *Life* that *Mr. Sammler's Planet* is his own favorite work: "I had a high degree of excitement writing it . . . and finished it in record time. It's my first thoroughly nonapologetic venture into ideas. In *Herzog* . . . and *Henderson the Rain King* I was kidding my way to Jesus, but here I'm baring myself nakedly." The novel and this statement about it marked a shift in proportion in Bellow's art, as abstraction began to overshadow concretion. The change has elicited mixed responses. Robert R. Dutton, in *Saul Bellow,* calls the novel "Bellow's highest technical achievement," and Brigitte Scheer-Schaezler, in support of what she calls "enlarged vision," describes the book as representative of "Bellow's effort to turn the novel into a medium of inquiry. In Bellow's most recent novels, experiences are not so much being undergone as discussed in a probing approach that may well be called essayistic." In the same vein, Nathan A. Scott, Jr., declares approvingly in *Three American Moralists: Mailer, Bellow, Trilling* that Bellow's "insistently didactic intention has had the effect of making rhetoric itself—rather than action and character—the main source of the essential energies in his fiction. And there is perhaps no other comparable body of work in the literature of the contemporary novel so drenched in ideas and speculations and theories, even commandments."

Other critics, however, have felt that Bellow's expository treatment of ideas in *Mr. Sammler's Planet* vitiates his art. David Galloway writes in *Modern Fiction Studies* that Bellow's emphasis on ideas leads to a failure of imagination, a too easy recourse to stock situations and well-worn character pairings. "The central problem in Bellow's novels," contends Galloway, is that "the imaginative structure fails to provide adequate support for the intellectual structure, so that at crucial moments the author's ideas fail to be organically embodied in character, action, or image." In her review in the *Nation*, Beverly Gross describes the scene at Columbia when Sammler is confronted by a heckler, a mere straw man in her view, as symptomatic of the fundamental flaw in the novel: "When an artist who is no blunderer—and Bellow is a supreme artist—furnishes so false a moment, it is something of a revelation. Bellow has failed to give credibility to the opposition." Benjamin DeMott, writing for *Saturday Review,* finds abstractions vivid in the novel but concretions pale. For example, Sammler's detachment, says DeMott, "attains insufficient substance for the reader, seemingly belonging only to the surface structure of Sammler's mind and story . . . whereas his scorn and vituperation come forth strongly as from the center."

Humboldt's Gift is the story of intellectual Chicagoan Charlie Citrine, Pulitzer Prize-winning biographer and dramatist, who approaches the completion of his sixth decade in the company of the nimbus of his deceased poetic mentor, Von Humboldt Fleisher, and the nemesis of his self-appointed materialistic advisor, Rinaldo Cantabile, both manic manipulators. The dead poet speaks to Citrine of his obligation to his creative spirit, art as power. The minor-league Mafioso Cantabile urges capitalistic enterprise, art as profit. Citrine ultimately frees himself from both figures, and at the end walks from the new grave he has provided for Humboldt into an ambivalently emerging spring to begin a meditative life away from the distractions of dissident voices and grotesque behavior. Charlie's compulsive flights into metaphysical explanations have to contend with the corrective pragmatism of his earthy mistress, Renata: "I prefer

to take things as billions of people have throughout history. You work, you get bread, you lose a leg, kiss some fellows, have a baby, you live to be eighty and bug hell out of everybody, or you get hung or drowned. But you don't spend years trying to dope your way out of the human condition. . . . I think when you're dead you're dead, and that's that." Such views lead Renata to abandon the hyperintellectual Citrine and choose an undertaker for a husband. Charlie resists Renata's reality-instructor text by clinging to a message from the dead poet: "Remember: we are not natural beings but supernatural beings," a spiritual reinforcement of Charlie's natural impulses that represents Humboldt's real gift to his protege.

"The novel therefore explores," says Judie Newman in *Saul Bellow and History,* "different approaches to history and retreats from history: pop history, instant history, history as nightmare, as tragedy, as farce, the retreat into myth or transcendence, or into the eternal present of the crisis mentality. By the novel's various structurings of time, Bellow succeeds in avoiding any one style of approach and thereby liberates the event to be judged in its total context, as it affects its participants, as it is recorded in public records, and as it is inherited, transformed and translated by succeeding generations." Bellow himself says in the *Newsweek* interview, "*Humboldt* is very much a comic book about death," and he sees it as an advance in his own authorial detachment and his function as social historian: "The nice thing about this book, which I was really struggling with in *Herzog,* is that I've really come into a cold air of objectivity about all the people in the book, including Charlie. It really came easily for me to see him as America saw him, and thereby America itself became clearer." Despite Bellow's claim of objectivity, the novel contains several elements of his own personal history—the poker game, for example, and the interest in Steinerian philosophy, which Bellow came to by way of Owen Barfield's *Saving the Appearances.* "Does he mean it?—all this business of the soul and an afterlife, and especially about [Rudolf] Steiner and his anthroposophy [or man-centered religious system]," asks Dutton in his revised *Saul Bellow.* "Yes," he answers, "Bellow does—at least figuratively. As far as Steiner is concerned, he is a figure for an illustration of Bellow's contention, through Charlie, that we must try new ideas, even ideas that are unscientific, and hence, that tend to inhibit us. . . . Charlie triumphs over his inhibitions and is able to go ahead with his irrational studies." Still, several critics have observed that there is a shrugging what-the-hell tone about Charlie's experimental commitment to anthroposophy as well as about his shifty character generally that undermines much of his compulsive philosophizing. The novel plays for laughs—and gets them—but it does so in large measure at the expense of its ostensibly serious purposes.

The humor that dominates *Humboldt's Gift* is absent in the ninth novel, *The Dean's December*. As a journalist turned academic, Dean Albert Corde has accompanied his Rumanian-born wife, Minna, to Bucharest to attend her dying mother, Valeria. Isolated in his room or cruising the streets as a "hungry observer" and a "moralist of seeing," Corde observes Bucharest and reflects on Chicago, a city whose "whirling lives" typify the chaotic American reality. The communist and the capitalist cities are grim places of different but related forms of disorder, injustice, repression, and destruction; they are yoked by violence together, for death is everywhere: "I imagine, sometimes," Corde thinks, "that if a film could be made of one's life, every other frame would be death." This macabre mood is sustained throughout the novel even though at the end, after Valeria's death, Corde is comforted briefly by a renewed closeness to his wife that somehow has its counterpart in his closeness to the heavens in the great telescope of the Mount Palomar Observatory. Although he is cold there, he tells his guide as they descend: "But I almost mind coming down more"—that is, coming down to earth, where robbery, rape, murder, prejudice, and political injustice mock the human quest for order, beauty, love, and justice.

Some of the darkness of *The Dean's December* grew out of Bellow's personal experience. Bellow told William Kennedy in *Esquire* that he wrote the novel "in a year and a half . . . and had no idea it was coming. One of these things that came over me. My wife's mother was dying in Bucharest, and I went with her to give her some support, which in that place one badly needs. The old mother died while we were there." Part of the grimness grew out of actual events, like a sensational Chicago rape case, and out of factual conditions, like the Cabrini Green housing project in Chicago, but most of the pessimism came from Bellow's increasing conviction that the decline of civilization is magnified in American cities. Malcolm Bradbury writes in *The Modern American Novel* that *The Dean's December* "confirms the later Bellow as the novelist of a world which has lost cultural bearings, moved into an age of boredom and terror, violence and indifference, private wealth and

public squalor." Bellow himself has been very explicit about his intentions in the novel. He told Matthew C. Roudane in an interview for *Contemporary Literature* that the decaying city has its counterpart in an "inner slum": "What I [mean is] there is a correspondence between outer and inner, between the brutalized city and the psyche of its citizens. Given their human resources I don't see how people today can experience life at all. Politicians, public figures, professors address 'modern problems' solely in terms of employment. They assume that unemployment causes incoherence, sexual disorders, the abandonment of children, robbery, rape and murder. Plainly, they have no imagination of these evils. They don't even *see* them." Ironically an exchange of styles seems to occur, in effect, between Corde and Bellow, for the passionate intensity that allows Corde's journalism to rise to the stature of art—as Bellow describes it here—leads Bellow's prose in the novel as a whole to assume the condition of journalism, the documentary, or, as Roudane observes, "a nonfiction novelistic style," an extension of the essayistic prose that has become more prominent in Bellow's later novels.

Bellow returns to the comic mode in his tenth novel, *More Die of Heartbreak,* a turgid, almost plotless story of two academics connected less by their blood kinship than by their similarly oblique relations to women and to everyday reality. The narrator is thirty-five-year-old Kenneth Tractenberg, a professor of Russian literature at a university in the Midwest. His beloved uncle, Benn Crader, is an internationally respected botanist whose specialty is Arctic lichens and whose patterns of practical misjudgment make him think of himself as "a phoenix who runs with arsonists." Kenneth, though, admires his uncle for reasons that are not clear. Kenneth's philandering father offers his son a sarcastic but perhaps accurate explanation: "you're one of those continuing-education types and you think Benn still has something to teach you." Although intelligent and ceaselessly introspective, Kenneth and Uncle Benn are curious naifs. Kenneth is at great pains to marry Treckie, the mother of his illegitimate daughter and a woman who rejects him to live with a sadist and travel the flea-market circuits. Uncle Benn marries a spoiled rich girl, Matilda Layamon, whose physician father maneuvers to recover Benn's lost inheritance from crooked Uncle Vilitzer so that Matilda can continue to live a life of pampered ease. Benn escapes both the solicitousness of Kenneth and the machinations of the Layamons, finally, by retreating to the North Pole to study lichens.

Critical response to *More Die of Heartbreak* has been characterized by qualified praise and reluctantly held reservations. "Kenneth's free-ranging mind allows Bellow to put just about everything real and imaginable into this novel," notes Robert Wilson in *USA Today*. "Even so, Kenneth does not seem to me to be among the best of Bellow's characters, nor this among the best of Bellow's comic novels. Kenneth wore me out, especially when his divagations took us so far from the plot that it was barely a memory." Clemons, in *Newsweek*, finds the supporting characters more appealing than the principals: "It's a slight drawback to *More Die of Heartbreak* that the innocents in the foreground, Uncle Benn and Kenneth, are upstaged by their captivating adversaries. . . . Our time with Benn and Kenneth is well spent for the sake of the rascals to whom they introduce us." Rhoda Koenig, reviewing for *New York*, contends that the sympathy implicit in the title is overshadowed by an intelligence that fails to sustain its own weight: "Bellow's heart seems to be more with the brutal comedy of the doctor than all his sodden mind games with Kenneth and Benn. In *More Die of Heartbreak*, despite the often voiced concern epitomized by the title, it is the mind that is given center stage, and fails to hold it." On the other hand, in the *New York Times Book Review*, William Gaddis judges the return of the wry Bellovian humor an ample trade-off for a makeshift plot: "In *More Die of Heartbreak* we welcome back the calamitous wit of *The Adventures of Augie March* and *Herzog* among people diligently struggling to rearrange one another's lives in their efforts to rescue or simply to define their own. . . . We hear their voices pour from the pages engulfing a plot that is comparatively simple, or would be if left to itself, a possibility this embattled narrator never entertains for a moment."

Although he has always been better known for his fictional explorations of contemporary life, Bellow has also confronted these issues through essays published in various periodicals and through lectures. Many of these are reprinted in Bellow's first collection of nonfiction writing, *It All Adds Up: From the Dim Past to the Uncertain Future*. "Here, in these nonfiction writings," notes Mark Harris in *Tribune Books*, "Saul Bellow draws upon those powers of observation basic to his fiction: his minutely detailed descriptions of people and places and striking conclusions about wonders of the world he has seen in many places." *Spectator* contributor Tom Shone also observes a kinship between these essays and Bellow's fiction. He writes: "Like his novels, Saul Bellow's journalism throngs with memorable grotesques."

According to Harris, "This book of selected essays, articles, travel accounts, lectures, historical recollections, character analysis, literary appreciations and cheerful obituaries . . . is no mere dutiful repository of tame pieces or curiosities." Rather, comments the reviewer, "These are vivid, vibrant documents telling us how we have lived during the life of Bellow's memory . . . and how we might yet perfect ourselves, how the world might become that place in which art reigns and thought becomes aesthetic pleasure." *New York Times Book Review* contributor Peter S. Prescott finds that "the best entries in *It All Adds Up* are autobiographical—sharp vignettes of the author at a certain time and in a specific place—or memories of friends and colleagues like John Berryman, John Cheever and Isaac Rosenfeld." Mordecai Richler offers a similar view in the *National Review*, writing that "a couple of the most enjoyable pieces in *It All Adds Up* are memoirs of Chicago. His prodigious gifts as a novelist beyond dispute, Mr. Bellow turns out to be a first-rate reporter as well." Ruben adds that this "collection is enriched by splendid accounts of Paris circa 1948, a journey through Franco's Spain, and reports from Tel Aviv and the Sinai in the aftermath of the Six-Day War."

Richler faults Bellow for the author's "touchingly mistaken belief that he is still addressing a literate rather than today's largely post-literate audience." *Christian Science Monitor* reviewer Merle Rubin also observes that "some of Bellow's pronouncements betray a sort of dismissive irritability toward the claims of feminists, homosexuals, and multiculturalists." Yet, as Richler concludes, *It All Adds Up* can be read as a "thoughtful, provocative, and only occasionally querulous addendum to the work of a novelist who has given us more aesthetic bliss than most."

BIOGRAPHICAL/CRITICAL SOURCES:

BOOKS

Aldridge, John W., *Time to Murder and Create*, McKay (New York City), 1966.

Ananad, Tarlochan Singh, *Saul Bellow: The Feminine Mystique*, ABS Publications (Jalandhar, India), 1993.

Authors in the News, Volume 2, Gale (Detroit), 1976.

Bach, Gerhard, and Jakob J. Kollhofer, editors, *Saul Bellow at Seventy-five: A Collection of Critical Essays*, G. Narr (Tubingen, Germany), 1991.

Bakker, J., *Fiction as Survival Strategy: A Comparative Study of the Major Works of Ernest Hemingway and Saul Bellow,* Humanities Press (Atlantic Highlands, NJ), 1983.

Baumbach, Jonathan, *The Landscape of Nightmare: Studies in the Contemporary Novel,* New York University Press, 1965.

Bellow, Saul, *Conversations with Saul Bellow,* edited by Gloria L. Cronin and Ben Siegel, University Press of Mississippi, 1994.

Bloom, Harold, editor, *Saul Bellow,* Chelsea House (New York City), 1986.

Bradbury, Malcolm, *The Modern American Novel,* Oxford University Press, 1983.

Braham, Jeanne, *A Sort of Columbus: The American Voyages of Saul Bellow's Fiction,* University of Georgia Press (Athens), 1984.

Breit, Harvey, *The Writer Observed,* World Publishing, 1956.

Clayton, John J., *Saul Bellow: In Defense of Man,* Indiana University Press (Bloomington), 1968, 2nd edition, 1979.

Cohen, Sarah Blacher, *Saul Bellow's Enigmatic Laughter,* University of Illinois Press (Champaign), 1974.

Concise Dictionary of American Literary Biography: The New Consciousness, 1941-1968, Gale, 1987.

Contemporary Authors Autobiography Series, Gale, Volume 1, 1984.

Contemporary Fiction in America and England, 1950-1970, Gale, 1976.

Contemporary Literary Criticism, Gale, Volume 1, 1973, Volume 2, 1974, Volume 3, 1975, Volume 6, 1976, Volume 8, 1978, Volume 10, 1979, Volume 13, 1980, Volume 15, 1980, Volume 25, 1983, Volume 33, 1985, Volume 34, 1985, Volume 63, 1991, Volume 79, 1993.

Conversations with Contemporary American Writers, Rodopi, 1985.

Cronin, Gloria L., and Blaine H. Hall, *Saul Bellow: An Annotated Bibliography,* 2nd edition, Garland Publishing (New York City), 1987.

Detweiler, Robert, *Saul Bellow: A Critical Essay,* Eerdmans, 1967.

Dictionary of Literary Biography, Gale, Volume 2: *American Novelists since World War II,* 1978, Volume 28: *Twentieth-Century American Jewish Fiction Writers,* 1984.

Dictionary of Literary Biography Yearbook, 1982, Gale, 1983.

Dutton, Robert R., *Saul Bellow,* Twayne (Boston), 1971, revised edition, 1982.

Eisinger, Chester E., *Fiction of the Forties,* University of Chicago Press, 1963.

Friedrich, Marianne M., *Character and Narration in the Short Fiction of Saul Bellow,* Peter Lang (New York City), 1995.

Fuchs, Daniel, *Saul Bellow: Vision and Revision,* Duke University Press (Durham, NC), 1984, p. 345.

Galloway, David D., *The Absurd Hero in American Fiction: Updike, Styron, Bellow, Salinger,* University of Texas Press (Austin), 1966, revised edition, 1970, 2nd revised edition, 1981.

Geismar, Maxwell, *American Moderns: From Rebellion to Conformity,* Hill & Wang (New York City), 1958.

Glenday, Michael K., *The Modern American Novella,* St. Martin's (New York City), 1989.

Glenday, *Saul Bellow and the Decline of Humanism,* St. Martin's, 1990.

Goldman, Cronin, and Ada Aharoni, compilers, *Saul Bellow: A Mosaic,* Peter Lang, 1992.

Goldman, L. H., *Saul Bellow's Moral Vision: A Critical Study of the Jewish Experience,* Irvington Publishers (New York City), 1983.

Gullette, Margaret Morganroth, *Safe at Last in the Middle Years: The Invention of the Midlife Progress Novel,* University of California Press (Berkeley), 1988.

Guttmann, Allen, *The Jewish Writer in America: Assimilation and the Crisis of Identity,* Oxford University Press (New York City), 1971.

Hall, James, *The Lunatic Giant in the Drawing Room,* Indiana University Press, 1968.

Handy, William J., *Modern Fiction: A Formalist Approach,* Southern Illinois University Press (Carbondale), 1971.

Harper, Howard, *Desperate Faith: A Study of Bellow, Salinger, Mailer, Baldwin, and Updike,* University of North Carolina Press (Chapel Hill), 1967.

Harris, Mark, *Saul Bellow: Drumlin Woodchuck,* University of Georgia Press (Athens), 1980.

Hassan, Ihab, *Radical Innocence: Studies in the Contemporary American Novel,* Harper, 1966.

Hendin, Josephine, *Vulnerable People: A View of American Fiction since 1945,* Oxford University Press, 1978.

Hollahan, Eugene, editor, *Saul Bellow and the Struggle at the Center,* AMS Press (New York City), 1994.

Howe, Irving, editor, *Saul Bellow: Herzog; Text and Criticism,* Viking, 1976.

Hyland, Peter, *Saul Bellow,* St. Martin's, 1992.

Iwayama, Tajiro, editor, *Saul Bellow,* Yamaguchi Shoten (Kyoto, Japan), 1982.

Kazin, Alfred, *Contemporaries,* Little, Brown (Boston), 1962.

Kiernan, Robert F., *Saul Bellow,* Continuum (New York City), 1989.

Kim, Kyung-Ae, *Quest for Salvation in Saul Bellow's Novels,* Lang (Frankfurt am Main, Germany), 1994.

Klein, Marcus, *After Alienation: American Novels in Mid-Century,* World Publishing, 1965.

Kulshrestha, Chirantan, *Saul Bellow: The Problem of Affirmation,* Arnold-Heinemann (New Delhi, India), 1978.

Lercangee, Francine, *Saul Bellow: A Bibliography of Secondary Sources,* Center for American Studies (Brussels, Belgium), 1977.

Malin, Irving, *Jews and Americans,* Southern Illinois University Press, 1965.

Malin, editor, *Saul Bellow and the Critics,* New York University Press, 1967.

Malin, *Saul Bellow's Fiction,* Southern Illinois University Press, 1969.

McCadden, Joseph F., *The Flight from Women in the Fiction of Saul Bellow,* University Press of America (Lanham, MD), 1980.

McConnell, Frank D., *Four Post-War American Novelists: Bellow, Mailer, Barth, and Pynchon,* Chicago University Press, 1977.

Melbourne, Lucy L., *Double Heart: Explicit and Implicit Texts in Bellow, Camus, and Kafka,* Peter Lang, 1986.

Miller, Ruth, *Saul Bellow: A Biography of the Imagination,* St. Martin's, 1991.

Moore, Harry T., editor, *Contemporary American Novelists,* Southern Illinois University Press, 1964.

Nault, Marianne, *Saul Bellow: His Works and His Critics; An Annotated International Bibliography,* Garland Publishing, 1977.

Nelson, Gerald B., *Ten Versions of America,* Knopf (New York City), 1972.

Newman, Judie, *Saul Bellow and History,* St. Martin's, 1984.

Noreen, Robert G., *Saul Bellow: A Reference Guide,* G. K. Hall (Boston), 1978.

Opdahl, Keith, *The Novels of Saul Bellow: An Introduction,* Pennsylvania State University Press (University Park), 1967.

Pifer, Ellen, *Saul Bellow against the Grain,* University of Pennsylvania Press (Philadelphia), 1990.

Porter, M. Gilbert, *Whence the Power?: The Artistry and Humanity of Saul Bellow,* University of Missouri Press (Columbia), 1974.

Rodrigues, Eusebio L., *Quest for the Human: An Exploration of Saul Bellow's Fiction,* Bucknell University Press (Cranbury, NJ), 1981.

Rovit, Earl, *Saul Bellow,* University of Minnesota Press (Minneapolis), 1967.

Rovit, editor, *Saul Bellow: A Collection of Critical Essays,* Prentice-Hall (Englewood Cliffs, NJ), 1975.

Rupp, Richard H., *Celebration in Postwar American Fiction,* University of Miami Press, 1970.

Schechner, Mark, *After the Revolution: Studies in the Contemporary Jewish American Imagination,* Indiana University Press, 1987.

Scheer-Schaezler, Brigitte, *Saul Bellow,* Ungar (New York City), 1972.

Schraepen, Edmond, editor, *Saul Bellow and His Work,* Free University of Brussels, 1978.

Schultz, Max F., *Radical Sophistication: Studies in Contemporary Jewish/American Novelists,* Ohio University Press (Athens), 1969.

Scott, Nathan A., Jr., *Three American Moralists: Mailer, Bellow, Trilling,* University of Notre Dame Press (Notre Dame, IN), 1968.

Siegel, Ben, *The American Writer and the University,* University of Delaware Press (Newark), 1989.

Singh, Sukhbir, *The Survivor in Contemporary American Fiction: Saul Bellow, Bernard Malamud, John Updike, Kurt Vonnegut, Jr.,* B. R. Publishing (Delhi, India), 1991.

Sokoloff, B. A., and Mark Posner, *Saul Bellow: A Comprehensive Bibliography,* Folcroft Library Editions (Folcroft, PA), 1972.

Tanner, Tony, *Saul Bellow,* Oliver & Boyd, 1965.

Tanner, *City of Words: American Fiction 1950-1970,* Harper, 1971.

Trachtenberg, Stanley, editor, *Critical Essays on Saul Bellow,* G. K. Hall, 1979.

Walden, Daniel, editor, *Studies in American Jewish Literature,* State University of New York Press (Albany), 1983.

Weinberg, Helen, *The New Novel in America: The Kafkan Mode in Contemporary Fiction,* Cornell University Press (Ithaca, NY), 1970.

Wilson, Jonathan, *On Bellow's Planet: Readings from the Dark Side,* Associated University Presses (Toronto), 1985, Fairleigh Dickinson University Press (East Brunswick, NJ), 1986.

Wilson, *Herzog: The Limits of Ideas,* Twayne, 1990.

PERIODICALS

Accent, Volume 18, 1958.

American Literature, Volume 43, number 2, 1971; July, 1989, p. 47.

American Spectator, September, 1987, p. 43.

Antioch Review, summer, 1982, p. 266.

Atlantic Monthly, January, 1965; October, 1995, p. 114.

Boston Globe, April 17, 1994, p. A14.

Centennial Review, Volume 22, 1978.

Chicago Jewish Forum, Volume 28, 1959.

Chicago Review, Volume 23, number 4, 1972; Volume 32, number 4, 1981, p. 92.

Chicago Tribune, April 18, 1990, sec. 5, p. 1; March 2, 1990, sec. 5, p. 1; May 25, 1993, sec. 2c, p. 1; June 19, 1994, sec. 10, p. 8.

Christian Science Monitor, November 1, 1985, p. B11; July 3, 1987, p. B1; April 28, 1994, p. 14.

College English, Volume 34, 1973.

College Language Association Journal, Volume 10, 1967.

Commentary, June, 1994, p. 37.

Commonweal, December 4, 1987, p. 715.

Comparative Literature Studies, Volume 3, number 2, 1966.

Contemporary Literature, Volume 25, number 3, 1984.

Critical Quarterly, Volume 15, 1973.

Criticism, Volume 15, number 3, 1973.

Critique: Studies in Modern Fiction, Volume 3, 1960; Volume 7, 1965; Volume 9, 1967; Volume 9, 1968.

Durham University Journal, Volume 72, number 1, 1979.

Encounter, Volume 24, number 2, 1965; Volume 45, number 5, 1975.

Esquire, February, 1982.

Essays in Literature, Volume 5, 1979.

Forum, Volume 7, 1969; Volume 14, number 1, 1976.

Georgia Review, winter, 1978.

Harper's, August, 1974.

Historical Reflections, Volume 3, number 2, 1976.

Hudson Review, Volume 12, 1959.

Indian Journal of American Studies, Volume 8, number 2, 1978.

Journal of American Studies, Volume 7, 1973; Volume 9, 1975; Volume 15, 1981.

Judaism, Volume 22, 1972.

Life, April 3, 1970.

Listener, February 13, 1975.

Literary Times, December, 1964.

London Review of Books, November 12, 1987, p. 3; March 30, 1989, p. 21; January 11, 1990, p. 11.

Los Angeles Times Book Review, November 17, 1985, p. 14; June 14, 1987, p. 1; March 19, 1989, p. 3.

Mature Outlook, Volume 1, number 3, 1984.

McNeese Review, Volume 24, 1977-78.

Midstream, Volume 10, number 4, 1964.

Modern Age, winter, 1984, p. 55.

Modern Fiction Studies, Volume 12, 1966-67; Volume 17, 1971; Volume 19, 1973; Volume 25, 1979.

Modern Language Studies, winter, 1986, p. 71.

Nation, February 9, 1970; May 15, 1989, p. 674; November 27, 1989, p. 652; August 8, 1994, p. 168.

National Review, July 17, 1987, p. 49; March 5, 1990, p. 52; August 1, 1994, p. 58.

New England Review, Volume 1, 1972.

New Republic, January 1, 1990, p. 37; May 2, 1994, p. 37.

New Statesman, October 23, 1987, p. 28; March 31, 1989, p. 35; October 20, 1989, p. 46.

Newsweek, September 1, 1975; June 8, 1987.

New York, June 8, 1987.

New Yorker, September 15, 1975; July 27, 1987, p. 89; May 1, 1989, p. 111; May 16, 1994, p. 109.

New York Review of Books, July 16, 1987, p. 3; April 27, 1989, p. 50; October 12, 1989, p. 34.

New York Times, May 21, 1987, p. 21; April 11, 1994, p. C15.

New York Times Book Review, February 15, 1959; May 9, 1971; October 27, 1985, p. 50; May 24, 1987, p. 1; March 5, 1989, p. 3; October 1, 1989, p. 11; April 10, 1994, p. 9.

New York Times Magazine, November 21, 1978; April 15, 1984, p 52.

Notes on Modern American Literature, Volume 2, number 4, 1978.

Observer, December 2, 1984, p. 19; April 2, 1989, p. 45; October 8, 1989, p. 46; September 11, 1994, p. 23.

Paris Review, Volume 9, number 36, 1966.

Partisan Review, Volume 26, number 3, 1959.

People, September 8, 1975.

Rolling Stone, March 4, 1982.

St. Louis Post-Dispatch, November 16, 1986.

Salmagundi (special Bellow issue), Volume 30, 1975.

Saturday Review, February 7, 1970.

Saturday Review of Literature, August 22, 1953; September 19, 1953; September 19, 1964.

Saul Bellow Journal, Volume 4, number 1, 1985; Volume 5, numbers 1 and 2, 1986; Volume 6, number 1, 1987.

Saul Bellow Newsletter, Volume 1, number 1, 1981.

Show, September, 1964.

South Carolina Review, Volume 6, number 1, 1973.

Southern Review, Volume 3, number 1, 1967.

Southwest Review, Volume 62, 1977.

Spectator, October 31, 1987, p. 36; April 15, 1989, p. 29; October 14, 1989, p. 34; September 17, 1994, p. 35.

Studies in Literature and Language, winter, 1987, p. 442.

Studies in Short Fiction, summer, 1974, p. 297.

Studies in the Literary Imagination (special Bellow issue), Volume 17, number 2, 1984, p. 59.

Studies in the Novel, Volume 1, number 3, 1969; Volume 15, number 3, 1983, p. 249.

Studies in the Twentieth Century, Volume 14, 1974.

Time, May 9, 1994, p. 80.

Times Literary Supplement, October 23, 1987, p. 71; March 24, 1989, p. 299; October 27, 1989, p. 1181; November 6, 1992, p. 20; September 23, 1994, p. 25.

Tribune Books, May 31, 1987, p. 1; March 5, 1989, p. 1; October 8, 1989, p. 3; April 10, 1994, p. 1.

Twentieth Century Literature, Volume 18, number 4, 1972.

University Review, Volume 37, number 1, 1970.

USA Today, June 5, 1987.

Voice Literary Supplement, March, 1990, p. 11.

Wascana Review, Volume 6, number 1, 1971.

Washington Post Book World, June 7, 1987, p. 1; December 3, 1989, p. 3; March 27, 1994, p. 3.

Western Humanities Review, Volume 14, 1960.

World Literature Today, autumn, 1992, p. 721.*

*   *   *

BERESFORD, Elisabeth

PERSONAL: Born in Paris, France; daughter of J. D. (a novelist) and Evelyn (Roskams) Beresford; married Maxwell Robertson (a sports commentator), 1949; children: Kate, Marcus. *Education:* Attended schools in Brighton, Sussex, England. *Avocational interests:* Reading, photography, surfing, gardening, "and not working, if at all possible."

ADDRESSES: Home—Alderney, Channel Islands. *Agent*—Juvenilia, Avington, Winchester, Hampshire, SO21 1DB, England.

CAREER: Writer; freelance journalist, beginning 1949; radio broadcaster. *Military service:* Radio operator in Women's Royal Naval Service during World War II.

WRITINGS:

FOR CHILDREN

The Television Mystery, Parrish (London), 1957.

The Flying Doctor Mystery, Parrish, 1958.

Trouble at Tullington Castle, Parrish, 1958.

Cocky and the Missing Castle, illustrated by Jennifer Miles, Constable (London), 1959.

Gappy Goes West, Parrish, 1959.

The Tullington Film-Makers, Parrish, 1960.

Two Gold Dolphins, illustrated by Peggy Fortnum, Constable, 1961, new edition illustrated by Janina Domanska, Bobbs-Merrill (Indianapolis, IN), 1964.

Danger on the Old Pull 'n Push, Parrish, 1962, White Lion, 1976.

Strange Hiding Place, Parrish, 1962.

Diana in Television, Collins (London), 1963.

The Missing Formula Mystery, Parrish, 1963.

The Mulberry Street Team (also see below), illustrated by Juliet Pannett, Friday Press (Penshurst, Kent), 1963.

Awkward Magic, illustrated by Judith Valpy, Hart-Davis (London), 1964, new edition illustrated by Domanska, published as *The Magic World,* Bobbs-Merrill, 1965, revised edition illustrated by Cathy Wood, published as *Strange Magic,* Methuen, 1986.

The Flying Doctor to the Rescue, Parrish, 1964.

Holiday for Slippy, illustrated by Pat Williams, Friday Press, 1964.

Game, Set, and Match, Parrish, 1965.

Knights of the Cardboard Castle, illustrated by C. R. Evans, Methuen, 1965, revised edition illustrated by Reginald Gray, 1976.

Travelling Magic, illustrated by Valpy, Hart-Davis, 1965, published as *The Vanishing Garden,* Funk (New York City), 1967.

The Hidden Mill, illustrated by Margery Gill, Benn (London), 1965, Meredith Press (New York City), 1967.

Peter Climbs a Tree, illustrated by Gill, Benn, 1966.

Fashion Girl, Collins, 1967.

The Black Mountain Mystery, Parrish, 1967.

Looking for a Friend, illustrated by Gill, Benn, 1967.

More Adventure Stories (includes *The Mulberry Street Team*), Benn, 1967.

The Island Bus, illustrated by Robert Hodgson, Methuen, 1968, revised edition illustrated by Gavin Rowe, 1977.

Sea-Green Magic, illustrated by Ann Tout, Hart-Davis, 1968.

David Goes Fishing, illustrated by Imre Hofbauer, Benn, 1969.

Gordon's Go-Kart, illustrated by Gill, McGraw (New York City), 1970.

Stephen and the Shaggy Dog, illustrated by Robert Hales, Methuen, 1970.

Vanishing Magic, illustrated by Tout, Hart-Davis, 1970.

Dangerous Magic, illustrated by Oliver Chadwick, Hart-Davis, 1972.

The Secret Railway, illustrated by James Hunt, Methuen, 1973.

Invisible Magic, illustrated by Gray, Hart-Davis, 1974.

Snuffle to the Rescue, illustrated by Gunvor Edwards, Kestrel (London), 1975.

Beginning to Read Storybook, Benn, 1977.

Toby's Luck, illustrated by Doreen Caldwell, Methuen, 1978.

Secret Magic, illustrated by Caroline Sharp, Hart Davis, 1978.

The Happy Ghost, illustrated by Joanna Carey, Methuen, 1979.

The Treasure Hunters, illustrated by Carey, Elsevier Nelson (New York City), 1980.

Curious Magic, illustrated by Claire Upsdale-Jones, Elsevier Nelson, 1980.

The Four of Us, illustrated by Trevor Stubley, Hutchinson (London), 1981.

The Animals Nobody Wanted, illustrated by Carey, Methuen, 1982.

(Adapter) *Jack and the Magic Stove* (folktale), illustrated by Rita van Bilsen, Hutchinson, 1982.

The Tovers, illustrated by Geoffrey Beitz, Methuen, 1982.

The Adventures of Poon, illustrated by Dinah Shedden, Hutchinson, 1984.

The Mysterious Island, illustrated by Carey, Methuen, 1984.

One of the Family, illustrated by Barrie Thorpe, Hutchinson, 1985.

The Ghosts of Lupus Street School, Methuen, 1986.

Emily and the Haunted Castle, illustrated by Kate Rogers, Hutchinson, 1987.

Once upon a Time Stories, illustrated by Alice Englander, Methuen, 1987.

The Secret Room, illustrated by Michael Bragg, Methuen, 1987.

The Armada Adventure, Methuen, 1988.

The Island Railway, illustrated by Maggie Harrison, Hamish Hamilton (London), 1988.

Rose, Hutchinson, 1989.

Charlie's Ark, Methuen, 1989.

The Wooden Gun, Hippo (London), 1989.

Tim the Trumpet, Blackie (London), 1992.

Jamie and the Rola Polar Bear, illustrated by Janet Robertson, Blackie, 1993.

Lizzie's War, illustrated by James Mayhew, Simon & Schuster (London), 1993.

Rola Polar Bear and the Heatwave, illustrated by Robertson, Blackie, 1994.

The Smallest Whale, illustrated by Susan Field, Orchard Books, 1996.

Lizzie's War, Part II, illustrated by Mayhew, Simon & Schuster, 1996.

"THE WOMBLES" SERIES; FOR CHILDREN

The Wombles (also see below), illustrated by Margaret Gordon, Benn, 1968, Meredith Press, 1969.

The Wandering Wombles (also see below), illustrated by Oliver Chadwick, Benn, 1970.

The Invisible Womble and Other Stories, illustrated by Ivor Wood, Benn, 1973.

The Wombles in Danger, Benn, 1973.

The Wombles at Work (also see below), illustrated by Gordon, Benn, 1973, revised edition illustrated by B. Leith, 1976.

The Wombles Go to the Seaside, World Distributors (London), 1974.

The Wombles Annual, 1975-1978 (four volumes) World Distributors, 1974-77.

The Wombles Book (includes *The Wombles* and *The Wandering Wombles*), Benn, 1975.

Tomsk and the Tired Tree, illustrated by Gordon, Benn, 1975.

Wellington and the Blue Balloon, illustrated by Gordon, Benn, 1975.

Orinoco Runs Away, illustrated by Gordon, Benn, 1975.

The Wombles Gift Book, illustrated by Gordon and Derek Collard, Benn, 1975.

The Snow Womble, illustrated by Gordon, Benn, 1975.

The Wombles Make a Clean Sweep, illustrated by Wood, Benn, 1975.

The Wombles to the Rescue (also see below), illustrated by Gordon, Benn, 1975.

Tobermory's Big Surprise, illustrated by Gordon, Benn, 1976.

Madame Cholet's Picnic Party, illustrated by Gordon, Benn, 1976.

Bungo Knows Best, illustrated by Gordon, Benn, 1976.

The Wombles of Wimbledon (includes *The Wombles at Work* and *The Wombles to the Rescue*), Benn, 1976.

The MacWomble's Pipe Band, illustrated by Gordon, Benn, 1976.

The Wombles Go round the World, illustrated by Gordon, Benn, 1976.

The World of the Wombles, illustrated by Edgar Hodges, World Distributors, 1976.

Wombling Free, illustrated by Hodges, Benn, 1978.

Also author of *The Wombles* (screenplay), 1971, sixty television scripts for *The Wombles* (series), from 1973, and of *The Wombles* (play), first produced in London, 1974.

NOVELS; FOR ADULTS

Paradise Island, Hale (London), 1963.
Escape to Happiness, Hale, 1964, Nordon (New York City), 1980.
Roses round the Door, Hale, 1964, Paperback Library (New York City), 1965.
Island of Shadows, Hale, 1966, Dale (New York City), 1980.
Veronica, Hale, 1967, Nordon, 1980.
A Tropical Affair, Hale, 1967, published as *Tropical Affairs,* Dell (New York City), 1978.
Saturday's Child, Hale, 1968, published as *Echoes of Love,* Dell, 1979.
Love Remembered, Hale, 1970, Dale, 1978.
Love and the S.S. Beatrice, Hale, 1972, published as *Thunder of Her Heart,* Dale, 1978.
Pandora, Hale, 1974.
The Steadfast Lover, Hale, 1980.
The Silver Chain, Hale, 1980.
The Restless Heart, Valueback (New York City), 1982.
Flight to Happiness, Hale, 1983.
A Passionate Adventure, Hale, 1983.

OTHER

(With Nick Renton) *Road to Albutal* (play), produced in Edinburgh, Scotland, 1976.
(With Peter Spence) *Move On,* BBC Publications, 1978.
The Best of Friends (play), produced in the Channel Islands, 1982.

Also contributor of short stories to magazines.

SIDELIGHTS: Elisabeth Beresford has achieved her greatest success as a writer through the creation of the "Wombles," a small race of creatures that inhabit her "Wombles" series of books for children. In over twenty-five books, this hard-working, fun-loving family, who live by the motto "make good use of bad rubbish," uphold old-fashioned virtues and introduce children to the more modern value of conservation.

Beresford was born in Paris, France, where her father, novelist J. D. Beresford, was living at the time. She returned to England and was educated in British schools. "Having a novelist for a father and two brothers who were successful writers I was brought up in a world of books," Beresford once recalled,

"so it seemed natural that I should become a writer too." She started off working as a journalist and eventually became a radio and television reporter for the BBC, a job that took her from the Outback in Australia to the jungles of South America. "Which, of course, all make wonderful backgrounds for books," she explained. "I've also met some extraordinary and unusual people; from goldminers to royalty, from Dukes to derelicts."

Beresford's furry "Wombles" creatures who live in burrows underneath the London suburb of Wimbledon, take their names from an atlas, are led by Great Uncle Bulgaria, and were introduced to young readers for the first time in 1969's *The Wombles.* As ardent collectors of things, words, and knowledge, Wombles are expert recyclers, intelligent, and, as Ginger Brauer observes in *Library Journal,* "generally superior in virtues to [Humans] . . . with whom they don't normally associate." In the over twenty books that followed—from *The Wombles at Work* and *Wellington and the Blue Balloon* to *Wombling Free,* the crowning book of the series—Beresford's engaging characters go beyond merely illustrating moral tales about picking up garbage and conserving natural resources. Their inventiveness and positive approach to many of society's growing problems have drawn praise from critics, and the author's sprightly prose keeps young readers interested. With the Wombles, Beresford "has done more than graft human characters on to animals," notes Margery Fisher in *Growing Point.* Instead the author "has created a new race, as consistent and plausible as the hobbits of Tolkien, whose likeness to ourselves is only one aspect of their existence."

The illustrations for Beresford's "Wombles" books were inspired by the puppetry magic of Ivor Wood, who designed the marionette figures used in the popular television series *The Wombles.* The majority of the books in the series have depicted Wood's original puppet characters—like Bungo, Tomsk, and Wellington—in vivid illustrations by Margaret Gordon. The Wombles have become somewhat of a legend in children's literature. The stories have been translated into twenty languages and made into both films and a television series.

Beresford has written many other novels for children including both fantasy and adventure. Beresford "shares in some degree the dilemma of [Arthur] Conan Doyle," contends Marcus Crouch in *Twentieth-Century Children's Writers.* Explaining that Conan Doyle's character of Sherlock Holmes "hung around his neck like a dead weight," forcing him to continue writing fiction featuring that famous detective long after he wanted to, Crouch goes on to say, "Beresford invented the Wombles. . . . There can be no doubt that, in writing these gently humorous tales, she is sharing with readers her own warm affection for these curious creatures. But, in achieving a runaway success with the Wombles, Beresford has distracted attention from her other, and not less important, writing."

The Animals Nobody Wanted is just one of Beresford's books of real-life adventure focusing on the concerns of young readers. Sharing the theme of conservation with the Wombles books, this 1982 novel tells about Rosa and Paul, who go on a seaside vacation and meet Granny Campbell, an old woman who lives in run-down Ballig Fort near the sea. Granny is dedicated to caring for the oil-soaked seabirds she finds near her door, as well as other sick animals who are gathered up by a local boy named Midge. Rosa and Paul bring their city-bred instincts for commerce to the aid of Granny and her animal hospital, gathering support from the nearby townspeople and getting funding for the woman's humanitarian efforts. "Elisabeth Beresford knows how to tell a good story and this one is nicely constructed [and] pleasantly readable," D. A. Young writes in *Junior Bookshelf*.

In *The Adventures of Poon* Beresford portrays the problems of an average family in dealing with a disabled child. Poon is profoundly deaf; when she is taken by her social worker to a farm in the country to allow her mother a chance to rest, Poon tries to run away. It's then that her adventures begin: in her quest for independence she helps the police by discovering an important piece of evidence in a police investigation into cattle rustling, uncovers a flint axehead for a local archaeologist, and, along the way, learns to cope with her own sense of isolation from speaking people and accept and to enjoy her new surroundings. In a *School Librarian* review, Sheila Armstrong comments that the characters are "likeable and amusing" but not idealized, and adds that Poon's adventures "are told with a lighthearted and sure touch."

Being uprooted and having to cope with a whole new set of people and circumstances is a situation that many children—not only those who are hearing-impaired or otherwise disabled—have to deal with sometime in their childhood, and it provides the subject of Beresford's 1988 novel *The Island Railway* as well. When Police Sergeant Stafford is transferred

from a busy town to a small, scantily populated island off the English coast, his son Thomas is not thrilled. Grudgingly, he seeks the friendship of Matthew, whose father is a fisherman, and together the two boys explore the small island with the help of Matthew's dog. When they find an old engine and a pair of abandoned railcars left behind after a local quarry shut down years before, the boy's stick-to-itiveness inspires the entire community—including a cantankerous elderly neighbor who alone has the knowledge to get the old engine moving again—to help set up a railroad on the island. "Beresford always fills her tales with vigorously drawn characters and this new story is no exception," commented Fisher in *Growing Point*. "Here is a most believable group of people linked in an unusual enterprise."

In Beresford's books, the everyday world can often stray into the realm of the fantastic, often at the most unpredictable times. Quite ordinary children can suddenly find themselves experiencing quite extraordinary things. "One of the many wonderful things about children is that *they* still live in a world where anything is possible," Beresford commented, "and the words 'once upon a time' can make it all happen." In the author's "Magic" books that began in 1964 with the publication of *Awkward Magic,* she weaves a spell of various impossibilities. In this first novel, for example, Beresford's characters journey through time. On his first day of school vacation, Joe finds a stray dog cowering in the basement of the flat where he lives with his father's landlady. The dog, who is actually an ancient griffin, has been sent from Antiquity to recover a lost treasure. Along the way, Joe and the Griffin gain an ally in Grace, a young girl who lives in the mansion where the treasure is finally located. "Beresford has the happily offhand, confident way with magic with which Edith Nesbit conducted her tales," comments *Growing Point*'s Fisher in her review of the book's 1986 update, titled *Strange Magic*. The critic adds that "comic fantasy is one of the trickiest outlets for imagination, demanding discipline, moderation, lightness of touch and complete confidence, all of which Elisabeth Beresford certainly has."

In 1978's *Secret Magic,* Beresford showcases her skills in the story of two boys who run a vegetable stand in the local farmer's market for their great uncle. When they discover a scruffy-looking cat haunting the market, they first react as typical boys and try to shoo it away. The cat begins to speak in its own defense and turns out to be a three-thousand-year-old Sphinx banished from his home for talkativeness. "Very well written indeed," B. Clark writes in *Junior Bookshelf,* "this is first-class reading." *Curious Magic,* published in 1980, repeats the time-travel motif as young Andy Jones comes to realize a striking similarity between the Mr. Dunk he knows as a neighbor on the island where he is spending his winter vacation, a Mr. Donkey from Roman days, and a Mr. Dunker from the Tudor period. The reason he knows so many people from ages past? His neighbor, the "white witch" Mrs. Tressida, and her niece Ella practice a form of magic that carries the three in and out of ages past to experience British history first-hand. *Curious Magic* "is warmed by humour and sharpened by the unexacting and intriguing shifts in time which Andy, a responsive but not over-emotional lad, takes in his stride," according to Fisher of *Growing Point.*

Although she has been a successful author for most of her adult life, Beresford is quick to note that it hasn't gotten any easier. "I hate typing the dreaded words 'Chapter One' as I find writing very hard work and will think up a dozen good reasons for *not* sitting down at the typewriter," she once confessed. "But one of the great bonuses is getting letters from children all over the world who sometimes just put 'The Wombles, England' on the envelope." "My pet peeve is the people who say, 'Of course I could write a book if I had the time,'" she once confessed. "If I had a sunny day for every time that's been said to me I should live in a world of perpetual sunshine." Despite her professed difficulty with writing, Beresford's love of her craft has inspired many others—including her own children: daughter Kate has written several children's books and son Marcus is a sports journalist.

"Children (and adults) write to me from all over the world," Beresford explained, "and quite often they seem to know more about my books than I do. I particularly like listening to children, because—fortunately—they still go on believing that anything is possible and that all kinds of adventures are just around the next corner. And when I put something funny into a story and it makes me laugh I know it will make a lot of children laugh. And there's no better sound in the world than children laughing."

BIOGRAPHICAL/CRITICAL SOURCES:

BOOKS

Something About the Author, Volume 86, Gale (Detroit), 1996.

Something About the Author Autobiography Series, Volume 20, Gale, 1995.
Twentieth-Century Children's Writers, 4th edition, St. James Press (Detroit), 1995.

PERIODICALS

Booklist, March 15, 1978, p. 1185.
Growing Point, January, 1976, p. 2785; March, 1979, p. 3467; July, 1980, p. 3716; July, 1981, p. 3910; July, 1986, p. 4641; September, 1988, p. 5026; July, 1989, p. 5096.
Horn Book, August, 1965, p. 390.
Junior Bookshelf, December, 1978, p. 298; August, 1982, p. 138; December, 1988, p. 287; February, 1990, p. 34; April, 1994, p. 54.
Library Journal, March 15, 1970, p. 1192.
Publishers Weekly, May 1, 1967, p. 56.
School Librarian, March, 1979, p. 34; December, 1982, p. 329; September, 1984, p. 233.
School Library Journal, May 15, 1967, p. 55, 74; August, 1980, p. 60; March, 1981, p. 140.
Times Educational Supplement, August 7, 1987, p. 19.
Times Literary Supplement, June 6, 1968, p. 584; June 15, 1972, p. 684; April 6, 1973, p. 386; July 11, 1975, p. 763; December 5, 1975, p. 1446; August 19-25, 1988, p. 917.

*   *   *

BLACKWOOD, Alan   1932-

PERSONAL: Born November 23, 1932, in London, England; son of William (an accountant) and Constance (Wingfield) Blackwood; divorced. *Education:* Attended secondary school in Brighton, England. *Politics:* "Social Democrat/moderate Labour." *Religion:* "Agnostic."

ADDRESSES: Home—18 Shelburne Ct., Carlton Dr., London SW15 2DQ, England.

CAREER: Evening Argus, Brighton, England, reporter, 1953-55; Hutchinson Publishing Group Ltd., London, England, editor, 1957-60; Odhams Books Ltd., Feltham, England, editor, 1960; Hamlyn Publishing Group Ltd., Feltham, editor, 1960-69; Thomas Nelson & Sons Ltd., Sunbury-on-Thames, England, children's picture book editor for "Nelson Young World" series, 1969-76; freelance writer and editor, 1976—. *Military service:* British Army, 1955-57, instructor in Royal Army Educational Corps; became sergeant.

WRITINGS:

The Pageant of Music, Barrie & Jenkins (Covent Garden, England), 1977.
Ward Lock Encyclopedia of Music, Ward, Lock (London), 1979.
Performing World of the Singer, Hamish Hamilton (London), 1981.
New Encyclopedia of Music, Ward, Lock, 1983.
Music and Cities/Music and Magic, Oxford University Press (New York City), 1989.
Music of the World, Facts on File (New York City), 1991.
A First Guide to the Orchestra, Oxford University Press, 1992.
Sir Thomas Beecham: The Man and the Music, Random House (New York City), 1994.

JUVENILES

(With Johannes Coenraad Van Hunnik) *My Super Book of Baby Animals in Colour,* Nelson (Surrey, England), 1973.
Dr. Crotchet's Symphony, Evans Brothers (London), 1977.
Gold and Silver, Wayland (Hove, East Sussex, England), 1979.
Musical Instruments, Wayland, 1986.
Twenty Names in Classical Music, Wayland, 1987.
Twenty Names in Art, Wayland, 1987.
Countries of the World: France, Wayland, 1988.
Young Musician Plays: Piano and Keyboards, F. Watts (New York City), 1992.

EDITOR

(And translator from the French) Jean Richartol, Pierre Chardon, and Giuseppe Grazzini, *Famous Battles of World History* (juvenile), Hamlyn (London), 1970.
Mulberry Bush Book of Nursery Rhymes (juvenile), Thomas Nelson (Nashville), 1974.
A-Z of Famous People, Octopus (London), 1982.

OTHER

Contributor to encyclopedias, including *The Hamlyn Children's Encyclopedia in Colour.* Also contributor to B.B.C. music publications and to periodicals.

WORK IN PROGRESS: A three-volume guide to western music, initially to be translated and published in Finland; *The Classical Selection,* part of a series, for Orbis Publishing; music entries for *Reader's Digest Great Illustrated Encyclopedia; Listener's Guide: The Classical Mood,* for International Masters Publishers; *Kingfisher Book of Music,* for Larousse.

SIDELIGHTS: Alan Blackwood told *CA:* "Music is my main interest, and I play the piano, though not professionally. I also have a small house in southern France, where I do some of my work. France is my favorite country, and I read and speak the language quite fluently. As a result, I think there is a slight bias in favor of French composers, notably Debussy and Ravel, in my music books. I have also visited Germany, Guadeloupe, Indonesia, Italy, the Soviet Union, Spain, Sri Lanka, and the United States."

*   *   *

BLUE, Zachary
See STINE, R(obert) L(awrence)

*   *   *

BOGGESS, Louise Bradford   1912-

PERSONAL: Surname is pronounced "*Bog*-gess," with hard g's; born March 28, 1912, in Sweetwater, TX; daughter of Giles Edward (a banker and rancher) and Hattie (Corbett) Bradford; married William Fannin Boggess, Jr. (an investigator with the U.S. Immigration and Naturalization Service), June 1, 1946; children: Patricia Anne, William Fannin III. *Education:* University of Texas, B.A., 1933, M.A., 1934, graduate study, summers, 1935-39; professional writing courses, University of Oklahoma. *Politics:* Democrat. *Religion:* Episcopalian.

ADDRESSES: Home—4016 Martin Dr., San Mateo, CA 94403.

CAREER: Junior high school teacher in Dallas, TX, 1937-39; high school teacher in Wichita Falls, TX, 1941-46; Texas College of Arts and Industry (now Texas A. & I. University), Kingsville, instructor in history and government, 1946-47; *Kingsville Record,* Kingsville, women's editor, 1947-51; College of San Mateo, San Mateo, CA, instructor in professional writing, 1956-79, teacher of televised courses for KCSM-TV, 1971-79. Teacher of correspondence courses for University of California, Berkeley, and Writer's Digest School. Served as editor of *HOBSTAR* (newsletter), started the catalog reprint program and matching service. Staff member of writers conferences and workshops.

MEMBER: American Cut Glass Association (co-founder; committee chair), American Association of University Women, Authors Guild, National Early American Glass Club, California Writers Club (former president), Burlingame Writers Club (former president), Scribblers Club, Phi Beta Kappa, Phi Lambda Theta, Phi Sigma Alpha.

AWARDS, HONORS: Jack London Award for outstanding service, California Writers Club; awards for outstanding service, American Cut Glass Association and American Cut Glass Association, Golden Gate chapter.

WRITINGS:

Fiction Techniques That Sell, Prentice-Hall (Englewood Cliffs, NJ), 1964.
Writing Articles That Sell, Prentice-Hall, 1965.
Writing Fillers That Sell, Funk (Mahwah, NJ), 1967.
Journey to Citizenship, Funk, 1968.
Your Social Security Benefits, Funk, 1969.
(With husband, Bill Boggess) *American Brilliant Cut Glass,* Crown (New York City), 1977.
Article Techniques That Sell, 2nd edition, B & B Press (Walworth, WI), 1978.
Writing Fiction That Sells, 2nd edition, B & B Press, 1978.
How to Write Short Stories That Sell, 3rd edition, Writer's Digest (Cincinnati, OH), 1980.
How to Write Fillers and Short Features That Sell, 2nd edition, Harper (New York City), 1981, 3rd edition, 1984.
(With B. Boggess) *Identifying American Brilliant Cut Glass,* Crown, 1984, 2nd edition, Schiffer (Atglen, PA), 1984.
(With B. Boggess) *Collecting American Brilliant Cut Glass,* Schiffer, 1993.
(With B. Boggess) *Reflections on American Brilliant Cut Glass,* Schiffer, 1995.

Author of columns "Reflections on Glass," *American Collector,* "Pressed Glass," *Antique Reporter,* and "Over the Coffee Cup," *Kingsville Record.* Author of video and audio tapes on "Fiction Techniques That Sell" and "Article Techniques That Sell" for KCSM-TV, College of San Mateo. Contributor to books, including *Law and the Writer,* Writer's Digest, 1978, 4th edition, 1988; *Fiction Writers Market,* edited by Jean M. Fredette and John Brady, Writer's Digest, 1981, 8th edition, 1988; and *Handbook of Short Story Writing,* edited by Fredette, 3rd edition, 1988. Also contributor to antique magazines.

WORK IN PROGRESS: Article Techniques That Sell, 3rd edition; *Writing Fiction That Sells,* 4th edition; *Identifying American Brilliant Cut Glass,* 3rd edition; a suspense novel; articles for antique and writing magazines.

SIDELIGHTS: Louise Bradford Boggess told *CA:* "Like many others I began writing because we needed an extra income, and writing enabled me to stay home with my children, a boy and a girl, until they were school age, and I could go back to teaching. I found teaching professional writing and writing myself blended beautifully. In all my books, whether on writing or collecting American cut glass, I try to help others avoid mistakes I made. I always urge anyone who turns to a career in writing to learn how to write, approach writing as a profession. A lawyer or a doctor doesn't practice until he has studied. Neither should a writer try to sell without learning professional techniques. Anyone starting to collect should read and talk to people so as to learn as much as possible about how to buy or sell. Learning to write or collect never ends, but from learning comes the excitement of achievement. Dare to make mistakes once, but not again. Impeccable research leads to success."

*   *   *

BOUCOLON, Maryse   1937(?)-
  (Maryse Conde)

PERSONAL: Born February 11, 1937 (one source says 1934), in Pointe-a-Pitre, Guadeloupe, French West Indies; daughter of Auguste and Jeanne (Quidal) Boucolon; married Mamadou Conde, 1958 (divorced, 1981); married Richard Philcox (a translator), 1982; children: (first marriage) Leila, Sylvie, Aicha, one other child. *Education:* Sorbonne, University of Paris, M.A., Ph.D., 1976.

ADDRESSES: Home—Montebello, 97170 Petit Bourg, Guadeloupe, French West Indies. *Agent*—Rosalie Siegel, Act III Productions, 711 Fifth St., New York, NY 10022.

CAREER: Ecole Normale Superieure, Conakry, Guinea, instructor, 1960-64; Ghana Institute of Languages, Accra, Ghana, instructor, 1964-66; Lycee Charles de Gaulle, Saint Louis, Senegal, instructor, 1966-68; French Services of the BBC, London, England, program producer, 1968-70; University of Paris, Paris, France, assistant at Jussieu, 1970-72, lecturer at Nanterre, 1972-80, charge de cours at Sorbonne, 1980-85; program producer, Radio France Internationale, France Culture, beginning in 1980. Bellagio Writer in Residence, Rockefeller Foundation, 1986; visiting professor, University of California, Berkeley, 1990-92; visiting professor, University of Virginia and University of Maryland, 1992—; lecturer in the United States, Africa, and the West Indies. Presenter of a literary program for Africa on Radio-France.

AWARDS, HONORS: Fulbright scholar, 1985-86; Prix Litteraire de la Femme, Prix Alain Boucheron, 1986, for *Moi, Tituba, Sorciere Noire de Salem;* Guggenheim fellow, 1987-88; Academie Francaise Prize, 1988, for *Tree of Life;* Puterbaugh fellow, University of Oklahoma, Norman, 1993.

WRITINGS:

(Editor) *Anthologie de la litterature africaine d'expression francaise,* Ghana Institute of Languages (Accra), 1966.
Dieu nous l'a donne (four-act play; title means "God Given"; first produced in Fort de France, Martinique, French West Indies, 1973), Oswald (Paris), 1972.
Mort d'Oluwemi d'Ajumako (four-act play; title means "Death of a King"; first produced in Haiti at Theatre d'Alliance Francaise, 1975), Oswald, 1973.
Heremakhonon (novel), Union Generale d'Editions (Paris), 1976, translation by husband, Richard Philcox, published under same title, Three Continents Press (Washington, DC), 1982.
(Translator into French with Philcox) Eric Williams, *From Columbus to Castro: The History of the Caribbean,* Presence Africaine (Paris), 1977.
(Editor) *La Poesie antillaise* (also see below), Nathan (Paris), 1977.
(Editor) *Le Roman antillais* (also see below), Nathan, 1977.

La Civilisation du bossale (criticism), Harmattan (Paris), 1978.
Le Profil d'une oeuvre: Cahier d'un retour au pays natal (criticism), Hatier (Paris), 1978.
La Parole des femmes (criticism), Harmattan, 1979.
Tim tim? Bois sec! Bloemlezing uit de Franstalige Caribsche Literatuur (contains revised and translated editions of *Le Roman antillais* and *La Poesie antillaise*), edited by Andries van der Wal, In de Knipscheer, 1980.
Une Saison a Rihata (novel), Robert Laffont (Paris), 1981, translation by Philcox published as *A Season in Rihata,* Heinemann (London), 1988.
Segou: Les Murailles de terre (novel), Robert Laffont, 1984, translation by Barbara Bray published as *Segu,* Viking (New York City), 1987.
Segou II: La Terre en miettes (novel), Robert Laffont, 1985, translation by Linda Coverdale published as *The Children of Segu,* Viking, 1989.
Pays mele (short stories), Hatier, 1985.
Moi, Tituba, Sorciere Noire de Salem (novel), Mercure de France (Paris), 1986, translation by Philcox published as *I, Tituba, Black Witch of Salem,* University Press of Virginia (Charlottesville), 1992.
La Vie scelerate (novel), Seghers, 1987, translation by Victoria Reiter published as *Tree of Life,* Ballantine (New York City), 1992.
Haiti cherie (juvenile), Bayard Presse (Paris), 1987.
Pension les Alizes (play; first produced in Pointe-a-Pitre, Guadeloupe, French West Indies), Mercure de France, 1988.
An Tan Revolisyon (play; first produced in Pointe-a-Pitre), Conseil Regional (Pointe-a-Pitre), 1989.
Victor et les barricades (juvenile), Bayard Presse, 1989.
Traversee de la mangrove (novel), Mercure de France, 1990, translation by Philcox published as *Crossing the Mangrove,* Anchor Books (New York City), 1995.
No Woman No Cry, Le Serpent a Plumes (Paris), 1991.
Hugo le terrible, Sepia (Saint Maur, France), 1991.
Les Derniers Rois mages (novel), Mercure de France, 1992.
(Editor) *L'Heritage de Caliban,* Jasor (Pointe-a-Pitre), 1992.
La Colonie du nouveau monde (novel), Robert Laffont, 1993.

Also author of recordings for Record CLEF and Radio France Internationale. Contributor to anthologies; contributor to journals, including *Presence Africaine* and *Recherche Pedagogique.*

SIDELIGHTS: West Indian author Maryse Boucolon, who writes under the name Maryse Conde, "is a tireless world traveler who refuses to write in order to illustrate any ideological construct," writes Hal Wylie in *World Literature Today.* "With Voltairean irony, she prefers to explore social realities with realism, always seeking out the lines of stress, the tension markers between sexes, races, cultures and languages." She often finds these lines of stress, note Charlotte and David Bruner in *World Literature Today,* in "the personal human complexities involved in holy wars, national rivalries, and migrations of peoples." Although she explores these larger issues, she does so through the lives of individuals and families.

Heremakhonon, for example, relates the journey of Veronica, an Antillean student searching for her roots in a newly liberated West African country. During her stay Veronica becomes involved with both a powerful government official and a young school director opposed to the new regime; "to her dismay," David Bruner summarizes, "she is unable to stay out of the political struggle, and yet she is aware that she does not know enough to understand what is happening."

The result of Veronica's exploration, which is told with an "insinuating prose [that] has a surreal, airless quality," as Carole Bovoso relates in the *Voice Literary Supplement,* is that "there were times I longed to rush in and break the spell, to shout at this black woman and shake her. But no one can rescue Veronica," the critic continues, "least of all herself; Conde conveys the seriousness of her plight by means of a tone of relentless irony and reproach." "Justly or not," write the Bruners, "one gains a comprehension of what a revolution is like, what new African nations are like, yet one is aware that this comprehension is nothing more than a feeling. The wise reader will go home as Veronica does," the critics conclude, "to continue more calmly to reflect, and to observe."

Conde expands her scope in *Segu,* "a wondrous novel about a period of African history few other writers have addressed," notes *New York Times Book Review* contributor Charles R. Larson. In tracing three generations of a West African family during the early and mid-1800s, "Conde has chosen for her subject . . . [a] chaotic stage, when the animism (which she calls fetishism) native to the region began to yield to Islam," the critic describes. "The result is the most significant historical novel about black Africa published in many a year." Beginning with

Dousika, a Bambara nobleman caught up in court intrigue, *Segu* trails the exploits of his family, from one son's conversion to Islam to another's enslavement to a third's successful career in commerce, connected with stories of their wives and concubines and servants. In addition, Conde's "knowledge of African history is prodigious, and she is equally versed in the continent's folklore," remarks Larson. "The unseen world haunts her characters and vibrates with the spirits of the dead."

Some critics, however, fault the author for an excess of detail; *Washington Post* contributor Harold Courlander, for example, comments that "the plethora of happenings in the book does not always make for easy reading." The critic explains that "the reader is sometimes uncertain whether history and culture are being used to illuminate the fiction or the novel exists to tell us about the culture and its history." While Howard Kaplan concurs with this assessment, he adds in the *Los Angeles Times Book Review* that *Segu* "glitters with nuggets of cultural fascination. . . . For those willing to make their way through this dense saga, genuine rewards will be reaped." "With such an overwhelming mass of data and with so extensive a literary objective, the risks of . . . producing a heavy, didactic treatise are, of course, great," the Bruners maintain. "The main reason that Conde has done neither is, perhaps, because she has written here essentially as she did in her two earlier novels: she has followed the lives of the fictional characters as individuals dominated by interests and concerns which are very personal and often selfish and petty, even when those characters are perceived by other characters as powerful leaders in significant national or religious movements." Because of this, the critics conclude, *Segu* is "a truly remarkable book. . . . To know [the subjects of her work] better, as well as to know Maryse Conde even better, would be a good thing."

Conde's novel *Tree of Life* is, in the words of *Los Angeles Times Book Review* critic Elaine Kendall "a potent mix of memory, legend and reality." Howard Frank Mosher describes the book in a *New York Times Book Review* piece as a "passionate, multigenerational novel . . . about the endlessly intriguing family of Albert Louis, born in Guadeloupe in the early 1870's, a patriarch as morally complex as he is simply stubborn." Mosher adds, "From 18th-century Africa to the America of the Rev. Dr. Martin Luther King Jr. and Malcolm X, Maryse Conde has chronicled in her wonderful fiction the lives of a series of remarkable individuals and the families that surround them." In addition to its characterization and plot, *Tree of Life*'s style has received critical attention. "Just as the Impressionist painters created their effects with minute, separate brush strokes," Kendall comments, "Conde uses vignettes to produce a similar literary unity." The result of Conde's efforts is "a grand account of the Caribbean, the politics of race and immigration, and the intricate, often sordid legacy of colonialism," Cristina Garcia concludes in *Tribune Books*.

I, Tituba, Black Witch of Salem is Conde's examination of how a young Barbadian woman's "skills as a healer ultimately made her an object of wonder and terror," observes Stephanie B. Goldberg in the *Chicago Tribune*. It is also an investigation of history and how historical themes resonate in the present. The story is based on a historical incident; in 1692, a black slave woman was tried as a part of the Salem, Massachusetts, witch hunts. Conde's Tituba is a mulatto, born from the rape of a African woman bound for the West Indies by an English sailor. After growing up and living a turbulent life on Barbados, Tituba is sold to a Puritan minister who takes her to New England. There because of some of her island ways, she is branded a witch and put on trial.

Conde goes to great lengths to capture the historical setting. Writing in the *Los Angeles Times Book Review*, Elaine Kendall finds that "though bolstered by diligent research into the customs and personalities of Puritan New England, *I, Tituba,* too often allows itself to slip into the cliches of Puritan life, a shortcoming bound to be more apparent to Americans than to the French." *Belles Lettres* reviewer Miller Newman does not see cliches, but rather skillful rendering of the historical milieu. "What is most affecting in this story," he writes, "is the chillingly realistic retelling of the Salem witch hunts. Conde weaves the fabric of her story so tightly that the reader is pulled through the Salem trials as if tied to the end of a spinner's shuttle."

Through this fictional retelling of a historical event, Conde raises issues that are very much a part of the present day. "Into a plot as action-packed as a romance novel," observes Jeanne Pimentel in the *San Francisco Review of Books*, "Conde introduces lively arguments not only on the themes of racism and feminism but on hypocrisy, intolerance, and exploitation." In this sense, Kendall maintains, "*I, Tituba, Black Witch of Salem* contrasts starkly with *Tree of Life*. Furious where *Tree of Life* is affectionate; didactic, polemical and passionately feminist, [*I,*

Tituba] is a work of another order entirely." The balancing of historical accuracy and modern issues raises a difficult challenge for the writer, according to some critics. As Mosher notes in the *New York Times Book Review*, "In less sure hands, this short, powerful novel . . . might well have become merely an extended denunciation of a perverted and evil society. What makes it larger and richer are Ms. Conde's gift for story telling and her unswerving focus on her characters, combined with her mordant sense of humor." In the end, Pimentel suggests that *I, Tituba* succeeds in reflecting Conde's "view of women today as well as the universality in time and space of issues from exploitation and political intrigue to the maternal urge and sexual betrayal."

Conde returns to her native Guadeloupe in *Crossing the Mangrove*. The title of this novel raises the image of an impossible act, crossing the thick jungle/swamp found along many Caribbean coasts. Behind the image is the story of Francis Sancher, a writer with a mysterious past who comes to live in a small village in Guadeloupe. As a *Publishers Weekly* reviewer explains, "Sancher, a handsome mulatto on an island besieged by concerns over skin color, turns everyone's hatreds and passions inside out." Through Sancher and the characters that he touches, Conde "vividly evokes the complexities of a color caste system . . . in a struggle for power and status," Paul E. Hutchinson remarks in *Library Journal*. Even after Sancher dies mysteriously, he dominates the lives of the villagers. At his wake, Conde follows the villagers as they discuss the departed. "Conde . . . intends to portray island life through Guadeloupeans talking among themselves," writes J. P. Slavin in the *Washington Post Book World*. "She magnificently succeeds in bringing realism to a novel which also portrays the rich spiritualism of the West Indies."

BIOGRAPHICAL/CRITICAL SOURCES:

BOOKS

Pfaff, Francoise, *Entretiens avec Maryse Conde,* Editions Karthala (Paris), 1993.
Townsel, Sylviane, *Negritude dans la litterature franco-antillaise: Conde et Cesaire, deux ecrivans baigne dans deux cultures differentes,* Pensee Universelle (Paris), 1992.

PERIODICALS

American Visions, February, 1991, p. 38.
Antioch Review, spring, 1987, p. 246.

Belles Lettres, spring, 1994, p. 48.

Bloomsbury Review, September, 1994, p. 12.

Boston Globe, September 20, 1992, p. B44; October 4, 1992, p. B38.

Callaloo, winter, 1989; winter, 1992, p. 147.

Chicago Tribune, September 22, 1992, sec. 5, p. 3.

Essence, May, 1995, p. 193.

Library Journal, March 15, 1995, p. 96.

Los Angeles Times Book Review, March 8, 1987, p. 4; December 2, 1990, p. 14; January 3, 1993, p. 3.

New York Times Book Review, May 31, 1987, p. 47; November 25, 1990, p. 32; October 25, 1992, p. 11; January 9, 1994, p. 28.

Publishers Weekly, January 23, 1995, p. 65.

San Francisco Review of Books, May/June, 1993, p. 19.

Tribune Books (Chicago), October 11, 1992, p. 6; November 21, 1993, p. 8; December 26, 1993, p. 2; April 23, 1995, p. 6.

Voice Literary Supplement, November, 1982.

Washington Post, March 3, 1987.

Washington Post Book World, June 19, 1988, p. 12; December 23, 1990, p. 12; September 6, 1992, p. 9; February 26, 1995, p. 5.

World Literature Today, winter, 1982; winter, 1985; spring, 1985, p. 309; summer, 1986, p. 509; spring, 1987, p. 337; summer, 1988, p. 498; autumn, 1993, p. 757; summer, 1994, p. 619.*

* * *

BOYNTON, Sandra (Keith) 1953-

PERSONAL: Born April 3, 1953, in Orange, NJ; daughter of Robert Whitney and Jeanne Carolyn (Ragsdale) Boynton; married James Patrick McEwan, October 18, 1978. *Education:* Yale University, B.A., 1974; graduate study at University of California, Berkeley, 1974-75, and Yale University, 1976-77. *Religion:* Society of Friends (Quakers).

CAREER: Author and illustrator of children's books. Recycled Paper Products, Inc., Chicago, IL, designer of greeting cards, 1974-94; Portal Publications, Ltd., Corte Madera, CA, 1996—.

MEMBER: Authors' Guild.

AWARDS, HONORS: Irma Simonton Black Award, 1986, for *Chloe and Maude;* National Parenting Publications Award, 1994, for *Barnyard Dance.*

WRITINGS:

SELF-ILLUSTRATED CHILDREN'S BOOKS

Hippos Go Berserk, Little, Brown (Boston, MA), 1977, revised, redrawn edition, Aladdin Books (New York City), 1996.

Hester in the Wild, Harper (New York City), 1979.

If at First. . ., Little, Brown, 1980.

A to Z, Simon & Schuster (New York City), 1982.

Blue Hat Green Hat, Simon & Schuster, 1982.

Doggies, Simon & Schuster, 1982.

Horns to Toes, Simon & Schuster, 1982.

But Not the Hippopotamus, Simon & Schuster, 1982, revised, redrawn edition, 1995.

The Going to Bed Book, Simon & Schuster, 1982.

Opposites, Simon & Schuster, 1982.

A Is for Angry: An Adjective and Animal Alphabet, Workman (New York City), 1983. *Moo Baa La La La!,* edited by Kate Klimo, Simon & Schuster, 1983, *Hey! What's That?,* Random House (New York City), 1985.

Chloe and Maude, Little, Brown, 1985.

Good Night, Good Night, Random House, 1985.

Grunt (children's book and CD recording), Workman, 1996.

Rhinoceros Tap (children's songbook and tape), Workman, 1996.

"BOYNTON ON BOARD" SERIES; JUVENILE; PUBLISHED BY WORKMAN

Barnyard Dance, 1993.

Birthday Monsters, 1993.

Oh My Oh My Oh Dinosaurs!, 1993.

One, Two, Three!, 1993.

OTHER BOOKS

Go For Baroque, and Other Beastly Conceits, Dutton (New York City), 1979.

The Compleat Turkey (adult), Little, Brown, 1980, revised edition published as *Don't Let the Turkeys Get You Down,* Workman, 1986.

Chocolate: The Consuming Passion (adult), Workman, 1982.

Christmastime (adult), Workman, 1987.

Boynton: The Classic Prints, Workman, 1990.

(Illustrator) James McEwan, *Grump & Pout,* Crown (New York City), 1988.

OTHER

Contributor to magazines, including *Redbook.*

SIDELIGHTS: Known for her best-selling greeting-card menagerie of whimsical animals displaying childlike behavior, Boynton is also an author who combines her talents as a cartoonist with clever and skillfully written texts. *Chocolate: The Consuming Passion,* for example, received much critical attention for its unique and irreverent look at chocolate. In her definitive guide to the popular confection Boynton profiles the numerous guises—from kisses to bunnies—of milk chocolate, offers proven methods for determining what's inside boxed candy, debunks such "insidious" myths as that chocolate is fattening or addictive, and even presents several recipes, all of which add up to what *Los Angeles Times Book Review* contributor Ben Reuven described as "a delightful little bonbon of a book. Sometimes playful, sometimes perfectly serious, always displaying a rich sense of wit and style."

Boynton has also written numerous books for younger children, including *Hippos Go Berserk,* in which she reveals her fine ear for nonsense rhyme. Not only a counting book but a visual tool as well, *Hippos Go Berserk* was described by *Wilson Library Bulletin* as "a small, unpretentious book" whose "total effect is light, airy, and tender." The old adage of "try, try again" is spotlighted in *If at First. . . ,* a story that chronicles the desperate attempts of a little brown mouse to push a giant, disinterested purple elephant up a hill. The mouse tries leading it, tempting it with a peanut, yelling, and pushing, but all tactics fail. Finally the mouse succeeds in startling the napping pachyderm awake and up the hill with the blast of a trumpet—only, however, to discover on the final page of text the word *again* and a view downhill of eight more purple elephants in line for the climb.

In *Chloe and Maude,* a 1985 Boynton publication, two cat friends star in a trio of brief stories, highlighting what *School Library Journal* called "the vicissitudes of friendship." The two felines have minor disagreements, but their friendship endures as each learns how to be a better friend. Calling Chloe and Maude "kissing cousins of the droll little animals in Boynton's greeting card line," the *School Library Journal* reviewer complimented Boynton on "mak[ing] the leap from card to book with considerable success."

BIOGRAPHICAL/CRITICAL SOURCES:

PERIODICALS

Booklist, March 1, 1986.
Chicago Tribune Book World, May 23, 1982.
Christian Science Monitor, February 7, 1986.
Globe and Mail (Toronto), March 16, 1985.
Los Angeles Times Book Review, June 27, 1982; January 15, 1984.
New York Times Book Review, June 13, 1982.
School Library Journal, March, 1983; March, 1986.
Washington Post Book World, February 12, 1984.
Wilson Library Bulletin, March, 1980.

* * *

BRADY, John (Mary)   1955-

PERSONAL: Born July 10, 1955, in Dublin, Ireland; son of Christopher (a civil servant) and Mary (a civil servant; maiden name, Carroll) Brady; married Johanna Wagner (a teacher), August 1, 1981; children: Julia, Michael. *Education:* Attended Oatlands College, 1972; Trinity College, Dublin, B.A., 1980; University of Toronto, B.Ed., 1981, M.Ed., 1985. *Avocational interests:* Swimming, walking, talking.

ADDRESSES: Office—St. Patrick's School, Western Ave., Schomberg, Ontario, Canada L0G 1TO.

CAREER: Bank of Ireland, Dublin, bank official, 1972-75; Royal Canadian Mounted Police, Yellowknife, Northwest Territories, police officer, 1975-76; schoolteacher in Terrace, British Columbia, 1981-84; employee of TV Ontario, 1985-86; St. Patrick's School, Schombey, Ontario, teacher, 1988—.

MEMBER: Trinity College, Dublin, Graduate Association (organizer of Canadian branch).

AWARDS, HONORS: Arthur Ellis Award, Crime Writers of Canada, 1989.

WRITINGS:

MYSTERY NOVELS

A Stone of the Heart, St. Martin's (New York City), 1988.
Unholy Ground, HarperCollins, 1989.
Kaddish in Dublin, St. Martin's, 1992.
All Souls, St. Martin's, 1993.
The Good Life, HarperCollins (Toronto), 1994, St. Martin's, 1995.

SIDELIGHTS: John Brady's mystery novels feature Dublin police inspector Matt Minogue, "a quintessential Irishman, with his keen wit, his own brand of sarcastic charm, and his dedicated, if occasionally world-weary, professionalism," as Emily Melton in *Booklist* describes him. Minogue's cases lead him into the heart of contemporary Ireland, with all its political and economic troubles. Marilyn Stasio in the *New York Times Book Review* calls the Minogue books a "superb series" in which "Brady adopts a tone of battered lyricism for Minogue's keening thoughts about the spiritual corruption he sees around him."

Inspector Minogue was first introduced in *A Stone of the Heart,* in which a Dublin college student is found murdered. Jarlath Walsh had no enemies, but he did tell his friends he suspected that the Irish Republican Army had agents on campus who were assisting the terrorist group in a campaign to murder policemen. Minogue must sort out the facts from the suspicions before more people are killed. Writing in the *Washington Post Book World,* Jean M. White calls *A Stone of the Heart* a "powerful, complex, compelling novel," while the critic for *Kirkus Reviews* describes the book as "a sad, introspective look at life on a tortured island" and finds Brady to be "a quietly powerful writer."

In *Unholy Ground* Minogue is assigned to find the killer of Arthur Combs, an elderly man who was once a British secret agent. Considered a security risk, Combs had been banned from England for some forty years. In the course of finding Combs' murderer, Minogue uncovers the truth about the agent's loyalty as well. Stasio maintains that Brady manages to keep "the narrative delicately balanced between a police procedural and a spy story" to produce "a nongeneric political novel rich in substance and raw with pain." The *Kirkus Reviews* critic states that "Brady is a master of the telling detail, and within the framework of the political novel, has created memorable characters, most especially the estimable Minogue."

In *Kaddish in Dublin,* the son of an Irish Supreme Court judge is murdered and Minogue must track down the killer. The judge is Jewish, and a terrorist group known as the League for Solidarity with the Palestinian People claims responsibility for his son's death. But the son was also investigating the activities of the Opus Dei, a secretive Catholic organization. Violent ecology groups, the IRA, and a plot to topple the Irish government also figure into the tangled plot. A *Kirkus Reviews* critic finds the novel to be "finely written, intellectually complex—and

further proof of Brady' ear for dialogue and skill in pricking the conscience of a country."

Again, in *All Souls* Minogue is vacationing in County Clare, when he finds himself embroiled in another murder case that involves a decades-old homicide and a current political scandal. Dick Adler in *Tribune Books* praises "Brady's elegant writing," while Stasio states that Brady's language "burns through the cold [of the winter setting] and lights up the dark."

In *The Good Life,* a murdered prostitute is pulled from a canal and Minogue finds himself investigating one of Dublin's most ruthless criminal gangs for her killer. The prostitute's rich accountant friend, her roommate's biker lover, and a pornographic photographer are among the suspects. "There is," Sheryl Halpern admits in *Books in Canada,* "some suspense. . . . But there's no mystery in the air—just the day-to-day tedium of police routine, run-of-the-gin-mill thuggery, prostitution, and drugs." Yet, even though the critic of *Publishers Weekly* claims that the plot is "as thin as weak tea," still s/he praises Brady for bringing "the contradictions of modern-day Dublin vividly to life."

BIOGRAPHICAL/CRITICAL SOURCES:

PERIODICALS

Armchair Detective, fall, 1993, p. 19; fall, 1994, p. 486.
Booklist, November 15, 1993, p. 605; July, 1995, p. 1863.
Books in Canada, August, 1989, p. 27; April, 1991, p. 46; summer, 1993, p. 35; November, 1994, p. 30.
Boston Globe, October 25, 1992, p. B14.
Globe and Mail (Toronto), April 15, 1989.
Kirkus Reviews, June 1, 1988, p. 792; November 1, 1991, p. 1376; August 1, 1992, p. 949; October 1, 1993, p. 1227.
Library Journal, June 1, 1995, p. 170.
Los Angeles Times Book Review, September 20, 1992, p. 8.
Maclean's, June 20, 1988, p. 54.
New York Times Book Review, February 16, 1992, p. 27; October 4, 1992, p. 26; November 28, 1993, p. 24; August 6, 1995, p. 23.
Observer, July 9, 1989, p. 47; November 4, 1990, p. 61.
Publishers Weekly, June 10, 1988, p. 71; December 6, 1991, p. 58; July 6, 1992, p. 40; September 20, 1993, p. 64; June 12, 1995, p. 51.

Punch, October 28, 1988, p. 64.
Quill and Quire, April, 1988, p. 25; May, 1993, p. 25; November, 1994, p. 29.
Tribune Books (Chicago), August 7, 1988, p. 6; November 7, 1993, p. 8.
Wall Street Journal, November 22, 1993, p. A12.
Washington Post Book World, July 17, 1988, p. 6.
Writer's Digest, February, 1989, p. 22.

* * *

BROCKMAN, James R(aymond) 1926-

PERSONAL: Born August 3, 1926, in Cincinnati, OH; son of Raymond J. and Rose (Gieske) Brockman. *Education:* Xavier University, Litt.B., 1951; West Baden College, Ph.L., 1955, S.T.B., 1961; Loyola University, M.A., 1959.

ADDRESSES: Home—P. O. Box 7565, Little Rock, AR 72217-7565.

CAREER: Entered Society of Jesus (Jesuits), 1947, ordained Roman Catholic priest, 1960; St. Ignatius High School, Cleveland, OH, teacher, 1952-53; Loyola Academy, Chicago, IL, teacher, 1955-56; St. Ignatius College Preparatory, Chicago, teacher, 1956-57; Colegio San Jose, Arequipa, Peru, teacher and administrator, 1963-72; Cook County Hospital, Chicago, chaplain, 1973-74; *America,* New York, NY, associate editor, 1974-80; writer, 1980—; Diocese of Gary, IN, pastoral minister to Hispanics, 1992-93; Diocese of Little Rock, AR, director of Hispanic ministry, 1993—. *Military service:* U.S. Army, 1945-46.

WRITINGS:

The Word Remains: A Life of Oscar Romero, Orbis (Maryknoll, NY), 1982, published as *Oscar Romero, Bishop and Martyr,* Sheed & Ward (London), 1982, revised edition published as *Romero: A Life,* Orbis, 1989.
(Translator) Juan Ramon Moreno, *Gospel and Mission,* Cardinal Bea Institute (Manila, Philippines), 1995.

EDITOR

(And translator) *The Church Is All of You: Thoughts of Archbishop Romero,* Winston Press (Minneapolis) 1984.

(And translator) *The Violence of Love: The Pastoral Wisdom of Archbishop Oscar Romero,* Harper (New York City), 1988.
Tiene que vencer el amor, CEP (Lima, Peru), 1988.
Asi habla Monsenor O. Romero, Ediciones Paulinas (Bogota, Colombia), 1992.

OTHER

Contributor to *The New Catholic Encyclopedia Supplement* and *The Modern Catholic Encyclopedia.* Also contributor to periodicals, including *Accion, America, Christian Century, Mensaje, Praying, Review for Religious, Sign, Spirituality Today, Third World Quarterly,* and *Thought.*

The Word Remains: A Life of Oscar Romero has been translated into French, Italian, Korean, Portuguese, and Spanish; *Romero: A Life* has been published in German.

WORK IN PROGRESS: A revised edition of the Spanish version of *Romero: A Life.*

SIDELIGHTS: James R. Brockman told *CA:* "In my writing I have tried to make the church and people of Latin America better understood in the United States and the world at large. In recent years my work has centered on Archbishop Oscar Romero, whose life and work symbolize and exemplify the transformation going on in the Latin American church. I think that a better understanding of that renewal can help us all to deepen our own religious dimension and can help the United States to form a more mature relationship with the people of Latin America."

* * *

BROPHY, Brigid (Antonia) 1929-1995

PERSONAL: Born June 12, 1929, in London, England; died August 7, 1995, in Louth, Lincolnshire, England; daughter of John (a novelist) and Charis Weare (Grundy) Brophy; married Michael Vincent Levey (former director of the National Gallery, London, and author), June 12, 1954; children: Katharine Jane. *Education:* St. Hugh's College, Oxford, 1947-48.

CAREER: Novelist, essayist, critic, biographer, and dramatist. Shorthand typist for camera firm, London;

journalist for *London Magazine;* co-organizer, Writers' Action Group campaign for Public Lending Right, 1972-82. Broadcaster on television and radio in the 1960s and 1970s.

MEMBER: Royal Society of Literature (fellow), Writers Guild of Great Britain (member of executive council, 1974-78), British Copyright Council (vice chair, 1976-80), Anti-Vivisection Society of Great Britain (vice president, beginning in 1974).

AWARDS, HONORS: Cheltenham Literary Festival first prize for a first novel, 1954, for *Hackenfeller's Ape; London Magazine* prize for prose, 1962, for *Black Ship to Hell;* fellow, Royal Society of Literature, 1973; Tony Godwin Award, 1985.

WRITINGS:

FICTION

The Crown Princess and Other Stories, Viking (New York City), 1953.
Hackenfeller's Ape, Hart-Davis (London), 1953, Random House (New York City), 1954.
The King of a Rainy Country, Secker & Warburg (London), 1956, Knopf (New York City), 1957, reprinted with afterword, Virago, 1990.
Flesh, Secker & Warburg, 1962, World (Cleveland, OH), 1963.
The Finishing Touch (also see below), Secker & Warburg, 1963, revised edition, GMP (London), 1987.
The Snow Ball (also see below), Secker & Warburg, 1964.
The Finishing Touch [and] *The Snow Ball,* World, 1964.
The Burglar (play; first produced in London at Vaudeville Theatre, February 22, 1967), Holt (New York City), 1968.
In Transit: An Heroicycle Novel, Macdonald & Co. (London), 1969, Putnam (New York City), 1970.
The Adventures of God in His Search for the Black Girl: A Novel and Some Fables, Macmillan (London), 1973, Little, Brown (Boston), 1974.
Pussy Owl: Superbeast (for children), illustrated by Hilary Hayton, BBC Publications (London), 1976.
Palace without Chairs: A Baroque Novel, Atheneum (New York City), 1978.

NONFICTION

Black Ship to Hell, Harcourt (New York City), 1962.

Mozart the Dramatist: A New View of Mozart, His Operas and His Age, Harcourt, 1964, revised edition, Da Capo (New York City), 1990.
Don't Never Forget: Collected Views and Reviews, Cape (London), 1966, Holt, 1967.
(With husband, Michael Levey, and Charles Osborne) *Fifty Works of English and American Literature We Could Do Without,* Rapp & Carroll (London), 1967, Stein & Day (New York City), 1968.
Religious Education in State Schools, Fabian Society (London), 1967.
Black and White: A Portrait of Aubrey Beardsley, Cape, 1968, Stein & Day, 1969.
The Rights of Animals, Animal Defence and Anti-Vivisection Society (London), 1969.
The Longford Threat to Freedom, National Secular Society (London), 1972.
Prancing Novelist: A Defence of Fiction in the Form of a Critical Biography in Praise of Ronald Firbank, Barnes & Noble (New York City), 1973.
Beardsley and His World, Harmony Books (New York City), 1976.
The Prince and the Wild Geese, pictures by Gregoire Gagarin, Hamish Hamilton (London), 1982, St. Martin's (New York City), 1983.
A Guide to Public Lending Right, Gower (Hampshire, England), 1983.
Baroque 'n' Roll and Other Essays, David & Charles (North Pomfret, VT), 1987.
Reads: A Collection of Essays, Cardinal (London), 1989.

OTHER

Contributor to books, including *Best Short Plays of the World Theatre, 1958-1967,* Crown (New York City), 1968; *Animals, Men and Morals,* edited by Godlovitch and J. Harris, Gollancz (London), 1971; *The Genius of Shaw,* edited by Michael Holroyd, Hodder & Stoughton (London), 1979; *Animal Rights: A Symposium,* edited by D. Paterson and R. D. Ryder, Centaur Press (West Sussex, England), 1979; and *Shakespeare Stories,* edited by Giles Gordon, Hamish Hamilton, 1982. Author of introduction to books, including *Pride and Prejudice,* by Jane Austen, Pan Books (London), 1967; *Sex Education: The Erroneous Zone,* by M. Hill and M. Lloyd-Jones, National Secular Society, 1970; and *Die Zauberfloete* [and] *Die Entfuehrung aus dem Serail* (libretti), translated by L. Salter, Cassell (London), 1971. Contributor to periodicals, including *London Magazine, Short Story Monthly, London Review of*

Books, Times Literary Supplement, Times (London), *New Statesman, New York Herald Tribune,* and *Texas Quarterly.* Also contributor to psychoanalytic journals.

A collection of Brophy's manuscripts are housed in Lilly Library at Indiana University at Bloomington.

ADAPTATIONS: The Snow Ball was televised by the British Broadcasting Corp. (BBC-TV), April, 1964; *Pussy Owl Superbeast* was televised by BBC-TV, March, 1976.

SIDELIGHTS: Brigid Brophy, British novelist, essayist, critic, advocate for writers and social causes, was described by S. J. Newman in the *Dictionary of Literary Biography: British Novelists since 1960,* as "one of the oddest, most brilliant, and most enduring of [the] 1960s symptoms." A feminist, pacifist, atheist, anti-vivisectionist, and vegetarian, among other things, Brophy had much to speak out on in that turbulent era. She expressed controversial opinions on marriage, the Vietnam War, religious education in schools, sex, and pornography. In response to her outspokenness, Brophy was labeled many things, including "one of our leading literary shrews" by a *Times Literary Supplement* reviewer. "A lonely, ubiquitous toiler in the weekend graveyards, she has scored some direct hits on massive targets: Kingsley Amis, Henry Miller, Professor Wilson Knight."

In turn, Brophy's enthusiasts, coined "brophiles" by *Life* critic Robert Phelps, envisioned her as "the arch-priestess of the permissive society, one of the rare and precious human beings who have done something positive, and a saint. Interviewers have been surprised to find a courteous and secluded hostess who claims that she becomes involved in controversies inadvertently," wrote Newman. As David Depledge commented in *Books and Bookmen,* "the unfortunate thing about . . . Brophy is that the Gods have cursed her with a facility for being misunderstood." Depledge believed this misunderstanding may have arisen, in part, from Brophy's many television appearances in the 1960s and 1970s. Brophy admitted to being a shy person and Depledge surmised that her shyness and nervousness in front of the cameras "makes her look solemn, and forbiddingly intense. . . . If her tenseness in front of the cameras could be wiped away we might see the mischievousness behind a large number of her dead-pan deliveries." But Brophy also revealed to Depledge that some of the misunderstanding was self-gener-

ated: "I sometimes can't resist the temptation to give fantasy answers to serious questions."

Brigid Brophy was the precocious daughter of novelist John Brophy. According to Newman, John Brophy wrote in 1940: "I have a daughter, ten years old, who excels me in everything, even in writing." From age three to nine, Brigid wrote numerous poetic dramas, inspired by Shakespeare and Sir Walter Scott, and then she stopped writing. However, beginning in the 1950s her skills and convictions produced a variety of works, including novels and novellas, essays, criticism, literary biography, various tracts, and additional dramas. And all this from a writer who insisted she hated to write: "You know, I don't like to write. I think I actually hate it. You see, it's so difficult. . . . I suffer terribly when I'm writing and I'm absolutely impossible," recorded Phyllis Meras in the *New York Times Book Review.*

Through the years, critics found Brophy's writing to be consistently clever and lucid. To Meras, Brophy's distinctions were her "vitriolic pen, penetrating intelligence and neat, sharp critical prose." Newman saw her as the "polymath, pundit and polemicist" and further remarked: "[Brophy] described herself Irishly as the highbrow's lowbrow and her work as a howl for tolerance. In a *Guardian* interview she called herself a most un-English writer: 'I am really most interested in intensity. I cannot stand anything that is lukewarm.'" Yet reviewers sometimes balked at the intensity of Brophy's prose. For example, in a *New Republic* assessment of Brophy's *The Adventures of God in His Search for the Black Girl,* Margaret Walters maintained: "Though she's both inventive and imaginative, Brophy has a tendency to try too hard. . . . Determined to mock and shock, she's so unrelentingly the *enfant terrible* that her flashes of genuine wit get lost. . . . She never misses a chance to throw us off balance, to discomfit and needle us into questioning our prejudices. . . . Bossily she divides us into sheep and goats. If you disagree you're cast into an irrational outer darkness and convicted of being humorless and non-literate."

In her youth, Brophy read the works of George Bernard Shaw, Oscar Wilde, James Joyce, and Ronald Firbank. She learned much about writing from both her novelist father and her mother, a teacher. Brophy studied classics on a Jubilee Scholarship at St. Hugh's College, Oxford, for four terms but was expelled for "sexual offenses that contravened the university's then-strict moral code," noted a *Washington Post* obituary. While working as a shorthand typist in London, she wrote stories that were eventually published in her collection *The Crown Princess and Other Stories.* A *Times Literary Supplement* reviewer responded to this collection: "Brophy's approach is quite unlike that of her fashionable British contemporaries; . . . it is more nearly related to that of such tough and sharp American talents as those of Miss Mary McCarthy and Miss Eleanor Clark."

Following *The Crown Princess,* Brophy moved into lengthier fiction and nonfiction works. *Hackenfeller's Ape* was her first novel. According to Brophy, "in my twenty-fifth year, I sat down to write a narrative poem and rose a fortnight later (a fortnight of which I have no memory) having written instead a brief novel called *Hackenfeller's Ape,* which is probably the best I shall ever write and which already displays at its most intense the violently romantic feeling in a precisely classical form to which most of my fiction aspires," recorded Newman. In this work, a professor of zoology sets an ape free from the London Zoo when he discovers this animal is destined for use in a rocket experiment. In the *Saturday Review,* Joseph Wood Krutch observed that "certainly there is a good deal of originality in [*Hackenfeller's Ape,* the tale of] a scientist with emotional conflicts who was trying to understand animals, humanity, and possibly even God by observing the behavior of [an ape]." Affected by what she herself saw at the London Zoo, Brophy explained that she "was trying to establish a parallel between shutting people up in prisons and shutting animals up in zoos," noted Newman. *Hackenfeller's Ape* garnered the Cheltenham Literary Festival first prize for a first novel in 1954.

In the early 1960s, Brophy wrote what some reviewers considered her best novels. One of the earliest of these is *Flesh,* a story drawing on the courtship and marriage of two young Jews. The sexually experienced Nancy opens the doors to a new world and, subsequently, a new lifestyle for her introverted husband, Marcus. Yet, to London *Observer* critic Hermione Lee, Marcus is transformed "into an obese, hedonistic aesthete: he *becomes* the kind of flesh he most admires, that of a Rubens woman. The nasty little tale, very smoothly told, is as much about second-generation North London Jews reacting against parental vulgarity and stuffiness as it is a pastiche of sensual awakening." Newman considered *Flesh* "clinical, but also poetic" and believed Brophy's writing, in this instance, paralleled her father's. As for *Saturday Review* contributor Manfred Wolf, he felt the book's subject was too narrow and that there

was not enough distance between Brophy and her characters: "*Flesh* would have been a better book if the author had not been so thoroughly taken in by it."

In her 1960s novella *The Finishing Touch,* Brophy presented what she called a "lesbian fantasy." This novella focuses on an English princess's stay at a finishing school on the French Riviera and the two English lesbians who run it. A number of reviewers detected Ronald Firbank's influence; indeed, Newman recorded one reviewer's opinion that the book was a posthumous monument to Firbank. Though some critics deemed *The Finishing Touch* a depraved work, *Best Sellers* contributor Joseph L. Quinn explained that "what Lionel Trilling said of Nabokov's grisly but beautifully written freak of a novel [*Lolita*] is also true of *The Finishing Touch;* the reader simply cannot work up sufficient indignation. Instead, he remains an amused observer, a sophisticated peeping Tom."

A third novella of this period, *The Snow Ball,* is a comedy of manners perceived by reviewers as Brophy's critique of middle-class morals and hypocrisies. It is a modern-day version of Mozart's opera *Don Giovanni.* Martin Tucker explained in the *New York Times Book Review* that in *The Snow Ball* "Brophy offers more than sex and seduction: she offers the commentary of a knowing ironist. Beneath her humor is, if not examination, then at least a stab at the hypocrisies of modern life." According to *New York Review of Books* contributor Eve Auchincloss, "the intellectual jokes [in *The Snow Ball*]—often either banal or irritatingly illegible—take precedence over the interplay of personalities (the people are no more than rather ugly dolls); yet under the surface one senses the beat of a sentimental, vindictive female heart." In Newman's opinion "there was a lot of uneasy praise from the critics, and even those who disliked the book conceded its effectiveness."

During the time that Brophy was publishing her succession of novels and novellas, she was also broadcasting on radio and television and crafting the critical works for which she has become known. A *Washington Post* writer called *Black Ship to Hell* an attack on "concepts of realism and naturalism in the English novel." Both this book and *Mozart the Dramatist: A New View of Mozart, His Operas and His Age* were seen as psychoanalytic studies much influenced by Freudian hypotheses. For instance, *New Yorker* contributor Naomi Bliven believed that in

Mozart the Dramatist Brophy "applies her own notions of psychoanalysis to the eighteenth century, to the Enlightenment, to Mozart, and to his librettos. She is looking for difficulties. . . . Brophy thinks [Mozart] is not only the greatest opera composer of the eighteenth century (and ever after) but the best expositor, in his operas, of that century's psychosexual problems. These, she believes, matter to us; I am not so certain." In addition, Brophy's *Don't Never Forget: Collected Views and Reviews* attests to her range and wit on a broad array of topics, from animal rights to contemporary writers.

One of Brophy's most controversial critical analyses, the one that induced a *Times Literary Supplement* reviewer to call her "one of our leading literary shrews," was *Fifty Works of English and American Literature We Could Do Without*. In this survey, Brophy, her husband, Michael Levey, and Charles Osborne devalued fifty works of fiction that had gained recognition over the years as classics of English and American literature. These include *Beowulf, Hamlet, Pilgrim's Progress, The Faerie Queene, Tom Jones,* Gray's *Elegy,* and the accomplishments of Daniel Defoe, T. S. Eliot, William Faulkner, and Gerard Manley Hopkins. The authors characterized Charlotte Bronte's *Jane Eyre* as an experience similar to "gobbling a jar-full of schoolgirl stick-jaw" candy.

Many reviewers were equally vehement in their denunciations of Brophy and her coauthors. In his *Encounter* assessment, for instance, Anthony Burgess called *Fifty Works* a "deplorable little work. . . . I . . . want to express my disquiet that this is what British literary criticism should have come to." Burgess then proposed why the authors published such a "vulgar" book: "one answer, a shameful one, is a hunger for notoriety. Their book, far from being ignored, . . . has had wide newspaper coverage. . . . Like children, they have shown off, and the showing-off has provoked attention." According to Burgess, the authors of *Fifty Works* failed to look at literature in a historic sense. Instead of viewing literature as a continuum over the centuries, Burgess felt Brophy and her collaborators erred when addressing the various literary works as isolated forms of entertainment. *Christian Science Monitor* reviewer Alan Levensohn described the book as "a collection of 50 brief, sneering essays. . . . Their sneering takes many forms, of which the most common is the direct, unsupported insult. . . . Where all else fails, the sneerers resort to amateur Freudianism. . . . The

book is not an utter waste. Three of the essays are worth skimming. . . . But the rest is merely relentless, irresponsible invective."

Other critics were not as displeased with *Fifty Works*. In the *Saturday Review* a writer admired the "poisonously delightful" book, and Edward Weeks concluded in *Atlantic* that "arbitrary and malicious as they are, the trio are protesting against the thoughtless acceptance of 'classics,' established by tradition and perpetuated by the reluctance of teachers and examiners to alter a system which everyone has learned to endure." Finally, a *New York Times Book Review* critic expressed disappointment because the authors did not direct enough of their attention to literary giants: "When the authors let fly at bigger game, notably T. S. Eliot, Hemingway and Faulkner, . . . they make one wish they had concentrated on more of these beefy sacred cows."

Brophy's avant-garde work *In Transit: An Heroicycle Novel* was a difficult book for some reviewers to characterize. In Newman's opinion, "though subtitled 'an heroicycle novel,' *In Transit* is less a novel than a cross between a neurotic essay in criticism and a farcical nightmare. . . . The book is best described as an anti-antinovel . . . [and] the protagonist . . . is nothing more than a voice." Though some reviewers could not discern a plot, those who did explain that a young girl, Patricia, is waiting at an airport, "a sort of Kennedy Terminal of the psyche," described Elizabeth Hardwick in *Vogue,* when a sudden amnesia sets in. The girl's identity fades; indeed, she cannot remember her name or her gender. The remainder of the story describes the girl's struggle for personal redefinition. According to Phelps, Brophy's *In Transit* brings to the forefront the concept of the multifaceted individual: "At his innermost center, . . . [a person] is many things, many appetites, all genders. . . . In his soul, he is as polymorphous as the angels. . . . Patricia's breakdown is actually a breakthrough: her tough little ego is fighting for its birthright, and on the last page of *In Transit,* she has died, been reborn, and is about to assume a more spacious selfhood." As for Guy Davenport in the *National Review,* "it is not at all clear just what's going on by way of action." Davenport, like others, found *In Transit*'s experimental style leads to confusion.

When interviewed by Bolivar Le France in *Books and Bookmen,* Brophy remarked that *In Transit* "attempts to be many dimensioned. . . . It is for me rather as if I'd gone on from writing concerti to writing symphony—with a big and rather brassy orchestra. . . . It was intended basically to give the reader something which could be read three or four times and still yield something." Brophy, known as a fine punster, utilized her talent to the utmost in *In Transit.* According to Hardwick, "from the first section . . . to the last . . . everything is in planned disorder, whirling with hallucination, disconnection, puns, fantasy, dreams, phantasmagoria, unexpected wit, and restless allusion. . . . [Brophy] is accompanied on every page by her fellow-traveller and Irishman, James Joyce." Other reviewers detected Joycean similarities as well. In *Books and Bookmen,* V. R. J. Clinton sensed Joyce's "anarchy," and Phelps found *In Transit* "robustly, joyously fertilized by James Joyce."

Following *In Transit,* Brophy authored the nearly six-hundred-page *Prancing Novelist: A Defence of Fiction in the Form of a Critical Biography in Praise of Ronald Firbank.* According to Newman, Philippa Pullar remarked in the *Sunday Times* that Brophy's "strength and beauty lies in her lyric brevity, writing a fat and heavy volume about someone whose own strength and beauty also lies in lyric brevity." In this lengthy defense of what most would consider a minor novelist, reviewers sensed unjustified admiration and a good deal of self-indulgence. "Inflating him beyond recognition, [Brophy] leaves Firbank a swollen, distorted hulk,. . ." offered Michael Rosenthal in the *New York Times Book Review.* "In its willfully perverse view of literary history and literary value, *Prancing Novelist* seems a document more self-serving than anything else, attesting to the uniqueness not of its subject but its author. . . . Those not already committed to Firbank will hardly be encouraged to sample him by the tendentiousness and irresponsibility of much of this book." In a similar vein, *New Republic* critic Lawrence Graver declared that the more Brophy "talks about lyric brevity, reverberating images, eloquent silence, textual spacing and novels that seal themselves in their own autonomy, the more convincing is the conventional wisdom that Firbank's talent is tiny. At times,. . . Brophy seems to glimpse the truth and her frantic language reveals the absurdity of erecting such a monument to a butterfly."

Brophy continued to write both fiction and nonfiction during the 1970s, but she devoted much of her time and energy to the establishment of the British Public Lending Right. With this goal in mind, Brophy and Maureen Duffy formed Writers' Action Group in the early 1970s as a lobbying tool. Brophy's father originated the idea of the Public Lending Right as a means of providing authors a small fee each time their books were loaned from libraries. Though it took a decade of work, in 1979 the Public Lending Right became law in England.

In the early 1980s, tragedy beset Brophy. Following years of good health, Brophy was stricken with multiple sclerosis. In her 1987 book *Baroque 'n' Roll and Other Essays,* Brophy relived the circumstances surrounding the onset and diagnosis of the disease in "A Case-Historical Fragment of Autobiography." As Brophy maintained, the chief "curse" of the disease is that "I must ask constant services of the people I love most closely, of whom I require my three meals a day and constant water and eternal coffee. . . . Sporadically it is, in its manifestations, a disgusting disease. . . . It is an illness accompanied by frustration. . . . It is an illness that inflicts awareness of loss. . . . Yet the past is, except through memory and imagination, irrecoverable in any case, whether or not your legs are strong enough to sprint after it. All that has happened to me is that I have in part died in advance of the total event." According to John Bayley in the *London Review of Books,* "A Case-Historical Fragment of Autobiography" is the most moving essay in Brophy's *Baroque 'n' Roll* collection: "To observe one's symptoms . . . and one's medical experiences for the benefit of others is a service rarely performed. Brigid Brophy does it with humour and stoicism, and in addition performs the almost impossible feat of thanking her husband and friends for all they have done for her. . . . That is as much a personal triumph as is her always creative criticism." London *Times* critic Peter Ackroyd likewise valued the humor and "clarity of judgement" evident in Brophy's personal essay. In addition, he found her continued argument against vivisection worthy of comment. Brophy "has always been an opponent of vivisection; but now she states that, in the search for the cure of her own disease, 'it is vital that no animal, human or non-human, be tortured or killed.' Under the circumstances this is an eloquent plea; but what is more eloquent still is that, in the course of this autobiographical essay, she has the humility . . . to turn aside from her own sufferings in order to address those of other creatures."

As Ackroyd noted, Brophy always displayed somewhat of an "anti-autobiographical temperament," thus making *Baroque 'n' Roll* a highly valued departure. Ronald Blythe explained in his *Sunday Telegraph* contribution: "I think that *Baroque 'n' Roll* allows us to view the work of Brigid Brophy in a way not previously possible . . . because she herself has chosen to use the material collected here specifically to illuminate who she is and what she stands for, something she has rather avoided or smudged until now. The result is moving and funny, persnickety and brave, erudite and pleasurable." Apart from her autobiographical account, Brophy revealed herself in essays on the baroque movement, from which the collection gets its title. In Bayley's opinion, "the linked essays on baroque which conclude [Brophy's] book are as fascinating as they are informed, and every sentence creates the author, on the one hand, while illuminating the spirit of baroque, on the other. The combination is rare, in every sense, and reveals what all its most devoted clients know by instinct: that art is both communal and personal; that it tells us we are individuals at the same time that it transcends individuality." Indeed, as Kris Kirk maintained in *Gay Times*, it was courage "which has helped [Brophy] give us the gift of this book."

Brophy's final offering for her readers was *Reads: A Collection of Essays,* comprised of works published between 1962 and 1989. Here, the author took on a wide variety of topics, including the literature of Louisa May Alcott, Georges Simenon, William Makepeace Thackeray, and Ronald Firbank, opera, and animal rights. Lorna Sage described the tone and style of these essays in an *Observer* review: "Maybe her loathing of the 'moral torture' of sentimentality (including religious belief) derives, by some law of opposites, from her Irishness. Her style surely does, rather more directly," added the reviewer. "She is entirely free from the English instinct for understatement and apology. Her most occasional piece will find something wholeheartedly to delight in or deplore." From these essays, noted Sage, the reader can get a feel for Brophy and for what made her unique. Sage concluded, "*Reads* is a tonic book, a medicine for mental weariness."

BIOGRAPHICAL/CRITICAL SOURCES:

BOOKS

Brophy, Brigid, *Baroque 'n' Roll and Other Essays,* David & Charles, 1987.
Contemporary Authors Autobiography Series, Volume 4, Gale, 1986.
Contemporary Literary Criticism, Gale, Volume 6, 1976, Volume 11, 1979, Volume 29, 1984.
Dick, Kay, *Friends and Friendship,* Sidgwick & Jackson (London), 1974.

Dictionary of Literary Biography, Volume 14: *British Novelists since 1960,* Gale, 1982.

PERIODICALS

Atlantic, April, 1957; March, 1968.
Best Sellers, July 15, 1964; March 15, 1970.
Books and Bookmen, July, 1967; January, 1969; December, 1969; March, 1974.
Book World, January 25, 1970.
Christian Science Monitor, February 15, 1968; February 14, 1970.
Encounter, August, 1967.
Gay Times, April, 1987.
Guardian, March 20, 1987.
Harper's, March, 1970.
Life, February 13, 1970.
Listener, March 21, 1968; December 6, 1973.
London Review of Books, March 17-31, 1983; March 5, 1987.
National Review, February 10, 1970.
New Republic, June 30, 1973; December 28, 1974.
New Statesman, February 16, 1962; May 26, 1967; April 28, 1978; January 25, 1980.
New Yorker, December 26, 1964.
New York Herald Tribune Book Review, September 27, 1953; February 17, 1957.
New York Review of Books, September 24, 1964.
New York Times, February 27, 1970.
New York Times Book Review, November 29, 1953; July 26, 1964; May 21, 1967; February 25, 1968; July 22, 1973; August 25, 1974; July 16, 1978.
Observer (London), January 13, 1980; March 26, 1989, p. 46.
Saturday Review, June 12, 1954; July 27, 1963; February 17, 1968; July 8, 1978.
Spectator, May 6, 1978; February 21, 1987.
Sunday Telegraph, February 15, 1987.
Sunday Times, February 15, 1987.
Time, February 2, 1970.
Times (London), March 10, 1983; February 19, 1987.
Times Educational Supplement, March 24, 1989, p. 22.
Times Literary Supplement, January 23, 1953; February 23, 1962; December 1, 1966; June 1, 1967; October 2, 1969; March 30, 1973; November 23, 1973; April 28, 1978; March 9, 1984; March 13, 1987.
Vogue, March 15, 1970.
Washington Post Book World, August 18, 1974; October 7, 1979.

OBITUARIES:

PERIODICALS

Chicago Tribune, August 10, 1995, sec. 3, p. 11.
New York Times, August 9, 1995, p. D20.
Washington Post, August 9, 1995, p. B4.*

*   *   *

BRUNETTE, Peter (Clark), Jr.   1943-

PERSONAL: Born September 18, 1943, in Richwood, WV; son of Peter Clark (a postal supervisor) and Mildred L. (Perkins) Brunette; married Lynne Ellen Johnson (a college teacher), August 10, 1974. *Education:* Duquesne University, B.A., 1965, M.A., 1967; University of Wisconsin—Madison, Ph.D., 1975.

ADDRESSES: Home—8911 Sudbury Rd., Silver Spring, MD 20901. *Office*—Department of English, George Mason University, Fairfax, VA 22030. *E-mail*—pbrunett@gmu.edu.

CAREER: University of Paris, Paris, France, lecturer in English, 1970-72; University of Maryland at College Park, instructor in English in European Division, 1972-73; University of Maryland Eastern Shore, Princess Anne, instructor in English and director of Basic Skills Center, 1974-75; George Mason University, Fairfax, VA, assistant professor, 1975-79, associate professor, 1979-88, professor of English, 1988—.

MEMBER: Modern Language Association of America, Society for Cinema Studies.

AWARDS, HONORS: Fellow of National Endowment for the Humanities, 1981-82, 1987-88; associate fellow at Center for Advanced Study in the Visual Arts, National Gallery of Art, 1981-82, senior fellow, 1992-93; fellow at School of Criticism and Theory, Northwestern University, 1982.

WRITINGS:

Roberto Rossellini, Oxford University Press (New York City), 1987, University of California Press (Berkeley), 1996.
(With David Wills) *Screen/Play: Derrida and Film Theory,* Princeton University Press (Princeton, NJ), 1989.

(Editor) Francois Truffaut, *Shoot the Piano Player,* Rutgers University Press (New Brunswick, NJ), 1993.
(Editor with David Wills) *Deconstruction and the Visual Arts: Art, Media, Architecture,* Cambridge University Press (New York City), 1994.

Contributor to books, including *The Classic American Novel and the Movies,* edited by Gerald Peary and Roger Shatzkin, Ungar (New York City), 1977; *The Modern American Novel and the Movies,* edited by Peary and Shatzkin, Ungar, 1978; *American Cartoon Animation,* edited by Gerald Peary and Dannis Peary, Dutton (New York City), 1978; *Modern European Filmmakers and the Art of Adaptation,* edited by Andrew Horton and Joan Magretta, Ungar, 1980; *Comedy/Cinema/Theory,* edited by Horton, University of California Press, 1991; and *Thinking Bodies,* edited by Juliet Flower MacCannell, Stanford University Press (Stanford, CA), 1994. Also contributor to magazines and newspapers, including *Cineaste, Film Quarterly, Boston Globe, Sight and Sound, Village Voice, New York Times,* and *Washington Post.*

WORK IN PROGRESS: A book on filmmaker Michelangelo Antonioni for Cambridge University Press; a book on filmmaker Luchino Visconti.

SIDELIGHTS: Peter Brunette told *CA:* "My work is rather schizophrenic, I'm afraid. On the one hand, I write film articles for various newspapers like the *New York Times,* the *Boston Globe,* and the *Village Voice.* I do this because I think it is important to reach large audiences in order to have at least some tiny effect on contemporary culture. On the other hand, my own intellectual interests are increasingly theoretical. So much of what is printed in newspapers and magazines, after all, is forgotten in days or even hours. It also sometimes seems that most of that sort of writing is really a matter of recycling the obvious, and trying to find new ways to say the same old boring stuff. Writing more academic pieces, however, gives me the chance to exercise my intellectual capabilities to their maximum, even if those books and essays will never be read by more than a handful of people. Granted, the work that post-structuralist thinkers like Jacques Derrida are engaged in is often difficult and daunting. But it also seems to presage a revolution in the ways we currently think about things—everything, from love to politics to movies—and therefore more than worth the effort."

BUCKLEY, William F(rank) Jr. 1925-

PERSONAL: Born November 24, 1925, in New York, NY; son of William Frank (a lawyer and oil-man) and Aloise (maiden name, Steiner) Buckley; married Patricia Austin Taylor, July 6, 1950; children: Christopher Taylor. *Education:* Attended University of Mexico, 1943-44; Yale University, B.A. (with honors), 1950. *Politics:* Republican. *Religion:* Roman Catholic.

ADDRESSES: Office—National Review, 150 East 35th St., New York, NY 10016.

CAREER: Yale University, New Haven, CT, instructor in Spanish, 1947-51; affiliated with the Central Intelligence Agency (C.I.A.) in Mexico, 1951-52; *American Mercury* (magazine), New York City, associate editor, 1952; freelance writer and editor, 1952-55; *National Review* (magazine), New York City, founder, president, and editor-in-chief, 1955-90, editor-at-large, 1990—; syndicated columnist, 1962—; host of *Firing Line* weekly television program, 1966—. Conservative Party candidate for mayor of New York City, 1965; member of National Advisory Commission on Information, U.S. Information Agency, 1969-72; public member of the U.S. delegation to the United Nations, 1973. Lecturer, New School for Social Research, 1967-68; Froman Distinguished Professor, Russell Sage College, 1973. Chairman of the board, Starr Broadcasting Group, Inc., 1969-78. *Military service:* U.S. Army, 1944-46; became second lieutenant.

MEMBER: Council on Foreign Relations, Century Club, Mont Pelerin Society, New York Yacht Club, Bohemian Club.

AWARDS, HONORS: Freedom Award, Order of Lafayette, 1966; George Sokolsky Award, American Jewish League against Communism, 1966; Best Columnist of the Year Award, 1967; University of Southern California Distinguished Achievement Award in Journalism, 1968; Liberty Bell Award, New Haven County Bar Association, 1969; Emmy Award, National Academy of Television Arts and Sciences, 1969, for *Firing Line;* Man of the Decade Award, Young Americans for Freedom, 1970; Cleveland Amory Award, *TV Guide,* 1974, for best interviewer/interviewee on television; fellow, Sigma Delta Chi, 1976; Bellarmine Medal, 1977; Americanism Award, Young Republican National Federation, 1979, for contributions to the American principles of freedom, individual liberty, and free enter-

prise; Carmel Award, American Friends of Haifa University, 1980, for journalism excellence; American Book Award for Best Mystery, 1980, for *Stained Glass;* New York University Creative Leadership Award, 1981; Lincoln Literary Award, Union League, 1985; Shelby Cullom Davis Award, 1986; Lowell Thomas Travel Journalism Award, 1989; Julius Award for Outstanding Public Service, University of Southern California School of Public Administration, 1990; Presidential Medal of Freedom, 1991; Gold Medal Award, National Institute of Social Sciences, 1992. Honorary degrees: L.H.D. from Seton Hall University, 1966, Niagara University, 1967, Mount Saint Mary's College, 1969, University of South Carolina, 1985, Converse College, 1988, and University of South Florida, 1992; LL.D. from St. Peter's College, 1969, Syracuse University, 1969, Ursinus College, 1969, Lehigh University, 1970, Lafayette College, 1972, St. Anselm's College, 1973, St. Bonaventure University, 1974, University of Notre Dame, 1978, New York Law School, 1981, and Colby College, 1985; D.Sc.O. from Curry College, 1970; Litt.D. from St. Vincent College, 1971, Fairleigh Dickinson University, 1973, Alfred University, 1974; College of William and Mary, 1981, William Jewell College, 1982, Albertus Magnus College, 1987, College of St. Thomas, 1987, Bowling Green State University, 1987, Coe College, 1989, Saint John's University (Minnesota), 1989, and Grove City College (Pennsylvania), 1991.

WRITINGS:

God and Man at Yale: The Superstitions of "Academic Freedom," Regnery, 1951, reprinted, Gateway Editions, 1977.
(With L. Brent Bozell) *McCarthy and His Enemies: The Record and Its Meaning,* Regnery, 1954.
Up from Liberalism, Obolensky, 1959.
Rumbles Left and Right: A Book about Troublesome People and Ideas, Putnam (New York City), 1963.
The Unmaking of a Mayor, Viking (New York City), 1966.
(Author of introduction) Edgar Smith, *Brief against Death,* Knopf (New York City), 1968.
The Jeweler's Eye: A Book of Irresistible Political Reflections, Putnam, 1968.
(Author of introduction) *Will Mrs. Major Go to Hell?: The Collected Work of Aloise Buckley Heath,* Arlington House (New York City), 1969.
Quotations from Chairman Bill: The Best of William F. Buckley, Jr., compiled by David Franke, Arlington House, 1970.

The Governor Listeth: A Book of Inspired Political Revelations, Putnam, 1970.

Cruising Speed: A Documentary, Putnam, 1971.

Taiwan: The West Berlin of China, St. John's University Center of Asian Studies, 1971.

Inveighing We Will Go, Putnam, 1972.

Four Reforms: A Guide for the Seventies, Putnam, 1973.

United Nations Journal: A Delegate's Odyssey, Putnam, 1974.

The Assault on the Free Market (lecture), Kansas State University (Manhattan, KS), 1974.

Execution Eve and Other Contemporary Ballads, Putnam, 1975.

Airborne: A Sentimental Journey, Macmillan (New York City), 1976.

A Hymnal: The Controversial Arts, Putnam, 1978.

Atlantic High: A Celebration, Doubleday (New York City), 1982.

Overdrive: A Personal Documentary, Doubleday, 1983.

Right Reason, Doubleday, 1985.

The Temptation of Wilfred Malachey (juvenile), Workman Publishing (New York City), 1985.

Racing through Paradise: A Pacific Passage, Random House (New York City), 1987.

On the Firing Line: The Public Life of Our Public Figures, Random House, 1989.

Gratitude: Reflections on What We Owe to Our Country, Random House, 1990.

Windfall: End of the Affair, Random House, 1992.

In Search of Anti-Semitism, Continuum (New York City), 1992.

Happy Days Were Here Again, Random House, 1993.

Lady Chatterly's Lover: Loss and Hope, Macmillan, 1993.

Brothers No More (novel), Doubleday, 1995.

Buckley: The Right Word, Random House, 1996.

EDITOR

(With others) *The Committee and Its Critics: A Calm Review of the House Committee on Un-American Activities,* Constructive Action (Whittier, CA), 1963.

Odyssey of a Friend: Whittaker Chambers' Letters to William F. Buckley, Jr., 1954-1961, Putnam, 1970.

(With Charles R. Kesler) *Did You Ever See a Dream Walking?: American Conservative Thought in the Twentieth Century,* Bobbs-Merrill (New York City), 1970, revised edition published as *Keeping the Tablets: Modern American Conservative Thought,* Perennial Library (New York City), 1988.

Also editor, with Stuart W. Little, of *The Buckley-Little Catalogue,* 1984-87.

ESPIONAGE NOVELS

Saving the Queen, Doubleday, 1976.

Stained Glass (also see below), Doubleday, 1978.

Who's On First, Doubleday, 1980.

Marco Polo, If You Can, Doubleday, 1982.

The Story of Henri Tod, Doubleday, 1984.

See You Later, Alligator, Doubleday, 1985.

High Jinx, Doubleday, 1986.

Mongoose, RIP (also see below), Random House, 1988.

Tucker's Last Stand, Random House, 1990.

A Very Private Plot, Morrow (New York City), 1994.

The Blackford Oakes Reader, Andrews & McNeel (Kansas City, MO), 1994.

CONTRIBUTOR

Ocean Racing, Van Nostrand (New York City), 1959.

George B. DeHuzar, editor, *The Intellectuals: A Conservative Portrait,* Free Press (New York City), 1960.

F. S. Meyer, editor, *What Is Conservatism?,* Holt (New York City), 1964.

Dialogues in Americanism, Regnery, 1964.

Edward D. Davis, editor, *The Beatles Book,* Cowles, 1968.

S. Endleman, editor, *Violence in the Streets,* Quadrangle, 1968.

R. Campbell, editor, *Spectrum of Catholic Attitudes,* Bruce Publishing, 1969.

Great Ideas Today Annual, 1970, Encyclopaedia Britannica (Chicago), 1970.

Fritz Machlup, editor, *Essays on Hayek,* New York University Press (New York City), 1976.

Mickey Is Sixty!, Time-Life (New York City), 1988.

OTHER

Mongoose, RIP (abridged recording of his book, read by the author), Sound Editions (Holmes, PA), 1988.

Stained Glass (play), produced by Actors Theatre of Louisville, 1989, Samuel French (New York City), 1989.

Also author of *Celestial Navigation,* a videocassette. Author of syndicated column "On the Right," 1962— . Contributor to *Esquire, Saturday Review, Harper's, Atlantic, Playboy, New Yorker, New York Times Magazine,* and other publications.

The Buckley Papers at the Beinecke Library at Yale University contain Buckley's correspondence since 1951 and material concerning the *National Review.*

SIDELIGHTS: William F. Buckley, Jr., is one of the most recognized and articulate spokesmen for American conservatives. On his television program *Firing Line,* in the pages of *National Review,* the magazine he founded, and through the books and syndicated columns he writes, Buckley argues for individual liberty, the free market, and the traditional moral values of Western culture. His eloquence, wit, and appealing personal style have made him palatable even to many of his political opponents. "The Buckley substance," a writer for *Time* reported, "is forgiven for the Buckley style."

Buckley's writings have been instrumental to the phenomenal growth of the American conservative movement. In the 1950s, when Buckley first appeared on the scene, conservatism was a peripheral presence on the national political spectrum. But in 1980 the conservatives elected Ronald Reagan, a longtime reader of Buckley's *National Review,* as president of the United States. "When the tide of intellectual and political history seemed headed inexorably leftward," Morton Kondracke wrote in the *New York Times Book Review,* "Mr. Buckley had the temerity to uphold the cause of Toryism. He and his magazine nurtured the movement . . . and gave it a rallying point and sounding board as it gradually gained the strength and respectability to win the Presidency. Conservatism is not far from the dominant intellectual force in the country today, but neither is liberalism. There is now a balance between the movements, a permanent contest, and Mr. Buckley deserves credit for helping make it so."

Buckley first came to public attention in 1951 when he published *God and Man at Yale: The Superstitions of "Academic Freedom,"* an attack against his alma mater, Yale University. The book accuses Yale of fostering values—such as atheism and collectivism—which are an anathema to the school's supporters. Further, Buckley claims that Yale stifled the political freedom of its more conservative students. Those students who spoke out against the liberal views of their professors were often ostracized. The book's charges stemmed from Buckley's own experiences while attending Yale, where his views on individualism, the free market, and communism found little support among the liberal academics.

God and Man at Yale raised a storm of controversy as Yale faculty members denounced the charges made against them. Some reviewers joined in the denunciation. McGeorge Bundy, writing in the *Atlantic,* called the book "dishonest in its use of facts, false in its theory, and a discredit to its author." Peter Viereck agreed with Buckley that "more conservatism and traditional morality" were needed at universities and wrote in the *New York Times* that "this important, symptomatic, and widely held book is a necessary counterbalance. However, its Old Guard antithesis to the outworn Marxist thesis is not the liberty security synthesis the future cries for." Frank D. Ashburn of the *Saturday Review of Literature* claimed that *God and Man at Yale* "has the glow and appeal of a fiery cross on a hillside at night. There will undoubtedly be robed figures who gather to it, but the hoods will not be academic. They will cover the face."

But other critics found *God and Man at Yale* to be a serious contribution to the political dialogue. Writing in the *American Mercury,* Max Eastman claimed that the book "is brilliant, sincere, well-informed, keenly reasoned, and exciting to read." Selden Rodman of the *Saturday Review of Literature* called it "an important book, perhaps the most thought-provoking that has appeared in the last decade on the subject of higher education in the United States. . . . That the author happens also to be a conservative, with whose specific religious and economic ideas I find myself not in sympathy, is less important than that he challenges forcefully that brand of 'liberal' materialism which, by making all values 'relative,' honors none." Because of the widespread controversy raised by *God and Man at Yale,* Buckley became well known among the nation's conservatives.

This position as conservative spokesman was vastly strengthened in 1955 when Buckley founded *National Review,* a magazine of conservative opinion. In a statement of purpose published in the magazine's first issue, Buckley stated: "The profound crisis of our era is, in essence, the conflict between the Social Engineers, who seek to adjust mankind to conform with scientific utopias, and the disciples of Truth, who defend the organic moral order." At the time of its founding, Richard Brookhiser remarked in *National Review*'s thirtieth anniversary issue, "the forces of conservatism in American thinking were insignificant." But Buckley used the magazine as a rallying point to consolidate the nation's conservatives. He formed a coalition, George H. Nash explained in his *The Conservative Intellectual Movement in America since 1945,* of "New Conservatives, libertarians, and anti-communists." From this core of supporters the *National Review* reached out to a larger audience. Buckley hoped, Nash wrote, "to establish a journal which would reach intellectuals." Buckley has said on other occasions that "what we are trying for is the maximum leverage that conservatives can exert."

Although *National Review,* in common with most other magazines of political opinion, has never made a profit (it is subsidized by reader contributions and Buckley's own money), it has become one of the most influential political journals in the country. Nash credited it with a central role in the growth of American conservative thought. "If *National Review* (or something like it) had not been founded," Nash wrote, "there would probably have been no interlocking intellectual force on the Right in the 1960's and 1970's. To a very substantial degree, the history of reflective conservatism in America after 1955 is the history of the individuals who collaborated in—or were discovered by—the magazine William F. Buckley, Jr. founded." Gene M. Moore pointed out in the *Dictionary of Literary Biography Yearbook: 1980* that over the years *National Review* has helped to "launch the careers of such authors and columnists as Renata Adler, Joan Didion, John Leonard, and Garry Wills."

With the growth of the conservative movement, *National Review* now enjoys a circulation of over 100,000, including some highly influential readers. Former president Ronald Reagan, for example, has declared that *National Review* is his favorite magazine. Speaking at the magazine's thirtieth anniversary celebration in 1985—a celebration attended by such notables as Charlton Heston, Tom Selleck, Jack Kemp, and Tom Wolfe—Reagan remarked: "If any of you doubt the impact of *National Review*'s verve and attractiveness, take a look around you this evening. The man standing before you now was a Democrat when he picked up his first issue in a plain brown wrapper; and even now, as an occupant of public housing, he awaits as anxiously as ever his biweekly edition—without the wrapper."

In addition to his writing and editing for the *National Review,* Buckley also writes a syndicated column, "On the Right," which appears in 350 newspapers three times weekly, as well as articles of opinion for various national magazines. Many of these columns and articles have been published in book-length col-

lections. These shorter pieces display Buckley's talent for political satire. John P. Roche of the *New York Times Book Review,* speaking of Buckley's articles in *Execution Eve and Other Contemporary Ballads,* claimed that "no commentator has a surer eye for the contradictions, the hypocrisies, the pretensions of liberal and radical pontiffs . . . even when you wince, reading Buckley is fun." A *Choice* critic, reviewing *A Hymnal: The Controversial Arts,* explained that "Buckley excels in the use of language, the sparkling epigram, and biting sarcasm that penetrates to the heart of a matter." And Steven R. Weisman of the *New York Times Book Review* maintained that "Bill Buckley certainly deserves his reputation as one of the wittiest political satirists writing today."

Happy Days Were Here Again, Buckley's 1993 collection, is a comprehensive primer of his ideas. It contains more than 120 articles and addresses written between 1985 and 1993. John Grimond commented in the *New York Times Book Review* that Buckley is "eloquent" on the subjects of anti-Communism, conservatism, sailing and illegitimacy. Yet Grimond continued: "It is a pity his range is not wider. A columnist needs to be able to say something interesting on many more issues than these if he is to delight his readers as much as himself. . . . Especially among the articles in which he is supposedly appreciating others, the self-serving references to himself occur with tedious frequency. The strongest single quality to emerge from this book is not percipience or wit; it is vanity." A more glowing endorsement came from Rush Limbaugh, who related in *National Review,* "I had read quite a few of these articles and columns before, in newspapers or in *NR.* As stand-alone pieces, they are stimulating and stirring. But nothing compares with a full, book-length dose of Buckley: nearly five hundred pages of witnessing, in Buckley's own words, 'the calisthenics of the free mind.' Reading these essays is like opening a window on history—recent history and the history of mankind."

Despite his status as one of the foremost leaders of conservatism, Buckley is a strong supporter of mandatory public service, a concept generally championed by liberals. In the book *Gratitude: Reflections on What We Owe to Our Country,* he set forth his ideas on the subject. He believes that young adults should spend a year in service to their country after completing high school—in the military, the Forest Service, or any federal program. Service would be voluntary, but those who chose not to participate would face penalties, such as denial of federal loans for college or loss of a driver's license. This year of service, Buckley stated, would do much to foster a sense of altruism in the young, and would be a source of inexpensive labor for federal programs. "John F. Kennedy summoning young Americans to the New Frontier was rarely more eloquent than Mr. Buckley articulating every citizen's obligation to ask what he can do for his country," stated Theodore C. Sorensen in the *New York Times Book Review.* Sorensen admits having some differences with Buckley's views, but concluded, "I have no difficulty understanding and embracing Mr. Buckley's underlying message. He is clearly devoted to this country, deeply grateful for the liberties and privileges it has afforded us and genuinely committed to recognizing and repaying that debt. After an American decade marred by greed and self-indulgence, this book, in reminding us all of our obligations, is a national service." Writing in *Christian Science Monitor,* R. Cort Kirkwood concurred that Buckley's book is the work of a great patriot: "In *Gratitude,* Buckley sets forth a vision of a truly heroic society in the tradition of those, such as George Washington, Edmund Burke, and other conservative luminaries, who fervently and correctly believed we owe a debt to our forebears for the heritage they bequeathed to us."

Buckley again showed his willingness to confront flaws in the conservative ranks with his book *In Search of Anti-Semitism.* It grew out of a special issue of *National Review*—December 30, 1991—in which he explored the subject of anti-Semitism in depth. Furthermore, he criticized two friends and conservative brethren, Joseph Sobran and Pat Buchanan, for anti-Semitic attitudes and remarks. The book is comprised of Buckley's original article, comment from readers, and additional comment from Buckley. "Leave it to William Buckley to see right to the heart of a complex issue," declared Jacob Neusner in *National Review.* "Instead of assuming that 'we all know' what anti-Semitism is, he takes up the burden of sorting matters out. This he does with wit, insight, common sense—and unfeigned affection for the Jews and appreciation of what the State of Israel stands for. . . . In sorting matters out with the obvious affection and respect for the Jews and Judaism that this book shows, Buckley should win from those most affected . . . the trust that is needed so that people can stop choosing up sides and start sorting out their conflicts—and resolving them." *New York Times Book Review* contributor Nathan Glazer also praised the book as "fascinating reading: some of our most skillful, subtle and elegant conservative

analysts of political trends can be read here, often in private correspondence with Mr. Buckley. He evokes very good letters—in part because he is such a good writer and letter-writer himself." Yet some reviewers found *In Search of Anti-Semitism* disturbing, in part because of what they perceive as Buckley's attempts to excuse his friends Sobran and Buchanan for their actions. Henry Grinberg castigated Buckley in the *American Book Review,* stating that "the effect of the whole presentation is chilling. Everyone, from Buckley on, is eloquent, graceful, and often witty— Buckley most of all—sometimes flippant—in a work that need not be gloomy, but would seem to call for some gravitas. This is Buckley the entertainer we all know, ever able to twinkle merrily at distress not his own. Soon you realize that Buckley indeed does not approve of what Buchanan and Sobran have done. But just as soon, you realize that he is not going to condemn them. Buchanan and Sobran are beloved old friends and comrades of the Right, and Buckley displays incredibly tortured thinking as he struggles to explain why he will not label the pair the bigots they clearly are." *Nation* contributor Micah L. Sifry also found Buckley's comments on his friends somewhat convoluted, yet he concluded, "for all his essay's slipperiness, . . . Buckley is at least trying to ask the right question."

In other books, Buckley turns from politics to his personal life. *Cruising Speed: A Documentary* is a diary-like account of a typical Buckley week. *Overdrive: A Personal Documentary* follows a similar format. Because of the many activities in which he is typically engaged, and the social opportunities afforded by his political connections and inherited wealth, Buckley's life makes fascinating reading. And he unabashedly shares it with his readers, moving some reviewers to criticize him. Nora Ephron of the *New York Times Book Review,* for example, called *Overdrive* "an astonishing glimpse of a life of privilege in America today." She complained that "it never seems to cross [Buckley's] mind that any of his remarks might be in poor taste, or his charm finite." And yet Carolyn See of the *Los Angeles Times* believed that the Buckley found in *Overdrive* "is a social butterfly, a gadabout, a mindless snob (or so he would have us believe). . . . Buckley shows us a brittle, acerbic, duty-bound, silly, 'conservative' semi-fudd, with a heart as vast and varicolored and wonderful to watch as a 1930s jukebox."

More universally appreciated are Buckley's sailing books. An avid yachtsman, he chronicles several of his sailing expeditions in *Airborne: A Sentimental*

Journey, Atlantic High: A Celebration, and *Racing through Paradise: A Pacific Passage.* These books are as much celebrations of the sailing life as they are the records of particular voyages. Speaking of *Atlantic High,* the account of Buckley's month-long journey from the Virgin Islands to Spain, Morton Hunt of the *New York Times Book Review* called it "more than an account of that trip, this is a book about a special and precious kind of human experience—the camaraderie of people who join together in a physical enterprise that is, at times, brutally demanding and hazardous and, at other times, idyllically tranquil and beautiful. . . . The shared experience of the sea . . . produces an intimacy and openness that life on shore might need years to achieve. And it is this, more than the experience of the sea itself, that Mr. Buckley is writing about."

When not writing about politics or sailing, Buckley has found time to pen a series of bestselling espionage novels featuring C.I.A. agent Blackford Oakes. The "arch and politically sophisticated" series, as Derrick Murdoch described the books in the Toronto *Globe and Mail,* is set in the Cold War years of the 1950s and 1960s and takes readers behind the scenes of the major political crises of the time. In doing so, the novels provide Buckley with the opportunity to dramatize some of his ideas concerning East-West relations. As Christopher Lehmann-Haupt of the *New York Times* remarked, "not only can Buckley execute the international thriller as well as nearly anyone working in the genre . . . he threatens to turn this form of fiction into effective propaganda for his ideas."

Saving the Queen, the first of the Blackford Oakes novels, is based in part on Buckley's own experiences in the C.I.A. "The training received by Blackford Oakes is, in exact detail, the training I received," Buckley explained. "In that sense, it's autobiographical." Oakes, a thinly disguised version of his creator, also shares Buckley's school years at an English public school and at Yale University. The story concerns a leak of classified information at the highest levels of the British government. Oakes is sent to locate the source of the leak and his investigation uncovers a treasonous cousin in the royal family. Robin W. Winks of the *New Republic* found *Saving the Queen* to be "replete with ambiguity, irony, suspense—all those qualities we associate with [Eric] Ambler, [Graham] Greene, [and John] le Carre." Amnon Kabatchnik of the *Armchair Detective* called *Saving the Queen* "an entertaining yarn,

graced with a literate style, keen knowledge and a twinkling sense of humor [that] injected a touch of sophistication and a flavor of sly irony to the genre of political intrigue."

Buckley's second novel, *Stained Glass,* is set in postwar Germany and revolves around the efforts of both East and West to prevent the reunification of Germany under the popular Count Axel Wintergrin. Both sides fear that a united Germany would be a military threat to the peace of Europe. Oakes penetrates Wintergrin's political organization disguised as an engineer hired to restore a local church. His restoring of broken church windows contrasts ironically with his efforts to keep Germany divided. "This novel is a work of history," Winks maintained, "for it parallels those options that might well have been open to the West [in the 1950s]. . . . *Stained Glass* is closer to the bone than le Carre has ever cut." Jane Larkin Crain of the *Saturday Review* called it a "first-rate spy story and . . . a disturbing lesson in the unsavory realities of international politics." *Stained Glass* won an American Book Award in 1980.

Later Blackford Oakes novels have concerned the Cuban missile showdown, the launching of Sputnik, and the construction of the Berlin Wall, among other Cold War crises. Buckley recounts these historical events faithfully. Anne Janette Johnson, speaking of *See You Later, Alligator,* which revolves around the Cuban missile crisis, asserted in the *Detroit Free Press* that "history buffs and spy-thriller enthusiasts alike should enjoy this in-depth portrayal of a unique moment in the history of the Western hemisphere." Stefan Kanfer of *Time* acknowledged that "it is to Buckley's credit that within his fiction, actual events are made as urgent and terrifying as they were."

But actual history is only a part of the Blackford Oakes novels. Oakes's missions take place behind the scenes of history. As Michael Malone explained in the *New York Times Book Review,* "Buckley slides his quite fascinatingly imagined, and appallingly conceivable, intrigues into the unknowns surrounding the secret skirmishes between *us* and *them.*" In several novels Buckley presents the case for an alternative policy from that which was actually followed. "He raises the sort of questions that only the most naive and the most sophisticated political observers would dare to ask," Anatole Broyard remarked in the *New York Times.* "He says, 'What if—' and then proposes something that is as attractive as it is preposterous, something so nearly commonsensical that it throws the entire Western world into pandemonium."

In building his novels around actual events Buckley is obliged to include historical figures in his cast of characters. Speaking of *See You Later, Alligator,* Murdoch believed that "the telling personal [details] are helping to make the Blackford Oakes series unique in spy fiction." In his review of *The Story of Henri Tod,* Broyard claims that "the best part . . . is [Buckley's] portrait of former President John F. Kennedy. His rendering of Nikita Khrushchev is quite good too, and this tempts me to suggest that Mr. Buckley seems most at home when he projects himself into the minds of heads of state." Similarly, Elaine Kendall of the *Los Angeles Times Book Review* speculated that Buckley may be evolving into "a psychic historian who can project himself into the most convoluted political minds."

A Very Private Plot, Buckley's tenth offering in the Blackford Oakes series, takes his hero to the conclusion of the Cold War. Commenting on the author's development as a novelist, D. Keith Mano wrote in the *National Review,* "He is a better fiction writer now by leagues than he was in 1976, when *Saving the Queen* took off. New directness and clarity jumpstart his prose. He has command of several voices and can modulate each. And, structurally, his later volumes . . . have had an arrow-shaped ease and *purpose.*" Furthermore, in Mano's opinion, "no one, Right or Left, has chronicled the Cold War period with more imagination or authority." Robin W. Winks mused in *Washington Post Book World:* "One wonders what Buckley would write, and what Oakes would do, were they to begin a 10-book trek now through the intricacies of intelligence in a post-Cold War world of enormously dangerous and very dirty small wars."

His next fiction effort was a departure from Blackford Oakes, however. *Brothers No More* was described as "an epic saga of doomed Yalies" by Joe Queenan in *New York Times Book Review.* The plot turns on the changing fortunes of two men who share a foxhole during World War II. One becomes a corrupt businessman; the other, a tenacious reporter. Years after their initial encounter, their paths cross again in a strange twist of fate. In Queenan's opinion, the book's plot is flimsy and contrived, and the book is "best thought of as patrician trash." He went on to say that Buckley's fine writing actually sabotages the novel: "For trash to work, the writing has

to be genuinely trashy, as in Jackie Collins, Danielle Steel, Judith Krantz. For trash to work, the writing has to be positively awful." Queenan believed that Buckley intended *Brothers No More* to be a genuinely serious book, but that it falls far short of that ambition. A *Publishers Weekly* reviewer rates the book as enjoyable, but concluded that "this is just a potboiler, deftly stirred but no match for Buckley's best."

Buckley's fiction usually has conservative political messages embedded in it, but his most influential popular means of spreading the conservative message may well be his weekly television program, *Firing Line,* which reaches several million viewers each week. It has been broadcast since 1966, and was the winner of an Emmy Award in 1969. The show presents debates between Buckley and selected guests from politics or the arts. His guests have ranged from Jorge Luis Borges to Jimmy Carter. "Whether the matter at hand is perfection of the soul or perfection of the state," Michiko Kakutani maintained in the *New York Times,* "exchanges on 'Firing Line' have always been animated by a love of language and a delight in logic."

An articulate and witty television host, Buckley nonetheless upsets some of his guests with his incisive questions. R. Z. Sheppard of *Time* called him a "TV Torquemada." Describing a typical *Firing Line* show, Phil Garner of the *Atlanta Journal & Constitution* observed that "Buckley's first question, characteristically, sought out the most likely weaknesses in his guests' most cherished positions." Frederick C. Kleig compared "the spectacle of William F. Buckley, Jr. spearing a foe" to "the sight of a cat stalking a bird. If you sympathize with the bird, you can still find it possible to admire the grace and ferocity of its pursuer." Buckley explained to Kakutani that many people are anxious to appear on *Firing Line,* but that "some people aren't so eager—people with positions not so easily defended in the face of rather relentless scrutiny."

Despite his long involvement in the nation's political life, Buckley has only once sought public office. In 1965 he ran for mayor of New York City in a highly visible, perhaps not-quite-serious campaign. Or maybe, as Buckley explained, it was just that he couldn't work up the "synthetic optimism" his followers expected. When asked, for example, what he would do if elected, Buckley replied: "Demand a recount." Although he lost the election, garnering 13.4 percent of the vote, Buckley managed to draw public attention to several issues he felt to be of importance, including welfare reform, the New York City traffic problem, and the treatment of criminals. Buckley now considers his political career over. "The only thing that would convince me to run again," he stated, "would be a direct order from my Maker, signed in triplicate by each member of the Trinity."

But in 1973 Buckley found himself in government office, this time as a public member of the U.S. delegation to the 28th General Assembly of the United Nations. He was appointed to the post by President Richard Nixon. Although a critic of the U.N. and skeptical of its effectiveness, Buckley took the job. "I saw myself there," Buckley wrote of his reasons for accepting the position, "in the center of the great assembly at the U.N. . . . holding the delegates spellbound . . . I would cajole, wheedle, parry, thrust, mesmerize, dismay, seduce, intimidate. The press of the world would rivet its attention on the case the American delegate was making for human rights." But Buckley's dream was not to be. "[If] the Gettysburg Address were to be delivered from the floor of the United Nations," Buckley later told an interviewer, "it would go unnoticed. . . . I soon became aware that the role of oratory was purely ceremonial. No one takes any notice of what is actually said. One listens for the overtones." Buckley has also served as a presidential appointee to the National Advisory Commission on Information, charged with assessing the work of the United States Information Agency. His only other brush with government work came in 1980 when President Reagan, who had just been elected, asked Buckley what position he would like to have in the new administration. "Ventriloquist," said Buckley.

As columnist, television host, novelist, and magazine editor, Buckley is known as "one of the most articulate, provocative, and entertaining spokesmen for American conservatism," as Moore wrote. For his role in the development of the modern conservative movement, Buckley "is a man who richly deserves praise," Kondrake believed. "He is generous, erudite, witty and courageous, and he has performed a service to the whole nation, even to those who disagree with him." Writing in the *Los Angeles Times Book Review*, John Haase called Buckley "witty, erudite, multifaceted, perhaps one of the few great exponents of the English language. He is politically contentious, a 'farceur,' I suspect, but we are willing to forgive all, because mostly Buckley is fun." Summing up Buckley's role in the nation's political life, Moore found that his "flickering tongue and flashing

wit have challenged a generation to remember the old truths while searching for the new, to abhor hypocrisy and to value logic, and to join in the worldwide struggle for human rights and human freedom."

BIOGRAPHICAL/CRITICAL SOURCES:

BOOKS

Buckley, William F., Jr., *The Unmaking of a Mayor,* Viking, 1966.
Buckley, *Cruising Speed: A Documentary,* Putnam, 1971.
Buckley, *United Nations Journal: A Delegate's Odyssey,* Putnam, 1974.
Buckley, *Overdrive: A Personal Documentary,* Doubleday, 1983.
Burner, David, and Thomas R. West, *Column Right: Conservative Journalists in the Service of Nationalism,* New York University Press, 1988.
Cain, Edward R., *They'd Rather Be Right: Youth and the Conservative Movement,* Macmillan, 1963.
Contemporary Issues Criticism, Volume I, Gale (Detroit), 1982.
Contemporary Literary Criticism, Gale, Volume 7, 1977, Volume 18, 1981, Volume 37, 1986.
Dictionary of Literary Biography, Volume 137: *American Magazine Journalists, 1900-1960, Second Series,* Gale, 1994.
Dictionary of Literary Biography Yearbook: 1980, Gale, 1980.
Forster, Arnold and B. R. Epstein, *Danger on the Right,* Random House, 1964.
Judis, John B., *William F. Buckley, Jr.: Patron Saint of the Conservatives,* Simon & Schuster (New York City), 1988.
Markmann, Charles L., *The Buckleys: A Family Examined,* Morrow, 1973.
Nash, George H., *The Conservative Intellectual Movement in America since 1945,* Basic Books (New York City), 1976.
Phelps, Donald, *Covering Ground: Essays for Now,* Croton Press, 1969.
Tuccille, J., *It Usually Begins with Ayn Rand: A Libertarian Odyssey,* Stein & Day (Briarcliff Manor, NY), 1972.

PERIODICALS

American Book Review, June 16, 1993.
American Mercury, December, 1951.
Armchair Detective, June, 1976.
Atlanta Journal & Constitution, March 3, 1974.
Atlantic, November, 1951; May, 1954; July, 1968.

Booklist, July, 1995, p. 1835.

Boston Globe, January 25, 1988, p. 28; August 20, 1988, p. 25; February 19, 1991, p. 30; September 7, 1991, p. 21.

Catholic World, November, 1959.

Chicago Tribune, November 8, 1959; January 10, 1988, p. B2; June 22, 1989, section 5, p. 1; October 26, 1990, section 5, p. 3; January 3, 1992, section 5, p. 5; March 20, 1994, section 5, p. 2; June 23, 1995, section 5, p. 3.

Choice, April, 1979.

Christian Century, July 3, 1968.

Christian Science Monitor, August 29, 1968; August 16, 1978; December 20, 1980; February 24, 1984; June 30, 1988, p. 29; July 18, 1988, p. 21; November 29, 1990, p. 19.

Commentary, April, 1974; November, 1983; February, 1992.

Commonweal, February 15, 1952; May 3, 1963; December 23, 1966; March 1, 1974.

Detroit Free Press, February 24, 1985.

Detroit News, September 19, 1982; August 21, 1983.

Esquire, January, 1961; November, 1966; January, 1968; August, 1969; September, 1969; February, 1972; July, 1976.

Forbes, October 10, 1994, pp. 60-69.

Globe and Mail (Toronto), February 18, 1984; April 13, 1985.

Harper's, March, 1967; November, 1971; October, 1983.

Life, September 17, 1965.

Listener, July 3, 1975; March 11, 1976.

Los Angeles Times, August 11, 1983; January 17, 1988, p. B10; July 1, 1988, p. VI25; July 14, 1988, p. V1; May 7, 1989, p. B1; November 11, 1990, p. E1; November 25, 1990, p. M4; July 6, 1991, p. F1; July 1, 1994, p. F34.

Los Angeles Times Book Review, February 7, 1982; September 12, 1982; January 22, 1984; April 7, 1985; March 23, 1986.

Mademoiselle, June, 1961.

Modern Age, summer, 1967; summer, 1974.

Nation, October 2, 1972; April 26, 1980; January 25, 1993, pp. 92-96, 98-99.

National Catholic Reporter, January 24, 1992.

National Observer, November 29, 1975.

National Review, May 7, 1963; November 15, 1966; July 30, 1968; September 13, 1974; October 24, 1975; December 5, 1975; February 20, 1976; May 13, 1977; June 9, 1978; November 24, 1978; April 4, 1980; January 22, 1982; October 15, 1982; September 2, 1983; February 24, 1984; December 31, 1985; July 31, 1987, pp. 44-46; January 6, 1992; May 11, 1992; December 28, 1992, pp. 40-42; October 4, 1993, pp. 55-57; February 21, 1994, pp. 58-60.

Negro Digest, April, 1969.

New Leader, January 19, 1976.

New Republic, October 19, 1959; June 10, 1978; February 10, 1992.

New Statesman, March 12, 1976.

Newsweek, October 17, 1966; March 25, 1968; August 2, 1971; September 30, 1974; January 5, 1976; February 19, 1979.

New Yorker, August 8, 1970; August 21, 1971; August 28, 1971; October 12, 1992, pp. 114-18.

New York Review of Books, July 18, 1974; October 13, 1983.

New York Times, November 4, 1951; April 4, 1954; October 6, 1971; April 5, 1978; February 6, 1980; February 25, 1981; December 28, 1981; August 18, 1983; December 21, 1983; February 4, 1985; March 27, 1986; January 24, 1988, section 7, p. 11; May 15, 1988, section 7, p. 12; August 16, 1988, p. B1; March 31, 1989, p. B2; May 28, 1989, section 7, p. 7; October 1, 1989, section 2, p. 27; October 13, 1988, p. B2; May 4, 1989, p. C24; October 12, 1990, p. B2; October 15, 1990, p. C16; September 6, 1991, p. B2; January 22, 1992, p. C20; July 13, 1992, p. C13; July 7, 1993, p. C18; January 5, 1994, p. B2.

New York Times (Connecticut edition), October 25, 1992, p. 14.

New York Times Book Review, March 25, 1962; April 28, 1963; October 30, 1966; September 15, 1968; August 2, 1970; September 26, 1971; October 8, 1972; January 13, 1974; September 28, 1975; December 26, 1976; January 11, 1978; May 14, 1978; November 19, 1978; February 17, 1980; March 30, 1980; January 24, 1982; March 7, 1982; September 5, 1982; August 7, 1983; February 5, 1984; March 3, 1985, pp. 12, 13; January 5, 1986, p. 14; February 9, 1986; April 6, 1986; May 31, 1987, p. 34; January 24, 1988, p. 11; May 15, 1988, p. 12; May 28, 1989, pp. 7, 8; October 28, 1990, pp. 1, 39; February 17, 1991, p. 15; September 27, 1992, pp. 3, 24; October 3, 1993, p. 14; February 6, 1994, p. 14; September 10, 1995, p. 16.

New York Times Magazine, September 5, 1965.

Observer, June 8, 1975.

Playboy, May, 1970.

Progressive, January, 1969.

Publishers Weekly, August 26, 1974; February 24, 1989, p. 211; August 7, 1995, p. 441.

Punch, July 12, 1978.

Quill and Quire, March, 1993, p. 78.

Reader's Digest, September, 1971.
San Francisco Review of Books, November-December, 1993, p. 28.
Saturday Evening Post, April, 1977.
Saturday Review, April 3, 1954; October 10, 1959; April 27, 1963; August 8, 1970; May 13, 1978; January, 1982.
Saturday Review of Literature, December 15, 1951.
Spectator, June 21, 1975.
Time, October 31, 1960; November 4, 1966; November 3, 1967; August 2, 1971; November 18, 1974; January 5, 1976; December 6, 1976; June 19, 1978; February 19, 1979; February 25, 1980; January 18, 1982; October 25, 1982; December 9, 1985; February 4, 1986; March 31, 1986; June 15, 1987.
Times Literary Supplement, March 12, 1976; July 27, 1984.
Town & Country Monthly, September, 1993.
Vanity Fair, September, 1993.
Village Voice, February 21, 1974; December 8, 1975.
Wall Street Journal, November 15, 1966; January 31, 1967; February 11, 1994, p. A11; April 29, 1994, p. A14.
Washington Post, February 12, 1980; October 6, 1990, p. C1; September 7, 1991, p. G1; December 12, 1991, p. B1; December 17, 1991, p. A21; June 29, 1992, pp. B1, B5.
Washington Post Book World, June 30, 1968; January 23, 1972; February 12, 1980; January 10, 1982; September 4, 1983; March 24, 1985; March 9, 1986; May 24, 1987; April 30, 1989, p. 4; October 28, 1990, p. 1; January 22, 1991, p. B3; June 29, 1992, p. B1; January 25, 1994, p. C2; August 7, 1994, p. 4.
Worldview, June, 1972.
Yale Review, December, 1959.

*   *   *

BURMAN, Jose Lionel   1917-1995

PERSONAL: Born April 10, 1917, in Jagersfontein, South Africa; died March 8, 1995; son of Elias Lewis and Dora (Loewenberg) Burman; married Ruth Valerie Herbert (deceased); married Cecily Kathleen Cheetham Robertson, August 28, 1939; children: (first marriage) Carol Lesley Burman Katz. *Education:* University of South Africa, B.A., 1938, LL.B., 1940. *Religion:* Jewish.

ADDRESSES: Home—P.O. Box 20, Hermanus, South Africa.

CAREER: Solicitor in Cape Town, South Africa, 1945-84; writer, 1960-94. *Military service:* South African Army, 1940-45.

MEMBER: International PEN, Mountain Club of South Africa, South African Spelaeological Association (president, 1967-77), Institute of Directors, South African Camping Club (chair, 1965-70), British Alpine Club, Historical Society of Cape Town (founder; chair, 1972), Masons (past district senior grand warden).

AWARDS, HONORS: Gold Medal from South African Spelaeological Association, 1965; award from International Wine Organization, 1980, for *Wine of Constantia.*

WRITINGS:

Safe to the Sea, Human & Rousseau (Cape Town, South Africa), 1962.
Peninsula Profile, Thomas Nelson (Nashville, TN), 1963.
So High the Road, Human & Rousseau, 1963.
The Garden Route, Human & Rousseau, 1964.
A Peak to Climb, Struik (South Africa), 1966.
Great Shipwrecks off the Coast of Southern Africa, Struik, 1967.
Where to Walk in the Cape Peninsula, Human & Rousseau, 1967.
Strange Shipwrecks of the Southern Seas, Struik, 1968.
Cape of Good Intent, Human & Rousseau, 1969.
Who Really Discovered South Africa, Struik, 1969.
Waters of the Western Cape, Human & Rousseau, 1970.
Disaster Struck South Africa, Struik, 1971.
Guide to the Garden Route, Human & Rousseau, 1972.
1652 and So Forth, Human & Rousseau, 1973.
The Saldanha Bay Story, Human & Rousseau, 1974.
Cape Drives and Places of Interest, Human & Rousseau, 1975.
Bay of Storms: Story of the Development of Table Bay, 1503-1860, Human & Rousseau, 1976.
The False Bay Story, Human & Rousseau, 1977.
Coastal Holiday, Human & Rousseau, 1978.
Wine of Constantia, Human & Rousseau, 1979.
Latest Walks in the Cape Peninsula, Human & Rousseau, 1979, revised and expanded edition, 1982.

Trails and Walks in the Southern Cape, Human & Rousseau, 1980.

The Little Karoo, Human & Rousseau, 1981.

Day Walks in the South-Western Cape, Human & Rousseau, 1984.

Early Railways at the Cape, Human & Rousseau, 1984.

Rediscovering the Garden Route, Human & Rousseau, 1985.

Shipwreck, Human & Rousseau, 1986.

Cape Trails and Wilderness Areas, Human & Rousseau, 1987.

Towards the Far Horizon, Human & Rousseau, 1988.

Hermanus: Riviera of the South, Human & Rousseau, 1989.

In the Footsteps of Lady Anne Barnard, Human & Rousseau, 1990.

The Table Mountain Book, Human & Rousseau, 1991.

The Unofficial History of the Cape, Human & Rousseau, 1992.

To Horse and Away, Human & Rousseau, 1993.

The Man in My Boots, Human & Rousseau, 1994.

Contributor to *Standard Encyclopedia of South Africa* and *Dictionary of South African Biography.* Also contributor of photography to *South African Wild Flower Guide #5: Hottentots Holland to Hermanus,* Botanical Society of South Africa, 1985.

SIDELIGHTS: Jose Lionel Burman told *CA:* "My interests are basically outdoor activities, and my writings are mostly a combination of the history and geography of South Africa. My driving motive is to let others share in enjoying the wildness and beauty of my country."

*　　*　　*

BURSTEIN, Chaya M(alamud)   1923-

PERSONAL: Born October 9, 1923, in New York, NY; daughter of Benjamin (a grocer) and Rivka (a grocer; maiden name, Zeile) Malamud; married Murray Burstein (an engineer), April 7, 1946; children: Ranan, Dina, Beth. *Education:* Hofstra University, B.A., 1968; State University of New York at Stony Brook, M.A., 1983. *Religion:* Jewish. *Avocational interests:* Gardening, hiking, writing letters, tutoring English.

ADDRESSES: Home—Mitzpeh Har Halutz, D.N. Bikat Bet Hakerem 25129, Israel.

CAREER: U.S. Geological Survey, Rolla, MO, draftsperson, 1950-54; mother and homemaker, 1954-70; writer and illustrator, 1970—. Volunteer teacher at Nassau County Jail, 1968-73, and Kiriat Chinuch, Maalot, Israel, 1987-90.

MEMBER: American Association of University Women, Hadassah, The Women's Zionist Organization of America.

AWARDS, HONORS: National Jewish book awards from Jewish Book Council, 1976, for *Rifka Grows Up,* and 1983, for *Jewish Kid's Catalogue.*

WRITINGS:

JUVENILE

Rifka Bangs the Teakettle, Harcourt (New York City), 1970.

Rifka Grows Up, Bonim Books, 1976.

A First Jewish Holiday Cookbook, Bonim Books, 1979.

Jewish Kid's Catalogue, Jewish Publication Society (Philadelphia), 1983.

What's an Israel?, Kar-Ben (Rockville, MD), 1983.

Joseph's and Anna's Time Capsule, Summit Books (New York City), 1984.

Hebrew Alphabet Coloring Book, Dover (Mineola, NY), 1986.

Kid's Catalogue of Israel, Jewish Publication Society, 1988.

The Secret of the Coins, Union of American Hebrew Congregations (New York City), 1988.

The Prophets, Union of American Hebrew Congregations, 1989.

Jewish Holidays and Traditions Coloring Book, Dover, 1990.

Kid's Catalog of Jewish Living, Union of American Hebrew Congregations, 1992.

The Jewish Kid's Hebrew-English Wordbook, Jewish Publication Society, 1993.

Our Land of Israel, Union of American Hebrew Congregations, 1995.

Daniel's Private War, Jewish Publication Society, 1996.

WORK IN PROGRESS: About the Bible, for Jewish Publication Society, completion expected in 1997.

SIDELIGHTS: Chaya M. Burstein told *CA:* "In my life and work I have struggled to balance my background of Jewish religion and culture with my American cultural environment. Jewish customs and holiday observances have always given me pleasure, so I have tried to impart a sense of fun as well as cultural richness in three juvenile 'how-to' books on Judaism. Because history fascinates me, I have chosen to write and illustrate stories and nonfiction about several historic periods. I hope that readers enjoy them, and at the same time gain a deeper understanding of their own origins.

"Ten years ago my husband and I moved to Israel—perhaps searching for origins—and now live in a tiny settlement in the Galilee mountains. The site, layered with Hebrew and Arab antiquities, ancient cisterns, crumbled towers, and potsherds, is full of history and current, challenging problems and provides endless material for thinking, illustrating, and writing."

*   *   *

BUTLER, Jack   1944-

PERSONAL: Born May 8, 1944, in Alligator, MS; son of Jack Butler (a Baptist preacher) and Dorothy (a homemaker; maiden name, Niland) Butler; married second wife, Jayme Thomas Tull (a purchasing manager), February 20, 1983; children: (first marriage) Lynnika, Sarah; (stepchildren) Sherri, Catherine. *Education:* Central Missouri State College (now University), B.S., 1966, B.A., 1966; University of Arkansas, Fayetteville, M.F.A., 1979.

ADDRESSES: Home—5820 Hawthorne, Little Rock, AR 72207. *Office*—Hendrix College, Conway, AR 72032. *Agent*—Ted Parkhurst, 1010 West Third, Little Rock, AR 72201.

CAREER: Joint Educational Consortium, Arkadelphia, AR, writer in residence, 1974-77; University of Arkansas, Fayetteville, instructor in English, 1977-79; Cancer Cooperative Group of Northwest Arkansas, Fayetteville, science writer and director of public relations, 1979-80; Blue Cross/Blue Shield of Arkansas, Little Rock, actuarial analyst, beginning 1980; Hendrix College, Conway, AR, assistant dean. Public speaker; actuarial consultant to Arkansas State Employees Insurance Commission.

AWARDS, HONORS: Award from Boatwright Literary Festival, 1971, for "Voices"; first prize for fic-

tion from *Black Warrior Review,* 1978, for "Without Any Ears," and 1981, for "A Country Girl."

WRITINGS:

West of Hollywood: Poems from a Hermitage, August House (Little Rock, AR), 1980.
Hawk Gumbo and Other Stories, August House, 1983.
The Kid Who Wanted to Be a Space Man, August House, 1984.
Jujitsu for Christ (novel), August House, 1986.
Nightshade (novel), Atlantic Monthly Press (New York City), 1989.
Living in Little Rock with Miss Little Rock (novel), Knopf (New York City), 1993.

Also author of "Voices" (poems), as yet unpublished. Work represented in anthologies, including *Best Poems of 1976,* edited by Joyce Carol Oates; *Ozark, Ozark,* edited by Miller Williams; and *Arkansas Voices.* Contributor of more than sixty poems to magazines, including *New Yorker, Atlantic Monthly, Poetry, Poetry Northwest, Cavalier, Southern Poetry Review, Mississippi Review,* and *New Orleans Review.*

SIDELIGHTS: Jack Butler lives, works, and writes in and around Little Rock, Arkansas, but his wide range of written work has attracted attention well beyond the Arkansas heartland. Butler once told *CA:* "I began writing as I might have begun baseball—because I wanted to do what I had seen others do so well and had moved me so powerfully. I write most of my stories from inside a character. We estimate each other very largely from voice: we listen for character in the ways people talk—richnesses, inconsistencies, secrets, fears, honesty, eagerness, confidence, humor. We may not all be story writers, but we are all judges of character. I like for my readers to discover my characters and their worlds in just the way that I discovered them. To me it does not seem that I am inventing so much as it seems that I am getting to know someone."

This concern for character, more than for event, is evident in *Hawk Gumbo and Other Stories,* according to David Jauss in a review for the *Arkansas Gazette.* "The book is particularly rich with voices," commented Jauss, ranging from the oblivious and uneducated to the self-conscious and intellectual. Maintaining that Butler handles the voice of his "country" characters best, Jauss praised him as having "an incredible gift for making colloquial language lyrical and poetic" and applauded the stories of *Hawk Gumbo* as "always competent and craftsmanlike and often exceptionally imaginative and beautifully written." Butler, Jauss concluded, is "a local author who deserves a national readership."

Butler earned a measure of national attention with his novel *Living in Little Rock with Miss Little Rock.* At its most basic level, it is the story of Charles Morrison, a lawyer, and his wife Lianne, a former Miss Little Rock. On this level, the novel "is territory we have explored with [John] Updike and [John] Cheever, among others," Patrick Anderson explained in the *Washington Post,* "but Butler's laser vision and word-wizardry make it fresh and fascinating." Besides the lives of his characters, Butler captures their city, and his city, Little Rock, Arkansas. As John and Carl Bellante pointed out in the *Bloomsbury Review,* "Little Rock is evoked with the same affection and attention to detail that James Joyce lavished on Dublin." Butler admitted in an interview with the Bellante brothers that in "*Living in Little Rock with Miss Little Rock,* I wanted to be accurate, because, among other things, it's a tribute to the town and to the state of Arkansas. For that reason I needed to get it as real as I could." Yet, as the Bellantes noted, "Butler's portrait isn't always entirely flattering" and some of the author's fellow citizens might have found reason to object.

For Anderson, however, it is not the characters, or the plot (which evolves into a murder mystery), or the setting which most sets *Living in Little Rock with Miss Little Rock* apart. Rather, it is the author's pyrotechnics. The reviewer called the novel "one of those books . . . that displays a full-blown novelistic

talent—in this case, a talent gleefully thumbing its nose at convention and causing this reader, at least, almost as much frustration as pleasure." *Chicago Tribune* contributor John Fink also struggled with the author's craft: "The opening of Butler's novel is so razzle-dazzle that it scared me half to death." And as reviewers pointed out, Butler's choice of narrator, an intrusive and irreverent Holy Ghost, can distract the reader from the novel's other concerns. "Fifty or so pages before the book's end, I had the feeling that I could have done nicely without that omniscient narrator, the Holy Ghost," Fink commented. "But then I read the final brilliant sermon . . . and finally saw how crucial the Holy Ghost is in all this." Concluded Anderson, "If you have the patience of a saint, a weakness for wordplay and a love of the language, this remarkable performance is not to be missed."

BIOGRAPHICAL/CRITICAL SOURCES:

PERIODICALS

Arkansas Gazette, February, 1983.
Bloomsbury Review, August, 1995, p. 3.
Chicago Tribune, May 10, 1993, sec. 5, p. 3.
Los Angeles Times Book Review, June 1, 1986, p. 6; August 27, 1989, p. 12; July 25, 1993, p. 3.
New Yorker, November 17, 1986, p. 151; November 13, 1989, p. 147.
New York Times Book Review, November 23, 1986, p. 9; September 3, 1989, p. 7; May 16, 1993, p. 32.
Rapport, Number 4, 1993, p. 24.
Science Fiction Chronicle, October, 1989, p. 44.
Small Press Review, April, 1983.
Voice Literary Supplement, April, 1987, p. 3.
Washington Post, April 12, 1993, p. B2.*

C

CAHILL, Thomas (Quinn) 1940-
(Tom Cahill)

PERSONAL: Born March 29, 1940, in New York, NY; son of Patrick Thomas (an insurance executive) and Margaret Mary (Buckley) Cahill; married Susan Jane Neunzig (a writer), November 4, 1966; children: Kristin Maria. *Education:* Fordham University, B.A., 1964, Ph.L., 1965; Columbia University, M.F.A., 1968.

ADDRESSES: Home—170-25 Highland Ave., Jamaica, NY 11432. *Office*—Doubleday and Company, 245 Park Ave., New York, NY 10017. *Agent*—Marcia Higgins, William Morris Agency, 1350 Avenue of the Americas, New York, NY 10019.

CAREER: New York Review of Books, New York City, advertising director for New York Review presentations, 1968-70; Seton Hall University, Center for Humanistic Studies, South Orange, NJ, instructor, 1968-73, assistant professor of humanistic studies, beginning 1973; Doubleday, New York City, currently director of religious publishing. Founder of the Cahill and Company Catalogue.

WRITINGS:

Jesus' Little Instruction Book: His Words to Your Heart, Bantam (New York City), 1994.
How the Irish Saved Civilization: The Untold Story of Ireland's Heroic Role from the Fall of Rome to the Rise of Medieval Europe, Nan A. Talese/ Doubleday (New York City), 1995.

WITH WIFE, SUSAN CAHILL

(Editor, under name Tom Cahill) *Big City Stories by Modern American Writers,* Bantam, 1971.
A Literary Guide to Ireland, Scribner (New York City), 1973.
A Literary Calendar: 1974 (Literary Guild selection), Universe Books (New York City), 1973.

Contributor to *Horizon.*

SIDELIGHTS: Thomas Cahill is perhaps best known to the publishing world for his work as the director of religious publishing for Doubleday and as the founder of the Cahill and Company Catalogue for bibliophiles. However, in the mid-1990s, he attracted the attention of readers, reviewers, and historians with his unique look at the important role played by Ireland following the collapse of the Roman Empire, *How the Irish Saved Civilization: The Untold Story of Ireland's Heroic Role from the Fall of Rome to the Rise of Medieval Europe.* In this book, Cahill recounts the dissolution of Roman civilization and the spread of the Germanic invaders on the European continent, events covered in nearly every history of this period. What is new in Cahill's account is his attention to Ireland, isolated and distant from the epicenter of this historic upheaval. According to Cahill, Peter Finn explains in the *New York Times Book Review,* in "those Dark Ages, between the classical and medieval worlds, remote Christian Ireland became the sanctuary of Western thought." Continues Finn: "Remarkably open-minded and uncensorial monks cherished the great books, beautifully and painstakingly copying them, before missionaries reintroduced them to the ignorant Continentals."

Cahill chronicles these events through the lives of those who shaped them: Ausonius (a Latin poet and philosopher from Bordeaux), St. Augustine, St. Patrick, Irish warrior Cuchulainn, Irish queen Medb, and others. In bringing together these lives, the writer "contrasts medieval Irish Catholicism—which after St. Patrick developed with virtually no influence from Rome—from that which was brought to the Angles and Saxons a century and a half later by the Roman missionary St. Augustine," notes Richard Eder in the *Los Angeles Times Book Review*. After the Irish reseeded Christianity and civilization on the continent, their influence was lost as Augustine's vision won the day, the church was centralized in Rome, and the English grew in power. With the loss of Irish influence also came, in Cahill's view, "the loss of gaiety, liberality, a celebration of the world's beauties, and even a touch of the bawdy," observes Eder.

Because it offers a different account of a well-traveled portion of history, and because its author is not a professional historian, *How the Irish Saved Civilization* has raised a stir of its own. Yet, as Richard Bernstein comments in the *New York Times,* "Mr. Cahill is a man of learning himself, and his writing is in the great Irish tradition he describes: lyrical, playful, penetrating and serious, but never too serious." "And," writes Bernstein, "even when his conclusions are not entirely persuasive—they do in places hang on rather slender reeds of evidence—they are always plausible and certainly interesting." Peter Finn finds that Cahill "has written a bracing book, brimming with freewheeling learning and unbridled enthusiasm. Professional historians might occasionally blanch at his exuberance, but his readers will revel in his deft and casual storytelling." Another value to this book suggested by Finn and by David Nyhan of the *Boston Globe* comes in the parallels that Cahill draws between that time of historic upheaval and our own. Concludes Bernstein: "Scholars, perhaps, will now evaluate these claims. But whatever they may find, Mr. Cahill's book will remain an entirely engaging, delectable voyage into the distant past, a small treasure."

BIOGRAPHICAL/CRITICAL SOURCES:

PERIODICALS

Atlanta Journal/Constitution, March 11, 1995, p. E6.
Boston Globe, December 30, 1994, p. 19.

Los Angeles Times Book Review, March 12, 1995, p. 3.
New York Times, April 5, 1995, p. C23.
New York Times Book Review, August 13, 1995, p. 15.*

*   *   *

CAHILL, Tom
  See CAHILL, Thomas (Quinn)

*   *   *

CAHN, Steven M.   1942-

PERSONAL: Born August 6, 1942, in Springfield, MA; son of Judah (an educator) and Evelyn (an educator; maiden name, Baum) Cahn; married Marilyn Ross (a physician). *Education:* Columbia University, A.B., 1963, Ph.D., 1966. *Religion:* Jewish.

ADDRESSES: Office—Graduate School and University Center, City University of New York, 33 West 42nd St., New York, NY 10036.

CAREER: Vassar College, Poughkeepsie, NY, assistant professor of philosophy, 1966-68; New York University, New York City, assistant professor, 1968-71, associate professor of philosophy, 1971-73; University of Vermont, Burlington, professor of philosophy and chairman of department, 1973-80, adjunct professor, 1980-83; City University of New York, Graduate School and University Center, New York City, professor of philosophy, 1983—, dean of graduate studies, 1983-84, provost and vice president for academic affairs, 1984-92, acting president, 1991. Visiting instructor in philosophy, Dartmouth College, 1966; visiting professor, University of Rochester 1967. Program officer, Exxon Education Foundation, 1977-79; Rockefeller Foundation, associate director of humanities, 1979-81, acting director, 1981-82. National Endowment for the Humanities, director of Division of General Programs, 1982-83, consultant panelist, Division of Fellowships and Stipends. Concert pianist.

MEMBER: American Association of University Professors, American Philosophical Association, Phi Beta Kappa.

WRITINGS:

Fate, Logic and Time, Yale University Press (New Haven, CT), 1967, Ridgeview Publishing Co. (Atascadero, CA), 1982.

A New Introduction to Philosophy, Harper (New York City), 1971, University Press of America (Lanham, MD), 1986.

The Eclipse of Excellence: A Critique of American Higher Education, with a foreword by Charles Frankel, Public Affairs Press (Washington, DC), 1973.

Education and the Democratic Idea, Nelson-Hall (Chicago, IL), 1979.

Saints and Scamps: Ethics in Academia, Rowman & Littlefield (Totowa, NJ), 1986, revised edition, 1993.

Philosophical Explorations: Freedom, God, and Goodness, Prometheus Books (Buffalo, NY), 1989.

EDITOR

(With Frank A. Tillman) *Philosophy of Art and Aesthetics,* Harper, 1969.

The Philosophical Foundations of Education, Harper, 1970.

Philosophy of Religion, Harper, 1970.

Classics of Western Philosophy, Hackett (Indianapolis, IN), 1977, 4th edition, 1995.

New Studies in the Philosophy of John Dewey, University Press of New England (Hanover, NH), 1977.

Scholars Who Teach: The Art of College Teaching, Nelson-Hall, 1978.

(With David Shatz) *Contemporary Philosophy of Religion,* Oxford University Press (New York City), 1982.

(With Patricia Kitcher and George Sher) *Reason at Work: Introductory Readings in Philosophy,* Harcourt (New York City), 1984, 3rd edition (with Kitcher, Sher and Peter J. Markie), 1995.

Morality, Responsibility and the University: Studies in Academic Ethics, Temple University Press (Philadelphia, PA), 1990.

Affirmative Action and the University: A Philosophical Inquiry, Temple University Press, 1993.

The Affirmative Action Debate, Rutledge (New York City), 1995.

(With Joram G. Haber) *Twentieth Century Ethical Theory,* Prentice-Hall (Englewood Cliffs, NJ), 1995.

OTHER

Contributor to *Encyclopedia of Philosophy.* Also contributor to periodicals including *American Philosophical Quarterly, Journal of Philosophy, New Republic,* and *New York Times.* General editor, *Issues in Academic Ethics,* 14-volume series, Rowman & Littlefield, 1993—.

WORK IN PROGRESS: Classic and Contemporary Readings in the Philosophy of Education, for McGraw-Hill; *Classics of Modern Political Theory,* for Oxford University Press; and (with Peter J. Markie) *The Moral Dimension,* for Oxford University Press.

*   *   *

CAMERON, Deborah   1958-

PERSONAL: Born November 10, 1958, in Glasgow, Scotland. *Ethnicity:* "Scottish European." *Education:* University of Newcastle upon Tyne, B.A. (with honors), 1980; Oxford University, M.Litt., 1985. *Politics:* "Feminist, socialist, and anti-racist." *Religion:* Atheist.

ADDRESSES: Home—London, England. *Office*—English Studies, Strathclyde University, 16 Richmond St., Glasgow G1 1QX, Scotland. *E-mail*—d.j.cameron @strath.ac.uk.

CAREER: Digby Stuart College, London, England, lecturer at Roehampton Institute of Higher Education, 1983-91; Strathclyde University, Glasgow, Scotland, senior lecturer, 1991—. Visiting professor at College of William and Mary, 1988-90, and Goetborgs University, 1995. Worked as teacher of English as a foreign language; active in British women's movement for more than fifteen years.

WRITINGS:

Feminism and Linguistic Theory, St. Martin's (New York City and London), 1985.

(With T. J. Taylor) *Analysing Conversation,* Pergamon (Oxford, England), 1987.

(With Elizabeth Frazer) *The Lust to Kill,* New York University Press (New York City), 1987.

(Editor) *The Feminist Critique of Language,* Routledge & Kegan Paul (London), 1989.

(Editor with Jennifer Coates) *Women in Their Speech Communities,* Longman (Essex, England), 1989.
Verbal Hygiene, Routledge & Kegan Paul, 1995.

Contributor of articles and reviews to magazines and newspapers, including *Language and Communication, City Limits,* and *Cosmopolitan.*

WORK IN PROGRESS: Research on language and gender.

SIDELIGHTS: Deborah Cameron told *CA:* "I write to entertain and to inform; the ideas which excite me intellectually I try to make accessible to people outside the charmed circle of professional academics. That is why I tend to write books for student and lay readers; it is also why I aim for a clear, plain style.

"The topics I choose to write about reflect a desire to make sense of my own experience as a Western woman—my own fear and fascination with sex murder, my sense of language as both restriction and liberation. This desire, I think, is common to all oppressed people as they come to political consciousness. It is fundamental to feminism: 'the personal is political.' For me, it transcends the boundaries of traditional academic disciplines and requires the writer instead to apply her intelligence and skill to whatever she feels strongly about."

BIOGRAPHICAL/CRITICAL SOURCES:

PERIODICALS

Times Literary Supplement, December 25, 1987.

*   *   *

CAMPBELL, Ewing   1940-

PERSONAL: Born December 26, 1940, in Alice, TX; son of James Vernon and Marie (Crofford) Campbell; married Lois R. Glenn (an editor), April, 1972 (divorced, 1980). *Education:* North Texas State University, B.B.A., 1968; University of Southern Mississippi, M.A., 1972; Oklahoma State University, Ph.D., 1980.

ADDRESSES: Home—1003 Magnolia, Hearne, TX 77859. *Office*—Department of English, Texas A & M University, College Station, TX 77843.

CAREER: Writer, 1967—. University of Texas at Austin, lecturer, 1981-82; Oklahoma State University, Stillwater, lecturer, 1982-83; Wharton County Junior College, Wharton, TX, lecturer, 1983-84; Texas A & M University, College Station, assistant professor, 1984-90, associate professor, 1990—. *Military service:* U.S. Army, 1959-62.

AWARDS, HONORS: First prize, *A. I. D. Review,* 1987, for "The Origin of a Metaphor"; National Endowment for the Humanities grant, 1987; Fulbright scholar in Argentina, 1989, and in Spain, 1996; National Endowment for the Arts fellowship, 1990; Dobie-Paisano Ralph A. Johnston Award for fiction, 1992.

WRITINGS:

Weave It Like Nightfall (novel; also see below), Nefertiti Head Press (Austin, TX), 1977.
(Translator) Julio Ortega, *The Land in the Day (Tierra en el dia),* New Latin Quarter Editions, 1978.
(Editor with Ortega) *The Plaza of Encounters,* Latitudes Press (Mansfield, TX), 1981.
The Way of Sequestered Places (novel; also see below), Nefertiti Head Press, 1982.
The Rincon Triptych (novel; includes *Weave It Like Nightfall, Cameo Illusion,* and *The Way of Sequestered Places*), Latitudes Press, 1984.
Piranesi's Dream: Stories (short stories), Nefertiti Head Press, 1986.
Raymond Carver: A Study of the Short Fiction (criticism), Macmillan (New York City), 1992.
The Tex-Mex Express (novel), Spectrum Press (Chicago), 1993.
Madonna, Maleva (novel), York Press (Fredericton, New Brunswick, Canada), 1995.

Contributor to periodicals, including *London Magazine, Cimarron Review, Cream City Review, New England Review, Kenyon Review, A. I. D. Review,* and *Chicago Review.*

*   *   *

CAMPBELL, Thomas M(oody)   1936-1993

PERSONAL: Born May 2, 1936, in Evanston, IL; died of heart failure, July 11, 1993, in Tallahassee, FL; son of Moody (a professor) and Cora (Rolfe) Campbell; married Julia Hickson, June 18, 1960 (divorced, 1971); married Cora Rolfe, 1973; children: (first marriage) Thomas M. III, David H., William H. *Education:* Randolph-Macon College, B.A. (cum laude), 1958; University of Virginia, M.A., 1960, Ph.D., 1964. *Religion:* Methodist.

ADDRESSES: Office—Department of History, Florida State University, Tallahassee, FL 32306.

CAREER: Florida State University, Tallahassee, instructor, 1963-65, assistant professor, 1965-72, associate professor, 1972-77, professor of history, 1977-93, assistant dean of Graduate School, 1965-67, member of Faculty Senate and chairman of the Rhodes Scholarship Committee.

MEMBER: Organization of American Historians, Society for the History of American Foreign Relations, Phi Beta Kappa, Omicron Delta Kappa.

AWARDS, HONORS: National Endowment for the Humanities fellowship, 1973-74; first recipient of the Edward R. Stettinius, Jr. fellowship; nomination for the Pulitzer Prize, 1975, for *The Diaries of Edward R. Stettinius, Jr., 1943-1946.*

WRITINGS:

Masquerade Peace: America's U.N. Policy, 1944-1945, University Presses of Florida (Gainesville, FL), 1973.
(Editor with George C. Herring) *The Diaries of Edward R. Stettinius, Jr., 1943-1946,* F. Watts (New York City), 1974.
(Contributor) *NATO after Thirty Years,* Scholarly Resources (Wilmington, DE), 1981.

Contributor to *International Organization, Journal of American History, American Historical Review* and other periodicals.

WORK IN PROGRESS: A biography of Edward R. Stettinius, Jr.

SIDELIGHTS: The late Thomas M. Campbell was a foreign policy scholar based at Florida State University. Over a thirty-year career of teaching and research, he published two important titles on Cold War diplomacy, *Masquerade Peace: America's U.N. Policy, 1944-1945* and *The Diaries of Edward R. Stettinius, Jr., 1943-1946.* Campbell based many of his scholarly conclusions on the extensive work he did with Stettinius's private and public papers, which he catalogued for the Library of Congress. In fact,

Campbell was at work on a biography of Stettinius—who served as Franklin Roosevelt's secretary of state—when he died of a heart attack in 1993.

Campbell's *Masquerade Peace* concerns the American role in the founding of the United Nations at the end of World War II. Concentrating on the early years of the Harry Truman presidency, Campbell argues that American relations with the United Nations became a "masquerade peace" behind which Truman sought more drastic security measures in a time of escalating anxiety. In the *American Historical Review,* James J. Dougherty called *Masquerade Peace* "a clearly written product of thorough research" and "an important contribution to the history of the period." *The Diaries of Edward R. Stettinius, Jr.* likewise elicited favorable reviews, and that volume—which Campbell edited with George C. Herring—was nominated for a Pulitzer Prize in 1975.

BIOGRAPHICAL/CRITICAL SOURCES:

PERIODICALS

American Historical Review, October, 1975, p. 1060.
Choice, December, 1973, p. 1620.
Journal of American History, December, 1994, p. 837.
Library Journal, January 15, 1974, p. 134.

OBITUARIES:

PERIODICALS

New York Times, July 22, 1993.*

*   *   *

CAREY, Peter 1943-

PERSONAL: Born May 7, 1943, in Bacchus Marsh, Victoria, Australia; son of Percival Stanley (an automobile dealer) and Helen Jean (an automobile dealer; maiden name, Warriner) Carey; married Alison Margaret Summers (a theater director), March 16, 1985; children: Sam, Charley. *Education:* Attended Monash University, 1961.

ADDRESSES: Home—New York, NY. *Agent*—Amanda Urban, International Creative Management, 40 W. 57th St., New York, NY 10019.

CAREER: Writer. Worked part-time in advertising in Australia from 1962 to 1988; also worked as a writing instructor at New York University and Princeton University.

AWARDS, HONORS: New South Wales Premier's Literary Award, 1980, for *War Crimes;* Miles Franklin Award, 1981, and New South Wales Premier's Literary Award and National Book Council Award, both 1982, all for *Bliss;* AWGIE Award and awards for best film and best screenplay from the Australian Film Institute, all 1985, all for *Bliss; The Age* Book of the Year Award and nomination for Booker Prize, both 1985, and Victorian Premier's Literary Award and National Book Council Award, both 1986, all for *Illywhacker;* Booker Prize, 1988, for *Oscar and Lucinda.*

WRITINGS:

SHORT FICTION

The Fat Man in History (includes "Crabs," "Peeling," "She Wakes," "Life and Death in the South Side Pavilion," "Room No. 5 (Escribo)," "Happy Story," "A Windmill in the West," "Withdrawal," "Report on the Shadow Industry," "Conversations with Unicorns," "American Dreams," and "The Fat Man in History"; also see below), University of Queensland Press (St. Lucia, Queensland, Australia), 1974.

War Crimes (includes "The Journey of a Lifetime," "Do You Love Me?" "The Uses of Williamson Wood," "The Last Days of a Famous Mime," "A Schoolboy Prank," "The Chance," "Fragrance of Roses," "The Puzzling Nature of Blue," "Ultra-violet Light," "Kristu-Du," "He Found Her in Late Summer," "Exotic Pleasures," and "War Crimes"; also see below), University of Queensland Press, 1979.

The Fat Man in History, and Other Stories (contains selections from *The Fat Man in History* and *War Crimes,* including "The Fat Man in History," "Peeling," "Do You Love Me?" "The Chance," "The Puzzling Nature of Blue," "Exotic Pleasures," "The Last Days of a Famous Mime," "A Windmill in the West," "American Dreams," and "War Crimes"), Random House (New York City), 1980, also published as *Exotic Pleasures,* Picador Books, 1981.

Collected Stories (includes "Do You Love Me?," "The Last Days of a Famous Mime," "Kristu-Du," "Crabs," "Life and Death in the South Side Pavilion," "Room No. 5," "Happy Story,"

"A Million Dollars Worth of Amphetamines," "Peeling," "A Windmill in the West," "Concerning the Greek Tyrant," and "Withdrawal"), University of Queensland Press, 1994.

NOVELS

Bliss, University of Queensland Press, 1981, Harper (New York City), 1982 (also see below).
Illywhacker, Harper, 1985.
Oscar and Lucinda, Harper, 1988.
The Tax Inspector, Faber & Faber (London), 1991, Knopf (New York City), 1992.
The Unusual Life of Tristan Smith, Knopf, 1995.

OTHER

(With Ray Lawrence) *Bliss* (screenplay; adapted from Carey's novel of the same title), Faber, 1986.
A Letter to Our Son, University of Queensland Press, 1994.
The Big Bazoohley, Holt (New York City), 1995.

Work represented in anthologies, including *The Most Beautiful Lies,* Angus & Robertson.

SIDELIGHTS: Peter Carey is an Australian writer who has earned substantial recognition for his quirky, inventive fiction. In his first short story collection, *The Fat Man in History,* published in 1974, he presented a matter-of-fact perspective on bizarre and occasionally grotesque subjects. Included in this book are "Conversations With Unicorns," in which the narrator recalls his various encounters with the extraordinary creatures, and "American Dreams," where a clerk succumbs to madness and isolates himself from his community. Upon his death, townspeople discover that in seclusion he constructed a model of their village. More gruesome are "Peeling," in which a character's quirky obsession results in a surreal mutilation, and "Withdrawal," in which the protagonist is a necrophile dealer of corpses and severed limbs. Among the curious figures in this tale is a pig who becomes dependent on narcotics after consuming an addict's excrement.

The publication of *The Fat Man in History* quickly established Carey as an important new figure in Australian literature. Carl Harrison-Ford wrote in *Stand* that Carey's first work was "the *succes d'estime* of 1974," and Bruce Bennett declared in *World Literature Written in English* that "Carey's first collection of stories . . . stamps him as the major talent among . . . new writers." Bennett found similarities between Carey's work and that of Kurt Vonnegut and Evelyn Waugh, but he added that "the shaping imagination is Carey's own." For Bennett, Carey was "a true fabulator . . ., one whose inventive, witty fictions both delight and instruct." Similarly, David Gilbey wrote in *Southerly* that *The Fat Man in History* was an "impressive volume," one that "dramatizes some of the dark myths beneath uncertainty and anxiety in contemporary life and does so with deadly, though not humourless, seriousness." Gilbey added that Carey's work was "intricately and surreally resonant and stands out markedly amongst contemporary Australian writing."

Equally unique was *War Crimes,* Carey's second collection of stories. The volume includes such vividly bizarre accounts as "The Chance," where a man vainly attempts to dissuade his lover from entering a lottery in which the major prize is a repulsive body. In the similarly disturbing title piece, a hippie-turned-businessman kills people threatening his profits from frozen food sales. Like Carey's first collection, *War Crimes* was immensely popular in Australia and received the New South Wales Premier's Literary Award in 1979.

Stories from both *The Fat Man in History* and *War Crimes* comprised Carey's third publication, *The Fat Man in History, and Other Stories.* This 1980 compilation brought Carey's unusual sensibility to American and British readers, many of whom readily acknowledged him as a unique and masterful storyteller. In his *Times Literary Supplement* review of the compilation, Peter Lewis called Carey an "outstanding writer" and praised his ability to write in a low-key but nonetheless compelling manner. "This naturalizing of the fantastic is probably Carey's most distinctive characteristic," Lewis wrote. "But he is also notable for his supposedly old-fashioned ability to hold the reader's attention." Similarly, *Saturday Review* critic Sandra Katz, who described Carey's work as "somewhere between science fiction and surrealism," declared that "the stories in [*The Fat Man in History*] are as brilliant as they are bizarre."

In 1981 Carey published his first novel, *Bliss.* Like his short stories, *Bliss* is fairly surreal, rendering the bizarre as if it is the norm. The novel's protagonist is Harry Joy, an overworked advertising executive who suffers a near-fatal heart attack. Upon recovering from the heart attack and equally life-threatening open-heart surgery, Joy believes that he is in Hell. He discovers that his wife is compromising him with

a close friend and that his seemingly lethargic son is actually a freewheeling drug dealer who forces his sister—Joy's daughter—to commit incest in return for drugs. Joy eventually forsakes his family for Honey Barbara, a worldly nature lover who regularly supports herself as a drug dealer and prostitute. Around the time that he befriends the charge-card accommodating prostitute, Joy also discovers that his advertising company maintains a map indicating cancer density for the area, with accountability traced to the company's clients. Aghast, Joy renounces his work and grows further remote from his family. Eventually, his wife has him committed to a mental institution, where he once again meets Honey Barbara, who has also been incarcerated. Together they escape to her home in a rain forest, where Joy finally finds happiness and fulfillment before meeting an unfortunate demise.

With *Bliss,* Carey gained further acclaim from American and British reviewers. In *British Book News,* Neil Philip referred to *Bliss* as "a rich, rewarding novel: crisply written, daringly conceived, brilliantly achieved," and in the *Washington Post Book World,* Judith Chettle wrote that Carey's novel possessed "all the virtues of a modern fable." For Chettle, Carey was "a writer of power and imagination." Even more impressed was *Spectator* critic Francis King. "In both the breadth of his vision of human life," wrote King, "in all its misery and happiness, and in the profundity of his insight into moral dilemmas, Mr. Carey makes the work of most of our 'promising' young and not so young novelists seem tinselly and trivial."

Carey collaborated with director Ray Lawrence on the 1985 film adaptation of *Bliss.* By visually rendering the novel's often grotesque and repellant imagery—including cockroaches that wander from a chest wound—the film *Bliss* proved controversial, offending many viewers at the 1985 Cannes Film Festival. But it also won top honors in Australia and developed an enthusiastic following in the United States. Among the film's strongest supporters was *Time*'s Richard Corliss, who commended its "outrage and ecstasy." Finding *Bliss* alternately "extravagant or exasperating," Corliss declared that it "puts nobody to sleep."

In 1985 Carey also published his second novel, *Illywhacker,* a wide-ranging comic work about Herbert Badgery, a 139-year-old trickster and liar. Badgery's life, which parallels the development of Australia following its independence from England, is full of odd adventures, including stints as a pilot, car salesman, and snakehandler. His accounts of his escapades, however, are not entirely reliable, and over the course of the novel's 600 pages Badgery often revels in tomfoolery and good-natured treachery. But he is hardly the novel's only unusual figure: Molly MaGrath maintains her sanity by periodically shocking herself with an "invigorator belt"; Emma, Badgery's daughter-in-law, lives in a lizard's cage; and an entire village proves gullible enough to cooperate with Badgery in his hastily organized plan to build an Australian airplane. By novel's end, Badgery has recounted many more mad schemes and regaled the reader with recollections of seemingly countless eccentrics.

Illywhacker, like Carey's previous publications, impressed many critics. In *Encounter,* D. J. Taylor called *Illywhacker* "a dazzling and hilarious book" and described the narrative as "a vast, diffuse plot chock-full of luminous characters and incident." Curt Suplee, who reviewed *Illywhacker* in the *Washington Post Book World,* recommended the novel as "huge and hugely rewarding" and added that it was a "rare and valuable" work. Howard Jacobson, writing in the *New York Times Book Review,* considered *Illywhacker* "a big, garrulous, funny novel, touching, farcical, and passionately bad-tempered." Jacobson also found *Illywhacker* a uniquely Australian work and contended that the experience of reading it was nearly the equivalent of visiting Australia. After noting occasional excesses in the narrative, Jacobson added: "Yet reading *Illywhacker* is not unlike spending a week in the company of the best kind of Australian. The stories keep coming, told with deceptive guilelessness and innocence. The talk is bawdy, the jokes are throwaways and rank, the sex is avid but democratic. Withal there is that haunting nostalgia and desolation that seems to be the immutable condition of the country. If you haven't been to Australia, read *Illywhacker.* It will give you the feeling of it like nothing else I know."

Carey's third novel, *Oscar and Lucinda,* is an extraordinary tale of two compulsive gamblers. The work begins in Victorian England, where the child Oscar endures life under the rigid rule of his intimidating father, a preacher. Later, Oscar breaks from his father and joins the conventional Anglican church, which he serves as a clergyman. Lucinda, meanwhile, has been raised in Australia by her mother, an intellectual who maintains the farm inherited from her late husband. Upon her mother's death, Lucinda inherits funds from the farm's sale. She also

becomes owner of a glassworks and consequently devises construction of a glass cathedral. Eventually, Oscar and Lucinda meet on a ship, where Lucinda reveals her own obsession with gambling. Together, Oscar and Lucinda commence an extensive gambling excursion through Australia while simultaneously attempting to spread Christianity throughout the still wild country. When Oscar discovers Lucinda's glass cathedral, he wagers with Lucinda that he can deliver the model to a faraway clergyman with whom he mistakenly believes she is in love. His sea voyage, in which he is accompanied by a memorably colorful crew, constitutes a crisis of faith and self-awareness.

Oscar and Lucinda resulted in still further praise for Carey and received the 1988 Booker Prize. Beryl Bainbridge, writing in the *New York Times Book Review,* was particularly impressed with those portions devoted to Oscar's traumatic childhood, though added that the remaining episodes were "racy with characters, teeming with invention and expressed in superlative language." Bainbridge also declared that Carey shared with Thomas Wolfe "that magnificent vitality, that ebullient delight in character, detail and language that turns a novel into an important book." Even more enthusiastic was *Los Angeles Times* reviewer Carolyn See, who wrote: "There's so much richness here. The sweetness of the star-crossed lovers. The goodness within the stifled English clergyman. The perfect irrationality of human behavior as it plays itself out in minor characters." See contended, "We have a great novelist living on the planet with us, and his name is Peter Carey."

Carey returned to writing about modern-day life with his fourth novel, *The Tax Inspector,* which describes four apocalyptic days in the life of the Catchprice family, proprietors of a crumbling auto dealership in a slummy suburb of Sydney, Australia. "Light-years beyond the merely dysfunctional, they're the Beverly Hillbillies on bad acid," stated Francine Prose in the *New York Times Book Review.* "The Catchprices are the sort of people you'd rather read about than spend time with." Granny Frieda Catchprice is a tough, half-senile widow who carries explosives in her pocketbook; her middle-aged daughter Cathy still dreams of leaving the family business to become a country-western singer; Cathy's brother Mort seems mild-mannered and harmless but has cruelly abused his two sons, as he himself was abused by Granny's late husband. One of Mort's children, 16-year-old Benny, listens religiously to "self-actualization" tapes until he comes to believe that he is an angel.

Suspecting that her children are about to put her in a nursing home, Granny reports them to the Australian Taxation Office, which sends Maria Takis—an unmarried, pregnant tax collector—to investigate. Maria's sympathy for Granny draws her into the Catchprices' malevolent vortex. "To summarize the novel's characters or its twisted plot is to risk making the book sound simply cartoonish, quirky and grotesque," warned Prose. "In fact, there's something extremely likable about all this, and especially about the way Mr. Carey gives the combative Catchprices great complexity and depth." Prose asserted that eventually, "the black hole these people call home" is transformed into "a dark mirror for the larger world outside."

Edmund White, reviewing for the *Times Literary Supplement,* also found much merit in the way the author made even his most unpleasant characters seem human. "Carey's triumph is that he doesn't ever turn his eccentrics into grotesques. We experience everything so intimately from several points of view that we scarcely judge anyone at all, any more than we ordinarily judge ourselves in the usual moments of just being. This suspension of moral discrimination is brought to our appalled attention only at the end of the book; the climax makes us recognize that we've dangerously misplaced our sympathies."

Richard B. Woodward, contributor to the *Village Voice,* described *The Tax Inspector* as "hard-bitten and close to the bone." Woodward continued that "it couldn't be more different from the arch cleverness and gentle fantasy of *The Unusual Life of Tristan Smith,*" Carey's next novel. *Tristan Smith* is a sprawling tale, set in the imaginary country of Efica—a tiny island nation colonized and exploited by Voorstand, a huge world power. Carey supplies a rich background for Efica, including a glossary of Efican dialect. The plot is typically convoluted, involving the Eficans' struggle to retain their own cultural identity. The Voorstanders attack that identity with a high-tech, semi-religious entertainment spectacle known as the Sirkus. The featured players in the Sirkus—Broder Mouse, Oncle Duck, and Hairy Man—bear more than a passing resemblance to three icons of the Walt Disney empire, Mickey Mouse, Donald Duck, and Goofy. The story is narrated by Tristan Smith, whose mother belongs to a radical theater group determined to resist the influence of the Sirkus. Hideously deformed at birth, Tristan finally finds love and acceptance after dis-

guising himself in an electronic Broder Mouse costume.

Writing in the *Chicago Tribune,* Douglas Glover found *Tristan Smith* "at once bizarre, comic and nauseating, . . . a deeply melancholy book about the Australia of the human heart. . . . Disturbing, wildly original and terribly sad, *The Unusual Life of Tristan Smith* is a book about the place where nation, myth and the personal intersect." Remarking on the novel's themes and relation to contemporary society, Michael Heyward, writing in the *New Republic,* stated: "If all the world is not a stage now but a themepark, we really are destined to become the residents of Voorstand and Efica. Could there be anything worse, Carey seems to be asking, than a situation in which practically everyone espoused the values of mass culture, especially in societies that did not create them?" The novel's driving force, Heyward continued, is "the savage irony of the provincial who has learned that the metropolis is merely a larger and more powerful province than his own." *Washington Post* contributor Carolyn See was also enthusiastic, declaring that "Peter Carey has attempted to do about 100 things in this very ambitious novel and—if I'm correct—has about a 90 percent success rate. This, combined with his always magical, absolutely lovable narrative voice, makes *The Unusual Life of Tristan Smith* an important contribution to contemporary fiction."

BIOGRAPHICAL/CRITICAL SOURCES:

BOOKS

Contemporary Literary Criticism, Gale (Detroit), Volume 40, 1986; Volume 55, 1989.
Hassall, Anthony J., *Dancing on Hot Macadam: Peter Carey's Fiction,* University of Queensland Press, 1994.
Krassnitzer, Hermine, *Aspects of Narration in Peter Carey's Novels: Deconstructing Colonialism,* E. Mellen Press (Lewiston, NY), 1995.

PERIODICALS

Boston Globe, January 12, 1992, section B, p. 43; March 14, 1995, p. 28.
British Book News, February, 1981; May, 1982.
Chicago Tribune, February 21, 1986; January 5, 1992, section 14, p. 1; February 19, 1995, section 14, p. 5.

Christian Science Monitor, February 9, 1989, p. 12.

Encounter, September-October, 1985.

Foundation, number 63, pp. 107-11.

Guardian Weekly, October 23, 1994, p. 28.

Listener, March 31, 1988, p. 29.

London Review of Books, April 18, 1985; April 21, 1988, p. 20; September 22, 1994, p. 5.

Los Angeles Times, October 2, 1980; August 29, 1985; February 21, 1986; June 19, 1988; June 11, 1989, p. B12.

Los Angeles Times Book Review, December 29, 1991, pp. 3, 8; February 5, 1995, pp. 3, 8.

Nation, March 16, 1992, pp. 346-48.

New Republic, April 10, 1995, pp. 38-41.

New Statesman, October 24, 1980; November 20, 1981; August 19, 1985; April 1, 1988, p. 28.

Newsweek, April 19, 1982; January 27, 1992, p. 60.

New York, January 13, 1992, p. 62.

New Yorker, August 23, 1982; November 11, 1985; February 24, 1992, p. 101; March 6, 1995, pp. 124-25.

New York Review of Books, June 25, 1992, p. 35-6.

New York Times, May 4, 1986; May 14, 1989; section 7, p. 1; January 28, 1992, p. C11, C15; January 16, 1992, p. C21.

New York Times Book Review, October 4, 1985; May 29, 1988; January 12, 1992, pp. 1, 26; February 28, 1993, p. 32; June 6, 1993, p. 56; February 12, 1995, p. 7.

Observer (London), November 15, 1981; April 14, 1985; March 27, 1988, p. 43; September 11, 1994, p. 18.

Partisan Review, spring, 1992, pp. 282-95.

Publishers Weekly, May 31, 1985.

Saturday Review, August, 1980.

Southerly, December, 1977.

Spectator, December 12, 1981.

Stand, Volume 16, number 3, 1975.

Time, March 17, 1986; January 20, 1992, p. 54.

Times (London), March 20, 1988, pp. 8-9.

Times Literary Supplement, October 31, 1980; November 20, 1981; May 3, 1985; August 30, 1991, p. 21; September 2, 1994, p. 10.

Tribune Books (Chicago), June 19, 1988, pp. 1, 11; December 6, 1992, p. 1; February 19, 1995, p. 5.

Village Voice, February 28, 1995, p. 59.

Voice Literary Supplement, February, 1982.

Washington Post, April 17, 1986; February 17, 1995, p. F7.

Washington Post Book World, May 2, 1982; August 18, 1985.

World Literature Written in English, November, 1976.*

CARPENTER, Delores Bird   1942-

PERSONAL: Born December 6, 1942, in Chattanooga, TN; daughter of Basil Ivan and Hazel (Hawkins) Bird; married Joe Keith Carpenter (a Methodist minister and elementary schoolteacher), December 27, 1959 (divorced July 21, 1987); children: Frederic Keith. *Ethnicity:* "Small part Cherokee." *Education:* Attended University of Mississippi; Boston University, B.A. (summa cum laude), 1967; University of Hartford, M.A., 1974; University of Massachusetts at Amherst, Ph.D., 1978. *Politics:* Democrat. *Religion:* "Spiritual."

ADDRESSES: Home—89 South Sandwich Rd., Mashpee, MA 02649. *Office*—Department of English, Cape Cod Community College, 2240 Iyanough Rd., West Barnstable, MA 02668.

CAREER: Junior high school English teacher in Shrewsbury, MA, 1967-70; University of Hartford, Hartford, CT, member of adjunct faculty, 1971-73; Tunxis Community College, Farmington, CT, member of adjunct faculty, 1973-74; Springfield College, Springfield, MA, member of adjunct faculty, 1974; Suffield High School, Suffield, CT, part-time teacher, 1974-75; Springfield Technical Community College, Springfield, member of adjunct faculty, 1975; University of Massachusetts at Amherst, member of adjunct faculty, 1976-77; Cape Cod Community College, West Barnstable, MA, instructor, 1977-80, assistant professor, 1980-84, associate professor of English, 1984-88, professor, 1988—. Southeastern Association for Cooperation in Higher Education Lecturer in southeastern Massachusetts, 1985-86.

MEMBER: Appalachian Mountain Club's 4000 Footer Club, Emily Dickinson Society, Ralph Waldo Emerson Society, Thoreau Society, Phi Beta Kappa.

WRITINGS:

(Editor) Ellen Tucker Emerson, *The Life of Lidian Jackson Emerson,* G. K. Hall (Boston, MA), 1980, revised edition, Michigan State University Press (East Lansing, MI), 1992.

(Editor and author of introduction) *The Selected Letters of Lidian Jackson Emerson,* University of Missouri Press (Columbia, MO), 1987.

The Early Days of Cape Cod Community College, Cape Cod Community College (W. Barnstable, MA), 1989.

Early Encounters: Native Americans and Europeans in New England from the Papers of W. Sears Nickerson, Michigan State University Press, 1994.

Also author of introduction to *Inside Out: The Poetry of George Hoar,* Sullwold Printer, 1994, and contributor to *Bulletin of the Massachusetts Archaeological Society.*

WORK IN PROGRESS: "Under contract with Michigan State University to edit an edition of Houghton Mifflin's 1931 printing of *Land Ho!—1620 A Seaman's Story of the Mayflower: Her Construction, Her Navigation and Her First Landfall* by W. Sears Nickerson. . . . It is copy-edited and waiting to be printed. I am looking for a publisher for an article entitled 'Grading Papers by Audio-Cassette Tapes.' Article accepted by *Cleveland Daily Banner* on a few pages from an autobiographical account by a family member describing the Dakotas and Cleveland, Tennessee in the late 1800s and the early 1900s."

SIDELIGHTS: Delores Bird Carpenter told *CA:* "Lidian Jackson Emerson was the wife of Ralph Waldo Emerson for forty-six years, the mother of their four children, and the hostess to the Transcendentalist circle. She gave herself to at least four causes, including active membership in the Massachusetts Society for the Prevention of Cruelty to Animals, serving as its vice-president for Concord in 1872. She could conjure up in her mind's eye real or imagined sufferings of animals, making their agonies more intense than her own. Something as inconsequential as the sun in Bossy's eye might distress her. The sufferings of humans also touched both her heart and mind. She worked for the Anti-Slavery Society, and got out of her sickbed to go to meetings in Boston. She worked on behalf of the Cherokee and Modoc Indians, and was an ardent advocate of woman's suffrage. Locally, for forty years she received school children at New Year's with gifts and admonitions concerning her favorite causes.

"A well-rounded woman of the nineteenth century emerges from Lidian Emerson's letters. They trace the growth of her independent and incisive mind, reveal her active influence on her husband's thought, and present a domestic view of the lives of the Emersons, their children, and their friends, including such notable contemporaries as Henry David Thoreau, Margaret Fuller, Thomas Carlyle, Amos Bronson Alcott, Jones Very, and many others."

BIOGRAPHICAL/CRITICAL SOURCES:

PERIODICALS

New England Quarterly, Vol. LXVIII, No. 3, September, 1995.
New York Times Book Review, November 29, 1987.

*   *   *

CARPENTER, Humphrey (William Bouverie) 1946-

PERSONAL: Born April 29, 1946, in Oxford, England; married Mari Prichard (a writer); children: two daughters. *Education:* Keble College, Oxford, M.A. and diploma in education. *Avocational interests:* Jazz (runs his own band playing popular music of the 1920s and '30s; he told *CA* he is "rather more proud of it than of my books!")

ADDRESSES: *Home*—6 Fardon Road, Oxford OX2 6R6, England. *Office*—c/o Allen & Unwin Ltd., 40 Museum St., London WC1A 1LU, England.

CAREER: British Broadcasting Corp. (BBC), London, England, radio producer and staff broadcaster, 1968-74; writer and freelance radio broadcaster, 1974—.

MEMBER: Royal Society of Literature (fellow).

AWARDS, HONORS: Somerset Maugham Award, Society of Authors, 1979, for *The Inklings: C. S. Lewis, J. R. R. Tolkien, Charles Williams, and Their Friends;* nominations for Whitbread Award for biography, 1981, and *Los Angeles Times* best biography, 1982, both for *W. H. Auden: A Biography;* E. M. Forster Award, American Academy and Institute of Arts and Letters, 1984.

WRITINGS:

BIOGRAPHIES

Tolkien: A Biography (Book-of-the-Month Club alternate selection), Houghton (Boston), 1977, published in England as *J. R. R. Tolkien: A Biography,* Allen & Unwin, 1977.
The Inklings: C. S. Lewis, J. R. R. Tolkien, Charles Williams, and Their Friends, Houghton, 1979.

W. H. Auden: A Biography, Houghton, 1981.
Geniuses Together: American Writers in Paris in the 1920s, Houghton, 1987.
A Serious Character: The Life of Ezra Pound, Houghton, 1988.
The Brideshead Generation: Evelyn Waugh and His Friends, Weidenfeld and Nicolson (London), 1989, Houghton, 1990.
Benjamin Britten, Scribner's (New York City), 1992.

JUVENILE

The Joshers; or, London to Birmingham with Albert and Victoria: A Story of the Canals, Allen & Unwin (London), 1977.
The Captain Hook Affair, Allen & Unwin, 1979.
Mr. Majeika, Viking Kestrel (London), 1984.
Mr. Majeika and the Music Teacher, Viking Kestrel, 1986.
Mr. Majeika and the Haunted Hotel, Viking Kestrel, 1987.
Mr. Majeika and the Dinner Lady, Viking Kestrel, 1989.
Further Television Adventures of Mr. Majeika, Puffin (London), 1990.
Mr. Majeika and the School Play, Viking (London), 1991.
Mr. Majeika and the School Book Week, Viking, 1992.
What Did You Do at School Today?, Orchard (London), 1992.
Charlie Crazee's Teevee, Pan (London), 1993.
Mr. Majeika and the School Inspector, Viking, 1993.
Mr. Majeika's Postbag, Viking, 1994.
Mr. Majeika and the Ghost Train, Viking, 1994.

OTHER

(With wife, Mari Prichard) *A Thames Companion,* Oxford Illustrated Press (Oxford), 1975.
Jesus, Hill & Wang, 1980.
(Editor with Christopher Tolkien) *The Letters of J.R.R. Tolkien,* Houghton, 1981.
(With Prichard) *The Oxford Companion to Children's Literature,* Oxford University Press (Oxford), 1984.
OUDS: A Centenary History of the Oxford University Dramatic Society, Oxford University Press, 1985.
Secret Gardens: A Study of the Golden Age of Children's Literature, Houghton, 1985.
Wellington and Boot, Macmillan (London), 1991.
Shakespeare without the Boring Bits, Viking, 1994.

Contributor of reviews to *Times Literary Supplement* and other periodicals. Also contributor to *Children and Their Books,* edited by Gillian Avery and Julia Briggs, Clarendon Press, (Oxford), 1989, and *Makers of Christianity,* Oxford University Press, 1993.

SIDELIGHTS: Humphrey Carpenter is an accomplished writer and editor whose forte is literary biography. A friend of the J. R. R. Tolkien family and a producer of several British Broadcasting Corp. (BBC) programs on The Hobbit's creator, he has written an authorized biography of Tolkien that, according to Robert Towers in *Newsweek,* appeals "not only to the cultists but a wider audience as well." Even more popular are *The Inklings: C. S. Lewis, J. R. R. Tolkien, Charles Williams, and Their Friends,* Carpenter's examination of the Oxford group that shared a Christian commitment and romantic literary interests, and his *W. H. Auden: A Biography,* a highly touted work that Alan Brownjohn says in *Encounter* "is almost certainly destined to provide the definitive account of [Auden's] life for the foreseeable future."

In writing *Tolkien: A Biography,* Carpenter, who first met John Ronald Reuel Tolkien while a student at Keble College, made use of extensive interviews with Tolkien's family and friends. But he was also allowed unrestricted access to the scholar's private papers, letters, photographs, and diaries. T. A. Shippey suggests in the *Times Literary Supplement* that Carpenter's "greatest achievement . . . is to have found his way through tangles of reminiscence, confusion, unordered manuscripts. His book ends with a complete bibliography containing many forgotten published works; his index offers a list of unpublished ones, each threaded into the line of a narrative complicated both by the intensity of his subject's inner life and by the uneventfulness of his public career."

Ironically, the man who wrote fantastic tales about hobbits, elves, dragons, and other creatures of Middle-Earth pursued a rather sedate career as an Oxford philologist. Several reviewers believe that Carpenter succeeds remarkably in making Tolkien's academic career as interesting as other facets of his life. Robert Towers, for example, writes: "Combining psychological insight with a tactful selectivity of detail, [Carpenter] makes Tolkien's public career as a professor of medieval literature and philology more dramatic than one might expect. He recreates the restrictively masculine world of Oxford in which Tolkien moved." Paul West points out in the *Wash-*

ington Post Book World that in the wrong hands, this biography "could have been a tame recital indeed, a monument of exalted outlines and dogged blather. Instead, it's a panorama of vignettes done with poise and exhaustive command. . . . Carpenter has an eye for the magic in what's pedestrian, and in his charge a 'quiet life,' such as Tolkien's, becomes an in-depth act of relish."

The Inklings: C. S. Lewis, J. R. R. Tolkien, Charles Williams, and Their Friends is "an amusing and insightful look at the birth of a literary movement," according to Christopher Willcox in the *Detroit News.* The book reconstructs the lives and exchanges of the Oxford group that met informally on Tuesday mornings at the "Bird and Baby" pub for beer and on Thursday evenings in C. S. "Jack" Lewis' Magdalen College quarters for rum and hot water. Drawn together by their commitment to Christianity and their obsession with elves, myths, and other romantic literary interests, the members—all male—initially devoted their meetings to the reading and discussion of Norse and Middle English poetry. Gradually, the meetings became a forum for the members to read out, and to talk out, their work in progress. At times, notes Christopher Ricks in the *New York Times Book Review,* the Inklings "were, in essence, a mutual-admiration society."

By far, the most influential members of the group were its founders, Tolkien and Lewis, and "for the reader interested in either," claims Willcox, "[*The Inklings*] is an essential text." A respected scholar of medieval studies, Tolkien helped revive the romance with the his *Lord of the Rings* trilogy and *The Hobbit,* which has been likened to Edmund Spenser's *Faerie Queene.* Lewis, too, contributed to this revival with his "Narnia" series, besides winning acclaim as a literary critic and popular Christian apologist. *The Inklings* illustrates how the group's influence, particularly their opposition to literary modernism, affected even the curriculum at Oxford. "To read *The Inklings,*" says Ricks, "is to learn about how some important things happened in the teaching of English literature at an important university . . . , especially . . . the weird 'reforms' that were perpetrated, such as the putsch that virtually abolished post-1830 literature from the syllabus. No wonder that the machinating Tolkien was called by Lewis (with disreputable respect) the 'Lord of the Strings.'"

Carpenter focuses on Lewis as the center of the group, delving into his personal as well as literary life. He documents Lewis' thirty years of non-roman-

tic cohabitation with Janie Moore, the mother of a friend killed in World War I. Carpenter also details Lewis' tragic relationship with Joy Gresham Davidman, an American Jew whom he married so that she could live in England. Lewis later fell in love with Davidman, and they renewed their vows in a more elaborate ritual than their previous civil ceremony. Unfortunately, Joy Lewis died of cancer three years later, perhaps never having consummated her marriage. "The end of Lewis' life, with his surprised love for Joy, is exceptionally touching, and her brave dying is enough to make you want to weep for them both," states Ricks.

Lewis was dismayed by Tolkien's ultimate dismissal of his "Narnia" series, but Carpenter attributes the eventual split of the Inklings to Lewis' enthusiasm for publisher and fabulist Charles Williams, whom Tolkien, suspicious and jealous, once called a "witch doctor." Kingsley Amis regards Carpenter's account of Williams, "beginning with a short memoir of his London days, [as] a triumph of skill and tact." Indeed, continues Amis in the *New Statesman,* "this could be said of the whole book, in which there is not one dull or slack sentence. [Carpenter] fuses his sources together off-stage, so to speak, and provides a smooth narrative unencumbered either with footnotes or with those horrid little numbers that refer you to a later page. The result is oddly vivid, as if the author must have known at first hand what he described."

In addition to the portraits of Lewis, Tolkien, and Williams, "Carpenter gives wonderful cameos of subsidiary members of the Inklings: of Charles L. Wrenn, Dr. R. E. Havard, Fr. Gervase Mathew, of John Wain, Nevill Coghill, and of the disputatious, incorrigible, and marvelous H. V. D. Dyson," writes Charles E. Lloyd in the *Sewanee Review.* "All, including those [Carpenter] did not know, come to life under his pen. He is an appreciator by nature; he reads letters and records with a quick imagination and a warm heart. We get a clear picture of men who encouraged one another to produce works of the imagination that will outlive our time."

Since the death of poet Wystan Hugh Auden in 1973, several biographies and tributes have appeared, most notably Stephen Spender's *W. H. Auden: A Tribute,* Charles Osborne's *W. H. Auden: The Life of a Poet,* and Edward Mendelson's *Early Auden.* But according to Paul Fussell in the *New York Times Book Review,* Carpenter's *W. H. Auden: A Biography* "is the best yet, so interesting, indeed, that it may have the effect of shifting attention from Auden's poems to his character and personality. More people may soon be enjoying anecdotes about Auden than reading his work." Other reviewers believe Carpenter's work to be the best, though for different reasons. "Carpenter triumphs where others have been so drawn to anecdote or exegesis that poetry (and, importantly, prose) seems diminished," states Lincoln Kirstein in the *New York Review of Books.* Describing Carpenter's book as the "definitive biography" of Auden, Ned Rorem maintains in the *Chicago Tribune Book World* that each page "echoes the games of the protagonist, forever sizing up society and art through contrast and metaphor, and emphasizing that the best reviews are made from quotes."

In praising Carpenter's *W. H. Auden,* critics frequently single out its completeness. "Carpenter's book amounts almost to an official biography," writes Peter Porter in the *Times Literary Supplement.* "It is very thorough and while sympathetic to Auden, does not gloss over his many peculiarities and occasional nastinesses." J. D. McClatchy points out in the *Yale Review* that although the book "has its errors of fact, its decorous oversights and distorting blind spots," Carpenter is nonetheless "a good journalist: old anecdotes are straightened out, new ones added, and a great many more facts made available. So, for instance, we learn a good deal more about [Auden's] anomalous but happy affair with Rhoda Jaffe; about his political marriage to [Thomas Mann's daughter,] Erika Mann, and of his real affection for her; about an early engagement to a woman known only as 'Sheilah,' and his two later [unsuccessful] proposals of marriage—one of them to Hannah Arendt."

One reason for the completeness of *W. H. Auden: A Biography* is that Carpenter had the full support of Edward Mendelson, Auden's literary executor and author of Early Auden. Carpenter was consequently given access to a wide range of personal correspondence, unpublished manuscripts, and family and personal memoirs—sources that were largely unavailable to previous biographers. In addition, notes Kirstein, "Auden's friends and lovers . . . felt free to confide in Carpenter, most of them without let or hindrance, and he responded with a generosity sparing nothing save grossness." As a result, continues Kirstein, "Auden the man, in his appetites, needs, satisfactions, or lack of them, is here, and from such just and vivid documentation of tastes and talents we comprehend the poetry from its wellsprings as never before. This book does not aim to, nor can it 'tell

everything,' but each and [every thing] related in depth and dignity may go far to convince those who misprize Auden's homogeneity in its largest sense to extend the accidental limits of their partial information."

Another of the book's merits, according to Fussell, is "its emphasis on Auden's essential career, that of teacher." Richard Howard concurs in the *Nation,* writing that the "growing image of Auden-as-schoolmaster is one of Carpenter's triumphs. All the skill gained in his treatment of the matter of Oxford—Tolkien, Lewis, Williams, . . . etc.—is deployed to advantage in accounts of Auden's classes at the various academies where he lodged, however erratically, for the delight of his students and the Muses' profit." "Auden was, and is, a wizard teacher for those whose curiosity and energy open themselves to quaint method," maintains Kirstein, "[and] Carpenter deftly describes his practice in suggestive dislocation of received ideas which teased students into thinking instead of allowing them to doze through an even flow of comestible opinion."

Carpenter's point of departure throughout the book is what Auden was writing at any given time, though his purpose is not to shed light on Auden's art but to use the works to illuminate the poet's life. (Auden himself believed that an artist's life will not explain his work, and he even told friends to burn his letters so that a biography could not be written.) In locating as many of Auden's works as possible in the exact circumstances that account for them, Carpenter charts the course of Auden's intellectual development in a way that, according to several reviewers, comes to terms with the poet's inward complexity. Brownjohn, for example, writes that Carpenter "traces Auden's month-by-month activities and rapid changes of personal philosophy in the '30s so carefully that the political connection [with Marxism] is now indisputably shown to have been extremely tenuous at best. . . . Similarly with his resumption of Christian beliefs in America in the 1940s: it was no simple question of remembering the shut churches of Barcelona during the Spanish Civil War, or falling among Protestant theologians in New York. Auden worked his way towards them through an elaborate self-catechism (the unpublished typescript has survived) in the mountains near Taos in July 1939."

Moreover, by quoting from Auden's own annotations to his poems, Carpenter identifies some of the people behind the pronouns and masks of the often cryptic works. Noting that Carpenter "has taken more trouble over his identifications than [Charles] Osborne did [in *W. H. Auden: The Life of a Poet*] and that he received more help from Auden's friends," Porter states that Carpenter is "to be applauded for honestly tracing those connections in Auden's life which emerged as salient shapes in his poetry."

But Brownjohn believes that as commendable as Carpenter's method is, it has the unintended effect of diminishing Auden's poetry: "Once launched on the inexorable relation of Auden's poems to specific people and situations, Carpenter is committed to the repetitive recital of those 'few things,' and the poetry—for all his reverence and enjoyment—is reduced. Lists of boys had in Berlin are boring; whereas to turn the pages of *Poems* or *Look, Stranger* is to experience a richness and strangeness of which this biographer gives little or no indication."

Other reviewers, too, see an unintentional diminishing of Auden's poetry. Howard attributes part of the problem to Auden's "terrible" life of drug dependency and unfulfilled homosexual love. "So carefully laid out," he says, "without gloating of any kind, is the dread tableau—the 'chemical life' of Benzedrine every morning, of Seconal every night; the loss of the very few friends [Auden] was so proud of . . . ; the crippling routines that finally became an embarrassment even to their inventor, their prisoner . . .—that I think there is a danger in this good book, there is a menace in the very modesty of its aspirations. . . . When there is a glint of the sensational on almost every page, and when the horrors and abjections are attached to the most revered and resonant names of our time (Stravinsky: 'soon we shall have to smooth him out to see who it is'), how easy, and how wicked, to forget the cause of our reading."

Porter claims an "inordinate amount of Mr. Carpenter's space is devoted to Auden's [homosexual] love-life: never pruriently, never stupidly and never completely irrelevantly—but not without discounting the surrounding seriousness of his life and work either." Carpenter describes in great detail Auden's sexual preferences, as well as those of his lover, Chester Kallman. "None of this is shocking or untoward," remarks Porter, "but it tends to get solemnized in a biography and to be made to explain more than it should."

But even Porter admits "it is partly Auden's own fault that one finishes Humphrey Carpenter's book impatient at all the exposure judged necessary after

the previous reticence." Andrew Motion also notes in the *New Statesman* that by "concentrating on the more intimate aspects of Auden's personal life, Carpenter admits the difficulties facing a biographer and, at the same time, attempts to see through the masks to the man. The result is candid, thorough and extremely readable—a book which flatly ignores Auden's objection that a writer's 'private life is, or should be, of no concern to anybody except himself, his family and his friends.'"

"Carpenter has had an extraordinarily volatile subject to account for," concludes Howard, "and to my sense of it as a loving reader of Auden's work and as one of the American poets Carpenter describes as 'seeking Auden out' once he made his residence in New York City as a U.S. citizen, how splendidly Carpenter has made his accounting. . . . I am grateful all over again to Humphrey Carpenter for his refreshment of the terms on which Auden lived among us."

In *Secret Gardens: A Study of the Golden Age of Children's Literature,* Carpenter presents an analysis of children's literature—focused primarily on British writers—from the mid-nineteenth-century through the early twentieth and argues that the works from this period often examine such serious adult struggles as religious faith and social constraints. Some of the major authors covered in the study include Lewis Carroll, Beatrix Potter, Kenneth Grahame, and Louisa May Alcott. On the surface, writes Jonathan Cott in the *New York Times Book Review,* the essays "first seem to be a series of pleasant and informally presented literary discussions," but they in fact have what Cott terms "a stimulating polemical edge." Invoking the book's title, Selma K. Richardson observes in the *Christian Science Monitor* that "Carpenter's work is a competent and provocative guide to these seemingly innocent places."

In reviewing Carpenter's next work, *Geniuses Together: American Writers in Paris in the 1920s,* John Taylor of the *New York Times Book Review* finds a paucity of truly original thought but commends the author nevertheless for "stressing points that are too often disregarded—for example, that most American writers living in Paris had little contact with the French and that the poverty in which some of them declared they had lived was often romantic fiction." Lachlan Mackinnon of the *Times Literary Supplement* notes that in *Geniuses Together,* "the best thing Carpenter offers are a rounded account of the background to Hemingway's *The Sun Also Rises* and some rightly acerbic comments on what many of the places his subjects freqented are now like. [*Geniuses Together*] is easy reading, but its use is as an introduction or a convenient *aide-memoire*."

In a return to biography, Carpenter's next work, *A Serious Character: The Life of Ezra Pound,* takes on the vilified Ezra Pound, creator of complex and often stunning poetry whose anti-Semitism at the height of World War II destroyed his career and landed him in a mental hospital for 13 years. "Reading Humphrey Carpenter's monumentally long yet absorbing biography of Pound, one comes away feeling that much of Pound's later life, like the 'Cantos,' were a terrible yet fascinating botch," writes Paul Mariani in the *Chicago Tribune Books*. Mariani describes Carpenter's approach as "sane, intelligent, witty," and adds that "Carpenter has dealt fairly with Pound's gifts, as well as with his very serious flaws." For Michiko Kakutani of the *New York Times*, Carpenter's biography puts Pound's defenders firmly in their place. "The one thing that Humphrey Carpenter's minutely researched new biography demonstrates . . . is that the artist and propagandist were one and the same man, that Pound's fascism was not some kind of aberration but an attitude with deep roots in the prejudices of his childhood and the elitism of his adult life." William H. Pritchard in the *New York Times Book Review* writes that Carpenter's "judgments are evenhanded, always sensible and usually unsurprising."

Carpenter chooses Evelyn Waugh as the subject of his next work, *The Brideshead Generation: Evelyn Waugh and His Friends.* Here again the author profiles a prickly, though much less controversial personality. "Evelyn Waugh was a very unhappy and very unpleasant little man," writes David Cannadine in the *New York Times Book Review*. Cannadine also notes that "at his best, [Waugh] wrote beautiful English prose, which was by turns moving and comical, evocative and captivating." In an effort to capture more of his subject, Cannadine notes that Carpenter's approach in *The Brideshead Generation* is to see Waugh through his contemporaries—J. R. R. Tolkien, W. H. Auden, and Ezra Pound. The result is a portrait of a man tortured by social resentment. "But although Humphrey Carpenter demonstrates this with vivid and searing clarity . . . he does not explain why Waugh . . . was afflicted by it." Peter Kemp observes in his review for the *Times Literary Supplement* that Carpenter's attempt to understand his subject centers on Waugh's relationship

to his father and his experiences moving through the British private school system. "Around this extensive territory Carpenter conducts the reader like some affable, acute and impeccably entertaining guide, bursting with good stories and epitomizing details." L.S. Klepp of the *Village Voice* calls Carpenter's narrative "leisurely and engaging," and one that "makes some effective excursions into literary criticism."

In *Benjamin Britten,* Carpenter's biography of the British composer, the author once again wrestles with a difficult subject whose artistic brilliance is shadowed by a lifelong internal battle with his homosexuality and callous treatment of his musical collaborators. Some critics find fault with Carpenter's heavy focus on Britten's personal torments. Robin Holloway, in a review for the *Times Literary Supplement,* describes the book as "a representative example of current 'full-undress biography,'" which ultimately works to demean the composer's art. David Blum of the *New York Times Book Review* notes that in writing about Britten's relationship with the singer Peter Pears, "Mr. Carpenter returns repeatedly to the problematic and the erotic aspects of the relationship." This preoccupation, in Blum's view, ignores that "the unique aspect of the relationship was the musical partnership, and I wish Mr. Carpenter had told us more about the ideas these two men exchanged." But Blum finds that the work does contain some "valuable passages." He writes: "It is refreshing when Mr. Carpenter allows us glimpses of Britten in various musical contexts: the expressivity of his piano playing and conducting, his work habits when composing, his guarded appreciation of the music of Sir Michael Tippett, his courage in putting off major heart surgery in order to complete *Death in Venice,* his last opera."

BIOGRAPHICAL/CRITICAL SOURCES:

BOOKS

Dictionary of Literary Biography, Volume 155: *Twentieth-Century British Literary Biographers,* Gale (Detroit), 1995.

PERIODICALS

American Scholar, autumn, 1982.
Antioch Review, summer, 1982.
Canadian Forum, June-July, 1979.

Christian Century, August 15, 1979; March 31, 1982.

Christian Science Monitor, August 2, 1985, p. B6.

Chicago Tribune Books, January 15, 1989, p. 6.

Chicago Tribune Book World, August 23, 1981; November 15, 1981.

Commonweal, November 6, 1981.

Critic, spring, 1978; May 1, 1979.

Detroit News, April 15, 1979.

Encounter, September, 1981.

Los Angeles Times Book Review, November 7, 1982.

Nation, October 24, 1981.

National Review, July 20, 1979.

New Statesman, May 13, 1977; October 20, 1978; April 4, 1980; July 3, 1981; October 30, 1981.

Newsweek, July 4, 1977; September 28, 1981.

New York Review of Books, December 17, 1981.

New York Times, March 29, 1979; September 14, 1981; December 14, 1988.

New York Times Book Review, August 14, 1977; April 8, 1979; October 4, 1981; November 15, 1981; July 25, 1985, p. 9; January 31, 1988, p. 25; December 18, 1988, pp. 3, 27; January 7, 1990, p. 11; July 11, 1993, pp. 9-11.

Observer (London), May 8, 1977; March 23, 1980; September 27, 1992.

Saturday Review, June 25, 1977; September, 1981.

Sewanee Review, January, 1978; April, 1981; January, 1982.

Spectator, May 14, 1977; October 17, 1987, pp. 37-9.

Times (London), August 27, 1981.

Times Literary Supplement, May 13, 1977; May 9, 1980; July 3, 1981; August 28, 1981; March 11-17, 1988, p. 285; January 13-19, 1989, pp. 27-8; September 8-14, 1989, p. 967; November 13, 1992, pp. 5-6.

Village Voice, March 20, 1990, p. 77.

Voice Literary Supplement, May, 1982.

Washington Post, March 26, 1979.

Washington Post Book World, June 26, 1977; October 5, 1980; September 13, 1981; October 18, 1981.

Yale Review, winter, 1982.*

*　　*　　*

CARPENTER, Lucas　1947-

PERSONAL: Born April 23, 1947, in Elberton, GA; son of Lucas Adams, Jr. (a U.S. civil servant) and Maria (Wasilenkov) Carpenter; married Judith Leidner (a counselor), September 2, 1972; children: Meredith Lauren. *Education:* College of Charleston, B.S., 1968; University of North Carolina at Chapel Hill, M.A., 1973; State University of New York at Stony Brook, Ph.D., 1982.

ADDRESSES: Home—2780 Club Forest Dr., Conyers, GA 30208. *Office*— Department of English, Oxford College, Emory University, Oxford, GA 30267.

CAREER: Suffolk Community College, Riverhead, NY, instructor, 1978-80, assistant professor of English, 1980-85, and editor of *Perspectives;* Emory University, Oxford College, Oxford, GA, associate professor of English, 1984—. Judge of annual awards of Poetry Society of Georgia, 1979. *Military service:* U.S. Army, 1968-71; served in Vietnam; became sergeant; received Bronze Star.

MEMBER: Poetry Society of America, National Council of Teachers of English, Southeast Modern Language Association.

WRITINGS:

A Year for the Spider (poems), University of North Carolina YMCA Press, 1972.

John Gould Fletcher and Southern Modernism, University of Arkansas Press (Fayetteville), 1990.

EDITOR

(With E. Leighton Rudolph, and coauthor of introduction) *The Selected Poems of John Gould Fletcher,* University of Arkansas Press, 1988.

The Autobiography of John Gould Fletcher, University of Arkansas Press, 1988.

John Gould Fletcher, *Arkansas: A History,* University of Arkansas Press, 1989.

Selected Essays of John Gould Fletcher, University of Arkansas Press, 1989.

(With E. Leighton Rudolph and Ethel Simpson) *Selected Letters of John Gould Fletcher,* University of Arkansas Press, 1996.

Work represented in anthologies, including *New Writing in South Carolina,* edited by William Peden and George Garrett, University of South Carolina Press (Columbia), 1970; and *Carolina Sun,* edited by Billy Mishoe and Ronald C. Midkiff, American Literary Associates, 1973. Contributor of more than one hundred-fifty poems, articles, stories, and reviews to magazines and newspapers, including *News-*

day, *Kansas Quarterly, Carolina Quarterly, Minnesota Review, Beloit Poetry Journal,* and *Atlanta Review.*

WORK IN PROGRESS: A collection of stories; a new volume of poetry; a critical study entitled *Addiction as Postmodern Metaphor.*

SIDELIGHTS: Lucas Carpenter told *CA:* "My ongoing interest in John Gould Fletcher was prompted by my study of the Imagist movement while I was a graduate student at the State University of New York at Stony Brook. I was immediately attracted to Fletcher's boldly experimental poetry and to his enormously interesting and highly influential career as a writer. Among the very first of the so-called modern American literary expatriates, the native Arkansan left the United States in 1908 for what would become a twenty-four year period of self-imposed exile spent for the most part in England. Along with Ezra Pound, F. S. Flint, T. E. Hulme, and Richard Aldington, Fletcher was one of the founders of the Imagist movement and was an active participant in the intellectual ferment that produced literary Modernism. He was responsible for introducing Ezra Pound to French symbolism and Amy Lowell to 'polyphonic prose' and was friends with such luminaries as T. S. Eliot, D. H. Lawrence, Ford Madox Ford, and Robert Frost.

"In the second half of his career, Fletcher turned his interest to southern regionalism. After meeting John Crowe Ransom, Donald Davidson, and Allen Tate in Nashville during a lecture tour in 1927, Fletcher began his connection with the southern Fugitive-Agrarian movement and contributed an essay on education to the controversial manifest *I'll Take My Stand* in 1930. He returned to the United States for good in 1933, and in 1938 his *Selected Poems* won the Pulitzer Prize. However, by the time of his suicide in 1950, Fletcher had been largely forgotten as a literary figure.

"In addition to his poetry, Fletcher was a prodigious art and literary critic, contributing scores of essays to such influential periodicals as the *Dial,* the *Little Review, The Criterion,* and *Poetry.* I have collected the best of these essays for *The Selected Essays of John Gould Fletcher* (1989). His *Autobiography* (originally published in 1937 as *Life Is My Song*) is a crucial document in charting the history of literary Modernism. Also of significance to the literary his-

torian is *The Selected Letters of John Gould Fletcher* (1996).

"My 'final say' on Fletcher is *John Gould Fletcher and Southern Modernism* (1990), where I contend that Fletcher can be legitimately regarded as the first southern Modernist writer and as perhaps the most representative poet of the entire Modernist movement. However, my primary objective as general editor of and principal contributor to this six-volume series devoted to Fletcher's life and work is to reawaken and stimulate interest in a writer who has been unjustly forgotten and neglected.

"With regard to my own poetry, my chief concern is the transfiguration of the common moment, the breaking forth of the infinite from the daily. This is more evident in my latest poems, than it is in my first publication, *A Year for the Spider,* which consists of poems coming out of my experience of the Vietnam War. I feel as if my writing has been influenced by virtually everything I've read, but I can identify William Wordsworth, William Butler Yeats, and Wallace Stevens as presences in my poetry. I believe that the role of the poet is to interpret reality, to read the world as a text of profound mystery presented through time, matter, space, energy, and, most importantly, imagination."

*   *   *

CARSON, Anne (Regina)   1950-

PERSONAL: Born December 16, 1950, in New York, NY; daughter of Eric R. I. (a teacher) and Katherine (a real estate agent; maiden name, Griffin) Carson; married David Price (an anthropologist, editor, and author), June 9, 1984; children: Catherine Clare. *Education:* Carnegie Mellon University, B.A., 1973; University of Pittsburgh, M.A., 1975, M.L.S., 1978. *Politics:* "Green." *Religion:* "Feminist."

ADDRESSES: Home—811 Mitchell St., Ithaca, NY 14850.

CAREER: University of Pittsburgh, Pittsburgh, PA, library assistant, 1976-80; Brown University, Providence, RI, rare book cataloger, 1980-82; Cornell University, Ithaca, NY, reference librarian and selector for philosophy and religion, 1983—.

MEMBER: American Library Association, Beta Phi Mu.

WRITINGS:

Feminist Spirituality and the Feminine Divine: An Annotated Bibliography, Crossing Press (Freedom, CA), 1986.

(Editor) *Spiritual Parenting in the New Age,* Crossing Press, 1989.

Goddesses and Wise Women—The Literature of Feminist Spirituality, 1980-1992: An Annotated Bibliography, Crossing Press, 1992.

Contributor to *Word of Mouth: Short-Short Writings by Women,* edited by Irene Zahava, Crossing Press, 1990. Also contributor of articles and reviews to magazines and newspapers, including *WomanSpirit, Off Our Backs,* and *SageWoman.*

SIDELIGHTS: Anne Carson told *CA:* "I studied karate for six years, earning a second degree black belt. I have also studied eight languages and traveled to Britain, Greece, Brazil, San Francisco, and points in between. My commitment is to women and the sacred feminine."

BIOGRAPHICAL/CRITICAL SOURCES:

PERIODICALS

Booklist, October 15, 1986, p. 336; June 15, 1989, p. 1756.

Choice, October, 1986, p. 276; October, 1992, p. 268.

Christian Century, September 24, 1986, p. 819.

Library Journal, August, 1986, p. 158; February 15, 1992, p. 156.

New Pages, spring, 1987, p. 10.

Small Press Book Review, spring, 1993, p. 17.*

*   *   *

CASE, Patricia J(une)   1952-

PERSONAL: Born July 24, 1952, in Hartford, CT; daughter of Howard C. (an automobile mechanic) and Virginia J. Case. *Education:* University of Connecticut, B.A., 1975; Southern Connecticut State College, M.L.S., 1981. *Politics:* None. *Religion:* None.

ADDRESSES: Home—1688 Oak St. N.W., Washington, DC 20010. *Office*—Federal Deposit Insurance Corporation, 550 17th St. N.W., Room H-1062, Washington, DC 20429.

CAREER: University of Connecticut, Storrs, special collections assistant, 1976-81, editor of *Harvest,* 1979-82; Temple University, Philadelphia, PA, curator of Contemporary Culture Collection, 1982-84; free-lance indexer, 1985—. Coordinator of Social Responsibilities Round Table's task force on alternatives in print, 1981-83; Federal Deposit Insurance Corporation, electronic information resources librarian, 1991—.

MEMBER: American Library Association, American Society of Indexers, Special Library Assocaition, Beta Phi Mu.

WRITINGS:

(Editor with Elliott Shore and Laura Daly) *Alternative Papers: Selections from the Alternative Press, 1979-1980,* Temple University Press (Philadelphia, PA), 1982.

(Contributor) Shore and James P. Danky, editors, *Alternative Materials in Libraries,* Scarecrow (Metuchen, NJ), 1982.

(Editor) *Field Guide to Alternative Media,* American Library Assocaition (Chicago), 1984.

(Editor) *Alternative Press Annuals 1983-86,* Temple University Press, 1984-87.

(Editor with Tim Ryan) *Whole Again Resource Guide 1986/87,* SourceNet (Santa Barbara, CA), 1986.

(Indexer) *The Krishnamurti Index,* Krishnamurti Foundation Trust, Ltd., 1992.

Compiler of "The Not in the *New York Times* Bibliography Series," Library, University of Connecticut (Storrs), 1979-81, and "Newsworthy," Library, Temple University, 1983-84. Contributing editor of *New Pages: News and Reviews of the Progressive Book Trade,* 1979-84.

BIOGRAPHICAL/CRITICAL SOURCES:

PERIODICALS

Village Voice Literary Supplement, February, 1983.

CAVALIERO, Glen   1927-

PERSONAL: Born June 7, 1927, in Eastbourne, England; son of Clarence John (a stockbroker) and Mildred (Tilburn) Cavaliero. *Education:* Oxford University, M.A., 1967, Ph.D., 1972; Cambridge University, M.A., 1971.

ADDRESSES: Home—29 Portugal Pl., Cambridge, England.

CAREER: Writer. Curate of Church of England parishes in Margate, 1952-55, and Canterbury, England, 1955-56; chaplain at Lincoln Theological College, 1956-60, and Edinburgh University, 1960-64; Cambridge University, Cambridge, England, fellow of St. Catharine's College, 1967-71, member of faculty of English, 1971—, fellow commoner, 1986. *Military service:* Royal Air Force, 1948-50.

WRITINGS:

John Cowper Powys: Novelist, Oxford University Press (Oxford, England, and New York City), 1973.
The Ancient People (poems), Carcanet (Manchester, England), 1973.
The Rural Tradition in the English Novel, 1900-1939, Macmillan (London and New York City), 1977.
Paradise Stairway (poems), Carcanet, 1977.
A Reading of E. M. Forster, Macmillan, 1979.
(Author of introduction) Charles Williams, *Witchcraft,* Aquarian Press (Wellingborough, Northamptonshire, England), 1980.
(Contributor) Belinda Humphrey, editor, *Recollections of the Powys Brothers,* Peter Owen (London), 1980.
Elegy for St. Anne's (poems), Warren House (Norfolk, England), 1982.
(Author of introduction) Edward Thomas, *The Happy-Go-Lucky Morgans,* Boydell & Brewer (Suffolk, England), 1983.
Charles Williams: Poet of Theology, Macmillan, 1983.
(Author of introduction) E. Lewis, *Dew on the Grass,* Boydell & Brewer, 1983.
(Author of introduction) *The Collected Poems of Gamel Woolsey,* Warren House, 1984.
(Author of afterword) John Cowper Powys, *Three Fantasies,* Carcanet, 1985.
(Contributor) Philip Dodd, editor, *Modern Selves,* Frank Cass (London), 1986.

(Author of introduction, abridgement, and notes) *Beatrix Potter's Journal,* Frederick Warne (London), 1986.
Out of Season, Olive Press (London), 1987.
(Author of introduction and notes) Lois Lang-Sims, *Letters to Lalage: The Letters of Charles Williams to Lois Lang-Sims,* Kent State University Press (Kent, OH), 1989.
The Supernatural and English Fiction, Oxford University Press, 1995.

WORK IN PROGRESS: A full length study on comedy in English fiction.

SIDELIGHTS: "Glen Cavaliero in his excellent study [*Charles Williams: Poet of Theology*]," says *Times Literary Supplement* critic Stephen Medcalf, "traces [the British author's] understanding that our lives are always bound up with an impossibility, from his personal life through his criticism to his theology of the Atonement, and indeed to the qualit of his belief in God. . . . Each of [Williams's] novels, as Dr Cavaliero well points out, is about paying the price: 'in each one the supernatural threatens to overwhelm the natural order, and equilibrium is only restored by those who can accept *both* aspects of reality.'"

BIOGRAPHICAL/CRITICAL SOURCES:

PERIODICALS

Times Literary Supplement, March 7, 1980, April 8, 1983, October 21, 1983, June 14, 1985.

*   *   *

CHAMBERS, Anne   1949-

PERSONAL: Born August 3, 1949, in County Mayo, Ireland; daughter of John (an undertaker) and Margaret (a bookkeeper; maiden name, Cruise) Chambers. *Education:* National University of Ireland, University College, Cork, M.A., 1985.

ADDRESSES: Home—Dublin, Ireland. *Office*—c/o Wolfhound Press, 68 Mount Joy Sq., Dublin, Ireland.

CAREER: Central Bank of Ireland, Dublin, senior executive officer, 1969-88; writer, 1988—. Guest lecturer in the United States for Irish American Cultural Institute, 1987; frequent lecturer in Ireland.

Designed the Grace O'Malley Visitor Centre, an exhibition on the life and times of Granuaile.

MEMBER: Writers Union of Ireland, Lansdowne Tennis Club (Dublin).

AWARDS, HONORS: As Wicked a Woman, Eleanor, Countess of Desmond (c. 1545-1636): A Heroine of Tudor Ireland was shortlisted for the Irish Book of the Year Award, 1987.

WRITINGS:

Granuaile: The Life and Times of Grace O'Malley, 1530-1603, Wolfhound Press (Dublin, Ireland), 1979.
Chieftain to Knight: Tibbott-ne-Long Bourke (1537-1629), First Viscount Mayo, Wolfhound Press, 1983.
As Wicked a Woman, Eleanor, Countess of Desmond (c. 1545-1636): A Heroine of Tudor Ireland, Wolfhound Press, 1986.
Adorable Diva, Margaret Burke Sheridan, Wolfhound Press, 1989.
The Geraldine Conspiracy (novel), Marino Press, 1995.

OTHER

The Pirate Queen (television documentary; based on Chambers's *Granuaile: The Life and Times of Grace O'Malley, 1530-1603*), RTE, 1983.

Author and presenter of introduction to Shaun Davey's *Granuaile at Greenwich Concert* (television special), RTE/Windmill, 1987. Coauthor with David Reilly of screenplays, including *Grace O'Malley: The Pirate Queen, The Rathdown Lottery, Melissa, To Bear Arms, Lorna Doone—The Western,* and *Bad Habits.* Contributor to books, including *Survival or Salvation,* Columba Press, 1994; and *Bold in Her Breeches,* Pandora Press, 1995. Contributor of articles and reviews to periodicals.

ADAPTATIONS: Adorable Diva, Margaret Burke Sheridan was adapted as a television documentary, broadcast as *Brief Butterfly,* RTE, 1989.

WORK IN PROGRESS: A biography of Grace O'Malley, for young readers; an historical novel.

SIDELIGHTS: Anne Chambers told *CA:* "I find the sixteenth century very rich in people and events for both biographical and fictional writing. In fact the factual circumstances relating to people and events in this colorful and eventful age provide the imagery and adventure which fiction would find difficult to match. It is a century of exploration and discovery, of rebellions and intrigue, of armadas and invasions, of glorious empires at the pinnacles of their powers, of the demise and overthrow of entire civilizations and the birth of others, the age of transition and change. It is an era full of great and exotic characters: Henry VIII, Silken Thomas, Philip of Spain, Grace O'Malley, the Earl of Essex, the Earl of Leicester, Hugh O'Neill, Red Hugh O'Donnell, Elizabeth I, Sir Walter Raleigh, Sir Francis Drake, the Countess of Desmond, Edmund Spenser, William Shakespeare. The list is endless and impressive.

"My first venture into the swash-and-buckle of the sixteenth century was, I thought, to be a once-off crusade to release from the bondage of historical neglect and fictional misrepresentation an extraordinary woman of legend and lore, Grace O'Malley (or 'Granuaile,' as she is more familiarly known in Ireland). From the faded contemporary manuscripts of the time, their age-darkened, spider-like writing evidence of the passage of four hundred years since their authors first put quill to parchment, the facts about this remarkable woman leapt from the flourishes and swirls on the brittle parchment which had imprisoned her for four centuries. Soon the story of this unique woman—pirate, chieftain, mercenary, wife, mother, lover, politician, admiral of a fleet of ships, and leader of a private army—emerged to emphatically prove the adage of fact being stranger than fiction.

"My second venture back in time was to unearth the facts about Toby-of-the-Ships, the youngest son of the pirate queen. His life story proved to be a unique commentary on a crucial period of transition and political change in Ireland. His story was representative of the minor chieftains who occupied the middle ground between the fixed battle lines of two fundamentally incompatible protagonists—the old order of Gaelic Ireland and the incoming new system of England. Many became pawns in this momentous game of strategy and intrigue and were duly sacrificed. A few like Toby plotted their own moves and, in a game within a deadly game, became intrepid knights charting their own survival.

"The life of Eleanor, Countess of Desmond, is the story of a heroic and indomitable woman, set against the background of one of the stormiest periods of Irish history. She was an active participant and vic-

tim of the Elizabethan re-conquest and final subjuga-
tion of Gaelic Ireland. But through it all she rises
phoenix-like, time after time, to bravely meet and
contend with every personal and political challenge
on the way."

* * *

CHESNEY, Marion 1936-
   (M. C. Beaton, Helen Crampton, Ann Fairfax,
   Jennie Tremaine, Charlotte Ward)

PERSONAL: Born June 10, 1936, in Glasgow, Scotland; married Harry Scott Gibbons (a writer and
editor); children: Charlie.

ADDRESSES: Home—5 Clarges Mews, London W1,
England. *Office*—c/o St. Martin's Press, 175 Fifth
Ave., New York, NY 10010.

CAREER: Writer. Worked as a fiction buyer for a
bookseller; women's fashion editor for *Scottish Field*
(magazine) in Glasgow, Scotland; theater critic and
reporter for *Scottish Daily Express* in Glasgow; chief
reporter for *Daily Express* in London.

WRITINGS:

HISTORICAL ROMANCES

Regency Gold, Fawcett (New York City), 1980.
Lady Margery's Intrigue, Fawcett, 1980.
The Constant Companion, Fawcett, 1980.
Quadrille, Fawcett, 1981.
My Lords, Ladies, and Marjorie, Fawcett, 1981.
Minerva (large print edition), G. K. Hall (Boston),
   1982.
Love and Lady Lovelace, Fawcett, 1982.
Duke's Diamonds, Fawcett, 1983.
The Westerby Sisters, Pinnacle Books (New York
   City), 1983.
The Viscount's Revenge, New American Library
   (New York City), 1983.
The Poor Relation, New American Library, 1983.
The French Affair, Fawcett, 1984.
Rake's Progress, St. Martin's (New York City),
   1984.
Sweet Masquerade, Fawcett, 1984.
The Education of Miss Paterson, New American Li-
   brary, 1985.
The Flirt, Fawcett, 1985.
Diana the Huntress, St. Martin's, 1985.
The Original Miss Honeyford, St. Martin's, 1986.

Those Endearing Young Charms, Fawcett, 1986.
To Dream of Love, Fawcett, 1986.
Lessons in Love, Fawcett, 1987.
Miss Fiona's Fancy, New American Library, 1987.
At the Sign of the Golden Pineapple, Fawcett, 1987.
The Perfect Gentleman, Ballantine, 1988.
The Savage Marquess, New American Library, 1988.
Silken Bonds, Fawcett, 1989.
Pretty Polly, Severn House (London), 1989.
The Scandalous Lady Wright, Fawcett, 1990.
The Love Match, Hale (London), 1992.
Her Grace's Passion, Hale, 1992.
Lady Lucy's Lover, Severn House, 1992.
The Glitter and the Gold, Fawcett, 1993.
The Desirable Duchess, Fawcett, 1993.
The Sins of Lady Dacey (large print edition), Chivers
   Press (Bath, England), 1995.

Also author of *The Ghost and Lady Alice* and *The
Dreadful Debutante.*

"SIX SISTERS" SERIES

Minerva: Being the First of Six Sisters, St. Martin's,
   1983.
The Taming of Annabelle, St. Martin's, 1983.
Deirdre and Desire, St. Martin's, 1984.
Daphne, St. Martin's, 1984.
Diana the Huntress, St. Martin's, 1985.
Frederica in Fashion, St. Martin's, 1985.

"A HOUSE FOR THE SEASON" SERIES

The Miser of Mayfair, St. Martin's, 1986.
Plain Jane, St. Martin's, 1986.
The Wicked Godmother, St. Martin's, 1987.
The Adventuress, St. Martin's, 1987.
Rake's Progress, St. Martin's, 1987.
Milady in Love, Ballantine, 1987.
Rainbird's Revenge, St. Martin's, 1988.

"SCHOOL FOR MANNERS" SERIES

Refining Felicity, St. Martin's, 1988.
Finessing Clarissa, St. Martin's, 1989.
Perfecting Fiona, St. Martin's, 1989.
Enlightening Delilah, St. Martin's, 1989.
Animating Maria, St. Martin's, 1990.
Marrying Harriet, St. Martin's, 1990.

"POOR RELATION" SERIES

Lady Fortescue Steps Out, St. Martin's, 1992.
Miss Tonks Turns to Crime, St. Martin's, 1993.

Mrs. Budley Falls from Grace, St. Martin's, 1993.
Sir Philip's Folly, St. Martin's, 1993.
Back in Society, St. Martin's, 1994.
Colonel Sandhurst to the Rescue, St. Martin's, 1994.

"DAUGHTERS OF MANNERING" SERIES

The Banishment, St. Martin's, 1995.
The Intrigue, St. Martin's, 1995.
The Deception, St. Martin's, 1996.
The Folly, St. Martin's, 1996.

"THE TRAVELLING MATCHMAKER" SERIES

Emily Goes to Exeter, St. Martin's, 1990.
Beatrice Goes to Brighton, St. Martin's, 1991.
Penelope Goes to Portsmouth, St. Martin's, 1991.
Belinda Goes to Bath, St. Martin's, 1991.
Deborah Goes to Dover, St. Martin's, 1992.
Yvonne Goes to York, St. Martin's, 1992.

UNDER PSEUDONYM M. C. BEATON

Death of a Gossip, St. Martin's, 1985.
Death of a Cad, St. Martin's, 1986.
Death of an Outsider, St. Martin's, 1988.
Death of a Perfect Wife, St. Martin's, 1989.
Death of a Glutton, St. Martin's, 1993.
Death of a Nag, Mysterious Press, 1995.

UNDER PSEUDONYM HELEN CRAMPTON

The Marquis Takes a Bride, Pocket Books, 1980.
The Highland Countess, Pocket Books, 1981.

UNDER PSEUDONYM ANN FAIRFAX

My Dear Duchess, Berkeley Publishing, 1979.
Henrietta, Jove, 1979.
Annabelle, Jove, 1981.
Penelope, Jove, 1981.

UNDER PSEUDONYM JENNIE TREMAINE

Kitty, Dell, 1979.
Daisy, Dell, 1980.
(Editor) *Lucy,* Dell, 1980.
Polly, Dell, 1980.
Molly, Dell, 1980.
Ginny, Dell, 1980.
Tilly, Dell, 1981.
Susie, Dell, 1981.
Poppy, Dell, 1982.
Sally, Dell, 1982.

Maggie, Dell, 1984.
Lady Anne's Deception, Fawcett, 1986.

UNDER PSEUDONYM CHARLOTTE WARD

The Westerby Inheritance, Pinnacle Books, 1982.

SIDELIGHTS: Marion Chesney is best known as the author of romance novels set during the English Regency—a period from 1811 to 1819, encompassing the regency of George, Prince of Wales (later King George IV). The Regency genre is generally marked by a light tone and careful attention to the social conventions of the period. Chesney's novels have been singled out for their accurate portrayal of such period details as clothing, decor, cuisine, manners, and idiosyncrasies of language. They are "frothy, light-hearted, fun and amusing," according to Marina Oliver, a contributor to *Twentieth-Century Romance and Historical Writers.* Oliver notes, however, that Chesney's novels have more substance than most in the genre: "Perhaps more than any other writer of Regency novels she uses contemporary events to good effect in weaving her plots and painting in the background setting. Unlike most authors she often portrays the lower life, the upstairs-downstairs contrast of high society and the servants' hall. There is real appreciation of the feelings of the poor and downtrodden."

Chesney explained to *CA* that she began writing fiction after her husband had a minor stroke. "He was working on a newspaper in Connecticut when we lived in Brooklyn, and the strain of commuting between there and New York was too much," she remembered. "I had to do something to help." She presented the draft of a novel she had been working on to an acquaintance who wrote gothic novels; he urged her to rewrite the first fifty pages, which he then presented to his agent, Barbara Lowenstein. Chesney recalled, "She phoned me up and said, 'In the first eleven pages, I don't understand who these people are. It's very confusing. If you change the first eleven pages, I'll sell it.' I did, and I gave it to her on the Friday. On the Monday she'd sold it. That was very exciting. Then other contracts began to come in. At that time writing was a bit like watching the stock market on Wall Street: Regencies are up, spies are down; mysteries are out, bodice-rippers are in. I think that's going, because the publishers seem to have realized that an author can't fake it. You can't cheat our reader; you must work awfully hard and never write down. It's no use looking at someone else making a lot of money writing something that just happens to be successful and thinking that you can do it and get the same money. All you'll do is turn out second best."

BIOGRAPHICAL/CRITICAL SOURCES:

BOOKS

Kathryn Falk, *Love's Leading Ladies,* Pinnacle Books, 1982.
Twentieth-Century Romance and Historical Writers, third edition, St. James (Detroit), 1994.

PERIODICALS

Booklist, November 1, 1992, pp. 488, 495; March 1, 1993, pp. 1155, 1219; July, 1993, pp. 1943, 1953; November 1, 1993, pp. 503, 509; June 1, 1994, pp. 1768, 1787; July, 1994, pp. 1921, 1931; July, 1995, pp. 1858, 1862.
Library Journal, November 15, 1993, p. 100; December, 1993, p. 169; May 1, 1994, p. 135; July, 1994, p. 125; November 15, 1994, p. 57.
Publishers Weekly, October 4, 1993, p. 68; May 23, 1994, p. 9; July 18, 1994, p. 236.
Washington Post Book World, August 6, 1989, p. 11.*

*   *   *

CLARK, Dennis J.   1927-1993

PERSONAL: Born June 30, 1927, in Philadelphia, PA; died of cancer, September 17, 1993, in Philadelphia, PA; son of John A. and Geraldine Clark; married Josepha T. O'Callaghan (a librarian), March 28, 1952; children: Conna, Brendan, Patrick, Ciaran, Brian, Drigid. *Education:* St. Joseph's College, B.S., 1951; Temple University, M.A., 1966, Ph.D., 1971. *Avocational interests:* Writing, folk song collections, camping.

ADDRESSES: Home—644 Bridle Rd., Glenside, PA 19038. *Office*—Samuel S. Fels Fund, 2 Penn Center, Philadelphia, PA 19102

CAREER: Philadelphia Housing Authority, Philadelphia, PA, information specialist, 1951-54; Philadelphia Fellowship Commission, Philadelphia, housing specialist, 1954-57; Philadelphia Commission on Human Relations, Philadelphia, supervisor in housing division, 1957-61; New York Catholic Interracial

Council, New York, NY, director, 1962-63; Temple University, Center for Community Studies, Philadelphia, staff member, 1964-71; Samuel S. Fels Fund, Philadelphia, secretary and executive director, 1971-93. Teacher in evening division, St. Joseph's College, 1956-57, 1964, and 1973; teacher, Pennsylvania State University, 1963. Consultant to National Association of Housing and Redevelopment Officials, 1966, U.S. Department of Health, Education, and Welfare, 1967, and Urban Poverty Neighborhood Data Resources Project, 1968. Lecturer. *Military service:* U.S. Army, 1945-47.

MEMBER: Organization of American Historians, National Catholic Conference for Interracial Justice (member of board), American Irish Historical Society, American Committee for Irish Studies, Historical Society of Pennsylvania.

WRITINGS:

Cities in Crisis: The Christian Response, Sheed, 1960.
The Ghetto Game, Sheed, 1962.
Work and the Human Spirit, Sheed, 1967.
The Irish in Philadelphia: Ten Generations of Urban Experience, Temple University Press (Philadelphia, PA), 1973.
(Editor) *Philadelphia, 1776-2076: A Three Hundred Year View,* National University Publications, 1976.
Irish Blood: Northern Ireland and the American Conscience, Kennikat (Port Washington, NY), 1977.
A History of the Society of the Friendly Sons of St. Patrick for the Relief of Emigrants from Ireland to Philadelphia, 1951-1981, with an Abridged Account of the Society from Its Founding in Philadelphia in 1771, Society of the Friendly Sons of St. Patrick (Philadelphia, PA), 1982.
The Irish Relations: Trials of an Immigrant Tradition, Fairleigh Dickinson University Press (Rutherford, NJ), 1982.
(With Merry Guben) *Future Bread: How Retail Workers Ransomed Their Jobs and Lives, with a Guide to Cooperative Ownership,* O & O Investment Fund (Philadelphia, PA), 1983.
Hibernia America: The Irish and Regional Cultures, Greenwood Press (New York City), 1986.
The Irish in Philadelphia: A People Share a Commonwealth (pamphlet), Pennsylvania Historical Association (University Park, PA), 1991.
Erin's Heirs: Irish Bonds of Community, University Press of Kentucky (Lexington, KY), 1991.

Also author of monographs. Contributor of articles to books and professional journals. Editor, *Interracial Review*, 1961-63.

SIDELIGHTS: "It would be hard to find anyone who has written more about the American Irish over the last two decades than Dennis [J.] Clark," according to Dale T. Knobel in the *American Historical Review.* An expert on the history of the Irish in America, Clark wrote several studies tracing the Irish experience from their arrival in this country as immigrants to their growth into a strong and vital community. Bruce Lambert, writing in the *New York Times,* quoted Clark explaining that the Irish culture was so diverse, "almost anything you say about them is both true and false."

The Irish in Philadelphia: Ten Generations of Urban Experience, Clark's first book on Irish-American history, focuses on the Irish immigrants in his hometown. He argues that the Irish created the first urban ghettoes in America as a means to insulate themselves from larger social forces. T. Kelly Fitzpatrick in *Book Sellers* contends that Clark attributes the cultural and financial success of the Irish in Philadelphia to "the development of a strong sub-culture which encouraged the attainment of upward social, economic, and educational mobility." And writing in *Commonweal,* Robert V. Remini notes that, according to the statistics compiled by Clark, the Irish in Philadelphia did better financially than did those in Boston and New York. This view contradicts the widely accepted opinion of many historians that Irish immigrants were often exploited.

In *Erin's Heirs: Irish Bonds of Community,* Clark focuses on the community-building efforts of Irish-Americans throughout America. Writing in *Choice,* P. I. Rose contends that "Clark makes a strong case for the belief that Gaelic traditions and political experiences . . . have continuing significance among the Irish in Philadelphia . . . and in many other cities," while Knobel praises *Erin's Heirs* as "a useful contribution to American ethnic history," which exemplifies "the product of Clark's scholarly range and . . . mature understanding of the nature of ethnicity in America."

Clark's *Hibernia America: The Irish and Regional Cultures,* on the other hand, examines the specific regional characteristics of various Irish-American communities. According to S. P. Metress in *Choice, Hibernia America* is "a well-organized and excep-

tionally well written model of fine scholarship . . . [by] one of the premier students of the Irish experience in America."

BIOGRAPHICAL/CRITICAL SOURCES:

PERIODICALS

America, September 23, 1967, pp. 325-326.
American Historical Review, February, 1986, p. 196; December, 1992, p. 1612.
Best Sellers, March 15, 1974, p. 558.
Booklist, November 1, 1967, p. 298.
Choice, June, 1974, p. 662; December, 1986, p. 679; February, 1992, p. 969.
Christian Century, August 23, 1967, pp. 1071-1072.
Commonweal, January 19, 1968, pp. 477-478; September 27, 1974, pp. 529-531.
Journal of American History, June, 1987, p. 186; September, 1993, p. 651.
Journal of Urban History, August, 1990, p. 428.
Library Journal, March 1, 1974, p. 653.

OBITUARIES:

PERIODICALS

Boston Globe, September 20, 1993, p. 21.
New York Times, September 19, 1993, p. 54.
Times (London), October 1, 1993, p. 23.*

*　　*　　*

CLIFFORD, Tony
See SLIDE, Anthony

*　　*　　*

CODRESCU, Andrei   1946-
(Betty Laredo, Maria Parfenie, Urmuz)

PERSONAL: Born December 20, 1946, in Sibiu, Romania; immigrated to the United States, 1966; naturalized U.S. citizen, 1981.

ADDRESSES: Office—Department of English, Louisiana State University, Baton Rouge, LA 70803. *Agent*—Jonathan Lazear, 930 First Ave. N., Suite 416, Minneapolis, MN 55401.

CAREER: Writer, journalist, editor, and translator. Louisiana State University, Baton Rouge, LA, professor of English, 1984—. Regular commentator on NPR's *All Things Considered,* and for Radio Free Europe's *The American Scene.* Appeared in documentary film *Road Scholar,* directed by Roger Weisberg, Metro-Goldwyn-Mayer, 1993.

MEMBER: American-Romanian Academy of Arts and Sciences, Modern Language Association of America, American Association of University Professors, Authors League of America, PEN American Chapter.

AWARDS, HONORS: Big Table Younger Poets Award, 1970, for *License to Carry a Gun;* National Endowment for the Arts fellowships, 1973, 1983; Pushcart Prize, 1980, for "Poet's Encyclopedia," and 1983, for novella *Samba de Los Agentes;* A. D. Emmart Humanities Award, 1982; National Public Radio fellowship, 1983; Towson University prize for literature, 1983, for *Selected Poems: 1970-1980;* National Endowment for the Arts grants, 1985, 1988; General Electric/CCLM Poetry Award, 1985, for "On Chicago Buildings"; American-Romanian Academy of Arts and Sciences Book Award, 1988; George Foster Peabody Award, Best Documentary Film, San Francisco Film Festival, Best Documentary Film, Seattle Film Festival, Cine Award, and Golden Eagle Award, all for *Road Scholar.*

WRITINGS:

POETRY

License to Carry a Gun, Big Table/Follett (Chicago), 1970.
A Serious Morning, Capra Press (Santa Barbara, CA), 1973.
The History of the Growth of Heaven, George Braziller (New York City), 1973, originally published in limited edition chapbook, Kingdom Kum Press (San Francisco), 1973.
For the Love of a Coat, Four Zoas Press (Boston), 1978.
The Lady Painter, Four Zoas Press, 1979.
Necrocorrida, Panjandrum (Los Angeles), 1982.
Selected Poems: 1970-1980, Sun Books (New York City), 1983.
Comrade Past and Mister Present, Coffee House Press (Minneapolis), 1986, second edition, 1991.
Belligerence, Coffee House Press, 1991.
Alien Candor: Selected Poems, 1970-1995, Black Sparrow Press (Santa Rosa, CA), 1996.

NOVELS

The Repentance of Lorraine, Pocket Books (New York City), 1976.
Monsieur Teste in America and Other Instances of Realism, Coffee House Press, 1987, Romanian edition translated by Traian Gardus and Lacrimioara Stoie, published as *Domnul Teste in America,* Editura Dacia (Cluj, Romania), 1993.
The Blood Countess, Simon & Schuster (New York City), 1995.

ESSAYS

A Craving for Swan, Ohio State University Press (Columbus), 1986.
Raised by Puppets Only to Be Killed by Research, Addison-Wesley (Reading, MA), 1988.
The Disappearance of the Outside: A Manifesto for Escape, Addison-Wesley, 1990, Romanian edition translated by Ruxandra Vasilescu, published as *Disparitia Lui Afara,* Editura Univers (Bucharest), 1995.
The Muse Is Always Half-Dressed in New Orleans and Other Essays, St. Martin's Press (New York City), 1993.
Zombification: Stories from NPR, St. Martin's Press, 1994.
The Dog with the Chip in His Neck: Essays from NPR and Elsewhere, St. Martin's Press, 1996.

CHAPBOOKS; LIMITED EDITION

Why I Can't Talk on the Telephone (stories), Kingdom Kum Press, 1972.
The Here What Where (poetry), Isthmus Press (San Francisco), 1972.
Grammar and Money (poetry), Arif Press (Berkeley, CA), 1973.
A Mote Suite for Jan and Anselm (poetry), Stone Pose Art (San Francisco), 1976.
Diapers On the Snow (poetry), Crowfoot Press (Ann Arbor, MI), 1981.

RADIO/AUDIO RECORDINGS

Traffic Au Bout Du Temps (poetry reading), Watershed Intermedia (Washington, DC), 1980.
American Life with Andrei Codrescu, National Public Radio (Washington, DC), 1984.
New Letters on the Air: Andrei Codrescu (poetry reading and interview), KSUR Radio (Kansas City), 1987.
An Exile's Return, National Public Radio, 1990.

Common Ground (radio series on world affairs), Stanley Foundation, 1991.

(With Spalding Grey, Linda Barry, Tom Bodett, and others) *First Words* (tape and compact disc; introductory recording to "Gang of Seven" spoken word series), BMG Distribution, 1992.

No Tacos for Saddam (tape and compact disc; "Gang of Seven" spoken word series), BMG Distribution, 1992.

Fax Your Prayers, Dove Audio (Los Angeles), 1995.

Plato Sucks, Dove Audio, 1996.

OTHER

(Editor with Pat Nolan) *The End over End,* privately printed, 1974.

(Translator) *For Max Jacob* (poetry), Tree Books (Berkeley, CA), 1974.

The Life and Times of an Involuntary Genius (autobiography), George Braziller, 1975.

In America's Shoes (autobiography), City Lights (San Francisco), 1975.

(Editor and contributor) *American Poetry since 1970: Up Late* (anthology), Four Walls Eight Windows (New York City), 1987, second edition, 1990.

(Translator) Lucian Blaga, *At the Court of Yearning: Poems by Lucian Blaga,* Ohio State University Press, 1988.

(Editor) *The Stiffest of the Corpse: An Exquisite Corpse Reader,* City Lights, 1988.

The Hole in the Flag: A Romanian Exile's Story of Return and Revolution, (reportage), Morrow (New York City), 1991.

Road Scholar (film; also see below), directed by Roger Weisberg, Metro-Goldwyn-Mayer, 1993.

Road Scholar: Coast to Coast Late in the Century (reportage), with photographs by David Graham, Hyperion (New York City), 1994.

(Editor with Laura Rosenthal) *American Poets Say Goodbye to the Twentieth Century,* Four Walls Eight Windows, 1996.

Also author, under pseudonym Betty Laredo, of *Meat from the Goldrush* and *36 Poems by Betty Laredo.* Author of novella *Samba de Los Agentes.* Contributor to anthologies, including *The World Anthology,* Bobbs-Merrill, 1969; *Another World,* Bobbs-Merrill, 1973; *The Fiction Collective Anthology,* Braziller, 1975; *Kaidmeon: An International Anthology,* Athens, 1976; *The Penguin Anthology of British and American Surrealism,* Penguin, 1978; *The Random House Anthology of British and American Surrealism,* Random House, 1979; *Longman Poetry Anthology,* Longman, 1985. Author of col-

umns "La Vie Boheme," 1979-82, and "The Last Word," 1981-85, and a bi-weekly editorial column, "The Penny Post," all for the Baltimore *Sun;* author of monthly book column "The Last Word," for *Sunday Sun* and *Philadelphia Inquirer,* 1982—; author of weekly column "Caveman Cry," for *Soho Arts Weekly,* 1985-86; author of weekly book column "Melville & Frisby," for the Baltimore and Washington, DC, *City Paper,* of the column "Actual Size," for *Organica,* and of weekly book review for National Public Radio's *Performance Today.*

Contributor of poetry, sometimes under pseudonyms Urmuz and Marie Parfenie, to periodicals, including *Poetry, Poetry Review, Chicago Review, World, Antaeus, Sun, Confrontation, Isthmus,* and *Editions Change;* also contributor of short stories and book reviews to periodicals, including *Washington Post Book World, New York Times Book Review, American Book Review, Chicago Review, Tri-Quarterly, Paris Review, Co-Evolution Quarterly,* and *New Directions Annual.* Poetry editor, *City Paper,* 1978-80, and Baltimore *Sun,* 1979-83; contributing editor, *San Francisco Review of Books,* 1978-83, and *American Book Review,* 1983—; editor, *Exquisite Corpse: A Journal of Books and Ideas,* 1983—; contributing editor, *Cover: The Arts,* 1986-88. Member of advisory board, *Performance Today* and *ARA: Journal of the American Romanian Academy of Arts and Sciences.*

Codrescu's writing has been translated into six languages. A collection of Codrescu's manuscripts is kept at the Hill Memorial Library, Louisiana State University.

ADAPTATIONS: The Blood Countess has been recorded by Simon & Schuster Audio, read by Codrescu and Suzanne Bartish, 1995.

SIDELIGHTS: A Romanian-born poet, fiction writer, editor, and journalist, Andrei Codrescu was expelled from the University of Bucharest for his criticism of the communist government and fled his homeland before he was conscripted into the army. Traveling to Rome, the young writer learned to speak fluent Italian; he then went to Paris and finally to the United States. Arriving in the U.S. in 1966 without any money or knowledge of English, Codrescu was nonetheless impressed with the social revolution that was occurring around the country. As *Village Voice* contributor M. G. Stephens relates, Codrescu quickly "hooked up with John Sinclair's Artist Workshop, and learned, as on a tabula rasa, the American language via the street, hippies, radical poets, rock records, and later from runaway girls he picked up on 8th Street." Within four years he had learned to speak colloquial English colorfully and fluently enough to write and publish his first poetry collection, *License to Carry a Gun.* The collection was hailed by many critics who recognized Codrescu to be a promising young poet, and, according to Thomas A. Wassmer in *Best Sellers,* he is now "considered by many writers to be one of this country's most imaginative poets, with talents similar to those of Walt Whitman and William Carlos Williams."

Echoing this comparison with Whitman and Williams, a *Choice* critic attests that like these American writers Codrescu "writes poems as if no one had written one before," but unlike them he is more interested in the "introspective, internal." John R. Carpenter feels there are advantages and disadvantages to Codrescu's tabula rasa approach. In a *Poetry* review, he notes that the poet "gains in spontaneity, but loses in participation; the freshness is specialized." Another feature of Codrescu's poetry is his unique perspective and interest in American English. His "greatest strength," asserts *New York Times Book Review* contributor John Krich, "lies in his outsider's appreciation for the succulence of American idioms. Where language is reinvented daily on billboards, it offers liberation from the chains of connotation."

But although Codrescu enjoys the artistic freedoms that exist in the United States, he is still as critical of bureaucracy in his adopted country as he was in his native Romania—a skepticism that is made evident in his poetry and his autobiographies, *The Life and Times of an Involuntary Genius* and *In America's Shoes.* "In Mr. Codrescu's native Transylvania," Bruce Schlain observes in a *New York Times Book Review* article on the author's poetry collection, *Comrade Past and Mister Present,* "poets are social spokesmen, and that perhaps explains his fearlessness of treading on the languages of philosophy, religion, politics, science or popular culture. His focus on a pet theme, oppression, is as much concerned with the private as with the public."

Just as *Comrade Past and Mister Present* compares East and West through poetry, in *The Disappearance of the Outside: A Manifesto for Escape* Codrescu discusses the matter in direct prose. He addresses here such subjects as the mind-numbing effects of television and mass marketing, the sexual and political implications that are a part of language, and the

use of drugs and alcohol. "In line with his literary modernism," writes Josephine Woll in the *Washington Post Book World,* "[Codrescu's] tastes run to the whimsical, the surreal (about which he writes with great understanding), even the perverse. He means to provoke, and he does. His ideas are worth thinking about." Codrescu's skill as an observant commentator about life in America has led critics like Wassmer to conclude that Codrescu has given his audience "a clearer penetration into the soul of America by a foreigner than any by a native American poet."

Codrescu returned to Romania after twenty-five years to observe firsthand the 1989 revolution which shook dictator Nicolai Ceausescu from power. The range of emotions Codrescu experienced during this time, from exhilaration to cynicism, are described in the volume *The Hole in the Flag: A Romanian Exile's Story of Return and Revolution.* Initially enthusiastic over the prospects of a new political system to replace Ceausescu's repressive police state, Codrescu became disheartened as neo-communists, led by Ion Iliescu, co-opted the revolution. Iliescu himself exhorted gangs of miners to beat student activists "who represented to Codrescu the most authentic part of the revolution in Bucharest," according to Alfred Stepan in the *Times Literary Supplement.* "It seemed to him the whole revolution had been a fake, a film scripted by the Romanian communists."

In preparation for the 1993 book and documentary film *Road Scholar: Coast to Coast Late in the Century,* Codrescu drove across the United States in a red Cadillac accompanied by photographer David Graham and a video crew. Encountering various aspects of the American persona in such cities as Detroit and Las Vegas, Codrescu filters his experiences through a distinctively wry point of view. "Codrescu is the sort of writer who feels obliged to satirize and interplay with reality and not just catalogue impressions," observes Francis X. Clines in the *New York Times Book Review,* who compares Codrescu's journey to the inspired traveling of "road novelist" Jack Kerouac and poet Walt Whitman. The reviewer points out that Codrescu "can redeem flagging curiosity in a single sentence, as when, returning to Detroit haunts he loved as a student, he finds he must wax more Mad Maxish than Whitmanesque: 'I see that when a city becomes extinct, its last inhabitants go crazy.'" Critical opinion is divided over *Road Scholar.* Although Christine Schwartz writes in the *Voice Literary Supplement* that "Codrescu's vision . . . is dated, condescending, and egocentric, based not on personal insight but persona," Clines states in the *New York Times Book Review* that the author "is a reminder that locomotion is not the heart of the matter; a decent imagination is."

The title of Codrescu's 1995 novel, *The Blood Countess,* refers to Elizabeth Bathory, a sixteenth-century Hungarian noblewoman notorious for bathing in the blood of hundreds of murdered girls. "While during the day she functions as administrator for her and her husband's estates . . . at night, in her private quarters, she rages at, tortures, and frequently kills the endless supply of peasant maidens. . . . Convinced that blood restores the youth of her skin, she installs a cage over her bath, in which young girls are pierced to death," informs Robert L. McLaughlin in the *American Book Review.*

Codrescu tells Bathory's gruesome story in tandem with a contemporary narrative about the countess's descendant, Drake Bathory-Kereshtur, an American reporter working in Budapest. Of royal lineage, Drake is called upon by Hungarian monarchists to become the next king (although the true goal of this group, which Drake soon suspects, is to install a fascist government). During the course of Drake's travels in Hungary, he meets up with various manifestations of Elizabeth and eventually is seduced by her spirit to commit murder. "Pleating the sixteenth century with the twentieth, Codrescu is nervously alert for recurrent patterns of evil and its handmaiden, absolute authority," points out *Time* contributor R. Z. Sheppard. "Both Elizabeth's and Drake's Hungarys are emerging from long periods of totalitarian culture," comments McLaughlin in the *American Book Review.* The critic further states, "These monolithic systems, by tolerating no heresy, were able to establish virtually unquestioned order and stability for a period of time. But when these periods end, the societies are thrown into chaos." During the era of communist repression in Hungary, the violence inextricably linked to the land was dormant. But in the words of Nina Auerbach in the *New York Times Book Review,* "ancient agents of savagery" are roused from sleep in *The Blood Countess* after the fall of communism and during the resultant political upheaval—these evil forces "overwhelm modernity and its representative, the bemused Drake."

While some reviewers comment on the horrific aspects of *The Blood Countess,* Bettina Drew points out in the *Washington Post Book World* that "Codrescu has done more than tap into a Western fascination, whipped up by Hollywood Draculas and vampires. . . . He has written a vivid narrative of the sixteenth century . . . [and] has made the history of Hungary and its shifting contemporary situation entertaining and compelling." Although McLaughlin observes in the *American Book Review* that *The Blood Countess*'s "historical foundation is interesting; the incidents of its parallel plots keep one turning the pages; it has much to say about our world." Sheppard observes in *Time* that "*The Blood Countess* offers stylish entertainment" while *Entertainment Weekly* contributor Margot Mifflin finds the book "beautifully written and meticulously researched."

BIOGRAPHICAL/CRITICAL SOURCES:

BOOKS

Contemporary Literary Criticism, Volume 46, Gale, 1988.

PERIODICALS

American Book Review, July-August, 1990; September-October, 1995, pp. 16, 23.
Best Sellers, June, 1975.
Booklist, July, 1994, p. 1915.
Chicago Tribune, July 12, 1990.
Choice, June, 1988, p. 1552; November, 1991, p. 514.
Entertainment Weekly, September 8, 1995, p. 76.
Kirkus Reviews, May 1, 1990.
Library Journal, July, 1970; May 11, 1990; May 15, 1990.
Los Angeles Times Book Review, August 21, 1983; November 15, 1987.
New Republic, August 16, 1993, p. 24.
New York Review of Books, March 5, 1992, p. 43.
New York Times, July 11, 1993, sec. 2, p. 22.
New York Times Book Review, January 25, 1987; January 10, 1988; June 30, 1993, p. 16; May 9, 1993, pp. 1, 22, 23; July 30, 1995, p. 7.
Poetry, December, 1974.
Publishers Weekly, May 4, 1990; May 10, 1991, p. 265; March 1, 1993, p. 97; June 21, 1993, p. 97; June 13, 1994, p. 58.
San Francisco Review of Books, winter, 1983-84; September/October, 1995.
Time, August 14, 1995, p. 70.
Times Literary Supplement, August 5, 1988; October 9, 1992, p. 26.
Variety, July 19, 1993, p. 72.
Village Voice, December 31, 1970; September 22, 1975.

Voice Literary Supplement, July, 1993, p. 10.
Washington Post, August 10, 1993, sec. B, pp. 1, 4.
Washington Post Book World, July 29, 1990; August 6, 1995, pp. 3, 10.

*   *   *

COHEN, Morris L(eo)   1927-

PERSONAL: Born November 2, 1927, in New York, NY; son of Emanuel (a manufacturer) and Anna (Frank) Cohen married Gloria Weitzner (a computer programmer) February 1, 1953; children: Havi, Daniel Asher. *Education:* University of Chicago, B.A., 1947; Columbia University, J.D., 1951; Pratt Institute, M.L.S., 1959. *Religion:* Jewish.

ADDRESSES: Home—84 McKinley Ave., New Haven, CT 06515. *Office*—Law School, Yale University, New Haven, CT 06520-8215. *E-mail*—cohen@mail.law.Yale.edu.

CAREER: Admitted to Bar of New York State, 1951; private practice in New York City, 1951-58; Rutgers University, New Brunswick, NJ, assistant law librarian, 1958-59; Columbia University, New York City, assistant law librarian, 1959-61; State University of New York at Buffalo, law librarian and associate professor of law, 1961-63; University of Pennsylvania, Philadelphia, Biddle Law Librarian, 1963-71, associate professor, 1963-67, professor of law, 1967-71; Harvard University, Cambridge, MA, law librarian and professor of law, 1971-81; Yale University, New Haven, CT, law librarian and professor of law, 1981-91, emeritus professor of law, 1991—. Lecturer at library school, Columbia University, 1963-70, and Drexel University, 1963-71; adjunct professor at library school, Simmons College, beginning 1976. Member of board of visitors, law school, Columbia University, 1977-95, and library school, Pratt Institute, beginning 1980. Consultant on law libraries to law schools and legal organizations.

MEMBER: International Association of Law Libraries, American Association of La Libraries (president, 1970-71), American Library Association, American Civil Liberties Union (member of executive board, Philadelphia chapter, 1965-71), American Bar Association, Bibliographical Society of America, American Association of University Professors, Jewish Publication Society.

AWARDS, HONORS: Grants from National Endowment for the Humanities, 1968-71, 1975-78, 1990-92.

WRITINGS:

Legal Bibliography Briefed, Graduate School of Library Sciences, Drexel Institute of Technology, 1965.
Legal Research in a Nutshell, West Publishing (St. Paul, MN), 1968, 6th edition, 1996.
(General editor) *How to Find the Law,* West Publishing, 7th edition, 1976, 9th edition, 1989.
(Compiler with Naomi Ronen and Jan Stepan; also author of introduction) *Law and Science: A Selected Bibliography,* Science, Technology, and Human Values, Harvard University (Cambridge, MA), 1978, revised edition (with Ronen), MIT Press (Cambridge, MA), 1980.
(With Robert C. Berring) *Finding the Law: An Abridged Edition of How to Find the Law, 8th Edition,* West Publishing, 1983.
Law: The Art of Justice, Hugh Lauter Levin Associates (Southport, CT), 1992.
(With Sharon H. O'Connor) *Guide to Early Reports of the Supreme Court of the United States,* Fred B. Rothman & Co. (Littleton, CO), 1995.

WORK IN PROGRESS: Editing *Bibliography of Early American Law,* six volumes, for William S. Hein & Co. (Buffalo, NY), expected in 1998.

*   *   *

CONARD, Robert C.   1933-

PERSONAL: Born August 10, 1933, in Cincinnati, OH; son of Robert G. (a pattern maker) and Antoinette Josephine (a homemaker; maiden name, Rielag) Conard; married Sheila Hancock (a professor), July 24, 1957; children: Christopher, Anthony, Nicholas, Angela. *Education:* University of Cincinnati, B.B.A., 1956, M.A., 1964, Ph.D., 1969; attended University of Vienna, 1956-57; St. Xavier (now Xavier) University, Teaching Certificate, 1958.

ADDRESSES: Home—416 Irving Ave., Dayton, OH 45409. *Office*—Department of Languages, University of Dayton, Dayton, OH 45469.

CAREER: Teacher of English and German at primary and secondary schools in Cincinnati, OH, 1958-66; University of Dayton, Dayton, OH, instructor, 1967-68, assistant professor, 1968-71, associate professor, 1971-75, professor of German, 1975—.

MEMBER: International Brecht Society, American Association of Teachers of German, German Studies Association, Modern Language Association of America.

AWARDS, HONORS: University of Dayton, summer research fellowships, 1971, 1972, 1974, 1975, 1991, 1992; grants from National Endowment for the Humanities, 1978, 1986; University of Dayton, College of Arts and Sciences Award for Outstanding Scholarship, 1994; University of Dayton Alumni Award, University Award for Outstanding Scholarship, 1995.

WRITINGS:

(Translator) Bero Rigauer, *Sport and Work,* New Critics Press (St. Louis, MO), 1972.
Heinrich Boell, G. K. Hall (Boston), 1981.
(Editor) Hermann Hesse, *Demian,* Suhrkamp/Insel (Boston), 1985.
Understanding Heinrich Boell: Understanding European and Latin American Literature, University of South Carolina Press (Columbia), 1992.
(Translator with Joanna Ratych and Ralph Ley) *Menschheitsdaemmerung: Ein Dokument des Expressionismus* (title means "Dawn of Humanity: A Document of Expressionism"), Camden House (Columbia, SC), 1994.

Contributor to *Heinrich Boell als Lyriker* (title means "Heinrich Boell as Lyric Poet"), edited by Gerhard Rademacher, Verlag Peter Lang, 1985. Also contributor of numerous articles and translations to literature and German studies periodicals, including various works to *University of Dayton Review.*

WORK IN PROGRESS: Brecht's Major Dramas: Literary Criticism in Perspective, for Camden House.

SIDELIGHTS: Robert C. Conrad once told *CA:* "I became interested in German language and literature by accident. After graduating from college with a degree in business and a major in accounting and after practicing accounting for four years, I was appalled at my ignorance of things that really mattered: foreign languages, literature, culture in a broad sense. I concluded that learning a foreign language and studying in Europe were the only medi-

cine for my miserable condition. The chance to study in Vienna was the first to come my way, and I jumped at it.

"Early in my reading of German literature, I realized that Heinrich Boell, because of his Catholic background and liberal, socialist, humanist commitment to society, was the writer who most interested me. Boell's main theme is simple and profound: only a collective moral memory can redeem a people. Boell's subject is always individual conscience placed in a dubious moral environment. Because he states over and over again in various ways the premise that Germany will never become a moral nation unless it deals individually and collectively with its recent history and converts the lessons of the Hitler years into a moral consciousness, his work creates a moral imperative for readers in all nations. Naturally, Boell's message is ultimately religious: but he is, because of the subtlety of his art, a religious writer in a nondidactic and unobtrusive manner.

"In general, Boell is easy to understand. His language, although poetically colloquial, deceptively refined, exact, and appropriate for each speaker and each occasion, is nonetheless accessible to the ordinary reader. In fact, his simple language is what gives his work its power. His concern for the right word and the correct tone for each voice, however, makes Boell's language difficult to translate, for the language that is correct in German often seems less natural in English. All translation has this problem, but it is more pronounced with Boell. It accounts, I believe, for the lack of success this Nobel laureate has had in English as compared to Russian, French, or Spanish. Additionally, his work may be received with some caution in the United States because of its apparent religious-moral commitment. The American reading public seems suspicious of religious ideas in fiction and of Boell's combination of piety and politics or the union of Christianity and socialism that has its home in his work. For this reason, interpreting Boell for the American reader is an extremely important task because his work has a message for twentieth century Americans from which we have much to learn."

*   *   *

CONDE, Maryse
See BOUCOLON, Maryse

CONIL, Jean (Marie Joseph)   1917-

PERSONAL: Born August 28, 1917, in Fontenay-le-Comte, France; son of Octave (a restaurateur) and Marie-Josephine (Gorriez) Conil; married October 10, 1942; children: Patricia, Christopher-Private. *Education:* Attended Stanislas College, Paris, France. *Politics:* Socialist-Liberal. *Religion:* Roman Catholic. *Philosophy:* "Spiritualist and Universalist."

ADDRESSES: Home and office—282 Dollis Hill Ln., London NW2 6HH, England.

CAREER: Executive master chef and senior manager, Fortnum & Mason, 1950-55; Atheneum Court Hotel, London England, catering director, 1955-58; Hurlingham Club, London, senior catering manager, 1962-64; food and cookery lecturer, Hendo College of Hotel Administration, 1965-70; Arts Club, London, currently executive chef; principal, Academy of Gastronomy. Lecturer. *Military service:* Served in British and French navies.

MEMBER: Society of Authors, International Academy of Chefs (president), Academie Culinaire de France, Cercle Epicurien (president), Epicurean World Master Chefs Society (president).

AWARDS, HONORS: Berne Exhibition, silver medal for cooking, 1950, London Exhibition, gold medal for cooking, 1951, 1952.

WRITINGS:

For Epicures Only, Laurie (London, England), 1953.
Haute Cuisine, Faber (Winchester, MA), 1955.
The Home Cookery, Methuen (New York City), 1956.
The Jean Conil Cookery Classes, P. Owen, 1957.
The Gastronomic Tour de France, Allen & Unwin (London, England), 1959.
The Epicurean Book, Allen & Unwin, 1961.
Oriental Cookery, Croom Helm (Beckenham, Kent, England), 1978.
(With Daphne MacCarthy) *Vegetarian Dishes,* Thorsons (Wellingborough, Northants, England), 1980.
(With Hugh Williams) *Variations on a Starter,* Piatkus Books (London, England), 1980.
(With Williams) *Variations on a Recipe: How to Create Your Own Original Dishes,* Piatkus Books, 1980.
(With Williams) *Variations on a Dessert,* Piatkus Books, 1981.

(With Williams) *Variations on a Main Course: How to Create Your Own Original Dishes,* Piatkus Books, 1981.
The French Vegetarian Cookery, Thorsons, 1985.
Cuisine Fraicheur, Aurum Press (London, England), 1987.
Fabulous Fruit Cuisine, Thorsons, 1988.
Dishes from the Great Chefs of the World, Epicurean Circle, 1989.
Cooking with Tofu, Foulsham (Bariebrook, Slough, England), 1990.
Passion for Food (in aid of National Children Society), Thornson, 1991.
French Cuisine, Foulsham, 1992.
Taste of the World (for Save the Children) Simon & Schuster (New York City), 1992.
Banquet Cuisine, Epicurean Master Chefs Society (London, England), 1993.
Meridional Cuisine, Foulsham, 1993.
Mediterranean Cuisine, Foulsham, 1994.
Flavours of France, HarperCollins (New York City), 1995.
Masterchef, Sunburst, 1995.
Hot Pot Cookery, Foulsham, 1996.
Jean Conil's Food Encyclopedia, Sunburst, 1996.

Also author of *French Home Cookery,* Methuen, *Magnum Cookery,* Methuen, *European Cookery,* and *Arab Cookery.* Executive editor, *Look 'n' Cook,* sixty volumes, Bay Books. Columnist for the *Sunday Times,* 1951-56, *Daily Sketch,* 1955-56, and *Modern Woman,* 1955-56. Contributor to magazines.

WORK IN PROGRESS: "In preparation," *Tropical Treasures,* "a major work on Creole cuisine and exotic products."

SIDELIGHTS: Jean Conil told *CA:* "Both my mother and grandmother were my tutors in teaching that food was the fuel of life. Bread was sacrosanct, symbolizing the fruit of hard work: 'at the sweat of your brow shall you earn your daily bread'. At our farmhouse the food was always freshly cooked and processed by the most basic methods. It was served when people were hungry and enjoyed mainly because hunger is the best stimulant of appetite. I have used the channel of food as the fuel of the body to project the principle of the three constituents of each individual: body, soul and spirit."

Referring to those who have inspired and influenced his career, Conil identifies "Tolstoy and Leibnitz on spiritual matters and Brillat Savarin on gastronomy, and Prosper Montagne and August Escoffier on cookery, and Louis Pasteur and Norman Potter on food technology and chemistry."

Commenting on his writings, Conil says, "I prefer to use a style of presentation that will excite the imagination and evoke a sentimental approach to personal relationships."

*   *   *

CONROY, (Donald) Pat(rick) 1945-

PERSONAL: Born October 26, 1945, in Atlanta, GA; son of Donald (a military officer) and Frances Dorothy "Peg" (Peek) Conroy; married Barbara Bolling, 1969 (divorced, 1977); married Lenore Gurewitz, March 21, 1981; children: (first marriage) Megan; Jessica, Melissa (stepdaughters); (second marriage) Susannah; Gregory, Emily (stepchildren). *Education:* The Citadel, B.A., 1967. *Politics:* Democrat.

ADDRESSES: Office—Old New York Book Shop, 1069 Juniper St. N.E., Atlanta, GA 30309. *Agent*—IMG-Bach Literary Agency, 22 E. 71 St., New York, NY 10021-4911.

CAREER: Writer. Worked as an elementary schoolteacher in Daufuski, SC, 1969, and as a high school teacher in Beaufort, SC, 1967-69.

MEMBER: Authors Guild, Authors League of America, Writers Guild, PEN.

AWARDS, HONORS: Anisfield-Wolf Award, Cleveland Foundation, 1972, for *The Water Is Wide;* National Endowment for the Arts award for achievement in education, 1974; Georgia Governor's Award for Arts, 1978; Lillian Smith Award for fiction, Southern Regional Council, 1981; *The Lords of Discipline* was nominated for the Robert Kennedy Book Award, Robert F. Kennedy Memorial, 1981; inducted into the South Carolina Hall of Fame, Academy of Authors, 1988; Thomas Cooper Society Literary Award, Thomas Coopper Library, University of South Carolina, 1995; South Carolina Governor's Award in the Humanities for Distinguished Achievement, South Carolina Humanities Council, 1996; Humanitarian Award, Georgia Commission on the Holocaust, 1996; The Lotos Medal of Merit in Recognition of Outstanding Literary Achievement, 1996.

WRITINGS:

The Boo, McClure Press (Verona, VA), 1970.
The Water Is Wide, Houghton (Boston), 1972.
The Great Santini, Houghton, 1976.
The Lords of Discipline, Houghton, 1980.
The Prince of Tides, Houghton, 1986.
Beach Music, Nan A. Talese/Doubleday (New York City), 1995.

Author of screenplay for television movie *Invictus,* 1988; also author with Becky Johnson of the Academy-Award nominated screenplay for the movie version of *The Prince of Tides.* Coauthor, with Doug Marlett, of the screenplay *Ex.*

ADAPTATIONS: The film *Conrack,* based on *The Water Is Wide,* was produced by Twentieth-Century Fox in 1974; the musical *Conrack* was adapted for the stage by Granville Burgess, and was first produced off-off Broadway at AMAS Repertory Theater, November, 1987; *The Great Santini* was produced by Warner Brothers in 1979; *The Lords of Discipline* was produced by Paramount in 1983; Barbra Streisand produced, directed, and starred in *The Prince of Tides,* a motion picture released in 1991.

SIDELIGHTS: Best-selling novelist Pat Conroy has worked some of his bitterest experiences into stories that present ironic, often jarring, yet humorous views of life and relationships in the contemporary South. Garry Abrams in the *Los Angeles Times* reports that "misfortune has been good to novelist Pat Conroy. It gave him a family of disciplinarians, misfits, eccentrics, liars and loudmouths. It gave him a Southern childhood in which the bizarre competed with the merely strange. It gave him a military school education apparently imported from Sparta by way of Prussia. It gave him a divorce and a breakdown followed by intensive therapy. It gave him everything he needed to write best sellers, make millions and live in Rome." Brigitte Weeks touches on Conroy's appeal in the *Washington Post:* "With his feet set firmly on his native earth, Conroy is, above all, a storyteller. His tales are full of the exaggeration and wild humor of stories told around a camp fire."

While his most recent works are fictional, critics frequently consider Conroy's novels autobiographical. Conroy's father was a Marine Corps pilot from Chicago who believed in strong discipline; his mother was an outwardly yielding Southerner who actually ran the household. "When he [Conroy's father] returned home from work my sister would yell, 'Godzilla's home' and the seven children would melt into whatever house we happened to be living in at the time. He was no match for my mother's byzantine and remarkable powers of intrigue. Neither were her children. It took me 30 years to realize that I had grown up in my mother's house and not my father's," Conroy is quoted in the *Book-of-the-Month Club News*. Still, critics frequently mention the ambivalent father-son relationships that appear in his novels. Gail Godwin in the *New York Times Book Review* describes Conroy's work: "The Southernboy protagonists of Pat Conroy's fiction have twin obsessions—oppressive fathers or father figures, and the South. Against both they fight furiously for selfhood and independence, yet they never manage to secede from their seductive entrappers. Some fatal combination of nostalgia and loyalty holds them back; they remain ambivalent sons of their families and their region, alternately railing against, then shamelessly romanticizing, the myths and strictures that imprison them."

Conroy's first work to receive national attention was openly autobiographical. After graduation, Conroy taught English in public high schools, but unsatisfied, he looked for a new challenge. When a desired position in the Peace Corps did not surface, he took a job teaching nearly illiterate black children on Daufuskie Island, a small, isolated area off the South Carolina coast. But he was not prepared for his new students. They did not know the name of their country, that they lived on the Atlantic Ocean, or that the world was round. On the other hand, Conroy found his pupils expected him to know how to set a trap, skin a muskrat, and plant okra. Conroy came to enjoy his unusual class, but eventually his unorthodox teaching methods, such as his unwillingness to allow corporal punishment of his students, and disregard for the school's administration turned numerous school officials against him and cost him his job. As a way of coping with his fury at the dismissal, Conroy wrote *The Water Is Wide,* an account of his experiences. As he told Ted Mahar for the *Oregonian,* "When you get fired like that, you have to do something. I couldn't get a job with the charges the school board leveled against me." The process of writing did more than cool him down however; he also gained a new perspective on his reasons for choosing Daufuskie (Yamacraw Island in the book) and on his own responses to racism. Anatole Broyard describes Conroy in the *New York Times Book Review* as "a former redneck and self-proclaimed racist,

[who] brought to Yamacraw the supererogatory fervor of the recently converted." In *The Water Is Wide,* Conroy agrees: "At this time of my life a black man could probably have handed me a bucket of cow p—, commanded me to drink it in order that I might rid my soul of the stench of racism, and I would only have asked for a straw. . . . It dawned on me that I came to Yamacraw for a fallacious reason: I needed to be cleansed, born again, resurrected by good works and suffering, purified of the dark cankers that grew like toadstools in my past."

After the successful publication of *The Water Is Wide,* Conroy began writing full-time. Although his following book, *The Great Santini,* was a novel, many critics think it represents his adolescence. An article in the *Virginia Quarterly Review* states that "the dialogue, anecdotes, and family atmosphere are pure Marine and probably autobiographical." Conroy did draw heavily on his family background to write the story of a tough Marine, Bull Meecham, his long-suffering wife, Lillian, and the eldest son Ben, who is striving for independence outside his father's control. Robert E. Burkholder writes in *Critique: Studies in Modern Fiction* that *The Great Santini* "is a curious blend of lurid reality and fantastic comedy, which deals with approximately one year in the life of Ben Meecham and his family. It is primarily a novel of initiation, but central to the concept of Ben's initiation into manhood and to the meaning of the whole novel is the idea that individual myths must be stripped away from Ben and the other major characters before Ben can approach reality with objectivity and maturity." Part of Ben's growing up involves rejecting the image of his father's infallibility. In one scene, Ben finally beats his father at a game of basketball. As the game ends, he tells him: "Do you know, Dad, that not one of us here has ever beaten you in a single game? Not checkers, not dominoes, not softball, nothing."

According to Robert M. Willingham in the *Dictionary of Literary Biography,* after his defeat, "Bull does not outwardly change. He still blusters, curses, flashes toughness and resoluteness, but his family has become more to him than before. When Colonel Meecham's plane crashes and he is killed, one learns that the crash was unavoidable, but Bull's death was not: 'Am commencing starboard turn to avoid populated area. Will attempt to punch out when wings are level. Wish me luck. Over.' The priority was to avoid populated areas, 'where people lived and slept, where families slept. Families like my family, wives like my wife, sons like my sons, daughters like my daughters.' He never punched out."

Bull Meecham is modeled on Conroy's father, Colonel Donald Conroy, who "would make John Wayne look like a pansy," as Conroy told Bill McDonald for the South Carolina *State.* Conroy reports that his father initially disliked *The Great Santini.* The author tells *Chicago Tribune* contributor Peer Gorner that "Dad could only read the book halfway through before throwing it across the room. Then people started telling him he actually was lovable. Now, he signs Christmas cards *The Great Santini,* and goes around talking about childrearing and how we need to have more discipline in the home—a sort of Nazi Dr. Spock."

The movie created from the novel helped to change the Colonel's attitude. *The Great Santini* starred Robert Duvall, and the Colonel liked the way "his" character came across. In a *Washington Post* interview, Conroy related an incident of one-upmanship that seems borrowed from the book. "He (the Colonel) came to the opening of 'The Great Santini' movie here in Washington. I introduced the film to the audience, and in the course of my remarks I pointed out why he had chosen the military as a career. It was, of course, something that occurred to him on the day when he discovered that his body temperature and his IQ were the same number. Then, when it was his turn to talk, all he said was, 'I want to say that my body temperature has always been 160 degrees.' People laughed harder. So you see, I still can't beat him." Conroy's father, however, says it is important to remember that *The Great Santini* is fiction. Willingham adds, "Colonel Conroy offers these comments: 'Pat embellished everything. Where's the truth in all these incidents? There is a moment of truth. Where it is, I suspect only Pat and I recognize.'"

Another period of Conroy's life appeared in his next book, *The Lords of Discipline.* According to his father's wishes, Conroy attended the Citadel, South Carolina's venerable military academy. "Quirky, eccentric, and unforgettable," Conroy describes the academy in the preface to *The Boo,* his first book, which gave a nostalgic look at the Citadel and its Commander of Cadets during the 1960s. But Willingham describes the Citadel in another way: "It is also an anachronism of the 1960s with a general disregard for the existence of the outside world." *The Lords of Discipline* paints an even bleaker picture of its fic-

tionalized institution, the Carolina Military Institute. This school, says Frank Rose in the *Washington Post Book World,* "combines some of the more quaint and murderous aspects of the Citadel, West Point, and Virginia Military Institute."

The Lords of Discipline concerns Will, the narrator, and his three roommates. Will is a senior cadet assigned to watch over the Institute's first black student. The novel's tension lies in the conflict between group loyalty and personal responsibility. Will eventually discovers the Ten, "a secret mafia whose existence has long been rumored but never proven, a silent and malevolent force dedicated . . . to maintain the purity of the Institute—racial purity included," comments Rose. He continues, "What Conroy has achieved is twofold; his book is at once a suspense-ridden duel between conflicting ideals of manhood and a paean to brother love that ends in betrayal and death. Out of the shards of broken friendship a blunted triumph emerges, and it is here, when the duel is won, that the reader finally comprehends the terrible price that any form of manhood can exact."

According to its author, *The Lords of Discipline* describes the love between men. "I wrote it because I wanted to tell about how little women understand about men," he explains in a *Washington Post* article. "The one cultural fact of life about military schools is that they are men living with men. And they love each other. The love between these men is shown only in obscure ways, which have to be learned by them. The four roommates who go through this book are very different from each other, but they have a powerful code. They have ways to prove their love to each other, and they're part of the rites of passage." And contradicting an old myth, Conroy adds, "There is no homosexuality under these conditions. If you smile, they'll kill you. You can imagine what would happen to a homosexual."

While *The Lords of Discipline* portrays deep friendships, it also contains a theme common to many of Conroy's books: the coexistence of love and brutality. "This book . . . makes *The Lord of the Flies* sound like *The Sound of Music,*" writes Christian Williams in the *Washington Post.* A *Chicago Tribune Book World* reviewer warns, "Conroy's chilling depictions of hazing are for strong stomachs only." And George Cohen in a later Chicago *Tribune Books* article describes the novel's pull for readers: "It is our attraction to violence—observed from the safest of places—together with our admiration for the rebel who beats the system, and Conroy's imposing ability as a storyteller that make the novel engrossing."

Conroy's wildest tale is *The Prince of Tides,* which follows Tom Wingo, an unemployed high school English teacher and football coach on a journey from coastal South Carolina to New York City to help his twin sister Savannah. Savannah, a well-known poet, is recovering from a nervous breakdown and suicide attempt. In an attempt to help Savannah's psychiatrist understand her patient, Tom relates the Wingo family's bizarre history. Despite the horrors the Wingos have suffered, including several rapes and the death of their brother, a sense of optimism prevails. Writes Judy Bass in Chicago *Tribune Books,* "Pat Conroy has fashioned a brilliant novel that ultimately affirms life, hope and the belief that one's future need not be contaminated by a monstrous past. In addition, Conroy . . . deals with the most prostrating crises in human experience—death of a loved one, parental brutality, injustice, insanity—without lapsing into pedantry or oppressive gloom."

The Prince of Tides's style drew more attention than that of Conroy's other books. Some critics felt the novel was overblown: Richard Eder in the *Los Angeles Times Book Review* claims that "inflation is the order of the day. The characters do too much, feel too much, suffer too much, eat too much, signify too much, and above all, talk too much. And, as with the classical American tomato, quantity is at the expense of quality." Godwin says that while "the ambition, invention and sheer irony in this book are admirable . . . , many readers will be put off by the turgid, high-flown rhetoric that the author must have decided would best match his grandiose designs. And as the bizarre, hyperbolic episodes of Wingo family life mount up, other readers are likely to feel they are being bombarded by whoppers told by an overwrought boy eager to impress or shock." But more critics have appreciated what *Detroit News* contributor Ruth Pollack Coughlin calls "spectacular, lyrical prose with a bitter sense of humor." The novel is long, says Weeks, "monstrously long, yet a pleasure to read, flawed yet stuffed to the endpapers with lyricism, melodrama, anguish and plain old suspense. Given all that, one can brush aside its lapses like troublesome flies."

In his long-awaited next novel, *Beach Music,* Conroy continues to mine his personal and family experience for the characters, events, and themes of his fiction. He weaves into this novel the difficulties of family relationships, the pain of a mother's death, changing friendships, and the personal impact of global events such as the Holocaust, Vietnam, and present-day terrorism. What Conroy creates is a story of family, betrayal, and place. As Don Paul writes in the *San Francisco Review of Books,* "In *Beach Music* Pat Conroy takes the theme of betrayal and fashions from it a story rambling and uneven and, like the family it portrays, erratic and flawed and magnificent. South Carolina overflows from his pages, sentimental and unforgiving, soft as sleepy pears and hard as turtle shells."

Beach Music is the story of Jack McCall. After his wife commits suicide, McCall leaves South Carolina and takes his young daughter to Italy to escape his memories and his strained relationships with his own and his wife's family. He returns to South Carolina when his mother becomes ill with leukemia. There, he finds himself caught up in the lives and intrigues of family and close friends. McCall and his friends are forced by current events to revisit the Vietnam era in their small South Carolina community. Some joined the military, some joined the anti-war movement, and some struggled with both. But, as Paul explains, "Central to the plot is the betrayal of the anti-war movement by a friend who turns out to be an FBI informer." The effect of this act continue to ripple into the novel's present.

The many characters, events, and themes make, in the opinion of *Detroit Free Press* contributor Barbara Holliday, for a long, convoluted book. She writes that "Conroy sets out to do too much and loses his focus in this novel. . . . But despite some fine passages, *Beach Music* finally becomes tiring, and that's too bad for one of the country's finer writers." A reviewer offers a more positive evaluation in *Publishers Weekly:* "Conroy has not lost his touch. His storytelling powers have not failed; neither has his fluid, poetic skill with words, nor his vivid imagination. His long-awaited sixth book sings with the familiar Southern cadences, his prose is sweepingly lyrical." And John Berendt, in a *Vanity Fair,* profile of Conroy calls *Beach Music* "a novel rich in haunting imagery and seductive, suspenseful storytelling, a worthy successor to *The Prince of Tides.*" Berendt adds, "In *Beach Music,* his most ambitious novel, Conroy proves once again that he is the master of place, that he can take possession of any local— Rome, Venice, South Carolina—merely by wrapping his sumptuous prose around it."

Because of the autobiographical nature of Conroy's work, his family often judges his novels more harshly than do reviewers. Although Conroy's mother is the inspiration for shrimper's wife Lila Wingo in *The Prince of Tides,* she died before he finished the novel and never read it. Conroy's sister, who did see the book, was offended. As Conroy told Rick Groen for the Toronto *Globe and Mail,* "Yes, my sister is also a poet in New York who has also had serious breakdowns. We were very close, but she has not spoken to me . . . since the book. I'm saddened, but when you write autobiography, this is one of the consequences. They're allowed to be mad at you. They have the right." This, however, was not the first time a family member reacted negatively to one of Conroy's books. *The Great Santini* infuriated his Chicago relatives: "My grandmother and grandfather told me they never wanted to see me or my children again," Conroy told Sam Staggs for *Publishers Weekly.* Conroy's Southern relatives have also responded to the sex scenes and "immodest" language in his books. Staggs relates, "After *The Lords of Discipline* was published, Conroy's Aunt Helen telephoned him and said, 'Pat, I hope someday you'll write a book a Christian can read.' 'How far did you get?' her nephew asked. 'Page four, and I declare, I've never been so embarrassed.'" Perhaps the most sobering moment for Conroy's autobiographical impulse was when a tragic event from his writing came true. In early manuscripts of *Beach Music,* Conroy had included a scene where one of the characters, based on one of his younger brothers, Tom, committed suicide. Tom Conroy, a paranoid schizophrenic, committed suicide in August of 1994. Devastated, Pat removed the scene from *Beach Music.*

Unlike his family, Hollywood has given Conroy's novels a warm reception. *The Great Santini* wasn't his only book to become a movie. *The Water Is Wide* was made into *Conrack,* starring Jon Voight, and later became a musical also entitled *Conrack.* *The Lords of Discipline* kept the same title as a film and featured David Keith. Conroy himself wrote a screenplay for *The Prince of Tides,* learning a lesson about Hollywood in the process. When producers offered him $100,000 to write the screenplay, he took it happily. They liked his work, but then decided to send it to an experienced Hollywood rewrite man—who received $500,000 for the job.

When Staggs asked why Conroy's books "make such entertaining movies," the author replied, "I always figure it's because I'm incredibly shallow. I write a straight story line, and I guess that's what they need. The dialogue also seems to be serviceable in a Hollywood way. But most important, I do the thing that

Southerners do naturally—I tell stories. I always try to make sure there's a good story going on in my books." Conroy further explained his method of writing to Gorner: "When I'm writing, I have no idea where I'm going. People get married, and I didn't realize they were engaged. People die in these novels and I'm surprised. They take on this little subterranean life of their own. They reveal secrets to me even as I'm doing it. Maybe this is a dangerous way to work, but for me it becomes the pleasure of writing. . . . Critics call me a popular novelist, but writing popular novels isn't what urges me on. If I could write like Faulkner or Thomas Wolfe, I surely would. I'd much rather write like them than like me. Each book has been more ambitious. I'm trying to be more courageous."

BIOGRAPHICAL/CRITICAL SOURCES:

BOOKS

Authors in the News, Volume 1, Gale (Detroit), 1976.
Contemporary Literary Criticism, Volume 30, Gale, 1984.
Dictionary of Literary Biography, Volume 6: *American Novelists since World War II, Second Series,* Gale, 1980.

PERIODICALS

Atlanta Journal-Constitution, March 27, 1988, p. J1.
Book-of-the-Month Club News, December, 1986.
Chicago Tribune, November 25, 1986.
Chicago Tribune Book World, October 19, 1980; September 14, 1986; October 19, 1986.
Cincinnati Enquirer, March 25, 1974.
Critique: Studies in Modern Fiction, Volume 21, number 1, 1979.
Detroit Free Press, July 9, 1995, p. 7G.
Detroit News, October 12, 1986; December 20, 1987.
Globe and Mail (Toronto), February 28, 1987; November 28, 1987.
Los Angeles Times, February 19, 1983; October 12, 1986; October 19, 1986; December 12, 1986.
Los Angeles Times Book Review, October 19, 1986, p. 3.
New York Times, January 10, 1987.
New York Times Book Review, July 13, 1972; September 24, 1972; December 7, 1980; October 12, 1986, p. 14.
Oregonian, April 28, 1974.
People, February 2, 1981, p. 67.

Publishers Weekly, May 15, 1972; September 5, 1986; May 8, 1995, p. 286: July 10, 1995, p. 16, July 31, 1995, p. 17.

San Francisco Review of Books, July-August, 1995, p. 24.

State (Columbia, South Carolina), March 31, 1974.

Time, October 13, 1986, p. 97; June 26, 1995, p. 77.

Tribune Books (Chicago), September 14, 1986, p. 23; October 19, 1986, p. 3; January 3, 1988, p. 3.

Vanity Fair, July, 1995, p. 108.

Virginia Quarterly Review, autumn, 1976.

Washington Post, October 23, 1980; March 9, 1992, p. B3.

Washington Post Book World, October 19, 1980; October 12, 1986.

*   *   *

COOLEY, Denton A(rthur)   1920-

PERSONAL: Born August 22, 1920, in Houston, TX; son of Ralph C. (a dentist) and Mary (Fraley) Cooley; married Louise Goldsborough Thomas, January 15, 1949; children: Mary, Susan, Louise, Florence, Helen. *Education:* University of Texas at Austin, B.A., 1941; Johns Hopkins University, M.D., 1944.

ADDRESSES: Home—Houston, TX. *Office*—Texas Heart Institute, P.O. Box 20345, Houston, TX 77030.

CAREER: Johns Hopkins University, Baltimore, MD, surgical intern at Johns Hopkins Hospital, 1944-45, resident in surgery, 1945-50; Brompton Hospital for Chest Diseases, London, senior surgical registrar in thoracic surgery, 1950-51; Baylor University, Houston, TX, associate professor, 1954-62, professor of surgery, 1962-69; Texas Heart Institute, Houston, founder and chief surgeon, 1962—, president, 1995—; University of Texas, Houston, clinical professor of surgery, 1975—. *Military service:* U.S. Army, Medical Corps, 1946-48; became captain.

MEMBER: International Cardiovascular Society, American Association of Thoracic Surgery, American College of Cardiology, American College of Chest Physicians, American College of Surgeons, American Surgical Association, Society of Thoracic Surgeons (president, 1993-94), Society of Thoracic Surgery, Society of University Surgeons, Society for Clinical Surgery, Society for Vascular Surgery, Western Surgical Association, Texas Surgical Society, Halsted Society.

AWARDS, HONORS: Named one of ten outstanding young men in the United States by U.S. Chamber of Commerce, 1955; man-of-the-year award from Kappa Sigma, 1964; Rene Leriche Prize from International Surgical Society, 1965-67; Billings Gold Medal from American Medical Association, 1967; Vishnevsky Medal from Vishnevsky Institute (Soviet Union), 1971; Theodore Roosevelt Award from National Collegiate Athletic Association, 1980; Presidential Medal of Freedom, 1984; gifted teacher award from American College of Cardiology, 1987. Honorary degrees from Hellenic College and Holy Cross Greek Orthodox School of Theology, Houston Baptist University, College of William and Mary, United States Sports Academy, and University of Turin.

WRITINGS:

Surgical Treatment of Congenital Heart Disease, Lea & Febiger (Philadelphia), 1966.

Techniques in Cardiac Surgery, Saunders (Philadelphia), 1975, 2nd edition, 1984.

Techniques in Vascular Surgery, Saunders, 1979.

Essays of Denton A. Cooley, M.D.: Reflections and Observations, Eakin Press (Austin, TX), 1984.

Surgical Treatment of Aortic Aneurysm, Saunders, 1986.

(With Carolyn E. Moore) *Eat Smart for a Healthy Heart Cookbook,* Barron's (Woodbury, NY), 1987.

Heart Owner's Handbook, Wiley (New York City), 1996.

Contributor to numerous surgical texts. Author or coauthor of more than 1,100 scientific articles.

WORK IN PROGRESS: "Ongoing research on all aspects of cardiovascular disease, with special interests in a total artificial heart and heart assist devices."

SIDELIGHTS: Denton A. Cooley, one of the greatest heart surgeons, is probably best known for performing the first transplant of an artificial heart into a human being. But he has also contributed to development of the heart-lung bypass device and has pioneered such extraordinary surgical techniques as the replacing of diseased heart valves and the removal of aortic aneurysms. He has been particularly active in combating congenital heart diseases in infants. In addition, he established the Texas Heart Institute at the Texas Medical Center in Houston.

Cooley told *CA:* "During my medical career, I have played a role in the development of what was, when I began, an entirely new specialty—cardiovascular surgery. After I received my medical degree from Johns Hopkins University in 1944 and as a surgical intern at Johns Hopkins Hospital, I had the unique privilege of participating in the first operation for tetralogy of Fallot (the famous 'blue baby' operation) performed by my chief, Dr. Alfred Blalock. This deeply dramatic experience impressed me and first introduced me to the excitement and opportunity ahead in cardiovascular surgery.

"Upon leaving Baltimore, I joined Mr. Russell (subsequently Lord) Brock of London for a year (1950-51), another leader in the field, who was operating on heart valves ravaged with disease. When I returned to Houston, I continued to perfect techniques for treatment of infants with heart defects. After the introduction of the heart-lung machine in the late 1950s, 'open' heart surgery became a reality, and patients began to flock to physicians who would operate on the heart. Thus, my interest led me to believe that the time had come for an institution devoted to diseases of the heart and blood vessels, and, in 1962, the Texas Heart Institute was born. During the next twenty-five years, the institute would become the largest cardiovascular surgical center in the world, and its staff would perform more than seventy thousand open-heart operations, including the first 'successful' heart transplant in the United States and the first implantation in man of a total artificial heart.

"Although a certain number of patients have hereditary factors that predispose them to heart disease, in many others, disease could have been prevented or lessened through the appropriate combination of work, exercise, relaxation, and rest—all in practice with good nutrition and healthful eating habits. *Eat Smart for a Healthy Heart Cookbook* resulted from my desire to work toward preventing much of the heart disease I see daily in my practice. The cookbook offers gourmet menus from some of Houston's

greatest chefs. The recipes, which have been modified to be 'heart healthy,' are low in sodium, fat, and cholesterol. A healthy and alert mind must be served by a fit and well-toned body. *Heart Owner's Handbook,* our most recent book, also stresses prevention and the importance of lifestyle modifications. The incidence of heart disease, the major killer in our society, will be reduced by attention to such a balanced lifestyle."

BIOGRAPHICAL/CRITICAL SOURCES:

BOOKS

Minetree, Harry, *Cooley: The Career of a Great Heart Surgeon,* Harper's Magazine Press, 1973.
Rapoport, Roger, *Superdoctors,* Playboy Press, 1975.
Thompson, Thomas, *Hearts: DeBakey and Cooley, Surgeons Extraordinary,* Saturday Review Press, 1971.

PERIODICALS

Esquire, December, 1969.
Good Housekeeping, March, 1996.
Life, August 2, 1968; April 10, 1970.
Time, October 25, 1971.
Town and Country, February, 1995.

*　　*　　*

COOPER, Louise   1952-

PERSONAL: Born May 29, 1952, in Barnet, Hertfordshire, England; daughter of Erle (an accountant) and Pat (a newspaper copyreader; maiden name, Papworth) Antell; married Gary Richard Cooper (an editor), December 5, 1970. *Education:* Educated in England. *Avocational interests:* Rock and folk music, the occult.

ADDRESSES: Agent—E. J. Carnell Literary Agency, 17 Burward Rd., Plumstead, London SE18, England.

CAREER: Writer. Worked as a secretary and a folk singer.

AWARDS, HONORS: The Sleep of Stone was named an American Library Association Notable Book for young adults in 1993.

WRITINGS:

FANTASY NOVELS

The Book of Paradox, Delacorte (New York City), 1973.
Nocturne, Tor Books (New York City), 1990.
The Sleep of Stone, Atheneum (New York City), 1991.
Avatar, Tor Books, 1992.
The Avenger, Bantam (New York City), 1992.
Revenant, Tor Books, 1993.
Star Ascendant, Tor Books, 1995.

Also author of *The Deceiver, Infanta, Inferno, The Initiate, The Master, Mirage, Nemesis, The Outcast, The Pretender, The Thorn Key, Aisling,* and *Troika.*

SIDELIGHTS: Louise Cooper's young adult fantasies have drawn consistent praise from reviewers. Discussing *Nocturne,* the fourth book in a series that includes *Nemesis, Inferno,* and *Infanta,* Joyce Yen wrote in *Voice of Youth Advocates:* "Overall it is excellent. This fantasy is brought to life so well even those who are not fantasy fans will enjoy it." The main character in the series, Indigo, once released seven demons from a place called the Tower of Regrets. Many of her adventures turn on her attempts to atone for her mistake and rid the world of the evil forces she inadvertently turned loose on the world. Yen pointed out the similarities between Cooper's tales and the myth of Pandora's box. She observed that "Cooper does an excellent job in conjuring a picture of the demon world through her words."

Discussing Cooper's "Chaos Gate" trilogy, *Locus* reviewer Tom Whitmore credited the author with making some deep philosophical points. "Cooper has strong women, uncommon men, and gods that are completely unconcerned with what mortals want," he related. He went on to say that out of the many unexpected plot twists in the series, the most "refreshing" was that the characters eventually realized their gods' indifference to them. Whitmore asserted that Cooper writes from a humanist perspective and sends readers the message that each person is responsible for his or her own life. "These books are subversive, and well done," he concluded. Another trilogy, "Time Master," was also singled out by a reviewer for *Publishers Weekly* for its subtle characterizations and avoidance of oversimplified moralizing.

Cooper won high praise for her style in *The Sleep of Stone*—the story of Ghysla, the last survivor of a shape-changing people who began to vanish from the earth when the age of humans commenced. "The narrative is elegant and stately, language that paints vivid images in the reader's mind," Donna L. Scanlon commented in *Kliatt.* "The fast-moving plot; several interesting characters; and the poignant description of Ghysla's loneliness, first love, and desperation add up to good reading," affirmed Carleen Blake Ryan in *Voice of Youth Advocates.*

BIOGRAPHICAL/CRITICAL SOURCES:

PERIODICALS

Locus, February, 1991, p. 29; March, 1992, p. 35; June, 1994, p. 57.
Kliatt, July, 1993, p. 16.
Publishers Weekly, October 16, 1995, p. 47.
Voice of Youth Advocates, December, 1990, p. 295; April, 1992, p. 41; August, 1992, p. 172.*

* * *

CORNWELL, Patricia Daniels   1956-

PERSONAL: Born June 9, 1956, in Miami, FL; daughter of Sam (an attorney) and Marilyn (a secretary; maiden name, Zenner) Daniels; married Charles Cornwell (a college professor), June 14, 1980 (divorced, 1990). *Education:* Davidson College, B.A., 1979. *Religion:* Presbyterian. *Avocational interests:* Tennis.

ADDRESSES: Home—Richmond, VA. *Office*—Cornwell Enterprises, P.O. Box 35686, Richmond, VA 23235. *Agent*—International Creative Management, 40 W. 57th St., New York, NY 10019.

CAREER: Charlotte Observer, Charlotte, NC, police reporter, 1979-81; Office of the Chief Medical Examiner, Richmond, VA, computer analyst, 1985-91. Volunteer police officer. Bell Vision Productions (film production company), president.

MEMBER: International Crime Writers Association, International Association of Chiefs of Police, International Association of Identification, National Association of Medical Examiners, Authors Guild.

AWARDS, HONORS: Investigative reporting award, North Carolina Press Association, 1980, for a series on prostitution; Gold Medallion Book Award for biography, Evangelical Christian Publishers Association, 1985, for *A Time for Remembering: The Story of Ruth Bell Graham;* John Creasy Award, British Crime Writers Association, Edgar Award, Mystery Writers of America, Anthony Award, Boucheron, World Mystery Convention, and Macavity Award, Mystery Readers International, all for best first crime novel, all 1990, and French Prix du Roman d'Aventure, 1991, all for *Postmortem;* Gold Dagger award, for *Cruel and Unusual.*

WRITINGS:

CRIME NOVELS

Postmortem, Scribner (New York City), 1990.
Body of Evidence, Scribner, 1991.
All That Remains, Scribner, 1992.
Cruel and Unusual, Scribner, 1993.
The Body Farm, Scribner, 1994.
From Potter's Field, Scribner, 1995.
Cause of Death, Putnam (New York City), 1996.
Hornet's Nest, Putnam, 1997.
Unnatural Exposure, Putnam, 1997.

OTHER

A Time for Remembering: The Story of Ruth Bell Graham (biography), Harper (New York City), 1983.

ADAPTATIONS: Brilliance Corp. released a sound recording of *Body of Evidence* in 1992; sound recordings are also available for *Postmortem, All That Remains, Cruel and Unusual, The Body Farm,* and *From Potter's Field.* Negotiations are in progress for the film rights to *From Potter's Field.*

SIDELIGHTS: Since 1990, Patricia Daniels Cornwell's novels have followed Dr. Kay Scarpetta, a medical examiner called upon to solve murders with forensic sleuthing. The novels are praised for their accurate detail based upon research Cornwell did in the Virginia medical examiner's office, witnessing scores of autopsies. In addition to this, Cornwell also went out on police homicide runs. "I'm not sure I could have read my last book if I hadn't written it," Cornwell told Sandra McElwaine in *Harper's Bazaar.* "The violence is so real, I think it would have scared me to death."

Cornwell began her book-writing career in 1983 with a biography of Ruth Graham, wife of evangelist Billy Graham. It was Graham who encouraged her to pursue writing. "I felt she had real ability," Graham told Joe Treen in *People.* "I've kept every note I ever got from her." With Graham's encouragement, Cornwell went back to school at Davidson College in North Carolina, majoring in English. Right after graduation she married Charles Cornwell, one of her former professors, and began working as a crime reporter for the *Charlotte Observer.*

"I had a compulsion to get close to every story. I really wanted to solve crimes," Cornwell told McElwaine. In 1980, Cornwell received an investigative reporting award from the North Carolina Press Association for a series she did on prostitution. Unfortunately, just when she felt her career was getting underway, her husband decided that he wanted to become a minister, and the couple moved to Richmond, Virginia, where he attended Union Theological Seminary. "I did not want to give up the *Observer,*" she told Treen. "It was a very bad time for me."

Cornwell began working on a biography of her good friend Graham, which kept her busy for a few years until it was published in 1983. She had always pictured herself as a novelist, so she decided to try writing crime novels with the information she had gathered as a reporter. She realized that she would need to do more in-depth research to make her murder plots seem more believable. A friend recommended that she might try talking to the deputy medical examiner at the Virginia Morgue. Cornwell took the advice and made an appointment with pathologist Dr. Marcella Fierro.

Her first appointment with Fierro was illuminating for Cornwell. There was a whole world of high-tech forensic procedures that she knew nothing about. "I was shocked by two things," Cornwell told Joanne Tangorra in *Publishers Weekly.* "One, by how fascinating it was, and two, by how absolutely little I knew about it. I realized I had no idea what a medical examiner would do—Did they put on gloves, wear lab coats and surgical greens? They do none of the above."

Cornwell soon became a regular visitor at the forensic center and also took on technical writing projects for the morgue to absorb more of the forensic knowledge she craved. The result was *Postmortem,* the first in a series of mysteries chronicling Cornwell's fictional investigative forensic pathologist, Dr. Kay Scarpetta.

Postmortem focuses on the rape and murder of several Richmond women by a serial killer. The book charts the work of Scarpetta, the chief medical examiner of Virginia, as she attempts to uncover the killer's identity. Frequently faced with sexism regarding her ability to handle a "man's job," Scarpetta aptly displays her knowledge of the innovative technologies of today's forensic medicine to crack the case. "Dr. Scarpetta has a terrible time with the chauvinists around her, one of whom in particular is malevolently eager for her to fail," writes Charles Champlin in the *Los Angeles Times Book Review.* "These passages have the ring of truth as experienced, and so does the portrait of an investigative reporter who abets the solving."

"*Postmortem* . . . won just about every mystery fiction award," declares *New York Times Book Review* contributor Bill Kent. "The follow-up novel, *Body of Evidence,* proved that Ms. Cornwell's success wasn't mere beginner's luck." *Body of Evidence* centers on Beryl Madison, a young woman who is writing a controversial book for which she has received death threats. Shortly after she reports these events she is murdered—apparently after allowing the killer to enter her home. Scarpetta must once again use tiny bits of evidence to track down the murderer.

In later novels, Cornwell introduces Temple Gault, a serial killer with intelligence to match Scarpetta's. Gault, who specializes in the murder of children, only narrowly escapes being captured by Scarpetta herself in *Cruel and Unusual.* "With his pale blue eyes and his ability to anticipate the best minds of law enforcement," writes Elise O'Shaughnessy in the *New York Times Book Review,* "Gault is a 'malignant genius' in the tradition of Hannibal Lecter," the cannibalistic character in Thomas Harris's *The Silence of the Lambs.* "Like Lecter's bond with Clarice Starling," O'Shaughnessy concludes, "Gault's relationship with Scarpetta is *personal.*"

In a column for *Mystery Scene* magazine, Cornwell shed some light on the nature of her heroine, Dr. Scarpetta. "Violence is filtered through her intellectual sophistication and inbred civility, meaning that the senseless cruelty of what she sees is all the more horrific," the author explained. She added that Dr. Scarpetta "approaches the cases with the sensitivity

of a physician, the rational thinking of a scientist, and the outrage of a humane woman who values, above all else, the sanctity of life. Through Dr. Scarpetta's character I began to struggle with an irony that had eluded me before: the more expert one gets in dismantling death, the less he understands it."

Scarpetta faces Temple Gault again in Cornwell's 1995 novel, *From Potter's Field,* set in New York City. Critics again note the research involved in the novel, as Mary B. W. Tabor comments in the *New York Times:* "There is something especially savory about novels set in real places, with real street names, real shops, real sights and smells that ring true for those who know the territory." Scarpetta is called in after Gault murders a young homeless woman on Christmas Eve in Central Park. *Booklist* reviewer Emily Melton compares reading *From Potter's Field* to "riding one of those amusement-park roller coasters . . . [that leave] the rider gasping and breathless." Melton lauds Cornwell's "magnificent plotting, masterful writing, and marvelous suspense," rating her among the top crime fiction writers.

BIOGRAPHICAL/CRITICAL SOURCES:

PERIODICALS

Armchair Detective, winter, 1991, p. 32.
Booklist, May 1, 1995.
Entertainment Weekly, June 26, 1992, p. 73.
Harper's Bazaar, August, 1992, pp. 46, 148.
Kirkus Reviews, June 1, 1995.
Library Journal, September 1, 1994, p. 213.
Los Angeles Times, March 28, 1991, p. F12.
Los Angeles Times Book Review, February 11, 1990, p. 5; February 10, 1991, p. 9; September 20, 1992, p. 8.
Mystery Scene, January, 1990, pp. 56-57.
Newsweek, August 3, 1992; July 5, 1993.
New York Times Book Review, January 7, 1990; February 24, 1991; August 23, 1992; April 4, 1993, p. 19; July 4, 1993; September 16, 1994, p. 38-39.
People, August 24, 1992, pp. 71-72; October 3, 1994, pp. 37-38.
Publisher's Weekly, December 7, 1990, p. 76; February 15, 1991, pp. 71-72; June 15, 1992, p. 89; September 12, 1994.
School Library Journal, December, 1992, pp. 146-147.
Time, September 14, 1992; October 3, 1994.
Times Literary Supplement, July 16, 1993, p. 22.

Washington Post Book World, January 21, 1990, p.
    6.
Wilson Library Bulletin, December, 1993.

*   *   *

CRAMPTON, Helen
    See CHESNEY, Marion

D

DARDIS, Tom 1926-

PERSONAL: Born August 19, 1926, in New York, NY; son of Michael Gregory (an accountant) and Josephine Coletta (O'Hara) Dardis; married Jane Buckelew (a nurse), October 25, 1947 (divorced, 1982); children: Anthony, Anne, Francis. *Education:* New York University, A.B., 1949; Columbia University, M.A., 1952, Ph.D., 1979.

CAREER: Avon Books, New York City, associate editor, 1952-55; Berkley Publishing Corp., New York City, executive editor, 1955-60, editor-in-chief, 1960-72; freelance writer, 1972-74; Adelphi University, Garden City, NY, adjunct professor of English, 1974-80; John Jay College of Criminal Justice of the City University of New York, New York City, assistant professor, associate professor of English, 1982—. *Military service:* U.S. Army, 1943-46; became sergeant.

WRITINGS:

(Editor) *Daughters of Eve,* Berkley Publishing (New York City), 1958.
(Editor) *Banned!,* Berkley Publishing, 1961.
(Editor) *Banned #2,* Berkley Publishing, 1962.
Some Time in the Sun: The Hollywood Years of Fitzgerald, Faulkner, Nathanael West, Aldous Huxley and James Agee, Scribner (New York City), 1976, revised edition, Penguin (New York City), 1981.
Keaton: The Man Who Wouldn't Lie Down, Scribner, 1979.
Harold Lloyd: The Man on the Clock, Viking (New York City), 1983.

The Thirsty Muse: Alcohol and the American Writer, Ticknor & Fields (New York City), 1989.
Firebrand: The Life of Horace Liveright, Random House (New York City), 1995.

Contributor to periodicals, including *American Film.*

SIDELIGHTS: Tom Dardis's books have explored the lives and works of several figures from the worlds of literature and show business, and are praised by several critics for their willingness to reexamine common myths and misconceptions. "Tom Dardis is a genuine film historian and not just a putter-together of Hollywood books for the fast buck," writes Ralph Tyler in *Chicago Tribune Book World.*

Some Time in the Sun: The Hollywood Years of Fitzgerald, Faulkner, Nathanael West, Aldous Huxley and James Agee is a study of the Hollywood years of several of America's brightest literati. Novelists William Faulkner, F. Scott Fitzgerald, Aldous Huxley, and Nathanael West, and critic James Agee, all served as studio screenwriters during the 1930s and 1940s. Rather than asking what Hollywood did to these talented writers, as do most writers on the subject, Dardis asks what did these writers "do to Hollywood when they had to work there?" says the *New York Times*'s John Leonard. According to Benny Green in *Spectator,* "Tom Dardis's book about the tribulations of creative writers in pre-war Hollywood is a wonderful read for anyone who has ever seen a lousy movie and then rushed home to read [F. Scott Fitzgerald's] *The Last Tycoon* in search of an explanation."

Some Time in the Sun seeks to dispel the common assumption that life in Hollywood destroyed these writers both morally and artistically. As Leonard comments, "We are more accustomed to hearing about what Hollywood did to them, a morality tale in which Hollywood usually plays the part of a venereal disease." Rather than relating tales of their personal lives, such as Faulkner's bouts of drunkenness or of Fitzgerald's affair with gossip columnist Sheilah Graham, Dardis instead concentrates on what his subjects actually accomplished in Hollywood and on the fact that not only did their studio work allow them to earn desperately needed money, but also to gain time to renew their creative forces and to return to the genres in which they began. As examples, Dardis cites Fitzgerald's unfinished *The Last Tycoon,* which some critics rank among his best work, and West's celebrated *The Day of the Locust.* Of *Some Time in the Sun,* Gavin writes in *Books and Bookmen:* "Dardis disposes of the myth that Hollywood 'destroyed' writers. He makes it clear that all his subjects were able to earn money that they vitally needed, and that if anyone destroyed Fitzgerald and Agee, it was Fitzgerald and Agee."

Gore Vidal in *New York Review of Books* considers Dardis to be "at his best when he shows his writers taking seriously their various 'assignments'" and in the way he "catches the ambivalence felt by the writers who had descended (but only temporarily) from literature's Parnassus to the swampy marketplace of the movies." However, some other critics consider the chief value of Dardis's book to lie in its attempt to verify, "as far as anyone can," as Green notes, "which lines of dialogue they did and didn't write." *Some Time in the Sun,* says Lambert, "is full of fascinating incidental research, of things I never knew and doubt that many other people did—especially concerning the movies on which these writers worked, at one stage or another, without receiving credit."

Dardis's biography of silent film star Buster Keaton contains what is considered the most detailed and definitive analysis of Keaton's career. *Keaton: The Man Who Wouldn't Lie Down* is, says Dwight McDonald in *New York Review of Books,* "the definitive life. I don't think it will ever be superseded except in the unlikely event someone discovers a new cache of important documentary material Dardis has overlooked. It is scholarly yet readable, the fullest, most objective and factually detailed book on virtually every aspect of Buster's career and personality: artistic, financial, and psychological." *Chicago Tribune Book World*'s Clarence Peterson calls the book

"a valuable reassessment of the great comic and an absorbing night's reading."

In preparation for *Keaton,* Dardis viewed all of the actor's films (the only biographer thought to have done so), spoke with one of Keaton's close friends, a sister, and an ex-wife, and pored over studio records of Keaton's career, digging up much information other film historians missed or ignored. Praised for his handling of sensitive material and for his insightful analysis, Dardis is, says McDonald, "no great respecter of *idees recues:* He's a genial iconoclast who doesn't hesitate to reverse (always with solid evidence) many of the most common assumptions about Buster's personal and professional life." Three years of preparation and "his careful research and skilled narration pay off in this biography of the master comedian with the tragic mask," comments Ralph Tyler in *Chicago Tribune Book World.* "Dardis's biography whets the appetite for a look at all of Keaton's movies."

In *The Thirsty Muse: Alcohol and the American Writer,* Dardis asserts that liquor contributed to the downfall of the writers Ernest Hemingway, F. Scott Fitzgerald, and William Faulkner. Each one, Dardis writes, was a problem drinker who romanticized his dependence as an aid to creativity. He also presents the playwright Eugene O'Neill as an example of a writer who overcame alcoholism and rejuvenated his career. Jay McInerney writes in the *Times Literary Supplement* that not all of Dardis's subjects fit neatly into his thesis. McInerney comments, ". . . in order to make his case that Faulkner lost his talent by the age of forty-five, Dardis has had to discount later books. . . ." To McInerney, the author also seems to suggest that giving up alcohol is the real creative inspiration, a conclusion that is easy to challenge. "For every writer who drank himself into a premature grave most of us can cite another who quit drinking and lost his creative spark," the reviewer says.

Phyllis Rose makes a similar complaint in the *Atlantic Monthly,* writing that Dardis's "case histories . . . don't neatly make the points he wants them to make." Both Faulkner and Fitzgerald, Rose opines, "wrote final works . . . that show no sign of withered talent." The reviewer notes that Dardis also ignores how age and time also work to exhaust creativity, and she points out that his "success story," O'Neill, attained sobriety but developed other problems, including depression and addiction to prescription drugs. But in spite of the author's "tut-tut moralism," Rose says "the cautionary tales of *The Thirsty Muse* make horrifying reading."

Kevin Jackson, who calls *The Thirsty Muse* "sober" and "agreeably written" in his review for *Punch,* remarks that the book is "a decent addition to the critical literature which pours icy water on the myth . . . that alcohol nurtures literary abilities." Writing for the *Los Angeles Times Book Review,* Sonja Bolle objects to Dardis's "narrow-mindedness" but also comments that his "point in writing the book is well taken," and "he rightly sees a need to de-glamorize intoxication and to point out the enormous cost of relying on this source of inspiration." Calvin Reid observes in the *Village Voice* that in tackling his subject, "Dardis plays, with equal aplomb, literary critic, biographer, and medical researcher. He marshals a great deal of information. . . ."

In *Firebrand: The Life of Horace Liveright,* Dardis once again profiles the alcoholic life, this time in the form of Liveright, the co-founder of and driving force behind the Boni & Liveright publishing company. While Liveright died broke after wasting his corporate profits on money-losing Broadway plays and gambling, he also published important American works such as *The Waste Land* by T. S. Eliot and *An American Tragedy* by Theodore Dreiser and established the Modern Library line of classic reprints. Liveright also is noted for fighting censorship, for introducing aggressive marketing techniques to book publishing, and for being one of the first Jews in his field. The book is "the model of what a popular biography should be: brisk, concise, sympathetic and unpedantic," writes Terry Teachout in the *New York Times Book Review.* But Teachout contends that Dardis falls prey to the biographer's lure of glamorizing his subject and that the work sometimes overestimates Liveright's importance to the growth of modern American fiction during the 1920s.

To Peter S. Prescott of the *Wall Street Journal, Firebrand* perfectly matches its subject. "Like the man himself, [the book is] overstated, a little slipshod, at times confused, but undeniably interesting," he writes. Despite Liveright's dissolute lifestyle and profligacy, Prescott points out, Dardis still finds the admirable qualities in his subject and "makes his rogue attractive." *Washington Post Book World*'s Jonathan Yardley considers Liveright merely "a footnote to literary history, but . . . both an interesting and significant one," so therefore Dardis's "workmanlike biography" is worthwhile and welcome. In the *New York Times,* Christopher Lehmann-Haupt

sees value in Dardis's analysis of Liveright's impact on publishing and concludes that while the book occasionally "sounds faintly condescending . . . it ultimately honors Liveright for his accomplishments."

BIOGRAPHICAL/CRITICAL SOURCES:

PERIODICALS

Atlantic Monthly, June, 1989, pp. 93-95.
Books and Bookmen, August, 1977, p. 60.
Chicago Tribune Book World, August 12, 1979; December 14, 1980.
Los Angeles Times Book Review, August 27, 1989, p. 6.
Newsweek, July 19, 1976, p. 71.
New Yorker, September 13, 1976, p. 163.
New York Review of Books, November 25, 1976, p. 35; October 9, 1980, p. 33.
New York Times, June 25, 1976; July 27, 1995, p. C16.
New York Times Book Review, January 18, 1981; July 16, 1995, pp. 11-12.
Punch, February 9, 1990, pp. 40-41.
Spectator, October 16, 1976, p. 23.
Times Literary Supplement, July 27-August 2, 1990, p. 792.
Village Voice, May 30, 1989, p. 55.
Wall Street Journal, August 8, 1995, p. A10.
Washington Post Book World, January 11, 1981; July 2, 1995, p. 3.*

*   *   *

DARNTON, John (Townsend) 1941-

PERSONAL: Born November 20, 1941, in New York, NY; son of Byron (a newsman) and Eleanor (an editor; maiden name, Choate) Darnton; married Nina Lieberman, August 21, 1966; children: Kyra, Liza, James. *Education:* Attended University of Paris IV (Sorbonne) and Alliance Francaise, Paris, 1960-61; University of Wisconsin, B.A., 1966. *Politics:* Democrat.

ADDRESSES: Office—New York Times, Foreign Desk, 229 West 43rd St., New York City, NY 10036.

CAREER: New York Times, New York City, copy boy, news clerk, and news assistant, 1966-68, city reporter, 1968-69, Connecticut correspondent, 1969-70, chief suburban correspondent, 1970-71, night rewriter, 1971-72, reporter for New York City fiscal crisis, 1972-75, correspondent in Lagos, Nigeria, 1976-77, and Nairobi, Kenya, 1977-79, bureau chief in Warsaw, Poland, 1979-82, and Madrid, Spain, 1982-84, deputy foreign editor, 1984-86, metropolitan editor, 1987-91, news editor, 1991-93, London bureau chief, 1993—. Correspondent and narrator for film, *Spain: Ten Years After.* Member of board of directors, New York State Associated Press.

MEMBER: Century Association, French American Institute.

AWARDS, HONORS: George Polk Award from Long Island University, 1979 and 1982, for foreign reporting; Pulitzer Prize in international reporting from Columbia University Graduate School of Journalism, 1982, for dispatches from Poland.

WRITINGS:

Neanderthal (novel), Random House (New York City), 1996.

Also author of *The Fat Lady Sings,* a film script about the Polish underground, and the introduction to *A Day in the Life of Spain.* Contributor to the *Readers Digest* and other periodicals.

Also contributor to *Assignment America: A Collection of Outstanding Writing From the New York Times* and *About Men: Reflections on the Male Experience.*

SIDELIGHTS: Pulitzer Prize winning journalist John Darnton also won the George Polk award in 1978 for his reports from Africa. In an article entitled "Nigeria's Dissident Superstar," Darnton covers the politically controversial career of Fela Anikulapo-Kuti, whose songs are highly critical of the Nigerian government. The article proved to be so embarassing to the government that Darnton was expelled from the country. In 1982, Darnton also received the George Polk award for his coverage of the political unrest in Poland. As the Warsaw bureau chief for the *New York Times,* he chronicled the rise of the industrial trade union Solidarity, and the wave of optimism which eventually swept away the Polish communist government. In a 1980 *New York Times* article, entitled "Sixty Days That Shook Poland," Darnton discusses the struggle between Solidarity and the Polish government, detailing the workers'

strike, which was lead by Lech Walesa to protest the rise in meat prices. Other articles followed, such as "Polish Awakening," which describes the intellectual, cultural, and spiritual renaissance that was the legacy of Solidarity's activities, and the less optimistic "Poland: Still Defiant," which examines the communist government's attempts to suppress the trade union movement by declaring martial law in December, 1981.

The award-winning journalist began writing novels, with the publication *Neanderthal* in 1996. The plot involves the discovery of two currently existing tribes of Neanderthals, and the scientists who study them, and work to keep them free from the intrusions of twentieth-century civilization. Edwin B. Burgess, in *Library Journal,* claims that Darnton's first novel "is very Indiana Jonesish," while Ian Tattersal in a *Time* magazine review comparing Darnton's *Neanderthal* to William Morrow's *Almost Adam,* suggests that both books are "pure fantasy constructs" and that "neither [author] even attempts to exploit the promising device of confronting human with almost human to explore the essence of our uniqueness as a species." Nevertheless, Tattersall admits that *Neanderthal* "might make an adequate companion on a plane ride."

BIOGRAPHICAL/CRITICAL SOURCES:

PERIODICALS

Detroit News, April 13, 1982.
Library Journal, May 15, 1996, p. 83.
New York Times, July 24, 1977; April 13, 1982; May 13, 1996, B2.
New York Times Book Review, April 14, 1996, p. 8.
Time, May 27, 1996, p. 79.*

*   *   *

DAVIS, Ossie   1917-

PERSONAL: Born December 18, 1917, in Cogdell, GA; son of Kince Charles (a railway construction engineer) and Laura (Cooper) Davis; married Ruby Ann Wallace (an actress and writer under name Ruby Dee), December 9, 1948; children: Nora, Guy, La Verne. *Education:* Attended Howard University, 1935-39, and Columbia University, 1948; trained for the stage with Paul Mann and Lloyd Richards.

ADDRESSES: Office—Emmalyn II Productions, P.O. Box 1318, New Rochelle, NY 10802. *Agent*—Artists Agency, 10000 Santa Monica Blvd., Suite 305, Los Angeles, CA 90067.

CAREER: Actor, playwright, screenwriter, novelist, director and producer of stage productions and motion pictures, civil rights activist. Worked as janitor, shipping clerk, and stock clerk in New York City, 1938-41. Actor in numerous stage productions, 1941—, including *Joy Exceeding Glory*, 1941, *Jeb*, 1946, *Anna Lucasta*, 1948, *Stevedore*, 1949, *The Green Pastures*, 1951, *No Time for Sergeants*, 1957, *A Raisin in the Sun*, 1959, *Purlie Victorious*, 1961, *Take It from the Top*, 1979, and *I'm Not Rappaport*, 1986. Actor in motion pictures and teleplays, including *The Joe Louis Story*, 1953, *The Emperor Jones*, 1955, *The Cardinal*, 1963, *Gone Are the Days*, 1963, *Man Called Adam*, 1966, *Teacher, Teacher* for Hallmark Hall of Fame, 1969, *Let's Do It Again*, 1976, *For Us the Living* for American Playhouse, 1983, *School Daze*, 1988, *Do the Right Thing*, 1989, *Jungle Fever*, 1991, *No Way Out*, *Harry and Son*, *Gladiator*, *Malcolm X*, *Grumpy Old Men*, and *The Client*, 1994; actor in television series *Evening Shade*, 1990-93; other television appearances include *Name of the Game*, *Night Gallery*, *Bonanza*, and *B. L. Stryker*.

Director of motion pictures, including *Cotton Comes to Harlem*, 1970, *Kongi's Harvest*, 1971, *Black Girl*, 1972, *Gordon's War*, 1973, and *Countdown at Kusini*, 1976. Cohost of radio program *Ossie Davis and Ruby Dee Story Hour*, 1974-78, and of television series *With Ossie and Ruby*, Public Broadcasting System (PBS-TV), 1981. Coproducer of stage production *Ballad for Bimshire*, 1963. Narrator of motion picture *From Dreams to Reality: A Tribute to Minority Inventors*, 1986, and of television movie *The American Experience: Goin' Back to T'Town*, 1993. Chairperson of the board, Institute for New Cinema Artists; founder with wife Ruby Dee of Emmalyn II Productions. Performer on recordings for Caedmon and Folkways Records. *Military service:* U.S. Army, 1942-45; served as surgical technician in Liberia, West Africa, and with Special Services Department.

MEMBER: Actor's Equity Association, Screen Actors Guild, American Federation of Radio and Television Artists, Director's Guild of America, National Association for the Advancement of Colored People (advisory board), Southern Christian Leadership Conference (advisory board), Congress of Racial Equality, Masons.

AWARDS, HONORS: First Mississippi Freedom Democratic Party Citation, 1965; Emmy Award nomination from Academy of Television Arts and Sciences, best actor in a special, 1969, for *Teacher, Teacher*, and nomination, c. 1978, for *King*; Antoinette Perry Award nomination, best musical, 1970, for *Purlie*; recipient with Dee of Frederick Douglass Award from New York Urban League, for "distinguished leadership toward equal opportunity," 1970; Paul Robeson Citation from Actor's Equity Association, 1975, for "outstanding creative contributions in the performing arts and in society at large"; Coretta Scott King Book Award from American Library Association, and Jane Addams Children's Book Award from Jane Addams Peace Association, both 1979, for *Escape to Freedom: A Play about Young Frederick Douglass*; Jury Award from Neil Simon Awards, 1983, for *For Us the Living*; Father of the Year Award, 1987; Image Award from National Association for the Advancement of Colored People, for best performance by a supporting actor, and Hall of Fame Award for outstanding artistic achievement, both 1989, both for *Do The Right Thing*; Monarch Award, 1990.

WRITINGS:

PLAYS

(And director) *Goldbrickers of 1944*, first produced in Liberia, West Africa, 1944.

Alice in Wonder (one-act), first produced in New York City at Elks Community Theatre, September 15, 1952; revised and expanded version produced as *The Big Deal in New York* at New Playwrights Theatre, March 7, 1953.

Purlie Victorious (first produced on Broadway at Cort Theatre, 1961; also see below), Samuel French (New York City), 1961.

Curtain Call, Mr. Aldridge, Sir (first produced in Santa Barbara at the University of California, summer, 1968), published in *The Black Teacher and the Dramatic Arts: A Dialogue, Bibliography, and Anthology*, edited by William R. Reardon and Thomas D. Pawley, Negro Universities Press, 1970.

(With Philip Rose, Peter Udell, and Gary Geld) *Purlie* (adaptation of *Purlie Victorious*; first produced on Broadway at Broadway Theatre, March 15, 1970), Samuel French, 1971.

Escape to Freedom: A Play about Young Frederick Douglass (first produced in New York City at the Town Hall, March 8, 1976), Viking (New York City), 1978.

Langston: A Play (first produced in New York City in 1982), Delacorte (New York City), 1982.

(With Hy Gilbert, and director) *Bingo* (baseball musical based on novel *The Bingo Long Traveling All-Stars and Motor Kings* by William Brashler), first produced in New York City at AMAS Repertory Theater, November, 1985.

Also author of *Last Dance for Sybil.*

SCREENPLAYS AND TELEPLAYS

Gone Are the Days (adaptation of *Purlie Victorious;* also released as *Purlie Victorious* and *The Man from C.O.T.T.O.N.),* Trans Lux, 1963.

(With Arnold Perl, and director) *Cotton Comes to Harlem* (based on a novel by Chester Himes), United Artists, 1970.

(And director) *Kongi's Harvest* (adapted from work by Wole Soyinka), Calpenny Films Nigeria Ltd., 1970.

Today Is Ours, Columbia Broadcasting System (CBS-TV), 1974.

(With Ladi Ladebo and Al Freeman, Jr.) *Countdown at Kusini* (based on a story by John Storm Roberts), CBS-TV, 1976.

Also writer of television episodes of *East Side/West Side,* 1963, *The Negro People,* 1965, *Just Say the Word,* 1969, *The Eleventh Hour, Bonanza,* and *N.Y.P.D.;* and for special *Alice in Wonder,* 1987.

FICTION

Just Like Martin (young adult novel), Simon & Schuster (New York City), 1992.

OTHER

(With others) *The Black Cinema: Foremost Representatives of the Black Film World Air Their Views* (sound recording), Center for Cassette Studies 30983, 1975.

(With wife Ruby Dee) *Hands upon the Heart* (two-volume videotape), Emmalyn Enterprises, 1994.

(Author of foreword) Langston Hughes, *Black Magic: A Pictorial History of the African-American in the Performing Arts,* Da Capo (New York City), 1990.

(Author of foreword) G. William Jones, *Black Cinema Treasures: Lost and Found,* University of North Texas (Denton), 1991.

(Author of afterword) Malcolm X, *The Autobiography of Malcom X* (with the assistance of Alex Haley; introduction by M. S. Handler; epilogue by Alex Haley), Ballantine (New York City), 1992.

(Author of foreword with Dee) Barbara Brandon, *Where I'm Coming From,* Andrews and McMeel (Kansas City), 1993.

Purlie Victorious: A Commemorative (with commentary by Dee), Emmalyn Enterprises (New Rochelle, NY), 1993.

Also author of "Ain't Now But It's Going to Be" (song), for *Cotton Comes to Harlem,* 1970. Contributor to journals and periodicals, including *Negro History Bulletin, Negro Digest,* and *Freedomways.*

SIDELIGHTS: "Ossie Davis is best known as an actor, but his accomplishments extend well beyond the stage," writes Michael E. Greene in the *Dictionary of Literary Biography.* "In the theater, in motion pictures, and in television he has won praise both for his individual performances and those he has given with his wife, Ruby Dee. He has, however, also been a writer, director, producer, social activist, and community leader." The bond uniting all of Davis's work, according to Jayne F. Mulvaney in the *Dictionary of Literary Biography,* is Davis's commitment to "creating works that would truthfully portray the black man's experience."

Long active in the cause of racial justice, Davis was a prominent figure in the civil rights movement of the 1960s. He gave the eulogies at the funerals of black leaders Malcolm X and Dr. Martin Luther King Jr., and he acted as master of ceremonies at the famous "March on Washington" in 1963—the site of Dr. King's "I Have a Dream" speech. Throughout his life, Davis has used his many talents and experiences to expose wide audiences to his views. As the actor explains to Calvin Reid in *Publishers Weekly:* "I am essentially a storyteller, and the story I want to tell is about black people. Sometimes I sing the story, sometimes I dance it, sometimes I tell tall tales about it, but I always want to share my great satisfaction at being a black man at this time in history."

A native of Cogdell, Georgia, Davis began his career after enrolling at Howard University, where Alain Locke, a drama critic and professor of philosophy, spurred his budding interest in the theater. On Locke's counseling, Davis became involved in several facets of stage life, including maintenance and set construction, while biding time as an actor. He first appeared on the stage as a member of Harlem's Ross McClendon Players in a 1941 production of *Joy*

Exceeding Glory. Few offers followed, however, and Davis was reduced to sleeping in parks and scrounging for food.

In 1942 in the midst of World War II, Davis was inducted into the U.S. Army, where he served as a medical technician in Liberia, West Africa. After his transfer to Special Services, he began writing and producing stage works to entertain military personnel. Upon discharge, though, Davis returned to his native Georgia. There he was reached by McClendon director Richard Campbell, who encouraged Davis to return to New York City and audition for Robert Ardrey's *Jeb.* Davis accepted Campbell's encouragement and eventually secured the title role in Ardrey's work. The play, which concerns a physically debilitated veteran's attempt to succeed as an adding machine operator in racist Louisiana, was poorly received, but Davis was exempted for his compelling performance.

Davis married fellow *Jeb* performer Ruby Dee in 1948 after they completed a stint with the touring company of *Anna Lucasta.* The pace of his acting career then accelerated as Davis received critical praise for his work in *Stevedore,* in which he played a servant who assumes a misplaced worldliness following a visit to Paris, and *The Green Pastures,* in which he portrayed one of several angels in a black-populated Heaven.

While acting, Davis also continued to devote attention to his writing. "As a playwright Davis was committed to creating works that would truthfully portray the black man's experience," says Mulvaney. In 1953, his play *Alice in Wonder,* which focused on McCarthy-era issues of integrity and blacklisting, was dimly received in Harlem; however, his 1961 opus *Purlie Victorious* generated a more favorable response. Mulvaney describes the play as a comedy about the schemes of an eloquent itinerant preacher who returns to his Georgia home with hopes of buying the old barn that once served as a black church, and establishing an integrated one. To realize his plan, he must secure the inheritance of his deceased aunt, a former slave, whose daughter has also died. Because Captain Cotchipee, the play's antagonist and holder of the inheritance, is unaware of the death of Purlie's cousin, Purlie plans to have a pretty young black girl impersonate his cousin so that he can claim the inheritance to finance the church of his dreams. "The action of the play involves the hilarious efforts of Purlie, his family, and the captain's liberal son, Charlie, to outwit the captain," says Mulvaney.

Many critics were especially pleased with Davis's humorous portrayal of the black preacher's efforts to swipe the $500 inheritance from the white plantation owner.

Greene calls *Purlie Victorious* a "Southern fable of right against wrong with Purlie's faith in the cause of equality triumphing over the bigotry of Ol' Cap'n Cotchipee, the local redneck aristocrat." Considering the comedy's brilliance to derive "chiefly from how cliches and stereotypes are blown out of proportion," Mulvaney suggests that *Purlie Victorious* is "satire which proceeds toward reconciliation rather than bitterness. Its invective is not venomous." "Unfortunately, despite the reviews, the endorsement of the National Association for the Advancement of Colored People, and the play's seven-and-a-half month run, neither playwright nor producer made money," notes Mulvaney. "The financial support of the black community was not enough; the white audiences did not come." Greene suggests that the play would have been considerably more successful had it been written either ten years before or after it was. "Davis himself recognized that his handling of stereotypes, black and white, would have been offensive had a white writer created them," Greene observes. He adds that Davis "argues that one of his purposes in the play was to present justice as an ideal, as something that is not always the same as traditional law-and-order, which allows the Ol' Cap'ns of American society to win too often."

Purlie Victorious was adapted by Davis as the motion picture *Gone Are the Days.* A. H. Weiler, writing in the *New York Times,* complains that the film rarely availed itself of cinematic techniques, but adds that the work "is still speaking out against injustice in low, broad, comic fashion." Weiler praises the performances of Davis, who played the preacher Purlie Victorious, and Ruby Dee, the title character's lover.

In 1970 Davis collaborated with Philip Rose and the songwriting team of Peter Udell and Gary Geld on *Purlie,* a musical adaptation of the play. *New York Times* critic Clive Barnes calls the new version "so strong . . . so magnificent" that audiences would respond by shouting "Hallelujah!" in praise. He deems it "by far the most successful and richest of all black musicals" and attributes its prominence to "the depth of the characterization and the salty wit of the dialogue."

For Davis himself, *Purlie* was not just another success—it was an experience in self-discovery. "Purlie told me," he writes, "I would never find my manhood by asking the white man to define it for me. That I would never become a man until I stopped measuring my black self by white standards."

Race relations are at the core of Davis's novel for young adults, *Just Like Martin.* A *Kirkus Reviews* contributor describes the story as "dramatic and simply told, with a cast of strong personalities." Set in 1963, the tale finds Isaac "Stone" and his father, Ike, struggling with their involvement in the civil rights movement. Ike will not let Stone, an all-A student, leave their Alabama home to go with a church youth group to a civil rights march in Washington, DC. Ike's fear that Stone would be harmed is compounded by his wife's recent death. Ike is also opposed to his son's devotion to nonviolence and belittles the boy's admiration of Martin Luther King. Stone, who hopes to become a preacher "just like Martin," eventually organizes a children's march after two friends are killed and another is maimed in a church bombing.

In *Just Like Martin,* the church's Reverend Cable asks Stone and other members in the Creative Nonviolence Workshop for Children if they have the strength to let people strike them and not strike back. Stone believes he can endure a beating without resorting to violence, yet finds himself "fist fighting in the house of the Lord," according to Reverend Cable. Anne Scott in *Washington Post Book World* praises Davis's characters, despite their flaws, as they fight off "injustice . . . not always knowing how to respond to the history in which they find themselves."

Other reviewers of Davis's novel comment on Ike's coming to terms with the values of his son. Watching the youth's efforts, along with the shock of hearing of President Kennedy's assassination, prompt Ike to resolve his inner conflict and lend his support to Stone. Lauding Davis's development of father and son, Lyn Miller-Lachmann notes in *Junior High Up* that the author "realistically portrays the boy's struggle to apply King's values in his personal life, and the ending is hopeful but not happy." *Booklist* contributor Hazel Rochman points out some minor flaws in the story, but deemed that "what is riveting here is the sense of history being made—of struggle and commitment in one community."

In addition to writing his novel, Davis has continued to appear in prominent movies and television programs. In 1989, for example, he co-starred with Burt Reynolds in the TV series *B. L. Stryker.* Though the series was only modestly successful, *New York* magazine reviewer John

Leonard calls Davis's performance as a wise retired boxer "brilliant." In 1990 Davis appeared in another TV series with Reynolds, the acclaimed situation comedy *Evening Shade.* Reynolds played a football coach in a rural town in Arkansas, and Davis played one of the town's interesting residents. According to Harry F. Waters in *Newsweek,* Davis provides the show with "the most high-powered cast ever assembled for a half-hour series."

Davis was also prominently featured in films such as Spike Lee's *School Daze, Do the Right Thing, Jungle Fever,* and *Malcolm X,* and the careers of Dee and Davis have remained intertwined as well. They have performed together in stage productions, films, and recordings; shared duties as hosts/performers on the brief PBS-TV series *With Ossie and Ruby;* and co-founded Emmalyn II Productions. When not on location, they live in New Rochelle, New York. In an article about the couple for *Modern Maturity,* Connie Goldman emphasizes that the two performers "have distinguished themselves not only as creative talents but as social activists with deep-rooted commitments to civil-rights organizations and causes." An *Ebony* magazine correspondent calls their marriage "a living argument against the popular notion that the theater is bound to wreck the homes of those couples who choose it as a profession."

In addition to his career and his status as a role model, Davis has also been a direct source of encouragement and support for other African American artists. He founded the Institute of Cinema Artists in 1973, providing black students with training for careers in television and film. In recognition of his achievements in this area, Mulvaney calls Davis "a force in the development of black culture." Davis explains his commitment to nurturing other artists in the *Dictionary of Literary Biography:* "For if we can, in fact, create for our own people; work for our own people; belong to our own people; we will no longer be forced into artistic prostitution and self-betrayal in the mad scramble, imposed upon us far too long, to belong to some other people . . . . Only then can we begin to take a truly independent position within the confines of American culture, a black position."

BIOGRAPHICAL/CRITICAL SOURCES:

BOOKS

Abramson, Doris E., *Negro Playwrights in the American Theatre, 1925-1959,* Columbia University Press (New York City), 1969.

Davis, Ossie, *Just Like Martin,* Simon and Schuster (New York City), 1992.

Dictionary of Literary Biography, Gale (Detroit), Volume 7: *Twentieth-Century American Dramatists,* 1981, Volume 38: *Afro-American Writers after 1955: Dramatists and Prose Writers,* 1985.

Funke, Lewis, *The Curtain Rises—The Story of Ossie Davis,* Grosset & Dunlap (New York City), 1971.

Patterson, Lindsay, editor, *Anthology of the American Negro in the Theatre,* Association for the Study of Life and History/Publishers Company, 1967.

PERIODICALS

Booklist, September 1, 1992.
Detroit Free Press, November 11, 1983.
Ebony, February, 1961; December, 1979.
Essence, December, 1994, p. 76.
Freedomways, spring, 1962; summer, 1965; summer, 1968.
Junior High Up, October, 1992.
Kirkus Reviews, September 15, 1992, p. 1185.
Modern Maturity, July-August, 1994, p. 64.
Nation, April 6, 1970; July 24-31, 1989, pp. 144-48.
National Observer, March 22, 1970.
Negro Digest, February, 1966; April, 1966.
Negro History Bulletin, April, 1967.
Newsweek, March 30, 1970; December 17, 1990, p. 64.
New York, April, 1970; February 13, 1989, p. 71.
New Yorker, October 7, 1961; July 24, 1989, p. 78; March 26, 1990, p. 79.
New York Times, September 24, 1963; May 5, 1968; October 12, 1969; March 10, 1970; November 11, 1985.
People, February 13, 1989, p. 13; September 24, 1990, p. 7; August 1, 1994, p. 16.
Publishers Weekly, December 28, 1992, p. 27.
Variety, March 5, 1969; January 28, 1970; March 28, 1970.
Voice of Youth Advocates, April, 1993, p. 24.
Washington Post Book World, December 6, 1992, p. 20.

*   *   *

DAVIS, William S(terling)   1943-

PERSONAL: Born April 18, 1943, in Pittston, PA; son of Sterling Q. (a postal supervisor) and Alice (an accountant; maiden name, Phethean) Davis; married Catherine A. Curcio, July 2, 1966; children: William, Theresa, Carla. *Education:* Lafayette College, B.S., 1965; State University of New York at Binghamton, M.A., 1968. *Politics:* Independent.

ADDRESSES: Home—4172 Via Mirada, Sarasota, FL 34238. *Office*—Department of Decision Sciences and Management Information Systems, Miami University, Oxford, OH 45056.

CAREER: International Business Machines Corp. (IBM), Vestal, NY, industrial engineer, 1965-67, Endicott, NY, systems analyst and programmer, 1968-71; Lafayette College, Easton, PA, instructor in industrial engineering, 1967-68; Miami University, Hamilton, OH, assistant professor of systems analysis, 1971-77, Oxford, OH, associate professor, 1977-81, professor of systems analysis, 1981-91, professor of Decision Sciences and Management Information Systems, 1991—. U.S. Navy Postgraduate School, Department of Administrative Science, Monterey, CA, adjunct professor, 1987. Business consultant 1971—.

MEMBER: Science Fiction Writers of America, Textbook and Academic Authors Association, Sarasota Fiction Writers.

WRITINGS:

Operating Systems: A Systematic View, Addison-Wesley (Reading, MA), 1977, 4th edition, Benjamin Cummings Publishing Co, Inc. 1992.
Information Processing Systems, Addison-Wesley, 1978, 2nd edition, 1981.
Business Data Processing, Addison-Wesley, 1978.
(With Richard H. Fisher) *COBOL: An Introduction to Structured Logic and Modular Program Design,* Addison-Wesley, 1979.
(With S. Allison McCormack) *The Information Age,* Addison-Wesley, 1979.
FORTRAN 77: Getting Started, Addison-Wesley, 1981.
BASIC: Getting Started, Addison-Wesley, 1981.
Computers and Business Information Processing, Addison-Wesley, 1981, 2nd edition, 1983.
Systems Analysis and Design: A Structured Approach, Addison-Wesley, 1983.
Tools and Techniques for Structured Systems Analysis and Design, Addison-Wesley, 1983.
The NECEN Voyage (fiction), Addison-Wesley, 1985.
True BASIC Primer, Addison-Wesley, 1986.

Fundamental Computer Concepts, Addison-Wesley, 1986, 2nd edition published as *Computing Fundamentals: Concepts,* 1989, 3rd edition, 1991.

PC BASIC: Getting Started, Addison-Wesley, 1988.

(With Paul Schreiner) *Computing Fundamentals: dBASE III Plus,* Addison-Wesley, 1989.

(With Schreiner) *Computing Fundamentals: dBASE IV,* Addison-Wesley, 1989.

(Editor and coauthor with others) *Computing Fundamentals: Productivity Tools,* Addison-Wesley, 1989.

Computing Fundamentals: WordPerfect, Addison-Wesley, 1989.

Computing Fundamentals: WordPerfect 5.0/5.1, Addison-Wesley, 1990.

(With D. Byrkett, Schreiner, and C. Wood) *Mastering Microcomputers,* Benjamin Cummings Publishing Co., Inc., 1993.

Business Systems Analysis and Design, Wadsworth Publishing Co. (Belmont, CA), 1994.

Management, Information, and Systems, West Publishing Co. (Minneapolis, MN), 1995.

Series editor, *Computing Fundamentals* series, Benjamin Cummings Publishing Co., Inc., 1988-93. Also contributor of fiction to *Analog Science Fiction Science Fact.*

Davis's books have been translated into Arabic, Chinese, Dutch, French, Greek, Indonesian, Japanese, Russian, and Spanish.

WORK IN PROGRESS: Fear Itself (novel); *Computers and Information Systems;* a new edition of *Business Systems Analysis and Design.*

SIDELIGHTS: William S. Davis told *CA:* "In 1957, the Russians launched the first artificial satellite, and science and mathematics moved to the fore throughout the United States. Consequently, when I entered college, there was little question that I would be an engineer. I really wanted to write, though. After several years with IBM, Miami University offered me an academic position. One of my first assignments was to teach operating systems; finding no acceptable text, I decided to write my own. The result, *Operating Systems: A Systematic View,* has since been translated into Russian, Spanish, and Bahasa-Indonesian.

"My writing is influenced by a number of factors. First, perhaps, is my engineering training; I worry about technical accuracy and precision, and tend to present concepts in an applied (rather than theoreti-

cal) context. Second, I am a self-taught computer person (academic computer training was not common in the sixties), and my writing tends to document my own learning experiences. Finally, I believe that technical literature should read like a novel, with a careful development of the 'story line' from beginning to end; the fact that a work is technical is no excuse for bad writing.

"I normally start a project by preparing a chapter outline, first at a very high level, and then in detail. I write one chapter at a time, using a word processor. A first draft is prepared in a day or two of intense, almost uninterrupted activity, after which I settle into a more regular work pattern to revise and polish the prose. This is where the word processor helps; I've found that I can complete five or six revisions in the time it used to take to finish two. At key points, for example at the end of a section, I print the material and go through another revision cycle, this time stressing consistency and continuity; similar revisions are made when the entire book is finished. The final steps involve preparing chapter exercises and an instructor's guide. Anyone who claims that writing is easy has never tried it—it's hard work. Still, I can't think of anything I would rather do."

*   *   *

DENNETT, Daniel C(lement)   1942-

PERSONAL: Born March 28, 1942, in Boston, MA; son of Daniel Clement Jr. (a historian and diplomat) and Ruth Marjorie (an editor and teacher; maiden name, Leck) Dennett; married Susan Elizabeth Bell, June 8, 1962; children: Andrea Elizabeth, Peter Nathaniel. *Education:* Harvard University, B.A. (cum laude), 1963; Oxford University, D.Phil., 1965. *Politics:* Democrat. *Avocational interests:* Sculpture, farming, sailing, scuba diving.

ADDRESSES: Home—68 Central St., Andover, MA 01810. *Office*—Center for Cognitive Studies, Tufts University, Medford, MA 02155.

CAREER: Oxford College of Technology, Oxford, England, lecturer in philosophy, 1964-65; University of California, Irvine, assistant professor, 1965-70, associate professor of philosophy, 1970-71; Tufts University, Medford, MA, visiting assistant professor, 1968, associate professor, 1971-75, professor of philosophy, 1975-85, Distinguished Arts and Sciences Professor, 1985—, head of philosophy department, 1976-82, director of Center for Cognitive Studies, 1985—, co-director, curricular software studio, 1985-89. Visiting professor or fellow at universities, including Harvard University, autumn, 1973, All Souls College, Oxford, 1979, and Center for Advanced Research in the Behavioral Sciences, 1979-80; lecturer at universities in the United States, Europe, and Australia.

MEMBER: American Academy of Arts and Sciences, American Association of University Professors, American Philosophical Association, Society for Philosophy and Psychology, Cognitive Science Society, Council for Philosophical Studies, Kollegewidgwok Yacht Club.

AWARDS, HONORS: Fellowships from National Endowment for the Humanities, 1974, and 1979, Fulbright Foundation, 1978, Center for Advanced Study in the Behavioral Sciences, 1979-80, and Guggenheim Foundation, 1986-87.

WRITINGS:

Content and Consciousness, Humanities Press (Atlantic Highlands, NJ), 1969, 2nd edition, Routledge & Kegan Paul (Boston), 1986.
Brainstorms: Philosophical Essays on Mind and Psychology, Bradford Books, 1978.
(Editor with Douglas R. Hofstadter) *The Mind's I: Fantasies and Reflections on Self and Soul,* Basic Books (New York City), 1981.
Elbow Room: The Varieties of Free Will Worth Wanting, MIT Press (Cambridge, MA), 1984.
The Intentional Stance, MIT Press, 1987.
Consciousness Explained, Little, Brown (Boston), 1991.
Darwin's Dangerous Idea: Evolution and the Meanings of Life, Simon & Schuster (New York City), 1995.

Contributor to philosophy journals. Associate editor, *Behavioral and Brain Sciences;* consulting editor, *Journal for the Theory of Social Behavior;* member of editorial board, *Cognitive Science.*

WORK IN PROGRESS: Research on theories of the mind, the foundations of artificial intelligence, and consciousness.

SIDELIGHTS: "When Daniel C. Dennett published *Content and Consciousness* in 1969," David

Papineau relates in a 1988 *Times Literary Supplement* article, "most professional philosophers felt that a book containing so much about brain mechanisms could not really be a work of philosophy." Since that time, however, "the mind-brain relation has become a central philosophical issue," the critic explains. Dennett has investigated issues of mind and consciousness through several books, including *The Mind's I: Fantasies and Reflections on Self and Soul,* which he edited with Douglas R. Hofstadter. Concerned with "the nuclear center of consciousness," as *New York Times Book Review* contributor William Barrett describes it, *The Mind's I* assembles "a very wide-ranging collection of pieces that come at the matter from quite different points of view. . . . The tone of the pieces is exploratory, questioning and on the whole undogmatic."

Dennett's own work uses a similarly open-minded approach; in *The Intentional Stance,* for example, "his writing is peppered with references to artificial intelligence, computer science, ethology and evolutionary biology," Papineau states. In addition, Dennett's engaging style leads critics to praise his writing even though they may dispute his theories. Galen Strawson observes in a *Times Literary Supplement* review of *Elbow Room: The Varieties of Free Will Worth Wanting* that "Dennett's fluent, informed, inventive and often elegant defence . . . makes as good a case as can be made for [his] view." The author "has a gift for vivid and memorable examples," the critic continues, and *Elbow Room* is "stimulating and effective." As Papineau concludes, through his "interesting and influential" work Dennett "has succeeded in persuading both philosophers and the practitioners of such allied sciences that they have much to learn from each other."

In *Consciousness Explained,* Dennett wrestles with questions about the link between mind and body. Applying a philosophy referred to as "materialism," Dennett holds that human experience and memory have a primarily physical basis, rejecting the idea that some sort of conduit—for instance, as seventeenth-century French philosopher Rene Descartes would have it, the pineal gland—transforms the physical into the mental. Galen Strawson's review in the *Times Literary Supplement* praises *Consciousness Explained* for the "lucidity and ingenuity with which it marshals and speculates about a great array of wonderful facts drawn mostly from neurophysiology and experimental psychology." Dennis O'Brien writes in *Commonweal* that the book "is a sprightly, intelligent, fascinating attack on a philosophical hardy perennial." In the end, however, O'Brien does not believe that Dennett fulfills the title's promise. "It is difficult to know if [consciousness] has been explained if one is not sure what [consciousness] is," the reviewer comments.

Dennett constructs another complex argument in *Darwin's Dangerous Idea: Evolution and the Meanings of Life,* this time taking aim at the revisionists who, he believes, indefensibly tamper with pure Darwinian theory of how the world and its inhabitants evolved. Darwinism's reach into every aspect of life is the "dangerous idea" of the title; Dennett calls it a "universal acid" that cuts through every traditional assumption. Dennett maintains that even developments that do not appear to fit into Darwin's concept of natural selection actually are outgrowths of this process, although he rejects the argument made by some Darwinians that human moral behavior has a purely genetic basis. Dennett's endorsement of Darwin's theory "does not deny the complexity of human culture, but seeks to comprehend how this complexity grew out of something far simpler," comments David Papineau in the *New York Times Book Review.* In the *Los Angeles Times Book Review,* Roger Lewin terms Dennett's effort "a bold work," of great interest whether or not one accepts the author's views, but providing perhaps an excess of information. Jim Holt, writing for the *Wall Street Journal,* notes that, "Mr. Dennett is a philosopher of rare originality, rigor and wit. Here he does one of the things philosophers are supposed to be good at: clearing up conceptual muddles in the sciences."

BIOGRAPHICAL/CRITICAL SOURCES:

BOOKS

Dahlbom, Bo, editor, *Dennett and His Critics: Demystifying Mind,* Blackwell (Oxford), 1993.

PERIODICALS

Commonweal, April 24, 1992, pp. 27-28.
London Review of Books, September 1, 1988, pp. 17-18.
Los Angeles Times Book Review, May 14, 1995, pp. 3, 7.
New Statesman and Society, March 20, 1992, p. 47.
New York Times Book Review, December 13, 1981; May 14, 1995, pp. 13-14.
Times Literary Supplement, February 12, 1970; April 19, 1985; August 19-25, 1988, p. 911; August 21, 1992, p. 5.

Voice Literary Supplement, October, 1981; October, 1984.
Wall Street Journal, August 4, 1995, p. A6.
Washington Post Book World, December 20, 1981.*

*   *   *

DENVER, Walt
  See SHERMAN, Jory (Tecumseh)

*   *   *

DESAI, Anita   1937-

PERSONAL: Born June 24, 1937, in Mussoorie, India; daughter of D. N. (a businessperson) and Toni (Nime) Mazumdar; married Ashvin Desai (an executive), December 13, 1958; children: Rahul, Tani, Arjun, Kiran. *Education:* Delhi University, B.A. (with honors), 1957.

ADDRESSES: Office—c/o Deborah Rogers Ltd., 20 Powis Mews, London W11 1JN, England; Department of English, Mount Holyoke College, South Hadley, MA 01075.

CAREER: Writer. Member of Advisory Board for English, Sahitya Akademi, New Delhi, India, 1972—. Smith College, Elizabeth Drew Professor, 1987-88; Mount Holyoke College, Purington Professor of English, 1988—.

MEMBER: Royal Society of Literature (fellow).

AWARDS, HONORS: Winifred Holtby Prize, Royal Society of Literature, 1978, for *Fire on the Mountain;* Sahitya Academy award, 1979; *Guardian* Prize for Children's Fiction, 1983, for *The Village by the Sea;* Girton College, University of Cambridge, Helen Cam Visiting fellow, 1986-87, honorary fellow, 1988; Clare Hall, University of Cambridge, Ashby fellow, 1989, honorary fellow, 1991; *Hadassah* Prize, *Hadassah* (magazine), 1989, for *Baumgartner's Bombay;* Padma Sri, 1990; Literary Lion Award, New York Public Library, 1993.

WRITINGS:

NOVELS

Cry, the Peacock, P. Owen (London), 1963.
Voices in the City, P. Owen, 1965.

Bye-Bye, Blackbird, Hind Pocket Books, 1968.
Where Shall We Go This Summer?, Vikas Publishing House (India), 1975.
Fire on the Mountain, Harper (New York City), 1977.
Clear Light of Day, Harper, 1980.
In Custody, Heinemann (London), 1984, Harper, 1985.
Baumgartner's Bombay, Knopf (New York City), 1989.
Journey to Ithaca, Knopf, 1995.

JUVENILE

The Peacock Garden, India Book House, 1974.
Cat on a Houseboat, Orient Longmans (India), 1976.
The Village by the Sea, Heinemann, 1982.

OTHER

Games at Twilight and Other Stories, Heinemann, 1978, Harper, 1980.
(Author of introduction) Lady Mary Wortley Montagu, *Turkish Embassy Letters,* edited by Malcolm Jack, University of Georgia Press (Athens), 1993.

Contributor of short stories to periodicals, including *Thought, Envoy, Writers Workshop, Quest, Indian Literature, Illustrated Weekly of India, Fesmina,* and *Harper's Bazaar.*

WORK IN PROGRESS: An untitled novel.

ADAPTATIONS: The Village by the Sea was filmed in 1992, and *In Custody* was filmed in 1993.

SIDELIGHTS: Indian writer Anita Desai focuses her novels upon the personal struggles of her Indian characters to cope with the problems of contemporary life. In this way, she manages to portray the cultural and social changes that her native country has undergone since the departure of the British. One of Desai's major themes is the relationships between family members, and especially the emotional tribulations of women whose independence is suppressed by Indian society. Her first novel, *Cry, the Peacock,* concerns a woman who finds it impossible to assert her individuality; the theme of the despairing woman is also explored in Desai's *Where Shall We Go This Summer?* Other novels explore life in urban India (*Voices in the City*), the clash between eastern and western cultures (*Bye-Bye, Blackbird*), and the differences between the generations (*Fire on the Mountain*).

Exile—physical as well as psychological—is also a prominent theme. In *Baumgartner's Bombay,* Desai (who is half-Indian and half-German) details the life of Hugo Baumgartner, a German Jew who flees Nazi Germany for India, where he "gradually drifts down through Indian society to settle, like sediment, somewhere near the bottom," writes Rosemary Dinnage in the *New York Review of Books.* She adds: "Baumgartner is a more thoroughly displaced person than Anglicized Indians, and more solitary, for Desai's Indian characters are still tied to family and community, however irksomely. She has drawn on her dual nationality to write on a subject new, I think, to English fiction—the experience of Jewish refugees in India." Pearl K. Bell makes a similar statement. "Baumgartner is the loneliest, saddest, most severely dislocated of Desai's fictional creatures," she notes in the *New Republic.* "But [he] is also a representative man, the German Jew to whom things happen, powerless to resist the evil wind that swept him like a vagrant weed from Berlin to India." Jean Sudrann of the *Yale Review* praises Desai's narrative skill "in making us feel the cumulative force of Hugo's alienation."

The author's descriptive powers are acclaimed by several critics. In the *New Leader* Betty Falkenberg calls *Baumgartner's Bombay* "a mathematical problem set and solved in exquisite prose." Bell observes that "there is a Dickensian rush and tumble to her portrayals of the bazaars, the crowded streets, the packed houses of an Indian metropolis." In general, Desai's "novels are quite short, but they convey a sharply detailed sense of the tangled complexities of Indian society, and an intimate view of the tug and pull of Indian family life."

While noting Desai's mixed German-Indian ancestry, *Spectator* contributor Caroline Moore nonetheless commends the author for the authentic Indian flavor of her works. "Westerners visiting India find themselves reeling under the outsider's sense of 'culture shock,' which is compounded more of shock than culture," the critic writes. "To Anita Desai, of course, the culture is second nature. Yet that intimacy never becomes mere familiarity: her achievement is to keep the shock of genuine freshness, the eyes of the perpetual outsider." This particular engagement with India is evident in many of Desai's novels, as A. G. Mojtabai notes in the *New York Times Book Review.* "Anita Desai is a writer of Bengali-German descent, who stands in a complicated but advantageous relation to India," says the reviewer. "Insiders rarely notice this much; outsiders cannot have this ease of reference." Mojtabai finds that Desai is able to delineate characters, settings, and feelings intricately yet economically, without extraneous detail or excessively populated scenes: "This author has no need of crowds. Properly observed, a roomful of people is crowd enough, and in the right hands—as Anita Desai so amply illustrates—*world* enough."

The complexities of outsiders facing Indian culture form the basis of Desai's 1995 novel, *Journey to Ithaca.* The story revolves around a hippie-era European couple who travel to India for quite different reasons—the husband to find enlightenment, the wife to enjoy a foreign experience. As the husband, Matteo, becomes involved with a spiritual guru known as the Mother, his wife, Sophie, goes on a quest of her own—to find the guru's roots in an effort either to debunk or to understand her. Calling the work "a kind of love triangle set against the madness of extreme spiritual searching," *New York Times* reviewer Richard Bernstein adds of *Journey to Ithaca:* "Ms. Desai writes with intelligence and power. She has a remarkable eye for substance, the things that give life its texture. Nothing escapes her power of observation, not the thickness of the drapes that blot out the light in a bourgeois Parisian home, or the enamel bowl in the office of an Indian doctor." Caroline Moore, in the *Spectator,* commends the book as "superbly powerful . . . emotionally and intellectually haunting, teasing and tugging our minds even through its imperfections." Among these imperfections, Moore says, is the fact that the main characters are drawn rather sketchily.

Gabriele Annan, reviewing for the *Times Literary Supplement,* finds other flaws in *Journey to Ithaca.* "This is a curiously inept book for a novelist of Desai's experience," Annan writes. "The narrative is full of gaps and improbabilities, as well as cliches . . . the dialogue is stagey and unconvincing." The *Wall Street Journal*'s Brooke Allen, while admiring Desai's writing style, also finds much of the story unbelievable. Spiritually inclined readers may find the action plausible, but "others will remain incredulous," Allen asserts.

Desai is frequently praised by critics for her ability to capture the local color of her country and the ways in which eastern and western cultures have blended together there and for developing this skill further with each successive novel. A large part of this skill is due to her use of imagery, one of the most important devices in Desai's novels. Because of this emphasis on imagery, Desai is referred to by such reviewers as *World Literature Today* contributor Madhusudan Prasad as an "imagist-novelist. . . . [Her use of imagery is] a remarkable quality of her craft that she has carefully maintained in all her later fiction" since *Cry, the Peacock.* Employing this imagery to suggest rather than overtly explain her themes, Desai's stories sometimes appear deceptively simple; but, as Anthony Thwaite points out in the *New Republic,* "she is such a consummate artist that she [is able to suggest], beyond the confines of the plot and the machinations of her characters, the immensities that lie beyond them—the immensities of India." In the *Observer,* Salman Rushdie describes Desai's books as being "illuminated by the author's perceptiveness, delicacy of language and sharp wit."

BIOGRAPHICAL/CRITICAL SOURCES:

BOOKS

Afzal-Khan, Fawzia, *Cultural Imperialism and the Indo-English Novel: Genre and Ideology in R. K. Narayan, Anita Desai, Kamala Markandaya, and Salman Rushdie,* Pennsylvania State University Press (University Park), 1993.

Bellioppa, Meena, *The Fiction of Anita Desai,* Writers Workshop, 1971.

Choudhury, Bidulata, *Women and Society in the novels of Anita Desai,* Creative Books (New Delhi), 1995.

Contemporary Literary Criticism, Gale (Detroit), Volume 19, 1981, Volume 37, 1986.

Khanna, Shashi, *Human Relationships in Anita Desai's Novels,* Sarup & Sons (New Delhi), 1995.

Mukheijee, Meenakshi, *The Twice-Born Fiction,* Heinemann, 1972.

Parker, Michael and Roger Starkey, editors, *Postcolonial Literature: Achebe, Ngugi, Desai, Walcott,* St. Martin's (New York City), 1995.

Pathania, Usha, *Human Bonds and Bondages: The Fiction of Anita Desai and Kamala Markandaya,* Kanishka Publishers (New Delhi), 1992.

Sharma, Kajali, *Symbolism in Anita Desai's Novels,* Abhinav Publications (New Delhi), 1991.

Singh, Sunaina, *The Novels of Margaret Atwood and Anita Desai: A Comparative study in Feminist Perspectives,* Creative Books, 1994.

Sivanna, Indira, *Anita Desai as an Artist: A Study in Image and Symbol,* Creative Books, 1994.

Solanki, Mrinalini, *Anita Desai's Fiction: Patterns of Survival Strategies,* Kanishka Publishers, 1992.

Srinivasa Iyengar, K. R., *Indian Writing in English,* Asia Publishing House, 1962.

Verghese, Paul, *Indian Writing in English,* Asia Publishing House, 1970.

PERIODICALS

Belles Lettres, summer, 1989, p. 4.
Boston Globe, August 15, 1995, p. 26.
Chicago Tribune, September 1, 1985.
Chicago Tribune Book World, August 23, 1981.
Globe and Mail (Toronto), August 20, 1988.
Los Angeles Times, July 31, 1980.
Los Angeles Times Book Review, March 3, 1985; April 9, 1989.
New Leader, May 1, 1989.
New Republic, March 18, 1985; April 3, 1989; April 6, 1992, p. 36; August 15, 1994, p. 43.
New York Review of Books, June 1, 1989; December 6, 1990, p. 53; January 16, 1992, p. 42; March 3, 1994, p. 41.
New York Times, November 24, 1980; February 22, 1985; March 14, 1989; August 30, 1995, p. B2.
New York Times Book Review, November 20, 1977; June 22, 1980; November 23, 1980; March 3, 1985, p. 7; April 9, 1989, p. 3; January 27, 1991, p. 23; September 17, 1995, p. 12.
Observer, (London) October 7, 1984, p. 22.
Spectator, June 3, 1995, pp. 41-42.
Time, July 1, 1985.
Times (London), September 4, 1980.
Times Literary Supplement, September 5, 1980; September 7, 1984; October 19, 1984; July 15-21, 1988, p. 787; June 2, 1995, p. 501.
Tribune Books (Chicago), March 5, 1989.
Wall Street Journal, August 24, 1995, p. A14.
Washington Post Book World, January 11, 1981, p. 3; October 7, 1984; March 31, 1985; February 26, 1989.
World Literature Today, summer, 1984, pp. 363-69.
Yale Review, Volume 79, spring, 1990, p. 414.

*   *   *

DEWDNEY, Christopher   1951-

PERSONAL: Born May 9, 1951, in London, Ontario, Canada; son of Selwyn (an ethnoarchaeologist) and Irene (an art therapist; maiden name, Donner) Dewdney; married Suzanne Dennison (marriage ended); married Lise Downe (an artist); children: Calla Xanthoria Kirk, Tristan Alexander Downe. *Education:* Attended art school and collegiate schools in London, Ontario.

ADDRESSES: Office—Winters College, York University, Downsview, Ontario, Canada M3J 1P3.

CAREER: Writer and artist, with solo and group exhibitions of sculpture and collages. Teacher of creative writing, 1984—; associate fellow of Winters College, York University; fellow, The McLuhan Program for Culture Technology, 1993.

AWARDS, HONORS: Award of Excellence from *Design Canada,* 1974, for *A Paleozoic Geology of London, Ontario: Poems and Collages;* finalist for Canadian Governor General's Award for poetry, 1984, 1987, 1989; first prize for poetry from Canadian Broadcasting Corp. (CBC) literary competition, 1986; writer in residence, University of Western Ontario, 1991.

WRITINGS:

POETRY, EXCEPT AS NOTED

Golders Green, privately printed, 1971, Coach House Press (Toronto), 1972.
A Paleozoic Geology of London, Ontario: Poems and Collages, Coach House Press, 1973, revised edition, 1974.
Fovea Centralis, Coach House Press, 1975.
Spring Trances in the Control Emerald Night, Figures, 1978.
Alter Sublime, Coach House Press, 1980.
The Cenozoic Asylum, Delires, 1983.
Predators of the Adoration: Selected Poems, 1972-1982, McClelland & Stewart (Toronto), 1983.
The Immaculate Perception (theoretical prose), self-illustrated, House of Anansi, 1986.
The Radiant Inventory, McClelland & Stewart, 1988.
The Secular Grail, Somerville House (Toronto), 1993.
Demon Pond, McClelland & Stewart, 1994.

Work represented in anthologies, including *The Contemporary Canadian Poem Anthology, From the Other Side of the Century: A New American Poetry, The New Oxford Book of Canadian Verse, The New Canadian Poets,* and *The Poets of Canada.* Contributor to periodicals in numerous countries, including *Capilano Review, Descant, Globe and Mail, Grand Street, Greenfield Review, Die Horen, Grosseteste Review,* and *Verse.*

WORK IN PROGRESS: A Natural History of South-western Ontario.

BIOGRAPHICAL/CRITICAL SOURCES:

BOOKS

Dictionary of Literary Biography, Volume 60: *Canadian Writers since 1960, Second Series,* Gale (Detroit), 1987.

PERIODICALS

Books in Canada, February, 1984.
Globe and Mail (Toronto), January 31, 1987.

* * *

DEXTER, (Norman) Colin 1930-
   (N. C. Dexter)

PERSONAL: Born September 29, 1930, in Stamford, Lincolnshire, England; son of Alfred (a taxi driver) and Dorothy (Towns) Dexter; married Dorothy Cooper (a physiotherapist), March 31, 1956; children: Sally, Jeremy. *Education:* Christ's College, Cambridge, B.A., 1953, M.A., 1958. *Politics:* Socialist ("lapsed"). *Religion:* Methodist ("lapsed").

ADDRESSES: Home—456 Banbury Rd., Oxford OX2 7RG, England.

CAREER: Wyggeston School, Leicester, England, assistant classics master, 1954-57; Loughborough Grammar School, Loughborough, England, sixth form classics master, 1957-59; Corby Grammar School, Corby, England, senior classics master, 1959-66; Oxford Local Examination Board, Oxford, England, assistant secretary, 1966-76, senior assistant secretary, 1976-87. *Military service:* Royal Corps of Signals, 1949-50.

MEMBER: Crime Writers Association, Detection Club.

AWARDS, HONORS: M.A., Oxford University, 1966; Silver Dagger Award, Crime Writers Association, 1979, for *Service of All the Dead,* and 1981, for *The Dead of Jericho;* Gold Dagger Award, Crime Writers Association, 1989, for *The Wench Is Dead,* and 1992, for *The Way through the Woods;* M.A., Leicester University, 1996; Medal of Merit, Lotus Club, 1996.

WRITINGS:

AS N. C. DEXTER

(With E. G. Rayner) *Liberal Studies: An Outline Course,* 2 volumes, Macmillan (New York City), 1964, revised edition, 1966.
(With Rayner) *Guide to Contemporary Politics,* Pergamon (London), 1966.

"INSPECTOR MORSE" MYSTERIES

Last Bus to Woodstock, St. Martin's (New York City), 1975.
Last Seen Wearing (also see below), St. Martin's, 1976.
The Silent World of Nicholas Quinn, St. Martin's, 1977.
Service of All the Dead, Macmillan (London), 1979, St. Martin's, 1980.
The Dead of Jericho, St. Martin's, 1981.
The Riddle of the Third Mile (also see below), Macmillan, 1983.
The Secret of Annexe 3 (also see below), Macmillan, 1986, St. Martin's, 1987.
The Wench Is Dead, Macmillan, 1989, St. Martin's, 1990.
The Jewel That Was Ours, Macmillan, 1991.
The Second Inspector Morse Omnibus (contains *The Secret of Annexe 3, The Riddle of the Third Mile,* and *Last Seen Wearing*) Macmillan, 1991.
The Way through the Woods, Macmillan, 1992.
Morse's Greatest Mystery (contains "As Good As Gold, Morse's Greatest Mystery, Evans Tries An O-Level, Dead as a Dodo, At the Lulu-Bar Motel, Neighbourhood Watch, A Case of Mis-Identity, The Inside Story, Monty's Revolver, The Carpet-Bagger," and "Last Call"), Macmillan, 1993.
The Daughters of Cain, Macmillan, 1994.
Death Is Now My Neighbour, Macmillan, 1996.

OTHER

Work represented in several anthologies, including *Murder Ink,* edited by Dilys Winn, Workman, 1977; *Winter's Crimes 9,* edited by George Hardinge, St. Martin's, 1978; *Winter's Crimes 13,* edited by Hardinge, St. Martin's, 1982; *Winter's Crimes 21,* edited by Hilary Hale, Macmillan, 1989.

ADAPTATIONS: Stories based on Dexter's Inspector Morse character have been adapted for television and shown in the United States on the PBS program

Mystery! Inspector Morse: Driven to Distraction by Anthony Minghella is a screenplay based on characters created by Dexter and was published by Unviersity of Cambridge (NY), 1994. Several of his novels have also been recorded and released as audio books.

SIDELIGHTS: "To most readers of Colin Dexter's books," writes *Dictionary of Literary Biography* contributor Bernard Benstock, "his major accomplishment is the creation of his particular detective hero, Detective Chief Inspector Morse of the Thames Valley Constabulary of Kidlington, Oxon." Inspector Morse is an irascible figure, fond of beer and tobacco, but nonetheless held in awe by his associate Detective Sergeant Lewis. "At times," Benstock reveals, "his seediness is similar to the seediness of a Graham Greene character, his bluster and swagger similar to John Mortimer's Rumpole of the Bailey, but always there is an element of the pathetic to counterbalance the braggadocio. Morse's vulnerable and remarkable character unfolds serially from book to book, so that eventually there are no mysteries about him—except for his given name."

Dexter introduced Inspector Morse in 1975 in *Last Bus to Woodstock,* which established many of the central characteristics of Dexter's work. "*Last Bus to Woodstock* concerns the brutal murder (and possible sex-murder) of a scantily clad female hitchhiker, whose companion at the bus stop fails to identify herself," writes Benstock. "Several young women are likely possibilities for the companion, but Morse is frustrated by their refusal to be honest with him." Morse finds himself sidetracked after having identified the wrong person as the murderer. "The grisly deaths of a husband and wife, each of whom had confessed to the murder," Benstock continues, "bring matters to a head, and Morse apprehends the woman murderer—an attractive young woman he had admired, who confesses that she has fallen in love with him—as she is taken away to stand trial." Dexter treats each of the Morse mysteries as a puzzle, complete with misleading clues, red herrings, and false trails. "Once you chose the wrong word," explains a *Virginia Quarterly Review* contributor, "the whole puzzle can be filled incorrectly."

Morse's irritability is complimented by his companion in mystery-solving, Detective Sergeant Lewis. Cushing Strout, writing in *Armchair Detective,* compares the relationship between Lewis and Morse to that of Arthur Conan Doyle's Sherlock Holmes and John Watson, calling Dexter's work "the best con-

temporary English example of adapting and updating Doyle's technique." Like Holmes, Strout continues, "Morse is a bachelor," but, "in spite of his generally cynical expectations about human nature and the world, unlike Holmes he is always romantically vulnerable (in spite of disappointing experience) to being smitten by love at first sight for some attractive and intelligent, but quite inappropriate woman." In contrast to Morse, Strout continues, Sergeant Lewis "is working class, a family man, and a competent policeman in a routine way. He has a refreshing common sense that Morse often sorely lacks, and the two men (like Holmes and Watson in this respect) know how to tease each other."

Dexter, Strout explains, "has collated his novels under the heading of 'what may be termed (though it sounds a bit posh) the exploitation of reader-mystification.'" This is a traditional attribute of English detective fiction: the ability to mislead the reader in identifying the culprit. The classic mystery novel, as set forth by one of the earliest practitioners of the genre, G. K. Chesterton, should present the reader with all the clues available to the detective, but in such a way that the reader fails to make the connection with the criminal until after the detective uncovers the guilty party. "Inferior writers," Strout continues, "tend to cast suspicion on so many characters that it is . . . like hiding one card amid the rest of the deck, rather than performing the much more difficult classic trick, wherein the 'money card' is one of only three cards." "Dexter," the critic concludes, "keeps shifting the pieces, like a conjuror misdirecting the audience by giving a specious explanation of his trick, until they finally make a coherent and credible picture with the lagniappe of a last surprise." In a review of *The Daughters of Cain* for the *New York Times Book Review,* Marilyn Stasio advises readers "to get out their pencils, timetables and aspirin."

As the series progresses, Dexter also begins to play highly literate games with his readers, ranging from apparently gratis references to literature, such as James Joyce's *Ulysses* in *The Riddle of the Third Mile* and Sophocles' Oedipus trilogy of plays in *The Dead of Jericho.* He also uses inscriptions and epigraphs at the beginning of each chapter like a chorus in a Greek play to comment on the story's action and the state of Morse's mind. "The basic norm in the Dexter novels," Benstock declares, "is best characterized by the epigraph to chapter 14 of *The Riddle of the Third Mile:* 'Preliminary investigations are now in full swing, and Morse appears unconcerned about the contradictory evidence that emerges.'"

Morse demonstrates his best points in the Gold Dagger award-winning novel *The Wench Is Dead.* Critics have compared the book to Josephine Tey's classic detective novel *The Daughter of Time,* in which her detective Alan Grant, immobilized in hospital with a fractured spine, tries to solve an historical mystery—the disappearance of young Edward V and his brother Richard of York in the Tower of London during the reign of Richard III. Like Grant, Morse is hospitalized, with a bleeding ulcer, and to ease his boredom he reopens a Victorian murder case that took place in Oxford: the death by drowning of a female passenger on a canal boat in the mid-nineteenth century. Morse's wits and temper, writes Stasio in the *New York Times Book Review,* "tug the reader into the detective's hospital bed to share his single-minded pursuit of the truth."

Dexter's "Inspector Morse" novels have established him as a pivotal figure in modern English detective fiction. Throughout the series, Benstock states, "the comic vies with the grotesque, pathos with the tragic, within an effective evocation of the mundane. The surface realities of ordinary life consistently color the criminal situations without impinging on the careful artifice of the usual murders and the bumbling but brilliant methods of investigation undertaken almost in spite of himself by Chief Inspector E. Morse." Strout declares that "fans of the [detective story] will be grateful to Dexter, for some of its greatest luminaries are showing signs of restlessness with the genre." Ruth Rendell, famous as an author of police-procedural novels, mixes social issues such as unemployment and racism in her detective fiction. P. D. James's poet-detective hero Adam Dalgliesh "seems to be headed for retirement," Strout explains, "not by his own or Scotland Yard's decision but by his creator's restlessness with the genre." Strout concludes that "it is much to our benefit that Dexter is still fond of the form."

BIOGRAPHICAL/CRITICAL SOURCES:

BOOKS

Dictionary of Literary Biography, Volume 87: *British Mystery and Thriller Writers since 1940, First Series,* Gale (Detroit), 1989.

PERIODICALS

Armchair Detective, winter, 1989, pp. 76-77; fall, 1990, p. 497; summer, 1994, p. 272; fall, 1995, pp. 434-37.

Listener, July 8, 1976, June 30, 1977.
New Republic, March 4, 1978.
New York Times Book Review, May 20, 1990, p. 53; April 4, 1993; April 16, 1995, p. 29.
Time, April 26, 1993, p. 65.
Times Literary Supplement, September 26, 1975; April 23, 1976; August 26, 1977; June 5, 1981; October 25, 1991, p. 21; October 23, 1992, p. 22.
Virginia Quarterly Review, autumn, 1992, p. 131.
Washington Post Book World, December 20, 1987, p. 8.

*   *   *

DEXTER, N. C.
    See DEXTER, (Norman) Colin

*   *   *

DOUGLAS, Carole Nelson   1944-

PERSONAL: Born November 5, 1944, in Everett, WA; daughter of Arnold Peter (a fisherman) and Agnes Olga (a teacher; maiden name, Lovchik) Nelson; married Sam Douglas (an artist), November 25, 1967. *Education:* College of St. Catherine, B.A., 1966. *Avocational interests:* Graphic design, designing and making silversmithed and strung jewelry, collecting fashion prints.

ADDRESSES: Home—3920 Singleleaf Lane, Fort Worth, TX 76113. *Agent*—Howard Morhaim, 175 Fifth Ave., 14th Floor, New York, NY 10010.

CAREER: St. Paul Pioneer Press & Dispatch (now *St. Paul Pioneer Press),* St. Paul, MN, reporter and feature writer, 1967-83, copy and layout editor and occasional editorialist for Opinion Pages, 1983-84; full-time writer, 1984—. Member of board of directors, Twin Cities Local of the Newspaper Guild, 1970-72; first woman chair of annual Gridiron show, 1971; honorary member of board of directors of St. Paul Public Library Centennial, 1981.

MEMBER: Mystery Writers of America, Science Fiction and Fantasy Writers of America, Romance Writers of America, Sisters in Crime.

AWARDS, HONORS: Finalist in *Vogue* Prix de Paris writing competition for college seniors, 1966; Page

One Award from the Newspaper Guild of the Twin Cities, 1969, 1971, 1972, 1973, 1974, and 1975; Catherine L. O'Brien Award honorable mention from Stanley Home Products, Inc., for outstanding achievement in women's interest newspaper reporting, and second place newswriting award from the Minnesota Associated Press, both 1975, both for an article on destitute elderly; president's citation from the American Society of Interior Designers (Minnesota chapter), 1980, for design and home furnishing reporting; Silver Medal, Sixth Annual West Coast Review of Books, 1982, for *Fair Wind, Fiery Star;* Golden Medallion Award finalist citation from Romance Writers of America for *Fair Wind, Fiery Star,* 1982, *In Her Prime,* 1983, *Lady Rogue,* 1984, and *The Exclusive,* 1987; Science Fiction/Fantasy Award from *Romantic Times,* 1984; Science Fiction Award from *Romantic Times,* 1986, for *Probe;* Nebula Award nomination from Science Fiction Writers of America, 1986, for *Probe;* Popular Fiction Award, 1987, and Lifetime Achievement Award for Versatility, 1991, both from *Romantic Times;* Best Novel of Romantic Suspense citation from American Mystery Awards, 1990, and *New York Times Book Review* notable book citation, 1991, both for *Good Night, Mr. Holmes.*

WRITINGS:

Amberleigh, Jove (New York City), 1980.
Fair Wind, Fiery Star, Jove, 1981.
The Best Man, Ballantine (New York City), 1983.
Lady Rogue, Ballantine, 1983.
Azure Days and Quicksilver Nights, Bantam (New York City), 1985.
Probe, Tor Books (New York City), 1985.
The Exclusive, Ballantine, 1986.
Counterprobe, Tor Books, 1988.
Crystal Days and Crystal Nights, two volumes, Bantam, 1990.

"SWORD AND CIRCLET" FANTASY SERIES

Six of Swords, Del Rey Books (New York City), 1982.
Exiles of the Rynth, Del Rey Books, 1984.
Keepers of Edanvant, Tor Books, 1987.
Heir of Rengarth, Tor Books, 1988.
Seven of Swords, Tor Books, 1989.

"IRENE ADLER" SERIES

Good Night, Mr. Holmes, Tor Books, 1990.
Good Morning, Irene, Tor Books, 1991.

Irene at Large, Tor Books, 1992.
Irene's Last Waltz, Forge, 1994.

"TALISWOMAN" FANTASY SERIES

Cup of Clay, Tor Books, 1991.
Seed upon the Wind, Tor Books, 1992.

"MIDNIGHT LOUIE" MYSTERY SERIES

Catnap, Tor Books, 1992.
Pussyfoot, Tor Books, 1993.
Cat on a Blue Monday, Forge, 1994.
Cat in a Crimson Haze, Forge, 1995.

OTHER

Also author of *In Her Prime* and *Her Own Person,* both 1982. Editorial writer for the *Fort Worth Star-Telegram,* 1985—; columnist for *Mystery Scene* magazine, 1991.

SIDELIGHTS: "An only child who often had to amuse myself, I used to think that everybody made up poems and descriptive sentences when lying on the grass and looking up at the clouds," Carole Nelson Douglas once explained. Spurred by her childhood creativity, Douglas studied journalism in college before turning to fiction. Since 1980, she has written novels in a variety of genres, including science fiction, romance, and fantasy.

After a career as a newspaper journalist, Douglas yearned to try her hand at fiction. In 1980 Douglas's first novel was published. "*Amberleigh,*" she told *CA,* "was my Victorian-set update of what has been a model for so-called women's fiction since *Jane Eyre*—the Gothic. I call mine a 'feminist' Gothic. Submitting *Amberleigh* to publishers unsolicited resulted in getting it returned unread (because it was considered 'off market'—no sex) until playwright-author Garson Kanin volunteered to take it to his publisher." Douglas and Kanin continued their friendship and it turned out to be a nurturing one for Douglas. "I interviewed Kanin on two separate occasions," she explained to *CA,* "and it was his enduring enthusiasm for my writing style that was the key to opening the door to publishing for me."

Douglas's second novel, *Fair Wind, Fiery Star,* was also an historical novel. After writing these two works, Douglas decided to try a different genre. She told *CA* that "although fiction directed at a woman's audience is extremely lucrative to publishers right now, this very popularity, I discovered, hampers writers who want to expand on the publishers' current limitations of formula. Frustrated by the fact that 'transcending a genre,' as my books do, is considered a handicap rather than an advantage, I turned to applying my same themes in a more veiled and symbolic manner with *Six of Swords,* a fantasy which showed up on national science fiction/fantasy top-ten-bestseller lists its first week out and is now in its twelfth printing. . . . I find [that] both fantasy and science fiction encourage originality and imagination, while so much of commercial fiction does not."

The "Sword and Circlet" fantasy series began with the publication of *Six of Swords.* She once explained that these books "document the [protagonists'] magical adventures, a means of exploring relationships and the search for self. I describe the series as a 'domestic epic,' because it examines how men and women can form lasting alliances without losing their individuality and independence. By the fifth book, Irissa and Kendric's children are teenagers confronting the same relationship quandaries as their parents. One child is magically gifted; the other not. Each has a special bond with the opposite parent. Fantasy novels offer a writer a subtle means of dealing with contemporary issues like gender role reversal, animal rights and ecology without getting on a soapbox."

With the publication of *Probe* in 1985 and *Counterprobe* in 1988, Douglas entered the science fiction market. "I want my books to appeal to a wide variety of readers on different levels, and to contain enough levels that they bear re-reading," Douglas once remarked. "Although labeled as science fiction novels, *Probe* and *Counterprobe* are contemporary-set suspense/psychological adventure stories with a strong feminist sub-text, the kind that husbands recommend to wives, and vice versa; teenagers to parents, and vice versa. To write books that cross common ground between the sexes and span the generation gap is rewarding, especially in this pigeon-holed publishing world."

With *Good Night, Mr. Holmes,* published in 1990, Douglas launched yet a new series of books. In this novel Douglas expands upon the character Irene Adler, the only woman to outwit Sherlock Holmes, an event which took place in Arthur Conan Doyle's *A Scandal in Bohemia.* "This book evolved the way most of my ideas come to me: I realized that all the recent novels set in the Sherlock Holmes world were written by men," Douglas once pointed out. "Yet I had loved the stories as a youngster. My years as a

newspaper reporter taught me that when men monopolize anything it's time for women to examine it from a female point of view."

Douglas wrote three more novels in this series, including *Good Morning, Irene, Irene at Large,* and *Irene's Last Waltz.* "My Irene Adler is as intelligent, self-sufficient and serious about her professional and personal integrity as Sherlock Holmes, and far too independent to be anyone's mistress but her own," Douglas explained. "She also moonlights as an inquiry agent while building her performing career, so she is a professional rival of Holmes's rather than a romantic interest. Her adventures intertwine with Holmes's, but she is definitely her own woman in these novels."

Good Night, Mr. Holmes takes place a short time after Irene bests Holmes at detective work. Irene finds herself becoming romantically interested in the king of Bohemia. But all is not well with that union, and, in the end, she has to outwit him as well as Holmes. By her side, Irene has assistant Nell Huxleigh, who is as steady and stable as Holmes's friend Watson. Critic Cynthia Ogorek writes in *Booklist* that *Good Night, Mr. Holmes* is "guaranteed to please Holmes fans or anyone who likes period mysteries."

In *Irene at Large,* Irene and Nell find themselves exiled in Paris when they happen upon an acquaintance who has been poisoned. Nell falls in love with the man, and they spend the rest of the book trying to untangle the intrigue around his murder attempt. Writing in the *New York Times Book Review,* Marilyn Stasio claims that in *Irene at Large* "the action never loses its jaunty, high-heeled pace."

In *Irene's Last Waltz,* Irene ventures to Prague to check on strange happenings there, as well as to meet up with her former boyfriend, the king of Bohemia. They investigate the murder of a young girl that seems to be connected to other strange happenings, including the haunting of the city by the Golem, a mythical monster. A *Kirkus Reviews* contributor calls the book "the best . . . of Irene's adventures to date."

In the "Taliswoman Trilogy" Douglas again turns to fantasy. The first novel in the trilogy, *Cup of Clay,* focuses on Alison Carver, a journalist who lives in Minnesota. Needing a break after working on a scandalous child-abuse trial, Carver goes to her own island in a mountain lake. Her vacation takes a strange twist as she finds herself transported into another world, where she wins the Cup of Earth. She becomes the Taliswoman, empowered with skills to save the world—if she decides such a depraved world deserves to be saved. Laura Staley comments in *Voice of Youth Advocates* that "the more serious themes of this book seem to have produced an even better story than usual."

The second book of the trilogy, *Seed upon the Wind,* finds Carver back in the world called Veil. Her friend Rowan Firemayne blames Carver for the mysterious blight that has come over Veil. The two begin to work out their differences, and form a deeper relationship as they set out to make a powerful talisman from the ashes of Rowan's brother. They find the danger to the world of Veil, and Alison finds that it is too similar to the evils in our own world. A *Publishers Weekly* reviewer comments that "Douglas's increasingly intricate fantasy raises disturbing issues about environmental depredations."

Douglas once wrote: "Another favorite character of mine is Midnight Louie, an 18-pound, crime-solving black tomcat who is the part-time narrator of a new mystery series. . . . Like many of my creations, Louie goes way back. He was a real if somewhat larger-than-life stray cat I wrote a feature story about for my newspaper in 1973." *Catnap,* published in 1992, follows the adventures of Temple Barr, a public relations person at an American Booksellers Association meeting in Las Vegas. Feline Midnight Louie is able to assist Barr in finding out more information about the murder of Chester Royal, a big time publisher. A *Publishers Weekly* contributor relates that "Douglas's fine-tuned sense of humor gives her tame plot enough of a spin to keep readers entertained."

In *Pussyfoot,* published in 1993, Temple Barr finds herself once again in a murder investigation. This time she has been employed to do publicity for a competition of exotic dancers. When one of the contestants is killed, Barr goes into action, and Louie helps her find the unsavory characters involved in the scheme. A *Kirkus Reviews* contributor criticizes the story, saying "dog lovers, and lovers of well-made plots and prose, need not apply." A *Publishers Weekly* reviewer, however, praises the characterization of Barr, noting that she is "a reasonably modern and liberated female."

Reflecting on her work, Douglas told *CA:* "Because of my undergraduate major in theater, I'm especially interested in fiction that captures and affects an audience with the immediacy of a stage play. For this reason, I prefer working in 'popular' fiction forms and find nothing unusual in the idea of fiction being 'entertaining' as well as enlightening. . . . I like to say that what I write is principally entertainment, but that the best entertainment always has principles." She went on to point out that "in effect, I write on a fine line between 'serious' fiction on one hand and sneered-at 'popular' fiction on the other. It is not a particularly comfortable position, but somebody has to do it; otherwise we will have nothing but serious writers that nobody knows how to read and popular writers that nobody ought to read."

BIOGRAPHICAL/CRITICAL SOURCES:

PERIODICALS

Booklist, October 15, 1990, p. 419.
Kirkus Reviews, February 1, 1993, p. 101; December 15, 1993, p. 1553.
Locus, August, 1982.
Minneapolis/St. Paul Magazine, November, 1981.
New York Times Book Review, August 9, 1992, p. 20.
Publishers Weekly, January 20, 1992, pp. 49-50; October 19, 1992, p. 62; January 25, 1993, p. 81.
St. Paul Sunday Pioneer Press, September 14, 1980.
Voice of Youth Advocates, February, 1992, pp. 380-381.
West Coast Review of Books, December, 1981.

*　　*　　*

DRAPER, Alfred　1924-

PERSONAL: Born October 26, 1924, in London, England; son of Richard and Florence (Wills) Draper; married Barbara Pilcher, March 31, 1951; children: Nicholas, Antony. *Education:* Studied four years at North West Polytechnic, London.

ADDRESSES: Home—31 Oakridge Ave., Radlett, Hertfordshire WD7 8EW, England.

CAREER: Daily Express and *Daily Mail,* London, England, journalist specializing in crime and murder trials at home and reporting from abroad, 1950-72. *Military service:* Royal Navy; served in Atlantic and Pacific theaters; became sub-lieutenant.

MEMBER: Society of Authors, National Union of Journalists.

AWARDS, HONORS: Runner-up in Macmillan/Panther first crime novel competition, 1970, for *Swansong for a Rare Bird.*

WRITINGS:

Swansong for a Rare Bird, Coward (New York City), 1969.
The Death Penalty, Macmillan (London and New York City), 1972.
Smoke without Fire, Arlington Books (London), 1974.
The Prince of Wales, New English Library (London), 1975.
The Story of the Goons, Everest, 1976.
Operation Fish, Cassell (London), 1978.
Armistar: The Massacre that Ended the Raj, Cassell, 1981, reprinted as *The Armistar Massacre: Twilight of the Raj,* Buchan & Enright (London), 1987.
Dawns Like Thunder, Leo Cooper (London), Arrow Books (London), 1988.
Scoops and Swindles, Buchan & Enright, 1988.
The Con Man, Piatkus Books (London), 1987, Doubleday (London and New York City), 1988.
A Crimson Splendour, Piatkus Books, 1991.
Operation Midas, Piatkus Books, 1993.

"GREY SEAL" SERIES

Grey Seal, Macdonald Futura (London), 1981.
Grey Seal: The Restless Waves, Macdonald Futura, 1983.
Grey Seal: The Raging of the Deep, Piatkus Books, 1985.
Grey Seal: Storm over Singapore, Piatkus Books, 1986.
Grey Seal: The Great Avenging Day, Piatkus Book, 1988.

OTHER

Contributor to British dailies and numerous magazines.

Some of Draper's novels have been translated into German, French, and Dutch.

ADAPTATIONS: The Death Penalty was made into a film shown in France.

WORK IN PROGRESS: A novel about Northern Ireland.

*   *   *

DUKORE, Bernard F.   1931-

PERSONAL: Born July 11, 1931, in New York, NY; married second wife, Barbara Cromwell, 1986. *Education:* Brooklyn College (now Brooklyn College of the City University of New York), A.B., 1952; Ohio State University, M.A., 1953; University of Illinois, Ph.D., 1957.

ADDRESSES: Home—2149 Stone Mill Dr., Salem, VA 24153. *Office*—Humanities Center, Virginia Polytechnic and State University, Blacksburg, VA 24061.

CAREER: Hunter College in the Bronx (now Herbert H. Lehman College of the City University of New York), Bronx, NY, instructor in drama, 1957-60; University of Southern California, Los Angeles, assistant professor of drama, 1960-62; California State College at Los Angeles (now California State University, Los Angeles), 1962-66, began as assistant professor, became associate professor of drama; City University of New York, New York City, 1966-72, began as associate professor, became professor of drama; University of Hawaii, Honolulu, professor of drama, 1972-86; Virginia Polytechnic and State University, Blacksburg, university distinguished professor of theatre arts and humanities, 1986-97. Visiting fellow at Humanities Research Centre, Australian National University, 1979. *Military service:* U.S. Army, 1954-56; became sergeant.

AWARDS, HONORS: Guggenheim fellow, 1969-70; American Theatre Association fellow, 1975 and 1989; National Endowment for the Humanities fellow, 1976-77, 1984-85; Fulbright scholarship, 1991-92.

WRITINGS:

(Editor and author of introduction) George Etherege, *The Man of Mode,* Chandler Publishing, 1962.
(Editor with Ruby Cohn) *Twentieth-Century Drama: England, Ireland, United States,* Random House (New York City), 1966.
Saint Joan: A Screenplay by Bernard Shaw, University of Washington Press (Seattle), 1968.

(Editor with Daniel C. Gerould) *Avant-Garde Drama: Major Plays and Documents, Post World War I,* Bantam (New York City), 1969.

(Editor with Robert O'Brien) *Tragedy: Ten Major Plays,* Bantam, 1969.

Bernard Shaw, Director, University of Washington Press, 1970.

(Editor) John Gassner, *A Treasury of the Theatre,* Volume 2, revised edition, Simon & Schuster (New York City), 1970.

(Compiler) *Drama and Revolution,* Holt (New York City), 1970.

(Compiler) *Documents for Drama and Revolution,* Holt, 1970.

Bernard Shaw, Playwright: Aspects of Shavian Drama, University of Missouri Press (Columbia), 1973.

Dramatic Theory and Criticism, Holt, 1974.

Seventeen Plays: Sophocles to Baraka, Crowell (New York City), 1976.

Where Laughter Stops: Pinter's Tragicomedy, University of Missouri Press, 1976.

Money and Politics in Ibsen, Shaw, and Brecht, University of Missouri Press, 1980.

(Editor and author of introduction) *The Collected Screenplays of Bernard Shaw,* University of Georgia Press (Athens), 1980.

The Theatre of Peter Barnes, Heinemann Educational (London), 1981.

(Compiler) *Bernard Shaw's "Arms and the Man": A Composite Production Book,* Southern Illinois University Press (Carbondale), 1982.

Harold Pinter, Grove (New York City), 1982.

American Dramatists, 1918-1945, Grove, 1984.

"Death of a Salesman" and "The Crucible": Text and Performance, Macmillan (New York City), 1989.

(Editor) *Alan Ayckbourn: A Casebook,* Garland (New York City), 1991.

(Editor) *Bernard Shaw: The Drama Observed,* 4 volumes, Pennsylvania State University Press (University Park), 1994.

Barnestorm: The Plays of Peter Barnes, Garland, 1995.

(Editor) *Bernard Shaw and Gabriel Pascal,* University of Toronto Press (Toronto), 1996.

Contributor to *Tulane Drama Review, Educational Theatre Journal, Modern Drama, Theatre Survey, New York Times Book Review,* and other drama journals.

WORK IN PROGRESS: Editing *He Who Can: The Columbia Book of Bernard Shaw Quotations,* for Columbia University Press, expected in 1997; *Drama!—Sam Peckinpah's Feature Films.*

* * *

DUNN, Stephen (Elliott) 1939-

PERSONAL: Born June 24, 1939, in New York, NY; son of Charles Francis (a salesperson) and Ellen Dorothy (maiden name, Fleishman) Dunn; married Lois Ann Kelly (a yoga teacher), September 26, 1964; children: Andrea Ellen, Susanne Rebecca. *Education:* Hofstra University, B.A., 1962; New School for Social Research, graduate study, 1964-66; Syracuse University, M.A., 1970.

ADDRESSES: Home—445 Chestnut Neck Rd., Port Republic, NJ 08241. *Office*—Stockton State College, Pomona, NJ 08240. *Agent*—Philip G. Spitzer Literary Agency, 111-25 76th Ave., Forest Hills, NY 11375.

CAREER: Williamsport Billies, Williamsport, PA, professional basketball player, 1962-63; National Biscuit Co., New York City, copywriter, 1963-66; Zipp-Davis Publishing Co., New York City, assistant editor, 1967-68; Southwestern State University, Marshall, MN, assistant professor of creative writing, 1970-73; Syracuse University, Syracuse, NY, lecturer in poetry, 1973-74; Stockton State College, Pomona, NJ, professor of creative writing, 1974—. Visiting professor, University of Washington, 1980; adjunct professor, Columbia University, 1983-87. *Military service:* U.S. Army, 1962.

MEMBER: American Association of University Professors; Associated Writing Programs; Director of Associated Writing Programs Poetry Series, 1980-82.

AWARDS, HONORS: Academy of American Poets Award, Syracuse University, 1970; New York Poetry Center "Discovery '71" Award; National Endowment for the Arts fellowship, 1973, 1983, 1989; Theodore Roethke Prize, 1977, and Helen Bullis Prize, 1983, both from *Poetry Northwest;* writing fellowships to Yaddo, 1979-89; Guggenheim fellow, 1984-85; Levinson Prize, *Poetry,* 1987; National Poetry Series winner, 1986, for *Local Time.*

WRITINGS:

POETRY

Five Impersonations, Ox Head Press, 1971.
Looking for Holes in the Ceiling, University of Massachusetts Press (Amherst), 1974.
Full of Lust and Good Usage, Carnegie-Mellon University Press (Pittsburgh, PA), 1976.
A Circus of Needs, Carnegie-Mellon University Press, 1978.
Work and Love, Carnegie-Mellon University Press, 1981.
Not Dancing, Carnegie-Mellon University Press, 1984.
Local Time, Quill/William Morrow & Co. (New York City), 1986.
Between Angels, Norton (New York City), 1989.
Landscape at the End of the Century, Norton, 1991.
New and Selected Poems: 1974-1994, Norton, 1994.
Loosestrife, W.W. Norton (New York City), 1996.

OTHER

Walking Light: Essays and Memoirs, Norton, 1993.
(Author of foreword) Juanita Tobin, *Ransom Street Quartet: Poems and Stories,* Parkway (Boone, NC), 1995.

Contributor to literary journals, including *American Poetry Review, Anteus, Boulevard, Georgia Review, Paris Review, Poetry, Virginia Quarterly Review,* and others.

SIDELIGHTS: Poet Stephen Dunn's biography is a common one for those raised in post-war America: he was raised in the suburbs, attended college, served in the armed forces, played professional sports, and worked in advertising, all before attending Syracuse to study writing with Philip Booth, Donald Justice and W. D. Snodgrass. As a result, Dunn writes poetry that reflects the social, cultural, psychological, and philosophical territory of the American middle class; his poems are considered intelligent and given neither to postmodern pessimism nor contemporary experimental excess. In his lyrical poems, Dunn is often his own protagonist, narrating the regular episodes of his growth both as an individual and as part of a married couple. His poetry often concerns the anxieties, fears, joys, and problems of how to co-exist in the world with all the others who are part of daily life.

When *Looking for Holes in the Ceiling* was published in 1974, Robert Wilson praised it in *New Letters* as

a "crash course in survival" and as "poems which strike a blow for life" in the midst of the prevailing confessional tone and suicidal themes of the time prevalent in the poetry of such writers as Sylvia Plath, Anne Sexton, and John Berryman. Dunn does not offer his readers "ready-made answers" for those "seeking survival in comfortable images," Wilson points out, but offers instead that, through the "vitality of poetry" life can be positive despite the concerns, doubts, and ruminations that are a part of existence. This first full-length collection displays Dunn's spare style, his evocative imagery, and his conversational voice which have been compared to the kind of plain, common-sense American dialect advocated by American poet William Carlos Williams.

In *Full of Lust and Good Usage,* Dunn continues his direct and personal poetry in what Cheryl Walker in *Parnassus* calls "a man's book" that is written with a "certain sense of ease," showing he is on "good terms with the universe." One dominant motif in this book is familial relationships. Ronald Wallace, writing in *Chowder Review,* also sees "the stuff of everyday life: small towns, houses, sidewalks, landlords, truck stops." *Full of Lust and Good Usage* is, says Wallace, "a good book, distinguished by [Dunn's] lean, honed lines, and the articulate music of his voice."

Dunn followed *Full of Lust and Good Usage* with *A Circus of Needs* in 1978. Peter Stitt, writing in *Georgia Review,* finds the collection to be "especially pleasing for the steady progress it shows in Dunn's career." In addition to the typical "poems that sound almost like parables," Stitt praises Dunn for poems that present "the mundane, the real world in which we live, work, and suffer." Stephen Yenser in the *Yale Review* calls Dunn "a remarkably resourceful poet" who writes "explicitly personal poems . . . ranging from the chiefly anecdotal to the chiefly meditative." These poems are also characterized by Dave Smith in *American Poetry Review* as peopled by "figures . . . bound into the archetype of the gambler. They are diverse, tight-rope walkers, adventurers, acolytes, and always lovers." With this collection, "rich with paradox and passion," Smith notes that Dunn "has become a philosophical poet of weight."

Dunn's next offering, *Work and Love,* published in 1981, received mixed critical responses. While Robert Shaw in a lukewarm review for *Poetry* finds "poems which are more often mildly likeable than they are moving or memorable," the *Virginia Quarterly Review* calls the book "surely . . . Dunn's finest," and praises the book for exploring how people are defined and affected by their jobs. Dunn calls these "poems in his own voice" that continue his examination of male-female relationships and other familial themes typical of his earlier work.

Local Time, chosen for the National Poetry Series by Dave Smith, presents Dunn, according to Andy Brumer in *New York Times Book Review,* as "everybody's friendly neighbor. He is what mothers want their sons to be. He is good, and his obsession with moral and ethical propriety both distinguishes his poetry and slightly alienates those . . . who cannot quite resolve problems with gentleness and understanding." This book continues to explore Dunn's motif of the modern marriage: how a marriage grows, and how couples grow together. Dunn also explores other contemporary (often suburban) concerns such as safety; the same person who has been mugged in "Round Trip" considers, in "Local Time," how "The house had double locks / but in the dark a wrong person / would understand: the windows / were made of glass." It is poems like these that lead J. P. White in *Poetry* to write that *Local Time* offers "language . . . [that] is always accessible and friendly" as well as a "moral quest—a desire to test limits and walk hard edges—that [is] inviting and authentic."

Between Angels, Dunn's widely acclaimed 1989 collection, writes Steve Kronen in *Kenyon Review,* "seems a culmination of Dunn's powers, wise in its insights, exquisitely modulated in its execution," developing the themes of "our human vulnerability and our quiet everyday tenacity, perhaps courage, in the face of those vulnerabilities." The book includes considerations of ten eternal verities, with poems entitled "Loneliness," "Sadness," "Happiness," "Cleanliness," and "Sweetness." The title poem continues the common Dunn themes of middle-class life and loving. Stephen Dobyns, writing in *New York Times Book Review* calls this a collection of poems in which "clarity is a virtue and strongly felt emotion is a reason for being," and Alfred Corn, in *Poetry,* commends Dunn for being "a poet primarily personal and, in a valuable sense, realistic," a writer who "has the rare gift of seeming trustworthy."

Landscape at the End of the Century, is written in three sections, the first of which, according to Steven Cramer in *Poetry,* "grapples with what it means to be a citizen—of a family, of a neighborhood, of a nation." In the second section, Dunn's focus is on domestic subjects: the politics of communications between men and women, elegies to adolescence, and what Cramer identifies as "the routine mysteries of marriage." Section three is a fourteen-page work entitled "Loves," an inventory of loving, luck, risk, intimacy, integrity, jazz, spontaneity, and inexhaustibility. Cramer praises the entire work, noting that "few poets write as unaffectedly about our middle class impulses to be decent—at times heroic—and our countervailing slippages toward apathy or self-interest."

In 1994, Dunn published *Walking Light: Essays and Memoirs,* an assortment of essays addressed to the literary establishment about the craft of poetry, among other topics. He followed the memoir with *New and Selected Poems: 1974-1994.* Anthony Libby, writing about the collection in the *New York Times Book Review,* notes that Dunn "is the American male as sensitive guy, full of love for women and the exquisite world." David Wojahn, in *Poetry,* calls Dunn "one of our most prolific and consistent poets," who is "level-headed, witty, conversational in his diction, and willing to see in domestic life his means of attaining and imparting wisdom." The book opens with several new works, including "The Snowmass Cycle," a sequence of eight meditative poems which Judith Kitchen in *Georgia Review* identifies as "written in self-imposed solitude." The poems in this collection, however, "give a clear retrospective," according to Kitchen, that allows "individual pieces to stand out." Deeming the poet a "spokesperson for the suburban middle class," Kitchen concludes that Dunn "continues to remind us that there is dignity in the mundane."

BIOGRAPHICAL/CRITICAL SOURCES:

BOOKS

Clark, LaVerne, *Focus 101,* Heidelberg Graphics (Chico, CA), 1979.
Contemporary Literary Criticism, Gale (Detroit), Volume 36, 1986.
Contemporary Poets, fifth edition, St. James Press (Chicago), 1991.
Dictionary of Literary Biography, Volume 105, *American Poets since World War II, Second Series,* Gale, 1991.

PERIODICALS

American Book Review, September-October, 1982, p. 16; June, 1991, p. 31.

American Poetry Review, June, 1979, pp. 29-33; March, 1987, p. 22.

Bloomsbury Review, November, 1993, p. 13.

Booklist, February 1, 1982, p. 694; June, 1986, p. 1430; May 1, 1989, p. 1506; April 15, 1991, p. 1616; May 1, 1994, p. 1577.

British Book News, January, 1985, p. 25.

Chowder Review, 1977, pp. 74-76; spring-summer, 1979, pp. 41-45.

Georgia Review, fall, 1977, pp. 764-766; fall, 1979, pp. 699-706; fall, 1989, p. 589; fall, 1991, p. 601; summer, 1995, p. 509-511.

Hudson Review, summer, 1979, pp. 252-268; winter, 1984, p. 657; autumn, 1986, p. 503.

Kenyon Review, spring, 1991, pp. 161-168.

Library Journal, March 1, 1986, p. 98; May 1, 1989, p. 80; March 15, 1991, p. 93; April 1, 1993, p. 98; March 1, 1994, p. 90.

Los Angeles Times Book Review, May 11, 1986, p. 1.

Missouri Review, spring, 1991, p. 130.

New England Review, spring, 1985, p. 147.

New Letters, June, 1975, pp. 103-107.

New Republic, June 2, 1986, p. 39.

New York Review of Books, October 23, 1986, p. 47.

New York Times Book Review, July 6, 1986, p. 23; January 28, 1990, p. 26; January 15, 1995, p. 15; February 12, 1995, p. 39.

North American Review, March, 1985, p. 65.

Parnassus, fall-winter, 1977, pp. 198-207.

Poetry, December, 1982, pp. 170-181; December, 1986, pp. 171-172; January, 1990, pp. 289-291; November, 1991, p. 111-116; January, 1995, p. 219-224.

Publishers Weekly, January 31, 1986, p. 362; March 3, 1989, p. 94; March 23, 1990, p. 74; February 22, 1991, p. 206; March 29, 1993, p. 42; March 28, 1994, p. 88.

Sewanee Review, April, 1994, pp. 3637.

Southern Review, winter, 1994, p. 165.

Times Literary Supplement, January 11, 1985, p. 35.

Virginia Quarterly Review, autumn, 1982, p. 135; autumn, 1986, p. 134; autumn, 1989, p. 13; autumn, 1994, p. 133.

Western Humanities Review, summer, 1985, pp. 162-64.

Yale Review, summer, 1979, pp. 557-577.*

—Sketch by Robert Miltner

E

EDDINGS, David (Carroll) 1931-

PERSONAL: Born July 7, 1931, in Spokane, WA; son of George Wayne and Theone (Berge) Eddings; married Judith Leigh Schall, October 27, 1962. *Education:* Attended Everett Junior College, 1950-52; Reed College, B.A., 1954; University of Washington, Seattle, M.A., 1961. *Politics:* "Unaffiliated." *Religion:* "Unaffiliated."

ADDRESSES: Agent—Eleanor Wood, Blasingame, McCauley, and Wood, 111 Eighth Ave., Suite 1501, New York, NY 10011.

CAREER: Writer; worked variously for Boeing Co., Seattle, WA, as a buyer; for a grocery store as a manager; and as a college English teacher. *Military service:* U.S. Army, 1954-56.

WRITINGS:

"BELGARIAD" FANTASY SERIES

Pawn of Prophecy, Del Rey Books (New York City), 1982.
Queen of Sorcery, Del Rey Books, 1982.
Magician's Gambit, Del Rey Books, 1984.
Castle of Wizardry, Del Rey Books, 1984.
Enchanter's Endgame, Del Rey Books, 1984.

"MALLOREON" FANTASY SERIES

Guardians of the West, Del Rey Books, 1987.
King of the Murgos, Del Rey Books, 1988.
Demon Lord of Karanda, Del Rey Books, 1988.

Sorceress of Darshiva, Del Rey Books, 1989.
The Seeress of Kell, Del Rey Books, 1991.

"ELENIUM" FANTASY SERIES

The Diamond Throne, Del Rey Books, 1989.
The Ruby Knight, Del Rey Books, 1990.
The Sapphire Rose, Del Rey Books, 1991.

"TAMULI" FANTASY SERIES

Domes of Fire, Del Rey Books, 1993.
The Shining Ones, Del Rey Books, 1993.
The Hidden City, Del Rey Books, 1994.

OTHER

High Hunt, Putnam (New York City), 1973.
The Losers, Fawcett (New York City), 1992.
Belgarath the Sorcerer, Ballantine (New York City), 1995.

SIDELIGHTS: David Eddings is a prolific and widely read fantasy writer whose books offer winning characters, persuasive dialogue, and plenty of humor. Though he has occasionally been taken to task for lacking originality, his well-plotted stories that feature war, politics, and intriguing situations have earned him a loyal readership. A *Publishers Weekly* reviewer notes that Eddings "is a good storyteller who never gets bogged down in the cliches and archaic language that often plague contemporary sword and sorcery." Likewise, in *Fantasy Review,* Dale F. Martin commends Eddings for his characters, "who are skillfully presented and deftly developed." The critic adds: "Along with the sorcery and derring-do, there is wry humor and loving domesticity and credible dialogue."

Born in Spokane, Washington, Eddings graduated from Reed College and got his M.A. at the University of Washington. His first book was *High Hunt,* an adventure set in the present. While working at a series of jobs that included teaching college English, working in a grocery store and a stint with the Boeing aircraft company, Eddings continued to write. As he once commented, "I have tried my hand at a wide variety of subgenres with more interest in the technical problems presented by each type than in commercial success." His advice to aspiring writers is blunt: "Never be afraid to discard a day's work—or a month's, or even a year's. Attachment to one's own brilliance is the worst form of juvenile self-indulgence."

Eddings's second novel, *Pawn of Prophecy,* which appeared nine years after *High Hunt,* was the first to have a fantasy setting. Its success allowed him to write full-time, and he launched both the "Belgariad" and "Malloreon" series. These series chronicle the adventures of Garion, a young orphan, who gradually recognizes his own magic abilities as extraordinary events begin to overtake the ordinary occurrences of his world. By accepting his own powers, Garion is able to enlist the aid of warriors and sorcerers to combat the followers of the evil god Torak. A *Publishers Weekly* reviewer remarks that *Pawn of Prophecy* was "obviously part of a longer work" and noted that Eddings's first volume was "a promising start."

The first book in the "Malloreon" series, *Guardians of the West,* was given a similarly positive reception. In the "Malloreon" books, King Garion is locked in battle with the sorceress Zandramas. A *Publishers Weekly* reviewer, considering the fourth book in the series, *The Sorceress of Darshiva,* notes of the author: "Eddings depicts a complex, believable and colorful society filled with nobles, rogues, and common people, the latter characters ringing particularly true." Michael Cule, however, reviewing the series in *Twentieth-Century Science-Fiction Writers,* finds that "there are few fresh characters," and "both plot and incident repeat themselves."

Critics have pointed out that Eddings's fantasy worlds and plots are fairly standard: parallels to Imperial Romans, ancient Egyptians, and Vikings are readily apparent, for example. For his part, Eddings stresses the credibility factor in any story. His "basic formula" for believable fantasy, as he once stated, is to "take a bit of magic, mix well with a few open-ended Jungian archetypal myths, make your people sweat and smell and get hungry at inopportune moments, throw in a ponderous prehistory, and let nature take its course."

His third series, the "Elenium" books, is hailed by *Booklist* contributor Roland Green for its "well-wrought world" and "originality." The trilogy depicts the adventures of Sparhawk, a knight on a quest for the jewel Bhelliom, whose powers will free the Queen Ehlana from prison. Reviewing *The Sapphire Rose,* the last book in the series, a *Publishers Weekly* critic notes that Eddings "adroitly mixes the exalted with the mundane in a tale that should satisfy his many fans." Cule finds that this series "is designed to be shorter . . . and is written with a greater emphasis on action. . . . Again the nature of magic and of the gods is a focus of interest, and destiny hangs heavy in the background, waiting to guide events."

Rather than embarking on another series, Eddings took a different direction with *The Losers.* The novel's protagonist, Raphael Taylor, is a present-day senior at Reed College in Portland, Oregon. Under the influence of his wealthy, reckless roommate, Damon Flood, Taylor plummets from the summit of academic and athletic success to an unhappy affair with an older woman and a series of alcoholic binges. Taylor then crashes his car, resulting in an amputated leg.

Eddings found little favor among critics for his foray into realistic fiction. Writing in *Voice of Youth Advocates,* Cecilia Swanson warns that readers looking for more of Eddings's "wonderful fantasies" would be disappointed and that the book was "basically a variation on good vs. evil," though she praises *The Losers* for being "well written." *Library Journal* correspondent Jackie Cassada claims that "stripped of their fantasy trappings, the author's opinions assume a heavy-handedness that verges on the polemic," and a critic in *Publishers Weekly* finds that the "simplistic, fable-like quality . . . patronizes its audiences."

The writer returned to fantasy for his next series, which he titled "Tamuli." The first of these books was *Domes of Fire,* which reprised Sir Sparhawk and Queen Ehlana of the "Elenium" series. The far-away Tamul Empire pleads with Sparhawk to help them, and he sets off with his wife Ehlana and their daughter in tow. They encounter several incidents that lead Sparhawk to suspect magical or godly opposition to his cause. *Publishers Weekly* welcomes the writer's "likable, spirited characters," which "reflect his original touch."

In the second book of the series, *The Shining Ones,* Eddings threw yet another obstacle in the way of Sparhawk and his entourage. The Shining Ones of the title seem human and friendly, but the knight strongly suspects that they are true to the Bhelliom stone rather than to him and his cause. *Booklist* reviewer Candace Smith highlights the "well-drawn, likable characters" and "complex but not unwieldy plots" of the story. In *Library Journal,* Cassada notes Eddings's "talent for creating appealing, erudite characters and vivid cultures" in this second installment of the trilogy, and a reviewer in *Publishers Weekly* terms the novel "vintage Eddings." The final installment of the "Tamuli" books is entitled *The Hidden City.* In it, Sir Sparhawk must rescue Queen Ehlana, now captive of the followers of the demented god Cyrgon. A *Publishers Weekly* reviewer remarks on a "new note of introspection" which gives "a fuller dimension to Eddings's rousing adventure."

Eddings has emphasized the need for total credibility in fantasy writing. As he once explained, "My magic is at best a kind of pragmatic cop-out. Many of my explanations of how magic is supposed to work are absurdities—*but* my characters all accept these explanations . . . and if the characters believe, then the readers seem also to believe."

Eddings told *CA:* "I have noted that no form is, of itself, trite or hackneyed. Those faults lie in the writer, not the form. The mystery, the western, the gothic horror, the thriller, the oversized historical novel—all are susceptible to that artistry which lifts the efforts of a given writer above those of his contemporaries, no matter what form he chooses.

"My advice to the young writer is likely to be unpalatable in an age of instant successes and meteoric falls. I tell the neophyte: Write a million words—the absolute best you can write, then throw it all away and bravely turn your back on what you have written. At that point, you're ready to begin.

"When you are with people, listen; don't talk. Writers are boring people. What are you going to talk about so brilliantly? Typewriters? The construction of paragraphs? Shut your mouth and listen. Listen to the cadences of speech. Engrave the sound of language on your mind. Language is our medium, and the spoken language is the sharp cutting edge of our art. Make your people sound human. The most tedious story will leap into life if the reader can hear the human voices in it. The most brilliant and profound of stories will sink unnoticed if the characters talk like sticks.

"Most of all, enjoy what you're doing. If you don't enjoy it, it's not worth doing at all. If hard and unrewarding work bothers you, do something else. If rejection withers your soul, do something else. If the work itself is not reward enough, stop wasting paper. But if you absolutely *have* to write—if you're compelled to do it even without hope of reward or recognition—then I welcome you to our sorry, exalted fraternity."

BIOGRAPHICAL/CRITICAL SOURCES:

BOOKS

Bestsellers 90, Issue 2, Gale (Detroit), 1990.
Watson, Noelle and Paul E. Schellinger, *Twentieth-Century Science-Fiction Writers,* St. James Press (Detroit), 1991.

PERIODICALS

Booklist, December 1, 1991, p. 659; October 15, 1992, p. 379; August, 1993, p. 2012.
Fantasy Review, June, 1987, pp. 35-36.
Library Journal, June 15, 1992, p. 100; September 15, 1993, p. 109.
New York Times Book Review, July 5, 1987.
Publishers Weekly, March 19, 1982, p. 69; October 27, 1989; October 25, 1991, p. 49; May 18, 1992, pp. 59-60; October 19, 1992, p. 62; August 2, 1993, p. 66; August 29, 1994, p. 65.
Voice of Youth Advocates, February, 1993, p. 348.
WB, May/June, 1989.

*   *   *

EISENBERG, Ronald L(ee)   1945-

PERSONAL: Born July 11, 1945, in Philadelphia, PA; son of Milton (a physician) and Betty (Klein) Eisenberg; married Zina Leah Schiff (a concert violinist), September 19, 1970; children: Avlana Kinneret, Cherina Carmel. *Education:* University of

Pennsylvania, A.B., 1965, M.D., 1969. *Avocational interests:* Playing the piano, collecting Israeli stamps (almost a complete set).

ADDRESSES: Office—Department of Radiology, Highland Hospital, 1411 E. 31st Street, Oakland, CA 94602.

CAREER: Mount Zion Hospital, San Francisco, CA, intern, 1969-70; Massachusetts General Hospital, Boston, MA, resident in radiology, 1970-71; University of California, San Francisco, resident in radiology, 1973-75, assistant professor of radiology, 1975-80; chief of gastrointestinal radiology at Veterans Administration Hospital (San Francisco), beginning 1975; Louisiana State University Medical Center, Shreveport, professor of radiology and chair of department, 1980-91; University of California, San Francisco, clinical professor of radiology, 1991—; Alameda County Medical Center, Oakland, CA, chair of radiology, 1991—. *Military service:* U.S. Army, 1971-73; became major.

MEMBER: American College of Radiology (fellow), American Roentgen Ray Society, Radiological Society of North America, Society of Gastrointestinal Radiology, San Francisco Radiology Society, Alpha Omega Alpha, Phi Beta Kappa.

AWARDS, HONORS: William Howard Taft University, J.D., 1996.

WRITINGS:

The Iguana Corps of the Haganah, Bloch Publishing (New York City), 1977.
Critical Diagnostic Pathways in Radiology, Lippincott (Philadelphia), 1981.
Gastrointestinal Radiology, Lippincott, 1983, 3rd edition, 1996.
Atlas of Signs in Radiology, Lippincott, 1984.
Veterans Compensation: An American Scandal, Pierremont, 1985.
Diagnostic Imaging in Internal Medicine, McGraw (New York City), 1985.
Diagnostic Imaging in Surgery, McGraw, 1986.
Clinical Imaging: Atlas of Differential Diagnosis, Aspen, 1988, 2nd edition, 1992.
Diagnostic Imaging: An Algorithmic Approach, Lippincott, 1988.
Radiology: An Illustrated History, Mosby (St. Louis, MO), 1992.
Radiology Pocket Reference, Lippincott, 1996.

Contributor to professional journals. Coauthor of newspaper column, "Doctor/Doctor" (appears three days per week). Editor of *The Radiologist* (journal), 1993—.

SIDELIGHTS: Ronald L. Eisenberg told *CA:* "The idea of writing seriously (other than medical articles) arose during my years in the Army. When I was on call every fourth night I had to remain on the base. Rarely was I called on to see a patient. With a great deal of time on my hands, I began to write.

"The subject of my writing was iguanas—primarily because we had one named Waverly. This, coupled with a visit to Israel and the reading of a work about a dog-parachutist by [a former] head of the Israeli Army, led me to write . . . *The Iguana Corps of the Haganah.* It is a story, probably fictitious, about the use of the large lizards to carry messages, guns, and explosives to the Israeli agents behind Arab lines."

*   *   *

ELLIS, Edward Robb   1911-

PERSONAL: Born February 22, 1911, in Kewanee, IL; son of John Talcott (a musician) and Lalla (Robb) Ellis; married Leatha Sparlin (divorced); married Ruth Kraus April 29, 1955 (died August 4, 1965); children: (first marriage) Sandra Gail. *Education:* University of Missouri, B.J., 1934. *Politics:* Independent. *Religion:* Pantheist.

ADDRESSES: Home—441 West 21st St., New York, NY 10011-2928. *Agent*—John Cushman Associates, Inc., 25 West 43rd St., New York, NY 10036.

CAREER: Feature writer and reporter for *Kewanee Daily Star-Courier,* Kewanee, IL, 1927-34, New Orleans bureau of Associated Press, 1934-35, *New Orleans Item,* New Orleans, LA, 1935-37, *Oklahoma City Times,* Oklahoma City, OK, 1937-40, *Peoria Journal-Transcript,* Peoria, IL, 1940-43, Chicago bureau of United Press, 1943-46, and *New York World-Telegram & Sun,* New York, NY, 1947-62; freelance writer, 1962—. *Military service:* U.S. Navy, World War II; based in Okinawa.

AWARDS, HONORS: Award for feature writing, Chicago Newspaper Guild, 1946; Friends of American Writers first prize, 1971, for *A Nation in Torment: The Great American Depression, 1929-1939.*

WRITINGS:

(With George N. Allen) *Traitor Within: Our Suicide Problem,* Doubleday (Garden City, NY), 1961.

(Contributor) *Accent,* Scott, Foresman (Chicago), 1965.

The Epic of New York City, Coward (New York City), 1966.

A Nation in Torment: The Great American Depression, 1929-1939, Coward, 1970.

Echoes of Distant Thunder: Life in the United States, 1914-1918, Coward, 1975.

A Diary of the Century: Tales from America's Greatest Diarist, 1927-1995, Kodansha (New York City), 1995.

Contributor to *New York Historical Quarterly.*

WORK IN PROGRESS: Work on an encyclopedia of New York City; a second volume of entries from his diary.

SIDELIGHTS: Diarist, journalist, and author Edward Robb Ellis lives and works in a walk-up apartment in a brownstone in the Chelsea area of Manhattan amid a private library of over fifteen thousand books. A newspaper and wire service reporter who experienced much of twentieth-century American history firsthand by covering breaking stories throughout the eastern United States—from Kewanee, Illinois, to New Orleans to New York—for over thirty-five years, he retired in 1962 and began a second career as a freelance writer and historian. His *Epic of New York City,* first published in 1966, remains one of the classic resources for students of the Big Apple; his diary, the longest on record, was published in 1995 in an abridged form as *A Diary of the Century: Tales from America's Greatest Diarist, 1927-1995.* The original manuscript—over sixty volumes, totalling twenty million words—was condensed to just under 600 pages, one percent of its original length, according to its author's calculations. It is a work that the critic for *Publishers Weekly* calls "a frank record [that] movingly captures the march of time both outward and inward."

Since December 27th, 1927, Ellis has kept the diary, undertaken as the result of a wager with friends made when he was a seventeen-year-old high school student working as a cub reporter for his hometown paper, the *Kewanee Daily Star-Courier.* On a bet to see who could keep a diary the longest, Ellis cracked his first composition book. Since that time, he has spent an hour a day, everyday, first writing long-

hand, then typing down all that he has encountered during the course of his eventful life. Every sight, feeling, thought, impression, or opinion, as well as an accompanying scrapbook of clips of his newspaper articles and letters he both wrote and received are included in the diary. A high school sophomore ranking the attributes of different girlfriends, recounting his first shave, and listing his favorite records; a young journalist with a boundless curiosity and strong political opinions describing newsworthy celebrities from Communist-hunting Senator Joseph McCarthy to songwriter Irving Berlin; a loving husband describing in intimate detail the last few hours spent watching his beloved wife die: Ellis's experiences have mirrored many of the social and political changes wrought upon his generation during the twentieth century. Candid about his faults as well as his triumphs, Ellis's writing is imbued with "a wry sense of humor and a falcon-sharp eye for details," according to John Elson in *Time* magazine.

Submitted by an archivist at the University of Wyoming's Archive of Contemporary History—to which Ellis has donated each completed volume of his massive work for safekeeping—for entry into the *Guiness Book of World Records* as the largest diary on record, Ellis's work eventually came to the attention of a New York City editor through the enthusiastic suggestion of a fellow booklover. The intimate view of sixty-eight years worth of informal twentieth-century history was edited and published as *A Diary of the Century:* "a great primitive painting . . . ," notes Elson, "limited in range but blessed with raw power."

BIOGRAPHICAL/CRITICAL SOURCES:

PERIODICALS

Best Sellers, July 1, 1970.
Christian Science Monitor, July 13, 1970.
New York Times, May 11, 1988, p. B1.
Publishers Weekly, August 7, 1995, pp. 454-55; September 11, 1995, pp. 64-65.
Time, September 4, 1995, p. 70.

*   *   *

ELLISON, Ralph (Waldo)   1914-1994

PERSONAL: Born March 1, 1914, in Oklahoma City, OK; died of cancer, April 16, 1994, in New York, NY; son of Lewis Alfred (a construction worker and tradesman) and Ida (Millsap) Ellison; married Fanny McConnell, July, 1946. *Education:* Attended Tuskegee Institute, 1933-36. *Avocational interests:* Jazz and classical music, photography, electronics, furniture-making, bird-watching, gardening.

CAREER: Writer, 1937-94. Worked as a researcher and writer on Federal Writers' Project in New York City, 1938-42; edited *Negro Quarterly,* 1942; lecture tour in Germany, 1954; lecturer at Salzburg Seminar, Austria, fall, 1954; U.S. Information Agency, tour of Italian cities, 1956; Bard College, Annandale-on-Hudson, NY, instructor in Russian and American literature, 1958-61; New York University, New York City, Albert Schweitzer Professor in Humanities, 1970-79, professor emeritus, 1979-94. Alexander White Visiting Professor, University of Chicago, 1961; visiting professor of writing, Rutgers University, 1962-64; visiting fellow in American studies, Yale University, 1966. Gertrude Whittall Lecturer, Library of Congress, January, 1964; delivered Ewing Lectures at University of California, Los Angeles, April, 1964. Lecturer in African-American culture, folklore, and creative writing at other colleges and universities throughout the United States, including Columbia University, Fisk University, Princeton University, Antioch University, and Bennington College.

Member of Carnegie Commission on Educational Television, 1966-67; honorary consultant in American letters, Library of Congress, 1966-72. Trustee, Colonial Williamsburg Foundation, John F. Kennedy Center for the Performing Arts, 1967-77, Educational Broadcasting Corp., 1968-69, New School for Social Research, 1969-83, Bennington College, 1970-75, and Museum of the City of New York, 1970-86. Charter member of National Council of the Arts, 1965-67, and of National Advisory Council, Hampshire College. *Military service:* U.S. Merchant Marine, World War II.

MEMBER: PEN (vice president, 1964), Authors Guild, Authors League of America, American Academy and Institute of Arts and Letters, Institute of Jazz Studies (member of board of advisors), Century Association (resident member).

AWARDS, HONORS: Rosenwald grant, 1945; National Book Award and National Newspaper Publishers' Russwurm Award, both 1953, both for *Invisible Man;* Certificate of Award, *Chicago Defender,* 1953; Rockefeller Foundation award, 1954; Prix de Rome fellowships, American Academy of Arts and Letters, 1955 and 1956; *Invisible Man* selected as the most

distinguished postwar American novel and Ellison as the sixth most influential novelist by *New York Herald Tribune Book Week* poll of two hundred authors, editors, and critics, 1965; recipient of award honoring well-known Oklahomans in the arts from governor of Oklahoma, 1966; Medal of Freedom, 1969; Chevalier de l'Ordre des Arts et Lettres (France), 1970; Ralph Ellison Public Library, Oklahoma City, named in his honor, 1975; National Medal of Arts, 1985, for *Invisible Man* and for his teaching at numerous universities; honorary doctorates from Tuskegee Institute, 1963, Rutgers University, 1966, Grinnell College, 1967, University of Michigan, 1967, Williams College, 1970, Long Island University, 1971, Adelphi University, 1971, College of William and Mary, 1972, Harvard University, 1974, Wake Forest College, 1974, University of Maryland, 1974, Bard College, 1978, Wesleyan University, 1980, and Brown University, 1980.

WRITINGS:

Invisible Man (novel), Random House (New York City), 1952, published in a limited edition with illustrations by Steven H. Stroud, Franklin Library, 1980, thirtieth-anniversary edition with new introduction by author, Random House, 1982.

(Author of introduction) Stephen Crane, *The Red Badge of Courage and Four Great Stories,* Dell (New York City), 1960.

Shadow and Act (essays), Random House, 1964.

(With Karl Shapiro) *The Writer's Experience* (lectures; includes "Hidden Names and Complex Fate: A Writer's Experience in the U.S.," by Ellison, and "American Poet?," by Shapiro), Gertrude Clarke Whittall Poetry and Literature Fund for Library of Congress, 1964.

(With Whitney M. Young and Herbert Gans) *The City in Crisis,* introduction by Bayard Rustin, A. Philip Randolph Education Fund, 1968.

(Author of introduction) Romare Bearden, *Paintings and Projections* (catalogue of exhibition, November 25-December 22, 1968), State University of New York at Albany, 1968.

(Author of foreword) Leon Forrest, *There Is a Tree More Ancient than Eden,* Random House, 1973.

Going to the Territory (essays), Random House, 1986.

The Collected Essays of Ralph Ellison, Modern Library, 1995.

Flying Home and Other Stories, preface by Saul Bellow, Random House, 1996.

Contributor to books, including *The Living Novel: A Symposium,* edited by Granville Hicks, Macmillan (New York City), 1957; *Education of the Deprived and Segregated* (report of seminar on education for culturally-different youth, Dedham, MA, September 3-15, 1963), Bank Street College of Education, 1965; *Who Speaks for the Negro?,* by Robert Penn Warren, Random House, 1965; *To Heal and to Build: The Programs of Lyndon B. Johnson,* edited by James MacGregor Burns, prologue by Howard K. Smith, epilogue by Eric Hoffer, McGraw (New York City), 1968; and *American Law: The Third Century, the Law Bicentennial Volume,* edited by Bernard Schwartz, F. B. Rothman for New York University School of Law, 1976. Work represented in numerous anthologies, including *American Writing,* edited by Hans Otto Storm and others, J. A. Decker, 1940; *Best Short Stories of World War II,* edited by Charles A. Fenton, Viking (New York City), 1957; *The Angry Black,* edited by John Alfred Williams, Lancer Books, 1962, 2nd edition published as *Beyond the Angry Black,* Cooper Square (Totowa, NJ), 1966; *Soon, One Morning: New Writing by American Negroes, 1940-1962* (includes previously unpublished section from original manuscript of *Invisible Man*), edited by Herbert Hill, Knopf (New York City), 1963, published in England as *Black Voices,* Elek Books (London), 1964; *Experience and Expression: Reading and Responding to Short Fiction,* edited by John L. Kimmey, Scott, Foresman (Glenview, IL), 1976; and *The Treasury of American Short Stories,* compiled by Nancy Sullivan, Doubleday (New York City), 1981.

OTHER

Ralph Ellison: An Interview with the Author of Invisible Man (sound recording), Center for Cassette Studies, 1974.
(With William Styron and James Baldwin) *Is the Novel Dead?: Ellison, Styron and Baldwin on Contemporary Fiction* (sound recording), Center for Cassette Studies, 1974.
Conversations with Ralph Ellison, edited by Maryemma Graham and Amritjit Singh, University Press of Mississippi (Jackson), 1995.

Contributor to *Proceedings, American Academy of Arts and Letters and the National Institute of Arts and Letters,* second series, 1965 and 1967. Also contributor of short fiction, critical essays, articles, and reviews to numerous journals and periodicals, including *American Scholar, Contemporary Literature, Iowa Review, New York Review of Books, New York Times Book Review, Noble Savage, Partisan Review, Quarterly Review of Literature, Reporter, Time,* and *Washington Post Book World.* Contributing editor, *Noble Savage,* 1960, and member of editorial board of *American Scholar,* 1966-69.

WORK IN PROGRESS: A second novel, as yet untitled, to be published by Random House, portions of which have been published under various titles, including "And Hickman Arrives" in *Noble Savage,* March, 1960, "The Roof, the Steeple, and the People" in *Quarterly Review of Literature,* Number 3, 1960, "It Always Breaks Out" in *Partisan Review,* spring, 1963, "Juneteenth" in *Quarterly Review of Literature,* Volume 13, numbers 3-4, 1969, "Song of Innocence" in *Iowa Review,* spring, 1970, and "Cadillac Flambe" in *American Review 16: The Magazine of New Writing,* edited by Theodore Solotaroff, Bantam, 1973.

SIDELIGHTS: Growing up in Oklahoma, a "frontier" state that "had no tradition of slavery" and where "relationships between the races were more fluid and thus more human than in the old slave states," Ralph Ellison became conscious of his obligation "to explore the full range of American Negro humanity and to affirm those qualities which are of value beyond any question of segregation, economics or previous condition of servitude." This sense of obligation, articulated in his 1964 collection of critical and biographical essays, *Shadow and Act,* led to his staunch refusal to limit his artistic vision to the "uneasy sanctuary of race" and commit instead to a literature that explores and affirms the complex, often contradictory frontier of an identity at once black and American and universally human. For Ellison, whom John F. Callahan in a *Chant of Saints: A Gathering of Afro-American Literature, Art, and Scholarship* essay called a "moral historian," the act of writing was fraught with both great possibility and grave responsibility. As Ellison asserted, writing "offers me the possibility of contributing not only to the growth of the literature but to the shaping of the culture as I should like it to be. The American novel is in this sense a conquest of the frontier; as it describes our experience, it creates it."

For Ellison, then, the task of the novelist was a moral and political one. In his preface to the thirtieth anniversary edition of *Invisible Man,* Ellison argued that the serious novel, like the best politics, "is a thrust toward a human ideal." Even when the ideal is not realized in the actual, he declared, "there is still available that fictional *vision* of an ideal democracy in which the actual combines with the ideal and gives us representations of a state of things in which the highly placed and the lowly, the black and the white, the Northerner and the Southerner, the native-born and the immigrant are combined to tell us of transcendent truths and possibilities such as those discovered when Mark Twain set Huck and Jim afloat on the raft." Ellison saw the novel as a "raft of hope" that may help readers stay above water as they try "to negotiate the snags and whirlpools that mark our nation's vacillating course toward and away from the democratic ideal."

This vision of pluralism and possibility as the basic definition of self and serious fiction has its roots in Ellison's personal history, a history marked by vacillations between the ideal and the real. He recalled in *Shadow and Act* that, as teenagers, he and his friends saw themselves as "Renaissance Men" unlimited by any sense of racial inferiority and determined to be recipients of the American Dream, to witness the ideal become the real. Ellison recounted two "accidents" that contributed to his sense of self as something beyond the external definition of race. The first occurred while he lived in a white, middle-class neighborhood where his mother worked as a building custodian. He became friends with a young white boy, a friendship based not on the "race question as such" but rather on their mutual loneliness and interest in radios. The other contact with "that world beyond the Negro community" came as his mother brought home discarded copies of magazines such as *Vanity Fair* and *Literary Digest* and old recordings of operas. Ellison remembered that these books and music "spoke to me of a life which was broader" and which "I could some day make my own."

This sense of a world beyond his but to which he would ultimately belong translated itself into his sense of the world that *was* his and to which he *did* belong. He was profoundly aware of the richness, vitality, and variety in his black community; he was aware, also, that the affirmative reality of black life was something he never found in the books he read, was never taught in the schools he attended. Ellison had experienced the nonverbal articulation of these qualities in the jazz and blues that were so much a part of his upbringing. In particular he recalls, in *Shadow and Act,* Jimmy Rushing, the blues singer who "represented, gave voice to, something which was very affirming of Negro life, feelings which you couldn't really put into words." But recording and preserving the value of black life only in this me-

dium did not satisfy Ellison; he was haunted, he admits, by a need "for other forms of transcendence and identification which I could only associate with classical music." As he explained, "I was taken very early with a passion to link together all I loved within the Negro community and all those things I felt in the world which lay beyond." This passion to join separate worlds and disparate selves into a unity of being infuses the content and style of *Invisible Man* and lies at the heart of Ellison's theory of fiction.

Early in his career, however, Ellison conceived of his vocation as a musician, as a composer of symphonies. When he entered Alabama's Tuskegee Institute in 1933 he enrolled as a music major; he wonders in *Shadow and Act* if he did so because, given his background, it was the only art "that seemed to offer some possibility for self-definition." The act of writing soon presented itself as an art through which he could link the disparate worlds he cherished, could verbally record and create the "affirmation of Negro life" he knew was so intrinsic a part of the universally human. To move beyond the old definitions that separated jazz from classical music, vernacular from literary language, the folk from the mythic, he would have to discover a prose style that could equal the integrative imagination of the "Renaissance Man."

Shadow and Act records that during 1935, his second year at Tuskegee, Ellison began his "conscious education in literature." Reading Emily Bronte's *Wuthering Heights* and Thomas Hardy's *Jude the Obscure* produced in him "an agony of unexpressible emotion," but T. S. Eliot's *The Waste Land* absolutely seized his imagination. He admits: "I was intrigued by its power to move me while eluding my understanding. Somehow its rhythms were often closer to those of jazz than were those of the Negro poets, and even though I could not understand then, its range of allusion was as mixed and varied as that of Louis Armstrong." Determined to understand the "hidden system of organization" that eluded him, Ellison began to explore the sources that Eliot had identified in the footnotes to the poem. This reading in ancient mythology, history, literature, and folklore led, in turn, to his reading of such twentieth-century writers as Ezra Pound, Ernest Hemingway, and Gertrude Stein, who led him back to the nineteenth-century authors Herman Melville and Mark Twain. The more Ellison read in literature and the sources of literature, the more he found that the details of his own history were "transformed." Local customs took on a "more universal meaning"; he became aware of the universal in the specific. His experience with *The Waste Land,* which forced him to wonder why he "had never read anything of equal intensity and sensibility by an American Negro writer," was his introduction to the universal power of the folk tradition as the foundation of literature.

During this same year, Ellison took a sociology course, an experience he describes in *Shadow and Act* as "humiliating." Presenting a reductive, unrealistic portrait of the American black as the "lady of the races," this sociological view denied the complex richness of black life that Ellison had so often experienced. In *The Craft of Ralph Ellison* Robert G. O'Meally argued that this encounter with a limited and limiting definition of blacks created in Ellison "an accelerated sense of urgency" to learn more about black culture and to find an artistic form to capture the vital reality of the black community that he had heard in the blues sessions, in the barbershops, and in the stories and jokes he had heard from some classmates as they returned from seasonal work in the cotton fields. Ironically, an accident intervened that propelled him on this course. Because of a mix-up about his scholarship, Ellison found himself without the money to return to Tuskegee. He went instead to New York, enacting the prototypical journey North, confident that he would return to Tuskegee after he had earned enough money.

Because Ellison did not get a job that paid him enough to save money for tuition, he stayed in New York, working and studying composition until his mother died in Dayton, Ohio. After his return to Dayton, he and his brother supported themselves by hunting. Though Ellison had hunted for years, he did not know how to wing-shoot; it was from Hemingway's fiction that he learned this process. Ellison studied Hemingway to learn writing techniques; from the older writer he also learned a lesson in descriptive accuracy and power, in the close relationship between fiction and reality. Like his narrator in *Invisible Man,* Ellison did not return to college; instead he began his long apprenticeship as a writer, his long and often difficult journey toward self-definition.

Ellison's early days in New York, before his return to Dayton, provided him with experiences that would later translate themselves into his theory of fiction. Two days after his arrival in "deceptively 'free' Harlem," he met black poet Langston Hughes who introduced him to the works of Andre Malraux, a French writer defined as Marxist. Though attracted to Marxism, Ellison sensed in Malraux something beyond a simplistic political sense of the human condition. Said Ellison: Malraux "was the artist-revolutionary rather than a politician when he wrote *Man's Fate,* and the book lives not because of a political position embraced at the time, but because of its larger concern with the tragic struggle of humanity." Ellison began to form his definition of the artist as a revolutionary concerned less with local injustice than with the timelessly tragic.

Ellison's view of art was furthered after he met black novelist Richard Wright. Wright urged him to read Joseph Conrad, Henry James, James Joyce, and Feodor Dostoevsky and invited Ellison to contribute a review essay and then a short story to the magazine he was editing. Wright was then in the process of writing *Native Son,* much of which Ellison read, he declared in *Shadow and Act,* "as it came out of the typewriter." Though awed by the process of writing and aware of the achievement of the novel, Ellison, who had just read Malraux, began to form his objections to the "sociological," deterministic ideology which informed the portrait of the work's protagonist, Bigger Thomas. In *Shadow and Act,* which Arthur P. Davis in *From the Dark Tower: Afro-American Writers, 1900 to 1960* described as partly an *apologia provita sua* (a defense of his life), Ellison articulated the basis of his objection: "I, for instance, found it disturbing that Bigger Thomas had none of the finer qualities of Richard Wright, none of the imagination, none of the sense of poetry, none of the gaiety." Ellison thus refuted the depiction of the black individual as an inarticulate victim whose life is one only of despair, anger, and pain. He insisted that art must capture instead the complex reality, the pain and the pleasure of black existence, thereby challenging the definition of the black person as something less than fully human. Such a vision of art, which is at the heart of *Invisible Man,* became the focal point of an extended debate between Ellison and Irving Howe, who in a 1963 *Dissent* article accused Ellison of disloyalty to Wright in particular and to "protest fiction" in general.

From 1938 to 1944, Ellison published a number of short stories and contributed essays to journals such as *New Masses.* As with other examples of Ellison's work, these stories have provoked disparate readings. In an essay in *Black World,* Ernest Kaiser called the earliest stories and the essays in *New Masses* "the healthiest" of Ellison's career. The critic praised the economic theories that inform the early fiction, and he found Ellison's language pure, emotional, and effective. Lamenting a change he attributed to Ellison's concern with literary technique, Kaiser charged the later stories, essays, and novel with being no longer concerned with people's problems and with being "unemotional." Other critics, like Marcus Klein in *After Alienation: American Novels in Mid-Century,* saw the early work as a progressive preparation for Ellison's mature fiction and theory. In the earliest of these stories, "Slick Gonna Learn," Ellison drew a character shaped largely by an ideological, naturalistic conception of existence, the very type of character he later repudiated. From this imitation of proletarian fiction, Ellison's work moved towards psychological and finally metaphysical explorations of the human condition. His characters thus were freed from restrictive definitions as Ellison developed a voice that was his own, Klein maintains.

In the two latest stories of the 1938-1944 period, "Flying Home" and "King of the Bingo Game," Ellison created characters congruent with his sense of pluralism and possibility and does so in a narrative style that begins to approach the complexity of *Invisible Man.* As Arthur P. Davis noted, in "Flying Home" Ellison combined realism, folk story, symbolism, and a touch of surrealism to present his protagonist, Todd. In a fictional world composed of myriad levels of the mythic and the folk, the classical and the modern, Todd fights to free himself of imposed definitions. In "King of the Bingo Game," Ellison experimented with integrating sources and techniques. As in all of Ellison's early stories, the protagonist is a young black man fighting for his freedom against forces and people that attempt to deny it. In "King of the Bingo Game," O'Meally argued, "the struggle is seen in its most abstracted form." This abstraction results from the "dreamlike shifts of time and levels of consciousness" that dominate the surrealistic story and also from the fact that "the King is Ellison's first character to sense the frightening absurdity of everyday American life." In an epiphany which frees him from illusion and which places him, even if for only a moment, in control, the King realizes "that his battle for freedom and identity must be waged not against individuals or even groups, but against no less than history and fate," O'Meally declared. The parameters of the fight for freedom and identity have been broadened. Ellison saw his black hero as one who wages the oldest battle in human history: the fight for freedom to be timelessly human, to engage in the "tragic

struggle of humanity," as the writer asserted in *Shadow and Act.*

Whereas The King achieves awareness for a moment, the Invisible Man not only becomes aware but is able to articulate fully the struggle. As Ellison noted in his preface to the anniversary edition of the novel, too often characters have been "figures caught up in the most intense forms of social struggle, subject to the most extreme forms of the human predicament but yet seldom able to articulate the issues which tortured them." The Invisible Man is endowed with eloquence; he is Ellison's radical experiment with a fiction that insists upon the full range and humanity of the black character.

Ellison began *Invisible Man* in 1945. Although he was at work on a never-completed war novel at the time, Ellison recalled in his 1982 preface that he could not ignore the "taunting, disembodied voice" he heard beckoning him to write *Invisible Man.* Published in 1952 after a seven-year creative struggle, and awarded the National Book Award in 1953, *Invisible Man* received critical acclaim. Although some early reviewers were puzzled or disappointed by the experimental narrative techniques, many now agree that these techniques give the work its lasting force and account for Ellison's influence on later fiction. The novel is a fugue of cultural fragments—echoes of Homer, Joyce, Eliot, and Hemingway join forces with the sounds of spirituals, blues, jazz, and nursery rhymes. The Invisible Man is as haunted by Louis Armstrong's "What did I do / To be so black / And blue?" as he is by Hemingway's bullfight scenes and his matadors' grace under pressure. The linking together of these disparate cultural elements allows the Invisible Man to draw the portrait of his inner face that is the way out of his wasteland.

In the novel, Ellison clearly employed the traditional motif of the *Bildungsroman,* or novel of education: the Invisible Man moves from innocence to experience, darkness to light, from blindness to sight. Complicating this linear journey, however, is the narrative frame provided by the Prologue and Epilogue which the narrator composes after the completion of his above-ground educational journey. Yet readers begin with the Prologue, written in his underground chamber on the "border area" of Harlem where he is waging a guerrilla war against the Monopolated Light & Power Company by invisibly draining their power. At first denied the story of his discovery, readers must be initiated through the act of re-experiencing the events that led them and the narrator to this hole. Armed with some suggestive hints and symbols, readers then start the journey toward a revisioning of the Invisible Man, America, and themselves.

The journey is a deliberate baptism by fire. From the Battle Royal where the Invisible Man swallows his own blood in the name of opportunity; to the madness of The Golden Day; to the protagonist's anguished expulsion from the College; to the horror of his lobotomy; to his dehumanization by the Brotherhood; to his jubilant discovery of the unseen people of Harlem; to the nightmare that is Ras and the riots; and finally to the descent underground and the ritualistic burning of the contents of his briefcase, readers are made to participate in the plot because they, finally, are a part of it. The novel is about plots: the plots against the Invisible Man by Bledsoe and the Brotherhood; the conspiracy against himself that is the inevitable result of his illusions; the plot of the American ideal that keeps him dodging the forces of the actual; the plot of the reader against the writer; and the plot, ultimately, against every human being by life itself. Like the Invisible Man, readers are duped, time and time again, resisting the reality before them.

In the Prologue and Epilogue the Invisible Man is the conscious, reflexive artist, recording his perceptions of self and other as he articulates the meaning of the journey and the descent. In the Epilogue he lets readers understand more clearly the preparatory hints and symbols he offered in the Prologue. He articulates his understanding of the old woman's words when she told him that freedom lay not in hating but in loving and in "knowing how to say" what is in one's head. Here too he unveils his insight into his grandfather, an ex-slave who "never had any doubts about his humanity" and who accepted the principle of America "in all its human and absurd diversity." As the Invisible Man records his journey through the underground America, he asserts a vision of America as it should be. He becomes the nation's moral conscience, embodying its greatest failure and its highest possibility. He reclaims his full humanity and freedom by accepting the world as a "concrete, ornery, vile and sublimely wonderful" reflection of the perceptive self.

The act of writing, of ordering and defining the self, is what gives the Invisible Man freedom and what allows him to manage the absurdity and chaos of everyday life. Writing frees the self from imposed definitions, from the straitjacket of all that would limit the productive possibilities of the self. Echoing the pluralism of the novel's form, the Invisible Man insists on the freedom to be ambivalent, to love and to hate, to denounce and to defend the America he inherits. Ellison himself was well-acquainted with the ambivalence of his American heritage; nowhere is it more evident than in his name. Named after the nineteenth-century essayist and poet Ralph Waldo Emerson, whom Ellison's father admired, the name created for Ellison embarrassment, confusion, and a desire to be the American writer his namesake called for. And Ellison placed such emphasis on his unnamed yet self-named narrator's breaking the shackles of restrictive definitions, of what others call reality or right, he also freed himself, as Robert B. Stepto in *From Behind the Veil: A Study of Afro-American Narrative* argued, from the strictures of the traditional slave narratives of Frederick Douglas and W. E. B. DuBois. By consciously invoking this form but then not bringing the motif of "ascent and immersion" to its traditional completion, Ellison revoiced the form, made it his own, and stepped outside it.

Within the novel, stepping outside of traditional form can be a dangerous act. In *Invisible Man,* Tod Clifton steps outside the historically powerful Brotherhood and is shot for "resisting reality." At the other extreme, Rinehart steps outside all definitions and becomes the embodiment of chaos. In *City of Words: American Fiction, 1950-1970* Tony Tanner noted that Ellison presented an overriding preoccupation of postmodern fiction: the fear of a rigid pattern that would limit all freedom of self, coupled with the fear of no pattern, of a chaotic void that would render illusory all sense of self. The Invisible Man is aware of form and formlessness. As he says, "Without light I am not only invisible but formless as well; and to be unaware of one's form is to live a death." The search for identity, which Ellison said in *Shadow and Act* is "*the* American theme," is the heart of the novel and the center of many critical debates over it. At novel's end, the journey is not complete; the Invisible Man must emerge from his hole and test the sense of self formed in hibernation. As he journeys toward this goal, toward the emergence of a sense of self that is at once black and American and universally human, questions recur: In his quest for pluralism, does he sacrifice his blackness? In his devotion to an imaginative rendering of self, does he lose his socially active self?

In her 1979 *PMLA* essay, Susan Blake argued that Ellison's insistence that black experience be ritualized as part of the larger human experience results in a denial of the unique social reality of black life. Because Ellison so thoroughly adapted black folklore into the Western tradition, Blake found that the definition of black life becomes "not black but white"; it "exchanges the self-definition of the folk for the definition of the masters." Thorpe Butler, in a 1984 *College Language Association Journal* essay, defended Ellison against Blake's criticism. He declared that Ellison's depiction of specific black experience as part of the universal does not "diminish the unique richness and anguish" of that experience and does not "diminish the force of Ellison's protest against the blind, cruel dehumanization of black Americans by white society." This debate extends arguments that have appeared since the publication of the novel. Underlying these controversies is the old, uneasy argument about the relationship of art and politics, of literary practice and social commitment.

Ellison repeatedly defended his view, here voiced in *Shadow and Act,* that "protest is an element of all art, though it does not necessarily take the form of speaking for a political or social program." In a 1970 *Time* essay, Ellison defined further his particular definition of protest, of the "soul" of his art and his people: "An expression of American diversity within unity, of blackness with whiteness, soul announces the presence of a creative struggle against the realities of existence." Insisting that the novelist is a "manipulator and depictor of moral problems," Ellison claimed that as novelist he does not try to escape the reality of black pain. He frequently reminded readers that he knows well the pain and anger that come with being black; his mother was arrested for violating Jim Crow housing laws, and in Alabama he was subjected daily to the outrageous policies of segregation. But for Ellison there needed to be more than even an eloquent depiction of this part of reality—he needed "to transform these elements into art . . . to transcend, as the blues transcend the painful conditions with which they deal." In *Invisible Man* he declared that Louis Armstrong "made poetry out of being invisible." Social reality may place the creator in the underground, render him invisible, but his art leads him out of the hole, eloquent, visible, and empowered by the very people who put him there.

Although the search for identity is the major theme of *Invisible Man,* other aspects of the novel have also received critical attention. Among them, as Joanne Giza noted in her essay in *Black American Writers:*

Bibliographical Essays, are literary debts and analogies, comic elements, the metaphor of vision, use of the blues, and folkloric elements. Although all of these concerns are part of the larger issue of identity, Ellison's use of blues and folklore has been singled out as a major contribution to contemporary literature and culture. Since the publication of *Invisible Man,* scores of articles have appeared on these two topics, a fact which in turn has led to a rediscovery and revisioning of the importance of blues and folklore to American literature and culture in general.

Much of Ellison's groundbreaking work is presented in *Shadow and Act.* Published in 1964, this collection of essays, said Ellison, is "concerned with three general themes: with literature and folklore, with Negro musical expression—especially jazz and the blues—and with the complex relationship between the Negro American subculture and North American culture as a whole." This volume has been hailed as one of the more prominent examples of cultural criticism of the century. Writing in *Commentary,* Robert Penn Warren praised the astuteness of Ellison's perceptions; in *New Leader,* Stanley Edgar Hyman proclaimed Ellison "the profoundest cultural critic we have." In the *New York Review of Books,* R. W. B. Lewis explored Ellison's study of black music as a form of power and found that "Ellison is not only a self-identifier but the source of self-definition in others." Published in 1986, *Going to the Territory* is a second collection of essays reprising many of the subjects and concerns treated in *Shadow and Act—* literature, art, music, the relationships of black and white cultures, fragments of autobiography, tributes to such noted black Americans as Richard Wright, Duke Ellington, and painter Romare Beardon. With the exception of "An Extravagance of Laughter," a lengthy examination of Ellison's response to Jack Kirkland's dramatization of Erskine Caldwell's novel *Tobacco Road,* the essays in *Going to the Territory* are reprints of previously published articles or speeches, most of them dating from the 1960s.

Ellison's influence as both novelist and critic, as artist and cultural historian, has been enormous. In special issues of *Black World* and *College Language Association Journal* devoted to Ellison, strident attacks appear alongside equally spirited accolades. Perhaps another measure of Ellison's stature and achievement is his readers' vigil for his long-awaited second novel. Although Ellison often refused to answer questions about the work-in-progress, there is enough evidence to suggest that the manuscript is very large, that all or part of it was destroyed in a fire and is being rewritten, and that its creation has been a long and painful task. Most readers wait expectantly, believing that Ellison, who has said in *Shadow and Act* that he "failed of eloquence" in *Invisible Man,* is waiting until his second novel equals his imaginative vision of the American novel as conqueror of the frontier, equals the Emersonian call for a literature to release all people from the bonds of oppression.

Eight excerpts from this novel-in-progress have been published in journals such as *Quarterly Review of Literature, Massachusetts Review,* and *Nobel Savage.* Set in the South in the years spanning the Jazz Age to the Civil Rights movement, these fragments seem an attempt to recreate modern American history and identity. The major characters are the Reverend Hickman, a one-time jazz musician, and Bliss, the light-skinned boy whom he adopts and who later passes into white society and becomes Senator Sun-raider, an advocate of white supremacy. As O'Meal-ly noted in *The Craft of Ralph Ellison,* the major difference between Bliss and Ellison's earlier young protagonists is that despite some harsh collisions with reality, Bliss refuses to divest himself of his illusions and accept his personal history. Said O'Meally: "Moreover, it is a renunciation of the blackness of American experience and culture, a refusal to accept the American past in all its complexity."

Like *Invisible Man,* this novel promises to be a broad and searching inquiry into identity, ideologies, culture, and history. The narrative form is similar as well; here, too, is the blending of popular and classical myth, of contradictory cultural memories, of an intricate pattern of images of birth, death, and rebirth. In *Shadow and Act* Ellison described the novel's form as "a realism extended beyond realism" in which he explores again the multifaceted meanings of the folk as the basis of all literature and culture. What the ultimate form of the novel will be—if, indeed, these excerpts are to be part of one novel—remains hidden.

In Ellison's excerpts, Bliss becomes a traitor to his own race and loses his hold on those things of transforming, affirmative value. Hickman, on the other hand, accepts and celebrates his heritage, his belief in the timeless value of his history. As O'Meally wrote in his book-length study of Ellison, Hickman "holds fast to personal and political goals and values." Ellison, too, held fast to his values in the often chaotic and chameleon world of art and politics. The tone of these excerpts is primarily tragicomic, a

mode well-suited to Ellison's definition of life. As he said in *Shadow and Act,* "I think that the mixture of the marvelous and the terrible is a basic condition of human life and that the persistence of human ideals represents the marvelous pulling itself up out of the chaos of the universe." Elsewhere in the book, Ellison argued that "true novels, even when most pessimistic and bitter, arise out of an impulse to celebrate human life," the "human and absurd" commixture of American life.

After Ellison's death on April 16, 1994, speculation about the existence of the second novel reignited. In an article in the *New York Times,* William Grimes assembled the information available on the subject. "Joe Fox, Mr. Ellison's editor at Random House, and close friends of the novelist say that Mr. Ellison has left a manuscript of somewhere between 1,000 and 2,000 pages," Grimes reported. "At the time of his death, he had been working on it every day and was close to completing the work, whose fate now rests with his widow, Fanny." A close friend of Ellison's, John F. Callahan, a college dean from Portland, Oregon, told Grimes that he had seen parts of the manuscript not already published in other sources. "From what I've read, if `Invisible Man' is akin to Joyce's `Portrait of the Artist,' then the novel in progress may be his `Ulysses.'" Callahan added that "it's a weaving together of all kinds of voices, and not simply voices in the black tradition, but white voices, too: all kinds of American voices." As Grimes suggested, "If Mr. Ellison, as his final creative act, were to top `Invisible Man,' it would be a stunning bequest," given that the first novel is considered a literary classic. *Invisible Man* "has never been out of print," Grimes pointed out. "It has sold millions of copies worldwide. On college campuses it is required reading in 20th-century American literature courses, and it has been the subject of hundreds of scholarly articles."

BIOGRAPHICAL/CRITICAL SOURCES:

BOOKS

Allen, Walter Ernest, *The Modern Novel in Britain and the United States,* Dutton (New York City), 1964.

Alvarez, A., editor, *Under Pressure: The Writer in Society; Eastern Europe and the U.S.A.,* Penguin (New York City), 1965.

Baker, Houston, A., Jr., *Long Black Song: Essays in Black American Literature and Culture,* University Press of Virginia, 1972.

Baumbach, Jonathan, *The Landscape of Nightmare: Studies in the Contemporary American Novel,* New York University Press, 1965.

Benstion, Kimberly W., editor, *Speaking for You: The Vision of Ralph Ellison,* Howard University Press (Washington, DC), 1987.

Bigsby, C. W. E., editor, *The Black American Writer,* Volume I, Everett Edwards, 1969.

Bishop, Jack, *Ralph Ellison,* Chelsea House (New York City), 1988.

Bloom, Harold, editor, *Ralph Ellison: Modern Critical Views,* Chelsea Publishing, 1986.

Bone, Robert, *The Negro Novel in America,* Yale University Press (New Haven, CT), revised edition, 1965.

Breit, Harvey, *The Writer Observed,* World Publishing, 1956.

Busby, Mark, *Ralph Ellison,* Twayne (Boston), 1991.

Callahan, John F., *In the African-American Grain: The Pursuit of Voice in Twentieth-Century Black Fiction,* University of Illinois Press (Urbana, IL), 1988.

Concise Dictionary of American Literary Biography: The New Consciousness, 1941-1948, Gale (Detroit), 1987.

Contemporary Fiction in America and England, 1950-1970, Gale, 1976.

Contemporary Literary Criticism, Gale, Volume 1, 1973, Volume 3, 1975, Volume 11, 1979, Volume 54, 1989.

Cooke, Michael, *Afro-American Literature in the Twentieth Century: The Achievement of Intimacy,* Yale University Press, 1984.

Covo, Jacqueline, *The Blinking Eye: Ralph Waldo Ellison and His American, French, German, and Italian Critics, 1952-1971: Bibliographic Essays and a Checklist,* Scarecrow (Metuchen, NJ), 1974.

Davis, Arthur P., *From the Dark Tower: Afro-American Writers (1900 to 1960),* Howard University Press, 1974.

Davis, Charles T., *Black Is the Color of the Cosmos: Essays on Afro-American Literature and Culture, 1942-1981,* edited by Henry Louis Gates, Jr., Garland Publishing (New York City), 1982.

Dictionary of Literary Biography, Gale, Volume 2: *American Novelists since World War II,* 1978, Volume 76: *Afro-American Writers, 1940-1955,* 1988.

Dietze, Rudolf F., *Ralph Ellison: The Genius of an Artist,* Carl (Nuremburg), 1982.

Ellison, Ralph, *Shadow and Act,* Random House, 1964.

Fabre, Michael, editor, *Delta Number 18: Ralph Ellison,* University Paul Valery (Paris), 1984.

Fischer-Hornung, Dorothea, *Folklore and Myth in Ralph Ellison's Early Works,* Hochschul (Stuttgart), 1979.

Fisher, Dexter, and Robert B. Stepto, editors, *Afro-American Literature: The Reconstruction of Instruction,* Modern Language Association of America (New York City), 1979.

Gayle, Addison, Jr., editor, *Black Expression: Essays by and about Americans in the Creative Arts,* Weybright & Talley, 1969.

Gayle, Addison, Jr., compiler, *The Black Aesthetic,* Doubleday, 1971.

Gayle, Addison, Jr., *The Way of the New World: The Black Novel in America,* Anchor Press (New York City), 1975.

Gibson, Donald B., compiler, *Five Black Writers: Essays on Wright, Ellison, Baldwin, Hughes, and Le Roi Jones,* New York University Press, 1970.

Gottesman, Ronald, editor, *Studies in Invisible Man,* Merrill, 1971.

Graham, John, *The Writer's Voice: Conversations with Contemporary Writers,* edited by George Garrett, Morrow (New York City), 1973.

Graham, Maryemma, and Amritjit Singh, editors, *Conversations with Ralph Ellison,* University Press of Mississippi (Jackson, MS), 1995.

Gross, Seymour L., and John Edward Hardy, editors, *Images of the Negro in American Literature,* University of Chicago Press, 1966.

Harper, Michael S., and R. B. Stepto, editors, *Chant of Saints: A Gathering of Afro-American Literature, Art, and Scholarship,* University of Illinois Press, 1979.

Henderson, Bill, editor, *The Pushcart Prize, III: Best of the Small Presses,* Avon (New York City), 1979.

Hersey, John, editor, *Ralph Ellison: A Collection of Critical Essays,* Prentice-Hall (Englewood Cliffs, NJ), 1974.

Hill, Herbert, editor, *Anger and Beyond: The Negro Writer in the United States,* Harper (New York City), 1966.

Inge, M. Thomas, and others, editors, *Black American Writers: Bibliographical Essays,* Volume II: *Richard Wright, Ralph Ellison, James Baldwin, and Amiri Baraka,* St. Martin's (New York City), 1978.

Jothiprakash, R., *Commitment as a Theme in African American Literature: A Study of James Baldwin and Ralph Ellison,* Wyndham Hall Press (Bristol, IN), 1994.

Kazin, Alfred, *Bright Book of Life: American Novelists and Storytellers from Hemingway to Mailer,* Atlantic-Little, Brown (Boston), 1973.

Klein, Marcus, *After Alienation: American Novels in Mid-Century,* World Publishing, 1964.

Kostelanetz, Richard, *On Contemporary Literature: An Anthology of Critical Essays on the Major Movements and Writers of Contemporary Literature,* Avon, 1964.

Kostelanetz, *Politics in the African-American Novel: James Weldon Johnson, W. E. B. DuBois, Richard Wright, and Ralph Ellison,* Greenwood Press (New York City), 1991.

Lynch, Michael F., *Creative Revolt: A Study of Wright, Ellison, and Dostevsky,* P. Lang (New York City), 1990.

Margolies, Edward, *Native Sons: A Critical Study of Twentieth-Century Negro American Authors,* Lippincott (Philadelphia, PA), 1968.

McSweeney, Kerry, *Invisible Man: Race and Identity,* Twayne (Boston), 1988.

Nadel, Alan, *Invisible Criticism: Ralph Ellison and the American Canon,* University of Iowa Press (Iowa City, IA), 1988.

O'Brien, John, *Interviews with Black Writers,* Liveright (New York City), 1973.

O'Meally, Robert G., *The Craft of Ralph Ellison,* Harvard University Press (Cambridge, MA), 1980.

O'Meally, *New Essays on Invisible Man,* Cambridge University Press (Cambridge, England), 1988.

Ottley, Roi, William J. Weatherby, and others, editors, *The Negro in New York: An Informal Social History,* New York Public Library, 1967.

Parr, Susan Resneck, and Pancho Savery, editors, *Approaches to Teaching Ellison's "Invisible Man,"* Modern Language Associates of America, 1989.

Plimpton, George, editor, *Writers at Work: The Paris Review Interviews,* second series, Viking (New York City), 1963.

Reilly, John M., editor, *Twentieth-Century Interpretations of Invisible Man: A Collection of Critical Essays,* Prentice-Hall, 1970.

Schor, Edith, *Visible Ellison: A Study of Ralph Ellison's Fiction,* Greenwood Press, 1993.

Stepto, R. B., *From Behind the Veil: A Study of Afro-American Narrative,* University of Illinois Press, 1979.

Sundquist, Eric J., editor, *Cultural Contexts for Ralph Ellison's Invisible Man,* Bedford Books (Boston), 1995.

Tanner, Tony, *City of Words: American Fiction, 1950-1970,* Harper, 1971.

Trimmer, Joseph F., editor, *A Casebook on Ralph Ellison's Invisible Man,* Crowell (New York City), 1972.

Waldmeir, Joseph J., editor, *Recent American Fiction: Some Critical Views,* Houghton (Boston), 1963.

Warren, Robert Penn, *Who Speaks for the Negro?,* Random House, 1965.

Watts, Jerry Gafio, *Heroism and the Black Intellectual: Ralph Ellison, Politics, and Afro-American Intellectual Life,* University of North Carolina Press (Chapel Hill, NC), 1994.

The Writer as Independent Spirit, [New York], 1968.

PERIODICALS

America, August 27, 1994, p. 26.
American Quarterly, March, 1972.
American Scholar, autumn, 1955.
Atlantic, July, 1952; December, 1970; August, 1986.
Barat Review, January, 1968.
Black Academy Review, winter, 1970.
Black American Literature Forum, summer, 1978.
Black Books Bulletin, winter, 1972.
Black Creation, summer, 1970.
Black World, December, 1970 (special Ellison issue).
Book Week, October 25, 1964.
Boundary 2, winter, 1978.
Brown Alumni Monthly, November, 1979.
Carleton Miscellany, winter, 1980 (special Ellison issue).
Chicago Review, Volume 19, number 2, 1967.
Chicago Tribune, June 18, 1992, p. 1.
Chicago Tribune Book World, August 10, 1986.
College Language Association Journal, December, 1963; June, 1967; March, 1970 (special Ellison issue); September, 1971; December, 1971; December, 1972; June, 1973; March, 1974; September, 1976; September, 1977; Number 25, 1982; Number 27, 1984.
Commentary, November, 1953; Number 39, 1965.
Commonweal, May 2, 1952.
Crisis, March, 1953; March, 1970.
Critique, Number 2, 1968.
Daedalus, winter, 1968.
Daily Oklahoman, August 23, 1953.
December, winter, 1961.
English Journal, September, 1969; May, 1973; November, 1984.
Entertainment Weekly, April 29, 1994, p. 73.
48 Magazine of the Year, May, 1948.
Grackle, Volume 4, 1977-78.
Harper's, October, 1959; March, 1967; July, 1967.
Journal of Black Studies, Number 7, 1976.
Los Angeles Times, August 8, 1986.
Massachusetts Review, autumn, 1967; autumn, 1977.
Modern Fiction Studies, winter, 1969-70.
Motive, April, 1966.
Muhammad Speaks, September, 1972; December, 1972.
Nation, May 10, 1952; September 9, 1964; November 9, 1964; September 20, 1965.

Negro American Literature Forum, July, 1970; summer, 1973; Number 9, 1975; spring, 1977.

Negro Digest, May, 1964; August, 1967.

Negro History Bulletin, May, 1953; October, 1953.

New Criterion, September, 1983.

New Leader, October 26, 1964.

New Republic, November 14, 1964; August 4, 1986.

Newsday, October, 1967.

Newsweek, August 12, 1963; October 26, 1964; May 2, 1994, p. 58.

New Yorker, May 31, 1952; November 22, 1976; March 14, 1994, p. 34.

New York Herald Tribune Book Review, April 13, 1952.

New York Review of Books, January 28, 1964; January 28, 1965.

New York Times, April 13, 1952; April 24, 1985; April 17, 1994, p. A38; April 20, 1994, p. C13; April 18, 1996, pp. B1, B2.

New York Times Book Review, April 13, 1952; May 4, 1952; October 25, 1964; January 24, 1982; August 3, 1986.

New York Times Magazine, November 20, 1966; January 1, 1995, p. 22.

Paris Review, spring, 1955; spring/summer, 1957.

Partisan Review, Number 25, 1958.

Phoenix, fall, 1961.

Phylon, winter, 1960; spring, 1970; spring, 1973; summer, 1973; summer, 1977.

PMLA, January, 1979.

Renascence, spring, 1974; winter, 1978.

Saturday Review, April 12, 1952; March 14, 1953; December 11, 1954; January 1, 1955; April 26, 1958; May 17, 1958; July 12, 1958; September 27, 1958; July 28, 1962; October 24, 1964.

Shenandoah, summer, 1969.

Smith Alumni Quarterly, July, 1964.

Southern Humanities Review, winter, 1970.

Southern Literary Journal, spring, 1969.

Southern Review, fall, 1974; summer, 1985.

Studies in American Fiction, spring, 1973.

Studies in Black Literature, autumn, 1971; autumn, 1972; spring, 1973; spring, 1975; spring, 1976; winter, 1976.

Tamarack Review, October, 1963; summer, 1964.

Time, April 14, 1952; February 9, 1959; February 1, 1963; April 6, 1970.

Times Literary Supplement, January 18, 1968.

Tribune Books (Chicago), April 24, 1994, p. 3.

Village Voice, November 19, 1964.

Washington Post, August 19-21, 1973; April 21, 1982; February 9, 1983; March 30, 1983; July 23, 1986; April 18, 1994, p. C1; April 25, 1994, p. C2.

Washington Post Book World, May 17, 1987.

Wisconsin Studies in Literature, winter, 1960; summer, 1966.

Y-Bird Reader, autumn, 1977.

OBITUARIES:

PERIODICALS

Atlanta Journal-Constitution, April 17, 1994, p. A1.

Boston Globe, April 17, 1994, p. 63.

Los Angeles Times, April 17, 1994, p. A1.

New York Times, April 17, 1994, p. A1.

Times (London), April 18, 1994, p. 17.

Washington Post, April 17, 1994, A1.*

* * *

EPSTEIN, Daniel Mark   1948-

PERSONAL: Born October 25, 1948, in Washington, DC; son of Donald David (a businessman) and Louise (Tilman) Epstein; married Wendy Roberts, May 29, 1976; children: Johanna Ruth, Benjamin Robert. *Education:* Kenyon College, B.A. (with highest honors), 1970; postgraduate study at University of Virginia, 1970-71.

ADDRESSES: Home—401 Wingate Road, Baltimore, MD 21201.

CAREER: Poet in residence, Maryland Arts Council, 1972-86; U.S. Information Service lecturer in Germany, 1977, and in Africa, 1978; Johns Hopkins University, Baltimore, MD, visiting assistant professor, 1979-82; Randolph-Macon Woman's College, Lynchburg, VA, distinguished writer in residence, 1982; Towson State University, Baltimore, writer in residence, 1983—. Consultant to National Endowment for the Humanities, 1973. Co-founder, Baltimore Poet's Theatre; member of board of directors, Baltimore Theatre Project. Has given numerous poetry readings.

MEMBER: Poetry Society of America, PEN, Phi Beta Kappa.

AWARDS, HONORS: Robert Frost Prize, 1969; Danforth Foundation and Woodrow Wilson fellowship, 1971; National Defense Education Art grant, 1972; National Endowment for the Arts fellow, 1974; Prix de Rome, American Academy and National Institute of Arts and Letters, 1977; Emily Clark Balch Award, *Virginia Quarterly,* 1981; Guggenheim fellowship, 1983; fellow, American Academy in Rome; Stephen Vincent Benet Prize for "Letter Concerning Yellow Fever."

WRITINGS:

POETRY

No Vacancies in Hell, Liveright (New York City), 1973.
The Follies, Overlook (Woodstock, New York), 1977.
Young Men's Gold, Overlook, 1978.
The Book of Fortune: Poems, Overlook, 1982.
Spirits, Overlook, 1987.
The Boy in the Well and Other Poems, Overlook, 1995.

Also author of poetry collection, *Appearances,* 1969.

OTHER

Jenny and the Phoenix (play), first produced at Baltimore Theatre Project, 1977.
Star of Wonder: American Stories and Memoirs (essays), Overlook, 1986.
(Compiler with David Bergman) *Heath Guide to Poetry,* D.C. Heath (Lexington, MA), 1983.
(Compiler with Bergman) *Heath Guide to Literature,* D.C. Heath, 1984, third edition, 1992.
Love's Compass: A Natural History of the Heart, Addison-Wesley (Reading, MA), 1990.
Sister Aimee: The Life of Aimee Semple McPherson, Harcourt (New York City), 1993.

Also author of play *The Gayety Burlesque,* 1978. Contributor of poems to magazines, including *New Yorker, Nation, Michigan Quarterly Review, Virginia Quarterly Review, Northwest Review,* and *Modern Occasions.*

SIDELIGHTS: Daniel Mark Epstein has distinguished himself as an American poet in a career that has spanned more than twenty-five years. From his second published collection of verse, 1973's *No Vacancies in Hell,* through *The Boy in the Well and Other Poems,* released in 1995, his works have consistently received critical praise. Speaking of *The Boy in the Well,* Ray Olson in *Booklist* finds that Epstein's "double-seeing characterizes all these poems, and, refreshingly in these brutal and cynical times, justice and mercy inform them." In addition to poetry, Epstein has written a short-story collection entitled *Star of Wonder,* the autobiographical *Love's Compass: A Natural History of the Heart,* and *Sister Aimee: The Life of Aimee Semple McPherson,* an acclaimed biography of the pre-Depression Era evangelist.

Epstein's *No Vacancies in Hell* first brought the poet to wide attention. If Epstein "learns to handle his large pack of skills, he may become one of the best poets of the century," reviewer Paul Ramsey remarked in the *Sewanee Review* in response to *No Vacancies in Hell.* While noting that the twenty-five-year-old poet had not completely reached his stylistic potential, several critics praised the volume for its young author's use of figurative language and abstracted narrative style. Reviewing the later collection *Young Men's Gold,* Jeffrey Hart in the *New Republic* claims that "with the publication of *The Follies* and now *Young Men's Gold,* [Epstein's] promise looks very close to being fulfilled." Hart singles out "In a Free Country," the first poem in *Young Men's Gold,* finding it "as good a love poem as has been written in this or any other century." The critic also points to the title poem, "Young Men's Gold," noting that "Romantic without reservation, both direct and richly textured, this verse narrative possesses great power and—dare one simply say it?—beauty." While finding that Epstein sometimes becomes almost self-congratulatory in *Young Men's Gold,* Susan Wood nevertheless comments in the *Washington Post* that "Epstein is basically a poet of love and celebration. His greatest strengths are wit and tenderness, a kind of energetic muscularity and great technical skill, qualities observed in the very first lines of this book."

In 1982's *The Book of Fortune,* Epstein paints poetic portraits of family, friends, and historical figures: from his own dying grandmother to the lonely and suicidal wife of noted historian Henry Adams. *Spirits,* which followed in 1987, found the poet continuing with this approach. "Everything in the world of this poet reveals a cornucopia of hidden surprises," states Philip Balla in the *Chicago Tribune,* "with spiraling processes embracing and infusing all." Translated and filtered by the language of music, dance, visual art, and storytelling, Epstein shows the calming effect of human creativity. While praising several of the poems in *Spirits, America* reviewer Robert E. Hosmer Jr. describes the collection as "an uneven performance, weakened by its lack of organization and the presence of a number of undistinguished poems." However, Hosmer adds, in the dramatic monologue "The Testament of Lakedion," "the narrative unfolds with haunting intensity and skill, demonstrating what is best in Epstein's poetry: sustained craftsmanship, lyrical intensity, . . . intellectual vigor, and integrity of vision."

Star of Wonder marked Epstein's first foray into prose fiction. In this collection of nine gently nostalgic essays, he recounts his boyhood—raised by a Christian mother and a Jewish father, Epstein was taught to both love people of diverse ethnic backgrounds and tolerate a variety of personal belief systems—and sets forth personal insights on the character and attributes of such public figures as magician Harry Houdini and musician Daniel Heifetz. More personal still is *Love's Compass,* described by a reviewer in the *West Coast Review of Books* as a "combination of history, philosophy and personal biography to define and describe the concept of love in all its forms." Love of parents and grandparents, love for wives, love for one's children: *Love's Compass* steers a course through Epstein's life as well as through his philosophic base rooted in the "love child" era of the 1960s. Although criticized by some reviewers for its author's one-sided view of relationships, Patrick H. Samway praises *Love's Compass* as a book of "depth and perspective . . . . a book you might want to read again before a roaring fire in the depths of winter."

Epstein has also written a biography of 1920s evangelist Aimee Semple McPherson, a controversial figure whose flamboyant style and reputed healings of the sick made her a national figure. At the height of her fame, McPherson presided over the Foursquare Gospel Church International based in Los Angeles. Her services, resembling Broadway shows more than traditional religious observances, made McPherson a favorite among the Hollywood set of the 1930s. Her church's radio station gave McPherson a national audience as well. Carol Flake in the *Washington Post Book World* finds that, "unlike most biographers of religious figures, [Epstein] is neither debunker, believer, nor scholar. He seems, rather, a curious and sympathetic admirer whose wonder increased with familiarity with his subject." According to William Martin in the *New York Times Book Review,* "*Sister Aimee* fills a significant gap in the history of revivalism. . . . A fascinating tale, well told."

BIOGRAPHICAL/CRITICAL SOURCES:

BOOKS

Contemporary Literary Criticism, Volume 7, Gale (Detroit), 1977.

PERIODICALS

America, May 7, 1988, pp. 490-91; May 12, 1990.
Best Sellers, March 1979.
Booklist, July 1995, p. 1855.
Boston Globe, April 6, 1993, p. 65.
Carolina Quarterly, winter 1974.
Chicago Tribune, September 13, 1987, p. 14.

National Review, December 24, 1982, pp. 1624-25.
New Republic, December 10, 1977, p. 34; September 16, 1978, pp. 25-26.
New York Times Book Review, March 14, 1993, p. 11.
Parnassus, fall/winter 1974.
Poetry, October 1974, pp. 44-52.
Sewanee Review, spring 1974, pp. 404-05.
Virginia Quarterly Review, summer 1974; winter 1979.
Washington Post, December 3, 1978, p. E6.
Washington Post Book World, March 14, 1993.
West Coast Review of Books, Volume 5, number 5, 1990.

*   *   *

EVANS, G. R.
See EVANS, Gillian (Rosemary)

*   *   *

EVANS, Gillian (Rosemary)   1944-
(G. R. Evans)

PERSONAL: Born October 26, 1944, in Birmingham, England; daughter of Arthur Raymond and Gertrude Elizabeth (Goodfellow) Evans. *Education:* St. Anne's College, Oxford, B.A., 1966, M.A., 1970, Ph.D., 1974, D.Litt., 1983, Litt.D., 1983.

ADDRESSES: Office—Faculty of History, Cambridge University, Cambridge, England.

CAREER: Associated with Queen Anne's School, Caversham, Reading, Berkshire, England, 1967-72; associated with department of history at University of Reading, Reading, Berkshire, England, 1972-78; associated with department of theology at University of Bristol, Bristol, Gloucestershire, England, 1978-80; Cambridge University, Cambridge, England, lecturer in history, 1980—. Research reader in theology for British Academy, 1986-88.

MEMBER: Royal Historical Society (fellow).

WRITINGS:

UNDER NAME G. R. EVANS

Anselm and Talking about God, Oxford University Press (Oxford, England and New York City), 1978.

Anselm and a New Generation, Oxford University Press, 1980.

Old Arts and New Theology: The Beginnings of Theology as an Academic Discipline, Oxford University Press, 1980.

Augustine on Evil, Cambridge University Press (Cambridge, England), 1982.

Alan of Lille: The Frontiers of Theology in the Later Twelfth Century, Cambridge University Press, 1983.

The Mind of St. Bernard of Clairvaux, Oxford University Press, 1983.

A Concordance to the Works of St. Anselm, Kraus International (Millwood, NY), c. 1984.

The Language and Logic of the Bible: The Earlier Middle Ages, Cambridge University Press, 1984.

The Language and Logic of the Bible: The Road to Reformation, Cambridge University Press, 1985.

The Thought of Gregory the Great, Cambridge University Press, 1986.

(Editor with Anna S. Abulafia) *The Works of Gilbert Crispin,* Oxford University Press, 1986.

(Editor with Henry Chadwick) *Atlas of the Christian Church,* Facts on File (New York City), 1987.

Problems of Authority in the Reformation Debates, Cambridge University Press, 1992.

The Church and the Churches, Cambridge University Press, 1994.

Philosophy and Theology in the Middle Ages, Routledge (London), 1994.

(Editor with Lorelei Fuchs and Diane C. Kessler) *Encounters for Unity,* Canterbury Press (Norwich, Norfolk, England), 1995.

Method in Ecumenical Theology, Cambridge University Press, 1996.

OTHER

(Under name Gillian Evans) *Chaucer,* Blackie & Son (Glasgow), 1977.

(Under name Gillian Evans) *The Age of the Metaphysicals,* Blackie & Son, 1978.

(With Alister E. McGrath and Allan D. Galloway) *The Science of Theology,* Eerdmans (Grand Rapids, MI), c. 1986.

WORK IN PROGRESS: The Theology of Reception; Sin and Crime in Medieval Canon Law.

F

FAIRFAX, Ann
  See CHESNEY, Marion

*　*　*

FATCHEN, Max   1920-

PERSONAL: Born August 3, 1920, in Adelaide, South Australia, Australia; son of Cecil William (a farmer) and Isabel (Ridgway) Fatchen; married Jean Wohlers (a teacher), May 15, 1942; children: Winsome Genevieve, Michael John, Timothy James. *Education:* Attended high school in South Australia. *Religion:* Methodist. *Avocational interests:* Fishing, travel.

ADDRESSES: Home—15 Jane St., Smithfield, South Australia 5114, Australia. *Agent*—John Johnson Ltd., 45-47 Clerkenwell Green, London EC1R 0HT, England.

CAREER: Adelaide News and *Sunday Mail,* Adelaide, South Australia, journalist and special writer, 1946-55; *Advertiser,* Adelaide, journalist, 1955-84, literary editor, 1971-81, special writer, 1981-84. *Military service:* Royal Australian Air Force, 1940-45.

MEMBER: Order of Australia.

AWARDS, HONORS: Book of the Year Younger Honor, Children's Book Council of Australia, 1988, for *A Paddock of Poems;* Advance Australia Award for literature, South Australia section, 1991; Walkley Award nomination, 1995; commendation, Children's Book Council of Australia, for *The River Kings;* Runner-up, Book of the Year Award, Children's Book Council of Australia, for *The Spirit Wind.*

WRITINGS:

JUVENILE FICTION

The River Kings, illustrated by Clyde Pearson, Hicks Smith (Sydney, Australia), 1966, St. Martin's (New York City), 1968.
Conquest of the River, illustrated by Pearson, Methuen (London), 1970.
The Spirit Wind, illustrated by Trevor Stubley, Methuen, 1973.
Chase through the Night, illustrated by Graham Humphreys, Methuen, 1977.
The Time Wave, illustrated by Edward Mortelmans, Methuen, 1978.
Closer to the Stars, Methuen, 1981.
Had Yer Jabs?, Methuen, 1987.

POETRY

Songs for My Dog and Other People, illustrated by Michael Atchison, Kestrel, 1980.
Wry Rhymes for Troublesome Times, illustrated by Atchison, Kestrel, 1983.
A Paddock of Poems, illustrated by Kerry Argent, Puffin (New York City), 1987.
A Pocketful of Rhymes, illustrated by Argent, Omnibus, 1989.
A Country Christmas, illustrated by Timothy Ide, Omnibus, 1990.
The Country Mail Is Coming: Poems from Down Under, illustrated by Catherine O'Neill, Joy Street Books, 1990.

(With Colin Thiele) *Tea for Three,* illustrated by Craig Smith, Moondrake, 1994.
Peculiar Rhymes and Lunatic Lines, illustrated by Lesley Bisseker, Orchard Books (New York City), 1995.

Contributor of light verse to the *Denver Post.*

VERSE; ILLUSTRATED BY IRIS MILLINGTON

Drivers and Trains, Longman (London), 1963.
Keepers and Lighthouses, Longman, 1963.
The Plumber, Longman, 1963.
The Electrician, Longman, 1963.
The Transport Driver, Longman, 1965.
The Carpenter, Longman, 1965.

ADULT COLLECTIONS

Peculia Australia: Verses, privately printed, 1965.
Just Fancy, Mr. Fatchen! A Collection of Verse, Prose and Fate's Cruel Blows, Rigby (Adelaide), 1967.
Forever Fatchen, Advertiser (Adelaide), 1983.
Mostly Max, Wakefield Press, 1995.

ADAPTATIONS: Chase through the Night was adapted as a television series by Independent Productions, 1983; *The River Kings* was adapted as a television miniseries by Prospect Productions and broadcast by Australian Broadcasting Corporation, 1991.

SIDELIGHTS: As a native Australian and journalist, Max Fatchen has traveled and lived throughout Australia. In his fiction and poetry for children, Fatchen shares his experiences and celebrates the Australian people and landscape. His adventure novels for teens, including *The River Kings* and *Chase through the Night,* and his poetry collections for younger readers, such as *Songs for My Dog and Other People* and *The Country Mail Is Coming: Poems from Down Under,* provide readers with an understanding of the land and language of Australia and the lives of young people there while addressing universal concerns and themes as well.

Fatchen wants his readers, he once explained, "to be standing beside me or running beside me, breathless with interest as we clamber up some old riverbank or hang onto a rail in the wild sea. A book is a voyage and I don't just want my readers to be passengers anxious to get off because they feel seasick with all the words, but eager members of the crew shouting, 'land ho' when we sight the islands of imagination

. . . . Stories must be honest, and honest stories are not always happy, but they can be moving, vivid, arresting, so that you never want to put them down . . . . That's what I want my stories to be."

During his years as a journalist for Australian newspapers, Fatchen discovered remote parts of his native land that fascinated him with their beauty. He recalled how he flew with "surveyors among the islands of the Gulf of Carpenteria" and "with helicopter pilots across swamps where the geese rose in living carpets or past muddy estuaries, where the seagoing crocodiles, drawn up like small canoes, lifted their heads as we came down low to buzz them as we passed.

"When I traveled along the Australian river, the Murray, with old riverboat men, again the feeling of the landscape, the movement of the river, the birds that congregated in small families on the long sandspit, and the river towns tucked around the bends all found their way into my books. When I was at sea with the trawler men, getting more stories for my paper, I watched the conflict between men and the sea, enjoyed the yarns in the fo'castle, wedged myself in the corner of the wheelhouse as the great grey-bearded waves went roaring past in the Australian bight."

Fatchen's adventure novels for teens draw upon his intimate knowledge of Australian history and geography. In several books, he wrote of the maritime life in old Australia. Set in nineteenth-century Australia, *The River Kings* concerns thirteen-year-old Shawn, who runs away from home to find work on the boats that trade goods up and down the Murray River. According to *Library Journal* contributor Joseph L. Buelna, Fatchen combined humor and "suspense" in an "entertaining mixture." *The River Kings* was adapted for Australian television in 1991. Shawn's further adventures on the Murray River are chronicled in *Conquest of the River,* which a *Times Literary Supplement* critic describes as a "tough racy book."

Encounters with kidnappers figure into the stories of two of Fatchen's more popular titles. In *The Time Wave,* Josef, the son of a millionaire, takes a vacation on a Pacific island that is periodically flooded by a gigantic wave. After he and his new friend Gina are kidnapped, the children attempt to escape their captors while the threat of the destructive wave looms over the island. *The Time Wave* contains some suspenseful moments. As the *Junior Bookshelf* critic noted, the scene in which a professional killer chases the children is "nerve-shattering" and "really quite something." *Chase through the Night* also involves a kidnapping. This time, Petra and her mother become the hostages of the thieves they have recognized. When they are taken to the small town where Petra's friend Ray lives, Ray tricks the thieves and foils their plans. Although *Times Literary Supplement* contributor David Bartlett complained about the story's "stereotyped characters," Margery Fisher, writing in *Growing Point*, admired the author's skillful use of setting and the "unity of atmosphere and plot."

Aside from his adventure fiction for children, Fatchen also writes poetry for a young audience. In the collection *Wry Rhymes for Troublesome Times*, for example, nonsense poems voice complaints about parents, aunts, and authority figures and describe the poet's pet peeves. Other poems toy with traditional nursery rhymes. According to *School Librarian* reviewer Colin Mills, Fatchen is "at his best with word play and mild satire" in this work. Similarly, *Songs for My Dog and Other People*, as *School Librarian* critic Marcus Crouch asserted, maintains the perspective of an Australian child but is "quite complex" technically, and Fatchen "handles rhymes and rhythms with professional ease."

The forty-one poems in *The Country Mail Is Coming* explore life in rural Australia as well as new babies, dinosaurs, haunted shipwrecks, and the letters in the mailman's bag. Although, as Ellen Fader related in *Horn Book*, the poems include Australian words like "takeaway," "heeler," and "bathers" that non-Australians might not understand, the meanings of the poems "are never obscured." Kathleen Whalin concluded in *School Library Journal* that *The Country Mail Is Coming* is "energetic" and "illuminating."

While Fatchen's books allow Australian children to take pride in their country's natural beauty and diverse cultures, they also inform other children about Australia. Fatchen told *CA:* "I am particularly interested in writing for children, and my children's verse is read throughout the English speaking world. I like children for their frankness and enthusiasm when they enjoy my work. I enjoy their criticisms too. They are very wise people." Fatchen once invited his readers to join him for adventure: "Come aboard my book. We're sailing in five minutes!"

BIOGRAPHICAL/CRITICAL SOURCES:

BOOKS

Something about the Author Autobiography Series, Volume 20, Gale (Detroit), 1995.

PERIODICALS

Booklist, April 1, 1990, p. 1548.
Growing Point, October, 1977, pp. 3185-86.
Horn Book, May/June, 1990, pp. 342-43.
Junior Bookshelf, February, 1979, p. 50.
Kirkus Reviews, September 1, 1968, p. 978.
Library Journal, November 15, 1968, pp. 4412-13.
School Librarian, March, 1979, p. 54; June, 1981, p. 143; March, 1984, p. 61.
School Library Journal, August, 1990, p. 153.
Times Literary Supplement, December 11, 1970, p. 1457; December 2, 1977, p. 1412.

*   *   *

FAXON, Alicia Craig   1931-

PERSONAL: Born July 27, 1931, in New York, NY; daughter of William Donald and Alicia (Harnecker) Craig; married Richard Bremer Faxon (a minister), February 21, 1953; children: Richard Paul, Thomas Hardwick. *Ethnicity:* "Caucasian." *Education:* Vassar College, B.A. (magna cum laude), 1952; Radcliffe College, M.A., 1953; Boston University, M.A., 1971, Ph.D., 1979. *Religion:* Episcopalian.

ADDRESSES: Office—8 Sullivan Lane, Bristol, RI 02809.

CAREER: Mt. Vernon High School, Washington, DC, teacher of English, 1955-56; American Historical Association, Washington, DC, research assistant, 1958; University of Maryland, College Park, instructor in American history, 1961-63; DeCordova Museum, member of print council, 1968-69; Boston University, Boston, MA, teaching fellow, 1970-71; DeCordova Museum School, Lincoln, MA, teacher of art history, 1972, 1973; New England School of Art, Boston, lecturer in art history, 1974-77; Massachusetts College of Art, Boston, instructor, 1975; Simmons College, Boston, instructor, 1979-80, assistant professor, 1980-86, associate professor, 1987-91, professor of art history, 1991-93, department chair, 1987-93, Alumnae Chair for the Humanities, 1992-93. Visiting lecturer, Tufts University, 1973. Danforth Museum, trustee, 1974-77, guest curator, 1975, acting director, 1977; art consultant to Microsoft Corporation, 1993.

MEMBER: College Art Association, Historians of British Art, National League of American Pen Women, Women's Caucus of Art, Boston Authors Club, Vassar Club (Boston; seminar chair), Rectory Club (Washington, DC; president, 1960-61), Phi Beta Kappa.

AWARDS, HONORS: Nan Award for art criticism, *Art New England,* 1987; National Endowment for the Humanities travel grant, 1989, and summer stipend grant, 1992; Women's Caucus for Art, national conference honoree, 1996.

WRITINGS:

Collecting Art on a Shoestring, Barre (New York City), 1969.
Women and Jesus, United Church Press (Philadelphia), 1973.
(With Yves Brayer) *Jean-Louis Forain: Artist, Realist, Humanist,* C. E. Tuttle (North Clarendon, VT), 1982.
Jean-Louis Forain: A Catalogue Raisonne of the Prints, Garland Publishing (New York City), 1982.
(Editor with Sylvia Moore) *Pilgrims and Pioneers: New England Women in the Arts,* Midmarch Arts-Women Artists News (New York City), 1987.
Dante Gabriel Rossetti as Artist, Abbeville Press (New York City), 1989.
(Editor with Susan Casteras) *Pre-Raphaelite Art in Its European Context,* Associated University Presses (London), 1995.

Contributor to local magazines and newspapers. Art critic, *Boston Phoenix,* 1970-71, Minute-Man Publications, 1971-73, *Real Paper,* 1975-76, and *Art New England,* 1985—; art writer, *Boston Globe,* 1971-73. Editor of *Women's Art Journal,* 1990—; regional editor for Rhode Island, *Art New England,* 1994—.

Some of Faxon's works have been translated into German, French, Italian, and Japanese.

SIDELIGHTS: Alicia Craig Faxon told *CA:* "My primary motivation is to share knowledge with others. My work as an art historian and art critic primarily influences my writing. Special areas of interest are nineteenth-century European art and women artists. Occasionally topics for art history symposia presentations influence my choice of subject. In my career as art critic, writing articles on current art world concerns and reviewing art exhibitions are the main influences on my writing.

"My writing process begins with research on the subject, usually taken on three-by-five cards. I then sort out the main topic interests and sequences and outline the article, lecture, or chapter of a book. These are also coded to visuals: slides for a paper or lecture and photographic sources for publication.

"I then resort to that latest technological innovation and write longhand on a yellow lined pad of paper. Slides are put in the margin for references, and photographs, with artist, title, date, and location provided in appropriate positions. (Getting the slides or photographs, if you don't have them, is one of the hardest tasks of art historical and critical writing—costly, time-consuming, and often frustrating.) Additions to the writing are put in by insert papers or, if small, on yellow sticky notes. The finished product is then edited and consigned to typewriter or computer.

"One of my main motivations to write on subjects I have chosen is a lack of material in the field. No one, for example, had written on Rossetti from an art historian's perspective and discipline, although there was a fine catalogue raisonne on his art and many biographies and literary appraisals of his career as poet, with incomplete material on his artistic career (which was his main occupation in terms of both time and monetary rewards). My interest in women artists was sparked by the disproportionate neglect of their careers and achievements."

*   *   *

FETTIG, Art(hur John)   1929-

PERSONAL: Born July 5, 1929, in Detroit, MI; son of Arthur J., Sr. (an inventor) and Jenny (Sands) Fettig; married Ruth R. Zepke (a registered nurse), September 11, 1955 (died, June, 1993); children: Nancy Lou, Daniel, Amy, David. *Education:* Attended high school in Detroit, MI. *Religion:* Roman Catholic.

ADDRESSES: Home—31 East Ave. S., Battle Creek, MI 49017. *Office*—Growth Unlimited, Inc., 36 Fairview Dr., Battle Creek, MI 49017.

CAREER: Grand Trunk Western Railroad Co., Battle Creek, MI, railroad claim agent in Detroit, 1948-60, and in Battle Creek, 1960-73, company relations officer, 1973-83; True-Fettig & Associates, Battle

Creek, president, 1975-78; Growth Unlimited (publisher), Battle Creek, president, 1983—. Conductor of seminars on personal growth, sales management, safety, public speaking, and creative writing, 1973—; designated certified speaking professional by National Speakers Association, 1980. *Military service:* U.S. Army, combat rifleman, 1951-53; served in Korea; received Purple Heart and five battle stars.

MEMBER: National Speakers Association, Professional Speakers Association of Michigan.

AWARDS, HONORS: Awards from American Association of Railroads, 1959, 1960; award from National Public Relations Association, 1977.

WRITINGS:

It Only Hurts When I Frown (humor), Liguori Publications (Liguori, MO), 1973, revised edition, Growth Unlimited (Battle Creek, MI), 1986.

Selling Lucky (true stories), Ovations Unlimited, 1977.

(Editor with Herb True) *Funny Bone,* Humor Guild of America, 1977.

How to Hold an Audience in the Hollow of Your Hand, Fell (New York City), 1979, revised edition, Growth Unlimited, 1988.

The Santa Train, Grand Trunk Western Railroad, 1980.

Mentor: Secret of the Ages, Fell, 1981, Growth Unlimited, 1993.

Remembering, Growth Unlimited, 1982.

The Pos Activity Book, Growth Unlimited, 1984.

"Pos" Parenting: A Guide to Greatness with Twenty-five Keys for Building Your Child's Self-Esteem, Growth Unlimited, 1986.

(With True) *How Funny Are You? The Humor Game,* Growth Unlimited, 1986.

Selling Luckier Yet, Growth Unlimited, 1987.

Unfit for Glory, Growth Unlimited, 1987.

The Pos "Just Say Yes" Activity Book, Growth Unlimited, 1987.

The Platinum Rule, Growth Unlimited, 1988.

Selling Safety in the 90's, Growth Unlimited, 1990.

World's Greatest Sales Meeting Idea Book, Growth Unlimited, 1990.

World's Greatest Safety Meeting Idea Book, Growth Unlimited, 1990.

More Great Safety Meeting Idea Book, Growth Unlimited, 1991.

Love Is the Target, An Answer for Troubled Americans Today, Growth Unlimited, 1992.

Serenity! Serenity!: Living the Serenity Prayer, Growth Unlimited, 1993.

Showtime: How to Make Thousands Vacationing in Hawaii, Growth Unlimited, 1994.

The New Pos Just Say Yes Activity Book, Growth Unlimited, 1994.

Welcome to the 21st Century: A Survival Guide for Workers, Growth Unlimited, 1996.

"THE THREE ROBOTS" SERIES

The Three Robots, Growth Unlimited, 1980.

The Three Robots and the Sandstorm, Growth Unlimited, 1983.

The Three Robots Find a Grandpa, Growth Unlimited, 1984.

The Three Robots Discover Their Pos-Abilities, Growth Unlimited, 1984.

The Three Robots Learn about Drugs, Growth Unlimited, 1987.

OTHER

Also author of three filmstrips, "They Can't Stop," for Grand Trunk Western Railroad, 1976, "Stages," 1976, and "No Place to Play," 1978. Contributor to *Forty Salutes to Michigan,* Poetry Society of Michigan. Contributor of more than a thousand articles, stories, and poems to a variety of magazines in the United States and abroad.

WORK IN PROGRESS: A book tentatively titled *One Hundred Tips on More Powerful Public Speaking* and a novel entitled *Rally.*

SIDELIGHTS: Art Fettig told *CA:* "If someone were to ask me why I write I would have to admit that I have no choice in the matter. In fact, I advise some would-be writers I meet, 'If you can possibly not write, then don't.' Unless you have a burning passion inside you to write, then I truly believe that you are probably not cut out to be a writer.

"Some people collect clutter around their homes. They hate to throw anything out. I'm the same way with new ideas. I like to capture everything new that I create in some form. Sometimes it is captured in an article or a verse. Maybe we capture it on a cassette tape of a speech.

"Although we are state-of-the-art with our computer, I write on a legal-sized yellow pad most of the time. I can still create and capture new ideas on my IBM Wheelwriter. My fingers fly across the keyboard, and I call this thinking through my fingertips. The computer itself still intimidates me, and I have an associate, Paula Hopkins, who translates my pen scratching into text.

"The variety of my interests seems to keep expanding. First I wrote humor, then books on sales and public speaking. Next came my work on children's books and books on parents and teachers. I keep returning to the children's field. I do so want to teach children how to say yes to positive living values.

"When I first began writing I visited a publisher in New York City, and in their lobby they had a wall of all the books they had published. Now I have my own wall crammed with my own books. We've run out of room on the wall and yet we keep on publishing new works. We are creeping over to the next wall and then around the corner. I've just begun.

"We get letters and phone calls every week from readers who report how a book or a verse had touched their life in some special way. That is all writing is for me. I want to capture a thought, a line, a feeling, in some way and share it with someone else to help them do a better job or perhaps ease their pain. When my work does that, when it touches one life, then it has succeeded beyond my wildest dreams."

*   *   *

FILTZER, Donald (Arthur) 1948-

PERSONAL: Born January 8, 1948, in Baltimore, MD; son of David L. (an orthopedic surgeon) and Frances (Sacks) Filtzer. *Education:* Wesleyan University, B.A. (cum laude), 1969; University of Glasgow, Ph.D., 1976. *Politics:* Marxist.

ADDRESSES: Office—Department of Sociology, University of East London, Longbridge Rd., Dagenham, Essex RM8 2AS, England.

CAREER: University of Birmingham, Birmingham, England, research fellow of Centre for Russian and East European Studies, c. 1978; Department of Sociology, University of East London, Dagenham, Essex, England, reader in European studies. School of Slavonic and East European Studies, University of London, honorary visiting fellow.

WRITINGS:

(Editor and author of introduction) E. A. Preobrazhensky, *The Crisis of Soviet Industrialization,* M. E. Sharpe (Armonk, NY), 1980.
(Editor and translator) I. I. Rubin, *A History of Economic Thought,* Ink Links (London, England), 1979.
Soviet Workers and Stalinist Industrialization: The Formation of Modern Soviet Production Relations, 1928-1941, Pluto Press (London, England), 1986.

Also author of *Soviet Workers and De-Stalinization: The Consolidation of the Modern System of Soviet Production Relations, 1953-1964* (Cambridge, England), 1992; *The Khrushchev Era: De-Stalinization and the Limits of Reform in the USSR, 1953-1964,* (London, England), 1993; *Soviet Workers and the Collapse of Perestroika: The Soviet Labour Process and Gorbachev's Reforms, 1985-1991,* (Cambridge, England), 1994. Contributor to anthologies, including *Labour in Transition: The Labour Process in Eastern Europe and China,* edited by Chris Smith and Paul Thompson, [London], 1992. Also contributor to periodicals, including *Challenge, Critique, Europe-Asia Studies, Slavonic and East European Review, Social History, Soviet Studies.*

WORK IN PROGRESS: Research on the social history of the U.S.S.R. in the immediate postwar period, 1945-1953.

SIDELIGHTS: In the *Times Literary Supplement,* reviewer Geoffrey Hosking hailed Donald Filtzer's *Soviet Workers and Stalinist Industrialization: The Formation of Modern Soviet Production Relations, 1928-1941* as "one of the most important contributions of recent years to Soviet social history." In the book, Filtzer asserted that Soviet workers of the 1930s assumed enough control over production to undermine all authoritarian attempts to govern them. The production demands of the young Soviet regime required an enormous work force, and this in itself forced planners to make concessions to the working class. Laziness, theft, and slipshod work habits had to be tolerated. Incentive programs to reward good workers were resented by other members of the work force. Treating work infringements as criminal offenses only encouraged middle-level management to cover up for their subordinates and peers. Filtzer concluded that the stalemate created by Soviet workers more than fifty years ago has not abated. It contributes to the Soviet Union's present reputation for waste and corruption in the workplace, poor quality of production, and an ongoing shortage of manual laborers. Hosking told his readers that Filtzer's "account of how the situation has arisen is vivid and instructive." He concluded: "This is a book which should be pondered by anyone who wants to understand the state of the Soviet Union today."

BIOGRAPHICAL/CRITICAL SOURCES:

PERIODICALS

Times Literary Supplement, May 27, 1987.

*   *   *

FINNIGAN, Joan   1925-
   (Michelle Bedard)

PERSONAL: Born November 23, 1925, in Ottawa, Ontario, Canada; daughter of Frank (a former National Hockey League player) and Maye (Horner) Finnigan; married Charles Grant MacKenzie (a psychiatrist), May 23, 1949 (died, August, 1965); children: Jonathan Alexander, Christopher Roderick, Martha Ruth. *Ethnicity:* "Celtic." *Education:* Queen's University, B.A. *Religion:* "Homegrown."

ADDRESSES: Home—Moore Farm, Hambly Lake, Hartington, Ontario, Canada K0H 1W0.

CAREER: Former school teacher and reporter for the Ottawa *Journal,* Ottawa, Ontario, Canada; freelance writer, 1965—.

AWARDS, HONORS: Borestone Mountain Poetry Prize, 1959, 1961, 1963; Centennial Prize for Poetry, 1967; President's Medal for Poetry, University of Western Ontario, 1969; Canadian Film Award (Genie) for best screenplay, 1969, for *The Best Damn Fiddler from Calabogie to Kaladar;* six Cana-da Council grants, including senior grant, 1973-74; Philemon Wright Award for History and Research in the Outaouais; Ottawa-Carleton Literary Award; Explorations Grant, Canada Council; Multiculturalism Grant; Ontario Heritage Foundation grant; Historical Society of the Gatineau grant; Ontario Arts Council grant; shortlisted for

Stephen Leacock Award for humour and Province of Ontario Trillium Award.

WRITINGS:

POETRY

Through the Glass, Darkly, Ryerson (Toronto), 1957.
A Dream of Lilies, University of New Brunswick Press (Fredericton), 1965.
Entrance to the Greenhouse, Ryerson, 1968.
It Was Warm and Sunny When We Set Out, Ryerson, 1970.
In the Brown Cottage on Loughborough Lake, CBC Learning Systems/Herzig Somerville (Toronto), 1970.
Living Together, Fiddlehead Poetry Books (Fredericton, New Brunswick), 1976.
A Reminder of Familiar Faces, NC Press (Toronto), 1978.
This Series Has Been Discontinued, University of New Brunswick Press 1981.
The Watershed Collection, introduction by Robert Weaver, Quarry Press (Kingston, Ontario), 1988.
Wintering Over, Quarry Press, 1992.

PROSE

(Under pseudonym Michelle Bedard) *Canada in Bed,* Pagurian Press (Toronto), 1969.
Kingston: Celebrate This City, McClelland & Stewart (Toronto), 1976.
"I Come from the Valley," NC Press, 1976.
Canadian Colonial Cooking, NC Press, 1976.
Canada: Country of the Giants, General Store Publishing (Burnstown, Ontario), 1981.
Some of the Stories I Told You Were True (oral history), Deneau Publishers (Ottawa), 1981.
Look! The Land Is Growing Giants, Tundra Press (Montreal), 1983.
Laughing All the Way Home (oral history), Deneau Publishers, 1984.
Legacies, Legends and Lies (oral history), Deneau Publishers, 1985.
Finnigan's Guide to the Ottawa Valley, Quarry Press, 1988.
Tell Me Another Story (oral history), McGraw-Hill Ryerson (Whitby, Ontario), 1988.
The Dog Who Wouldn't Be Left Behind, Douglas & McIntyre (Vancouver), 1989.
Witches, Ghosts and Loups-zaroies, Quarry Press, 1994.
Dancing at the Crossroads, Quarry Press, 1995.

PLAYS AND SCREENPLAYS

The Best Damn Fiddler from Calabogie to Kaladar (screenplay), first produced by National Film Board of Canada and first shown on Canadian television 1969, Quarry Press, 1990.

Up the Vallee! (play), produced in Toronto at Tarragon Theatre, 1978.

Songs from Both Sides of the River (play), produced in Ottawa at National Art Centre, 1987.

Wintering Over (play), produced in Ottawa and at Museum of Civilization, 1988-92.

*   *   *

FISHBEIN, Harold D(ennis)   1938-

PERSONAL: Born May 13, 1938, in Milwaukee, WI; married, 1962; children: two. *Education:* University of Illinois at Urbana-Champaign, B.A., 1959; University of Pennsylvania, M.A., 1961, Ph.D., 1963.

ADDRESSES: Office—Department of Psychology, McMicken College of Arts and Sciences, University of Cincinnati, Cincinnati, OH 45221-0376. *E-mail*—Harold.Fishbein@UC.Edu.

CAREER: Indiana University—Bloomington, research fellow in psychology, 1963-64; University of Cincinnati, Cincinnati, OH, assistant professor, 1964-68, associate professor of psychology, 1968-72, professor, 1972—, associate dean of McMicken College of Arts and Sciences, 1971—. National Institutes of Health and National Science Foundation research fellow, Philadelphia Child Guidance Clinic, 1977-79.

MEMBER: American Psychological Association, Society for Research in Child Development, Sigma Xi.

AWARDS, HONORS: Grants from National Institutes of Health, 1965-66 and 1970-71, National Science Foundation, 1966-68, and U.S. Office of Education, 1972-73; Fulbright senior lecturer, Bombay, India, 1994.

WRITINGS:

Evolution, Development, and Children's Learning, Goodyear Publishing, 1976.

The Psychology of Infancy and Childhood: Evolutionary and Cross-Cultural Perspectives, Lawrence Erlbaum (Hillsdale, NJ), 1984.

Peer Prejudice and Discrimination: Evolutionary, Cultural, and Developmental Dynamics, Westview Press (Boulder, CO), 1996.

Author of text for sound recordings on auditory perception.

*   *   *

FRASER, J(ulius) T(homas)   1923-

PERSONAL: Born May 7, 1923, in Budapest, Hungary; immigrated to United States, 1946, naturalized citizen, 1953; son of Francis (an attorney) and Olga (Szigethy) Fraser; married Margaret Cameron (a musician), 1948 (divorced, 1970); married Jane Hunsicker (a teacher), 1973; children: Thomas C. Fraser, Anne-Marie C. Fraser, Carol Hunsicker, Margaret C. Fraser, Ann Hunsicker. *Education:* Cooper Union School of Engineering, B.E.E., 1951; Technische Universitaet Hannover, Ph.D., 1970. *Politics:* "A Jeffersonian independent." *Religion:* "Christian by private creed."

ADDRESSES: Office—International Society for the Study of Time, P.O. Box 815, Westport, CT 06881.

CAREER: Worked as a machinist, technician, and draftsman in Budapest, Hungary, 1941-44; Allied Control Commission, Rome, Italy, English correspondent, 1945-46; cataloger at Columbia University Libraries, contract inspector for Electrolux Vacuum Cleaners, and laboratory foreman at North American Philips, Inc., 1947-50; Rangertone, Inc., Newark, NJ, design draftsman, 1950-51; Westinghouse Electric Corp., Baltimore, MD, junior engineer, 1951-53; General Precision Laboratory (now Singer-Kearfott, Inc.), Pleasantville, NY, staff member, 1955-57, senior staff member, 1957-62, senior scientist in physics department of Research Division, 1962-71; independent scholar in the study of time, 1971—. Visiting lecturer, Massachusetts Institute of Technology, 1966-67, and Mt. Holyoke College, 1967-69; visiting professor, University of Maryland, 1969-70; adjunct professor, Fordham University, 1971-84. Has lectured extensively on various aspects of the study of time.

MEMBER: International Society for the Study of Time (founder, 1966).

WRITINGS:

EDITOR AND CONTRIBUTOR

The Voices of Time: A Cooperative Survey of Man's Views of Time as Expressed by the Sciences and the Humanities, Braziller, 1966, 2nd enlarged edition, University of Massachusetts Press, 1981.

(With F. C. Haber and G. H. Mueller) *The Study of Time I,* Springer-Verlag (New York City), 1972.

(With N. Lawrence) *The Study of Time II,* Springer-Verlag, 1975.

(With Lawrence and D. Park) *The Study of Time III,* Springer-Verlag, 1978.

(With Lawrence and Park) *The Study of Time IV,* Springer-Verlag, 1981.

(With Lawrence) *Time, Science, and Society in China and the West (The Study of Time V),* University of Massachusetts Press, 1986.

Time and Mind: Interdisciplinary Issues (The Study of Time VI), International Universities Press (Madison, CT), 1989.

(With Lewis Rowell) *Time and Process (The Study of Time VII),* International Universities Press, 1992.

(With Marlene Soulsby) *Dimensions of Time and Life (The Study of Time VI),* International Universities Press, 1994.

OTHER

Of Time, Passion, and Knowledge: Reflections on the Strategy of Existence, Braziller (New York City), 1975, 2nd edition, Princeton University Press (Princeton, NJ), 1990.

Time as Conflict: A Scientific and Humanistic Study, Birkhauser (Boston), 1978.

The Genesis and Evolution of Time: A Critique of Interpretation in Physics, University of Massachusetts Press (Amherst, MA), 1982.

Time, the Familiar Stranger, University of Massachusetts Press, 1987.

Contributor to *Britannica Yearbook of Science and the Future,* 1970, and to numerous scientific and scholarly books, including *Time, Cultures, and Development,* edited by C. A. Mallmann and Oscar Nudler, Fundacion Bariloche, 1986. Contributor to periodicals, including *Main Currents in Modern Thought* and *Time and Society.* Fraser's books have been translated into German, Italian, and Spanish.

WORK IN PROGRESS: Time, Conflict and Human Values, "a study of the profound changes, brought about by the time-compactness of the globe, in attitudes toward time, toward conflict and toward traditional judgments about what is true, good, and beautiful."

SIDELIGHTS: "In an age of relentless specialization," reported the *Times Higher Education Supplement,* J. T. Fraser "has worked against the academic grain to sustain an inquiry which is best classified under an older term. He is a natural philosopher of time. . . . His achievement, after 40 years of reading and thinking, is an outline of a theory of time which takes the subject out of the hands of the physicists."

In his pioneering 1966 work *The Voices of Time: A Cooperative Survey of Man's Views of Time as Expressed by the Sciences and the Humanities,* Fraser "managed to bring together a most impressive collection of materials bearing on his subject, such as notions of time in the history of philosophy and religions, the rhythms of language and music, time-perception in children," and many other areas, notes J. Ben Lieberman in the *Saturday Review.* In gathering together various studies of time, "what Fraser is really after is an interdisciplinary understanding of time itself, and he has broken new ground in bringing out its role in almost every conceivable field of study," adds Lieberman. Despite the work's scholarly nature, *Observer Review* contributor Philip Toynbee finds *The Voices of Time* accessible to the general reader: "For a non-scientist reader a principal source of pleasure comes from having his mind stretched to the uttermost limits of its capacity." Lieberman concurs, asserting that the lay reader "can still profit from the book"; in addition, the critic finds that "the ramifications of time are both so profound and so superficial, so pervasive and so personal, that the sensitive reader or conversationalist may well find himself pursuing the subject more and more deeply, until he is confronted with all those questions about the meaning of his own life." Toynbee concludes that *The Voices of Time* is "one of the most fascinating books I have read for a long time."

Fraser founded the International Society for the Study of Time in 1966. He has also written numerous books on the nature of time. *Of Time, Passion, and Knowledge: Reflections on the Strategy of Existence,* his first, covers much of the same ground as *The Voices of Time* but attempts to integrate the various themes into a single theory. "J. T. Fraser would have earned our gratitude if his new book provided a lucid and encompassing guide to this complex topic—period! But that is only one of his achievements," claims Robert Kastenbaum in *Social Science.* "More than a scholarly treatise, this volume delights with its play of mind upon the most varied and challenging of materials." The critic notes Fraser's "style and wit, his gift for integrating unexpected elements, and the enthusiasm he obviously feels for this topic," adding that Fraser makes an additional contribution by including "the outlines of a systematic theory of time. It is a bold and welcome attempt."

Fraser's *Time, the Familiar Stranger,* "is the best available discussion of time for a general audience," remarks H. C. Byerly in a *Choice* review, adding that the work "provides an excellent introduction to more specialized studies." Discussing the use of time in different cultures, *Time, the Familiar Stranger*'s "unifying theme is the difference between psychological time and time in modern physics," describes David Gordon in *Library Journal*. "It is not a new idea that time is multiple, that there is more than one structure to which the word refers," notes *Nature* contributor C. J. S. Clarke; "this explains why the discussion of time is so fraught with paradox. But Fraser is the first to have developed the idea into a universal vision, condensed into the modest space of this book." Concludes the critic: "As well as setting the context for future work on time, this book will add to our understanding of the choice before us for the future direction of humanity."

"As a young child growing up in the Hungarian countryside, I liked to tell people that I would be a blacksmith, explorer, and everyone's friend," J. T. Fraser told *CA*. "The 'blacksmith' progressed through technician, draftsman, engineer, inventor, physicist and philosopher to the writer of both fiction and nonfiction. The 'explorer' still travels around the world, in search of ideas and feelings. The 'friend' is manifest in a profound empathy for people and in an unremitting concern with the responsibility of being human.

"All three parts are joined in my dedication to the study of time, which spans over thirty-five years. In my early writings I formulated a new system of natural philosophy—the theory of time as conflict. In my subsequent writings I have been working out the practical significance of the new philosophical system for our understanding of matter, life, and society.

"The moving power of this single passion—the analysis of time—to which I have given my life, is, not surprisingly, experiential. As an adolescent in World War II, I watched the clash of cultures and the attendant release of primordial emotions. As a young man I observed America, this land of promise, through extensive travels—but always returning in body and spirit to my home along the Hudson.

"Integrating these two families of impressions, I could not help but note how thoroughly the spectacular achievements of science and industry have undermined all traditional assessments of the position of man in the scheme of things. The consequent absence of ideals, inspiring as well as intelligible to the majority of people, makes our epoch an uninformed one.

"An analysis of the social forces at work, carried out through the theory of time as conflict, suggests that this regression is, metaphorically, a withdrawal before the leap. We are witnessing around the earth a 'revolt of the caged mind,' a radical alteration in the texture of human life itself. The march is not to the medieval Dies Irae, an expression of atonement and hope in heaven, nor to the 20th century's Communist International promising a final conflict followed by heaven on earth, but to a more elemental call. A new drummer has announced a crisis in needs and means: man, the measure of time, is being driven by the unresolvable conflicts of his individual and collective being toward a new level of incipient complexity, that of the time-compact globe.

"As a writer, philosopher, and scientist I see my task as one of chronicling and interpreting these profound changes, becoming a part of the motive forces behind them, and pursuing them toward their unknown end."

BIOGRAPHICAL/CRITICAL SOURCES:

BOOKS

Samuel L. Macey, editor, *Encyclopedia of Time,* Garland Publishing (New York City), 1994, pp. 223-24.

PERIODICALS

Choice, March, 1983; May, 1988.
Contemporary Psychology, Volume 34, number 4, 1989.
Library Journal, November 15, 1987.
Nature, December 24, 1987.
Observer Review, February 18, 1968.
Saturday Review, January 29, 1966.
Social Science, autumn, 1975.
Times Higher Education Supplement, November 23, 1990.
Washington Post Book World, August 17, 1975.

FULLER, Roy (Broadbent)   1912-1991

PERSONAL: Born February 11, 1912, in Failsworth, Lancashire, England; died September 27, 1991, in London, England; son of Leopold Charles (a factory manager) and Nellie (Broadbent) Fuller; married Kathleen Smith, 1936; children: John. *Education:* Attended Blackpool High School, Lancashire.

CAREER: Poet, novelist, and critic. Qualified as solicitor, 1934; staff member of various legal firms, 1934-38; Woolwich Equitable Building Society, London, assistant solicitor, 1938-58, solicitor, 1958-69, director, 1969-88; Oxford University, professor of poetry, 1968-73. Building Societies Association, London, chair of Legal Advisory Panel, 1958-69, vice president, 1969-91. Member of board of Governors, British Broadcasting Corp. (BBC), 1972-79. *Military service:* Royal Navy, 1941-46; Royal Naval Volunteer Reserve, lieutenant.

AWARDS, HONORS: Royal Society of Literature fellow, 1958; Arts Council Poetry Award, 1959; Duff Cooper Memorial Prize for Poetry, 1968; Queen's Gold Medal for Poetry, 1970; Commander, Order of the British Empire, 1970; Cholmondeley Award for poetry, 1980; honorary M.A., Oxford University; honorary D.Litt., University of Kent, Canterbury, 1986.

WRITINGS:

FOR CHILDREN

Savage Gold: A Story of Adventure, illustrated by Robert Medley, Lehmann (London), 1946, new edition illustrated by Douglas Hall, Hutchinson Educational, 1960.
With My Little Eye, illustrated by Alan Lindsay, Lehmann, 1948, Macmillan (New York City), 1957.
Catspaw, illustrated by David Gollins, Alan Ross (London), 1966.
Seen Grandpa Lately? (verse), illustrated by Joan Hickson, Deutsch (London), 1972.
Poor Roy (verse), illustrated by Nicolas Bentley, Deutsch, 1977.
The Other Planet and Three Other Fables, illustrated by Paul Peter Piech, Keepsake Press (Surrey), 1979.
More about Tompkins and Other Light Verse, Tragara Press (Edinburgh), 1981.
(With Barbara Giles and Adrian Rumble) *Upright, Downfall* (verse), Oxford University Press (Oxford), 1983.

The World through the Window: Collected Poems for Children, illustrated by Nick Duffy, Blackie (Glasgow), 1989.

POETRY FOR ADULTS

Poems, Fortune (London), 1940.
The Middle of a War, Hogarth Press (London), 1942.
A Lost Season, Hogarth Press, 1944.
Epitaphs and Occasions, Lehmann, 1949.
Counterparts, Verschoyle (London), 1954.
Brutus's Orchard, Deutsch, 1957, Macmillan, 1958.
Collected Poems 1936-1961, Dufour (Philadelphia), 1962.
Buff, Dufour, 1965.
New Poems, Dufour, 1968.
Off Course, Turret (London), 1969.
To an Unknown Reader, Poem-of-the-Month Club (London), 1970.
Song Cycle from a Record Sleeve, Sycamore Press (Oxford), 1972.
Tiny Tears, Deutsch, 1973.
An Old War, Tragara Press, 1974.
Waiting for the Barbarians: A Poem, Keepsake Press, 1974.
From the Joke Shop, Deutsch, 1975.
The Joke Shop Annexe, Tragara Press, 1975.
An Ill-Governed Coast, Ceolfrith Press (Sunderland), 1976.
Re-treads, Tragara Press, 1979.
The Reign of Sparrows, London Magazine Editions (London), 1980.
The Individual and His Times: A Selection of the Poetry of Roy Fuller, edited by V. J. Lee, Athlone Press (London), 1982.
House and Shop, Tragara Press, 1982.
As from the Thirties, Tragara Press, 1983.
Mianserin Sonnets, Tragara Press, 1984.
New and Collected Poems 1934-1984, Secker and Warburg (London), 1985.
Subsequent to Summer, Salamander Press (London), 1985.
Outside the Canon, Tragara Press, 1986.
Consolations, Secker and Warburg, 1987.
Available for Dreams, Collins, 1989.

Contributor to books, including *Pergamon Poets 1,* edited by Evan Owen, Pergamon Press, 1968; and *Penguin Modern Poets 18,* Penguin, 1970.

FICTION FOR ADULTS

The Second Curtain, Verschoyle, 1953, Macmillan, 1956.

Fantasy and Fugue, Verschoyle, 1954, Macmillan, 1956, published as *Murder in Mind,* Academy (Chicago), 1986.

Image of a Society, Deutsch, 1956, Macmillan, 1957.

The Ruined Boys, Deutsch, 1959, published as *That Distant Afternoon,* Macmillan, 1957.

The Father's Comedy, Deutsch, 1961.

The Perfect Fool, Deutsch, 1963.

My Child, My Sister, Deutsch, 1965.

The Carnal Island, Deutsch, 1970.

Omnibus (contains *With My Little Eye, The Second Curtain,* and *Fantasy and Fugue*), Carcanet (Manchester), 1988.

Stares, Sinclair-Stevenson, 1990.

NONFICTION FOR ADULTS

Owls and Artificers: Oxford Lectures on Poetry, Deutsch, 1971, Library Press (LaSalle, IL), 1971.

Professors and Gods: Last Oxford Lectures on Poetry, Deutsch, 1973, St. Martin's Press (New York City), 1974.

Souvenirs (memoirs), London Magazine Editions, 1980.

Vamp till Ready: Further Memoirs, London Magazine Editions, 1982.

Home and Dry: Memoirs 3, London Magazine Editions, 1984.

Twelfth Night: A Personal View, Tragara Press, 1985.

The Strange and the Good: Collected Memoirs, Collins Harvill (London), 1989.

Spanner and Pen: Post-War Memoirs, Sinclair-Stevenson, 1991.

EDITOR

Byron for Today, Porcupine Press (Philadelphia), 1948.

(With Clifford Dyment and Montagu Slater) *New Poems 1952,* Joseph, 1952.

The Building Societies Acts 1874-1960: Great Britain and Northern Ireland, Franey, 1957, 6th edition, 1962.

Supplement of New Poetry, Poetry Book Society, 1964.

Fellow Mortals: An Anthology of Animal Verse, illustrated by David Koster, Macdonald & Evans, 1981.

(With John Lehmann) *The Penguin New Writing 1940-1950: An Anthology,* Penguin, 1985.

OTHER

Legal correspondent for *Building Societies' Gazette.*

Contributor to periodicals, including *Listener, New Statesman,* and *Times Literary Supplement.*

Fuller's papers are housed in manuscript collections at the Brotherton Collection, Leeds University, the State University of New York, Buffalo, and the British Library, London.

SIDELIGHTS: According to Stephen Spender in *Dictionary of Literary Biography,* Roy Fuller is the norm against which "other poets of the past thirty years may be judged." Clear, lucid verses were Fuller's trademark, something that became unfashionable in the later twentieth century. Fuller was also a well respected novelist, turning his hand to stories about sensitive individuals fighting against the forces of an uncaring society or corporation. Less well known are Fuller's works for young readers. In the four fiction books and the five collections of poetry he wrote for a juvenile audience, Fuller explored many of the same themes and with much the same linguistic sophistication as his adult works. "There is no talking-down to a youthful audience here," Peter Reading commented in the *Times Literary Supplement* in a review of Fuller's collected poems for children, *The World through the Window.*

Fuller was a family man involved in corporate life, serving for thirty years as a solicitor for a British savings and loan association. He once described his life as "part managerial, part poetic," and he balanced both aspects well enough to leave behind, at his death in 1991, a body of work including thirty-one volumes of poetry, nine novels, eleven nonfiction works, and a score of edited works and reviews.

Born into a lower-middle-class home in Failsworth, Lancashire, in 1912, Fuller was one of two children, and his father worked as manager of a rubber-proofing mill. With the death of his father when he was only eight, Fuller and his family moved to Black-pool. At sixteen Fuller was articled, or apprenticed, to a solicitor from whom he learned the law, and by age twenty-one he passed his qualifying law exams. As quoted in *Dictionary of Literary Biography,* Fuller described his background as "provincial . . . [and] unliterary" and his schooling as "uninspired . . . [and] truncated." He worked for various law firms, married in 1936, and by the time of the outbreak of World War II had moved his family to the outskirts of London where he took a post with the Woolwich Equitable Building Society. Except for serving in the Royal Navy during the war, Fuller remained with this firm until his retirement in 1968 and stayed in Blackheath, his London suburb, until his death.

During the war, Fuller worked in the newly emerging field of radar and spent several years in Kenya as a radar technician. He had already begun to write poetry before the war and published his first volume in 1939. But it was during the war years that he gained some renown with *The Middle of a War* and *A Lost Season*. Influenced by W. H. Auden and Stephen Spender, these early poems are characterized by a liberal political slant—Fuller considered himself a Marxist at the time—and a concern for the individual in modern technological society. Some critics have mentioned these two volumes as among the best war poetry of the time.

With the end of the war and his return to England, Fuller wrote his first fiction. His son, John, later a poet in his own right, stimulated Fuller to write books for younger readers. The first of these, *Savage Gold: A Story of Adventure,* revolves around two young boys who become involved in a rivalry between two mining companies. Alan Edwin Day, writing in *Twentieth-Century Children's Writers,* characterized *Savage Gold* as "well told" and with "a fast and exciting pace." In 1948, Fuller wrote his first mystery novel, *With My Little Eye.* Its youthful protagonist, Frederick French, the only son of a county judge, plays detective with a courtroom murder trial. Both literate and sophisticated, the book is "in its small way a perfect example of a modern crime story," according to Julian Symons, writing in *Mortal Consequences: A History—From the Detective Story to the Crime Novel.* But it is this very sophistication that bothered Day. For Day, this sophistication and plot complexity were too much for young readers: "We can only conclude that Fuller sadly misdirected his inventiveness," Day noted. In the same article, Fuller himself commented that "though writing for children has always given me a certain sense of freedom, I have never thought of my children's books as 'written down' to an audience. Indeed, I have erred the other way."

As his son grew up, Fuller's inspirations changed, and he returned to adult fiction and poetry for almost twenty years. During this time he secured his reputation with such poetry collections as *Epitaphs and Occasions, Counterparts,* and *Brutus's Orchard.* By the 1960s Fuller was considered one of the foremost British poets of his time. He also continued his experiments in the mystery fiction genre in the 1950s with *The Second Curtain* and *Fantasy and Fugue.* By the late 1960s both Fuller's poetry and prose had reached a new and more personal level, exploring themes of death, loss, aging and the role of the art-

ist. Much of the poetry is infused with a quiet and suburban enjoyment of nature, as well, influenced by back-garden musings at his home on Blackheath. *Collected Poems* and *The Individual and His Times* are considered by some critics to be touchstones of this middle to late period of Fuller's poetic development. His novels also took on more private, personal themes, as in *My Child, My Sister,* which Fuller considered his best structured poetry.

With retirement from Woolwich Equitable in 1968, Fuller's public life did not diminish. He became a professor of poetry at Oxford University and served as governor on the board of the British Broadcasting Corporation (BBC). It was during this part of his career that Fuller returned to children's books. "The separation in time between the two groups of children's books," Fuller explained in *Twentieth-Century Children's Writers,* "is to be accounted for by the fact that I was stimulated to write them first by my son's childhood, then my grandchildren's." Fuller's first return to juvenile fiction was *Catspaw,* in which his character Victoria wanders into a land populated only by dogs who are continually worried about the machinations of the country called Pussia, populated only by cats—an allegory of the Cold War, then at its height.

With the publication of *Seen Grandpa Lately?,* Fuller made his first verse contribution to children's literature. Judith Nichols, writing in *Books for Your Children,* commented on the "gentle pleasures" of this volume. In part comic and nonsensical, the volume also contains serious poems exploring many of Fuller's adult themes such as death and loss. Throughout the 1970s, Fuller made further periodic sallies into juvenile fiction and verse. A second volume of children's verse, *Poor Roy,* appeared in 1977, followed by a book of stories, *The Other Planet and Three Other Fables,* in 1979. Fuller's output for young readers in the 1980s was confined to verse: *More about Tompkins and Other Light Verse* in 1981 and *Upright, Downfall* in 1983. The latter was written with two other poets, which, according to a reviewer for *Book Report,* provides "a broad range of experience, discovery and delight."

New and Collected Poems 1934-1984 successfully reintroduced the poet to a new generation of adult readers. Other volumes of poetry followed, *Consolations* and *Available for Dreams* among them. He also wrote several volumes of memoirs as well as making a return to fiction with the 1990 *Stares,* which Lachlan Mackinnon, writing in the *Times Literary Supplement,* called a "frightening and memorable novel." Fuller's verse for children was gathered together in *The World through the Window: Collected Poems for Children* in 1989. Peter Reading, in his *Times Literary Supplement* review of the collection, noted that it "is at once enjoyable and informative" but also that because of its "wit, imagery, sophistication" it would probably not find the wide readership that other simpler texts do. An *Observer Review* writer commented on Fuller's "light and genial touch" evident in his collected poems, while Nichols, in *Books for Your Children,* concluded that *The World through the Window* would be "an ideal opportunity to catch up" on Fuller's work.

BIOGRAPHICAL/CRITICAL SOURCES:

BOOKS

Austin, Alan E., *Roy Fuller,* Twayne (New York City), 1979.

Contemporary Authors Autobiography Series, Volume 10, Gale (Detroit), 1989.

Contemporary Literary Criticism, Gale, Volume 4, 1975, Volume 28, 1984.

Dictionary of Literary Biography, Gale, Volume 15: *British Novelists, 1930-1959,* 1983, Volume 20: *British Poets, 1914-1945,* 1983.

Fuller, Roy, *The World through the Window: Collected Poems for Children,* illustrated by Nick Duffy, Blackie, 1989.

Symons, Julian, *Mortal Consequences: A History—From the Detective Story to the Crime Novel,* Harper (New York City), 1972.

Twentieth-Century Children's Writers, fourth edition, St. James Press (Detroit), 1995.

PERIODICALS

Book Report, May-June, 1986, p. 36.

Books for Your Children, spring, 1990, p. 19.

New York Times Book Review, April 13, 1986, p. 38.

Observer (London), September 5, 1965, p. 26; June 23, 1985, p. 23; February 8, 1987, p. 28; March 22, 1987, p. 27; April 23, 1989, p. 44; November 11, 1990, p. 67; March 10, 1991, p. 61.

Observer Review, August 6, 1989, p. 40.

Times Literary Supplement, November 1, 1985, p. 1223; April 25, 1986, p. 450; March 6, 1987, p. 244; June 23, 1989, p. 694; December 1, 1989, p. 1344; January 11, 1991, p. 17; February 1, 1991, p. 21.

OBITUARIES:

PERIODICALS

Los Angeles Times, September 30, 1991, p. A20.

Times (London), September 28, 1991, p. 14.

Washington Post, September 29, 1991, p. B7.*

G

GABBARD, Glen O(wens) 1949-

PERSONAL: Born August 8, 1949, in Charleston, IL; son of E. G. (an actor) and Lucina (an actress; maiden name, Paquet) Gabbard; married Joyce Davidson (a psychiatrist), June 14, 1985; children: Matthew, Abigail, Amanda, Allison. *Education:* Eastern Illinois University, B.S., 1972; Rush Medical College, M.D., 1975; postdoctoral study at Karl Menninger School of Psychiatry, 1975-78; and Topeka Institute of Psychoanalysis, 1977-84.

ADDRESSES: Home—5410 Southwest Mission, Topeka, KS 66610-0829. *Office*—The Menninger Clinic, P. O. Box 829, Topeka, KS 66601-0829.

CAREER: Kansas Correctional Vocational Training Center, Topeka, KS, penal physician and psychiatric consultant, 1976-82; C. F. Menninger Memorial Hospital, Topeka, staff psychiatrist, 1978-83, section chief, 1984-89, director, 1989-94, vice president for adult services at the Menninger Clinic, 1991-94. Instructor at Topeka Institute for Psychoanalysis, 1981-89, training and supervising analyst, 1989—; Karl Menninger School of Psychiatry, J. Cotter Hirschberg Professorship in Clinical Psychology, 1986-87, Karl and Mona Malden Professorship, 1993-94, Bessie Walker Callaway Distinguished Professor of Psychoanalysis and Education, 1994—; University of Kansas School of Medicine, professor of clinical psychiatry, 1991—. President of board of directors of Topeka Civic Theater, 1982-83.

Distinguished visiting professor, Wilford Hall Air Force Hospital, San Antonio, TX, 1991, University of Hawaii, 1993; Hall Mercer visiting scholar, Pennsylvania Hospital, 1992; William Orr lecturer, Vanderbilt University School of Medicine, 1992; Distinguished visiting scholar, Beth Israel Medical Center, 1993; visiting professor, Hershey Medical Center, Penn State College of Medicine, 1993; Ben Weisel lecturer, Hartford Hospital, 1994; G. Henry Katz visiting professor, Institute of the Pennsylvania, 1994; Serota lecturer, San Diego Psychoanalytic Institute, 1994; visiting scholar, Southern California Psychoanalytic Institute, 1994; Jacob E. Finesinger visiting professor, University of Maryland, 1995; Prager visiting professor and lecturer in psychoanalytic psychiatry, George Washington University, 1995; Windholz lecturer, San Francisco Psychoanalytic Institute, 1995.

MEMBER: International Association for Near-Death Studies, International Psycho-Analytic Association, Academia, Medicina & Psychiatria Foundation, American Association for the Advancement of Science, American College of Psychiatrists (fellow and member of board of regents, 1994—), American College of Psychoanalysts (fellow, 1988), American Medical Association (member, task force on sexual misconduct, 1993—), American Psychiatric Association (fellow, 1988—; member, ethics committee, 1993—; member, committee on the practice of psychotherapy, 1994—), American Psychoanalytic Association (member, program committee, 1988—; member, ethics subcommittee, 1994—), American Society of Psychoanalytic Physicians, Benjamin Rush Society, Committee on the Practice of Psychotherapy (member of Council on Psychiatric Services, 1994-97), Forum for the Psychoanalytic Study of Film, Group for the Advancement of Psychiatry, Society for Psychotherapy Research, Central Neuropsychiatric Hospital Association (president, 1992), Kansas Medical Society, Shawnee County Medical Society, Topeka

Psychoanalytic Society (president, 1991-93), Sigma Xi, Alpha Omega Alpha.

AWARDS, HONORS: Falk fellow of American Psychiatric Association, 1976; Topeka Institute for Psychoanalysis Publications award, 1978, 1982, 1986; Wood-Prince Award, 1980, 1983, 1984, 1985; Edward Hoedemaker Award, Seattle Psychoanalytic Society, 1986, for article "The Treatment of the 'Special' Patient in a Psychoanalytic Hospital"; named Menninger Foundation Distinguished Clinical Researcher, 1987; Alumni Award for Scientific Writing, Karl Menninger School of Psychiatry and Mental Health Sciences, 1989, and William C. Menninger Teacher of the Year award, 1989 and 1990, I. Arthur Marshall Distinguished Alumnus award, 1992; Wolfe Adler award, Sheppard & Pratt Hospital, 1991; *Psychiatric Times* Teacher of the Year award, 1992; Sigmund Freud Award, American Society of Psychoanalytic Physicians, 1992; Edward A. Strecker Award, Institute of Pennsylvania Hospital, 1994; Menninger professional writing award, Menninger Alumni Association, 1994; distinguished alumnus award, Eastern Illinois University, 1994.

WRITINGS:

(With Stuart W. Twemlow) *With the Eyes of the Mind: An Empirical Analysis of Out-of-Body States,* Praeger (New York City), 1984.

(With brother, Krin Gabbard) *Psychiatry and the Cinema,* University of Chicago Press (Chicago), 1987.

Psychodynamic Psychiatry in Clinical Practice: The DSM-IV Edition, American Psychiatric Press (Washington, DC), 1990.

(With S. Wilkinson) *Management of Countertransference with Borderline Patients,* American Psychiatric Press, 1994.

(With E. P. Lester) *Boundaries and Boundary Violations in Psychoanalysis,* Basic Books (New York City), 1995.

(With S. D. Adkinson) *Synopsis of Treatments of Psychiatric Disorders: The Second Edition,* American Psychiatric Press, in press.

(With Adkinson) *Study Guide for Treatments of Psychiatric Disorders: The DSM-IV Edition,* American Psychiatric Press, in press.

Love and Hate in the Analytic Setting, Jason Aronson (Northvale, NJ), in press.

EDITOR

(With Roy W. Menninger, and contributor) *Medical Marriages,* American Psychiatric Press, 1988.

Sexual Exploitation in Professional Relationships, American Psychiatric Press, 1989.

(Contributing editor) Harold Kaplan and Benjamin Sadock, *Synopsis of Psychiatry,* 7th edition, William & Wilkins (Baltimore, MD), 1994.

(Editor in chief) *Treatments of Psychiatric Disorders: The Second Edition,* American Psychiatric Press, 1995.

OTHER

Also author and director of videotape, *The Royal Road: Psychoanalytic Approaches to the Dream,* Menninger Video Productions, 1988. Author of audiotapes, *Management of Countertransference in the Psychotherapy of Borderline Patients,* 1992, and *Professional Boundaries in Psychiatric Practice,* 1995, both from American College of Psychiatrists Update Series. Member of editorial boards for various journals, including *American Journal of Psychotherapy, American Psychoanalyst* (newsletter of the American Psychoanalytic Association), *Ethics and Behavior, Journal of the American Psychoanalytic Association, Journal of Near-Death Studies, Journal of Psychotherapy Practice and Research, Journal of Sex and Marital Therapy,* and *Psychoanalytic Quarterly.* Editor of *The Menninger Letter,* 1992-96, and associate editor of *Journal of the American Psychoanalytic Association,* 1994—.

SIDELIGHTS: Glen O. Gabbard once told *CA:* "I grew up in a theatrical family and majored in drama as an undergraduate. At some ill-defined point in my college career, I became more interested in analyzing the psychology of the characters I was playing than in performing on stage. I switched to a premedical emphasis, but I was rejected by a registration computer because premedical studies and a drama major were deemed incompatible. I persevered nonetheless and eventually combined my interests in my writings on stage fright and the interface between psychiatry and movies. My interest in film culminated in *Psychiatry and the Cinema,* which I wrote in collaboration with my brother and fellow film buff, Krin Gabbard. This book will require frequent updates to keep abreast of current developments in film, so I anticipate work on future editions for the rest of my professional career."

BIOGRAPHICAL/CRITICAL SOURCES:

PERIODICALS

New York Times, July 24, 1987.
San Francisco Chronicle, August 9, 1987.

GAGNIER, Regenia (A.)   1953-

PERSONAL: Born June 24, 1953; daughter of Clenton J. (an industrial machinist) and Jean (a painter; maiden name, Young) Gagnier; married John Austin Dupre, 1989; children: Gabriel, Julian. *Education:* University of California, Berkeley, Ph.D., 1981. *Politics:* "Socialist and Feminist."

ADDRESSES: Home—860 San Jude Ave., Palo Alto, CA 94305. *Office*—Department of English, Stanford University, Stanford, CA 94305. *E-mail*—Gagnier@leland.stanford.edu

CAREER: Stanford University, Stanford, CA, assistant professor of English, 1982-89, associate professor, 1989-92, professor, 1993—.

MEMBER: Modern Language Association of America.

AWARDS, HONORS: Fellow of Humanities Center at Stanford University, 1985-86; Guggenheim fellow, 1991-92.

WRITINGS:

Idylls of the Marketplace: Oscar Wilde and the Victorian Public, Stanford University Press (Stanford, CA), 1986.
Subjectivities: A History of Self-Representation in Britain, 1832-1920, Oxford University Press (New York City), 1991.
(Editor and contributor) *Critical Essays on Oscar Wilde,* Macmillan/G. K. Hall (New York City), 1991.

Contributor to literature and women's studies journals.

WORK IN PROGRESS: Comparative study of the histories of economics and aesthetics in the development of market societies.

BIOGRAPHICAL/CRITICAL SOURCES:

PERIODICALS

Times Literary Supplement, June 19, 1987.

GANNON, Frank   1952-

PERSONAL: Born August 30, 1952, in Camden, NJ; son of Bernard (a bar owner) and Anne (a homemaker; maiden name, Forde) Gannon; married Paulette Piquet (a teacher), April 2, 1971; children: Aimee, Anne, Frank. *Education:* University of Georgia, B.A. (magna cum laude), 1974, M.A., 1977. *Politics:* Democrat. *Religion:* Roman Catholic.

ADDRESSES: Home and office—P. O. Box 547, Demorest, GA 30535. *Agent*—Kristine Dahl, 137 Fifth Ave., New York, NY 10010.

CAREER: Writer.

WRITINGS:

Yo, Poe (humor), Viking (New York City), 1987.
Vanna Karenina (humor), Viking, 1988.
All About Man, Longstreet, 1993.

Contributor to magazines, including *Atlantic, Gentleman's Quarterly, Harper's,* and *New Yorker,* and a regular contributor to *New York Times Magazine.* Contributor editor of *Southern.*

SIDELIGHTS: Frank Gannon told *CA:* "I'm a humorist. I'm not a very talented writer, but I do what I can. I would rather be one of these guys on the Left Bank looking out into the Parisian night and having profound thoughts, but I'm not smart enough to do that. I started out to be a serious artist person but it didn't work out because I don't have anything to say. I lack depth, like the serving dishes in certain Chinese restaurants, but, like those dishes, I try my best to give the illusion of depth. I like what Joe Orton said about all this: 'I was born without a soul, but I've tried to develop very good manners to compensate.'

"I guess that my two books, and the one I'm writing now, are about my hopeless inability to have values, thoughts, and beliefs like other writers. I had a very happy childhood, and I've had a very nice life, so I can't really blame anybody. But, given enough time, I probably will."

More recently, Gannon added: "My primary motivation for writing has changed over the years. Originally I wanted self expression, then I wanted money, then I wanted self expression, etc. The biggest kick I ever got was the first check. It was for the first story I ever even tried to write. I wrote it in the guard shack at Anaconda Wire and Cable Company in Watkinsville, Georgia. I read it over and thought, 'That's pretty good.' I felt real good as I went around on my hourly trip through the plant.

"At first I was influenced by Yukio Mishima. Then Hemingway and Fitzgerald. Then Joe Orton. Then S. J. Perelman. I am influenced by dead people. Nothing I read now can have as big an effect on me as things I read when I was young. I think almost everyone is like this.

"I write every day except Sunday. I use a word processor now. I used to think that the first typewriter I used when I first started to make money was 'magic', but I got over that. I always write in the same room, but I know that if it burned down, I would get another one. And then that would be 'magic'.

"I have realized, over the years, that the biggest 'inspiration' isn't something good. It's a horrible, painful realization of the quiet human agony that goes on forever. For me, my deepest response to this is 'funny' or 'comic.' This probably means that there is something lacking deep in my soul. To those who read this, I can only say, if you too feel something dark and ghastly embedded in the very essence of life, whoa! better throw that thing out or take it home!"

*   *   *

GARRETT, Gerald R.   1940-

PERSONAL: Born September 21, 1940, in Mount Vernon, WA; son of Kenneth J. and Pearl Odessa (Wells) Garrett; married Marcia Pope (a professor of sociology and a lawyer), June 10, 1967 (divorced June 10, 1976). *Education:* Whitman College, A.B., 1962; Washington State University, M.A., 1966, Ph.D., 1970.

ADDRESSES: Office—Department of Sociology, University of Massachusetts-Boston, 100 Morrissey Blvd., Boston, MA 02125-3393.

CAREER: University of Wisconsin—Whitewater, instructor in sociology, 1966-67; Carroll College, Waukesha, WI, assistant professor of sociology, 1967-68; Washington State University, Pullman, re-

search fellow in sociology, 1968-70; University of Massachusetts—Boston, professor of sociology, 1970—, director, Graduate Program in Applied Sociology, 1982-85, director, Alcohol and Substance Abuse Studies, 1986—, and Center for Criminal Justice, 1988—. Senior research associate at Columbia University, 1969, 1970; lecturer at University of Maryland, European Division, Heidelberg, Germany, 1976-77, and Boston University Overseas Programs, Seckenheim, Germany, 1978-84; visiting associate professor at Washington State University, 1977-78, and University of Alaska, Fairbanks, 1978; visiting professor, Troy State University/European Region, Wiesbaden, Germany, 1978-79; visiting professor, Washington State University-Spokane, Graduate Center, 1994. Member of National Task Force on Higher Education and Criminal Justice, 1975-76; technical consultant, alcohol and substance abuse training services, 1978-88; visiting scholar, National Institute on Alcohol Abuse and Alcoholism, Rockville, MD, 1988-89; consultant, Center for Substance Abuse Treatment, Substance Abuse Mental Health Administration, 1990—; member of board of directors, Massachusetts Halfway Houses, Inc., Boston, 1994—.

MEMBER: International Coalition of Addiction Studies Educators (president, 1995-96), American Sociological Association, American Society of Criminology, Eastern Sociological Society, Northeastern Academy of Criminal Justice Sciences, Academy of Criminal Justice Sciences, Society for the Study of Social Problems.

WRITINGS:

(With D. H. Volk) *Homeless Women in New York City,* Columbia, 1970.

Problem Drinking among Women, Columbia, 1970.

(With H. M. Bahr) *Disaffiliation among Urban Women,* Columbia, 1971.

(With Bahr) *Women Alone,* Heath (Lexington, MA), 1976.

(With Richard Rettig and Manuel J. Torres) *Manny: A Criminal-Addict's Story,* Houghton (Boston), 1977, revised edition, in press.

(With R. Schutt) *Working with the Homeless: A Video-Based Training Experience* (book and video), Center for Communications Media, 1987.

(With Schutt) *Responding to the Homeless,* Plenum (New York City), 1992.

(With C. J. Larson) *Crime, Justice, and Society* (2nd edition), General Hall (Bayside, NY), 1996.

Contributor to books, including *Skid Row: An Introduction to Disaffiliation,* edited by Bahr, Oxford University Press, 1973; *Professionalization in Amer-ica: Police Roles in the 1970s,* edited by Jack Kinton, Social Science & Sociological Resources (Aurora, IL), 1975; *Intimate Life Styles,* edited by Jack and Joann Delora, Goodyear Publishing, 1972, 2nd edition, 1978; *Criminal Justice Planning,* edited by Joseph Scott and Simon Dinitz, Praeger (New York City), 1978; *Military Families: Adaptation to Stress,* edited by E. J. Hunter and Steven Nice, Praeger, 1979; *Women and Alcohol,* edited by C. Ford and J. Eddy, W. C. Brown (Dubuque, IA), 1980; *Homelessness: Critical Issues in Policy and Practice,* Boston Foundation, 1987; *Research Agenda: The Homeless with Alcohol and Drug Problems,* edited by J. Baumohl, National Institute on Alcohol Abuse and Alcoholism, 1987; (with Schutt) *Homelessness in the United States,* edited by J. Momeni, Greenwood (Westport, CT), Volume 1, 1989, Volume 2, 1990; (with Schutt) *Homelessness: The National Perspective,* edited by M. Robertson and M. Greenblatt, Plenum, 1990; and *Homelessness: New England and Beyond,* edited by Padraig O'Malley, University of Massachusetts Press (Amherst), 1993. Also contributor to numerous professional journals. Guest editor of "Alcohol, Drugs, and Criminal Justice Policy" issue of *Criminal Justice Policy Review,* 1989.

SIDELIGHTS: Gerald R. Garrett once told *CA:* "The crisis of homelessness in the 1980s and 1990s touches the life of every American. It is a social problem that cuts across the fabric of American life—social services and welfare, criminal justice, health care, employment, education, housing, and federal, state and local government. Most of all, homelessness offends our sense of humanity and compassion for others. For both personal and professional reasons, my work in the 1980s focused on issues related to homelessness and on how we can return the homeless to stable and productive life-styles. My research interests in alcohol problems and substance abuse are especially relevant, since as many as half of the homeless suffer from alcohol and other drug disorders. In the course of my research work, it is increasingly clear to me that alcohol and drug dependency among the homeless is not just a treatment issue. It is also a political and economic issue. Therapeutic successes are short-lived without efforts that provide opportunities for education, job training and placement, access to health care services, and affordable housing. The homelessness-addiction cycle will continue unless we adopt a broader approach in our recovery programs."

Garrett more recently added, "In addition to my work and research on homelessness, I am also spending considerable time on alcohol and addictions education. Much of this work is connected to my position as president of the International Coalition of Addiction Studies Educators (INCASE), which is dedicated to enhancing addiction education programs and research."

*   *   *

GATES, Henry Louis, Jr. 1950-

PERSONAL: Born September 16, 1950, in Keyser, WV; son of Henry Louis and Pauline Augusta (Coleman) Gates; married Sharon Adams (a potter), September 1, 1979; children: Maude, Elizabeth. *Education:* Yale University, B.A. (summa cum laude), 1973; Clare College, Cambridge, M.A., 1974, Ph.D., 1979.

ADDRESSES: Office—Department of Afro-American Studies, Harvard University, 1430 Massachusetts Ave., Cambridge, MA 02138; W. E. B. Du Bois Institute for Afro-American Research, Harvard University, 26 Church St., Cambridge, MA 02138. *Agent*—Carl Brandt, Brandt & Brandt Literary Agents, Inc., 1501 Broadway, New York, NY 10036.

CAREER: Anglican Mission Hospital, Kilimatinde, Tanzania, general anesthetist, 1970-71; John D. Rockefeller gubernatorial campaign, Charleston, WV, director of student affairs, 1971, director of research, 1972; *Time,* London Bureau, London, England, staff correspondent, 1973-75; Yale University, New Haven, CT, lecturer, 1976-79, assistant professor, 1979-84, associate professor of English, 1984-85, director of undergraduate Afro-American studies, 1976-79; Cornell University, Ithaca, NY, professor of English, comparative literature, and African studies, 1985-88, W. E. B. DuBois Professor of Literature, 1988-90; Duke University, Durham, NC, John Spencer Bassett Professor of English and Literature, 1990—; Harvard University, Cambridge, MA, W. E. B. DuBois Professor of the Humanities, professor of English, chair of Afro-American studies, and director of W. E. B. DuBois Institute for Afro-American Research, 1991—. Virginia Commonwealth, visiting professor, 1987. Created the television series *The Image of the Black in the Western Imagination,* Public Broadcasting Service (PBS), 1982. Committees include National Book Award, PBS Adult Learning Series, Cultural Diversity, Ritz

Paris Hemingway Prize Selection Committee, and the Schomburg Commission for the Preservation of Black Culture. Member of board of directors of African-American Newspapers and Periodicals: *A National Bibliography and Union List, African Labour History, American Council of Learned Societies, Center for the Study of Black Literature and Culture, Diacritics, European Institute for Literary and Cultural Studies, Everyman Library, Lincoln Center Theater Project, LIT Literature in Transition, Museum of Afro-American History, Museum of Science, New Museum of Contemporary Arts, Proceedings of the American Antiquarian Society, Studio Museum in Harlem,* and UMI Research Press's "Challenging the American Canon" series.

MEMBER: Council on Foreign Relations; American Antiquarian Society; Union of Writers of the African Peoples; Association for Documentary Editing; African Roundtable; African Literature Association; Afro-American Academy; American Studies Association; Trans Africa Forum Scholars Council; Association for the Study of Afro-American Life and History (life); Caribbean Studies Association; College Language Association (life); Modern Language Association; Stone Trust; Zora Neale Hurston Society; Cambridge Scientific Club; American Civil Liberties Union National Advisory Council; German American Studies Association; National Coalition Against Censorship; American Philosophical Society; Saturday Club; New England Historic Genealogical Society; Phi Beta Kappa.

AWARDS, HONORS: Carnegie Foundation Fellowship for Africa, 1970-71; Phelps Fellowship, Yale University, 1970-71; Mellon fellowships, Cambridge University, 1973-75, and National Humanities Center, 1989-90; grants from Ford Foundation, 1976-77 and 1984-85, and National Endowment for the Humanities, 1980-86; A. Whitney Griswold Fellowship, 1980; Rockefeller Foundation fellowships, 1981 and 1990; MacArthur Prize Fellowship, MacArthur Foundation, 1981-86; Yale Afro-American teaching prize, 1983; award from Whitney Humanities Center, 1983-85; Princeton University Council of the Humanities lectureship, 1985; Award for Creative Scholarship, Zora Neale Hurston Society, 1986; associate fellowship from W. E. B. DuBois Institute, Harvard University, 1987-88 and 1988-89; John Hope Franklin Prize honorable mention, American Studies Association, 1988; Woodrow Wilson National Fellow, 1988-89 and 1989-90; Candle Award, Morehouse College, 1989; American Book Award and Anisfield-Wolf Book Award for Race Relations, both 1989, both for *The Signifying Monkey: Towards a Theory of Afro-American Literary Criticism;* recipient

of honorary degrees from Dartmouth College, 1989, University of West Virginia, 1990, University of Rochester, 1990, Pratt Institute, 1990, University of Bridgeport, 1991 (declined), University of New Hampshire, 1991, Bryant College, 1992, Manhattan Community College, 1992, George Washington University, 1993, University of Massachusetts at Amherst, 1993, Williams College, 1993, Emory University, 1995, Colby College, 1995, Bard College, 1995, and Bates College, 1995; Richard Wright Lecturer, Center for the Study of Black Literature and Culture, University of Pennsylvania, 1990; Potomac State College Alumni Award, 1991; Bellagio Conference Center Fellowship, 1992; Clarendon Lecturer, Oxford University, 1992; Best New Journal of the Year award (in the humanities and the social sciences), Association of American Publishers, 1992; elected to the American Academy of Arts and Sciences, 1993; Golden Plate Achievement Award, 1993; African American Students Faculty Award, 1993; George Polk Award for Social Commentary, 1993; Heartland Prize for Nonfiction, 1994, for *Colored People: A Memoir;* Lillian Smith Book Award, 1994; West Virginian of the Year, 1995; Humanities Award, West Virginia Humanities Council, 1995; Ethics Award, *Tikun* (magazine), 1996; Distinguished Editorial Achievement, *Critical Inquiry,* 1996; W. D. Weatherford Award.

WRITINGS:

Figures in Black: Words, Signs, and the Racial Self, Oxford University Press (New York City), 1987.
The Signifying Monkey: Towards a Theory of Afro-American Literary Criticism, Oxford University Press, 1988.
Loose Canons: Notes on the Culture Wars (essays), Oxford University Press, 1992.
Colored People: A Memoir, Knopf (New York City), 1994.
(With Cornel West) *The Future of the Race,* Knopf, 1996.

EDITOR

(And author of introduction) *Black Is the Color of the Cosmos: Charles T. Davis's Essays on Afro-American Literature and Culture, 1942-1981,* Garland Publishing (New York City), 1982.
(And author of introduction) Harriet E. Wilson, *Our Nig; or, Sketches from the Life of a Free Black,* Random House (New York City), 1983.
(And author of introduction) *Black Literature and Literary Theory,* Methuen (New York City), 1984.

(And author of introduction with Charles T. Davis) *The Slave's Narrative: Texts and Contexts,* Oxford University Press, 1986.

(And author of introduction) *"Race," Writing, and Difference,* University of Chicago Press (Chicago), 1986.

(And author of introduction) *The Classic Slave Narratives,* New American Library (New York City), 1987.

(And author of introduction) *In the House of Oshugbo: A Collection of Essays on Wole Soyinka,* Oxford University Press, 1988.

(Series editor) *The Oxford-Schomburg Library of Nineteenth-Century Black Women Writers,* 30 volumes, Oxford University Press, 1988.

W. E. B. DuBois, *The Souls of Black Folk,* Bantam Books (New York City), 1989.

James Weldon Johnson, *The Autobiography of an Ex-Coloured Man,* Vintage, 1989.

Three Classic African American Novels, Vintage, 1990.

Zora Neale Hurston, *Their Eyes Were Watching God* (introduction by Mary Helen Washington), Harper (New York City), 1990.

Hurston, *Jonah's Gourd Vine* (introduction by Rita Dove), Harper, 1990.

Hurston, *Tell My Horse* (introduction by Ishmael Reed), Harper, 1990.

Hurston, *Mules and Men* (introduction by Arnold Rampersad), Harper, 1990.

Reading Black, Reading Feminist: A Critical Anthology, Meridian Book, 1990.

Voodoo Gods of Haiti (introduction by Ishmael Reed), Harper and Row, 1991.

The Schomburg Library of Nineteenth-Century Black Women Writers, 10 volume supplement, Oxford University Press, 1991.

(With Randall K. Burkett and Nancy Hall Burkett) *Black Biography, 1790-1950: A Cumulative Index,* Chadwyck-Healey (Teaneck, NJ), 1991.

(With George Bass) Langston Hughes and Zora Neale Hurston, *Mulebone: A Comedy of Negro Life,* HarperPerennial (New York City), 1991.

Bearing Witness: Selections from African American Autobiography in the Twentieth Century, Pantheon Books (New York City), 1991.

(With Anthony Appiah) *Gloria Naylor: Critical Perspectives Past and Present,* Amistad (New York City), 1993.

(With Appiah) *Alice Walker: Critical Perspectives Past and Present,* Amistad, 1993.

(With Appiah) *Langston Hughes: Critical Perspectives Past and Present,* Amistad, 1993.

(With Appiah) *Richard Wright: Critical Perspectives Past and Present,* Amistad, 1993.

(With Appiah) *Toni Morrison: Critical Perspectives Past and Present,* Amistad, 1993.

(With Appiah) *Zora Neale Hurston: Critical Perspectives Past and Present,* Amistad, 1993.

The Amistad Chronology of African American History from 1445-1990, Amistad, 1993.

(And annotations)*Frederick Douglass: Autobiographies,* Library of America, 1994.

(With Appiah) *The Dictionary of Global Culture,* Knopf, 1995.

The Complete Stories of Zora Neale Hurston, Harper Collins, 1995.

(With Appiah) *Identities,* University of Chicago, 1996.

Also editor, with Appiah, of "Amistad Critical Studies in African American Literature" series, 1993, and editor of the Black Periodical Literature Project. Advisory editor of "Contributions to African and Afro-American Studies" series for Greenwood Press (Westport, CT), "Critical Studies in Black Life and Culture" series for Garland Press, and "Perspectives on the Black World" series for G. K. Hall (Boston). General editor of *The Norton Anthology of Afro-American Literature; A Dictionary of Cultural and Critical Theory; Middle-Atlantic Writers Association Review.* Coeditor of *Transition.* Associate editor of *Journal of American Folklore.* Member of editorial boards including, *Critical Inquiry, Studies in American Fiction, Black American Literature Forum, PMLA, Stanford Humanities Review,* and *Yale Journal of Law and Liberation.*

OTHER

(Compiler with James Gibb and Ketu H. Katrak) *Wole Soyinka: A Bibliography of Primary and Secondary Sources,* Greenwood Press, 1986.

Contributor of articles and reviews to numerous periodicals and journals, including *American Book Review, Black Scholar, Chronicle of Higher Education, Harper's, New Republic, New Yorker, Saturday Review, Village Voice Literary Supplement,* and *Yale Review.* Contributor to numerous books, including *Millenarianism and Messianism in English Literature and Thought, 1650-1800,* edited by Richard Popkin, E. J. Brill (Long Island City, NY), 1988; *Literature, Language, and Politics,* edited by Betty Jean Craige, University of Georgia (Athens, GA), 1988; *Facing History: The Black Image in American Art, 1710-1940,* edited by Guy C. McElroy, Bedford Arts (San Francisco, CA), 1990; and *Speaking of Race, Speaking of Sex: Hate Speech, Civil Rights, and Civil Liberties,* New York University Press (New York City), 1994.

WORK IN PROGRESS:Race and Reason: Black Letters in the Enlightenment, Oxford University Press.

SIDELIGHTS: Henry Louis Gates, Jr. is one of the most controversial, and respected scholars in the field of African-American studies. Gates was recognized early on by an English instructor at Potomac State Community College, who encouraged his student to transfer to Yale University. Gates graduated from that institution with highest honors in 1973. While in Africa on a Carnegie Foundation Fellowship and a Phelps Fellowship during 1970-1971, he visited fifteen countries and became familiar with various aspects of African culture. His knowledge of Africa deepened when the celebrated African writer Wole Soyinka became his tutor at Cambridge University, where Gates worked on his master's and doctoral degrees. In 1981 he was awarded one of the so-called "genius grants" from the MacArthur Foundation. He moved quickly from a teaching post at Yale to a full professorship at Cornell to an endowed chair at Duke, and in 1991, he became the W. E. B. DuBois Professor of the Humanities at Harvard and head of its Afro-American Studies program. Gates breathed new life and enthusiasm into the program and hired lecturers, such as film director Spike Lee and authors Jamaica Kincaid and Wole Soyinka. Under Gates's leadership, the number of students in the program tripled within a few years.

Gates has his detractors as well as his admirers, however. Some of his colleagues have faulted him for being insufficiently Afro-centric, while others have criticized his high-profile activities—such as publicly testifying at the obscenity trial of rap group 2 Live Crew—as inappropriate self-promotion. Yet even those who take exception to Gates's showmanship cannot argue with his credentials or deny his prolific contributions to Afro-American scholarship, as he has written and edited numerous books of literary and social criticism. According to James Olney in the *Dictionary of Literary Biography,* Gates's mission is to reorder and reinterpret "the literary and critical history of Afro-Americans in the context of a tradition that is fully modern but also continuous with Yoruba modes of interpretation that are firmly settled and at home in the world of black Americans."

In his approach to literary criticism, Gates is avowedly eclectic and defines himself as a centrist who rejects extreme positions, whether they be on the right (guardians of a Western tradition) or on the left (Afrocentricists). Gates insists that we need to tran-

scend "ethnic absolutism" of all kinds. Like the American novelist Ralph Ellison, Gates sees the fluid, indeed porous, relationship between black and white culture in the United States. Gates argues that our conception of the literary canon needs to be enlarged accordingly.

Gates's *Black Literature and Literary Theory,* which he edited, is considered by many reviewers to be an important contribution to the study of black literature. Calling it "an exciting, important volume," Reed Way Dasenbrock wrote in *World Literature Today:* "It is a collection of essays . . . that attempts to explore the relevance of contemporary literary theory, especially structuralism and poststructuralism, to African and Afro-American literature. . . . Anyone seriously interested in contemporary critical theory, in Afro-American and African literature, and in black and African studies generally will need to read and absorb this book." R. G. O'Meally wrote in *Choice* that in *Black Literature and Literary Theory* Gates "brings together thirteen superb essays in which the most modern literary theory is applied to black literature of Africa and the U.S. . . . For those interested in [the] crucial issues—and for those interested in fresh and challenging readings of key texts in black literature—this book is indispensable." Finally, Terry Eagleton remarked in the *New York Times Book Review* that "the most thought-provoking contributions to [this] collection are those that not only enrich our understanding of black literary works but in doing so implicitly question the authoritarianism of a literary 'canon.'"

One of Gates's best-known works is *Loose Canons: Notes on the Culture Wars,* in which he discusses gender, literature, and multiculturalism and argues for greater diversity in American arts and letters. Writing in the *Virginia Quarterly Review,* Sanford Pinsker noted that according to Gates "the cultural right . . . is guilty of 'intellectual protectionism,' of defending the best that has been thought and said within the Western Tradition because they are threatened by America's rapidly changing demographic profile; while the cultural left 'demands changes to accord with population shifts in gender and ethnicity.' *Loose Canons* makes it clear that Gates has problems with both positions." "The society we have made," Gates argues in *Loose Canons,* "simply won't survive without the values of tolerance. And cultural tolerance comes to nothing without cultural understanding. . . . If we relinquish the ideal of America as a plural nation, we've abandoned the very experiment that America represents." Writing in the *Los Angeles Times,* Jonathan Kirsch praised the humor and wit that infused Gates's arguments. *Loose Can-*

ons, Kirsch concluded, is "the work of a man who has mastered the arcane politics and encoded language of the canon makers; it's an arsenal of ideas in the cultural wars. But it is also the outpouring of a humane, witty and truly civilized mind."

Colored People: A Memoir played to a wider audience than did *Loose Canons.* In it, Gates recalls his youth in Piedmont, West Virginia, at a time when the town was becoming integrated. It "explores the tension between the racially segregated past and the integrated modernity that the author himself represents," commented David Lionel Smith in *America.* While affirming the progress brought by desegregation, Gates also laments the loss of the strong, united community feeling that segregation created among blacks—a feeling epitomized in the annual all-black picnic sponsored by the paper mill that provided jobs to most of Piedmont's citizens. Numerous reviewers pointed out the gentle, reminiscent tone of Gates's narrative, but some considered this a weakness in light of the momentous changes Gates lived through. Smith remarked: "From an author of Gates's sophistication, we expect more than unreflective nostalgia." Comparing it to other recent African-American memoirs and autobiographies, he concluded, "Some of them address social issues more cogently and others are more self-analytical, but none is more vivid and pleasant to read than *Colored People.*" *Los Angeles Times Book Review* contributor Richard Eder affirmed that *Colored People* was an "affecting, beautifully written and morally complex memoir," and Joyce Carol Oates, in her *London Review of Books* assessment, described it as an "eloquent document to set beside the grittier contemporary testimonies of black male urban memoirists; in essence a work of filial gratitude, paying homage to such virtues as courage, loyalty, integrity, kindness; a pleasure to read and, in the best sense, inspiring."

Gates wrote *The Future of the Race* with Cornel West, a professor of Afro-American studies at Harvard University. This work contains an essay by Gates, an essay by West, and two essays by black intellectual W. E. B. DuBois, the latter of which are preceded by a foreword by Gates. Writing in *The New York Times Book Review,* Gerald Early noted: "The question...that the authors wish to answer—what is their duty to the lower or less fortunate class of blacks?—indicates the black bourgeoisie's inability to understand precisely what their success means to themselves or blacks generally." Early also observed that while "the pieces seem hastily written," Gates's essay is "engagingly witty and journalistic" as well as "charming and coherent."

BIOGRAPHICAL/CRITICAL SOURCES:

BOOKS

Dictionary of Literary Biography, Volume 67: *Modern American Critics since 1955,* Gale (Detroit), 1988.
Gates, Henry Louis, Jr., *Loose Canons: Notes on the Culture Wars,* Oxford University Press, 1992.

PERIODICALS

America, December 31, 1994, p. 24.
Boston Globe, October 20, 1990, p. 3; May 12, 1991, p. 12; April 23, 1992, p. 70; November 7, 1992, p. 15; December 1, 1992, p. 23; April 29, 1993, p. 53; May 29, 1994, p. A13.
Callaloo, spring, 1991.
Chicago Tribune, February 18, 1993, section 5, p. 3; November 18, 1993, section 1, p. 32; July 17, 1994, section 14, p. 3; August 24, 1994, section 5, p. 1.
Choice, May, 1985; March, 1995, p. 1059.
Christian Century, January 19, 1994, p. 53-54.
Christian Science Monitor, April 10, 1992, p. 11; June 7, 1994, p. 13.
Commonweal, December 18, 1992, pp. 22-23.
Criticism, winter, 1994, pp. 155-61.
Emerge, November, 1990, p. 76.
Humanities Magazine, July/August, 1991, pp. 4-10 .
London Review of Books, July 21, 1994, p. 22-23; January 12, 1995, p. 14.
Los Angeles Times, October 29, 1990, p. A20; March 25, 1992, p. E2; June 3, 1994, p. E1.
Los Angeles Times Book Review, May 8, 1994, pp. 3, 12.
New Leader, September 12, 1994, pp. 12-13.
New Literary History, autumn, 1991.
New Statesman & Society, February 10, 1995, p. 43.
New York Times, December 6, 1989, p. B14; April 1, 1990, section 6, p. 25; June 3, 1992, p. B7; May 16, 1994, p. C16.
New York Times Book Review, December 9, 1984; August 9, 1992, p. 21; June 19, 1994, p. 10; April 21, 1996, p. 7.
New York Times Magazine, April 1, 1990.
Spectator, February 18, 1995, pp. 31-32.
Time, April 22, 1991, pp. 16, 18; May 23, 1994, p. 73.
Times Literary Supplement, May 17, 1985; February 24, 1995, p. 26.
Tribune Books (Chicago), July 17, 1994, pp. 3, 5; October 9, 1994, p. 11.
U.S. News and World Report, March, 1992.

Village Voice, July 5, 1994, p. 82.
Virginia Quarterly Review, summer, 1993, pp. 562-68.
Voice Literary Supplement, June, 1985.
U. S. News and World Report, March, 1992.
Washington Post, October 20, 1990, p. D1; August 11, 1992, p. A17.
Washington Post Book World, July 3, 1983; June 7, 1992, p. 6; May 15, 1994, p. 3.
World Literature Today, summer, 1985.

* * *

GEISMAR, Ludwig L(eo)   1921-

PERSONAL: Born February 25, 1921, in Mannheim, Germany; son of Heinrich (in sales) and Lina Geismar; married Shirley Ann Cooperman (an editor), September 18, 1948; children: Layah, Deborah, Aviva. *Ethnicity:* "Jewish." *Education:* University of Minnesota, B.A. (cum laude), 1947, M.A., 1950; Hebrew University of Jerusalem, Ph.D., 1956. *Religion:* Jewish.

ADDRESSES: Home—347 Valentine St., Highland Park, NJ 08904. *Office*—Graduate School of Social Work, Rutgers University, New Brunswick NJ 08903.

CAREER: Ministry of Social Welfare, Jerusalem, Israel, coordinator of social research, 1954-56; Family Centered Project, St. Paul, MN, director, 1956-59; Rutgers University, New Brunswick, NJ, associate professor, 1959-62, professor of social work and sociology, 1962-74, distinguished professor of social work and sociology, 1974-91, distinguished professor emeritus of social work and sociology, 1992—, director of Rutgers University Social Work Research Center. Visiting professor and director of a cross-national family study, University of Melbourne, 1975-76; lecturer at Columbia University School of Social Work, summers, 1963-66, 1968, and at Brandeis University, University of Sydney, University of New South Wales, and Flinders University (Australia). Project director of a cross-national family study in Stockholm, 1969-73. Member of review team in Mediterranean countries, United Nations, 1955; member of Social Welfare Administration grant review panel, U.S. Department of Health, Education, and Welfare, 1963. Member of Raritan Valley Community Welfare Council, 1960-62, and Middlesex County Mental Health Board, 1962-64. Consultant, Area Development Project, Vancouver, 1962-67. *Military service:* U.S. Army, 1942-45; served in North Africa and Europe; became sergeant.

MEMBER: American Association of University Professors, American Sociological Association (fellow), Council on Social Work Education (member of accreditation commission, 1965—), National Association of Social Workers, National Council on Family Relations, Society for the Study of Social Problems.

AWARDS, HONORS: Research grants from Australian Department of Social Security, Buckland Foundation (University of Melbourne, Australia), Ford Foundation, National Institute of Mental Health, New Haven Foundation, Office of Child Development of the U.S. Department of Health, Education, and Welfare, Rutgers Research Council, Tri-Centenary Fund of the Bank of Sweden, U.S. Social and Rehabilitation Service, and Victorian Family Council (Australia); Rutgers University Presidential Citation, 1990.

WRITINGS:

Community Organization in Israel, Israel Ministry of Social Welfare, 1955.
Family Centered Project, Family Centered Project (St. Paul, MN), 1957.
Report on a Check List Survey, Family Centered Project, 1957.
(With Beverly Ayres) *Families in Trouble,* Family Centered Project, 1958.
(With Ayres) *Patterns of Change in Problem Families,* Family Centered Project, 1959.
(With Ayres) *Measuring Family Functioning,* Family Centered Project, 1960.
(With Michael La Sorte) *Understanding the Multi-Problem Family: A Conceptual Analysis and Exploration in Identification,* Association Press (New York City), 1964.
(With Jane Krisberg) *The Forgotten Neighborhood: Site of an Early Skirmish in the War on Poverty,* Scarecrow (Metuchen, NJ), 1967.
Preventive Intervention in Social Work, Scarecrow, 1968.
Family and Community Functioning, Scarecrow, 1971, revised edition, 1980.
(With Bruce Lagey and others) *Early Supports for Family Life,* Scarecrow, 1972.
555 Families: A Social Psychological Study of Young Families in Transition, Transaction Books (New Brunswick, NJ), 1973.
(With wife, Shirley Geismar) *Families in an Urban Mold,* Pergamon (Elmsford, NY), 1979.
(Coeditor and contributor) *A Quarter Century of Social Work Education,* National Association of Social Workers and ABC-Clio (Silver Springs, MD), 1984.

(With Katherine Wood) *Family and Delinquency,* Human Sciences (New York City), 1986.

(With K. Wood) *Families at Risk,* Human Sciences, 1989.

(With Michael Camasso) *The Family Functioning Scale,* Springer Publishing Co. (New York City), 1993.

Contributor to professional journals, including *Australian Social Research, Health and Social Work, Journal of Comparative Family Studies, Journal of Social Service Research, Social Casework,* and *Social Service Review.* Member of editorial committee, *Social Casework,* 1964-65, 1978-80; member of editorial advisory panel, *Contemporary Social Work Education* (Australia).

SIDELIGHTS: Ludwig L. Geismar told *CA* that the primary motive of his writing is "to share the results of my research with fellow professionals and, occasionally, the community at large." Geismar noted that "the work, past and present, of researchers in the fields of the social and behavioral sciences and social work/social welfare," have influenced him. "In my own field of interest I wish to cite particularly the influences of Professor F. Ivan Nye and the late Professor Reuben Hill."

*   *   *

GLOER, (William) Hulitt   1950-

PERSONAL: Born December 23, 1950 in Atlanta, GA; son of William Talmadge (a retailer) and Francis (Lancaster) Gloer; married Sheila Katherine Rogers (a teacher), December 29, 1972; children: Jeremy Hulitt, Joshua William. *Education:* Baylor University, B.A., 1972; Pittsburgh Theological Seminary, M.Div., 1975; Southern Baptist Theological Seminary, Ph.D., 1981; post-graduate study at the University of Tuebingen, 1987-88, and at University of Cambridge, 1993. *Religion:* Baptist. *Avocational interests:* Peacemaking activities, travel.

ADDRESSES: Home—8604 North Flora, Kansas City, MO 64155. *Office*—Department of the New Testament, Midwestern Baptist Theological Seminary, 5001 North Oak St., Kansas City, MO 64118.

CAREER: Southern Baptist Theological Seminary, Louisville, KY, instructor, 1979-81; North American Baptist Seminary, Sioux Falls, SD, assistant professor, 1981-83; Midwestern Baptist Theological Seminary, Kansas City, MO, associate professor, 1983—, became professor. Adjunct faculty member of Sha-

lom-Ecumenical Center for Continuing Education, Augustana College, Sioux Falls, SD, 1982-83; participant in the National Endowment for the Humanities summer seminar series, 1986.

MEMBER: Catholic Biblical Association, Institute for Biblical Research, National Association of Baptist Professors of Religion, Society of Biblical Literature.

AWARDS, HONORS: Michael Wilson Keith Prize in Homiletics, 1975, from Pittsburgh Theological Seminary.

WRITINGS:

As We Go: Honest Reflections on the First Disciples of Jesus, Smyth-Helwys (Macon, GA), 1996.

An Exegetical and Theological Study of Paul's Concept of Resurrection and New Creation in 2 Corinthians 5:14-21, Mellen Biblical Press (Lewiston, NY), 1996.

EDITOR

Jesus Christ: The Man From Nazareth and the Exalted Lord, Mercer University Press (Macon, GA), 1987.

Eschatology and the Kingdom of God, Hendrikson, 1988.

Following Jesus: Sermons on Discipleship from Priests and Professors, Smyth-Helwys, 1993.

OTHER

Contributor to *Holman Bible Dictionary, International Standard Bible Encyclopedia* (revised edition), *Layman's Bible Dictionary, Mercer Commentary on the Bible, Mercer Dictionary of the Bible,* and *Perspectives on John.* Contributor of articles to periodicals, including *Baptist Peacemaker, Biblical Illustrator, Biblical Theology Bulletin, Perspectives in Religious Studies,* and *Review and Expositor.*

WORK IN PROGRESS: Commentary on the Gospel of Matthew; Cross-Purposes: Discipleship in the Gospels and Acts.

SIDELIGHTS: Hulitt Gloer told *CA:* "I have a special interest in the theme of discipleship in the New Testament and church history and the history and practice of Christian spirituality. My aim in writing is to wed the concerns of academic studies with the concerns of the life of the church."

GLUCK, Carol 1941-

PERSONAL: Born November 12, 1941, in Newark, NJ; married Peter L. Gluck (an architect), 1966; children: Thomas, William. *Ethnicity:* "Caucasian." *Education:* Attended University of Munich, 1960-61; Wellesley College, B.A. (with special honors), 1962; Columbia University, M.A. and Certificate in East Asian Studies, 1970, Ph.D., 1977; attended Tokyo University, 1972-74.

ADDRESSES: Home—440 Riverside Dr., New York, NY 10027. *Office*—912 International Affairs Building, East Asian Institute, Columbia University, New York, NY 10027. *E-mail*—cg9@columbia.edu.

CAREER: Columbia University, New York City, assistant professor, 1975-83, associate professor, 1983-86, professor of Japanese history, 1986-88, George Sansom Professor of History, 1988—, chair of Undergraduate Program in East Asian Studies, 1977-87. Visiting professor of Japanese history to Harvard University, 1991, Tokyo University, 1993, and l'Ecole des Hautes Etudes en Sciences Sociales, Paris, 1995. Visiting research associate in law at Tokyo University, 1978-79, 1985-86, and spring, 1992. Member of advisory committee for Senior Fulbright Awards Program, Council for the International Exchange of Scholars, 1981-84; member of American Council of Learned Societies and Social Science Research Council Joint Committee on Japanese Studies, 1984-89; member of American advisory committee of Japan Foundation, 1986—, chair, 1990-96; codirector of National Endowment for the Humanities seminar "Asia in the Core Curriculum," 1987—; member of committee on research libraries at New York Public Library, 1987—.

MEMBER: International Commission for the History of Historiography, American Historical Association (member of council, 1987—), Association for Asian Studies (member of Northeast Area council, 1981-84, president, 1996-97), Society for Historians of American Foreign Relations, Asia Society (board of trustees, 1992—, member of executive committee, 1996—), Japan Society (board of directors and member of executive committee, 1990—), Council on Foreign Relations, Japan-U.S. Friendship Commission (appointed, 1994, member of executive committee, 1994—, CULCON, 1995—), Phi Beta Kappa.

AWARDS, HONORS: Woodrow Wilson fellow, 1963-64; Social Science Research Council foreign area fellow in Japan, 1972-74; grants from Council for Research in the Social Sciences, 1978, 1980, 1982, and American Council of Learned Societies and Social Science Research Council, 1978-79; Japan Foundation fellow, 1978-79; Mark Van Doren Award for teaching from Columbia College, 1982; Fulbright grant, 1985-86; John King Fairbank Prize in East Asian History from American Historical Association, 1986, and Lionel Trilling Award from Columbia University, 1987, both for *Japan's Modern Myths;* distinguished lectureship, Northeast Asia Council, Association for Asian Studies, 1988; Japan Society for the Promotion of Science research fellowship and traveling lectureship, 1989; Great Teacher Award, Society of Columbia Graduates, 1989; elected fellow of the American Academy of Arts and Sciences, 1991; Alumna Achievement Award, Wellesley College, 1993.

WRITINGS:

Japan's Modern Myths: Ideology in the Late Meiji Period, Princeton University Press (Princeton, NJ), 1985.

(Coeditor) *Showa: The Japan of Hirohito,* Norton (New York City), 1992.

(Coeditor) *Asia in Western and World History,* M. E. Sharpe (Armonk, NY), 1996.

Coeditor of series "The United States and Pacific Asia: Studies in Social, Economics, and Political Interaction," Columbia University Press (New York City), 1987—. Contributor to books, including *New Frontiers in American-East Asian Relations,* edited by Warren Cohen, Columbia University Press, 1983; *Sengo Nihon seishinshi no saikento* (title means "Reevaluations of Postwar Japanese Intellectual History"), edited by M. Takebatake and A. Igarashi, Iwanami shoten, 1988; *Rethinking Japan,* Paul Norbury, 1990; *Legacies and Ambiguities: Postwar Fiction and Culture in West Germany and Japan,* edited by Ernestine Schlant and J. Thomas Rimer, Johns Hopkins University Press (Baltimore, MD), 1991; and *Postwar Japan as History,* edited by Andrew Gordon, University of California Press (Berkeley), 1993. Also contributor to *Encyclopedia of Asian History.* Contributor of articles and reviews to scholarly journals and Japanese newspapers.

WORK IN PROGRESS: Versions of the Past: The Japanese and Their Modern History, on historical consciousness in twentieth-century Japan; editing *Varieties of Japanese History,* translations of Happiness writings on history writing.

SIDELIGHTS: Carol Gluck told *CA* that she has focused her attention on the intellectual and social history of nineteenth-and twentieth-century Japan. She also expressed an interest in the history of international relations, comparative (European, American, and Japanese) historiography, and recent issues in war and public memory. The author's languages include Japanese, German, Spanish, and French.

*   *   *

GOEDICKE, Patricia (McKenna) 1931-

PERSONAL: Born June 21, 1931, in Boston, MA; daughter of John Bernard (a psychiatrist) and Helen (Mulvey) McKenna; married Victor Goedicke (a professor), September 12, 1956 (divorced, 1968); married Leonard Wallace Robinson (a writer), June 3, 1971. *Education:* Middlebury College, Middlebury, VT, B.A. (cum laude), 1953; studied under W. H. Auden at Young Men's Hebrew Association, New York City, 1955; Ohio University, M.A. in creative writing and poetry, 1965.

ADDRESSES: Home—310 McLeod Ave., Missoula, MT 59801. *Office*—Department of English, University of Montana, Missoula, MT 59812.

CAREER: Harcourt, Brace & World, New York City, editorial assistant, 1953-54; T. Y. Crowell (publishers), New York City, editorial assistant, 1955-56; coeditor, *Page* (poetry broadsheet), 1961-66; Ohio University, Athens, instructor in English, 1963-68; Book-of-the-Month Club, reader/writer, 1968-69; Hunter College of the City University of New York, New York City, lecturer in English, 1969-71; Instituto Allende, Guanajuato, Mexico, associate professor of creative writing, 1972-79; Sarah Lawrence College, Bronxville, NY, guest faculty member in writing program, 1980-81; University of Montana, Missoula, visiting poet in residence, 1981-83, associate professor of English, 1983-89, professor, 1990—. Has given poetry readings at the Library of Congress, the Young Men's Hebrew Association Poetry Center in New York, the New England Poetry Club, and the San Francisco State Poetry Center, as well as at colleges and universities, including State University of New York College at Brockport, Columbia University, New York University, Dartmouth College, Kalamazoo College, Washington University, Lake Forest College, San Francisco State University, Queens College of the City University of New York, Bucknell University, Wells College, and the Universities of Kansas, Arkansas,

Alaska, Oregon, Minnesota, and Nevada. Panel member, Ohio Poetry Association annual meeting, 1974.

MEMBER: PEN, Academy of American Poets, Associated Writing Programs, Poetry Society of America, MacDowell Colony (fellow, 1968—), Phi Beta Kappa.

AWARDS, HONORS: Virginia Clark Balch Poetry Contest second prize and National Endowment for the Arts award, both 1968, both for poem "You Could Pick It Up"; National Endowment for the Arts creative writing fellowship, 1976-77; Coordinating Council of Literary Magazines prize, 1976, for poem "Lost"; Duncan Frazier Prize, *Loon,* fall, 1976; William Carlos Williams Prize for poetry, *New Letters,* spring, 1977; *Quarterly West* Prize for poetry, 1977; Pushcart Prize, 1977; Carolyn Kizer Prize, Monmouth Institute, 1987; Strousse Award, *Prairie Schooner,* 1987; Hohenberg Award, *Memphis State Review,* 1988; research grant from University of Montana, 1989; *The Tongues We Speak: New and Selected Poems* was named a *New York Times* "Notable Book of the Year" for 1990; Distinguished Scholar Award, University of Montana, 1991; Edward Stanley Award for poems "Whatever Happens" and "Dead Baby," 1992; Walter Hall Award, *Hubbub,* 1995, for "These Words" and "Who Goes There."

WRITINGS:

POETRY

Between Oceans, Harcourt (San Diego, CA), 1968.
For the Four Corners, Ithaca House (Ithaca, NY), 1976.
The Trail That Turns on Itself, Ithaca House, 1978.
The Dog That Was Barking Yesterday, Lynx (Amherst, MA), 1980.
Crossing the Same River, University of Massachusetts Press (Amherst), 1980.
The Wind of Our Going, Copper Canyon Press (Port Townsend, WA), 1985.
Listen, Love, Barnwood (Daleville, IN), 1986.
The Tongues We Speak: New and Selected Poems, Milkweed Editions (Minneapolis), 1989.
Paul Bunyan's Bearskin, Milkweed Editions, 1992.
Invisible Horses, Milkweed Editions, 1996.

CONTRIBUTOR

The American Literary Anthology, Volume 3, Viking (New York City), 1970.

William Cole, editor, *And Be Merry,* Grossman (New York City), 1972.

Psyche: The Feminine Poetic Consciousness, Dell (New York City), 1976.

William Cole, editor, *The Ardis Anthology of New American Poetry,* Ardis (Ann Arbor, MI), 1976.

Bill Henderson, editor, *The Pushcart Prize, II: Best of the Small Presses,* Pushcart (New York City), 1978.

Tangled Vines, Beacon Press (Boston, MA), 1978.

The Treasury of American Poetry, Doubleday (New York City), 1978.

A Geography of Poets, Bantam (New York City), 1979.

Editor's Choice, Spirit That Moves Us (Iowa City, Iowa), 1980.

Walt Whitman: The Measure of His Song, Holy Cow Press (Minneapolis, MN), 1981.

Of Silence and Solitude, Beacon Press, 1982.

New Letters Reader 1: Anthology of Contemporary Poetry, New Letters (Kansas City, MO), 1983.

Jim Schley, editor, *Writing in a Nuclear Age,* University Press of New England (Hanover, NH), 1984.

Margaret Randall, editor, *Women Brave in the Face of Danger: Photographs of and Writings by Latin and North American Women,* Crossing Press (Trumansburg, NY), 1985.

Dacey and Lundgren, editors, *Strong Measures,* Harper (New York City), 1986.

Buchwald and Roston, editors, *This Sporting Life,* Milkweed Editions, 1987.

The Discovery of Poetry, Harcourt, 1987.

Ray Gonzalez, editor, *Crossing the River: Poets of the Western U.S.,* Permanent Press (Sag Harbor, NY), 1987.

Jon Mukand, editor, *Sutured Words,* Aviva Press, 1988.

Lea Lifshitz, editor, *Her Soul beneath the Bone,* University of Illinois Press (Champaign), 1988.

William Kittredge and Annick Smith, senior editors, *The Last Best Place,* University of Washington Press (Seattle), 1988.

Ronald Wallace, editor, *Vital Signs,* University of Wisconsin Press (Madison), 1989.

Participating in the Poem, Center for Learning, 1989.

Richard Reynolds and John Stone, editors, *On Doctoring,* Simon & Schuster (New York City), 1991.

Buchwald and Roston, editors, *Mixed Voices,* Milkweed Editions, 1991.

Mark Sanders, editor, *Decade Dance,* Sandhills Press, 1991.

Anderson and Gildzen, editors, *A Gathering of Poets,* Kent State University Press (Kent, OH), 1992.

Michael Blumenthal, editor, *To Woo and to Wed,* Poseidon Press (New York City), 1992.

Lyn Lifshin, editor, *Tangled Vines,* Harcourt, 1992.

Forrest Gander, editor, *Mouth to Mouth,* Milkweed Editions, 1993.

Florence Howe, editor, *No More Masks!,* HarperCollins (New York City), 1993.

John Bradley, editor, *Atomic Ghost: Poets Respond to the Nuclear Age,* Coffee House Press, 1995.

Also contributor to *Arvon International Poetry Competition Anthology for 1987,* Arvon Foundation Publishers (Todmorden, England), 1987, *Seneca Review Twenty-Fifth Anniversary Anthology,* 1995, *Hampden-Sydney Poetry Review Anthology, 1975-1990,* and *Spreading the Word.*

OTHER

(Contributor of translations) *IXOK AMARGO* (poems), Granite Press, 1987.

Contributing editor, *Chowder Review.* Contributor to periodicals, including *Open Places, New Yorker, American Poetry Review, Antioch Review, Saturday Review, Nation,* and *Harper's.*

SIDELIGHTS: Patricia Goedicke's poetry is described in the *Times Literary Supplement* by David Kirby as "intensely emotional, intensely physical." "More than any contemporary woman poet, perhaps, she exhibits a Whitmanesque exuberance," claims *Small Press Review* contributor Hans Ostrom. According to Peter Schjeldahl in the *New York Times Book Review,* Goedicke "bears down hard on the language, frequently producing exact ambiguities of phrasing that are startling and funny." And *Harper's* reviewer Hayden Carruth believes that Goedicke's poems "have a hard truthful ring, like parables of survival." Goedicke's collection, *The Wind of Our Going,* "is distinguished by its use of lavish images and multiple comparisons," describes Lex Runciman in *Western American Literature.* "Her poems delight in their connections, in the sheer physical length and amplitude of their sentences." Ostrom also likes the book, and writes, "*The Wind of Our Going* shows [Goedicke] to be a confident poet and a poet who has reason to be confident. Although she could benefit from a lighter touch and more varied forms, this is an engaging, vital book."

BIOGRAPHICAL/CRITICAL SOURCES:

PERIODICALS

Bloomsbury Review, March/April, 1990.
Chicago Sun-Times, July 9, 1978.
Harper's, December, 1980.
Hudson Review, summer, 1994.
Los Angeles Times Book Review, April 27, 1980.
Missoulian, July 28-August 3, 1989.
Modern Poetry Studies, winter, 1976.
New York Times Book Review, December 17, 1978; February 9, 1986; January 28, 1990.
Small Press Review, November, 1985.
Southern Humanities Review, fall, 1971.
Southern Review, October, 1993.
Tar River Poetry Review, fall, 1985.
Times Literary Supplement, June 13, 1980.
Western American Literature, fall, 1986.

* * *

GOODWIN, Doris (Helen) Kearns 1943-
    (Doris Helen Kearns)

PERSONAL: Born January 4, 1943, in Rockville Centre, NY; daughter of Michael Alouisius (a bank examiner) and Helen Witt (Miller) Kearns; married Richard Goodwin (a writer and political consultant), 1975; children: three sons. *Education:* Colby College, B.A. (magna cum laude), Harvard University, Ph.D., 1968. *Religion:* Roman Catholic.

ADDRESSES: Home—Concord, MA.

CAREER: U.S. Government, Washington, DC, State Department intern, 1963, House of Representatives intern, 1965, Department of Health, Education, and Welfare, research associate, 1966, special assistant to Willard Wirtz, Department of Labor, 1967, special assistant to President Lyndon Johnson, 1968; Harvard University, Cambridge, MA, assistant professor, 1969-71, associate professor of government, beginning 1972, assistant director of Institute of Politics, beginning 1971, member of faculty council. Special consultant to President Johnson, 1969-73. Hostess of television show, *What's the Big Idea,* WGBH-TV, Boston, MA, 1972; political analyst for news desk, WBZ-TV, Boston, Member of Democratic party platform committee, 1972; member of Women's Political Caucus in Massachusetts (member of steering committee, beginning 1972). Trustee of Wesleyan University, Colby College, and Robert F. Kennedy Foundation.

MEMBER: American Political Science Association, Council on Foreign Relations (member of nominating and reform committees, 1972), Women Involved (chairman and member of board of advisers), Group for Applied Psychoanalysis, Phi Beta Kappa, Phi Sigma Iota, Signet Society.

AWARDS, HONORS: Fulbright fellow, 1966; Outstanding Young Woman of the Year award from Phi Beta Kappa, 1966; White House fellow, 1967; Pulitzer Prize, 1995, for *No Ordinary Time: Franklin and Eleanor Roosevelt; The Home Front in World War II.*

WRITINGS:

(Under name Doris Helen Kearns) *Lyndon Johnson and the American Dream,* Harper (New York City), 1976, published under name Doris Kearns Goodwin, St. Martin's (New York City), 1991.
(Contributor) Marc Pachter, editor, *Telling Lives: The Biographer's Art,* New Republic Books, 1979.
The Fitzgeralds and the Kennedys: An American Saga, Simon & Schuster (New York City), 1987.
No Ordinary Time: Franklin and Eleanor Roosevelt; The Home Front in World War II, Simon & Schuster, 1994.

Also contributor of articles to *New Republic.*

WORK IN PROGRESS: A memoir about growing up in the 1950s and the influence of baseball on her life; a view of the Civil War from the perspective of the Lincoln White House; a study, co-written with her husband, of the modern presidency and its most important actions.

ADAPTATIONS: American Broadcasting Companies, Inc. has purchased the television rights to *The Fitzgeralds and the Kennedys: An American Saga.*

SIDELIGHTS: Doris Kearns Goodwin, a former professor of government at Harvard University, is the author of highly acclaimed biographies. *Lyndon Johnson and the American Dream* is a political and psychological study of the thirty-sixth president, while *The Fitzgeralds and the Kennedys: An American Saga* examines the life of John F. Kennedy as well as the two generations that preceded him. *No Ordinary Time: Franklin and Eleanor Roosevelt; The Home Front in World War II* looks at the difficult and often stormy relationship between Franklin and Eleanor Roosevelt during World War II. "I realize," Goodwin states in *Publishers Weekly,* "that to be a historian is to discover the facts in context, to discover what things mean, to lay before the reader your reconstruction of time, place, mood, to empathize even when you disagree. You read all the relevant material, you synthesize all the books, you speak to all the people you can, and then you write down what you known about the period. You feel you own it."

The circumstances surrounding the writing of *Lyndon Johnson and the American Dream* are interesting and somewhat unusual. Goodwin first met Johnson at a White House dance in 1967. At the time, she was a White House fellow working as a special assistant to Willard Wirtz. She had recently coauthored an article for *New Republic* entitled "How to Remove LBJ in 1968," in which she was sharply critical of Johnson's foreign policy. Johnson was aware of her feelings when he met her but instead of arguing with her, he asked her to dance. At the end of the evening, he suggested that she be assigned to work with him in the White House. According to *Nation* reviewer Ronnie Dugger, in befriending Goodwin, Johnson had apparently heeded the advice of John Roche, one of his aides, who told him that having a White House fellow who was critical of the administration would cause him to appear open-minded and unthreatened by the growing anti-war sentiment in America. When Johnson eventually asked Goodwin to help him write his memoirs, she agreed; after his retirement, she traveled to the Johnson ranch in Austin, Texas, on weekends, holidays and vacations to help Johnson write the "official" version of his presidency.

Johnson's choice of Goodwin as his biographer was one many observers found noteworthy. In addition to being critical of his administration, she was, as *New York Times Book Review* contributor David Halberstam notes, "respected in the Eastern intellectual world which Johnson was sure despised him." With Goodwin (as one of their own) telling his story, he believed that the group he felt excluded from would finally, if not accept him, then at least listen to his story. He had, as a writer for the *New Yorker* put it, become "preoccupied with the verdict of history." He wanted to be remembered as a successful president; he sought out writers who would be friendly in their judgment of him. According to *New Republic* contributor Robert Coles, Johnson is reported to have told Goodwin that she reminded him of his mother, and as he spent more and more time with her, he apparently came to believe that she felt sympathetic towards him and that she would write a flattering portrayal of him.

Published in 1976, three years after Johnson's death, *Lyndon Johnson and the American Dream* met with a good deal of acclaim. Halberstam calls the book "a fascinating and unusual addition to the Johnson shelf." Christopher Lehmann-Haupt of the *New York Times* deems it "the most penetrating, fascinating political biography I have ever read." Reviewers also found favor with Goodwin's writing. In his *Washington Post Book World* review, Horace Busby describes the author's prose as "vivid and sensitive" and her portrait of the ex-president "the most fascinating and absorbing and, yes, sympathetic to appear in contemporary literature." The quality that many critics admired in the book was Goodwin's objectivity. Coles sees her "open-eyed restraint" as one of the book's greatest assets. Similarly, Halberstam describes Goodwin as "a good listener . . . at once intelligent and sympathetic, and yet strong and independent enough to make her story credible."

In *Lyndon Johnson and the American Dream,* Goodwin does more than recount the details of Johnson's personal life and political career; she also offers a probing study of the former president's personality, examining in particular how his early years were integral in making him the politician he became. As Goodwin sees it, Johnson's political ambitions, his quest for power, and his plans for the "Great Society" all stemmed from an effort to free himself from the conflict he felt torn by from birth. His mother was shy, genteel, and dignified; his father was easygoing, flamboyant, and frequently ill-mannered. As *Saturday Review* contributor Larry McMurtry explains, Goodwin "demonstrates again and again how Johnson's youthful need to keep the peace between his parents affected his style as a politician, a style dependent upon endless and often very subtle personal negotiation." This psychobiographical approach drew quite a bit of critical attention, much of it positive. In his *Newsweek* review Paul D. Zimmerman praises Goodwin for "producing a sensible, scrupulous compassionate study of the connections between Lyndon Johnson's psychological drives and his political fortunes." He adds, "Other books, pitched at a greater distance from their subject, will undoubtedly offer a more definitive social and political appraisal of the Johnson Presidency. But none is likely to offer a sharper, more intimate portrait of Lyndon Johnson in full psychic undress." Writes McMurtry, "the effort she has made to untangle the psychic knots of his character and relate them to his actions as a leader is . . . extremely loyal, requiring much empathy and a long application of effort and intelligence."

One of the more controversial aspects of the book was Goodwin's analysis of Johnson's dreams; several critics wondered about the validity of these interpretations. "She seems," writes *New York Review of Books* contributor Gary Wills, "insufficiently aware of the fact that dreams told in a persuasive context cannot have the evidentiary value of those discussed in analysis." McMurtry, on the other hand, claims that Goodwin "makes a tentative, fair, never very dogmatic use of the tools of psychoanalysis." James M. Perry writes in the *National Observer* that although Goodwin presents "some pretty heavy character analysis amounting to psychohistory" in her book, "she is honest enough to admit that there are vast empty spaces in what we know about the human mind and human behavior."

In a *New Republic* article, Goodwin wrote that she would rather have waited a number of years before writing *Lyndon Johnson and the American Dream,* so that she could "really understand and convey its human value." But she was a young Harvard professor, and as she said, "I had to publish." In spite of Goodwin's disclaimers, many reviewers tend to side with McMurtry when he calls *Lyndon Johnson and the American Dream* "a triumph—partly [Goodwin's] and partly Lyndon Johnson's" and deems the book "by far the most significant we have of Johnson."

Six months after *Lyndon Johnson and the American Dream* was published, Simon & Schuster contracted Goodwin to write a biography of Johnson's predecessor, John F. Kennedy. Goodwin began work in late 1977 but what she initially envisioned as a three-year project on Kennedy's life evolved into a multi-generational saga of two Irish-American families. As she explained to the *Detroit News:* "As I got into the project, I realized I wanted to do a book about my own heritage, something different than just a biography of Jack. I wanted to look at the whole assimilation of an immigrant group, the Irish, over a period of time, an assimilation that ended up in the most dramatic way by having Kennedy becoming the president of the United States." Divided into three parts and spanning nearly a century, *The Fitzgeralds and the Kennedys: An American Saga* chronicles three generations of Fitzgeralds and Kennedys—from the baptism of John "Honey Fitz" Fitzgerald in 1863 to the inauguration of his grandson and namesake John F. Kennedy in 1961.

The enormous amount of research entailed in a work of such scope was one reason it took Goodwin nearly a decade to complete her second book. Another factor was her decision to spend more time with her family. The birth of her youngest son, Joey, "changed my whole feeling toward the project," Goodwin told Judith Michaelson in the *Los Angeles Times.* "When I was writing the Johnson book and was still single, it was probably the most important thing in my life, and I would stay up if I wanted to, until midnight. With this book when I started it, the kids were so little that I could spend only two or three hours on it at the beginning. It was deeper than that. I wasn't panicked about it. It wasn't the thing I was obsessed about. I was obsessed about the kids." Goodwin also sees another fundamental difference between the writing of these two books—her contact with the subjects themselves. In writing the Johnson book, "I was aware of being captive to him," Goodwin told the *Washington Post.* On the other hand, she says of the Fitzgerald-Kennedy book: "these were not people that I knew. I had to recreate them for myself first, in order to render them to the reader. Part of what gave me the confidence to write honestly . . . is that I began to feel I knew them."

Although quite a few books have been written about the Kennedys in recent years, Goodwin was able to add fresh material to her work as a result of her access to two valuable sources. One of these was her husband, Richard, a former speechwriter for and advisor to Lyndon Johnson and Robert and John Kennedy. Having known the Kennedys for over twenty-five years, Richard Goodwin was able to provide his wife with an insider's view of the family. Through her husband's close ties to the Kennedys, Goodwin also came upon a mine of information untapped by previous biographers—one hundred and fifty cartons of Joseph Kennedy's personal correspondence. These letters not only permitted Goodwin to fill in important details concerning Joseph's business dealings, they also allowed her to gain insight into his relationships with his wife and children. Goodwin in turn was able to use the contents of these letters to stimulate the latent memories of Joseph's wife, Rose. In doing so she was able to dispel certain notions about John and his father as well as offer new perspectives on existing knowledge about other family members.

Critical reaction to *The Fitzgeralds and the Kennedys* was enthusiastic, with many critics praising Goodwin's treatment of what has become a rather well-traversed subject. Writes Christopher Lehmann-Haupt of the *New York Times:* "The story is familiar enough. We've read its various parts in at least a dozen books over the past quarter century. . . . Yet rarely has this familiar saga seemed so fresh and dramatic. Rarely have its characters been so alive and individual. Rarely has popular history rung so authentic, or, conversely, fresh scholarship struck us as so captivating." Similarly, *Los Angeles Times Book Review* contributor Robert Dallek notes: "The elevation of the Kennedys to the status of a royal family has led to an outpouring of articles and books on the entire clan. Doris Kearns Goodwin's new study is now the best book on the subject." Goodwin's writing style also met with acclaim. *Washington Post* critic George V. Higgins calls *The Fitzgeralds and the Kennedys* "an anecdotal, thoughtful genealogy" and deems Goodwin "a meticulous and felicitous writer." Geoffrey C. Ward, writing in the *New York Times Book Review* describes Goodwin's portrayal of the book's main characters as "remarkably rich and fully rounded," adding, "her accounts of the events through which they all lived [are] unusually complex and elegantly rendered."

In his *New York Times* review Lehmann-Haupt comments on the trigenerational approach the author employs in *The Fitzgeralds and the Kennedys,* deeming it "deceptively simple," and commends Goodwin on the book's attention to detail and "thematic coherence." What gives *The Fitzgeralds and the Kennedys* thematic unity is largely its emphasis on the concept of the family. As Goodwin told the *New York Times,* it is through this multigenerational approach that "the reader will, I hope, be able to see more clearly the inescapable impact of family relationships over time, the repeated patterns of behaviour, both enviable and dubious, the same strengths and the same weaknesses that crop up again and again." Ward praises Goodwin for her adherence to such an approach, noting that Goodwin "does not so much excuse the less attractive chapters of the Kennedy saga as attempt to understand them, while providing the kind of informed historical context without which no family's history can ever be understood. She never loses sight of the fact that family *matters,* that what happens within one generation inevitably has its impact on the next."

While *The Fitzgeralds and the Kennedys* was generally well-received, some critics had mixed reactions to the book. Ward, for example, finds fault with Goodwin's rendering of the voices of those she interviewed during her research. He writes: "Ms. Goodwin is a serious, sensitive biographer, and she has clearly mined a good deal of important new material from those with whom she talked. But the impact of much that they told her is vitiated by the artful way in which she seems to have sculptured their memories." He adds, "In *The Fitzgeralds and the Kennedys*

it is too frequently true that when key witnesses to important events are heard from, the reader cannot help wondering who is really talking, whose conclusions are being reached." Similarly, though he admires Goodwin's "tact and scholarship," *Time* contributor R. Z. Sheppard claims: "The author overextends herself when she tries to occupy high critical ground. She is on much firmer ground when sticking to her own preconception, an alluring vision of history as romance."

Many critics were aware of Goodwin's close personal and political ties to the Kennedy family, and a good number praised Goodwin for her ability to write *The Fitzgeralds and the Kennedys* objectively, or as Dallek puts it, "with compassion and understanding." Commending Goodwin for "deftly eliding the problem implicit in the fact that her husband, Richard Goodwin, has been a Kennedy confidant for about three decades—while employing the advantage of that relationship," Higgins goes on to note: "I think she dealt brilliantly with the potential problem. She has ended her chronicle at JFK's inauguration, in 1961. While I think a stranger to the living family might have employed harsher rhetoric to deliver the moral and ethical estimates she renders, her verdicts are—though mercifully couched—just, complete and unsparing." "Mrs. Goodwin pulls no punches when it comes to the faults and frailties of the Fitzgerald and Kennedy families," writes Lehmann-Haupt, adding, "because Mrs. Goodwin examines their characters so intelligently, and because she places them all in the broader sweep of history, she never appears to be debunking her subjects. . . . In short, the legend remains intact in both its triumphant and tragic aspects. We get the Fitzgeralds and the Kennedys with and without tears. We are permitted to envy them, and yet also to be grateful that most of us, at least, have not been cursed with their radiant gifts and their ambition to reach and grasp the sun."

In 1995, Goodwin received the Pulitzer Prize in biography for her third book, *No Ordinary Time: Franklin and Eleanor Roosevelt; The Home Front in World War II.* The book's strong points and the "glowing reviews" it received, according to *Chicago Tribune* reporter Barbara B. Buchholz, "are in large part due to Goodwin's ability to bring to life complex personal relationships." These relationships ranged from Franklin Roosevelt's "friendships with the women in his life: Lucy Mercer Rutherford (the woman who almost broke up the Roosevelt marriage in 1918), Marguerite (Missy) LeHand (his secretary and companion for over 20 years) and Princess

Martha of Norway," explains Blanche Wiesen Cook in the *Los Angeles Times Book Review*. For her part, states *New Republic* reviewer Joe Klein, Eleanor Roosevelt "hir[ed] close friends—the actor Melvyn Douglas and the dancer Mayris Chaney, among others—as public morale boosters" in her brief stint as assistant director of the Office of Civil Defense. She also carried on close—Goodwin does *not* say intimate—relationships with Associated Press reporter Lorena Hickock, her secretary Malvina "Tommy" Thompson, and social activist Joseph Lash. However, Keith Henderson of the *Christian Science Monitor* emphasizes that "the central relationship between the wartime president and his irrepressible wife drives the book."

"'No Ordinary Time' is no ordinary book," declares *New York Times Book Review* contributor David M. Kennedy. Besides being one of the few biographies to present a joint picture of the presidential couple during the war years, it also shows a unique picture of the two working together as a political, if not a romantic, team. "To Goodwin, though such a partnership made good political sense," states James Bowman in the *Washington Post Book World*, "it was founded upon an essential truth about the partners' respective natures. Eleanor, the daughter of a neglectful mother and a loving but alcoholic father, never felt at home in a domestic role—partly because Franklin's mother, on whom he was emotionally dependent, prevented her from being mistress in her own house." For his part, Franklin was deeply sensitive about his paraplegia and dreamed about the days before he was stricken with polio, when he could walk alone and unassisted. "It is a measure of Doris Kearns Goodwin's success," Klein asserts, "that the subtle sources of FDR's greatness become manifest in the course of this book."

Despite their effective partnership, Goodwin depicts both Eleanor and Franklin Roosevelt as alienated from each other. "In the final pages of this book, Franklin, broken in health and isolated, appears unspeakably lonely. So too does Eleanor," Kennedy states. "She still loved Franklin, Ms. Goodwin insists, but could no longer touch his soul nor be touched by his. . . . The constricting band of history reached even her, in the inner chambers of the heart." "In weaving together private and public contexts," concludes *Tribune Books* reviewer Linda Simon, "Goodwin shows that history is not a chronicle of major events but the cumulative, quirky responses of idiosyncratic human beings to the demands and challenges of their time."

BIOGRAPHICAL/CRITICAL SOURCES:

PERIODICALS

Atlanta Constitution, April 11, 1995, p. E1.
Boston Globe, July 25, 1994, p. 2; April 19, 1995, p. 1.
Chicago Tribune, October 30, 1994, p. 5.
Chicago Tribune Books, October 2, 1994, section 14, p. 1, 13.
Christian Science Monitor, October 18, 1994, p. 3.
Commentary, August, 1976.
Detroit News, March 27, 1987.
Los Angeles Times, March 4, 1987; October 23, 1994, p. M3.
Los Angeles Times Book Review, March 1, 1987; October 9, 1994, pp. 2, 13.
Nation, September 4, 1976.
National Observer, June 19, 1976.
National Review, November 21, 1994, pp. 63-64.
New Republic, August 7 & 14, 1976; March 23, 1979; November 21, 1993, pp. 63-64; October 10, 1994, pp. 42-47.
New Statesman, October 8, 1976.
Newsweek, May 31, 1976; February 9, 1987.
New Yorker, June 7, 1976.
New York Review of Books, June 24, 1976; January 14, 1993, pp. 3-7.
New York Times, June 7, 1976; February 2, 1987.
New York Times Book Review, June 6, 1976; February 15, 1987; September 11, 1994, pp. 9, 11.
Publishers Weekly, October 3, 1986, pp. 64-65.
Saturday Review, June 12, 1976.
Spectator, October 16, 1976.
Time, February 16, 1987.
Times Literary Supplement, December 10, 1976; July 17, 1987.
Tribune Books (Chicago), October 2, 1994, pp. 1, 13.
TV Guide, July 18-24, 1987, pp. 12-13.
Washington Post, January 20, 1987.
Washington Post Book World, December 12, 1976; September 18, 1994, pp. 1, 11.*

* * *

GREAVES, Margaret 1914-

PERSONAL: Born June 13, 1914, in Birmingham, England; daughter of Joseph William (a clergyman) and Jessie May (Greenup) Greaves. *Education:* St. Hugh's College, Oxford, B.A. (with honors), 1936, B. Litt., 1938, M.A., 1947. *Religion:* Church of England.

ADDRESSES: Home—8 Greenways, Winchcombe, Cheltenham, Gloucestershire GL54 5LG, England.

CAREER: Writer, 1970—. Lincoln High School for Girls, English teacher, 1938-40; Priory School, Shrewsbury, England, English teacher, 1940-41; Pate's Grammar School for Girls, Cheltenham, England, English teacher, 1943-46; St. Mary's College, Cheltenham, lecturer, 1946-60, principal lecturer and head of English department, 1960-70. *Military service:* British Women's Land Army, 1941-43.

MEMBER: English Association, School Library Association.

WRITINGS:

CHILDREN'S FICTION

The Dagger and the Bird: A Story of Suspense, illustrated by Jill McDonald, Methuen (London), 1971, illustrated by Laszlo Kubinyi, Harper (New York City), 1975.

The Grandmother Stone, Methuen, 1972, published in the United States as *Stone of Terror,* Harper, 1974.

Little Jacko and the Wolf People, illustrated by McDonald, Methuen, 1973.

The Gryphon Quest, Methuen, 1974.

Curfew, Methuen, 1975.

The Night of the Goat, illustrated by Trevor Ridley, Abelard, Schuman (London), 1976.

Nothing Ever Happens on Sundays, illustrated by Gareth Floyd, BBC Publications (London), 1976.

A Net to Catch the Wind, illustrated by Stephen Gammell, Harper, 1979.

The Abbotsbury Ring, illustrated by Laszlo Acs, Methuen, 1979.

Cat's Magic, illustrated by Joanna Carey, Methuen, 1980, Harper, 1981.

Charlie, Emma, and Alberic, illustrated by Eileen Browne, Methuen, 1979.

The Snake Whistle, illustrated by Floyd, BBC Publications, 1980.

Charlie, Emma, and the Dragon Family, illustrated by Browne, Methuen, 1982.

Charlie, Emma, and the School Dragon, illustrated by Browne, Methuen, 1984.

The Monster of Roundwater, illustrated by Michael Bragg, Methuen, 1984.

(Reteller) *A Little Box of Witches* (four volumes), illustrated by Francesca Crespi, Dial (New York City), 1985.

(Reteller) *Fairy Tale* (four volumes), illustrated by Annegart Fuchschuber, Michele Lemieux, Renate Mortl-Rangnick, and Eva Scherbarth, Methuen, 1985.

Once There Were No Pandas: A Chinese Legend, illustrated by Beverley Gooding, Dutton (New York City), 1985.

(Reteller) *A Little Box of Ballet Stories* (three volumes), illustrated by Crespi, Dial, 1986.

Little Bear and the Papagini Circus, illustrated by Crespi, Dial, 1986.

Charlie, Emma, and Dragons to the Rescue, illustrated by Browne, Methuen, 1986.

(Reteller) *Goldilocks and the Three Bears,* illustrated by Maria Claret, Methuen, 1987.

Hetty Pegler, Half-Witch, illustrated by Derek Crowe, Methuen, 1987.

Charlie, Emma, and the Juggling Dragon, Methuen, 1989.

Mouse Mischief, illustrated by Jane Pinkney, M. Malin/Deutsch (London), 1989.

The Magic Flute: The Story of Mozart's Opera, illustrated by Crespi, Greenwillow (New York City), 1989.

Juniper's Journey, Methuen, 1990.

(Reteller) *Tattercoats,* illustrated by Margaret Chamberlain, Crown (New York City), 1990.

Magic from the Ground, Dent (London), 1990.

The Lucky Coin, illustrated by Liz Underhill, -, Tabori & Chang (New York City), 1990.

Henry's Wild Morning, illustrated by Teresa O'Brien, Dent, 1990, Dial, 1991.

Amanda and the Star Child, illustrated by Diane Catchpole, Dent, 1991.

The Lost Ones (short stories), illustrated by Honey de Lacey, Dent, 1991.

Charlie, Emma, and the Runaway Dragon, Methuen, 1991.

Rosie's Lion, Dent, 1992.

The Naming, illustrated by Pauline Baynes, Dent, 1992, Harcourt (San Diego), 1993.

The Star Horse, illustrated by Jan Nesbitt, Dent, 1992.

Littlemouse Alone, Scholastic (New York City), 1992.

Sarah's Lion, illustrated by de Lacey, Barron's Educational (Hauppauge, New York), 1992.

The Ice Journey, illustrated by Alison Claire Darke, Dent, 1993.

Henry in the Dark, illustrated by O'Brien, Dent, 1993.

The Serpent Shell, illustrated by Nesbitt, Barron's Educational, 1993.

Stories from the Ballet, illustrated by Lisa Kopper, Lincoln (London), 1993.

CHILDREN'S POETRY

Nicky's Knitting Granny and the Cat, illustrated by Alice Englander, Methuen, 1985.

The Mice of Nibbling Village, illustrated by Jane Pinkney, Dutton, 1986.

"ENGLISH FOR JUNIORS" SERIES

Your Turn Next, illustrated by McDonald, Methuen, 1966.

One World and Another, illustrated by McDonald, Methuen, 1967.

(Editor) *Gallery* (short stories), illustrated by McDonald, Methuen, 1968.

Two at Number Twenty, illustrated by McDonald, Methuen, 1970.

What Am I? illustrated by McDonald, Methuen, 1972.

Gallery Wonders (compilation), Bowmar (Glendale, CA), 1975.

"GALLIMAUFRY" SERIES

The Great Bell of Peking, illustrated by McDonald, Methuen, 1971, Bowmar, 1975.

King Solomon and the Hoopoes, illustrated by McDonald, Methuen, 1971, Bowmar, 1975.

The Rainbow Sun, illustrated by McDonald, Methuen, 1971, Bowmar, 1975.

The Snowman of Biddle, illustrated by McDonald, Methuen, 1971, Bowmar, 1975.

OTHER

The Blazon of Honor: A Study in Renaissance Magnanimity, Barnes & Noble (New York City), 1964.

Regency Patron: Sir George Beaumont, Methuen, 1966.

(Compiler) *Scrap-Box: Poems for Grown-ups to Share with Children,* illustrated by McDonald, Methuen, 1969.

A Star for My Son (teleplay), produced by British Broadcast Corp., 1980.

Contributor of reviews to *Renaissance Quarterly.*

SIDELIGHTS: "Few children's writers have commanded the range, assurance, and depth of Margaret Greaves," notes Myles McDowell in an essay for *Twentieth-Century Children's Writers.* In many of her novels, Greaves presents her young protagonists with real-life dilemmas in which they must make hard choices. From historical novels such as *Curfew,*

where a young boy must question the meaning of justice in nineteenth-century Britain, to adaptations of stories as familiar as *Goldilocks and the Three Bears* and as sophisticated as *The Magic Flute: The Story of Mozart's Opera,* Greaves concentrates on the relationships between good and evil, and between fantasy and reality.

The Dagger and the Bird: A Story of Suspense combines history and fantasy in a suspenseful tale that has been praised by reviewers. The story focuses on the abusive Simon, younger brother to Bridget and Luke. When it is revealed that Simon is really a changeling, left in place of their real brother, Bridget and Luke must undertake a dangerous journey to rescue the real Simon. Greaves denies her readers a tidy ending; it is clear, instead, that the aftershocks of the children's adventures will continue to affect each of them, and the reader has witnessed only a small part of their story. "If Greaves has the courage to leave her heroes (and readers!) in uncertainty and nagging doubt," comments McDowell in *Twentieth-Century Children's Writers,* "it is because, enriched in self-knowledge, they emerge from adventure equipped to face a more complex world."

The Grandmother Stone, published in the United States as *Stone of Terror,* also combines history and fantasy to tell of the personal growth of its young protagonist. Sent to live with his grandfather on a small Channel Island, Philip finds that an ancient stone idol exerts a strong and menacing influence on him. J. G. Gray, writing in *Best Sellers,* calls *Stone of Terror* "a haunting tale of witchcraft, mob cruelty, and the poignancy of young love." Philip's "rationalism is strengthened," writes Gloris Levitas in the *New York Times Book Review,* "when he comes to understand that demons are produced by love, hatred and social constraints rather than by supernatural power."

Greaves enters the world of the fantastic even more fully in *Cat's Magic.* When Louise Higgs saves a cat from drowning, she wins the gratitude of Bast, the Egyptian cat goddess, who rewards the girl by sending her on a journey a hundred years into the past. Although Jessica Yates in the *Times Literary Supplement* finds the book to be "hackneyed" and containing "children's book cliches," she nonetheless calls *Cat's Magic* "ambitious and expansive" and, for some children, "it could be a very enjoyable read." Writing in *Growing Point,* Margery Fisher believes that "surprise and tension are well sustained" to make *Cat's Magic* "more than a casual adventure."

While many of her books have been aimed at older readers, Greaves has also written stories for younger children. In *The Mice of Nibbling Village,* fourteen poems by Greaves are combined with gentle watercolor drawings by illustrator Jane Pinkney. The poems concern the mice who have an entire village under the floorboards of an old country house. Linda Wicher, writing in *School Library Journal,* describes Greaves's poems as having "strong rhythms and solid rhyme patterns." Fisher notes that Greaves's poems "vary from the lightly satirical to the cosily affectionate." "Children," Nita Kurmins Gilson states in the *Christian Science Monitor,* "should enjoy poring over every detail in the drawings while listening to the tales of Nibbling Village characters." Also designed to be read aloud, *The Naming* is Greaves's account of how animals first got their names. To this Old Testament story is added a drop of magic as Greaves adds a single unicorn into the crowd of animals that appear in pairs before Adam to receive their names. "Wonderful moments are described in musical, precise language," reviewer Patricia Pearl Dole states in *School Library Journal.*

The Naming is one of several adaptations of traditional stories that Greaves has done during her writing career. Her story collection *The Lost Ones* contains a dozen folktales meant to be read aloud. "These are carefully turned pieces, lightly done so that the pathos of lost or enchanted children breathes through the settings of seashore or woodland, of riverside or ancient dwelling," notes Fisher. The eerie fantasy stories collected in *The Lost Ones* are followed by *Once There Were No Pandas,* Greaves's retelling of a Chinese legend about how panda bears came to have black spots, and *Tattercoats,* a classic folktale about a princess who is cast out of her home and befriended by a gooseherd and his flock. In addition to folk and fairy tales from many cultures, Greaves has transformed a personal love for the ballet into several books for young readers, including *A Little Box of Ballet Stories,* which contains the stories of "Firebird," "Petrushka," and "Coppelia," each in their own tiny volume. *Stories from the Ballet* expands the theme with outlines of seven of the most widely-viewed ballets. "The Magic Flute," an opera popular with children, is outlined by Greaves in *The Magic Flute: The Story of Mozart's Opera.*

Wide-ranging interests and an enthusiasm for sharing those interests with young readers have made Greaves's books lasting favorites. "My ideas," Greaves once explained, "spring from an interest in human relationships and a deep love of the countryside in which I have always lived, and from a heritage of folklore and history. My books often grow from a single image that comes to me quite unexpectedly—an ancient statue seen at a church gate in the Channel Islands, or a mental picture of the desolation of a changeling in a human household; and I recognize the image as the germ of a story that may become clear to me if I wait quietly and patiently. It is as if the story is there already and only waiting to be discovered."

BIOGRAPHICAL/CRITICAL SOURCES:

BOOKS

Twentieth-Century Children's Writers, St. James Press (Detroit), 1994.

PERIODICALS

Best Sellers, November 15, 1974, p. 378.
Booklist, December 1, 1992, p. 675.
Christian Science Monitor, April 17, 1987, p. 26.
Growing Point, July, 1980, p. 3716; March, 1987, p. 4754; July, 1991, pp. 5538-41.
Horn Book, October, 1974; April, 1975.
Junior Bookshelf, June, 1982, p. 97; April, 1986, p. 67; October, 1990, p. 231; February, 1993, pp. 12-13; April, 1993, p. 60; December, 1993, p. 233; April, 1994, pp. 49-50.
New York Times Book Review, November 10, 1974, p. 10; April 8, 1979, pp. 32-33; December 8, 1985, p. 74.
Publishers Weekly, October 14, 1974, p. 57; August 2, 1985, pp. 66-67.
School Library Journal, September, 1979, p. 110; April, 1981, p. 127; January, 1987, p. 63; February, 1987, p. 68; May, 1993, p. 84.
Times Literary Supplement, April 2, 1971; September 20, 1974; March 28, 1980, p. 361; March 30, 1984.
Voice of Youth Advocates, June, 1981, p. 38.
Wilson Library Bulletin, February, 1988, pp. 76-77.

*　　　*　　　*

GREEN, Sheila Ellen　　1934-
(Sheila Greenwald)

PERSONAL: Born May 26, 1934, in New York, NY; daughter of Julius (a manufacturer) and Florence

(Friedman) Greenwald; married George Green (a surgeon), February 18, 1960; children: Samuel, Benjamin. *Education:* Sarah Lawrence College, B.A., 1956. *Politics:* Democrat. *Religion:* Jewish.

ADDRESSES: Home—175 Riverside Dr., New York, NY 10024.

CAREER: Writer and illustrator.

AWARDS, HONORS: Notable Children's Book, American Library Association (ALA), 1981, for *Give Us a Great Big Smile, Rosy Cole;* Junior Library Guild Selection, 1983, for *Will the Real Gertrude Hollings Please Stand Up?* and 1989, for *Rosy's Romance;* Parents Choice selection, 1985, for *Rosy Cole's Great American Guilt Club.*

WRITINGS:

SELF-ILLUSTRATED FICTION UNDER NAME SHEILA GREEN-WALD

A Metropolitan Love Story, Doubleday (New York City), 1962.
Willie Bryant and the Flying Otis, Grosset (New York City), 1971.
The Hot Day, Bobbs-Merrill (New York City), 1972.
Miss Amanda Snap, Bobbs-Merrill, 1972.
Mat Pit and the Tunnel Tenants, Lippincott (New York City), 1972.
The Secret Museum, Lippincott, 1974.
The Secret in Miranda's Closet, Houghton (Boston), 1977.
The Mariah Delany Lending Library Disaster, Houghton, 1977.
The Atrocious Two, Houghton, 1978.
All the Way to Wits' End, Little, Brown (Boston), 1979.
It All Began with Jane Eyre; or, the Secret Life of Franny Dillman, Little, Brown, 1980.
Give Us a Great Big Smile, Rosy Cole, Atlantic/ Little, Brown, 1981.
Blissful Joy and the SATs: A Multiple-Choice Romance, Atlantic/Little, Brown, 1982.
Will the Real Gertrude Hollings Please Stand Up?, Atlantic/Little, Brown, 1983.
Valentine Rosy, Atlantic/Little Brown, 1984.
Rosy Cole's Great American Guilt Club, Atlantic/ Little Brown, 1985.
Alvin Webster's Sure Fire Plan for Success and How It Failed, Little, Brown, 1987.
Write On, Rosy!: A Young Author in Crisis, Little, Brown, 1988.
Rosy's Romance, Little, Brown, 1989.

Mariah Delany's Author-of-the-Month Club, Little, Brown, 1990.
Here's Hermione: A Rosy Cole Production, Little, Brown, 1991.
Rosy Cole Discovers America!, Little, Brown, 1992.
My Fabulous New Life, Browndeer Press, 1993.
Rosy Cole: She Walks in Beauty, Little, Brown, 1994.
Emerald House, Browndeer Press, 1996.
The Rose Grows, Orchard Books (Danbury, CT), 1996.

ILLUSTRATOR UNDER NAME SHEILA GREENWALD

Marie L. Allen, *Pocketful of Poems,* Harper (New York City), 1957.
Carol Ryrie Brink, *The Pink Motel,* Macmillan (New York City), 1959.
Florence Laughlin, *The Little Leftover Witch,* Macmillan, 1960.
Miriam Dreifus, *Brave Betsy,* Putnam (New York City), 1961.
Grace V. Curl, *Come A-Witching,* Bobbs-Merrill, 1964.
Laura H. Fisher, *Amy and the Sorrel Summer,* Holt (New York City), 1964.
Barbara Rinkoff, *The Remarkable Ramsey,* Morrow (New York City), 1965.
Hila Colman, *The Boy Who Couldn't Make Up His Mind,* Macmillan, 1965.
Anne Mallet, *Who'll Mind Henry?,* Doubleday, 1965.
Florence Laughlin, *The Seventh Cousin,* Macmillan, 1966.
Mary J. Roth, *The Pretender Princess,* Morrow, 1967.
James Playsted Wood, *When I Was Jersey,* Pantheon (New York City), 1967.
Emma V. Worstell, *Jump the Rope Jingles,* Macmillan, 1967.
Jean Bothwell, *The Mystery Cup,* Dial (New York City), 1968.
M. Jean Craig, *The New Boy on the Sidewalk,* Norton (New York City), 1968.
Nancy K. Robinson, *Veronica the Show Off,* Scholastic Inc. (New York City), 1982.
Henny Youngman, *Henny Youngman's Book of Jokes,* Carol Publishers, 1992.

OTHER

Contributor to *Cricket, New York Times, Harper's, Gourmet,* and *Reporter.*

SIDELIGHTS: Humorous and sensitive are the adjectives most often used to describe the work of Sheila Ellen Green, best known under the name Sheila Greenwald. Her "Rosy Cole" stories trace the adventures and misadventures of the eponymous preteen heroine through the trials of romance, violin playing and self-beautification schemes. Greenwald's books for middle readers and young adults deal with contemporary problems—divorce, mental illness, anorexia, unwanted pregnancy—but with a sense of humor. Her characters are thus able, as Maryclare O'Donnell Himmel writes in *Twentieth-Century Young Adult Writers,* "to laugh at themselves and their seemingly hopeless situations."

Greenwald's books are marked by an ironic and whimsical vision of the world. Her scratchy pen and ink drawings complement her word portraits of characters slightly offbeat, full of bravado, and just mischievous enough to feel like old friends to the reader. Though she does not necessarily write autobiographically, Greenwald confesses to exploring and expanding with her fiction the situations that touch her life. "My challenge," Greenwald once explained, "is to invent characters, plots and scenes which will develop and define my feelings and opinions. In fact, my books often begin with strong opinions which I then have to soften and obscure so they aren't boring and polemical."

"I write down ideas that appeal to me—some work out, some don't," she has said of her writing method. "*The Hot Day* was based on an incident from my father's childhood." One of her earliest books, *The Hot Day* tells the story of a family sweltering in summer heat, before the days of air conditioning, and of their roomer who remains cool because he has the only fan in the house. One night the kids decide to scare the roomer by blowing talcum powder over themselves in the breeze from the fan, making themselves look like ghosts. "A mischievous idea," notes the critic for *Kirkus Reviews.* Much of Greenwald's juvenile fiction depends upon similar mischief. In *Miss Amanda Snap,* for example, Greenwald tells of a children's book writer whose main character—Kirby the mouse—comes to life, changes into a man, and marries the author. There is no happy ending, however, for the next Kirby-the-mouse book is a flop. *Miss Amanda Snap* contains "a witty and imaginative plot and pictures," comments a critic for *Publishers Weekly.*

Mischievous young girls play a prominent role in Greenwald's fiction, none more prominently than the popular Rosy Cole. In the first novel featuring the character, *Give Us a Great Big Smile, Rosy Cole,* ten-year-old Rosy has the spotlight turned on her by her photographer uncle who wants to create a book of photographs about her. The book will feature Rosy as a violinist. For a time Rosy enjoys the attention, but she is crushed after hearing a recording of her own terrible violin playing and realizing how bad she really is. She then tries to stop publication of her uncle's book. Kate M. Flanagan in *Horn Book* calls Rosy "a refreshingly ordinary child whose basic good sense saves her from the foibles of adults." Marilyn Kaye, writing in *School Library Journal,* finds this first Rosy Cole adventure "a cheerful, zesty story with a potential for wide appeal."

In several Rosy adventures the pre-teen character learns lessons in love and romance. In *Valentine Rosy,* for example, she is surprised to find that she will have to invite boys to her Valentine's Day party. "Rosy is an exceedingly likable heroine, and her realization that everyone grows up at his or her own pace strikes a reassuring note," comments a critic for *Booklist,* while the reviewer for *Bulletin of the Center for Children's Books* finds that Greenwald's creation is "shrewdly perceptive on pre-teens." Karen Jameyson in *Horn Book* concludes that the author "has created another wholly successful book about her refreshingly down-to-earth heroine." In *Rosy's Romance,* Rosy and her buddy Hermione become obsessed with romance novels and try to turn Rosy's sisters into the kind of teens they have been reading about. Rosy is so busy trying to get her sisters dates, that she almost misses romance staring her in the face. Partly a spoof on juvenile series books and their lack of depth, *Rosy's Romance* might prove the antidote to such books, according to Sylvia S. Margantz in *School Library Journal:* "If anyone can woo girls from series books to a bit more substantial plotting and character depiction, it will be Rosy."

While the Rosy Cole books are popular, Greenwald is perhaps best known for her young adult novel, *Blissful Joy and the SATs: A Multiple-Choice Romance.* A multi-layered and complex novel, it tells the story of 16-year-old Blissful Joy Bowman, who sees herself as a practical person until low scores on the SAT test shakes her self-confidence. Befriending a stray dog helps in the process of self-discovery, as do the cast of quirky individuals the dog brings into her well-organized life. Himmel concludes that "Greenwald's expert use of irony and satire is one of the qualities that lifts this novel above other, more mundane 'problem novels.'" A *Publishers Weekly* critic finds that "Greenwald's piquant wit and velvety prose transform stories into delights, although she does not underestimate the dilemmas that teens face."

BIOGRAPHICAL/CRITICAL SOURCES:

BOOKS

Twentieth-Century Young Adult Writers, St. James Press (Detroit), 1994, pp. 259-60.

PERIODICALS

Booklist, March 1, 1985, p. 982; December 15, 1994, p. 753.
Bulletin of the Center for Children's Books, December, 1972, p. 56; July, 1974, p. 177; September, 1977, p. 15; February, 1978, p. 93; September, 1980, p. 10; July, 1981, p. 193; December, 1983, p. 67; January, 1985, p. 84; January, 1986, p. 86; January, 1989, p. 121; July, 1989, p. 276; September, 1991, p. 11; January, 1993, p. 146; January, 1995, p. 165.
Horn Book, February, 1978, p. 45; February, 1980, p. 55; August, 1980, p. 407; August, 1981, pp. 421-22; August, 1982, p. 412; August, 1983, p. 443; January-February, 1985, p. 50; January, 1986, p. 58; March, 1988, p. 201; March, 1989, p. 233; September, 1989, p. 647; November, 1991, p. 735.
Kirkus Reviews, March 15, 1972, p. 320; March 1, 1977, p. 223.
Publishers Weekly, August 7, 1972, p. 50; March 25, 1974, p. 56; March 19, 1982, p. 71.
School Library Journal, May, 1977, p. 61; November, 1977, p. 56; March, 1981, p. 108; September, 1981, p. 125; August, 1983, p. 65; December, 1984, p. 80; January, 1986, p. 67; January, 1988, p. 74; January, 1989, p. 77; August, 1989, pp. 139-40; November, 1991, p. 96; December, 1991, p. 114; January, 1993, p. 98; October, 1993, p. 124; January, 1995, p. 106.
Voice of Youth Advocates, January, 1982, p. 33; October, 1983, p. 202; June, 1994, p. 82.

* * *

GREENWALD, Sheila
See GREEN, Sheila Ellen

* * *

GRENVILLE, Kate   1950-

PERSONAL: Born October 14, 1950, in Sydney, Australia; daughter of Kenneth Grenville (a lawyer) and Isobel (a teacher; maiden name, Russell) Gee; married Bruce Petty (an editorial cartoonist); chil-

dren: Tom, Alice. *Education:* University of Sydney, B.A. (with honors), 1972; University of Colorado, M.A., 1982. *Avocational interests:* Playing the piano.

ADDRESSES: Agent—C. Lurie, 26 Yarraford Ave., Alphington, Victoria 3067, Australia.

CAREER: Writer. Worked for Australia Council (arts administration), Sydney, 1973-74; Film Australia, Sydney, worked on documentary film production, 1974-77; worked as freelance film editor and writer in London, England, 1974-80; Multicultural TV (subtitling firm), Sydney, subeditor, 1983-85. Script consultant for the Australian films *Sleeping Partner* and *Bronco.* Instructor in writing at University of Sydney.

MEMBER: Australian Society of Authors.

AWARDS, HONORS: Fellowship from International Association of University Women, 1981; grant from Australia Council, 1983; Australian/Vogel Award for *Lilian's Story,* 1984; writer's fellowship from Australia Council, 1985.

WRITINGS:

Bearded Ladies (short stories), University of Queensland Press (St. Lucia, Queensland, Australia), 1984.
Lilian's Story (novel), Allen & Unwin (North Sydney, Australia), 1984, Viking (New York City), 1986.
Dreamhouse (novel), University of Queensland Press, 1986, Viking, 1987.
Joan Makes History (novel), British American Publishers (Latham, NY), 1988.
The Writing Book: A Workbook for Fiction Writers, Allen & Unwin (Australia), 1990.
(With Sue Woolfe) *Making Stories: How Ten Australian Novels Were Written,* Allen & Unwin, 1993.
Albion's Story (novel), Harcourt (New York City), 1994, published in England as *Dark Places,* Picador (London), 1994.

SIDELIGHTS: "Like her heroines," declares Norman Oder in *Publishers Weekly,* "Australian novelist Kate Grenville has learned to confront convention. She hasn't just questioned sex roles in the land of 'blokes.' She's also resisted the rules of story-telling—at least, the former rules—that long stifled her voice." Grenville is best known for her satirical feminist novels and short stories, which look at poor relationships between men and women, many of them based on power rather than love and affection. She uses language inventively, relying more on short vignettes, dialogue, and imagery rather than narration—a technique she may have derived from the years she worked as a film editor. She also has a strong sense of Australian history, revealed in *Joan Makes History,* and the relationship between literature and history. "Grenville possesses a rare and beautiful gift for words," writes Constance Markey in *Tribune Book,* "a delicacy of description, and an awareness of nature rare to present-day fiction. These qualities, plus an abiding intuition of life's eternal conflicts, distinguish her as a writer of great strength and sensitivity."

Grenville's first published work was the collection *Bearded Ladies.* Many of the stories in the book are experimental in form. "When I left Australia and started writing seriously," Grenville states in an interview with Gerry Turcotte of *Southerly* magazine, "I felt that there were huge gaps in human experience—female experience—that had never been written about, and that there was no way you could write about them in conventional terms. It somehow just wasn't adequate to talk about them in terms of the conventional, and in nice neat language. The forces operating—anger, frustration, pain, loneliness—couldn't be written about truthfully in neatly ordered fiction." The completed volume, according to Oder, "shows her testing form, voice and narrative." *Bearded Ladies* is, according to a *Publishers Weekly* reviewer, "a collection to be savored as much for the colloquial ease of the writing as for the hypocrisy it exposes."

Many reviewers find a strong feminist ideology in *Bearded Ladies.* The "bearded ladies" of the title are, according to Joanna Motion in the *Times Literary Supplement,* "contemporary Australian women . . . who find themselves out of step with their surroundings and respond by slipping away from other people's expectations." "The 'ladies' we meet are bearded by virtue of their personalities and pursuits," writes the *Publishers Weekly* critic, "the soft skin of their femininity roughened with the effort of moving away from conventional behavior and expectations." They travel to exotic locations, to Italy and India, only to encounter the same oppressive concepts. "*Bearded Ladies* is the sort of angry place where feminism actually begins, when you suddenly *see* how the world is really working," Grenville tells Turcotte, "which is why I was obsessed with that sort of photographic clarity—people *must know* this is what's really happening underneath the nice rhetoric of romance."

Lilian's Story, Grenville's first published novel, takes a deeper look at a woman's attempts to escape from other people's expectations. Loosely based on a street person named Bee Miles, who roamed the streets of Sydney, Australia, during the middle of the twentieth century, *Lilian's Story* is "a remarkable journey from childhood to madness," declares *Los Angeles Times* contributor Elaine Kendall. The title character is "at odds with her world from infancy," the reviewer continues. "A large, intellectually precocious child, she resists every attempt to turn her into the prevailing vapid and docile image of Australian womanhood." "She grows up loud and fat and unladylike," explains Margaret Walters in the London *Observer,* "acutely aware that she doesn't fit in. All her attempts to escape—to make friends, to take pleasure in her own body—are blocked by her sadistic bully of a father." Lilian Singer remains committed to her individuality, quoting Shakespeare loudly in public after her father rapes her and has her shut up for ten years in an insane asylum. "She has remained herself through all vicissitudes," writes James Purdy in the *New York Times Book Review,* "unrepentant, in her own way victorious."

Dreamhouse paints quite a different portrait of a trapped woman. Louise Dufrey is a secretary, slender and beautiful, who moves to the Italian countryside for a season with her husband Rennie so he can complete his doctoral dissertation. The villa (which belongs to Daniel, a friend of Louise's husband) turns out to be a decaying monstrosity, infested with mice and birds. "The state of the villa," writes *Los Angeles Times Book Review* contributor Judith Freeman, "can aptly be said to be a metaphor for the state of their marriage—pretty crumbly." Soon Louise and Rennie are forced to move in with Daniel's grown children, Hugo and Viola, next door. "Is conformity worth the price of freedom?" asks Markey. "Or more specifically, is Louise's image of traditional womanhood . . . worth salvaging if it spells the loss of personal fulfillment? Wisely, Grenville does not decide these dilemmas for the reader." "With a less talented writer," declares Hariclea Zengos in *Belles Lettres,* "*Dreamhouse* could have been yet another ordinary novel concerning the dissolution of a marriage. But with Grenville nothing is ever ordinary; small yet significant details betray her extraordinary talent as a novelist."

In *Joan Makes History,* Grenville "employs a highly imaginative splicing technique to weave a double plot," declares Elizabeth Ward in the *Washington Post Book World.* "The story of a contemporary Australian Joan, born to an immigrant couple in

1901, the year of Federation, whose life is narrowed down by successive hard choices; and, alternating with hers, the stories of a whole string of historical Joans, whom the modern Joan either dreams, imagines or remembers (it doesn't matter which, the point being that Joan, like Whitman, contains multitudes)." "Their stories make one story, told in different voices," states *New York Times Book Review* contributor Nancy Willard. "This is really more a collection of stories connected by the idea that we are reading history from the perspective of the women who never make the history books, the ones who cooked dinner, washed socks, and swept floors, those 'who will melt away like mud when they die,'" explains *Los Angeles Times* contributor Judith Freeman. "The history of the world is the male version. It seems perfect that Grenville has made Joan not an individual but an archetype of the 'whole tribe of humanity keeping the generations flowing along,' the women and the workers."

Grenville returns to the Singer family of Sydney in *Albion's Story*, which tells how Lilian's father became the sort of person to abuse his daughter. "Albion Gidley Singer properly graduates from son to husband to father, and becomes a thriving businessman, 'always a gentleman,'" states Lynn Knight in the *Times Literary Supplement*. "This solid figure is tormented by the fear that he will be exposed as a mere 'husk,' a 'hollow shell.' From childhood, Albion has rebuffed this image by pursuing an encyclopedic knowledge of facts: with his sexual initiation he discovers that he can merge his inner and outer selves in the 'blossoming epiphany' of orgasm. This temporary satisfaction immediately induces the emptiness he dreads, locking him in a cycle of craving." "In Albion Gidley Singer," Knight concludes, "Grenville has created the supreme misogynist." "The author explores every avenue here," asserts Carolyn See in the *Washington Post*. "Was Albion simply a repressed homosexual? Was he the oppressed product of the late-Victorian patriarchy or just terrified by the sexual folklore of the day? Having deprived himself of his family's affection, was he forced to commit an awful act just to make an impression on them? Or did cosmic loneliness force him to live as a sociopath, absolutely unable to think of anyone's feelings but his own?"

Kate Grenville told *CA:* "I started writing because I was struggling to understand how to be a woman in the 1960's and 1970's—the heady years of the women's movement. I had no message, nothing to preach: I wanted just to lay out contemporary sexual politics for examination and satire, not to suggest answers but to show things as they really were. I also wanted to do something more stylistically and formally interesting than the kind of social realism—sociology masquerading as fiction—that the women's movement was producing so much of. I wanted to dignify the dilemmas of contemporary women by making them into art (whatever, exactly, that might be).

"Now I write for the excitement of discovery. It seems that I can only find out most of what I think or feel in the process of writing. To paraphrase Flannery O'Connor, I only know what I think after I've said it. The process of writing is therefore one of constant surprise. In many ways the pleasure of writing is the same as the pleasure of reading: the suspense of not knowing what the next page might reveal. These days I feel privileged to be a woman and a writer because centuries of comparative silence by women means that for us, today, there are still enormous areas of women's experience and sensibility that have hardly been touched on in fiction. The more I write about women, the more I feel I understand about men as well, and I feel a tremendous compassion for all of us, locked into our different systems.

"The other impulse that keeps me writing is the delight of style and form. Each new fictional project presents a new challenge and demands the invention of a style and shape that is precisely and individually made to fit that particular work. Since I never feel I get it absolutely 100 percent right, the lure or goad of unattainable perfection keeps me going."

BIOGRAPHICAL/CRITICAL SOURCES:

BOOKS

Contemporary Literary Criticism, Volume 61, Gale (Detroit), 1990.

PERIODICALS

Australian Book Review, July, 1994, p. 8.
Belles Letters, July-August, 1988, p. 5.
Los Angeles Times, December 18, 1988, p. 9; November 17, 1994, p. E9.
Los Angeles Times Book Review, November 22, 1987, p. 13.
New Yorker, February 6, 1995, p. 91.
New York Times Book Review, September 7, 1986, p. 27; December 18, 1988, pp. 7, 9; December 11, 1994, p. 7.

Observer (London), September 14, 1986, p. 27;
April 3, 1988, p. 42; September 18, 1994, p.
19.
Publishers Weekly, November 23, 1984, p. 67; October 31, 1994, pp. 40-41.
Southerly, Volume 47, number 3, 1987, pp. 284-99.
Times Literary Supplement, October 18, 1985, p.
1173; September 2, 1994, p. 11.
Tribune Books (Chicago), November 8, 1987, p. 5.
Washington Post, October 14, 1994, p. F2.
Washington Post Book World, November 20, 1988,
p. 7.

*   *   *

GRIFFITH-JONES, Stephany   1947-

PERSONAL: Born June 5, 1947, in Prague, Czechoslovakia; daughter of Francisco (a factory owner) and Clara (a homemaker; maiden name, Kafka) Novy; married Robert Griffith-Jones (an educator), April 23, 1977; children: Edward, David. *Education:* University of Chile, B.A. (with distinction), 1969; Cambridge University, Ph.D., 1981.

ADDRESSES: Home—12 Lenham Rd. E., Brighton, Sussex, England. *Office*—Institute of Development Studies, University of Sussex, Brighton, Sussex BN1 9RE, England.

CAREER: Corporacion de Fomento, Santiago de Chile, research officer in Division of Industrial Planning, 1969-70; Central Bank of Chile, Santiago de Chile, member of section of credit and savings policy, 1970-72, head of department of credit for the public sector, 1972; University of Sussex, Brighton, England, research officer at Institute for Development Studies, 1978-81, research fellow, 1982—. Professor of economic analysis at Inter-American Center of Statistics, 1971; has lectured at Cambridge University, London School of Economics and Political Science, London, University of Warwick, and University of Birmingham; interviewed on British and Scottish radio programs. Member of board of directors of Banco O'Higgins, 1971-72; adviser to Barclays Bank International, 1977; consultant to World Bank, UNICEF, UNCTAD, UNIDO, PHARE, and European Economic Community, senior consultant on development finance to ECLAC, 1994; Institute of Developmental Studies, research officer, 1978-81, fellow, 1982—; visiting professor at CIEPIAN, Chile, 1990.

MEMBER: Society for International Development (member of executive committee).

AWARDS, HONORS: Alide Prize from Association of Latin American Financial Institutions, 1983, for essay "International Finance and Latin America."

WRITINGS:

The Role of Finance in the Transition, Allanheld, Osmun, 1981.
International Finance and Latin America, Croom Helm (Beckenham, Kent, England), 1984.
(With Osvaldo Sunkel) *The Crisis of International Debt and National Development,* Oxford University Press (Oxford, England), 1986.
Managing World Debt, St. Martin's (New York City), 1987.
Chile to 1991, Economist Intelligence Unit, 1987.
Third World Debt: Managing the Consequences, International Financing Review (London), 1989.
Loan Guarantees for Large Infrastructure Projects: The Issues and Possible Lessons for a European Facility, EEC Office for Official Publications of the European Community (Luxembourg), 1994.

EDITOR

(With Charles Harvey) *World Prices and Development,* Gower (Brookfield, VT), 1985.
(With E. Rodriguez) *Debt, Cross-Conditionality and Banking Regulations,* Macmillan, 1992.
(With Z. Drabek) *Financial Sector Reform in Central and Eastern Europe,* Macmillan, 1994.
(With R. Ffrench-Davies) *Surges in Capital Flows to Latin America,* Lynn Rienner and F.C.E. (Swengel, PA), 1995.

OTHER

Also author with H. Singer, C. Stevens and A. Puyana of *IDS Research Report No. 25: Evaluation of IDB Lending to the Latin Americas and Caribbean,* 1994.

Contributor to magazines and journals, including *Banker, Case Western Journal of International Law, Chile-America* (Rome, Italy), *Comercio Exterior* (Mexico), *Development and Change, Development Policy Review, Estudios Internacionales* (Santiago, Chile), *IDS Bulletin, Journal of Developmental Studies, Oxford Review of Economic Policy, Revista Interamericana de Planificacion* (Venezuela), *South, World Development,* and to newspapers, including *Guardian* and *Kuala Lumpur Business Times.*

WORK IN PROGRESS: Research on "cross-conditionality" and its impact on developing countries, with a book expected to result.

SIDELIGHTS: Stephany Griffith-Jones told *CA:* "My area of interest in writing and research is the impact of international finance and external debt, and the impact of adjustment policies on the development of poorer countries, with a view to defining better alternatives to those currently in operation. I also write stories for children; some were published in the main Chilean newspaper in the sixties. I have traveled to Latin America, the United States, and Europe to exchange ideas and to learn from policymakers and other academics.

"I write in the hope that my writings can help improve understanding of the world we live in, and above all, lead to *some improvements*. I focus very much on issues of international finance, and its impact on development (this is a relatively rare combination, as those concerned with finance normally do not look at its impact on growth, development, or poverty alleviation!).

"I believe liberalization of capital flows, though having beneficial effects, may have gone in some ways too far, and some additional regulation and/or taxation of such flows may be needed. This would enhance the efficiency of international capital markets.

"I am influenced by my discussions with political leaders, policy-makers and other academics, in different parts of the world. I am also much influenced by leading economic thinkers who have written on related subjects. I could perhaps highlight the influence of Keynes, of James Tobin and of Joseph Stiglitz."

Griffith-Jones is fluent in English, Spanish and Czech, and rates herself as "fair" in both German and French.

BIOGRAPHICAL/CRITICAL SOURCES:

PERIODICALS

Times Literary Supplement, October 9, 1984.

*   *   *

GROSS, Martin L(ouis) 1925-

PERSONAL: Born August 15, 1925, in New York, NY; son of Samuel and Anna (Bachrach) Gross; married Anita Grail, November 24, 1946 (deceased); married Anita Klang Rush (an interior decorator), September 1, 1974; children: Army, Ellen; stepchildren: Louis, Jane, William. *Education:* College of City of New York (now City College of the City University of New York), B.S.S., 1947; Columbia University, graduate study, 1950-52.

CAREER: Writer and editor. New School for Social Research, New York City, teacher of modern social criticism, beginning 1963; New York University, New York City, adjunct assistant professor of social history, beginning 1974. Alternate delegate, Democratic National Convention, 1956; moderator, *Protest,* WNBC Radio, New York City, 1963-64; president, Empire Books. *Military service:* U.S. Army Air Corps, 1943-46; became flight officer.

MEMBER: PEN International, Authors League of America, Authors Guild, Society of Magazine Writers.

AWARDS, HONORS: Writing award, American Heritage Foundation, 1955; School Bell Award, National Education Association, 1959.

WRITINGS:

The Brain Watchers, Random House (New York City), 1962.
The Doctors, Random House, 1966.
The Psychological Society: A Critical Analysis of Psychiatry, Psychotherapy, Psychoanalysis and the Psychological Revolution, Random House, 1978.
The Red President (novel), Doubleday (New York City), 1987.
The Red Defector (novel), Berkley (New York City), 1991.
The Government Racket: Washington Waste from A to Z, Bantam (New York City), 1992.
The Fourth House (novel), Berkley, 1993.
A Call for Revolution: How Government Is Strangling America and How to Stop It, Ballantine (New York City), 1993.
The Great Whitewater Fiasco, Ballantine, 1994.
The Tax Racket: Government Extortion from A to Z, Ballantine, 1995.

Columnist for Publishers Hall Syndicate, 1968-70. Contributor of more than 150 articles to magazines, including *Life, Saturday Evening Post, Reader's Digest, Good Housekeeping,* and *New Republic.* Founder and editor-in-chief of *Intellectual Digest,* 1970-72, and *Book Digest,* 1973-78.

SIDELIGHTS: In his bestselling books, social critic Martin L. Gross exposes hidden corruption or malfeasance in both government and various professions. Gross's exposes on government spending, including *The Government Racket: Washington Waste from A to Z,* examine what Gross considers the waste, corruption, and abuses of power among those in the nation's federal government. In addition to his writing, Gross has also been a successful publisher, founding and later selling *Book Digest* during the 1970s.

In *The Psychological Society: A Critical Analysis of Psychiatry, Psychotherapy, Psychoanalysis, and the Psychological Revolution* Gross attacks the influence of modern psychology on American society. As Gross states in the book: "The marketing of normality is the sales device which sustains the new Society. Underlying its success is a well-merchandised axiom that *unhappiness is synonymous with sickness.* It is a popular but false premise which has taught millions to view their insecurity, even their failure in life, as an *abnormality,* thus shaping the neurotic profile of the second half of the twentieth century." E. Fuller Torrey notes in *Psychology Today* that the psychological society's "gurus are not only psychiatrists, clinical psychologists, psychoanalysts, social workers, psychiatric nurses, guidance counselors, and marriage and family therapists, but also an assortment of self-anointed sensitivity-group leaders and recycled encyclopedia salesmen. They sell 'sickness' in place of what used to be called sin." Writing in *Human Behavior,* David Graber comments: "Gross is savage in his evaluation of both the scientific quality of psychology today and its effects on society. He denounces Freud and his successors for claiming to have created a science and thence a therapy when in fact all they spawned was a collection of unsubstantiated notions and a faith (now a plethora of competing faiths)."

In 1992 Gross turned his attention to the federal government with *The Government Racket,* the first of three books detailing federal government actions and expenditures. Gross explained his basic philosophy of politics to *People* magazine: "The government is a giant slush fund, many politicians are pathological liars, and what they are doing is nothing less than evil." Organized alphabetically in encyclopedia fashion, *The Government Racket* lists such outrageous examples of spending as the $3 billion spent on 1,300 government airplanes, many of which cannot be located, a half million dollars spent to build a replica of the Great Pyramid of Egypt in Indiana, and $1 billion spent on maintaining vast reserves of helium. Joseph Sobran in *National Review* calls *The Government Racket* "a great little piece of detective work, far more significant than most of what passes for investigative reporting." Writing in the *Wall Street Journal,* Kevin Pritchett was surprised to learn in the book that "U.S. government overhead—travel, telephone, rent—is more than the entire budget of France." Gross ends the book by arguing for a fifty percent cut in the federal payroll and the closing of twenty nonessential agencies as the best way to reduce the excessive costs of the federal government.

Gross returned to the topic of government spending in two other exposes of government waste: *A Call for Revolution: How Government Is Strangling America and How to Stop It* and *The Tax Racket: Government Extortion from A to Z. A Call for Revolution* uncovers more examples of government waste and examines governmental programs such as welfare and governmental policies including immigration. As Ray Olson notes in *Booklist,* "This book's so full of fetching notions and spirited argument that you want to send it to all your political representatives." In *The Tax Racket,* Gross details a score of state and federal tax policies and recounts the damage they have caused to the economy. Gross argues, for example, that the 1990 yacht tax was devastating to the domestic boat construction industry. "Gross's antidotes," writes Gilbert Taylor in *Booklist,* "are radically astringent," calling for a single national sales tax, the closing down of the Internal Revenue Service and dramatic cutbacks in the size of government.

In *The Great Whitewater Fiasco,* Gross turns from larger governmental abuses to the alleged financial misdoings of President Bill Clinton and his political allies and former business partners in the state of Arkansas. A review of the interlocking series of land development and bank fraud scandals popularly known as Whitewater (named after the Whitewater land development), the book reveals Gross's "investigating and reporting powers [to be] excellent," according to the critic for *Rapport.* Despite finding Gross a disappointing political analyst, the reviewer concludes: "Those of us who have been bewildered by . . . Whitewater . . . must be grateful to Gross for dedicated research and up-to-date reporting on this subject."

BIOGRAPHICAL/CRITICAL SOURCES:

BOOKS

Gross, Martin L., *The Psychological Society: A Critical Analysis of Psychiatry,* Random House, 1978.

PERIODICALS

American Spectator, June, 1987, p. 46.
Booklist, January 1, 1987, p. 686; December 15, 1993,
    p. 722; July, 1995, p. 1843.
Book World, April 9, 1978.
Human Behavior, October, 1978.
Human Events, October 6, 1978.
National Review, March 13, 1987, p. 50; September
    14, 1992, pp. 67-68.
New York Times, May 5, 1978.
New York Times Book Review, January 18, 1987, p. 19;
    October 25, 1992, p. 8.
People, September 9, 1993, pp. 63-64.
Psychology Today, March, 1978; December, 1978.
Publishers Weekly, December 12, 1986, p. 40; September
    ber 13, 1991, p. 73.
Rapport, Volume 18, number 4, 1994, p. 38.
Wall Street Journal, May 22, 1978; October 23, 1992.
Washington Post Book World, February 1, 1987, p. 11.*

* * *

GUNLICKS, Arthur B. 1936-

PERSONAL: Born July 7, 1936, in North Platte, NE;
son of Anfin B. and Verna M. (Waltemath) Gunlicks;
married Regine J. Sattler (a teacher), July 19, 1962;
children: Michael, Lars. *Education:* University of Denver, B.A., 1958; attended University of Freiburg,
1958-59, and University of Goettingen, 1964-66;
Georgetown University, Ph.D., 1967. *Religion:*
Lutheran.

ADDRESSES: Home—602 Ridge Top Rd., Richmond,
VA 23229. *Office*—Department of Political Science,
University of Richmond, Richmond, VA 23173.

CAREER: East Tennessee State University, Johnson
City, TN, assistant professor of political science,
1966-68; University of Richmond, Richmond, VA,
assistant professor, 1968-71, associate professor,
1971-81, department chair, 1971-75, dean of graduate studies and associate dean of faculty, 1977-80,
professor of political science, 1981—, department
chair, 1987-89. Visiting professor in Germany,
1980, 1982-83, 1989, 1992. President of Virginia
Social Science Association, 1976; Conference Group
on German Politics, vice president and president-
elect, 1994-96, president, 1996-98; member, board of
directors, German Institute of Federalism Studies,
Hanover, Germany. President of College Hills Neigh-

borhood Association, 1981-82, 1985-86, and Ridgetop
Recreation Association, 1985-86. *Military service:* U.S.
Army, 1959-61; became first lieutenant.

MEMBER: Deutsche Vereinigung fuer Parlaments-
fragen, American Association of University Professors,
American Political Science Association, Conference
Group on German Politics, Council of European Studies, European Communities Studies Association, German Studies Association, Southern Political Science
Association, Virginia Social Science Association, Fulbright Alumni Association.

AWARDS, HONORS: Scholarship from the German
Academic Exchange Service, 1958-59, 1980, 1990;
Fulbright scholar, 1964-66, 1975-76, 1990; scholar
of Virginia Social Science Association, 1987.

WRITINGS:

(Editor and contributor) *Local Government Reform
    and Reorganization: An International Perspec-
    tive,* Kennikat (Port Washington, NY), 1981.
Local Government in the German Federal System,
    Duke University Press (Durham, NC), 1986.
(Editor with John D. Treadway) *The Soviet Union
    Under Gorbachev: Assessing the First Year,*
    Praeger (New York City), 1987.
(Editor and contributor) *Campaign and Party Fi-
    nance in North America and Western Europe,*
    Westview (Boulder, CO), 1993.

Editor of special issue on German Federalism, *Publius:
Journal of Federalism;* editor and contributor with
Ruediger Voight, *Foderalismus in der
Dewahrungsprobe,* Universtaetsverlag Dr. N. Brock-
meyer, 1991 and 1994.

WORK IN PROGRESS: A book on the German states.

* * *

GUTHRIE, Arlo (Davy) 1947-

PERSONAL: Born July 10, 1947, in Brooklyn, NY; son
of Woody (a folksinger) and Marjorie Mazia (a dancer
and teacher; maiden name, Greenblatt) Guthrie; married Jacklyn Hyde (a waitress), October 9, 1969; children: Abraham, Cathyalicia, Annie Hays, Sarah Lee.
Education: Attended Rocky Mountain College.

ADDRESSES: Home—P.O. Box 6573, Housatonic, MA
10236. *Agent*—Harold Leventhal Management Co., 250
West 57th St., Suite 1304, New York, NY 10019.

CAREER: Singer, recording artist, and composer. Office boy for Harold Leventhal Management Co. Performer in concerts, including Newport Folk Festival, 1967. Appeared in the motion picture *Alice's Restaurant,* 1969. Appeared on television programs, including *The Johnny Cash Show, The Dick Cavett Show, The Tonight Show Starring Johnny Carson, The David Frost Show,* and *The Muppet Show.* Affiliated with Black Panthers, with American Indian, antinuclear, and ecological movements, with Senator Fred Harris's campaign for Democratic presidential nomination, and with economic and industrial development programs in Massachusetts. Founder with mother, Marjorie Guthrie, of Committee to Combat Huntington's Disease. Host of film *Woody Guthrie, Hard Travelin',* Wombat Films & Video, 1985. Publisher, *Rolling Blunder Review* (newsletter). Founder, Rising Son Records.

AWARDS, HONORS: Gold Record Award from Recording Industry Association of America, 1967, for album *Alice's Restaurant;* the Governor of Massachusetts instituted an Arlo Guthrie Day in November, 1976.

WRITINGS:

Alice's Restaurant (adaptation of Guthrie's original song [also see below]; includes melody with words), illustrations by Marvin Glass, Grove Press (New York City), 1968.
This Is the Arlo Guthrie Book (music), Amsco, 1969.
(Author of introduction) Henrietta Yurchenco, *A Mighty Hard Road: The Life of Woody Guthrie,* McGraw, 1970.
Mooses Come Walking (children's book), Chronicle Books (San Francisco), 1995.

RECORDINGS

Alice's Restaurant, Reprise, 1967, motion picture sound track, 1970.
Arlo, Reprise, 1968.
Running Down the Road, Reprise, 1969.
Washington County, Reprise, 1970.
Hobo's Lullaby, Reprise, 1972.
Last of the Brooklyn Cowboys, Reprise, 1973.
Arlo Guthrie, Reprise, 1974.
Pete Seeger and Arlo Guthrie Together in Concert, Reprise, 1975.
Amigo, Reprise, 1976. (Contributor)
A Tribute to Leadbelly: His Songs Sung by His Friends, Tomato, 1977.
Outlasting the Blues, Warner Bros., 1979.
Power of Love, Warner Bros., 1981.

Arlo Guthrie and Pete Seeger: Precious Friend (two-record set), Warner Bros., 1982.
(With Holly Near and others) *Harp,* Redwood Records (Oakland, CA), 1985.
(With sisters, Nora and Joady) *Woody's 20 Grow Big Songs,* Warner Bros., 1992.

ADAPTATIONS: United Artists released a film adaptation of Guthrie's "Alice's Restaurant" in 1969, and the screenplay by Venable Herndon and Arthur Penn was published under the same title by Doubleday in 1970.

SIDELIGHTS: Folksinger Arlo Guthrie is best known for his song "Alice's Restaurant," the humorous and autobiographical account of a young man arrested for littering who is then ineligible for the draft because of his criminal record. Long active in leftist political causes, Guthrie has often used his music to promote his beliefs. The son of celebrated 1930s folksinger Woody Guthrie—composer of such songs as "This Land Is Your Land"—Arlo Guthrie carries on the family tradition of mixing politics and entertainment.

The song "Alice's Restaurant" grew out of a Thanksgiving outing in which Guthrie helped collect refuse from a friend's restaurant, packed it in a Volkswagen van, and drove it to the city dump, which was closed. Guthrie left the refuse on a mound of trash outside of the dump and was arrested and incarcerated for littering. Over a period of two years Guthrie worked on the song until it became a long, rambling story with the refrain "You can get anything you want at Alice's Restaurant." The song propelled him to national prominence and a film adaptation of the song's story, starring Guthrie, was released in 1969. In 1992, Guthrie purchased the church building which housed the original Alice's Restaurant to use as offices for his Rising Son Records.

Like his father, who wrote some 1,000 songs about the people he met during his many travels across the country, Arlo Guthrie has written of the people he has met. Speaking of his approach to songwriting, Guthrie tells Ken Franckling in the *Chicago Tribune:* "I always write from the perspective of the little guy in the big world. I like to write to the best common denominator, which is one person lookin' at the world—the things that happen to everybody." Also like his father, who was an activist in the union and communist movements of the 1930s, Guthrie has written songs about causes he believes in. But Susan Baudy writes in the *New York Times Magazine* that Guthrie "adds a certain whimsy and contemporary irony to his radical message, and he delivers it with a self-parodying humor that makes even unsympathetic audiences laugh along with him."

"Even though," Joe Klein reveals in *Rolling Stone*, "[Guthrie has] played more than his share of benefits . . . and even though he's one of the few major performers to sing songs against things like fascism in Chile, Arlo isn't a very radical person. His politics seem intuitive, a part of the tradition he was born into. He does what he feels is right and doesn't have much patience with the purists who expect, because of the songs he sings and the family heritage, that he'll follow a strict anticapitalist line."

Guthrie's early involvement with politics eventually led him to a spiritual path. Speaking to Claudia Dreifus in the *Progressive,* the singer explains: "There are a lot of people who grew up in the kind of world I grew up in . . . left-wing politics, New York . . . for whom that has not been wholly fulfilling. There are a lot of people . . . who did not ask themselves, 'What does it further a man to gain the world and lose his own soul?' I came to a point where I really needed to ask myself that question— and I did." He explained to Debra Rae Cohen in *Rolling Stone:* "I guess a lot of things changed for me, when I finally realized that I could see myself, all along, being utilized for things that I believed in. Not just peace and love, but even justice and compassion. I realized that I had the decision whether or not to pursue these qualities in myself; I decided to pursue God in whatever way he would allow me to." In 1977 Guthrie converted to Catholicism, becoming a lay brother in the Order of St. Francis shortly thereafter, and even traveling with two Franciscans while touring. He has since become a follower of Ma Jaya Bhagavati, an Eastern spiritual teacher.

Although he is best known for songs like "Alice's Restaurant" and "The City of New Orleans," Guthrie has also recorded a number of songs for children. In 1992, he recorded *Woody's 20 Grow Big Songs,* a collection of songs his father wrote many years before. The informal recordings—some of them done in living rooms among friends—had been rediscovered in 1989 in the library of Sarah Lawrence College. Together with his sisters Nora and Joady, Arlo took the recordings his father had made and remixed them so that Woody's children could sing along with him. According to Lynne Heffley in the *Los Angeles Times,* the record is "a celebration of childhood."

In 1995 Guthrie published a book for children as well, *Mooses Come Walking,* which tells in verse the story of moose coming out at night to walk through a town and peek in at sleeping humans. The book grew out of a poem Guthrie wrote as part of his live concert show. With illustrations by Alice M. Brock—the same Alice who owned the restaurant of Guthrie's famous song—*Mooses Come Walking* is, according to Alice Miller Bregman in the *New York Times Book Review,* "a perfect bedtime story for city and country kids alike."

BIOGRAPHICAL/CRITICAL SOURCES:

BOOKS

Baggelaar, Kristin, and Donald Milton, *Folk Music: More Than a Song,* Crowell (New York City), 1976.

Cronkite, Kathy, *On the Edge of the Spotlight,* Morrow (New York City), 1981.

Miller, Edwin, *Seventeen Interviews,* Macmillan, 1970.

Okun, Milton, *Something to Sing About,* Macmillan (New York City), 1968.

PERIODICALS

Boston Globe, July 24, 1987, p. 83; December 7, 1988, p. 73; December 14, 1991, p. 21.

Chicago Tribune, February 13, 1986, p. J9.

Christian Science Monitor, March 30, 1978.

Life, March 28, 1969.

Look, February 4, 1969.

Los Angeles Times, May 1, 1989; August 24, 1992, p. F12.

Maclean's, March 17, 1986, pp. 10-11.

Newsday, August 23, 1969.

Newsweek, May 26, 1966; September 29, 1969; October 20, 1969; October 30, 1978.

New Yorker, January 6, 1968.

New York Sunday News Magazine, November 16, 1969.

New York Times, August 25, 1969; September 28, 1969; December 6, 1991, p. A14.

New York Times Book Review, November 12, 1995.

New York Times Magazine, April 27, 1969.

Progressive, February, 1993, pp. 32-35.

Rolling Stone, March 10, 1977; September 6, 1979.

Sight and Sound, spring, 1969.

Stereo Review, July, 1982.

Time, August 29, 1969; October 17, 1969.

Variety, August 13, 1969.

Village Voice, August 29, 1977.*

H-J

HARRISON, Barbara 1941-
(Alexandra Lyle)

PERSONAL: Born January 22, 1941, in New York, NY; daughter of Alexander (in hotel management) and Ann (Sokol) Harrison. *Education:* Attended schools in New York and Vermont. *Politics:* Independent. *Religion:* Roman Catholic. *Avocational interests:* "Reading, especially murder mysteries."

ADDRESSES: Home and office—400 East 57th St., New York, NY 10022.

WRITINGS:

The Pagans, Avon (New York City), 1970.
City Hospital, Avon, 1975.
The Gorlin Clinic, Avon, 1975.
Rhinelander Center, Zebra Books (New York City), 1980.
This Cherished Dream, Zebra Books, 1984.
Passion's Price, Zebra Books, 1985.
Impulse, Zebra Books, 1987.
Society Princess, Zebra Books, 1989.

UNDER PSEUDONYM ALEXANDRA LYLE

Stolen Dreams, Pinnacle (New York City), 1990.
Keepsakes, Pinnacle, 1991.
All Her Dreams, Pinnacle, 1993.

OTHER

Also author of *The Wildings,* for Dell, and of novelizations *Mr. Cool* and *A Cold Night's Death.*

WORK IN PROGRESS: A novel.

SIDELIGHTS: Barbara Harrison told *CA:* "I hope that my books are entertaining—brief respites from the terrors of today's world. I'm always happy to hear from my readers, and especially happy to hear what they like in my work, and what they don't like."

Her books have been published in Australia, England, Ireland, Israel, Norway, and Romania as well as the United States.

*   *   *

HARVEY, Brett 1936-

PERSONAL: Born April 28, 1936, in New York, NY; daughter of Robert (a stockbroker) and Marjorie (a writer; maiden name, Abbott) Harvey; married Louis Vuolo, 1960 (divorced, 1971); children: Robert, Katherine. *Education:* Attended Northwestern University, 1956-59.

ADDRESSES: Home—305 8th Ave., Brooklyn, NY 11215.

CAREER: WBAI-FM, New York, NY, drama and literature director, 1971-74; *The Feminist Press,* Old Westbury, NY, publicity and promotion director, 1974-80; free-lance journalist, book critic, and children's book author, 1980—.

MEMBER: Authors Guild, National Writers' Union (Eastern Regional Grievance Officer).

AWARDS, HONORS: Named notable children's book by the American Library Association, 1986, named to the William Allen White Award Master List for 1988-89, award from Philadelphia Children's Reading Round Table, 1986, and Golden Sower Award nomination from Nebraska Library Association, 1988, all for *My Prairie Year;* named to American Library Association's list of notable children's books, 1988, for *Cassie's Journey,* and 1990, for *My Prairie Christmas.*

WRITINGS:

JUVENILE

My Prairie Year, Holiday House (New York City), 1986.
Immigrant Girl, Holiday House, 1987.
Cassie's Journey, Holiday House, 1988.
My Prairie Christmas, Holiday House, 1990.
Farmers and Ranchers ("Settling the West" series), Twentieth-Century Books (New York City), 1995.

OTHER

(Editor and author of introduction) *Various Gifts: Brooklyn Fiction of the 1980s,* Fund for Borough of Brooklyn, 1988.
The Fifties: A Women's Oral History, HarperCollins (New York City), 1993.

Contributor of articles to periodicals, including *Village Voice, New York Times Book Review, Psychology Today, Voice Literary Supplement,* and *Mademoiselle.*

SIDELIGHTS: Brett Harvey told *CA:* "An incorrigible activist, the moment I became a freelancer in 1981 I realized that isolation and low pay were my deadly enemies, and joined the then-fledgling National Writers' Union (NWU) to remedy both. I now juggle my writing with my work as Eastern Regional Grievance Officer for magazines of the NWU, now 4,000 members strong."

BIOGRAPHICAL/CRITICAL SOURCES:

PERIODICALS

Kliatt Young Adult Paperback Book Guide, September, 1994, p. 39.
Los Angeles Times Book Review, April 10, 1994, p. 8.
New York Times Book Review, September 13, 1987.
Off Our Backs, July, 1994, p. 14.

HARWOOD, Gina
See BATTISCOMBE, E(sther) Georgina (Harwood)

*   *   *

HAUSER, Frank
See WIEMER, Rudolf Otto

*   *   *

HAVIS, Allan 1951-

PERSONAL: Born September 26, 1951, in New York City, NY; son of Meyer (in business) an Estelle (Heitner) Havis. *Education:* City College of the City University of New York, B.A., 1973; Hunter College of the City University of New York, M.A., 1976; Yale University, M.F.A., 1980. *Avocational interests:* Foreign travel, horseback and motorcycle riding.

ADDRESSES: Office—Department of Theatre, University of California, San Diego, La Jolla, CA 92037. *Agent*—William Craver, Writers & Artists, 19 W. 44th St., Ste. 1000, New York, NY 10036.

CAREER: Guggenheim Museum, New York City, film instructor, 1974-76; Foundation of the Dramatist Guild, New York City, playwriting instructor, 1985-87; Ulster County Community College, Stone Ridge, NY, playwriting instructor, 1985-87; University of California, San Diego, professor of theatre, 1988—.

MEMBER: Circle Rep Writers Lab, Literary Managers and Dramaturgs of America (LMDA).

AWARDS, HONORS: John Golden Award for playwriting from Hunter College, 1974 and 1975; Marc A. Klein Award, Case Western Reserve University, 1976, for *Oedipus Again;* Foundation of the Dramatist Guild/CBS Award, 1985; Playwrights USA Award (HBO grant), 1986, for *Morocco;* National Endowment for the Arts fellowship, 1986; Rockefeller fellowship, 1987; Guggenheim fellowship, 1987; New York State Foundation for the Arts fellowship, 1987; Edward Albee Foundation for the Arts fellowship,

1987; Kennedy Center/American Express Production grant, 1987; MacDowell residency fellowship, 1988; McKnight fellowship, 1989; Hawthornden fellowship, 1989; University of California faculty summer fellowship, 1989; California Arts Council playwriting fellowship, 1991; Bellagio Center/Rockefeller fellowship, 1991; Camargo fellowship (France), 1993.

WRITINGS:

PLAYS

The Boarder and Mrs. Rifkin (two-act), first produced in New York City at Hunter Playwrights, December, 1974.

Oedipus Again (two-act), first produced in Cleveland, OH, at Case Western Reserve University, February, 1976.

Interludes (one-act), first produced in New Haven, CT, at Yale Center Cabaret, December, 1978.

Family Rites (one-act), first produced in New Haven, CT, at Yale Drama School, December, 1979.

The Road from Jerusalem, first produced in Cambridge, MA, at American Repertory Theatre, 1984.

Morocco (first produced in Cambridge, MA, at American Repertory Theatre, 1984), published in *Plays in Process,* Volume 6, number 5, Theatre Communications Group (New York City), 1985.

Haut Gout (first produced in Norfolk, VA, at Virginia State Company, 1987), published in *Plays in Process,* Volume 8, number 5, Theatre Communications Group, 1987.

Mink Sonata (two-act), first produced at BACA Downtown, New York City, 1986.

Duet for Three, first produced at West Bank Cafe, New York City, 1986.

Mother's Aria, first produced at West Bank Cafe, New York City, 1986.

Hospitality, first produced in Philadelphia, PA, at Philadelphia Theatre Company, 1988.

A Daring Bride, first produced in New Haven, CT, at Long Wharf Theatre, 1990.

Lilith (first produced in New York City, at Home for Contemporary Arts, 1990), Broadway Play Publishing (New York City), 1991.

Heaven & Earth (radio play), first produced by LA Theatre Works, 1991.

Ladies of Fisher Cove, first produced in New York City, at Ohio Theatre, 1993.

Adoring the Madonna, first produced in New York City, at Circle Rep Lab, 1994.

A Vow of Silence, Penguin (New York City), 1996.

OTHER

Albert the Astronomer (juvenile novel), Harper (New York City), 1979.

WORK IN PROGRESS: A full-length play, tentatively entitled *The Gift.*

SIDELIGHTS: Allan Havis told *CA:* "In several of my plays I have attempted to build a drama without the mechanics of predictable plotting. I wanted to deal with little scenes, as if I were working in a film editing room, organizing old anti-climatic dialogues, putting them together in stories that begin harmlessly and end wickedly. These plays were meant to stir and shock the casual audience.

"These plays were also an experiment in economy. I wanted to take out as much verbiage as possible, leaving only essential dialogue that comes from looking inside people's minds and hearts."

*   *   *

HEALY, Dermot   1947-

PERSONAL: Born November 9, 1947, in Westmeath, Ireland; son of Jack (a civic guard) and Winnie (a cafe and bakery worker; maiden name, Slacke) Healy; married Anne Mari Cusack (a designer and cook), 1974; children: Dallan Cusack, Inor O'Brien. *Politics:* Irish.

ADDRESSES: Home—c/o Una Smith, Riverside House, Cootehill, County Cavan, Ireland. *Agent*—c/o Allison & Busby Ltd., 6A Noel St., London W1V 3RB, England.

CAREER: Writer. Has worked as laborer and insurance underwriter in England and Ireland. Owner and editor, *Drumlin* magazine, 1978-79; Hacklers Drama group, director, 1980-81.

AWARDS, HONORS: Hennessy Literary Awards, 1974, for the story "First Snow of the Year," and 1976, for *Banished Misfortune;* Arts Council of Ireland bursaries, 1978 and 1983; Tom Gallan Award, Society of Authors, 1983, for the story "The Tenant"; All-Ireland Athlone Award for Hacklers Drama group production of Samuel Beckett's *Waiting for Godot.*

WRITINGS:

NOVELS

Fighting with Shadows; or, Sciamachy, Allison &
    Busby (London), 1984.
A Goat's Song, HarperCollins (London), 1994, Vi-
    king (New York City), 1995.

OTHER

Banished Misfortune (short story collection; includes
    "First Snow of the Year" and "The Tenant"),
    Allison & Busby, 1982.
Poverty of Localities, Allison & Busby, 1985.
The Ballyconnell Colours (poetry), Gallery Press
    (Loughcrew, Ireland), 1992.

Also author of *The Turn for Home,* 1987. Author of
the screenplay *Our Boys,* 1979, and the radio play
Interrogations, 1980.

Work represented in anthologies, including *Soft Day,*
edited by Sean Golden and Peter Fallon, Wolfhound,
1977; *Paddy No More,* edited by William Vorm,
Wolfhound, 1978; *Firebird,* Penguin
(Harmondsworth), 1982; and *A Feast of Christmas
Stories,* Macmillan (London), 1983.

ADAPTATIONS: Our Boys was made into a film directed by Cathal Black in 1981.

SIDELIGHTS: For playwright and novelist Dermot
Healy, Ireland is more than just his native country;
the land around him acts as a backdrop for his novels
and other creative works, which have included short
fiction, plays and screenplays, and even a book of
poetry, *The Ballyconnell Colours,* published in 1992.
"I can only live or survive here, in the present
minute," Healy once told *CA,* "for if I try to imagine
what's ahead I'll be dishonest, and if I look back I'll
try to correct what's gone before." Through his
writing he attempts to "reflect the way people have
of looking into mirrors as if they were trying to find
out who's behind them. I mean there is always someone behind the observer, not [behind] the mirror.
And the closer they look the greater the illusion
grows. I try to turn around and see who's there."

Illusions play a large part in the stories in Healy's
1982 collection, *Banished Misfortune.* These tales
range from the sordid lives of London's street people
to accounts of equally miserable lives in the Irish
countryside. According to *Times Literary Supplement*

reviewer Patricia Craig, Healy inverts romanticism
to accommodate bleakness. "The lives he evokes are
shady and off-key," explains Craig. The critic also
notes that "Healy can startle us with the vigour and
perceptiveness of his observations"; the "intense,
wayward and romantic feeling [that he creates] pre-
dominates over simple craftsmanship."

Fighting with Shadows; or, Sciamachy, Healy's first
novel, focuses on the Allen family, headed by twin
brothers Frank and George. The brothers are hard-
working Catholics who strive to keep food on the
table and avoid the political turmoil roiling in their
Northern Irish village. Healy brings to life the indis-
criminate violence between Irish Catholics and Prot-
estants that has raged in his country for generations.
Surrounding the Allen's home—in one of the most
beautiful areas of southern Ulster county—a war zone
has developed and residents must attend to their daily
business at their peril. Rather than a linear narrative,
Fighting with Shadows reads like a collection of short
stories, each tale imbued with the personality and
Gaelic dialect of its narrator—often a "colorful" local
whose life touches the Allen family in some way. As
the family's saga unwinds, it moves from their village south to Dublin, and then to Belfast, where the
legal wrongs done the Allens as a result of the violence are righted. Despite the seriousness of his subject, Healy has been praised for his lyrical prose, and
for interjecting both humor and poignancy into what
would otherwise be a darkly tragic tale. As Brian
Morton notes in the *Times Literary Supplement,* "in
a situation where only pessimism seems appropriate,
[Healy] manages to inject a convincing spark of
hope."

Ireland is again the setting for Healy's second novel,
1994's *A Goat's Song.* From its opening sequence, in
which a part-time Catholic playwright loses himself
to alcoholic oblivion on the heels of a doomed love
affair with a young Protestant actress, the novel
looks at the last fifty years of Irish history, bringing
into focus the changing attitudes of the many men
and women who have long contested the land. Healy
reveals the changes wrought in one man by time,
experience, and a liberal wife as Jonathan Adams—
a Protestant policeman—begins to examine his sometimes violent past and rethink many of his bigoted
attitudes about "the enemy." By depicting Jonathan's
efforts to learn the Irish language, study ancient Irish
myths, and learn the history of his church—as well
as his sensitive portrayal of Jonathan's developing
friendship with a Catholic neighbor—Healy has
"braid[ed] together four divergent aspects of Irish

society," according to James McManus in the *New York Times Book Review:* "Dublin, the cities of the Protestant North, agrarian counties on either side of the border, and the Gaeltacht, the Irish-speaking areas on the westernmost edges of the republic."

BIOGRAPHICAL/CRITICAL SOURCES:

PERIODICALS

London Review of Books, June 23, 1994, p. 23.
New York Times Book Review, November 12, 1995, p. 66.
Times Literary Supplement, June 11, 1982; March 1, 1985, p. 41; April 22, 1994, p. 22.

*   *   *

HEATH, Robert L.   1941-

PERSONAL: Born November 3, 1941, in Hotchkiss, CO; son of James L. (a farmer) and Mary A. (a homemaker; maiden name, Houseweart) Heath; married Mary V. Bradley (an expediter), September 11, 1965; children: Janna Marie. *Education:* Western State College of Colorado, B.A., 1963; University of New Mexico, M.A., 1965; University of Illinois at Urbana-Champaign, Ph.D., 1971.

ADDRESSES: Home—11815 S. Nottingham, Houston, TX 77071. *Office*—School of Communication, University of Houston Central Campus, University Park, 4800 Calhoun Rd., Houston, TX 77004.

CAREER: University of New Mexico, Albuquerque, instructor in communication, 1965-66; Purdue University, Fort Wayne Campus (now Indiana University—Purdue University at Fort Wayne), Fort Wayne, IN, instructor in communication and director of forensics, 1966-68; University of Houston, Houston, TX, assistant professor, 1971-75, associate professor, 1975-87, professor of communication, 1987—, founding director of the Institute for the Study of Issues Management, director of graduate studies and curriculum development, 1983-86, director of graduate studies, 1977-86, 1993-96. Chair of Planning Commission of Missouri City, TX, 1977—; advisory director, Churchill Research Group (professional public relations firm).

MEMBER: International Communication Association, Association for Education in Journalism and Mass Communications, Speech Communication Association, Southern Speech Communication Association.

AWARDS, HONORS: Mortar Board Top Prof, 1974, 1979, 1985, 1990, and director's award for outstanding service to the school of communications, 1982, all from University of Houston; Grant from Edison Electric Institute, 1987; Pathfinder Award from Institute for Public Relations Research and Education, 1992, for original scholarly contribution to public relations; PRIDE Award from the Speech Communication Association, 1992, for *Rhetorical and Critical Approaches to Public Relations.*

WRITINGS:

(With Richard Alan Nelson) *Issues Management: Corporate Public Policymaking in an Information Society,* Sage Publications (Newbury Park, CA), 1986.
Realism and Relativism: A Perspective on Kenneth Burke, Mercer University Press (Macon, GA), 1986.
Strategic Issues Management, Jossey-Bass (San Francisco, CA), 1988.
(With Jennings Bryant) *Human Communication Theories and Research: Concepts, Contexts, and Challenges,* Lawrence Erlbaum Publications (Hillsdale, NJ), 1992.
(With Elizabeth Toth) *Rhetorical and Critical Approaches to Public Relations,* Lawrence Erlbaum Publications, 1992.
Management of Corporate Communication: From Interpersonal Contacts to External Affairs, Lawrence Erlbaum Publications, 1994.
(With Richard Allen Nelson) *Strategic Issues Management: Organizations and Public Policy Challenges,* Sage Publications, 1996.

Contributor of more than fifty articles, reviews, and editorials to communication journals, including *Central States Speech Journal, Journal of Applied Communication, Journal of Mass Media Ethics, Journal of Public Relations Research, Public Relations Review, Public Relations Quarterly, Southern Speech Communication Journal,* and to newspapers, including *Beumont Enterprise, Dallas Morning News, Houston Chronicle,* and the *Houston Post.*

SIDELIGHTS: Robert L. Heath told *CA:* "Three writers have been extraordinarily influential upon my work. Aristotle offered sage advice upon the tactics of rhetoric and the role of rhetoric in society. Kenneth Burke provided insight into how motivation is tied to language. He argued that people are best understood by examining their unique ability to use words. James Madison's writings on government laid out a solid rationale justifying the importance of public discussion of controversial issues.

"Writing for me has three purposes. One is to strive to be at the cutting edge of crucial issues. If you can publish on topics in advance of others, that is a test of your foresight and ingenuity. The second is to draw together key lines of research and analysis. One test of the huge output of research and theory is how well it can be integrated. That which is unimportant gets ignored. The third is cathartic. In today's academic environment, university awards are so minimal that I write to get a sense of self-efficacy.

"I am inspired to write on topics I cover by a conviction that communication is a central human experience that is often slighted, ignored, or even assumed because it is such a universal experience. But many people lack substantial insight into how communication occurs and how to be effective. That is especially true in public policy battles and in the decisions in communities where technological risks collide with personal concerns for health and safety.

"My writing process is simple: research, think, imagine, challenge, listen, argue, write, edit, and rewrite—each day."

*   *   *

HEATH, Roy A(ubrey) K(elvin)   1926-

PERSONAL: Born August 13, 1926, in Georgetown, British Guiana (now Guyana); son of Melrose A. (a teacher) and Jessie R. (a teacher) Heath; married Aemilia Oberli; children: three. *Education:* University of London, B.A., 1956.

ADDRESSES: Agent—Bill Hamilton, A. M. Heath and Company. Ltd., 40-42 William IV St., London WC2N 4DD, England.

CAREER: Called to the Bar, Lincolns Inn, 1964. Worked in civil service in British Guiana, 1942-50; held various clerical jobs in London, England, 1951-58; teacher of French and German in London, 1959—.

AWARDS, HONORS: Drama award, Theatre Guild of Guyana, 1971, for *Inez Combray;* fiction prize, London *Guardian,* 1978, for *The Murderer;* Guyana Award for Literature, 1989, for *The Shadow Bride.*

WRITINGS:

NOVELS

A Man Come Home, Longman (Port of Spain), 1974.
The Murderer, Allison & Busby (London), 1978, Persea (New York City), 1992.
From the Heat of the Day (also see below), Allison & Busby, 1979, Persea, 1993.
One Generation (also see below), Allison & Busby (New York City), 1980.
Genetha (also see below), Allison & Busby, 1981.
Kwaku; or, The Man Who Could Not Keep His Mouth Shut, Allison & Busby, 1982.
Orealla, Allison & Busby, 1984.
The Shadow Bride, Collins (London), 1988.
The Armstrong Trilogy (contains *From the Heat of the Day, One Generation,* and *Genetha*), Persea, 1994.

OTHER

The Reasonable Adventurer, University of Pittsburgh Press (Pittsburgh, PA), 1964.
Inez Combray (stage play), produced in Georgetown, Guyana, 1972.
Princeton Retrospectives: Twenty-Fifth-Year Reflections on a College Education, Darwin Press, 1979.
Art and History (lectures), Ministry of Education (Georgetown, Guyana), 1983.
Shadows round the Moon: Caribbean Memoirs, Collins, 1990.

Contributor of short stories to anthologies, including *Firebird 2,* edited by T. J. Binding, Penguin (London), 1983; *Colours of a New Day: New Writing for South Africa,* edited by Sarah Lefanu and Stephen Hayward, Pantheon (New York City), 1990; and *So Very English,* edited by Marsha Rowe, Serpents Tail, 1991. Contributor of short stories to periodicals, including *London, Savacou,* and *Kaie.*

SIDELIGHTS: Though a London resident since 1951, Roy A. K. Heath sets his fiction in Georgetown, British Guiana (now Guyana), where he was born in 1926. "My work is intended to be a chronicle of twentieth-century Guyana," he once told *CA.* By providing detailed descriptions of Georgetown streets, slums, brothels, and suburbs, combined with insights on local colonial roots, Heath not only educates readers about life in contemporary Guyana but also reveals a deeper, more historical concern. "His reference to ancestors illustrates a vital aspect of Heath's vision as a novelist," comments Ian H. Munro in the *Dictionary of Literary Biography,* "for though the surface of his work is naturalistic, his narrative technique relentlessly probes the hidden realities of Guyanese life, the complex web of myths, dreams, customs, and prejudices arising from the aboriginal, African, and East Indian legacies."

Published in 1974, Heath's first novel, *A Man Come Home,* is a tale "pungent with the sex, sweat and wit of Georgetown's 'yard society,'" explains Sally Emerson in *Books and Bookmen.* Loutish protagonist Bird Foster relies for a living on the financial generosity of his mistress. Seeking to escape this dependence, he is finally motivated to gain monetary independence and vanishes from the area, only to return as a wealthy man. Given his reputation as a layabout, local wisdom credits Foster's fortune to the magic of Fair Maid, a local river spirit. In the nature of such tales, Foster's happiness is short-lived; his mistress discovers and removes a gold chain given to her lover by the river spirit, thus enraging Fair Maid, who conjures forth the circumstances of Foster's death. A multilayered novel, *A Man Comes Home* sets Foster's tale against that of his father, whose hopes for independence for both his children and for Guyana are destroyed by violence and a breakdown of morality. Interweaving contemporary drama with the harsh, uncompromising justice born of ancient myths, Heath's "occasional allusions to Guyana's tormented history are reminders that the explosive, unexamined emotions [of his characters] have counterparts in the larger world," observes Munro.

The Murderer, winner of the 1978 *Guardian* prize for fiction, depicts the mental turmoil of one Galton Flood, a man who kills his wife, Gemma, after discovering that she had engaged in a sexual relationship with another man before their marriage. Heath's protagonist battles "the web of domination and subservience lying at the heart of Guyanese society," according to Munro, as "the flood of repressed emotion he feels when he kills her is his one moment of emotional truth." "It is the geography of Guyana . . . that determines the disposition of her people," adds Shena Mackay, also commenting on the political allegory inherent in Heath's work in the *Times Educational Supplement.* "Trapped between the oceans and the forest, . . . people are isolated and frustrated;

friendships founder, resentments and misunderstandings smoulder, good intentions explode into violence; love and regrets cannot be expressed."

Heath's *The Armstrong Trilogy,* which was released in a single volume in 1994, focuses on "irredeemably paranoid men and the women they destroy in their madness," according to James Polk in the *Washington Post Book World.* Tracing Guyanese culture from the 1920s to the 1950s, the trilogy begins with 1979's *From the Heat of the Day,* which opens during the wedding of Sonny Armstrong and Gladys Davis. *One Generation,* published in 1980, focuses on the life of the couple's son, Rohan; *Genetha,* published a year later, charts the life of their daughter.

From the Heat of the Day presents a foredoomed marriage: Gladys comes from an upper-class family that scorns Sonny, a mere civil servant. He, in turn, reacts by being abusive to Gladys, riding the emotional pendulum between his natural compassion and the urge to belittle her because of his feelings of inferiority. The novel "is nicely evocative of the mood of [the 1930s,] that paralysed decade," comments John Naughton in *Listener,* "and nicely evocative also of the sultry hopelessness of a society where few people have anything, and where the men have the lion's share of what little is going."

One Generation continues the history of Sonny and his family following the death of his wife. The novel focuses on his son, Rohan, who becomes an aimless civil servant and a frequenter of pool halls alongside a ne'er-do-well calling himself Fingers. After Fingers gets involved with Rohan's sister, Genetha, Rohan flees from Georgetown society and recoils into a tragic affair with an East Indian woman. *Genetha* explores the dysfunctional relationship between Rohan's sister and Fingers, which results in her growing poverty and degradation. Sheltered by a prostitute who once worked as Sonny's servant, Genetha is drawn down into the ultimate degradation afforded in the world of sex-for-money. Although she is aware of the depravity she has fallen into, Genetha finds it strangely satisfying.

The protagonist of Heath's 1982 novel *Kwaku; or, The Man Who Could Not Keep His Mouth Shut* is a shoemaker who lives with his wife and eight children in a small Guyanese village and dreams of one day becoming successful. He leaves his family and travels to the town of New Amsterdam, where he passes himself off as a medicine man. The recovery of several patients, which accidentally coincides with their use of one of his concoctions, transforms Kwaku into an instant success. A variant of the Native American trickster character, Kwaku is able to ride the crest of this fluke of fate through cleverness and sheer brazenness. His newfound success and social status are challenged, however, after Kwaku returns to his native village: His wife succumbs to an illness her husband cannot cure, and a new medicine man begins to challenge Kwaku's monopoly on the enterprise. Ultimately, the once distant Kwaku learns to appreciate family, both supporting and gaining support from his wife. "Heath puts all of his considerable skills—of narration, characterization and description—on display in a book that conveys its comic vision with wisdom as well as wit," concludes Alan Bold in the *Times Literary Supplement.*

Orealla takes place in 1920's Georgetown, a capitalist society where "the aura of gas lamps, shadows, burning sun, and horses passing on rain-sodden streets provides a haunting background to this most disturbing of Heath's novels," comments Munro. In *Orealla* Heath tells the story of Ben, a black freelance journalist who craves freedom but is forced by circumstance to sideline as a private coachman. Ben also moonlights as a burglar. Robbing the homes of wealthy citizens is, in fact, his way of striking out against the class and racial prejudice rife in Guyanese society. Caught and forced to work for a petty civil servant, Ben dreams of attaining his freedom by traveling to the village of Orealla. Instead, he kills his overbearing employer, thereby gaining a measure of freedom without making the dreamed-of journey.

Taking as its subject the condition of East Indians living in Guyana, Heath's 1988 novel, *The Shadow Bride,* focuses on the well-to-do Singh family. One of the children, Betta, dedicates his life to healing the poor and sickly. However, the young man's noble efforts are sabotaged by the efforts of his widowed mother, who emerges as the novel's destructive force. Brought from India to Guyana by her husband, the widowed mother is the "shadow bride" who rages against her exile, influencing her hapless son to identify with his Indian heritage and destroy his compassion for his fellow Guyanese. Although torn by this conflict, Betta ultimately comes to accept the contradictions of his birth and avoids ultimate despair. Calling the novel a tale of "the tragic isolation of this Indian version of Medea," John Spurling in the London *Observer* notes that the mother character "is as fully explored and credible as that of the place, time and people amongst which he sets her."

Although his works focus on his native country, Heath's appeal as a novelist has extended to his adopted home of England. While sometimes criticized for his dry prose style, Clive Davis praises Heath's work in *New Statesman and Society*. "At his best," notes Davis, "he evokes the arbitrary, almost fantastical atmosphere of life in a British possession teetering on the edge of South America." Evoking compassion for the land of his birth—its language, its vistas, and its society—through his fiction, Heath continues to enlighten readers' understanding of his homeland; he has, in Munro's opinion, "added a new dimension to the literary map of Guyana."

BIOGRAPHICAL/CRITICAL SOURCES:

BOOKS

Dictionary of Literary Biography, Volume 117: *Twentieth-Century Caribbean and Black African Writers, First Series,* Gale (Detroit), 1992, pp. 198-203.
Smilowitz, Erika Sollish and Roberta Quarles Knowles, editors, *Critical Issues in West Indian Literature,* Caribbean (Parkersburg, IA), 1984, pp. 54-64.

PERIODICALS

American Book Review, August/September, 1993, p. 25.
Booklist, September, 1982.
Books and Bookmen, April, 1975.
Listener, December 13, 1979.
London Review of Books, July 12, 1990, pp. 19-20.
Los Angeles Times, January 21, 1993, p. E5.
Los Angeles Times Book Review, April 12, 1992.
New Statesman and Society, December 7, 1979; May 11, 1990, p. 38.
New York Times, June 22, 1994, p. C12.
New York Times Book Review, January 15, 1984; August 23, 1992, p. 9; June 27, 1993, p. 19.
Observer (London), April 17, 1988.
Publishers Weekly, June 25, 1982; January 6, 1992.
Times Educational Supplement, February 22, 1985, p. 22.
Times Literary Supplement, December 27, 1974; November 12, 1982; July 27, 1984; September 14, 1990, p. 979.
Washington Post Book World, August 21, 1994, p. 4; February 18, 1996, p. 7.
World Literature Today, winter, 1989, pp. 151-52; autumn, 1991, pp. 753-54; spring, 1993, pp. 427-28.

World Literature Written in English, spring, 1989, pp. 103-10.

* * *

HEINLEIN, Robert A(nson)   1907-1988
(Anson MacDonald, Lyle Monroe, John Riverside, Caleb Saunders, Simon York)

PERSONAL: Surname rhymes with "fine line"; born July 7, 1907, in Butler, MO; died of heart failure, May 8, 1988, in Carmel, CA; cremated and ashes scattered at sea with military honors; son of Rex Ivar (an accountant) and Bam (Lyle) Heinlein; married Leslyn McDonald (divorced, 1947); married Virginia Doris Gerstenfeld, October 21, 1948. *Education:* Attended University of Missouri, 1925; U.S. Naval Academy, graduate, 1929; University of California, Los Angeles, graduate study (physics and mathematics), 1934.

CAREER: Writer, 1939-88. Owner of Shively & Sophie Lodes silver mine, 1934-35; candidate for California State Assembly, 1938; also worked as a real estate agent during the 1930s; aviation engineer at Naval Air Experimental Station, Philadelphia, PA, 1942-45; guest commentator during Apollo 11 lunar landing, Columbia Broadcasting System, 1969; James V. Forrestal Lecturer, U.S. Naval Academy, 1973. *Military service:* Commissioned ensign, U.S. Navy, 1929, became lieutenant, junior grade; retired due to physical disability, 1934.

AWARDS, HONORS: Guest of Honor, World Science Fiction Convention, 1941, 1961, and 1976; Hugo Award, World Science Fiction Convention, 1956, for *Double Star,* 1960, for *Starship Troopers,* 1962, for *Stranger in a Strange Land,* and 1967, for *The Moon Is a Harsh Mistress;* Boys' Clubs of America Book Award, 1959; Sequoyah Children's Book Award of Oklahoma, Oklahoma Library Association, 1961, for *Have Space Suit—Will Travel;* named best all-time author, *Locus* magazine readers' poll, 1973 and 1975; National Rare Blood Club Humanitarian Award, 1974; Nebula Award, Grand Master, Science Fiction and Fantasy Writers of America, 1975; Council of Community Blood Centers Award, 1977; American Association of Blood Banks Award, 1977; Inkpot Award, 1977; L.H.D., Eastern Michigan University, 1977; Distinguished Public Service Medal, National Aeronautics and Space Administration (NASA), 1988 (posthumously awarded), "in recognition of his meritorious service to the nation and mankind in advocat-

ing and promoting the exploration of space"; the Rhysling Award of the Science Fiction Poetry Association is named after the character in Heinlein's story "The Green Hills of Earth"; Tomorrow Starts Here Award, Delta Vee Society; numerous awards for work with blood drives.

WRITINGS:

SCIENCE FICTION NOVELS

Beyond This Horizon (originally serialized under pseudonym Anson MacDonald in *Astounding Science Fiction,* April and May, 1942), Fantasy Press (Reading, PA), 1948.

Sixth Column, Gnome Press (Hicksville, NY), 1949, published as *The Day After Tomorrow,* New American Library (New York City), 1951.

Waldo [and] *Magic, Inc.* (also see below), Doubleday (New York City), 1950, published as *Waldo: Genius in Orbit,* Avon (New York City), 1958.

Universe, Dell (New York City), 1951, published as *Orphans of the Sky,* Gollancz (London), 1963.

The Puppet Masters (also see below; originally serialized in *Galaxy Science Fiction,* September-November, 1951), Doubleday, 1951.

Revolt in 2100, Shasta (Chicago), 1953.

Double Star (originally serialized in *Astounding Science Fiction,* February-April, 1956), Doubleday, 1956.

The Door into Summer (originally serialized in *Magazine of Fantasy and Science Fiction,* October-December, 1956), Doubleday, 1957.

Methuselah's Children (originally serialized in *Astounding Science Fiction,* July-September, 1941), Gnome Press, 1958.

Stranger in a Strange Land, Putnam, 1961, revised and uncut edition with preface by wife Virginia Heinlein, 1990.

Glory Road (originally serialized in *Magazine of Fantasy and Science Fiction,* July-September, 1963), Putnam, 1963.

Farnham's Freehold (originally serialized in *If,* July, August, and October, 1964), Putnam, 1964.

Three by Heinlein (contains *The Puppet Masters, Waldo,* and *Magic, Inc.*), Doubleday, 1965, published in England as *A Heinlein Triad,* Gollancz, 1966.

A Robert Heinlein Omnibus, Sidgwick & Jackson (London), 1966.

The Moon Is a Harsh Mistress (originally serialized in *If,* December, 1965, January-April, 1966), Putnam, 1966.

I Will Fear No Evil (originally serialized in *Galaxy,* July, August, October, and December, 1970), Putnam, 1971.

Time Enough for Love: The Lives of Lazarus Long, Putnam, 1973.

The Notebooks of Lazarus Long (excerpted from *Time Enough for Love: The Lives of Lazarus Long*), Putnam, 1978.

The Number of the Beast, Fawcett (New York City), 1980.

Friday, Holt (New York City), 1982.

Job: A Comedy of Justice, Ballantine (New York City), 1984.

The Cat Who Walks through Walls: A Comedy of Manners, Putnam, 1985.

To Sail beyond the Sunset: The Life and Loves of Maureen Johnson, Being the Memoirs of a Somewhat Irregular Lady, Putnam, 1987.

JUVENILE SCIENCE FICTION NOVELS

Rocket Ship Galileo (also see below), Scribner (New York City), 1947.

Space Cadet (also see below), Scribner, 1948.

Red Planet, Scribner, 1949, new paperback edition including previously unpublished passages, Del Rey, 1989.

Farmer in the Sky (originally serialized as "Satellite Scout" in *Boy's Life,* August-November, 1950), Scribner, 1950.

Between Planets (originally serialized as "Planets in Combat" in *Blue Book,* September and October, 1951), Scribner, 1951.

The Rolling Stones (originally serialized as "Tramp Space Ship" in *Boy's Life,* September-December, 1952), Scribner, 1952, published in England as *Space Family Stone,* Gollancz, 1969.

Starman Jones, Scribner, 1953.

Star Beast (originally serialized as "The Star Lummox" in *Magazine of Fantasy and Science Fiction,* May-July, 1954), Scribner, 1954.

Tunnel in the Sky, Scribner, 1955.

Time for the Stars, Scribner, 1956.

Citizen of the Galaxy (originally serialized in *Astounding Science Fiction,* September-December, 1957), Scribner, 1957.

Have Space Suit—Will Travel (originally serialized in *Magazine of Fantasy and Science Fiction,* August-October, 1958), Scribner, 1958.

Starship Troopers (originally serialized as "Starship Soldier" in *Magazine of Fantasy and Science Fiction,* October and November, 1959), Putnam, 1959.

Podkayne of Mars: Her Life and Times (originally serialized in *Worlds of If,* November, 1962, January and March, 1963), Putnam, 1963, published as *Podkayne of Mars,* Baen (Riverdale, NY), 1993.

STORY COLLECTIONS

The Man Who Sold the Moon, Shasta, 1950.

The Green Hills of Earth, Shasta, 1951.

Assignment in Eternity, Fantasy Press, 1953.

The Menace from Earth, Gnome Press, 1959.

The Unpleasant Profession of Jonathan Hoag, Gnome Press, 1959, published as *6 x H,* Pyramid Publications (New York City), 1962.

The Worlds of Robert A. Heinlein, Ace Books, 1966.

The Past through Tomorrow: Future History Stories, Putnam, 1967.

The Best of Robert Heinlein, 1939-1959, two volumes, edited by Angus Wells, Sidgwick & Jackson, 1973.

Destination Moon, Gregg (Boston), 1979.

Expanded Universe: The New Worlds of Robert A. Heinlein, Ace Books, 1980.

Requiem: New Collected Words by Robert A. Heinlein and Tributes to the Grand Master, edited by Yoji Kondo, Tom Doherty Associates (New York City), 1992.

SCREENPLAYS

(With Rip Van Ronkel and James O' Hanlon) *Destination Moon* (based on *Rocket Ship Galileo;* produced and directed by George Pal/Eagle Lion, 1950), edited by David G. Hartwell, Gregg, 1979.

(With Jack Seaman) *Project Moonbase,* Galaxy Pictures/Lippert Productions, 1953.

Also author of scripts for television and radio programs.

OTHER

(Editor) *Tomorrow, the Stars,* Doubleday, 1952.

(With others) *Famous Science Fiction Stories,* Random House (New York City), 1957.

(With others) *The Science Fiction Novel: Imagination and Social Criticism,* Advent (Chicago), 1959.

(Author of preface) Daniel O. Graham, *High Frontier: A Strategy for National Survival,* Pinnacle Books (New York City), 1983.

Grumbles from the Grave (collected correspondence), edited by Virginia Heinlein, Ballantine, 1989.

Take Back Your Government: A Practical Handbook for the Private Citizen Who Wants Democracy to Work (political commentary), with introduction by Jerry Pournelle, Baen, 1992.

Tramp Royale (autobiographical fiction), Ace, 1992.

Also author of engineering report, *Test Procedures for Plastic Materials Intended for Structural and Semi-Structural Aircraft Uses,* 1944. Contributor to books, including *Of Worlds Beyond: The Science of Science Fiction,* edited by Lloyd Arthur Eshbach, Fantasy Press, 1947. Also contributor to anthologies and to the *Encyclopaedia Britannica.* Contributor of over 150 short stories and articles, sometimes under pseudonyms, to *Saturday Evening Post, Analog, Galaxy, Astounding Science Fiction,* and other publications.

ADAPTATIONS: The television series *Tom Corbett: Space Cadet,* which aired from 1951-56, was based on Heinlein's novel *Space Cadet;* a military simulation boardgame was created based upon *Starship Troopers; Starship Troopers* was released as an animated feature in Japan; *Red Planet* was adapted as a three-part cartoon mini-series, released as *Robert A. Heinlein's Red Planet; The Puppet Masters* was filmed in 1994, released as *Robert A. Heinlein's The Puppet Masters,* starring Donald Sutherland; *Starship Troopers* was filmed in 1996, directed by Paul Verhoeven; television, radio, and film rights to many of Heinlein's works have been sold.

SIDELIGHTS: "The one author who has raised science fiction from the gutter of pulp space opera . . . to the altitude of original and breathtaking concepts," Alfred Bester maintained in *Publishers Weekly,* "is Robert A. Heinlein." Heinlein's influence in his field was so great that Alexei Panshin stated in his *Heinlein in Dimension: A Critical Analysis* that "the last twenty-five years of science fiction may even be taken in large part as an exploration by many writers of the possibilities inherent in Heinlein's techniques." Some critics compared Heinlein's influence on the genre to that of H. G. Wells. Writer Robert Silverberg, for example, wrote in a *Locus* obituary on Heinlein that like "no one else but H. G. Wells, he gave science fiction its definition," adding that Heinlein "utterly transformed our notions of how to tell a science fiction story, and the transformation has been a permanent and irreversible one."

Heinlein gave credibility to the science fiction genre by taking "the science in science fiction out of the realm of fantasy and bas[ing] his extrapolations on research then going on in the nation's laboratories," according to Frank Robinson in another *Locus* obituary. "And it was Heinlein who decided that science fiction stories would be more believable if believable people did all those unbelievable things." Heinlein's

earlier work often revolved around teen-age boys living in high-tech civilizations of the future. In his later works, Heinlein became increasingly concerned with philosophical issues and his work was criticized by some critics for preaching the author's personal ideas. "It will be remembered that after 1957," wrote *Dictionary of Literary Biography* contributor Joseph Patrouch, "Heinlein began to write about unpopular, conservative causes . . . and unpopular, liberal sexual causes." This made Heinlein an ever more controversial figure in science fiction during his later years.

Heinlein's influence began with his fiction of the 1940s and, as Panshin pointed out, derives from his "insistence in talking clearly, knowledgeably, and dramatically about the real world [which] destroyed forever the sweet, pure, wonderful innocence that science fiction once had. . . . In a sense, Heinlein may be said to have offered science fiction a road to adulthood." Speaking of this early work, Daniel Dickinson wrote in *Modern Fiction Studies* that Heinlein possessed "a vast knowledge of science, military affairs, and politics" which enabled him to write "stories that shimmered gemlike amid the vast mass of middling, amateurish tales that choked the pulp SF journals. Heinlein's influence was enormous; dozens of young writers strove to imitate his style, and editors refashioned their publications to reflect the new sense of sophistication Heinlein and a few others were bringing to the field." In a poll taken by *Astounding Science Fiction* magazine in 1953, eighteen top science fiction writers of the time cited Heinlein as the major influence on their work.

Despite his great importance in science fiction, Heinlein's explanations of his work belie his own stature. He explained in several interviews that he only began to write when his career as a naval officer was cut short by tuberculosis. After his forced retirement from the Navy, Heinlein tried his hand at several unsuccessful ventures, including a silver mine in Colorado. In 1939, to supplement his modest retirement pay, he wrote and submitted the short story "Life-Line" to *Astounding Science Fiction* magazine. They sent him a check for seventy dollars, and Heinlein began his career. He told *CA:* "I started writing for a reason many writers have had: I was in poor health and unable to work steadily. I continued because it turned out to be a gratifying way of supporting myself and my dependents." "Look," Heinlein told Curt Suplee of the *Washington Post,* "I write stories for money. What I wanted to be was an admiral."

"Heinlein's following was ardent and instant with the appearance of his first short story in *Astounding Science Fiction* magazine," Theodore Sturgeon explained in the *Los Angeles Times Book Review*. In his early stories, Heinlein concentrated on a particular kind of science fiction—logically extrapolating current science into the near-future. His speculations were so accurate that his work of this time predicts a host of developments years before they came to be, including the atom bomb, nuclear power plants, the waterbed, moving sidewalks, and an electronic space defense shield. As Suplee explained, Heinlein "pioneered the extrapolative story format, in which present trends are projected into a plausible future, [and] couched his scientific problems in human terms."

After working as an engineer during World War II, Heinlein returned to writing in the late 1940s. It was during this time that he moved from the genre magazines in which he had made his reputation to more mainstream periodicals, particularly the *Saturday Evening Post*. As Patrouch wrote, "Heinlein was the first major science-fiction writer to break out of category and reach the larger general-fiction market, and therefore he was the first to start breaking down the walls that had isolated science fiction for so long."

Heinlein also began to publish novels for young people in the late 1940s. Dickinson called this work "a series of well-crafted novels that continue to attract readers both young and old." Sturgeon believed that Heinlein's "series of 'juveniles' had a great deal to do with raising that category from childish to what is now called YA—'Young adult'." Several reviewers deemed Heinlein's ostensibly "juvenile" books to be better than much of what is marketed as adult science fiction. H. H. Holmes, for example, wrote in the *New York Herald Tribune Book Review* that "the nominally 'teen-age' science-fiction novels of Robert A. Heinlein stand so far apart from even their best competitors as to deserve a separate classification. These are no easy, adventurous, first-steps-to-space boys' books, but mature and complex novels, far above the level of most adult science fiction both in characterization and in scientific thought." "A Heinlein book," Villiers Gerson observed in the *New York Times Book Review,* "is still better than 99 per cent of the science-fiction adventures produced every year." Heinlein's novels of this time have been reprinted and marketed to adult readers since their initial appearances.

In the 1950s, Heinlein entered the field of television and motion pictures. His novel *Space Cadet* was adapted as the television program *Tom Corbett: Space Cadet*. He wrote the screenplay and served as technical advisor for the film *Destination Moon,* described by Peter R. Weston as "the first serious and commercially successful space flight film" which "helped to pave the way" for the Apollo space program of the 1960s. Heinlein also wrote an original television pilot, "Ring around the Moon," which was expanded without his approval by Jack Seaman into the screenplay for the film *Project Moonbase*. The 1956 movie *The Brain Eaters* was based on Heinlein's *The Puppet Masters,* also without his knowledge or approval, and in an out-of-court settlement, Heinlein received compensation and the right to demand that certain material be removed from the film.

Heinlein's belief in man's eventual exploration of outer space, and his proselytizing on behalf of space travel, was a primary concern in his postwar fiction. Donald A. Wollheim noted in his *The Universe Makers: Science Fiction Today* that Heinlein "believes in the future of mankind and in the endless frontier of the galactic civilization that is to be." Writing in *Extrapolation,* Diane Parkin-Speer commented that "Heinlein assumes that technology will continue to develop, [that] the cosmos is infinite, [and that] with increased scientific knowledge man may roam the universe."

By writing for young people about space travel, Heinlein hoped to prepare them for the future. Patrouch quoted Heinlein explaining: "Youths who build hot-rods are not dismayed by spaceships; in their adult years they will build such ships. In the meantime they will read stories of interplanetary travel." Patrouch maintained that Heinlein was essentially correct about the effect he had on his young readers: "Heinlein's stories convinced a whole generation that man will really be able to do things he can only imagine now—and that generation grew up and sent Apollo to the moon."

In the late 1950s Heinlein turned away from his juvenile fiction and published the first of what became a string of controversial novels. *Starship Troopers,* the first of Heinlein's books to speculate not on future scientific changes, but on future societal changes, postulates a world run by military veterans. The novel's protagonist is an army infantryman. Military law takes precedent over civil law in this world, and military discipline is the norm. As Heinlein explained to Suplee, the society depicted in the novel is "a democracy in which the poll tax is putting in a term of voluntary service—which could be as a garbage collector." *Starship Troopers* has been attacked by some critics for its supposed fascistic and militaristic tendencies and earned Heinlein a reputation as a rightwinger. But Dennis E. Showalter countered critical attacks on *Starship Troopers* in an article for *Extrapolation.* Although he agreed that the pervasive military presence in the hypothetical society would "chill the heart of the civil libertarian," Showalter maintained that the novel is "neither militaristic nor fascist in the scholarly sense of these concepts." Despite the controversy, *Starship Troopers* is still one of Heinlein's most popular novels. It won a Hugo Award and has remained in print for more than three decades.

Heinlein followed *Starship Troopers* with another controversial novel which met with strong opposition, this one quite different in its speculations about the future. *Stranger in a Strange Land* tells the story of Valentine Michael Smith, a Martian with psi powers who establishes a religious movement on Earth. Members of his Church of All Worlds practice group sex and live in small communes. *Stranger in a Strange Land* is perhaps Heinlein's best known work. It has sold over three million copies, won a Hugo Award, created an intense cult following, and even inspired a real-life Church of All Worlds, founded by some devoted readers of the book.

Stranger in a Strange Land was, David N. Samuelson wrote in *Critical Encounters: Writers and Themes in Science Fiction,* "in some ways emblematic of the Sixties. . . . It fit the iconoclastic mood of the time, attacking human folly under several guises, especially in the person or persons of the Establishment: government, the military, organized religion. By many of its readers, too, it was taken to advocate a religion of love, and of incalculable power, which could revolutionize human affairs and bring about an apocalyptic change, presumably for the better." Robert Scholes and Eric S. Rabkin wrote in their *Science Fiction: History, Science, Vision* that "the values of the sixties could hardly have found a more congenial expression."

Heinlein explained to R. A. Jelliffe in the *Chicago Tribune* that, in *Stranger in a Strange Land,* he intended to "examine every major axiom of the western culture, to question each axiom, throw doubt on it—and, if possible, to make the anti-thesis of each axiom appear a possible and perhaps desirable thing—rather than unthinkable." This ambitious attack caused a major upheaval in science fiction. *Stranger in a Strange Land,* Patrouch explained,

"forced a reevaluation of what science fiction could be and do. As he had done immediately before World War II, Heinlein helped to reshape the genre and make it more significant and valuable than it had been."

Stranger in a Strange Land was reissued in an uncut edition in 1990. Author Kurt Vonnegut, in a piece in the *New York Times Book Review,* argued that in "the Soviet Union before glasnost the Writers Union regularly said that some writers weren't really writers, no matter how much and how well they had written, since they were politically incorrect. In this country the same thing is done to writers like Robert A. Heinlein because they are socially incorrect." Though Vonnegut refrained from declaring whether the uncut version was better or worse than the original, leaving it to "someone else to compare the two versions line by line," Rudy Rucker in the *Los Angeles Times Book Review* commented that most "of the material added to this new edition seems to consist of speeches by Jubal, and the rest of the new material includes nominally 'shocking' sections that, aired in 1990, are glaringly sexist." Rucker concluded that the publisher and Heinlein's widow Virginia, who wrote the introduction to the uncut edition, "should have let the book be." Vonnegut, however, claimed that the approximately 60,000 words that were restored in the new edition were "at last taking their rightful place in the body of world literature."

In subsequent novels Heinlein continued to speculate on social changes of the future, dealing with such controversial subjects as group marriage and incest. In *The Moon Is a Harsh Mistress,* lunar colonists practice a variety of marriage forms because of the shortage of women on the moon. Variations on group marriage are necessary. In *I Will Fear No Evil,* an elderly, dying businessman has his brain transplanted into the body of a young woman. He then impregnates himself with his own sperm, previously stored in a sperm bank. *Time Enough for Love: The Lives of Lazarus Long* explores varieties of future incest through the immortal character Lazarus Long. Long rescues a young girl from a fire, raises her as his daughter, then marries her and has children. He also creates two female clones of himself with whom he has sex. In another episode, Lazarus travels back in time two thousand years and has intercourse with his own mother. In these novels of the 1960s and 1970s, Parkin-Speer wrote, "a defense of unconventional sexual love is [Heinlein's] central theme. . . . The ideal sexual love relationship, first presented in

Stranger in a Strange Land, is heterosexual, non-monogamous, and patriarchal, with an emphasis on procreation. The protagonists of the novels and their various sexual partners express unorthodox sexual views and have no inhibitions or guilt."

Although several of these more controversial novels won major awards, some critics expressed misgivings about Heinlein's work from this period. "Instead of concerning himself with facts," Panshin said of several of these books, Heinlein "treated his opinions as though they were facts. More than that, he has so concentrated on presenting his opinions with every narrative device he knows that he has neglected story construction, characterization, and plot." Parkin-Speer believed that "as Heinlein the preacher has come to the forefront, the quality of his fiction has declined." Norman Spinrad allowed in a *Washington Post Book World* review that some critics "have used these latter-day works as springboards for a rather extreme revisionism which seeks to discredit [Heinlein's] entire oeuvre." But Elizabeth Anne Hull insisted in *Extrapolation* that in his controversial novels Heinlein does not force his opinions on his reader. Hull believed that he "raises issues for the serious adult mind to consider and trusts the reader to draw his or her own conclusions."

Beginning with his novel *Friday,* published in 1982, Heinlein tempered his social speculations by presenting them in the context of a science fiction adventure. The novel tells the story of Friday, a female "artificial person"—a genetically-designed human—working for a government spy agency of the next century. In her interplanetary travels as a courier of secret documents, Friday enjoys sexual exploits with both men and women. But as an artificial person, she is insecure about herself and uneasy about the role she must play to pass in human society. When assassinations and terrorism rock the Earth, Friday must fight her way back home across several foreign countries. This journey becomes a symbolic quest for her own identity. Many critics welcomed the change in Heinlein's writing. Dickinson called it a "paean to tolerance that Heinlein sings through the Friday persona. . . . With this book, Heinlein once again pulled the rug out from under those who had him pegged." Sturgeon found Friday a "remarkable and most welcome book" that is "as joyous to read as it is provocative."

In *Job: A Comedy of Justice* and *The Cat Who Walks through Walls: A Comedy of Manners,* Heinlein con-

tinued to combine serious subject matter with rollicking interplanetary adventure. *Job* is a science fiction cover of the biblical story of a man who is tested by God. In this novel, Alex Hergensheimer shifts between alternate worlds without warning. These jarring disruptions force him to continually reassess himself and adapt his behavior to new and sometimes dangerous conditions. Gerald Jonas of the *New York Times Book Review,* while finding *Job* not as fine as earlier, "classic Heinlein," still described the book as "an exhilarating romp through the author's mental universe (or rather universes), with special emphasis on cultural relativism, dogmatic religion (treated with surprising sympathy) and the philosophical conundrum of solipsism. . . . Heinlein has chosen to confront head on the question posed by the original story: why do bad things happen to good people?" Although Sue Martin of the *Los Angeles Times Book Review* called *Job* "another dreadful wallow in the muddy fringe of a once-great, if not the greatest, SF imagination," Kelvin Johnston of the London *Observer* claimed that Heinlein is a "veteran raconteur who couldn't bore you if he tried."

The Cat Who Walks through Walls also ranges through vast stretches of time and space. When Colonel Colin Campbell is wrongly accused of murder, he and his wife escape in a spaceship, hide out on the moon, and eventually join the Time Corps, a group of time-travellers who revise human history by intervening at crucial moments. David Bradley of the *New York Times Book Review* found that *The Cat Who Walks through Walls* contains "dialogue as witty as Oscar Wilde's, action as rollicking as Edgar Rice Burroughs' and satire as spicy as Jonathan Swift's, and it gives a troubling glimpse of the future that may be ours." James and Eugene Sloan, writing of the novel in the *Chicago Tribune Book World,* claimed that "no writer is better or clearer with science and technology. When Heinlein describes the physics of an airless landing (you speed up to slow down), it's like an old cowboy telling you how to break broncos."

In 1989, Virginia Heinlein collected and published some of Robert's correspondence in *Grumbles from the Grave.* "Most of the letters are to Heinlein's agent, Lurton Blasingame, and relate the details of the Heinleins' lives in addition to telling of Heinlein's experiences in writing and publishing," commented Darren Harris-Fain in *Extrapolation.* Robert Silverberg in a *Locus* review called the collection "essential reading," arguing that what emerges from the letters is "a depiction of a gifted man who is tough, determined, fierce in the defense of his own integrity, [and] amiably willing to compromise where compromise makes sense." Charles Solomon, however, found the portrait of Heinlein revealed by the collection was that of a "censorious arch-conservative, furiously railing at anything that incurs his disapproval, from gun control to Freudian psychoanalysis," and concluded that the letters would "tarnish Heinlein's reputation."

Some critics faulted *Grumbles from the Grave* for having an incomplete index, arranging the letters by subject rather than chronologically, and omitting certain key details. Gregory Feeley, despite finding the book "fascinating for anyone who reads science fiction, and essential for anyone interested in the genre's history," found the book "poorly produced by [publisher] Del Rey: The index is shoddy and incomplete, misspellings abound—including, amazingly, that of Scribners, which is gotten wrong throughout—and individuals named in the text are sometimes identified only upon their second appearances, sometimes not at all." Harris-Fain concurred, arguing that "enjoyable as it is, Heinlein is important enough as a literary figure to warrant even fuller attention."

Evaluations of Heinlein's career often point out the polarized critical reaction to his work. Though Heinlein "set the tone for much of modern science fiction," as Jonas reported, and Sturgeon believed "his influence on science fiction has been immense," there are critics who characterized him as right wing or even fascistic and, based on their reaction to his politics, denigrated the value of Heinlein's work. Heinlein's belief in self-reliance, liberty, individualism, and patriotism made him appear, Joseph D. Olander and Martin Harry Greenberg admitted in their *Robert A. Heinlein,* "to adopt positions favored by the American political right."

Bud Foote of the *Detroit News* defined Heinlein's political thought, which he saw as having stayed consistent since the 1950s, in this way: "The greatest thing to which a human can aspire is living free. Enslaving one's fellow-human physically, mentally or spiritually is the unforgivable sin; allowing oneself so to be enslaved is nearly as bad. Honorable people meet their obligations; there's no such thing as a free lunch. All systems are suspect; all forms of government are terrible, with rule by the majority low on the list." Suplee saw much of Heinlein's fiction as concerned with "how freedom of will and

libertarian self-reliance can coexist with devotion to authority and love of country." Olander and Greenberg found "some of the perennial concerns of philosophy, such as the best form of government, whether and to what extent political utopias are possible, and the dimensions of power, liberty, equality, justice, and order" to be confronted in Heinlein's best work.

Central to Heinlein's vision was the strong and independent hero found in much of his fiction. The Heinlein hero, Olander and Greenberg maintain, "is always tough, just, relatively fearless when it counts, and endowed with extraordinary skills and physical prowess." Johnston described the typical Heinlein protagonist as a "lone male genius on the Last Frontier who prevails against any organized authority that dares to restrict his potential." Writing in his study *The Classic Years of Robert A. Heinlein,* George Edgar Slusser argued that Heinlein's protagonists are "elite" men born with inherently superior traits. "Heinlein's elite are not known by physical signs, nor do they bear the traditional hero's stamp," Slusser wrote. "[They possess] a common mental disposition: they believe in individual freedom, and are willing to band together to fight entangling bureaucracy and mass strictures."

Although Heinlein "remains the most controversial" of science fiction writers, as H. Bruce Franklin wrote in the *New York Times Book Review,* he is undoubtedly one of the most popular and influential writers in the field. His books have sold over forty million copies and have been translated into twenty-nine languages, and virtually everything he has published is still in print. Heinlein's influence in the field of science fiction continues to be enormous. Olander and Greenberg described him as "an outstanding figure in modern American science fiction." Jonas maintained that he "has probably influenced the development of science fiction more than any other writer." And, because of his importance in shaping the modern science fiction genre, Bradley believed that Heinlein "is gradually being recognized as one of the most influential writers in American literature."

BIOGRAPHICAL/CRITICAL SOURCES:

BOOKS

Aldiss, Brian W., *Billion Year Spree: The True History of Science Fiction,* Doubleday, 1973.
Atheling, William, Jr., *The Issue at Hand,* Advent, 1964.

Atheling, *More Issues at Hand,* Advent, 1970.

Clareson, Thomas D., editor, *Voices for the Future: Essays on Major Science Fiction Writers,* Volume 1, Bowling Green University (Bowling Green, OH), 1976.

Contemporary Literary Criticism, Gale (Detroit), Volume 1, 1973, Volume 3, 1975, Volume 8, 1978, Volume 14, 1980, Volume 26, 1983, Volume 55, 1989.

Dictionary of Literary Biography, Volume 8: *Twentieth Century American Science Fiction Writers,* Gale, 1981.

Downing, Nancy Bailey, *A Robert A. Heinlein Cyclopedia: A Complete Guide to the People, Places, and Things in the Fiction of Robert A. Heinlein,* Borgo Press (San Bernardino, CA), 1989.

Franklin, H. Bruce, *Robert A. Heinlein: America as Science Fiction,* Oxford University Press (New York City), 1980.

Gunn, James, *The Road to Science Fiction: From Heinlein to the Present,* New American Library, 1979.

Knight, Damon, *In Search of Wonder: Critical Essays on Science Fiction,* Advent, 1956.

Maskowitz, Sam, *Seekers of Tomorrow: Masters of Modern Science Fiction,* World Publishing, 1966.

Nicholls, Peter, *Robert A. Heinlein,* Scribner, 1982.

Olander, Joseph D., and Martin Harry Greenberg, editors, *Robert A. Heinlein,* Taplinger (New York City), 1978.

Panshin, Alexei, *Heinlein in Dimension: A Critical Analysis,* Advent, 1968.

Riley, Dick, editor, *Critical Encounters: Writers and Themes in Science Fiction,* Ungar (New York City), 1978.

Rose, Lois, and Stephen Rose, *The Shattered Ring: Science Fiction and the Quest for Meaning,* John Knox (Atlanta, GA), 1970.

Scholes, Robert, and Eric S. Rabkin, *Science Fiction: History, Science, Vision,* Oxford University Press, 1977.

Slusser, George Edgar, *Robert A. Heinlein: Stranger in His Own Land,* Borgo, 1976.

Slusser, *The Classic Years of Robert A. Heinlein,* Borgo, 1977.

Slusser, and Robert Reginald, editors, *Yesterday or Tomorrow?: Questions of Vision in the Fiction of Robert A. Heinlein,* Borgo, 1995.

Usher, Robin, *Self-Begetting, Self-Devouring: Jungian Archetypes in the Fiction of Robert A. Heinlein,* Borgo Press, 1995.

Wollheim, Donald A., *The Universe Makers: Science Fiction Today,* Harper (New York City), 1971.

PERIODICALS

American Mercury, October, 1960.

Analog, May, 1954; September, 1964.

Author and Journalist, January, 1963.

CEA Critic, March, 1968.

Chicago Tribune, August 6, 1961.

Chicago Tribune Book World, August 17, 1980; January 7, 1984.

Christian Science Monitor, November 7, 1957.

Detroit News, July 25, 1982.

Extrapolation, December, 1970; May, 1975; spring, 1979; fall, 1979; fall, 1982; fall, 1990, p. 287.

Galaxy, February, 1952; December, 1966.

Journal of Popular Culture, spring, 1972.

Locus, May, 1989, p. 46; November, 1989, p. 23; January, 1991, p. 43.

Los Angeles Times, December 19, 1985.

Los Angeles Times Book Review, June 20, 1982; October 21, 1984; December 16, 1990, p. 10; December 23, 1990, p. 7; December 30, 1990, p. 10.

Magazine of Fantasy and Science Fiction, June, 1956; November, 1961; March, 1971; October, 1980.

Modern Fiction Studies, spring, 1986.

National Observer, November 16, 1970.

National Review, March 26, 1963; November 16, 1970; December 12, 1980.

New Statesman, July 30, 1965.

New Worlds, June, 1962.

New Yorker, July 1, 1974.

New York Herald Tribune Book Review, November 28, 1954; November 13, 1955; November 18, 1956; May 12, 1962.

New York Times, March 3, 1957; August 22, 1973.

New York Times Book Review, October 23, 1949; November 14, 1954; December 29, 1957; December 14, 1958; January 31, 1960; March 23, 1975; August 24, 1980; September 14, 1980; July 4, 1982; November 11, 1984; December 22, 1985; December 9, 1990, p. 13.

Observer (London), December 23, 1984.

Publishers Weekly, July 2, 1973; June 28, 1993, p. 72.

Punch, August 25, 1965; November 22, 1967.

Saturday Review, November 1, 1958.

Science Fiction Chronicle, September, 1988, p. 45.

Science Fiction Review, November, 1970.

SF Commentary, May, 1976.

Spectator, June 3, 1966; July 30, 1977.

Speculation, August, 1969.

Times Literary Supplement, October 16, 1969; December 11, 1970; April 2, 1971; June 14, 1974.

Washington Post, September 5, 1984.
Washington Post Book World, May 11, 1975; June 27, 1982; December 31, 1989, p. 4; December 30, 1990.

OBITUARIES:

PERIODICALS

Chicago Tribune, May 11, 1988.
Detroit News, May 10, 1988.
Locus, June, 1988.
Los Angeles Times, May 10, 1988.
New York Times, May 10, 1988.
Times (London), May 11, 1988.
Washington Post, May 10, 1988.*

*   *   *

HENBEST, Nigel   1951-

PERSONAL: Born May 6, 1951, in Manchester, Lancashire, England; son of Harold Bernard (a professor) and Rosalind Eve Skone (a psychiatrist; maiden name, James) Henbest. *Education:* University of Leicester, B.S. (with first class honors), 1972; Cambridge University, M.S., 1975. *Avocational interests:* Travel, good and homemade wine, vegetarian food, and music.

ADDRESSES: Home and office—Collins Cottage, Lower Road, Loosley Row, Bucks, HP27 0PF England.

CAREER: University of Leicester, Leicester, England, research assistant at Mount Etna, Sicily, 1976-77; *New Scientist,* London, England, astronomy consultant, beginning 1980; Royal Greenwich Observatory, Sussex, England, consultant, 1982-85; *Journal of the British Astronomical Association,* London, editor, 1985-87; British Broadcasting Corp. (BBC), London, presenter of radio program *Seeing Stars.* Founder and director of Hencoup Enterprises (consultants) and of Pioneer Productions (film production company). Former public relations officer, British Astronomical Association, and former media consultant, Science and Engineering Research Council.

MEMBER: British Astronomical Association, Royal Astronomical Society, Association of British Science Writers.

AWARDS, HONORS: Special award for a series on engineering and technology from the New York Academy of Sciences, 1978, for *Space Frontiers;* Gold Medal for Science and Technology, New York TV Awards, 1994 and 1996; Banff Rockie Award, 1995, for popular science programs; has also received Children's Science Book Award, New York Academy of Science and Senior Information Book Award, *Times Educational Supplement.*

WRITINGS:

The Exploding Universe, Macmillan (New York City), 1979.
Spotter's Guide to the Night Sky (juvenile), illustrations by Michael Roffe, Mayflower (London), 1979.
Mysteries of the Universe, Van Nostrand (New York City), 1981 (published in England as *The Mysterious Universe,* Ebury Press, 1981).
(With Michael Marten) *The New Astronomy,* Cambridge University Press (New York City), 1983, revised 2nd edition, 1996.
(Editor) *Exploring the Universe,* Blackwell/New Scientist (London), 1984.
Comets, Stars, Planets, Admiral, 1985.
(Editor) *Halley's Comet,* New Science Publications, 1985.
The Universe, Weidenfeld & Nicolson, 1992.
The Planets, Viking (New York City), 1992.
The Planets, Ladybird, 1996.

WITH HEATHER COUPER

Space Frontiers (juvenile), edited by Christopher Cooper, Viking, 1978.
All About Space (juvenile), edited by Cooper, Cavendish, Marshall (Freeport, NY), 1981.
The Restless Universe, Philip & Son, 1982.
Astronomy (juvenile), F. Watts (New York City), 1983.
Physics (juvenile), F. Watts, 1983.
The Planets, Pan Books (London), 1985, published as *New Worlds: In Search of Planets,* Addison-Wesley (Reading, MA), 1986.
The Sun, F. Watts, 1986.
The Moon, F. Watts, 1986.
Galaxies and Quasars, F. Watts, 1986.
Telescopes and Observatories, F. Watts, 1987.
Spaceprobes and Satellites, F. Watts, 1987.
Guide to the Galaxy, Cambridge University Press, 1988.
The Stars, Pan Books, 1988.

The Space Atlas, Dorling Kindersley (New York City), 1992.

The Guide to the Galaxy, Cambridge University Press, 1994.

How the Universe Works, Dorling Kindersley, 1994.

Black Holes, Dorling Kindersley, 1996.

TELEVISION SCRIPTS

(With G. Jones) *IRAS: The Infrared Eye,* British Broadcasting Corporation (BBC-TV), 1985.

(With Couper) *The Planets* (based on Couper and Henbest's book of the same name), Moving Picture Company, 1986.

Space Shuttle Discovery, Channel 4, 1993.

PLAYS

(With Michael Bennett) *It's All in the Stars!,* Molecule Theatre of Science, 1989.

OTHER

Columnist for *The Independent.* Former columnist for *The European* and *Focus.* Contributor to encyclopedias, including *Encyclopaedia Britannica, Encyclopedia of Astronomy and Space,* and *Encyclopedia of Space Travel and Astronomy.* Contributor to periodicals, including *Sunday Times, Guardian, Popular Astronomy, Astronomy, Christian Science Monitor,* and *Newton.* Contributor of research papers to scholarly journals, including *Journal of Vulcanology, Geothermal Research,* and *Journal of Physics.*

SIDELIGHTS: Considered clear and understandable by critics, Nigel Henbest's books fill a literary black hole by guiding the reader through many of the most important achievements in astronomy and science in the past twenty-five years. In *The Exploding Universe,* Henbest provides a synopsis of the most outstanding developments in the sciences, from cosmology to physics, in the 1970's. Henbest and coauthor Heather Couper, in *New Worlds: In Search of the Planets,* provide new information about the planets gathered by the fleet of interplanetary spaceprobes sent out during the 1980's and update current information in language understandable to the general reading public.

In *Observing the Universe,* Henbest compiles a selection of astronomical articles by acknowledged authorities which appeared in *New Scientist* from 1980 to 1983. The focus of this book is on observational techniques—optical and radio telescopes, highly so-phisticated spaceprobes, devices to detect gravity waves—but also includes historical articles, works on radio astronomy, and a piece on cosmic chemistry. *The New Astronomy* also concentrates on observational techniques and provides depictions of new findings gathered by radio, infrared, ultraviolet, X-ray, and gamma ray exploration of space. Colin Ronan, writing for the *Times Literary Supplement,* claimed that Henbest's *New Astronomy* is "the first [book] to present and explain 'new astronomy' to a wide public—[and] deserves every success."

Henbest told *CA:* "Astronomy is one of the few areas of science that the average person finds fascinating. By writing about the sky, its beauty and its mysteries, an author can not only grip his audience, but also impart—in a most gentle way—an understanding of how science and scientists work.

"When I began my career as an author, I was doing research at Cambridge, under the then Astronomer Royal. As a research scientist, I was learning more and more—about less and less! In my case, that meant the exploding gases from a supernova that went off over four hundred years ago.

"At the same time, there were very few people with a professional background who could—or who wanted to—explain astronomy to the public. So I moved into the field, and (somewhat to my surprise) found a virtually unlimited market for astronomy titles."

BIOGRAPHICAL/CRITICAL SOURCES:

PERIODICALS

Times Literary Supplement, February 17, 1984.

*   *   *

HOCHSCHILD, Adam   1942-

PERSONAL: Born October 5, 1942, in New York, NY; son of Harold K. (in business) and Mary (an artist; maiden name, Marquand) Hochschild; married Arlie Russell (a sociology professor), June 26, 1965; children: David, Gabriel. *Education:* Harvard University, A.B. (cum laude), 1963. *Politics:* "Non-denominational progressive." *Religion:* None.

ADDRESSES: Home—84 Seward St., San Francisco, CA 94114. *Agent*—Georges Borchardt, Inc., 136 East 57th St., New York, NY 10022.

CAREER: Freelance writer, 1965—; *San Francisco Chronicle,* San Francisco, CA, reporter, 1965-66; *Ramparts,* magazine, San Francisco, writer and editor, 1966-68, 1973-74; *Mother Jones,* magazine, San Francisco, cofounder, 1974, editor and writer, 1976-81, 1986-87. Presidential campaign staff member for Sen. George McGovern, 1972; commentator for National Public Radio in Washington, DC, 1982-83; regents lecturer at University of California at Santa Cruz, 1987-88; commentator for Public Interest Radio in New York City, 1987—; lecturer, graduate school of journalism, University of California at Berkeley, 1992, 1995. *Military service:* U.S. Army Reserve, 1964-70.

MEMBER: National Writers Union, Overseas Press Club, National Book Critics Circle, Media Alliance.

AWARDS, HONORS: Certificate of Excellence from Overseas Press Club of America, 1981, for *Mother Jones* article on South Africa; Bryant Spann Memorial Prize from Eugene V. Debs Foundation, 1984, for *Mother Jones* article on El Salvador; *Half the Way Home: A Memoir of Father and Son* was named a Notable Book of the Year for 1986 by the *New York Times Book Review* and the American Library Association; Thomas M. Storke International Journalism Award, World Affairs Council, 1987; *The Unquiet Ghost: Russians Remember Stalin* was named a Notable Book of the Year for 1995 by the *New York Times Book Review* and *Library Journal;* Madeline Dane Ross Award, Overseas Press Club of America, 1995, for *The Unquiet Ghost.*

WRITINGS:

Half the Way Home: A Memoir of Father and Son, Viking (New York City), 1986.
The Mirror at Midnight: A South African Journey, Viking Penguin, 1990.
The Unquiet Ghost: Russians Remember Stalin, Viking Penguin, 1994.

Contributor of articles and reviews to periodicals, including *Harper's New Republic, Village Voice, Nation, Washington Monthly, New York Times, New York Times Review of Books,* and *Los Angeles Times.*

WORK IN PROGRESS: Magazine essays and reviews; several works for children; non-fiction book for Houghton Mifflin.

SIDELIGHTS: Cofounder, contributor and editor of *Mother Jones* magazine, Adam Hochschild has earned respect and achieved success in the world of the alternative press. It is a success different from that envisioned by his father, however, as Hochschild recounts in his 1986 autobiography, *Half the Way Home: A Memoir of Father and Son.* His memoir is "by turns nostalgic and regretful, lyrical and melancholy," according to *New York Times* reviewer Michiko Kakutani. She added: "[Hochschild] creates a deeply felt portrait of a man and a boy" narrated with "Proustian detail and affection." "Mr. Hochschild illuminates, with rare tact, the situations of fathers and sons," professed Mary Gordon in *New York Times Book Review,* "and he avoids the traps of sentimentality and rancor both."

Hochschild's grandfather, Berthold Hochschild, came from Germany to New York in 1886, where he was one of the founders of a company that eventually became AMAX, Inc., a worldwide mining empire. The Hochschilds rejected their Jewish heritage to better assimilate into the white Gentile majority. Clinching his acceptance into the WASP elite, Berthold's son Harold married Mary Marquand, a white Protestant with excellent social and political connections, when he was forty-nine and she was forty-one. A year later they had a son, Adam.

An only child, Adam Hochschild grew up with all the servants, fine homes, travel, and quality education wealth could provide, and also with all the expectations his anxious parents could place on him. In Gordon's words, Harold Hochschild "believed that the world was a difficult place and that his son was born to run it." Recognized for his benevolence, sound judgment, and irrefutable reason, Harold Hochschild raised his son with the same quiet reserve and emotional detachment he employed with business associates. But although such authoritative tactics worked smoothly with business executives, they came across to Harold's son as domineering, patriarchal, and intimidating. Adam Hochschild's mother adored both her husband and son, but while young Adam was encouraged by her devotion, he also felt betrayed by her failure to intercede on his behalf. "For," as Gordon explained, "he had to believe the justice of his father's criticisms if the mother who adored him went along with them."

Hochschild's break from his father's authority and his parents' world began after a visit to the mines owned by the company his father headed in central Africa. Concern over racial injustice there and in the

United States led Hochschild as a young man to join the civil rights movement. A political activist during the 1960s, Hochschild demonstrated against the Vietnam War and joined the leftist ranks of the alternative press, eventually helping to found *Mother Jones,* named after labor organizer Mary Harris Jones. The self-proclaimed "magazine for the rest of us," *Mother Jones* brought the goals of progressive politics—disarmament, the non-involvement of the United States in the internal affairs of other countries, race and gender equality, and other ideals of social justice—to a large and diverse audience.

The differences between Adam and Harold Hochschild on the surface seem apparent, critics point out, but they are in fact difficult to define. While Adam Hochschild fairly clearly led the life of a 1960s radical, Harold Hochschild was not a stereotypical ruthless entrepreneur. The company the elder Hochschild directed had major holdings in central and southern Africa, where the mines often ran under the oppressive contract labor system, yet, like his peace-activist son, he publicly opposed the Vietnam War. Though he had many business contacts in China, he supported the Communist Revolution there. And, unlike many other corporate tycoons, as an ecologist he brought about some of the most effective environmental legislation in New York State. His fatherly disapproval, then, was not so much of his son's political and social beliefs as of his ways of expressing those beliefs. In Richard Eder's words in *Los Angeles Times Book Review,* Harold Hochschild's criticism grew "out of concern that Adam was wasting his life."

That Adam Hochschild can so readily illustrate his and his father's similarities as well as their differences adds credibility and depth to his story in critics' eyes. Gordon observed, for example, that "it would indeed have been easy [for Hochschild] to present himself as the hero of the piece and his father as the villain, but he does not."

Also adding depth, according to reviewers, is Hochschild's realistic portrayal of the relative peace he and his father attained during the last few years of the elder Hochschild's life. *"Half the Way Home* isn't only a story of flight. It's also a story of a son's reconciliation with his father," Suzanne Gordon asserted in *Washington Post Book World.* Hochschild remembers fondly that eventually his father, in the words of reviewer Kakutani, "even hands out gift subscriptions to [*Mother Jones],* as an unspoken gesture that he approves, perhaps even takes pride, in

his son's vocation." Like other critics, Kakutani noted with relief that there "are no tearful reconciliation scenes between father and son—just as there were never any declarations of overt hostility." The reconciliation takes place quietly, the reviewer observed, and "by the time Harold Hochschild lies dying in a hospital bed, Adam has been able to move toward an acceptance of this difficult man, and even to acknowledge his own love."

Critics compared Hochschild's book favorably with other parent-child reminiscences; Roger W. Fromm, for example, writing in *Library Journal,* deemed the book "an honest, sensitive, fascinating portrait of a father-son relationship that is unique, yet one of universal experience." And *Newsday* contributor Merin Wexler praised *Half the Way Home* as "an intriguing memoir, gently told," adding that Hochschild's book contains memories which are "in themselves remarkable, but his telling makes them doubly so."

Hochschild told *CA:* "I seem to be one of these people who writes a book on a totally different subject each time. I also tend to get stuck between books, and to think I'm never going to find the right subject for the next one. Although when I do find each subject, I realize that, in one way or another, it is something that's been obsessing me for a long time, even if I haven't recognized it before . . . I find that there's a sort of magnetic attraction that takes over, that pulls me towards certain people, episodes, bits of history. A person or a situation that seems to embody some moral dilemma."

BIOGRAPHICAL/CRITICAL SOURCES:

BOOKS

Mary Gordon, *Good Boys and Dead Girls and Other Essays,* Viking Penguin, 1991, pp. 72-76.

PERIODICALS

Kirkus Reviews, January 1, 1994.
Library Journal, May 15, 1986, January, 1995.
London Daily Telegraph, September 3, 1991.
Los Angeles Times, June 21, 1987.
Los Angeles Times Book Review, June 15, 1986; April 3, 1994.
Mother Jones, July/August, 1986.
Newsday, July 6, 1986; March 20, 1994.
New York Times, June 21, 1986.
New York Times Book Review, June 15, 1986; March 27, 1994.

The Progressive, July 1994.
Publisher's Weekly, October 5, 1990.
San Francisco Chronicle, November 11, 1990.
Village Voice, August 12, 1986.
Washington Post Book World, May 11, 1986.

*   *   *

HOLCOMBE, Randall G(regory)   1950-

PERSONAL: Born June 4, 1950, in Bridgeport, CT; son of L. M. Holcombe and R. E. Ledbetter; married. *Education:* University of Florida, B.S. and B.A. (with honors), 1972; Virginia Polytechnic Institute and State University, M.A., 1974, Ph.D., 1976.

ADDRESSES: Home—3514 Limerick Dr., Tallahassee, FL 32308. *Office*—Department of Economics, Florida State University, Tallahassee, FL 32306. *E-mail*—holcombe@coss.fsu.edu.

CAREER: Texas A & M University, College Station, assistant professor of economics, 1975-77; Auburn University, Auburn, AL, assistant professor, 1977-81, associate professor, 1981-85, professor of economics, 1985-88; Florida State University, Tallahassee, professor of economics, 1988—. Adjunct scholar, Ludwig von Mises Institute, 1982—; James Madison Institute, research advisory council, member, 1987—, chairman, 1991—.

AWARDS, HONORS: Earhart Foundation fellow, summers, 1979-80, 1983, 1989; Georgescu-Roegen Prize, *Southern Economic Journal,* 1992, for best article to appear that year; Ludwig von Mises prize, 1992, for scholarship in Austrian economics; undergraduate teaching award, Florida State University, 1994.

WRITINGS:

Public Finance and the Political Process, Southern Illinois University Press (Carbondale, IL), 1983.
An Economic Analysis of Democracy, Southern Illinois University Press, 1985.
Public Sector Economics, Wadsworth Publishing (Belmont, CA), 1988.
Economic Models and Methodology, Greenwood Press (Westport, CT), 1989.
The Economic Foundations of Government, Macmillan (New York City), 1994.

Public Policy and the Quality of Life, Greenwood Press, 1995.
Public Finance: Government Revenues and Expenditures in the United States Economy, West Publishing Company (St. Paul, MN), 1996.

Contributor of more than 100 articles and reviews to economics and political science journals. Member of editorial board, *Review of Austrian Economics,* 1987—, and *Public Finance Quarterly,* 1995—.

SIDELIGHTS: Randall G. Holcombe told *CA:* "Most of my writing has been analyzing the effects of decision making by majority rule. The government is a major factor in modern economies, but the way in which democracies make economic decisions is not well enough understood. Too often, the result has been government policies that are well intentioned but are unable to accomplish what they intended. I hope that my writing can contribute to understanding the economic effect of political decisions."

*   *   *

HOLMES, John
See SOUSTER, (Holmes) Raymond

*   *   *

HOLMES, Raymond
See SOUSTER, (Holmes) Raymond

*   *   *

HOOBLER, Thomas

PERSONAL: Born in Cincinnati, OH; son of John T. (a printer) and Jane Frances (Pachoud) Hoobler; married Dorothy Law (a writer), December 18, 1971; children: Ellen Marie. *Education:* University of Notre Dame, A.B., 1964; attended University of Iowa, Writer's Workshop, 1965. *Avocational interests:* Oriental, American, and European medieval history, music, photography, gardening, and travel.

ADDRESSES: Home—320 West 83rd St., Apt. 6-C, New York, NY 10024.

CAREER: Worked in various positions at private schools in Cincinnati, OH, including teacher of English and photography, audio-visual coordinator, and basketball coach, 1965-70; trade magazine editor, 1971-76; freelance writer and editor, 1976—.

WRITINGS:

(With Burt Wetanson) *The Hunters,* Doubleday (New York City), 1978.
(With Wetanson) *The Treasure Hunters,* Playboy Press, 1983.
Dr. Chill's Project, Putnam (New York City), 1987.
The Revenge of Ho-tai, Walker (Louisville, KY), 1989.

NONFICTION; WITH WIFE, DOROTHY HOOBLER

Frontier Diary, Macmillan (New York City), 1974.
Margaret Mead: A Life in Science, Macmillan, 1974.
House Plants, Grosset, 1975.
Vegetable Gardening and Cooking, Grosset, 1975.
Pruning, Grosset, 1975.
An Album of World War I, F. Watts (New York City), 1976.
The Year in Bloom, Bantam (New York City), 1977.
Photographing History: The Career of Mathew Brady, Putnam, 1977.
An Album of World War II, F. Watts, 1977.
The Trenches: Fighting on the Western Front in World War I, Putnam, 1978.
Photographing the Frontier, Putnam, 1980.
U.S.-China Relations since World War II, F. Watts, 1981.
An Album of the Seventies, F. Watts, 1981.
The Social Security System, F. Watts, 1982.
The Voyages of Captain Cook, Putnam, 1983.
Stalin, Chelsea House (New York City), 1985.
Your Right to Privacy, F. Watts, 1986.
Zhou Enlai, Chelsea House, 1986.
Cleopatra, Chelsea House, 1986.
Nelson and Winnie Mandela, F. Watts, 1987.
Drugs and Crime, Chelsea House, 1988.
Toussaint L'Ouverture, Chelsea House, 1989.
George Washington, Silver Press, 1990.
Vietnam: Why We Fought, Knopf (New York City), 1990.
Showa: The Age of Hirohito, Walker, 1990.
Vanished!, Walker, 1991.
Lost Civilizations, Walker, 1992.
Mandela: The Man, the Struggle, the Triumph, F. Watts, 1992.

Confucianism, Facts on File (New York City), 1993.

"IMAGES ACROSS THE AGES" NONFICTION SERIES; PUBLISHED BY STECK-VAUGHN; WITH D. HOOBLER

African Portraits, 1993.
Chinese Portraits, 1993.
Mexican Portraits, 1993.
Italian Portraits, 1993.
Japanese Portraits, 1994.
Russian Portraits, 1994.
South American Portraits, 1994.
French Portraits, 1994.

"AMERICAN FAMILY ALBUM" NONFICTION SERIES; PUBLISHED BY OXFORD UNIVERSITY PRESS; WITH D. HOOBLER

The Chinese American Family Album, 1994.
The Italian American Family Album, 1994.
The Mexican American Family Album, 1994.
The Irish American Family Album, 1995.
The African American Family Album, 1995.
The Jewish American Family Album, 1995.
The Japanese American Family Album, 1995.
The German American Family Album, 1996.
The Cuban American Family Album, 1996.
The Scandinavian American Family Album, 1996.

"HER STORY" CHILDREN'S HISTORICAL FICTION SERIES; PUBLISHED BY SILVER BURDETT PRESS; WITH D. HOOBLER

The Sign-Painter's Secret, 1991.
Next Stop: Freedom, 1991.
Treasure in the Stream, 1991.
Aloha Means Come Back, 1991.
And Now, a Word from Our Sponsor, 1992.
A Promise at the Alamo, 1992.
The Trail on Which They Wept, 1992.
The Summer of Dreams, 1993.

TEXTBOOKS; WITH D. HOOBLER

China: History, Culture, Geography, Globe (Cleveland, OH), 1986.
Blacks in American History: 1877 to the Present, Globe, 1989.
The Pacific Rim, Scholastic (New York City), 1990.
The Soviet Union and Eastern Europe, Scholastic, 1990.
Latin America: Tradition and Change, Longman (New York City), 1991.

HOWES, Barbara 1914-1996

PERSONAL: Born May 1, 1914, in New York, NY; died February 24, 1996, in Bennington, VT; daughter of Osborne (a stock broker) and Mildred (Cox) Howes; married William Jay Smith (a teacher and writer), October 1, 1947 (divorced, 1964); children: David E., Gregory Jay. *Education:* Attended Beaver Country Day School, Chestnut Hill, MA; Bennington College, B.A., 1937. *Politics:* Democrat. *Religion:* Episcopalian.

ADDRESSES: Agent—c/o Gregory Smith (literary estate executor), RR1, Box 175, North Pownal, VT 05260.

CAREER: Writer.

AWARDS, HONORS: Bess Hokin Prize, *Poetry* magazine, 1949; Guggenheim fellowship, 1955; Brandeis University poetry grant, 1958; Eunice Tietjens Memorial Prize, 1959; award in literature from the National Institute of Arts and Letters, 1971; National Book Award nomination, 1995, for *The Collected Poems of Barbara Howes, 1945-1990.*

WRITINGS:

POETRY

The Undersea Farmer, Banyan Press (Pawlet, VT), 1948.
In the Cold Country, Bonacio & Saul/Grove Press (New York City), 1954.
Light and Dark, Wesleyan University Press (Middletown, CT), 1959.
Looking Up at Leaves, Knopf (New York City), 1966.
The Blue Garden, Wesleyan University Press, 1972.
A Private Signal: Poems New and Selected, Wesleyan University Press, 1977.
Moving, Elysian Press (New York City), 1983.
The Collected Poems of Barbara Howes, 1945-1990, University of Arkansas Press (Fayetteville), 1995.

Poems anthologized in *New Poems by American Poets,* Ballantine (New York City), 1957; *Modern Verse in English,* Macmillan, 1958; *Modern American Poetry,* Harcourt (New York City), 1962; *Poet's Choice,* Dial (New York City), 1962; *Modern Poets,* McGraw (New York City), 1963; *Of Poetry and Power,* Basic Books (New York City), 1964; *The Girl in the Black Raincoat,* edited by George Garrett,

Duell, Sloane & Pierce, 1966; *The Marvelous Light,* edited by Helen Plotz, Crowell (New York City), 1970; *Inside Outer Space,* edited by Robert Vas Dias, Anchor Books (New York City), 1970.

EDITOR

23 Modern Stories, Vintage (New York City), 1963.
From the Green Antilles: Writings of the Caribbean, Macmillan (New York City), 1966.
(With son, Gregory Jay Smith) *The Sea-Green Horse* (juvenile short stories), Macmillan, 1970.
The Eye of the Heart: Short Stories from Latin America, Bobbs-Merrill (Indianapolis, IN), 1973.

Editor, *Chimera: A Literary Magazine,* 1943-47.

OTHER

The Road Commissioner and Other Stories, illustrated by Gregory Smith, Stinehour Press, 1983.

Contributor to periodicals, including *American Scholar, Atlantic, Chicago Review, New Directions, New Republic, New Yorker, New York Times Book Review, Poetry, Saturday Review, Southern Review, University of Kansas Review, Virginia Quarterly Review,* and *Yale Review.*

SIDELIGHTS: Despite being nominated for the 1995 National Book Award for her *The Collected Poems of Barbara Howes, 1945-1990,* the work of poet Barbara Howes has received relatively little publicity; Robert Richman, writing in the *New York Times,* called Howes "as obscure a worthy poet as I can think of." Usually alternating her backdrop between the gentle climate of the West Indies and the harsher landscape of her native New England, Howes's verses paint a world of family, natural surroundings, and the wisdom inherent in natural inclinations. "I might say that my poems are about relationships," she would write by way of explanation in an essay published in *Contemporary Authors Autobiography Series (CAAS)*—"the relation of the poet's eye, mind, and heart to reality."

Born in 1914, Howes was raised in a suburb of Boston. Educated at Bennington College, Vermont, she moved to New York City after graduation. While submitting her poetry to magazines, Howes got a job editing *Chimera: A Literary Magazine* from 1944 to 1947. Although the job kept her from her own writing for several years, it would prove to be valuable, not only because it put her in contact with numerous other writers living in the city, but also because of the editorial skills Howes developed. These skills would be put to good use several years later when she edited several acclaimed short story anthologies: 1966's *From the Green Antilles: Writings of the Caribbean;* 1973's *The Eye of the Heart: Short Stories from Latin America;* and *The Sea-Green Horse,* a young-adult short story anthology Howes compiled with her son, Gregory Jay Smith, in 1970.

Howes's first collection of verse, *The Undersea Farmer,* was published in 1948. While recognizing that hers was a young talent, reviewers were quick to see it as the work of an accomplished poet. 1954's *In the Cold Country* would further refine Howes's considerable abilities, drawing even more critical acclaim. Praising her as "the most accomplished women poet of the younger writing generation," Louise Bogan commented in the *New Yorker* on Howes's "strong, positive emotions that continually resolve into a major key." "We sense the possibility of a new reconciliation in modern verse," concluded Bogan, "for so long filled with division and dissent."

Comparing Howes's verse to that of British poet Wallace Stevens, Thom Gunn noted in the *Yale Review* that "at her best . . . the very indirection of her style contributes to her meaning. Her most considerable power is in her control over language." This control would be exhibited throughout Howes's work, in volumes that include *Light and Dark, Looking Up at Leaves,* and *The Blue Garden,* which Robert B. Shaw termed remarkable "for the clarity of its descriptive passages" in a review in *Poetry.* Her best work would be anthologized in *Collected Poems* in 1990.

Although she has been acknowledged for her skill as a stylist, Howes has always been quick to explain that her abilities are not the obvious outlet of "God-given" talent. "One does not own one's talent . . . and should not identify with it," she explained in her essay for *CAAS;* "rather, one works at it, is responsible for tending this blithe or gloomy spirit which can flash in and fade out in its own inexplicable way. . . . [T]alent, and the artist who houses and labors over it, are not one." Although recognizing that the possession of talent is necessary to any poetic endeavor, "the other base from which any art springs is simply real, steady work. If one sits around waiting for the lightning of inspiration to strike, it will surely descend over the way, where another poet is hard at it."

BIOGRAPHICAL/CRITICAL SOURCES:

BOOKS

Contemporary Authors Autobiography Series, Volume 3, Gale (Detroit), 1986.
Nemerov, Howard, editor, *Poets on Poetry,* Basic Books (New York City), 1966.
Untermeyer, Louis, editor, *Modern American Poetry,* Harcourt (New York City), 1962.

PERIODICALS

Kenyon Review, June, 1966.
Nation, January 15, 1949.
New Yorker, June 5, 1954, pp. 133-35.
New York Times, April 4, 1954.
New York Times Book Review, February 20, 1966, pp. 4, 33; April 1, 1967, p. 22; July 19, 1970, p. 22; December 17, 1995, p. 16.
Poetry, June, 1949; September, 1973, pp. 344-50; January, 1967.
Saturday Review, March 19, 1949; October 9, 1954; December 31, 1956.
Times Literary Supplement, June 29, 1967, p. 583.
Virginia Quarterly Review, autumn, 1966.
Yale Review, December, 1959, pp. 295-304.

OBITUARIES:

PERIODICALS

New York Times, February 25, 1996.

[Sketch reviewed by son, Gregory Smith.]

*   *   *

HURT, Ray Douglas   1946-

PERSONAL: Born July 11, 1946, in Hays, KS; son of Ray Kent (a laborer) and Margaret Jane (a secretary; maiden name, Miller) Hurt; married Mary Ellen Cox (a housewife), August 20, 1980; children: Adlai Andrew, John Austin. *Education:* Fort Hays Kansas State College (now Fort Hays State University), B.A., 1969, M.A., 1971; Kansas State University, Ph.D., 1975.

ADDRESSES: Home—1904 Bel-Air Dr., Ames, IA 50010. *Office*—Department of History, 603 Ross Hall, Iowa State University, Ames, IA 50010.

CAREER: University of Mid-America, Lincoln, NE, researcher in Great Plains history, 1975-76; Smithsonian Institution, Washington, DC, fellow in history of science and technology, 1976-77; Texas Tech University, Lubbock, visiting assistant professor of American history, 1977-78; Ohio Historical Society, Columbus, curator of agricultural history, 1978-86; State Historical Society of Missouri, Columbia, associate director, 1986-89; Iowa State University, Ames, IA, professor and director of graduate program in agricultural history and rural studies, 1989—. Curator of agricultural history and associate editor of *Timeline,* Ohio Agricultural Society, 1978-86; adjunct associate professor of history, Ohio State University, 1981-86; associate director, State Historical Society of Missouri, 1986-89; adjunct professor of history, University of Missouri-Columbia, 1986-89.

MEMBER: Agricultural History Society, American Historical Association, Organization of American Historians, Southern Historical Association, Western History Association, Phi Alpha Theta, Phi Kappa Phi.

AWARDS, HONORS: Young Alumni Award, Fort Hays State University, 1979; course development grant, Iowa State University, 1990; Teaching Excellence Award, Sigma Phi Chapter of the Order of Omega at Iowa State University, 1991; co-winner of Theodore Saloutos Award, Agricultural History Society, for best book in the field, 1992, and winner of the Missouri History Book Award, from State Historical Society of Missouri, for best book in the field, 1993, both for *Agriculture and Slavery in Missouri's Little Dixie;* research travel grant, American Heritage Center, University of Wyoming, 1993; Richard E. Brownlee Research Award, State Historical Society of Missouri, 1994.

WRITINGS:

The Dust Bowl: An Agricultural and Social History, Nelson-Hall (Chicago, IL), 1981.

American Farm Tools: From Hand Power to Steam Power, Sunflower University Press, 1982.

Indian Agriculture in America: Prehistory to the Present, University Press of Kansas (Lawrence, KS), 1988.

The Department of Agriculture, Chelsea House (New York City), 1988.

(Editor with Mary K. Dains) *Thomas Hart Benton: Artist, Writer and Intellectual,* State Historical Society of Missouri, 1989.

Agricultural Technology in the Twentieth Century, Sunflower Press (Manhattan, KS), 1991.

Agriculture and Slavery in Missouri's Little Dixie, University of Missouri Press (Columbia, MO), 1992.

The History of Agricultural Science and Technology: An Annotated International Bibliography, Garland Publishing (New York City), 1994.

American Agriculture: A Brief History, Iowa State University Press (Ames, IA), 1994.

American Farms: Exploring Their History, Krieger, 1996.

The Ohio Frontier: Crucible of the Old Northwest, 1720-1830, Indiana University Press, 1996.

Editor, The Henry A. Wallace Series on Agricultural History and Rural Life, Iowa State University Press, 1993—. Author of foreword, Lawrence Svobida, *Farming in the Dust Bowl,* University Press of Kansas, 1986. Contributor to books, including *The Great Plains: Environment and Culture,* edited by Brian W. Blouet and Frederick C. Luebke, University of Nebraska Press (Lincoln, NE), 1979; *Technology in the Twentieth Century,* edited by Frank H. Coppa and Richard P. Harmond, Kendall Hunt Publishing Co. (Dubuque, IA), 1983; *Heartland: Comparative Histories of the Midwestern States,* edited by James H. Madison, Indiana University Press (Bloomington, IN), 1988; *Historians of the American Frontier: A Bio-Bibliographical Sourcebook,* edited by John R. Wunder, Greenwood Press (Westport, CT), 1988; *Agriculture and National Development: Views on the Nineteenth Century,* edited by Louis Ferleger, Iowa State University Press, 1990.

Contributor to encyclopedias and dictionaries, including *Encyclopedia of American Social History, Encyclopedia of Southern Culture, Encyclopedia of the United States Congress, Encyclopedia USA, History of Science in the United States: An Encyclopedia, Native America in the Twentieth Century: An Encyclopedia, Political Parties and Elections in the United States: An Encyclopedia, World Book Encyclopedia,* and *Dictionary of American Biography.*

Contributor of articles and reviews to history and education journals, including *Agricultural Archaeology, Agricultural History, Agriculture and Human Values, American Heritage, American West, Cincinnati Historical Society Bulletin, Curator, Gateway Heritage, Great Plains Journal, Heritage of the Great Plains, History Teacher, Journal of the West, Kansas Historical Quarterly, Kansas History, Midwest Review, Missouri Historical Review, Northwest*

Ohio Quarterly, OAH Magazine of History, Ohio History, Old Northwest, Panhandle: Plains Historical Review, Peabody Journal of Education, Red River Valley Historical Review, Timeline, True West, and *Western Historical Quarterly.* Editor, *Agricultural History,* 1994—; member of editorial advisory board, *Journal of the West,* 1981-88, 1990-92.

SIDELIGHTS: Ray Douglas Hurt told *CA:* "As a boy I hauled hay, plowed, and seeded crops for farmers near my home town. I thoroughly enjoyed the work. During my undergraduate years I became fascinated with the populist movement that swept the Great Plains during the late nineteenth century. The study of agricultural history seemed to be an excellent way to combine two things that I loved—farming and history.

"I have a compulsive need to know how things have come to be as they are. The study of agricultural history helps me satisfy that need.

"For me, agricultural history is the story of innovation, adaptation, and perseverance combined with science, technology, economics, politics, and the art of daily living. It is an incredibly diverse and exciting field of study."

*   *   *

HUSEN, Torsten   1916-

PERSONAL: Born March 1, 1916, in Lund, Sweden; son of Johan S. (an executive director) and Betty Maria (Prawitz) Husen; married Ingrid Joensson (a language teacher), April 10, 1940; children: Sven-Torsten, Mats O., Goerel. *Education:* University of Lund, B.A., 1937, M.A., 1938, Fil.lic., 1941, Ph.D., 1944. *Avocational interests:* Collecting old books.

ADDRESSES: Home—Armfeltsgatan 10, S-11534 Stockholm, Sweden. *Office*—University of Stockholm, S-10691 Stockholm, Sweden.

CAREER: University of Lund, Lund, Sweden, instructor and research assistant, 1938-44; University of Stockholm, Stockholm, Sweden, associate professor, 1947-52, professor of educational psychology, 1953-56, professor of education and director of Institute of Educational Research, 1959-71, professor of international education, 1971-81, professor emeritus, 1982—.

Visiting professor, University of Chicago, 1959, University of Hawaii, 1968, Ontario Institute for Studies in Education, 1971, Stanford University, 1981, and University of California, Berkeley, 1984. Chair of governing boards of universities and of international education associations. Participant in international seminars; expert and consultant on various Swedish government commissions; consultant to many world organizations. *Military service:* Swedish Armed Forces, psychologist, 1942-44, senior psychologist, 1944-51.

MEMBER: International Association for the Evaluation of Educational Achievement (chair), International Council for Educational Development, International Academy of Education (chair), American Academy of Arts and Sciences, National Academy of Education (United States; foreign associate), Swedish Royal Academy of Sciences, Finnish Academy, Polish Academy.

AWARDS, HONORS: Prize for educational authorship, Swedish Literary Foundation, 1961; fellow, Center for Advanced Study of the Behavioral Sciences, 1965-66, and 1973-74; honorary degrees from University of Chicago, 1967, Brunel University, 1974, University of Glasgow, 1974, University of Rhode Island, 1975, University of Joensuu, 1979, University of Amsterdam, 1982, and Ohio State University, 1985; medal for distinguished service, Teachers College, Columbia University, 1969; fellow, National Center for the Humanities, 1978-79; Swedish cultural prize, Natur & Kultur Publishing House, 1979; Gold Medal, National Institute of Educational Research (Tokyo), 1983; named honorary professor, University of Shanghai, 1984; Comenius Medal, UNESCO, 1993.

WRITINGS:

Psykologisk krigfoering, C.W.K. Gleerup, 1942.
Adolescensen: Undersoekningar roerande manlig svensk ungdom i aaldern 17-20 aar, Almqvist & Wiksell, 1944.
Studier roerande de eidetiska fenomenen, C.W.K. Gleerup, Volume I, 1946, Volume II, 1952.
Begavning och miljoe: Studier i begaavningsutvecklingens och begaavningsurvalets psykologiskpedagogiska och sociala problem, H. Geber, 1948.
Om innerboerden av psykologiska maetningar: Naagra bidrag till psykometrikans metodlaera, C.W.K. Gleerup, 1949.
Anders Berg under folkskolans pionjaeraar, Erlanders Bookstore, 1949.

Raettstavningsfoermaagans psykologi: Naagra experimentella bidrag, Svensk Laeraretidnings Foerlag, 1950.

Testresultatens prognosvaerde: En Undersoekning av den teoretiska skolningens inverkan paa testresultaten, intelligenstedens prognosvaerde och de sociala faktorernas inverkan pa urvalet till hogre laroanstalter, H. Geber, 1950.

(With Sven-Eric Henricson) *Some Principles of Construction of Group Intelligence Tests for Adults: A Report on Construction and Standardization of the Swedish Induction Test (the I-test),* Almqvist & Wiksell, 1951.

Tvillingstudier: Undersoekningar roerande begaavningsfoerhaallanden, skolprestationer, intraparrelationer, antropometriska maatt, handstilslikhet samt diagnosproblem m.m. inom e reprensentativ population likkoenade tvillingar, Almqvist & Wiksell, 1953.

Pskologi, Svenska Bokfoerlaget, 1954, 5th edition with Lars Larsson, 1966.

(With others) *Betyg och standardprov: En orientering for foraeldrar och laerare,* Almqvist & Wiksell, 1956.

(With others) *Standardproven: En redogoerelse foer konstruktion och standardisering,* Almqvist & Wiksell, 1956.

Militaert och civilt, Norstedt, 1956.

Ur psykologisk synvinkel, Almqvist & Wiksell, 1957.

Pedagogisk psykologi, Svenska Bokfoerlaget, 1957, 4th edition, 1968.

(With Artur Olsson) *Akademiska studier: Studieteknik for studenter,* Svenska Bokfoerlaget, 1958.

Psychological Twin Research: A Methodological Study, Almqvist & Wiksell, 1959.

Att undervisa studenter, Almqvist & Wiksell, 1959.

(Editor with Sten Henrysson) *Differentiation and Guidance in the Comprehensive School: Report on the Sigtuna Course Organized by the Swedish Government under the Auspices of the Council of Europe, August, 1958,* Almqvist & Wiksell, 1959.

(With Urban Dahlloef) *Matematik och modersmaalet i skola och yrkesliv: Studier av kunskapskrav, kunskapbehaallning och undervisningens upplaeggning,* Studieforbundet Naeringsliv och Samhaelle, 1960, translation published as *Mathematics and Communication Skills in School and Society: An Empirical Approach to the Problem of Curriculum Contest,* Industrial Council for Social and Economic Studies, 1960.

Psykologi, introduktion til psykologien af i dag, A. Busck, 1960.

Skolan i ett foraenderligt samhaelle, Almqvist & Wiksell, 1961, 2nd edition, 1963.

De Farliga psykologerna, Raben & Sjogren, 1961.

Studieteknik foer gymnasiet, Svenska Bokforlaget, 1961.

(With Elvy Johanson) *Fysik och kemi i skola och yrkesliv,* Studienfoerbundet Naeringsliv och Samhaelle, 1961.

School Reform in Sweden, U.S. Department of Health, Education, and Welfare, 1961.

Tonaaringarna i utbildningssamhaellet—Studier i Amerikansk pedagogik, Almqvist & Wiksell, 1962.

(With Goesta Ekman) *Att studera psykologi och pedagogik,* Svenska Bokfoerlaget, 1962.

Problems of Differentiation in Swedish Compulsory Schooling, Svenska Bokforlaget, 1962.

(With Malcolm Shepherd Knowles) *Erwachsene lernen,* E. Klett, 1963.

Skola foer 60-talet, Almqvist & Wiksell, 1963.

(With Gunnar Boalt) *Skolans sociologi,* Almqvist & Wiksell, 1964, 3rd edition, 1967.

Det nya gymnasiet: Information och debatt, Almqvist & Wiksell, 1964.

(With Karl-Erik Waerneryd) *Psykologi for fackskolan,* Svenska Bokforlaget, 1966.

Skola i foervandling, Almqvist & Wiksell, 1966.

(Editor with Ingvar Carlson) *Tonaaringarna och skolan,* Almqvist & Wiksell, 1966.

(Editor) *International Study of Achievement in Mathematics: A Comparison of Twelve Countries,* Wiley, 1967.

(With Boalt) *Educational Research and Educational Change: The Case of Sweden,* Wiley, 1968.

Skola foer 80-talet, Almqvist & Wiksell, 1968.

(Compiler) *Livsaaskaadning och religion,* Svenska Bokforlaget, 1968.

Talent, Opportunity and Career: A Twenty-Six Year Follow-up of 1500 Individuals, Almqvist & Wiksell, 1969.

(Compiler with Sune Askaner) *Literatur: Konst och musik,* Laeromedelsfoerlaget, 1969.

(Contributor) D. F. Swift, editor, *Basic Readings in the Sociology of Education,* Routledge & Kegan Paul, 1970.

(Compiler with Ulf Hard af Segerstad) *Samhaellsfraagor: Planering ocho miljoe,* Laromedelsforlaget, 1971.

Present Trends and Future Developments in Education: A European Perspective, Ontario Institute for Studies in Education, 1971.

Utbildning aar 2000, Bonniers, 1971.

Social Background and Educational Career: Research Perspectives on Equality of Educational Opportunity, Organization for Economic Co-operation and Development, 1972.

Skolans kris och andra uppsatser om utbildning, Almqvist & Wiksell, 1972.

Svensk skola i internationell belysning: Naturorienterande aemnen, Almqvist & Wiksell, 1973.

Talent, Equality and Meritocracy, Nijhoff, 1974.

The Learning Society, Methuen, 1974.

Social Influences on Educational Attainment, Organization for Economic Co-operation and Development, 1975.

Universiteten och forskningen, Natur och Kultur, 1975.

(Contributor) Jerome Karabel and A. H. Halsey, *Power and Ideology in Education,* Oxford University Press, 1977.

The School in Question, Oxford University Press, 1979.

The Future of Formal Education, Almqvist & Wiksell, 1980.

En obotlig akademiker: En professors memoarer, Natur och Kultur, 1981, translation published as *An Incurable Academic: Memoirs of a Professor,* Pergamon Press, 1983.

(Contributor) Manfred Niessen and Jules Peschar, *International Comparative Research: Problems of Theory, methodology, and Organization in Eastern and Western Europe,* Pergamon Press, 1982.

(Editor with S. Opper) *Multicultural and Multilingual Education in Immigrant Countries,* Pergamon Press, 1983.

(Editor with M. Kogan) *Educational Research and Policy: How Do They Relate?,* Pergamon Press, 1984.

Devenir Adulte dans une societe en mutation, OECD, 1985, translation published as *Becoming Adult in a Changing Society,* OECD, 1985.

(Contributor) Bjoern Engholm, editor, *Demokratie faengt in der Schule an,* Eichborn Verlag, 1985.

Utbildning i internationellt perspektiv: En inledning till den jamforande pedagogiken, Liber Utbildningfoerlaget, 1985.

The Learning Society Revisited: Essays, Pergamon Press, 1986.

Higher Education and Social Stratification, UNESCO, 1987.

Femtio ar som utbildningsforskare, Royal Swedish Academy of Sciences, 1988.

Skolreformerna och forskningen: Psykologisk pedagogik under reformaren, Verbum, 1988.

Skolan i focus: Kritiska betraktelser, Almqvist & Wiksell, 1989.

Education and Global Concern, Pergamon Press, 1990.

(Editor with John Keeves) *Issues in Science Education,* Pergamon Press, 1991.

Moeten, Wiken, 1991.

(Editor with A. J. Tuijnman and W. D. Halls) *Schooling in Modern European Society,* Pergamon Press, 1992.

(Editor) *The Role of the University: A Global Perspective,* United Nations University (Tokyo), 1994.

Skola och universitet infor 2000-talet, Atlantis, 1995.

Also contributor of chapters, introductions, and forewords to many studies in psychology and education. Co-editor-in-chief, *International Encyclopedia of Education: Research and Studies;* editor, *Scandinavian Encyclopedia of Psychology and Education;* member, international board of consultants, *World Book Encyclopedia.*

Some of Husen's works have been translated into Polish, Russian, Arabic, Hindi, Hungarian, Dutch, Italian, Spanish, Portuguese, Chinese, French, German, and Japanese.

WORK IN PROGRESS: Education Activities in Connection with UNESCO, 1946-1996.

SIDELIGHTS: In an article entitled "Marriage to Higher Education" in the *Journal of Higher Education,* Torsten Husen writes, "I can hardly think of any other group in society to which the principle of lifelong learning applies more adequately than to academics involved in advanced teaching and research. In essence, to be involved in research means that one constantly has to revise ideas and restructure models of reality and incessantly move into new intellectual territory. A university professor is never 'fully prepared' or 'competent.' One has to prove oneself continuously. The most salient feature of the professorial role is that of a permanent student who is involved in continuous learning, not least from one's own students of whom the more able often are the initiators of new paradigms of thinking in the discipline."

BIOGRAPHICAL/CRITICAL SOURCES:

BOOKS

Faegerlind, Ingemar, and others, editors, *Torsten Husen: An Educator,* Institute of International Education, Stockholm University, 1991.

Husen, Torsten, *An Incurable Academic: Memoirs of a Professor,* Pergamon Press, 1983.

Husen, *Moten,* Wiken, 1992.

PERIODICALS

Journal of Higher Education, Volume 51, number 6, 1980.

*   *   *

IQBAL, Afzal   1919-1994

PERSONAL: Born August 14, 1919, in Lahore, Pakistan; died November 14, 1994. *Education:* Government College, Lahore, Pakistan, B.A. (with honors), 1939; University of the Punjab, M.A., 1941.

CAREER: Ministry of Foreign Affairs, Islamabad, Pakistan, 1950—, served as second secretary at embassies in Iran, 1950, and Burma, 1952; first secretary in Spain, 1955-57, and England, 1957-58; deputy secretary for external publicity, 1959-61; served at embassies in Thailand, 1961-63, and Syria, 1963-64; deputy high commissioner at embassy in India, 1964-66; minister in London, 1966-69; ambassador to Switzerland and the Holy See, 1969-71, to Brazil, Bolivia, Colombia, and Paraguay, 1971-73, to Sweden and Norway, 1973-76, to Canada, Guyana, and Trinidad and Tobago, 1976-79. Guest lecturer at Universities of London, Durham, Manchester, Toronto, Minnesota, Delhi, Geneva, Berne, Rio de Janeiro, Sao Paulo, Bangkok, Stockholm, Uppsala, Oslo, Ankara, Istanbul, Konya, and Azamgarh, and at Oxford, Cambridge, and Yale Universities.

MEMBER: Royal Society of Arts (fellow).

AWARDS, HONORS: Decorated by Order of Istihquq (Syrian Arab Republic), Order of Humayun and Order of Sipas (both Iran), Order of Pius IX (Holy See), and Order of the Grand Cruz do Sul (Brazil); honorary Ph.D., University of the Punjab, 1970; Award for Best Book in English, Academy of Letters, 1986, for *Diary of a Diplomat;* Sitara-i-Imtiaz, government of Pakistan, 1993, for contributions to the field of literature.

WRITINGS:

(Editor) *My Life: A Fragment* (on the life of Mohamed Ali, leader of the Khilafat Movement of the 1920s), Muhammad Ashraf, 1942, 4th edition, 1966.

(Editor) *Select Writings and Speeches of Maulana Mohamed Ali,* two volumes, Muhammad Ashraf, 1944, 3rd edition, 1969.
The Life and Work of Maulana Jalaluddin Rumi, Institute of Islamic Culture (Lahore), 1956, 5th revised edition, Octagon Press (London), 1983.
Diplomacy in Islam, Institute of Islamic Culture, 1961, 2nd edition, 1965.
The Culture of Islam, Institute of Islamic Culture, 1967, 3rd revised edition, 1981.
The Life and Times of Maulana Mohamed Ali, Institute of Islamic Culture, 1974, 2nd edition, 1979.
The Impact of Maulana Jalaluddin Rumi on Islamic Culture, Regional Cultural Institute (Tehran), 1975.
The Prophet's Diplomacy, Claude Stark, 1975.
Circumstances Leading to the First Afghan War, Research Society of Pakistan and University of the Punjab, 1975, 2nd edition, 1975.
(Translator) Albert Camus, *Ajnabi* (Urdu translation of *L'Etranger*), Ayeena-i-adab, 1975.
Contemporary Muslim World, Hurriyet, 1983.
Islamisation of Pakistan, [Delhi], 1984, Vanguard Books, 1986.
Dimensions of Islam, [Delhi], 1986.
Diplomacy in Islam: The First Forty Years, Institute of Islamic Culture, 1988.
Kitab (poetry), Rawalpindi, 1985.
Diary of a Diplomat, Hamdard Foundation, 1986.
Puppet on a String (essay collection), National Book Foundation, 1993.
(Editor and translator) Hamidullah, *Emergence of Islam,* Islamic Research Institute (Islamabad), 1993.

Also author of *Reflections on Rumi* and a volume of Urdu verse, both in press. Contributor of over 500 articles to various books, magazines and newspapers.

SIDELIGHTS: Afzal Iqbal was an authority on Islam in general and on Maulana Jalaluddin and Mohamed Ali of the Khilafat movement in particular. *The Life and Work of Maulana Jalaluddin Rumi* has been translated into Urdu and Turkish. Other works have been published in the United States, Great Britain, Iran, Turkey, India, and Pakistan.

*   *   *

JACOB, John   1950-

PERSONAL: Born August 27, 1950, in Chicago, IL; son of Bertram Frank (an insurance agent) and

Eleanor (Addy) Jacob; children: Lucas John, Kathleen Rebecca. *Ethnicity:* "Caucasian." *Education:* University of Michigan, A.B., 1972; University of Illinois at Chicago, M.A., 1973, Ph.D., 1989.

ADDRESSES: Home and office—417 S. Taylor, #3B, Oak Park, IL 60302.

CAREER: Northwestern University, Evanston, IL, instructor in English, 1974-79; Illinois Legislative Investigating Commission, Chicago, chief writer, 1979-82; Northwestern University, instructor in English, 1984—. Development director for Community Advancement Programs, Chicago, 1973-77. Lecturer at Roosevelt University, 1975—; assistant professor at North Central College, Naperville, IL, 1987-94. Member of board of directors of domestic violence support group, Sarah's Inn. Consultant to Illinois Arts Council.

MEMBER: International PEN, Modern Language Association of America, Associated Writing Programs, Authors Guild.

AWARDS, HONORS: Carl Sandburg Award from Friends of Chicago Public Library, 1980, for *Scatter: Selected Poems;* grants from Illinois Arts Council, 1985 and 1987; Burlington Northern Award, 1988; PEN Discovery Award, 1989; *Whetstone* Fiction Award, 1991; Distinguished Teaching Award, Northwestern University, 1992.

WRITINGS:

POETRY

Scatter: Selected Poems, Wine Press, 1979.
Hawk Spin, Pentagram Press (Markesan, WI), 1983.
Summerbook, Spoon River Poetry Press (Peroria, IL), 1983.
Wooden Indian, Kestrel Editions, 1987.
Hungers, Lake Shore Publishing, 1995.

OTHER

The Light Fandango (short stories), Another Chicago Press (Oak Park, IL), 1988.
Long Ride Back (novel), Thunder's Mouth Press (New York City), 1988.

Columnist for *Margins.* Reviewer for *ALA Booklist,* 1976-86.

WORK IN PROGRESS: A second novel, for Another Chicago Press; research on the poetry of Charles Olson.

SIDELIGHTS: John Jacob told *CA:* "I've been interested in subjects from a 'non-literary' point of view: anthropology, social work, philosophy, psychology, and psychiatry. Urban scenes and life interest me a great deal, and so does the American Indian.

"Most of my poetry is concerned with concrete ways of looking at abstract concepts. My recent work is more narrative. Some of the work has the urban experience as a theme.

"My novel, *Long Ride Back,* ostensibly is about the war in Vietnam, the antiwar movement, and a particular man's involvement in both and his life in the 1980s. I consider it a personal rather than a universal statement. My personal view in my fiction is that random activity governs the 'order' we try to create in our worlds. Obviously, we do not always succeed. My second novel will attempt to trace this theme or point of view in a smaller, less obvious, and shorter format."

Jacob later told *CA:* "I have very different writing processes depending on whether I am writing fiction or poetry. I wrote my first two novels whenever I had a chance, in train stations, when I finished grading papers, when I was traveling and staying in a hotel. But I put my third novel on a word processor, making very few changes but having to be in my office to write. I have been told that my best fiction is in the third book, though it remains unpublished. I think that subject matter, point of view, and approach will dictate publishability.

"Poetry is 95% spontaneous with me. I occasionally will sit to write a sestine or villanelle, or use a blues form, but the subjects almost always incubate for long periods of time. I may not write for three months and then write five poems. I consider that substantial.

"I have been influenced by film, both in subject matter, occasionally, and in style. I jump-cut scenes in my poetry and in some of my short stories. I find that I use a rapid, speedy approach to almost all of my writing, including my essays, unless they have been heavily researched.

"Like many writers, I find the writing process to be both terribly demanding and exhilarating. I find it hard to start writing a short story, for instance, but once into it, I want to get it done. At the same time, I know I can't cut corners. My last long story ended up as a 31-page manuscript. I had in mind a 15-page story, but I knew that would not do justice to the subject. I started another story months ago and because I know it will be long, have not returned to it. I am spending time reading in its place. I have far too many unpublished stories. I need someone to take away all distractions, to give me time at a writers' colony, and force me to do it.

"I have been most inspired by the really good writing students I have had, especially Tracy Harris, and by Charles Olson and Michael Anania, both poets. I have been inspired in my fiction by experimental fiction writers and by the best of the young adult authors, like Robert Cormier and Francesca Lia Block. I have started such a book but, again, it is sitting undone.

"I won my first award when I was 15. I haven't looked back. One way or another, I plan to write until I die."

BIOGRAPHICAL/CRITICAL SOURCES:

PERIODICALS

Chicago Tribune, June 28, 1988.

*   *   *

JEFFERSON, Alan 1921-

PERSONAL: Born March 20, 1921, in Surrey, England; son of H. E. and Dorothy (Clark) Jefferson; married Elisabeth Ann Grogan (a dancer), 1944 (divorced, 1949); married Joan Pamela Bailey (a singer), July 22, 1955 (divorced, 1976); married Antonia Raebur (an artist and author), 1976; children: (first marriage) one son; (second marriage) two sons, one daughter; (third marriage) two sons. *Education:* Attended Rydal School 1935-37, and Old Vic Theatre School, 1947-48.

ADDRESSES: c/o The Society of Authors, 84 Drayton Gardens, London, SW10 9SB, England.

CAREER: Stage manager and producer in theaters in London and Stratford-on-Avon, England, 1948-54;

worked for various advertising agencies in London, 1954-62, and for Shell-Mex and B. P. Ltd., London, 1962-66; London Symphony Orchestra, London administrator, 1967-68; British Broadcasting Corp. (BBC), London, orchestral and concerts manager, 1968-73; Guildhall School of Music and Drama, professor of vocal interpretation, 1967-74; deputy registrar of births and deaths, 1974-84; full-time author, music reviewer, 1984—. *Military service:* British Army, 1939-46, served in Duke of Cornwall's Light Infantry, Reconnaissance Corps, and Parachute Regiment; became captain.

MEMBER: Richard Strauss Society of Great Britain, Parachute Regimental Association.

WRITINGS:

The Operas of Richard Strauss in Great Britain: 1910-1963, Putnam (New York City), 1964.
The Leider of Richard Strauss, Praeger (New York City), 1971.
Delius, Octagon (New York City), 1972.
The Life of Richard Strauss (biography), David & Charles (North Pomfret, VT), 1973.
Inside the Orchestra, Reid , 1974.
Strauss, Macmillan (New York City), 1975.
The Glory of Opera, Putnam, 1976.
Sir Thomas Beecham: A Centenary Tribute, Macdonald & Jane's (London), 1979.
The Complete Gilbert and Sullivan Opera Guide, Webb & Bower (New York City), 1984.
Richard Strauss: Der Rosenkavalier, Cambridge University Press (New York City), 1986.
Assault of the Guns of Merville: D-Day and After, J. Murray, 1987.
Lotte Lehman: A Centenary Biography, Julia Macrae (New York City), 1988.
Elizabeth Schwarzkopf, Northeastern University Press (Boston), 1996.
The Attica Guide to Classical Music (CD Rom), Airtew Ltd. (Oxford, England), 1996.

Also music reviewer for British publications.

*   *   *

JENKINS, John (Robert Graham) 1928-

PERSONAL: Born June 20, 1928, in Pontypridd, Wales; son of J. Henry (in business) and Olwen

(Prys-Jones) Jenkins. *Education:* Cambridge University, B.A., 1950, M.A., 1955; University of Toronto, M.B.A., 1953; Harvard University, D.B.A., 1968; Oxford University, D.Phil., 1981.

ADDRESSES: Office—Fisher Graduate School of International Management, Monterey Institute of International Studies, 425 Van Buren St., Monterey, CA 93940.

CAREER: Marketing supervisor, Procter & Gamble of Canada, 1953-56; account executive, Foster Advertising, 1956-57; media director, McKim Advertising, 1957-59; director of market and media planning, Batten, Barton, Durstine & Osborn (Canada), 1959-62; director of marketing research, Canadian Television Network, 1962-64; Northeastern University, Boston, MA, associate professor of marketing, 1967-70; Wilfrid Laurier University, Waterloo, Ontario, dean of School of Business and Economics, 1970-74, professor of business administration, 1970-92, emeritus professor, 1992—; Monterey Institute of International Studies, profesor of international management, 1992—. Visiting scholar, Manchester Business School, 1975-76; visiting professor, University of Waikato, New Zealand, 1983, University of New South Wales, Australia, 1984, Monterey Institute of International Studies, 1985-86, and Huazhong University, People's Republic of China, 1989. Appointed public member of Advertising Standards Council, Canadian Advertising Federation, 1988—.

MEMBER: Academy of International Business, International Council for Small Business, Administrative Sciences Association of Canada, American Academy of Advertising, American Marketing Association (former vice president, Boston chapter).

WRITINGS:

(With J. J. Zif) *Planning the Advertising Campaign* (player's manual and instructor's guide; business simulation game), Macmillan (New York City), 1971.

Marketing and Customer Behavior, Pergamon (Elmsford, NY), 1973.

(With Robert D. Wilson) *Planning the Advertising Campaign: A Canadian Simulation Game* (player's manual and instructor's guide), Collier Macmillan (Canada), 1983.

(Editor with Walter B. Herbert) *Public Relations in Canada: Some Perspectives,* Fitzhenry & Whiteside, 1984.

Jura Separatism in Switzerland, Clarendon Press (Oxford, England), 1985.

(With Hugh F. Dow) *Canadplan,* Ginn (Lexington, MA), 1994.

Contributor to *Marketing Management,* Wiley, 1976, and *Advertising in Canada,* McGraw-Hill Ryerson, 1980. Author of over forty cases and over fifty research articles and papers. Also contributor to numerous academic and professional journals.

K

KAHANE, Claire 1935-

PERSONAL: Surname originally Katz; name legally changed in 1974; born February 18, 1935, in New York, NY; daughter of Max (a retailer) and Diana (a housewife; maiden name, Rubinstein) Katz; married Ronald Hauser (a professor), February 14, 1976; children: Lukas. *Education:* City College (now of the City University of New York), B.A. (cum laude), 1956; University of California, Berkeley, M.A., 1963, Ph.D., 1975.

ADDRESSES: Home—48 Woodward Ave., Buffalo, NY 14222. *Office*—Department of English, State University of New York at Buffalo, Buffalo, NY 14260. *E-mail*—ckahane@ubvms.cc.buffalo.edu.

CAREER: Queens College of the City University of New York, Flushing, NY, lecturer in English, 1963-64; Brooklyn College of the City University of New York, Brooklyn, NY, lecturer in English, 1964-66; University of San Francisco, San Francisco, CA, lecturer in English, 1969-71, 1972-73; University of California, Berkeley, associate lecturer, 1971-73; State University of New York at Buffalo, assistant professor, 1974-81, associate professor of English, 1981-94, professor of English, 1995—.

MEMBER: Modern Language Association of America.

WRITINGS:

(Editor, contributor, and author of introduction) *Psychoanalyse und das Unheimliche: Essays aus der amerikanischen Literaturkritik,* Bouvier Press, 1981.

(Editor with Charles Bernheimer) *In Dora's Case: Freud, Hysteria, Feminism,* Columbia University Press (New York City), 1985.

(Editor with Shirley Nelson Garner and Madelon Sprengnether; and contributor) *The M/Other Tongue: Essays in Feminist Psychoanalytic Interpretation,* Cornell University Press (Ithaca, NY), 1985.

Passions of the Voice: Hysteria, Narrative and the Figure of the Speaking Woman, 1850-1915, John Hopkins University Press (Baltimore, MD), 1995.

Also contributor to a number of books, including *The Female Gothic,* edited by Juliann Fleenor, Eden Press, 1983; *Critical Essays on Flannery O'Connor,* edited by Beverly Lyon Clark and Melvin J. Friedman, G. K. Hall, 1985; and *Feminism and Psychoanalysis,* edited by Richard Feldstein and Judith Roof, Cornell University Press, 1989. Contributor of articles and reviews to periodicals, including *Studies in American Fiction, Literature and Psychology, Centennial Review, Massachusetts Review, American Literature,* and *Journal of English and German Philology.*

WORK IN PROGRESS: Geographies of Loss: Mourning, Writing, and the Spaces of Recuperation.

SIDELIGHTS: Claire Kahane told *CA:* "Both feminism and psychoanalysis were empowering systems of thought in my life. They also became the means by which I engage literary texts."

KAISER, Daniel H. 1945-

PERSONAL: Born July 20, 1945, in Philadelphia, PA; son of Walter Christian (a farmer and carpenter) and Estelle Evelyn (a homemaker; maiden name, Jaworsky) Kaiser; married Jonelle Marie Marwin, August 10, 1968; children: Nina Marie, Andrew Eliot. *Education:* Wheaton College, Wheaton, IL, A.B., 1967; University of Chicago, A.M., 1970, Ph.D., 1977; also attended Moscow State University, 1974. *Religion:* Presbyterian.

ADDRESSES: Home—1433 Main St., Grinnell, IA 50112. *Office*—Department of History, Grinnell College, P.O. Box 805, Grinnell, IA 50112-0806; fax 515-269-4985. *E-mail*—kaiser@ac.grin.edu.

CAREER: King's College, Briarcliff Manor, NY, instructor in history, 1968-71; Trinity College, Deerfield, IL, assistant professor of history, 1971-73; University of Chicago, Chicago, IL, visiting assistant professor of history, 1977-78; Grinnell College, Grinnell, IA, assistant professor, 1979-84, associate professor, 1984-87, professor of history, 1987—, Joseph F. Rosenfield Professor of Social Studies, 1984—. Darwin College, Cambridge University, England, research associate in Slavonic studies, and visiting member, 1992-93; University of California, Los Angeles, visiting professor of Slavonic language and literature, 1996.

MEMBER: American Historical Association, American Association for the Advancement of Slavic Studies, Early Slavic Studies Association (vice-president; president-elect, 1995-97), Eighteenth Century Russian Studies Association, Study Group for Eighteenth-Century Russia, Medieval Slavic Study Group (UK).

AWARDS, HONORS: John Nicholas Brown Prize from Medieval Academy of America, 1984, for *The Growth of the Law in Medieval Russia.*

WRITINGS:

The Growth of the Law in Medieval Russia, Princeton University Press (Princeton, NJ), 1980.
(Editor) *The Workers' Revolution in Russia,* Cambridge University Press (New York City), 1987.
(Translator) *The Laws of Russia, Tenth to Fifteenth Centuries,* Charles Schlacks, 1992.
(Editor with Gary Marker) *Reinterpreting Russian History 860-1860,* Oxford University Press (New York City), 1994.

WORK IN PROGRESS: Family Life in Early Modern Russia; City Life in Early Modern Russia.

SIDELIGHTS: Daniel H. Kaiser told *CA:* "*The Workers' Revolution in Russia* differs from most such books by emphasizing the social legitimacy of Bolshevik political success in the cities of Russia. As such, the book corrects the image dominant in both American scholarly and popular opinion that in some fundamental way the Bolsheviks usurped power.

"Certainly there were many places in the Russian Empire where Bolshevism was unwelcome, but it is equally true—and less well known—that there were many places where Bolsheviks were very welcome, and this book attempts to tell that story for the general reader.

"My chief interest, however, continues to be in early Russia, to which I was drawn long ago. My present work on family life derives from my first book in which I discovered a legal system suitable for a social system quite different from that normally depicted in the histories of Russia. There was, for example, almost no trace of a 'court' in the sense in which we normally understand that term; most justice depended exclusively upon the initiative of the aggrieved parties. In cases of homicide, they could practice revenge or exact compensation; in cases of property loss, the victims sought compensation directly from the responsible party. But the available materials say very little about the social structure that undergirded this legal system, although historians have fashioned some very detailed descriptions of early Russian society. The available materials do not permit, however, a serious examination of any of the fundamental social units of early Russia, so I turned my attention to the sixteenth and seventeenth centuries, employing methodologies developed for family history in early modern Europe. In many respects the sources are still wanting (in comparison with French and English parish registers, for example), but I have been able to collect a substantial body of testaments and dowry contracts together with other related materials in order to write a history of family life in this period.

"Of course, these themes are by their very nature of interest whether the time is the sixteenth or twentieth century, and I continue to spend considerable time reading not only about family life in other parts of the world but especially about family life in the contemporary U.S.S.R. One of the chief concerns of family historians has been to determine whether and when a significant change in family life took place. In Russia this issue becomes especially important immediately on the heels of the 1917 Revolution, so that a historian can follow the development of this issue all the way through the historical process. As a result, we learn a good deal not only about Russian family life, but about the way that family life affects each of us."

*   *   *

KAMINSKY, Stuart M(elvin)   1934-

PERSONAL: Born September 29, 1934, in Chicago, IL; son of Leo and Dorothy (Zelac) Kaminsky; married Merle Gordon, August 30, 1959; married Enid Lisa Perll, January 7, 1986; children: (first marriage) Peter Michael, Toby Arthur, Lucy Irene; (second marriage) Natasha Melisa Perll. *Education:* University of Illinois, B.S., 1957, M.A., 1959; Northwestern University, Ph.D., 1972. *Avocational interests:* Athletics (especially basketball and football), reading detective fiction and media history/criticism.

ADDRESSES: Home—7644 North Keduale, Skokie, IL 60016. *Office*—Northwestern University School of Speech, Evanston, IL 60201. *Agent*—Dominick Abel Literary Agency, Inc., 498 West End Ave., New York, NY 10024.

CAREER: University of Illinois at Urbana-Champaign, Champaign, science writer, 1962-64; University of Illinois at Chicago, medical writer, 1965-68; University of Michigan, Ann Arbor, editor of News Service, 1968-69; University of Chicago, director of public relations and assistant to the vice-president for public affairs, 1969-72; Northwestern University, Evanston, IL, assistant professor, 1973-75, associate professor of speech, 1975-79, professor of radio, television and film and head of Film Division, 1979—. Chicago Film Festival, chair, 1972-74, board member, 1974-75; member of film and creative arts panel, Illinois Arts Council, 1978—; consultant, National Endowment for the Humanities. *Military service:* U.S. Army, 1957-59.

MEMBER: International Crime Writers Association, Writers Guild of America, Private Eye Writers of America, Mystery Writers of America, Popular Culture Association of America, Society for Cinema Studies.

AWARDS, HONORS: Edgar Award nomination, Mystery Writers of America, 1984, for *Black Knight in Red Square;* Edgar Award, Mystery Writers of America, 1989, for *A Cold Red Sunrise.*

WRITINGS:

MYSTERY NOVELS

Bullet for a Star, St. Martin's (New York City), 1977.
Murder on the Yellow Brick Road, St. Martin's, 1978.
You Bet Your Life, St. Martin's, 1979.
The Howard Hughes Affair, St. Martin's, 1980.
Never Cross a Vampire, St. Martin's, 1980.
Death of a Dissident, Ace Books/Charter Books, 1981, reprinted, Armchair Detective Library, 1991.
High Midnight, St. Martin's, 1981.
Catch a Falling Clown, St. Martin's, 1982.
He Done Her Wrong: A Toby Peters Mystery, St. Martin's, 1983.
When the Dark Man Calls (also see below), St. Martin's, 1983.
The Fala Factor, St. Martin's, 1984.
Black Night in Red Square, Charter Books, 1984.
Down for the Count, G. K. Hall (Boston, MA), 1985.
Red Chameleon, Scribner, 1985.
Exercise in Terror, St. Martin's, 1985.
Smart Moves, St. Martin's, 1986.
The Man Who Shot Lewis Vance, St. Martin's, 1986.
Think Fast, Mr. Peters, St. Martin's, 1987.
A Fine, Red Rain, Scribner, 1987.
A Cold Red Sunrise, Scribner, 1988.
Buried Caesars, Mysterious Press, 1989.
Poor Butterfly, Mysterious Press, 1990.
The Man Who Walked Like a Bear: A Porfiry Rostnikov Novel, Scribner, 1990.
Lieberman's Folly, St. Martin's, 1991.
The Melting Clock, Mysterious Press, 1991.
Rostnikov's Vacation: An Inspector Porfiry Rostnikov Novel, Scribner, 1991.
Death of a Russian Priest, Fawcett Columbine, 1992.
The Devil Met a Lady, Mysterious Press, 1993.
Lieberman's Choice, St. Martin's, 1993.
Lieberman's Day, Holt, 1994.
Hard Currency, Fawcett Columbine, 1995.
Lieberman's Thief, Holt, 1995.
Tomorrow Is Another Day, Mysterious Press, 1995.
Dancing in the Dark, Mysterious Press, 1996.

OTHER

Here Comes the Interesting Part (one-act play), first produced in New York City at New York Academy of Arts and Sciences, 1968.

Don Siegel, Director (biography), Curtis Books, 1974.

American Film Genres: Approaches to a Critical Theory of Popular Film (textbook), Pflaum/Standard (Fairfield, NJ), 1974, 2nd revised edition, Nelson-Hall (Chicago, IL), 1984.

Clint Eastwood (biography), New American Library, 1975.

(Editor with Joseph F. Hill) *Ingmar Bergman: Essays in Criticism,* Oxford University Press, 1976.

John Huston: Maker of Magic (biography), Houghton (Boston), 1978.

Coop: The Life and Legend of Gary Cooper (biography), St. Martin's, 1980.

(With Dana Hodgdon) *Basic Filmmaking* (textbook), Arco, 1981.

(With Jeffrey Mahan) *American Television Genres* (textbook), Nelson-Hall, 1985.

Writing for Television, Dell, 1988.

Also author of dialogue for the film *Once upon a Time in America,* 1984; author of story and screenplay for the film *Enemy Territory,* 1987; author of screenplay for the film *A Woman in the Wind,* 1988. Contributor to books, including *Hal in the Classroom,* edited by Ralph Amelio, Pflaum/Standard, 1976; *Graphic Violence on the Screen,* edited by Thomas Atkins, Simon & Schuster, 1976; and *Science Fiction Film,* edited by Atkins, Simon & Schuster, 1976. Contributor to cinema journals and other magazines, including *The Man from U.N.C.L.E. Magazine, Positif, Take One, Journal of Popular Film, Journal of the Literary Imagination, Wooster Review,* and *New Mexico Quarterly.*

ADAPTATIONS: When the Dark Man Calls was adapted as a film entitled *Frequence Meurtre* for Geuville Pictures in 1988.

SIDELIGHTS: A film historian and head of the Radio/Television/Film Department at Northwestern University in Illinois, Stuart M. Kaminsky is best known for his mystery novels featuring detective Toby Peters. The Peters books, including *Murder on the Yellow Brick Road, Catch a Falling Clown,* and *Think Fast, Mr. Peters,* involve famous real-life characters (often of Hollywood renown) in fictional situations during the 1930s and 1940s. Kaminsky uses his vast knowledge of the time period to fill his books with nostalgic references to things past, such

as Beechnut Gum and the *Dagwood and Blondie* radio show. Concerning his interest in radio, television, and film history, the author once told *CA:* "I am interested in fostering a concern for serious study of those aspects of our cultural life which are seldom considered seriously. I think our objects of nostalgia and entertainment merit serious attention."

In a review of *Catch a Falling Clown, Los Angeles Times* book editor Art Seidenbaum remarks that "the fun of Kaminsky comes in dollops of nostalgia and sometimes drops of literary insights." *Catch a Falling Clown* concerns a series of murders at a circus. The famous clown Emmett Kelley is portrayed as Toby Peters's client, while one of the suspects is none other than Alfred Hitchcock. Other novels by Kaminsky feature film stars like Mae West, in *He Done Her Wrong,* and Judy Garland, in *Murder on the Yellow Brick Road.* Well-known names like Howard Hughes, Joe Louis, Albert Einstein, and Salvador Dali also become victims of plots against their lives or reputations in the Peters novels.

Remarking on the author's characters, Seidebaum believes that "Kaminsky creates people who perform a nice balancing act, between sympathy and cynicism," adding that the author's portrayal of Emmett Kelley is "credible and engaging." *New York Times Book Review* critic Newgate Callendar, however, thinks that "Kaminsky is too obvious in his nostalgia kick." Margaret Cannon also objects to the author's frequent use of trivia. In a *Globe and Mail* article, Cannon says that Kaminsky "has a talent for nicely developed plot, but he buries it under in-group jokes and period references." Conversely, in a review of *Poor Butterfly* for *Publishers Weekly,* a critic concludes that the "frightful, madly comic and nostalgic incidents [are] made believable and entertaining in Kaminsky's artful handling."

Although Kaminsky is better known for his books which have Peters as the main character, he has written a series of novels about Russian inspector Porfiry Rostnikov, too, including *Death of a Dissident, Red Chameleon,* and *A Cold Red Sunrise.* It is the Rostnikov series that has established Kaminsky's literary reputation, winning him a coveted Edgar Award for best mystery novel in 1989 for *A Cold Red Sunrise.* Reviewers have found particularly praiseworthy Kaminsky's depiction of the vagaries of police work in a Russia that has changed its political stripes over the past decades. Rostnikov not only has to solve baffling murders in such far-flung locales as Moscow and Siberia, he also has to answer to bureaucratic bosses, sidestep the KGB, and struggle to get a broken toilet repaired. A wounded veteran of World War II, he likes American mystery novels and weight-lifting, and he is an apolitical pragmatist. According to a *Virginia Quarterly Review* contributor, "the murky and constantly shifting moral ground of contemporary Russia is a perfect background for Kaminsky's detective Porfiry Rostnikov." Likewise, *Washington Post Book World* correspondent Jean M. White notes that the author "has staked a claim to a piece of the Russian turf. His stories are laced with fascinating tidbits of Russian history. He captures the Russian scene and character in rich detail."

Chicago Tribune Books correspondent Anthony Olcott cites Kaminsky's Rostnikov books for staking a claim "on a rich virgin territory for mysteries, a kind of 87th Precinctski crammed with maniacs, cowards, heroes and just plain oddities." The critic adds: "Kaminsky draws his Soviet police force as the sort of place where Rostnikov can use virtually any sleuthing tricks he wishes to, provided it will help to solve his case; yet when his tactics succeed and justice is done, jail yawns as wide for him as for the bad guys. Even by itself this marriage of the hard-boiled genre and the police procedural would be a clever stroke, because of the fresh and funny possibilities it presents." In a *Booklist* review of *Death of a Russian Priest*, Peter Robertson concludes: "Kaminsky's pacing never falters, but it is his richly layered characterizations and surprising twists of plot that have been the shining jewels in this justly acclaimed series."

Comfortable in many genres, Kaminsky has written screenplays, textbooks, and biographies. Regarding his writing in general, he once told *CA*: "In my fiction writing, I am particularly interested in avoiding pretension. In my nonfiction, I am particularly concerned with being provocative and readable."

BIOGRAPHICAL/CRITICAL SOURCES:

BOOKS

Contemporary Literary Criticism, Volume 59, Gale (Detroit), 1992.

PERIODICALS

Armchair Detective, Volume XIII, 1980, pp. 338-341.
Booklist, November 15, 1988, p. 542; May 15, 1990, p. 1783; July, 1992, p. 1923.
Chicago Tribune Books, June 24, 1990, p. 5.

Christian Science Monitor, August 4, 1989, pp. 12-13.
Globe and Mail (Toronto), April 11, 1987; April 9, 1988.
Los Angeles Times, January 20, 1982.
Los Angeles Times Book Review, December 2, 1979, p. 3.
New Yorker, October 12, 1987, p. 146.
New York Times Book Review, April 22, 1979; December 22, 1991, p. 21.
Publishers Weekly, October 4, 1985, p. 70; October 28, 1988, p. 64; April 13, 1990, p. 57; April 27, 1990, p. 55.
Virginia Quarterly Review, spring, 1992, p. 60.
Washington Post Book World, December 18, 1988, p. 8.

*   *   *

KAPLAN, William   1957-

PERSONAL: Born May 24, 1957, in Toronto, Ontario, Canada; son of Igor (a lawyer) and Cara (Cherniak) Kaplan; married Susan Mardane Krever (an editor), July 8, 1985. *Education:* University of Toronto, B.A. (with honors), 1980, M.A., 1985; Osgoode Hall Law School, LL.B., 1983; Stanford Law School, J.S.D., 1985. *Religion:* Jewish.

ADDRESSES: Office—Faculty of Law, University of Ottawa, 550 Cumberland St., Ottawa, Ontario K1N 6N5, Canada; 70 Bond St., Suite 200, Toronto, Ontario M5B 1X3, Canada; fax 416-365-7702. *E-mail*—wkaplan@io.org. *Agent*—Westwood Creative Artists, 10 St. Mary St., Toronto, Ontario M4Y 1P9, Canada.

CAREER: University of Ottawa, Faculty of Law, Ottawa, Ontario, assistant professor, 1986-91, associate professor, 1991— (on leave beginning 1995), associate director of graduate studies in law, 1993-94; arbitrator and mediator in private practice, 1995—. Faculty editor of *Ottawa Law Review,* 1987-89. Barrister and solicitor.

MEMBER: Association of Canadian Law Teachers, Canadian Civil Liberties Association, Canadian Committee for the History of the Second World War, Law Society of Upper Canada, Ontario Labour Management Arbitrator's Association.

AWARDS, HONORS: Osgoode Society Fellowship, 1989-90.

WRITINGS:

Everything That Floats: Pat Sullivan, Hal Banks and the Seamen's Unions of Canada, University of Toronto Press (Toronto), 1987.

State and Salvation: The Jehovah's Witnesses and their Fight for Civil Rights, University of Toronto Press, 1989.

Bad Judgment: The Case of Mr. Justice Leo Landreville, University Press and The Osgoode Society (Toronto), 1995.

Contributor to books, including *Belonging: The Meaning and Future of Canadian Citizenship,* McGill-Queen's University Press (Montreal and Kingston), 1993.

EDITOR

(With Dean Beeby) *Moscow Despatches: Inside Cold War Russia,* Lorimer (Toronto), 1987.

(With Jeffrey Sack and Morley Gunderson) *Labor Arbitration Yearbook* (Volumes I-IV), Butterworths (Toronto), 1991-93, Volume V, Lancaster House (Toronto), 1995.

(With Donald McRae; and contributor) *Law Policy and International Justice: Essays in Honour of Maxwell Cohen,* McGill-Queen's University Press, 1993.

OTHER

Also contributor to *"English Canada" Speaks Out,* edited by J. L. Granatstein and Kenneth McNaught, Doubleday Canada, 1991. Contributor of articles and book reviews to law and history journals, including *Australian-Canadian Studies, Canadian Bar Review, Canadian Historical Review, Stanford Journal of International Law, Ottawa Law Review,* and *Policy Options.*

BIOGRAPHICAL/CRITICAL SOURCES:

PERIODICALS

Globe and Mail (Toronto), February 15, 1988.

* * *

KEARNS, Doris Helen
   See GOODWIN, Doris (Helen) Kearns

KELLEHER, Catherine McArdle   1939-
   (Catherine McArdle)

PERSONAL: Born January 19, 1939, in Boston, MA; daughter of Francis X. and Catherine (Roche) McArdle; married James J. Kelleher, 1966; children: Michael, Diane. *Education:* Mount Holyoke College, A.B., 1960; attended Free University of Berlin, 1960-61; Massachusetts Institute of Technology, Ph.D., 1967.

ADDRESSES: Office—United States Mission to the North Atlantic Treaty Organization, PSC 81, Box 150, APO AE 09724.

CAREER: Columbia University, Barnard College, New York, NY, assistant professor of political science, 1967-69; University of Illinois at Chicago Circle, Chicago, assistant professor, 1969-71, associate professor of political science, 1972-73; University of Michigan, Ann Arbor, associate professor of political science, 1973-78; University of Denver, Denver, CO, professor of international studies, 1979-83; National War College, Washington, DC, professor of military strategy, 1980-82; University of Maryland at College Park, professor of public policy, 1982-91, director of Center for International Security Studies, 1985-91; Brookings Institute, senior fellow, 1990-94, personal advisor in Europe to the U.S. Secretary of Defense, 1995—; defense advisor to the U.S. Ambassador to NATO, 1995—.

Research associate at Columbia University, 1967-69, Harvard University, 1969-70, and Institute for Social Research, 1973-78; fellow of International Institute for Strategic Studies, London, England, 1975-76; member of staff of National Security Council, 1977-78; member of research council of Centre d'Etudes et Recherches sur l'Armee, of the Committee for International Security and Arms Control, and of the advisory board of National Security Archives, WGBH Nuclear Era Project, Institute for Peace at Notre Dame University; director of Maryland International Security Project. Consultant to National Defense University, National Security Council, Office of Secretary of Defense, Arms Control and Disarmament Agency, U.S. Information Agency, Brookings Institution, Ford Foundation, and the MacArthur Foundation.

MEMBER: International Institute for Strategic Studies, Women in International Security (founder and board member), Hesse Foundation for Peace and

Conflict Research, Council on Foreign Relations, and Committee for National Security.

AWARDS, HONORS: Fulbright fellow, 1960-61; Ford Foreign Area Fellowship, 1961-67; fellow at Institute for War and Peace Studies, Columbia University, 1967-69, and Center for West European Studies, Harvard University, 1969-70; fellow of Council on Foreign Relations, 1976-77, and North Atlantic Treaty Organization (NATO), 1980-82; D.Litt. from Mount Holyoke College, 1980; Ford Foundation grant, 1981-85; diploma from National War College, 1981; Kistiakowsky fellow, American Academy of Arts and Sciences, 1988-89; visiting fellow, All Souls College, Oxford, 1992; National Defense Education Act Fellowship.

WRITINGS:

(With Norman Padelford) *The Financing of Future Peace and Security Operations Under the United Nations,* Center for International Studies, Massachusetts Institute of Technology (Cambridge, MA), 1962.

(Under name Catherine McArdle) *The Role of Military Assistance in the Problems of Arms Control: The Middle East, Latin America, and Africa,* Center for International Studies, Massachusetts Institute of Technology, 1963, revised edition, 1964.

The Nature of Political-Military Gaming, Deutsche Gesellschaft fuer Auswaertige Politik, 1965.

(With Warren R. Schilling and others) *American Arms and a Changing Europe,* Columbia University Press (New York City), 1973.

Germany and the Politics of Nuclear Weapons, Columbia University Press, 1975.

Germany, Nuclear Weapons, and Alliance Relations, 1954-1966, Columbia University Press, 1975.

Weapons, Verification Issues and Global Security, United Nations Department for Disarmament (New York City), 1988.

The Future of European Security: An Interim Assessment, The Brookings Institution (Washington, D.C.), 1995.

EDITOR

Political-Military Systems: Comparative Perspectives, Sage Publications (Beverly Hills, CA), 1974.

(With Betty A. Nesvold) *SETUPS II: Cross-National and World Politics* (9 volumes), APSA (Washington, D.C.), 1976-78.

(With Wolf Dieter Eberwein; also contributor) *Sicherheit: Zum welchem Preis?* (title means "Security: At What Price?"), Olzog Verlag, 1983.

(With Frank Kerr and George Quester) *Nuclear Deterrence: New Risks, New Opportunities,* Pergamon-Brassey (New York City), 1986.

(With Gale A. Mattox, and contributor) *Evolving European Defense Policies,* Heath (Lexington, MA), 1987.

(With Leokadia Drobizheva, Rose Gottemoeller, and Lee Walker) *Ethnic Conflict in the Post-Soviet World,* M. E. Sharpe (Armonk, NY), 1996.

(With Lawrence Freedman Jane M. O. Sharp) *The Treaty on Conventional Forces in Europe: The Politics of Post-Wall Arms Control,* Nomos Verlagsgesellschaft (Baden-Baden, Germany), in press.

OTHER

Also contributor to many books on arms, arms control, military strategy and international relations, including *Non-Nuclear Conflicts in the Nuclear Age,* edited by Sam C. Sarkesian, Praeger, 1980; *The Art and Practice of Military Strategy,* edited by George E. Thibault, National Defense University Press, 1984; *Nuclear Winter, Deterrence, and the Prevention of Nuclear War,* edited by Peter C. Sederberg, Praeger, 1986; *The Future of Nuclear Weapons in Europe,* edited by Beatrice Heuser, Center for Defense Studies (London), 1991; and *Global Engagement: Cooperative Security in the 21st Century,* edited by Janne E. Nolan, The Brookings Institution, 1994. Contributor to political science and international studies journals, including *Brookings Review, Arms Control Today,* and *World Politics.* Member of editorial board of *Armed Forces and Society,* 1974—, *International Security,* 1979—, and *Information Studies Quarterly,* 1984—.

*   *   *

KELLMAN, Steven G.   1947-

PERSONAL: Born November 15, 1947, in Brooklyn, NY; son of Max (an electronics technician) and Pearl (an insurance broker; maiden name, Pomerantz) Kellman. *Education:* State University of New York at Binghamton, B.A. (summa cum laude), 1967; University of California at Berkeley, M.A., 1969, Ph.D., 1972.

ADDRESSES: Home—302 Fawn Dr., San Antonio, TX 78231-1519. *Office*—Division of Foreign Languages, University of Texas at San Antonio, San Antonio, TX 78285-0644.

CAREER: University of California, Berkeley, acting instructor in comparative literature, 1972; Bemidji State College (now University), Bemidji, MN, assistant professor of English, 1972-73; Tel-Aviv University, Tel-Aviv, Israel, lecturer in poetics and comparative literature, 1973-75; University of California, Irvine, visiting lecturer in English and comparative literature, 1975-76; University of Texas at San Antonio, assistant professor, 1976-80, associate professor, 1980-85, professor of comparative literature, 1985—, Ashbel Smith Professor, 1995—. Fulbright senior lecturer at Tbilisi State University, U.S.S.R., and at other Soviet institutions, 1980; visiting associate professor at University of California, Berkeley, 1982; Partners of the Americas lecturer in Peru, 1985. Member of numerous committees at University of Texas at San Antonio. Guest on television and radio programs; advisor and juror, CineFestival; moderator on Internet; workshop leader and guest speaker. Editorial consultant; consultant to Israel Institute for Poetics and Semiotics. Delegate to the Democratic national convention, 1992.

MEMBER: Popular Culture Association, American Culture Association, PEN American Center, National Book Critics Circle, Modern Language Association of America (Romance Literary Relations executive committee, 1988-93), National Society of Arts and Letters, South Central Modern Language Association (secretary of Comparative Literature Section, 1981-82, chair, 1982-83), PEN Center USA West.

AWARDS, HONORS: Ford Foundation special career fellow, 1967-72; Shrout Short Story Award, University of California, 1972; Danforth Teaching Associate, 1981-86; American Council of Learned Societies Travel Grant, 1984; National Book Critics Circle Citation nomination, 1984, 1990, 1992, 1993, 1994, 1996; Amoco Teaching Award, 1985-86; H. L. Mencken Writing Award, *Baltimore Sun,* 1986; first place award, San Antonio Sigma Delta Chi magazine column competition, 1987; President's Distinguished Achievement Award in Recognition of Research Excellence, University of San Antonio, 1990-91; study grant to China, Fulbright-Hays, 1995.

WRITINGS:

(Translator) Jean Anouilh, *Antigone,* first produced in New York by Gallery Players of Park Slope, March, 1979.
The Self-Begetting Novel, Columbia University Press (New York City), 1980.
(Editor) *Approaches to Teaching Camus's "The Plague,"* Modern Language Association of America (New York City), 1985.
Loving Reading: Erotics of the Text, Archon Books (Hamden, CT), 1985.
The Modern American Novel, Salem Press (Englewood Cliffs, NJ), 1991.
The Plague: Fiction and Resistance, Twayne (Boston), 1993.
(Editor) *Perspectives on Raging Bull,* G. K. Hall (New York City), 1994.

Contributor to many anthologies on literature and film, including *Critical Survey of Long Fiction,* edited by Walton Beacham, Salem Press 1983; *Film/Literature,* edited by George E. Toles, Mosaic, 1983; and *Winners of the Nobel Prize for Literature,* edited by Frank N. Magill, Salem Press, 1988. Contributor to *Dictionary of Literary Biography,* Volume 9, Gale, 1981; contributing editor, *Contemporary Authors,* Gale, 1987. Contributor of hundreds of articles, poems, stories, translations, and reviews to magazines and newspapers, including *Newsweek, USA Today, Nation, Saturday Review, Washington Post,* and *New Republic.* Translator of poetry, drama, and essays. Arts columnist and reviewer, for *San Antonio Light,* 1983—; film critic for *San Antonio Current,* 1986—. *Occident* magazine, member of editorial board, 1967-68, assistant editor, 1968-69, editor in chief, 1969-70, advisory editor, 1970-72; staff contributor to *Abstracts of English Studies,* 1971—; editorial secretary, *Poetics and Theory of Literature,* 1973-75; member of editorial board, *Newark Review,* 1982-85, and *Jewish Journal of San Antonio,* 1987—; literary scene editor, *USA Today* magazine, 1985—.

SIDELIGHTS: Steven G. Kellman once told *CA:* "*The Self-Begetting Novel* is an account of how so much of the most compelling fiction is a record of its own invention. All sentences are an attempt to reinvent the real, a further contribution to consciousness's vast reclamation project. Though I would not want Aeolus, the god of wind, as my patron, I would contribute to that project.

"I admit to writing for recognition, and what I recognize is the enormity of the task for both reader and writer. My weekly newspaper column has provided me the precious opportunity to discuss whatever in the arts and culture tackles my fancy. Whether I am writing for a deadline or for eternity, for a mass audience or for specialists, I dread the dead line. I suppose I write, like a prospector, for acclaim, but I am willing to settle for wisdom."

*   *   *

KENNEDY, Adrienne (Lita) 1931-

PERSONAL: Born September 13, 1931, in Pittsburgh, PA; daughter of Cornell Wallace (an executive secretary of the YMCA) and Etta (a teacher, maiden name, Haugabook) Hawkins; married Joseph C. Kennedy, May 15, 1953 (divorced, 1966); children: Joseph C., Adam Patrice. *Education:* Ohio State University, B.A., 1953; graduate study at Columbia University, 1954-56; also studied at New School for Social Research, American Theatre Wing, Circle in the Square Theatre School, and Edward Albee's workshop.

ADDRESSES: Home—New York, NY. *Office*—Department of Afro-American Studies, Princeton University, Princeton, NJ 08544. *Agent*—Bridget Aschenberg, 40 West 57th St., New York, NY 10019.

CAREER: Playwright. Yale University, New Haven, CT, lecturer, 1972-74; Princeton University, Princeton, NJ, lecturer, 1977; Brown University, Providence, RI, visiting associate professor, 1979-80; University of California, Berkeley, distinguished lecturer, 1980, 1986; Harvard University, Cambridge, MA, visiting lecturer, 1990-91; Signature Theatre Company, New York City, playwright-in-residence, 1995-96. Member of playwriting unit, Actors Studio, New York, 1962-65. International Theatre Institute representative, Budapest, 1978.

MEMBER: PEN (member of board of directors, 1976-77).

AWARDS, HONORS: Obie Award from *Village Voice,* 1964, for *Funnyhouse of a Negro;* Guggenheim memorial fellowship, 1967; Rockefeller grants, 1967-69, 1974, 1976; National Endowment for the Arts grant, 1973; CBS fellow, School of Drama, 1973; Creative Artists Public Service grant, 1974;

Yale fellow, 1974-75; Stanley Award for play writing; New England Theatre Conference grant; Manhattan Borough President's award, 1988, for *People Who Led to My Plays.*

WRITINGS:

PLAYS

Funnyhouse of a Negro (one-act; first produced Off-Broadway at Circle in the Square Theatre, 1962), Samuel French (New York City), 1969.

The Owl Answers (one-act; also see below), first produced in Westport, CT, at White Barn Theatre, 1963, produced Off-Broadway at Public Theatre, January 12, 1969.

A Lesson in a Dead Language, first produced in 1964.

A Rat's Mass, first produced in Boston, MA, by the Theatre Company, April, 1966, produced Off-Broadway at La Mama Experimental Theatre Club, November, 1969.

A Beast Story (one-act; also see below), first produced in 1966, produced Off-Broadway at Public Theatre, January 12, 1969.

(With John Lennon and Victor Spinetti) *The Lennon Play: In His Own Write* (adapted from Lennon's books *In His Own Write* and *A Spaniard in the Works;* first produced in London by National Theatre, 1967; produced in Albany, NY, at Arena Summer Theatre, August, 1969), Simon & Schuster (New York City), 1969.

Sun: A Poem for Malcolm X Inspired by His Murder, first produced on the West End, London, at Royal Court Theatre, 1968, produced in New York at La Mama Experimental Theatre Club, 1970.

Cities in Bezique (contains *The Owl Answers* and *A Beast Story;* first produced in New York at Shakespeare Festival, 1969), Samuel French, 1969.

Boats, first produced in Los Angeles at the Forum, 1969.

An Evening With Dead Essex, first produced in New York by American Place Theatre Workshop, 1973.

A Movie Star Has to Star in Black and White, first produced in New York by Public Theatre Workshop, 1976.

A Lancashire Lad (for children), first produced in Albany, NY, at Governor Nelson A. Rockefeller Empire State Plaza Performing Arts Center, May, 1980.

Orestes and Electra, first produced in New York at Juilliard School of Music, 1980.

Black Children's Day, first produced in Providence, RI, at Brown University, November, 1980.

Diary of Lights, first produced at City College in New York, June 5, 1987.

The Alexander Plays (contains *She Talks to Beethoven, The Ohio State Murders, The Film Club,* and *The Dramatic Circle*), University of Minnesota Press (Minneapolis), 1992.

Also author of *In One Act,* a collection of plays, and (with son, Adam Patrice Kennedy) *Sleep Deprivation Chamber,* a play. Contributor to numerous anthologies, including *New American Plays,* edited by William M. Hoffman, Hill & Wang (New York City), 1968; *New Black Playwrights,* edited by William Couch, Jr., Louisiana State University Press (Baton Rouge), 1968; *Kuntu Drama,* edited by Paul C. Harrison, Grove (New York City), 1974; and *Wordplay 3,* Performing Arts Journal (New York City), 1984. Contributor of plays to periodicals, including *Scripts 1.*

OTHER

People Who Led to My Plays (memoir), Knopf (New York City), 1987.

Deadly Triplets: A Theatre Mystery and Journal (novel), University of Minnesota Press, 1990.

ADAPTATIONS: Solo Voyages, an adaptation by Joseph Chaikin of three monologues from *The Owl Answers, A Rat's Mass,* and *A Movie Star Has to Star in Black and White,* was produced in New York and Washington, 1985.

SIDELIGHTS: "While almost every black playwright in the country is fundamentally concerned with realism . . . Miss [Adrienne] Kennedy is weaving some kind of dramatic fabric of poetry," Clive Barnes comments in the *New York Times.* "What she writes is a mosaic of feeling, with each tiny stone stained with the blood of the gray experience. Of all our black writers, Miss Kennedy is most concerned with white, with white relationship, with white blood. She thinks black, but she remembers white. It gives her work an eddying ambiguity."

In her complex and introspective plays, Martin Duberman remarks in *Partisan Review,* Kennedy is "absorbed by her private fantasies, her interior world. She disdains narrative, 'everyday' language and human interaction; the dream, the myth, the poem are her domain." James Hatch and Ted Shine also note that "in a tradition in which the major style

has long been realism, Adrienne Kennedy has done what few black playwrights have attempted: used form to project an interior reality and thereby created a rich and demanding theatrical style."

Kennedy's first play, *Funnyhouse of a Negro,* examines the psychological problems of Sarah, a young mulatto woman who lives with a Jewish poet in a boarding house run by a white landlady. Dealing with the last moments before Sarah's suicide, the play consists of scenes of the young woman's struggle with herself. Tortured by an identity crisis, Sarah is "lost in a nightmare world where black is evil and white is good, where various personages, including Queen Victoria, Patrice Lumumba, and Jesus Himself, materialize to mock her," says *New Yorker*'s Edith Oliver. *Funnyhouse of a Negro* earned Kennedy an Obie award, and, notes a *Variety* reviewer, a reputation as "a gifted writer with a distinctive dramatic imagination."

Oliver describes *The Owl Answers* as another fantasy of "a forbidden and glorious white world, viewed with a passion and frustration that shred the spirit and nerves and mind of the dispossessed heroine." The illegitimate child of a black cook and the wealthiest white man in Georgia, the heroine is riding on a New York subway. The subway doors become the doors to the chapel of the Tower of London through which appear masked historical characters, including Chaucer, Shakespeare, Anne Boleyn, and the Virgin Mary, who at times unmask to become other characters, such as the heroine's mother and father.

A Beast Story, produced with *The Owl Answers* under the title *Cities in Bezique,* was described as more elaborate, hallucinatory and obscure than the first play. It draws analogies, says Steve Tennen in *Show Business,* "between inhuman beings and man's bestial tendencies." Kennedy's later play, *A Rat's Mass,* staged as a parody mass, is also abstract, centering around the relationship between a black brother and sister and their childhood involvement with the white girl next door.

In all of these plays, Kennedy's writing is poetic and symbolic; plot and dialogue are secondary to effect. Her reliance on such devices as masks, characters who become other characters, characters played by more than one actor, and Christian symbolism makes her work difficult to understand, and her plays have been seen as both nightmarish rituals and poetic dances.

Marilyn Stasio explains in *Cue:* "Kennedy is a poet, working with disjointed time sequences, evocative images, internalized half-thoughts, and incantatory language to create a netherworld of submerged emotions surfacing only in fragments. Events are crucial only for the articulated feelings they evoke."

During 1971, Kennedy joined five other women playwrights to found the Women's Theatre Council, a theatre cooperative devoted to producing the works of women playwrights and providing opportunities for women in other aspects of the theatre, such as directing and acting. Mel Gussow of the *New York Times* notes that the council's "founding sisters all come from Off Off Broadway. . . . Each has a distinctive voice, but their work is related in being largely non-realistic and experimental. The women feel unified as innovators and by their artistic consciousness."

Kennedy branched out into juvenile theatre in 1980 after being commissioned by the Empire State Youth Theatre Institute. *A Lancashire Lad,* her first play for children, is a fictionalized version of Charles Chaplin's childhood. Narrated by the hero, the play traces his life growing up in Dickensian England and beginning his career in the British music halls. Although an entertaining musical, the show confronts the poverty and pain of Chaplin's youth. Praising Kennedy's language for achieving "powerful emotional effects with the sparest of means," *New York Times* reviewer Frank Rich concludes: "The difference between *A Lancashire Lad* and an adult play is, perhaps, the intellectual simplicity of its ambitions. Yet that simplicity can also be theater magic in its purest and most eloquent form."

During the latter half of the 1980s, Kennedy worked on a quartet of plays illuminating the life of a woman named Suzanne Alexander—a character several commentators believe is a fictionalized version of Kennedy herself. *She Talks to Beethoven, The Ohio State Murders, The Film Club,* and *The Dramatic Circle* were collected in 1992 under the title *The Alexander Plays.* According to *Theatre Journal* reviewer Nicole R. King, this collection of one-acts "will further [Kennedy's] brilliant reputation and characteristically introduce the theatre world to something altogether new."

In *The Ohio State Murders,* which some critics have singled out as the best of the Alexander plays, Suzanne recalls her tenure as a student at an Ohio college. Kennedy has often related that her years at Ohio State University during the early period of integration were an ordeal; in the play, Alexander summons up memories of trauma similar to Kennedy's, and worse. During the course of the drama, it is revealed that Alexander was seduced by a professor and gave birth to twins, who were later murdered. Years later, after becoming a successful writer, she returns to the college to lecture on the origins of her work's frequently violent imagery. King relates: "Typically, the answer is imbedded in the multiple experiences of violence, racism and emotional abuse." *She Talks to Beethoven, The Dramatic Circle,* and *The Film Club* show Alexander in England and Africa, where her husband mysteriously vanishes. There are references to various aspects of African and European culture, and the contrast between the two; through it all, the power of love and the fight against oppression provide the plays' grounding, critics observe.

King notes that while these plays are typical of Kennedy's work in that they are highly unconventional, they also "demonstrate a palpable shift in [her] creative style." There is little action, points out Rosemary Keefe Curb in *Belles Lettres;* instead, Suzanne is seen "waiting, dreading, hoping, remembering, and reading aloud from literature and letters. Since nothing happens in the dramatized present except a layering of voices, spectators must create a dramatic context."

Like all of Kennedy's best work, each of *The Alexander Plays* is "short and powerful," relates King. Kennedy's style in these plays is "no less powerful" but "markedly less frenetic" than in her previous efforts, King comments. The critic finds that many of Kennedy's trademark techniques, such as the use of striking and contrasting images, are present in *The Alexander Plays,* but they are used in fresh, startling ways. "For Kennedy fans," King summarizes, "the poignancy of this quartet will seem new although the multiple levels of consciousness and instability of time frame will not."

BIOGRAPHICAL/CRITICAL SOURCES:

BOOKS

Abramson, Doris E., *Negro Playwrights in the American Theatre, 1925-1959,* Columbia University Press (New York City), 1969.

Betsko, Kathleen, and Rachel Koenig, *Interviews with Contemporary Women Playwrights,* Beech Tree Books, 1987.

Black Literature Criticism, Gale (Detroit), Volume 2, 1992.

Bryant-Jackson, Paul K., and Lois More Overbeck, editors, *Intersecting Boundaries: The Theatre of Adrienne Kennedy,* University of Minnesota Press, 1992.

Cohn, Ruby, *New American Dramatists: 1960-1980,* Grove (New York City), 1982, pp. 95, 108-15.

Contemporary Authors Autobiography Series, Volume 20, Gale, 1994.

Contemporary Literary Criticism, Gale, Volume 66, 1991.

Dictionary of Literary Biography, Volume 38: *Afro-American Writers after 1955: Dramatists and Prose Writers,* Gale, 1985.

Drama Criticism, Volume 5, Gale, 1995.

Harrison, Paul Carter, *The Drama of Nommo,* Grove, 1972.

Hatch, James V., and Ted Shine, editors, *Black Theater U.S.A.,* Free Press (New York City), 1974.

Kintz, Linda, *The Subject's Tragedy: Political Poetics, Feminist Theory, and Drama,* University of Michigan Press (Ann Arbor), 1992.

Mitchell, Loften, *Black Drama,* Hawthorn Books, 1967.

Oliver, Clinton, and Stephanie Sills, *Contemporary Black Drama,* Scribner (New York City), 1971, pp. 189-205.

Schlueter, June, *Modern American Drama: The Female Canon,* Fairleigh Dickinson University Press (East Brunswick, NJ), 1990, pp. 172-83.

PERIODICALS

Belles Lettres, spring, 1989, p. 23; summer, 1993, pp. 49-50.

City Arts Monthly, February, 1982.

CLA Journal, December, 1976, pp. 235-44.

Cue, January 18, 1969; October 4, 1969.

Drama Review, December, 1977, pp. 41-48.

International Times, September 22, 1968.

Los Angeles Times Book Review, July 12, 1987.

Modern Drama, December, 1989, pp. 520-39.

Ms., June, 1987.

Multicultural Review, April, 1992, p. 76.

New Yorker, January 25, 1964, pp. 76-78; January 25, 1969.

New York Times, January 15, 1964; June 20, 1968; July 9, 1968; January 13, 1969, p. 26; January 19, 1969; November 1, 1969; February 22, 1972; May 21, 1980; February 15, 1981; September 11, 1985; September 20, 1985; January 27, 1991, p. CN12; July 25, 1995, pp. C13, C14.

New York Times Book Review, October 14, 1990, p. 48.

Observer Review, June 23, 1968.

Partisan Review, Number 3, 1969.

Show Business, January 25, 1969; October 4, 1969.

Studies in Black Literature, summer, 1975, pp. 1-5.

Theatre Journal, October, 1985, pp. 302-316; March, 1991, pp. 125-28; March, 1992, pp. 67-86; October, 1993, pp. 406-408.

Variety, January 29, 1969.

Village Voice, August 14, 1969; September 25, 1969; November 3, 1987, pp. 61, 65.

Voice Literary Supplement, October, 1990, p. 2.

Washington Post Book World, November 20, 1988, p. 12.

Women's Review of Books, October, 1987, pp. 14-15.*

* * *

KERCHEVAL, Jesse Lee 1956-

PERSONAL: Born July 27, 1956, in Fontainebleau, France; daughter of Edwin Gregory (an American army officer) and Mary (an American army officer; maiden name, Boggess) Beggs; married Dan Hughes Fuller (a photographer), June, 1984. *Education:* Florida State University, B.A., 1983; University of Iowa, M.F.A., 1986.

ADDRESSES: Home—Madison, WI. *Office*—Department of English, White Building, 600 N. Park St., University of Wisconsin—Madison, Madison, WI 53706. *Agent*—Gail Hochman, Brandt & Brandt, 1501 Broadway, New York, NY 10036.

CAREER: DePauw University, Greencastle, IN, assistant professor of English, 1986-87; University of Wisconsin—Madison, associate professor of English, 1987—.

AWARDS, HONORS: Literary award, Iowa Arts Council, 1986; short fiction award, Associated Writing Programs, 1987, for *The Dogeater;* Granville Hicks fellow at Yaddo Colony, 1987; James A. Michener fellow, Copernicus Society, 1987-88; creative writing fellow, National Endowment for the Arts, 1989; Mary Ingraham Bunting fellow, Bunting Institute, Harvard, 1989-91; creative writing fellow, Wisconsin Arts Board, 1991.

WRITINGS:

The Dogeater (stories), University of Missouri Press (Columbia, MO), 1987.
The Museum of Happiness (novel), Faber and Faber (Boston), 1993.

Work represented in anthologies, including *Twenty Under Thirty: Best Stories by America's New Young Writers,* edited by Debra Spark, Scribner, 1986; *Writing Fiction: A Guide to Narrative Craft,* edited by Janet Burroway, Little, Brown, 1986; *How We Live Now: Contemporary Multicultural Literature,* edited by John Repp, Bedford Books, 1992; *Sister to Sister: Women Write about the Unbreakable Bond,* edited by Patricia Foster, Anchor Books, 1995; and *New Stories From the South.* Contributor of stories, nonfiction, and poems to numerous magazines in the United States and abroad, including *American Short Fiction, Carolina Quarterly, Fiction, Indiana Review, London Magazine, Massachusetts Review, New England Review, Ohio Review, Ploughshares, Poetry Northwest, Poetry Wales, Prairie Schooner, Redbook, Stand,* and *Southern Review.*

WORK IN PROGRESS: Space, memoir, for Algonquin Press; *Plot and Structure in Fiction,* book on writing, for Story Press; *The History of the Church in America,* novel.

* * *

KNOBLAUCH, C(yril) H. 1945-

PERSONAL: Surname is pronounced "Knob-lock"; born October 5, 1945, in Minneapolis, MN; son of Cyril H. and Helen I. Knoblauch; married Lil Borop Brannon (a university professor), July 14, 1984. *Education:* College of St. Thomas, B.A., 1967; Brown University, M.A., 1969, Ph.D., 1973.

ADDRESSES: Home—30 Linda Lane, Niskayuna, NY 12309. *Office*—Dean of Arts and Sciences, State University of New York at Albany, Albany, NY 12222.

CAREER: Brown University, Providence, RI, instructor in English, 1972-74; Columbia University, New York City, assistant professor of English, 1974-79; New York University, New York City, assistant professor of English, 1979-82; State University of New York at Albany, Albany, associate professor,

1982-89, professor of English, 1992—, interim Dean of College of Arts and Sciences, 1995—. *Military service:* U.S. Army, 1969-71; became sergeant.

MEMBER: Modern Language Association of America, National Council of Teachers of English.

WRITINGS:

(With A. D. Van Nostrand) *Functional Writing,* Houghton (Boston), 1978.
(With Van Nostrand) *The Process of Writing: Discovery and Control,* Houghton, 1982.
(With wife, Lil Brannon) *Rhetorical Traditions and the Teaching of Writing,* Boynton Cook (Upper Montclair, NJ), 1984.
(With Brannon) *Critical Teaching and the Idea of Literacy,* Boynton Cook, 1994.

Contributor to literature and composition journals.

BIOGRAPHICAL/CRITICAL SOURCES:

PERIODICALS

New York Times, July 27, 1984.

* * *

KNOEPFLE, John   1923-

PERSONAL: Surname pronounced "Know-full"; born February 4, 1923, in Cincinnati, OH; son of Rudolph (a salesperson) and Catherine (Brickley) Knoepfle; married Margaret Godfrey Sower, December 26, 1956; children: John Michael, Mary Catherine, David Edmund, James Girard (deceased), Christopher Brickley. *Education:* Xavier University, Cincinnati, OH, Ph.B., 1947, M.A., 1949; St. Louis University, Ph.D., 1967. *Politics:* Democrat. *Religion:* Catholic.

ADDRESSES: Home—1008 West Adams, Auburn IL 62615.

CAREER: WCET (educational television), Cincinnati, OH, producer-director, 1953-55; College of Music, Cincinnati, lecturer, 1954-55; Ohio State University, Columbus, assistant instructor, 1956-57; Southern Illinois University, East St. Louis, lecturer, 1957-60; St. Louis University High School, St. Louis, MO, lecturer in English, 1961-62; Maryville

College of the Sacred Heart, St. Louis, MO, assistant professor of English, 1962-66; St. Louis University, St. Louis, MO, assistant professor, 1966-70, associate professor and director for creative writing, 1970-72; Sangamon State University, Springfield, IL, professor of literature, 1972-91. Also affiliated with Mark Twain Summer Institute, 1962-64, and Washington University College, 1963-66. Consultant to Project Upward Bound, 1966-70. *Military service:* U.S. Navy, 1943-46; became lieutenant junior grade; received Purple Heart.

MEMBER: Modern Language Association, American Studies Association.

AWARDS, HONORS: Rockefeller Foundation fellowship, 1967; National Endowment for the Art fellowship, 1980; Mark Twain Award, Society for the Study of Midwestern Literature, 1986, for distinguished contributions to Midwestern literature; Illinois Author of the Year, Illinois Association of Teachers of English, 1986; Illinois Arts Council fellowship, 1986; fellow, Springfield Area Arts Council, 1994; Illinois Literary Heritage Award, Center for the Book, 1995; Doctor of Humane Letters (honorary), Maryville University, 1996.

WRITINGS:

(Translator with James Wright and Robert Bly) *Twenty Poems of Cesar Vallejo,* Sixties Press, 1961, also published as *Neruda and Vallejo: Selected Poems,* Beacon Press (Boston), 1971.

Rivers into Islands, University of Chicago Press (Chicago), 1965.

An Affair of Culture and Other Poems, Juniper (New York City), 1969.

After Gray Days and Other Poems, Crabgrass Press, 1969.

Songs for Gail Guidry's Guitar, New Rivers Press (St. Paul, MN), 1969.

The Intricate Land, New Rivers Press, 1970.

Dogs and Cats and Things like That: A Book of Poems for Children, McGraw (New York City), 1971.

The Ten-Fifteen Community Poems, Back Door (Edmonds, WA), 1971.

Our Street Feels Good: A Book of Poems for Children, McGraw, 1972.

Whetstone: A Book of Poems, BkMk (Kansas City, MO), 1972.

Deep Winter Poems, Three Sheets, 1972.

Thinking of Offerings: Poems 1970-1973, Juniper, 1975.

A Box of Sandalwood: Love Poems, Juniper, 1978.

A Gathering of Voices, Rook, 1978.

(Editor with Dan Jaffe) *Frontier Literature: Images of the American West,* McGraw, 1979.

Poems for the Hours, Uzzano (Menomonie, WI), 1979.

Selected Poems, BkMk, 1985.

Poems from the Sangamon, University of Illinois Press (Champaign, IL), 1985, 2nd edition, 1995.

Dim Tales, Stormline Press, 1989.

Begging an Amnesty, Druid Press (Ephraim, WI), 1994.

The Chinkapin Oak Poems 1993-95, Rose Hill Press (Waynesboro, PA), 1995.

Also contributor of poems and essays to numerous anthologies, including *Poems at the Gate,* 1964; *Voyages to the Inland Sea,* edited by John Judson, Juniper, 1971; *Five Missouri Poets,* edited by Jim Barnes, Chariton Press, 1979; *A Reader's Guide to Illinois Literature,* Read Illinois Program, 1985; *Inheriting the Land: Contemporary Voices from the Midwest,* University of Minnesota Press, 1993; and *Gone to Croatan: Origins of North American Dropout Culture,* Autonomedia/AK Press, 1993. Contributor of poems, interviews, and articles to periodicals, including *Minnesota Review, Kansas Quarterly, The Spoon River Quarterly, Illinois Writers Review,* and *The Centennial Review.* Collector of "The Knoepfle Collection," fifty one-hour recordings of steamboat men of the inland rivers, Division of Inland Rivers, Public Library of Cincinnati and Hamilton County, 1954-60. Collector of "The Peoria-Miami Language Collection," copies of historical documents and records in an attempt to gather source materials for the meeting of three cultures: Central Algonquian, French-Metis, and Anglo-American, housed at Illinois State Museum, Dixon Mounds Museum, and with Miami and Peoria tribes of Oklahoma, 1996. Appearances in films, including *Inland Voyages: The Poetry of John Knoepfle,* produced by James Scott, 1995.

SIDELIGHTS: John Knoepfle's poetry speaks of his life in the Midwest. Midwestern poetry is rarely studied by modern critics, states Dan Jaffe in *Great Lakes Review;* Knoepfle, therefore, who "has been producing poems of enormous resonance," remains generally unknown.

Knoepfle, writes Jaffe, "does not write one or two kinds of poems. One of the indications of his strength is the variety of textures, attitudes, subjects, and tactics found in his poems. He can be cryptically epigrammatic, journalistically surreal, and religiously sardonic. So those sound like paradoxes? He is a landscape poet and a political poet. At times he searches our history and our folklore, at others creates nightmares. He is a poet of gentleness who probes the inhumane. He lays it out without comment in one poem; the next poem is a riddle. To be sure there is a Knoepfle personality, a quality of language and concern that marks all of the poems, but I hesitate to label it."

BIOGRAPHICAL/CRITICAL SOURCES:

PERIODICALS

Focus Midwest, number 14, 1980.
Great Lakes Review, number 3, 1976.
Minnesota Review, number 3, 1968.

OTHER

Inland Voyages: The Poetry of John Knoepfle (video), produced by James Scott, 1995.

*   *   *

KRISTOF, Nicholas D(onabet)   1959-

PERSONAL: Born April 27, 1959, in Chicago, IL; son of Ladis K. D. (a professor) and Jane (a professor; maiden name, McWilliams) Kristof; married Sheryl WuDunn (a journalist), 1988; children: Gregory, Geoffrey. *Education:* Harvard University, B.A., 1981; Oxford University, Law Degree, 1983; American University in Cairo, Arabic Language Diploma, 1984.

ADDRESSES: Office—New York Times, Foreign Desk, 229 West 43rd St., New York, NY 10036. *E-mail—* kristof@nytimes.com.

CAREER: New York Times, New York, NY, economics reporter, 1984-85, Los Angeles correspondent, 1985-86, Hong Kong bureau chief, 1986-87, Beijing bureau chief, 1988-93, Tokyo bureau chief, 1995—.

AWARDS, HONORS: Rhodes Scholar, 1983; Pulitzer Prize, 1990, for international reporting; Overseas Press Club Award, 1990, for foreign reporting; George Polk Award, 1990.

WRITINGS:

China Wakes: The Struggle for the Soul of a Rising Power, Times Books (New York City), 1994.

WORK IN PROGRESS: A children's book about two escaped slaves, set in the year 1858; research on Japan.

SIDELIGHTS: Nicholas D. Kristof told *CA:* "Since my student days, when I began to travel with a backpack around Africa and Asia, I have had a fascination with foreign lands, cultures, and languages. In Cairo I studied Arabic and exulted in meeting Bedouin camel herders. Then came the overwhelming experience of China, and now I'm exploring Japan with my wife and children."

*   *   *

KUEN, Alfred (F.) 1921-

PERSONAL: Born August 31, 1921, in Strasbourg, France; son of Albert (a painter) and Line (Kaetzel) Kuen; married Mimosa Schelterle, April 1, 1947; children: Daniel Paul, Nelly-Rose. *Education:* Ecole Normale, Strasbourg, teaching certificate; attended Institut Emmaus. *Religion:* Evangelical.

*ADDRESSES: Home and office—*Institut Emmaus, C.H. 1806, St. Legier, Switzerland.

CAREER: Teacher at teacher training school in Strasbourg, France, 1950-76; Institut Emmaus, St. Legier, Switzerland, teacher, 1976—. *Military service:* French Army, 1944-45.

AWARDS, HONORS: Chevalier and Officier des Palmes academiques.

WRITINGS:

Que tous soient un (title means "That All May Be One"), Edit. Litt. Bibl., 1964.
Je batirai mon Eglise, Emmaus, 1967, translation published as *I Will Build My Church,* Moody, 1971.
Le Bapteme, S.P.B., 1974.
Choeurs joyeux (songs), Ligue pour la Lecture de la Bible, 1975.
Comment etudier la Bible (title means "How to Study the Bible"), Ligue pour la Lecture de la Bible, 1976.

Comment lire la Bible (title means "How to Read the Bible"), Ligue pour la Lecture de la Bible, 1976.

Le Renouveau charismatique, Emmaus, 1977.

(Translator) *Parole vivante* (New Testament), Edit. Litt. Bibl., 1978.

Il faut que vous naissiez de nouveau, Ligue pour la Lecture de la Bible, 1978.

Le Saint-Esprit: Bapteme et plenitude, Emmaus, 1978.

L'Art de vivre selon Dieu: Concordance thematique du livre des proverbes (title means "The Art of Living According to God: Proverbs Clarified"), Emmaus, 1980.

Louanges pour notre temps (rhythmic translation of the Psalms), Edit. Litt. Bibl., 1980.

Pourquoi l'Englise?, Emmaus, 1981.

L'audace de la foi (biography of George Mueller; title means "Audacious Faith"), Emmaus, 1982.

Les Lettres de Paul: Introduction au Nouveau Testament (introduction to the Pauline Epistles), Emmaus, 1982.

Dons pour le service (title means "Gifts of Service"), Emmaus, 1982.

Sagesse et poesie pour notre temps (translation of the poetical books of the Old Testament), Edit. Litt. Bibl., 1982.

Se former pour mieux servir Dieu (title means "Training for the Ministry"), Emmaus, 1982.

Ministeres dans l'Eglise (title means "Ministries in the Church"), Emmaus, 1983.

Comment etudier (title means "How to Study"), Emmaus, 1986.

Oui a la musique (title means "Music in the Bible and the Church"), Emmaus, 1986.

Prophetes pour notre temps (translation of the prophetical books of the Bible, with introduction and notes), Edit. Litt. Bibl., 1987.

SIDELIGHTS: Alfred Kuen once told *CA:* "For many years, my writing was only a side activity. It is only since my retirement that I have been able to devote myself to writing, editing, and Bible teaching."

*   *   *

KUHN, Annette   1945-

PERSONAL: Born September 29, 1945, in London, England; daughter of Henry Philip Kuhn (a bus conductor) and Betty Saunders (a bus conductor); mar-

ried Brodnax Moore (divorced). *Ethnicity:* "Anglo-Saxon-Celtic." *Education:* University of Sheffield, B.A. (with honors), 1969, M.A., 1975; University of London, Ph.D., 1987.

ADDRESSES: Home—London, England; fax 0141-330-4142. *Office*—Department of Theatre Film and TV Studies, University of Glasgow, Glasgow G12 8QF, Scotland. *E-mail*—afk@arts.gla.ac.uk.

CAREER: University of Sheffield, Sheffield, England, independent research worker in sociology, 1969-73; University of London, Goldsmith's College, London, England, lecturer in sociology, 1974-77; freelance writer and teacher of film studies, 1977-88; University of Glasgow, Glasgow, Scotland, lecturer, beginning 1989, currently reader in film and TV studies. Visiting professor at University of Iowa and University of Wisconsin—Madison, 1979-80.

MEMBER: Society for Cinema Studies, Society of Authors.

AWARDS, HONORS: Economic and Social Research Council award.

WRITINGS:

Women's Pictures: Feminism and Cinema, Routledge & Kegan Paul (London), 1982, revised edition, Verso (New York City), 1995.

The Power of the Image: Essays on Representation and Sexuality, Routledge & Kegan Paul, 1985.

Cinema, Censorship and Sexuality, 1909-1925, Routledge & Kegan Paul, 1988.

Family Secrets: Acts of Memory and Imagination, Verso, 1995.

EDITOR

(With AnneMarie Wolpe) *Feminism and Materialism: Women and Modes of Production,* Routledge & Kegan Paul, 1978.

(With Michele Barrett, Philip Corrigan, and Janet Wolff) *Ideology and Cultural Production,* Croom Helm (London), 1979.

Women's Companion Guide to International Film, Virago, 1990.

Alien Zone: Cultural Theory and Contemporary Science Fiction Cinema, Verso, 1991.

Queen of the Bs: Ida Lupino Behind the Camera, Flicks Books, 1995.

OTHER

Contributor to magazines, including *Signs* and *Wide Angle. Screen,* member of editorial board, 1976-1985, coeditor, 1989—; member of editorial board, *Feminist Review,* 1977-80.

WORK IN PROGRESS: An historical study of cinema culture in Britain in the 1930s.

SIDELIGHTS: Annette Kuhn told *CA:* "To be described as an author is rather strange, perhaps because I feel a little uneasy with the authority the title confers. For, to the extent that the work I do is best motivated by a will to knowledge, scholarship rather than authorship is what lies behind it. That is, I enjoy trying to understand—a curiosity that goes in all sorts of directions, not the least of which is cin-ema. Aside from its continuing importance as a medium of communication, writing is but a moment in the quest for knowledge. A crucial moment, though: a writing project provides both the opportunity and the necessity to question, to work ideas through as nothing else—except possibly the best kind of teaching—can."

BIOGRAPHICAL/CRITICAL SOURCES:

PERIODICALS

New Society, November 9, 1978.
New Statesman, August 20, 1982.
San Francisco Examiner-Chronicle, October 10, 1982.
Signs, Volume 5, 1980.

L

LANGBEIN, John H(arriss) 1941-

PERSONAL: Born November 17, 1941, in Washington, DC; son of I. L. (a lawyer) and M. V. (a statistician; maiden name, Harriss) Langbein; married Kirsti M. Hiekka (a legal administrator), June 24, 1973; children: Christopher H., Julia L., Anne K. *Education:* Columbia University, A.B., 1964; Harvard University, LL.B. (magna cum laude), 1968; Trinity Hall, Cambridge, LL.B. (with first class honors), 1969, Ph.D., 1971. *Politics:* Republican. *Religion:* Episcopalian.

ADDRESSES: Home—127 Wall St., New Haven, CT 06511. *Office*—Yale Law School, P.O. Box 208215, New Haven, CT 06520-8215.

CAREER: Admitted to the Bar of the District of Columbia, 1969, of Inner Temple, 1970, and of Florida, 1971; University of Chicago, Chicago, IL, assistant professor, 1971-73, associate professor, 1973-74, professor, 1974-80, Max Pam Professor of American and Foreign Law, 1980-90; Yale University, New Haven, CT, Chancellor Kent Professor of Law and Legal History, 1990—. Visiting scholar at Max Planck Institute for European Legal History, Frankfurt, West Germany, 1969-70, 1977, and Max Planck Institute for Criminal Law, Freiburg, West Germany, 1973; visiting fellow at All Soul's College, Oxford, 1977; visiting professor at University of Michigan Law School, 1976, Stanford University Law School, 1985-86, and Yale Law School, 1989-90. Commissioner, National Conference of Commissioners of Uniform State Laws, 1984—; advisor, American Law Institute, 1987—; reporter, Uniform Law Commission, 1990—; member of U.S. Secretary of State's Advisory Committee on Private Inter-

national Law, 1984—, of Joint Editorial Board on the Uniform Probate Code, 1985—, and of Connecticut Law Revision Commission, 1990—.

MEMBER: International Academy of Comparative Law, International Academy of Estate and Trust Law, International Association of Penal Law, International Commission for the History of Representative and Parliamentary Institutions, Association Internationale de Droit Judiciare, American Academy of Arts and Sciences, American Association for the Comparative Study of Law, American Bar Association, American College of Trust and Estate Counsel, American Historical Association, American Society for Legal History, American Academy of Foreign Law, American Law Institute, Wagner Society of America, Society of Public Teachers of Law, Connecticut Bar Association, Selden Society, Gesellschaft fuer Rechtsvergleichung, Iuris Canonici Medii Aevi Consociatio.

AWARDS, HONORS: Yorke Prize from Cambridge University, 1974, for *Prosecuting Crime in the Renaissance: England, Germany, France;* honorary M.A., Yale University, 1990.

WRITINGS:

Prosecuting Crime in the Renaissance: England, Germany, France, Harvard University Press (Cambridge, MA), 1974.
Torture and the Law of Proof: Europe and England in the Ancien Regime, University of Chicago Press (Chicago), 1977.
Comparative Criminal Procedure: Germany, West Publishing (St. Paul, MN), 1977.

(With Lawrence Waggoner) *Selected Statutes on Trusts and Estates,* Foundation Press (St. Paul, MN), 1987.

(With Bruce Walker) *Pension and Employee Benefit Law,* Foundation Press, 1990, 2nd edition, 1995.

Contributor of chapters to books. Contributor to periodicals, including *American Bar Association Journal, Yale Law Journal, University of Chicago Law Review, Harvard Law Review, American Journal of Legal History, Public Interest, Planning for Higher Education, Newsweek* and *Michigan Law Review.*

BIOGRAPHICAL/CRITICAL SOURCES:

PERIODICALS

Times Literary Supplement, September 20, 1974; February 17, 1978.

*   *   *

LANGDALE, Cecily   1939-

PERSONAL: Born July 27, 1939, in New York, NY; daughter of A. Barnett (an educator) and Elizabeth (a teacher and librarian; maiden name, Armstrong) Langdale; married Roy Davis (an art dealer), July 24, 1972. *Education:* Swarthmore College, B.A., 1961.

*ADDRESSES: Home and office—*231 East 60th St., New York, NY 10022.

CAREER: Davis Galleries, New York, NY, gallery assistant, 1961-63, 1964-67; Hirschl & Adler Galleries, New York City, assistant director of American Department, 1967-73; Davis & Long Co. (art gallery), New York City, associate director, 1973-80; Davis & Langdale Co. (art gallery), New York City, partner, 1980—.

MEMBER: Art Dealers Association of America (board of executives, 1994—), Cosmopolitan Club of New York.

WRITINGS:

(With Betsy G. Fryberger) *Gwen John: Paintings and Drawings From the Collection of John Quinn and Others,* Stanford University Press (Palo Alto, CA), 1982.

Monotypes by Maurice Prendergast in the Terra Museum of American Art, Terra Museum (Chicago), 1984.

(With David Fraser Jenkins) *Gwen John: An Interior Life,* Phaidon (London), 1985, Rizzoli International (New York City), 1986.

Gwen John: With a Catalogue Raisonne of the Paintings and a Selection of the Drawings, Yale University Press (New Haven, CT), 1987.

Contributor to *Maurice Brazil Prendergast, Charles Prendergast: A Catalogue Raisonne,* Williams College Museum of Art (Williamstown, MA) and Prestel-Verlag (Munich), 1990. Contributor to periodicals, including *The Connoisseur, Antiques,* and *Drawing.*

WORK IN PROGRESS: Research on the monotypes of Maurice Prendergast.

BIOGRAPHICAL/CRITICAL SOURCES:

PERIODICALS

Times Literary Supplement, December 18, 1987.

*   *   *

LANSKY, Vicki   1942-

PERSONAL: Born January 6, 1942, in Louisville, KY; daughter of Arthur (an executive in the men's ready-to-wear business) and Mary (Kaplan) Rogosin; married Bruce Lansky (a publisher and literary agent), June 13, 1967 (divorced, 1983); children: Douglas, Dana. *Education:* Connecticut College, B.A., 1963. *Avocational interests:* Tending plants and children, swimming, travel and "running my own publishing company."

*ADDRESSES: Home—*3342 Robinson Bay Rd., Deephaven, MN 55391. *Office—*The Book Peddlers, 18326B Minnetonka Blvd., Deephaven, MN 55391-3275.

CAREER: Lord & Taylor and Mercantile Stores, New York City, sportswear buyer, 1965-69; freelance photographer, 1968-72; Childbirth Education Association, Minneapolis, MN, teaching assistant, 1971-74; Meadowbrook Press, Wayzata, MN, founder, treasurer and executive vice-president in charge of operations, beginning 1975; *Practical*

Parenting (newsletter), Deephaven, MN, editor and publisher, 1979-87; The Book Peddlers (publisher and literary agency), Deephaven, owner, 1983—. Daily radio commentator, Associated Press Broadcast Features, 1981-82; has appeared on a number of television programs, including *Donahue* and *Today.* Former member, Pillsbury/Green Giant Consumer Advisory Panel. Member of advisory board, Catholic Charities Office for Divorced and Separated, Parenthood Cable TV, National Parenting Center, and Children's Rights Council.

AWARDS, HONORS: Parents Choice Award, 1990, for *Vicki Lansky's Divorce Book for Parents: Helping Children Cope with Divorce and Its Aftermath.*

WRITINGS:

(With others) *Feed Me! I'm Yours,* Meadowbrook Press (Deephaven, MN), 1974, revised edition, 1994.

The Taming of the C.A.N.D.Y. Monster, Meadowbrook Press, 1978.

(Editor with Bruce Lansky) *The Best Baby Name Book in the Whole World,* Meadowbrook Press, 1979.

(Editor with B. Lansky) *Watch Me Grow: The Baby Memory and Record Book,* Meadowbrook Press, 1979.

Vicki Lansky's Best Practical Parenting Tips, edited by Kathe Grooms, Meadowbrook Press, 1980, revised edition published as *Vicki Lansky's Practical Parenting Tips,* edited by Kathryn Ring, 1982.

(Editor with others) *Free Stuff for Parents* (catalog), Meadowbrook Press, 1981.

Dear Babysitter, edited by Ring, Meadowbrook Press, 1982.

Practical Parenting Tips, Meadowbrook Press, 1982.

Toilet Training, Bantam (New York City), 1984.

Welcoming Your Second Baby, Bantam, 1984, revised edition, Book Peddlers (Deephaven, MN), 1991.

Practical Parenting Tips for the School Age Years, Bantam, 1985.

Traveling with Your Baby, Bantam, 1985.

Getting Your Baby to Sleep (and Back to Sleep), Bantam, 1985, published as *Getting Your Child to Sleep . . . and Back to Sleep,* Book Peddlers, 1991.

Birthday Parties, Bantam, 1986, published as *Birthday Parties: Best Party Tips and Ideas for Ages 1-8,* Book Peddlers, 1989.

The Best of Vicki Lansky's Practical Parenting, Book Peddlers, 1987.

Fat-Proofing Your Kids, Bantam, 1987, published as *Fat-Proofing Your Children . . . So That They Never Become Diet-Addicted Adults,* 1988.

101 Ways to Tell Your Child 'I Love You,' Contemporary Books (Chicago), 1988.

Vicki Lansky's Divorce Book for Parents: Helping Children Cope with Divorce and Its Aftermath, New American Library (New York City), 1989.

101 Ways to Make Your Child Feel Special, Contemporary Books, 1991.

Another Use for . . . 101 Common Household Items, Book Peddlers, 1991.

Games Babies Play from Birth to 12 Months, Book Peddlers, 1993.

Don't Throw That Out!: A Pennywise Parent's Guide to Creative Uses for Over 200 Household Items, Book Peddlers, 1994.

101 Ways to Be a Special Mom, Contemporary Books, 1995.

101 Ways to Be a Special Dad, Contemporary Books, 1995.

Baking Soda: Over 500 Fabulous, Fun and Frugal Uses You've Probably Never Thought Of, Book Peddlers, 1995.

Transparent Tape: Over 350 Super, Simple and Surprising Uses You've Probably Never Thought Of, Book Peddlers, 1995.

FOR CHILDREN

Koko Bear's New Potty, Bantam, 1986.

Koko Bear's New Babysitter, Bantam, 1987.

A New Baby at Koko Bear's House, Bantam, 1987.

Vicki Lansky's Kids Cooking, Scholastic, Inc. (New York City), 1987.

Koko Bear's Big Earache (juvenile), Bantam, 1988.

Sing Along as You Ride Along (book and cassette tape), Scholastic, Inc., 1988.

Sing Along Birthday Fun (book and cassette tape), Scholastic, Inc., 1988.

OTHER

Also author of *Vicki Lansky's Microwave Cooking for Kids,* Scholastic, Inc., *Trouble-Free Travel with Children: Helpful Hints for Parents on the Go,* Book Peddlers, *101 Ways to Say 'I Love You,'* Simon & Schuster, and, with *Consumer Guide* editors, *Complete Pregnancy and Baby Book,* Publications International. Sunday newspaper columnist, Minneapolis *Star and Tribune.* Contributing editor, *Family Circle,* 1988—; columnist, *Sesame Street Parents Magazine,* 1988—.

WORK IN PROGRESS: Helpful hints books; two books on grandparenting; repackaging some earlier works.

SIDELIGHTS: In 1974 Vicki Lansky and several other mothers from a local Childbirth Education Association chapter wrote a baby food cookbook for new mothers. Although she believed the book to have commercial appeal, no publisher was interested in it. Undaunted, Lansky and her husband turned their back porch into their own publishing company and began producing *Feed Me! I'm Yours* for distribution. Their creative promotional efforts and appearances on television talk shows made *Feed Me! I'm Yours* America's best selling baby food and toddler cookbook.

As her children grew older, Lansky found the struggle to maintain good nutritional habits intensifying. Saturday morning television commercials for junk food permeated her children's minds along with their fare of cartoons, and she perceived the need to counter this offensive with tasty alternative recipes for young children. In *The Taming of the C.A.N.D.Y. Monster* she sought to provide parents with practical ideas to improve their children's eating habits. The book rose quickly to the number one spot on the *New York Times* Trade Paperback Bestseller list.

In 1979, Lansky began publishing *Practical Parenting,* a bimonthly newsletter consisting of articles and tips on different issues of childrearing. The newsletter has grown into a nationally syndicated radio feature and a series of "Practical Parenting" books. Lansky designs each book to cover a single topic, providing a quick and easy source of information for inexperienced parents. As Sue MacDonald reports in the *Cincinnati Enquirer:* Lansky said "'a lot of these books [are] a replacement for the support group,' . . . pointing out that many new parents have no family or close friends in whom to confide—or feel too stupid to ask their own mothers for advice."

Lansky told *CA:* "I continue to be fascinated by the world of household trivia, the challenges of book publishing, my young adult children's entry into the world of responsibility, the changing world of divorce social services, computer on-line services as well as desktop publishing and, of course, the ever evolving nature of the human condition and relationships.

"I feel very lucky to be around at this point in time. I doubt that I could have made a living with this type of material 75 years ago and I am not sure of the need for it 75 years hence. Despite the fact that my titles have probably sold over four million copies, I have no illusions about the literary value of my work. There is none. But I have touched many people's lives and hopefully made it a little better or easier for them."

BIOGRAPHICAL/CRITICAL SOURCES:

PERIODICALS

Cincinnati Enquirer, August 3, 1984.
Los Angeles Times Book Review, July 25, 1982.
New York Times Book Review, April 2, 1978.
Us, June 27, 1978.

*   *   *

LAREDO, Betty
    See CODRESCU, Andrei

*   *   *

LAWLESS, Elaine J.   1947-

PERSONAL: Born September 29, 1947, in Poplar Bluff, MO; daughter of James (a farmer) and Angie Mae (a homemaker; maiden name, Dunlap) Lawless; married James Rikoon (a folklorist); children: Alexander Keller, Jesse, Kate. *Ethnicity:* "Anglo." *Education:* Attended Southeast Missouri State College (now University), 1965-69; University of Illinois at Urbana-Champaign, 1971-75; Indiana University—Bloomington, 1977-82.

ADDRESSES: Office—Department of English, 107 Tate Hall, University of Missouri—Columbia, Columbia, MO 65211. *E-mail*—engle1@showme.missouri.edu.

CAREER: University of Missouri—Columbia, assistant professor of English, 1983-88, professor, 1988—. Co-producer of television documentary "Joy Unspeakable," for Indiana University—Bloomington, 1981.

WRITINGS:

God's Peculiar People: Women's Voices and Folk Tradition in a Pentecostal Church, University Press of Kentucky (Lexington, KY), 1987.

Handmaidens of the Lord: Pentecostal Women Preachers and Traditional Religion, American Folklore Society and University of Pennsylvania Press (Philadelphia, PA), 1988.

Holy Women, Wholly Women: Sharing Ministries of Wholeness Through Life Stories and Reciprocal Ethnography, American Folklore Society and University of Pennsylvania Press, 1993.

Women Preaching Revolution: Calling for Connection in a Disconnected Time, University of Pennsylvania Press, 1996.

Contributor to folklore, women's studies, religious studies, and literary journals.

*   *   *

LEE, James A(lvin) 1922-

PERSONAL: Born August 7, 1922, in Breckenridge, TX; son of James Arlington (an oil field superintendent) and Aultna Lee; married Frances Irene Smith (a linguist), in 1949; children: five. *Education:* Trinity College of Music, London, Diploma in Composition, 1946; Fresno State College (now California State University, Fresno), A.B., 1950; University of Utah, M.S., 1951; Harvard University, D.B.A., 1968. *Avocational interests:* Squash racquets, music, antique British sports cars.

ADDRESSES: Home—30 N. May Ave., Athens, OH 45701.

CAREER: Douglas Aircraft, Long Beach, CA, and Oklahoma City, OK, tool designer, 1941-43; North American Aviation, Inglewood, CA, tool designer, 1943-44; Kennecott Copper Corp., Arizona Division, Ray, AZ, director of industrial relations, 1951-55; O. S. Stapley Co., Phoenix, AZ, personnel director, 1955-56; Sperry Rand, Flight Systems Division, Phoenix, personnel director, 1956-60; University of Wisconsin—Madison, Madison, associate professor of industrial relations, 1960-61; University of Southern California, Los Angeles, associate professor of management, attached to University of Karachi, 1961-64; Harvard University, Cambridge, MA, research associate in personnel administration, 1965-66; Haile Selassie I University, Addis Ababa, Ethiopia, professor of business and dean of College of Business, 1966-69; Ohio University, Athens, professor of management, 1969-92, chairman of department of organizational science, 1969-72, chairman of

graduate programs, 1976-78 and 1981-83, director of Ohio Programs in Malaysia, 1983-85. Professor, chairman of department of industrial management, and founding dean of College of Industrial Management at Saudi Arabia's University of Petroleum and Minerals, Dhahran, 1974-76. International Management Development Institute, Inc., cofounder, vice president, academic head, and member of board of directors, 1970—; consultant to Kinetics Technology International, U.S. Civil Service Commission, and Shell Oil Co. *Military service:* U.S. Army Air Forces, 1944-46, served in Europe.

MEMBER: Academy of Management.

WRITINGS:

The Gold and Garbage in Management Theories and Prescriptions, Ohio University Press (Athens, OH), 1980.

(With Phillip L. Martin) *Contemporary Labor Relations* (2nd edition), CT Publications (Redding, CA), 1990.

America's Terminal Disease—Societal Aids—the Destruction of Our Mechanisms for Solving Our Societal Problems, Minerva Press (London), in press.

Contributor to business and management journals. Editor and publisher of bimonthly newsletter, *Newsletter from Athens.*

WORK IN PROGRESS: Evaluating and Applying Management Theories.

SIDELIGHTS: James A. Lee told *CA:* "*The Gold and Garbage in Management Theories and Prescriptions* was prompted by my astonishment at the proliferation of theories about how to manage that had little or no scientific support. The book is the result of about two thousand hours of research looking for such support. Little was found.

"The first edition of *Contemporary Labor Relations* was written by Phillip L. Martin. I had used it for two years as a basic text in a labor relations course I taught at Ohio University, but it was getting out of date by 1988. I phoned the publisher who told me that Professor Martin had no interest in doing a 2nd edition. Would he mind if I did? No. So I did the 2nd edition, updating all the numbers and adding several new chapters. My interest in using the book in the first place was its small size—190 pages. Since I augment my course with extensive case analysis, my students wouldn't have had time to read a 700-page typical labor relations text and do the case analyses plus contract bargaining simulation. I am now working on a 3rd edition to be out by the end of the year."

*   *   *

LEE, Tanith 1947-

PERSONAL: Born September 19, 1947, in London, England; daughter of Bernard and Hylda (Moore) Lee. *Education:* Attended secondary school in London, England; studied at an art college. *Avocational interests:* Past civilizations (Egyptian, Roman, Incan), psychic powers (their development, use, and misuse), music.

ADDRESSES: c/o Macmillan London Ltd., 4 Little Essex St., London WC2R 3LF, England.

CAREER: Writer. Has also worked as a librarian.

AWARDS, HONORS: August Derleth Award, 1980; World Fantasy Convention Award, 1983.

WRITINGS:

NOVELS

Volkhavaar, DAW (New York City), 1977.
Electric Forest, Doubleday (Garden City, NY), 1979.
Kill the Dead, DAW, 1980.
Sabella; or, The Blood Stone, DAW, 1980.
Day by Night, DAW, 1980.
Lycanthia; or, The Children of Wolves, DAW, 1981, Legend (London), 1990.
Sometimes, after Sunset (includes *Sabella* and *Kill the Dead*), Doubleday, 1981.
The Silver Metal Lover, DAW, 1982.
Sung in Shadow, DAW, 1983.
Days of Grass, DAW, 1985.
Dark Castle, White Horse, DAW, 1986.
Madame Two Swords, illustrated by Thomas Canty, Donald M. Grant (West Kingston, RI), 1988.
A Heroine of the World, DAW, 1989.
The Blood of Roses, Century, 1990.
Heart-Beast, Headline (London), 1992, Dell (New York City), 1993.
Elephantasm, Headline, 1993.
Eva Fairdeath, Headline, 1994.
Reigning Cats and Dogs, Headline, 1995.

"BIRTHGRAVE" SERIES

The Birthgrave, DAW, 1975.
Vazkor, Son of Vaskor, DAW, 1978, published in England as *Shadowfire,* Futura, 1979.
Quest for the White Witch, DAW, 1978.

"BLOOD OPERA" SERIES

Dark Dance, Dell, 1992.
Personal Darkness, Little, Brown (London), 1993, Dell, 1994.
Darkness, I, Little, Brown, 1994.

"DARK CASTLE" SERIES; JUVENILE NOVELS

The Castle of Dark, Macmillan (London), 1978.
Prince on a White Horse, Macmillan, 1982.

"DON'T BITE THE SUN" SERIES

Don't Bite the Sun, DAW, 1976, reprinted, Starmont House (Mercer Island, WA), 1987.
Drinking Sapphire Wine, DAW, 1977, published with *Don't Bite the Sun,* Hamlyn (London), 1979.

"DRAGONFLIGHT" SERIES

Black Unicorn, illustrated by Heather Cooper, Atheneum (New York City), 1991.
Gold Unicorn, Atheneum, 1994.

"SECRET BOOKS OF PARADYS" SERIES

The Book of the Damned (short stories), Unwin (London), 1988, Overlook Press, 1990.
The Book of the Beast, Unwin, 1988, Overlook Press (Woodstock, NY), 1991.
The Book of the Dead (short stories), Overlook Press, 1991.
The Book of the Mad, Overlook Press, 1993.

"TALES FROM THE FLAT EARTH" SERIES

Night's Master, DAW, 1978.
Death's Master, DAW, 1979.
Delusion's Master, DAW, 1981.
Delirium's Mistress, DAW, 1986.
Night's Sorceries (short stories), DAW, 1987.
Tales from the Flat Earth: Night's Daughter (short stories), Doubleday, 1987.

"WARS OF VIS" SERIES

The Storm Lord, DAW, 1976.
Anackire, DAW, 1983.
The Wars of Vis (contains *The Storm Lord* and *Anackire*), Doubleday, 1984.
The White Serpent, DAW, 1988.

JUVENILE NOVELS

The Dragon Hoard, Farrar, Straus (New York City), 1971.
Animal Castle, Farrar, Straus, 1972.
Companions on the Road, Macmillan, 1975.
The Winter Players, Macmillan, 1976.
East of Midnight, Macmillan, 1977, St. Martin's (New York City), 1978.
Shon the Taken, Macmillan, 1979.

SHORT STORY COLLECTIONS

The Betrothed, Slughorn Press (Sidcup, Kent), 1968.
Princess Hynchatti and Some Other Surprises (juvenile), Macmillan, 1972, Farrar, Straus, 1973.
Unsilent Night, NESFA Press (Cambridge, MA), 1981.
Cyrion, DAW, 1982.
Red as Blood; or, Tales from the Sisters Grimmer, DAW, 1983.
The Beautiful Biting Machine, Cheap Street (New Castle, VA), 1984.
Tamastara; or, The Indian Nights, DAW, 1984.
The Gorgon and Other Beastly Tales, DAW, 1985.
Dreams of Dark and Light: The Great Short Fiction of Tanith Lee, Arkham House (Sauk City, WI), 1986.
Forests of the Night, Unwin, 1989.
Nightshades: Thirteen Journeys into Shadow, Headline, 1993.

NONFICTION

Women as Demons: The Male Perception of Women through Space and Time, Women's Press (London), 1989.

PLAYS

Bitter Gate (radio play), BBC Radio, 1977.
Red Wine (radio play), BBC Radio, 1977.
Death is King (radio play), 1979.
The Silver Sky (radio play), 1980.
Sarcophagus (television play), "Blake's Seven" series, 1980.
Sand (television play), "Blake's Seven" series, 1981.

SIDELIGHTS: Tanith Lee's many works of fiction reveal a dark and erotic imagination at work in fields as varied as horror, science fiction, and fantasy. Through novels, short story collections, and series, such as "The Secret Books of Paradys" and "Tales from the Flat Earth," Lee grapples with such perplexing questions as the fate of the universe, the individual's ability to control events, and the nature of morality. Her work has been cited by critics for its vivid imagery and unique cast of larger-than-life characters. *Voice Literary Supplement* reviewer Peter Stampfel calls Lee the "Princess Royal of Heroic Fantasy and Goddess-Empress of the Hot Read" and states that her writing "dazzles and intoxicates."

Lee was born, raised, and educated in London. She began her writing career with books for children, such as *The Dragon Hoard* and *Animal Castle.* Her first novel for adults, *The Birthgrave,* appeared in 1975. Since then she has published at least one novel or story collection a year, and many years she produces multiple works. "I intend my books for anyone who will enjoy them," Tanith commented. "Frankly, I write for me, I can't help it. My books are expressions of my private inner world. I love the idea that other people may read and perhaps relish them, but that, if it happens, is a delightful by-product."

Lee has never shied from depictions of the bizarre. Whether human or god, her heroes and heroines struggle against the madness and morbidity of their worlds. Their travails allow the author to expose human society and its failures as well as the ambiguities in the relationship between behavior and morality. Some of her novels and stories, such as the well-known *Red as Blood; or, Tales from the Sisters Grimmer,* turn popular fairy tales upside-down to reveal darker and more diabolic suggestions. Myths and legends also form the basis of the "Tales from the Flat Earth" series, which includes *Night's Master, Death's Master,* and *Delirium's Mistress.* In the *Washington Post Book World,* Michael Swanwick describes such works as "darkly, lushly romantic stuff, with silvery veins of eroticism and sinister beauty. . . . Her prose practically shimmers on the page."

Another well-known Lee series is "The Secret Books of Paradys," a selection of linked works that include stories, novellas, and novels. These books reveal the depraved lives of characters in a fictitious French town, variously named Paradys, Paradis, and Paradise. The parallel cities and their various malignant characters allow the author to ruminate on the frailties of modern society, especially in relationship to its younger members and its artists. Reviewing Tanith's 1993 series release, *The Book of the Mad* for *Los Angeles Times Book Review,* Sue Martin notes: "This is Gothic writing at the extreme end of weirdness." The critic maintains that the writing succeeds because "its dream-drenched, spaced-out characters are compelling as they flit ghost-like on their errands." A *Washington Post Book World* reviewer finds in *The Book of the Mad* that Lee "has given us a map to the outer limits of imagination, and then dares us to find our way home." *Locus* contributor Faren Miller argues that the "Secret Books of Paradys" series reveals a writer at the height of her powers. Miller observes: "[Lee] began as a good writer, developed into an elegant, ironic stylist, and has now matured still further to become one of our very best authors of short fiction."

Tanith Lee once told *CA:* "I began to write, and continue to write, out of the sheer compulsion to fantasize. I can claim no noble motives, no aspirations that what comes galloping from my Biro will overthrow tyranny, unite nations or cause roses to bloom in the winter snow. I just want to write, can't stop, don't want to stop, and hope I never shall.

"As a writer who has been lucky enough to make writing her profession, I am most undisciplined and erratic. One day I will commence work at four in the afternoon and persevere until four the next morning. Sometimes I start at four in the morning, and go on until physical stamina gives out. Sometimes I get stuck on some knotty problem, (how do you describe the emotions of a man who finds he is a god? What will he do now he knows? Is there any point in his doing anything? Yes. What?) and worry about said problem for days, pen poised, eyes glazed. Frequently I race through 150 pages in a month, and then stick for three months over one page. It's wonder to me I get anything done. But I do, so presumably it's all right.

"I admire far too many writers to make a list. I'm always discovering new ones to admire. Some operate in the Fantasy/Science Fiction field; a lot don't. I think I can say that I've been influenced by everything I've read and liked. But I'm influenced by symphonies and concertos, too, by paintings and by films. And sometimes by people. A character. A sentence."

Don't Bite the Sun has been translated into Swedish. Several other books are "in the pipeline" for Italy, France, and Germany.

BIOGRAPHICAL/CRITICAL SOURCES:

BOOKS

Contemporary Literary Criticism, Volume 46, Gale, 1987.
St. James Guide to Science Fiction Writers, fourth edition, St. James Press, 1996.

PERIODICALS

Books and Bookmen, May, 1972.
Fantasy Macabre 4 [London], 1983.
Fantasy Review, April, 1986, p. 25.
History Today, December, 1975.
Locus, January, 1989, pp. 15, 17; August, 1991, p. 15; February, 1992, p. 57; June, 1993, p. 57; November, 1993, p. 54; February, 1994, pp. 36-37; June, 1994, p. 63.
Los Angeles Times Book Review, June 6, 1993, p. 11.
Observer (London), November 26, 1972; February 15, 1976; November 28, 1976.
Publishers Weekly, July 21, 1989, p. 55; October 26, 1990, p. 58; January 1, 1992, p. 50.
Review of Contemporary Fiction, fall, 1993, pp. 238-39.
Spectator, April 22, 1972; November 11, 1972.
Times Literary Supplement, July 14, 1972; November 3, 1972; April 2, 1976; October 1, 1976.
Voice Literary Supplement, October 1981, p. 6.
Voice of Youth Advocates, February, 1990, p. 372; December, 1991, p. 324.
Washington Post Book World, July 27, 1986, p. 4; May 30, 1993, p. 9.
Wilson Library Bulletin, April, 1992, pp. 96-97.*

*　　*　　*

LEECH, Geoffrey N(eil)   1936-

PERSONAL: Born January 16, 1936, in Gloucester, England; son of Charles Richard (a bank employee) and Dorothy (Foster) Leech; married Frances Berman, July 29, 1961; children: Thomas Camilla. *Ethnicity:* Caucasian. *Education:* University College, London, B.A., 1959, M.A., 1962, Ph.D. 1969; additional study, Massachusetts Institute of Technology, 1964-65. *Religion:* Church of England. *Avocational interests:* Music (playing piano and organ).

ADDRESSES: Home—Old Manor House, Mill Brow, Kirkby Lonsdale, Cumbria, LA6 2AT, England. *E-mail*—g.leech@lancaster.ac.uk. *Office*—Department of Linguistics and Modern English Language, University of Lancaster, Bailrigg, Lancaster, LA1 4YT England.

CAREER: Clarendon School, South Oxhey, Hertfordshire, England, assistant schoolmaster, 1960-61; University of London, University College, London, England, assistant lecturer, 1962-65, lecturer in English, 1965-69; University of Lancaster, Bailrigg, Lancaster, England, reader in English, 1969-74, professor of linguistics and modern English languages, 1974—. Harkness fellow, Massachusetts Institute of Technology, 1964-65. *Military service:* Royal Air Force, 1954-56; became senior aircraftsman.

MEMBER: Academia Europea, Philological Society, Linguistic Association of Great Britain, Norske Videnskaps-Akademi.

AWARDS, HONORS: Doctor of Philosophy, Lund University, Sweden, 1987; fellow of British Academy, 1987; fellow of University College, London, 1989; named Honorary Professor, Beijing Foreign Studies University.

WRITINGS:

English in Advertising: A Linguistic Study of Advertising in Great Britain, Longmans, Green (London), 1966.
A Linguistic Guide to English Poetry, Longmans, Green, 1969.
Towards a Semantic Description of English, Longmans, Green, 1969, Indiana University Press (Bloomington, IN), 1970.
Meaning and the English Verb, Longman (New York City), 1971, revised edition, 1987.
(With Randolph Quirk, Sidney Greenbaum, and Jan Svartvik) *A Grammar of Contemporary English,* Longman, 1972.
Semantics, Penguin Books (New York City), 1974, revised edition, 1981.
(With Svartvik) *A Communicative Grammar of English,* Longman, 1975, revised edition, 1994.
Explorations in Semantics and Pragmatics, Benjamins, 1980.
(With Michael H. Short) *Style in Fiction,* Longman, 1981.
(With Margaret Deuchar and Robert Hoogenraad) *English Grammar for Today,* Macmillan (New York City), 1982.

Principles of Pragmatics, Longman, 1983.
(With Quirk, Greenbaum, and Svartvik) *A Comprehensive Grammar of the English Language,* Longman, 1985.
An A-Z Guide to English Grammar and Usage, Longman, 1989.
Introducing English Grammar, Penguin Books, 1992.

EDITOR

(With Greenbaum and Svartvik) *Studies in English Linguistics: For Randolph Quirk,* Longman, 1980.
(With Christopher N. Candlin) *Computers in English Language Teaching and Research,* Longman, 1986.
(With Roger Garside and Geoffrey Sampson) *The Computational Analysis of English: A Corpus-based Approach,* Longman, 1987.
(With Ezra Black and Garside) *Statistically-Driven Computer Grammars of English,* Rodopi (Amsterdam), 1993.
(With Greg Myers and Jenny Thomas) *Spoken English on Computer: Transcription, Mark-up and Application,* Longman, 1995.

OTHER

Contributor of articles and essays to journals and edited collections.

*   *   *

LEONARD, Elmore (John, Jr.)   1925-

PERSONAL: Born October 11, 1925, in New Orleans, LA; son of Elmore John (an automotive executive) and Flora Amelia (Rive) Leonard; married Beverly Cline, July 30, 1949 (divorced May 24, 1977); married Joan Shepard, September 15, 1979 (died January 13, 1993); married Christine Kent, August 19, 1993; children: (first marriage) Jane Jones, Peter, Christopher, William, Katherine Dudley. *Education:* University of Detroit, Ph.B., 1950. *Religion:* Roman Catholic.

ADDRESSES: Home—Bloomfield Village, MI. *Agent*—Michael Siegel, Creative Artists Agency, Beverly Hills, CA 90212.

CAREER: Full-time writer, 1967—. Campbell-Ewald Advertising Agency, Detroit, MI, copywriter, 1950-

61; freelance copywriter and author of educational and industrial films, 1961-63; head of Elmore Leonard Advertising Company, 1963-66. *Military service:* U.S. Naval Reserve, 1943-46.

MEMBER: Writers Guild of America West, Mystery Writers of America, Western Writers of America, Authors League of America, Authors Guild.

AWARDS, HONORS: Hombre was named one of the twenty-five best western novels of all time by the Western Writers of America, 1977; Edgar Allan Poe Award, Mystery Writers of America, 1984, for *LaBrava;* Michigan Foundation of the Arts Award, 1985; Mystery Writers of America, Grand Master Award, 1992; Doctor of Human Letters, Florida Atlantic University, 1996.

WRITINGS:

WESTERN NOVELS

The Bounty Hunters, Houghton (Boston), 1953, reprinted, Bantam (New York City), 1985.
The Law at Randado, Houghton, 1955, reprinted, Bantam, 1985.
Escape from 5 Shadows, Houghton, 1956, reprinted, Bantam, 1985.
Last Stand at Saber River, Dell (New York City), 1957, reprinted, Bantam, 1985 (published in England as *Lawless River,* R. Hale, 1959, and as *Stand on the Saber,* Corgi, 1960).
Hombre, Ballantine (New York City), 1961, reprinted, 1984.
Valdez Is Coming, Gold Medal (New York City), 1970.
Forty Lashes Less One, Bantam (New York City), 1972.
Gunsights, Bantam, 1979.

CRIME NOVELS

The Big Bounce, Gold Medal, 1969, revised edition, Armchair Detective, 1989.
The Moonshine War (also see below), Doubleday (New York City), 1969, reprinted, Dell, 1988.
Mr. Majestyk (also see below), Dell, 1974.
Fifty-Two Pickup (also see below), Delacorte (New York City), 1974.
Swag (also see below), Delacorte, 1976, published as *Ryan's Rules,* Dell, 1976.
Unknown Man, No. 89, Delacorte, 1977.
The Hunted (also see below), Dell, 1977.
The Switch, Bantam, 1978.

City Primeval: High Noon in Detroit (also see below), Arbor House (New York City), 1980.
Gold Coast (also see below), Bantam, 1980, revised edition, 1985.
Split Images (also see below), Arbor House, 1981.
Cat Chaser (also see below), Arbor House, 1982.
Stick (also see below; Book-of-the-Month Club alternate selection), Arbor House, 1983.
LaBrava (also see below), Arbor House, 1983.
Glitz (Book-of-the-Month Club selection), Arbor House, 1985.
Bandits, Arbor House, 1987.
Touch, Arbor House, 1987.
Freaky Deaky (Book-of-the-Month Club selection), Morrow (New York City), 1988.
Killshot (Literary Guild selection), Morrow, 1989.
Get Shorty (Book-of-the-Month Club selection), Delacorte, 1990.
Maximum Bob, Delacorte, 1991.
Rum Punch, Delacorte, 1992.
Pronto, Delacorte, 1993.
Riding the Rap, Delacorte, 1995.
Out of Sight, Delacorte, 1996.

OMNIBUS VOLUMES

Elmore Leonard's Dutch Treat (contains *The Hunted, Swag,* and *Mr. Majestyk*), introduction by George F. Will, Arbor House, 1985.
Elmore Leonard's Double Dutch Treat (contains *City Primeval: High Noon in Detroit, The Moonshine War,* and *Gold Coast*), introduction by Bob Greene, Arbor House, 1986.
Three Complete Novels (contains *LaBrava, Cat Chaser,* and *Split Images*), Wings Books (New York City), 1992.

SCREENPLAYS

The Moonshine War (based on Leonard's novel of the same title), Metro-Goldwyn-Mayer (MGM), 1970.
Joe Kidd, Universal, 1972.
Mr. Majestyk (based on Leonard's novel of the same title), United Artists (UA), 1974.
High Noon, Part 2: The Return of Will Kane, Columbia Broadcasting System (CBS), 1980.
(With Joseph C. Stinson) *Stick* (based on Leonard's novel of the same title), Universal, 1985.
(With John Steppling) *52 Pick-Up* (based on Leonard's novel of the same title), Cannon Group, 1986.
(With Fred Walton) *The Rosary Murders* (based on the novel by William X. Kienzle), New Line Cinema, 1987.

Desperado, National Broadcasting Corp. (NBC), 1988.

(With Joe Borrelli) *Cat Chaser* (based on Leonard's novel of the same title), Viacom, 1989.

Also author of filmscripts for Encyclopaedia Britannica Films, including *Settlement of the Mississippi Valley, Boy of Spain, Frontier Boy,* and *Julius Caesar,* and of a recruiting film for the Franciscans.

OTHER

Contributor to books, including *The Courage to Change: Personal Conversations about Alcoholism,* edited by Dennis Wholey, Houghton, 1984. Contributor of about thirty short stories and novelettes to *Dime Western, Argosy, Saturday Evening Post, Zane Grey's Western Magazine,* and other publications during the 1950s.

ADAPTATIONS: The novelette *3:10 to Yuma* was filmed by Columbia Pictures, 1957; the story "The Tall T" was filmed by Columbia, 1957; *Hombre* was filmed by Twentieth Century-Fox, 1967; *The Big Bounce* was filmed by Warner Bros., 1969; *Valdez Is Coming* was filmed by United Artists, 1970; *Glitz* was filmed for television by the National Broadcasting Corp.; *Get Shorty* was filmed by MGM/UA, 1995; *Touch* was filmed by Lumiere, 1996; the film rights to most of Leonard's other novels have been sold.

SIDELIGHTS: "After writing 23 novels, Elmore Leonard has been discovered," Herbert Mitgang remarked in the *New York Times* in 1983. Following three decades of moderate success with his novels and short stories, Leonard began in the early 1980s to receive the kind of attention from reviewers befitting an author whom Richard Herzfelder in the *Chicago Tribune* calls "a writer of thrillers whose vision goes deeper than thrill." While the plots of Leonard's books remain inherently action-packed and suspenseful, he is, says *Washington Post Book World* critic Jonathan Yardley, now being "praised for accomplishments rather more substantial than that of keeping the reader on tenterhooks." These accomplishments, which Yardley describes as raising "the hard-boiled suspense novel beyond the limits of genre and into social commentary," have led critics previously inclined to pigeonhole Leonard as a crime or mystery novelist to dispense with such labels in their assessments of his work. In the process, several critics have chosen to mention Leonard's name alongside those of other writers whose literary works

transcend their genre, among them Ross Macdonald and Dashiell Hammett. Such comparisons are "flattering, but hardly accurate," according to Grover Sales in the *Los Angeles Times Book Review.* "Leonard is an original," Sales believes. "His uncanny sense of plot, pace and his inexhaustible flair for the nervous rhythms of contemporary urban speech have caught the spirit of the '80s."

Leonard began his career in the early 1950s as a writer of western stories for magazines. His first sale was a novelette entitled *Apache Agent* to *Argosy* magazine for $90. He eventually turned his hand to novels in the genre, publishing five of them while pursuing a career as an advertising copywriter for a firm in Detroit. Copywriter was not an occupation much to Leonard's liking. "He says matter-of-factly that he hated the work," notes Bill Dunn in a *Publishers Weekly* interview, "but it allowed him precious time and a steady paycheck to experiment with fiction, which he did in the early morning before going off to work." Leonard told Dunn: "Sometimes I would write a little fiction at work, too. I would write in my desk drawer and close the drawer if somebody came in."

Western fiction appealed to Leonard for two reasons: he had always liked western movies, and he was determined that his writing should be a lucrative as well as a creative pursuit. "I decided I wasn't going to be a literary writer, that I wouldn't end up in the quarterlies," he tells Beaufort Cranford in *Michigan Magazine.* "So if I was going to be a commercial writer, I had to learn how to do it." His decidedly professional approach to writing paid off. During the 1950s Leonard sold some thirty short stories and five novels. And two of his stories were also sold to Hollywood: *3:10 to Yuma,* a novelette that first appeared in *Dime Western* magazine, starred actor Glenn Ford; *The Tall T* starred Randolph Scott and Richard Boone.

By the early 1960s the western genre had peaked in popularity, and Leonard found that the market for his fiction had dried up. For several years he wrote no fiction at all, devoting his time to freelance copywriting, primarily for Hurst gear shifters, a popular feature in hot rod cars. He also wrote industrial films for Detroit-area companies and educational films for Encyclopaedia Britannica at a thousand dollars apiece. Finally in 1965, when his agent sold the film rights to his last western novel, *Hombre,* for ten thousand dollars, Leonard had the financial leeway to write fiction again. This time he focused on the mystery-suspense genre. As he tells Gay Rubin of *Detroiter:* "I began writing westerns because there was a market for them. Now of course there is an interest in police stories . . . suspense, mystery, crime."

Despite the shift in genre, Leonard's fiction has remained in many ways the same. In both his western and crime fiction there is an overriding interest in seeing that justice is done. Leonard's prose, lean and hard, has consistently been of the same high quality. And his gunfighters and urban detectives approach their work with the same glib, wisecracking attitude. Writing in *Esquire,* Mike Lupica claims that despite their apparent diversity, all of Leonard's main characters are essentially the same, but "with a different name and a different job. . . . They have all been beat on by life, they all can drop a cool, wise-guy line on you, they are all tough, don't try to push them around." Leonard's first crime novel, *The Big Bounce,* was rejected by some eighty-four publishers and film producers before being published as a paperback original by Gold Medal. Unsure about his switch to crime writing because of the trouble he had selling the book, Leonard turned again to westerns, publishing two more novels in the genre. But when the film rights to *The Big Bounce* were sold for $50,000, Leonard abandoned the western genre for good. Since making that decision, all of his subsequent novels have enjoyed both hardcover and paperback editions and have been sold to Hollywood.

The typical Leonard novel, Michael Kernan of the *Washington Post* maintains, is distinguished by "guns, a killing or two or three, fights and chases and sex. Tight, clean prose, ear-perfect, whip-smart dialogue. And, just beneath the surface, an acute sense of the ridiculous." Leonard has said on several occasions that he has been less influenced by other crime writers than by such writers as Ernest Hemingway, John Steinbeck, and John O'Hara. Their lean, unadorned writing style and ability to remain in the background of their stories appealed to Leonard. He tells Charles Champlin of the *Los Angeles Times:* "I became a stylist by intentionally avoiding style. When I go back and edit and something sounds like *writing,* I rewrite it. I rewrite constantly, four pages in the basket for every one that survives." The result impresses Ken Tucker of the *Village Voice,* who calls Leonard "the finest thriller writer alive primarily because he does his best to efface style."

To get his dialogue right, Leonard listens to the way people really talk and copies it down as faithfully as possible. When writing the novel *City Primeval: High Noon in Detroit,* Leonard even sat in at the Detroit police department's homicide squad room for several months, listening to the way that police officers, lawyers, and suspects spoke. His writing is full of slang terms and peculiarities of speech that mark each of his characters as a one-of-a-kind individual. More importantly, he captures the speech rhythms of his characters. Leonard recreates speech so well, Alan Cheuse writes in the *Los Angeles Times Book Review,* that "it's difficult to say . . . who among this novelist's contemporaries has a better ear." Herbert Mitgang of the *New York Times* agrees. The conversations in Leonard's books, Mitgang writes, "sound absolutely authentic." Avoiding narration and description, Leonard moves his novels along with dialogue, letting his characters' conversations tell the story. Speaking of the novel *Freaky Deaky,* Jonathan Kirsch writes in the *Los Angeles Times* that the book "is all dialogue—cool banter, jive talk, interior monologue. Virtually everything we learn about the plot and the characters is imparted through conversation, and so the book reads like a radio script."

When plotting his novels, Leonard allows his characters full rein to create their own story. Before beginning a new book, Leonard creates a handful of vividly imagined characters, the relationships between them, and their basic situation, and then he sets them in action. Leonard has, Michael Kernan remarks in the *Washington Post,* "no idea how it will end." He tells Michael Ruhlman in the *New York Times Book Review:* "I see my characters as being most important, how they bounce off one another, how they talk to each other, and the plot just sort of comes along." This spontaneous plotting technique works well for Leonard but has caused at least one reviewer occasional difficulty. Ben Yagoda of the *Chicago Tribune* describes Leonard's crime novels as being "smoky improvisations grouped around a set of reliable elements. . . . Eventually, the elements congeal into a taut climax, but for the first two-thirds or so of the book, the characters, the reader and, it turns out, the author simmer on the low burner and, in Huckleberry Finn style, 'swap juices,' trying to figure out what's going on."

Many of Leonard's crime novels feature lower-class characters trying to make fast money with a big heist or quick scam. They "fall into crime," according to Tucker, "because it's an easier way to make money than that tedious nine-to-five." George Stade of the *New York Times Book Review* calls Leonard's villains "treacherous and tricky, smart enough to outsmart themselves, driven, audacious and outrageous, capable of anything, paranoid-cunning and casually vicious—and rousing fun." Dick Roraback of the *Los Angeles Times Book Review* claims that "it is the mark of the author's craft that his characters do not seem to be created, 'written.' They simply are there, stalking, posturing, playing, loving, scheming, and we watch and listen and are fascinated. And appalled, yes, or approving, but always absorbed. They never let us off the hook."

Often partially set in Leonard's hometown of Detroit, his stories take place in locations ranging from Florida, where Leonard vacations and where his mother owns a motel, to New Orleans, where he was born. But Leonard shows only the seedy parts of these towns, the places where his characters are likely to be conducting their criminal business or avoiding their pursuers. He has, according to Marcel Berlins of the London *Times,* "a feel for the losers of this world, and for the shabby world they inhabit, with its own rules and its own noble principles." As Yardley explains, "Leonard's viewpoint is not exactly cynical, inasmuch as he admits the possibility of something approximating redemption, but it certainly is worldly and unsentimental. In his world nobody gets a free ticket and the victories that people win, such as they are, are limited and costly; which is to say that his world bears a striking resemblance to the real one."

Although he had been writing critically acclaimed crime novels for a decade, and his work was being adapted for the screen, Leonard had only a small cadre of fans until the early 1980s, when his novels began to attract the attention of a larger audience. With the novel *Stick* in 1982, Leonard suddenly became a bestselling writer. One sign of this sudden success can be seen in the agreeable change in Leonard's finances that year. The paperback rights for *Split Images* earned him $7,000 in 1981; the rights for *Stick* a year later earned $50,000. Then, in 1983, *LaBrava* won an Edgar Award from the Mystery Writers of America as the best novel of the year. And the book sold over 400,000 copies. Leonard's next novel, *Glitz,* hit the bestseller lists in 1985 and was a Book-of-the-Month Club selection.

Leonard's popularity continued to increase throughout the 1990s. In *Get Shorty,* he used his years of experience as a screenwriter to create an intricate story full of inside jokes about the seamy underbelly of Hollywood. The protagonist is Chili Palmer, a Miami loan shark who travels to California in pursuit

of a man. He is also being pursued, and in the course of the action, he becomes entangled with a third-rate producer, a washed-up actress, and some cocaine dealers. Writing in the *Los Angeles Times Book Review,* Charles Champlin applauds the accuracy of Leonard's portrait of the movie business, calling it "less angry than 'Day of the Locust' but not less devastating in its tour of the industry's soiled follies and the gaminess beneath the grandeurs." Even more sweeping praise comes from Whitney Balliett of the *New Yorker,* who declares that "book by book (he publishes almost one a year), the tireless and ingenious genre novelist Elmore Leonard is painting an intimate, precise, funny, frightening, and irresistible mural of the American underworld. . . . Leonard treats [his characters] with the understanding and the detailed attention that Jane Austen gives her Darcys and Emma Woodhouses."

The publication of *Maximum Bob* in 1991 spurred reviewers on to even greater superlatives. Barry Gifford announces in the *New York Times Book Review:* "Leonard confirms with this, his 29th novel, his right to a prominent place in the American *noir* writers' hall of fame. . . . Nobody I've ever read sets up pace, mood and sound better than Elmore Leonard. . . . [He] is the greatest living writer of crime fiction." The title character is a Florida judge whose nickname comes from his fondness for the electric chair. Having tired of his wife, who believes she is possessed by the spirit of a girl eaten by an alligator 130 years before, the judge attempts to drive her out of his life so that he can pursue another woman. Thus begins the story, described by Robert Carver in *New Statesman & Society* as "a murder chase in reverse, where the killing hasn't yet happened, so you keep trying to guess both victim and perpetrator." Carver asserts that "this is a brilliant, funny, hugely enjoyable black comedy." Clifford Irving remarks in the *Los Angeles Times Book Review* on the profound aspects of the humor found in *Maximum Bob,* stating that "Leonard, like any true comic, has a melancholy view of the world and its primitive denizens. Without moralizing, he is telling us—no, he is showing us—how rotten life is in the heartland of the USA. In 'Maximum Bob,' more than ever, he is the great delineator of the macho redneck, the professional thug, the semi-mindless street-wise slob who kills and maims and rapes because it's part of the American mystique of violence and seems like fun. . . . Elmore Leonard's prose, in its way, is as good as anything being written in this country." Yet not every critic is so sure of the worth of Leonard's work. Savkar Altinel contends in *Times Literary*

Supplement that "certainly, this piece of Florida gothic displays not only his indisputable talents but also his limitations. The plot is good, the characters are well-drawn, the dialogue crackles; what is missing is compassion, any sense that Leonard cares for the [people] he describes, or is even curious about them."

Such objections are the exception, however. *Rum Punch,* published in 1992, inspired Ann Arensberg to write in the *New York Times Book Review:* "I didn't know it was possible to be as good as Elmore Leonard. . . . Outpacing the classic hard-boiled novel, leaving the British detective novel in the dust, Elmore Leonard has compressed *Rum Punch* into almost pure drama, as close to playwriting as novel writing can get (and get away with)." *Washington Post Book World* contributor Michael Dirda calls it "as unputdownable as anyone could wish," as well as "a novel about growing old, about the way that time changes us, about the old dream of starting over again and its cost."

Discussing Leonard's 1993 offering, *Pronto,* Teresa Carpenter laments the fact that "somewhere along the line, it became fashionable to discuss Elmore Leonard in terms formerly reserved for the likes of [French novelist Gustave] Flaubert," but she readily admits in her *New York Times Book Review* piece that his books often "make insightful observations on contemporary culture," "contain sharply drawn portraits of characters on the fringe of society," and, most importantly, that they are fun to read. Still, other reviewers continue to find much more than simple fun in Leonard's books. "Elmore Leonard is a literary genius," Martin Amis states simply in his *New York Times Book Review* assessment of *Riding the Rap.* "[He] possesses gifts—of ear and eye, of timing and phrasing—that even the most indolent and snobbish masters of the mainstream must vigorously covet."

BIOGRAPHICAL/CRITICAL SOURCES:

BOOKS

Authors in the News, Volume 1, Gale (Detroit), 1976.
Contemporary Literary Criticism, Gale, Volume 28, 1984, Volume 34, 1985, Volume 71, 1992.
Geherin, David, *Elmore Leonard,* Continuum (New York City), 1989.

PERIODICALS

American Film, December, 1984.
Armchair Detective, winter, 1986; spring, 1986; winter, 1989.
Boston Globe, July 30, 1992, p. 80; November 14, 1993, p. 7.
Chicago Tribune, February 4, 1981; April 8, 1983; December 8, 1983; February 7, 1985.
Chicago Tribune Book World, April 10, 1983; October 30, 1983; May 21, 1995, section 14, p. 5.
Christian Science Monitor, November 4, 1983.
Commentary, May, 1985, pp. 64, 66-67.
Detroiter, June, 1974.
Detroit News, February 23, 1982; October 23, 1983.
Esquire, April, 1987, pp. 169-74.
Globe and Mail (Toronto), December 14, 1985.
Listener, April 9, 1987, p. 28; October 4, 1990, pp. 30-31.
London Review of Books, September 5, 1985, p. 16.
Los Angeles Times, June 28, 1984; May 4, 1988.
Los Angeles Times Book Review, February 27, 1983;, December 4, 1983; January 13, 1985; August 30, 1987, pp. 2, 8; April 23, 1989, p. 14; July 29, 1990, p. 9; August 4, 1991, pp. 2, 9; October 24, 1994, p. 8; May 14, 1995, p. 1.
Maclean's, January 19, 1987.
Michigan Magazine (Sunday magazine of the *Detroit News*), October 9, 1983.
New Statesman & Society, October 11, 1991; November 13, 1992.
Newsweek, March 22, 1982; July 11, 1983; November 14, 1983; April 22, 1985, pp. 62-64, 67.
New York, May 2, 1988, p. 86.
New Yorker, September 3, 1990, pp. 106-107.
New York Times, June 11, 1982; April 28, 1983; October 7, 1983; October 29, 1983; April 26, 1985; May 2, 1988; July 25, 1991, p. C18; September 23, 1993, p. C18; May 11, 1995; August 15, 1996.
New York Times Book Review, May 22, 1977; September 5, 1982; March 6, 1983; December 27, 1983; February 10, 1985, p. 7; January 4, 1987, p. 7; July 29, 1990, pp. 1, 28; July 28, 1991, p. 8; August 16, 1992, p. 13; October 17, 1993, p. 39; May 14, 1995, p. 7.
Observer (London), September 22, 1991, p. 59; August 16, 1992, p. 13.
People, March 4, 1985.
Publishers Weekly, February 25, 1983; June 15, 1990, p. 55.
Rolling Stone, February 28, 1985.
Spectator, November 27, 1993, p. 42.
Time, May 28, 1984, pp. 84, 86.

Times (London), April 23, 1987.

Times Literary Supplement, December 5, 1986, p. 1370; November 30, 1990, p. 1287; September 27, 1991, p. 24; October 30, 1992, p. 21; November 5, 1993, p. 20.

Tribune Books (Chicago), April 9, 1989, pp. 1, 4.

U.S. News & World Report, March 9, 1987.

Village Voice, February 23, 1982.

Voice Literary Supplement, February, 1985, p. 4.

Washington Post, October 6, 1980; February 6, 1985.

Washington Post Book World, February 7, 1982; July 4, 1982; February 20, 1983; November 13, 1983; December 28, 1986, p. 3; August 23, 1987, pp. 1-2; May 1, 1988; July 14, 1991, pp. 1-2; July 19, 1992, p. 2.

—*Sketch by Joan Goldsworthy*

*   *   *

LEONARD, Thomas C(harles)   1944-

PERSONAL: Born October 17, 1944, in Detroit, MI; son of Vincent C. (a certified public accountant) and Virginia (a librarian; maiden name, Damm) Leonard; married Carol Hurlbut (a psychologist), August 25, 1969; children: Peter S., Anne S. *Education:* University of Michigan, B.A. (high honors), 1966; graduate study at Queens University, Belfast, 1966-67; University of California, Berkeley, Ph.D., 1973.

ADDRESSES: Home—1315 McGee, Berkeley, CA 94703. *Office*—School of Journalism, University of California, 607 Evans, Berkeley, CA 94720.

CAREER: Columbia University, New York City, assistant professor of history, 1973-76; University of California, Berkeley, 1976—, began as assistant professor of journalism, currently associate dean of the Graduate School of Journalism and Director of the Mass Communications program.

MEMBER: American Historical Association, Organization of American Historians.

AWARDS, HONORS: Woodrow Wilson fellow, 1967-68; Ford Foundation fellow, 1967-72.

WRITINGS:

Above the Battle: War-Making in America from Appomattox to Versailles, Oxford University Press (New York City), 1978.

The Power of the Press: The Birth of American Political Reporting, Oxford University Press, 1986.

News for All: America's Coming-of-Age with the Press, Oxford University Press, 1995.

Contributor to *American Quarterly, American Heritage, Media Studies Journal,* and the *Journal of American History;* associate editor, *American National Biography.*

SIDELIGHTS: Cultural historian Thomas C. Leonard explores the history of American journalism and its impact on American politics and society in two of his books, *The Power of the Press: The Birth of American Political Reporting* and *News for All: America's Coming-of-Age with the Press.* As David Armstrong reports in the *Chicago Tribune,* the first book is "a well-written and generally well-researched history of American political reporting before World War I, in which [Leonard] recounts how a scattered handful of tiny newspapers grew into a major force in U.S. political life." Leonard's history outlines some of the major trends in political reporting during this period. In colonial times and the early days of the new nation, journalists often had to battle local authoritarian leaders and a national government reluctant to let journalists into their sphere. Events were reported poorly if at all. In the mid-1800s, political journalism flourished and fed the citizenry's interest in public policy, often exposing social ills and corruption. The twentieth century saw the growth of muckraking. In the end, Leonard "suggests that changing styles of political reporting contributed to the fabulous political participation of the nineteenth century and to the much-lamented apathy that followed in the Progressive era and that continues to this day," notes Mark E. Neely, Jr., in the *American Historical Review.*

In *The Power of the Press,* "Leonard is at his best when he recounts the birth of the Fourth Estate," comments Armstrong. "He has a reporter's eye for detail and a historian's gift for re-creating the past." *New York Times* contributor John Gross finds that Leonard "keeps close to events and personalities, and enlivens his narrative with diverting detail." He adds that some of the author's case studies are especially effective. "Mr. Leonard gives an excellent, unhackneyed account of how Boss Tweed was toppled by *Harper's Weekly* and the *New York Times,* subjecting the editorial strategies of both publications to a more searching examination than they usually receive."

A number of reviewers question Leonard's connection of reporting style to public participation in the political process. For some, he fails to adequately prove his conclusions. *Times Literary Supplement* contributor Kenneth O. Morgan writes: "In some ways, this book is unsatisfactory. It is too brief, hardly allowing the author to develop major elements in his theme." Samuel Kernell argues in *Political Science Quarterly* that "the author's methodology is insufficient to make the kind of case needed to sustain his theory." He maintains: "Rather than systematically examining trends in political reporting or reporters' professional development, Leonard offers us a series of disjointed case studies that merely illustrate his point." Others disagree with Leonard's conclusion that the muckrakers of the early part of this century turned Americans away from an interest in politics. Morgan offers a view shared by other critics: "[Leonard] fails to cover other aspects of the period, including the growth of American society, the explosive expansion of its cities, and the huge immigration from Europe, which left the parties, like most other institutions, beleaguered." The result, in Armstrong's opinion is that this lack of "a broader view of political reporting and political life constricts his vision in this sometimes insightful book."

Still, as other reviewers such as John Kentleton of the *Journal of American Studies* note, "Professor Leonard, if not always very readable, raises a lot of issues; even the full notes are interesting though the index is somewhat economical; but the book itself is, perhaps, more a thoughtful introduction than a final conclusion." And, in the opinion of Neely, "few historians have stopped to think that political reporting even has a history and have used its results without much reflection on its conventions." He concludes, "Leonard offers a fresh perspective on the whole phenomenon and many original and useful observations along the way."

BIOGRAPHICAL/CRITICAL SOURCES:

PERIODICALS

American Historical Review, April, 1987, p. 474.
Best Sellers, July, 1986, p. 146.
Chicago Tribune, December 31, 1986, p. 3.
Journalism Quarterly, spring, 1987, pp. 216-17.
Journal of American Studies, April, 1988, p. 118.
Los Angeles Times Book Review, June 22, 1986, p. 1.
New York Times, March 25, 1986, p. C21.
New York Times Book Review, November 12, 1995, p. 58.
Philadelphia Inquirer, June 8, 1986, p. 7.
Political Science Quarterly, spring, 1987, p. 149.
Publishers Weekly, January 24, 1986, p. 69.
Times Literary Supplement, March 13, 1987, p. 268.

*　　*　　*

LEVIN, Betty 1927-

PERSONAL: Born September 10, 1927, in New York, NY; daughter of Max (a lawyer) and Eleanor (a musician; maiden name, Mack) Lowenthal; married Alvin Levin (a lawyer), August 3, 1947; children: Katherine, Bara, Jennifer. *Education:* University of Rochester, A.B. (high honors), 1949; Radcliffe College, M.A., 1951; Harvard University, A.M.T., 1951.

ADDRESSES: Home—Old Winter St., Lincoln, MA 01773.

CAREER: Museum of Fine Arts, Boston, MA, assistant in research, 1951-52; part-time teaching fellow, Harvard Graduate School of Education, 1953; creative writing fellow, Radcliffe Institute, 1968-70; Massachusetts coordinator, McCarthy Historical Archive, 1969; Pine Manor Open College, Chestnut Hill, MA, instructor in literature, 1970-75; Minute Man Publications, Lexington, MA, feature writer, 1972; Center for the Study of Children's Literature, Simmons College, Boston, special instructor in children's literature, 1975-77, adjunct professor of children's literature, 1977-87; instructor at Emmanuel College, Boston, 1975, and at Radcliffe College, Cambridge, MA, 1976—. Member of the steering committee, Children's Literature New England. Sheep farmer.

MEMBER: Authors Guild, Authors League of America, Masterworks Chorale, Children's Books Authors (Boston), Middlesex Sheep Breeders Association.

AWARDS, HONORS: Judy Lopez Memorial Award, 1989, for *The Trouble with Gramary*; Best Book for Young Adults citation, American Library Association, 1990, for *Brother Moose*; New York Public Library Books for the Teen Age list, 1993, for *Mercy's Mill*; Parents' Choice Story Book Award, 1994, for *Away to Me, Moss!*

WRITINGS:

CHILDREN'S NOVELS

The Zoo Conspiracy, illustrated by Marian Parry, Hastings House (New York City), 1973.

The Sword of Culann, Macmillan (New York City), 1973.

A Griffon's Nest (sequel to *The Sword of Culann*), Macmillan, 1975.

The Forespoken (sequel to *A Griffon's Nest*), Macmillan, 1976.

Landfall, Atheneum (New York City), 1979.

The Beast on the Brink, illustrated by Parry, Avon (New York City), 1980.

The Keeping-Room, Greenwillow (New York City), 1981.

A Binding Spell, Lodestar/Dutton (New York City), 1984.

Put on My Crown, Lodestar/Dutton, 1985.

The Ice Bear, Greenwillow, 1986, MacRae (London), 1987.

The Trouble with Gramary, Greenwillow, 1988.

Brother Moose, Greenwillow, 1990.

Mercy's Mill, Greenwillow, 1992.

Starshine and Sunglow, illustrated by Joseph A. Smith, Greenwillow, 1994.

Away to Me, Moss!, Greenwillow, 1994.

Fire in the Wind, Greenwillow, 1995.

Gift Horse, Greenwillow, 1996.

OTHER

Contributor to books, including *Innocence and Experience: Essays and Conversations on Children's Literature,* compiled and edited by Barbara Harrison and Gregory Maguire, Lothrop (New York City), 1987; and *Proceedings for Travelers in Time,* Green Bay Press, 1990. Contributor of articles to periodicals, including *Harvard Educational Review, Horn Book,* and *Children's Literature in Education.* Levin's manuscripts are housed in the Kerlan Collection, University of Minnesota, Minneapolis.

WORK IN PROGRESS: Island Bound.

SIDELIGHTS: Betty Levin "is not an easy writer," states Adele M. Fasick in *Twentieth-Century Children's Writers,* but she adds that "readers who are willing to immerse themselves in the strange settings and to struggle to understand the significance of mysterious events will find themselves embarking on an enriching experience. Levin's work grows in strength and scope with each book published."

Levin drew upon Celtic and Norse mythology in writing the fantasy trilogy consisting of *The Sword of Culann, A Griffon's Nest,* and *The Forespoken.* In all three novels, Claudia, who lives on an island off the coast of Maine, travels back in time through the use of an ancient sword hilt, visiting Ireland and the Orkney Islands during medieval times. "Levin is skillful in writing of the physical realities of both worlds, especially the cold, dampness, dirt, and hard physical labour," states Fasick. A *Kirkus Reviews* contributor writes of *The Sword of Culann:* "The characters are stirring creations, . . . and although the plot is labyrinthian it's well worth staying on for the surprises and layered revelations at every turn." Finding the use of symbols, magic, and historical events to be implausible in *A Griffon's Nest,* another *Kirkus Reviews* contributor concludes that "for the agile mind" the story is "an unusual adventure in time travel." In a *School Library Journal* review of the final novel of the trilogy, *The Forespoken,* Andrew K. Stevenson finds the numerous subplots confusing, but asserts that the "characterization is good, and the mystery and brutality of the islands is powerfully conveyed."

In the novel *The Trouble with Gramary,* Maine is again the setting. In this story a young girl named Merkka lives in a seaside village. As the town becomes a tourist attraction, Merkka's family is pressured by neighbors to leave their home because of the welding business her grandmother, Gramary, runs out of the backyard. Struggling to understand her grandmother's ways, Merkka eventually learns to appreciate her nonconformity. "Although Merkka doesn't always understand her grandmother, the natural affinity between the two is unmistakable," notes Nancy Vasilakis in *Horn Book.* Eleanor K. MacDonald mentions in her *School Library Journal* review that *The Trouble with Gramary* is "a novel in which place, character, and circumstance mesh into a believable and satisfying whole."

Starshine and Sunglow also has a realistic fusing of character and setting. The story concerns the Flint family, whose sweet corn the whole neighborhood enjoys eating. When they experience trouble with scavenging wildlife, the Flints decide they will no longer grow corn. In an effort to prevent this, neighborhood children band together to keep the wild animals away from the crop by setting up two scarecrows. "Accurate information about the challenges of farming are woven into the plot," observes Lee Bock in *School Library Journal.* A *Kirkus Reviews* contributor points out that the focus in *Starshine and*

Sunglow "is on the nurturing of community spirit," concluding that "Levin has honed her easily read story with a grace and subtle humor."

Although Levin has been writing since the early 1970s, it is only in recent years that awards have been given to her works, including *Mercy's Mill*, which was listed on the New York Public Library's Books for the Teen Age, and *Away to Me, Moss!*, which received a *Parents' Choice* Story Book Award in 1994. *Mercy's Mill* is a time-travel story in which three characters from different periods are able to meet one another at an old mill in Massachusetts. Although the present-day Sarah must discover the secret of a 19th-century boy she meets, the story is primarily about how Sarah grows to become less self-involved and more caring about her family through her experiences at the mill.

In the same way that *Mercy's Mill* is not merely a time-travel story, *Away to Me, Moss!* is not just another dog story. Using her own extensive knowledge of sheep dogs and herding, Levin creates a "heartfelt and satisfying portrayal" of the bond between dogs and people in this novel, as Wendy E. Betts states in her *Five Owls* review. Levin tells the story of a young girl, Zanna, who helps out when a local sheep herder, Rob, has suffered a stroke and needs assistance with his sheep dog. The novel also concerns Zanna's family problems as her parents face divorce. Critics praised Levin's adept handling of such a complicated plot: "The stress of both Zanna's and Rob's families is skillfully paralleled," according to Betsy Hearne in the *Bulletin of the Center for Children's Books*. "Levin sketches adult problems adroitly," remarks a *Kirkus Reviews* contributor.

Levin notes in her essay for *Something about the Author Autobiography Series:* "The themes I'm drawn to and the situations I explore through fiction reflect not only the places and people and ways of life I love, but also the baffling aspects of the human condition—human traits that sadden and trouble me. I see connections between some of the tiny experiences in my early childhood and unavoidable truths about callousness and cruelty."

BIOGRAPHICAL/CRITICAL SOURCES:

BOOKS

Something about the Author Autobiography Series, Volume 11, Gale (Detroit), 1991.

Twentieth-Century Children's Writers, 4th edition, St. James Press (Detroit), 1995.

PERIODICALS

Booklist, November 15, 1984, p. 449; May 1, 1990, p. 1598; December 1, 1992, p. 670.

Bulletin of the Center for Children's Books, January, 1976, p. 81; April, 1981, p. 155; July/August, 1985; January, 1987, pp. 91-92; May, 1990, p. 219; December, 1994, pp. 135-36.

Fantasy Review, January, 1987, p. 45.

Five Owls, February, 1995, pp. 63-64.

Horn Book, February, 1977; December, 1979, pp. 669-70; May/June, 1988, pp. 353-54; January/February, 1993, p. 92; September/October, 1994, pp. 587-88.

Kirkus Reviews, November 1, 1973, pp. 1212-13; April 15, 1975, p. 465; July 15, 1976, p. 799; August 15, 1992, p. 1064; May 15, 1994, p. 702; October 15, 1994, pp. 1410-11.

Learning Teacher, May, 1993, p. 33.

Publishers Weekly, June 18, 1973, p. 70; September 21, 1992, p. 95.

Quill and Quire, February, 1991, p. 25.

School Library Journal, September, 1973, p. 71; October, 1973, p. 126; October, 1976, p. 118; November, 1979, pp. 89-90; December, 1984, p. 101; October, 1986, p. 192; April, 1988, p. 102; July, 1990, p. 77; September, 1992, p. 278; June, 1994, p. 132.

Times Educational Supplement, June 5, 1987, p. 64.

Times Literary Supplement, July 24, 1987, p. 804.

Voice of Youth Advocates, August, 1981, pp. 29-30; August, 1988, p. 132.

Wilson Library Bulletin, October, 1988, p. 78.*

*   *   *

LEVIN, Gail

PERSONAL: Born in Atlanta, GA; daughter of Barron W. and Shirley (Sunshine) Levin. *Education:* Attended Sorbonne, University of Paris, 1968; Simmons College, B.A. (with honors), 1969; Tufts University, M.A., 1970; Rutgers University, Ph.D., 1976. *Avocational interests:* International travel, gardening.

ADDRESSES: Office—Baruch College, City University of New York, 17 Lexington Ave., New York, NY 10010.

CAREER: Rutgers University, New Brunswick, NJ, junior instructor, 1970-71, instructor in art history at Newark College of Arts and Sciences, 1972-73; New School for Social Research, New York City, instructor in art history, 1973-75; Connecticut College, New London, assistant professor of art history, 1975-76; Whitney Museum of American Art, New York City, curator of the Edward Hopper Collection, 1976-84; Bernard M. Baruch College and the Graduate School, City University of New York, New York City, professor of art history, 1986—. Instructor at Drew University, spring, 1973. Organizes panels, symposia, and art exhibitions.

MEMBER: College Art Association of America.

AWARDS, HONORS: Citation of excellence from Art Libraries Society of New York, 1979, for *Synchromism and American Color Abstraction, 1910-1925;* D.L. (honoris causa), Simmons College, 1996; received special mention at the George Wittenborn Memorial Awards, Art Libraries Society of North America (ARLIS/NA), for *Edward Hopper: A Catalogue Raisonne,* 1996.

WRITINGS:

Synchromism and American Color Abstraction, 1910-1925, Braziller (New York City), 1978.

(With Robert C. Hobbs) *Abstract Expressionism: The Formative Years,* Whitney Museum of American Art (New York City), 1978.

Edward Hopper: The Complete Prints, Norton (New York City), 1979.

Edward Hopper as Illustrator, Norton, 1979.

Edward Hopper: The Art and the Artist, Norton, 1980.

(Contributor) Tom Wolf, *Konrad Cramer: A Retrospective,* Bard College Center (Annandale-on-Hudson, NY), 1981.

(With Dewey F. Mosby) *Alex Katz, Process and Development: Small Paintings from the Collection of Paul J. Schupf '58,* Picker Art Gallery, Colgate University (Hamilton, NY), 1984.

Edward Hopper, Crown (New York City), 1984.

Hopper's Places, Knopf (New York City), 1985.

Twentieth Century American Painting: The Thyssen-Bornemisza Collection, Sothby Publications (London), 1987.

Marsden Hartley in Bavaria, University Press of New England, Hannover, and London, 1989.

Theme and Improvisation: Kandinsky and the American Avant-Garde, 1912-1915, Little, Brown (Boston), 1992.

Edward Hopper: A Catalogue Raisonne (three volumes and a CD-ROM), Norton, 1995.

Edward Hopper: An Intimate Biography, Knopf, 1995.

(Editor) *The Poetry of Solitude: A Tribute to Edward Hopper,* Universe, 1995.

Author of exhibition brochures and catalogues. Contributor to over thirty books and of more than fifty articles to art journals, including *Connoisseur, Museum, Woman's Art Journal, Arts,* and *Criticism.*

SIDELIGHTS: Art historian and museum curator Gail Levin has made a career of bringing the world of twentieth-century art and artists to the American public. Her most notable achievements in this field deal with the career and work of the American realist painter Edward Hopper. Regarding Hopper, Arthur C. Danto in a *Nation* review comments: "more than any artist in our history—more than Inness or Eakins or Homer—Hopper found a way of showing not just how America looks but how America *is.*" In addition to her past work as curator of the Whitney Museum of American Art's Hopper collection, Levin has published eight books on the painter. In *Hopper's Places,* Levin compares and contrasts a selection of Hopper's paintings of buildings in New York, Massachusetts, and Maine with photographs of the actual buildings. "To compare photographs of unmemorable structures with the saturate, intensely lighted paintings . . . is to see how realism is much more than mere depiction," comments Renee Gernand in the *New York Times Book Review.* The images and Levin's discussion create "a beautiful, intriguing portfolio," according to a contributor to *Booklist.*

Levin's most detailed and significant account of the painter is her 1995 book, *Edward Hopper: An Intimate Biography.* Drawing largely from the journals of Hopper's wife, Josephine ("Jo") Nivison, and comments from friends, art critics, and the painter himself, as well as her own scholarship, Levin offers a portrait of the painter and his art. Michael Kammen suggests in the *New York Times Book Review* that this book "should reach a wide readership for many reasons: it is a compelling and accessible narrative for anyone even remotely interested in modern American art." Kammen finds the biography "a nearly flawless account of a remarkable artist scarred by an absolutely dismal temperament."

This insight into Hopper the man may offer some surprises to his admiring public. In a description of

Jo, Hopper's wife, Robert Coles writes in the *Washington Post Book World:* "Wisely, generously, [Levin] lets Jo herself present her day-to-day struggles with her mighty, inscrutable, tenaciously determined husband—a continuing, detailed narrative by a protagonist, and at times, an antagonist. For over four decades these two artists lived together, loved and inspired one another, and not least, locked horns." Danto similarly explains that the relationship "was a deep but terrifying marriage, as frustrating as it was fulfilling," and that Hopper "existed on two planes at once, and must have been hell to live with on both. But the complex interplay between engagement and detachment is the glory of his art." Kammen sums up the impact of Levin's portrait of the artist and his art: "Readers of this masterly but chilling book will never again view with quite the same feelings a picture by Edward Hopper, perhaps the most powerful American 'realist' painter of the 20th century."

Levin once told *CA* about the primary aims of her work: "Art history can be at once scholarly and accessible to a general audience. I write about art and artists with the belief that I can explain important concepts and interpret essential ideas while making art more comprehensible to a larger public. The study of art offers insights into the cultural fabric of a society. Art history at its best investigates related developments in music, literature, theatre, popular art forms, and science."

BIOGRAPHICAL/CRITICAL SOURCES:

PERIODICALS

Atlanta Journal and Constitution, December 1, 1985, p. J1; March 21, 1993, p. N8.
Booklist, December 1, 1984, p. 474; December 1, 1985, p. 522.
Chicago Tribune Book World, December 7, 1980.
Library Journal, September 15, 1992, p. 37; September 1, 1995.
Los Angeles Times Book Review, November 5, 1995, p. 2.
Nation, October 2, 1995, pp. 355-58.
Newsweek, August 7, 1995, pp. 58-59.
New Yorker, November 13, 1995, p. 127.
New York Times, June 26, 1976; January 27, 1978.
New York Times Book Review, January 19, 1986, p. 21; October 8, 1995, p. 15.
School Library Journal, December, 1995, p. 31.
Venice, January/February, 1996, pp. 72-73.
Washington Post Book World, October 15, 1995, pp. 1, 11.
Women Artists News, spring, 1996, pp. 31-32.

LEYNER, Mark 1956-

PERSONAL: Born January 4, 1956, in Jersey City, NJ; son of Joel (a lawyer) and Muriel (a real estate agent; maiden name, Chasan) Leyner; married Arleen Portada (a psychotherapist; marriage ended); married second wife, Mercedes; children: Gabrielle. *Education:* Brandeis University, B.A., 1977; University of Colorado, M.F.A., 1979. *Religion:* Jewish.

ADDRESSES: Agent—Amanda Urban, International Creative Management, 40 W. 57th St., New York, NY 10019.

CAREER: Panasonic Co., Secaucus, NJ, advertising copywriter, 1981-82; Brooklyn College of the City University of New York, Brooklyn, NY, lecturer in English, 1982; lecturer, Jersey City State College, 1982-84; freelance copywriter, 1984-88; freelance writer and novelist, 1989—.

WRITINGS:

I Smell Esther Williams and Other Stories, Fiction Collective (New York City), 1983.
(Editor with Curtis White and Thomas Glynn) *American Made,* Fiction Collective, 1986.
My Cousin, My Gastroenterologist, Fiction Collective, 1989.
Et Tu, Babe, Harmony Books (New York City), 1992.
Tooth Imprints on a Corn Dog, Harmony Books, 1995.

Contributor of stories, articles, plays, and poems to magazines, including *Fictional International, Esquire, Mississippi Review, Rolling Stone, Semiotexte,* and *Between C and D.*

ADAPTATIONS: My Cousin, My Gastroenterologist, I Smell Esther Williams and Other Stories, and *Et Tu, Babe* were all released as sound recordings (read by the author) by Dove Audio in 1990, 1991, and 1992 respectively.

SIDELIGHTS: "I feel like I'm living a writer's life at warp speed," Mark Leyner tells *Boston Globe* contributor Joseph P. Kahn. "In three years I've gone from being a fringe avant-gardist to a cult object to mainstream novelist." Leyner's novels and short story collections to date—*I Smell Esther Williams and Other Stories, My Cousin, My Gastroenterologist, Et Tu, Babe,* and *Tooth Imprints on a Corn Dog*—depict a warped, gonzo world in which literally anything can happen, and usually does. "Reading his books," states Jonathan Yardley in the *Washington Post Book World,* "is like watching a blend of *Saturday Night Live* and *Monty Python;* they have the energy and insouciance of high-risk, off-the-wall performance." "When you have been called America's best-built comic novelist by *The New York Times,* personal trainer to pop-culture heavyweights everywhere," Kahn argues, "you are liable to say, do and write almost anything."

Leyner began his writing career as a poet at his New Jersey high school. When he moved on to Brandeis University, he began experimenting with using poetic techniques in fiction. "I thought, 'Wouldn't it be wonderful to have the kind of fiction that was as dense with imagery and dense with excitement and pleasure as poetry is,'" Leyner tells *Los Angeles Times* contributor Irene Lacher, "'and have a kind of fiction that didn't have all kinds of dumb transitional pages where you're getting people off a plane to a hotel?'" Leyner's first venture into this type of prose was *I Smell Esther Williams and Other Stories,* which "was written in graduate school" at the University of Colorado, Kahn explains, "and is regarded today by its author rather like an old prom date who rebuffed his advances in the back seat of her father's convertible."

Leyner's second book, *My Cousin, My Gastroenterologist,* was published in 1989 and established him as a favorite of the collegiate undergraduate literati. "That manic volume of surreal prose poetry," writes Lacher, "offered cameo appearances from the Pope's *valet de chambre* and Nazi filmmaker Leni Riefenstahl—not to mention such unlikely inventions as Le Corbusier-designed jeans and the fearfully sexually over-mature Joey D., who at 4 1/2 revved a tricycle with a turbo-charged V-8 engine." "Leyner is regarded as the Writer for the MTV Generation," Lacher explains, "the spiritual stepson of William Burroughs and Lenny Bruce, only with a high-tech sheen."

The author explains in a clip reprinted in *Harper's* magazine that he supported himself "by doing advertising copywriting" while working on *My Cousin, My Gastroenterologist.* The novel's success allowed Leyner to devote himself full-time to writing and also gave him a theme for his next book, *Et Tu, Babe.* "The novel (using the term in the loosest imaginable sense)," states Yardley, "is about 'the most intense and, in a certain sense, the most significant young prose writer in America.' His name is Mark Leyner." The character Leyner, who in many respects resembles the author Leyner, is obsessed with self-promotion. He has even gathered a group of enthusiasts, called Team Leyner, to assist him in his publicity stunts. *New York Times* reviewer Michiko Kakutani writes, "The reader learns of such bizarre phenomena as weight-loss camps for terrorists, penile-growth hormones; medical cheese sculptures (sculptures of human organs, made of mozzarella and havarti), interactive computerized laser-video players that insert Mr. Schwarzenegger as the actor in any movie . . . and 'visceral tattoos,' that is, tattoos inscribed on people's internal organs with radioactive isotopes."

"I figured Team Leyner would reach some kind of apogee in the middle of the book, when it would be most powerful," Leyner tells *Bloomsbury Review* interviewers John and Carl Bellante. "The Leyner character would be at his most megalomaniacal. His delusions of grandeur would be full-blown. Then gradually, the Team Leyner minions, personnel, and staff would start deserting him." In the end the Leyner character is left alone, and finally even he vanishes—mourned in passing by such celebrities as Connie Chung and Carl Sagan. "If the world is a leopard-print cocktail lounge on the Titanic," declares Carol Anshaw in the *Village Voice Literary Supplement,* "Leyner is at the piano, noodling out 'My Way.'" "Mr. Leyner," concludes *New York Times Book Review* contributor Lewis Burke Frumkes, "is a very funny man who has written a very twisted book."

Leyner's 1995 collection of short stories, *Tooth Imprints on a Corn Dog,* continues his exploration through the manic world he perceives around him. "*Tooth Imprints,*" explains Kristan Schiller in the *New York Times,* "is based on occurrences in Mr. Leyner's life . . . spun into surreal tales that satirize the media-crazed, image-obsessed society he beholds—and accepts." "The results are intermittently hilarious," Kakutani states, "but also silly and highly sophomoric." The work "lacks the abrasive, experimental edge of his previous fiction," writes Jonathan Bing in *Publishers Weekly,* but "it nevertheless exhibits all the whimsy, irreverence and biting satire of his best work. The protagonist is still, much of the time, Mark Leyner; yet his persona is gentler, more circumspect, given to tender reflections about the pressures of fatherhood and professional free-lancing." Rick Marin argues in a *Newsweek* review of *Tooth Imprints* that though the novel is "Leyner's most accessible opus to date, it is emphatically not for everyone. Then again, what good book is?"

Mark Leyner told *CA:* "My work isn't animated by a desire to be experimental or post-modernist or aesthetically subversive or even 'innovative'—it is animated by a desire to craft a kind of writing that is at every single moment exhilarating for the reader; where each phrase, each sentence is an event. That's what I'm trying for, at least. This, I think, is what gives my work its peculiar shape and feel—it's because I want every little surface to shimmer and gyrate that I haven't patience for those lax transitional devices of plot, setting, character, and so on, that characterize a lot of traditional fiction. I'm after the gaudiness, self-consciousness, laughter, encoded sadness of public language (public because language is the sea in which all our minds swim).

"I don't feel part of any artistic movement or 'ism.' But I feel linked to artists who launched their careers reading billboards aloud in the back seats on family trips, who spent their formative Saturday mornings cemented to their television screens with Crazy Glue, who grew up fascinated by the rhetoric of pentecostal preachers, dictators, game show hosts, and other assorted demagogues, who were entranced by the outlandishly superfluous chatter of baseball announcers filling air-time during rain delays, and who could never figure out the qualitative difference between Thackeray's *Vanity Fair* and E. C. Segar's *Popeye the Sailor.*

"I said in an article once that we need a kind of writing that the brain can dance to. Well, that's the kind of writing I'm trying to write—thrashing the smoky air of the cerebral ballroom with a very American ball-point baton."

BIOGRAPHICAL/CRITICAL SOURCES:

PERIODICALS

Bloomsbury Review, July/August, 1993, pp. 5-7.
Boston Globe, November 9, 1993, p. 29.
Harper's, July, 1990, pp. 43-44.
Los Angeles Times, November 6, 1992, pp. E1, E4.
Los Angeles Times Book Review, October 11, 1992, p. 6.
Newsweek, March 27, 1995, p. 68.
New York Times, October 13, 1992, p. C17; February 19, 1995, p. J13; March 7, 1995, p. C18.
New York Times Book Review, September 27, 1992, p. 14; April 23, 1995, p. 12.

Publishers Weekly, March 6, 1995, pp. 44-45.
San Francisco Review of Books, winter, 1992, p. 40.
Village Voice Literary Supplement, November, 1992, pp. 25-27.
Washington Post Book World, October 4, 1992, p. 3.*

* * *

LINDEY, Christine 1947-

PERSONAL: Born in 1947 in France; daughter of J. C. A. and M. M. (Taillhardat) Chaimowicz; married Raymond Lindey (a caretaker), 1967. *Ethnicity:* "Human being." *Education:* Courtauld Institute of Art, London, B.A., 1973.

ADDRESSES: Home—London, England. *Office*—West Herts College, The Art School, Leavesden Rd., Watford, Hertfordshire, WD2 5EF, England.

CAREER: Part-time lecturer in art history at art schools in England, 1973—. Lecturer at Watford School of Art, 1976—.

WRITINGS:

Surrealist Painting and Sculpture, Morrow (New York City), 1980.
Twentieth-Century Painting: Bonnard to Rothko, Warne (New York City), 1981.
Art in the Cold War: From Vladivostok to Kalamazoo, 1945-62, The Herbert Press (London), 1990.

WORK IN PROGRESS: An autobiographical novel; an exploration of the relationship between painting and creative writing.

SIDELIGHTS: Christine Lindey told *CA:* "My current area of interest is art since World War II. I aim to write in a manner which is accessible to the non-specialist, and I try to avoid unnecessarily obtuse terms. My concern is with public response and the context within which art operates, as well as the aims of the artists themselves."

* * *

Lo BELLO, Nino 1921-

PERSONAL: Born September 8, 1921, in Brooklyn, NY; son of Joseph and Rosalie (Moscarelli) Lo

Bello; married Irene Helen Rooney, February 22, 1948; children: Susan, Thomas. *Education:* Queens College (now Queens College of the City University of New York), B.A., 1947; New York University, M.A., 1948, graduate study, 1948-50. *Politics:* Liberal. *Religion:* Roman Catholic. *Avocational interests:* Opera ("opera buff supreme").

ADDRESSES: Home—Loquai Platz II/A-1060 Vienna, Austria. *Office*—Foreign Press Club of Vienna, 8 Bank Gasse, Vienna, Austria. *Agent*—McIntosh & Otis, Inc., 310 Madison Ave., New York, NY 10017.

CAREER: Newspaper reporter in Brooklyn, NY, 1946-50; University of Kansas, Lawrence, instructor in sociology, 1950-56; Rome correspondent for *Business Week* and McGraw-Hill's *World News,* 1957-62, and *New York Journal of Commerce,* 1962-64; *New York Herald Tribune,* New York City, economic correspondent in Vienna, Austria, 1964-66; freelance journalist. Visiting professor at Denison University, 1956, and University of Alaska, 1974. *Military service:* U.S. Army, 1942-46.

MEMBER: Overseas Press Club of America, Foreign Press Club of Vienna, Foreign Press Club of Rome.

WRITINGS:

The Vatican Empire, Simon & Schuster (New York City), 1968.
The Vatican's Wealth, Bruce & Watson, 1971.
Vatican, U.S.A., Simon & Schuster, 1972.
European Detours, Hammond, Inc. (Maplewood, NJ), 1981.
The Vatican Papers, New English Library (London, England), 1982.
Vatikan im Zwielicht, Econ-Verlag, 1983, revised edition (with four new chapters), Heine-Verlag, 1990.
Nino Lo Bello's Guide to Offbeat Europe, Chicago Review Press (Chicago, IL), 1985.
English Well Speeched Here, Price, Stern (Los Angeles, CA), 1986.
Nino Lo Bello's Guide to the Vatican, Chicago Review Press, 1987.
Der Vatikan, HPT-Verlagsgesellschaft, 1988.
The Travel Trivia Handbook of European Sights, Citadel Press (Secaucus, NJ), 1992.

WORK IN PROGRESS: Twelve-volume encyclopedic work; a travel book about the Danube River.

SIDELIGHTS: Nino Lo Bello once told *CA:* "It has not been my purpose, in writing frequently about the Vatican, to demean the Roman Catholic religion (the one I grew up with and practice), either in the eyes of Catholics or non-Catholics. I make no judgment on the validity of the faith, for I recognize that the religion gives many people solace and joy. Furthermore, though I have not sought to rebut any Catholic tenets, I have concerned myself with certain imperfections and failings among the men who run the Church. As a journalist I have attempted in my books always to be as professionally objective as is humanly possible and let the facts speak for themselves.

"Whoever takes it upon himself to write about the Vatican could easily give the impression that he is an expert. There are, in my opinion, no experts on the Vatican. There are, indeed, Vatican-watchers, Vatican theorists, and Vaticanologists—but there are no Vatican experts. This reminds me of a story: During an audience one day when a dozen cardinals, bishops, and assorted clerics were present, and Pope Pius XII was in one of his rare good moods, he asked two young priests the same question: 'How long have you been in the Vatican?' The first man replied, 'Three weeks.' 'Then,' said the pope, 'you are an expert on the Vatican!' The second man gave as his reply, 'Three years.' 'Then,' said the pope, 'you know nothing about the Vatican!'"

BIOGRAPHICAL/CRITICAL SOURCES:

PERIODICALS

Christian Science Monitor, July 31, 1969.
Commonweal, February 28, 1969.
New York Times, February 3, 1969.
New York Times Book Review, June 29, 1969.
Saturday Review, February 8, 1969.

*   *   *

LOCKE, Elsie 1912-

PERSONAL: Born August 17, 1912, in Hamilton, New Zealand; daughter of William John (a builder) and Ellen (Bryan) Farrelly; married John Gibson Locke (a meat worker); children: Donald Bryan, Keith James, Maire Frances, Alison Gwyneth. *Education:* University of Auckland, B.A., 1932. *Politics:* "No political affiliation." *Religion:* "Agnostic-humanist."

ADDRESSES: Home—392 Oxford Ter., Christchurch 1, New Zealand.

CAREER: Writer. Former worker in New Zealand libraries.

AWARDS, HONORS: Katherine Mansfield Award, 1959, for essay "Looking for Answers," published in *Landfall,* December, 1958; D.Litt., University of Canterbury, Christchurch, 1987, for work in children's literature and history.

WRITINGS:

The Runaway Settlers (juvenile historical novel), J. Cape (London), 1965, Dutton (New York City), 1966.

The End of the Harbour (juvenile historical novel), J. Cape, 1968.

Maori King and British Queen, Hulton Educational (London), 1974.

Look under the Leaves, Pumpkin Press (Christchurch, New Zealand), 1975.

Moko's Hideout, Whitcoulls (Christchurch), 1976.

(With Ken Dawson) *The Boy with the Snowgrass Hair* (juvenile adventure novel), Whitcoulls, 1976, Price Milburn, 1983.

Explorer Zach (juvenile novel), Pumpkin Press, 1978.

The Gaoler (adult history), Dunmore Press, 1978.

Student at the Gates (personal experience), Whitcoulls, 1981.

Journey under Warning (juvenile historical novel), Oxford University Press, 1983.

The Kauri and the Willow, Government Printer (New Zealand), 1984.

A Canoe in the Mist (juvenile historical novel), J. Cape, 1984.

Two Peoples, One Land (history), Government Printer, 1988.

Peace People, Hazard Press (Christchurch), 1992.

Joe's Ruby, Cape Catley (Picton, New Zealand), 1995.

Also author of radio scripts, articles, and poems.

SIDELIGHTS: Of European descent from early New Zealand settlers on both sides of her family, Elsie Locke told *CA* that she is "also very interested in the Maori (Polynesian) side of New Zealand life, and the human relationship with the earth and all it bears." She adds: "Children are to be enjoyed, their individuality respected, their imaginations cherished; and writing for them is a privilege and a pleasure. To

defend their world from the threat of nuclear and/or ecological disaster, and to secure a fully human life for those now deprived, are aims I share with millions of others; but I am optimistic and not solemn in my writings. I would like all children to enjoy their childhood as much as I did mine."

*   *   *

LOCKE, Ralph P(aul)   1949-

PERSONAL: Born March 9, 1949, in Boston, MA; son of Merle I. and Doris (Tobis) Locke; married Lona M. Farhi, May 26, 1979; children: Martha Deborah, Susannah Felicia. *Education:* Harvard University, B.A., 1970; University of Chicago, M.A., 1974, Ph.D., 1980.

ADDRESSES: Home—Rochester, NY. *Office*—Department of Musicology, Eastman School of Music, University of Rochester, 26 Gibbs St., Rochester, NY 14604.

CAREER: University of Rochester, Eastman School of Music, Rochester, NY, instructor, 1975-80, assistant professor, 1980-84, associate professor, 1984-88, professor of musicology, 1988—.

MEMBER: American Musicological Society (member of council, 1985-87; member of board of directors, 1994-96), Societe Francaise de Musicologie, Association Nationale Hector Berlioz, Sonneck Society.

AWARDS, HONORS: Grant from Deutscher Akademischer Austauschdienst, 1970; French government exchange fellow, 1974, and Bourse d'Ete, 1976; "Best Article of a Bibliographic Nature" award from Music Library Association, 1982, for "New Schumann Material in Upstate New York"; American Council of Learned Societies research fellowship, 1984; Deems Taylor Award, 1992, for excellence in writing about music; grants from American Musicological Society, 1986 and 1995, and from Sonneck Society, 1995.

WRITINGS:

Music, Musicians, and the Saint-Simonians, University of Chicago Press (Chicago), 1986.

(Editor with Cyrilla Barr) *Cultivating Music in America: Women Patrons and Activists since 1860,* University of California Press (Berkeley), in press.

Contributor to books. Contributor to *New Harvard Dictionary of Music, New Grove Dictionary of Music, New Grove Dictionary of American Music, New Grove Dictionary of Opera, Norton/Grove Dictionary of Woman Composers* and *Encyclopaedia Britannica.* Contributor of articles and reviews to music journals, including *Cambridge Opera Journal* and *Opera Quarterly.*

WORK IN PROGRESS: Research on musical exoticism from Rameau to Messiaen, text-music relations in the settings of Emily Dickinson's poems, musical patronage and institutions in America, the symphony in France, the Walton viola concerto, and the relationship between music scholarship and issues of social concern and social justice.

SIDELIGHTS: Ralph P. Locke told *CA:* "My research focuses in varying ways on the relationship between music and society. In my book on the Saint-Simonians I sought to reveal the intricate and previously unknown ties that connected this major social movement of the 1830s to the music and musicians of its day, including Berlioz, Felicien David, Halevy, Liszt, and Mendelssohn.

"My ongoing work on musical exoticism broadens the focus of my 'music and society' studies to include a wide range of music: operas of such composers as Rameau, Mozart, Bizet, Verdi, and Puccini, but also instrumental music of Saint-Saens, Debussy and others. Looking at these composers' evocation of the exotic also leads me to touch upon a number of intriguing issues, notably the ways in which musical portrayals of distant regions, especially the Middle East, contributed to the cultural self-definition of the Western European. And since we are in many ways the heirs of that European, my studies carry some implications for understanding such present-day concerns as the hidden messages in 'high culture,' the Western view of the non-Western world generally, and the meanings that music, that supposedly abstract and pure art, transmits from composer and performer to listener.

"Finally, I have been giving a lot of attention to the concrete problems of how music and the arts generally are supported by various social institutions, including government and coalitions of private citizens.

"I might mention that, as a writer, I try to write as directly and flavorfully as possible, but also try to avoid making simplistic assertions about complex phenomena. It is a tricky balancing act, and it needs to be handled differently in publications aimed at different kinds of readers."

* * *

LODGE, David (John) 1935-

PERSONAL: Born January 28, 1935, in England; son of William Frederick (a musician) and Rosalie (Murphy) Lodge; married Mary Frances Jacob, May 16, 1959; children: Julia, Stephen, Christopher. *Education:* University College, London, B.A. (with first class honors), 1955, M.A., 1959; University of Birmingham, Ph.D., 1967. *Religion:* Roman Catholic.

ADDRESSES: Office—Department of English, University of Birmingham, Birmingham B15 2TT, England. *Agent*—Curtis Brown Ltd., 28-29 Haymarket, London SW1Y 4SP, England.

CAREER: British Council, London, England, assistant, 1959-60; University of Birmingham, Birmingham, England, lecturer, 1960-71, senior lecturer, 1971-73, reader, 1973-76, professor of modern English literature, 1976-87, honorary professor, 1987—. Visiting associate professor, University of California, Berkeley, 1969. *Military service:* British Army, 1955-57.

AWARDS, HONORS: Harkness Commonwealth fellowship, 1964-65, for study and travel in the United States; *Yorkshire Post* fiction prize and Hawthornden Prize, both 1975, for *Changing Places: A Tale of Two Campuses;* Royal Society of Literature fellowship, 1976; Whitbread Award for fiction and for book of the year, 1980, for *How Far Can You Go?;* Sunday Express Book of the Year, 1989, for *Nice Work;* Royal Television Society award for best drama serial and Silver Nymph for best mini-series screenplay Monte Carlo International TV Festival, both 1990, for *Nice Work.*

WRITINGS:

CRITICISM

Language of Fiction, Columbia University Press (New York City), 1966.
Graham Greene, Columbia University Press, 1966.

The Novelist at the Crossroads and Other Essays on Fiction and Criticism, Cornell University Press (Ithaca, NY), 1971.

Evelyn Waugh, Columbia University Press, 1971.

The Modes of Modern Writing: Metaphor, Metonymy and the Typology of Modern Literature, Cornell University Press, 1977, University of Chicago Press (Chicago, IL), 1988.

Working with Structuralism: Essays and Reviews on Nineteenth and Twentieth-Century Literature, Routledge & Kegan Paul (Boston), 1981.

Write On: Occasional Essays, Secker & Warburg (London), 1986.

After Bakhtin: Essays on Fiction and Criticism, Routledge (London), 1990.

The Art of Fiction: Illustrated from Classic and Modern Texts, Secker & Warburg, 1992, Viking (New York City), 1993.

The Practice of Writing: Essays, Lectures, Reviews, and a Diary, Secker & Warburg, 1996.

NOVELS

The Picturegoers, MacGibbon & Kee, 1960, new edition, Penguin (London), 1993.

Ginger, You're Barmy, MacGibbon & Kee, 1962, Doubleday (New York City), 1965, reprinted with a new introduction by the author, Secker & Warburg, 1982.

The British Museum Is Falling Down, MacGibbon & Kee, 1965, Holt, 1967, reprinted with a new introduction by the author, Secker & Warburg, 1981.

Out of the Shelter, Macmillan (Basingstoke, England), 1970, revised edition, Secker & Warburg, 1985, revised edition with an introduction by the author, Penguin (New York City), 1989.

Changing Places: A Tale of Two Campuses, Secker & Warburg, 1975, Penguin, 1979.

How Far Can You Go?, Secker & Warburg, 1980, published as *Souls and Bodies,* Morrow (New York City), 1982.

Small World: An Academic Romance, Secker & Warburg, 1984, Macmillan, 1985.

Nice Work, Secker & Warburg, 1988, Viking (New York City), 1989.

Paradise News, Secker & Warburg, 1991, Viking, 1992.

Therapy, Secker & Warburg, 1995, Viking, 1995.

EDITOR

Jane Austen's "Emma": A Casebook, Macmillan, 1968.

(And author of introduction) Jane Austen, *Emma,* Oxford University Press, 1971, revised edition, Macmillan, 1991.

Twentieth Century Literary Criticism: A Reader, Longman (London), 1972.

George Eliot, *Scenes of Clerical Life,* Penguin, 1973.

Thomas Hardy, *The Woodlanders,* Macmillan, 1974.

Henry James, *The Spoils of Poynton,* Penguin, 1987.

Modern Criticism and Theory: A Reader, Longman, 1988.

PLAYS

(With Malcolm Bradbury and James Duckett) *Between These Four Walls,* produced in Birmingham, England, 1963.

(With Duckett and David Turner) *Slap in the Middle,* produced in Birmingham, England, 1965.

The Writing Game, produced in Birmingham, England, 1990, and Cambridge, MA, 1991.

OTHER

About Catholic Authors (juvenile), St. Paul Press, 1958.

(Author of introduction) *The Best of Ring Lardner,* Dent, 1984.

Contributor to *The State of the Language,* edited by Leonard Michaels and Christopher Ricks, University of California Press (Berkeley), 1980. Also contributor of articles and reviews to *Critical Quarterly, Tablet, Times Literary Supplement, New Republic, New York Times Book Review, New York Review of Books,* and *Encounter.*

ADAPTATIONS: Nice Work was adapted by the British Broadcasting Corp. as a television mini-series in 1989; *The Writing Game* was adapted for television, 1996.

SIDELIGHTS: David Lodge is known to general readers as a novelist whose works, while often treating serious themes, are "exuberant" and "marvelously funny," in the words of *New York Times Book Review* contributor Michael Rosenthal. The settings and characters of Lodge's novels reflect his own life experiences, including a childhood in wartime London, a stint in the British Army, study as a graduate student, and work as a university professor. His Roman Catholic upbringing has profoundly influenced his fiction as well. "Most of his novels have at least some Catholic statement in them," notes Dennis Jackson in *Dictionary of Literary Biography,* and "one of the recurrent themes in Lodge's stories is the struggle of his Catholic characters to reconcile their spiritual and sensual desires."

Lodge began work on his first published novel while completing his service in the British army. Published in 1960 as *The Picturegoers*, this book describes a group of Catholics living in a dingy London suburb and the changes they experience over the course of a year. The thoughts and dreams of over a dozen characters are revealed through their reactions to the films they watch regularly in the crumbling local cinema, focusing most sharply on Mark Underwood, a thoughtful young literature student who has fallen away from the church. While finishing school, Mark boards with the Mallory family and becomes enamored of Clare Mallory, a former convent novice. As he attempts to seduce her, she attempts to reawaken his faith. In an ironic conclusion, Clare, having fallen in love with Mark, offers herself to him, but he rejects her to join the priesthood. Some reviewers fault the book as disconnected and overburdened with characters, but "for a first novel, *The Picturegoers* is eminently lively and readable," believes Jackson. Lodge's "alternation of diction, tone, and rhythm as he shifts from . . . the inner thoughts of one character to those of another seems particularly impressive." In addition, "a lot of it is quite funny," writes Maurice Richardson in *New Statesman*.

An "act of revenge" is Lodge's description of his next book, writes Jackson. *Ginger, You're Barmy* grew out of the author's years in the army, an experience he bitterly resented. The tedium, brutality and dehumanizing atmosphere of life in the service are evoked with a "total recall" that is "unnerving," according to *New Statesman* contributor Christopher Ricks. The novel's tension is provided by the contrast between the narrator, Jonathan Browne, and his friend, Mike "Ginger" Brady. Jonathan is a cynical intellectual, a former university student who concentrates on living through his two-year hitch with as little trouble as possible. Mike, on the other hand, is a passionate, idealistic fighter who eventually becomes involved with the Irish Revolutionary Army. Ultimately, Jonathan betrays Mike, stealing his girlfriend and playing a key part in his arrest. Critics have noted similarities in style and subject matter between Lodge's novels and Graham Greene's, and Lodge later acknowledged that he had modeled *Ginger, You're Barmy* after Greene's *The Quiet American*.

Some reviewers, while conceding that Lodge has portrayed army life convincingly, feel that *Ginger,*

You're Barmy is plagued by stereotypes and a predictable storyline. "The story has been told so often that merely to tell it again is not enough," maintains Chad Walsh in *Washington Post Book World*. But Thomas P. McDonnell counters in a *Commonweal* review: "Some reviewers have passed off *Ginger, You're Barmy* as the same old thing about life in the army, but it is a much better book than they are readers. They are certainly unknowing in the ways of military life if they do not realize that extreme regimentation all but forces a reversion to types. . . . They have missed, certainly, that it is a beautifully written book, and that its marvelously controlled first-person orientation lifts it out of the mere melodrama that they were no doubt expecting to read in just another book about life in the army. . . . Mostly, I think, they have missed . . . a poignancy in crisis and denouement, no less, that you will be hard put to it to find anywhere in the reams of overblown nihilism which passes for fiction today."

Lodge followed *Ginger, You're Barmy* with *The British Museum Is Falling Down*, a book which "represented a real development in his career as a writer of fiction," according to Dennis Jackson. It was the first of the highly comic, satiric novels which were to become his trademark, and it embodies one of Lodge's recurring themes, that of the sincere Catholic struggling with the difficulties imposed on him by the rigid doctrines of his church—specifically, the complexities of the unreliable "rhythm" method of birth control, the only form of contraception permitted to Catholics. The novel details one day in the life of Adam Appleby, a harried graduate student who has already fathered three children while using the rhythm method. When Adam awakes that day, his wife Barbara confides that she may again be pregnant, sending Adam out into a day of pandemonium much like Leopold Bloom's in James Joyce's *Ulysses*. "Like Leopold Bloom, Adam—because of the domestic and academic pressures he is facing—becomes increasingly disoriented as his day progresses, and his perceptions of life around him become increasingly phantasmagoric," writes Jackson.

After a day of countless mishaps, hallucinations, and anxious telephone calls to Barbara, Adam returns home to make love to his wife. Immediately thereafter, their "day of alarm [is] clinched by the arrival of her period," notes *Commonweal* contributor Paul West. The book concludes with a long, one-sentence monologue by Barbara (patterned after Molly Bloom's in *Ulysses*). West reports that this "night-reverie . . . twists the preceding comedy by the tail, gives it a depth and resonance." Lodge's skillful blend of humor and thoughtful discourse is also praised by Jackson, who writes: "*The British Museum Is Falling Down* is unceasingly and vigorously funny. . . . Yet throughout the book serious undertones give emphasis and point to the author's general levity. His comic and satiric treatment of the current Catholic indecision over family planning is not a frontal attack on the church itself but rather a good-natured tickling meant to evoke laughter and a serious new consideration of the effect of the Catholic ban on artificial contraception on couples such as the Applebys."

A strong Joycean influence is again evident in Lodge's fourth novel, *Out of the Shelter*. This story of a young man's maturation opens with a stream-of-consciousness narrative inspired by the beginning of Joyce's *Portrait of the Artist as a Young Man*. The plot follows Timothy Anderson through his childhood in London during the Blitzkrieg to his coming of age on a summer holiday in postwar Germany. Jackson judges this to be Lodge's least successful novel, pointing out that "the book lacks intensity; it has no sharply drawn conflict or dramatic tension, and, for most of the story, the only real suspense has to do with this question of how and when Timothy will learn about sex." Nevertheless, *Times Literary Supplement* critic Christopher Hawtree finds that "Timothy's development is chronicled with a fine sense of pace, the tone of the narrative reflecting his changing attitudes," and Philip Howard calls *Out of the Shelter* "a charming period piece, heavy with nostalgia for vanished childhood" in the London *Times*.

Immediately after finishing *Out of the Shelter* in 1969, Lodge and his family travelled to the United States, where the author was to be a visiting professor for two terms at the University of California in Berkeley. It was a time of unrest on campuses everywhere, and Lodge's American stay was punctuated by student strikes and sometimes-bloody altercations between students and National Guardsmen. Although student protests were also occurring in England, they were of a much milder nature. Lodge's fascination with the differences between the two cultures led to his fifth novel, *Changing Places: A Tale of Two Campuses*. Eliciting positive responses from almost all reviewers, *Changing Places* won two major prizes and boosted Lodge's popularity considerably.

A university exchange program provides the premise for *Changing Places*. Aggressive, flamboyant Morris

Zapp leaves his post at the State University of Euphoria (a thinly-disguised Berkeley) to trade places with timid, unambitious Philip Swallow from the dreary University of Rummidge in the English Midlands. Eventually they exchange cars, homes, and wives as well. Prior to the switch, both Zapp and Swallow have suffered from failing marriages and stagnating careers, but each finds a new identity and flourishes in his new surroundings. Neil Hepburn writes in *Listener* that Zapp and Swallow's parallel stories provide "a series of reflections, both on and of the two worlds—reflections on symmetry, on the novel as a reflection of reality, on the way real troubles like Vietnam and the Prague Spring are reflected in unreal ones like student unrest, on narrative techniques and literary styles . . . and, finally, on America and England as reflections of each other. No funnier or more penetrating account of the special relationship is likely to come your way for a long time."

Zapp and Swallow appear again in *Small World: An Academic Romance*, another "campus novel"—and Lodge's best-selling book up to this time. In *Small World*, they are only two of the many characters who jet around the globe from one academic conference to another in search of glory, romantic trysts, and the UNESCO chair of literary criticism—a job with virtually no responsibilities and a $100,000 tax-free salary. Mark Rosenthal writes in the *New York Times Book Review*: "[This] exuberant, marvelously funny novel demonstrates [that] no one is better able to treat the peripatetic quality of current academic life than the British writer David Lodge. . . . Despite the novel's breathless pace, profusion of incident and geographic scope, Mr. Lodge never loses control of his material. His deliberately outrageous manipulation of character and event is entirely successful."

While *Changing Places* cemented Lodge's reputation as a popular novelist in England, it was only the first of his books to attract much notice in the United States. Widespread attention in America did not come to Lodge until the publication of his sixth novel, *How Far Can You Go?*, which appeared in the U.S. under the title *Souls and Bodies*. Jackson believes that *How Far Can You Go?* represents a "circling back over thematic grounds covered in [Lodge's] earlier novels," now handled in a more accomplished fashion by the mature novelist. As in *The Picturegoers*, *The British Museum Is Falling Down*, and *Out of the Shelter*, the focus is on the sexual and religious evolution of a group of English Catholic characters, treated in a comic fashion. The changes that Lodge's characters experience over the book's twenty-year time span present "a panoramic view of the vast changes effected inside the church during the era spanning the 1950s up to Pope John Paul II's installation in the late 1970s," writes Jackson.

Lodge used a large cast of characters to illuminate the many aspects of a Catholic upbringing in *How Far Can You Go?* Some critics dislike what they see as a collection of stereotypes, but Le Anne Schreiber points out in the *New York Times:* "By drafting his characters . . . into service as prototypes of every variant of Catholic experience, the author does at times lose something vital, but, in recompense, we get a very thorough crash course in modern Catholicism, including an introduction to process theology, the charismatic movement and the debates over priestly celibacy and the ordination of women. . . . Mr. Lodge has written a book full of his own energy, intelligence, wit, compassion and anger."

To incorporate explications of Catholic doctrine, Lodge also used narrative asides and other unconventional fictional devices in *How Far Can You Go?* Some critics find these intrusive, such as Paul Theroux, whose *New York Times Book Review* article indicates that the book is best when Lodge "forgets he is a Professor of Modern English literature, ditches the arch tone and all the mannerisms and begins to believe in these characters." Others feel that Lodge's narrative musings give his book added depth and power. Nicholas Shrimpton explains in a *New Statesman* piece: "*How Far Can You Go?* is at its best at those moments when an intimate link is established between theological debate and personal life. The real hero of the novel is the pill, and Lodge's picture of these couples struggling to come to terms with it hovers delicately between tragedy and farce."

Lodge's next campus novel, *Nice Work,* is set in Rummidge, England, in 1986 and centers on Robyn Penrose, a temporary university literature teacher who is in search of a permanent teaching position. The year 1986 is deemed "Industry Year," and Penrose has been chosen by the university vice-chancellor to visit Vic Wilcox, the manager of a local engineering firm, once a week to learn more about the world of work. Vic, writes Hilary Mantel in the *New York Review of Books,* "is a repository of ridiculous prejudices at which Lodge invites us to laugh, as elsewhere he invites us to laugh at Robyn's pretensions, at her equally naive world view." An-

thony Quinn further comments on the contrast between the two characters in *New Statesman,* stating that "Robyn is erudite and sophisticated, a justice-for-all idealogue, yet she's also snobbish and doctrinaire. Vic is a hard-headed, *Daily Mail*-reading chauvinist whom we ought to dislike, but beneath his boorishness lurks a gruff sort of chivalry." While some critics fault *Nice Work,* calling the plot, as Quinn states, "a convenient device for a face-off between two disparate ideologies," others applaud its humor and even-handed treatment of two contradictory personalities.

Writing about *Paradise News,* Lodge's next novel, Susan Miron of the *Christian Science Monitor* states, "Lodge's fascination with the complex social rift between classes, between men and women, and between Americans and the British continues." The work centers on Bernard Walsh, a former Catholic priest and now a theology teacher, who receives a telephone call from his long-lost aunt Ursula asking him to come to Hawaii, where she is dying of cancer. Bernard travels with his father, who, while on the island, gets hit by a car driven by a middle-aged woman named Yolande. By the end of the novel, Yolande and Bernard become involved and Bernard's father reconciles with his sister. Bette Pesetsky observes in the *New York Times Book Review* that Lodge "bravely uses coincidence and contrivance to tie up loose ends. And just under the surface of the spirited and often comic adventures of his travelers he runs an undercurrent of understanding about their longings for the perfection of paradise." Michael Dirda of *Washington Post Book World* also notes that Lodge "persistently takes on some of the grimmest of subjects,. . . death, the loss of faith, sexual dysfunction, and unhappy families being unhappy in their own ways."

"Like his characters, Lodge is searching for faith and his religion," writes John Podhoretz in *New Republic.* "We have grown so accustomed to those highly praised novels in which adolescents discover sexual freedom, irrational violence wreaks its consequences on a wise but hapless hero, and the struggle of life is reduced to a battle between superego and id, that a good novel about a few people merely trying to *get by* may seem a rather small achievement. If so, then perhaps we have lost sight of the value and purpose of fiction. . . . The modern popular novel has devoted itself to the body alone; Lodge joins an honorable and great tradition by restoring the primacy of the soul in fiction."

Lodge's recent works of literary criticism include *After Bakhtin: Essays on Fiction and Criticism* and *The Art of Fiction: Illustrated from Classic and Modern Texts*. The first work is more academic and, as Lee Zimmerman notes in *San Francisco Review of Books,* "moves from 'fairly long broad-ranging exercises in Bakhtinian criticism' to more or less Bakhtinian studies of particular texts and authors illustrative of developments in the novel between the nineteenth and twentieth centuries." The latter work, according to Hilary Mantel in the *Spectator,* "is a kind of readers' handbook, a book about literary criticism for the not-too-critical." Critical reaction to *After Bakhtin* was generally favorable, with Zimmerman observing that if "Lodge hasn't completely solved the 'puzzle' at the heart of Bakhtin's thought, in my view, he has produced a provocative and engaging piece of work—'critical theory and all that' at its unpedantic best." Reviewers also praise *The Art of Fiction: Illustrated from Classic and Modern Texts,* albeit for different reasons. This work, notes Mantel, "can be seen as a brave attempt to build a bridge between today's reader and today's writer—whose interests, sometimes, seem irreconcilable. It is almost jargon-free, and it is entertaining, wise and well-organised."

Regarding his career as a novelist and a literary critic, Lodge noted in a 1985 *CA* interview: "I've always maintained the two careers more or less in tandem, and I've tried to write a novel and a book of criticism alternately over the last twenty years. It grew out of the fact that my interest in writing was triggered by reading, as with most people, and getting some pleasure and satisfaction out of criticism as well as writing my own work and then wanting to continue the study of literature. All along I think I saw my literary career as a writer-critic, alternating and combining both types of discourse. As I get older, in a way I find creative writing more interesting, more of a challenge, more unpredictable—and more anxiety-making, but in the end, more satisfying."

BIOGRAPHICAL/CRITICAL SOURCES:

BOOKS

Contemporary Literary Criticism, Volume 36, Gale (Detroit), 1986.

Dictionary of Literary Biography, Volume 14: *British Novelists since 1960,* Gale, 1983.

Lodge, David, *How Far Can You Go?,* Secker & Warburg, 1980, published as *Souls and Bodies,* Morrow, 1982.

PERIODICALS

Christian Science Monitor, April 14, 1992, p. 13.
Commonweal, November 26, 1965; September 30, 1966; June 16, 1967.
Critique, summer, 1994, p. 237.
Encounter, August-September, 1980.
Globe and Mail (Toronto), September 8, 1981; July 7, 1984.
Guardian Weekly, December 2, 1990, p. 29.
Listener, February 27, 1975; May 1, 1980; March 29, 1984.
London Review of Books, September 29, 1988, p. 11.
Modern Fiction Studies, summer, 1982.
Modern Language Review, October, 1972.
Month, February, 1970.
New Republic, April 7, 1982.
New Statesman, July 30, 1960; November 9, 1962; December 17, 1971; December 9, 1977; May 16, 1980; June 26, 1981; August 13, 1982; September 23, 1988, p. 37.
Newsweek, December 28, 1981.
New York Herald Tribune, July 25, 1965.
New York Times, January 1, 1982; March 8, 1985; July 8, 1993, p. C17.
New York Times Book Review, January 31, 1982; March 17, 1985; July 23, 1989, p. 1; April 5, 1992, p. 6.
Novel: A Forum on Fiction, winter, 1972.
Observer (London), March 18, 1984.
Punch, March 21, 1984.
San Francisco Review of Books, January, 1990, p. 23.
Spectator, March 25, 1966; May 3, 1980; July 31, 1982; April 7, 1984; October 10, 1992, p. 29.
Tablet, October 3, 1970.
Time, April 15, 1985.
Times (London), March 22, 1984; April 4, 1985; June 29, 1985.
Times Literary Supplement, February 14, 1975; May 2, 1980; June 26, 1981; March 23, 1984; May 31, 1985; September 23, 1988, p. 1040; August 10, 1990, p. 839; October 23, 1992, p. 23.
Voice Literary Supplement, May, 1992, pp. 31-32.
Washington Post Book World, February 7, 1982; March 3, 1985; April 5, 1992, p. 4.
World Literature Today, autumn, 1991, p. 780; winter, 1993, p. 181.
Yale Review, December, 1966; December, 1977; January, 1993, p. 148.

LOUDON, Irvine 1924-

PERSONAL: Born August 1, 1924, in Cardiff, Wales; son of Andrew and Morag (Lees) Loudon; married Jean Norman; children: Andrew, Michael, Catherine, Elizabeth, Mary. *Ethnicity:* "White." *Education:* Oxford University, B.A., 1948, B.M., B.Ch., 1951, D.M., 1973; Royal College of Obstetrics and Gynecology, D.Obst., 1961. *Politics:* Neutral. *Religion:* None.

ADDRESSES: Home—The Mill House, Locks Lane Wantage, Oxfordshire OX12 9EH, England. *E-mail*—irvine.loudon@wuhmo.oxford.ac.uk.

CAREER: General medical practitioner in Wantage, England, 1952-81; Oxford University, Oxford, England, medical historian at Wellcome Unit, 1981—. Member of Green College, Oxford. Also works as a professional etcher. *Military service:* Royal Air Force, pilot, 1942-45; became flying officer.

MEMBER: Royal Society of Medicine, British Medical Association, Royal College of General Practitioners (fellow), Royal Society of Painter-Printmakers (associate).

WRITINGS:

The Demand for Hospital Care, United Oxford Hospitals, 1970.
Medical Care and the General Practitioner, 1750-1850, Oxford University Press (New York City), 1986.
Death in Childbirth: An International Study of Maternal Care and Maternal Mortality, 1800-1950, Clarendon Press (Oxford), 1992.
(Editor) *Childbed Fever: A Documentary History,* Garland Press (New York City), 1995.
(Editor) *The Oxford Illustrated History of Western Medicine,* Oxford University Press, in press.

Contributor to periodicals.

WORK IN PROGRESS: A History of Puperal Fever, for Oxford University Press; *General Practice under the National Health Service,* with John Horder and Charles Webster.

SIDELIGHTS: Irvine Loudon told *CA:* "I became seriously interested in research into medical history as a result of undertaking an analysis of hospital care and primary care in Oxfordshire in 1970. This analysis was the subject of my first book, *The Demand for Hospital Care.* It became clear to me that one could not understand the organization of medical care today except in a historical context. This led me to undertake a series of investigations into the history of hospitals and dispensaries, most of which were undertaken on a part-time basis while I was still in clinical practice. Historical research came to dominate my life to such an extent that I took the opportunity, as a result of being awarded a Wellcome Research Fellowship in 1981, to resign from general practice after thirty years as a clinician and devote my time totally to historical research."

*   *   *

LOUIS, Father M.
See MERTON, Thomas

*   *   *

LUKES, Steven (Michael) 1941-

PERSONAL: Born March 8, 1941, in Newcastle-on-Tyne, England; son of Stanley and Martha Lukes; married Nina Stanger (a barrister-at-law), 1977; children: Daniel, Michael, Alexandra. *Education:* Balliol College, Oxford, B.A. (with first class honors), 1962; Nuffield College, Oxford, D.Phil., 1968.

ADDRESSES: Home—138 Woodstock Rd., Oxford, England. *Office*—Balliol College, Oxford University, Oxford OX1 3BJ, England. *Agent*—Michael Sissons, A.D. Peters & Co. Ltd., 10 Buckingham St., London WC2N 6BU, England.

CAREER: University of Keele, Keele, England, assistant lecturer in philosophy, 1963; Oxford University, Oxford, England, lecturer in politics at Worcester College, 1964-66, fellow and tutor in politics and sociology at Balliol College, 1966—, fellow of Nuffield College, 1964-66. Visiting lecturer in Canada, the United States, and Europe, including Sorbonne, University of Paris, Free University of Berlin, Harvard University, and Princeton University; director of studies at Ecole Pratique des Hautes Etudes, 1972; associate professor of public law at University of Paris, 1974; participant in scholarly meetings in England and the United States.

MEMBER: International Sociological Association (president of research committee on history of sociology, 1974-83), Groupe d'Etudes Durkheimiennes.

WRITINGS:

(Editor with Anthony Arblaster) *The Good Society: A Book of Readings,* Harper (New York City), 1971.

Emile Durkheim, His Life and Work: A Historical and Critical Study, Harper, 1973.

Individualism, Harper, 1973.

Power: A Radical View, Macmillan (England), 1974, Humanities (Atlantic Highlands, NJ), 1975.

Essays in Social Theory, Macmillan, 1976.

(Editor with Michael Carrithers and Steven Collins) *The Category of the Person: Anthropology, Philosophy, History,* Cambridge University Press (Cambridge, England), 1985.

Marxism and Morality, Clarendon Press (Oxford, England), 1985.

(Editor with Itzhak Galnoor) *No Laughing Matter: A Collection of Political Jokes,* Routledge & Kegan Paul (London), 1985.

(Editor) *Power,* New York University Press (New York City), 1986.

Moral Conflict and Politics, Clarendon Press, 1991.

The Curious Enlightenment of Professor Caritat: A Comedy of Ideas (novel), Verso (New York City), 1995.

CONTRIBUTOR

H. S. Kariel, editor, *Frontiers of Democratic Theory,* Random House (New York City) 1970.

B. R. Wilson, editor, *Rationality,* Basil Blackwell (Oxford, England), 1970.

Dorothy Emmet and Alasdair Macintyre, editors, *Sociological Theory and Philosophical Analysis,* Macmillan, 1970.

Geoffrey Mortimore, editor, *Weakness of the Will,* Macmillan, 1971.

A. W. Finifter, editor, *Alienation and the Social System,* Wiley (New York City), 1972.

Robin Horton and Ruth Finnegan, editors, *Modes of Thought: Essays Presented to E. E. Evans-Pritchard,* Faber & Faber (London), 1973.

Leszek Kolakowski and Stuart Hampshire, editors, *The Socialist Idea: A Reappraisal,* Weidenfeld & Nicolson (London), 1974.

T. B. Bottomore and Robert A. Nisbet, editors, *A History of Sociological Analysis,* Basic Books (New York City), 1978.

Stuart Brown, editor, *Philosophical Disputes in the Social Sciences,* Harvester (Brighton, England), 1979.

Alkis Kontos, editor, *Festschrift for C. B. Macpherson,* University of Toronto Press, 1979.

G. H. R. Parkinson, editor, *Marx and Marxism,* Cambridge University Press, 1982.

John B. Thompson and David Held, editors, *Habermas: Critical Debates,* Beacon (Boston), 1982.

David Miller and Larry Siedentop, editors, *The Nature of Political Theory,* Clarendon Press, 1983.

Ben Pimlott, editor, *Fabian Essays in Socialist Thought,* Heinemann Educational (Exeter, NH), 1984.

OTHER

Coeditor of *Marxism and . . . ,* a series published by Clarendon Press. Contributor to *International Encyclopedia of the Social Sciences, Dictionary of the History of Ideas, Dictionary of World History,* and *Dictionary of Ancient Thought.* Contributor of more than twenty-five articles and reviews to sociology, history, and philosophy journals. Associate editor of *Political Studies,* 1976-81; member of editorial board of *Archives europeennes de sociologie.*

SIDELIGHTS: In his book *Marxism and Morality,* one of a series of books on Marxism published by Clarendon Press, Steven Lukes explores one of the most significant inconsistencies in the social and political theories that have emerged from the work of Karl Marx. The problem, as Alan Ryan describes it in the *Partisan Review,* is this: "How could Marx simultaneously think that 'morality' was nonsense and spend forty years as the scathing moral critic he undoubtedly was?" As Arthur C. Danto puts it in a *Times Literary Supplement* article, "Marx . . . moralized without restraint and behaved as though he lived in a universe stained with objective good and evil. It was as though he were blind to the consequence that his own moral judgments must be vacuous if his metamoral theory were true." To address this issue, observes Eugene Kamenka in the *New York Times Book Review,* "Lukes turns to a question that has occupied a number of outstanding minds on a variety of levels—ethical theory, moral psychology, and practical and political outcomes."

Kamenka finds that "Mr. Lukes is conscious of and well informed on all of these [who have discussed this topic], without having anything new or important to say, especially about ethical theory." The reviewer also comments that "*Marxism and Morality* is at one level a serious, scholarly book—fairly lightly, if not elegantly, written and full of references to and quotations from the extensive literature." Yet, Kamenka believes that "It never questions deeply enough. . . . Clarity and fair-mindedness, not logical sharpness, are his virtues; politics, not philosophy, is his game." *New Statesman* contributor James Bentley credits Lukes for his ability to turn a critical eye on Marxism and its proponents. He writes: "The chapter on 'Means and Ends' in *Marxism and Morality* displays Steven Lukes's masterly ability to expound and criticise the arguments of other theorists." Bentley also finds merit in Lukes's balancing of the issues and of scholarship and accessibility. "Lukes's analyses of political concepts . . . contain dense and occasionally dry arguments, but they never lapse into the irritating private language of some professional philosophers," comments Bentley. "And passion soon bursts through again. This academically scrupulous book treats of a subject that is far from merely academic." The result, in Ryan's opinion, is "a brisk little book on a very large topic. If it isn't the last word on its subject, it is certainly one of the best."

Lukes continued to explore the relationship between morality and politics in books such as *Moral Conflict and Politics*. These eighteen essays previously published during the 1980s "add up to a strong and urgent plea for the recognition of the reality and importance of the moral element in political decisions and an equally strong plea that any such recognition must involve an acknowledgment of an ineradicable conflict of values," writes Jack Lively in the *Times Literary Supplement*. Norman Geras maintains in the *New Statesman* that "the essays display a remarkable breadth of interest, perspective and erudition." He adds: "Lukes pursues a clear, analytically discriminating path through the conceptual fields of moral diversity itself, the incommensurability of values, equality and liberty, power and authority." Lively allows that "*Moral Conflict and Politics* has a few of the recurrent faults of the genre: several of the occasional pieces are too tied to particular circumstances to be of permanent interest; there is some repetition of ideas and arguments." Still, the reviewer admits, "The collection avoids one common fault of the genre: it has a general, unifying theme."

BIOGRAPHICAL/CRITICAL SOURCES:

PERIODICALS

Contemporary Sociology, March, 1987, p. 249.
New Statesman, August 23, 1985, p. 26; June 7, 1991, p. 43.

New York Times Book Review, February 2, 1986, p. 20; November 19, 1995, p. 36.
Partisan Review, March, 1986, p. 486.
Times Literary Supplement, September 27, 1985, p. 1052; May 30, 1986, p. 580; September 6, 1991, p. 26.*

*   *   *

LUX, Thomas 1946-

PERSONAL: Born December 10, 1946, in Northampton, MA; son of N. O. (a milkman) and Eleanor (Healey) Lux; divorced; children: Claudia. *Education:* Emerson College, B.A., 1970; University of Iowa, graduate study, 1971.

ADDRESSES: Office—Department of English, Sarah Lawrence College, Bronxville, NY.

CAREER: Emerson College, Boston, MA, poet in residence, 1972-75; Sarah Lawrence College, Bronxville, NY, member of faculty, 1975—. Visiting professor, University of California, Irvine, 1995. Editor, Born Dream Press.

AWARDS, HONORS: Bread Loaf scholarship, 1970; MacDowell Colony fellowship, 1973; Kingsley Tufts Poetry Award, 1995, for *Split Horizon*.

WRITINGS:

The Land Sighted, Pym-Randall (Roslindale, MA), 1970.
Memory's Handgrenade, Pym-Randall, 1972.
Poems: The Glassblower's Breath, Cleveland State University (Cleveland, OH), 1976.
Sunday: Poems, Houghton (Boston), 1979.
Half Promised Land, Houghton, 1986.
The Drowned River: New Poems, Houghton, 1990.
A Boat in the Forest, Adastra Press (Easthampton, MA), 1992.
Pecked to Death by Swans, Adastra Press, 1993.
Split Horizon, Houghton, 1994.
(Coeditor and author of foreword) *The Sanity of Earth and Grass*, Tilbury House (Gardiner, ME), 1994.

Managing editor, *Iowa Review*, 1971-72, and *Ploughshares*, 1973.

SIDELIGHTS: Since his first collections of poetry were published in the 1970s, Thomas Lux has been receiving critical appreciation for his "compelling rhythms, his biting irony and his steady devotion to a craft that often seems thankless," according to Elizabeth Mehren in the *Los Angeles Times*. One sign of this appreciation came in 1995 when Lux was awarded the $50,000 Kingsley Tufts Poetry Award (one of the nation's richest poetry prizes) for *Split Horizon*. Perhaps behind the poet's success is his penchant for "pairing humor with hard-edged serious themes," comments Mehren. As Lux told Mehren, "I like to make the reader laugh—and then steal that laugh, right out of the throat. Because I think life is like that, tragedy right alongside humor."

In his 1979 collection, *Sunday: Poems,* Lux offers such poems as "Elegy for Frank Stanford," "The Green," "Portrait of the Man Who Drowned Wearing His Best Suit and Shoes," "Gold on Mule," "Farmers," "Barrett and Browning," "Flying Noises," and "Spiders Wanting." The individuals who live in the poetic world created in *Sunday* share a feeling of being out of place. "Lux's solo native is always strange to the world," observes Elizabeth Macklin in *Parnassus,* "always on the verge of extradition, always beset with allergies to the native element, 'like a simple vase not tolerating water.'" These characters find themselves expressing anger and humor in their attempts to cope with their world. As Peter Stitt writes in the *Georgia Review,* "There is a deep tenderness at the heart of Lux's work, born of vulnerability and terror. It issues in a stance both bitter and cynical, and directs its anger against the imperatives of reality—time, degeneration, death." Stitt finds that Lux's strongest poems ("Elegy for Frank Stanford" is one) "are those written in his most difficult tone— an ironic mingling of humor and sincerity which betrays a ferocious anger at necessity."

Half Promised Land, published in 1986, reflects some of the same stylistic and thematic concerns found in Lux's earlier poems but, as Lynne McMahon points out in the *New York Times Book Review,* there are also differences. "The jazzy syncopated phrasings are still often present, as well as the burlesquing of grand emotions," she writes. "There are still glimpses of the high-wire artist who requires for grounding only the thinnest narrative line. But here Mr. Lux foregoes the collision of the surreal and the mundane, so characteristic of his earlier work, for a more somber tone." Sam Cornish also comments on Lux's style and themes. He notes in the *Christian Science Monitor,* "Here the poetry has the assurance of a short story, with sharp, focused character sketches, and his observations of human behavior and youth are honest and moving." *Partisan*

Review contributor Stuart Dischell finds Lux's willingness to look outside the self to be refreshing. He observes that many of the poems in this collection "concern social relations, especially work: not just the dull labor we do to survive in this world, but also the work we must do to survive ourselves." Dischell concludes, "In a decade in which much of the poetry being published seems merely decorative, solipsistic, or willfully obscure, it is a pleasure to read poems that quicken the senses and challenge the reader. *Half Promised Land* is an excellent book."

In *The Drowned River: New Poems,* which appeared in 1990, Lux once again turns his poetic eye on individuals in conflict with the world around them. As the *Nation*'s Beatrix Gates puts it, the collection "tells the story and struggle of plain and magnificent humans." A *Washington Post Book World* reviewer explains that "among his subjects are lifestyles of the poor and obscure, the powerless, invisible millions who comprise history." And, as Jack Anderson observes in *American Book Review,* the lot drawn by these invisible millions is far from an easy one. "Lux stares at the world, and what he sees dismays him," notes the reviewer. "Nature is not necessarily kind to human beings." Though his people are poor and obscure, Lux makes their struggles the reader's struggle; and though these struggles seem overwhelming, Lux sees a way out. Gates writes that "the poems in *The Drowned River* are made from the lives we cannot ignore. He makes them our own." Moreover, suggests the *Washington Post Book World* reviewer, "Though selfishness, cruelty and mortality drive him wild, this is a poet who can't stop hoping." Anderson concludes that Lux "makes his small hopes as convincing as his grand doubts."

Lux conveys human struggles against nature in a conversational style. According to Anderson, "These poems often sound like a man talking to himself, recording impressions of events almost as quickly as they occur." A *Publishers Weekly* reviewer faults this approach, arguing that Lux's "propensity for repetition and reiteration deflates the impact of his observations." Yet, the *Washington Post Book World* reviewer offers a different evaluation: "Lux's rhetoric is so striking that the subject never becomes ponderous. The most touching poems (and there are many) frame their large questions in riveting terms: . . . Like good conversation, this poetry thinks as it moves. Its urgency is due in part to the poet's fervor and in part to his distinctive style."

In the end, Lux offers a poetic vision that challenges the reader. "There are terrible songs in this book, terrible because their construction is so beautiful, the message so savage in its demand that the reader is open in kind," comments Gates. She adds that "these powerful poems are the deadly currents and riptides of the 'drowned,' a song present in any river if you can hear it. The clear-eyed detail in his poems stuns, and eventually does render a cumulative, unshiny faith."

Split Horizon, Lux's award-winning collection, "thrives on dislocations," writes Fred Muratori in *Library Journal.* It also casts a critical eye on contemporary life and current trends. "Wearing irreverence like a uniform, Lux skewers received literary symbols . . . medical science . . . and God . . . with equal deadpanache," Muratori explains. He carries all this off in a way not common among contemporary poets. In the view of a *Publishers Weekly* reviewer, "With Lux, the wonders of the world can be communicated in the jangling noise of his language and in his amazing manipulation of tone to suit his poetry's matter. He is singular among his peers in his ability to convey with a deceptive lightness the paradoxes of human emotion."

Lux has been praised for his poetry, but as he told Mehren, "This is not something one chooses to do. . . . It is something I was drawn to. I do it because I love to do it, and because I don't have any choice. If I don't write, I feel empty and lost." He added, "Poetry exists because there is no other way to say the things that get said in good poems except in poems. There is something about the right combination of metaphor or image connected to the business of being alive that only poems can do. To me, it makes me feel more alive, reading good poetry."

BIOGRAPHICAL/CRITICAL SOURCES:

PERIODICALS

American Book Review, summer, 1979, p. 11; January-March, 1991, p. 28.
American Poetry Review, January-February, 1988, p. 17.
Boston Globe, October 2, 1994, p. B16.
Christian Science Monitor, July 16, 1986.
Georgia Review, summer, 1980, p. 428; spring, 1991, p. 154.
Library Journal, August, 1994, p. 91.
Los Angeles Times, April 10, 1995, p. E1.
Nation, January 21, 1991, p. 64.
New York Times Book Review, May 4, 1980, p. 15; April 19, 1987, p. 20.
Parnassus, Volume 8, number 2, p. 210.
Partisan Review, February, 1987, p. 341.
Publishers Weekly, January 19, 1990, p. 102; June 27, 1994, p. 67.
Virginia Quarterly Review, spring, 1993, p. 64.
Washington Post Book World, June 17, 1990, p. 10.*

*   *   *

LYLE, Alexandra
 See HARRISON, Barbara

*   *   *

LYLE, Katie Letcher   1938-

PERSONAL: Born May 12, 1938, in Peking, China; daughter of John Seymour (a U.S. Marine Corps brigadier general) and Elizabeth (an artist; maiden name, Marston) Letcher; married Royster Lyle, Jr. (associate director of a research foundation), March 16, 1963; children: Royster Cochran, Virginia. *Ethnicity:* Caucasian. *Education:* Hollins College, B.A., 1959; Johns Hopkins University, M.A., 1960; graduate study at Vanderbilt University, 1961-62. *Avocational interests:* Acting, European travel, mycology, foreign cooking, and archaeology, particularly Aegean.

ADDRESSES: Home—110 W. McDowell, Lexington, VA 24450. *Agent*—Sally Hill McMillan, 429 E. Kingston Ave., Charlotte, NC 28203.

CAREER: Teacher in Baltimore, MD, 1960-61, 1962-63; Southern Seminary Junior College, Buena Vista, VA, member of English faculty, 1963-87, chair of English department, 1968-80, chair of liberal arts division, 1971-73. Instructor for Elderhostel on various subjects, 1983—; instructor, Washington and Lee University, 1984-86; Hollins College, writer in residence, 1989, guest adjunct professor, 1989-93; guest adjunct professor, Randolph-Macon Women's College, 1992. Consultant for Dell Laurel Books, 1974-84. Has served on many boards and commissions, including the Virginia Commission for the Arts, 1982-86, Special Education Advisory Committee for the Lexington Public School System, and the Rockridge Concert-Theatre Series.

AWARDS, HONORS: Bread Loaf fellowship, 1973, 1974; Newbery Award finalist, 1973, 1974; Irene Leach Memorial Essay Award, 1984.

WRITINGS:

(With Maude Rubin and May Miller) *Lyrics of Three Women,* Linden Press (New York City), 1964.

I Will Go Barefoot All Summer for You (young adult), Lippincott (Philadelphia, PA), 1973.

Fair Day, and Another Step Begun (young adult), Lippincott, 1974.

The Golden Shores of Heaven (young adult), Lippincott, 1976.

Dark but Full of Diamonds (young adult), Coward (New York City), 1981.

Finders Weepers (young adult), Coward, 1982.

Scalded to Death by the Steam: Authentic Stories of Railroad Disasters and the Ballads That Were Written about Them, Algonquin Books (New York City), 1983.

The Man Who Wanted Seven Wives, Algonquin Books, 1986.

The Wild Berry Book, North Word, 1994.

(Editor with Roger Jeans) *Letters from Peking,* U.S. Marine Corps Historical Society, 1996.

The Wild Gourmet, Lyons & Burford (New York City), in press.

Also author of *Footsteps,* a television series on parenting. Work represented in anthologies, including *Beyond the Square,* edited by Robert K. Rosenburg, Linden Press, 1972; *A Guide to Chessie Trail,* 1988; and *Virginia Wild Rivers Study,* edited by Paul Dulaney, 1970. Author of "A Foreign Flavor," a weekly column on food and humor, for *Roanoke Times,* 1970-74. Contributor of poems and short stories to *Shenandoah, Virginia Quarterly Review,* and other literary magazines, and of articles and reviews to many newspapers and magazines, including *Newsweek.*

WORK IN PROGRESS: All Together Again: American Camping, 1900 to the Present; a book of excerpts from the diaries of Virginia women, 1800-1850; *The Good Hater,* a memoir about growing up in Virginia.

*   *   *

LYNN, (Dorcas) Joanne (Harley)   1951-

PERSONAL: Born July 2, 1951, in Oakland, MD; daughter of John B. (a physician) and Mary Dorcas (a physician; maiden name, Clark) Harley; married Barry W. Lynn (an attorney), June 6, 1970; children: Christina, Nicholas. *Education:* Dickinson College, B.S., 1970; Boston University, M.D., 1974; George Washington University, M.A., 1984; Dartmouth College, M.S., 1995.

ADDRESSES: Home—11711 Amkin Dr., Clifton, VA 22024. *Office*—Center to Improve Care of the Dying, George Washington University, 1001 22nd St. NW, Suite 820, Washington, DC 20037.

CAREER: Private practice in Clinton, MD, 1978; George Washington University, Washington, DC, faculty associate for medicine and humanities in Division of Experimental Programs, 1978-81, associate professor of health care sciences and medicine in Division of Geriatric Medicine, 1979-91, professor of health sciences, 1991-92, professor of health sciences and medicine, 1995—, co-director of Division of ICU Research, 1986-92, director of Center to Improve Care of the Dying, 1995—; Dartmouth Medical School, Hanover, NH, professor of medicine and community and family medicine, 1992-95, associate director of Center for the Aging, 1992-95, senior associate of Center for the Evaluative Clinical Sciences, 1992-95.

Medical director of Washington Home, 1983-89, Hospice of Washington, 1979-91, G. W. Cancer Home Care Program and Home Health Services, 1990-92, all Washington, DC. Member of research ethics task force, National Institute on Aging's Senile Dementia of the Alzheimer's Type, 1981-82; member of governing council, Society for Health and Human Values, 1981-84; assistant director of medical studies for President's Commission for the Study of Ethical Problems in Medicine and Biomedical and Behavioral Research, 1981-83; member of board of directors, American Society of Law and Medicine, 1983-84; member of physician's advisory committee, International Hospice Institute, 1984-86; member of advisory panel on life-sustaining technology in the elderly, Office of Technology Assessment, 1985-86; member of board of directors, Concern for Dying (now Choice in Dying), 1985-89; commissioner, American Bar Association Commission on Legal Problems of the Elderly, 1985-92; member of task force on AIDS, American Health Care Association, 1987-89; member of national advisory committee on wandering patients, American College of Health Care Administrators, 1987-88; member of coordinating council on life-sustaining medical treatment decision-making by the courts, National Center for State

Courts, 1989-93; member of ethics task force, Society for Critical Care Medicine, 1989-96; member of National Clinical Panel on High-Cost Hospice Care, Washington, DC, 1991; member of advisory board of project on death in America, Open Society Institute Foundation, 1993—; member of advisory committee to Project on Community Based Acute Care, John Hopkins Medical Center, 1994—; member of Milbank Memorial Fund committee on care at the end of life, 1995—.

MEMBER: American Association for the Advancement of Science, American College of Physicians (member of subcommittee on aging, 1986-91), American Geriatrics Society (member of committee on public policy, 1983—, and of review of abstracts, 1996—; chair of ethics committee, 1991—; member of board of directors, 1991—), American Hospital Association (member of special committee on biomedical ethics, 1983-85, of governing committee on aging and long-term care, 1996—), American Medical Directors Association, Hastings Institute (member of working group on ethical issues in dementia, 1995—), Institute of Medicine (member of committee on care at the end of life, 1996—), Kennedy Institute of Ethics, Medical and Chirurgical Faculty of the State of Maryland, Medical Society of the District of Columbia, Society for Health and Human Values, Society for Research and Education in Primary Care Internal Medicine, Veterans Health Administration (member of geriatrics and gerontology advisory committee to the Department of Veterans Affairs, 1991—).

AWARDS, HONORS: Grand Prize overall and in veterinary medicine from International Science Fair, 1967; Robert Wood Johnson Clinical Scholar, 1976-78; honorary M.S., Dartmouth College, 1991; National Board Award from Medical College of Pennsylvania (annual award for a distinguished woman physician/scientist), 1992; honorable mention, Nellie Westerman Prize for Excellence in Ethics in Clinical Research, 1993; fellow, American College of Physicians, American Geriatrics Society, Hastings Institute and Kennedy Institute of Ethics.

WRITINGS:

(Editor and contributor) *By No Extraordinary Means: The Choice to Forego Life-Sustaining Food and Water,* Indiana University, Press (Bloomington, IN), 1986, 2nd edition (revised with updated chapter by Lynn and J. Glover), 1989.

Contributor of chapters to over thirty books. Contributor of articles to professional journals, including *Journal of Medical Education, Medical Ethics for the Physician, Patient Care, Hospice Journal, Caring, Journal of Clinical Ethics, Journal of the American Medical Association, Hastings Center Report, Generations, Annals of Internal Medicine,* and *New England Journal of Medicine.* Member of editorial board of journals and books, including *Biolaw* (formerly *Bioethics Reporter*), 1983, *Hospice Journal,* 1984, *Medical Ethics for the Physician,* 1985-92, *Medical Humanities Review,* 1986-91, *Journal of General Internal Medicine,* 1988-91, *Cambridge Quarterly,* 1991—, and *The Encyclopedia of Bioethics,* 2nd edition, 1994-95.

WORK IN PROGRESS: Research on prognosis and decision-making for critically ill, hospitalized adults; development of guidelines for the care of dying persons in health care facilities.

SIDELIGHTS: Joanne Lynn told *CA:* "By No Extraordinary Means: The Choice to Forego Life-Sustaining Food and Water* grew out of a very rewarding conference sponsored by the Society for Health and Human Values. It addresses what is probably the most commonly identified problem in nursing homes: whether or not patients must be artificially fed.

"While I have resolved some aspects of the issue, on others I am quite uncertain. There are people whose lives are rendered miserable or meaningless by being force-fed and we should learn to abstain from causing that. However, what we should do in regard to permanently unconscious or severely demented persons is more troubling.

"Since publication of the book, there have been a large number of court cases, legislative actions, and publications on the issue. We do seem, as a society, to be moving toward intelligent discussion of the issues and possibly toward resolution of the range of options that will be open to patients."

BIOGRAPHICAL/CRITICAL SOURCES:

PERIODICALS

Medical Humanities Review, Issue 1, 1987, pp. 26-29.
New England Journal of Medicine, Number 316, 1987, p. 171.
New York Times Book Review, March 1, 1987.

M

MACAROV, David   1918-

PERSONAL: Born November 20, 1918, in Savannah, GA; son of Isaac (a manufacturer) and Fannie (Schoenberg) Macarov; married Frieda Rabinowitz (a registered nurse), December 5, 1946; children: Varda, Frances, Raanan, Annette. *Education:* University of Pittsburgh, B.Sc., 1951; Western Reserve University (now Case Western Reserve University), M.Sc., 1954; Brandeis University, Ph.D., 1968. *Religion:* Jewish.

ADDRESSES: Home—Nayot 8, Jerusalem, Israel. *Office*—Paul Baerwald School of Social Work, Hebrew University, Jerusalem, Israel.

CAREER: Hebrew University, Paul Baerwald School of Social Work, Jerusalem, professor of social welfare and planning, 1959—, director of Joseph J. Schwartz Graduate Program for Training Directors and Senior Personnel for Community Centers, 1970-75. Visiting professor at Adelphi University, 1975-77, and University of Melbourne, 1977. Member, National Conference of Jewish Communal Service, Council on Social Work Education. *Military service:* U.S. Air Force, 1942-45; received Distinguished Unit Citation and battle cluster. Israel Defence Forces, 1947-49; became squadron leader.

MEMBER: International Association of Social Workers, International Society for Social Economics (member of board), World Future Society (Israel coordinator), Society for the Reduction of Human Labor (chairperson), National Association of Social Workers, American Council on Social Work, Society for Human Development, Industrial Relations Research Association.

WRITINGS:

Incentives to Work: The Effects of Unearned Income, Jossey-Bass (San Francisco, CA), 1970.
The Short Course in Development Training, Massada, 1973.
Administration in the Social Work Curriculum, Council on Social Work Education, 1976.
Work and Welfare: The Unholy Alliance, Sage Publications (Beverly Hills, CA), 1980.
Worker Productivity: Myths and Reality, Sage Publications, 1982.
(Editor and contributor) *People, Work, and Human Services in the Future,* School of Social Work, Adelphi University (Garden City, NY), 1982.
Quitting Time: The End of Work, MCB University Press, 1988.
(Editor) *Computers in the Social Services,* MCB University Press, 1990.
(Editor) *Persisting Unemployment,* MCB University Press, 1991.
Certain Change, National Association of Social Workers, 1991.
(Editor) *Social Welfare in Socialist Countries,* Croom Helm (Beckenham, Kent, England), 1992.
Social Welfare: Structure and Practice, Sage Publications, 1995.

Contributor to various books, including *Meeting Human Needs: An Overview of Nine Countries,* edited by D. Thursz and J. L. Vigilante, Sage Publications, Volume 1, 1975, Volume 2, 1977; *Working Now and in the Future,* edited by H. Didsbury, World Future Society (Bethesda, MD), 1983; *Social Welfare in the Middle East,* edited by J. Dixon, Croom Helm, 1987; and *Careers Tomorrow: The Outlook for Work in a Changing World,* edited by E. Cornish, World Future Society, 1988.

* * *

MacDONALD, Anson
   See HEINLEIN, Robert A(nson)

* * *

MacNEIL, Robert (Breckenridge Ware)   1931-

PERSONAL: Born January 19, 1931, in Montreal, Quebec, Canada; son of Robert A. S. (in Canadian foreign service) and Margaret Virginia (maiden name, Oxner) MacNeil; married Rosemarie Anne Copland, 1956 (divorced, 1964); married Jane J. Doherty, May 29, 1965 (divorced, 1983); married Donna P. Richards, October 20, 1984; children: (first marriage) Catherine Anne, Ian B.; (second marriage) Alison N., William H. *Education:* Attended Dalhousie University, 1949-51; Carleton University, B.A., 1955.

*ADDRESSES: Home—*Manhattan, NY; Connecticut; and Jordan Bay, Nova Scotia, Canada. *Agent—*Bill Adler, 551 Fifth Ave., Suite 923, New York, NY 10017.

CAREER: Canadian Broadcasting Corp. (CBC), Halifax, Nova Scotia, radio actor, 1950-52; Station CJCH, Halifax, all-night disc jockey, 1951-52; Station CFRA, Ottawa, Ontario, announcer and newswriter, 1952-54; CBC, Ottawa, radio and television host, 1954-55; Reuters News Agency (wire service), London, England, subeditor to filing editor, 1955-60; National Broadcasting Co. (NBC), New York City, foreign news correspondent in London, 1960-63, news correspondent at Washington, DC, bureau, 1963-65, nightly news anchor for WNBC-TV in New York City and co-anchor of *The Scherer-MacNeil Report,* 1965-67; British Broadcasting Corp. (BBC), London, reporter for *Panorama,* 1967-72; Public Broadcasting Service (PBS), Washington, DC, senior correspondent for National Public Affairs Center for Television (NPACT) and co-moderator of *Washington Week in Review,* 1972-73; BBC, reporter for *Panorama,* 1973-75; PBS, executive editor and

co-anchor of *The Robert MacNeil Report* (later became *The MacNeil/Lehrer Report;* became *The MacNeil/Lehrer News Hour,* September, 1983) for WNET/WETA-TV, 1975-95.

Stringer for CBC, 1955-60; newscaster for NBC-Radio, 1965-67; co-anchor of *A Public-Affair/Election '72, America '73,* and Senate Watergate hearings, 1973, all for PBS. The MacDowell Colony, fellow and chairperson, 1993—; fellow, American Association for the Advancement of Science.

MEMBER: American Federation of Television and Radio Artists, Association of Radio and Television News Analysts, Writers Guild of America, Century Association, American Yacht Club.

AWARDS, HONORS: Emmy Award from Academy of Television Arts and Sciences, 1974, for coverage of Senate Watergate hearings; George Foster Peabody Award from University of Georgia, 1977; Alfred I. DuPont Award from Columbia School of Journalism, 1977; medal of honor from University of Missouri, 1980; William Allen White Award from University of Kansas, 1982; Paul White Award, RTNDA, 1990; Broadcaster of the Year Award, IRTS, 1991. L.H.D. from William Patterson College, 1977, Beaver College and Bates College, both 1979, Lawrence University, 1981, Bucknell University, 1982, George Washington University, Trinity College (Hartford), and University of Maine, all 1983, Brown University, 1984, Colby College, Carleton College, and University of South Carolina, all 1985, Franklin and Marshall College, 1987, Nazareth College and Washington College, both 1988, Kenyon College, 1990, and University of Western Ontario, 1992.

WRITINGS:

The People Machine: The Influence of Television on American Politics, Harper (New York City), 1968.
The Right Place at the Right Time, Little, Brown (Boston), 1982.
(With Robert McCrum and William Cran) *The Story of English* (narrative to accompany nine-part public television series), Viking (New York City), 1986, revised edition, Penguin Books (New York City), 1993.
(Editor) *The Way We Were: 1963, The Year Kennedy Was Shot* (Book of the Month Club selection), Carroll & Graf (New York City), 1988.
Wordstruck: A Memoir, Viking, 1989.

Eudora Welty: Seeing Black and White, University Press of Mississippi (Jackson), 1990.

Burden of Desire (novel), Doubleday (Garden City, NY), 1992.

The Voyage (novel), Doubleday, 1995.

Correspondent for television documentaries, including *The Big Ear,* NBC; *The Right to Bear Arms,* NBC; *The Whole World Is Watching,* Public Broadcasting Laboratories; and *The Impeachment of Andrew Johnson,* BBC, 1974; host of videocassette series *The Story of English* (nine-part series broadcast on PBS-TV; has accompanying book of the same title), Part 1: "An English Speaking World," Part 2: "Mother Tongue," Part 3: "A Muse of Fire," Part 4: "The Grid Scots Tongue," Part 5: "Black on White," Part 6: "Pioneers, O Pioneers!," Part 7: "The Muvver Tongue," Part 8: "The Loaded Weapon," Part 9: "Next Year's Words: A Look into the Future," Films Inc. (Chicago), 1986; narrator of motion picture (also released as video recording and videocassette under same title), *Slow Fires: On the Preservation of the Human Record,* American Film Foundation, 1987; author of sound cassette recording of *Wordstruck* (audio adaptation of his book of the same title), Simon & Schuster Audioworks, 1989; host with Jim Lehrer of anniversary special videocassette *Fifteen Years of MacNeil/Lehrer,* WNET-TV (New York City) and WETA-TV (Washington), 1990.

Contributor of chapters to books. Contributor of articles to periodicals, including *Harpers Magazine, Nation, Listener, TV Guide,* and *Travel and Leisure.*

WORK IN PROGRESS: Looking for My Country, about his personal search for a Canadian identity.

SIDELIGHTS: Some years after his retirement, Robert MacNeil is still best known as the former co-host of *The MacNeil/Lehrer News Hour,* an influential and award-winning newscast aired by the Public Broadcasting System. For MacNeil, a veteran broadcast journalist whose work as a correspondent included on-site coverage of the John F. Kennedy assassination, *The MacNeil/Lehrer News Hour* and its predecessor, *The MacNeil/Lehrer Report* provided the opportunity to delve into stories at greater depth than network newscasts might. For twenty years MacNeil co-hosted the show out of studios in New York City, and also made time to write several well-received nonfiction books and a novel. Since leaving his post with PBS he has continued to write, calling his new occupation "another level of liberation."

MacNeil has chronicled his life and work in two memoirs, *The Right Place at the Right Time* and *Wordstruck.* He was born in Montreal, Quebec in 1931 and learned his love for literature and drama at his mother's knee. In his teen years he was drawn to the stage, and he began his broadcasting career as a radio actor for the Canadian Broadcasting Corporation. After stints as a radio announcer and disc jockey, he moved on to television in 1954 as the host of CBC's weekly show *Let's Go to the Museum.* The following year he moved to London and joined the Reuters News Service bureau there.

From Reuters, MacNeil moved in 1960 to the National Broadcasting Company, where he served first as a roving foreign correspondent and then as a national reporter based in Washington, D.C. MacNeil was one of the first on-scene journalists to report the assassination of John F. Kennedy—indeed, legend has it that MacNeil may have bumped into Kennedy's assassin, Lee Harvey Oswald, in his haste to report the story.

Growing disillusioned with network television, MacNeil moved to London in 1966 and joined the British Broadcasting Corporation as host of the documentary series *Panorama.* Some years later, MacNeil told *CA* that his experience with the BBC helped him to make the transition to America's PBS. "The most important thing I think British television could teach American television . . . is that there can be a really healthy competition and creative tension between public broadcasting and commercial broadcasting," he said.

MacNeil helped to introduce that "creative tension" to America when he joined PBS in 1975 as host of a news analysis program called *The Robert MacNeil Report.* The show was soon re-named *The MacNeil/Lehrer Report* in a nod to MacNeil's Washington-based co-anchor, James Lehrer. Exploring such diverse subjects as nuclear reactor safety, white collar crime, Iranian militancy, and the deteriorating taste of tomatoes, the *MacNeil/Lehrer Report* enlisted public figures and those whom MacNeil called "people who really know—the staff assistant, and not necessarily the senator" in an hour of questioning and discussion. MacNeil believes that the show's popularity sprang from the need of television viewers to have more depth than network television could provide. "Our feeling is that perhaps people are becoming bored by these rushed recitals," he told Dennis Duggan in *Newsday.* MacNeil commented further in *New York:* "Network people who contend that you have sixty seconds to make a point before viewers begin to lose interest, said it couldn't and shouldn't be done in television. Now . . . while we aren't giving them any sleepless nights over our ratings, we have proved, at least, that in-depth journalism has its place on TV."

MacNeil wrote about the television news medium in his 1968 work, *The People Machine: The Influence of Television on American Politics.* The book examines the frailties of television news organizations, which "are dependent and often at the mercy of a corporate body whose prime motive is profit," Laurence Goldstein noted in the *Nation,* as well as the more serious problem of the interplay between television and politics: the politicians' use of television, the television industry's strong influence in Washington, and the control exerted by the White House on television networks. "[MacNeil] has written a wide-ranging and frequently disconcerting account of how television news operates *vis-a-vis* politicians, special interest groups, and the entertainment side of TV," noted *New Leader* critic Herbert Dorfman.

The People Machine was praised as valuable reading by other critics as well. In the *New York Times,* Elliot Fremont-Smith called it an "acute, detailed and quite damning book. . . . It should make someone who counts in television to more than wince off-screen." A *Saturday Review* critic remarked that the book "offers a full, fair, critical, informed, and fascinating look into the techniques of the business and how they influence the public." Joseph O. Dougherty, writing in *Best Sellers,* described *The People Machine* as "a provocative book, to say the least, and should be a 'must' for every person who wants to be known as 'well-read.'" And Goldstein concluded: "The value of MacNeil's book is its overwhelming concern for the integrity of television, his excellent research into its problems, and his ability to point out many of the hidden defects within its present structure."

In 1982 MacNeil wrote *The Right Place at the Right Time,* a volume of memoirs that recounts his journalism career in England and America. The title reflects the author's ready acknowledgment that few journalists have had the consistent good fortune that he has enjoyed over the past twenty-five years; according to Betty Lukas in the *Los Angeles Times Book Review,* MacNeil has had "access" throughout his career, and he has known how to use it. "His short book of memoirs contains roughly what one would expect

from a liberal Canadian with a brow in the upper middle," reflected Christopher Hitchens in the *Times Literary Supplement.* "It is a humane and worthy story, quite deftly told, and it derives most of its interest from the scenes (Katanga, Cuba, Teheran, Washington) in which the action takes place."

Some critics expressed disappointment that this book of recollections shared so little of the man himself. Lukas noted that "aside from being lucky . . . and aside from certain political and professional positions, there is little here about Robert MacNeil the person." *Washington Post Book World* reviewer Christopher Lydon concurred, writing that "as an autobiography the book has grave flaws. . . . MacNeil is shy about himself." Still, Lydon did find MacNeil's discussion of his medium's handling of the Vietnam War "frank and . . . redeeming." Similarly, Neil Hickey pointed out in a *Columbia Journalism Review* critique that the author's chapter on the Kennedy assassination "has a fine narrative drive that makes it worth the scrutiny of both aspiring and working journalists" and that his meditations on the nature of television news early in the book are so apt "that I hereby recommend they be committed to a parchment scroll and copies sent to all television newsrooms and schools of journalism." Hickey concluded that *The Right Place at the Right Time* is "a richly detailed and rollicking good job of picaresque storytelling."

In 1986 MacNeil provided the narration for a nine-part PBS television series entitled *The Story of English.* MacNeil went on to coauthor a book based on the show with Robert McCrum and William Cran. In a review of the print version of *The Story of English,* Douglas Balz of the *Chicago Tribune* called the work "an admirable undertaking: explaining our language to the people who use it every day. . . . *The Story of English* is handsomely illustrated, lavishly displayed and competently, occasionally eloquently, written." Balz also deemed both the television series and the book "an honorable project, well worth a reader's or viewer's attention."

Although born in Montreal, MacNeil grew up in Halifax, and it is this locale he remembers so fondly in *Wordstruck: A Memoir.* A *Time* critic declared that at its best, the book evokes "the salty tang of fog descending on proud, poky Halifax as winter comes." Acclaimed by Gillian MacKay in *Maclean's* as "a thoughtful, charming chronicle of a lifelong romance with words," the book examines the newsman's "abiding passion for the English language." MacNeil describes vivid memories of his mother's voice telling him stories and reading aloud children's classics, including *Winnie the Pooh, Peter Pan, A Child's Garden of Verses,* and *Treasure Island.* Helen Benedict remarked in the *New York Times Book Review* that MacNeil "re-explores these works with care, turning their words over as sensuously as if they were rare Oriental delicacies and recapturing their power." MacKay added: "In his own prose, MacNeil employs the straightforward, soothing style of the broadcaster effectively, rising to more poetic heights in his evocation of a happy childhood. He is most touching when he describes his parents." Benedict concluded in the *New York Times Book Review,* "Mostly the book draws us into an appreciation of language that seems rare in this crass and overbearing age."

Halifax also serves as the setting for MacNeil's first novel, *Burden of Desire.* John DeMont stated in *Maclean's* that the book explores "the lives of two men and a woman buffeted by the winds of change blowing through Halifax in the years during the First World War." DeMont explains further: "The novel touches on weighty matters: sexual morality, religious faith, the psychiatric theories of Freud and Carl Jung, and the emergence of a Canadian identity during the carnage of the First World War." Constructed around an actual event—the 1917 collision and subsequent explosion of two freighters in the Halifax harbor, resulting in massive death and property destruction—the book focuses on Julia Robertson, who keeps a diary of her private sexual thoughts while her husband is overseas fighting in the war. After the harbor explosion, her diary disappears, ending up in the hands of a cleric, who falls in love with the woman revealed on the pages. In attempting to trace the owner of the diary, the cleric shares it with his psychologist friend, who reads it and also learns to love her. Together they discover Julia's identity.

Susan Fromberg Schaeffer observed in the *New York Times Book Review* that the novel "is at once an intricate, satisfying romance and an exploration of how difficult it is for a society to give up its well-loved ideas. . . . It is a novel filled with riches and alight with understanding of the small events that lead to the huge upheavals in life." She additionally commented that *Burden of Desire* "is at once a wonderful romance involving one of the more appealing triangles in recent fiction and a thoughtful dissection of the glacial pace of social change."

For years MacNeil successfully combined his duties as a broadcast journalist with his work as a writer. The critical reception for *Burden of Desire* and his urge to write more fiction certainly contributed to his decision to retire from *The MacNeil/Lehrer News Hour* on October 20, 1995, his twentieth anniversary with the show. MacNeil told the *Los Angeles Times:* "My colleagues know that I've been thinking about when to retire, and the twentieth anniversary provides a nice symmetry. . . . But what confirmed me was the coincidence of our [station's] need to save money. We were faced with a budget shortfall in our funding." MacNeil made little secret about his future career plans. "I set out to be a writer, not a journalist," he told *Maclean's.*

A number of MacNeil's projects have examined the nature of Canadian citizenship and the Canadian's place in the wider world. In his 1995 novel *The Voyage,* for instance, MacNeil tells the story of political tensions between Canada and America as reflected in the actions of David Lyon, who serves in the book as Canada's Consul-General in New York. *The Voyage* is not the first of MacNeil's novels to use historical figures and incidents, but it is the first to provide characterizations of living Canadian and American politicians. "I wondered at first whether I should use real people, then I decided to go ahead, because I do think it makes it seem more authentic," MacNeil explained in *Publishers Weekly.* "I don't know, of course, how they'll respond to finding themselves in a novel."

MacNeil calls his forays into fiction "a liberation" after all his years as an objective journalist and news commentator. "You need a lot of discontent to write on the side," he told *Publishers Weekly.* "When someone's sending you around the world to exciting places it's hard to say that you're not really doing what you want to do." He added, however, that working with the printed page allows him to be graphic and uncompromising in a way that the subtle censorship of television news never allowed. "Journalism is still euphemistic in many ways. It daren't show the worst," he said. With his fictional stories, he concluded, "I can make it real *myself.*"

BIOGRAPHICAL/CRITICAL SOURCES:

BOOKS

MacNeil, Robert, *Robert MacNeil, Journalist* (sound cassette recording), National Public Radio (Washington, D.C.), 1986.

MacNeil, *The Right Place at the Right Time,* Little, Brown, 1982.

MacNeil, *Wordstruck: A Memoir,* Viking, 1989.

PERIODICALS

Best Sellers, December 1, 1968.
Bestsellers 89, Issue 3, 1989, pp. 53-54.
Chicago Tribune, September 29, 1986, section 5, p. 3.
Christian Science Monitor, May 26, 1992, p. 14.
Columbia Journalism Review, July/August, 1982.
Detroit News, June 8, 1982.
Library Journal, November 1, 1988, p. 95.
Los Angeles Times, October 11, 1994, pp. F2, 9.
Los Angeles Times Book Review, September 19, 1982.
Maclean's, April 10, 1989, p. 79; March 16, 1992, p. 53.
Nation, April 14, 1969.
New Leader, November 18, 1968.
Newsday, May 10, 1976.
New York, August 27, 1979.
New Yorker, September 6, 1982.
New York Times, October 7, 1968; October 11, 1994.
New York Times Book Review, March 26, 1989, p. 6; March 8, 1992, pp. 10-11.
Observer Review, June 7, 1970.
Publishers Weekly, September 30, 1988, p. 54; October 16, 1995, pp. 38-39.
Quill and Quire, January 1992, p. 26.
Saturday Night, March 1992, pp. 24-26, 60-63.
Saturday Review, December 14, 1968; May 15, 1976.
Time, April 24, 1989, p. 87.
Times Literary Supplement, October 7, 1983; April 6, 1990, p. 366.
Virginia Quarterly Review, spring, 1969.
Washington Post Book World, June 20, 1982.*

* * *

MAGUIRE, Gregory (Peter) 1954-

PERSONAL: Born June 9, 1954, in Albany, NY; son of John (a journalist) and Helen (Gregory) Maguire. *Education:* State University of New York at Albany, B.A., 1976; Simmons College, M.A., 1978; Tufts University, Ph.D., 1990. *Religion:* Roman Catholic.

ADDRESSES: Agent—c/o William Reiss, John Hawkins Associates, 71 West 23rd St., Suite 1600, New York, NY 10010.

CAREER: Vincentian Grade School, Albany, NY, teacher of English, 1976-77; freelance writer and educator, 1977—; Center for the Study of Children's Literature, Simmons College, Boston, staff member, 1979-83, then associate director and assistant professor, 1983-87. Director of contemporary music at Roman Catholic church in Albany, NY, 1972-77; codirector, Children's Literature New England, 1987—. Artist-in-residence, Isabella Stewart Gardner Museum, 1994.

AWARDS, HONORS: Fellow, Bread Loaf Writers' Conference, 1978; Blue Mountain Center fellowship, 1986, 1987, 1988, 1989, 1990, and 1995.

WRITINGS:

FOR CHILDREN

The Lightning Time, Farrar, Straus (New York City), 1978.
The Daughter of the Moon, Farrar, Straus, 1980.
Lights on the Lake, Farrar, Straus, 1981.
The Dream Stealer, Harper (New York City), 1983.
The Peace and Quiet Diner, illustrated by David Perry, Parents' Magazine Press (New York City), 1988.
I Feel like the Morning Star, Harper, 1989.
Lucas Fishbone, illustrated by Frank Gargiulo, Harper, 1990.
Seven Spiders Spinning, Clarion (New York City), 1994.
Missing Sisters, M. K. McEldery Books (New York City), 1994.
Oasis, Clarion, 1996.
Six Haunted Hairdos, Clarion, 1997.

OTHER

(Editor, with Barbara Harrison) *Innocence and Experience: Essays and Conversations on Children's Literature,* Lothrop (New York City), 1987.
Wicked: The Life and Times of the Wicked Witch of the West (novel), HarperCollins (New York City), 1995.

SIDELIGHTS: After writing fantasy books for children for over fifteen years, author and educator Gregory Maguire decided to turn his sights to one of the classics of children's literature and examine it from an adult point of view. His study of the development of the Wicked Witch of the West, the despicable character from L. Frank Baum's *The Wizard of Oz,* resulted in *Wicked: The Life and Times of the*

Wicked Witch of the West, a fictional work that, in the words of a *Publishers Weekly* reviewer, "combines puckish humor and bracing pessimism in [a] fantastical meditation on good and evil."

In Maguire's novel, the Wicked Witch has a name—Elphaba (El-pha-ba: L-F-B, the initials of L. Frank Baum)—and a past. The daughter of a compulsive missionary and his self-absorbed wife, young, green-complected Elphaba grows up in a loveless, detached environment in an Oz ruled by an autocratic wizard intent on subjugating the citizenry and gaining control of most of the land in the kingdom. Not until her first year at Shiz University, where she rooms with the air-headed and status-conscious Glinda, is Elphaba emotionally able to involve herself in anything. Politics becomes her passion; she breaks from her shell and joins a group of radical young underground activists in their fight to depose the despotic Wizard and promote the cause of animal rights. A plot to kill the Wizard's closest advisor calls forth her total commitment; neither romance nor parenthood can command the same dedication from Elphaba. "Far from evil, Elphaba is an extremely likeable character," notes Peter Galvin in the *Advocate.* "She's a truth-teller in a world of sycophants, phonies, and charlatans, and she spends her entire life battling the forces of evil—personal, theological, and political."

Maguire drew on several inspirations in writing *Wicked.* "When I was a child, I used to get the neighborhood kids together, and we would do a re-enactment of the movie the day after it was on television," he told Galvin. "I always had to play the Scarecrow," the author added, "because obviously I couldn't be Dorothy." His other inspiration was the way Iraqi leader Saddam Hussein was vilified by the media during the Gulf War. "I began to be interested in the idea of evil and I wanted to explore it in fictional form," he remarked. The Wicked Witch of the West, which through the skill of actress Margaret Hamilton in the 1939 film production of *The Wizard of Oz* became one of the classic incarnations of evil in U.S. popular culture, was an obvious choice for a subject.

Overall critical reaction to *Wicked* was largely enthusiastic. Robert Rodi praised the novel in the *Los Angeles Times Book Review,* calling it a "fully realized fantasy realm that coheres politically, culturally, sexually—and magically," and hailing it as "a staggering feat of wordcraft, made no less so by the fact that its boundaries were set decades ago by somebody else." Michiko Kakutani, however, asserted

that Maguire strays far from the traditional boundaries of Baum's classic story, and remarked in the *New York Times Book Review* that Maguire's "alterations, annotations and embroideries have so little to do with the original story that they're neither amusing nor provocative; to make matters worse, they're relentlessly politically correct."

In addition to his adult novel, *Wicked,* Maguire has written several fantasy novels for children, including 1983's highly praised *The Dream Stealer,* as well as others in a more realistic vein. *I Feel like the Morning Star,* published in 1989, is a futuristic novel featuring three teenagers who are among a community of people confined to a fallout shelter, not knowing what has happened since they moved below ground. Fleeing the ostensibly democratic but ultimately oppressive environment underground, they eventually return safely to the Earth's surface. In 1994's *Missing Sisters* Maguire draws on his Roman Catholic heritage in a story of a shy orphaned girl suffering from speech and hearing impediments whose view of the world changes through the discovery of a twin sister and the simple wisdom of the nuns at the orphanage where she lives.

Maguire told *CA:* "There are twin concerns that emerge in nearly all my work, from the more light-hearted farcical romps of the Hamlet Chronicles (which include *Seven Spiders Spinning* and *Six Haunted Hairdos*) up through the dark comic novels for adults like *Wicked* and other works in progress. The first concern is the search for parents, particularly the missing mother, an obsession that clearly derives from my own early life experience as an infant whose mother died in childbirth. The second concern is broader but no less pressing: the struggle of a child or an adult to claim autonomy and accept personal responsibility while maintaining identity as a member of a larger group—a family, a club, a religious denomination, a neighborhood, a nation."

BIOGRAPHICAL/CRITICAL SOURCES:

BOOKS

Twentieth-Century Children's Writers, St. James Press (Detroit), 1995.

PERIODICALS

Advocate, October 17, 1995, pp. 56-58.
Los Angeles Times Book Review, October 29, 1995, p. 4.

New York Times Book Review, October 24, 1995, p.
  C17.
Publishers Weekly, August 21, 1995, p. 45.
Voice of Youth Advocates, December, 1994, pp. 277-
  78.

*   *   *

MAILLOUX, Steven   1950-

PERSONAL: Born March 23, 1950, in La Jolla, CA;
son of Edmund Joseph (an electronics supervisor)
and Nell (in sales; maiden name, Gasca) Mailloux;
married Mary Ann Young (an elementary school
teacher), August 3, 1975; children: Mary Nell, Roman Edmund, Teresa Elizabeth. *Education:* Loyola
University, Los Angeles, CA, B.A., 1972; University of Southern California, M.A., 1974, Ph.D.,
1977. *Politics:* Independent. *Religion:* Roman Catholic.

ADDRESSES: Home—20 Lewis, Irvine, CA 92760.
Office—Department of English and Comparative Literature, University of California, Irvine, CA 92720.

CAREER: Temple University, Philadelphia, PA, assistant professor of English, 1977-79; University of
Miami, Coral Gables, FL, assistant professor, 1979-
82, associate professor of English, 1982-86; Syracuse University, Syracuse, NY, professor of English,
1986-91; University of California—Irvine, Irvine,
CA, professor of English, 1991—. Faculty member,
National Endowment for the Humanities summer institute on recent literary criticism and the core literature course, 1985, and National Council of Teachers
of English summer institute on teaching literature to
undergraduates, 1987.

MEMBER: International Society for the History of
Rhetoric, Modern Language Association of America,
Rhetoric Society of America, American Literature
Association, Society for Critical Exchange, National
Council of Teachers of English, Speech Communica-
tion Association, Kenneth Burke Society.

AWARDS, HONORS: National Endowment for the
Humanities grant, 1979-80; fellowship for School of
Criticism and Theory, Northwestern University,
1982; Stanford Humanities Center fellowship, 1985-86.

WRITINGS:

*Interpretive Conventions: The Reader in the Study of
  American Fiction,* Cornell University Press
  (Ithaca, NY), 1982.
(Editor with Sanford Levinson) *Interpreting Law and
  Literature,* Northwestern University Press
  (Evanston, IL), 1988.
Rhetorical Power, Cornell University Press, 1989.
(Editor) *Rhetoric, Sophistry, Pragmatism,* Cambridge
  University Press (New York City), 1995.

Contributor to *Critical Terms,* University of Chicago
Press (Chicago), 1989, *Readers in History: American
Literature and the Context of Response,* Johns
Hopkins University Press (Baltimore), 1993, and
*English Studies/Culture Studies: Institutionalizing
Dissent,* University of Illinois Press (Urbana), 1994.
Contributor to journals, including *Critical Inquiry*
and *Text and Performance Quarterly.*

*WORK IN PROGRESS: Reception Histories: Rheto-
ric, Critical Theory and Cultural Studies.*

*   *   *

MAJOR, Clarence   1936-

PERSONAL: Born December 31, 1936, in Atlanta,
GA; son of Clarence and Inez (Huff) Major; married
Joyce Sparrow, 1958 (divorced, 1964); married
Pamela Jane Ritter, May 8, 1980. *Education:* State
University of New York at Albany, B.S.; Union for
Experimenting Colleges and Universities, Ph.D.,
1978.

ADDRESSES: Office—Department of English, University of California at Davis, 211 Sproul Hall,
Davis, CA 95616. *Agent*—Susan Bergholz, 17 W.
10th St. #5, New York, NY 10011-8769.

CAREER: Writer. Brooklyn College, City University
of New York, SEEK program lecturer, 1968-69, lecturer, 1973-75; Sarah Lawrence College, Bronxville,
NY, lecturer, 1972-75; Queens College, City University of New York, lecturer, 1972-73, 1975, adjunct lecturer for New York Board of Higher Education, ACE program, 1973; Howard University,
Washington, DC, assistant professor, 1974-76; University of Washington, Seattle, assistant professor,

1976-77; University of Colorado, Boulder, associate professor, 1977-81, professor of English, 1981-89; University of California at Davis, professor of English, 1989—, director of creative writing, 1991-93. Visiting professor, University of Nice, France, 1981-82 and 1983; visiting assistant professor, University of Maryland at College Park and State University of New York at Binghamton, 1987. Writer in residence at colleges and universities. Research analyst for Simulmatics Corp., New York City, 1967; newspaper reporter, 1968. Lecturer and guest lecturer at colleges, universities, libraries, and other institutions in the United States, Europe, and Africa. Judge for various literary competitions. Artist; has exhibited and published his photographs and paintings. Member of advisory board, Reading Program, New York Public School District 5, 1970. *Military service:* U.S. Air Force, 1955-57; served as record specialist.

AWARDS, HONORS: Recipient of numerous grants; National Council on the Arts Award, Association of American University Presses, 1970; National Council on the Arts Award, 1970, for *Swallow the Lake;* Pushcart Prize, 1976, for poem "Funeral," from *The Syncopated Cakewalk,* and 1989, for story "My Mother and Mitch"; Fulbright-Hays Inter-University Exchange Award, Franco-American Commission for Education Exchange, Nice, France, 1981-83; Le Prix Maurice Edgar Coindreau nomination, 1982, for French version of *Reflex and Bone Structure;* Western States Book Award for fiction, 1986, for *My Amputations; New York Times Book Review* notable book of the year citation, 1988, for *Painted Turtle: Woman with Guitar; Los Angeles Times* Book Critics Award nomination, 1990, for *Fun & Games.*

WRITINGS:

POETRY

The Fires that Burn in Heaven, [Chicago], 1954.
Love Poems of a Black Man, Coercion (Omaha, NE), 1965.
Human Juices, Coercion, 1966.
Swallow the Lake, Wesleyan University Press (Middletown, CT), 1970.
Symptoms and Madness, Corinth Books (New York City), 1971.
Private Line, Paul Breman (London), 1971.
The Cotton Club, Broadside Press (Detroit, MI), 1972.
The Syncopated Cakewalk, Barlenmir (New York City), 1974.

Inside Diameter: The France Poems, Permanent Press (London and New York City), 1985.
Surfaces and Masks, Coffee House Press (Minneapolis, MN), 1987.
Some Observations of a Stranger at Zuni in the Latter Part of the Century, Sun & Moon (Los Angeles, CA), 1988.
Parking Lots, illustrated by Laura Dronzek, Perishable Press (Mount Horeb, WI), 1992.

Contributor of poetry to anthologies and to numerous periodicals, including *American Poetry Review, Kenyon Review, Michigan Quarterly Review, Folger Poetry Broadside, Poetry Miscellany, Unmuzzled Ox, Yardbird Reader,* and *Black Orpheus* (Nigeria).

NOVELS

All-Night Visitors, Olympia (New York City), 1969.
No, Emerson Hall (New York City), 1973.
Reflex and Bone Structure, Fiction Collective (New York City), 1975.
Emergency Exit, Fiction Collective, 1979.
My Amputations, Fiction Collective, 1986.
Such Was the Season (Literary Guild alternate selection), Mercury House (San Francisco, CA), 1987.
Painted Turtle: Woman with Guitar, Sun & Moon, 1988.

NONFICTION

The Dark and Feeling: Black American Writers and Their Work (essays), Third Press (New York City), 1974.

Contributor of articles, essays, reviews, and other nonfiction prose to books, anthologies, and numerous periodicals, including *New York Times Book Review, Washington Post Book World, Los Angeles Times Book Review, American Poetry Review, Epoch, American Book Review, John O'Hara Journal, Essence, Negro Digest, Black Scholar, Journal of Black Studies and Research,* and *Black Orpheus* (Nigeria).

EDITOR

Writers Workshop Anthology, Harlem Education Program, 1967.
Man Is Like a Child: An Anthology of Creative Writing by Students, Macomb Junior High School, 1968.
(And author of introduction) *The New Black Poetry,* International Publications, 1969.

Dictionary of Afro-American Slang, International Publications (New York City), 1970, published in England as *Black Slang: A Dictionary of Afro-American Talk,* Routledge & Kegan Paul (London), 1971, new edition with introduction by Major published as *Juba to Jive: A Dictionary of African-American Slang,* Viking (New York City), 1994.

Jerry Bumpus, *Things in Place* (short stories), Fiction Collective, 1975.

(And author of introduction) *Calling the Wind: Twentieth-Century African-American Short Stories* (Book-of-the-Month Club selection), HarperCollins/Burlingame (New York City), 1993.

The Garden Thrives: Twentieth-Century African-American Poetry, HarperCollins (New York City), 1995.

SHORT STORIES

Fun & Games, Holy Cow! Press (Duluth, MN), 1990.

Contributor of short fiction to anthologies and to numerous periodicals, including *Massachusetts Review, Essence, Zyzzyva, Witness, Boulevard, Fiction, Chelsea, Baltimore Sun, Black Scholar, Black American Literature Forum, Agni Review, Seattle Review, Hambone,* and *Callaloo.*

OTHER

Also author of television script, *Africa Speaks to New York,* 1970. Distinguished contributing editor to *The Pushcart Prize: The Best of the Small Presses,* Pushcart Press (Wainscott, NY), 1977—. Columnist, *American Poetry Review,* 1973-76. Editor, *Coercion Review,* 1958-66; staff writer, *Proof,* 1960-61; associate editor, *Caw,* 1967-70, and *Journal of Black Poetry,* 1967-70; member of board of directors, *What's Happening* magazine, Columbia University, 1969; contributing editor, *American Poetry Review,* 1976—, and *Dark Waters,* 1977; *American Book Review,* editor, 1977-78, associate editor, 1978—; associate editor, *Bopp,* 1977-78, *Gumbo,* 1978, *Departures,* 1979, and *par rapport,* 1979—; member of editorial board, *Umojo: A Scholarly Journal of Black Studies,* 1979; committee member, *Signes,* 1983—; fiction editor, *High Plains Literary Review,* 1986—.

All-Night Visitors has been translated into Italian and German; *Reflex and Bone Structure* has been translated into French; *Such Was the Season* has been translated into German.

SIDELIGHTS: American writer Clarence Major "has been in the forefront of experimental poetry and prose," Eugene B. Redmond writes in *Parnassus.* "In prose he fits 'loosely' into a category with William Melvin Kelley and Ishmael Reed. But his influences and antecedents are not so easy to identify." Perhaps best known for his novels, Major draws on his experience as a Southern African-American to "[defy] the white-imposed 'traditions' of black literature [and] to develop a brilliant lyricism in new forms of fiction," states Jerome Klinkowitz in *The Life of Fiction.* But Major's art, continues Klinkowitz, "inevitably turns back to the basic social and personal concerns which must remain at the heart of any literary experience." Noting the high incidence of violent scenes in Major's work, *Black Creation* critic Jim Walker comments, "Major has filled [his work] with the violence we expect of Southern life; violence of whites against Blacks, and more unfortunately, violence of Blacks against Blacks. . . . But the point Major is obviously trying to make with these kinds of scenes is that violence is an integral part of life for Southern Blacks and moreover, that it helps shape their lives and attitudes."

Critics praise Major's unique use of language in *My Amputations,* for which he received the Western States Book Award in 1986. *My Amputations* follows well-read parolee Mason Ellis as he impersonates an African-American novelist named Clarence McKay, whom he has taken hostage. McKay's literary agent plays along, and almost no one who meets the imposter on his world-wide lecture tour can tell the difference between Mason and the author whose identity he has usurped. "Major has fashioned a parable of the black writer as the most invisible and misrepresented of us all," notes Greg Tate in a *Washington Post Book World* review. *New York Times Book Review* contributor Richard Perry finds *My Amputations* "a book in which the question of identity throbs like an infected tooth,. . . . a picaresque novel that comes wailing out of the blues tradition: it is ironic, irreverent, sexy, on a first-name basis with the human condition, and defined in part by exaggeration and laughter." In a *Nation* review, Stuart Klawans writes: "Mere description cannot convey the wild humor and audacity to be found here, nor the anxiety and cunning. . . . When a writer loads a book with so many references, the reader is entitled to ask whether he knows what he's doing. Believe me, Clarence Major knows. He has fashioned a novel that is simultaneously a deception and one great, roaring self-revelation." Tate comments, "Major feels particular ardor for mixing the rhythms of American slang with those of historical, scientific, mythological and occult texts. . . . The integration of such alchemical language into the mundane human affairs of its subjects is part of what makes *My Amputations* such a provocative advance in contemporary American writing."

Such Was the Season is "more structured and accessible" than Major's earlier novels, writes David Nicholson in the *Washington Post Book World.* To Nicholson, it "seems rooted in Major's experience, and much of the book's success has to do with the warmth of the central character. . . . Annie Eliza . . . speaks to us for more than 200 pages of things past and present in a voice that is always uniquely hers." In this matriarch of a black middle-class Atlanta family who speaks authentic vernacular, "Major has created a delightfully lifelike, storytelling woman whose candor is matched only by her devotion to truth and her down-to-earth yea-saying to life," Al Young writes in the *New York Times Book Review.* "It is as if Clarence Major, the avid *avant-gardiste,* has himself come home to touch base with the blues and spirituals that continue to nourish and express the lives of those people he writes about so knowingly, and with contagious affection." *Such Was the Season,* Young summarizes, is a "straight-ahead narrative crammed with action, a dramatic storyline and meaty characterization." In the one week described by Annie Eliza, several scandals touching family members erupt in the wake of her daughter-in-law's candidacy for the state senate. Even so, "the book's pleasures have less to do with what happens and more with Annie Eliza and her tale," Nicholson maintains. "Though at first glance Major seems to have abandoned his postmodern explorations, *Such Was the Season* actually has much in common with those earlier works."

In *Fun & Games,* Major's 1990 collection of short "fictions," the author continues to bend and twist social realism around experimental narratives and prose. Writing in the *New York Times Book Review,* Karen Brailsford takes note of Major's "eloquent" prose, but finds that his "plots are frequently pointless, and ultimately disappointing." But while commenting that some of the stories in *Fun & Games* lack "the thematic and technical complexities that are Major's trademark," Maurice Bennett asserts in the *Washington Post Book World* that Major "is still here doing what he has done for the past 25 years: producing some of the very best experimental fiction." He adds, "Major remains at heart the poet he was at

the beginning of his career, importing into his fictions a poetic fascination with the 'word' and its power to create realities, whether they be realities of identity, relationship, or phenomena." Merle Rubin, writing in the *Los Angeles Times Book Review,* suggests that Major uses the "realist mode" to comment on the way we construct reality. "In Major's hands, straightforward realism has a way of wandering off into the labyrinths of literary self-awareness. . . . Major's 'short fictions' remind us that reality is not simply something out there: Ours, as he puts it, is a 'man-made world,' influenced by our ability to reflect, re-imagine, re-interpret and reform it."

Major's nonfiction has also garnered acclaim. *Calling the Wind: Twentieth-Century African-American Short Stories,* edited and with an introduction by Major, is an anthology of short fiction by African-American writers which "charts both the evolution of the short-story form and the evolution of African American consciousness," comments Howard Junker in the *San Francisco Review of Books. Calling the Wind* includes short fiction from writers such as Charles Chesnutt, Ralph Ellison, Toni Cade Bambara and Terry McMillan. Junker argues that *Calling the Wind* "should be required reading."

Major also edited and authored the introduction to *Juba to Jive: A Dictionary of African-American Slang,* an updated and expanded version of *Dictionary of Afro-American Slang* published originally in 1970. *Juba to Jive,* in the words of Ipeling Kgositsile in the *Village Voice Literary Supplement,* is a "no-nonsense guide to African American verbal expression." Kira Hall in the *Washington Post Book World* finds *Juba to Jive* an "exciting [introduction] to African-American *languaculture,* drawing the reader into an active world of words and phrases which might never appear in the American Heritage Dictionary," despite being spoken daily by many Americans. Applauding Major's ample etymological information on each term, Kgositsile calls *Juba to Jive* a "must buy; read it and learn the roots of a mother tongue."

Major's work has "provided a series of systematic searches into different sources of identity—sexual, literary, cultural, visual, socio-economic, familial, regional, national, and personal, as well as ethnic," argues Lisa C. Roney in the *African American Review.* "When he is at his best," Doug Bolling remarks in the *Black American Literature Forum,* "Major helps us to see that fiction created within an aesthetic of fluidity and denial of 'closure' and verbal freedom can generate an excitement and awareness of great value; that the rigidities of plot, characterization, and illusioned depth can be softened and, finally, dropped in favor of new and valid rhythms." Major's achievement, according to Klinkowitz in an *African American Review* overview of Major's career and works, "has been to show just how concretely we live within the imagination—how our lives are shaped by language and how by a simple act of self-awareness we can seize control of the world and reshape it to our liking and benefit."

BIOGRAPHICAL/CRITICAL SOURCES:

BOOKS

Bell, Bernard W., *The Afro-American Novel and Its Tradition,* University of Massachusetts Press (Amherst), 1987.

Blacks in America: Bibliographical Essays, Doubleday (New York City), 1971.

Byerman, Keith E., *Fingering the Jogged Grain: Tradition and Form in Recent Black Fiction,* University of Georgia Press (Athens), 1985.

Chapman, A., editor, *New Black Voices: An Anthology of Contemporary Afro-American Literature,* New American Library (New York City), 1972.

Contemporary Authors Autobiography Series, Volume 6, Gale (Detroit), 1988.

Contemporary Black Biography, Volume 9, Gale, 1995.

Contemporary Literary Criticism, Gale, Volume 3, 1975, Volume 19, 1981, Volume 48, 1987.

Critical Survey of Short Fiction: Current Writers, Salem Press (Englewood Cliffs, NJ), 1981.

Dictionary of Literary Biography, Volume 33: *Afro-American Writers since 1955,* Gale, 1984.

Dillard, J. L., *Lexicon of Black English,* Seabury Press (New York City), 1977.

Finding the Words: Conversations with Writers Who Teach, Ohio University Press (Athens), 1984.

Henderson, Bill, editor, *Pushcart Prize: The Best of the Small Presses, 1976-77,* Pushcart Press, 1976.

Hoffman, Daniel, editor, *The Harvard Guide to Contemporary American Writing,* Harvard University Press (Cambridge, MA), 1979.

Johnson, Charles, *Being and Race,* Indiana University Press (Bloomington), 1988.

Kiernan, Robert F., *American Writing since 1945: A Critical Survey,* Ungar (New York City), 1983.

Klinkowitz, Jerome, *The Life of Fiction,* University of Illinois Press (Champaign), 1977.

Klinkowitz, Jerome, *The Practice of Fiction in America: Writers from Hawthorne to the Present,* Iowa State University Press (Ames), 1980.

Klinkowitz, Jerome, *Literary Disruptions: The Making of a Post-Contemporary American Fiction,* revised edition, University of Illinois, 1980.

Major, Clarence, *The Dark and Feeling: Black American Writers and Their Work,* Third Press, 1974.

O'Brien, John, *Interviews with Black Writers,* Liveright (New York City), 1973.

Redmond, Eugene B., *Drumvoices: The Mission of Afro-American Poetry—A Critical History,* Anchor/Doubleday (New York City), 1976.

Shapiro, Nancy, and Ron Padgett, editors, *The Point: Where Teaching and Writing Intersect,* Teachers and Writers (New York City), 1983.

Wepman, Dennis, and others, *The Life: The Lore and Folk Poetry of the Black Hustler,* University of Pennsylvania Press (Philadelphia), 1976.

Williams, Sherley Anne, *Give Birth to Brightness: A Thematic Study in Neo-Black Literature,* Dial (New York City), 1972.

World Literature since 1945: Critical Surveys of the Contemporary Literatures of Europe and the Americas, Ungar, 1973.

PERIODICALS

African American Review, spring, 1994.
American Anthropologist, June, 1975.
American Book Review, September/October, 1982; September, 1986.
Best Sellers, June 1, 1973.
Black American Literature Forum, Number 12, 1978; Volume 12, number 2, 1979; fall, 1983.
Black Creation, summer, 1973.
Black Scholar, January, 1971.
Chicago Sun-Times, April 28, 1974.
Chicago Tribune, October 6, 1986.
Chicago Tribune Books, October 6, 1986; April 3, 1994, p. 8.
Essence, November, 1970.
Greenfield Review, winter, 1971.
Los Angeles Times Book Review, February 18, 1990; April 29, 1990, p. 14.
Ms., July, 1977.
Nation, January 24, 1987.
Negro Digest, December, 1969.
Newsday, November 1, 1987.
New York Times, April 7, 1969.
New York Times Book Review, February 13, 1972; July 1, 1973; November 30, 1975; September 28, 1986; December 13, 1987; May 20, 1990.

Observer (London), May 1, 1994, p. 26.

Obsidian, Volume 4, number 2, 1978.

Parnassus, spring/summer, 1975.

par rapport, Volume 2, number 1, 1979.

Penthouse, February, 1971.

Phylon, winter, 1972.

Plain Dealer (Cleveland), December 3, 1987.

Poetry, August, 1971.

Publishers Weekly, March 24, 1969; March 19, 1973; May 9, 1986; July 4, 1986; July 31, 1987.

Quarterly Journal of Speech, April, 1977.

San Francisco Review of Books, Volume 1, number 12, 1976; Volume 7, number 3, 1982; March/April, 1993, p. 14.

Saturday Review, December 5, 1970; April 3, 1971.

Village Voice Literary Supplement, February, 1987; July 26, 1994, p. 81.

Virginia Quarterly Review, winter, 1971.

Washington Post Book World, September, 13, 1986; January 10, 1988; February 18, 1990; January 10, 1993, p. 12; July 24, 1994, p. 8.

*   *   *

MANUEL, Frank Edward   1910-

PERSONAL: Born September 12, 1910, in Boston, MA; son of Morris and Jessica (Fredson) Manuel; married Fritzie Prigohzy, October 6, 1936. *Education:* Harvard University, A.B., 1930, M.A., 1931, Ph.D., 1933; additional graduate study at Ecole des Hautes Etudes Politiques et Sociales, Paris, France, 1933.

ADDRESSES: Home—10 Emerson Pl., No. 21E, Boston, MA 02114.

CAREER: Harvard University, Cambridge, MA, member of department of history, government, and economics, 1935-37; research and administrative positions with National Defense Commission and Office of Price Administration, 1940-43, 1945-47; Western Reserve University (now Case Western Reserve University), Cleveland, OH, professor of history, 1947; Brandeis University, Waltham, MA, professor of history and moral psychology, 1949-65; New York University, New York City, professor, 1965-76, Kenan Professor of History, 1970-76; Brandeis University, Alfred and Viola Hart University Professor, 1977-86. Visiting professor at various universities, including Harvard University, 1960, Hebrew University of Jerusalem, 1972, Oxford Uni-

versity (Eastman visiting professor), 1972-73, University of Chicago, 1975, University of California at Los Angeles, 1976, and Boston University, 1986-88; visiting research fellow at Australian National University, 1974. Member of Institute for Advanced Study, 1976-77. *Military service:* U.S. Army, 1943-45; served as combat intelligence officer with Twenty-First Corps; received Bronze Star.

MEMBER: American Academy of Arts and Sciences (fellow), Phi Beta Kappa.

AWARDS, HONORS: Guggenheim fellow, 1957-58; Center for Advanced Study in the Behavioral Sciences fellow, 1962-63; Phi Beta Kappa visiting scholar, 1978; Litt.D., Jewish Theological Seminary, 1979; Melcher Prize, 1980, Phi Beta Kappa Emerson Award, 1980, and American Book Award, paperback history, 1983, all for *Utopian Thought in the Western World;* Doctor of Humane Letters, Brandeis University, 1986.

WRITINGS:

The Politics of Modern Spain, McGraw (New York City), 1938.

The Realities of American-Palestine Relations, Public Affairs Press, 1949.

The Age of Reason, Cornell University Press (Ithaca, NY), 1951, reprinted, Greenwood Press (Westport, CT), 1982.

The New World of Henri Saint-Simon, Harvard University Press (Cambridge, MA), 1956.

The Eighteenth Century Confronts the Gods, Harvard University Press, 1959.

The Prophets of Paris, Harvard University Press, 1962.

Isaac Newton: Historian, Harvard University Press, 1963.

Shapes of Philosophical History, Stanford University Press (Stanford, CA), 1965.

A Portrait of Isaac Newton, Harvard University Press, 1968.

Freedom from History, and Other Untimely Essays, New York University Press (New York City), 1971.

The Religion of Isaac Newton, Clarendon Press (Oxford, England), 1974.

(With wife, Fritzie P. Manuel) *Utopian Thought in the Western World,* Harvard University Press, 1979.

The Changing of the Gods, University Press of New England (Hanover, NH), 1983.

The Broken Staff: Judaism through Christian Eyes, Harvard University Press, 1992.

A Requiem for Karl Marx, Harvard University Press, 1995.

EDITOR

The Enlightenment, Prentice-Hall (Englewood Cliffs, NJ), 1965.

Utopias and Utopian Thought, Houghton (Boston), 1966.

(Translator, and author of introduction with F. P. Manuel) *French Utopias: An Anthology of Ideal Societies,* Free Press (New York City), 1966.

Johann Gottfried von Herder, Reflections on the Philosophy of the History of Mankind, University of Chicago Press (Chicago), 1968.

OTHER

Member of board of editors, *Dictionary of the History of Ideas,* 1969-71; consulting editor, *Psychoanalysis and Contemporary Science,* 1970—; advisory editor, *Clio,* 1971—.

SIDELIGHTS: "Frank [Edward] Manuel has long been distinguished for the depth and diversity of his interest in European intellectual history of the eighteenth and nineteenth centuries; and to this we must add his two books on Newton and his various anthologies of thinkers of the Enlightenment and of the classical utopian writers," comments Robert Brown in the *Times Literary Supplement.* "Now he has joined with his wife [Fritzie P. Manuel] to produce" *Utopian Thought in the Western World,* "a highly informative study which is both a summary of, and reflection upon, the results of their many years of shared work on the ideas of utopian writers." "Since the Renaissance, many of the most gifted Western intellectuals . . . have exhibited a striking 'utopian propensity,'" summarizes *New York Times Book Review* contributor Leo Marx, "and the Manuels set out to describe and, if possible, explain that curious habit of mind." The result, asserts Marx, "is a work of monumental scope, written with authority, wit and unfailing lucidity. *Utopian Thought in the Western World* challenges received ideas about an entire mode of expression and, by implication, about creativity itself." In his *New Republic* review, Robert Nisbet similarly claims that the American Book Award-winning *Utopian Thought in the Western World* "is without any doubt the finest single history of Western utopias to be found anywhere. It is comprehensive, covering the last 2500 years, from early Hebrew and Greek texts, richly detailed, and written with a verve and an unerring eye for the illuminating essence of whatever the authors happen to be dealing with."

In providing such an extensive overview of utopian thought, the Manuels first arrange their subjects into seven "constellations," groups which contain clusters of important writers, with minor writers of the same general area attached to the main cluster. In addition, the Manuels "are interested in bringing to life all of the circumstances, outward, and inward, public and private, that bear upon the making of utopias, and much of this book reads like traditional narrative biography or history," notes Marx. These biographies, adds the critic, "are gems of concise, detached yet sympathetic analysis, never condescending, seldom reductive and invariably engaging. The book's essence lies in these audacious character studies in which a particular life and work and cultural milieu is connected to the overall history of the mode. For all the idiosyncratic diversity of the utopians—and the study is based on many examples," continues Marx, "the Manuels succeed in sketching a compelling profile of their characteristic neurotic style." And Nisbet finds that in particular, "the authors' treatment of Sir Thomas More and his classic [*Utopia*] is masterly and a pure distillation of some of the finest recent scholarship on this complex mind."

Brown, however, while acknowledging the magnitude of *Utopian Thought,* also faults the authors for not presenting enough connections to support their "constellation" groupings: "Useful generalizations about all the members of a given constellation are conspicuously scarce. This is not surprising since the Manuels nowhere give us much reason to believe that they have found common elements of the desired sort." The critic continues by observing that unless the few generalizations that are made "are to be used by the authors in the course of developing an argument or as a test of theory—which they are not—there is no work for them to do." David McLellan similarly remarks in the *New Statesman* that he "get[s] the impression that the book is really a set of separate chapters rather than an overall study within a single, united framework. . . . The book obviously raises a number of difficulties about the whole concept of Utopia—how it is related to political philosophy and social science, and how it should be studied." The critic adds that while "Manuel's almost belletristic style and treatment is extremely readable and at times utterly captivating, nevertheless I feel the lack ultimately of a rigorous framework of analysis."

Nisbet, however, believes that this separation into clusters helps the book achieve overall consistency; he maintains that "it is not simply utopias the authors write about; what they refer to as 'constellations' of utopias are the real subject of the book, its 'underlying pattern.' Thus conventional, linear, event-by-event narrative is happily avoided," concludes the critic, "its place taken by a more comparative and sociological approach to the history of utopias." Marx, while commenting that "the Manuels may have a political blind spot" in their selection of utopians, nevertheless concludes that these reservations "do not drastically diminish my admiration for the Manuels' achievement. *Utopian Thought* is a triumph of old-fashioned personal scholarship. Anyone who bothers to contemplate the size and complexity of the materials they mastered will have trouble believing, as I do, that it was the work of two people." The critic concludes that "no group effort could possibly produce a work of such force and empathy. What the Manuel accomplish is rooted in self-knowledge, and above all in their profound ambivalence about the imagining and writing of utopias." "What is of overriding and overwhelming importance is that the Manuels have given us a book of ideas and personages, written in a style often brilliant and never less than graceful, and filled with more wit than one usually finds in half a hundred work of scholarship," declares Nisbet. "I repeat: it is by far the best and the grandest of histories of the utopian mind."

BIOGRAPHICAL/CRITICAL SOURCES:

PERIODICALS

New Republic, March 1, 1975; November 10, 1979.
New Statesman, March 21, 1969; January 25, 1980.
New York Review of Books, April 10, 1969; March 6, 1980.
New York Times, December 1, 1979.
New York Times Book Review, February 25, 1968; October 21, 1979.
Religious Studies Review, July, 1993, p. 275.
Sixteenth-Century Journal, winter, 1993, p. 937.
Spectator, February 2, 1980.
Times Literary Supplement, June 1, 1973; June 20, 1975; June 6, 1980.

* * *

MANUS, Willard   1930-

PERSONAL: Born September 28, 1930, in New York, NY; son of Isidore (a merchant) and Henriette (Lewine) Manus; married Mavis Ross (a cookbook writer), October 26, 1960; children: Lisa Jennifer,

Ross Saul. *Education:* Adelphi College (now University), B.A., 1952. *Politics:* Independent. *Religion:* Jewish.

ADDRESSES: Home and office—248 Lasky Dr., Beverly Hills, CA 90212; and Lindos, Rhodes, Greece. *Agent*—Carole Abel, Literary Agent, 160 West 87th St., New York, NY 10024.

CAREER: Yonkers Daily Times, Yonkers, NY, reporter, 1953; Columbia Broadcasting System, Inc. (CBS-Radio), New York City, writer for *John Henry Faulk Show,* 1953-54; *Bounty* (magazine), New York City, managing editor, 1955; Cecilwood Summer Playhouse, Fishkill, NY, publicity director, 1956-59; Macmillan Publishing Co., Inc., New York City, publicity director, 1962-64; freelance writer in Lindos, Rhodes, Greece, 1965-70; *Financial Post,* Toronto, Ontario, foreign correspondent in the Mediterranean, 1970-78; film and theatre critic for *Century City News, Daily News, Star News, Evening Outlook, Northeast Newspapers, Happening Magazine,* and *This Month on Stage,* 1980—.

MEMBER: American Theatre Critics Association, Writers Guild of America (West), Los Angeles Film Critics Association, Los Angeles Playwright's Group.

AWARDS, HONORS: Golden Apple Award, National Educational Film and Video Festival, 1990, for video version of play *Walt: Sweet Bird of Freedom.*

WRITINGS:

This Is Lindos (nonfiction), Anglo-Hellenic (Athens), 1974.
This Way to Paradise: Dancing on the Tables (memoirs), Lycabettus Press (Athens), 1996.

NOVELS

The Fixers, Ace Books (New York City), 1957.
Mott the Hoople, McGraw (New York City), 1967, reprinted, Pinnacle Books (New York City), 1980.
The Fighting Men, Panjandrum (Los Angeles), 1982.
Connubial Bliss, Panjandrum, 1990.

FOR CHILDREN

The Proud Rebel, Teenage Book Club, 1959.
Sea Treasure, illustrations by Lee J. Ames, Doubleday (New York City), 1962.

The Mystery of the Flooded Mine, illustrations by James Dwyer, Doubleday, 1964.
The Island Kids, Anglo-Hellenic, 1974.

PLAYS

Creatures of the Chase (also see below), published in *Adelphi Quarterly,* 1967.
The Bleachers (one-act), first produced in New York City at Public Theatre, 1975.
Junk Food (new version of *Creatures of the Chase;* one-act), first produced in Los Angeles at Actors Theatre, 1981, published in *Best One-Act Plays of L.A. Actors Theatre,* Pajandrum, 1985; two-act version published in *Plays and Progress* series, Theatre Communications Group (New York City), 1982.
(With Brian Maeda) *The Kendo Master* (one-act), first produced in Los Angeles at Company of Angels Theatre, 1981.
The Deepest Hunger (adapted from David Ray's *The Orphans of Mingo*), produced in North Hollywood, CA, at Group Repertory Theatre, 1984.
Bon Appetit (one-act), produced in North Hollywood at Group Repertory Theatre, 1984.
Walt: Sweet Bird of Freedom (also see below), first produced in Los Angeles at Chamber Theatre, 1985.
Diamonds, first produced in Los Angeles at Richmond Shepard Theatre, 1986.
The Love Boutique (one-act), first produced in Los Angeles at Skylight Theatre, 1987, published in *Sex in the Afternoon: Seven One-Act Plays from L.A. Actors Theatre,* Great Jones Press, 1987.
(With Ed Metzger) *Hemingway: On the Edge,* first produced in Ottawa, KS, at Ottawa Theatre, 1987.
MM at 58, first produced in Los Angeles at Zephyr Theatre, 1990.
The Electronic Lincoln (one-act), first produced in Los Angeles at Theatre of Note, 1991.
Their Finest Hour: Murrow and Churchill, first produced in New Orleans at Nunemaker Auditorium, 1995.
The Jack London Story (radio play), California Artists Radio Theatre for National Public Radio, 1996.

TELEVISION SCRIPTS

Secrets of Midland Heights, first broadcast by Columbia Broadcasting System (CBS-TV), 1980.
Shannon, first broadcast by CBS-TV, 1981.
Too Close for Comfort, first broadcast by American Broadcasting Company (ABC-TV), 1984.

OTHER

Contributor of stories and articles to numerous periodicals, including *Nation, New Leader, Observer, Confrontation, New Letters, Chicago Tribune, Blues Access, New York Times,* and the *Washington Post.*

Some of Manus's work has been published in Italian, Czech, and German.

ADAPTATIONS: Walt: Sweet Bird of Freedom was produced as a half-hour video by Turtle on the Move Productions (Hollywood, CA).

WORK IN PROGRESS: The Pigskin Rabbi, a novel; *Congo Square,* an opera.

SIDELIGHTS: Willard Manus told *CA:* "For me—a writer who has not yet won important critical or financial recognition—one of the few sustaining pleasures of the craft is to be able to do something new each time out. Each of my published novels is different from the last, and intentionally so, because I cannot understand how and why a writer would want to go on writing and publishing the same kind of work year after year the way many of our so-called best writers do. What a failure of nerve and imagination.

"*The Fixers,* my first novel, was based on the college basketball scandals of the 1950s and dealt with my deep disillusionment with the way sport has been corrupted in this society. Next time around, in *Mott the Hoople,* a book on which I labored for seven years, I went for wild, Rabelasian comedy and a bigger-than-life hero who could laugh at the insanities he encountered during his brief, bizarre stay on Earth. Number three was *The Fighting Men,* a tough, gritty story about a bunch of men who were in Vietnam together and who meet for a reunion in an unnamed South American country and get caught up in a gunfight with a left-wing guerrilla band.

"My book *Connubial Bliss* bears no relation whatsoever to any of the above. It is a tragicomic exploration of sexual obsession.

"As for my plays, they too look radically unlike each other. Their settings range from a sex shop to a dirt farm in Oklahoma to a garbage dump in Pittsburgh. Just recently I changed gears even more and wrote a memoir, *This Way to Paradise: Dancing on the Tables,* dealing with my experiences living on a

Greek island from 1965 to 1979. Enough, though. I shouldn't go on talking about my work because, to paraphrase Samuel Beckett, I doubt whether I'm qualified to do so."

BIOGRAPHICAL/CRITICAL SOURCES:

BOOKS

Manus, Willard, *This Way to Paradise: Dancing on the Tables* (memoirs), Lycabettus Press, 1996.

PERIODICALS

Los Angeles Times, June 21, 1985.
Observer, August 6, 1967.

*　　*　　*

MARCHANT, Anyda   1911-
(Sarah Aldridge)

PERSONAL: Name is pronounced "*Annee*-da Marchant"; born January 27, 1911, in Rio de Janeiro, Brazil; daughter of Langworthy (an educator and editor) and Maude Henrietta (Annett) Marchant. *Education:* National University (now George Washington University), Washington, DC, A.B. (with distinction), 1931, M.A. 1933, LL.B., 1936. *Politics:* Democrat. *Religion:* Episcopalian. *Avocational interests:* "The feminist agenda; the history of feminism."

ADDRESSES: Home—212 Laurel St., Rehoboth Beach, DE 19971. *Office*—A & M Books, P. O. Box 283, Rehoboth Beach, DE 19971.

CAREER: Writer. Admitted to the bars of Virginia, District of Columbia, and U.S. Supreme Court. Former attorney with law firms Schuster & Feuille, New York City, and Covington & Burling, Washington, DC; Library of Congress, Washington, staff member of Law Library, 1940-45; Light & Power Co., Rio de Janeiro, Brazil, member of legal staff, 1947-48; U.S. Department of Commerce, Washington, staff member of Bureau of Foreign and Domestic Commerce, 1951-53; International Bank for Reconstruction and Development, Washington, member of legal staff, 1954-73. Founder, with Muriel Crawford, Barbara Grier, and Donna McBride, of Naiad Press, 1974; founder, with Crawford, of A & M Books, 1995.

AWARDS, HONORS: Recipient of Jeanine Rae Award for the advancement of women's culture by the National Women's Music Festival, Bloomington, IN, 1992.

WRITINGS:

NOVELS; UNDER PSEUDONYM SARAH ALDRIDGE

The Latecomer, Naiad Press (Tallahassee, FL), 1974.
Tottie: The Tale of the Sixties, Naiad Press, 1975.
Cytherea's Breath, Naiad Press, 1976.
All True Lovers, Naiad Press, 1978.
The Nesting Place, Naiad Press, 1982.
Madame Aurora, Naiad Press, 1983.
Misfortune's Friend, Naiad Press, 1985.
Magdalena, Naiad Press, 1987.
Keep to Me Stranger, Naiad Press, 1989.
A Flight of Angels, Naiad Press, 1992.
Michaela, Naiad Press, 1994.
Amantha, A & M Books (Rehoboth Beach, DE), 1995.

OTHER

Contributor to *Brazil: Portrait of Half a Continent,* edited by T. Lynn Smith and Alexander Marchant, Dryden Press, 1951, revised edition, University of Florida Press, 1966; and *Viscount Maua and the Empire of Brazil,* University of California Press, 1965. Contributor to journals, including *Americas, Frontiers, Hispanic American Historical Review* and *Southwest Review.*

WORK IN PROGRESS: A new novel.

SIDELIGHTS: Anyda Marchant told *CA:* "I began writing in my teens, both short stories and novels, but novels were my chief concern. For financial reasons, when I graduated from college, I had to abandon the idea of pursuing a career as a writer and went to law school instead. This was 1930 and the economic condition of the country was at its worst. I was not a pioneer but I was nevertheless among the first women who sought to enter the legal profession in the United States. When I retired in 1972 I decided to make another effort to establish myself as a writer; I had never ceased to write but did not publish. In the early '70s it was extremely difficult to find a publisher interested in serious fiction written from a feminist and lesbian viewpoint. The idea of establishing a publishing house for such books occurred to me. With the collaboration of two other women this came about and in 1974 my companion

Muriel Crawford and I incorporated the Naiad Press with two other shareholders. Its first publication was my novel *The Latecomer*. In the next twenty years the Naiad Press published my next ten novels. In 1995 Muriel Crawford and I decided to sever our connection with the Naiad Press and to found our own publishing company, A & M Books. Its first publication was my twelfth novel, *Amantha*.

"I write because it is the activity that brings me the most satisfaction. I write novels because I find the observation of human beings most fascinating. I believe that the considerable success that my novels have enjoyed is in part due to my own attitude in writing them. The exercise of whatever gift one has, great or small, cannot be denied without a crippling effect on one's own life, as every artist will attest. I have always been a feminist and the subject matter of my novels is simply the problems that women generally encounter in their lives, dictated by the limitations traditionally imposed upon them as women. The struggle of women to free themselves from these shackles so as to be able to think, speak and act as independent individuals is one that has gone on throughout the ages anywhere. In the western world as a result of the organized feminist movement women are finding more opportunities and the conflict between the desire to seize them and their attachment to the traditional roles assigned them by society form the basis of my novels."

BIOGRAPHICAL/CRITICAL SOURCES:

PERIODICALS

Front Page, August 11, 1995, pp. 23, 27.
News Journal (Wilmington, DE), June 16, 1994, p. D1.

*   *   *

MARTIN, Cort
   See SHERMAN, Jory (Tecumseh)

*   *   *

MARTIN, James Kirby   1943-

PERSONAL: Born May 26, 1943, in Akron, OH; son of Paul E. (in business) and Dorothy (a homemaker;

maiden name, Garrett) Martin; married Karen Wierwille (a book editor), August 7, 1965; children: Darcy Elizabeth, Sarah Marie, Joelle Kathryn Garrett. *Education:* Hiram College, B.A. (summa cum laude), 1965; University of Wisconsin—Madison, M.A., 1967, Ph.D., 1969.

ADDRESSES: Home—Houston, TX. *Office*—Department of History, University of Houston, 4800 Calhoun Rd., Houston, TX 77204-3785. *Agent*—Gerard W. McCauley, Gerard McCauley Agency, Inc., P.O. Box 844, Katonah, NY 10536.

CAREER: Rutgers University, New Brunswick, NJ, assistant professor, 1969-73, associate professor, 1973-79, professor of history, 1979-80, assistant provost for administration, 1972-74, vice-president for academic affairs, 1977-79; University of Houston, Houston, TX, professor of history, 1980—, chairperson of department, 1980-83. Visiting associate professor and professor of alcohol studies, Rutgers Center of Alcohol Studies, 1978-88; visiting professor of history, Rice University, fall, 1992; scholar in residence, David Library of the American Revolution, and research fellow, Philadelphia Center for Early American Studies, University of Pennsylvania, winter, 1988.

MEMBER: American Historical Association, Organization of American Historians, Society for Historians of the Early American Republic, Southern Historical Association, Texas State Historical Association, Texas Association for the Advancement of History (vice-president, 1986-91), New Jersey Historical Society, Phi Beta Kappa, Phi Kappa Phi, Phi Alpha Theta, Pi Gamma Mu, Omicron Delta Kappa.

AWARDS, HONORS: A Respectable Army: The Military Origins of the Republic, 1763-1789 appeared on the U.S. Army's "Contemporary Military Reading List," 1982; R. P. McCormick Prize, New Jersey Historical Commission, 1984, for *Citizen-Soldier: The Revolutionary War Journal of Joseph Bloomfield;* New Jersey Society of the Cincinnati Prize, 1995, for distinguished achievement in advancing the knowledge, understanding, and appreciation of American history.

WRITINGS:

Men in Rebellion: Higher Governmental Leaders and the Coming of the American Revolution, Rutgers University Press (New Brunswick, NJ), 1973.

(Editor) *Interpreting Colonial America: Selected Readings,* Dodd (New York City), 1973, 2nd edition, Harper (New York City), 1978.

The Human Dimensions of Nation Making: Essays on Colonial and Revolutionary America, Wisconsin State Historical Society, 1976.

(Editor with K. R. Stubaus) *The American Revolution: Whose Revolution?,* Robert E. Krieger (Melbourne, FL), 1977, revised edition, 1981.

In the Course of Human Events: An Interpretive Exploration of the American Revolution, Harlan Davidson, 1979.

(With Mark Edward Lender) *A Respectable Army: The Military Origins of the Republic, 1763-1789,* Harlan Davidson, 1982.

(Editor with Mark Edward Lender) *Citizen-Soldier: The Revolutionary War Journal of Joseph Bloomfield,* New Jersey Historical Society (Newark), 1982.

(With Mark Edward Lender) *Drinking in America: A History, 1620-1980,* Free Press (New York City), 1982, revised and expanded edition, 1987.

(With Randy Roberts, Steven Mintz, and others) *America and Its People,* Scott, Foresman (Glenview, IL), 1989, 3rd edition, HarperCollins (New York City), 1997.

(Editor) *Ordinary Courage: The Revolutionary War Adventures of Joseph Plumb Martin,* Brandywine Press (New York City), 1993.

(With Mark Edward Lender) *Prohibitionism: Smoking, Drinking, and Coercive Reform in America,* New York University Press (New York City), in press.

The Rise of Benedict Arnold, an American Hero, New York University Press, in press.

General editor of "American Social Experience" series, New York University Press; past member of editorial board of "Conversations with the Past" series, Brandywine Press. Member of editorial board of *New Jersey* and *Houston Review;* past member of editorial board of *Papers of William Livingston,* and *Papers of Thomas Edison.* Also coauthor of film *Drinking in America,* released by Gary Whiteaker Co., 1984.

WORK IN PROGRESS: A revisionist study of George Washington and the Conway Cabal; a study of the "battles" among political and military leaders that shaped the outcome of the great martial victory by American rebels at Saratoga; a study of Peggy Shippen, "temptress of the Revolution"; a study of the persistent conflict over smoking in America.

SIDELIGHTS: James Kirby Martin's book *Drinking in America: A History, 1620-1980* was hailed as a "brilliant social history" by Anatole Broyard of the *New York Times.* The history begins in colonial times, when Americans consumed more than six gallons of alcoholic beverages per person per year. These Americans regarded ordinary water with suspicion, and they believed their cider and beer would not only protect them from the cold and disease, but strengthen their constitutions and improve their general health. In 1784 Dr. Benjamin Rush, a signer of the Declaration of Independence, tried to promulgate the idea that alcoholism was a disease, but his advice was little heeded, and Americans steadily increased their per capita consumption to more than seven gallons over the next thirty years.

Temperance movements were established as early as 1808, but they lost their influence during the crisis of the Civil War. When Prohibition was finally approved in 1919, many people hoped that only "hard liquor" would be affected by the new law. The severity of the legislation that was enacted outraged Americans who might have accepted a milder version of the law. In addition, according to Martin and coauthor Mark Edward Lender, the coming of the Depression required the federal government to increase its tax revenues, and Prohibition was doomed.

Over the years, drinking was not considered to be a national or even a social problem, but rather a personal, individual, and relatively infrequent one. It was not until the 1950s that the American Medical Association declared that alcoholism was a physical disease. Since then drinking has become as much a part of daily life as it once was in the colonies, and scores of government agencies and private organizations like Alcoholics Anonymous have dedicated their work to eradicating the disease.

Such is the story that Martin and Lender relate in their scholarly book. In Broyard's opinion: "Besides being highly readable and filled with witty and interesting asides, 'Drinking in America' is almost amazingly free of prejudice or special pleading. It's the best kind of social history." Similarly, Ben Irwin wrote in the *Los Angeles Times,* "This is a scholarly, informative book," adding that it "covers an astonishing amount of ground; one does not need to be an alcoholic . . . to appreciate its scholarship and dedication."

Martin once told *CA:* "Pursuing the craft of history can be both frustrating and rewarding. The well-trained historian understands that there are never enough documents to comprehend past events. Writing good history, from my point of view, involves unleashing one's creative energy in prose after carefully assembling the data. Despite what some historians assert, the past does not interpret itself.

"In my own career as an academic historian, I have been influenced by a number of outstanding professors who taught me the value of mastering the art of critical analysis and interpretation. The production of good history, one of my professors argued, will always depend upon ongoing research in the archives and the creative act of interpretation. Clear writing, something sorely lacking in most academic history, is also essential to the production of useful history.

"Getting at the sources is the first step, and the second is to put aside personal opinion and political prejudice in assessing the behavior of past generations of human actors. Too often—in the rush to identify and define forces, trends, concepts, and ideologies—historians forget that human beings of all types and kinds, ordinary as well as extraordinary, initiate and direct movements and events. Thus in my own history, people are at the center. Further, the sources demonstrate that these actors rarely operate in some sort of celestial harmony. Rather, human conflict gives form to the past and drives it forward toward a meaningful present. Those who frame their history in terms of human consensus miss the fundamental reality of what provokes change over time.

"In my own writing, human conflict has been a persistent theme. Studying such grand events as the American Revolution, or looking at such recurring reform efforts as temperance and Prohibition, it is impossible to ignore conflict as the formative ingredient of the past. The analysis of human conflict allows the historian to bring perspective to the present.

"In recent years my work has stretched beyond my initial specialization in early American history with a primary focus on the American Revolution. Too often, from my point of view, academically trained historians keep digging into smaller and smaller topics. My decision had been to go the other way, to reach into new fields, including U.S. military history and the social history of alcohol and drug use as well as the ongoing historical conflict over smoking in America. Further, some of my future work will have much more of a biographical orientation, featuring ordinary as well as extraordinary lives. If this is fleeing from overspecialization, so let it be. After all, virtually no one, except for a few specialists,

reads academic history anymore. As an old beer commercial once stated, 'we only go around once,' so why not take some chances along the way? The product, in the end, might even find a wide readership and have some influence, however slight, in the search to find meaning in life."

BIOGRAPHICAL/CRITICAL SOURCES:

PERIODICALS

American Historical Review, December, 1984.
Annals of the American Academy of Political and Social Science, March, 1984.
Los Angeles Times, November 16, 1982.
New York Times, January 8, 1983.
New York Times Book Review, January 9, 1983.

*   *   *

MCARDLE, Catherine
   See KELLEHER, Catherine McArdle

*   *   *

McCLURE, Charles R(obert)   1949-

PERSONAL: Born May 24, 1949, in Syracuse, NY; son of Robert C. and Doris C. (Gordon) McClure; married Victoria Anne (a librarian), 1970; children: Gwendolyn Anne. *Education:* Oklahoma State University, B.A., 1970, M.A., 1971; University of Oklahoma, M.L.S., 1972; Rutgers University, Ph.D., 1977.

ADDRESSES: Home—Manlius, NY. *Office*—School of Information Studies, Syracuse University, Syracuse, NY 13244. *E-mail*—cmcclure@mailbox.syr.edu.

CAREER: University of Oklahoma, Norman, archival assistant in Western History Collection, 1972; University of Texas, El Paso, head of library's history and government department, 1972-74; Rutgers University, New Brunswick, NJ, director of audio-visual laboratory of Graduate School of Library Service, 1974-75, instructor in library service, 1976-77; University of Oklahoma, assistant professor, 1977-81, associate professor, 1981-83, professor of library science, 1983-86; Syracuse University, Syracuse, NY, professor of information studies, 1986-94, distinguished professor, 1994—. President of Information/Management Consultant Services, Inc., 1978—; consultant to government agencies and to businesses, including National Technical Information Service, U.S. Government Printing Office, U.S. International Communication Agency, De Witt Wallace-*Reader's Digest* Fund, National Commission on Libraries and Information Science, and NYSERNet.

MEMBER: American Library Association, American Society for Information Science, Association of Library Information Science Educators, Association of College and Research Libraries, Information Industry Association, New York Library Association, Beta Phi Mu.

AWARDS, HONORS: Award from American Library Association, 1979, for paper "Evaluation of Information Sources for Library Decision Making"; best research paper of the year, 1985 and 1990; Best Book of the Year Award in information science from American Society for Information Science, 1988; distinguished researcher, National Commission on Libraries and Information Science, 1993; distinguished alumnus, University of Oklahoma, 1994; distinguished alumnus, Rutgers University, 1996.

WRITINGS:

Information for Academic Library Decision Making: The Case for Organizational Information Management, Greenwood Press (Westport, CT), 1980.

(With Peter Hernon) *Improving the Quality of Reference Services for Government Publications,* American Library Association (Chicago), 1983.

Public Access to Government Information, Ablex Publishing (Norwood, NJ), 1984, 2nd edition, 1988.

Action Research for Library Decision Making, American Library Association, 1984.

State Library Services and Issues, Ablex Publishing, 1986.

Unobtrusive Testing of Library Reference Service, Ablex Publishing, 1987.

Planning and Role Setting for Public Libraries, American Library Association, 1987.

Output Measures for Public Libraries, American Library Association, 1987.

Federal Information Policies in the 1980s, Ablex Publishing, 1987.

U.S. Government Information Policies: Views and Perspectives, Ablex Publishing, 1989.

U.S. Scientific and Technical Information Policies: Views and Perspectives, Ablex Publishing, 1989.

The National Research and Education Network, Ablex Publishing, 1991.

Libraries and the Internet/NREN: Perspectives, Issues, and Challenges, Mecklermedia (Westport, CT), 1993.

Public Libraries and the Internet, National Commission on Libraries and Information Science (Washington, DC), 1994.

Assessing the Academic Network Environment, Coalition for Networked Information, 1996.

EDITOR

Planning for Library Services: A Guide to Utilizing Planning Methods for Library Management, Haworth Press (Binghampton, NY), 1982.

(With Alan Samuels) *Approaches to Library Administration: Strategies and Concepts,* Libraries Unlimited (Littleton, CO), 1982.

Federal Information Policies in the 1990s, Ablex Publishing, 1996.

OTHER

Also coeditor of book series "Information Management, Policy, and Services," Ablex Publishing, 1987-95. Author or coauthor of more than 150 articles and reports on such topics as librarianship, information science, management, the Internet and national networking, and information policy. Coeditor and founder of *Government Information Quarterly,* 1984—; founder and editor of *Internet Research,* 1991-95.

SIDELIGHTS: Charles R. McClure wrote to *CA:* "The emphasis of my writings is on 1) increasing the effectiveness with which libraries and other information centers can respond to and resolve the information needs of their clientele, 2) increasing the public's access to and use of U.S. government information, and 3) utilizing the Internet and the global information infrastructure for better communication and public access to electronic information. As we all struggle to cope with the various impacts of living in the 'information age,' concern for the individual's ability to exploit and access information is essential. Assisting in that process of making necessary information accessible to individuals, managing information resources, and controlling technology to serve *our* needs are themes that I try to stress [with] my publishing activities. We all need to better understand how to transition effectively into the evolving networked information environment and how to promote public policies that increase access to and use of electronic information."

＊　　＊　　＊

McCULLOUGH, David (Gaub) 1933-

PERSONAL: Born July 7, 1933, in Pittsburgh, PA; son of Christian Hax (a businessman) and Ruth (maiden name, Rankin) McCullough; married Rosalee Ingram Barnes, December 18, 1954; children: Melissa (Mrs. John E. McDonald, Jr.), David Jr., William Barnes, Geoffrey Barnes, Doreen Kane. *Education:* Yale University, B.A., 1955.

ADDRESSES: Home and office—Music Street, West Tisbury, MA 02575. *Agent*—Janklow & Nesbit Associates, 598 Madison Ave., New York, NY 10022.

CAREER: Editor and writer for Time, Inc., New York City, 1956-61, U.S. Information Agency, Washington, DC, 1961-64, and American Heritage Publishing Co., New York City, 1964-70; freelance writer, 1970—. Host of television series *Smithsonian World,* 1984-88, and *The American Experience,* 1988—, for Public Broadcasting Service Television (PBS-TV). Narrator of numerous documentaries, including *The Civil War, Huey Long, The Statue of Liberty, The Shakers,* and *Brooklyn Bridge.* Scholar in residence, University of New Mexico, 1979, Wesleyan University Writers Conference, 1982-83; Newman Visiting Professor of American Civilization, Cornell University, 1989. Member, Bennington College Writers Workshop, 1978-79; member of advisory board, Center for the Book, Library of Congress; member, Harry S Truman Centennial Commission; trustee, Shady Side Academy, Pittsburgh, PA.

MEMBER: Society of American Historians (president, beginning in 1991), American Society of Civil Engineers (honorary).

AWARDS, HONORS: Special citation for excellence, Society of American Historians, 1973, Diamond Jubilee medal for excellence, City of New York, 1973, and certificate of merit, Municipal Art Society of New York, 1974, all for *The Great Bridge;* National Book Award for history, Francis Parkman Award from Society of American Historians, Samuel Eliot Morison Award, and Cornelius Ryan Award, all

1978, all for *The Path between the Seas: The Creation of the Panama Canal, 1870-1914;* Civil Engineering History and Heritage award, 1978; *Los Angeles Times* Award for biography, 1981, American Book Award for biography, 1982, and Pulitzer Prize nomination in biography, 1982, all for *Mornings on Horseback;* Emmy Award, for interview with Anne Morrow Lindbergh on *Smithsonian World;* Guggenheim Fellowship, 1987; Pulitzer Prize for Biography, 1993, for *Truman;* Harry S Truman Public Service Award, 1993; St. Louis Literary Award, 1993; honorary degrees include H.L.D., Rensselaer Polytechnic Institute, 1983, D.Eng., Villanova University, 1984, Litt.D., Allegheny College, 1984, L.H.D, Wesleyan University, Middletown, CT, 1984, and Litt.D., Middlebury College, 1986.

WRITINGS:

(Editor) C. L. Sulzberger, *The American Heritage Picture History of World War II,* American Heritage Publishing (New York City), 1967, revised edition published as *World War II,* McGraw (New York City), 1970, reprinted, Houghton (Boston), 1985.

(Editor) *Smithsonian Library,* six volumes, Smithsonian Institution Press/American Heritage Publishing, 1968-70.

The Johnstown Flood (*Readers Digest* Condensed Book), Simon & Schuster (New York City), 1968.

The Great Bridge (*Readers Digest* Condensed Book), Simon & Schuster, 1972.

The Path between the Seas: The Creation of the Panama Canal, 1870-1914 (Book-of-the-Month Club selection; *Readers Digest* Condensed Book), Simon & Schuster, 1977.

Mornings on Horseback (biography), Simon & Schuster, 1981.

(Contributor) *A Sense of History: The Best Writing from the Pages of American Heritage,* American Heritage Publishing/Houghton, 1985.

(With others) William Zinsser, editor, *Extraordinary Lives: The Art and Craft of American Biography,* American Heritage Publishing, 1986.

(And host) "A Man, a Plan, a Canal—Panama" (episode of *Nova*), first broadcast on PBS-TV, November 3, 1987.

(Editor with others) Michael E. Shapiro and Peter H. Frederick, *Remington: The Masterworks,* Abrams (New York City), 1988.

Brave Companions: Portraits in History, Prentice Hall (New York City), 1992.

Truman (biography), Simon & Schuster, 1992.

Contributor to periodicals, including *Audubon, Architectural Forum, American Heritage, Geo, Smithsonian, New York Times, New Republic, Psychology Today,* and *Washington Post.* Senior contributing editor, *American Heritage;* contributing editor, *Parade.*

SIDELIGHTS: David McCullough is known to many Americans as an important disseminator of history not only through his award-winning books, but also through his appearances as host of the PBS television programs *Smithsonian World* and *The American Experience.* Recognition for his abilities ranges from an Academy Award nomination for a film on the Brooklyn Bridge to the Pulitzer Prize for his biography of Harry S Truman to two National Book Awards for his narrative histories *The Path between the Seas: The Creation of the Panama Canal, 1870-1914* and *Mornings on Horseback.* Richard Robbins writes in the Pittsburgh *Tribune-Review* that in these histories, "David McCullough combines a powerful narrative style with an exhaustive concern for the details of a story."

McCullough began his first book, *The Johnstown Flood,* when he wanted to learn more about the 1889 bursting of a Pennsylvania dam that claimed the lives of more than two thousand people and was one of the most widely reported stories of the late nineteenth century. None of the volumes McCullough consulted proved satisfactory, however, and he finally decided he would have to write the book himself. Upon its publication, critics hailed *The Johnstown Flood* as an important addition to the field of social history. For example, Alden Whitman, writing in the *New York Times,* calls it "a superb job, scholarly yet vivid, balanced yet incisive."

In 1972 McCullough published *The Great Bridge,* a history of the building of the Brooklyn Bridge. Considered by contemporaries and historians to be the greatest engineering feat of America's "Gilded Age," the Brooklyn Bridge was the dream of one man—John Roebling, a wealthy steel cable manufacturer. When he died in 1869, before construction of the bridge actually began, his son Washington A. Roebling became chief engineer, and, over the next thirteen years, saw the bridge completed. McCullough traces the dangers that the younger Roebling faced and the problems he overcame, ranging from corrupt politicians in Boss Tweed's Tammany Hall to cases of the "bends" that afflicted workers and left Roebling himself a semi-invalid for the rest of his life.

The Great Bridge covers both the engineering and social aspects of the bridge's construction. "The

whole story is told in David McCullough's admirably written, definitive and highly entertaining book," remarks L. J. Davis in the *Washington Post Book World.* "He is especially adept at weaving in those disparate but relevant details that bring an age to life, from the Cardiff giant to the scandal of Henry Ward Beecher's infidelity. It is hard to see how the story could be better or more thoroughly told." "McCullough does justice to this gamy background," declares Justin Kaplan in *Saturday Review,* "but never allows it to get the better of his subject or his narrative or to turn into that familiar historical stereotype that obscures the fact that the Gilded Age was a period of enormous achievement in virtually every area of activity."

McCullough shifted settings from Brooklyn to Panama for *The Path between the Seas: The Creation of the Panama Canal, 1870-1914.* Once again the author mixes engineering with social, political, and economic history, this time to create a panorama of the canal project from its origins to the day it finally opened. Beginning with the dream of Suez Canal entrepreneur Ferdinand de Lesseps, McCullough describes how political corruption, disease, anti-Semitism, and bankruptcy put an end to French efforts to dig a sea-level canal across the isthmus of Panama. Later, McCullough continues, the Americans under the leadership of Theodore Roosevelt connived to "liberate" Panama from an uncooperative Colombia, conquered the yellow fever and malaria that had plagued the French, and over a ten-year period created the largest and costliest engineering project the world had ever seen—and, as R. Z. Sheppard points out in *Time,* completed it "six months ahead of schedule and below the estimated cost."

The Path between the Seas won the National Book Award as well as several important awards from historical associations. Critics hailed the book for its vivid portrayal of the many issues that surrounded the canal's construction. "There are scores of previous volumes on the subject," reports *New York Times Book Review* contributor Gaddis Smith, "but none is so thorough, readable, fair or graceful in the handling of myriad intricately connected elements: French national pride and humiliation, personal courage and corruption, disease and death, medical and engineering genius, political and financial chicanery, and the unsung contribution of tens of thousands of black laborers recruited from the West Indies to do the heavy work." McCullough, declares Walter Clemons in *Newsweek,* "is a storyteller with the capacity to steer readers through political, financial and engineering intricacies without fatigue or muddle. This is grand-scale, expert work."

In his next book, *Mornings on Horseback,* McCullough examines the early years of the Panama Canal's greatest supporter—Theodore Roosevelt. Unlike many biographies of the Republican Roosevelt, however, McCullough's work encompasses the entire family: Theodore, Sr., philanthropic scion of an old New York Dutch clan, his wife Martha ("Mittie") Bulloch, a Georgia belle whose family mansion may have been the inspiration for Tara in Margaret Mitchell's *Gone with the Wind,* their daughters Anna ("Bamie") and Corinne ("Conie"), and sons Theodore, Jr. and Elliott. Moreover, in its depiction of the Roosevelts, *Mornings on Horseback* affords a glimpse of American society in the years following the Civil War, "a period that has always seemed remote and cartoonlike," explains James Lardner in the *New Republic.* "It introduces us to a collection of fascinating people and makes their society vivid, plausible, and even a tempting destination for anyone planning a trip back in time."

McCullough also breaks new ground by exploring neglected aspects of Theodore Jr.'s youth, including his bouts of psychosomatic illness and his fascination with killing and preserving animals. As a child "Teddie" suffered from violent attacks of asthma, probably brought on by feelings of inadequacy, that occurred "almost invariably on a Saturday night [in order] to secure a Sunday with his father," reports John Leonard in the *New York Times Book Review.* McCullough notes that the boy's asthma disappeared as soon as he left home to begin studying at Harvard. Roosevelt's enchantment with shooting and the Wild West, the author suggests, in part stemmed from his mother's stories about the Old South and his relatives' exploits in the Confederate Army. McCullough combines these images to create a portrait of a man who, as *Saturday Review* contributor Gary Wills puts it, "never felt more alive than when killing something."

McCullough next attempted to write a biography of the painter Pablo Picasso, but after only a few months' work, he developed such a loathing for the artist's personality that he abandoned the project. When an editor suggested that he take on the story of Franklin Delano Roosevelt, McCullough immediately replied, "If I were going to do a 20th-century President, I would do Harry Truman," Lynn Karpen quotes him as saying in the *New York Times Book*

Review. The comment seemed to come "from somewhere deep inside of me," he remembered. Speaking to John Budris of the *Christian Science Monitor,* McCullough recalled that Truman was the first president he had ever seen in person. It happened in 1956, in New York City, where McCullough had just begun work as a staff member of the newly-created *Sports Illustrated* magazine. "A small crowd had gathered on the sidewalk awaiting the Governor, who was attending a dinner party," Karpen quotes him as saying. "A limousine pulled up and out stepped . . . Harry Truman. My first thought was, 'My God, he's in color!'" Discussing the incident further with Budris, he added, "He looked so human. He was not bigger than life. . . . I might have tapped him on the shoulder and said 'I thought you should know, Mr. President, that in 30 years I'm going to write your biography, and I'm just wondering if there's anything you want to tell me in advance.'"

Once started, McCullough's Truman project took ten full years to finish. "In those 10 years, my youngest daughter changed from a girl into a woman, both my parents died, grandchildren were born, we moved our residence twice, we put a child through college and law school, and paid off a mortgage," Esther B. Fein quotes the author as saying in the *New York Times.* "Meanwhile, the world we knew was changing. The cold war ended. My God! That cast a completely different light on certain things that Harry Truman said and did." McCullough's dedication to his subject paid off. *Truman,* described by *Time* reviewer Walter Isaacson as a "loving and richly detailed megabiography," earned its author a Pulitzer Prize.

Truman was a plain man who never attended college and might never have left his family's farm if not for World War I. He served in Europe, then returned to his home town of Independence, Missouri to marry his long-time sweetheart, Bess Wallace—a woman whose family was convinced that she had married beneath her. Truman was a hard worker, yet he failed both as a farmer and as a haberdasher. He went into politics simply because he needed a job. A tenuous connection with Tom Pendergast, a powerful Democratic leader of the 1920s, led to Truman's appointment as a county judge and, eventually, a place in the Senate. When he stepped into the presidency upon Franklin Delano Roosevelt's death in 1945, he remarked that there were a million men better qualified for the job than him. Many Americans agreed with him. During his term in office, he was highly unpopular, but his stature has risen in the decades since his presidency. "He was intelligent. He worked hard, read widely, and was always willing to listen to ideas and advice. . . . The same plainness of manner and directness of speech that led so many to dismiss him as a 'little man' helped him win the deep respect, loyalty and affection of such figures as Winston Churchill, George Marshall and Dean Acheson," describes Alan Brinkley in the *New York Times Book Review.* "Perhaps most important, Mr. McCullough argues, he was a decent man with common sense."

McCullough chose to tell Truman's story in a plain, straightforward style that reflected that character of his subject. "I did not want to be tricky or contrived or in fashion because that's not the way Harry Truman was," the author told Budris. "I wanted the book to unfold like *David Copperfield* and the old style biographies. . . . He is an ordinary man faced with extraordinary problems. He is the part Jimmy Stewart plays in American movies." McCullough's deep admiration for Truman comes through in his book's pages, yet he provides an even-handed portrait, according to Brinkley: "McCullough manages to keep Truman himself at the center of the story . . . rather than allowing him to become obscured by the complexity of events and institutions that surrounded him. And he deals openly with Truman's many mistakes and weaknesses as a leader."

Isaacson finds that "McCullough's main weakness is one he shares with Truman: he occasionally fails to wrestle with the moral complexities of policy." Instead, he provides "a sense of historic sweep" and a "marvelous feel for history" that is based on "an appreciation of colorful tales and an insight into personalities. In this compelling saga of America's greatest common-man President, McCullough adds luster to an old-fashioned historical approach that is regaining respect: the sweeping narrative, filled with telling details and an appreciation of the role individuals play in shaping the world."

In all his work McCullough emphasizes the value history has for modern Americans. "We're not being quite selfish enough if we don't know history, not that history is likely to repeat itself," McCullough told Robbins. "Besides, there is the matter of commiserating in the agonies and basking in the glories of our fellow human beings from long ago, of not being provincial, of opening our minds and hearts to generations once alive. . . . Why should we deny ourselves the chance to experience life in another time if its available to us? There is a wonderful

world called the past, and for heavens sake don't miss it, because if you do you'll be denying yourself a big part of being alive."

BIOGRAPHICAL/CRITICAL SOURCES:

PERIODICALS

Atlantic, July, 1977.
Boston Globe, August 10, 1992, p. 32; October 6, 1992, p. 29; May 23, 1993, p. 38; April 14, 1993, p. 1; March 17, 1995, p. 81; April 27, 1995, p. 37.
Chicago Tribune, June 7, 1992, section 14, p. 1; May 2, 1993, section 14, p. 8; November 28, 1993, section 13, p. 2.
Christian Science Monitor, June 12, 1992, p. 13; October 13, 1992, p. 18.
Los Angeles Times, September 30, 1991, p. F1.
Los Angeles Times Book Review, June 7, 1992, p. 1; July 7, 1992, pp. 1, 9.
Nation, May 10, 1993, pp. 640-41.
New Republic, July 4, 1981.
Newsweek, June 13, 1977; June 22, 1981.
New Yorker, June 20, 1977.
New York Times, April 24, 1968; May 24, 1977; June 18, 1981; April 14, 1991; June 15, 1992, p. C20; June 21, 1992, section 7, p. 19; August 12, 1992, pp. C1, C10; April 14, 1993, p. B6.
New York Times Book Review, October 15, 1972; June 19, 1977; July 26, 1981; December 15, 1991, p. 18; June 21, 1992, pp. 1, 19, 20.
Saturday Review, September 30, 1972; June 11, 1977; June, 1981.
Time, June 6, 1977; July 20, 1981; June 29, 1992, p. 80.
Tribune-Review (Pittsburgh), November 11, 1984.
Washington Post, June 1, 1992, p. B2; June 23, 1994, p. B1; February 17, 1995, p. F2.
Washington Post Book World, October 1, 1972; June 12, 1977; June 14, 1981; July 15, 1986; June 7, 1992, p. 1.*

* * *

McNAMARA, Eugene (Joseph)   1930-

PERSONAL: Born March 18, 1930, in Oak Park, IL; son of Martin Joseph (an office worker) and Anna (Ryan) McNamara; married Margaret Lindstrom, July 19, 1952; children: Michael, Mary, David, Brian, Christopher. *Education:* DePaul University,

B.A., 1953, M.A., 1955; Northwestern University, Ph.D., 1964. *Religion:* Roman Catholic.

ADDRESSES: Home—289 Bellepercue Pl., Windsor, Ontario, Canada. *Office*—Department of English, University of Windsor, Windsor, Ontario N9B 3P4, Canada.

CAREER: Fenwick High School, Oak Park, IL, English teacher, 1953-55; University of Illinois at Chicago Circle, instructor in English, 1955-59; University of Windsor, Windsor, Ontario, 1959—, began as associate professor, currently professor of English, director of graduate program in creative writing, 1967—.

MEMBER: National Council of Teachers of English, Canadian Association of American Studies, Canadian Association of University Teachers of English, League of Canadian Poets.

WRITINGS:

Discovery: Voyage of Exploration (twenty-four scripts of radio talks given over the Canadian Broadcasting Corp.), Assumption University Press, 1962.
(Editor) *The Interior Landscape: The Literary Criticism of Marshall McLuhan, 1934-1962,* McGraw (New York City), 1969.
Laura: As Novel, Film and Myth, Edwin Mellen (Lewiston, NY), 1992.

POETRY

For the Mean Time, Gryphon Press (Windsor), 1965.
Outerings, Delta Canada, 1970.
Love Scene, Hellric House, 1970.
Dillinger Poems, Black Moss Press (Windsor), 1971.
Hard Words, Fiddlehead, 1972.
Passages and Other Poems, Sono Nis Press, 1972.
Diving for the Body, Borealis Press, 1974.
In Transit, Pennyworth Press, 1975.
Screens, Coach House Press (Toronto), 1977.
Forcing the Field, Sesame Press, 1981.
Call It a Day, blewointment press, 1984.
The Moving Light, Wolsak & Wynn, 1986.

FICTION

Salt: Short Stories, Sono Nis Press, 1975.
Search for Sarah Grace and Other Stories, Black Moss Press, 1977.
Spectral Evidence: Short Stories, Black Moss Press, 1986.

Fox Trot: Stories, Black Moss Press, 1994.

OTHER

Also author of television script "The Stranger," with James Hurley, for ABC-TV series *Johnny Ringo.* Also contributor to anthologies, including *Best American Short Stories,* 1975, *Best Canadian Stories,* 1979, 1986, 1991, and 1994, and *Die Weite Reise.* Author of weekly column "Flicks" for *Windsor Star.* Contributor of poems, articles, and short stories to periodicals, including *America, Critic, Western Humanities Review, Midwestern University Quarterly, Vagabond, Films in Review, Canadian Forum, Ontario Review,* and *Texas Quarterly.* Editor, *University of Windsor Review,* 1966—.

ADAPTATIONS: Some of McNamara's stories have been read on the Canadian Broadcasting Corp. series *Anthology.*

WORK IN PROGRESS: Poems, short stories.

SIDELIGHTS: Eugene McNamara has established a reputation as both a poet and a short-story writer. Born in the United States and a resident of Canada since 1959, McNamara told *CA* that "much of my poetry and fiction deals with crossing the border—the bifocal experience of living in two countries, being 'home' and away from 'home' in the same moment." Louise Longo in *Quill & Quire* finds that in his collection *Spectral Evidence: Short Stories,* "McNamara demonstrates his considerable skill, wit, and peculiar brand of gentle wisdom. . . . His real strength lies in his graceful, emotionally subdued prose style, which carries the reader along effortlessly." In a *Windsor Star* review of the poetry collection *The Moving Light,* Judith Fitzgerald explains that McNamara "possesses ample creative powers, terrific imaginative gifts. He writes and the world around him blossoms; he writes and the world within him bursts forth. The mark of a master distinguishes these poems."

McNamara is interested in contemporary American literature and lists as influences Thomas Wolfe, Walt Whitman, William Carlos Williams, and Robinson Jeffers.

BIOGRAPHICAL/CRITICAL SOURCES:

PERIODICALS

Canadian Fiction Magazine, Volume 46, 1983.

Canadian Forum, July, 1971; August, 1973; June, 1975.
Globe and Mail (Toronto), February 22, 1986.
Quill and Quire, May, 1986.
Toronto Star, July 8, 1984.
Windsor Star, June 27, 1987.

* * *

MEADE, Marion 1934-

PERSONAL: Born January 7, 1934, in Pittsburgh, PA; daughter of Surain (a physicist) and Mary (Homeny) Sidhu; children: Alison Linkhorn. *Education:* Northwestern University, B.S., 1955; Columbia University, M.S., 1956.

ADDRESSES: Home—New York, NY. *Agent*—Julia Coopersmith Literary Agency, 10 West 15th St., New York, NY 10011.

CAREER: Novelist; biographer.

WRITINGS:

Bitching, Prentice-Hall (Englewood Cliffs, NJ), 1973.
Stealing Heaven: The Love Story of Heloise and Abelard (novel), Morrow (New York City), 1979.
Sybille, Morrow, 1983.

BIOGRAPHIES

Eleanor of Aquitaine, Dutton (New York City), 1977.
Madame Blavatsky: The Woman behind the Myth, Putnam (New York City), 1980.
Dorothy Parker: What Fresh Hell Is This?, Villard Books (New York City), 1988.
Buster Keaton: Cut to the Chase, HarperCollins (New York City), 1995.

JUVENILE

Free Woman: The Life and Times of Victoria Woodhull, Knopf (New York City), 1976.
Little Book of Big Riddles, Harvey House (New York City), 1976.
Little Book of Big Bad Jokes, Harvey House, 1977.

OTHER

Contributor to various periodicals, including the *New York Times, Village Voice, McCall's, Commonweal,* and *Cosmopolitan.*

SIDELIGHTS: According to *Spectator* critic David Wright, Marion Meade's biography *Dorothy Parker: What Fresh Hell Is This?* is "a lively book, an entertaining read and a memorable portrait" of Dorothy Parker, the author who ultimately became more famous for her cutting humor and wit than for her actual writings. Parker was a member of the New York group known as the Algonquin Round Table. Many of her fellows in this clique, which flowered during the Prohibition era, were, like her, associated with the newly-created *New Yorker* magazine. Robert Benchley, Robert Sherwood, Edmund Wilson, and Alexander Wolcott were some of her more illustrious associates. Many died young, burnt out from hard drinking and other excesses. Parker was as indulgent as any of them, but lived to a lonely old age. Her rapier wit, never tempered by kindness, was feared even by her friends; the subtitle to Meade's biography was Parker's standard response whenever her doorbell announced a visitor.

Parker's life was filled with dramatic events—including suicide attempts, failed marriages, long drinking binges, and misadventures with numerous notable literary figures. Reviewer Emily Toth praised Mead for avoiding a sensationalistic approach to her subject, writing in the *Women's Review of Books* that the biography "does not build up to punch-lines (rising action, climax, falling action—a masculine approach). Rather, it follows what feminist theorists might call a feminine approach: moments of consciousness, a lyrical portrayal of the dailiness of life." Mead also explained that "*Dorothy Parker* is a sad book: like many women's biographies, it concentrates on losses, and it would be dishonest to make Parker's disintegration anything but painful to read about."

Michiko Kakutani of the *New York Times,* less impressed with *Dorothy Parker,* complained that Meade did not penetrate deeply enough into her subject, demonstrating instead "a tendency to dwell on the details of Parker's and her friends' private lives, filling us in on their sexual predilections, their drinking habits and their continuing quarrels with one another. This makes for fast but not very illuminating reading; indeed, the reader ends with the feeling of having plowed through several decades worth of gossip columns." Other reviewers were more generous in their assessments, however. Diana Eden, writing in *New Statesman,* declared that "Marion Meade is to be congratulated upon a detailed and balanced reconstruction of a life based on interviews, insight, and research," and *Times Literary Supplement* contributor Shena Mackay credited the author with creating "a balanced and generally sympathetic study of an artist and her era, rich in detail and gossip." Meade was also given high marks for the scope of her work by Anne Chamberlin, who wrote in the *Washington Post Book World,* "Dorothy Parker . . . left no clues behind her when she died. No letters, no manuscripts, no memorabilia, no private papers of any kind. . . . Undismayed by this daunting void, biographer Marion Meade . . . has peered into every cranny that is left. No crumbling shard escaped her gaze."

Meade looked deeply into the background of another famous American in her 1995 biography, *Buster Keaton: Cut to the Chase.* First attaining fame as a star of silent comedies, Keaton, according to Joseph McBride in the *New York Times Book Review,* "developed a stoicism that set him apart from the more sentimental comedy of his contemporaries." In her book, Meade revealed the macabre roots of Keaton's comic artistry. As a child, he was featured in his family's vaudeville act, the Three Keatons. Young Buster was billed as "the Human Mop," "the Little Boy Who Can't Be Damaged," and "Mr. Black and Blue." His part in the show was to remain stoic while his sadistic and frequently drunken father dragged, kicked, and threw him about the stage.

As an adult, Keaton became a famous silent film star, only to have his career go into a tailspin with the advent of talking pictures. According to McBride, Meade "chillingly details Keaton's headlong collapse with the coming of sound and gives a full and sympathetic account of his remaining decades as a dogged journeyman comic on television and in such movie potboilers as *Beach Blanket Bingo* and *How to Stuff a Wild Bikini.*" In the words of a *Publishers Weekly* reviewer, "this is an engrossing portrait of a tormented comedic genius."

BIOGRAPHICAL/CRITICAL SOURCES:

PERIODICALS

Belles Lettres, spring, 1995, p. 102.
Chicago Tribune, January 24, 1988, section 14, p. 6.

Christian Science Monitor, May 25, 1988, p. 20.
Library Journal, July, 1994, p. 134.
Listener, April 21, 1988, p. 33.
Los Angeles Times Book Review, March 26, 1989, p. 10.
New Statesman, April 22, 1988, p. 28.
New Yorker, April 25, 1988, p. 109.
New York Times, January 9, 1988, p. A17; April 25, 1988, p. 109; February 26, 1995, section LI, p. 8.
New York Times Book Review, October 8, 1995, p. 12.
Publishers Weekly, March 11, 1983, pp. 26-27; July 13, 1994, p. 466; September 4, 1995, p. 59.
Spectator, April 23, 1988, pp. 30-31.
Times Literary Supplement, November 30, 1973, p. 1473; May 6, 1988, p. 497.
Washington Post Book World, February 14, 1988, pp. 4, 7.
Women's Review of Books, May, 1988, p. 4.*

*   *   *

MEINKE, Peter   1932-

PERSONAL: Surname is pronounced "*Mine*-key"; born December 29, 1932, in Brooklyn, NY; son of Harry Frederick (a salesman) and Kathleen (McDonald) Lewis; married Jeanne Clark (an artist), December 14, 1957; children: Perrie, Peter, Gretchen, Timothy. *Education:* Hamilton College, A.B., 1955; University of Michigan, M.A., 1961; University of Minnesota, Ph.D., 1965. *Avocational interests:* Sports, movies, music.

ADDRESSES: Home—147 Wildwood Lane S.E., St. Petersburg, FL 33705.

CAREER: High school English teacher in Mountain Lakes, NJ, 1958-60; Hamline University, St. Paul, MN, instructor, 1961-65, assistant professor of English, 1965-66, poet in residence, 1973; Eckerd College, St. Petersburg, FL, assistant professor, 1966-68, associate professor, 1968-72, professor of English literature and director of writing workshop, 1972-93. Visiting professor and lecturer at numerous colleges and universities, including term as McGee Writer in Residence at Davidson College, 1989. Director of Mid-Florida Colleges in Neuchatel, Switzerland, and of Emory University Writing Institute, summer, 1982. Distinguished visiting professor,

University of Hawaii, 1993; writer in residence, Austin Peay State University (TN), 1995; distinguished writer in residence, University of North Carolina, Greensboro, NC, 1996. *Military service:* U.S. Army, 1955-57.

MEMBER: Academy of American Poets, Poetry Society of America.

AWARDS, HONORS: First prize, Olivet National Sonnet Competition, 1965; Gustav Davidson Memorial Award, 1976, Lucille Medick Memorial Award, 1984, and Emily Dickinson Award, 1992, all from Poetry Society of America; First prize in poetry, *Writer's Digest* competition, 1976; O. Henry Award for short fiction, 1983, for "The Ponoes," and 1986, for "Uncle George and Uncle Stefan"; Emily Clark Balch Prize for short fiction, *Virginia Quarterly,* for "A Decent Life," 1984; PEN Syndicated Fiction Award, 1984, for "Leicester Square," 1986, for "Woman Like That," and 1988, for "The Cranes"; Flannery O'Connor Award for short fiction, 1986, and LSU/Southern Review Award, 1987, both for *The Piano Tuner;* "Campocorto" winner of Sow's Ear Press chapbook competition, 1995; also recipient of numerous grants and fellowships, including National Endowment for the Arts fellowships, 1974, 1989; Robert A. Staub Distinguished Teacher Award, Eckerd College, 1990; Paumanok Poetry Award, 1993; Provincetown Master Artist's fellowship, 1995.

WRITINGS:

Howard Nemerov (criticism), University of Minnesota Press (Minneapolis, MN), 1968.
The Legend of Larry the Lizard (children's verse), illustrations by wife, Jeanne Meinke, John Knox, 1968.
Very Seldom Animals (children's verse), Possum Press, 1970, 2nd edition, 1972.
Lines from Neuchatel (poetry), illustrations by J. Meinke, Konglomerati Press (Gulfport, FL), 1974.
The Night Train and the Golden Bird (poetry), University of Pittsburgh Press (Pittsburgh, PA), 1977.
The Rat Poems, illustrations by J. Meinke, Bits Press (Cleveland, OH), 1978.
Trying to Surprise God (poetry), University of Pittsburgh Press, 1981.
The Piano Tuner (short stories), University of Georgia Press (Athens, GA), 1986, paperback edition, 1994.

Night Watch on the Chesapeake (poetry), University of Pittsburgh Press, 1986.
Underneath the Lantern (poetry), illustrations by J. Meinke, Heatherstone Press, 1986.
Far from Home (poetry), illustrations by J. Meinke, Heatherstone Press, 1988.
Liquid Paper: New & Selected Poems (poetry), University of Pittsburgh Press, 1991.
Campocorto (poetry), illustrations by J. Meinke, Sow's Ear Press, 1996.
Scars (poetry), University of Pittsburgh Press, 1996.

Contributor of poems, essays, and reviews to periodicals, including *Georgia Review, Gettysburg Review, Grand Street, Nation, New Republic, New Yorker, Poetry,* and *Virginia Quarterly Review.*

WORK IN PROGRESS: Songs from the Wrong Bay (poetry).

SIDELIGHTS: "As opposed to much of today's literature, which is experimental, obscure, and even at times shows a conscious disregard for its audience, Peter Meinke's poems are accessible to a broad group of readers," Deno Trakas asserts in the *Dictionary of Literary Biography.* This is the poet's specific intent, for as he once told *CA,* clarity is "a chief virtue that my writing strives for, an avoidance of academic bookishness that restricts the audience for serious literature to a handful of similarly trained critics." Trakas describes Meinke's work as "sometimes bright with joy, sometimes pale with despair," and notes that the poems "are rarely abstract or intellectual and never pretentious." Although the poet's verse is both funny and witty, Trakas observes that "Meinke does not write 'light' verse; rather, his talent is in mixing levity with gravity in a single poem." As the critic concludes, Meinke's "poems are not always successful, but despite blemishes, his work . . . is mature, varied, and vigorous."

Peter Meinke more recently told *CA:* "It's been all right, writing in this quiet town and teaching at a small school on the west coast of Florida for thirty years (with time off for good behavior). While in some ways I've felt isolated, out of touch—it must be almost the opposite of living in New York or San Francisco—in most ways I have felt unpressured, free to write and live how I choose.

"Now that the children have flown, I have my own study, and try to work there most mornings. I thought when I retired that I might do more stories, but instead poems have been coming, and I've been following them.

"I work very slowly, doing many drafts, trying to see if the poem wants to be formal in some way (about half my poems have formal elements: sestinas and syllabic poems, rhymed forms, sonnets, blank verse, etc.). I've always done this, so it's interesting to me that form has come back in favor; in fact, it makes me a little nervous! But I like the tension between colloquial language and traditional forms. These forms to me are no more dead than clay is to the hand of the potter.

"While many people read poems for their novelty and surprise—perfectly valid reasons—I think most readers are still drawn to poems that 'teach and delight.' These aren't contradictory qualities, of course; it's a matter of emphasis. In my poems I try to draw out meaning, or at least resonance, from our everyday chaotic experiences. It's been a nasty half-century in many ways, and yet most of us Americans muddle along contentedly enough. My poems often come about when that inner contentment brushes against the thin wall between it and the dangerous outer world.

"One of my major satisfactions has been having two artists in the family, and working with them. Our daughter Perrie's work is on the cover of *Liquid Paper* and *Scars,* and my wife Jeanne has illustrated all five of my chapbooks, and my children's book, *The Legend of Larry the Lizard.* I'm much affected by the visual arts; I've done a series of poems on one of my favorite artists, Camille Pissarro—we made a pilgrimage to his house outside of Paris—and would like to do more."

BIOGRAPHICAL/CRITICAL SOURCES:

BOOKS

Berke, Roberta, *Bounds out of Bounds,* Oxford University Press, 1981.
Dictionary of Literary Biography, Volume 5: *American Poets since World War II,* Gale, 1980.

PERIODICALS

Chattahoochie Review, winter, 1988.

Columbus Dispatch, July 12, 1987.

* * *

MERTON, Thomas   1915-1968
(Father M. Louis)

PERSONAL: One source cites name as Tom Feverel Merton; name in religious life, Father M. Louis; born January 31, 1915, in Prades, Pyrennes-Orientales, France; brought to the United States, 1916; returned to France, 1925; came to the United States, 1939; naturalized citizen, 1951; fatally electrocuted in Bangkok, Thailand, December 10, 1968; buried in monastic cemetery at Abbey of Our Lady of Gethsemani, near Bardstown, KY; son of Owen Heathcote (an artist) and Ruth (an artist; maiden name, Jenkins) Merton. *Education:* Attended Clare College, Cambridge, 1933-34; Columbia University, B.A., 1938, M.A., 1939. *Politics:* "No party; generally liberal." *Avocational interests:* Merton reportedly told his publishers: "Zen. Indians. Wood. Birds. Beer. Anglican friends. Subversive tape recordings for nuns. Tea. Bob Dylan."

CAREER: Instructor in English, Columbia University Extension Division, New York City, 1938-39, and St. Bonaventure University, Allegany, NY, 1939-41; Abbey of Our Lady of Gethsemani, near Bardstown, KY, Roman Catholic monk of Cistercians of the Strict Observance (Trappists), 1941-68, ordained Roman Catholic priest, 1949, master of scholastics, 1951-55, monastic forester, beginning 1951, novice master, 1955-65, lived as a hermit on grounds of monastery, 1965-68. Drawings exhibited in Louisville, KY; St. Louis, MO; New Orleans, LA; Milwaukee, WI; and Santa Barbara, CA, 1964-65.

MEMBER: Fellowship of Reconciliation.

AWARDS, HONORS: Mariana Griswold Van Rensselaer Award, 1939; citation from Literary Awards Committee of the Catholic Press Association of the United States, 1948, for *Figures for an Apocalypse;* Catholic Literary Award from the Gallery of Living Catholic Authors, 1949, for *The Seven Storey Mountain;* Catholic Writers Guild Golden Book Award for the best spiritual book by an American writer, 1951, for *The Ascent to the Truth;* Columbia University Medal for Excellence, 1961; LL.D., University of Kentucky, 1963; Pax Medal, 1963; Religious Book Award, Catholic Press Association, 1973, for *The Asian Journal of Thomas Merton.*

WRITINGS:

POETRY

Thirty Poems (also see below), New Directions (New York City), 1944.

A Man in the Divided Sea (includes poems from *Thirty Poems*), New Directions, 1946.

Figures for an Apocalypse (also contains an essay), New Directions, 1948.

The Tears of Blind Lions, New Directions, 1949.

Selected Poems of Thomas Merton, Hollis & Carter (London), 1950.

The Strange Islands: Poems (also see below), New Directions, 1957.

Selected Poems of Thomas Merton, New Directions, 1959, revised edition, 1967.

The Solitary Life, limited edition, Anvil Press (Lexington, KY), 1960.

Emblems of a Season of Fury (also contains some prose and Merton's translations of other poets), New Directions, 1963.

Cables to the Ace; or, Familiar Liturgies of Misunderstanding, New Directions, 1968, reprinted, Unicorn Press (Greensboro, NC), 1986.

Landscape, Prophet and Wild-Dog, [Syracuse, NY], 1968.

The Geography of Lograire, New Directions, 1969.

Early Poems: 1940-42, Anvil Press, 1972.

He Is Risen: Selections from Thomas Merton, Argus Communications, 1975.

The Collected Poems of Thomas Merton, New Directions, 1977.

ESSAYS

What Is Contemplation? (also see below), Saint Mary's College, Notre Dame (Holy Cross, IN), 1948, revised edition, Templegate (Springfield, IL), 1981.

Seeds of Contemplation, New Directions, 1949, revised and expanded edition published as *New Seeds of Contemplation,* 1962.

The Ascent to the Truth, Harcourt (San Diego), 1951.

Bread in the Wilderness, New Directions, 1953.

No Man Is an Island, Harcourt, 1955.

The Living Bread, Farrar, Straus (New York City), 1956.

Praying the Psalms, Liturgical Press (Collegeville, MN), 1956, published as *The Psalms Are Our Prayer,* Burns & Oates, 1957, published as *Thomas Merton on the Psalms,* Sheldon Press (London), 1970.

The Silent Life, Farrar, Straus, 1957.

Thoughts in Solitude, Farrar, Straus, 1958.

The Christmas Sermons of Bl. Guerric of Igny (essay), Abbey of Our Lady of Gethsemani (Bardstown, KY), 1959.

Spiritual Direction and Meditation (also see below), Liturgical Press, 1960.

Disputed Questions (also see below), Farrar, Straus, 1960.

The Behavior of Titans (also see below), New Directions, 1961.

The New Man, Farrar, Straus, 1962.

Life and Holiness, Herder & Herder, 1963.

Seeds of Destruction (also includes several letters), Farrar, Straus, 1964, abridged edition published as *Redeeming the Time,* Burns & Oates, 1966.

Seasons of Celebration, Farrar, Straus, 1965, published as *Meditations on Liturgy,* Mowbrays (London), 1976.

Mystics and Zen Masters (includes "The Ox Mountain Parable of Meng Tzu" [also see below]), Farrar, Straus, 1967.

Zen and the Birds of Appetite, New Directions, 1968.

Faith and Violence: Christian Teaching and Christian Practice, University of Notre Dame Press, 1968.

The Climate of Monastic Prayer, Cistercian Publications (Kalamazoo, MI), 1969, published as *Contemplative Prayer,* Herder & Herder, 1969.

True Solitude: Selections from the Writings of Thomas Merton, Hallmark Editions (Kansas City, MO), 1969.

Three Essays, Unicorn Press, 1969.

Opening the Bible, Liturgical Press, 1970, revised edition, 1983.

Contemplation in a World of Action, Doubleday (New York City), 1971.

The Zen Revival, Buddhist Society (London), 1971.

Thomas Merton on Peace, McCall Publishing Co., 1971, revised edition published as *The Nonviolent Alternative,* edited and with an introduction by Gordon C. Zahn, Farrar, Straus, 1980.

Spiritual Direction and Meditation; and, What Is Contemplation?, A. Clarke (Westhampstead), 1975.

Thomas Merton on Zen, Sheldon Press, 1976.

The Power and Meaning of Love (includes six essays originally published in *Disputed Questions*), Sheldon Press, 1976.

Ishi Means Man: Essays on Native Americans, foreword by Dorothy Day, Unicorn Press, 1976.

The Monastic Journey, edited by Patrick Hart, Sheed, Andrews & McMeel, 1977.

Love and Living, edited by Naomi Burton Stone and Hart, Farrar, Straus, 1979.

Thomas Merton on St. Bernard, Cistercian Publications, 1980.

The Literary Essays of Thomas Merton, edited by Hart, New Directions, 1981.

Passion for Peace: The Social Essays, edited by William Henry Shannon, Crossroad Publishing (New York City), 1995.

AUTOBIOGRAPHIES

The Seven Storey Mountain, Harcourt, 1948, abridged edition published as *Elected Silence: The Autobiography of Thomas Merton,* with an introduction by Evelyn Waugh, Hollis & Carter, 1949.

The Sign of Jonas (journal), Harcourt, 1953.

The Secular Journal of Thomas Merton, Farrar, Straus, 1959.

Conjectures of a Guilty Bystander (journal), Doubleday, 1966, 2nd edition, Sheldon Press, 1977.

The Asian Journal of Thomas Merton, edited by Stone, Hart, and James Laughlin, New Directions, 1973.

Woods, Shore, Desert: A Notebook, May, 1968, with photographs by Merton, Museum of New Mexico Press (Santa Fe), 1982.

A Vow of Conversation: Journals, 1964-65, edited by Stone, Farrar, Straus, 1988.

BIOGRAPHIES

Exile Ends in Glory: The Life of a Trappistine, Mother M. Berchmans, O.C.S.O., Bruce (Milwaukee), 1948.

What Are These Wounds?: The Life of a Cistercian Mystic, Saint Lutgarde of Aywieres, Clonmore & Reynolds (Dublin), 1949, Bruce, 1950.

The Last of the Fathers: Saint Bernard of Clairvaux and the Encyclical Letter "Doctor Mellifluus," Harcourt, 1954.

LETTERS

Six Letters: Boris Pasternak, Thomas Merton, edited by Stone, King Library Press, University of Kentucky, 1973.

(With Robert Lax) *A Catch of Anti-Letters,* Sheed, Andrews & McMeel, 1978.

Letters from Tom: A Selection of Letters from Father Thomas Merton, Monk of Gethsemani, to W. H. Ferry, 1961-1968, edited by W. H. Ferry, Fort Hill Press (Scarsdale, NY), 1983.

The Hidden Ground of Love: The Letters of Thomas Merton on Religious Experience and Social Concerns, selected and edited by Shannon, Farrar, Straus, 1985.

The Road to Joy: The Letters of Thomas Merton to New and Old Friends, edited by Robert E. Daggy, Farrar, Straus, 1989.

The School of Charity: The Letters of Thomas Merton on Religious Renewal and Spiritual Direction, edited by Hart, Farrar, Straus, 1990.

The Courage for Truth: The Letters of Thomas Merton to Writers, edited by Christine M. Bochen, Farrar, Straus, 1993.

Witness to Freedom: The Letters of Thomas Merton in Times of Crisis, edited by Shannon, Farrar, Straus, 1994.

At Home in the World: The Letters of Thomas Merton and Rosemary Radford Ruether, edited by Mary Tardiff, Orbis Books (Maryknoll, NY), 1995.

LYRICS

Four Freedom Songs, G.I.A. Publications (Chicago), 1968.

The Niles-Merton Songs: Opus 171 and 172, Mark Foster Museum, 1981.

EDITOR

What Ought I Do?: Sayings of the Desert Fathers, Stamperia del Santuccio (Lexington, KY), 1959, revised and expanded edition published as *The Wisdom of the Desert Fathers of the Fourth Century,* New Directions, 1961.

The Ox Mountain Parable of Meng Tzu, Stamperia del Santuccio, 1960.

(And contributor and author of introduction) *Breakthrough to Peace: Twelve Views on the Threat of Thermonuclear Extermination,* New Directions, 1962.

(And author of introduction) Mohandas Gandhi, *Gandhi on Non-violence: Selected Texts from Gandhi's "Non-violence in Peace and War,"* New Directions, 1965.

(And author of introductory essays) *The Way of Chuang Tzu,* New Directions, 1965.

(And author of introduction and commentary) Albert Camus, *The Plague,* Seabury (New York City), 1968.

TRANSLATOR

(From the French) Jean-Baptiste Chautard, *The Soul of the Apostolate,* Abbey of Our Lady of Gethsemani, 1946, new edition with introduction by Merton, Image Books (New York City), 1961.

(From the French) Saint John Eudes, *The Life and the Kingdom of Jesus in Christian Souls for the Use by Clergy or Laity,* P. J. Kennedy & Sons, 1946.

(And author of commentary) *The Spirit of Simplicity Characteristic of the Cistercian Order: An Official Report, Demanded and Approved by the General Chapter Together with Texts from St. Bernard Clairvaux on Interior Simplicity,* Abbey of Our Lady of Gethsemani, 1948.

(And author of preface) Cassiodorus, *A Prayer from the Treatise 'De anima,'* Stanbrook Abbey Press (Worcester, England), 1956.

(And author of explanatory essay) Clement of Alexandria, *Selections from the Protreptikos,* New Directions, 1963.

(From the Latin; and author of introduction) Guigo I, *The Solitary Life: A Letter from Guigo,* Stanbrook Abbey Press, 1963, published as *On the Solitary Life,* Banyan Press (Pawlet, VT), 1977.

(From the Spanish; with others) Nicanor Parra, *Poems and Antipoems,* edited by Miller Williams, New Directions, 1967.

Pablo Antonio Cuadra, *El jaguar y la luna/The Jaguar and the Moon* (bilingual edition), Unicorn Press, 1974.

ILLUSTRATOR

A Hidden Wholeness: The Visual World of Thomas Merton, edited by John Howard Griffin, Houghton, 1970.

Geography of Holiness: The Photography of Thomas Merton, edited by Deba Prasad Patnaik, Pilgrim Press, 1980.

OTHER

Cistercian Contemplatives: Monks of the Strict Observance at Our Lady of Gethsemani, Kentucky, Our Lady of the Holy Ghost, Georgia, Our Lady of the Holy Trinity, Utah—A Guide to the Trappist Life, Abbey of Our Lady of Gethsemani, 1948.

Gethsemani Magnificat: Centenary of Gethsemani Abbey, Abbey of Our Lady of Gethsemani, 1949.

The Waters of Siloe (history), Harcourt, 1949, reprinted, 1979, revised edition published as *The Waters of Silence,* Hollis & Carter, 1950, deluxe limited edition, Theodore Brun Limited, 1950.

Silence in Heaven: A Book of the Monastic Life, Studio Publications and Crowell (New York City), 1956.

The Tower of Babel (a morality play in two acts), [Hamburg], 1957, New Directions, 1958.

Monastic Peace, Abbey of Our Lady of Gethsemani, 1958.

Hagia Sophia (prose poems), Stamperia del Santuccio, 1962.

A Thomas Merton Reader, edited by Thomas P. McDonnell, Harcourt, 1962, revised and enlarged edition, Image Books, 1974.

Original Child Bomb: Points for Meditation to Be Scratched on the Walls of a Cave (prose poem), New Directions, 1962.

Come to the Mountain: New Ways and Living Traditions in the Monastic Life, Saint Benedict's Cistercian Monastery (Snowmass, CO), 1964.

The Poorer Means: A Meditation on Ways to Unity, Abbey of Our Lady of Gethsemani, 1965.

Gethsemani: A Life of Praise, Abbey of Our Lady of Gethsemani, 1966.

(Author of introductory essay) George A. Panichas, editor, *Mansions of the Spirit: Essays in Religion and Literature,* Hawthorn (New York City), 1967.

Christ in the Desert, Monastery of Christ in the Desert (Abiquiu, NM), 1968.

My Argument with the Gestapo: A Macaronic Journal (novel), Doubleday, 1969.

Cistercian Life, Cistercian Book Service (Spenser, MA), 1974.

Introductions East and West: The Foreign Prefaces of Thomas Merton, edited by Daggy, Unicorn Press, 1981, revised edition published as *Honorable Reader: Reflections on My Work,* Crossroad Publishing, 1989.

Blaze of Recognition: Through the Year with Thomas Merton: Daily Meditations, selected and edited by McDonnell, with illustrations by Merton, Doubleday, 1983, published as *Through the Year with Thomas Merton: Daily Meditations from His Writings,* Image Books, 1985.

Monks Pond: Thomas Merton's Little Magazine (collected issues), edited by Daggy, University Press of Kentucky (Lexington), 1989.

Thomas Merton: Preview of the Asian Journey, edited by Walter H. Capps, Crossroad Publishing, 1989.

Thomas Merton in Alaska: Prelude to the Asian Journal: The Alaskan Conferences, Journals, and Letters, New Directions, 1989.

Thomas Merton's Rewritings: The Five Versions of Seeds / New Seeds of Contemplation as a Key to the Development of His Thought, edited by Donald Grayson, Edwin Mellen Press (Lewiston, NY), 1989.

The Springs of Contemplation: A Retreat at the Abbey of Gethsemani, edited by Jane Marie Richardson, Farrar, Straus, 1992.

Thomas Merton, Spiritual Master: The Essential Writings, edited by Lawrence S. Cunningham, Paulist Press, 1992.

Ways of the Christian Mystics, Shambhala (Boston), 1994.

Run to the Mountain: The Story of a Vocation, edited by Hart, HarperSanFrancisco, 1995.

Thoughts on the East, New Directions, 1995.

Also author of numerous shorter works and pamphlets, including *A Balanced Life of Prayer,* 1951, *Basic Principles of Monastic Spirituality,* 1957, *Prometheus: A Meditation,* 1958, *Nativity Kerygma,* 1958, *Monastic Vocation and the Background of Modern Secular Thought,* 1964, and *Notes on the Future of Monasticism,* 1968. Contributor to books, including Selden Rodman, editor, *New Anthology of Modern Poetry,* revised edition, Modern Library, 1946; James E. Tobin, compiler, *The Happy Crusaders,* McMullen Books, 1952; and Fallon Evans, compiler, *J. F. Powers,* Herder & Herder, 1968. Contributor of book reviews, articles, and poetry to *New York Herald Tribune, New York Times Book Review, Commonweal, Catholic World,* and *Catholic Worker.* Editor, *Monks Pond* (quarterly), 1968. The largest collection of Merton's manuscripts is held at the Thomas Merton Studies Center, Bellarmine College, Louisville, KY.

ADAPTATIONS: The Tower of Babel, condensed and adapted by Richard J. Walsh, was televised by National Broadcasting Corporation (NBC-TV) in 1957.

SIDELIGHTS: A monk who lived in isolation for several years, Thomas Merton was a prolific poet, religious writer, and essayist whose diversity of work has rendered a precise definition of his life and an estimation of the significance of his career difficult. In *The Seven Mountains of Thomas Merton,* Michael Mott called Merton a "poet, writer, activist, contemplative, . . . reformer of monastic life, artist, [and] bridge between Western and Eastern religious thought." In the *New York Times Book Review,* however, Mott admitted to D. J. R. Brucker that he "was never able to categorize [Merton]. The breadth and freshness of his interests [were] simply amazing."

Paradoxical is perhaps the word that best summarizes Merton's life and works. In a *Publishers Weekly* interview with Ellen Mangin, for example, Mott noted that although Merton had been a contemplative who led a life dedicated to meditation, Mott was able to write a nearly 600-page biography on him. Not only was Merton a contemplative, but he was also a Trappist, a member of a branch of Roman Catholic monks known for their severely simple living conditions and their vow of silence in which all conversation is forbidden. Merton's accomplishments as an author are even more remarkable considering that when he entered the Trappist monastery in Kentucky in 1941, the monks were allowed to write only two half-page letters four times a year and nothing more. In the *Dictionary of Literary Biography,* Victor A. Kramer also commented on the contradictory aspects of Merton's life and work, observing that "Merton's dual career as a cloistered monk and prolific writer, a career of silence yet one which allowed him to speak to thousands of readers world wide, was a paradox." The significance of this contrasting need in Merton for both silence and fellowship with the people outside the monastery walls "was a source of anxiety to Merton himself," stated Ross Labrie in the *Dictionary of Literary Biography Yearbook: 1981.* But according to Labrie, "it is one of the strongest centers of excitement in approaching his work as well as being one of the clearest ways to see his role in twentieth-century letters." James Thomas Baker agreed that the dichotomy of monk/writer in Merton's personality was an essential ingredient in his writing. As Baker stated in *Thomas Merton: Social Critic,* "There was . . . an oriental paradox about his life and thought, the paradox of a monk speaking to the world, which gave it the quality that was uniquely Merton, and any other career would have robbed his work of that quality."

Due to the abundant autobiographical material Merton produced (at his death, he left 800,000 words of unpublished writings—mainly journals and letters—as well as hundreds of taped talks), we know a great deal about how Merton dealt with the anxiety produced by his paradoxical desire to be both a contemplative and a social activist. Mott's research revealed that by 1940 Merton was actually keeping two sets of journals, private journals handwritten in bound notebooks and edited typewritten journals that he showed to others. Although not a journal, *The Seven Storey Mountain,* an autobiography Merton published in 1948 when he was only thirty-three years old, is probably the book for which he is best remembered. It was an instant success, selling 6,000 copies in the first month of publication and nearly 300,000 copies the first year. It has been consistently in print since its initial publication.

Even before publication, *The Seven Storey Mountain* had caused considerable excitement for its publisher.

Looking for recommendations to print on the book's jacket, Robert Giroux, Merton's editor, sent galley proofs to Evelyn Waugh, Graham Greene, and Clare Boothe Luce for their opinions. According to Mott, Waugh said *The Seven Storey Mountain* "may well prove to be of permanent interest in the history of religious experience." Greene wrote that the autobiography had "a pattern and meaning valid for all of us." And Clare Boothe Luce declared, "It is to a book like this that men will turn a hundred years from now to find out what went on in the heart of men in this cruel century." These enthusiastic replies led Harcourt, Brace & Co. to increase the first printing order from five thousand to twenty thousand copies and to order a second printing before publication.

Post-publication reviewers admired *The Seven Storey Mountain* as well. In *Catholic World,* F. X. Connolly noted: "The book is bracing in its realism, sincere, direct and challenging. . . . *The Seven Storey Mountain* is a prolonged prayer as well as a great book." Commenting in the *New York Herald Tribune Weekly Book Review,* George Shuster wrote: "The fervor of [Merton's] progress to the monastery of Gethsemani is deeply moving. It is a difficult matter to write about, but I think there will be many who, however alien the experience may remain to them personally, will put the narrative down with wonder and respect." George Miles observed in a *Commonweal* review that "the book is written simply; the sensory images of boyhood are wonderful, and the incisive quality of his criticism, that tartness of his humor have not been sentimentalized by Merton's entry into a monastery. . . . *The Seven Storey Mountain* is a book that deeply impresses the mind and the heart for days. It fills one with love and hope."

Reviewers and readers were moved by the intriguing story of Merton's undisciplined youth, conversion to Catholicism, and subsequent entry into the Trappist monastery. "With publication of his autobiography," noted Kenneth L. Woodward in *Newsweek,* "Merton became a cult figure among pious Catholics." According to Edward Rice in his biography of Merton, *The Man in the Sycamore Tree: The Good Times and Hard Life of Thomas Merton, An Entertainment,* "[the book] was forceful enough to cause a quiet revolution among American Catholics, and then among people of many beliefs throughout the world." A *Time* writer reported that "under its spell disillusioned veterans, students, even teenagers flocked to monasteries across the country either to stay or visit as retreatants." As Richard Kostelanetz

observed in the *New York Times Book Review,* "[Merton's] example made credible an extreme religious option that would strike many as unthinkable."

Rice theorized that the success of *The Seven Storey Mountain* was not only due to interest in Merton's story but also to the way the events in his life reflected the feelings of a whole society recovering from the shock of a world war. Explained Rice: "What [made *The Seven Storey Mountain*] different from [other books like it was] its great evocation of a young man in an age when the soul of mankind had been laid open as never before during world depression and unrest and the rise of both Communism and Fascism. . . . It became a symbol and a guide to the plight of the contemporary world, touching Catholics and non-Catholics alike in their deep, alienated unconsciousness."

The popularity of the book brought money to the Abbey of Gethsemani that was used for much-needed improvements and expansion. As Rice noted, however, it also "catapulted Merton into the eyes of the world," making a celebrity of a man who wanted to live in solitude. Mott wrote: "Without the publication of this . . . autobiography . . . it is just possible . . . that Thomas Merton might have achieved . . . obscurity and oblivion." But that was not to be; for the rest of his life Merton was to deal with the consequences of having written such a popular book.

In an interview with Thomas P. McDonnell that appeared in *Motive* in 1967, Merton commented on being an author of a best-seller. "I left [*The Seven Storey Mountain*] behind many years ago. Certainly, it was a book I had to write, and it says a great deal of what I have to say; but if I had to write it over again, it would be handled in a very different way. . . . Unfortunately, the book was a best-seller, and it has become a kind of edifying legend or something. . . . I am doing my best to live it down. The legend is stronger than I am."

Merton's love of writing started early in his life, as Israel Shenker noted in the *New York Times.* "He wrote his first book at the age of ten," wrote Shenker, "and followed it with ten more unpublished novels." (One of these early novels was published posthumously as *My Argument with the Gestapo: A Macaronic Journal.*) By 1939, when Merton was teaching university extension classes at night, writing and re-writing novels and articles occupied most of his days. That same year, according to Mott, Merton also "wrote the first poem that would continue to mean something to him." Although Merton had already written quite a few poems, he explained in *The Seven Storey Mountain,* "I had never been able to write verse before I became a Catholic [in 1938]. I had tried, but I had never really succeeded, and it was impossible to keep alive enough ambition to go on trying."

Merton became well known as a poet during his first years in the monastery. His first book of poetry, *Thirty Poems,* was published in 1944. It included poems he composed before and after entering the abbey. According to Baker, Merton felt "that the poetry which he wrote at that time was the best of his career." The book received favorable reviews, including one written by poet Robert Lowell for *Commonweal* in which the critic called Merton "easily the most promising of our American Catholic poets."

Merton's next book of poems included all the poems from his first book plus fifty-six more written during the same period. This book, *A Man in the Divided Sea,* was equally praised by critics. Calling it "brilliant" and "provocative" in *Poetry,* John Nerber commented, "It is, without doubt, one of the important books of the year." In the *New Yorker* Louise Bogan wrote that although Merton "has not yet developed a real synthesis between his poetic gifts and his religious ones . . . the possibility of his becoming a religious poet of stature is evident."

Despite the stature of his religious writings and essays, the literary value of Merton's poetry is still in question. As Kostelanetz wrote: "Merton's poems are scarcely anthologized, and his name rarely appears in histories of American literature." Writing in *Commonweal,* William Henry Shannon argued that Merton's poetry, consisting of "over a thousand pages," contained "a fair amount of . . . mediocre or just plain bad" writing, "but one will also find fine poetry there." Speaking of the religious content of Merton's work, Therese Lentfoehr, writing in her *Words and Silence: On the Poetry of Thomas Merton,* explained that "only about a third of the poems might be viewed as having specific religious themes." Many of the other poems were accessible to a larger audience because Merton enjoyed writing about children, the natural world, and the larger world outside the monastery. In the 1960s he also wrote poems about social issues of the day.

After his poetry writing in the 1940s, Merton was not able to write poems in such quantities again until the 1960s. With his appointment in 1951 as master of scholastics, many of his works—such as *The Living Bread, No Man Is an Island,* and *The Silent Life*—expanded on ideas expressed in the monastery classes he conducted for the young monks studying for the priesthood.

Several critics, including Kramer and Baker, noted a change in Merton's writing style sometime between the end of the 1950s and the early 1960s. Whereas Merton previously appeared to advocate isolation from society as the answer to the question of how a Christian should respond to the unspirituality of the world, his writing began to suggest the need to deal with social injustice through social activism. Baker explained, "By the mid-1960s [Merton's] attitude toward the world had changed so dramatically that Merton-watchers were speaking of the 'early Merton' and the 'later Merton' to distinguish between his two careers, the one as a silent mystic who celebrated the virtues of monastic life in glowing prose and poetry, the other as a social commentator."

Kramer chose three Merton books to demonstrate "the significant changes in awareness" in Merton's writing. The first of these books, *Seeds of Contemplation,* published in 1949, was entirely spiritual in focus. *New Seeds of Contemplation,* published in 1961, was a revised version of the same book, and it reflected what Kramer called Merton's "greater concern for the problems of living in the world." The third book Kramer mentioned, *Seeds of Destruction,* published in 1964, was a collection of essays on world problems, including racism. According to Kramer, the changing themes illustrated in these three books reflect Merton's movement from solitary monk in a monastery cell to social activist. While unable to join the sit-ins and protest marches of the 1960s, Merton was able to express his support for such activities with his writing.

Mott explained the change in Merton's style by noting that at the end of the 1950s, "after sixteen years of isolation from social issues, Merton was beginning to feel cut off from what he needed to know." Since radios, televisions, and newspapers were forbidden in the monastery, only chance readings of magazines and books brought to the abbey by Merton's friends enabled him to keep up with world events. Belatedly, found out about the suffering caused by the U.S. atomic bomb attacks on Japan and the horrors of Nazi concentration camps. He learned of social injustice in Latin America by reading Latin American poets, including Nicaraguan Ernesto Cardenal, who spent some time at the Abbey of Gethsemani himself in the late 1950s. Mott continued: "[Merton] was unsure of himself, certain only that the time had come to move from the role of bystander . . . to that of declared witness." His poetic works *Original Child Bomb: Points for Meditation to Be Scratched on the Walls of a Cave* (about the atomic bomb) and "Chants to be Used in Processions around a Site with Furnaces" (about the ovens of the Nazi extermination camps) were products of his awakening social conscience.

Merton's increasing concern with racial injustice, the immorality of war—particularly of the Vietnam conflict—and the plight of the world's poor caused more and more censorship problems. Actually, he had had problems with monastic censors throughout his stay at Gethsemani. When originally confronted with the manuscript version of *The Seven Storey Mountain,* for instance, the censors rejected it because of the numerous references to sex and drinking it contained. In a section of Merton's journal published as *The Sign of Jonas* the monk complained that one of the censors even "held [that Merton was] incapable of writing an autobiography 'with his present literary equipment' and . . . advised [Merton] to take a correspondence course in English grammar." Although the debate over *The Seven Storey Mountain* was eventually resolved, censors became even more concerned about Merton's writings on war and peace. Frustrated, Merton circulated some of his work in mimeographed form. These came to be known as "The Cold War Letters." In 1962, Merton was forbidden by his superiors to write about war, but he could write about peace. Mott quoted a letter Merton wrote that year: "Did I tell you that the decision of the higher ups has become final and conclusive? . . . Too controversial, doesn't give a nice image of monk. Monk concerned with peace. Bad image."

Despite censorship and isolation Merton became, according to Kenneth L. Woodward in *Newsweek,* "a prophet to the peace movement [and] a conscience to the counterculture." At the height of the escalation of the Vietnam War, he welcomed a Vietnamese Buddhist monk to speak at the abbey, met with peace activist Joan Baez, corresponded with Daniel Berrigan (a Catholic priest arrested for burning draft cards), and planned a retreat for Dr. Martin Luther King Jr., a plan thwarted by King's assassination. Controversial comedian Lenny Bruce often closed his nightclub act by reading from an essay Merton wrote

about German Nazi leader Adolf Eichmann in which Merton questioned the sanity of the world.

Much of this activity occurred after Merton began living as a hermit in a cabin located in the woods on the monastery grounds. Just as his desire to be removed from the world became greatest so did his need to speak out on social problems. In his writings, he attempted to explain this paradox as much to himself as to others.

In *Best Sellers,* Sister Joseph Marie Anderson wrote that in Merton's *Contemplation in a World of Action* the monk stressed "that the contemplative is not exempt from the problem of the world nor is the monastic life an escape from reality." In a review of Merton's *The Climate of Monastic Prayer,* a *Times Literary Supplement* critic noted, "Merton came to see that the monk is not exempt from the agonies of the world outside his walls: he is involved at another level." The reviewer offered this quote from Merton's book: "The monk searches not only his own heart: he plunges deep into the heart of that world of which he remains a part although he seems to have 'left' it. In reality the monk abandons the world only in order to listen more intently to the deepest and most neglected voices that proceed from the inner depth." According to Lawrence S. Cunningham, writing in *Commonweal,* Merton saw the contemplative as someone who "should be able to communicate . . . from the deep center or *ground* which is God."

Along with social activism, Merton became increasingly interested in the study of other religions, particularly Zen Buddhism. His books *Mystics and Zen Masters* and *Zen and the Birds of Appetite* acknowledged his love for Eastern thought. In the *New York Times Book Review* Nancy Wilson Ross wrote, "In *Mystics and Zen Masters* . . . Merton . . . has made a vital, sensitive and timely contribution to the growing worldwide effort . . . to shed new light on mankind's common spiritual heritage." She added: "Merton's reasons for writing this [book] . . . might be summed up in a single quotation: 'If the West continues to underestimate and to neglect the spiritual heritage of the East, it may well hasten the tragedy that threatens man and his civilization.'" In the *New York Times Book Review* Edward Rice explained further: "Merton's first notion was to pluck whatever 'Christian' gems he could out of the East that might fit into the Catholic theological structure. Later he abandoned this attempt and accepted Buddhism, Hinduism and Islam on their own equally valid terms . . . without compromising his own Christianity."

Merton died in 1968 while hoping to expand his understanding of Eastern thought at an ecumenical conference in Bangkok, Thailand, his first extended journey outside the monastery walls since his entry in 1941. His death came 27 years to the day from when he first became a member of the Gethsemani community, and was the result of an electrical shock from a faulty fan.

Merton's writings on peace, war, social injustice, and Eastern thought created controversy both inside and outside the abbey. In the revised edition of *Thomas Merton: Monk,* Daniel Berrigan noted that many people refused to accept the work of the "new" Merton and that they preferred "rather a Merton in their own image, a Merton who [was] safe, and cornered, contemplative in a terribly wrong sense, and therefore manageable." However, as J. M. Cameron remarked in the *New York Review of Books,* it is most likely these later writings will stand out as Merton's most important work. According to Cameron, "Merton will be remembered for two things: his place . . . in the thinking about the morality of war. . . ; and his partially successful attempt to bring out, through study and personal encounter, what is common to Asian and West monasticism and . . . contemplative life." Rice agreed with this observation, noting in *The Man in the Sycamore Tree,* "It [was] the later writings on war and peace, nonviolence, race, . . . and above all on Buddhism, that show Merton at his best and most creative." Robert E. Daggy is quoted by Carl Simmons in *AB Bookman's Weekly* as attributing Merton's continuing popularity to the "great deal of interest in Merton as a human being, sort of struggling through the 20th century, struggling through a period where traditions and roots seem to be lost, where people don't know quite what they believe or what they believe in."

Thomas Merton was, as Shannon noted, "one of those persons people instinctively like[d]" and, it appears, Merton's personal attraction is still felt decades after his death. His works and life seem to have relevance to a new generation of Catholics and non-Catholics. "His influence," wrote Mitch Finley in *Our Sunday Visitor,* a national Catholic weekly, "is, if anything, on the increase." His ideas on war and peace contained in his writing from the 1960s were echoed in the U.S. Catholic bishops' statement

on nuclear war published in the 1980s. His life, too, continues to reveal, Monica Furlong noted in *Merton: A Biography,* "much about the twentieth century and, in particular, the role of religion in it."

"Perhaps the best indicator of the continuing interest in Thomas Merton," wrote Simmons, "besides the dozens of posthumously published works, is the existence of several centers specifically dedicated to the study of Merton, including those in New York, Pittsburgh, Denver, and Magog, Quebec." Another site, the Thomas Merton Studies Center at Bellarmine College in Louisville, Kentucky, contains over 10,000 items related to Merton and some 3,000 of his manuscripts. The Merton Legacy Trust, devoted to gathering all future Merton scholarship, is also located at Bellarmine. The International Thomas Merton Society was founded in 1987 and reports a membership of over 1,500.

BIOGRAPHICAL/CRITICAL SOURCES:

BOOKS

Adams, Daniel J., *Thomas Merton's Shared Contemplation: A Protestant Perspective,* edited by Teresa A. Doyle, Cistercian Publications, 1979.

Baker, James Thomas, *Thomas Merton: Social Critic,* University of Kentucky, 1971.

Breit, Marquita E., editor, *Thomas Merton: A Bibliography,* Scarecrow Press (Metuchen, NJ), 1974, revised edition published as *Thomas Merton: A Comprehensive Bibliography,* Garland Press (New York City), 1986.

Carr, Anne E., *A Search for Wisdom and Spirit: Thomas Merton's Theology of the Self,* University of Notre Dame Press (Notre Dame, IN), 1988.

Contemporary Literary Criticism, Gale (Detroit), Volume 1, 1973, Volume 3, 1975, Volume 11, 1979, Volume 34, 1985, Volume 83, 1994.

Cooper, David D., *Thomas Merton's Art of Denial: The Evolution of a Radical Humanist,* University of Georgia Press (Athens, GA), 1989.

Del Prete, Thomas, *Thomas Merton and the Education of the Whole Person,* Religious Education Press (Birmingham, AL), 1990.

De Waal, Esther, *A Seven-Day Journey with Thomas Merton,* Servant Publications (Ann Arbor, MI), 1992.

Dictionary of Literary Biography, Volume 48: *American Poets, 1880-1945, Second Series,* Gale, 1986.

Dictionary of Literary Biography Yearbook: 1981, Gale, 1982.

Finley, James, *Merton's Palace of Nowhere,* Ave Maria Press, 1978.

Forest, James H., *Thomas Merton: A Pictorial Biography,* Paulist Press, 1980.

Forest, James H., *Living with Wisdom: A Life of Thomas Merton,* Orbis Books, 1991.

Furlong, Monica, *Merton: A Biography,* Harper (New York City), 1980.

Grayston, Donald, *Thomas Merton: The Development of a Spiritual Theologian,* Edwin Mellen Press, 1985.

Griffin, John Howard, *Follow the Ecstasy: The Hermitage Years of Thomas Merton,* edited by Robert Bonazzi, JHG Editions/Latitudes Press (Fort Worth, TX), 1983, published as *Thomas Merton: The Hermitage Years, a Biographical Study,* Orbis Books, 1993.

Groves, Gerald, *Up and Down Merton's Mountain,* CBP Press (St. Louis, MO), 1988.

Hart, Patrick, editor, *The Message of Thomas Merton,* Cistercian Publications, 1981.

Hart, Patrick, *Thomas Merton: Monk,* Sheed & Ward, 1974, revised and enlarged edition, Cistercian Publications, 1983.

Hart, Patrick, editor, *The Legacy of Thomas Merton,* Cistercian Publications, 1985.

Kilcourse, George, *Ace of Freedoms: Thomas Merton's Christ,* University of Notre Dame Press, 1993.

King, Thomas Mulvihill, *Merton: Mystic at the Center of America,* Liturgical Press, 1992.

Kountz, Peter, *Thomas Merton as Writer and Monk: A Cultural Study, 1915-1951,* Carlson Publishing (Brooklyn), 1991.

Kramer, Victor A., *Thomas Merton,* Twayne (New York City), 1984.

Labrie, Ross, *The Art of Thomas Merton,* Texas Christian University Press, 1979.

Lawlor, Patrick T., editor, *Thomas Merton: The Poet and the Contemplative Life; An Exhibition,* Columbia University Libraries (New York City), 1990.

Lentfoehr, Therese, *Words and Silence: On the Poetry of Thomas Merton,* New Directions, 1979.

Lipski, Alexander, *Thomas Merton and Asia: His Quest for Utopia,* Cistercian Publications, 1983.

Maltis, Elena, *The Solitary Explorer: Thomas Merton's Transforming Journey,* Harper, 1980.

McInerny, Dennis Q., *Thomas Merton: The Man and His Work,* Consortium Press (Washington, DC), 1974.

Meatyard, Ralph Eugene, *Father Louie: Photographs of Thomas Merton,* Timken Publishers (New York City), 1991.

Merton, Thomas, *The Seven Storey Mountain,* Harcourt, 1948.

Merton, Thomas, *The Sign of Jonas,* Harcourt, 1953.

Merton, Thomas, *Letters from Tom: A Selection of Letters from Father Thomas Merton, Monk of Gethsemani,* edited by W. H. Ferry, Fort Hill Press, 1983.

The Merton Annual, AMS Press (New York City), 1988—.

Mott, Michael, *The Seven Mountains of Thomas Merton,* Houghton (Boston), 1984.

Mulhearn, Timothy, editor, *Getting It All Together: The Heritage of Thomas Merton,* M. Glazier, 1984.

Nouwen, Henri J. M., *Pray to Live; Thomas Merton: A Contemplative Critic,* Fides Publishers (Notre Dame, IN), 1972.

Pennington, M. Basil, *A Retreat with Thomas Merton,* Amity House (Warwick, NY), 1988.

Pennington, M. Basil, editor, *Toward an Integrated Humanity: Thomas Merton's Journey,* Cistercian Publications, 1988.

Powaski, Ronald E., *Thomas Merton on Nuclear Weapons,* Loyola University Press (Chicago), 1988.

Rice, Edward, *The Man in the Sycamore Tree: The Good Times and Hard Life of Thomas Merton, An Entertainment,* Doubleday, 1970.

Seitz, Ron, *Song for Nobody: A Memory Vision of Thomas Merton,* Triumph Books (Ligouri, MO), 1993.

Shannon, William Henry, *Thomas Merton's Dark Path: The Inner Experience of a Contemplative,* Farrar, Straus, 1981, revised edition, 1986.

Shannon, William Henry, *Silent Lamp: The Thomas Merton Story,* Crossroad Publishing, 1992.

Stull, Bradford T., *Religious Dialectics of Pain and Imagination,* State University of New York Press (Albany), 1994.

Sussman, Cornelia and Irving Sussman, *Thomas Merton,* Doubleday, 1980.

Waldron, Robert G., *Thomas Merton in Search of His Soul: A Jungian Perspective,* Ave Maria Press (Notre Dame, IN), 1994.

Wilkes, Paul, *Merton: By Those Who Knew Him Best,* Harper, 1984.

Woodcock, George, *Thomas Merton: Monk and Poet, a Critical Study,* Farrar, Straus, 1978.

PERIODICALS

AB Bookman's Weekly, November 16, 1992, pp. 1832-46.

America, October 25, 1969; November 24, 1984; October 22, 1988, pp. 277, 280, 288, 290; November 12, 1988, p. 387; October 21, 1989, p. 267; November 18, 1989, p. 358; February 3, 1990, p. 76; October 6, 1990, p. 218; October 27, 1990, p. 309; January 1, 1994, p. 6; February 11, 1995, p. 26.

American Book Review, March, 1990, p. 16.

Atlantic, May, 1949.

Best Sellers, November 15, 1970; April 15, 1971; August 15, 1973.

Bloomsbury Review, July, 1989, p. 23.

Booklist, May 1, 1985, p. 1220; March 15, 1989, p. 1222; May 1, 1995, p. 1533.

Boston Globe, August 22, 1993, p. B14; December 7, 1993, p. 19.

Boston Review, February, 1985.

Catholic World, October, 1948; November, 1948; October, 1949; December, 1949, pp. 198-203; June, 1950; November, 1951; March, 1953; June, 1955; February, 1957; July, 1958; November, 1960; August, 1961; April, 1962; May-June, 1990, pp. 126, 133; May, 1994, p. 148.

Chicago Tribune, January 27, 1985; May 22, 1992, p. C9.

Christian Century, March 9, 1988, p. 242; March 22, 1995, p. 330.

Columbia Literary Columns, November, 1989, pp. 18-30.

Commentary, April, 1965, pp. 90, 92-4.

Commonweal, June 22, 1945, pp. 240-42; December 27, 1946; August 13, 1948; April 15, 1949; October 14, 1949; October 26, 1951; February 27, 1953; May 13, 1955, pp. 155-59; July 6, 1956; June 9, 1961; March 16, 1962; April 19, 1963; March 12, 1965; January 10, 1969; October 17, 1969; February 27, 1970; January 22, 1971; October 12, 1973; February 3, 1978; November 18, 1983, pp. 634-37; October 19, 1984; February 28, 1986, p. 118; December 2, 1988, pp. 649-52; April 19, 1991, p. 270; February 25, 1994, pp. 26-8; September 9, 1994, p. 18.

Contemporary Literature, winter, 1973.

Critic, April, 1963; February, 1966; January, 1970; May, 1971; February 15, 1981.

Detroit Free Press, February 11, 1969.

Hudson Review, spring, 1970, pp. 187-88; summer, 1978.

Kentucky Review, summer, 1987, pp. 1-145.

Los Angeles Times Book Review, December 14, 1980; December 30, 1984; October 13, 1985.

Motive, October, 1967.

Nation, November 6, 1948.

National Catholic Reporter, January 29, 1988, p. 7; July 14, 1989, p. 2; September 22, 1989, p. 17; April 12, 1991, p. 24; December 10, 1993, pp. 22-3.

National Review, May 31, 1985, p. 42; December 5, 1994, p. 80.

Negro Digest, December, 1967.

New Republic, October 4, 1948; September 12, 1949.

Newsweek, December 10, 1984.

New Yorker, October 5, 1946; October 9, 1948; October 8, 1949.

New York Herald Tribune Weekly Book Review, October 24, 1948.

New York Review of Books, February 11, 1965; April 10, 1969; September 27, 1979.

New York Times, March 18, 1945; October 3, 1948; March 20, 1949; September 18, 1949; March 26, 1950; September 23, 1951; February 8, 1953; March 27, 1955; March 11, 1956; July 10, 1969; December 10, 1984; December 20, 1984.

New York Times Book Review, October 3, 1948, pp. 4, 33; February 8, 1953, pp. 1, 30; February 14, 1965; April 17, 1966; July 2, 1967; March 30, 1969; March 15, 1970; March 14, 1971; July 8, 1973; February 5, 1978, p. 20; May 23, 1982, p. 15; December 23, 1984; September 17, 1989, p. 25; February 12, 1995, p. 22.

Our Sunday Visitor, January 25, 1987.

Parabola, February, 1991, p. 124.

Poetry, February, 1945; December, 1946; October, 1948; July, 1950.

Publishers Weekly, December 7, 1984.

Renascence, winter, 1974; spring, 1978.

Saturday Review of Literature, October 9, 1948; April 16, 1949; September 17, 1949; February 11, 1950.

Sewanee Review, summer, 1969; winter, 1973; autumn, 1973.

Thought, September, 1974.

Time, January 24, 1968; December 31, 1984.

Times Literary Supplement, December 23, 1949; May 22, 1959; February 12, 1970; May 5, 1972.

U.S. Catholic, January, 1993, p. 20; December, 1993, p. 20; June, 1994, p. 33.

Virginia Quarterly Review, summer, 1968.

Wall Street Journal, June 4, 1985, p. 30.

Washington Post, September 4, 1969.

Washington Post Book World, December 16, 1984; June 30, 1985.

World Literature Today, spring, 1989, p. 311; summer, 1990, p. 469.

OBITUARIES:

PERIODICALS

Antiquarian Bookman, December 23-30, 1968.
Books Abroad, spring, 1969.
Detroit Free Press, December 11, 1968.
Newsweek, December 23, 1968.
New York Times, December 11, 1968.
Publishers Weekly, December 30, 1968.
Time, December 20, 1968.
Times (London), December 12, 1968.
Washington Post, December 12, 1968.*

*   *   *

MESA-LAGO, Carmelo   1934-

PERSONAL: Surname is pronounced "Mayseh-Lahgo"; born August 11, 1934, in Havana, Cuba; son of Rogelio (in legal field) and Ana Maria (Lago) Mesa; married Elena Gross, September 3, 1966; children: Elizabeth, Ingrid, Helena. *Education:* University of Havana, Master in Law, 1957; University of Madrid, LL.D., 1958; University of Miami, M.A. (economics), 1965; Cornell University, Ph.D., 1968. *Religion:* Roman Catholic.

ADDRESSES: Office—4M38 Forbes Quadrangle, Department of Economics, University of Pittsburgh, Pittsburgh, PA 15260.

CAREER: University of Pittsburgh, Pittsburgh, PA, assistant professor, 1967-70, associate professor, 1970-76, professor of economics, 1976-80, distinguished service professor, 1980—, assistant director of Center for Latin American Studies, 1967-70, associate director, beginning 1970, director, 1976-86. Emilio Bacardi Chair, University of Miami, fall, 1994. Consultant to Hispanic Foundation, Library of Congress, 1969, State Department, 1972, 1975, 1976-77, 1980, 1992-93, International Labour Organization, 1973, 1986-88, 1991, Organization of American States, 1981, 1982, 1983, World Bank, 1982, 1983, 1985-89, 1992, United Nations Economic Commission for Latin America, 1983-84, 1993-94, Inter-American Development Bank, 1985, 1991-94, USAID, 1985-88, 1992-94, Pan American Health Organization, 1985, 1990, 1993-94, and UNCTAD, 1993.

MEMBER: International Association of Labor Law and Social Security, Association for Comparative Economic Studies, Latin American Studies Association (president, 1980), American Economic Association, Caribbean Studies Association (member of executive council, 1973), National Academy of Social Insurance, Council on Foreign Relations.

AWARDS, HONORS: Arthur Whitaker Prize, 1982, for *The Economy of Socialist Cuba: A Two-Decade Appraisal;* Hoover Institution Prize, 1986, for best article on Latin America; Chancellor Distinguished Research and Public Service Award, University of Pittsburgh, 1991 and 1995; Alexander von Humboldt Senior Research Award, 1991-92.

WRITINGS:

(Coauthor) *Labor Conditions in Communist Cuba,* University of Miami Press (Miami, FL), 1963.
The Labor Sector and Socialist Distribution in Cuba, Praeger (New York City), 1968.
(Editor) *Revolutionary Change in Cuba,* University of Pittsburgh Press (Pittsburgh, PA), 1971.
Cuba in the 1970s: Pragmatism and Institutionalization, University of New Mexico Press (Albuquerque), 1974, 2nd edition, 1978.
(Editor) *Comparative Socialist Systems: Essays in Politics and Economics,* Center for International Studies, University of Pittsburgh, 1975.
Social Security in Latin America: Pressure Groups, Stratification and Inequality, University of Pittsburgh Press, 1978.
The Economy of Socialist Cuba: A Two-Decade Appraisal, University of New Mexico Press, 1981.
(Editor) *Cuba in Africa,* University of Pittsburgh Press, 1982.
El desarrollo de la seguridad social en America Latina, CEPAL, 1985.
(Editor) *The Crisis of Social Security and Health Care,* Center for Latin American Studies, University of Pittsburgh Press, 1985.
Ascent to Bankruptcy: Social Security Financing and Development in Latin America, University of Pittsburgh Press, 1989.
La segurid social y el sector informal, ILO-PREALC (Geneva, Switzerland, and Santiago, Chile), 1990.
Portfolio Performance of Selected Social Security Institutes in Latin America, World Bank (Washington, DC), 1991.
Health Care for the Poor in Latin America and the Caribbean, Pan American Health Organization (Washington, DC), 1992.

(Editor) *Cuba after the Cold War,* University of Pittsburgh Press, 1993.

Changing Social Security in Latin America: Towards the Alleviation of Social Costs of Economic Reform, Lynne Reinner (Boulder, CO), 1994.

Breve historia economica de Cuba socialista, Allianza Editorial (Madrid), 1994.

Are Economic Reforms Propelling Cuba to the Market?, North-South Center, University of Miami, 1994.

Alternative Models of Economic Development and Performance: Chile, Costa Rica and Cuba, EDC Publishing (Tulsa), 1996.

Contributor to journals. Editor, *Cuban Studies* (yearbook), 1986-90.

*   *   *

MILLER, Anita   1926-

PERSONAL: Born August 31, 1926, in Chicago, IL; daughter of Louis and Clara (Ruttenberg) Wolfberg; married Jordan Miller (a publisher), December 19, 1948; children: Mark Crispin, Bruce Joshua, Eric Lincoln. *Education:* Roosevelt University, B.A., 1948; Northwestern University, M.A., Ph.D., 1972.

ADDRESSES: Home—334 Hawthorn, Glencoe, IL 60022. *Office*—Academy Chicago, 213 West Institute Pl., Chicago, IL 60610.

CAREER: University of Wisconsin—Parkside, Kenosha, lecturer in English, 1969-70; Northwestern University, Evanston, IL, lecturer in English, 1970-77; Academy Chicago Publishers, Chicago, IL, editorial director, 1976—.

WRITINGS:

Arnold Bennett: An Annotated Bibliography, 1887-1932, Garland Publishing (New York City), 1972.

(With Jean M. Weiman) *The Fair Women,* Academy Chicago (Chicago), 1981.

EDITOR

Beyond the Front Page, Academy Chicago, 1983.
Feminismo!, Academy Chicago, 1988.
The Trial of Levi Weeks, Academy Chicago, 1989.

Four Classic Ghostly Tales, Academy Chicago, 1993.

Complete Transcripts of the Clarence Thomas-Anita Hill Hearings, Academy Chicago, 1994.

(With J. Papp) Augustus Hare, *Peculiar People: The Story of My Life,* Academy Chicago, 1995.

TRANSLATOR

Hella S. Haasse, *In a Dark Wood Wandering: A Novel of the Middle Ages,* Academy Chicago, 1989.

Haasse, *The Scarlet City: A Novel of 16th Century Italy,* Academy Chicago, 1990.

(With Nina Blinstrub) Haasse, *Threshold of Fire: A Novel of Fifth Century Rome,* Academy Chicago, 1994.

OTHER

Editor, *Arnold Bennett Newsletter;* contributing editor, *English Literature in Translation.*

WORK IN PROGRESS: Uncollecting Cheever, a nonfiction narrative about a literary lawsuit; *Tea and Antipathy,* a nonfiction memoir of swinging London in the sixties.

SIDELIGHTS: Anita Miller told *CA:* "I have been writing since I was in grade school. I became a translator of Dutch literature by accident, when I was sent a poorly translated historical novel by Hella Haasse, and went to a dictionary to attempt to improve the translation; eventually I completely rewrote the English version. This was followed by two other Haasse novels, the English versions of which have been well received by critics and the public. As the moment I am working on two nonfiction projects: I prefer a light, humorous approach to nonfiction. I am also interested in reviving interest in worthwhile but now neglected writers, by writing critical introductions to their work and seeing that they are reprinted."

*   *   *

MILLER, Danny   1947-

PERSONAL: Born November 15, 1947, in Montreal, Quebec, Canada; son of Morris and Maria (Verbruggen) Miller. *Education:* Sir George Williams University, B.Com. (with distinction), 1968; University of Toronto, M.B.A., 1970; McGill University, Ph.D., 1976.

ADDRESSES: Office—4642 Melrose Ave., Montreal, Quebec, Canada H4A 2S9. *E-mail*—Danny.Miller@ hec.ca.

CAREER: Bank of Montreal, Montreal, Quebec, administrative manager, 1968-69, senior project analyst, 1970-72; McGill University, Montreal, Quebec, postdoctoral research associate, 1976-82, associate professor of management, 1982-90, visiting professor, 1990-96. University of Montreal, Ecole des Hautes Etudes Commerciales, associate professor, 1980-86, professor, 1986—. Columbia University, Graduate School of Business, visiting professor, 1996—. Consultant to public and private organizations and foundations.

MEMBER: Macro-Organizational Behavior Society.

AWARDS, HONORS: Grants from Canada Council, Social Science and Humanities Research Council of Canada, Government of Quebec, Federal Department of Industry, Trade, and Commerce, and private industry; Glueck Best Paper Award, Academy of Management, 1995; Wiley Prize, Strategic Management Society, 1995, for most important contribution to the *Strategic Management Journal* for the decade 1980-90.

WRITINGS:

(With Lawrence Gordon and Henry Mintzberg) *Normative Models of Managerial Decision Making,* National Association of Accountants (New York City), 1975.

(With Gordon, Robert Cooper, and Haim Falk) *The Pricing Decision,* National Association of Accountants, 1980.

(With Peter H. Friesen and Mintzberg) *Organizations: A Quantum View,* Prentice-Hall (Englewood Cliffs, NJ), 1984.

(With Manfred F. R. Kets de Vries) *The Neurotic Organization: Diagnosing and Changing Counterproductive Styles of Management,* Jossey-Bass (San Francisco, CA), 1984.

(With Kets de Vries) *Unstable at the Top,* New American Library (New York City), 1988.

The Icarus Paradox, Harper (New York City), 1990.

Contributor to books on business and economics, including *Beyond Method,* edited by Gareth Morgan, Sage Publications, 1983, and *Advances in Applied Business Strategy,* edited by Robert Lamb, JAI

Press, 1988. Contributor of about seventy-five articles and reviews to academic journals, including *Psychology Today, Harper's, Administrative Science Quarterly, Management Science, Academy of Management Journal,* and *Academy of Management Review.* Member of editorial board of *Journal of Management,* 1983-86, *Academy of Management Journal,* 1986-90, *Strategic Management Journal,* 1986—, *Administrative Science Quarterly,* 1987-93, *Industrial Crisis Quarterly,* 1987—, *Organization Science,* 1988—, *Canadian Journal of Administrative Sciences,* 1990—, *Journal of Management Studies,* 1991—, and *International Management,* 1995—.

WORK IN PROGRESS: Research topics include organizational strategy and change; the relationships among executive personality, strategy, decision making, and administrative structure; the differential applicability of paradigms of organizational theory to common types of organizations; organizational simplicity and configuration; and sociological views of markets.

SIDELIGHTS: Danny Miller told *CA:* "The work closest to my heart is *Organizations: A Quantum View.* Its themes are simple, although their articulation in the book is somewhat abstract and technical. First, organizational reality is too complex to be described by generalizing across all organizations. Distinctions must be made and the only way to discover those that are most important is through taxonomy. Second, the variety of organizations is limited by internally reinforcing complementarities among a multitude of managerial, strategic, and structural factors. These form common configurations or gestalts that allow for a better understanding and more accurate prediction of organizational behavior. Finally, since configurations resist change, firms undergo long periods of stability punctuated by brief intervals of revolutionary change as they move quickly to a different configuration.

"Subsequent work with psychoanalyst Manfred Kets de Vries probed into pathological configurations and found that in many cases, their roots could be traced to the personalities of top executives. *The Neurotic Organization: Diagnosing and Changing Counterproductive Styles of Management* lays out the theoretical and conceptual basis for failing, personality-driven firms, and *Unstable at the Top* presents examples of the common failure configurations. These configurations include the bold *dramatic* firms run by impulsive and narcissistic managers who expand operations too rapidly and recklessly; *detached* firms that are really fragmented fiefdoms beset by political infighting; as well as organizations that are *compulsive, suspicious,* or *depressive.* Organizational problems are very deeply embedded in the culture, structure, strategy, and executive personality of organizations, all of which are in varying degrees mutually reinforcing. Change is rarely possible without extensive administrative overhauls, which almost never take place until performance declines manifestly and until top managers depart.

"My last book, *The Icarus Paradox,* details how success itself and the characteristics that cause it lead frequently to an organization's downfall. I identified four very common evolutionary trajectories along which highly successful American businesses developed over the last century. These paths transformed firms from robust and healthy configurations built around an important talent, to forms that lacked resilience and were narrowly obsessive. Most successful firms ultimately became caricatures or more extreme and simpler versions of their former selves. For example, many 'Craftsman' type organizations became compulsive 'Tinkerers,' innovative 'Pioneers' became utopian 'Escapists,' and ambitious 'Builders' became reckless 'Imperialists.' Many well-known firms were portrayed as complex systems with highly interdependent parts and as being much subject to dangerous forces of internal Darwinism and momentum. *Icarus* attracted a good deal of attention from journalists and business executives alike, perhaps because of widespread concern in the early 1990s with the threat of foreign competition and the loss of international competitiveness."

BIOGRAPHICAL/CRITICAL SOURCES:

PERIODICALS

Academy of Management Journal, October, 1984.
Canadian Business, February, 1991.
Financial Times of Canada, January 28, 1991.
Financial Times of London, January 25, 1991.
Globe and Mail (Toronto), February 27, 1988; March 23, 1991.
Maclean's, July 15, 1985.
Montreal Gazette, March 27, 1987.
New York Times, October 28, 1990.
Ottawa Citizen, July 14, 1987; December 16, 1990.
La Presse, November 5, 1995, p. A8.
Revue Gestion, March, 1996, pp. 42-56.
Wall Street Journal, May 12, 1992, p. A22.

MILLETT, Kate   1934-

PERSONAL: Given name Katherine Murray Millett; born September 14, 1934, in St. Paul, MN; daughter of James Albert (an engineer) and Helen (a teacher; maiden name, Feely) Millett; married Fumio Yoshimura (a sculptor), 1965 (divorced, 1985). *Education:* University of Minnesota, B.A. (magna cum laude), 1956; St. Hilda's College, Oxford University, M.A. (first class honors), 1958; Columbia University, Ph.D. (with distinction), 1970. *Politics:* "Left, feminist, liberationist."

ADDRESSES: Home—295 Bowery St., New York, NY 10003. *Agent*—Georges Borchardt, 136 East 57th St., New York, NY.

CAREER: Sculptor, photographer, and painter, 1959—, with numerous exhibitions, including Minami Gallery, Tokyo, Japan, 1963, Judson Gallery, Greenwich Village, NY, 1967, Los Angeles Womens Building, Los Angeles, CA, 1977, and Courtland Jessup Gallery, Provincetown, MA, 1991-94; writer, 1970—. Professor of English at University of North Carolina at Greensboro, 1958; kindergarten teacher in Harlem, NY, 1960-61; English teacher at Waseda University, Tokyo, 1961-63; professor of English and philosophy at Barnard College, New York City, 1964-69; professor of sociology, Bryn Mawr College, 1971; distinguished visiting professor at State College of Sacramento, 1973—. Founder, Women's Art Colony Farm, Poughkeepsie, NY.

MEMBER: National Organization of Women (chair of education committee, 1965-68), Congress of Racial Equality (CORE), Phi Beta Kappa.

WRITINGS:

NONFICTION

Token Learning, National Organization for Women, 1967.
Sexual Politics, Doubleday (Garden City, NY), 1970.
Prostitution Papers, Banc Books (New York City), 1971.
The Basement: Meditations on Human Sacrifice, Simon & Schuster (New York City), 1980, revised edition with new introduction, 1991.
Going to Iran, Coward (New York City), 1981.

The Politics of Cruelty: An Essay on the Literature of Political Imprisonment, Viking (New York City), 1994.

AUTOBIOGRAPHY

Flying, Knopf (New York City), 1974.
Sita, Farrar, Straus (New York City), 1977, revised edition with a new introduction by Millett, Simon & Schuster, 1992.
The Loony-Bin Trip, Simon & Schuster, 1990.
A.D.: A Memoir, Norton (New York City), 1995.

OTHER

(And director) *Three Lives* (documentary film strip), Impact Films, 1971.
(Contributor) *Caterpillars: Journal Entries by 11 Women,* Epona, 1977.

Contributor of essays to numerous magazines, including *Ms.*

SIDELIGHTS: Author and artist Kate Millett has been an acknowledged leader of the women's liberation movement since 1970, when her book *Sexual Politics* was hailed as a manifesto on the inequity of gender distinctions in Western culture. Millett, who has described herself as an "unknown sculptor" who was transformed into a "media nut in a matter of weeks," approaches the topics of feminism and homosexuality from scholarly, personal, and artistic perspectives. Her books, including *Flying, Sita,* and *The Basement: Meditations on Human Sacrifice,* explore the dilemmas and dangers of growing up female in America. According to Susan Paynter in the *Seattle Post-Intelligencer,* "National Leader" is a label that has stuck with Millett since *Sexual Politics* "won her a Ph.D. at Columbia University and the wrath of much of the nation." Paynter adds, however, that "overall social, not just sexual, change is Millett's concern, and she uses her teaching, writing and speaking talents to make her contribution."

Millett was born Katherine Murray Millett in St. Paul, Minnesota in 1934. When she was fourteen, her father left the family and her mother was forced to look for work in order to support the household. Millett recalled in the New York *Post* that despite a college degree, her mother faced nearly insurmountable odds in the postwar job market, eventually finding only commission work selling insurance. "We went hungry," Millett said. "We lived on fear largely." Her family's difficult circumstances notwithstanding, Millett was able to attend the University of Minnesota, where she graduated in 1956 magna cum laude and Phi Beta Kappa distinctions.

With the help of her beloved Aunt Dorothy, Millett then went to Oxford University for two years of graduate study, earning honors grades there as well. A rebellious young woman who enjoyed flouting convention, she decided in 1959 that she wanted to pursue painting and sculpting. Supporting herself by teaching kindergarten in Harlem, New York, Millett went to work crafting art in a Bowery studio. In 1961 she went to Japan, where she taught English at Waseda University and studied sculpting. Her first show was held in Tokyo in 1963, at the Minami Gallery. While in Japan Millett met her future husband, Fumio Yoshimura, also a sculptor.

Returning to the United States in 1963, Millett became a lecturer in English at Barnard College, a division of Columbia University. She also became passionately involved with the burgeoning civil rights movement. First she joined the Congress of Racial Equality (CORE), then, in 1965, the National Organization for Women, where she served as chair of the education committee. Millett's fiery speeches on behalf of women's liberation, abortion reform, and other progressive causes did not endear her to the Barnard administration; she would be relieved of her duties in 1968. When she returned to teaching in 1969, she was hard at work on a doctoral thesis aimed at dissecting the way literature and political philosophy subtly conspire against sexual equality. The thesis, *Sexual Politics,* won her a Ph.D. "with distinction" from Columbia in 1970.

Few doctoral dissertations see publication outside of the academic community. Fewer still become bestsellers. Millett's *Sexual Politics* was a rare success, going through seven printings and selling 80,000 copies in its first year of publication alone. *New York Times Book Review* correspondent Jane Wilson describes the work as "an original and useful book . . . that imposed a moratorium on reiterated, dead-end feminist complaint against the male chauvinist pig in the street. Millett's oblique approach to the problem of women's liberation—concentrating on the incidence of sexism in literature, as opposed to life—made cooler and somewhat more productive discussion possible." Although some reviews of

Sexual Politics were decidedly hostile, most critics found the book a reasonable and scholarly political analysis of the sex war. In the *Saturday Review,* Muriel Haynes describes the work as "an impressively informed, controlled polemic against the patriarchal order, launched in dead seriousness and high spirits, the expression of a young radical sensibility, nurtured by intellectual and social developments that could barely be glimpsed even twenty years ago." *Sexual Politics* lifted Millett from the anonymity of the New York art world and ensconced her as a widely interviewed spokesperson for the growing feminist movement. Within months, Wilson observes, the author "came up hard against the fact that she could not control the image of herself that was projected by the press and on television. . . . Once recognized as an articulate member of the movement, she somehow ceased to be a free agent. In her uncomfortable new spokeswoman status she was urged on by her sisters to do her duty in speaking out on their behalf, while also being browbeaten and harassed for her arrogance and 'elitism in presuming to do so.'"

Millett's autobiographical book *Flying,* published in 1974, details her struggle to remain self-aware, personally happy, and productive in the face of such overwhelming publicity. The central theme of *Flying,* as well as that of 1977's *Sita* and 1995's *A.D.: A Memoir,* is the author's avowed lesbianism and the effect her "coming out" had on her public and private life—especially among family members and lovers. "The publicity that has attached to figures such as Kate Millett in America is unimaginable," notes Emma Tennant in the *Times Literary Supplement.* "Her greatest desire . . . was to reconstruct some sort of personality for herself after the glare of the cameras had begun to fade."

Millett's battle to retain control over her life was a difficult one in the face of the reception of *Sexual Politics,* made even more difficult by the fact that she suffered from manic depressive disorder. Despite her attempts to remain unaffected by the public fallout, the experience would take its toll, not only in terms of her productivity as a writer and artist, but also in terms of her sanity. In 1980, with the support of her lover, Millett took herself off lithium, a drug she had used to control her depression. When her behavior began to become erratic, her family did what they thought was the right thing and had her institutionalized. Millett used her skills as a writer therapeutically and between 1982 and 1985 recorded

her experiences of the drug-enamored American mental health industry. She would publish these revealing journals five years later as *The Loony-Bin Trip.* Comparing its exploration of mental illness to *One Flew over the Cuckoo's Nest* by Ken Kesey, Marilyn Yalom notes of the book in the *Washington Post Book World:* "Millett's prose is rich, her passion compelling. . . . [She] takes us into internal landscapes where no one goes by choice." And as Karen Malpede explains in *Women's Review of Books,* "This is a harrowing, hallucinatory, heroic book. . . . It is written in the style of vision and rhapsody, the tongue of a super-agile mind spilling out rivers of image and thought, emotion, sexual desire, fantasy, historical or linguistic fact."

However, Millett's candidness would receive a mixed response from most mainstream reviewers. Joy Williams writes of *The Loony-Bin Trip* in *Tribune Books:* "The title tells a great deal about the tone of this book—plucky, breezy, a flip bravado masking a quavery confidence. The book actually is quite incoherent; there seems a disinclination here to focus, to shape a truth. . . . There is no sense of the mind examining itself, of the judgement of the present upon the past." Indeed, reviewer Liam Hudson goes beyond a critique of *The Loony-Bin Trip* in his commentary in the *Times Literary Supplement.* Recalling the widespread Freudian-inspired backlash to the feminist position set forth in *Sexual Politics*—"Women like [Millett], it was claimed, were acting out at society's expense the unresolved conflicts implicit in their relations with their fathers"—Hudson maintains that "*The Loony-Bin Trip* reveals that the stock response was uncannily accurate; in fact, it reads at times like a case history made up by a male chauvinist in order to discredit her views. . . . [Millett] describes her realization that, all along, she has been obsessed with her father, and that the nature of her obsession has been incestuous."

In addition to such candidly autobiographical works, Millett has also turned her attention to numerous social ills. In 1980's *The Basement,* she explores a topic that had haunted her for over ten years: the brutal torture-death of an Indianapolis teenager named Sylvia Likens. *The Basement* offers a chilling chronology of Sylvia's final months, from her point of view as well as that of her killers. A *Ms.* reviewer contends that what emerges is "not just a story of an isolated incident, but of the powerlessness of children, the imposition of sexual shame on adolescent girls, [and] the ways in which a woman is used to break the spirit and the body of younger women." In *The Politics of Cruelty: An Essay on the Literature of Political Imprisonment,* Millett expresses her horror at the modern manifestation of the Spanish Inquisition: the torture that is a matter of government policy in almost half the nations of the world. "The knowledge of torture is itself a political act . . . ," she writes in her conclusion. "To speak of the unspeakable is the beginning of action." Finding *The Politics of Cruelty* both engaging and frustrating by turns, critic Elissa Gelfand notes in *Women's Review of Books* that "not everyone will share Millett's belief that exposing and condemning the continued global acquiescence in state-sponsored violence constitute political action. . . . [T]hose looking for a blueprint for collective resistance will not find it in this book." While praising her choice of subject in the *New Republic,* reviewer Michael Scammell takes the author to task for "blurring the boundaries" between real and fictional events, endowing each "with equal ontological weight and validity." Citing Millett's tendency to interweave her reactions to the horrific events that she describes, he credits this "narcissism" with her initial success as a writer. "[A]nd if so it is a terrible pity," adds Scammell, "for if ever there was a subject that demanded discipline, self-restraint and humility, that subject is torture."

Still active in the civil rights arena as well as in the world of the arts, Millett continues to divide her time between her art studio in New York City and a seventy-five acre Christmas tree farm she has established north of Poughkeepsie, New York. The farm also serves as a summer retreat for artists—Millett describes it in *Ms.* as "26,000 trees and the company of good women." She and her guests farm the land in the morning and spend the afternoon hours making prints, paintings, and sculptures, and writing. Reflecting on her hectic years as a crusader for women's rights, Millett tells *Life* magazine: "I hope I pointed out to men how truly inhuman it is for them to think of women the way they do, to treat them that way, to act that way toward them. All I was trying to say was, look, brother, I'm human."

BIOGRAPHICAL/CRITICAL SOURCES:

BOOKS

Authors in the News, Volume 1, Gale (Detroit), 1976.

Smith, Sharon, *Women Who Make Movies,* Hopkinson & Blake, 1975.

PERIODICALS

Books and Bookmen, June, 1971.
Book World, November 22, 1970.
Canadian Forum, November/December, 1970.
Kirkus Reviews, March 1, 1977.
Life, September 4, 1970.
Listener, March 25, 1971.
Los Angeles Times Book Review, September 16, 1979; July 7, 1991, p. 10.
Mademoiselle, February, 1971.
Ms., February, 1981; May, 1988.
Nation, April 17, 1982.
National Review, August 30, 1974.
New Leader, December 14, 1970.
New Republic, August 1, 1970; July 6-13, 1974; July 7-14, 1979; May 16, 1994, pp. 33-38.
New Statesmen & Society, August 5, 1994, p. 38.
Newsweek, July 27, 1970; July 15, 1974.
New Yorker, August 9, 1974.
New York Times, July 20, 1970; August 5, 1970; August 6, 1970; August 27, 1970; September 6, 1970; December 18, 1970; November 5, 1971; May 13, 1977.
New York Times Book Review, September 6, 1970; June 23, 1974; May 29, 1977; September 9, 1979; May 16, 1982; June 3, 1990, p. 12; June 16, 1991, p. 28; August 13, 1995, p. 17.
Observer, November 20, 1994, p. 719.
People, April 2, 1979.
Post (New York City), August 1, 1970.
Ramparts, November, 1970.
Saturday Review, August 29, 1970; June 15, 1974; May 28, 1977.
Seattle Post-Intelligencer, March 4, 1973.
Time, August 31, 1970; December 14, 1970; July 26, 1971; July 1, 1974; May 9, 1977.
Times Literary Supplement, April 9, 1971; October 7, 1977; November 8, 1991, p. 10; September 2, 1994, p. 32.
Tribune Books (Chicago), June 3, 1990, p. 5.
Washington Post, July 30, 1970.
Washington Post Book World, January 8, 1978; May 13, 1990, p. 7.
Women's Review of Books, October, 1990, pp. 7-8; June, 1994, pp. 1, 3-4.

*   *   *

MITCHUM, Hank
See SHERMAN, Jory (Tecumseh)

MONROE, Lyle
  See HEINLEIN, Robert A(nson)

*   *   *

MUNRO, Alice   1931-

PERSONAL: Born July 10, 1931, in Wingham, Ontario, Canada; daughter of Robert Eric (a farmer) and Ann Clarke (Chamney) Laidlaw; married James Armstrong Munro (a bookseller), December 29, 1951 (divorced, 1976); married Gerald Fremlin (a geographer), 1976; children: (first marriage) Sheila, Jenny, Andrea. *Education:* University of Western Ontario, B.A., 1952. *Politics:* New Democratic Party. *Religion:* Unitarian Universalist.

ADDRESSES: Home—P.O. Box 1133, Clinton, Ontario, Canada N0M 1LO. *Office*—Alfred A. Knopf, Inc., 201 East 50th St., New York, NY 10022-7703.

CAREER: Writer. Artist-in-residence, University of Western Ontario, 1974-75, and University of British Columbia, 1980.

MEMBER: Writers Union of Canada.

AWARDS, HONORS: Governor General's Literary Award, 1969, for *Dance of the Happy Shades,* 1979, for *The Beggar Maid: Stories of Flo and Rose,* and 1987, for *The Progress of Love;* Canadian Bookseller's Award, 1972, for *Lives of Girls and Women;* D. Litt., University of Western Ontario, 1976; Canada-Australia Literary Prize, 1977, and 1994; Marian Engel Award, 1986; Lannan Literary Award, W. H. Smith Award, and Canadian Booksellers' Award, all 1995.

WRITINGS:

SHORT STORIES

Dance of the Happy Shades, Ryerson (Toronto), 1968, McGraw (New York City), 1973.
Lives of Girls and Women, McGraw-Hill Ryerson, 1971, McGraw, 1972.
Something I've Been Meaning to Tell You: Thirteen Stories, McGraw-Hill Ryerson, 1974, McGraw, 1974.
Who Do You Think You Are?: Stories, Macmillan (Toronto), 1978, published in the United States as *The Beggar Maid: Stories of Flo and Rose,* Knopf (New York City), 1979.
The Moons of Jupiter: Stories, Macmillan, 1982, Knopf, 1983.
The Progress of Love, Knopf, 1986.
Friend of My Youth: Stories, Knopf, 1991.
Open Secrets: Stories, Knopf, 1994.

Contributor to books, including *Canadian Short Stories,* second series, Oxford University Press, 1968; *Sixteen by Twelve: Short Stories by Canadian Writers,* edited by John Metcalf, Ryerson, 1970; *The Narrative Voice: Stories and Reflections by Canadian Authors,* edited by David Helwig and Joan Harcourt, Oberon (Ottawa, Ontario, Canada), 1974; *Here and Now,* Oberon, 1977; *Personal Fictions,* Oxford University Press, 1977; *Night Light: Stories of Aging,* Oxford University Press, 1986; and *Best American Short Stories, 1989.* Also contributor to periodicals, including *Atlantic, Canadian Forum, Chatelaine, Grand Street, Queen's Quarterly,* and *New Yorker.*

TELEPLAYS

"A Trip to the Coast," in *To See Ourselves* Canadian Broadcasting Corp. (CBC), 1973.
"Thanks for the Ride," in *To See Ourselves,* CBC, 1973.
"How I Met My Husband," in *The Plays the Thing,* CBC, 1974, Macmillan, 1976.
"1847: The Irish," in *The Newcomers: Inhabiting a New Land,* CBC, 1978.

ADAPTATIONS: "Baptising," in *Lives of Girls and Women,* was adapted and filmed for the CBC *Performance* series, 1975.

SIDELIGHTS: Usually concerned with characters living in the small towns of southwestern Ontario, the stories of Alice Munro present "ordinary experiences so that they appear extraordinary, invested with a kind of magic," according to Catherine Sheldrick Ross in *Dictionary of Literary Biography.* Considered one of Canada's major writers, Munro's work is characterized by a refusal to imbue events with moral overtones: her stories offer no resolution, leaving readers to draw their own conclusions regarding the actions of her unpredictable protagonists. "Few people writing today," critic Beverley Slopen claims in *Publishers Weekly,* "can bring a character, a mood or a scene to life with such economy. And [Munro] has an exhilarating ability to make the readers see the familiar with fresh insight and compassion."

In a review of *Dance of the Happy Shades* in the *New York Times Book Review,* contributor Martin Levin writes that "the short story is alive and well in Canada. . . . Alice Munro creates a solid habitat for her fiction—southwestern Ontario, a generation or more in the past—and is in sympathetic vibration with the farmers and townspeople who live there." Peter Prince, writing in the *New Statesman,* calls the stories in *Dance of the Happy Shades* "beautifully controlled and precise. And always this precision appears unstrained. The proportions so exactly fit the writer's thematic aims that in almost every case it seems that really no other words *could* have been used, certainly no more or less."

Reviewing 1974's *Something I've Been Meaning to Tell You* in *Saturday Night,* Kildare Dobbs writes: "Readers who enjoyed the earlier books because they confirmed the reality of the Canadian small-town experience for a certain generation, or because they seemed to reinforce some of the ideology of the women's movement, will find more of the same. . . . All the stories are told with the skill which the author has perfected over the years, narrated with meticulous precision in a voice that is unmistakably Ontarian in its lack of emphasis, its sly humour and willingness to live with a mystery." Joyce Carol Oates argues that readers will be "most impressed by the feeling behind [Munro's] stories—the evocation of emotions, ranging from bitter hatred to love, from bewilderment and resentment to awe." "In all her work," Oates adds in the *Ontario Review,* ". . . there is an effortless, almost conversational tone, and we know we are in the presence of an art that works to conceal itself, in order to celebrate its subject."

Munro "has the ability to isolate the one detail that will evoke the rest of the landscape," writes Urjo Kareda in *Saturday Night,* calling *Who Do You Think You Are?*—published in the United States as *The Beggar Maid: Stories of Flo and Rose*—a "remarkable, immensely pleasurable collection." A volume of related short stories, *Who Do You Think You Are?* introduces readers to Rose—a wealthy, middle-aged divorcee who grew up in poverty in Hanratty, Ontario—as she fits the pieces of her life together. Julia O'Faolain, writing in the *New York Times Book Review,* adds that "Munro captures a kaleidoscope of lights and depths. Through the lens of Rose's eye, she manages to reproduce the vibrant prance of life while scrutinizing the working of her own narrative art. This is an exhilarating collection."

"In *The Progress of Love,* the focus has changed," contends Anne Tyler in the *New Republic.* "The

characters in these 11 stories are concerned not so much with the journey as with the journey's hidden meaning—how to view the journey, how to make sense of it. . . . In the most successful of the stories, the end result is a satisfying click as everything settles precisely into place." Munro "is concerned not only with the different configurations of love that occur in the wake of divorces, separations and deaths, but also with the 'progress of love,' the ways in which it endures or changes through time," explains Michiko Kakutani in the *New York Times.* "The results are pictures of life, or relationships, of love, glimpsed from a succession of mirrors and frames—pictures that possess both the pain and immediacy of life and the clear, hard radiance of art." And Oates declares in the *New York Times Book Review* that "Munro writes stories that have the density—moral, emotional, sometimes historical—of other writer's novels"—a claim echoed by several other critics. "*The Progress of Love* is a volume of unflinching audacious honesty," Oates continues, "uncompromisingly downright in its dissection of the ways in which we deceive ourselves in the name of love; the bleakness of its vision is enriched by the author's exquisite eye and ear for detail. Life is heartbreak, but it is also uncharted moments of kindness and reconciliation."

The success of 1990's *Friend of My Youth: Stories* won Munro significant critical acclaim. In *Time,* Stefan Kanfer compares her to the great Russian short story writer and dramatist, Anton Chekhov, while the *New York Times Book Review* included the collection among their "Best Books of 1990." In *Friend of My Youth,* Munro continues her exploration of the movements of relationships and characters with respect to time. "Movement is central to all Munro's stories," writes Kate Walbert in the *Nation.* "That endings give way to beginnings is the one constant in the lives of these characters." Walbert also asserts that for Munro, "self-identity . . . is a commodity to wage battles for," and for her female protagonists, "self-scrutinization . . . is as habitual as breathing." According to Walbert, the issue for these women is not so much the events of their past— "first marriages, lonely childhoods, severed friendships"—but "who they were in relation to that event." As they trace "their footsteps with . . . How did-I-get-here? wonder," the attempt "to extract the 'I' from a time when who they were was defined *for* them seems a Sisyphean task," since "so many of [their] actions were taken in observance of patriarchal rules."

The 1994 publication of *Open Secrets* prompted Ted Solataroff to call Munro "the mother figure of Canadian fiction" in his review in the *Nation,* placing her writing in the tradition of "the great stylist of 1920's realism, a Katherine Anne Porter brought up to date." Josephine Humphreys, writing in the *New York Times Book Review* also remarks on Munro's stylistic achievements. She notes that every story in *Open Secrets* contains "a startling leap"—in time, place, or point of view—which "explod[es]—the fictional context," thereby allowing Munro to reach "toward difficult truths." For, as Humphreys claims, "Ms. Munro's fiction is out to seize—to apprehend—the mystery of existence within time, 'the unforeseen intervention,' the unique quality of a person's fate."

Like her previous collections, *Open Secrets* is largely concerned with the politics of sex. Solataroff finds that the stories in *Open Secrets* "develop Munro's master theme from various points in time and from dramatically unexpected angles." Praising "A Wilderness Station"—an epistolary story concerning two brothers, an unsolved murder, and a woman's oppression and descent into madness amid a rough-hewn existence on the Canadian frontier,—as "extraordinary writing," he also lauds Munro for her ability to capture what he terms "the male shadow on women's lives": "Carried Away" is a "three-part variation on the theme of being carried away, in its double meaning of love and death"; and "The Albanian Virgin," which first appeared in the *New Yorker,* the critic proclaims a "masterpiece . . . written with the guts of a burglar."

"I never intended to be a short story writer," Munro explains to Mervyn Rothstein of the *New York Times.* "I started writing them because I didn't have time to write anything else—I had three children. And then I got used to writing stories, so I saw my material that way, and I don't think I'll ever write a novel." Indeed, Munro has noted that she feels the coherence required of a novel does not reflect the transitory attitudes and actions she perceives in those around her; a quirky human nature that she depicts to best effect in short fictional vignettes.

A compulsive writer for much of her adult life, Munro views within her work the essence of her ability to transcend ageing. "I'm a little panicked at the idea of stopping—," she told Jeanne McCulloch and Mona Simpson in *Paris Review,* "as if, if I stopped I could be stopped for good. . . . There are parts of a story where the story fails. . . . The story fails but your faith in the importance of doing the story doesn't fail. That it might is the danger."

BIOGRAPHICAL/CRITICAL SOURCES:

BOOKS

Authors in the News, Volume 2, Gale (Detroit), 1976.

Contemporary Literary Criticism, Gale, Volume 6, 1976; Volume 10, 1979; Volume 19, 1981; Volume 50, 1988; Volume 94, 1996.

Dahlie, Hallvard, *Alice Munro and Her Works,* ECW Press (Toronto), 1985.

Dictionary of Literary Biography, Volume 53: *Canadian Writers since 1960,* Gale, 1986.

MacKendrick, Louis K., editor, *Probable Fictions: Alice Munro's Narrative Acts,* ECW Press, 1984.

MacKendrick, *Some Other Reality: Alice Munro's "Something I've Been Meaning to Tell You,"* ECW Press, 1993.

Martin, W. R., *Alice Munro,* University of Alberta Press (Edmonton), 1987.

Redekop, Magdalene, *Mothers and Other Clowns: The Stories of Alice Munro,* Routledge (London), 1992.

Smythe, Karen E., *Figuring Grief: Gallant, Munro, and the Poetics of Elegy,* McGill-Queen's University Press (Montreal), 1992.

PERIODICALS

Belles Lettres, summer, 1990.

Canadian Fiction Magazine, number 43, 1982, pp. 74-114.

Canadian Forum, February, 1969.

Chatelaine, August, 1975, pp. 42-43; July, 1990, p. 10.

Journal of Canadian Studies, spring, 1991, pp. 5-21; summer, 1991, pp. 156-69; summer, 1994, pp. 184-94.

Listener, June 13, 1974; January 29, 1987, pp. 22-23.

Los Angeles Times Book Review, April 1, 1990, p. 4.

Maclean's, September 22, 1986; May 7, 1990, p. 66; October 17, 1994, pp. 46-49.

Meanjin, Volume 54, number 2, 1995, pp. 222-40.

Nation, May 14, 1990, pp. 678-80; November 28, 1994, pp. 665-68.

New Republic, September 15, 1986; pp. 54-55; May 14, 1990, pp. 50-53; November 31, 1994, pp. 51-53.

New Statesman, May 3, 1974.

Newsweek, April 2, 1990, pp. 56-57; September 26, 1994, p. 63.

New Yorker, December 17, 1990, p. 123.

New York Review of Books, May 17, 1990, pp. 38-39; December 22, 1994, pp. 59-60.

New York Times, February 16, 1983; September 3, 1986, p. C22; November 10, 1986; April 17, 1990.

New York Times Book Review, September 23, 1973; September 16, 1979, p. 12; September 14, 1986, pp. 7, 9; March 18, 1990, pp. 1, 31; December 2, 1990, p. 3; September 11, 1994, pp. 1, 36-37.

Ontario Review, fall, 1974; fall/winter, 1979-80, pp. 87-90.

Paris Review, summer, 1994, pp. 227-64.

Publishers Weekly, August 22, 1986; August 1, 1994, p. 72.

Quill and Quire, June, 1990, p. 29.

Saturday Night, July, 1974, p. 28; January/February, 1979, pp. 62-63.

Spectator, October 20, 1990, pp. 37-38; October 29, 1994, pp. 35-36.

Time, January 15, 1973; July 2, 1990, pp. 66-67; October 3, 1994, p. 80.

Times Literary Supplement, November 14, 1994, p. 24.

Washington Post Book World, March 18, 1990, pp. 1-2; September 18, 1994, p. 2.

*   *   *

MUTO, Susan Annette   1942-

PERSONAL: Born December 11, 1942, in Pittsburgh, PA; daughter of Frank and Helen (Scardamalia) Muto. *Education:* Duquesne University, B.A., 1964; University of Pittsburgh, M.A., 1967, Ph.D., 1970. *Politics:* Democrat. *Religion:* Roman Catholic.

ADDRESSES: Home—2223 Wenzell Ave., Pittsburgh, PA 15216. *Office*—Epiphany Association, 948 Tropical Ave., Pittsburgh, PA 15216-3032.

CAREER: United Jewish Federation, Pittsburgh, PA, assistant director of public relations, 1964-65; *Jewish Chronicle,* Pittsburgh, society editor, 1965-66 Duquesne University, Pittsburgh, professor, 1965—, assistant director of Institute of Man, 1966-80, member of institute workshop and conference team, 1971—, director of Institute of Formative Spirituality, 1980-88, Graduate School of Arts and Sciences, adjunct professor of literature and spirituality, 1988—; Epiphany Association (ecumenical lay center), Pittsburgh, executive director, 1988—. Guest lecturer at numerous colleges, universities, work-shops, and seminars throughout the U.S. and Canada. Member of Pittsburgh Advisory Council, Project for Moral and Spiritual Development in the Workplace, 1987—.

MEMBER: Society for Scientific Study of Religion, Edith Stein Guild (lifetime member), Phi Kappa Phi.

WRITINGS:

Approaching the Sacred: An Introduction to Spiritual Reading, Dimension (Wilkes-Barre, PA), 1973.

Steps along the Way: The Path of Spiritual Reading, Dimension, 1975.

A Practical Guide to Spiritual Reading, Dimension, 1976.

The Journey Homeward: On the Road of Spiritual Reading, Dimension, 1977.

Renewed at Each Awakening: The Formative Power of Sacred Words, Dimension, 1979.

Celebrating the Single Life: A Spirituality for Single Persons in Today's World, Doubleday (New York City), 1982.

Blessings That Make Us Be: Living the Beatitudes, Crossroad/Continuum (New York City), 1982.

Pathways of Spiritual Living, Doubleday, 1984.

Meditation in Motion, Doubleday, 1986.

John of the Cross for Today: The Ascent, Ave Maria Press (Notre Dame, IN), 1991.

Womenspirit, Crossroad (New York City), 1992.

John of the Cross for Today: The Dark Night, Ave Maria Press, 1994.

A Practical Guide to Spiritual Reading, St. Bede's Publications (Petersham, MA), 1994.

Words of Wisdom for Our World: The Precautions and Counsels of St. John of the Cross, ICS Publications (Washington, DC), 1996.

WITH ADRIAN VAN KAAM

The Emergent Self, Dimension, 1968.

The Participant Self, Dimension, 1969.

Tell Me Who I Am, Dimension, 1977.

Am I Living a Spiritual Life?, Dimension, 1978.

Practicing the Prayer of Presence, Dimension, 1980.

(Coeditor) *Creative Formation of Life and World,* University Press of America (Lanham, MD), 1982.

Commitment: Key to Christian Maturity, Paulist Press (Mahwah, NJ), 1989.

Commitment: Key to Christian Maturity: A Workbook and Study Guide, Paulist Press, 1991.

Harnessing Stress: A Spiritual Quest, Resurrection Press (Williston Park, NY), 1993.

Healthy and Holy Under Stress: A Royal Road to Wise Living, Resurrection Press, 1993.

Stress and the Search for Happiness: A New Challenge for Christian Spirituality, Resurrection Press, 1993.

The Power of Appreciation, Crossroad, 1993.

Divine Guidance: Seeking to Find and Follow the Will of God, Servant (Ann Arbor, MI)), 1994.

The Commandments: Ten Ways to a Happy Life and a Healthy Soul, Servant, 1996.

Praying with the New Catechism: A Compendium of Its Teachings and Inspirational Treasures, Liguori Publications (Liguori, MO), 1996.

OTHER

Contributor of approximately sixty articles to religious magazines and theology journals, including *Spiritual Life, Cross and Crown,* and *Contemplative Review.* Managing editor of *Envoy* and *Humanitas,* both 1966-79, and of *Studies in Formative Spirituality,* 1979—.

SIDELIGHTS: Susan Muto told *CA:* "After a brief career in journalism and public relations, I became assistant director of the Institute of Man, a position that changed the direction of my life and led me into my present dedication to teaching, speaking, writing, and research in the field of foundational formation. As a single laywoman living my vocation in the world and supported by over twenty-one years of experience at the Institute, I am qualified to address the formation concerns of laity, clergy, and religious. My time is spent doing what I love most—

reading and writing within the framework of the Christian formation tradition, especially as it is recorded in the writings of both pre-and post-Reformation spiritual masters. This work continues in a marvelous way in my new position as executive director of the ecumenical lay center with which I am affiliated in Pittsburgh, the Epiphany Association.

"The aim of one of my best-known books, *Celebrating the Single Life,* is to suggest—on the basis of lived experience—concrete dynamic ways and means in which men and women are formed in this vocation to the single life as fully human, fully Christian people. Most of its contents are applicable to anyone who wants to live a seriously committed, spiritually-grounded single life. Their formation as single persons enables them to participate in a special way in the transformation of self and world.

"The single state is the foundation of all human formation. We are born single (that is, unique), and we die single. In this world, before one chooses any other state of life, he or she is single. Only to the degree that persons accept this blessing of uniqueness can they enjoy the togetherness offered by marriage or community membership. Married couples, who really love one another, know how much the preservation of their relationship depends on respect for their spouse's uniqueness. Vowed religious agree that their solidarity as a community finds its greatest resource in each one's solitude before God. He calls them all to give witness temporarily or for a lifetime to the originating uniqueness that is his gift to every human being."

N-O

NELSON, Esther L. 1928-

PERSONAL: Born September 9, 1928, in New York, NY; daughter of Rubin (a fabric cutter) and Freda (a nurse; maiden name, Seligman) Nelson; married Leon Sokolsky (an art teacher), November 18, 1949; children: Mara, Risa. *Education:* Brooklyn College (now Brooklyn College of the City University of New York), B.A., 1949; New York University, M.A., 1951; attended New School for Social Research and Bank Street College of Education. *Avocational interests:* International travel, "singing and dancing with my granddaughters, . . . and always on the lookout for new songs and dances to add to my collection."

ADDRESSES: Home—3605 Sedgwick Ave., Bronx, NY 10463. *Office*—Dimension Five, P.O. Box 403, Kingsbridge Station, Bronx, NY 10463.

CAREER: Knollwood School, Elmsford, NY, dance teacher, 1953-56; Scarsdale Dance Inc., Scarsdale, NY, dance teacher, 1953-70; Fieldston School, Riverdale, NY, dance teacher, 1958-63; Dimension Five (book distribution, cassette, and recording company), Bronx, NY, partner with composer Bruce Haack, 1963—. Music and dance teacher, 1953-78; teacher at Horace Mann Nursery Years, New York City; lecturer at Brooklyn College of the City University of New York, Shippensburg College, and Millersville State College. Conductor of dance and music workshops throughout the country for teachers and librarians; keynote speaker at meetings of numerous professional organizations throughout the country. Performer on records for children.

MEMBER: American Dance Guild, American Alliance for Health, Physical Education and Recreation (Dance Division), Dance Library (Israel).

AWARDS, HONORS: Nelson's record "Dance, Sing and Listen Again" was named one of the best children's recordings of 1979 by the American Library Association.

WRITINGS:

Dancing Games for Children of All Ages (Instructor Book Club selection), Sterling, 1973.
Movement Games for Children of All Ages (Instructor Book Club selection), Sterling, 1975.
Musical Games for Children of All Ages (Instructor Book Club selection), Sterling, 1976.
Singing and Dancing Games for the Very Young, Sterling, 1977.
Holiday Singing and Dancing Games, Sterling, 1980.
The Silly Songbook, Sterling, 1981.
The Funny Songbook, Sterling, 1984.
The Great Rounds Songbook, Sterling, 1985.
The Fun-to-Sing Songbook, Sterling, 1986.
The World's Best Funny Songs, Sterling, 1988.
Everybody Sing and Dance, Scholastic (New York City), 1989.

Also author of children's record, "Dance, Sing, and Listen Again," 1979. Author of children's records and cassettes with Bruce Haack. Contributor to *Dance Magazine* and *Early Childhood Day Care.*

SIDELIGHTS: Esther L. Nelson once told *CA:* "I have always loved and been involved with music and dance, and so it was natural for me to continue into adulthood and to get a masters degree in dance education. I thank my mother, Freda Nelson, for sharing her love of music with me (two of my books are dedicated to her). My branching into the fields of recordings and books was a natural progression, and both times came at the suggestion of parents of children in my dance classes.

"Dimension Five now has a totally equipped sound studio where we record and produce our records and cassettes. We have sold more than 100,000 of our childrens' music and dance participation records and cassettes to schools, libraries, book clubs, and stores and parents all over the country."

About getting started in her career, Nelson adds: "After getting my master's degree in dance education and starting to teach, I went to the library to look for material and found that it did not exist. I had to create much of my work with young children in music and dance, and so after perfecting my craft I started to write books to share what I had found to be successful. My first book, *Dancing Games for Children of All Ages,* was a huge success with more than thirteen printings, and that encouraged me to go on and write ten more books. They have sold more than half a million copies and are used and enjoyed here and abroad.

"Also founding a cassette company called Dimension Five (the dimension of the imagination) with composer Bruce Haack, we created music and dance participation records as well as cassettes to match five of my songbooks. Being well-known in the childrens' librarian community for my books and cassettes, I began giving workshops for them (in twenty-six states) on how to use music and movement in their story hours. I reached thousands of librarians who were then able to carry my message of the importance of music and dance in the life of the young child directly to their young readers."

*   *   *

NEMEROV, Howard (Stanley)   1920-1991

PERSONAL: Born March 1, 1920, in New York, NY; died of cancer of the esophagus, July 5, 1991, in University City, MO; son of David and Gertrude (Russek) Nemerov; married Margaret Russell, January 26, 1944; children: David, Alexander Michael,

Jeremy Seth. *Education:* Harvard University, A.B., 1941.

CAREER: Hamilton College, Clinton, NY, instructor, 1946-48; Bennington College, Bennington, VT, member of faculty in literature, 1948-66; Brandeis University, Waltham, MA, professor of English, 1966-69; Washington University, St. Louis, MO, visiting Hurst Professor of English, 1969-70, professor of English, 1970-76, Edward Mallinckrodt Distinguished University Professor of English, 1976-90. Visiting lecturer in English University of Minnesota, 1958-59; writer in residence, Hollins College, 1962-64; consultant in poetry, Library of Congress, 1963-64; chancellor, American Academy of Poets, beginning 1976. *Military service:* Royal Canadian Air Force, 1942-44; became flying officer; U.S. Army Air Forces, 1944-45; became first lieutenant.

AWARDS, HONORS: Bowdoin Prize, Harvard University, 1940; *Kenyon Review* fellowship in fiction, 1955; Oscar Blumenthal Prize, 1958, Harriet Monroe Memorial Prize, 1959, Frank O'Hara Memorial Prize, 1971, Levinson Prize, 1975, all from *Poetry* magazine; second prize, *Virginia Quarterly Review* short story competition, 1958; National Institute of Arts and Letters Grant, 1961; Golden Rose Trophy, New England Poetry Club, 1962; Brandeis Creative Arts Award, 1963; D.L., Lawrence University, 1964, and Tufts University, 1969; National Endowment for the Arts Grant, 1966-67; First Theodore Roethke Memorial Award, 1968, for *The Blue Swallows;* St. Botolph's Club (Boston) Prize for Poetry, 1968; Guggenheim fellow, 1968-69; Academy of American Poets fellowship, 1970; O'Hara Prize, 1971; Pulitzer Prize and National Book award, 1978, and Bollingen Prize, 1981, Yale University, all for *The Collected Poems of Howard Nemerov;* the first Aiken Taylor Award for Modern Poetry, 1987, from *Sewanee Review* and University of the South; National Medal of the Arts, 1987, for promoting "excellence, growth, support and availability of the arts in the United States"; poet laureate of the United States, 1988-90; honorary degree from Washington and Lee University.

WRITINGS:

The Melodramatists (novel), Random House (New York City), 1949.
Federigo: Or the Power of Love (novel), Little, Brown (Boston), 1954.
The Homecoming Game (novel), Simon & Schuster (New York City), 1957.

A Commodity of Dreams and Other Stories, Simon & Schuster, 1959.

(Editor and author of introduction) Henry Wadsworth Longfellow, *Longfellow: Selected Poetry,* Dell (New York City), 1959.

Poetry and Fiction: Essays, Rutgers University Press (New Brunswick, NJ), 1963.

Journal of the Fictive Life (autobiography), Rutgers University Press, 1965, reprinted with a new preface, University of Chicago Press (Chicago), 1981.

(Editor and contributor) *Poets on Poetry,* Basic Books (New York City), 1965.

(Editor) Marianne Moore, *Poetry and Criticism,* Adams House & Lowell House Printers, 1965.

Stories, Fables and Other Diversions, David R. Godine, 1971.

Reflexions on Poetry and Poetics, Rutgers University Press, 1972.

Figures of Thought: Speculations on the Meaning of Poetry and Other Essays, David R. Godine, 1978.

New and Selected Essays, with foreword by Kenneth Burke, Southern Illinois University Press (Carbondale), 1985.

The Oak in the Acorn: On Remembrance of Things Past and on Teaching Proust, Who Will Never Learn, Louisiana State University Press (Baton Rouge), 1987.

A Howard Nemerov Reader, University of Missouri Press (Columbia), 1991.

POETRY

The Image and the Law, Holt (New York City), 1947.

Guide to the Ruins, Random House, 1950.

The Salt Garden, Little, Brown, 1955.

Small Moment, Ward Ritchie Press, 1957.

Mirrors and Windows, University of Chicago Press, 1958.

New and Selected Poems, University of Chicago Press, 1960.

Endor: Drama in One Act (verse play; also see below), Abingdon (Nashville), 1961.

The Next Room of the Dream: Poems and Two Plays (includes the verse plays "Endor" and "Cain"), University of Chicago Press, 1962.

The Blue Swallows, University of Chicago Press, 1967.

A Sequence of Seven with a Drawing by Ron Slaughter, Tinker Press, 1967.

The Winter Lightning: Selected Poems, Rapp & Whiting, 1968.

The Painter Dreaming in the Scholar's House (limited edition), Phoenix Book Shop (New York City), 1968.

Gnomes and Occasions, University of Chicago Press, 1973.

The Western Approaches: Poems, 1973-75, University of Chicago Press, 1975.

The Collected Poems of Howard Nemerov, University of Chicago Press, 1977.

Sentences, University of Chicago Press, 1980.

Inside the Onion, University of Chicago Press, 1984.

Trying Conclusions: New and Selected Poems, 1961-1991, University of Chicago Press, 1991.

Also author of *War Stories: Poems about Long Ago and Now,* 1987. Contributor of poems to *Five American Poets,* edited by Ted Hughes and Thom Gunn, Faber, 1963, and numerous periodicals, including *Harvard Advocate, Kenyon Review, Poetry, New Yorker, Nation* and *Polemic.*

SOUND RECORDINGS

"The Poetry of Howard Nemerov" (two audio cassettes), Jeffrey Norton, 1962.

"Howard Nemerov," Tapes for Readers, 1978.

"Howard Nemerov," Tapes for Readers, 1979.

(Contributor of introduction) "Surly Verses for the Holidays: From D. H. Lawrence to E. E. Cummings and Far Beyond," read by Reed Whittemore, Library of Congress, 1989.

"Science and Stories: A Lecture," Library of Congress, 1989.

"Language, Nonsense and Poetry," Library of Congress, 1989.

"Prosser Gifford Interviews Howard Nemerov," Library of Congress, 1990.

"The Poet and the Poem," Library of Congress, 1990.

"Howard Nemerov Reading from His Work," Library of Congress, 1990.

"The Junction on a Warm Afternoon" (musical score), music by William Bolcom, poem by Howard Nemerov, E. B. Marks, 1990.

OTHER

Associate editor of *Furioso,* 1946-51. Contributor of essays, introductions or commentaries to several books. Contributor of essays, articles and reviews to literary journals, including *Hudson Review, Poetry, Atlantic, Partisan Review,* and *Virginia Quarterly Review.* Contributor of short fiction to *Harvard*

Advocate, Story, Esquire, Carleton Miscellany, Reporter, and *Virginia Quarterly Review.*

ADAPTATIONS: The Homecoming Game was adapted as a play entitled *Tall Story* and filmed by Warner Bros. in 1959.

SIDELIGHTS: Howard Nemerov was a highly acclaimed poet often cited for the range of his capabilities and subject matter, "from the profound to the poignant to the comic," James Billington remarked in his frequently quoted announcement of Nemerov's appointment to the post of United States poet laureate. A distinguished professor at Washington University in St. Louis from 1969 to 1990, Nemerov wrote poetry and fiction that managed to engage the reader's mind without becoming academic, many reviewers reported. Though his works showed a consistent emphasis on thought—the process of thinking and ideas themselves—his poems related a broad spectrum of emotion and a variety of concerns. As Joyce Carol Oates remarked in the *New Republic,* "Romantic, realist, comedian, satirist, relentless and indefatigable brooder upon the most ancient mysteries—Nemerov is not to be classified." Writing in the study *Howard Nemerov,* Peter Meinke stated that these contrasting qualities are due to Nemerov's "deeply divided personality." Meinke pointed out that Nemerov himself spoke of a duality in his nature in *Journal of the Fictive Life* in which he said that "it has seemed to me that I must attempt to bring together the opposed elements of my character represented by poetry and fiction." Commented Meinke, "These 'opposed elements' in Howard Nemerov's character are reflected in his life and work: in the tensions between his romantic and realistic visions, his belief and unbelief, his heart and mind."

If Nemerov harbored impulses toward both poetry and fiction, he expressed them as opposites suspended in balanced co-existence rather than dissonance. A direct expression of this equilibrium is his poem "Because You Asked about the Line between Prose and Poetry." Wrote *Poetry* contributor Mary Kinzie, "It is about rain gradually turning into snow, but still acting like rain (only somehow lighter and thicker), until—there is suddenly snow flying instead of rain falling." As the poem states, "There came a moment that you couldn't tell. / And then they clearly flew instead of fell." Kinzie continued, "What clearly flew? Clearly, the pieces of snow, now soft and crowded flakes," but these words also leave room to suggest the sudden upward flight of some dark swallows Nemerov had mentioned earlier in the poem. These birds, Kinzie said, are "the suggestive warrant for any kind of flight. . . . So is the poem launched. Not going straight to its goal—not falling like rain—a poem imperceptibly thickens itself out of the visible stream of prose." The choice—the crossing of the line that separates opposing impulses—is not consciously traceable, Nemerov told Melinda Miller of the *Washington Post:* "It's like a fairy tale. You're allowed to do it as long as you don't know too much about it."

The Harvard graduate's first book of poems, *The Image and the Law,* characteristically is based on opposed elements, on a duality of vision. As F. C. Golffing explained in *Poetry,* "Mr. Nemerov tells us that he dichotomizes the 'poetry of the eye' and the 'poetry of the mind,' and that he attempts to exhibit in his verse the 'ever-present dispute between two ways of looking at the world.'" Some reviewers have found that this dichotomy leads to a lack of coherence in the verse. *New York Times* writer Milton Crane, for example, felt that the poems "unfortunately show no unity of conception such as their author attributes to them." The book was also criticized for being derivative of earlier modern poets such as T. S. Eliot, W. H. Auden, W. B. Yeats, and Wallace Stevens.

After reading *Guide to the Ruins,* Nemerov's second book of verse, *Saturday Review* contributor I. L. Salomon asserted that Nemerov "suffers from a dichotomy of personality." Within Nemerov, Salomon claimed, an "instinct for perfection" and unity contends with a modern "carelessness in expression." Yet Crane noticed not so much modern "carelessness" as praiseworthy modern sensibility; he believed that *Ruins* "is the work of an original and sensitive mind, alive to the thousand anxieties and agonies of our age." And Meinke contended that it is Nemerov's "modern awareness of contemporary man's alienation and fragmentation combined with a breadth of wit in the eighteenth century sense of the word" which "sets Nemerov's writing apart from other modern writers."

Like *Image and the Law* and *Guide to the Ruins, The Salt Garden,* when published, drew criticism for being derivative. "The accents of Auden and [John Crowe] Ransom," observed Louis Untermeyer, "occasionally twist his utterance into a curious poetic patois." Similarly, Randall Jarrell found that "you can see where he found out how to do some of the things he does—he isn't, as yet, a very individual poet." Years later, when asked if his work had changed in character or style, Nemerov replied in *Poets on Poetry,* "In style,. . . for I began and for a long time remained imitative, and poems in my first books . . . show more than traces of admired modern masters—Eliot, Auden, Stevens, [E. E.] Cummings, Yeats." Meinke, too, maintained that Nemerov in his early work was "writing Eliot, Yeats, and Stevens out of his system." Yet at the same time that Untermeyer and Jarrell faulted Nemerov for his imitation, like other readers, they were impressed by his growth as a poet. Jarrell commented that "as you read *The Salt Garden* you are impressed with how much the poet has learned, how well he has developed," while Hayden Carruth remarked, "Nemerov's new book is his third . . . and his best; steady improvement, I take it, is one sign of formidable ability."

The Salt Garden, many critics felt, marked the beginning of other changes in Nemerov's work, as well. Meinke observed that in this volume "Nemerov has found his most characteristic voice: a quiet intelligent voice brooding lyrically on the strange beauty and tragic loneliness of life." In a review of *The Collected Poems of Howard Nemerov,* Willard Spiegelman, like Meinke, discovered in the poems from *The Salt Garden* "Nemerov's characteristic manner and tone." Spiegelman still found opposed elements, but in balance; he described Nemerov's manner as "genuinely Horatian according to Auden's marvelous definition of looking at 'this world with a happy eye / but from a sober perspective.' Nemerov's *aurea mediocritas* [golden mean] sails between philosophical skepticism . . . and social satire on one side, and, on the other, an open-eyed, child-like appreciation of the world's miracles."

Another change that began with *The Salt Garden* and continued in *Mirrors and Windows, The Next Room of the Dream,* and *The Blue Swallows* was Nemerov's growing concern with nature. In 1966, Nemerov wrote in *Poets on Poetry* of the impact of the natural world on his work: "During the war and since, I have lived in the country, chiefly in Vermont, and while my relation to the landscape has been contemplative rather than practical, the landscape nevertheless has in large part taken over my poetry." This interest in the landscape has led Chad Walsh to say of *The Blue Swallows* that "in its quiet lyricism and sensitivity to nature it suggests Robert Frost." The comparison to Frost, suggested by many other critics, was also made on the grounds that Nemerov, like Frost, brought philosophical issues into his poetry. As he said in *Poets on Poetry,* he was not so

much an observer of nature as its medium, bringing into speech "an unknowably large part of a material world whose independent existence might be likened to that of the human unconscious, a sleep of causes, a chaos of the possible-impossible." Phrasing it differently in the poem "A Spell before Winter," Nemerov wrote, "And I speak to you now with the land's voice, / It is the cold, wild land that says to you / A knowledge glimmers in the sleep of things: / The old hills hunch before the north wind blows."

A feature of the poems more frequently pointed out by critics is a witty, ironic manner and a serious, perhaps pessimistic, philosophy. James Dickey observed the seriousness that underlies Nemerov's wit. Nemerov, Dickey maintained, "is one of the wittiest and funniest poets we have. . . . But the enveloping emotion that arises from his writing is helplessness: the helplessness we all feel in the face of the events of our time, and of life itself. . . . And beneath even this feeling is a sort of hopelessly involved acceptance and resignation which has in it more of the truly tragic than most poetry which deliberately sets out in quest of tragedy." At the same time, Julia A. Bartholomay detected a somewhat different dichotomy. She contended that in Nemerov's poetry a basic dualism "underlies the two different . . . attitudes which appear consistently in the poet's work. On the one hand, he is very much the witty, sophisticated man of his time. . . . Nemerov often views life with a humorous but bitter irony. . . . On the other hand, the poet perceives the world ontologically. His experience may be philosophical, subjective, lyrical, or even mystical." Bartholomay argued that Nemerov's double view was expressed in his poetry through the use of paradox. The paradoxes reflect the "divisiveness, fragmentation, complexity, and absurdity of modern existence."

Not all critics applauded the tragic irony which Dickey and many others have found in Nemerov's poetry. Carruth, for example, commented: "No one would deny that famous and marvelous poems have been written in the manner of poetic irony. . . . But today this manner is an exceedingly tired poetic attitude. . . . And Nemerov's tired attitude is revealed in tired poetry: spent meters, predictable rhymes, and metaphors haggard with use." *New York Times* critic Thomas Lask also objected to Nemerov's irony, but for different reasons. He believed that in *The Blue Swallows* it has turned bitter, expressing "loathing and contempt for man and his work." In contrast to both these views, Laurence Lieberman, writing in the *Yale Review,* felt that "Howard Nemerov has perfected the poem as an instrument for exercising brilliance of wit. Searching, discursive, clear-sighted, he has learned to make the poem serve his relaxed manner and humane insights so expertly, I can only admire the clean purposefulness of his statements, his thoughtful care, the measure and grace of his lines."

However strong his ironic voice, Nemerov mellowed with age, according to many reviewers. Meinke claimed that "Nemerov has progressed steadily in his poetry to a broader, more tolerant view, less bitter and more sad." Likewise, Harvey Gilman found in a review of *Gnomes and Occasions* that "Nemerov's tone modulates as saving wit gives way to wistful contemplation, reminiscence, and prayer. The mask of irony is lowered and Nemerov writes a more sustained elegiac verse. . . . True, the epigrammatic manner remains in evidence . . . but the wit is here tinged with whimsy and warmth." Similarly, Spiegelman observed: "Nemerov, growing old, becomes younger as he adopts the manner of an ancient sage. Cynicism barely touches his voice; the occasional sardonic moments are offset by feeling and sympathy. . . . In the 40's and 50's Nemerov was rabbinically fixated on sin and redemption. What was, early on, a source of prophetic despair . . ., becomes in the poems of his middle age the cause of poetic variety and energy, metaphysical delight, and emotional equilibrium." And Helen Vendler discerned in a critique of *Collected Poems* that as "the echoes of the *grand maitres* fade, the poems get steadily better. The severity of attitude is itself chastened by a growing humanity, and the forms of the earth grow ever more distinct."

Gnomes and Occasions indulged Nemerov's penchant for short, aphoristic verses in which the images carry the burden of persuasion. In these "gnomes," Nemerov achieved a "Biblical resonance," said Kenneth Burke in his introduction to Nemerov's early poems, which are still ranked with the best postwar American poetry. More than one critic has referred to Nemerov's writings as wisdom literature. For example, Helen Vendler reported in *Part of Nature, Part of Us* that Nemerov's "mind plays with epigram, gnome, riddle, rune, advice, meditation, notes, dialectic, prophecy, reflection, views, knowledge, questions, speculation—all the forms of thought. His wishes go homing to origins and ends." Scholars linked this stylistic tendency to the poet's Jewish heritage. Meinke described the early Nemerov as a "non-practicing Jew engaged in a continual dialogue with Christianity . . . testing its relevance

in the modern world." In addition to the influence of Dante and St. Augustine, that of W. B. Yeats left its mark on the poems, said *Dictionary of Literary Biography* contributor Robert W. Hill, "not so much in form or style as in subject matter and in a decidedly religious quality of the language." For instance, one of Nemerov's definitions of poetry given in "Thirteen Ways of Looking at a Skylark" stated: "In the highest range the theory of poetry would be the theory of the Incarnation, which seeks to explain how the Word became Flesh."

Nemerov, however, did not reconstruct the world with imagination as other poets have done. Explained Hill, "While Yeats went about his way inventing new religion and culling the cabala for hints and signs, Nemerov's poems show him to be a critic of the secularizers: coming from the Jewish tradition, his sense of the decline of religion is not so easily pacified by new contrivances as Yeats's was. But the connections Nemerov feels with the seers of the past are clearly modern, clearly attached with the threads of the naturalistic modes, the beliefs in touchable things rather than in the untouchable." Thus Nemerov used acts of the imagination not to alter the world but to make it known. To the extent that this process is magical, "Our proper magic is the magic of language," claimed the poet, according to *Contemporary Authors Bibliography Series* contributor Gloria Young.

Poetry as a link between the material and spiritual worlds emerged as the theme of *Sentences*. In this volume, Nemerov achieved thematic coherence by organizing the poems into three sections, "Beneath," "Above," and "Beyond." Bonnie Costello, writing in *Parnassus: Poetry in Review,* related that the sections "mark off, respectively, poems of low diction and subject (our social sphere of sex and power), poems of higher diction and subject (metaphysics and poetry), and those of middle diction and subject (our origin and fate)." Critics approved the last two sections more than the first, which they claimed was beneath the level of quality they had come to expect from Nemerov. The section castigated the purveyors of low artistic, social and political values, related Ronald Baughman in the *Dictionary of Literary Biography Yearbook, 1983:* "The reviewers damn the writer for accomplishing the goal which he has set for himself—the portrayal of man acting beneath dignity." Looking over the entire book, Baughman offered, "*Sentences* contains a wide range of poems, extending from the mocking, bitter verse of section one to the interesting but restrained appraisals of section two to the deeply moving contemplations of section three. The volume's theme—the order art gives to the randomness of life—develops with this movement from beginning to end. Nemerov's title is reminiscent of Stephen Spender's poem 'Subject: Object: Sentence,' in which Spender states, 'A sentence is condemned to stay as stated—/ As in *life-sentence, death-sentence,*' for example. As Howard Nemerov dramatizes his life and death sentences, he reveals his attempts to connect, through the power of his art, with the world below, nature above, and the spirit beyond."

The Collected Poems of Howard Nemerov presented verse from all of the earlier volumes and its publication in 1977 spurred a re-evaluation of Nemerov's work. Phoebe Pettingell noted in the *New Leader* that the book showed "a gradual intensifying of a unified perspective," the poet's obsession with the theme of "man's sometimes tragic, sometimes ludicrous relation to history, death and the universe." Robert B. Shaw, writing in the *Nation,* related, "To what extent, he repeatedly wonders, is the world we see our own creation? . . . Is the poem a mirror reflecting the appearances of the world in responsible detail, or is it a window, a transparent medium through which we may see . . .? Or might it begin in one and with care and luck become the other? Nemerov never fully unravels these aesthetic and metaphysical knots. They provide him the material for endless reflection." Tom Johnson offered this assessment in the *Sewanee Review:* "Nemerov has written more incisively of science and its place in our imaginations than anyone else has yet managed to do in good (or even readable) poems. . . . The breadth of accomplishment and depth of insight are one's most striking impressions from first readings of the *Collected Poems,* enriched later by the humor, in intricacy, the grace." Shaw recommended *Collected Poems* to readers whose interest in poetry stems more from curiosity than from experience with the genre. "Such readers," Shaw said, "can expect to be charmed by the easy flow of Nemerov's reasoned discourse, and moved by those fine moments in his poems in which reason is overcome by awe."

Several reviewers also found much of value in *Trying Conclusions: New and Selected Poems, 1961-1991,* published the year of Nemerov's death. Sidney Burris, writing in the *Southern Review,* found the collection significant because, in addition to containing a dozen new poems, it provided an excellent selection of Nemerov's work beginning with *The*

Next Room of the Dream, with *Collected Poems* containing much of the poet's earlier output and therefore functioning as a "companion volume." Burris went on, "The poetry selected for *Trying Conclusions* issues from what Nemerov continually described as a simple respect for an audience who has—or at least ought to have, he always added—more pressing things to do than read his poems. . . . The deepest wish of Nemerov's poetry, particularly of the poems gathered together in *Trying Conclusions,* is that his poems aim ultimately to dignify the world of our recognizably common experience." D. G. Myers, in a review for *Commentary,* deemed the volume's short poems, "in which [Nemerov] wonders about the things in this world which are least wondered about: waiting rooms . . . people driving fast cars . . . pockets," to be the "most characteristic" of the poet's work, while the most powerful poems were "the longer essayistic ones in which he speculates on the theme of art." Christopher Benfey, writing in *Partisan Review,* found something to appreciate in all the poems—"even the slacker, longer ones"—and expressed a "special gratitude for the ten or fifteen that one promises oneself to remember and return to." Several reviewers also saw in the collection the humor and versatility frequently associated with Nemerov. Phoebe Pettingell, in *Sewanee Review,* noted the poet's "mean, satirical wit," and pointed out that the title, *Trying Conclusions,* could be interpreted in many ways, in keeping with Nemerov's penchant for plays on words. Myers commented that Nemerov "never shied away from trying something new, experimenting with forms and subjects."

Nemerov's prose has also been commended, especially for displaying an irony and wit similar to that of his poems. His novels, as Meinke remarked, "like his poems,. . . are basically pessimistic. The condition of man is not an enviable one: we act foolishly and understand imperfectly. Nemerov's dark viewpoint, which in his poetry is redeemed by beauty,. . . in his fiction is redeemed by humor." Meinke termed *The Melodramatists* "a highly successful first novel," and in the *Nation* Diana Trilling seconded him, commenting that after a slow start, it is "a considerable first novel—literate and entertaining, with a nice satiric barb." *Federigo: Or the Power of Love* and *The Homecoming Game* were also well received. For example, Richard Sullivan called the latter book a "beautifully controlled satire" with characters "rendered with authentic irony," and *Atlantic Monthly* reviewer C. J. Rolo found that it has "wit, dash, and point."

Through the characters in these novels, Nemerov explored "the consequences of the overactive imagination," wrote Carl Rapp in the *Dictionary of Literary Biography: Novelists since World War II.* Characters with romantic expectations of finding meaningful action and self-realization amid the social pressures of their times instead realize that they are the victims of their own fantasies. Thus, the novels, like the poetry, comment on the relationship between imagination and reality.

Nemerov published his last novel, *The Homecoming Game* (about a professor who discovers his limits when faced with opposing groups on campus), in 1957. Rapp suggested, "Nemerov has perhaps come to feel that the novelist himself, with his own incorrigible tendency to fantasize melodramatic scenes and situations, presents a spectacle as ridiculous as that of his own characters. In recent poems such as 'Novelists' and 'Reflexions of a Novelist,' he observes that it is, of course, the novelist who is preeminently the man with the overactive imagination, the egomaniac, the voyeur." Nemerov told Robert Boyers in a *Salmagundi* interview that he left off being a novelist when Bennington College chose to retain him as its poet and hired Bernard Malamud to be its novelist.

Though through with the novel form, Nemerov continued to work with prose in short stories and literary criticism. Like his poetry and fiction, Nemerov's essays won him the respect of many well-known writers and critics. To *Figures of Thought: Speculations on the Meaning of Poetry and Other Essays,* Benjamin DeMott responded: "Taken as a whole . . . these 'speculations' are uncommonly stimulating and persuasive. . . . [This book] communicates throughout a vivid sense of the possibility of a richer kind of knowing in all areas than we're in the process of settling for. . . . Like the high art it salutes, it hums with the life of things." Moreover, Joyce Carol Oates added: "The book is a marvelous one, rewarding not only for what it tells us about poetry in general . . ., but for what it tells us about the processes of the imagination. Nemerov is, quite simply, a brilliant mind."

New and Selected Essays, a later collection of essays spanning thirty years of Nemerov's criticism, was also considered valuable upon publication. "It is the *texture* of [Nemerov's] thinking that is exhilarating, and not the Grand Propositions—though one of the latter (his favorite) is sturdy indeed: 'Poetry is getting something right in language.' . . . The theoretical essays and the studies of particular writers are the

ones most wealthy in serviceable lore," offered Richard Wertime in the *Yale Review.* Deborah S. Murphy and Gloria Young stated in the *Contemporary Authors Bibliography Series* that since "Nemerov is a poet who is continually changing and growing, becoming more complex in subject matter and apparently simpler in style," the body of his work has only begun to receive the serious critical attention it merits.

Several of Nemerov's essays and works of fiction, along with a smattering of poems, were collected in 1991 into *A Howard Nemerov Reader. Southern Review*'s Sidney Burris found the volume important chiefly because of its reprint of *Federigo: Or the Power of Love* as the rest of its contents could be found in other collections; he added, however, that the book served as a testament to Nemerov's ability "to provide poetry, criticism, and fiction, all of an extraordinarily high degree of sophistication." Doug Anderson, writing in the *New York Times Book Review,* said the book would be valuable to those who know Nemerov only as a poet, as "his fiction . . . allows him a much wider emotional and imaginative range than do his poems, and his essays . . . reveal Mr. Nemerov as brilliantly incisive, if occasionally curmudgeonly." And in *Poetry,* Robert B. Shaw pronounced, "This volume amply serves its purpose as an introduction to the spectrum of Nemerov's writing in its several forms."

Nemerov's books brought him many major awards for poetry, including the National Book Award, the Pulitzer Prize, the Bollingen Prize, and the National Medal of Art. Regarding his fame, he told Jake Thompson of the *Chicago Tribune,* "You do the best you can and really don't worry about immortality all that much, especially as you have to be dead to achieve it. . . . Oh, you want praise and recognition and above all money. But if that was your true motive, you would have done something else. All this fame and honor is a very nice thing, as long as you don't believe it."

BIOGRAPHICAL/CRITICAL SOURCES:

BOOKS

Bartholomay, Julia A., *The Shield of Perseus: The Vision and Imagination of Howard Nemerov,* University of Florida Press (Gainesville), 1972.
Boyers, Robert, editor, *Contemporary Poetry in America: Essays and Interviews,* Schocken (New York City), 1974.

Boyers, editor, *Excursions: Selected Literary Essays,* Kennikat Press (Port Washington, NY), 1975.

Contemporary Authors Bibliography Series, Volume 2, Gale (Detroit), 1986.

Contemporary Literary Criticism, Gale, Volume 2, 1974, Volume 6, 1976, Volume 9, 1978, Volume 36, 1986.

DeMott, Robert J., and Sanford E. Marovits, editors, *Artful Thunder: Versions of the Romantic Tradition in American Literature in Honor of Howard P. Vincent,* Kent State University Press (Kent, OH), 1975.

Dickey, James, *Babel to Byzantium,* Farrar, Straus (New York City), 1968.

Dictionary of Literary Biography, Gale, Volume 5: *American Poets since World War II,* 1980, Volume 6: *American Novelists since World War II, Second Series,* 1980.

Dictionary of Literary Biography Yearbook, 1983, Gale, 1984.

Donoghue, Denis, editor, *Seven American Poets from MacLeish to Nemerov,* University of Minnesota Press (Minneapolis), 1975.

Duncan, Bowie, editor, *The Critical Reception of Howard Nemerov: A Selection of Essays and a Bibliography,* Scarecrow (Metuchen, NJ), 1971.

Howard, Richard, editor, *Preferences,* Viking (New York City), 1974.

Hungerford, Edward, editor, *Poets in Progress: Critical Prefaces to Ten Contemporary Americans,* Northwestern University Press (Evanston, IL), 1962.

Hutton, Charles, editor, *Imagination and the Spirit: Essays in Literature and the Christian Faith Presented to Clyde S. Kilby,* Eerdmans (Grand Rapids, MI), 1971.

Kumin, Maxine, *To Make a Prairie: Essays on Poets, Poetry and Country Living,* University of Michigan Press (Ann Arbor), 1979.

Labrie, Ross, *Howard Nemerov,* Twayne (Boston), 1980.

Lieberman, Laurence, editor, *Unassigned Frequencies: American Poetry in Review, 1964-77,* University of Illinois Press (Champaign), 1977.

Maxfield, Melinda R., editor, *Images and Innovations: Update 1970's,* Center for the Humanities, Converse College, 1979.

Meinke, Peter, *Howard Nemerov,* University of Minnesota Press, 1968.

Mills, William, *The Stillness in Moving Things: The World of Howard Nemerov,* Memphis State University Press (Memphis, TN), 1975.

Nemerov, Howard, *The Next Room of the Dream,* University of Chicago Press (Chicago), 1962.

Nemerov, *Poets on Poetry,* Basic Books, 1966.

Nemerov, *Journal of the Fictive Life* (autobiography), Rutgers University Press, 1965, reprinted with a new preface, University of Chicago Press, 1981.

Nemerov, *New and Selected Essays,* Southern Illinois University Press (Carbondale), 1985.

Potts, Donna L., *Howard Nemerov and Objective Idealism: The Influence of Owen Barfield,* University of Missouri Press, 1994.

Rosenthal, M. L., *The Modern Poets: A Critical Introduction,* Oxford University Press (New York City), 1961.

Vendler, Helen, *Part of Nature, Part of Us: Modern American Poets,* Howard University Press (Washington, DC), 1980.

Waggoner, Hyatt, *American Poets from the Puritans to the Present,* Houghton (Boston), 1968.

Wyllie, Diana E., *Elizabeth Bishop and Howard Nemerov: A Reference Guide,* Hall (Boston), 1983.

PERIODICALS

America, October 5, 1974; April 8, 1978; February 1, 1986; May 7, 1988.

American Book Review, March, 1979.

American Poetry Review, May/June, 1975; January, 1976.

American Scholar, summer, 1959; summer, 1968; autumn, 1993, pp. 551-561.

Antioch Review, spring, 1963; summer, 1987.

Atlantic Monthly, November, 1954; May, 1957; November, 1961; February, 1968.

Chicago Review, Volume XXV, number 1, 1973.

Chicago Tribune, July 4, 1988.

Chicago Tribune Book World, March 29, 1981.

Christian Science Monitor, January 29, 1964.

Commentary, November, 1991, p. 60.

Commonweal, February 13, 1959.

Encounter, February, 1969.

Georgia Review, winter, 1976; fall, 1985.

Harper's, September, 1963.

Hudson Review, summer, 1963; spring, 1964; spring, 1976; autumn, 1984.

Island, fall, 1966.

Journal of Aesthetics and Art Criticism, spring, 1979.

Kenyon Review, winter, 1952.

London Review of Books, February 21-February 27, 1985.

Los Angeles Times, June 19, 1987.

Massachusetts Review, spring, 1981.

Modern Language Notes, December, 1978.

Nation, July 13, 1963; November 8, 1975; February 25, 1978; November 11, 1978.

New Leader, December 5, 1977; April 30, 1984; December 30, 1991.

New Republic, June 23, 1958; April 28, 1973; April 8, 1978.

New Yorker, March 14, 1959; April 1, 1961; September 18, 1989, p. 133.

New York Herald Tribune Book Review, March 1, 1959; July 30, 1961.

New York Times, August 1, 1947; May 21, 1950; March 3, 1957; March 30, 1968; April 28, 1968; December 26, 1978; June 5, 1987; June 11, 1987; May 18, 1988.

New York Times Book Review, April 3, 1949; May 21, 1950; July 17, 1955; February 8, 1959; March 1, 1959; January 8, 1961; July 21, 1963; November 8, 1975; December 18, 1977; April 16, 1978; April 28, 1991, p. 15.

Parnassus: Poetry in Review, fall/winter, 1973; spring/summer, 1975; spring/summer, 1976; fall/winter, 1977; fall/winter, 1981.

Partisan Review, winter, 1961; winter, 1965; winter, 1994, pp. 176-180.

Poet and Critic, number 11, 1979.

Poetry, November, 1947; June, 1955; December, 1958; September, 1963; March, 1965; February, 1967; December, 1976; September, 1978; September, 1981; February, 1988; May, 1992, pp. 346-58.

Poets and Writers, May/June, 1987.

Prairie Schooner, spring, 1965.

Reporter, September 12, 1963.

Salmagundi, fall/winter, 1975; fall, 1978.

San Francisco Review of Books, July, 1984.

Saturday Review, July 1, 1950; May 21, 1955; September 27, 1958; February 21, 1959; February 11, 1961; July 6, 1963.

Sewanee Review, winter, 1952; spring, 1961; fall, 1968; summer, 1978; October, 1985; January, 1988; October, 1991, pp. 669-673; October, 1992, pp. 706-15.

Southern Review, winter, 1974; summer, 1975; fall, 1976; summer, 1979; winter, 1979; winter, 1992, pp. 184-201.

Thought, summer, 1979.

Times Literary Supplement, February 19, 1960; June 11, 1976; October 6, 1978; April 3, 1992, p. 7.

University of Windsor Review, spring, 1969.

Virginia Quarterly Review, spring, 1978; autumn, 1984; spring, 1988.

Washington Post, January 15, 1981; March 31, 1987; June 11, 1987; October 25, 1990, p. D1.

Washington Post Book World, December 24, 1967; December 25, 1977; June 11, 1987; May 18, 1988; April 21, 1991, p. 9.

Webster Review, spring, 1974; fall, 1980.

World Literature Today, summer, 1981; autumn, 1984; winter, 1986.

Yale Review, autumn, 1954; autumn, 1955; summer, 1961; summer, 1964; autumn, 1968; spring, 1976; summer, 1985.

OTHER

One on One (filmed interview), Kent State University Television Center, October 5, 1979.

OBITUARIES:

PERIODICALS

Boston Globe, July 7, 1991, p. 63.
Current Biography, September, 1991, p. 59.
Los Angeles Times, July 8, 1991.
New York Times, July 7, 1991, section 1, p. 18.
Time, July 15, 1991, p. 61.
USA Today, July 8, 1991, p. A2.
Washington Post, July 7, 1991, p. C5.*

* * *

NI CHUILLEANAIN, Eilean 1942-

PERSONAL: Surname is pronounced "Nee-Quillenoin"; born November 28, 1942, in Cork, Ireland; daughter of Cormac (a university professor) and Eilis (a writer; maiden name, Dillon) O'Cuilleanain; married Macdara Woods (a poet and editor), June 27, 1978; children: Niall. *Education:* University College, National University of Ireland, B.A., 1962, M.A., 1964; Lady Margaret Hall, Oxford, B.Litt., 1968.

ADDRESSES: Office—Department of English, University of Dublin Trinity College, Dublin 2, Ireland. *E-mail*—enchullnn@tcd.ie.

CAREER: University of Dublin Trinity College, Dublin, Ireland, lecturer, beginning 1966, senior lecturer in English, 1984—. Founder of *Cyphers* literary magazine, 1975.

AWARDS, HONORS: Irish Times Poetry Award, 1966, for poems, including "Ars Poetica"; Patrick Kavanagh Award for Poetry, 1973, for *Acts and*

Monuments; Books Ireland Publishers' Award, 1975, for *Site of Ambush;* O'Shaughnessy Prize, Irish-American Cultural Foundation, 1992.

WRITINGS:

POETRY

Acts and Monuments, Gallery Books, 1972.
Site of Ambush, Gallery Books, 1975.
The Second Voyage, Wake Forest University Press (Chapel Hill, NC), 1977.
(With Brian Lalor) *Cork,* illustrations by Lalor, Gallery Books, 1977.
The Rose-Geranium, Gallery Books, 1981.
The Magdalene Sermon, Gallery Press, 1989, 2nd edition, 1994, Wake Forest University Press, 1990.
The Brazen Serpent, Wake Forest University Press, 1995.

EDITOR

Irish Women: Image and Achievement, Arlen House, 1985.
(With J. D. Pheifer) *Noble and Joyous Histories: English Romances, 1350-1650,* Irish Academic Press, 1993.

Poems represented in anthologies, including *Choice,* edited by Desmond Egan and Michael Hartnett, Goldsmith Press, 1973, and *The Pleasures of Gaelic Poetry,* edited by Sean Mac Reamoinn, Allen Lane, 1982. Contributor to periodicals, including *Aquarius, Broadsheet, Irish Press, Irish Times,* and *Ploughshares.* Coeditor of *Cyphers,* 1975—.

WORK IN PROGRESS: Research on religious poetry of the English Renaissance; a new collection of poems.

SIDELIGHTS: Eilean Ni Chuilleanain, who helped found the distinguished Irish literary magazine *Cyphers,* has become known for her own "intensely imagined, private, and frequently mysterious" poetry, asserts Joseph Browne in the *Dictionary of Literary Biography.* A sense of connection between past and present characterizes her work, which draws on legend and mythology in its examination of being and death as well as the poet's struggle to reveal her self. Ni Chuilleanain's distant style has drawn criticism from some reviewers, but in Browne's opinion, "Her poetry's creative vigor, thematic depth, and technical range are consistently and sufficiently evident to authenticate its artistic worth. . . . In her more than one hundred published poems, . . . [Ni Chuilleanain] has, like the Gaelic poetry she so admires, provided us with a body of work 'full of suggestions and fascinating patterns.'"

In such early poems as "The Second Voyage," Ni Chuilleanain's awareness of history and isolation figure strongly. Her choice of the Greek hero Odysseus as a protagonist demonstrates her historical orientation; Odysseus's isolation, as a traveler at sea, expresses one of her common themes. As Ni Chuilleanain identifies memory and connection with the earth, in her early poems the sea becomes a symbol of separation and forgetting. "The Second Voyage" bears this out through Odysseus's yearning to leave the lonely sea for a settled home on land. Remarks Browne, "Odysseus is so thoroughly realized as a human being that the poem becomes brilliantly immediate and harmonious in the poet's blending of subject, theme, language, structure, and personal vision."

The problem of self has dominated Ni Chuilleanain's poetry and criticism. Her unwillingness to identify herself with female characters or even to write in an intimate, personal voice leads some reviewers to judge her poems unemotional, asexual, and elusive. Yet in Browne's opinion, "what has been misconstrued as 'paralytic politeness' may actually be a unique blend of intentional and unintentional mystery, anonymity, and reticence." In her essays, Ni Chuilleanain expresses support for the poet's right to reveal only what she chooses in order to deal with the corresponding mystery of life. Thus, suggests Browne, the important question is whether the reader is "convinced that a poem's specific mystery reflects the general mystery of humanity."

In poems such as "The Lady's Tower," from Ni Chuilleanain's second volume, *Site of Ambush,* the poet reveals herself more fully in a feminine persona isolated from, yet caught up in, the world around her. Observes Browne, "Unlike earlier poems, which were often obscured by a vague or incompletely realized persona that excluded the reader, 'The Lady's Tower' is an entirety because its persona and her world complement and complete one another, thereby engaging the reader in their existence." Ni Chuilleanain's use of a female protagonist is considered significant; Browne quoted the poet as saying she believed she had succeeded in "partly solving the female 'I' problem" with this poem.

Written to accompany Brian Lalor's drawings, the poems in *Cork* sometimes seem to reviewers to lack the originality and vigor of Ni Chuilleanain's independent writings about humanity. "Ironically," reports Browne, "it is when she deals with the natural world in her personal, imaginative fashion that Ni Chuilleanain is at her best" in this collection. *The Rose-Geranium,* in contrast, offers a vivid and personal perspective on human concerns and relationships. "The themes of time, change, aging, and death which previously had been simply characteristics of mythology, legend, history, and the natural world, that is, of the world outside her, are now observed as an intimate part of her own being and of her relations with others," Browne writes.

Ni Chuilleanain told *CA:* "My motivation is obscure, connected with the stimulus of mythology, folklore, and religious writing (which is also an academic interest). The problem of addressing the special (Irish) audience in a special (female) voice remains unsolved and many of my poems are attempts to solve it.

"I have traveled and lived at various times in Italy, with shorter expeditions elsewhere in Europe and Morocco. All are important to my writing. I speak Irish, Italian, and French, read Latin, and hope to learn Arabic."

BIOGRAPHICAL/CRITICAL SOURCES:

BOOKS

Dictionary of Literary Biography, Volume 40: *Poets of Great Britain and Ireland since 1960,* Gale (Detroit), 1985.

PERIODICALS

Poetry Ireland Review, summer, 1995.
Times Literary Supplement, July 27, 1973; December 25-31, 1987; July 7, 1995.

*   *   *

NIN, Anais   1903-1977

PERSONAL: First name is pronounced "anna-*ees*"; surname is pronounced "neen"; born February 21, 1903, in Paris, France; brought to the United States in 1914, became an American citizen; died January 14, 1977, of cancer, in Los Angeles, CA; daughter of Joaquin (a pianist and composer) and Rosa (a singer; maiden name Culmell) Nin; married Hugh Guiler (a banker; later, under the name Ian Hugo, a film maker and illustrator of Nin's books), 1920; also married Rupert Pole. *Education:* Attended public schools in New York; self-educated after grammar school.

CAREER: Writer. Worked as a fashion and artist's model; studied Spanish dance, giving one recital in Paris during the 1930s; studied psychoanalysis and practiced under Otto Rank in Europe, and briefly in New York City, during the mid-1930s, returning to France in 1935; established Siana Editions with Villa Seurat group (Henry Miller, Alfred Perles and Michael Franekel), about 1935; returned to the United States in 1939; published her own books for four years under various imprints, principally Gemor Press. Frequent lecturer at colleges and universities, including Harvard University, University of Chicago, Dartmouth College, University of Michigan, University of California at Berkeley, and Duke University. Also taught creative writing and acted in films. Member of advisory board, Feminist Book Club, Los Angeles, and Women's History Library, Berkeley, CA.

MEMBER: National Institute of Arts and Letters.

AWARDS, HONORS: Prix Sevigne, 1971.

WRITINGS:

NONFICTION

D. H. Lawrence: An Unprofessional Study, E. W. Titus (Paris), 1932, Spearman (London), 1961, A. Swallow, 1964.
Realism and Reality, Alicat, 1946.
On Writing, O. Baradinsky, 1947.
The Novel of the Future (also see below), Macmillan (New York City), 1968.
Nuances, Sans Souci Press, 1970.
Anais Nin Reader, edited by Philip K. Jason, Swallow Press (Athens, OH), 1973.
(With Duane Schneider) *An Interview with Anais Nin,* Village Press (Unionville, CT), 1973.
A Woman Speaks: The Lectures, Seminars, and Interviews of Anais Nin, edited by Evelyn Hinz, Swallow Press, 1975.
In Favor of the Sensitive Man and Other Essays, Harcourt (San Diego), 1976.

Letters to a Friend in Australia, Nosukumo (Melbourne), 1992.

Conversations with Anais Nin, edited by Wendy M. DuBow, University of Mississippi Press (Jackson), 1994.

The Mystic of Sex: A First Look at D. H. Lawrence, Uncollected Writings, 1931-1974, Capra (Santa Barbara, CA), 1995.

NOVELS

Winter of Artifice, Obelisk Press (Paris), 1939, published as *Winter of Artifice: Three Novelettes,* Swallow Press (Athens, OH), 1961, revised edition published as *Winter of Artifice* [and] *House of Incest* (also see below), P. Owen (London), 1974.

This Hunger, Gemor Press (New York City), 1945.

Ladders to Fire (also see below), Dutton (New York City), 1946.

Children of the Albatross (also see below), Dutton, 1947.

The Four-Chambered Heart (also see below), Duell (New York City), 1950.

A Spy in the House of Love (also see below), British Book Centre (New York City), 1954.

Solar Barque (also see below), Swallow Press, 1958, enlarged edition published as *Seduction of the Minotaur* (also see below), Swallow Press, 1961.

Cities of the Interior (contains *Ladders to Fire, Children of the Albatross, The Four-Chambered Heart, A Spy in the House of Love,* and *Solar Barque*), Swallow Press, 1959, reprinted, with *Seduction of the Minotaur* replacing *Solar Barque,* Swallow Press, 1961, published with an introduction by Sharon Spencer, Swallow Press, 1974.

JOURNALS

The Diary of Anais Nin (also see below), edited by Gunther Stuhlmann, Harcourt (first two volumes published in conjunction with Swallow Press), Volume 1: *1931-1934* (also see below), 1966, Volume 2: *1934-1939,* 1967, Volume 3: *1939-1944,* 1969, Volume 4: *1944-1947,* 1971, Volume 5: *1947-1955* (also see below), 1974, Volume 6: *1955-1966,* 1977, Volume 7: *1966-1974,* 1981 (published in England as *The Journals of Anais Nin,* P. Owen, Volume 1, 1966, Volume 2, 1967, Volume 3, 1970, Volume 4, 1972, Volume 5, 1974, Volume 6, 1977, Volume 7, 1980).

Unpublished Selections from the Diary (contains excerpts from Volume 1 of *The Diary of Anais Nin*), edited by Duane Schneider, D. Schneider Press, 1968.

Paris Revisited (contains excerpts from Volume 5 of *The Diary of Anais Nin*), Capra, 1972.

Eidolons (contains diary excerpts written in 1971), edited by Rochelle Holt, Ragnarok Press, 1973.

The Early Diary of Anais Nin, Harcourt, Volume 1: *Linotte: The Early Diary of Anais Nin, 1914-1920* (translated from the French by Jean L. Sherman), 1980, Volume 2: *1920-1923,* 1983, Volume 3: *1923-1927,* 1983, Volume 4: *1927-1931,* 1985.

Henry and June: From the Unexpurgated Diary of Anais Nin, Harcourt, 1986, published as *Henry and June: From 'A Journal of Love': The Unexpurgated Diary of Anais Nin, 1931-32,* 1992.

Incest: From 'A Journal of Love': The Unexpurgated Diary of Anais Nin, 1932-1934, Harcourt, 1992.

Fire: From 'A Journal of Love': The Unexpurgated Diary of Anais Nin, 1934-1937, Harcourt, 1995.

SHORT STORIES

Under a Glass Bell, Gemor Press, 1944, published as *Under a Glass Bell and Other Stories,* Dutton, 1948.

Collages (also see below), Swallow Press, 1964.

Waste of Timelessness, and Other Early Stories, Magic Circle Press, 1977.

Delta of Venus (erotica), Harcourt, 1977, published with photographs by Bob Carlos Clarke as *The Illustrated Delta of Venus,* W. H. Allen, 1980.

Little Birds (erotica), Harcourt, 1979.

SOUND RECORDINGS

An Evening with Anais Nin, Big Sur Recordings, 1972.

Anais Nin Discusses "The Diary of Anais Nin, 1944-1947, Volume 4, 'A Journal of Self-Discovery,'" Center for Cassette Studies, 1972.

Craft of Writing, Big Sur Recordings, 1973.

Anais Nin: The Author Explains the Purpose Behind Her Writing, Center for Cassette Studies, 1975.

Anais Nin in Recital: Diary Excerpts and Comments, Caedmon, 1979.

OTHER

House of Incest (prose poem), Siana Editions (Paris), 1936, Gemor Press, 1947, Swallow Press, 1961.

(With John Boyce) *Aphrodisiac* (erotic drawings), Quartet Books, 1976.

Portrait in Three Dimensions (contains excerpts from *The Diary of Anais Nin, The Novel of the Future,* and *Collages*), Concentric Circle Press, 1979.

The White Blackbird, Capra, 1985.

Author of introduction to *Tropic of Cancer,* by Henry Miller, Obelisk Press, 1934; *Antonin Artaud: A Man of Vision,* by Bettina L. Knapp, David Lewis, 1969; and *The Sun's Birthday,* by John Pearson, Doubleday (New York City), 1973. Work is included in numerous anthologies. Contributor to periodicals, including *Massachusetts Review, New York Times, Village Voice, Saturday Review, Ms.,* and the *New York Times Book Review. Booster* and *Delta* (both Paris), society editor, 1937, associate editor, 1937-38, member of editorial board, 1939; *Two Cities,* general editor, 1959, honorary editor, 1960; member of advisory board, *Voyages.*

The University of California has a large collection of Nin's papers and literary manuscripts, including her diaries. Much of Nin's published and unpublished work has also been collected at Northwestern University Library. *Under the Sign of Pisces,* a literary journal devoted to Anais Nin and her circle, is produced at Ohio State University. Nin's work is studied in Paris by the group Les Amis de Anais Nin.

ADAPTATIONS: Walter Carrol adapted the short story "Under a Glass Bell" for a film of the same title in 1967; John McLean and Sharon Bunn adapted Volume 1 of *The Diary of Anais Nin* as a play entitled *The Voice of a Woman,* first produced in Dallas, TX, at Poverty Playhouse, 1970; Danielle Suissa acquired film rights to *A Spy in the House of Love* in 1970; several stories were adapted as *Erotica: Delta of Venus,* a play produced in Chicago in 1987; *Henry & June,* directed by Philip Kaufman and starring Maria de Medeiros as Anais Nin, Fred Ward as Henry Miller, and Uma Thurman as June Miller, was released by Universal in 1990; *Erotica: Little Birds,* a play written by Karen Goodman and based on stories by Nin, was produced in Chicago in 1991.

SIDELIGHTS: On a ship bound for New York from Barcelona in 1914, eleven-year-old Anais Nin began writing the journal that would gradually evolve into the most acclaimed work of her literary career, a journal that Henry Miller, writing in the *Criterion,* predicted would someday "take its place beside the revelations of St. Augustine, Petronius, Abelard, Rousseau, Proust, and others." Aboard the ship with

young Anais were her two brothers, Thorvald and Joaquin, and her mother, Rosa Culmell Nin, a classical singer of Danish and French descent. Absent was Anais's father, Joaquin Nin. A respected Spanish composer and pianist, he was, Rosa told her children, on an extended concert tour and would join them in New York City later. In fact, Joaquin had deserted his wife and three children forever. Suspecting the truth, Anais began her diary as an extended letter to her father, one intended to coax him back to his family.

For the first ten years of her life Anais moved in some of Europe's most glittering circles. Her parents were from aristocratic families, and their musical careers enabled them to associate with the finest artists of their day. While Anais enjoyed this cosmopolitan life, she was also shaken by her parents' private battles at home—violent arguments that stemmed from Joaquin's endless infidelities. When he finally deserted Rosa, she decided it would be best to take their children as far away from him as possible. Although Anais had feared her harsh, critical father, she also idealized him and suffered keenly from his absence.

Trained only as a musician, Rosa Nin managed to support her children by taking in boarders and giving singing lessons in New York. The family led a life that was poor and drab compared to the one they had left behind in Europe. Anais was isolated by her limited knowledge of English as well as by her deep sadness over the changes in her life. She turned to her journal for companionship and escape. "I hate New York," she confided in its pages at the age of eleven. "I find it too big, too superficial, everything goes too fast. It is just *hell.*" Although filled with a strong desire for learning, Anais did poorly in school, preferring to educate herself by reading alphabetically through the books in the public library. When a teacher criticized her writing style as stilted, the sixteen-year-old dropped out of public school permanently. She remarked to her diary, "I leave . . . with the greatest pleasure in the world, the pleasure that a prisoner feels on leaving his prison after a sentence of a thousand years." When not studying in the library, Anais helped to support her family by working as a model for artists, illustrators, and fashion designers.

Nin married Hugh Guiler, a banker, when she was twenty. Not long after their marriage, Guiler was transferred to a bank in Paris. Nin had been writing regularly in her journal since 1914, but it wasn't until her return to Paris as an adult that she began to work seriously at writing for publication. As she struggled with her early fiction, she began to feel a powerful inner conflict between "her desire to be a woman—as she saw it, one who gives, is involved in relationships—and an artist—one who takes, is unfaithful and abandons loved ones (like her concert pianist father)," noted *New York Times Book Review* contributor Sharon Spencer. Nin felt unable to follow her artistic inclinations while also carrying out her duties as a banker's wife. Guiler's work kept the couple in conservative circles, and Nin, who craved the company of artists, found herself stifled by long hours spent in social intercourse with bank employees. But although she was beginning to "acknowledge disappointment with her marriage to the banker . . . Hugh Guiler," explained Spencer, Nin maintained a "madly romantic ideal of married love with remarkable tenacity."

In spite of her personal difficulties, Nin managed at this time to publish her first book, a commentary on D. H. Lawrence. Nin had been strongly influenced by Lawrence's style and "shared with him belief in the value of the subconscious, myth, progression, and the recognition of the physical," stated Benjamin Franklin V in the *Dictionary of Literary Biography*. While Nin's book *D. H. Lawrence: An Unprofessional Study* is still recognized as a sensitive and original discussion of the English novelist's work, its greatest importance was probably the change it helped bring about in Nin's private life. The lawyer she engaged to negotiate the contract for her book introduced her to a poor, unpublished American writer living in Paris named Henry Miller, whose works *Tropic of Cancer* and *Tropic of Capricorn* would later be widely banned as obscene.

Miller lived in an underground world different from any Nin had ever known. His companions were the gangsters, prostitutes, and drug addicts of Paris. He and his wife June lived a life of extremes, and it seemed to Nin that they were fully alive in a way that she was not. Franklin pointed out their differences in his essay: "Nin was personally elegant, Miller was not; she was selective, Miller voracious; in their writings Nin was implicit, Miller explicit; she was sensual, he sexual. But despite these and other differences Nin and Miller inspired each other, and each performed as a sounding board for the other's ideas." As Nin became increasingly involved with Henry and June Miller, the tension she felt between her life as Hugh Guiler's wife and her life as Anais Nin the artist became intolerable. In 1932 she sought

to resolve her conflicts through therapy with the prominent Parisian psychoanalyst, Rene Allendy, and later with Otto Rank, a brilliant though unorthodox student of Sigmund Freud.

Spencer believed that the insights Nin gained through "therapy with Otto Rank and a love affair with Henry Miller freed her to live a greatly expanded life—without sacrificing the marriage that had such great psychological and spiritual value for her." Details on how she accomplished this were for many years not known, for Nin heavily edited her published journals from those years and omitted all references to her husband at his request. It is known that he later established a secondary career as an artist and film maker under the pseudonym Ian Hugo. Nin appeared in some of his films, and his engravings illustrated some of her books. They remained legally married until her death, but they may have established an open relationship. During her lifetime, "Nin refused to discuss her marriage or even name her husband in interviews," revealed Rose Marie Cutting in *Anais Nin: A Reference Guide*. Psychoanalysis became a lifelong fascination for Nin. She studied it under Rank and eventually practiced with him in New York City. Its influence on her fiction was profound, for in all her novels she attempted to illustrate her characters' inner landscapes rather than to describe their external lives.

The first work to show evidence of Nin's liberation was a long prose poem entitled *House of Incest*. In a surrealistic style, the narrator recounts her nightmare of wounded souls, trapped by their unresolved inner conflicts in the dark, airless "house of incest." Only one inhabitant can find an exit from this sealed environment—a dancer who has lost her arms as punishment for clinging to all she loved in life. When she learns to accept her flaws, she is able to dance her way to the daylight outside the house. Incorporating Nin's own recurring dreams, *House of Incest* was symbolic of her feelings of suffocation from childhood traumas and her rebirth through psychoanalysis. "Nin's message is clear," explained Benjamin Franklin V in one of his *Dictionary of Literary Biography* essays. "The nature of man's existence is multiple and imperfect. Every individual has many parts, the sum of which is something less than one's ideal self. But if one ignores that multiplicity or demands perfection, that person will not be able to function in life. . . . Nin never expressed these basic concerns as eloquently or convincingly as she did in this first volume of her fiction, even though almost all the rest of her fiction is similar to it thematically." Franklin added: "Such an esoteric book doubtless could not have been written or published in the United States at that time."

Indeed, Nin had trouble finding a publisher for *House of Incest* even in France. Eventually Nin, Miller, and the other writers with whom they associated (a group sometimes called the Villa Seurat circle) established Siana Editions to publish their own works and those of other avant-garde writers. With the encouragement of the Villa Seurat writers, Nin's style continued to develop, and by the time she published *Winter of Artifice* in 1939, her prose showed much less of an obvious debt to surrealism. While *House of Incest* cautions against the danger of becoming trapped in one's dreams, *Winter of Artifice* stresses that "dreams have to be probed, not to the exclusion of conscious reality, but rather to nourish it," wrote Franklin. The story centers on Djuna and her reunion with the father she has not seen for twenty years. Nin's narrative recreates Djuna's yearning to penetrate the many illusions with which both father and daughter have surrounded themselves. Little by little, she succeeds in exposing the true nature of their relationship.

Besides illuminating the psychological drama played out between Djuna and her father, Nin's intent in *Winter of Artifice* was to create prose that would provoke the immediate emotional response usually associated with music. Her success is unquestioned by Spencer, who wrote in *Collage of Dreams: The Writings of Anais Nin* that "*Winter of Artifice* is a mature work, very sophisticated technically, in which Anais Nin first fully displays her talent for adapting the structure of the non-verbal arts to fiction. It is a ballet of words in which music and movement are . . . skillfully balanced and . . . subtly interwoven." Bettina L. Knapp, in her critical volume entitled *Anais Nin,* praised the author's skillful use of "the literary devices of repetitions, omissions, ellipses, dream sequences, and stream-of-consciousness" that have the cumulative effect of "jarring the reader into a new state of awareness."

Both *House of Incest* and *Winter of Artifice* were well-received in Europe's avant-garde literary circles. But the rich cultural atmosphere that helped Nin to create those first books disintegrated as World War II drew closer. In 1939, Hugh Guiler was called back to the United States and Nin chose to accompany him. Just as she had in childhood, Nin found New York City cold and sterile in comparison to Europe. She also discovered that American publish-

ers were unreceptive to her work, which they considered unhealthy, decadent surrealism. After a few years of consistent rejections by American publishers, Nin bought a secondhand, foot-operated printing press and began to set the type for her own books. In this way she produced limited editions of *House of Incest* and *Winter of Artifice,* as well as a volume of short stories, *Under a Glass Bell,* and another novel, *This Hunger.* In time she attracted the attention of Edmund Wilson, a highly respected critic. He praised *Under a Glass Bell* in the *New Yorker:* "The pieces in this collection belong to a peculiar genre sometimes cultivated by the late Virginia Woolf. They are half short stories, half dreams, and they mix a sometimes exquisite poetry with a homely realistic observation. They take place in a special world, a world of feminine perception and fancy. . . . The main thing to say is that Miss Nin is a very good artist." It was through Wilson's influence that Nin was finally able to place her work with a commercial publisher in the United States.

In novels such as *Ladders to Fire, The Four-Chambered Heart* and *A Spy in the House of Love* Nin continued the exploration of the feminine psyche she had begun in *House of Incest* and *Winter of Artifice.* Her novels have a fluid quality, found *Spectator* contributor Emma Fisher, "because her female characters are all faces of Woman. . . . The characters melt and dissolve into each other," even exchanging names as they reappear from one novel to the next. William Goyen, who rated Nin "one of the most fiercely passionate practitioners of the experimental novel in America," stated in the *New York Times Book Review* that as Nin "follows the inner flow of her characters' drives and motivations . . . she occasionally directs the flow to the surface where she freezes it into something as plain and dazzling as ice." Reviews such as these helped to bring Nin greater acceptance in the United States.

But her fiction was still misunderstood and attacked by some critics, who objected to her experimental style as "murky and precious," to quote Audrey C. Foote in *Washington Post Book World.* "She covers her canvas too thickly," declared Herbert Lyons in the *New York Times Book Review.* "It tends to look like a used palette: the resulting abstraction is murky, meaningless and too often in bad taste." Some reviewers felt the absence of conventional plot and characters rendered Nin's books inaccessible. Others found her recurrent themes and characters tedious. For example, Blake Morrison wrote in his *New Statesman* review of the five-volume "continuous novel," *Cities of the Interior,* "Nin herself described *Cities of the Interior* as 'an endless novel,' and for anyone wading faithfully through 589 pages of such sub-Lawrentian wisdom as 'A breast touched for the first time is a breast never touched before' the description is going to sound all too appropriate."

Franklin suggested that while Nin's fiction was very accomplished, it "was never popular, but understandably so: she wrote about psychological reality, not the surface reality that she called realism and that most readers desire." Franklin believed that "while her fiction may at first seem impenetrable because of its lack of surface reality, an attentive reading reveals a powerful psychological reality that is the hallmark of her writing." He concluded: "She was a great writer of psychological fiction. . . . Her work challenges the reader and involves him in the creative act."

When Nin finally achieved widespread acceptance it was with the work she never intended to publish—the diary she began on the ship to New York. Writing in the journal had developed into an obsessive activity which Nin sometimes compared to a drug addiction. She eventually filled more than two hundred manuscript volumes with the record of her transatlantic crossings, relationships with artists both famous and unknown, struggles with publishers, and efforts toward artistic success and self-fulfillment. Many of those closest to her had at one time urged her to abandon her journal, including Allendy, Rank, and Miller. They felt that it was a hindrance to her career as a fiction writer, but the journal continued to grow. Eventually, Nin's supporters began to urge her to publish portions of it, believing that her finest writing was contained therein.

After long deliberation, Nin consented. Her aim in editing her journal was similar to her objective in fiction: to illuminate the drama of individual growth. Volume One of *The Diary of Anais Nin* was published in 1966 and was received far more enthusiastically than any of the author's previous novels. Readers, particularly women and young people, identified strongly with Nin's quest for self-knowledge and personal freedom. Many critics called the *Diary* a far stronger literary work than anything Nin had published previously. For example, Jean Garrigue noted in the *New York Times Book Review:* "The best parts of this diary are written with a daylight energy and sharpness that are in marked contrast to the frangibilities and antennaed delicacy of Miss Nin's stories and novels. . . . This diary has the elusive

fluidity of life. Its author-subject is neither moralizer nor judge but a witness, vulnerable, susceptible, subtle, critical. . . . It is a rich, various, and fascinating work."

Eventually seven volumes of *The Diary of Anais Nin* were published. Its success was summarized by Duane Schneider in the *Southern Review:* "The *Diary* stands as Miss Nin's most remarkable artistic achievement because its literary form provides the author with a more effective means to reveal her characters than her novels do. The *Diary* symbolizes a quest for complete self-introspection and understanding; the result of the quest is a coherent, organic, revelatory work of art." *Shenandoah* contributor Lynn Sukenick called Nin's diaries "books of wisdom which have elevated their author to the status of a sage and have had a healing effect on many of her readers."

The Diary of Anais Nin received some negative attention. Susan Manso remarked in the *New Boston Republic* that the journal's size was "matched only by its vacuity," and Susan Heath wrote in *Saturday Review:* "Only the self-absorbed will be fascinated by this solipsistic quest for healing and wholeness, for they will see themselves in the mirror Miss Nin has held to her soul. And the disenchanted will recognize it as the tiresome work of a querulous bore who cultivates neurosis in hopes of achieving self-realization." But for the most part, *The Diary of Anais Nin* was accepted as an important document, both for Nin's insight into the development of individual personality and for her sketches of the many artists she associated with in her lifetime of world traveling.

After the publication of the *Diary,* Nin found herself in great demand as a lecturer. She became a controversial figure in the woman's movement, alternately praised for writing from a uniquely feminine perspective and denounced as a supporter of archaic feminine values. Anais Nin died of cancer in 1977 and, in accordance with her wishes, her ashes were scattered over the Pacific. After her death, a number of books appeared which she had refused to have published during her lifetime. The first to appear were two volumes of erotica she wrote for a dollar a page in the early 1940s. Rosalind Thomas explained in *Room of One's Own* that Miller had first been approached to write erotica for a private collector willing to pay one hundred dollars a month for the material. Miller soon got bored with the arrangement, however, and "suggested that Nin write the stories instead. Like some of her other artist friends who needed money, she accepted the offer. She became what she called the 'Madame' of an unusual house of literary prostitution." Her erotic fiction from this arrangement, the books *Delta of Venus* and *Little Birds,* put her name on the *New York Times* best-seller list for the first time. Both books were praised by Alice Walker in *Ms.* as "so distinct an advance in the depiction of female sensuality that I felt, on reading it, enormous gratitude." Thomas remarked that "No one has suggested that Nin's erotica is great art. Its interest resides primarily in its feminine perspective and in its unmistakable poetical quality."

In addition to Nin's erotic fiction, full, unexpurgated versions of her diaries were also published after her death. These versions of the diaries, long suppressed by the author to spare the feelings of her husband and others, revealed a private life of immense passion. In the volumes *Henry and June: From the Unexpurgated Diary of Anais Nin, Incest: From 'A Journal of Love': The Unexpurgated Diary of Anais Nin, 1932-1934,* and *Fire: From 'A Journal of Love': The Unexpurgated Diary of Anais Nin, 1934-1937* Nin details the numerous affairs of her life, including those with Miller, Miller's wife June, her psychiatrists Allendy and Rank, with playwright Antonin Artaud and with her father. At one time in the 1930s, Nin was sexually active with three men and her husband at once, none of them aware of the others. During the 1960s, she was married to Hugh Guiler and Rupert Pole at the same time, and she traveled cross country to spend time with them both. As Joseph Coates remarked in the *Chicago Tribune,* "not till the unexpurgated Journal of Love series began . . . did we see the full emotional and sexual drama of a life lived on the line." Writing in the *Times Literary Supplement,* Erica Jong called the journals "unlike any ever published before." Nin, Jong believed, "has created here . . . nothing less than a mirror of life. The fluctuations of moods, from hate to love that mark our frail humanity are seen in *process,* as never before."

Nin's literary reputation is still unsettled. Among feminists who at first admired her work in the 1960s, she now seems "out of fashion," as Jong noted. Nin, Jong explained, "is a seductress in a time when all seduction is presumed to be rape, a sensitive chronicler of inner emotion and psychoanalytic transformation when all that is wanted from women writers is angry agitprop which repudiates Freud and all 'dead

white males.'" In *Anais Nin: A Biography,* Deirdre Bair called her "a major minor writer" who explored "sex, the self, and psychoanalysis" in her writings.

BIOGRAPHICAL/CRITICAL SOURCES:

BOOKS

Anais Nin Observed: From a Film Portrait of a Woman as Artist, Swallow Press, 1976.
Authors in the News, Gale (Detroit), Volume 2, 1976.
Bair, Deirdre, *Anais Nin: A Biography,* Putnam (New York City), 1995.
Benstock, Shari, editor, *The Private Self: Theory and Practice of Women's Autobiographical Writings,* University of North Carolina Press (Chapel Hill), 1988, pp. 34-62.
Contemporary Literary Criticism, Gale, Volume 1, 1973, Volume 4, 1975, Volume 8, 1978, Volume 11, 1979, Volume 14, 1980, Volume 60, 1990.
Cutting, Rose Marie, *Anais Nin: A Reference Guide,* G. K. Hall (Boston), 1978.
Dictionary of Literary Biography, Gale, Volume 2: *American Novelists since World War II,* 1978, Volume 4: *American Writers in Paris,* 1980, Volume 152: *American Novelists since World War II,* 1995.
Evans, Oliver, *Anais Nin,* Southern Illinois University Press (Carbondale), 1968.
Fitch, Noel Riley, *Anais: The Erotic Life of Anais Nin,* Little, Brown (Boston), 1993.
Franklin, Benjamin V, *Anais Nin: A Bibliography,* Kent State University Press (Kent, OH), 1973.
Franklin and Duane Schneider, *Anais Nin: An Introduction,* Ohio University Press (Athens), 1979.
Freidman, Ellen G. and Miriam Fuchs, editors, *Breaking the Sequence: Women's Experimental Fiction,* Princeton University Press (Princeton, NJ), 1989.
Harms, Valerie, editor, *Celebration with Anais Nin,* Magic Circle Press, 1973.
Hinz, Evelyn J., *The Mirror and the Garden: Realism and Reality in the Writings of Anais Nin,* Harcourt, 1973.
Jason, Philip K., *Anais Nin and Her Critics,* Camden House (Columbia, SC), 1993.
Knapp, Bettina L., *Anais Nin,* Ungar (New York City), 1978.
Merchant, Hoshang, *In-discretions: Anais Nin,* Writers Workshop (Calcutta), 1990.
Miller, Henry, *Letters to Anais Nin,* edited by Gunther Stuhlmann, Putnam, 1965.

Nalbantian, Suzanne, *Aesthetic Autobiography: From Life to Art in Marcel Proust, James Joyce, Virginia Woolf, and Anais Nin,* St. Martin's (New York City), 1994.

Nin, Anais, *The Diary of Anais Nin,* Harcourt (first two volumes published in conjunction with Swallow Press), Volume 1: *1931-34,* 1966, Volume 2: *1934-1939,* 1967, Volume 3: *1939-1944,* 1969, Volume 4: *1944-1947,* 1971, Volume 5: *1947-1955,* 1974, Volume 6: *1955-1966,* 1977, Volume 7: *1966-1974,* 1981 (published in England as *The Journals of Anais Nin,* P. Owen, Volume 1, 1966, Volume 2, 1967, Volume 3, 1970, Volume 4, 1972, Volume 5, 1974, Volume 6, 1977, Volume 7, 1980).

Nin, *Paris Revisited,* Capra Press, 1972.

Nin, *The Early Diary of Anais Nin,* Harcourt, Volume 1: *Linotte: The Early Diary of Anais Nin, 1914-1920,* 1980, Volume 2: *1920-1923,* 1983, Volume 3: *1923-1927,* 1983, Volume 4: *1927-1931,* 1985.

A Photographic Supplement to the Diary of Anais Nin, Harcourt, 1974.

Realism, Reality and the Fictional Theory of Alain Robbe-Grillet and Anais Nin, University Presses of America, 1983.

Schneider, *Unpublished Selections from the Diary,* D. Schneider Press, 1968.

Schneider and Nin, *An Interview with Anais Nin,* D. Schneider Press, 1970.

Spencer, Sharon, *Collage of Dreams: The Writings of Anais Nin,* Swallow Press, 1977.

Spencer, *Space, Time and Structure in the Modern Novel,* New York University Press, 1971.

Zaller, Robert, editor, *A Casebook on Anais Nin,* World, 1974.

PERIODICALS

American Poetry Review, January-February, 1973.

Anais: An International Journal (annual), 1983—.

Booklist, May 1, 1995, pp. 1547-48.

Books Abroad, summer, 1963.

Books and Bookmen, April, 1975.

Carleton Miscellany, fall/winter, 1973-74.

Chicago Review, Volume 24, number 2, 1972.

Chicago Tribune, April 8, 1979; October 22, 1992.

Chicago Tribune Book World, October 24, 1982.

Christian Science Monitor, November 1, 1978.

Contemporary Literature, spring, 1972.

Cosmopolitan, October, 1992, p. 38.

Criterion, October, 1937.

Economist, January 25, 1992, p. 92.

L'Express, February 28, 1963.

Los Angeles Free Press, November 26, 1964.

Los Angeles Times Book Review, September 26, 1971; September 5, 1982; January 8, 1984; November 8, 1987, p. 14; November 8, 1992, p. 6.

Mademoiselle, March, 1965.

Minnesota Review, spring, 1982, pp. 86-101.

Mosaic, winter, 1978, pp. 163-70.

Ms., April, 1977; October, 1980.

Nation, January 26, 1946, pp. 105-07; July 24, 1954; November 30, 1974.

New Boston Republic, fall, 1976.

New Directions in Prose and Poetry, Number 7, 1942, pp. 429-36.

New Republic, June 15, 1974.

New Statesman, October 4, 1974; November 10, 1978.

New Yorker, April 1, 1944, pp. 71-4; March 1, 1993, p. 74.

New York Herald Tribune, May 1, 1966.

New York Review of Books, June 26, 1980, p. 21.

New York Times, December 4, 1992, p. C27.

New York Times Book Review, November 29, 1964; April 24, 1966; July 17, 1966; November 23, 1969; January 16, 1972; September 9, 1973; April 14, 1974; June 27, 1976; July 10, 1977; August 13, 1978; April 8, 1979; June 16, 1985; September 28, 1986, p. 27; January 17, 1988, p. 15; November 22, 1992, p. 3; June 4, 1995, p. 29.

Observer (London), March 22, 1987, p. 26.

Outcast Chapbooks, Number 11.

Oz, July, 1970.

Playboy, November, 1993, p. 33.

Prairie Schooner, fall, 1962; summer, 1971; summer, 1972.

Publishers Weekly, April 3, 1995, p. 54.

Review of Contemporary Fiction, summer, 1993, p. 264.

Room of One's Own, Volume 7, number 4, 1982, pp. 57-69.

San Francisco Review of Books, July/August, 1995, pp. 37-8.

Saturday Review, November 30, 1946; May 7, 1966; July 22, 1967; May 4, 1974; May 29, 1976.

Second Wave, summer, 1971.

Shenandoah, spring, 1967; spring, 1976.

Southern Review, spring, 1970.

Spectator, January 20, 1979; November 12, 1988, p. 43.

Times (London), August 12, 1985.

Times Literary Supplement, April 30, 1964; June 11, 1970; January 29, 1971; May 12, 1972; June 25, 1993, pp. 3-4.

Tribune Books (Chicago), September 14, 1986, p. 24; November 29, 1987, p. 6.

Under the Sign of Pisces: Anais Nin and Her Circle (quarterly journal), 1970—.

Village Voice, January 6, 1975; July 26, 1976.

Virginia Quarterly Review, spring, 1987, p. 56.

Vogue, October 15, 1971.

Washington Post Book World, October 29, 1978; August 29, 1985.

West Coast Review of Books, July, 1979.

Woman's Journal, December, 1994, p. 44.

World Literature Today, winter, 1986, p. 114; autumn, 1988, p. 663; spring, 1993, p. 392.

OTHER

Anais Observed (film), Robert Snyder, 1973.

OBITUARIES:

PERIODICALS

Newsweek, January 24, 1977.

New York Times, January 16, 1977.

Time, January 24, 1977.

Washington Post, January 16, 1977.*

*   *   *

NORRIS, Christopher (Charles) 1947-

PERSONAL: Born November 6, 1947, in London, England; son of Charles F. (an accountant) and Edith E. (Ward) Norris; married Alison Newton (a teacher), 1971; children: Clare, Jennifer. *Education:* University of London, B.A. (first class honors), 1970; Ph.D., 1975. *Politics:* Socialist (Labour). *Religion:* None.

ADDRESSES: Home—14 Belle Vue Terrace, Penarth, South Glamorgan CF64 1DB Wales. *Office*—Philosophy Section, SECAP, University of Wales, P.O. Box 94, Cardiff CF1 3XB, Wales.

CAREER: University lecturer in English in Duisburg, West Germany (now Germany), 1974-76; *Books and Bookmen,* London, assistant editor, 1976-78; University of Wales Institute of Science and Technology, Cardiff, Wales, lecturer in English, 1978-94, appointed to personal chair, 1987, professor of philoso-

phy, 1994—. Visiting fellow at Northwestern University, 1983; visiting professor at University of California, Berkley, 1986, City University of New York, 1988, and University of Sunderland; faculty member at School of Criticism and Theory, Dartmouth College, 1994; associate fellow at Centre for Research in Philosophy and Literature, University of Warwick.

WRITINGS:

William Empson and the Philosophy of Literary Criticism, Athlone Press (London), 1978.

Deconstruction: Theory and Practice, Methuen (London), 1982; second edition, Routledge & Kegan Paul (London), 1991.

(Editor) *Shostakovich: The Man and His Music,* Lawrence & Wishart (London), 1982.

The Deconstructive Turn: Essays in the Rhetoric of Philosophy, Methuen, 1983.

(Editor) *Inside the Myth: George Orwell—Views from the Left,* Lawrence & Wishart, 1984.

The Contest of Faculties: Philosophy and Theory after Deconstruction, Methuen, 1985.

Jacques Derrida, Harvard University Press (Cambridge, MA), 1987, second edition, 1995.

(Editor with Richard Machin) *Post-Structuralist Readings of English Poetry,* Cambridge University Press (Cambridge), 1987.

Paul de Man: Deconstruction and the Critique of Aesthetic Ideology, Routledge & Kegan Paul (New York City), 1988.

Deconstruction and the Interests of Theory, Oklahoma University Press (Norman), 1988.

(Editor) *Music and the Politics of Culture,* Lawrence & Wishart, 1989.

(With Andrew Benjamin) *What Is Deconstruction?,* Academy Editions (London), 1989.

Spinoza and the Origins of Modern Critical Theory, Basil Blackwell (Oxford), 1990.

Uncritical Theory: Postmodernism, Intellectuals and the Gulf War, University of Massachusetts (Amherst), 1992.

The Truth about Postmodernism, Basil Blackwell, 1993.

(Editor with Nigel Mapp) *William Empson: The Critical Achievement,* Cambridge University Press, 1993.

Truth and the Ethics of Criticism, Manchester University Press (Manchester), 1994.

Reclaiming Truth: Contribution to a Critique of Cultural Relativism, Duke University Press (Durham, NC), 1996.

Resources of Realism: Truth, Meaning, and Interpretation, Macmillan (London), 1996.

On the Limits of Anti-Realism: Deconstruction, Hermeneutics, and Philosophy of Science, Manchester University Press, 1996.

Also author of *What's Wrong with Postmodernism: Critical Theory and the Ends of Philosophy,* Johns Hopkins University Press (Baltimore, MD). Contributor to periodicals, including *Times Literary Supplement, London Review of Books, Essays in Criticism, Mind, Philosophy and Literature,* and *Critical Quarterly.* General editor of Routledge's "Critics of the Twentieth Century" series

SIDELIGHTS: Christopher Norris told *CA:* "My interests have changed quite a lot over the past few years. Having written a half-dozen books about deconstruction and another five on various aspects of postmodernism it did seem time to start out in a new direction. At about the same time (1994), I moved from the English to the Philosophy Department in my home university at Cardiff. So I am now working mainly on issues in philosophy of science and philosophical semantics. . . . For the rest, my chief spare-time activities are singing (with Cor Cochion, a Cardiff-based socialist choir), flying model-aircraft—an old interest lately revived—and travelling."

BIOGRAPHICAL/CRITICAL SOURCES:

PERIODICALS

London Review of Books, October 21, 1982; April 23, 1993.
Times Literary Supplement, June 4, 1982; July 2, 1982.

* * *

NOVA, Craig 1945-

PERSONAL: Born July 5, 1945, in Los Angeles, CA; son of Karl and Elizabeth (Sinclair) Nova; married Christina Barnes, July 2, 1977; children: Abigail, Tate. *Education:* University of California, Berkeley, B.A. (with honors), 1967; Columbia University, M.F.A. (with distinction), 1969.

CAREER: Writer. Has held jobs as farm hand, truck driver, computer salesman, editor, real estate manager, painter, reporter, proofreader, and gas station attendant.

AWARDS, HONORS: Harper-Saxton Prize, 1971, for *Turkey Hash;* National Endowment for the Arts fellowships, 1973 and 1975; New York State Council on the Arts fellowship, 1974; Guggenheim fellowship, 1977; American Academy and Institute of Arts and Letters award in literature, 1984; National Endowment for the Arts fellowship, 1985.

WRITINGS:

NOVELS

Turkey Hash, Harper (New York City), 1972.
The Geek, Harper, 1975.
Incandescence, Harper, 1979.
The Good Son, Delacorte (New York City), 1982.
The Congressman's Daughter, Delacorte, 1986.
Tornado Alley, Delacorte, 1989.
Trombone, Grove Weidenfeld (New York City), 1992.
The Book of Dreams, Ticknor & Fields (New York City), 1994.

SIDELIGHTS: John Domini writes in the *New York Times Book Review* that Craig Nova's "themes do not merely live; they burn. . . . Nova has proved that nothing gives off sparks like hard living struck against surfaces even harder: the passing of time and our relentless struggle to make it stop." While Nova is heralded by some critics, including William O'Rourke in the *Village Voice,* as "one of the finest writers of his generation (post World War II) and, more importantly, one of the few in possession of an entirely unique voice," others have a different view; for instance, Anatole Broyard of the *New York Times* writes that Nova's work "is just one bad joke after another, an itch that Mr. Nova cannot seem to scratch."

The difference of opinion regarding Nova's novels tends to center around his surrealistic characters and unusual dialogue. In his review of Nova's first book, *Turkey Hash,* Martin Levin writes in the *New York Times Book Review* that the book is filled with "mental defectives, maimed drifters who think with their appetites, geek material, random assassins and their victims—these float in and out of Craig Nova's harsh spotlight. The center of attention is Niles Cabro, an L.A. youth whom the publisher bills as 'borderline' psychotic. Tut. Anyone whose idea of fun is to be beaten nearly senseless in an offal orgy is hardly 'borderline.'" However, Jerry G. Bowles writes in *Saturday Review* that Nova "is a fine writer. His style is telegraphic and minimal, yet strangely evocative of landscape. His characters appear both real and surreal as they act out strange rituals and plot insane acts. His handling of pace and dialogue is superb, and the writing in general has the feel of a polished hand. Despite its ultimate coldness, [*Turkey Hash*] is a remarkably accomplished first novel."

Nova's second novel, *The Geek,* observes a group of misfits on a Greek island. *New York Review of Books* critic Michael Wood feels that "there is something too cryptic about a lot of the novel's transactions, a suggestion of dialogue out of Henry James shifted to a dusty taverna, and . . . the writing keeps reaching for effects that are more than a little lurid. But the blending of emblematic and literal truth . . . is remarkable. The specificity of the island landscape, the clear characters and past history of the individual islanders . . . all help to pitch *The Geek* somewhere between reality and nightmare." C. D. B. Bryan, discussing *The Geek* in the *New York Times Book Review,* writes that "there is no point in summarizing this plot; it isn't what happens that makes this book so strong. In fact, I find it difficult to articulate where exactly Craig Nova's genius lies. I know only that it has been a long time—a very long time—since I have come across a novel so gripping, a talent so exciting, so immense and so pure that I am ashamed I have not read him before. This book is so powerful, so alive, it is a wonder that turning its pages doesn't somehow burn one's hands."

In *Incandescence,* Nova again deals with assorted drifters and lowlifes; central among them is a formerly brilliant inventor now barely eking out a living as a New York City cab driver. While several critics praise the novel's style—"brisk and often funny," says Tim O'Brien in the *Saturday Review*—some also express reservations about the lack of growth of the characters and the absence of a credible plot. "The author has merely strung together a series of throwaway vignettes," writes Randall Rothenberg in the *New Leader.*

In *The Good Son* Nova leaves the seedy milieu of his earlier novels to tell the story of an upper-middle-class father and son in conflict. The story is narrated by a number of different characters as the novel progresses. While Carol L. Cardozo of *Library Journal* calls it "a well-written work," she finds that "the Faulknerian obliqueness and unrelieved atmosphere of menace are sometimes overdone." Similarly, Hermione Lee in the *Observer* claims that *The Good Son* "reads as though Faulkner had been cloned with the script-writer for 'Dynasty'." But John Irving,

writing in the *New York Times Book Review,* praises the novel: "[*The Good Son*] is not only Mr. Nova's best novel; it is the richest and most expert novel in my recent reading by any writer now under 40."

Where *The Good Son* focuses on the relationship between a father and son, *The Congressman's Daughter* examines the relationship between a father and daughter. When her controlling father dies, Alexandra Pearson discovers that she is bound by strict codicils in her father's will. These restrictions limit the scope of her life for the next twenty years, driving her finally into a love affair to escape the husband chosen for her by her late father. "A dry, credible bitterness pervades this latest novel by [Nova]," asserts a *Publishers Weekly* critic. Christopher Lehman-Haupt, reviewing the book for the *New York Times,* calls *The Congressman's Daughter* an "unlikely yet strangely plausible tale" and "a penetrating comment on American life."

In *Tornado Alley* Nova focuses his attention on small-town American life, telling the story of two doomed lovers. The "first two-thirds" of the book, according to Paul Stuewe in *Quill & Quire,* tells "an engrossing tale of mainstream American life, firmly grounded in an understanding of small-town mores and big-time dreams," but Stuewe finds the novel's violent ending less than credible. Andrei Codrescu, writing in the *New York Times Book Review,* praises the realism of the novel's setting. "Its world is painstakingly needlepointed in every detail," he writes. He considers the plot, however, ultimately unbelievable, although he points out "splendid moments that in themselves would have made beautiful small books." A critic for *Publishers Weekly,* though, concludes that *Tornado Alley* is a "riveting American tragedy comparable to that of Dreiser or Cain."

With *Trombone* Nova returns to an examination of a father and son relationship, this time between a minor hoodlum who works as an arsonist for the mob and his teenaged son, "two of the most vivid, appealing and surprising characters to appear in recent American fiction," Jonathan Yardley claims in the *Washington Post Book World. Trombone* is set in California and Nevada and, Bruce Cook notes in Chicago *Tribune Books,* is written with "an aridity that is altogether consistent with the setting . . . and with [the] characters, who seem as dry and emotionally withered as the landscapes in which they move." Lehmann-Haupt, writing in the *New York Times,* finds *Trombone* fascinatingly unpredictable, if not wholly successful: "you get the feeling . . . that with just a few more twists and a good hard shake, its pieces could fall into place to form something completely original." But George Stade in the *New York Times Book Review* believes that Nova "manages his imagery, his plot and his characters, pathetic or vicious or both, with impressive skill."

Nova writes of Hollywood in *The Book of Dreams,* following Warren Hodges, a film producer, Marta Brooks, his girlfriend, and Victor Shaw, an ex-con turned blackmailer. When Brooks accidentally kills a man who attacked her, Shaw uses the incident to force her into squeezing money from Hodges. Although Lawrence Thornton in the *New York Times Book Review* finds *The Book of Dreams* to be "a trip down a noirish memory lane" and "far too familiar," a critic for *Publishers Weekly* believes that "Nova deftly interweaves a glitzy Hollywood background with some good noir atmosphere." Carolyn See, reviewing for the *Washington Post,* finds the book unconvincing and excessively imitative of Hollywood chronicles by other authors, such as F. Scott Fitzgerald and Nathanael West. But Lehmann-Haupt, in the *New York Times,* concludes *The Book of Dreams* is "a powerful if ultimately comic nightmare."

BIOGRAPHICAL/CRITICAL SOURCES:

BOOKS

Contemporary Literary Criticism, Gale (Detroit), Volume 7, 1977, Volume 31, 1985.

PERIODICALS

Chicago Tribune Book World, February 25, 1979.
Library Journal, July, 1982, p. 1346; April 15, 1986, p. 96.
Los Angeles Times, June 16, 1994, p. E6.
New Leader, April 23, 1979, p. 20.
New York Review of Books, June 10, 1976.
New York Times, February 21, 1979; April 24, 1986, p. C21; July 23, 1992, p. C21; April 28, 1994, p. C22.
New York Times Book Review, October 29, 1972; December 21, 1973; February 11, 1979; October 3, 1982, p. 3; May 25, 1986, p. 6; July 23, 1989, pp. 7, 9; July 12, 1992, p. 10; June 5, 1994, p. 41.
Observer (London), February 6, 1983, p. 33.
Publishers Weekly, February 14, 1986, p. 70; March 17, 1989, p. 77; June 22, 1992, pp. 42-43; March 14, 1994, p. 61.
Punch, February 16, 1983, p. 41.

Quill & Quire, December, 1982, p. 30; July, 1989, p. 47.
Saturday Review, September 23, 1972; February 17, 1979, pp. 53-54.
Tribune Books (Chicago), June 21, 1992, p. 7.
Village Voice, November 3, 1975.
Washington Post, April 7, 1979; April 29, 1994, p. C2.
Washington Post Book World, June 28, 1992, p. 3.*

*   *   *

NOYCE, Gaylord B.   1926-

PERSONAL: Born July 8, 1926, in Burlington, Iowa; son of Ralph Brewster (a member of the clergy) and Harriet (Norton) Noyce; married Dorothy Caldwell (a school psychologist), May 25, 1949; children: Elizabeth Ann, Karen Virginia, Timothy Brewster. *Education:* Miami University, Oxford, Ohio, B.A., 1947; Yale University, M.Div., 1952.

ADDRESSES: Home—75 Washington Ave., Hamden, CT 06518. *Office*—Divinity School, Yale University, 409 Prospect St., New Haven, CT 06510.

CAREER: Member of the clegy of United Church of Christ; Robert College, Istanbul, Turkey, instructor in mathematics, 1947-49; assistant minister of congregational church in Lexington, MA, 1952-54; pastor of United Community Church in Raleigh, NC, 1954-60; Yale University, Divinity School, New Haven, CT, assistant professor 1960-65, associate professor, 1965-80, professor of pastoral theology, 1980-94, emeritus professor, 1994—. *Military service:* U.S. Navy, 1944-46.

WRITINGS:

The Church Is Not Expendable, Westminster (Philadelphia, PA), 1969.
The Responsible Suburban Church, Westminster, 1970.
Survival and Mission for the City Church, Westminster, 1975.
New Perspectives on Parish Ministry: A View from the Third World, Judson (Valley Forge, PA), 1981.
The Art of Pastoral Conversation, John Knox (Atlanta, GA), 1981.
(With Parker Rossman) *Helping People Care on the Job,* Judson, 1985.

Pastoral Ethics: Professional Responsibilities of the Clergy, Abingdon (Nashville, TN), 1988.
The Minister As Moral Counselor, Abingdon, 1989.
Church Meetings That Work, Alban Institute, 1994.

SIDELIGHTS: Gaylord B. Noyce wrote *CA,* "Most of my work is an attempt to enhance the religious vision and competence of congregations, their pastors, and the individuals in the pews."

*   *   *

OAKLEY, Allen   1943-

PERSONAL: Born July 22, 1943, in Adelaide, Australia; married Renate Rosenauer (a language teacher), February 1, 1982; children: Tania. *Education:* University of Adelaide, B.Ec. (with first class honors), 1972, Ph.D., 1980. *Politics:* "Democratic Socialist."

ADDRESSES: Office—Department of Economics, University of Newcastle, Newcastle, New South Wales 2308, Australia. *E-mail*—ecaco@cc.newcastle.edu.au

CAREER: Adelaide College of Advanced Education, Adelaide, Australia, lecturer in economics, 1973-77; University of Newcastle, Newcastle, Australia, lecturer, 1977-82, senior lecturer, 1983-89, associate professor of economics, 1990—.

MEMBER: International Network for Economic Method, History of Economic Thought Society (Australia), Association for Social Economics, History of Economics Society.

WRITINGS:

The Making of Marx's Critical Theory: A Bibliographical Analysis, Routledge & Kegan Paul (Boston, MA), 1983.
Marx's Critique of Political Economy: Intellectual Sources and Evolution, Routledge & Kegan Paul, volume 1, 1984, volume 2, 1985.
(Editor) Adolph Lowe, *Essays in Political Economics: Public Control in a Democratic Society,* New York University Press (New York City), 1987.
Schumpeter's Theory of Capitalist Motion: A Critical Exposition and Reassessment, Edward Elgar Publishing, 1990.
Classical Economic Man: Human Agency and Methodology in the Political Economy of Adam Smith and J. S. Mill, Edward Elgar Publishing, 1994.
The Foundations of Austrian Economics from Menger to Mises: A Critico-historical Retrospective of Subjectivism, Edward Elgar Publishing, 1996.

Contributor to economic journals.

WORK IN PROGRESS: The Revival of Modern Austrian Economics: A Critical Reassessment and Reconstruction of Subjectivism for Edward Elgar Publishing.

P-Q

PAREEK, Udai (Narain) 1925-

PERSONAL: Born January 21, 1925, in Jaipur, India; son of Vijailal and Gaindi Pareek; married Rama Sharma, May 13, 1945; children: Sushama, Surabhi, Anagat. *Education:* St. Johns College, Agra, India, B.A., 1944; Teachers Training College, Ajmer, India, B.T., 1945; Calcutta University, M.A., 1950; Agra University, M.A., 1952; University of Delhi, Ph.D., 1956.

ADDRESSES: Home—1 Yamuna Path, Suraj Nagar W., Jaipur 302006, India.

CAREER: Teachers Training School, Jaipur, India, teacher of psychology, 1945-48; Teachers Training College, Bikaner, India, lecturer in psychology, 1953-54; Delhi School of Social Work, Delhi, India, lecturer in psychology, 1954-55; National Institute of Basic Education, New Delhi, India, psychologist, 1956-62; Indian Agricultural Research Institute, New Delhi, psychologist, 1962-64; Small Industry Extension Training Institute, Hyderabad, India, director of extension education, 1964-66; University of North Carolina at Chapel Hill, visiting associate professor of psychology, 1966-68; National Institute of Health Administration and Education, New Delhi, professor of social sciences, 1968-70; University of Udaipur, Udaipur, India, director of School of Basic Sciences and Humanities and dean of faculty of social sciences, 1970-73; Indian Institute of Management, Ahmedabad, Larsen and Toubro Professor of Organisational Behaviour, 1973-85; Ministry of Health, Government of Indonesia, organization development advisor, 1985-88; University of North Carolina at Chapel Hill, adjunct professor of health policy, 1993—.

Chair of Institute of Development Studies; member of governing board, National Institute of Motivational and Institutional Development, National Insurance Academy, and Indian Institute of Health Management Research; member of advisory committee, Family Planning Foundation of India.

MEMBER: Society for the Psychological Study of Social Issues, National HRD Network (president, 1992-94), Indian Psychological Association, Madras Psychological Association, Andhra Pradesh Psychological Association (president, 1964-66), Indian Society of Applied Behavioural Science (president, 1987).

AWARDS, HONORS: Escorts Award, 1981, for *Designing and Managing Human Resource Systems,* and 1993, for *Making Organizational Roles Effective.*

WRITINGS:

Developmental Patterns in Reaction to Frustration, Asia Publishing House (Bombay), 1964.

(With S. R. Mittal) *A Guide to the Literature of Research Methodology in Behavioural Sciences,* Behavioural Sciences Centre (Delhi), 1965.

(Editor) *Studies in Rural Leadership,* Behavioural Sciences Centre, 1966.

Behavioural Science Research in India: A Directory, 1925-1965, Acharan Sahkar, 1966.

A Guide to Indian Behavioural Science Periodicals, Behavioural Sciences Centre, 1966.

(With Rolf P. Lynton) *Training for Development,* Irwin (Homewood, IL), 1967, 2nd edition, Kumarian (West Hartford, CT), 1991.

(With S. R. Devi and Saul Rosenzweig) *Manual of the Indian Adaptation of the Adult Form of the Rosenzweig P. F. Study,* Roopa Psychological Corp., 1968.

(With Willis H. Griffin) *The Process of Planned Change in Education,* Somaiya, 1969.

Foreign Behavioural Research on India: A Directory of Research and Researchers, Acharan Sahkar, 1970.

(With T. V. Rao) *A Status Study on Population Research in India,* Volume 1, McGraw (New York City), 1974.

(With Rao) *Handbook of Psychological and Social Instruments,* Samashti, 1974.

(With Y. P. Singh and D. R. Arora) *Diffusion of an Interdiscipline,* Bookhive, 1974.

(With Rao and Ravi Matthai) *Institution Building in Education and Research: From Stagnation to Self-Renewal,* All India Management Association, 1977.

(With Rao) *Performance Appraisal and Review: Trainers Manual, Operating Manual, and Skills Workbook,* Learning Systems, 1978.

(With Rao) *Developing Entrepreneurship,* Learning Systems, 1978.

Survey of Psychological Research in India, 1971-1976, Popular Prakashan, Part 1, 1980, Part 2, 1982.

(With Rao) *Designing and Managing Human Resource Systems,* Oxford University Press (Oxford, England), 1981, 2nd edition, 1991.

Beyond Management: Essays on the Processes of Institution Building, Oxford University Press, 1981, revised enlarged edition, 1993.

(With Rao and D. M. Pestonjee) *Behavioural Processes in Organisations,* Oxford University Press, 1981.

(With Rao) *Handbook for Trainers in Educational Management,* UNESCO Regional Office for Education in Asia and the Pacific, 1981.

(With Rao) *Developing Motivation through Experiencing,* Oxford University Press, 1982, 2nd edition, 1992.

(With Somnath Chattopadhyay) *Managing Organisational Change,* Oxford University Press, 1982.

Managing Conflict and Collaboration, Oxford University Press, 1982, revised edition published as *Conflict and Collaboration in Organizations,* 1992.

Education and Rural Development in Asia, Oxford University Press, 1982.

Role Stress Scales, Navin Publishers, 1982.

Role Pics: Coping with Role Stress, Navin Publishers, 1982.

Perilaku Organisasi (title means "Organizational Behaviour"), Pustak Binaman Pressindo (Jakarta, Indonesia), 1984.

(With Lynton) *Pelatihan dan Pengembangan Tenaga Kerja* (title means "Training and Manpower Development"), Pustak Binaman Pressindo, 1984.

Memahami Proses Perilaku Organisasi (title means "Teaching Organizational Behaviour"), Pustak Binaman Pressindo, 1985.

Medayagunakan Peran-Peran Keorganisasian (title means "Motivating Organizational Roles"), Pustak Binaman Pressindo, 1985.

Motivating Organizational Roles: Role Efficacy Approach, Rawat Publications (Jaipur, India), 1987.

Organizational Behaviour Processes, Rawat Publications, 1988.

(With R. Padaki and R. R. Nair) *Managing Transition: The HRD Response,* Tata McGraw-Hill (India), 1992.

(With Lynton) *Facilitating Development: Readings for Trainers, Consultants and Policy-Makers,* Sage Publications (Beverly Hills, CA), 1992.

(With Matthai and Rao) *Management Processes in Universities,* Oxford University Press and IBH, 1992.

Making Organizational Roles Effective, Tata McGraw-Hill, 1993.

(With Rao) *Redesigning Performance Appraisal,* Tata McGraw-Hill, 1996.

Instruments for Human Resource Development, Tata McGraw-Hill, 1996.

OTHER

Contributor to books, including *Consultants and Consulting Styles,* edited by Dharni P. Sinha, Vision Books (Coos Bay, OR), 1979; *Manpower Management,* edited by R. S. Dwivedi, Prentice-Hall (India), 1980; and *Instrumentation Kit,* edited by Pfeiffer and A. C. Ballew, University Associates (San Diego, CA), 1988. Also contributor to human resource and group facilitator annuals, edited by Pfeiffer. Editor of *Indian Psychological Abstracts* and *Manas.* Member of editorial board, *Psychologia, Managerial Psychology, Group and Organization Studies, Psychological Panorama,* and *New Trends in Education;* member of advisory group for *Theory and Models Kit,* University Associates.

SIDELIGHTS: Udai Pareek once told *CA:* "My current work and writings are concerned with helping individuals, groups, and organizations to take charge of shaping their own destinies, and develop pro-social behavior. My main contribution has been to approach motivation from the point of view of hope (contrasted with fear), and the concept of "extension motive'—an urge to be relevant to a larger group or cause, in a way extending oneself to others. I have been working on extension motive and empowering in organizations, so critical for developing countries."

*   *   *

PARFENIE, Maria
  See CODRESCU, Andrei

*   *   *

PAVLOWITCH, Stevan K. 1933-

PERSONAL: Born September 7, 1933, in Belgrade, Yugoslavia; son of Kosta (a diplomat) and Mara (Dyoukitch) Pavlowitch; married France Raffray; children: Kosta (a son). *Education:* University of Paris and University of Lille, licence es lettres, 1956; King's College, London, B.A., 1956; School of Slavonic and Eastern European Studies, London, M.A., 1959.

ADDRESSES: Office—Department of History, University of Southampton, Highfield, Southampton S017 1BJ, England.

CAREER: Employed in field of public relations as a journalist in Brussels, Stockholm, Milan, and London, 1958-65; University of Southampton, Highfield, Southampton, England, 1965—, began as lecturer, currently professor in Balkan history, department of history and Mountbatten Centre for International Studies.

WRITINGS:

Anglo-Russian Rivalry in Serbia, 1837-1839: The Mission of Colonel Hodges, Mouton, 1961.
Yugoslavia, Praeger, 1971.
Bijou d'Art: Histoires de la vie, de l'ouvre et du milieu de Bojidar Karageorgevitch, artiste parisien et prince balkanique, L'Age d'Homme, 1978.
(Contributor) R. Clogg, editor, *Balkan Society in the Age of Greek Independence,* Macmillan, 1981.
The Albanian Problem in Yugoslavia: Two Views, Institute for Study of Conflict, 1982.

Unconventional Perceptions of Yugoslavia, 1940-45, Columbia University Press (New York City), 1985.
(Contributor) L. Kaplan and others, editors, *NATO and the Mediterranean,* Scholarly Resources (Wilmington, DE), 1985.
The Improbable Survivor: Yugoslavia and Its Problems, 1918-88, Hurst and Ohio State University Press (Columbus), 1988.
(Contributor) P. Ramet, editor, *Eastern Christianity and Politics in the Twentieth Century,* Duke University Press (Durham, NC), 1988.
Yugoslavia's Great Dictator, Tito: A Reassessment, Hurst and Ohio State University Press, 1992.
(Contributor) J. Ruprik, editor, *De Sarajevo a Sarajevo—L'echec yougoslave,* Editions complete, 1992.
(Contributor) Ruprik, editor, *Le Dechirement des nations,* Seuil, 1995.

Contributor to numerous periodicals, including *Daedalus, Journal of Contemporary History, War and Society, European History Review, European Journal of International Affairs, L'Autre Europe, Commentaire,* and *Vingtieme Siecle.*

WORK IN PROGRESS: A history of the Balkans, 1804-1945.

*   *   *

PICKERING, James H(enry) 1937-

PERSONAL: Born July 11, 1937, in New York, NY; son of James Henry and Anita (Felber) Pickering; married Patricia Paterson, August 18, 1962; children: David Scott, Susan Elizabeth. *Education:* Williams College, B.A., 1959; Northwestern University, M.A., 1960, Ph.D., 1964. *Religion:* Protestant.

ADDRESSES: Home—13602 Queensbury Lane, Houston, TX 77079. *Office*—Department of English, University of Houston, Houston, TX 77204-2162.

CAREER: Michigan State University, East Lansing, assistant professor, 1965-68, associate professor, 1968-72, professor of English, 1972-81, associate chair of department and director of graduate study, 1968-75, director of Honors College, 1975-81; University of Houston, Houston, TX, dean of College of Humanities and Fine Arts, and professor of English, 1981-90, senior vice president and provost, 1990-92, president, 1992-95. Consultant.

MEMBER: Phi Beta Kappa, Omicron Delta Kappa, Phi Kappa Phi, Golden Key.

WRITINGS:

(Editor) Herman Melville, *Five Tales,* Dodd (New York City), 1967.

(Editor with E. Fred Carlisle) *The Harper Reader,* Harper (New York City), 1971.

(Editor) James Fenimore Cooper, *The Spy: A Tale of the Neutral Ground,* College & University Press (New Haven, CT), 1971.

(Compiler) *Fiction 100: An Anthology of Short Stories,* Macmillan (New York City), 1974, 7th edition, 1995.

(Editor) *The World Turned Upside Down: The Prose and Poetry of the American Revolution,* Kennikat (Washington, NY), 1975.

(Editor) H. L. Barnum, *The Spy Unmasked,* Harbor Hill (Harrison, NY), 1975.

(Editor) *The City in American Literature,* Harper (New York City), 1977.

(With Jeffrey D. Hoeper) *Concise Companion to Literature,* Macmillan, 1981.

(With Hoeper) *Literature: An Anthology,* Macmillan, 1982, 5th edition, in press.

(Editor) Frederick H. Chapin, *Mountaineering in Colorado: The Peaks about Estes Park,* University of Nebraska Press (Lincoln), 1987.

(Editor) Joe Mills, *A Mountain Boyhood,* University of Nebraska Press 1988.

(Editor) Enos Abijah Mills, *Wild Life on the Rockies,* University of Nebraska Press, 1988.

(Editor) Enos Abijah Mills, *Spell of the Rockies,* University of Nebraska Press, 1989.

(With Hoeper) *Purpose and Process,* Macmillan, 1989.

(With Hoeper) *Poetry,* Macmillan, 1990.

(Editor) Enos Abijah Mills, *In Beaver World,* University of Nebraska Press, 1990.

(Editor) Enos Abijah Mills, *The Rocky Mountain Wonderland,* University of Nebraska Press, 1991.

(Editor) Samuel Bowles, *The Switzerland of America: A Summer Vacation in the Parks and Mountains of Colorado,* University of Oklahoma Press (Norman), 1992.

(Compiler) *Fiction 50: An Anthology of Short Stories,* Macmillan, 1993.

(With Hoeper and Deborah Chappel) *Drama,* Macmillan, 1994.

(Editor) Ernest Ingersoll, *Knocking around the Rockies,* University of Oklahoma Press, 1994.

(Editor) Frederick H. Chapin, *Frederick Chapin's Colorado: The Peaks about Estes Park and Other Writings,* University Press of Colorado, 1995.

Contributor to history and literature journals, including *Colorado Heritage* and *New York History.* Member of editorial board, *Journal of the American Studies Association of Texas,* 1988-90.

WORK IN PROGRESS: "This Blue Hollow": The Annals of Estes Park, A Colorado Reader; research on nineteenth-century American literature, Western American history and literature, and higher education.

*   *   *

PIERSEN, William D.   1942-

PERSONAL: Born April 15, 1942, in Highland Park, IL; son of Benjamin G. (a real estate broker) and Katherine A. (a homemaker; maiden name, Dillon) Piersen; married Charlotte L. Graham (a librarian), August 3, 1968; children: Katherine L. *Education:* Grinnell College, B.A., 1964; Indiana University— Bloomington, M.A., 1967, M.A., 1968, Ph.D., 1975.

ADDRESSES: Home—405 Arrowwood Dr., Nashville, TN 37211. *Office*—Department of History, Fisk University, 17th Ave. N., Nashville, TN 37208.

CAREER: Purdue University, Calumet Campus, Hammond, IN, instructor in history, 1971-73; Springfield College, Springfield, MA, instructor in history, 1974-75; Texas Tech University, Lubbock, visiting assistant professor of history, 1976-77; Fisk University, Nashville, TN, assistant professor, 1977- 84, associate professor, 1985-88, professor of history, 1988—, chair of department, 1980-87.

MEMBER: American Historical Association, Organization of American Historians, Association for the Study of Afro-American Life and History, American Studies Association.

WRITINGS:

Black Yankees: The Development of an Afro-American Subculture in Eighteenth-Century New England, University of Massachusetts Press (Amherst), 1988.

Black Legacy: America's Hidden Heritage, University of Massachusetts Press, 1993.

From Africa to America: African-American History from the Colonial Era to the Early Republic, 1526-1790, Twayne (Boston), 1996.

Contributor of more than 370 articles and abstracts to history journals.

WORK IN PROGRESS: A monograph on African and Afro-American royalty in the Americas; a brief introductory world history textbook.

SIDELIGHTS: William D. Piersen told *CA:* "All my books argue that the cultural legacy of Africa was formative in the building of America. Nominally historical, my work is equally informed with the social and cultural interests of my folkloristic background. I have come to understand that my choice of topics and approach mirrors the era of my youth when the civil rights struggle and the questioning of American values asked us all, 'Which side are you on?' My answer, as it turned out, came later in unexpected life choices and writing decisions. Because my books wander into the topics that interest me, rather than following some narrow chronological subject, they reflect their author far more than I ever understood when I was writing them. I most enjoy their signifying humor.

"I have tried in each book to write with a clear style devoid of social science jargon and scholarly pretentiousness. I think of myself more as a writer than as an historian. I spend a lot of time on metaphors I later reject. Like most writers I hate the empty page and love the process of revision. I learned more about rewriting from Robert H. Ferrell of Indiana University than from anyone else, and I try to repay my debt by continuing to teach freshman writing sections while a Professor of History at Fisk.

"Research and writing are solitary pursuits with an oddly social intent. Writing is a Janus-like art that can mask or reveal. In my case, I have tried to rewrite history, to change the past irrevocably without altering it at all. To write is to possess magic."

*   *   *

PLAIN, Belva 1919-

PERSONAL: Born October 9, 1919, in New York, NY; daughter of Oscar and Eleanor Offenberg; married Irving Plain (a physician), June 14, 1941 (died December, 1982); children: three. *Education:* Graduated from Barnard College.

ADDRESSES: Home—77 Slope Drive, Short Hills, NJ 07078. *Office*—c/o Delacorte Press, 666 Fifth Ave., New York, NY 10103.

CAREER: Writer.

WRITINGS:

NOVELS

Evergreen (Literary Guild selection), Delacorte (New York City), 1978.
Random Winds, Delacorte, 1980.
Eden Burning, Delacorte, 1982.
Crescent City, Delacorte, 1984.
The Golden Cup, Delacorte, 1987.
Tapestry, Delacorte, 1988.
Blessings, Delacorte, 1989.
Harvest, Delacorte, 1990.
Treasures, Delacorte, 1992.
Whispers, Delacorte, 1993.
Daybreak, Delacorte, 1994.
The Carousel, Delacorte, 1995.
Promises, Delacorte, 1996.

OTHER

Contributor of several dozen short stories to periodicals, including *McCall's, Good Housekeeping, Redbook,* and *Cosmopolitan.*

ADAPTATIONS: Evergreen was produced as a miniseries by the National Broadcasting Co. (NBC) in 1985.

SIDELIGHTS: Best-selling author Belva Plain began her career by writing formula fiction for women's magazines in the 1940s. *Cosmopolitan* and *Good Housekeeping* printed her stories of women in love, some of whom toyed with the idea of having extramarital affairs but chose in the end to honor their vows. Her enthusiasm for writing such stories then took second place to the activities of family life, and for about twelve years she wrote almost nothing for publication. However, she remained an avid reader. Jewish characters in novels she read during that time were slight variations on stereotypes that she found repugnant and inaccurate, and by the 1950s, she was moved to provide an alternative view of Jewish American life in her first book-length work. *Evergreen*—the story of a young immigrant maid, Anna, who falls in love with her boss's son Paul—became the first of many best-sellers for Plain. There are now more than eleven million copies of this book in a dozen languages.

Unlike the dominating, hysterical Jewish mothers of contemporary myth, Plain's women characters are good mothers, discreet lovers, and emotionally strong. As capable in business as in domestic affairs, they make the best of unchangeable circumstances, finding fulfillment despite repeated disappointment. They often have to overcome the problems of immigration and other challenges related to their heritage, yet they elicit the interest of many readers outside the ethnic circle. Laura Kavesh notes in the *Chicago Tribune* that "Plain characters march through life courageously and usually with great success—but bearing private, searing aches over love just out of reach, the kind that sneaks along behind its slaves forever, jumping out in front of them now and again to shake things up."

Plain's novels also take readers to other places and times. *Eden Burning* takes place on a Caribbean island, and *Crescent City* goes back to the Civil War era. "It's all here," writes Gay Courter in the *Washington Post,* "moss and mansions, languid afternoons and clandestine evenings, repressed old maids and irresistible quadroons, the glamour and gore of war, chance encounters and missed opportunities." Furthermore, the novel uncovers little-known details about Jewish life during that period of American history. For example, Jews stood on both sides of the conflict over slavery, but only those on the Confederate side were allowed to have chaplains until Lincoln learned of this inequity among the Northern troops. The surprise ending, remarks Courter, lends a seldom-seen view of "American Jewry and southern history" that incites readers to further research on historical figures of the Civil War era.

Following the same sense of fair play that inspired *Evergreen,* Plain takes a second look at Anna's life in *The Golden Cup,* this time to fully explore her story from Paul's point of view. *Tapestry,* the third book in the Werner family saga, looks at the lives of Anna's grandchildren. The chronicle is informed by the author's own family experiences, she told *CA:* "I had always been curious about my own grandmother, who came here from Europe at the age of sixteen. Such courage! I think of her still saying a final good-bye and sailing toward an unknown world so long ago. She never saw her people again. Of course, all that is a common American adventure: the loneliness, the struggles and failures—and sometimes, the rise to shining affluence. *Evergreen* is everybody's story whether he be of Irish, Italian, Polish, or any other stock."

Plain told *CA* that she has visited all the many foreign settings featured in her novels: "I've never really written about any place that I haven't seen, because I think that's artificial; it's phony. Readers are intelligent. They can sense when you've made something up. Even for the one book that took place far back in history, a time I couldn't have known firsthand, the Civil War, still I went through Louisiana plantations that have been restored and opened to the public. You can see from them exactly how people lived—the wash basins in the bedrooms, the chamber pots, everything as it was. I always do write about what I have actually seen."

When asked to explain the popularity of her characters, Plain told Kavesh, "I think I show real people and a real understanding of human nature, how people function and react to their environment. And there's a good story line." Plain's approach to writing a story is inspired by the sprawling Victorian novels of the 19th century. She told *CA:* "I've always liked books, especially the Victorians, that start with a person almost at birth and show you his growth, like a vine that spreads and puts out tendrils. You see people grow up, marry—or not marry!—and go through a whole series of events, reach out to other areas and other people; yet you always have the background of childhood in your mind, so you know the character quite thoroughly and know how he's going to react to whatever happens. I enjoy reading books like that, and I enjoy writing them."

Plain writes for about five hours every morning and then reads her work into a tape recorder, after which a secretary types it. She has told *CA,* "My primary motive for writing is the same as a painter's or a musician's: for love of it." Her inspiration comes from people she meets and events she reads about in newspapers. Further, she has explained, "Odd glimpses of characters and personalities in public places give rise to story-weaving in my head. . . . The world is fascinating. There is a story in every human life if you look for it."

BIOGRAPHICAL/CRITICAL SOURCES:

PERIODICALS

Best Sellers, August, 1978; August, 1980; September, 1982; November, 1984; December, 1986.
Books, February, 1988.
Chicago Tribune, October 12, 1984.

New York Times Book Review, July 30, 1978; August 22, 1982; October 7, 1984; June 19, 1988; May 17, 1992; May 8, 1994.
Publishers Weekly, May 21, 1979; March 28, 1980; March 18, 1988.
Washington Post, September 28, 1984.
West Coast Review of Books, July, 1978.
Woman's Day, February 16, 1988.

* * *

PLASKOW, Judith (Ellen) 1947-

PERSONAL: Born March 14, 1947, in Brooklyn, NY; married, 1969 (divorced, 1986); children: one. *Education:* Clark University, A.B., 1968; Yale University, M.Phil., 1971, Ph.D., 1975.

ADDRESSES: Home—75-75 Utopia Parkway, Fresh Meadows, NY 11366. *Office*—Department of Religious Studies, Manhattan College, College Parkway, Riverdale, NY 10471.

CAREER: New York University, New York, NY, assistant professor of religion, 1974-75; Wichita State University, Wichita, KS, assistant professor of religion, 1976-79; Manhattan College, Riverdale, NY, assistant professor, 1979-84, associate professor, 1984-90, professor of religion, 1990—. Visiting appointments as lecturer or professor at colleges and universities, including New York University, University of Southern California, Harvard Divinity School, and Union Theological Seminary, 1981-1995.

MEMBER: American Academy of Religion (secretary and member of executive committee, 1980-84; associate director, 1992-94; vice president, 1995-96), American Theological Society, Women's Caucus for Religious Studies, New York Feminist Scholars in Religion.

WRITINGS:

Sex, Sin, and Grace: Women's Experience and the Theologies of Reinhold Niebuhr and Paul Tillich, University Press of America (Lanham, MD), 1980.
Standing Again at Sinai: Judaism from a Feminist Perspective, Harper (New York City), 1990.

EDITOR

Women and Religion 1972, American Academy of Religion, 1972.
(With Joan Arnold Romero) *Women and Religion 1974,* American Academy of Religion, 1974.
(With Carol P. Christ) *Womanspirit Rising: A Feminist Reader in Religion,* Harper, 1979.
(With Christ) *Weaving the Visions: New Patterns in Feminist Spirituality,* Harper, 1989.

OTHER

Contributor of articles to books, including *Women's Spirit Bounding,* edited by Janet Kalven and Mary Buckley, Pilgrim Press, 1984, and *On Being a Jewish Feminist: A Reader,* edited by Susannah Heschel, Schocken Books, 1983. Contributor of numerous articles to journals, including *Response, Manna, Reconstructionist, Tikkun* and *Cross Currents.* Co-founder and coeditor, *Journal of Feminist Studies,* 1983-94; member of editorial board and columnist, *Tikkun.* Plaskow's books have been translated into German, Japanese and Dutch.

BIOGRAPHICAL/CRITICAL SOURCES:

PERIODICALS

New York Times Book Review, July 29, 1979.

* * *

POTEET, G(eorge) Howard 1935-

PERSONAL: Born March 31, 1935, in Baltimore, MD; son of G. Howard (a computer operator) and Catherine (Aro) Poteet; married Hilda Klock, January 21, 1956 (divorced, 1961); married Frances Rosenthal (a teacher), October 3, 1961 (divorced, 1983); married Anna Cheng, October 21, 1983; children: Cynthia, Christopher, Jennifer. *Education:* Shippensburg State College, B.S., 1961; Columbia University, M.A., 1964, Prof.Dip., 1965, Ed.D., 1971. *Avocational interests:* Photography, bicycling, antiques, electronics, computers.

ADDRESSES: Home—21 Princeton St., Nutley, NJ 07110. *Office*—Department of English, Essex County College, 303 University Ave., Newark NJ 07102.

CAREER: English teacher in public schools in Pennsylvania and New Jersey, 1957-68; Essex County College, Newark, NJ, associate professor, 1968-74, professor of English, 1974—, head of department, 1968-75. President, G. Howard Poteet, Inc. (publishing firm), 1974—. Film and linguistics consultant to schools and businesses; educational consultant to various distance education schools.

MEMBER: National Council of Teachers of English (chair of committee on film study), Modern Language Association of America, National Education Association.

AWARDS, HONORS: Award of Excellence, Sixteenth Annual Exhibition of *Communications Arts* (magazine), 1975, for *Tom Swift and His Electric English Teacher.*

WRITINGS:

Film Criticism in Popular American Periodicals: 1933-1967, Revisionist Press (Brooklyn, NY), 1971.

Sentence Strategies: Writing for College, Harcourt (San Diego, CA), 1971.

The Complete Guide to Film Study, National Council of Teachers of English (Urbana, IL), 1972.

Tom Swift and His Electric English Teacher, Pflaum/Standard (Fairfield, NJ), 1974.

Radio!, Pflaum/Standard, 1975.

Death and Dying: A Bibliography, Whitston Publishing (Troy, NY), 1976, supplement, 1978.

How to Live in Your Van and Love It!, Trail-R-Club of America (Escondido, CA), 1976.

Published Radio, TV, and Film Scripts: A Bibliography, Whitston Publishing, 1976.

Workbench Guide to Tape Recorder Servicing, Parker Publishing (Englewood Cliffs, NJ), 1976.

The Complete Guide to Making Money, G. Howard Poteet, Inc., 1976.

Treasure Hunting in the City, Ram Publishing (Salt Lake City, UT), 1977.

Your Career in Chiropractic, Richard Rosen (New York City), 1977, revised edition, 1985.

Suicide, Whitston Publishing, 1978.

Complete Guide to the Use and Maintenance of Hand and Power Tools, Parker Publishing, 1978.

There's a School in Your Mailbox, National Home Study Council, 1979, revised edition, 1980.

Complete Illustrated Guide to Basic Carpentry, Parker Publishing, 1980.

Professional Photography, SCI, 1986.

We Succeeded through Home Study, National Home Study Council, 1986.

Powerboating, PC, 1987.

Starting Up Your Own Business, McGraw (New York City), 1991.

Making Your Small Business a Success, McGraw, 1991.

How to Speak and Write English Correctly, The Center for Research in English, 1993.

Tips, Tricks, and Hints for Effective Business and Professional Writing, The Center for Research in English, 1995.

Practical Tips, Tricks, and Hints to Help You Master Correct English!, The Center for Research in English, 1996.

1,000 Words that Every Educated Person Must Know, The Center for Research in English, 1996.

Also author of *The Complete Guide to Making Money from Your Writing,* 1996, and *How to Use Your Computer to Write Effectively,* 1996. Author of tape-and-text series "The English Program," Williamsville Publishing, 1976, revised edition, 1993; also author of numerous other lessons, tapes, and texts for distance education schools in photography, locksmithing, and building trades. Contributor of poetry, short stories, and articles to periodicals, including *English Journal, Media and Methods, Reading Instruction Journal, Mechanix Illustrated,* and the *New York Times.* Member of editorial board, *New Jersey Audio-Visual News;* contributing editor, *Film Journal Newsletter;* editor in chief, *College English Notes, Printing Trade Secrets* newsletter; and *How to Make Extra Money Newsletter.*

SIDELIGHTS: G. Howard Poteet told *CA:* "I have always wanted to write. When I was a young child, I took delight in writing stories. In the seventh grade I wrote a short story a week. My first published article, a description of winter in the country, was published during the summer between when I was in the eighth and ninth grades. I wrote for my high school papers in various schools that I attended and wrote for the newspaper and literary magazine while attending Shippensburg State College.

"However, I have always wanted to write for money and even today, I think that that is what proves a writer's worth. Even Shakespeare wrote for money, didn't he? Fame and all the trappings are less important than being paid cash for words. I know that most of my colleagues who are scholars will disagree. However, I have spent my life as a scholar. I have the doctoral degree, which is a union card and have made it to tenured full professor. I have published in scholarly journals and have been active in scholarly organizations. In sum, I fail to see why writers shouldn't be proud of the fact that someone is willing to pay to read what they've written."

*　*　*

QUELCH, John A(nthony)   1951-

PERSONAL: Born August 8, 1951, in London, England; came to the United States in 1972; son of Norman (an accountant) and Laura S. (a nurse; maiden name, Jones) Quelch; married Joyce Ann Huntley. *Education:* Oxford University, B.A., 1972, M.A., 1976; University of Pennsylvania, M.B.A., 1974; Harvard University, D.B.A., 1977, M.S., 1978.

ADDRESSES: Home—57 Baker Bridge Rd., Lincoln, MA 01773. *Office*—Harvard Business School, Harvard University, Soldiers Field, Boston, MA 02163.

CAREER: University of Western Ontario, London, assistant professor of business 1977-79; Harvard Business School, Harvard University, Boston, assistant professor, 1979-84, associate professor, 1984-88, professor of business, 1988-93, Sebastian S. Kresge Professor of Marketing, 1993—. President of Marque Associates, Inc.; director of Reebok International Ltd., WPP Group PLC, U.S. Office Products Company, Council of Better Business Bureaus.

WRITINGS:

Advertising and Promotion Management, Chilton (Radnor, PA), 1983, 2nd edition, Robert E. Krieger (Melbourne, FL), 1987.

Cases in Advertising and Promotion Management, Business Publications (Plano, TX), 1983, 4th edition, Irwin (Homewood, IL), 1994.

Consumer Behavior for Marketing Managers, Allyn & Bacon (Newton, MA), 1984.

Marketing Management, three volumes, Irwin, 1985, 2nd edition, 1993.

Cases in Consumer Behavior, 2nd edition, Prentice-Hall (Englewood Cliffs, NJ), 1986.

Multinational Marketing Management, Addison-Wesley (Reading, MA), 1988, 3rd edition republished as *Global Marketing Management,* 1995.

Sales Promotion Management, Prentice-Hall, 1989.

How to Market to Consumers, Wiley (New York City), 1989.

The Marketing Challenge of 1992, 2nd edition, Addison-Wesley, 1991.

Ethics in Marketing, Irwin, 1992.

Cases in European Marketing Management, Irwin, 1994.

Cases in Product Management, Irwin, 1995.

Contributor to business journals.

BIOGRAPHICAL/CRITICAL SOURCES:

PERIODICALS

Harvard Business School Bulletin, December, 1983.

R

RAMPLING, Anne
See RICE, Anne

* * *

RICE, Anne 1941-
(Anne Rampling, A. N. Roquelaure)

PERSONAL: Original given name, Howard Allen; name changed, c. 1947; born October 4, 1941, in New Orleans, LA; daughter of Howard (a postal worker, novelist, and sculptor) and Katherine (Allen) O'Brien; married Stan Rice (a poet and painter), October 14, 1961; children: Michele (deceased), Christopher. *Education:* Attended Texas Woman's University, 1959-60; San Francisco State College (now University), B.A., 1964, M.A., 1971; graduate study at University of California, Berkeley, 1969-70. *Avocational interests:* Traveling, ancient Greek history, archaeology, social history since the beginning of recorded time, old movies on television, and "going to boxing matches—am fascinated by performers of all kinds, and by sports which involve one man against another or against a force."

ADDRESSES: Home—1239 First St., New Orleans, LA 70130. *Office*—c/o Alfred A. Knopf, 201 East 50th St., New York, NY 10022. *Agent*—Jacklyn Nesbit Associates, 598 Madison Ave., New York, NY 10022.

CAREER: Writer. Held a variety of jobs, including waitress, cook, theater usherette, and insurance claims examiner.

MEMBER: Authors Guild.

AWARDS, HONORS: Joseph Henry Jackson Award (honorable mention), 1970.

WRITINGS:

NOVELS

The Feast of All Saints, Simon & Schuster (New York City), 1980.
Cry to Heaven, Knopf (New York City), 1982.
The Mummy: or, Ramses the Damned (Book-of-the-Month Club main selection), Ballantine (New York City), 1989.
Servant of the Bones, Knopf, 1996.

"VAMPIRE CHRONICLES" SERIES

Interview with the Vampire (Book-of-the-Month Club alternate selection; also see below), Knopf, 1976.
The Vampire Lestat (also see below), Ballantine, 1985.
The Queen of the Damned (Literary Guild main selection; also see below), Knopf, 1988.
Vampire Chronicles (contains *Interview with the Vampire, The Vampire Lestat,* and *The Queen of the Damned*), Ballantine, 1989, hardcover edition, Random House (New York City), 1990.
The Tale of the Body Thief, Knopf, 1992.
Memnoch the Devil, Knopf, 1995.

"LIVES OF THE MAYFAIR WITCHES" SERIES

The Witching Hour (Book-of-the-Month Club main selection), Knopf, 1990.

Lasher, Knopf, 1993.
Taltos, Knopf, 1994.

EROTIC NOVELS; UNDER PSEUDONYM A. N. ROQUELAURE

The Claiming of Sleeping Beauty, Dutton (New York City), 1983.
Beauty's Punishment, Dutton, 1984.
Beauty's Release: The Continued Erotic Adventures of Sleeping Beauty, Dutton, 1985.
The Sleeping Beauty Novels (contains *The Claiming of Sleeping Beauty, Beauty's Punishment,* and *Beauty's Release: The Continued Erotic Adventures of Sleeping Beauty*), New American Library (New York City), 1991.

NOVELS; UNDER PSEUDONYM ANNE RAMPLING

Exit to Eden, Arbor House (New York City), 1985.
Belinda, Arbor House, 1986.

SCREENPLAY

Interview with the Vampire (adapted from her novel; starring Tom Cruise and Brad Pitt; directed by Neil Jordan), Geffen Pictures, 1994.

OTHER

Contributor of numerous book reviews to *San Francisco Chronicle* and *San Francisco Bay Guardian.*

ADAPTATIONS: Many of Rice's novels have been recorded on audiocassette and released by Random House AudioBooks, including *Interview with the Vampire* (read by F. Murray Abraham), 1986, *The Queen of the Damned,* 1988, *The Vampire Lestat* (read by Michael York), 1989, and *The Mummy: Or Ramses the Damned* (read by York), 1990. *Exit to Eden* was adapted for film by Deborah Amelon and Bob Brunner and released as a motion picture in 1994. *The Vampire Lestat* was adapted into a graphic novel by Faye Perozich, painted by Daerick Gross, Ballantine, 1991.

SIDELIGHTS: "Anne Rice, a novelist so prolific she needs two pseudonyms—Anne Rampling and A. N. Roquelaure—to distinguish the disparate voices in her books, has won both critical acclaim and a readership of cult proportions," says Bob Summer in *Publishers Weekly.* Under her own name, Rice crafts novels about the bizarre and the supernatural; under the Rampling pseudonym, she writes contemporary and mainstream fiction; and under the Roquelaure *nom*

de plume she depicts sadomasochistic fantasies. Rice embraces all of her voices now, realizing that each one represents a part of what she perceives as her divided self. In a *New York Times* interview with Stewart Kellerman, Rice indicates that she's "a divided person with different voices, like an actor playing different roles." She also explains in a *Washington Post* interview with Sarah Booth Conroy: "I think sometimes that if I had had perhaps a few more genes, or whatever, I would have been truly mad, a multiple personality whose selves didn't recognize each other."

"Anne Rice has been looking for—and inventing—herself all her life," contends Susan Ferraro in *New York Times Magazine.* "She was named Howard Allen O'Brien—the Howard after her father, even though he didn't much like the name. She hated it. By the time she was in the first grade, she had changed it to Anne." Rice grew up with three sisters in an area of New Orleans called the Irish Channel, which "was, culturally speaking, light-years removed from the aristocratic, mansion-filled Garden District just a few blocks away," write Joyce Wadler and Johnny Greene in *People.* Imagining what life would be like in these majestic homes, Rice felt like an outsider, as do many of the characters she creates. "She loved the sensuous and sinister streets of her hometown," says Kellerman. Daydreams filled the hours of Rice's childhood, and she developed a vivid imagination. In a *Rolling Stone* article, Gerri Hirshey points out that Rice "was a fifth grader at the Holy Name of Jesus School when she filled a notebook with her first novel about two kids from Mars who commit suicide."

Rice's storytelling skills have evolved since childhood and are especially evident in her inventive stories, intricate plots, descriptive passages, and vibrant characters. "Growing up in an Irish Catholic family, you hear people using language to the hilt," explains Rice in a *Lear's* interview with W. Kenneth Holditch. "They dramatize the simplest story: Their timing is perfect, the phrasing has real bite. . . . Some of us must have a chemical in our heads that causes us to create plots, tell stories, have daydreams. With too much of that you wind up crazy. I think I have just under that amount."

At the age of fourteen, Rice lost her mother to alcoholism; soon after, the family relocated to Texas. She fled from the Catholic Church four years later, and explains to Ferraro: "It struck me as really evil—the idea you could go to hell for French-kissing someone. I just didn't believe it was the one true Church established by Christ to give grace. I didn't believe God existed. I didn't believe Jesus Christ was the Son. I didn't believe one had to be Catholic in order to go to heaven. I didn't believe heaven existed either." Creating an ethical code to replace this lost religious code, Rice suggests in her *Lear's* interview that "even if we live in a godless world, we can search for love and maintain it and believe it." Emphasizing the importance of ethics, she adds that "we can found a code of morality on ethics rather than outmoded religious concepts. We can base our sexual mores on ethics rather than on religious beliefs."

Rice married her high school sweetheart, poet Stan Rice, at the age of twenty; and despite their ferocious arguments, they are devoted to each other. "I fell completely in love with Stan, and I'm still completely in love with him," declares Rice in her *New York Times* interview, adding that "it's a passionate, stormy love. The ferocity of our arguments frightens away many people, and our affection for each other inspires them." A year after they were married they moved from Texas to San Francisco, where Rice gave birth to Michele. It was there that she had a prophetic dream: "I dreamed my daughter, Michele, was dying—that there was something wrong with her blood," she recalls in her *People* interview. Several months later, Michele was diagnosed with a rare form of leukemia and died shortly before her sixth birthday. "Two years later, her image was reincarnated as the child vampire Claudia in [*Interview with the Vampire*], Anne's first published work," writes Hirshey, noting that like Michele, Claudia is beautiful and blond but is granted eternal life at the age of six. "It was written out of grief, the author says, in five weeks of 'white-hot, access-the-subconscious' sessions between 10:00 p.m. and dawn," adds Hirshey.

As its title describes, *Interview with the Vampire* is the result of an evening in which Louis, the vampire, tells a young reporter his life story. The novel, which actually began in the late 1960s as a short story, developed into something much larger. "I got to the point where the vampire began describing his brother's death, and the whole thing just exploded! Suddenly, in the guise of Louis, a fantasy figure, I was able to touch the reality that was mine. . . .," explains Rice in her *Publishers Weekly* interview. "Through Louis' eyes, everything became accessible."

Critics are intrigued by Rice's unusual treatment of vampires: "Rice brings a fresh and powerful imagination to the staples of vampire lore; she makes well-worn coffins and crucifixes tell new tales that compose a chillingly original myth," observes Nina Auerbach in the *New York Times Book Review*. "Because Rice identifies with the vampire instead of the victim (reversing the usual focus), the horror for the reader springs from the realization of the monster within the self," writes Ferraro. "Moreover, Rice's vampires are loquacious philosophers who spend much of eternity debating the nature of good and evil. Trapped in immortality, they suffer human regret. They are lonely, prisoners of circumstance, compulsive sinners, full of self-loathing and doubt. They are, in short, Everyman Eternal." All that separates the vampires from humans and makes them outsiders is their hunt for human blood and indestructible bodies. Presented with flawless, alabaster skin, colorful glinting eyes, and hair that shimmers and seems to take on a life of its own, they are described by H. J. Kirchhoff in a Toronto *Globe and Mail* review as "romantic figures, super-humanly strong and fast, brilliant and subtle of thought and flamboyant of manner."

Walter Kendrick praises the scope of *Interview with the Vampire* in the *Voice Literary Supplement*, saying that "it would have been a notable tour de force even if its characters had been human." Kendrick also suggests that "Rice's most effective accomplishment, though, was to link up sex and fear again." Conroy maintains that "not since Mary Shelley's *Frankenstein* and Louisa May Alcott's penny dreadful novelettes has a woman written so strongly about death and sex." Similarly, in a *New York Times Book Review* article, Leo Braudy observes that "Rice exploits all the sexual elements in [vampire myths] with a firm self-consciousness of their meaning." The sensuous description of Louis' first kill is an example: "I knelt beside the bent, struggling man and, clamping both my hands on his shoulders, I went into his neck. My teeth had only just begun to change, and I had to tear his flesh, not puncture it; but once the wound was made, the blood flowed. . . . The sucking mesmerized me, the warm struggling of the man was soothing to the tension of my hands; and there came the beating of the drum again, which was the drumbeat of his heart."

When the novel was completed, Rice knew it would be her first published work; many rejection letters later her goal was accomplished. Success was not immediate; *Interview with the Vampire* did not instantly find its cult audience. When it did, "the book pierced and possessed those who by choice or rejection stand apart from society—heretics, moon worshipers, gays and lovers of the night, the supernatural, the erotic and the exotic," explains Conroy. Gay readers in particular saw the vampires and their relationships as "an original metaphor for gay society—an underworld of the undead that functions within society, yet, of necessity, outside of it," writes Chicago *Tribune Books* reviewer Richard Panek. Summer asserts that Rice's readership developed by "word-of-mouth" which "pushed the novel into the realm of success." The initial reviews were mixed, though, and sometimes scathing. "What a scope for farce! For satire! For, God help us, whimsey!," exclaims Edith Milton in *New Republic,* adding that "although one hopes at first that this may all be a hoax, the realization comes at length, painfully, that we are in a serious novel here." However, *Village Voice* contributor Irma Pascal Heldman suggests that "Rice pulls off her unique tale with a low-key style that is almost mundane in the presentation of the horrific. She has created a preternatural world that parallels the natural one." Adding that "while not for the squeamish," Heldman maintains that "it is spellbinding, eerie, original in conception, and deserving of the popular attention it appears destined to receive." Ferraro remarks that "Rice, who can quote bad reviews years after they have disappeared onto microfilm, refuses to quit."

The Vampire Lestat appeared in 1985, continuing the saga of the vampires. Kendrick finds that "In Anne Rice's hands, vampires have come of age. They now have a history and a vital new tradition; instead of creeping about in charnel houses, they stand center stage, with a thousand spotlights on them. And they smile straight at the camera, licking without shame their voluptuous lips and white, sharp teeth." In this second novel of the "Vampire Chronicles," Lestat, creator of Louis in *Interview with the Vampire,* awakens from a sleep of many years to find himself in the 1980s. A rock band practicing in a house nearby rouses him, and a few days later, he is dressed in leather and roaring around on a big, black Harley Davidson motorcycle.

The Vampire Lestat assumes the form of an autobiography written as part of the marketing campaign to launch Lestat's new rock and roll career. It takes the reader through "a history of vampirism, from its beginnings in ancient Egypt, through its manifestations in Roman Gaul, Renaissance Italy, pre-Revolutionary Paris and *belle epoque* New Orleans, and a

further discussion of the philosophical, ethical and theological implications of vampirism," writes Kirchhoff, adding that "Rice is a beautiful writer. Her prose glitters and every character in Lestat's dark odyssey is unique." Although the *New York Times*'s Michiko Kakutani believes that Rice recounts this history "in lugubrious, cliche-ridden sentences that repeat every idea and sentiment a couple or more times," Auerbach finds the novel to be "ornate and pungently witty," explaining that "in the classic tradition of Gothic fiction, it teases and tantalizes us into accepting its kaleidoscopic world. Even when they annoy us or tell us more than we want to know, its undead characters are utterly alive."

Kendrick asserts that "*Lestat* is more than a sequel to *Interview;* it's also a prequel and a supplement, swallowing the earlier novel whole." While the novel ends with Lestat's concert in San Francisco, where, scattered throughout the crowd, hundreds of vampires wait to destroy him for revealing secrets and names in his songs and autobiography, *The Queen of the Damned,* the third book in the "Vampire Chronicles," opens before the concert, with the wrathful vampires plotting Lestat's destruction. He has some supporters, though, among them Akasha, the mother of all vampires and queen of the damned, who has been awakened by Lestat from a several centuries-long sleep. Far from a nurturing character, Akasha wants to bring peace to the world by killing ninety percent of all males and creating a kingdom ruled by women.

A chorus of vampires narrates *The Queen of the Damned,* and many of the pages are devoted to answering the questions of how and when vampires were created. "Although the events that comprise this prehistory of vampire life are often ludicrous, Rice relates them with authority, verve and a well-developed sense of fun," maintains Kakutani. Conversely, Kendrick believes that the novel is "verbose, sluggish, and *boring,*" and written as if "Rice didn't believe her fantasies anymore." Laurence Coven, in his *Los Angeles Times Book Review* article, concludes that Rice "provides an exhilarating blend of philosophic questing and pure, wondrous adventure." The last words of *The Queen of the Damned* are: "The Vampire Chronicles will continue."

That promise was fulfilled with *The Tale of the Body Thief,* which finds Lestat so weary of his immortality that he attempts suicide. He fails, but is soon approached by a mortal who offers to exchange bodies for a few days. Eager for even a taste of mortality,

Lestat agrees, only to have his partner in this transaction vanish with his immortal body. "Rice is in good form with 'The Tale of the Body Thief,'" Sarah Smith appraises in *Washington Post Book World.* Smith lauds the book's "whiplash speed," "page-turner plot," "beautifully realized atmosphere," and "real storytelling intelligence." The passages in which Lestat, confined to the night for two centuries, once again experiences daylight are "Rice at her best, looking through the outsider's eyes with all the outsider's alienated power," Smith adds. Writing in the *Chicago Tribune,* Dan Greenberg terms Rice's description of the body exchange "brilliant," and goes on to say that "Lestat's reactions to pulling on a mortal body like a suit of ill-fitting clothes and suddenly having to re-learn vulgar, unvampirelike bodily functions—urinating, eating, defecating, making love—are downright dazzling."

Both Smith and Greenberg suggest that Rice fell short of her capabilities, however, with Smith commenting that the book is "both exhilarating and frustrating . . . because it might so easily have been better." Certain aspects of the plot are implausible, Smith writes, saying the book could have used "three more weeks of really vicious editing and rewrites" to develop "an already strong story into consistent brilliance." Greenberg notes that "real action languishes in its coffin for more than 100 pages," but adds that patient readers will be rewarded once they get past the book's slow start. Bob Summers awards Rice unqualified praise, stating in the *Atlanta Journal and Constitution* that "no one writing today—straight, gay or in between—matches her deftness with the erotic. When combined with storytelling mastery and a penchant for developing characters that engage the imagination, that's a sure-fire route to success."

To the dismay of Lestat's fans everywhere, Rice announced that the adventures of her star vampire would end with her 1995 novel *Memnoch the Devil.* In this story, Lestat, accustomed to being the hunter, finds that he is the prey. His pursuer is none other than Satan, who tries to enlist Lestat to become his assistant. Lestat refuses, but accepts the Devil's offer for a tour of heaven, hell, and purgatory. After seeing all this, his guide tells him that he will have another chance to accept the job offer. "With the stage thus set, the book transmogrifies into a modern *Paradise Lost,* The Universe According to Rice," explains Kevin Allman in *Washington Post Book World.* "Many, many pages of *Memnoch* are devoted to her personal cosmology and angelology, to her versions of creation, evolution and the Crucifixion.

It's a tour that's interesting at times and poky at others."

Other reviewers also complain that *Memnoch* contains too much talk, and that Rice took on more than she could handle with this novel. A *Publishers Weekly* reviewer finds that Rice's attempt to answer meaning-of-life questions overshadows her narrative, and also makes the criticism that "God and the Devil . . . too often end up sounding like arguing philosophy majors." For Michael McLeod in the *Chicago Tribune, Memnoch* proves a disappointing conclusion to the Lestat saga. He notes that the book deals with the mysteries of life, death, and eternity more "dramatically and directly" than any other installment in Rice's vampire series. "But the proportions of the author's writing are so epic that her dark hero gets lost among them," he maintains. "If Rice really is retiring her flagship vampire . . . it's puzzling she made him play out his last scene as Satan's sidekick." Allman, however, concludes with a more positive assessment of *Memnoch,* stating that "Rice has penned an ambitious close to this long-running series, as well as a classy exit for a classic horror character."

The erotic overtones featured in the "Vampire Chronicles" are given full range in the books Rice published under the pseudonym A. N. Roquelaure. *The Claiming of Sleeping Beauty, Beauty's Punishment,* and *Beauty's Release: The Continued Erotic Adventures of Sleeping Beauty* are loosely based on the story of Sleeping Beauty and are described as sadomasochistic pornography by some critics. "A. N. Roquelaure is an S&M pornographer with a shocking penchant for leather collars . . . and other kinky bijoux," states Hirshey. Conroy asserts, however, that "despite the content, all is presented with something of the breathless, innocent, gingham-ruffled voice of fairy tales." Rice counters the critical assessment of these works as pornographic in a *People* interview: "I wrote about the fantasy that interested me personally and that I couldn't find in bookstores. I wanted to create a Disneyland of S&M. Most porno is written by hacks. I meant it to be erotic and nothing else—to turn people on. Sex is good. Nothing about sex is evil or to be ashamed of." Moreover, in a *Lear's* interview Rice maintains, "they're of high quality . . . and I'm very proud that I wrote them."

Writing under the pseudonym Anne Rampling, Rice has written two conventional novels, *Exit to Eden* and *Belinda,* which combine erotica and romance.

Carolyn See contends in the *Los Angeles Times* that "Rampling attempts a fascinating middle ground" between the "straight erotica" of Roquelaure, and the "semi-serious literature" of Rice. *Exit to Eden* tells the story of Lisa Kelly, a gorgeous young woman in skimpy lace and high leather boots who exudes sexuality. Raised by an Irish Catholic family that abhors the idea of sex, she discovers at an early age that she is obsessed by sadomasochism. This obsession, combined with her executive skills, leads Lisa to an island on the Caribbean where she opens the Club—a resort "which is something between a luxury hotel and an S-M brothel," says See. The second half of the novel relates Lisa's exit with Elliott from a lifestyle they once perceived as Edenic. They settle in New Orleans and start dating, proving "that one man and one woman can make a happy life together and be transformed by love, the most seductive fantasy of all," writes See, adding that "'Anne Rampling' makes a lovely case here. Let's take what we've learned of sex and bring it back into the real world, she suggests. It's time, isn't it?"

Belinda is divided into three parts, the first describing the life of Jeremy Walker, a famous author and illustrator of children's books, who lives alone in an old house. Not only is he desperately lonely, but he is also cut off from his sexuality until Belinda comes along. She is a fifteen-year-old runaway who smokes, drinks, and is willing to partake in every erotic fantasy Jeremy concocts. Although Belinda urges him not to search for clues to her past, he does. She runs away and the second part of the novel describes her childhood and her relationship with her mother. The final part of the book contains the search for Belinda and several happy endings—"True love triumphs," claims See in a *Los Angeles Times* review of *Belinda*. "Sex is as nice as champagne and friendship, Rampling earnestly instructs us. Value it! Don't be puritanical morons *all* your life."

During the early 1980s, Rice published two historical novels "of great depth, research and enchantment," remarks Conroy. In *The Feast of All Saints,* Rice writes about the free people of color, the mulattoes who numbered about 18,000 in nineteenth-century Louisiana. The novel centers around the Ferronaire family, focusing on golden-colored Marcel and his sister Marie who could pass for white. Living in the midst of the antebellum South, they are never really a part of it, and the novel examines this discrimination and the choices the characters must make because of it. Penelope Mesic, in a *Chicago Tribune Book World* review, considers it "an honest book, a

gifted book, the substantial execution of a known design," and *Los Angeles Times Book Review* contributor Valerie Miner suggests that "this new book is rare, combining a 'real story,' a profound theme and exquisite literary grace."

Cry to Heaven, another historical novel, enters the world of the Italian castrati, famous male sopranos who were castrated as boys so their voices would remain high. Tonio Treschi, the hero, is a Venetian heir whose brother has him abducted, castrated, and exiled from his home. The rest of the novel relates the pursuit of the goals that obsess him—to become one of the best singers in Europe, and to take his revenge on his brother. Alice Hoffman describes *Cry to Heaven* in a *New York Times Book Review* article as "bold and erotic, laced with luxury, sexual tension, music," adding that "here passion is all, desires are overwhelming, gender is blurred." Hoffman concludes that "this is a novel dazzling in its darkness, and there are times when Rice seems like nothing less than a magician: It is a pure and uncanny talent that can give a voice to monsters and angels both."

Rice returned to New Orleans in 1988 and to writing about the supernatural world under her own name. In 1989, she released *The Mummy: or, Ramses the Damned,* and *The Witching Hour* soon followed. *The Mummy* tells the story of Ramses the Great, who ruled Egypt 3,000 years ago. Having taken an elixir that gives him eternal life, Ramses is awakened from his sleep by an Egyptologist who finds his tomb and brings him to London. Although James Blair Lovell, writing in the *Washington Post Book World,* says *The Mummy* is "episodic, predictable and, worse, artless," Frank J. Prial, writing in the *New York Times Book Review,* asserts that "if you liked her vampires, you're going to love her mummies."

Rice uses her large, antebellum mansion in New Orleans as the setting for another novel, *The Witching Hour*. The mansion in the novel belongs to the Mayfair family and its generations of witches. Rowan, the thirteenth witch, has extrasensory powers and must defend herself from Lasher, the personification of evil. Leading Ferraro through a tour of her home, Rice describes the scenes that took place in each of the rooms: "'There's the fireplace where Rowan and Lasher sat on Christmas morning,' she says matter-of-factly, a smile tugging at her lips. . . . Up a flight of stairs, to Rice's office, where she ignores the messy desk and points dramatically to an ornate bed—'where Deirdre died,' she says, of another of the book's characters."

"What is unnerving about all this is not that Rice switches back and forth between her fictional and factual worlds, but that they seem to coexist, with equal intensity. It is as if she has somehow brought about the haunting of her own house," writes Ferraro. Although Patrick McGrath indicates in the *New York Times Book Review* that, "despite its tireless narrative energy, despite its relentless inventiveness, the book is bloated, grown to elephantine proportions because more is included than is needed," Susan Isaacs, in her *Washington Post Book World* review, believes that "Rice offers more than just a story; she creates myth. In *The Witching Hour,* she presents a rich, complicated universe that operates by both natural and supernatural law, and she does so with . . . consummate skill."

The Mayfair story expanded to a trilogy with the publication of *Lasher* and *Taltos.* In the former, the title character, whose presence in spirit was a key to *The Witching Hour,* assumes human form as the son of Rowan Mayfair and seeks a woman with whom he can reproduce. *Taltos* centers on a kindly immortal giant named Ashlar who becomes involved with the Mayfair clan. Numerous reviewers mention the books' huge casts of characters and baroque plotlines as weaknesses, and find the series as a whole to be less compelling than the "Vampire Chronicles." "You might . . . need a scorecard to keep all the Mayfair witches separate," writes Dick Adler in his *Tribune Books* review of *Lasher.* Paul West, critiquing *Lasher* for the *New York Times Book Review,* says Rice narrates her story "in plodding prose, but she does tell it as if it interested her." But Elizabeth Hand of *Washington Post Book World,* find much to praise in Rice's Mayfair series. Hand exclaims: "With *Lasher* [Rice] concocts a heady and potent salmagundi of contemporary witchcraft, Caribbean voodoo, aristocratic decadence and good old-fashioned Celtic paganism, and makes what should be an unpalatable mess as wickedly irresistible as a Halloween stash of Baby Ruths." Even though its characters are supernatural, *Lasher* is actually "an old-fashioned family saga," Hand writes. "Rice's Mayfairs are as gorgeous and doomed and steeped in the South as Scarlett O'Hara."

As for *Taltos,* several reviewers note that the story is difficult to follow without knowledge of the two previous Mayfair books. *Washington Post Book World* critic Douglas E. Winter finds *Taltos* too similar, in theme and action, to other Rice works, conveying a sensation "of covering old ground." The *Boston Globe*'s Clea Simon finds the characters in *Taltos* underdeveloped and the book as a whole "too damned nice," while Gahan Wilson of the *New York Times Book Review* sees "very little sense of the otherworldly" in the book's ostensibly supernatural beings and events. The book, Winter concludes, "demands both a taste—and a patience—that has been refined by prior experience. *Taltos* is thus certain to please the many fans of Anne Rice, but it is not likely to gain her any new readers. And this is a shame, because Rice is a formidable talent among writers of the fantastique."

Devils, witches, mummies, vampires, eroticism, and a dash of New Orleans are all parts of Rice's literary creations. Intermingled with these fictional creations are aspects of her personal life—a childhood spent in New Orleans, the loss of her mother and of her daughter, an absence of a belief in God, and the feeling of being an outsider. "The passionate energy that infuses Rice's prose is personal," observes Ferraro, and Rice declares in a *People* interview: "When I'm writing, the darkness is always there. I go where the pain is." Ferraro describes this writing as "florid, both lurid and lyrical, and full of sensuous detail. She supports her fantasies with superb narrative, unabashed eroticism and a queasy but ultimately cathartic indulgence in the forbidden." Even though she puts much of herself into her works, the world in which Rice lives contrasts sharply with the fantasy worlds she creates. "If it is true, as Rice says, that we each wear a cloak of respectability while in our hearts we are all monsters, her cloak is pulled very tightly indeed," write Wadler and Greene. Spending most of her time with her husband and son, Christopher, and the rest writing, Rice seeks immortality through her books. "I want people to carry dog-eared copies of *Interview with the Vampire* in their backpacks," says Rice in her *Lear's* interview. "I want my books to live, to be read after I'm dead. That will be justification enough for all the pain and work and struggling and doubt."

BIOGRAPHICAL/CRITICAL SOURCES:

BOOKS

Contemporary Literary Criticism, Volume 41, Gale (Detroit), 1987.

Ramsland, Katherine M., *Prism of the Night: A Biography of Anne Rice,* Dutton, 1991.

Ramsland, Katherine M., *The Vampire Companion: The Official Guide to Anne Rice's The Vampire Chronicles,* Ballantine, 1993.

Ramsland, Katherine M., *The Witches' Companion: The Official Guide to Anne Rice's Lives of the Mayfair Witches,* Ballantine, 1994.

Riley, Michael, *Conversations with Anne Rice,* Ballantine, 1996.

Roberts, Bette B., *Anne Rice,* Twayne (New York City), 1994.

Smith, Jennifer, *Anne Rice: A Critical Companion,* Greenwood, 1996.

Twentieth Century Young Adult Writers, St. James Press (Detroit), 1994.

PERIODICALS

Atlanta Constitution, November 11, 1994, p. P5; July 31, 1995, p. B1.

Atlanta Journal and Constitution, October 4, 1992, p. N8; January 27, 1993, p. A3; June 27, 1993, p. A3; October 3, 1993, p. N10.

Book-of-the-Month Club News, December, 1990.

Boston Globe, September 30, 1994, p. 64.

Chicago Tribune, October 15, 1993, section 1, p. 22; October 26, 1993, section 5, pp. 1, 2; March 5, 1995, section 12, p. 1; August 31, 1995, section 5, p. 2.

Chicago Tribune Book World, January 27, 1980; February 10, 1980.

Christian Science Monitor, November 14, 1994, p. 13.

Globe and Mail (Toronto), March 15, 1986; November 5, 1988.

Kirkus Reviews, August 15, 1990.

Lear's, October, 1989.

Locus, September, 1992, pp. 17, 19; October, 1993, p. 25.

Los Angeles Times, August 18, 1988; August 15, 1993; September 21, 1994, p. F1; November 28, 1994, p. B7.

Los Angeles Times Book Review, February 3, 1980; December 19, 1982; July 1, 1985; October 27, 1986; November 6, 1988; October 25, 1992, pp. 1, 9; August 15, 1993, p. 10; October 31, 1993, p. 3.

MacLean's, November 16, 1992, p. 68.

Metro Times Literary Quarterly (Detroit), August 16, 1995, pp. 1-2.

National Review, September 3, 1976.

New Republic, May 8, 1976, pp. 29-30.

Newsweek, November 5, 1990.

New York Times, September 8, 1982; September 9, 1982, p. C25; October 19, 1985, p. 16; October 15, 1988; November 7, 1988; October 28, 1993, pp. C15, C20; November 11, 1994, p. A51.

New York Times Book Review, March 2, 1976; May 2, 1976, pp. 7, 14; February 17, 1980, p. 17; October 10, 1980; October 10, 1982, p. 14; October 27, 1985, p. 15; November 27, 1988; June 11, 1989; November 4, 1990; October 24, 1993, p. 38; December 4, 1994, p. 82; July 23, 1995, p.14.

New York Times Magazine, October 14, 1990.

People, December 5, 1988.

Publishers Weekly, October 28, 1988; February 10, 1989; November 3, 1989; June 5, 1995, p. 51.

Rolling Stone, November 20, 1986.

Saturday Review, February 2, 1980, p. 37.

Spectator, December 3, 1994, pp. 56-57.

Time, September 9, 1989.

Tribune Books (Chicago), October 27, 1988; May 28, 1989; November 11, 1990; October 18, 1992, p. 3; October 17, 1993, p. 3; October 9, 1994, p. 5.

TV Guide, October 22, 1994, pp. 24-27.

Village Voice, May 10, 1976, p. 50.

Voice Literary Supplement, June, 1982; November, 1987; November, 1988.

Wall Street Journal, June 17, 1976, p. 14.

Washington Post, November 6, 1988; October 30, 1992, p. B1.

Washington Post Book World, January 27, 1980, p. 6; October 3, 1982, pp. 7, 9; December 1, 1985, pp. 1, 7; October 26, 1986; November 6, 1988; June 18, 1989; February 11, 1990; October 28, 1990; October 30, 1992, p. 1; October 4, 1993, pp. 4-5; October 10, 1993, p. 4; October 9, 1994, p. 4; January 15, 1995, p. 4; August 6, 1995, p. 2.*

*   *   *

RICH, Adrienne (Cecile)   1929-

PERSONAL: Born May 16, in Baltimore, MD; daughter of Arnold Rice (a physician) and Helen Elizabeth (a musician; maiden name, Jones) Rich; married Alfred Haskell Conrad (an economist), June 26, 1953 (died, 1970); children: David, Paul, Jacob. *Education:* Radcliffe College, A.B. (cum laude), 1951.

ADDRESSES: Agent—c/o W. W. Norton Co., 500 Fifth Avenue, New York, NY 10110.

CAREER: Poet and writer. Conductor of workshop, YM-YWHA Poetry Center, New York City, 1966-

67; visiting lecturer, Swarthmore College, Swarthmore, PA, 1967-69; adjunct professor in writing division, Columbia University, Graduate School of the Arts, New York City, 1967-69; City College of the City University of New York, New York City, lecturer in SEEK English program, 1968-70, instructor in creative writing program, 1970-71, assistant professor of English, 1971-72, and 1974-75; Fannie Hurst Visiting Professor of Creative Literature, Brandeis University, Waltham, MA, 1972-73; Lucy Martin Donnelly fellow, Bryn Mawr College, 1975; professor of English, Douglass College, Rutgers University, New Brunswick, NJ, 1976-78; A. D. White Professor-at-Large, Cornell University, Ithaca, NY, 1982-85; Clark Lecturer and distinguished visiting professor, Scripps College, Claremont, CA, 1983, 1984; visiting professor, San Jose State University, CA, 1984-96; Burgess Lecturer, Pacific Oaks College, Pasadena, CA, 1986; professor of English and feminist studies, Stanford University, Stanford, CA, 1986-92; Marjorie Kovler visiting fellow, University of Chicago, 1989; National Director, The National Writers' Voice Project, 1992—. Member of advisory board, Boston Woman's Fund, National Writers Union, Sisterhood in Support of Sisters in South Africa and New Jewish Agenda.

MEMBER: PEN, Modern Language Association (honorary fellow, 1985—), National Writers Union, Poetry Society of America, American Academy of Arts and Letters, Amercian Academy of Arts and Sciences, Phi Beta Kappa.

AWARDS, HONORS: Yale Series of Younger Poets award for *A Change of World,* 1951; Guggenheim fellowships, 1952 and 1961; Ridgely Torrence Memorial Award, Poetry Society of America, 1955; Grace Thayer Bradley award, Friends of Literature (Chicago) for *The Diamond Cutters and Other Poems,* 1956; Phi Beta Kappa Poet, College of William and Mary, 1960, Swarthmore College, 1965, and Harvard University, 1966; National Institute of Arts and Letters award for poetry, 1961; Amy Lowell travelling fellowship, 1962; Bollingen Foundation translation grant, 1962; Bess Hokin Prize, *Poetry* magazine, 1963; Litt.D., Wheaton College, 1967; National Translation Center grant, 1968; Eunice Tietjens Memorial Prize, *Poetry* magazine, 1968; National Endowment for the Arts grant, 1970, for poems in *American Literary Anthology: 3;* Shelley Memorial Award, Poetry Society of America, 1971; Ingram Merrill Foundation grant, 1973-74; National Book Award, 1974, for *Diving into the Wreck: Poems, 1971-1972;* National Book Critics Circle Award

in Poetry nomination, 1978, for *The Dream of a Common Language: Poems, 1974-1977;* Litt.D., Smith College, 1979; Fund for Human Dignity Award, National Gay Task Force, 1981; *Los Angeles Times* Book Prize nomination, 1982, for *A Wild Patience Has Taken Me This Far: Poems, 1978-1981;* Ruth Lilly Poetry Prize, Modern Poetry Association and American Council for the Arts, 1986; Brandeis University Creative Arts Medal in Poetry, 1987; National Poetry Association Award, 1989, for distinguished service to the art of poetry; Elmer Holmes Bobst Award in Arts and Letters, New York University Library, 1989; Bay Area Book Reviewers Award in Poetry, 1990, 1996; Litt.D., Harvard University, 1990; The Common Wealth Award in Literature, 1991; Robert Frost Silver Medal for Lifetime Achievement in Poetry, Poetry Society of America, 1992; William Whitehead Award of the Gay and Lesbian Publishing Triangle for Lifetime Achievement in Letters, 1992; Lambda Book Award in Lesbian Poetry, 1992, for *An Atlas of the Difficult World: Poems, 1988-1991*, and 1996, for *Dark Fields of the Republic, 1991-1995;* Lenore Marshall/ *Nation* Poetry Prize and *Los Angeles Times* Book Award, 1992, and The Poets' Prize, 1993, all for *An Atlas of the Difficult World: Poems, 1988-1991.*

WRITINGS:

POETRY

A Change of World, with foreword by W. H. Auden, Yale University Press (New Haven, CT), 1951.

Poems, Oxford University Poetry Society, 1952.

The Diamond Cutters and Other Poems, Harper (New York City), 1955.

Snapshots of a Daughter-in-Law: Poems, 1954-1962, Harper, 1963, revised edition, Norton (New York City), 1967.

Necessities of Life, Norton, 1966.

Selected Poems, Chatto & Windus, 1967.

Leaflets: Poems, 1965-1968, Norton, 1969.

The Will to Change: Poems, 1968-1970 (also see below), Norton, 1971.

Diving into the Wreck: Poems, 1971-1972, Norton, 1973.

Poems: Selected and New, 1950-1974, Norton, 1974.

Twenty-One Love Poems (also see below), Effie's Press (Emeryville, CA), 1977.

The Dream of a Common Language: Poems, 1974-1977, Norton, 1978.

A Wild Patience Has Taken Me This Far: Poems, 1978-1981, Norton, 1981.

Sources, Heyeck Press (Woodside, CA), 1983.

The Fact of a Doorframe: Poems Selected and New, 1950-1984, Norton, 1984.

Your Native Land, Your Life, Norton, 1986.

Time's Power: Poems, 1985-1988, Norton, 1988.

An Atlas of the Difficult World: Poems, 1988-1991, Norton, 1991.

Collected Early Poems, 1950-1970, Norton, 1993.

Dark Fields of the Republic, 1991-1995, Norton, 1995.

Also guest editor for *Best American Poetry of 1996,* Scribner, 1996.

PROSE

Of Woman Born: Motherhood as Experience and Institution, Norton, 1976, tenth anniversary edition with a revised introduction, 1986.

Women and Honor: Some Notes on Lying (pamphlet), Motheroot Publishing (Pittsburgh, PA), Pittsburgh Women Writers, 1977.

On Lies, Secrets and Silence: Selected Prose, 1966-1978, Norton, 1979.

Compulsory Heterosexuality and Lesbian Existence (pamphlet), Antelope Publications (Denver, CO), 1980.

Blood, Bread and Poetry: Selected Prose, 1979-1986, Norton, 1986.

What Is Found There: Notebooks on Poetry and Politics, Norton, 1993.

TRANSLATOR

(With Aijaz Ahmad and William Stafford) Ahmad, editor, *Poems by Ghalib,* Hudson Review, 1969.

Mark Insingel, *Reflections,* Red Dust (New York City), 1973.

Also contributor of translations to *Poets on Street Corners: Portraits of 15 Russian Poets,* edited by Olga Carlisle, Random House (New York City), 1968; *A Treasury of Yiddish Poetry,* edited by Irving Howe and Eliezer Greenberg, Holt, 1969; and *Selected Poems of Mirza Ghalib,* edited by Ahmad, Columbia University Press (New York City), 1971, World Treasury of Poetry, 1996.

OTHER

Ariadne: A Play in Three Acts and Poems, J. H. Furst (Baltimore, MD), 1939.

Not I, But Death, A Play in One Act, J. H. Furst, 1941.

Also contributor to numerous books and anthologies, including *The Poet As Critic,* edited by Anthony Ostroff, Little, Brown (Boston, MA), 1965; *Randall Jarrell, 1914-1965,* edited by Robert Lowell, Peter Taylor, and Robert Penn Warren, Farrar, Straus (New York City), 1967; *The Contemporary American Poets: American Poetry since 1940,* edited by Mark Strand, New American Library (New York City), 1969; *The Voice That Is Great Within Us: American Poetry of the Twentieth Century,* edited by Hayden Carruth, Bantam (New York City), 1970; *Gay and Lesbian Poetry in Our Time,* edited by Carl Marge and Joan Larkin, St. Martin's, 1989; and *No More Masks!: An Anthology of Twentieth-Century American Women Poets,* edited by Florence Howe, Harper, 1993. Contributor of reviews and critical articles to *Poetry, Nation, New York Review of Books, Partisan Review, Boston Review, Women's Review of Books, Freedomways, New York Times Book Review, Hungry Mind Review, Southwest Review, Village Voice,* and other publications. Columnist, *American Poetry Review,* 1972-73. Coeditor, *Sinister Wisdom,* 1981-84; contributing editor, *Chrysalis: A Magazine of Women's Culture;* founding coeditor, *Bridges: A Journal of Jewish Feminists and Our Friends,* 1989-92.

SIDELIGHTS: "Adrienne Rich is not just one of America's best feminist poets," writes Margaret Atwood in *Second Words: Selected Critical Prose,* "or one of America's best woman poets, she is one of America's best poets." Rich's poetry has not always been described as "feminist." She "began as [a] poet-ingenue," according to Carol Muske in the *New York Times Book Review,* "polite copyist of Yeats and Auden, wife and mother. She has progressed in life (and in her poems . . .) from young widow and disenchanted formalist, to spiritual and rhetorical convalescent, to feminist leader . . . and *doyenne* of a newly-defined female literature." In *Poet and Critic* David Zuger describes a similar metamorphosis in Rich's work. He writes, "The 20-year-old author of painstaking, decorous poems that are eager to 'maturely' accept the world they are given becomes a . . . poet of prophetic intensity and 'visionary anger' bitterly unable to feel at home in a world 'that gives no room / to be what we dreamt of being.'"

Albert Gelpi observes that Rich's stance in her early poems is far from feminist. In *American Poetry since*

1960: Some Critical Perspectives Gelpi notes that in W. H. Auden's foreword to *A Change of World,* Rich's introductory book of poetry, Auden said her poems "are neatly and modestly dressed, speak quietly but do not mumble, respect their elders but are not cowed by them, and do not tell fibs." "In other words," Gelpi comments, "[the poems reflect] the stereotype—prim, fussy and schoolmarmish—that has corseted and strait-laced women-poets into 'poetesses' whom men could deprecate with admiration." In *Writing Like a Woman,* Alicia Ostriker states, "Rich at this point [was] a cautious good poet in the sense of being a good girl, a quality noted with approval by her early reviewers."

Critics Ruth Whitman and Le Anne Schreiber see Rich's development as a reflection of the changing consciousness of women in general during the last half of the twentieth century. In *Harvard Magazine* Whitman observes, "Rich's process of transformation over the years has been an astonishing phenomenon to watch: in one woman the history of women in our country, from careful and traditional obedience (that was Auden's description of her) to cosmic awareness." Schreiber notes in the *New York Times:* "[Rich] has written through youth, fame, marriage, motherhood, separation, solitude, political rage, [and] feminist awakening. In its broad outlines . . . her progress through the decades has paralleled that of her generation of women."

The evolution in Rich's work is a result of the poet's growth from imitation to personal discovery and disclosure. In the *Dictionary of Literary Biography,* Anne Newman observes that Rich's first book contains "many echoes of her masters" but only "muted notes of her personal voice," while in the *Michigan Quarterly Review,* Laurence Goldstein declares, "Rich's career really began when she emerged from the shadow of influence and began to speak in the impassioned rhythms of her own reveries."

Many critics find in Rich's book *Snapshots of a Daughter-in-Law: Poems, 1954-1962* the first indication of both the end of Rich's imitative efforts and the beginning of her concern with feminist issues. In *Southwest Review,* Willard Spiegelman calls *Snapshots* "the liminal volume, attempting a journey from one self, world, poetic form, to another." Spiegelman notes that the poem "Roof-walker" articulates Rich's precarious position as a poet balancing between two modes of writing: "exposed, larger than life, / and due to break my neck." Ostriker also

comments on the change in Rich's poetry evident in *Snapshots.* Calling the collection "Rich's breakthrough volume," Ostriker notes that the book's title poem "consists of fragmentary and odd-shaped sections instead of stanzas, and has the immediacy and force which Rich did not attempt earlier."

Snapshots offers the reader a change in the form of Rich's poetry as Ostriker observes. This change, according to Newman, includes "dropping the initial capital letter in each line, increasing enjambment, using speech cadences in place of formal meters, limiting the use of rhyme, and varying stanza length." The content of Rich's poetry changes also. Her work begins to reflect her personal confrontation with what it means to be female in a male-dominated society. In Rich's 1971 essay, "When We Dead Awaken: Writing as Re-vision," quoted by Newman, the poet comments: "In the late fifties I was able to write, for the first time, directly about experiencing myself as a woman—Until then I had tried very hard *not* to identify myself as a female poet. Over two years I wrote . . . 'Snapshots of a Daughter-in-Law' (1958-60), in a longer, looser mode than I'd ever trusted myself with before. It was an extraordinary relief to write that poem."

Negative criticism soon crept into the reviews of previously enthusiastic critics. In "Blood, Bread and Poetry," an essay which first appeared in the *Massachusetts Review,* Rich explains what happened: "In the fifties and early sixties there was much shaking of heads if an artist was found meddling in politics; art was mystical and universal but the artist was also, apparently irresponsible and emotional, and politically naive. . . . In my own case, as soon as I published . . . a book of poems which was informed by any conscious sexual politics [*Snapshots*], I was told, in print, that this work was 'bitter,' 'personal'; and I had sacrificed the sweetly flowing measures of my earlier books for a ragged line and a coarsened voice."

A *Times Literary Supplement* reviewer states, for example, that while the poet "began as an elegant American," she has since then "lost a great deal of her intensity." In the *New York Review of Books* Rosemary Tonks writes: "In . . . Rich's work, the moral proportions are valid, the protagonists are sane, responsible persons, and the themes are moving on their courses. Why is it then that we are still waiting for the poetry?. . . She has taken on too much, and the imagination is exhausted by the effort required to familiarize itself with all the burdens of the modern world." And, in the *New Republic,* Barbara Grizzuti Harrison calls Rich "a polemicist . . . [whose] respect and love for the written word [is] betrayed by her ideology."

Rich has been criticized for the harsh depictions of males in her poetry. This is especially true in reviews of *Diving into the Wreck: Poems, 1971-1972* and *A Wild Patience Has Taken Me This Far: Poems, 1978-1981.* Ostriker comments on what she calls Rich's "partisanship" and observes, "Men in [*Diving into the Wreck*] are depicted universally and exclusively as parisitic on women, emotionally threatened by them, brutal . . . and undeserving of pity." In *Parnassus: Poetry in Review,* Helen Vendler notes that the poem "Rape" from *Diving into the Wreck,* seems to bestow on all men the image of the sadistic rapist portrayed in the work. "This poem," she writes, "like some others [in the volume], is a deliberate refusal of the modulations of intelligence in favor of . . . propaganda." Similarly, in the *Voice Literary Supplement,* Kathryn Kilgore calls *A Wild Patience* "a ritual of man-hatred" while in the *Times Literary Supplement* Jay Parini states that in some of the poems in the volume Rich "wilfully misrepresents men, committing the same act of distortions that she complains about elsewhere."

On the other hand, *Diving into the Wreck* was granted the prestigious National Book Award (Rich, along with Audre Lorde and Alice Walker, declined the award as an individual but accepted it on behalf of women whose voices have been silenced, and donated the cash award to the Sisterhood of Black Single Mothers). The book was praised by many critics. Goldstein, for example, believes it is "Rich's finest single volume," and observes that the title poem is "a modern classic." In *Harvard Magazine,* Ruth Whitman calls the same piece "one of the great poems of our time." In her *Ms.* review of the book, Erica Jong declares that Rich handles political issues well in her poetry. "Rich is one of the few poets," she states, "who can deal with political issues in her poems without letting them degenerate into social realism." Focusing on the title poem, Jong also denies that Rich is anti-male. A portion of the poem reads: "And I am here, the mermaid whose dark hair / streams black, the merman in his armored body. / We circle silently / about the wreck. / We dive into the hold. / I am she: I am he." Jong comments, "This stranger-poet-survivor carries 'a book of myths' in which her/his 'names do not appear.'

These are the old myths . . . that perpetuate the battle between the sexes. Implicit in Rich's image of the androgyne is the idea that we must write new myths, create new definitions of humanity which will not glorify this angry chasm but heal it." *A Wild Patience* received similar if not as abundant praise. For instance, Sara Mandlebaum notes in *Ms.* that in the volume "the radicalism of [Rich's] vision . . . remains strong and invigorating: the writing as lyrical . . . and moving as ever—and even more honest."

Rich's prose has caused as much controversy as her poetry. Newman discusses the reception of *Of Woman Born: Motherhood as Experience and Institution,* Rich's study of the concept of motherhood. "Some critical reactions to the book," Newman observes, "are almost vehement, claiming Rich's perspective has been clouded by a rage that has led her into biased statements and a strident style. Others, who have read it with more sympathy, call it scholarly and well researched and insist that it should not be read . . . for polemics." In her *New York Times Book Review* critique of the volume, for example, Francine du Plessix Gray writes, "It is vexing to see such a dedicated feminist playing the dangerous game of using the oppressor's tactics. Going from mythologization of history to remythologization of male and female character traits, Rich indulges in stereotypes throughout the book." Speaking of the same book, but representative of the other half of the critics, Laura E. Casari comments in *Prairie Schooner:* "[In *Of Woman Born* Rich] thoroughly documents the powerlessness of women in a patriarchal culture and vividly depicts its results."

Rich's second prose work, *On Lies, Secrets and Silence: Selected Prose, 1966-1978,* furthers her feminist aesthetic. This volume contains one of Rich's most-noted essays, "When We Dead Awaken: Writing as Re-Vision," in which Rich clarifies the need for female self-definition. It was during this time, in 1976, that Rich also came out as a lesbian. In *Blood, Bread and Poetry: Selected Prose, 1979-1986,* Rich continues to explore issues of lesbianism while addressing such topics as racial identity and racism. Rich's fourth book of prose, *What Is Found There: Notebooks on Poetry and Politics,* contains meditations on politics, poetry, and poets. Focusing on such writers as Muriel Rukeyser, Audre Lorde, Wallace Stevens, and June Jordan, Rich emphasizes her belief that poetry is inevitably political and that "poetry can break open locked chambers of possibility, restore numbed zones to feeling, recharge desire." Rich, according to *Nation* writer Jan Montefiore, goes on to "address the social, ecological, and political dilemmas and contradictions of the United States, defining and identifying herself with a specifically American stream of radical poetry."

In the verse collections *Your Native Land, Your Life; Time's Power: Poems, 1985-1988;* and *An Atlas of the Difficult World: Poems, 1988-1991,* Rich addresses new issues while continuing to develop feminist themes. The long sequence titled "Sources" in *Your Native Land, Your Life* is Rich's first major attempt to confront her Jewish heritage and the effects of the Holocaust on her life and work. In "Living Memory," a long poem in *Time's Power,* Rich faces the consequences of time and aging and also meditates on her bond to the American landscape. Marilyn Hacker writes in the *Nation* that this volume ranges "backward through personal and international history, geographically from southern California to Vermont to the Golan Heights. These texts present a variety of dramatis personae, and do not flinch at the knottiest moral conundrums." *An Atlas of the Difficult World* focuses on such issues as poverty, the Persian Gulf War, and the exploitation of minorities and women. Rich's use of personal experience, first-person narratives, and language prompted critics to compare this collection to the works of Emily Dickinson and Walt Whitman. *Hudson Review* critic Dick Allen observes, "Rich's book is truly a small atlas; but it is also the mature poetry of a writer who knows her own power, who speaks in the passionate, ambitious blending of the personal and the universal forever present in major work. She will be read and studied for centuries to come."

Critical commentary on Rich's work has reflected the polemics of her verse; critics who adhere to Rich's politics frequently commend her poems unconditionally, while those who disagree with her politics disavow her work. Additionally, there has been no conclusive appraisal of her canon as Rich continually develops her views and asserts new approaches to contemporary issues. Most critics concur, however, that Rich's intelligent and innovative portrayals of women have contributed significantly to the feminist movement. Wendy Martin notes in *An American Triptych: Anne Bradstreet, Emily Dickinson, Adrienne Rich* that Rich "establishes a coherent point of view, a feminist identity and poetic vision which becomes part of the composite reality of a community. Her poetry, then, like all good poetry changes the way we perceive and experience the world."

BIOGRAPHICAL/CRITICAL SOURCES:

BOOKS

Altieri, Charles, *Self and Sensibility in Contemporary American Poetry,* Cambridge University Press, 1984.

Atwood, Margaret, *Second Words: Selected Critical Prose,* House of Anansi Press, 1982.

Contemporary Literary Criticism, Gale (Detroit), Volume 3, 1975, Volume 5, 1976, Volume 7, 1977, Volume 11, 1979, Volume 18, 1981, Volume 36, 1986, Volume 73, 1993, Volume 76, 1993.

Cooper, Jane Roberta, editor, *Reading Adrienne Rich: Reviews and Re-Visions, 1951-81,* University of Michigan Press, 1984.

Dictionary of Literary Biography, Gale, Volume 5: *American Poets since World War II,* 1980, Volume 67: *Modern American Critics since 1955,* 1988.

Gelpi, Barbara Charlesworth, and Albert Gelpi, editors, *Adrienne Rich's Poetry, Prose, Reviews and Criticism,* Norton, 1993.

Kalstone, David, *Five Temperaments: Elizabeth Bishop, Robert Lowell, James Merrill, Adrienne Rich, John Ashbery,* Oxford University Press, 1977.

Martin, Wendy, *An American Triptych: Anne Bradstreet, Emily Dickinson, Adrienne Rich,* University of North Carolina Press, 1984.

McDaniel, Judith, *Reconstituting the World: The Poetry and Vision of Adrienne Rich,* Spinsters Ink (Argyle, NY), 1979.

Ostriker, Alicia, *Writing Like a Woman,* University of Michigan Press, 1983.

Plath, Sylvia, *The Journals of Sylvia Plath,* edited by Ted Hughes and Frances McCullough, Dial Press, 1982.

Poetry Criticism, Volume 5, Gale, 1992.

Rich, Adrienne, *A Change of World,* foreword by W. H. Auden, Yale University Press (New Haven, CT), 1951.

Rich, Adrienne, *Snapshots of a Daughter-in-Law: Poems, 1954-1962,* Harper, 1963.

Rich, Adrienne, *Diving into the Wreck: Poems, 1971-1972,* Norton, 1973.

Shaw, Robert B., editor, *American Poetry since 1960: Some Critical Perspectives,* Carcanet, 1973.

Templeton, Alice, *The Dream and the Dialogue: Adrienne Rich's Feminist Poetics,* University of Tennessee Press, 1994.

Vendler, Helen, *Part of Nature, Part of Us: Modern American Poets,* Harvard University Press, 1980.

Wagner, Linda W., *American Modern: Essays in Fiction and Poetry,* Kennikat, 1980.

Werner, Craig Hansen, *Adrienne Rich: The Poet and Her Critics,* American Library Association, 1988.

PERIODICALS

America, February 26, 1977.

American Book Review, August, 1994, p. 16.

American Poetry Review, September/October, 1973; March/April, 1975; July/August, 1979; July/August, 1992, pp. 35-8.

Atlantic, June, 1978.

Atlantis: A Women's Studies Journal, fall, 1982, pp. 97-110.

Belles Lettres, fall, 1994, p. 37.

Christian Science Monitor, August 18, 1966; July 24, 1969; January 26, 1977.

Contemporary Literature, winter, 1975.

Harper's, December, 1973; November, 1978.

Harvard Magazine, July-August, 1975; January-February, 1977.

Hudson Review, autumn, 1971; autumn, 1975; summer, 1992, pp. 319-30.

Los Angeles Times, April 23, 1986; June 7, 1986.

Los Angeles Times Book Review, October 17, 1982; March 25, 1984.

Massachusetts Review, autumn, 1983.

Michigan Quarterly Review, summer, 1976; winter, 1983.

Modern Poetry Studies, autumn, 1977.

Ms., July, 1973; December, 1981.

Nation, July 28, 1951; October 8, 1973; July 1, 1978; December 23, 1978; June 7, 1986, pp. 797-98; October 23, 1989; November 30, 1992, pp. 673-74.

New Leader, May 26, 1975.

New Republic, November 6, 1976; December 9, 1978; June 2, 1979; January 7-14, 1985.

Newsweek, October 18, 1976.

New Yorker, November 3, 1951; April 25, 1994, p. 111.

New York Review of Books, May 7, 1970; October 4, 1973; September 30, 1976; December 17, 1981; November 21, 1991, pp. 50-6.

New York Times, May 13, 1951; August 25, 1973.

New York Times Book Review, July 17, 1966; May 23, 1971; December 30, 1973; April 27, 1975; October 10, 1976; June 11, 1978; April 22, 1979; December 9, 1981; December 20, 1981;

January 7, 1985; January 20, 1985; December 8, 1991, p. 7; November 7, 1993, p. 7; April 21, 1996, pp. 32-33.

Parnassus: Poetry in Review, fall-winter, 1973; spring-summer, 1979.

Partisan Review, winter, 1978.

Poet and Critic, Volume 9, number 2, 1976; Volume 10, number 2, 1978.

Poetry, February, 1955; July, 1963; March, 1970; February, 1976; August, 1992, pp. 284-304.

Prairie Schooner, summer, 1978.

Salmagundi, spring-summer, 1973; spring-summer, 1979.

Saturday Review, December 18, 1971; November 13, 1976.

Southern Review, April, 1969.

Southwest Review, autumn, 1975.

Times Literary Supplement, November 23, 1967; June 9, 1972; April 20, 1973; November 12, 1982; July 20, 1984; July 8, 1994, p. 9.

Village Voice, November 8, 1976.

Voice Literary Supplement, December, 1981.

Washington Post Book World, December 23, 1973; November 14, 1976; December 5, 1976; December 3, 1978; May 6, 1979; May 20, 1982.

Western Humanities Review, autumn, 1975.

Women's Review of Books, December, 1983; April, 1987, pp. 5-6; March, 1990, pp. 12-13.

World Literature Today, winter, 1979.

Yale Review, autumn, 1956; autumn, 1978.

*   *   *

RICHARDS, Todd
See SUTPHEN, Richard Charles

*   *   *

RICKS, Chip
See RICKS, Nadine

*   *   *

RICKS, Nadine   1925-
(Chip Ricks)

PERSONAL: Born February 20, 1925, in Texas; daughter of Sidney Leeman (a rancher) and Mabel

(Bollinger) Wilson; married Albert Conwell Ricks (a stockbroker), May 5, 1944; children: Cynthia Ann, Connie Jean, Richard Alan. *Education:* University of Texas, B.A., 1954; University of Nebraska, M.A., 1964. *Religion:* Baptist.

ADDRESSES: Home—505 St. Andrews Way, Lompoc, CA 93436.

CAREER: Aroostook State Teachers College (now University of Maine at Presque Isle), Presque Isle, ME, instructor in English, 1960; University of Nebraska, Lincoln, instructor in English, 1964-67; Allan Hancock College, Santa Maria, CA, instructor in English, 1967-84; Trinity Nazarene Church, Lompoc, CA, director of adult education, 1984-87.

WRITINGS:

(With Marilyn Marsh) *Patterns in English,* Scribner (New York City), 1969.
(With Marsh) *How to Write Your First Research Paper,* Wadsworth Publishing (Belmont, CA), 1971, revised edition, Kendall/Hunt (Dubuque, IA), 1982.

UNDER PSEUDONYM CHIP RICKS

Beyond the Clouds, Tyndale (Wheaton, IL), 1979.
Carol's Story, Tyndale, 1980.
John and 1st John, Tyndale, 1982.
How to Write for Christian Magazines, Broadman (Nashville, TN), 1985.
Understanding the Bible, Volume 1: *The Five Books of Moses;* Volume 2: *The Twelve History Books;* Volume 3: *The Poetry and Major Prophets;* Volume 4, *The Twelve Minor Prophets,* Hensley, 1989-91.
Exploring the New Testament: The Four Gospels, Hensley, 1992.
The Plans of His Heart, Broadman, 1996.

SIDELIGHTS: Nadine Ricks, also known to readers as Chip Ricks, told *CA:* "As a Christian writer, I am deeply concerned about the direction our nation is moving and the choices we as individuals are making. I firmly believe that there is one God who created heaven and earth, and that he has a purpose and a plan for mankind. That plan is laid out for us in the Bible. It threads through the sixty-six books from Genesis to Revelation, teaching us right from wrong

with no room for compromise. Yet, we as a people are daily compromising God's laws. My purpose as a writer is to help readers see the deep love of our God who calls us to follow in the footsteps of Jesus, His Son. But, he will never take away our free will. We must make the choice to either accept or reject his plan. This is the essence of all my writing."

*   *   *

RINVOLUCRI, Mario (Francesco Giuseppe) 1940-

PERSONAL: Surname is pronounced "Rin-*vo*-luke-ree"; born June 9, 1940, in Cardiff, Wales; son of Giuseppe and Mina (Moore) Rinvolucri; married Sophie Laure Gabrielle Leyris; children: Lola-Agnes, Martin, Bruno. *Education:* Queen's College, Oxford, B.A., 1961. *Politics:* Labour Party. *Religion:* Agnostic ("ex-Roman Catholic").

ADDRESSES: Home—26 London Rd., Faversham, ME13 8RX, England.

CAREER: Reuters (news agency), London, England, journalist, 1961-62; magazine correspondent in Athens, Greece, 1962-65, and part-time teacher of English in Athens; teacher of English and part-time writer, Cambridge, England, 1965-70; University of Valdivia, Valdivia, Chile, teacher of English, 1971-73; Pilgrims Language Courses, Canterbury, England, teacher of English as a foreign language, 1974—.

WRITINGS:

Anatomy of a Church: Greek Orthodoxy Today, Burns & Oates, 1966.
(Translator) Sotiris Spatharis, *Behind the White Screen,* London Magazine Editions (London), 1967.
Hitch-Hiking, Cambridge (New York City), 1975.
(With James Dixey) *Well Said,* Pilgrims, 1977.
(With Dixey) *Get Up and Do It,* Longman (London), 1977.
(With Margaret Berer) *Mazes,* Heinemann, 1981.
(With Berer and M. Frank) *Challenge to Think,* Oxford University Press (New York City), 1982.

(With Frank) *Grammar in Action,* Prentice-Hall (Englewood Cliffs, NJ), 1983.

(With John Morgan) *Once Upon a Time: Using Stories in the Language Classroom,* Cambridge University Press, 1983.

Grammar Games: Cognitive, Affective, and Drama Activities for EFL Students, Cambridge University Press, 1984.

(With Morgan) *Vocabulary,* Oxford University Press, 1986.

(With Paul Davis) *Dictation,* Cambridge University Press, 1988.

(With Morgan) *The Q Book,* Longman, 1988.

(With Davis) *The Confidence Book,* Longman, 1990.

(With Richard Cooper and Mike Lavery) *Video,* Oxford University Press, 1991.

(With Davis) *More Grammar Games,* Cambridge University Press, 1995.

(With Nicky Burbidge, Peta Gray, and Sheila Levy) *Letters,* Oxford University Press, 1996.

Contributor to books, including *Methods That Work,* edited by J. W. Oller, Newbury House, 1983, and *Recipes for Tired Teachers,* edited by C. Sion, Addison-Wesley, 1985.

SIDELIGHTS: Mario Rinvolucri told *CA:* "I belong to a team of people, associated with Pilgrims Language Courses, Canterbury, U.K., who are determined to make the learning of foreign languages a pleasurable and energetic business. We believe in offering the student 'frames' in which she can learn a language, rather than imposing a set progression on all students. All the language books I have coauthored see the student as a person first and a technical learner second."

*   *   *

RIVERSIDE, John
   See HEINLEIN, Robert A(nson)

*   *   *

ROBINSON, W. Stitt
   See ROBINSON, W. Stitt, Jr.

ROBINSON, W(alter) Stitt, Jr. 1917-
   (W. Stitt Robinson)

PERSONAL: Born August 28, 1917, in Matthews, NC; son of Walter Stitt and Mary Irene (Jamison) Robinson; married Constance Lee Mock, March 18, 1944; children: Ethel Barry, Walter Lee. *Education:* Davidson College, B.A. (summa cum laude), 1939; University of Virginia, M.A., 1941, Ph.D., 1950. *Religion:* Methodist.

ADDRESSES: Home—801 Broadview Dr., Lawrence, KS 66044. *Office*—Department of History, 3001 Wescoe, University of Kansas, Lawrence, KS 66045.

CAREER: Florence State Teachers College (now University of North Alabama), Florence, assistant professor, 1946-47, associate professor of history, 1947-48; University of Kansas, Lawrence, assistant professor, 1950-54, associate professor, 1954-59, professor of history, 1959—, chairman of department, 1968-73. Member of National Civil War Centennial Commission, 1961-65; Kansas Committee for the Humanities, member of committee, 1971-78, chairman, 1975-77; Kansas School of Religion, president, 1983-86, member of executive committee and board of directors. *Military service:* U.S. Army, 1941-45; became captain; received Bronze Star.

MEMBER: American Historical Association, Organization of American Historians, Southern Historical Association, Kansas State Historical Society (member of board of directors and executive committee; vice-president, 1996), Douglas County Historical Society (president, 1979-81, 1995-96), Raven Society, Phi Beta Kappa, Phi Alpha Theta (member of international council, 1978-80; president, 1984-85).

AWARDS, HONORS: Grants from Social Science Research Council, 1959-60, American Philosophical Society, 1967, 1983, and National Endowment for the Humanities, 1994; Distinguished Scholarship Award from University of Kansas, 1976.

WRITINGS:

(Editor and contributor) Richard Oswald, *Memorandum on the Folly of Invading Virginia, the Strategic Importance of Portsmouth, and the Need for Civilian Control of the Military: Written in 1781 by the British Negotiator of the First American Treaty of Peace,* University Press of Virginia (Charlottesville, VA), 1953.

Mother Earth: Land Grants in Virginia, 1607-1699, University Press of Virginia, 1957.

The Southern Colonial Frontier, 1607-1763, University of New Mexico Press (Albuquerque, NM), 1979.

James Glen: From Scottish Provost to Royal Governor of South Carolina, Greenwood Press (Westport, CT), 1996.

Also editor of *Indian Treaties of Colonial Virginia* (two volumes) and *Indian Treaties of Colonial Maryland,* and contributor to history books and journals, including *The Old Dominion,* edited by D. B. Rutman, University Press of Virginia, 1964. Member of editorial board of *Philosophical Quarterly,* 1975-78.

* * *

ROOKE, Leon 1934-

PERSONAL: Born September 11, 1934, in Roanoke Rapids, NC. *Education:* Attended University of North Carolina, 1955-58, 1961-62. *Politics:* New Democrat.

ADDRESSES: Home—1019 Terrace Ave., Victoria, British Columbia, Canada V8S 3V2. *Agent*—Liz Darhansoff, 1220 Park Ave., New York, NY 10128.

CAREER: Short story writer, novelist, and dramatist. University of North Carolina at Chapel Hill, writer in residence, 1965-66; University of Victoria, Victoria, British Columbia, lecturer in creative writing, 1971-72, visiting professor, 1980-81; Southwest Minnesota State College, Marshall, writer in residence, 1975-76; University of Toronto, Toronto, Ontario, writer in residence, 1984-85; University of Western Ontario, 1990-91. *Military service:* U.S. Army, Infantry, 1958-60, served in Alaska.

MEMBER: PEN, Writers' Union of Canada.

AWARDS, HONORS: MacDowell fellowship, 1974; Canada Council theater and fiction grants, 1974, 1975, 1976, 1979, 1983, and 1985; Yaddo fellowship, 1976; National Endowment for the Arts fellowship, 1978; Best Paperback Novel of the Year, 1981, for *Fat Woman;* Canada/Australia Literary Prize, 1981, for overall body of work; Governor General's Literary Award for fiction, Canada Council, 1984, for *Shakespeare's Dog;* Author's Award for short

fiction, Foundation for the Advancement of Canadian Letters, 1986; North Carolina Award for Literature, 1990.

WRITINGS:

STORY COLLECTIONS

Last One Home Sleeps in the Yellow Bed, Louisiana State University Press (Baton Rouge), 1968.

The Love Parlour: Stories, Oberon, 1977.

The Broad Back of the Angel, Fiction Collective (Brooklyn, NY), 1977.

Cry Evil, Oberon, 1980.

Death Suite, ECW Press (Toronto), 1981.

The Birth Control King of the Upper Volta, ECW Press, 1982.

Sing Me No Love Songs, I'll Say You No Prayers: Selected Stories, Ecco Press (New York City), 1984.

A Bolt of White Cloth, Ecco Press, 1985.

The Happiness of Others, Porcupine's Quill (Erin, Ontario), 1991.

Who Do You Love?, McClelland & Stewart (Toronto), 1992.

NOVELS

Fat Woman, Knopf (New York City), 1981.

The Magician in Love, Aya Press (Toronto), 1981.

Shakespeare's Dog, Knopf, 1983.

How I Saved the Province, Colichan (Lantzville, British Columbia), 1989.

A Good Baby, McClelland & Stewart, 1989, Knopf, 1990.

PLAYS

Lady Physhie's Cafe, produced in Louisville, Kentucky, at Louisville Art Center, 1960.

Krokodile, Playwrights Co-op (Toronto), 1973.

Ms. America (three-act play), first produced in Toronto, 1974.

Sword Play (one-act; first produced in Vancouver, British Columbia, at New Play Centre, March, 1973; produced Off-Off Broadway, 1975), Playwrights Co-op, 1974.

Of Ice and Men (two-act), produced in Toronto at Theatre Passe Muraille, 1985.

Shakespeare's Dog (one-man show), produced in Toronto at Theatre Passe Muraille, 1985.

The Good Baby (two-act), produced by Caravan Stage Company for British Columbia tour, 1987.

Also author of the play *Evening Meeting of the Club of Suicide,* New Play Centre and *The Coming* (1991). Author of radio plays for Canadian Broadcasting Corporation (CBC), 1986-87.

Contributor to anthologies, including *Prize Stories of 1965: The O. Henry Awards,* edited by William Abrahams and Richard Poirier, Doubleday, 1965; *Chapel Hill Carousel,* edited by Jessie Rehder, University of North Carolina Press, 1967; *76: New Canadian Stories,* edited by John Metcalf, Oberon, 1977; *Statements,* Fiction Collective, 1977; *The North Carolina Short Story,* edited by Guy Owen, University of North Carolina Press, 1977; *Here and Now,* edited by Metcalf and Clark Blaise, Oberon, 1977; *Transitions II,* edited by Edward Peck, Comancept, 1978; *Stories Plus,* edited by Metcalf, McGraw, 1979; *Best American Short Stories, 1980,* edited by Stanley Elkin and Shannon Ravenel, Houghton, 1980; *Magic Realism,* edited by Geoff Hancock, Aya Press, 1980; *80: Best Canadian Stories,* edited by Metcalf, Oberon, 1980; *Illusions,* edited by Hancock, Aya Press, 1981; *Canadian Short Fiction Anthology,* edited by Paul Belserene, Intermedia Press, 1982; *Rainshadow: Stories from Vancouver Island,* edited by Ron Smith and Stephen Guppy, Oolichon Books/Sono Nis Press, 1982; *West of Fiction,* edited by Leah Flater, Aritha Van Herk, and Ruby Wiebe, NeWest Press, 1982; *Elements of Fiction,* edited by Scholes and Sullivan, Oxford University Press, 1982; *Introduction to Fiction,* edited by Jack David and John Redfern, Holt, 1982; *An Anthology of Canadian Literature in English,* Volume II, edited by Donna Bennett and Russell Brown, Oxford University Press, 1983; *Making It New,* edited by Metcalf, Methuen, 1983; *The Shoe Anthology,* edited by Hancock, Aya Press, 1984; *New: West Coast Fiction,* WCR/Pulp Press, 1984; *Canadian Short Stories,* Oxford University Press, 1985; *Skeleton at Sixty,* edited by Barbara E. Turner, Porcupine's Quill, 1986; *The Art of the Tale: An International Anthology of Short Stories, 1945-1985,* edited by Daniel Halpern, Viking, 1986; *The Oxford Book of Canadian Short Stories,* edited by Margaret Atwood and Robert Weaver, Oxford University Press, 1986; *Canadian Short Stories: From Myth to Modern,* edited by W. H. New, Prentice-Hall, 1986; *A Grand Street Reader,* edited by Ben Sonnenberg, Summit Books, 1986; *The Arch of Experience,* edited by Ian W. Mills and Judith H. Mills, Holt, 1986; *Magic Realism and Canadian Literature: Essays and Stories,* edited by Peter Hinchcliffe and Ed Jewinski, University of Waterloo Press, 1986; *86: Best Canadian Stories,* edited by David Helwig and Sandra

Martin, Oberon, 1987; *Tesseracts 2: Canadian Science Fiction,* Press Porcepic, 1987; and *87: Best Canadian Short Stories,* edited by D. Helwig and Maggie Helwig, Oberon, 1988.

OTHER

Vault, a Story in Three Parts: Conjugal Precepts, Dinner with the Swardians, and Break and Enter, Lillabulero Press, 1973.

(Editor with Metcalf) *81: Best Canadian Stories,* Oberon, 1981.

(Editor with Metcalf) *82: Best Canadian Stories,* Oberon, 1982.

(Editor with Metcalf) *The New Press Anthology: Best Canadian Short Fiction,* General Publishing (Toronto), 1984.

(Editor with Metcalf) *The Macmillan Anthology One,* Macmillan of Canada, 1988.

Contributor of short novels to *Carolina Quarterly, Noble Savage,* and *Descant.* Contributor of about 250 short stories to Canadian and U.S. literary magazines, including *Southern Review, Canadian Fiction Magazine, Antaeus, Yale Review, Mississippi Review,* and *Malahat Review.*

SIDELIGHTS: According to Toronto *Globe and Mail* reviewer William French, "Leon Rooke is unquestionably the most imaginative fiction writer currently practising in Canada. His closest competitor is probably Jacques Ferron, the Montreal fantasist, but Rooke is far more prolific than Ferron." Rooke has authored several volumes of short stories and a growing list of plays, and among his novels are *Fat Woman* and *Shakespeare's Dog.* In the *New York Times Book Review,* Alberto Manguel finds Rooke hard to classify: "[Rooke's] style varies greatly not only from book to book but sometimes from page to page. It is impossible to speak of a typical Leon Rooke paragraph; each one sets out to explore different voices and textures."

Rooke's earliest short story collections, including *Last One Home Sleeps in the Yellow Bed, The Broad Back of the Angel,* and *The Love Parlour: Stories,* are noted for their experimental qualities and their intertwining of realism and surrealism. *Sewanee Review* critic George Garrett finds the collection *The Broad Back of the Angel* "mildly surrealist in matter and in manner . . . [like] a French surrealist movie of the late thirties, afflicted with poor subtitles. But Rooke is good at it and knows what he is doing well enough." Lesley Hogan comments in the *Canadian*

Fiction Magazine that *The Broad Back of the Angel* and *The Love Parlour* "show masterful control of a variety of techniques. Rooke's concern is with love and the importance of personal relationships in an ever-increasingly impersonal society. . . . He maintains a delicate balance between the realms of reality and fantasy which gives his stories their double impact of strangeness and familiarity." In this same vein, Stephen Scobie claims in *Books in Canada* that "[one] feature of Rooke's fiction has been the way the ordinary lives of ordinary people coexist with the most extravagant and bizarre events and are presented in exuberantly experimental forms. . . . One key to such an approach is Rooke's insistence on *voice*. . . . Whooping and hollering, cajoling or complaining, Rooke's characters meet the world at an interface of language; their perception *is* their rhetoric."

Although reviewers generally find Rooke's earlier story collections impressive, they acknowledge the unevenness of these volumes and the fact that Rooke's avant-garde style, at times, fails. Regarding *The Broad Back of the Angel*, *Fiddlehead* contributor John Mills notes that although Rooke "writes excellent and sometimes poetic prose," *The Broad Back of the Angel* contains three stories about a magician that "are experimental, and in my opinion they fail—there is a coy air of self-congratulation about them." In turn, Sally Beauman expresses in her *New York Times Book Review* assessment of *Last One Home Sleeps in the Yellow Bed* that "there is a feeling of frustration" about these stories, "as if [Rooke] wanted to write, not short stories at all, but a novel. Not that it's such a bad fault to have themes which are too big for your medium."

With the advent of Rooke's collection *Cry Evil* in 1980, critics detected a change in Rooke's posture. "From the very first words of [*Cry Evil*]," writes Russell M. Brown in the *Canadian Forum*, ". . . it becomes clear that we are dealing with a writer who is now trying out the self-conscious and self-reflexive mode of post-modernism. As we move through this book, we encounter something of the exhaustion, the labyrinths and the narrative games of writers like Barth." In *Canadian Literature*, Jerry Wasserman concurs: "The stories in *Cry Evil* are . . . [baroque and make great] demands on the reader, echoing Barth and Borges, Dostoevsky, Kafka, and Poe. They are not recommended for chronic depressives." Whereas the narrators in Rooke's earlier story collections were conventional, Brown finds that Rooke has informed *Cry Evil* with "a series of ingenious narra-

tive variations that are evidence of the search for renewed creative energy." The story called "The Deacons Tale," for instance, presents a deacon who has trouble telling his tale, partly due to his wife's incessant harping from the sidelines. Though Brown expresses a degree of distaste for Rooke's drive toward inventive storytelling, he simultaneously maintains that "there is still emotion embedded in these stories, still human compulsions and neuroses," and he believes Rooke's stories contain a valuable depth beyond their wit.

Rooke's succeeding story collections, *Death Suite*, *The Birth Control King of the Upper Volta*, *Sing Me No Love Songs, I'll Say You No Prayers: Selected Stories*, and *A Bolt of White Cloth*, have also sparked varied critical responses. "Rooke's hyperactive imagination occasionally betrays him, but the general quality of his output remains at an impressively high level," observes French. Of Rooke's 1985 endeavor *A Bolt of White Cloth*, *Canadian Forum* reviewer Barry Dempster feels Rooke "invents occurrences that are disappointingly unbelievable, endings that stumble and freeze in the unwelcome air." But Paul Steuwe declares in *Books in Canada* that "if for any reason you've been holding back from experiencing the world of Leon Rooke, this is as good a place as any to begin getting acquainted with a master craftsman of Canadian literature."

In the midst of Rooke's additions to his short story collections, he published his first novel, *Fat Woman*, in 1981. *Fat Woman* "is a slim novel with a big heart and a sizable funny bone," according to David Quammen in the *New York Times Book Review*. "Rooke puts us inside the copious body of Ella Mae Hopkins—an obese wife . . .—and we waddle with her through one traumatic day, sharing her secret worries and consolations, . . . her battles of gastronomic will. . . . The small miracle about *Fat Woman* is that it remains entertaining despite its extreme simplicity of event. One large reason for this is the richness and rhythms and humor of Southern country language, which Rooke has captured wonderfully." Conversely, Timothy Down Adams notes in his *American Book Review* article that Rooke's "tampering with the slapstick humor characteristic of the worst of Southern fiction" almost kept *Fat Woman* from getting off the ground. Adams maintains that the book is redeemed by the development of the tender and humorous love relationship between the leading fat woman and her thin husband. "However," stresses Adams, "like its heroine, *Fat Woman* would have been easier to love if it were reduced by a third and tightened overall." For Tom Marshall in *Canadian Literature, Fat Woman* "is an enjoyable and absorbing read, and . . . has as a central aim an exploration of the dignity and even complexity of the lives of quite ordinary or socially marginal people."

Rooke's award-winning novel, *Shakespeare's Dog,* is a "real sleeper, a veritable find, a novel to thoroughly delight and amuse the most jaded of readers," states a reviewer for *Publishers Weekly.* As winner of the Governor General's Literary Award for fiction in 1984, this highly imaginative tale aims at exposing Shakespeare during his married life with Anne Hathaway before he had ventured to London. The splendor of it all is that Shakespeare's philosophical cur, Mr. Hooker, is narrator. In what *New York Times Book Review* critic Jerome Charyn perceives as Rooke's "sad and funny novel about the ultimate talking dog[,] Hooker has caught Shakespeare's disease. His head is puffed with language, and the other dogs of Stratford poke fun at him. . . . [*Shakespeare's Dog*] would be a silly novel, imprisoned by its own narrow concerns, were it not for the vitality that . . . Rooke brings to the squabbling household of Hooker, Will Shakespeare and Anne Hathaway. . . . It parodies all the mysteries surrounding Master Will and seems to suggest that the real author of *Hamlet* and *Lear* was Hooker himself." Other reviewers proclaim that much of the novel's success stems from Rooke's gamble with language. John Bemrose writes in *Maclean's* that "*Shakespeare's Dog* is a triumph of Rooke's delight in the language, in how it can be twisted and even reinvented. It is written in pseudo-Elizabethan tongue that effortlessly carries its rich cargo of bawdy epithets and street poetry." A reviewer in *Vogue* praises Rooke's language as "a breathless, randy mix of Joycean teasers, Elizabethan bawdies, newly-minted Rookisms—even a sprinkling of Shakespeare—that makes for a dark, ferocious lyricism and a whopping good story."

Although there are reviewers who consider *Shakespeare's Dog* short on plot, overall the work is praised as yet another surprise from a writer whose range of talent seemingly knows no bounds. S. Schoenbaum declares in the *Washington Post Book World* that "if there is a better novel than Rooke's dealing with Shakespeare's early days I'm not aware of it, although in fairness I'd have to add that his competition isn't that formidable. He has a highly original conception, and his spokespooch is a feisty (as well as intellectual) hound. . . . Through Hooker's eyes, sixteenth-century Stratford lives."

In *A Good Baby,* Rooke spins a characteristically twisted plot. Set in North Carolina, the story commences with the murder of a woman by her boyfriend shortly after she successfully gives birth to a baby girl. The infant is abandoned but found by a kindly man named Toker. But the infant is no ordinary baby, as Douglas Bauer points out in the *New York Times Book Review:* "She is not merely good, she is plainly fabulous—a quality one assumes Mr. Rooke intends, for the novel is filled with the spectral and the mythic, often rendered in a singing language of dialect and invention. . . ." Doug Bell, writing for *Quill and Quire,* observes that Rooke's ear for Appalachian speech requires that *A Good Baby* "be read aloud" because "the rhythm and tone of the tale never hit a false note." Katherine Dieckmann writes in the *Voice Literary Supplement* that "Rooke's backwoods is so creepy it makes Faulkner's *Sanctuary* seem like a playground."

In the collections *Who Do You Love?* and *The Happiness of Others,* Rooke shows himself "a writer on the crest of his craft," notes Stephen Smith in *Quill and Quire.* Both collections introduce more of Rooke's "sordid" characters, who despite their problems are "so fully alive, so clearly not caricatures," Smith says. He adds, "if instant moral uplift and happy outlook are what you want from a story, then it would be best to forsake the terrific rewards of reading Rooke and go elsewhere." To Robin Britt of *Books in Canada,* readers of *Who Do You Love?* "can count on revealingly oblique points of view and compellingly polyrhythmic narratives as given in these unpredictable tales." Writing for *Canadian Literature,* Elaine Auerbach states that the collection succeeds in "developing raw and tender evocations of emotional truth."

The stories in *The Happiness of Others,* writes Douglas Glover in *Books in Canada,* are "harsh, dark, brooding, and extremely funny." These stories, Glover continues, feature some of Rooke's most inventive fictive signatures, including "inter-woven voices, bizarre or fantastic situations, and morally ambiguous or outrageously evil characters." The common theme of this collection, Glover concludes, is "the idea of innocence under assault."

BIOGRAPHICAL/CRITICAL SOURCES:

BOOKS

Contemporary Literary Criticism, Gale (Detroit), Volume 25, 1983; Volume 34, 1985.

PERIODICALS

American Book Review, March-April, 1982.
Books in Canada, November, 1981; May, 1983; May, 1985; March, 1992, p. 38; October, 1992, p. 48; October, 1995, pp. 6-10.
Canadian Fiction Magazine, Numbers 30-31, 1979.
Canadian Forum, August, 1980; April, 1985; September, 1992, pp. 30-31.
Canadian Literature, summer, 1981; winter, 1981; spring, 1994, pp. 115-17.
Fiddlehead, spring, 1978.
Globe and Mail (Toronto), January 5, 1985.
Harpers, May, 1983.
Kirkus Reviews, March 1, 1983.
Los Angeles Times, May 4, 1981.
Maclean's, January 11, 1982; May 16, 1983.
New Yorker, November 19, 1990, pp. 155-56.
New York Times Book Review, March 2, 1969; January 1, 1978; May 17, 1981; May 29, 1983; April 1, 1984; September 30, 1990, p. 12.
Publishers Weekly, March 11, 1983.
Quill and Quire, June, 1983; November, 1989, p. 22; May, 1992, p. 19.
Sewanee Review, summer, 1978.
Vogue, June, 1983.
Voice Literary Supplement, November, 1991, p. 32.
Washington Post Book World, June 7, 1981; May 22, 1983; August 5, 1984.
WAVES, winter, 1982.

—*Sketch by Cheryl Gottler*

*   *   *

ROQUELAURE, A. N.
   See RICE, Anne

*   *   *

ROSENBERG, Tina   1960-

PERSONAL: Born April 14, 1960, in Brooklyn, NY; daughter of Barnett (a biophysicist) and Ritta Rosenberg. *Education:* Northwestern University, B.S., 1981, M.S., 1982. *Religion:* Jewish.

ADDRESSES: Agent—Gail Ross, Lichtman, Trister, Singer, & Ross, 1666 Connecticut Ave. N.W., Washington, DC 20036.

CAREER: Roosevelt Center for American Policy Studies, Washington, DC, staff writer, 1982-83; Walter Mondale for president campaign, Washington, DC, speech writer, 1983; freelance writer, Managua, Nicaragua, 1985-87, and Santiago, Chile, 1987-90; Carnegie Endowment for International Peace, Washington, DC, resident associate, 1990; Overseas Development Council, Washington, DC, visiting fellow, 1991—; member of editorial board, *New York Times,* 1996—.

AWARDS, HONORS: MacArthur fellow, 1987; National Book Award for nonfiction, 1995, and Pulitzer Prize for general nonfiction, 1996, both for *The Haunted Land: Facing Europe's Ghosts after Communism.*

WRITINGS:

Children of Cain: Violence and the Violent in Latin America, Morrow (New York City), 1991.
The Haunted Land: Facing Europe's Ghosts after Communism, Random House (New York City), 1995.

SIDELIGHTS: Tina Rosenberg's first book, *Children of Cain: Violence and the Violent in Latin America,* grew out of her experiences as a journalist in Central and South America from 1985 to 1990. The book deals with regions that were especially troubled during that period, including Nicaragua, El Salvador, Colombia, and Chile. In the *New York Times Book Review,* Kevin Buckley pronounces the book "insightful" and thoroughly researched.

Rosenberg moved on to Central and Eastern Europe in 1991 to observe the countries in that region as they tried to come to terms with their past and build new, democratic institutions following the collapse of Communism. Her findings are contained in *The Haunted Land: Facing Europe's Ghosts after Communism.* The book focuses on the former Czechoslovakia, Poland, and the former East Germany. Rosenberg reports that in the Czech Republic, people believed—sometimes wrongly—to have been secret police informants under the Communist government are commonly persecuted. In Slovakia, she notes, no such persecution is occurring, but those who held power under Communism remain in power. In her coverage of Poland, she analyzes General Wojciech Jaruzelski, who imposed martial law in 1981, and the extensive debate about his motives in doing so. Her section on East Germany discusses the trials of various agents of the state, ranging from top political leaders to border guards, and the opening of security files kept by the Communist regime. In all the regions, she finds people struggling, not always successfully, with the questions of who was to blame for repressive government actions and how they should be dealt with in a freer system.

Several critics praise Rosenberg for the scope of her research and depth of her understanding. Timothy Garton Ash, writing in the *New York Review of Books,* calls the book "a genuine achievement: rich, vivid, and stimulating. Though not convincing in all its arguments or conclusions, *The Haunted Land* will teach you more about the real life of post-Communist Central Europe than many a multi-author volume of academic transitology." According to Blaine Harden, reviewing for the *Washington Monthly,* "Rosenberg's considerable success lies in the subtlety of the questions she asks and in the diligence with which she has dug up human stories." In the *Los Angeles Times Book Review,* David Rieff describes *The Haunted Land* as "the definitive account of what the transition away from communism in Eastern Europe has meant in moral terms."

These and other critics laud Rosenberg's focus on individual, personal stories. "In each of three geographically organized sections she builds from a dramatic tale at the center, embellishing and layering it with discursive accounts of other lives, other experiences, that reflect that society's approach to the past," Michael T. Kaufman observes in the *New York Times Book Review.* Marc Fisher, reviewer for the *Washington Post Book World,* believes Rosenberg focuses on the wrong individuals, however. By concentrating on "government officials, prominent dissidents and others with experiences far from those of everyday citizens, Rosenberg . . . lends too much credence to the bitterness and disappointment of those who will never adjust to western ways." Fisher also perceives a lack of immediacy in the book, perhaps because Rosenberg did not come to Europe until nearly two years after Communism's collapse, and suggests that the three regions she explores are too disparate to be considered in the same book. Harden, though, points out that the three are similar in a significant way—they have made the transition from authoritarian to democratic government without violence. This may be a reason, Harden says, for Rosenberg's digressions to complain about past U.S. policy toward Eastern Europe: "I . . . suspect she grew a bit impatient with her narrow focus on peaceful change, while a hot war raged on in the former Yugoslavia." Harden opines that peaceful change is

more typical of the Eastern European experience than is civil war and that the key message of *The Haunted Land*—whether or not Rosenberg intended to send it—is that, while mistakes have been made along the way, "the changes in Eastern Europe have been spectacularly beneficial."

BIOGRAPHICAL/CRITICAL SOURCES:

PERIODICALS

Los Angeles Times Book Review, August 13, 1995, p. 11.
New York Review of Books, July 13, 1995, pp. 21-23.
New York Times Book Review, November 29, 1992, p. 32; May 14, 1995, p.8.
Washington Monthly, June, 1995, pp. 48-50.
Washington Post Book World, May 28, 1995, p. 7.*

—*Sketch by Trudy Ring*

* * *

RUTTER, Michael (Llewellyn) 1933-

PERSONAL: Born August 15, 1933, in Brummana, Lebanon; son of Llewellyn Charles (a medical practitioner) and Winifred (Barber) Rutter; married Majorie Heys (a nurse practitioner and psychosexual counselor), December 27, 1958; children: Sheila Carol Rutter Mellish, Stephen Michael, Christine Ann. *Education:* University of Birmingham, M.B., Ch.B. (with distinction), 1955, M.D. (with honors), 1963; University of London, D.P.M. (with distinction), 1961.

ADDRESSES: Home—London, England. *Office*—Department of Child and Adolescent Psychiatry, Institute of Psychiatry, University of London, De Crespigny Park, London SE5 8AF, England.

CAREER: Held various training positions in pediatrics, neurology, and internal medicine, 1955-58; Maudsley Hospital, London, registrar, 1958-61, senior registrar, 1961, member of scientific staff of Medical Research Council Social Psychiatry Research Unit, 1962-65, honorary consultant child psychiatrist, 1966—; Institute of Psychiatry, University of London, London, senior lecturer, 1965-68, reader, 1968-73, professor, 1973—, honorary director of Medical Research Council Psychiatry Unit, 1984—, honorary director of the Social, Genetic and

Developmental Psychiatry Research Centre, 1994—. Fellow of Center for Advanced Study in the Behavioral Sciences, Palo Alto, CA, 1979-80.

MEMBER: Association for Child Psychology and Psychiatry (chair, 1973-74), British Paediatric Association, Royal College of Physicians (fellow), Royal College of Psychiatrists (fellow), Royal Society of Medicine (fellow), British Psychological Society (honorary fellow), American Academy of Pediatrics (honorary fellow), American Academy of Child Psychiatry (honorary member).

AWARDS, HONORS: Nuffield medical traveling fellow, Yeshiva University, 1961-62; Belding traveling scholar in United States, 1963; Goulstonian Lecturer, Royal College of Physicians, 1973; research award, American Association on Mental Deficiency, 1975; Rock Carling fellow, Nuffield Provincial Hospitals Trust, 1979; C. Anderson Aldrich Award, American Academy of Pediatrics, 1981; Commander of the Order of the British Empire, 1985; Fellow of the Royal Society, 1987; honorary degrees from University of Leiden, 1985, Catholic University of Louvain, 1990, University of Birmingham, 1990, University of Edinburgh, 1990, University of Chicago, 1991, University of Minnesota, 1993, University of Ghent, 1994, and University of Jyvaskyla, Finland, 1996.

WRITINGS:

Children of Sick Parents: An Environmental and Psychiatric Study, Oxford University Press (Oxford), 1966.

(With Philip Graham and William Yule) *A Neuropsychiatric Study in Childhood,* Heinemann (London), 1970.

(Editor with Jack Tizard and Kingsley Whitmore) *Education, Health, and Behaviour,* Longmans, Green, 1970, Robert E. Krieger (Melbourne, FL), 1981.

(Editor) *Infantile Autism: Concepts, Characteristics, and Treatment,* Churchill Livingstone (Edinburgh), 1970.

Maternal Deprivation Reassessed, Penguin (West Drayton, Middlesex), 1972, second edition, 1981, published as *The Qualities of Mothering: Maternal Deprivation Reassessed,* Jason Aronson, 1974.

(Editor with J. A. M. Martin) *The Child with Delayed Speech,* Heinemann, 1972.

(With David Shaffer and Michael Shepherd) *A Multi-Axial Classification of Child Psychiatric Disor-*

ders, World Health Organization (Albany, NY), 1975.

Helping Troubled Children, Penguin, 1975, Plenum (New York City), 1976.

(With Nicola Madge) *Cycles of Disadvantage,* Heinemann Educational (London), 1976.

(Editor with Lionel Abraham Hersov) *Child Psychiatry: Modern Approaches,* Blackwell Scientific Publications (Oxford), 1977, second edition published as *Child and Adolescent Psychiatry: Modern Approaches,* 1985, third edition, 1994.

(Editor with Eric Schopler) *Autism: A Reappraisal of Concepts and Treatment,* Plenum, 1978.

(With Barbara Maughan, Peter Mortimer, and others) *Fifteen Thousand Hours: Secondary Schools and Their Effects on Children,* Harvard University Press (Cambridge, MA), 1979.

Changing Youth in a Changing Society: Patterns of Adolescent Development and Disorder, Nuffield Provincial Hospital Trust (London), 1979, Harvard University Press, 1980.

(Editor) *Scientific Foundation of Developmental Psychiatry,* Heinemann Medical Books (London), 1980.

(With Henri Giller) *Juvenile Delinquency: Trends and Perspectives,* Penguin, 1983.

(Editor with Norman Garmezy) *Stress, Coping, and Development in Children,* McGraw (New York City), 1983.

(Editor) *Developmental Neuropsychiatry,* Guilford (New York City), 1983.

(Editor with R. Russell Jones) *Lead versus Health: Sources and Effects of Low Level Lead Exposure,* Wiley (New York City), 1983.

(Contributor) E. M. Hetherington, editor, *Carmichael's Manual of Child Psychology,* Volume 4: *Social and Personality Development,* Wiley, 1983.

A Measure of Our Values: Goals and Dilemmas in the Upbringing of Children, Quaker Home Service Committee (London), 1983.

(Editor with Carroll Izard and Peter Read) *Depression in Young People: Developmental and Clinical Perspectives,* Guilford, 1986.

(With Patricia Howlin) *Treatment of Autistic Children,* Wiley, 1987.

(With Yule) *Language Development and Disorders,* MacKeith, 1987.

(Editor with A. Hussain Tuma and Irma S. Lann) *Assessment and Diagnosis in Child Psychopathology,* Guilford, 1988.

(With David Quinton) *Parenting Breakdown: The Making and Breaking of Inter-generational Links,* Avebury (Brookefield, VT), 1988.

(Editor) *Studies of Psychosocial Risk: The Power of Longitudinal Data,* Cambridge University Press (New York City), 1989.

(Editor with Lee Robins) *Straight and Devious Pathways from Childhood to Adulthood,* Cambridge University Press, 1990.

(Editor with Paul Casaer) *Biological Risk Factors for Psychosocial Disorders,* Cambridge University Press, 1991.

(With Marjorie Rutter) *Developing Minds: Challenge and Continuity across the Lifespan,* Penguin Books/Blackwell Scientific Publications, 1994.

(Editor with Dale Hay) *Development through Life: A Handbook for Clinicians,* Blackwell Scientific Publications, 1994.

(Editor with Robert Haggerty, Lonnie Sherrod, Norman Garmezy) *Stress, Risk, and Resilience in Children and Adolescents: Processes, Mechanisms, and Interventions,* Cambridge University Press, 1994.

(Editor) *Psychosocial Disturbances in Young People: Challenges for Prevention,* Cambridge University Press, 1995.

(Editor with David Smith) *Psychosocial Disorders in Young People: Time Trends and Their Causes,* Wiley, 1995.

Member of numerous editorial boards.

WORK IN PROGRESS: Conducting a study of "normal and abnormal child development, with particular focus on the links between experiences in childhood and functioning in adult life, factors in the child and in his environment leading to resilience in the face of adversity, the characteristics that make for effective schooling, the skills involved in interviewing, the characteristics of good parenting and the factors that facilitate it, and the study of autistic, depressed, and hyperkinetic children."

BIOGRAPHICAL/CRITICAL SOURCES:

PERIODICALS

APA Monitor, June, 1980.
New Society, Volume 62, number 1049/50, 1982.

S

SAATKAMP, Herman J(oseph), Jr.   1942-

PERSONAL: Born September 29, 1942, in Knoxville, TN; son of Herman Joseph (a pharmacist) and Geneva May (a homemaker) Saatkamp; married Dorothy Tyre (a teacher), June 13, 1964; children: Barbara, Joseph. *Education:* Carson-Newman College, B.A., 1964; Southern Seminary, M.Div., 1967; Vanderbilt University, M.A., 1970, Ph.D., 1972.

ADDRESSES: Home—1203 Merry Oaks Dr., College Station, TX 77840. *Office*—Department of Philosophy and Humanities, Texas A & M University, College Station, TX 77843-4237.

CAREER: University of Tampa, Tampa, FL, assistant professor, 1970-73, associate professor, 1973-78, professor of philosophy, 1978-80, Dana Professor of Philosophy, 1981-85, chair of Philosophy/Religion Area, 1975-83, and Humanities Division, 1983-85; Texas A & M University, College Station, professor of philosophy, 1985—, head of department, 1985-94, founder and chair of University Chamber Music Series, 1985-88. Adjunct lecturer at University of South Florida, Tampa, 1971-72. Brazos Valley Symphony Society, first vice president, 1987-88; chair of finance committee, 1986-88.

MEMBER: American Philosophical Association, Association of Documentary Editing (president-elect, 1995-96), Modern Language Association of America, Opera and Performing Arts Society, Santayana Society, Society for the Advancement of American Philosophy, Association for Computers and the Humanities, Society for Textual Scholarship, Texas Committee for the Humanities (board of directors, 1992—, vice chair, 1995-96), Word-Processors Topical Study Group (chair, 1985-87), Bibliographical Society of the University of Virginia, Alpha Chi (honorary member), Omicron Delta Kappa.

AWARDS, HONORS: Grants from National Endowment for the Humanities, 1975-96, General Electric Co., 1976, Council for Philosophical Studies, 1976, Penrose Fund of the American Philosophical Society, 1977, and Conn Foundation, 1982.

WRITINGS:

(Contributor) Peter Caws, editor, *Two Centuries of Philosophy,* Littlefield (Totowa, NJ), 1980.

(With John Jones) *George Santayana: A Bibliographical Checklist, 1880-1980,* Philosophy Documentation Center, Bowling Green State University (Bowling Green, OH), 1982.

(Editor with William G. Holzberger) *The Works of George Santayana,* MIT Press (Cambridge, MA), Volume 1: *Persons and Places,* 1987, Volume 2: *The Sense of Beauty,* 1988, Volume 3: *Interpretations of Poetry and Religion,* 1989, Volume 4: *The Last Puritan,* 1994.

(Editor with Robert Burch) *Frontiers in American Philosophy,* Texas A & M University Press (College Station), Volume 1, 1992, Volume 2, 1996.

(Editor and author of introduction) *Rorty and Pragmatism: The Philosopher Responds to His Critics,* Vanderbilt University Press (Nashville, TN), 1995.

Contributor to philosophy journals; general editor of *The Works of George Santayana,* MIT Press, and *The Vanderbilt Library of American Philosophy,* Vanderbilt University Press; coeditor of *Overhead in Seville: Bulletin of the Santayana Society;* associate editor of *American National Biography*, Oxford University Press.

WORK IN PROGRESS: Editing *The Works of George Santayana*, Volume V: *The Letters of George Santayana*, publication by MIT Press expected in 1997-98; Volume VI: *The Life of Reason* (five books); *Don't Forget Your Loving Father: Augustin to George Santayana*, letters from father to son; *George Santayana*, a monograph on his philosophy; *Under Avila's Skies*, essays from the 1992 International Congress of George Santayana.

* * *

SALMOND, John A(lexander) 1937-

PERSONAL: Born September 28, 1937, in Dunedin, New Zealand; son of James D. (a clergyman) and Margaret (a teacher; maiden name, McKenzie) Salmond; divorced; children: Kerry Salmond Washington, Nicola, Paul, Mark. *Education:* University of Otago, B.A., 1958, M.A., 1960; Duke University, Ph.D., 1964.

ADDRESSES: Home—45 Ramsay Ave., East Kew, Victoria 3107, Australia. *Office*—Department of History, La Trobe University, Melbourne 3083, Australia.

CAREER: Otago Daily Times, Dunedin, New Zealand, sub-editor, 1959-60; Victoria University of Wellington, Wellington, New Zealand, lecturer, 1963-66, senior lecturer in history, 1966-67; La Trobe University, Melbourne, Australia, senior lecturer in history, 1968-69, professor of American history, 1970—, chairman of department, 1971-73, 1979-80, and 1982-83, dean of School of Humanities, 1974-75.

AWARDS, HONORS: James B. Duke Commonwealth fellow at Duke University.

WRITINGS:

The Civilian Conservation Corps: A New Deal Case Study, Duke University Press (Durham, NC), 1967.

(With W. T. Breen) *An Ideal of Freedom: A History of the United States of America*, Longman (London), 1978.

A Southern Rebel: The Life and Times of Aubrey Willis Williams, 1890-1965, University of North Carolina Press (Chapel Hill), 1983.

(Editor with Bruce Clayton) *The South Is Another Land: Essays on the Twentieth-Century South*, Greenwood Press (New York City), 1987.

Miss Lucy of the CIO: The Life and Times of Lucy Randolph Mason, 1882-1959, University of Georgia Press (Athens), 1988.

The Conscience of a Lawyer: Clifford J. Durr and American Civil Liberties, 1899-1975, University of Alabama Press (Tuscaloosa), 1990.

Gastonia, 1929: The Story of the Loray Mill Strike, University of North Carolina Press, 1995.

SIDELIGHTS: Australian writer John A. Salmond specializes in American labor history, particularly when it involves the American South. His *Miss Lucy of the CIO: The Life and Times of Lucy Randolph Mason, 1882-1959* is the biography of a prominent labor leader and social activist, while *The Conscience of a Lawyer: Clifford J. Durr and American Civil Liberties, 1899-1975* presents the career of the left-wing civil rights activist and president of the National Lawyers Guild. In *Gastonia, 1929: The Story of the Loray Mill Strike* Salmond examines a doomed strike led by the American Communist Party against a North Carolina textile company.

Miss Lucy of the CIO details the life of Lucy Randolph Mason, a descendent of a prominent Southern family who held positions in such groups as the Young Women's Christian Association (YWCA), the League of Women Voters, the National Consumers League, and finally with the Congress of Industrial Organizations (CIO), one of the nation's leading labor organizations. Mason was inspired in her social activism by a strong faith and a desire to improve her native South. "Salmond's study shows," writes R. F. Zeidel in *Choice*, "that [Mason's] career . . . was a natural outgrowth of both her piety and her concern for the South." Salmond's book also, Zeidel notes, "provides an excellent description and assessment" of Mason's close personal friendship with Eleanor Roosevelt. Although Ann Schofield in the *Journal of American History* finds that "the book is ultimately disappointing, for we come to know more of the times than the life of Lucy Randolph Mason," she nonetheless concludes that the biography is "a welcome addition to a growing literature on twentieth-century female reformers."

In *The Conscience of a Lawyer* Salmond examines the life of Clifford J. Durr, a long-time activist in leftist political causes. A New Deal attorney in the 1930s and president of the radical National Lawyers Guild from 1949, Durr went on to defend Communists accused of disloyalty in the 1950s. He was also a strong advocate for civil rights, a cause he believed furthered the civil liberties of all Americans. Salmond's work is "a moving and informative biography of a truly remarkable American lawyer," according to Michal R. Belknap in the *American Historical Review.* Writing in the *Journal of American History,* William A. Donohue wonders why "Salmond never explains why someone who is cast as a champion of liberty came to the defense of those who sought to sunder civil liberties. After all, liberals such as Abe Fortas refused to defend known Communists. Why didn't Durr?" Donohue also questions Durr's membership in "the notorious National Lawyers Guild instead of the more moderate American Civil Liberties Union." Donohue concludes that "none of these questions is answered . . . an omission that detracts from an otherwise excellent effort."

Salmond tells the story of a textile strike in *Gastonia, 1929.* Because the violent strike was organized by a vocal American Communist Party, Gastonia led many people in the South to equate labor unions with Communism and violence, a linkage that has done much harm to union organizing efforts in the region. Gastonia, explains Maurice Isserman in the *New York Times Book Review,* "took on mythic proportions in subsequent years." Isserman finds that "implicit throughout *Gastonia, 1929* is the counter-factual proposition that had someone other than the Communists played the leading role . . . then Gastonia might have proved a triumph." Isserman argues, however, that the failure of more moderate labor unions to organize the Southern textile industry since Gastonia shows how resistant the region is to unions. Yardley concludes that Salmond "presents the facts as he finds them, not as he wills them to be, with the result that he has written a fair, dispassionate book."

Salmond told *CA:* "My interest in United States history predated my coming to the United States for doctoral work at Duke University on a James B. Duke Commonwealth fellowship. I lived in the South during the years of great change between 1960 and 1964. It was that experience that has drawn me to people like Aubrey Williams, Lucy Mason, and Virginia Durr, all Southerners, and all people who fought valiantly for Southern change before it was popular to do so."

BIOGRAPHICAL/CRITICAL SOURCES:

PERIODICALS

American Historical Review, April, 1990, p. 612; October, 1991, p. 1317.
Boston Globe, December 31, 1995, p. 48.
Choice, December, 1988, pp. 702, 704; March, 1994, p. 1079.
Historian, February, 1985, p. 294.
Journal of American History, June, 1989, p. 297; September, 1991, p. 700.
New Directions for Women, September, 1988, p. 19.
New York Times Book Review, December 10, 1995, p. 33.
South Atlantic Quarterly, winter, 1985, p. 108.
Southern Historical Review, summer, 1985, p. 245.
Washington Post Book World, November 22, 1995, p. B2.

*   *   *

SALTMAN, Judith   1947-

PERSONAL: Born May 11, 1947, in Vancouver, British Columbia, Canada; daughter of Harry and Ruth (Berezovsky) Saltman; children: Anne. *Ethnicity:* "Jewish." *Education:* University of British Columbia, B.A., 1969, B.L.S., 1970; Simmons College, M.A., 1982. *Politics:* Social Democrat.

ADDRESSES: Home—101-3189 Camosun St., Vancouver, British Columbia, Canada, VGR 3X2. *Office*—School of Library, Archival, and Information Studies, University of British Columbia, 831-1956 Main Mall, Vancouver, British Columbia, Canada V6T 1Y3. *E-mail*—saltman@unixg.ubc.ca.

CAREER: Toronto Public Library, Toronto, Ontario, children's librarian, 1970-72; West Vancouver Memorial Library, West Vancouver, British Columbia, children's librarian, 1973-79; Vancouver Public Library, Vancouver, British Columbia, children's librarian, 1980-83; University of British Columbia, Vancouver, assistant professor, 1983-88, associate professor of children's literature and librarianship, 1988—. Member of International Board on Books for Young People.

MEMBER: Canadian Library Association, American Library Association, Association for Library and

Information Science Education, British Columbia Library Association.

AWARDS, HONORS: Howard V. Phalin-World Book scholar of Canadian Library Association, 1981; Frances E. Russell Memorial Award from Canadian section of International Board on Books for Young People, 1986.

WRITINGS:

(Editor) *Riverside Anthology of Children's Literature,* 6th edition, Houghton (Boston), 1985.
Goldie and the Sea (juvenile), Groundwood Books (Toronto), 1987.
Modern Canadian Children's Books, Oxford University Press (New York City), 1987.
(With Sheila Egoff) *The New Republic of Childhood: A Critical Guide to Canadian Children's Literature in English,* Oxford University Press, 1990.

SIDELIGHTS: Judith Saltman told *CA:* "All my work as a writer, teacher, and librarian has been devoted to the creation of quality children's literature and the promotion and mediation of literature with children. This is a very exciting time to be working in this field in Canada. Canadian authors and illustrators are interpreting Canadian life and values, telling our children about our culture, history, and ourselves as members of the human community."

*   *   *

SANDERSON, Lennox, Jr.
  See SLIDE, Anthony

*   *   *

SAPIRO, Virginia 1951-

PERSONAL: Born February 28, 1951, in East Orange, NJ; daughter of William H. (a scriptwriter) and Florence (an educator; maiden name, Michaels) Sapiro; married Graham K. Wilson (a professor), 1981; children: Adam. *Education:* Clark University, B.A. (with high honors), 1972; University of Michigan, M.A. and Ph.D., both 1976.

ADDRESSES: Office—Department of Political Science, University of Wisconsin-Madison, 1050 Bascom Mall, Madison, WI 53706. *E-mail*—sapiro @polisci.wisc.edu.

CAREER: Clark University, Worcester, MA, instructor in political science, summer, 1974; University of Michigan, Ann Arbor, instructor in political science, summer, 1975; University of Wisconsin-Madison, assistant professor, 1976-81, associate professor, 1981-86, professor of political science and women's studies, 1986—, Sophonisba P. Breckinridge Professor of political science and women's studies, 1995—. University of Essex (England), department of government, visiting lecturer, 1979-80, visiting professor, 1989.

MEMBER: International Society for Political Psychology, American Political Science Association (chairperson of Committee on the Status of Women, 1985-86; founding president of Organized Section on Women and Politics, 1986), Women's Caucus in Political Science, Midwest Political Science Association (member of executive council, 1984-86), Phi Beta Kappa.

AWARDS, HONORS: Chastain Award from Southern Political Science Association, 1975, for paper "New Pride, Old Prejudice: Political Ambition and Role Orientations among Female Partisan Elites"; award from Western Political Science Association's Committee on the Status of Women, 1978, for article "News from the Front: Inter-Sex and Inter-generational Conflict over the Status of Women"; Sophonisba Breckinridge Award from Midwest Political Science Association, 1983, for paper "Women, Citizenship, and Immigration Policy in the United States"; Erik Erikson Award for Early Career Contribution to Political Psychology from International Society for Political Psychology, 1986; Victoria Schuck Award for best book on women and politics, from American Political Science Association, 1993, for *A Vindication of Political Virtue: The Political Theory of Mary Wollstonecraft;* named Mentor of Distinction, American Political Science Association, 1993.

WRITINGS:

The Political Integration of Women: Roles, Socialization, and Politics, University of Illinois Press (Urbana, IL), 1983.
Women, Political Action, and Political Participation, American Political Science Association (Washington, DC), 1983.

(Editor and contributor) *Women, Biology, and Public Policy,* Sage Publications (Beverly Hills, CA), 1985.

Women in American Society: An Introduction to Women's Studies, Mayfield Publishing (Mountain View, CA), 1986, 3rd edition, 1994.

A Vindication of Political Virtue: The Political Theory of Mary Wollstonecraft, University of Chicago Press (Chicago, IL), 1992.

Member of editorial board of *American Journal of Political Science,* 1979-82, 1991-94, *Woman and Politics,* 1980—, *Political Psychology,* 1981—, *Youth and Society,* 1982—, *Political Science Quarterly,* 1984—, and *American Science Review,* 1995—.

Also contributor of articles and reviews to political science and women's studies journals.

WORK IN PROGRESS: A history of political action in the United States.

SIDELIGHTS: Virginia Sapiro told *CA:* "My primary concern is a feminist analysis of the relationship of women to the political world. Although my work is scholarly and employs the methods of contemporary social science, my view is that writing in the social sciences should be intelligible and even enjoyable to read."

*   *   *

SAUNDERS, Caleb
    See HEINLEIN, Robert A(nson)

*   *   *

SCARF, Maggi
    See SCARF, Maggie

*   *   *

SCARF, Maggie   1932-
    (Maggi Scarf)

PERSONAL: Born May 13, 1932, in Philadelphia, PA; daughter of Benjamin and Helen (Rotbin) Klein;

married Herbert E. Scarf (a professor at Yale University), June 23, 1953; children: Martha, Elizabeth, Susan. *Education:* Attended Temple University, 1950-53, Stanford University, 1955-56, and Southern Connecticut State College, 1963-64. *Politics:* Democrat. *Religion:* Jewish.

ADDRESSES: Home—88 Blake Rd., Hamden, CT 06517. *Office*—c/o Jonathan Edwards College, Yale University, 68 High St., New Haven, CT 06520. *Agent*—Brandt & Brandt, 1501 Broadway, New York, NY 10036.

CAREER: Writer. Yale University, Jonathan Edwards College, associate fellow, 1979, 1981, 1983—. Senior fellow, Bush Center in Child Development.

AWARDS, HONORS: National Media Awards from American Psychological Foundation, 1971 and 1974, for articles, and 1977, for *Body, Mind, Behavior;* Ford Foundation fellow, 1973-74; Nieman fellow in journalism at Harvard University, 1975-76; fellow at Center for Advanced Study in the Behavioral Sciences, 1977-78, 1985-86; Alicia Patterson Foundation fellow, 1978-79.

WRITINGS:

(Under name Maggi Scarf) *Meet Benjamin Franklin* (juvenile), Random House (New York City), 1968, reprinted, 1989.

Antarctica: Exploring the Frozen Continent (juvenile), Random House, 1970.

Body, Mind, Behavior, New Republic (Washington, DC), 1976.

Unfinished Business: Pressure Points in the Lives of Women, Doubleday (New York City), 1981.

Intimate Partners: Patterns in Love and Marriage, Random House, 1987.

Intimate Worlds: Life inside the Family, Random House, 1995.

Contributor of articles and book reviews to *New York Times, Psychology Today, New Republic, Redbook, Cosmopolitan,* and *New York Times Book Review.* Contributing editor, *New Republic* and *Self.*

SIDELIGHTS: Maggie Scarf "is a respected science writer whose specialty is the relationship between body and mind—in sickness and in health," writes *Nation* contributor Susan Jacoby. Scarf has spent much of her writing career exploring the complex interactions between men and women, between family members, and within individuals' psyches, taking into account how a person's past can affect his or her present dilemmas. According to *New York Times Book Review* contributor Sandra Blakeslee, Scarf's work "at the very least, . . . gets you thinking about the skeletons in your closet—and how you might lay them to rest."

One of Scarf's best known books is a study of women and depression entitled *Unfinished Business: Pressure Points in the Lives of Women.* Scarf's premise is that every woman, beginning with adolescence and each decade thereafter, experiences a "pressure point." At these "key points all women must make and break a series of emotional bonds," observes Cynthia H. Wilson and Eric Gelman in *Newsweek.* "If they fail to do so, if they become emotionally stranded, their 'unfinished business' almost inevitably leads to depression."

The research on depression indicates that there are two to six times as many depressed women as men. In a *Los Angeles Times* interview with Lisa Connolly, Scarf explains that women are more vulnerable to depression because of their concern "with the search for security within the context of a vitally significant relationship." She adds, however, that there are also "differences in the ways men and women express psychological trouble. For men in trouble, you'd look in the courts and jails. For women, you'd look in psychiatric clinics. Men hurt other people. Women hurt themselves."

Unfinished Business includes lengthy profiles of ten of the over 150 women Scarf interviewed at the Dartmouth-Hitchcock Mental Health Center, the University of Pennsylvania's Mood Clinic, and the Yale Depression Research Unit. Observes Maya Pines in the *New York Times Book Review:* "One gets caught up in the stories of the 10 women whom Mrs. Scarf describes, with their intimate details and quirks that, nevertheless, bring a shock of recognition. . . . The stories have the immediacy and fascination of good television drama. At the same time they act as sugarcoating for the solid bits of information that the author slips in deftly here and there: information about the signs of depression, the kinds of treatment that are available, how they work, where to find them." Expressing a similar opinion, *Washington Post Book World* contributor Ursula K. LeGuin notes that "each voice, each woman [is] a facet of the dark

jewel: Loss, Mourning, Terror, Despair, Anger, Loneliness." She concludes: "Depression might be a depressing subject, but the voices of women from the darkness are very moving, and *Unfinished Business* is, in its firmness and intelligence and charity, an invigorating, hope-giving book."

Scarf has also drawn attention for her voluminous work on marriage, entitled *Intimate Partners: Patterns in Love and Marriage.* Once again the author uses in-depth interviews, this time with 32 married couples, to illustrate her conclusions on how marriages can be destroyed by—or how they can survive—stressful events. In the *Christian Science Monitor,* Marilyn Gardner calls *Intimate Partners* "one of the most sobering appraisals of marital relationships since Ingmar Bergman's 'Scenes from a Marriage,'" adding that Scarf "throws buckets of cold realism on the flames of romantic idealism." In addition to outlining the stages that marriages progress through, Scarf reveals how childhood experiences influence the choice of a mate as well as the way a spouse reacts to that mate. "Scarf is at her best when she offers her own considerable insights on marriage," Gardner concludes. " . . . With this volume, [she] joins a growing list of authors who are expanding the genre of 'relationship books.'"

After publishing *Intimate Partners,* Scarf spent the next eight years researching the American family. She interviewed numerous families of different sorts, took further psychology and sociology courses, and spent time at institutions where research into the family is currently being conducted. Her 1995 title *Intimate Worlds: Life inside the Family* reveals "how to determine your family's level of emotional health by analyzing how it handles power, intimacy and conflict," according to *USA Today* correspondent Karen S. Peterson.

In *Intimate Worlds,* Scarf uses the Beavers Systems Model, a clinical scale developed in the 1970s to classify families according to their relative levels of health and function. The book offers case studies for each of five different levels designated by the Beavers System and, while Scarf's goals are scientific, her approach is aimed at the general reader. Blakeslee writes: "'Intimate Worlds' will appeal to many readers who are not familiar with . . . psychoanalytic concepts. From Ms. Scarf's case studies they will learn how families can betray important personal boundaries, develop tyrants, choose scapegoats and build or erode self-esteem. She includes self-examination exercises for readers to help them discover these unhealthy patterns at home." *Washington Post* reviewer Jon Katz notes of the work: "Scarf knows the intricacies of the family structure and, even better, knows how to write well about them. . . . In 'Intimate Worlds,' as in most of our lives, family is riveting, white-knuckle stuff."

BIOGRAPHICAL/CRITICAL SOURCES:

PERIODICALS

Christian Science Monitor, February 6, 1987, pp. B1, B4.
Los Angeles Times, October 23, 1980.
Los Angeles Times Book Review, December 24, 1995, p. 4.
Ms., November, 1980.
Nation, October 4, 1980.
Newsweek, September 8, 1980.
New York Times Book Review, August 24, 1980; November 9, 1980; March 1, 1987, pp. 15-16; November 26, 1995, p. 28.
Saturday Review, August, 1980.
USA Today, February 13, 1987, p. D4; October 24, 1995, p. D6.
Washington Post, October 26, 1995, p. C2.
Washington Post Book World, August 24, 1980; February 15, 1987; October 26, 1995, p. 2.

*   *   *

SCHLISSEL, Lillian   1930-

PERSONAL: Born February 22, 1930, in New York, NY; daughter of Abraham and Mae (Isaacson) Fischer; children: Rebecca Claire, Daniel. *Education:* Brooklyn College (now Brooklyn College of the City University of New York), B.A., 1951; Yale University, Ph.D., 1957.

ADDRESSES: Office—Department of English, Brooklyn College of the City University of New York, Brooklyn, NY 11210.

CAREER: Brooklyn College of the City University of New York, Brooklyn, NY, instructor, 1957-65, assistant professor, 1965-69, associate professor, 1969-71, professor of English, 1971—, director of American studies program, 1974—.

MEMBER: American Studies Association, Organization of American Historians, Western Historical Association.

WRITINGS:

(Editor) *The World of Randolph Bourne,* Dutton (New York City), 1965.
(Editor) *Conscience in America: A Documentary History of Conscientious Objection in the United States, 1757-1967,* Dutton, 1968.
(With Walter Reigart) *The Journals of Washington Irving,* Volume 2, Twayne (Boston, MA), 1981.
Women's Diaries of the Westward Journey, preface by Carl N. Delger, Schocken (New York City), 1982.
(Editor with V. Ruiz and J. Monk) *Western Women: Their Land, Their Lives,* University of New Mexico Press (Albuquerque, NM), 1988.
(With Byrd Gibbens and E. Hampsten) *Far from Home: Families of the Westward Journey,* preface by Robert Coles, Schocken, 1989.
(Author of introduction) Ken Holmes, editor, *Covered Wagon Women,* University of Nebraska Press (Lincoln, NE), 1996.

Contributor to books, including *Woman's Being, Woman's Place: Female Identity and Vocation,* edited by Mary Kelley, G. K. Hall (Boston), 1979; *The American Self,* edited by Sam Girgus, University of New Mexico Press, 1981; and *Making America, the Society and Culture of O. S.,* edited by Luther S. Luedtke, 1987. Also contributor to periodicals, including *Frontiers, Culturefront, Western Historical Quarterly,* and *American Studies.*

WORK IN PROGRESS: A book on the women of vaudeville between 1865 and 1935.

SIDELIGHTS: "The most astonishing revelation of Lillian Schlissel's marvelous book about the women of the Westward migration is that they didn't want to go," *Ms.* contributor Susan Dworkin explains in discussing *Women's Diaries of the Westward Journey.* The book is a collection of letters and diaries written by women traveling to California and Oregon between 1840 and 1870 via the Overland Trail. In the *New York Times,* Emid Nemy notes that while the "story of the covered wagons wending their way West has been told before. . ., it is doubtful if anything available in the past has been more accurate or revealing than this compilation from actual diaries.

The excerpts . . . provide a stark day-by-day account." *Christian Science Monitor* contributor S. R. Williams applauds Schlissel's approach, which focuses on men's and women's contrasting roles and emotions on the journey, and claims that the author "has moved scholarship ahead by two giant steps." And while Nemy remarks that the book "is not light summer reading," she continues that "it is important for anyone who wants a clear understanding of the people, and particularly the women, who shaped a good part of the nation."

Lillian Schlissel told *CA:* "My new project is about the women of vaudeville who worked between 1865 and 1935. My interest is in closing the circle between 'high' and 'low' comedy, to show how often these circles came together, and how women used the vaudeville stage as a public space to learn the speech they would need for life in the modern world."

BIOGRAPHICAL/CRITICAL SOURCES:

PERIODICALS

Booklist, November 15, 1993, p. 618.
Christian Science Monitor, April 14, 1982.
Horn Book Guide, spring, 1994, p. 158.
Kirkus Reviews, October 15, 1993, p. 1331.
Ms., April, 1982.
New York Times, July 21, 1982.
Publishers Weekly, November 1, 1993, p. 79.
Washington Post Book World, December 5, 1993, p. 24.

*   *   *

SCHMALENBACH, Werner   1920-

PERSONAL: Born September 13, 1920, in Goettingen, Germany; son of Herman and Sala (Muentz) Schmalenbach; married Esther Grey, December 15, 1950; children: Peggy, Corinne. *Education:* Attended Basel University.

ADDRESSES: Home—Poststrasse 17, 40667 Meerbusch, West Germany. *Office*—Marketplatz 3, 40213 Duesseldorf, West Germany.

CAREER: Gewerbemuseum Basel, Basel, Switzerland, curator, 1945-55; Kestner-Gesellschaft Hannover, Hannover, West Germany, director, 1955-62; Kunstsammlung Nordrhein-Westfalen, Duesseldorf, West Germany, director, 1962-90.

MEMBER: PEN, Sotheby's International (member of advisory board, 1991—).

WRITINGS:

(With Peter Baechlin and Georg Schmidt) *Der Film: Wirtschaftlich, Gesellschaftlich, Kuenstlerisch,* Holbein-Verlag, 1947, translation by Hugo Weber and Roger Manvell published as *The Film: Its Economic, Social and Artistic Problems,* Falcon Press (Helena, MT), 1948.
Die Kunst Afrikas, Holbein-Verlag, 1953, translation by Glyn T. Hughes published as *African Art,* Macmillan (New York City), 1954.
Adel des Pferdes: Kleiner Galopp durch die Kunstgeschichte, Walter-Verlag, 1959, translation by Daphne M. Goodall published as *The Noble Horse: A Journey through the History of Art,* Allen, J. A. (Canaan, NY), 1962.
Julius Bissier: Farbige Miniaturen, Piper Books (Boston), 1960.
Bissier, Abrams (New York City), 1963.
Kurt Schwitters, Verlag DuMont Schauberg, 1967, English translation published under same title, Abrams, 1970.
Die Kunstsammlung Nordrhein-Westfalen in Duesseldorf, Verlag DuMont Schauberg, 1970, translation by Sarah Twohig published as *Picasso to Lichtenstein: Masterpieces of Twentieth-Century Art from the Nordrhein-Westfalen Collection in Duesseldorf,* Tate Gallery Publications (London), 1974.
Antoni Tapies: Zeichen und Strukturen, Propylaeen Verlag, 1974.
Fernand Leger, Abrams, 1976.
Eduardo Chillida: Zeichnungen, Propylaeen Verlag, 1977.
Julius Bissier: Tuschen und Aquarelle (text in German, French, and English), Propylaeen Verlag, 1978.
Emil Schumacher (text in German and English), Verlag DuMont Schauberg, 1981.
Joan Miro: Zeichnungen aus den spaeten Jahren, Propylaeen Verlag, 1982.
Bilder des zwanzigsten Jahrhunderts, Prestel Verlag, 1986.
Paul Klee, Prestel Verlag, 1986.
Afrikanische Kunst, Prestel Verlag, 1988.
Amedeo Modigliana, Prestel Verlag, 1990, Abrams, 1990.

Die Lust auf das Bild. Ein Leben mit der Kunst, Siedler Verlag, 1996.

*   *   *

SCOTT, Joanna 1960-

PERSONAL: Born June 22, 1960, in Greenwich, CT; daughter of Walter Lee and Yvonne (a psychologist; maiden name, DePotter) Scott; married James Longenbach; children: Kathryn, Alice. *Education:* Trinity College, B.A. (with honors), 1983; Brown University, M.A., 1985.

ADDRESSES: Office—Department of English, University of Rochester, Rochester, NY 14627. *E-mail*—JSCT@dbl.cc.rochester.edu. *Agent*—Elaine Markson Literary Agency, Inc., 44 Greenwich Ave., New York, NY 10011.

CAREER: Elaine Markson Literary Agency, Inc., New York City, assistant, 1984-85; Brown University, Providence, RI, adjunct lecturer in creative writing, 1986-87; University of Maryland, College Park, assistant professor of English, 1987-88; University of Rochester, Rochester, NY, instructor, 1987, assistant professor, 1988-92, associate professor, 1992-95, professor of English, 1995—. Judge for various literary awards, including the PEN-Hemingway Award, Katherine Anne Porter Prize, Drue Heinz Award, Janet Kafka Award, William Peden Prize, and literature fellowships of the National Endowment for the Arts. Guest lecturer and reader at various universities, bookstores, libraries, theaters, writers' workshops, and conferences.

MEMBER: PEN.

AWARDS, HONORS: William Peden Prize for best fiction, *Missouri Review,* 1988; Guggenheim fellowship, 1988-89; Lillian Fairchild Award for contribution to the arts, 1990; Richard and Hilda Rosenthal Award, American Academy and Institute of Arts and Letters, 1991; PEN-Faulkner award nomination, 1991, for *Arrogance;*MacArthur fellowship, 1992-97; Aga Khan Award, 1992, and National Magazine Award in fiction, 1993, both from the *Paris Review,* both for "A Borderline Case"; Pushcart Prize, 1993, for "Convicta et Combusta"; first annual Rochester Writer's Award, 1994; named "one of the twenty-five best books of the year," *Voice Literary Supplement,* Short Fiction Prize, *Southern Review,* and

PEN-Faulkner award nomination, all 1995, for *Various Antidotes.*

WRITINGS:

Fading, My Parmacheene Belle (novel), Ticknor & Fields (New York City), 1987.
The Closest Possible Union (novel), Ticknor & Fields, 1988.
Arrogance (novel), Linden/Simon & Schuster (New York City), 1990.
Various Antidotes (short fiction collection), Holt (New York City), 1994.
Speakeasy (one-act play), first produced at the University of Rochester, 1994.
The Manikin (novel), Holt, 1996.

Contributor of short stories, essays, and reviews to numerous literary magazines, newspapers, and anthologies.

SIDELIGHTS: Joanna Scott is an American novelist whose first work, *Fading, My Parmacheene Belle,* garnered praise from critics, many of whom lauded the original dialect of Scott's narrator, an unnamed, aged man whose wife of fifty-three years has recently died. Scott's narrator embarks on a journey to the place of his wife's childhood accompanied by a fifteen-year-old runaway. "The old man's history is tortured and extravagant, and the novel fashions it in an unrelenting prose that is by turns precise and visionary. The world it conjures up is grimy and infected, but the author stops short of impassioned polemic, and focuses on the pathetic and the human," comments David Profumo in the *Spectator.* Chris Gordon Owen summarizes in *New Directions for Women:* "Youth is seeking a kind of atonement; age is winding back through 53 years of marital memories and doubts."

"What sets Joanna Scott's novel apart . . . is its particularity, its emotional intensity and its extraordinary language," finds Catherine Petroski in Chicago *Tribune Books.* Petroski lauds Scott's use of language, arguing that reading the novel is "like encountering a new strain of English." Profumo calls the novel an "honorable exception" to what he considers the usually unsuccessful metaphoric use of fishing, "combining as it does astute psychology with a vein of dark humour which maintains a constant and intriguing tension." Petroski comments that while some readers "may not survive" the language of *Fading, My Parmacheene Belle,* "those who do will witness a virtuoso performance." Nancy Ramsey in the *New York Times Book Review* calls *Fading* a "moving, wise novel."

Scott's second novel, *The Closest Possible Union,* is the story of fourteen-year-old Tom, a young man apprenticed to the captain of his father's slave ship. Cynthia Johnson Whealler notes in *Library Journal* that the voyage becomes both a "geographic and spiritual" journey to Africa and back, resembling Joseph Conrad's *Heart of Darkness.* A reviewer for *Kirkus Reviews* concurs, commenting that *The Closest Possible Union* is one of the "eeriest and most romantic stories about coming of age in moral darkness since the 19th century." Whealler calls the novel "beautifully written, but complex and disturbing."

Scott's next novel, *Arrogance,* garnered her a nomination for the prestigious PEN-Faulkner Award. The novel is a fictionalized account of the life of Egon Schiele, a controversial Austrian expressionist painter. Hunter Drohojowska in the *Los Angeles Times Book Review* summarizes: "[This] is an impressionistic and fictional sketch of Schiele's life, a selection of vignettes woven together with turn-of-the-century ambience." The narrative of *Arrogance* is not strictly chronological, but rather intersperses events from different time periods in "a collage whereby one gleans the sense of Schiele's grim life," notes Drohojowska. "Much of the novel turns on Schiele's imprisonment and trial, and Scott powerfully evokes the artist's prison cell, a metaphor for both society and his genius," comments J. D. McClatchy in the *Washington Post Book World.*

Despite finding that in some ways "the reader doesn't have a sense of the innocence or malevolence of" Schiele's painting of adolescent models, Drohojowska nevertheless concludes that with *Arrogance,* Scott "emerges as a writer who should not be ignored." McClatchy argues that, unlike some contemporary writers, Scott "undertake[s] narrative challenges of a high order." The critic concludes: "Scott's flair for poetic detail, her ability to render extreme psychological states, her sensitivity to the making of art and the unmaking of the artist—all of this helps make *Arrogance* a compelling tale."

In 1994, Scott published a collection of short fiction entitled *Various Antidotes,* for which she received a second nomination for the PEN-Faulkner Award. As Stephen Stark explains in the *Washington Post Book World,* the stories in *Various Antidotes* are compiled "chronologically from the 18th century through contemporary times . . . [and] feature historical and quasi-historical figures from the annals of truth-is-stranger-than-fiction." Among the stories in the collection is "Chloroform Jags," concerning a 19th century midwife who claims a newborn baby as her own, which Stark deems the "most fully realized" story in the collection. Though Stark finds that the short story form allows Scott only "enough room to explore her subjects in a cursory manner," Liza Pennywitt Taylor in the *Los Angeles Times Book Review* calls the entire collection "absorbing and entertaining." "[The collection's] grim super-realism may reflect Scott's absorption with the pathos and solitude of an exploring mind, and can serve to ask the question of how possible it is to exist as a thinking human in anything except a solitary state," comments Taylor. Peter S. Prescott in the *New York Times Book Review* calls *Various Antidotes* "a collection of distinctive and highly charged short stories."

Scott's 1996 novel *The Manikin* is the story of life on the estate of the late Henry Craxton, who earned his fortune as a taxidermist, at one time supplying museums the world over. His mansion, referred to as "The Manikin," is now inhabited by his widow Mary, Boggio—the master taxidermist—and an assortment of other characters, including a small staff who maintain what is left of the Craxton collection. Anna Mundow in the *Los Angeles Times Book Review* summarizes: "Now only flea-bitten members of the collection and of the Craxton family remain, preserved by a staff that is reduced in every sense of the word." Various major events change the lives of the inhabitants of the estate, including the sexual awakening of Peg, the housekeeper's daughter, and the death of Mary, who has recently written her son completely out of her will. "All of these events," comments Louise Titchener in the *Washington Post Book World,* "like stones tossed into a quiet pool, send out ripples that affect everything and everyone surrounding them." Prescott describes *The Manikin* as "a full-bore, old-fashioned Gothic romance, a foreboding melodrama that pulses with greed, mean-spiritedness and illicit sex (decorously wrought) . . . preparing the stage for the catastrophes to come."

Critical response to *The Manikin* was largely positive. Titchener calls Scott's prose "sensitive and beautifully crafted," concluding that "no reader who finished reading *The Manikin* will regret the experience." Concerning various potentially over-melodramatic elements of the Gothic romance, Prescott writes: "[How], without camping it up, can Ms. Scott make such a romance acceptable to discriminating readers? Make no mistake: she does." Mundow argues that both "character and plot in *The Manikin* risk being similarly crushed by the weight of the author's ideas. It is difficult to make human specimens engaging or to maintain a story's urgency when the actors are diminished by their creator's quirky objectivity." Prescott disagrees, arguing that the novel works because of this objectivity. The critic admires Scott's "intensely vivid prose," and ultimately compares the narrative voice of the novel to that of Ovid's *Metamorphoses*.

BIOGRAPHICAL/CRITICAL SOURCES:

BOOKS

Contemporary Literary Criticism, Volume 50, Gale (Detroit), 1988.

PERIODICALS

Belles Lettres, September-October, 1987, pp. 9, 15.
Kirkus Reviews, March 15, 1988, p. 400.
Library Journal, April 1, 1988, p. 99.
Los Angeles Times Book Review, August 12, 1990, pp. 1, 9; April 24, 1994, pp. 3, 11; March 10, 1996, p. 4.
New Directions for Women, September-October, 1987, p. 17.
New York Times, March 26, 1987, p. 21.
New York Times Book Review, March 22, 1987, p. 28; August 14, 1988, p. 20; April 14, 1996, p. 28.
Publishers Weekly, January 30, 1987, p. 369.
Spectator, April 9, 1988, p. 34.
Tribune Books (Chicago), March 8, 1987, pp. 6-7.
Washington Post Book World, July 22, 1990, p. 9; February 6, 1994, p. 4; March 24, 1996, p. 4.

* * *

SELZ, Peter (Howard)   1919-

PERSONAL: Born March 27, 1919, in Munich, Germany; came to the United States, 1936; became naturalized citizen, 1942; son of Eugene and Edith (Drey) Selz; married Thalia Cheronis, 1948 (divorced, 1965); married Carole Schemmerling, December 18, 1983; children: (first marriage) Tanya Nicole Eugenia, Gabrielle Hamlin. *Education:* Attended Columbia University, 1937-38, and Univer-

sity of Paris, 1949-50; University of Chicago, M.A., 1949, Ph.D., 1954.

ADDRESSES: Office—Department of Art History, University of California, Berkeley, CA 94720.

CAREER: University of Chicago, Chicago, IL, instructor, 1949-53; Institute of Design, Chicago, assistant professor of art history and head of art education department, 1949-55; Pomona College, Claremont, CA, chair of art department and director of art gallery, 1955-58; Museum of Modern Art, New York City, curator of department of painting and sculpture exhibitions, 1958-65; University of California, Berkeley, founding director of university art museum, 1965-72, professor of art history, 1965—; guest professor, University of Jerusalem, 1976, and City University of New York, 1987; lecturer at universities and museums in the United States, Europe, and China; director of numerous art exhibitions touring museums in the United States and Europe; member of president's council on art and architecture, Yale University, 1971-76, acquisitions committee, Museums of Fine Arts, San Francisco, 1993—; trustee, American Craft Council, 1980-86, Marin Museum Association, 1990—. *Military service:* U.S. Army, Office of Strategic Services, 1941-46.

MEMBER: International Art Critics Association, College Art Association of America (director, 1958-64, 1966-71), American Association of University Professors.

AWARDS, HONORS: Fulbright grant for University of Paris and Ecole de Louvre, 1949-50, and Musees Royaux d'Art et d'Histoire, 1953; Belgian-American Educational Foundation fellowship, 1953; Medal for American Scholars, New York Public Library, 1961; Order of Merit, Federal Republic of Germany, 1967; D.F.A., California College of Arts and Crafts, 1967; National Endowment for the Humanities senior fellowship, 1972-73; residency, Rockefeller Study Center, Bellagio, Italy, 1994.

WRITINGS:

German Expressionist Painting, University of California Press (Berkeley), 1957.
New Images of Man, Doubleday for the Museum of Modern Art (New York City), 1959.
(Editor with Mildred Constantine) *Art Nouveau: Art and Design at the Turn of the Century,* Doubleday for the Museum of Modern Art, 1960, Ayer Co. (Salem, NY), 1976.

Mark Rothko, Doubleday for the Museum of Modern Art, 1961.

Fifteen Polish Painters, Doubleday for the Museum of Modern Art, 1961.

The Work of Jean Dubuffet, Doubleday for the Museum of Modern Art, 1962, Arno Press, 1980.

Emil Nolde, Doubleday for the Museum of Modern Art, 1963, Arno Press, 1980.

Max Beckmann, Doubleday for the Museum of Modern Art, 1964, Abbeville Press (New York City), 1996.

(Editor) *Alberto Giacometti,* Doubleday for the Museum of Modern Art, 1965.

Directions in Kinetic Sculpture, University of California Press, 1966.

Seven Decades of Modern Art, 1895-1965: Cross-currents in Modern Art, [New York City], 1966.

Funk, University of California Press, 1967.

Ferdinand Hodler, University of California Press, 1972.

Harold Paris: The California Years, University of California Press, 1972.

Sam Francis, Abrams (New York City), 1975, revised edition, 1982.

(With Thomas C. Blaisdell) *The American Presidency in Political Cartoons, 1776-1976,* Peregrine Smith (Layton, UT), 1976.

Zwei Jahrzehnte amerikanische Malerei, 1920-1940, Kunsthalle (Duesseldorf, Germany), 1979.

Art in Our Times: A Pictorial History, 1890-1980, Harcourt (San Diego, CA), 1981.

Art in a Turbulent Era, edited by Donald Kuspit, UMI Research Press (Ann Arbor, MI), 1985.

Chillida, Abrams, 1986.

(With Friedrich Duerrenmatt) *Varlin, 1900-1977: Paintings,* translated by Felice Ross and Mimi Levitt, C. Bernard Gallery, 1986.

Dramas of Human Encounter: The Work of Bedri Baykam, Screen Productions, 1986.

Max Beckmann: The Self Portraits, Rizzoli International (New York City), 1992.

(With Fred Licht) *William Congdon,* Milano Jaca Books, 1992.

(With Kristine Stiles) *Theories and Documents of Contemporary Art,* University of California Press, 1996.

Beyond the Mainstream, Cambridge University Press (New York City), 1997.

Contributor to *Theories of Modern Art: A Source Book by Artists and Critics,* by Herschel Browning Chipp, University of California Press, 1968. Also contributor of articles and reviews to various publications, including *Art Bulletin, Art Journal, Art in America, Art International, Arts, Artspace, Cimaise, Massachusetts Review,* and *Art and Artists.*

SIDELIGHTS: Peter Selz's first major publication was *German Expressionist Painting* and throughout his career his principal interest has been modernist figurative painting and sculpture, although he has written books on major abstract artists, including Mark Rothko, Sam Francis and Eduardo Chillida.

An early opponent to Formalist aesthetics, Selz is a staunch believer in placing art into a socio-political-economic contest without resorting to Neo-Marxist theory. His book *Art in Our Times: A Pictorial History, 1890-1980* examines twentieth-century art and architecture by locating the works in each decade and comparing them in terms of content (or building types) rather than simply placing the art into the Formalist constructs of movements and isms.

In his interests Selz has never followed trends or fashions, but has, both as curator and writer, studied art which was (or is) on the periphery of attention. His most recent collection of essays is, in fact, entitled *Beyond the Mainstream.*

BIOGRAPHICAL/CRITICAL SOURCES:

PERIODICALS

New York Times Book Review, May 24, 1981.
Publishers Weekly, May 6, 1996, p. 62.

* * *

SENIOR, Donald 1940-

PERSONAL: Born January 1, 1940, in Philadelphia, PA; son of Vincent E. (a business executive) and Margaret (Tiernan) Senior. *Education:* Passionist Seminary College, Chicago, IL, B.A. 1963; University of Louvain, lic. theology, 1970, S.T.D., 1972; postdoctoral study at Harvard University and Hebrew Union College, Cincinnati, OH.

ADDRESSES: Home—5401 South Cornell Ave., Chicago, IL 60615. *Office*—Catholic Theological Union, 5401 South Cornell Ave., Chicago, IL 60615.

CAREER: Entered Passionist Religious Congregation, 1960, ordained Roman Catholic priest, 1967; Catholic Theological Union, Chicago, IL, assistant professor, 1972-77, associate professor, 1977-82, professor of New Testament studies and director of Israel Study Program, 1982-87, president, 1987-95. Member of board of directors of Sadlier Publishing Company and board of advisors of the Auburn Center for Theological Education. Lecturer and conductor of retreats in the United States, Canada, Israel, Asia, and Africa. Member of Roman Catholic/Southern Baptist Scholars Dialogue, 1977-80. Has appeared on Chicago's Catholic television network (CTN/C).

MEMBER: Pax Christi International, Society of Biblical Literature, Catholic Biblical Association of America, Catholic Theological Society of America, Chicago Society of Biblical Research, Studiorum Novi Testamenti Societas, International Association of Missiological Studies.

AWARDS, HONORS: Jerome Award, Catholic Library Association, 1994, for outstanding scholarship; Bishop Loras Lane Award, National Catholic Education Association, 1996, for his contribution to theological education.

WRITINGS:

Matthew: A Gospel for the Church, Franciscan Herald (Chicago), 1973.
Matthew: Read and Pray, Franciscan Herald, 1974.
Jesus: A Gospel Portrait, Pflaum (Fairfield, NJ), 1975, revised edition, 1992.
The Passion Narrative according to Matthew, University of Louvain Press, 1975.
Invitation to Matthew, Doubleday (New York City), 1977.
Loving and Dying, NCR Publications, 1979.
(Editor) Wilfrid Harrington, *Mark,* Michael Glazier (Wilmington, DE), 1980.
I and II Peter, Michael Glazier, 1980.
God the Son, Argus (Hemel Hempstead), 1981.
What Are They Saying about Matthew?, Paulist Press (Ramsey, NJ), 1983, revised edition, 1996.
(With Carroll Stuhlmueller) *The Biblical Foundations for Mission,* Orbis, 1983.
(Coeditor) *Biblical and Theological Reflections on the Challenge to Peace,* Michael Glazier, 1984.
The Passion of Jesus in the Gospel of Mark, Michael Glazier, 1984.
The Passion of Jesus in the Gospel of Matthew, Michael Glazier, 1985.
(Coeditor) *Economic Justice,* Pastoral Press, 1988.
(Coeditor) *Scripture and Prayer,* Michael Glazier, 1988.

The Passion of Jesus in the Gospel of Luke, Michael Glazier, 1989.
(General Editor) *The Catholic Study Bible,* Oxford University Press (Oxford), 1990.
The Passion of Jesus in the Gospel of John, Liturgical Press (Collegeville, MN), 1991.
(Coeditor) *The Collegeville Pastoral Dictionary of the Bible,* Liturgical Press, 1996.

EDITOR WITH W. HARRINGTON; PUBLISHED BY MICHAEL GLAZIER

Adela Y. Collins, *Apocalypse,* 1979.
Daniel J. Harrington, *Interpreting the New Testament: A Practical Guide,* 1979.
Robert J. Karris, *Pastoral Epistles,* 1979.
James McPolin, *John,* 1979.
Jerome Crowe, *The Acts,* 1980.
Eugene H. Maly, *Romans,* 1980.
Pheme Perkins, *Johannine Epistles,* 1980.

OTHER

General editor with W. Harrington of "New Testament Message" series, twenty-two volumes. Creator of tape cassette series "The Gospel of Mark" and "The Gospel of Matthew." Contributor of articles and reviews to periodicals, including *American Benedictine Review, Bible Today, Biblical Research, Biblical Theology Bulletin, Catholic Biblical Quarterly, Catechist, Commonweal, Cross and Crown, Emmanuel, Interpretation, New Theology Review, Worship, U.S. Catholic, Horizons, St. Anthony's Messenger,* and *Spirituality Today.* Associate editor of *Bible Today.*

WORK IN PROGRESS: Research on the Gospels, particularly on their presentation of the death of Jesus, and on the biblical attitudes to body and health.

SIDELIGHTS: Donald Senior told *CA:* "My career has been shaped by two main influences: my professional training in critical biblical scholarship and my vocation as a Catholic priest. I have tried to keep faith with both by serious scholarship and by a heavy schedule of lectures and writings to disseminate the results of biblical scholarship for the sake of Christians interested in contemporary interpretation of the Bible. I have had the opportunity to travel and lecture throughout the United States and Canada, have spent five years in Europe, and in 1977, spent five months in Korea, Japan, and the Philippines lecturing to and learning from people there. All of this helps me understand more about the art of interpreting a treasured tradition in a new world."

*   *   *

SHERMAN, Charlotte A.
   See SHERMAN, Jory (Tecumseh)

*   *   *

SHERMAN, Jory (Tecumseh) 1932-
   (Frank Anvic, Cort Martin, Hank Mitchum, Charlotte A. Sherman, Wilma Tarrant; Walt Denver, a house pseudonym)

PERSONAL: Born October 20, 1932, in St. Paul, MN; son of Keith Edward (a franchise consultant) and Mercedes (a stenographer; maiden name, Sheplee) Sherman; married Remy Montes Roxas, June 10, 1951 (deceased); married Felicia, August 15, 1958 (divorced December, 1967); married Charlotte Balcom (a writer), March 2, 1968; children: Francis Antonio, Jory Vittorio, Forrest Redmond, Gina Felice, Misty April, Marcus Tecumseh; (stepchildren) Gerald LeRoy Wilhite, David Dean Wilhite, Janet Lynn Wilhite. *Education:* Attended San Francisco State College (now University) and University of Minnesota. *Politics:* Democrat. *Avocational interests:* Black powder guns, hunting, fishing, canoeing, computer programming, local and western history.

ADDRESSES: Home—Ste. 642, 3044 Shepherd Hills Exp., Branson, MO 65616.

CAREER: Writer. Denver Dry Goods, Denver, CO, advertising copywriter, 1949-50; American President Lines, San Francisco, CA, computer programmer, 1953-54; Great Plays Co., Lethbridge, Alberta, Canada, actor, 1954-55; *San Francisco Examiner,* San Francisco, editor, 1960-61; American Art Enterprise, North Hollywood, CA, magazine editor, 1961-65; freelance editor, 1965-67; newspaper columnist, 1965—. San Bernardino County press chairperson for Gerald Brown; press chairperson for John Tunney and Jesse Unruh. Teacher of creative writing for adults at Southwest Missouri State University and elsewhere. President, MicroDramas Co., Rialto, CA,

1969-71. Editor, Academy Press, Chatsworth, CA, 1971-72. *Military service:* U.S. Navy, 1950-53.

MEMBER: Writers Guild of America, Authors League of America, Authors Guild, Western Writers of America, Ozark Writers League (co-founder), Missouri Writers Guild, Twin Counties Press Club (member of board of directors, 1966-70), Desert-Mountain Press Club, Baja California Writers Association.

AWARDS, HONORS: Best Newspaper Column Award, 1970, Best Radio Station Public Service Program Award, 1970 and 1971, all from Twin Counties Press Club; Best Newspaper Column Award, 1985, Best Novel Award, 1985, Best Magazine Article Award, 1985, Best Major Work Award, 1988, for *Song of the Cheyenne,* Best Major Work Award, 1992, for *The Medicine Horn,* and award for best book, 1995, for *Trapper's Moon,* all from Missouri Writers Guild; Best Novel of the West Award, Western Writers of America, 1992, for *The Medicine Horn;* nomination for Pulitzer Prize in Letters, 1994, for *Grass Kingdom.*

WRITINGS:

So Many Rooms, Galley Sail Publications, 1960.
My Face in Wax, Windfall Press, 1965.
Lust on Canvas, Anchor Publications, 1965.
The October Scarf, Challenge Books, 1966.
The Sculptor, Private Edition Books, 1966.
The Fires of Autumn, All Star Books, 1967.
Nightsong, All Star Books, 1968.
Blood Jungle, Triumph News, 1968.
(Under pseudonym Cort Martin) *The Star,* Dominion (San Marcos, CA), 1968.
(Under pseudonym Cort Martin) *Quest,* Powell Publications, 1969.
(Under pseudonym Cort Martin) *The Edge of Passion,* Saber Books, 1969.
The Love Rain, Tecumseh Press, 1971.
(Under pseudonym Frank Anvic) *The All Girl Crew,* Barclay, 1973.
(Under pseudonym Frank Anvic) *The Hard Riders,* Barclay, 1973.
There Are Ways of Making Love to You, Tecumseh Press, 1974.
(Under pseudonym Frank Anvic) *We Have Your Daughter,* Brandon Books, 1974.
(Under pseudonym Frank Anvic) *Bride of Satan,* Brandon Books, 1974.
Gun for Hire, Major (Canoga Park, CA), 1975.

(Under pseudonym Charlotte A. Sherman) *The Shuttered Room,* Major, 1975.

Ride Hard, Ride Fast, Major, 1976.

(Under pseudonym Wilma Tarrant) *Her Strange Needs,* Carlyle Communications, 1976.

(Under pseudonym Wilma Tarrant) *Trying Out Tricia,* Carlyle Communications, 1976.

Buzzard Bait, Major, 1977.

Satan's Seed, Pinnacle Books (New York City), 1978.

Chill, Pinnacle Books, 1978.

The Bamboo Demons, Pinnacle Books, 1979.

Hellfire Trail, Leisure Books (Norwalk, CT), 1979.

The Reincarnation of Jenny James, Carlyle Books, 1979.

The Fugitive Gun, Leisure Books, 1980.

Vegas Vampire, Pinnacle Books, 1980.

The Phoenix Man, Pinnacle Books, 1980.

House of Scorpions, Pinnacle Books, 1980.

Shadows, Pinnacle Books, 1980.

Dawn of Revenge, Zebra Books (New York City), 1980.

Mexican Showdown, Zebra Books, 1980.

Death's Head Trail, Zebra Books, 1980.

Blood Justice, Zebra Books, 1980.

Winter Hell, Zebra Books, 1980.

Bukowski: Friendship, Fame, and Bestial Myth, Blue Horse Publications, 1981.

Duel in Purgatory, Zebra Books, 1981.

Law of the Rope, Zebra Books, 1981.

Apache Arrows, Zebra Books, 1981.

Boothill Bounty, Zebra Books, 1981.

Hard Bullets, Zebra Books, 1981.

Trial by Sixgun, Zebra Books, 1981.

(Under pseudonym Cort Martin) *First Blood,* Zebra Books, 1981.

My Heart Is in the Ozarks, First Ozark (Harrison, AR), 1982.

The Widow Maker, Zebra Books, 1982.

Arizona Hardcase, Zebra Books, 1982.

The Buff Runners, Zebra Books, 1982.

Gunman's Curse, Pinnacle Books, 1983.

Dry-Gulched, Zebra Books, 1983.

Wyoming Wanton, Zebra Books, 1983.

Tucson Twosome, Zebra Books, 1983.

Blood Warriors, Zebra Books, 1983.

(Under pseudonym Walt Denver) *Pistolero,* Zebra Books, 1983.

(Under pseudonym Hank Mitchum) *Stagecoach Station 8: Fort Yuma,* Bantam (New York City), 1983.

Death Valley, Zebra Books, 1984.

Red Tomahawk, Zebra Books, 1984.

Blood Trail South, Zebra Books, 1984.

Song of the Cheyenne, Doubleday (New York City), 1987.

Winter of the Wolf, Walker & Co. (New York City), 1987.

Horn's Law, Walker & Co., 1988.

Eagles of Destiny, Zebra Books, 1990.

The Arkansas River, Bantam, 1991.

The Medicine Horn, Tor Books (New York City), 1991.

An Early Frost, White Oak (Redwood City, CA), 1992.

Grass Kingdom, Tor Books, 1994.

Trapper's Moon, Tor Books, 1994.

The Rio Grande, Bantam, 1994.

The Columbia River, Bantam, 1996.

Also creator and producer of "Hellrider" series, Pinnacle Books, 1985, "Killsquad" series, Avon (New York City), 1986, "Remington" series, Avon, 1986, "Powell's Army" series, Zebra Books, 1986, "Brazo" series, Zebra Books, 1986, "Dateline" series, Paperjacks, 1987, and "Rivers West" series, Bantam, 1987—. Author of columns, "View on Living," *Grand Terrace Living,* 1966-67, "Ensenada at Bay," *Ensenada Hello,* 1966-67, "The New Notebook," *San Bernardino Independent,* 1970-71, "Baja Notebook," *Fiesta,* 1972-75, "Bear with Me," *Big Bear News,* 1972-75, and a column in *San Bernardino Mountain Highlander,* 1975-76. Author of two series of educational tapes for radio, "Youth and Drugs" and "Youth and Alcohol," distributed by Classroom World Productions. Contributor of poetry and articles to periodicals, including *Roundup, Branson Living, Ozarks Mountaineer,* and *Midwest Quarterly.* West Coast editor, *Outsider;* advisory editor, *Black Cat Review.*

WORK IN PROGRESS: The Barons of Texas, Rendezvous, Greensleeves, and "The Way West" series, all for Tor Books; *The South Platte, The Brazos, The Widow's Journey, The Mississippi River,* and the "Frontier Rivers" series, all for Bantam Books.

SIDELIGHTS: Jory Sherman told *CA:* "My goal in writing novels of the West is to push the story of America's westward expansion into the mainstream of American literature. The category western novel has fallen by the wayside. Those of us still publishing have [dug] deeper into our history, producing books that rise above category. Women writers of the West are coming into their own, at last, and there is an entire new body of literature that should last for generations. In the vanguard of the new wave of novels of the West are my publishers, Bantam and

Tor/Forge. There is some fine writing out there, and many of us are waiting for the general public to not only discover it, but to embrace it wholeheartedly. For the western is our only native literature and deserves much more respect than it has garnered in the past. This is an exciting time for me and my fellow novelists who are telling the story of America's push westward into new lands, unknown territories. It is a grand story, exclusive to us, and will never be fully told. I am proud to be among those writers who are forging new paths in western literature and to be associated with publishers who are not afraid to venture beyond the boundaries of category fiction. They, too, are among the pioneers who people the new literature of the West."

BIOGRAPHICAL/CRITICAL SOURCES:

PERIODICALS

Listen, April, 1971.

*　　*　　*

SHULMAN, Neil B(arnett)　1945-

PERSONAL: Born March 18, 1945, in Washington, DC. *Education:* George Washington University, B.S., 1967; Emory University, M.D., 1971; also attended Harvard University, 1974, and Georgetown University, summer, 1976.

ADDRESSES: Home—2272 Vistamont Dr., Decatur, GA 30033.

CAREER: Intern at Emory University Hospital, Veterans Administration Hospital, and Grady Memorial Hospital, all Atlanta, GA, all 1971-72; Grady Memorial Hospital, fellow in nephrology and associate in department of medicine, 1972-74; Emory University School of Medicine, Atlanta, assistant professor of nephrology, 1974-80, associate professor in Division of Hypertension, 1981—, co-director of First and Second International Interdisciplinary Conferences on Hypertension in Blacks, 1986, 1987; Pine Knoll Nursing Home, Carrollton, GA, medical director, 1976—; Georgia Department of Human Resources, Atlanta, staff member in Division of Physical Health, 1977-78, primary and rural health care developer, 1977—.

American Heart Association-Georgia affiliate, chairman of state high blood pressure education program, 1973, member of hypertension task force, 1974, member of health education in the young committee, 1975; National Institutes of Health, conferee for national patient education task force on hypertension, 1973, member of community consultation team for national high blood pressure education program, 1975; member of technical review board, California Regional Medical Program, 1974-76; member of task force to review health care delivery in state prisons, Georgia Department of Human Resources, 1976; reviewer of grants for hypertension education and research, National Heart, Lung and Blood Institute, 1977—; chairman of statewide information sharing committee on primary health care, 1977-80; member of board of directors, Georgia Association of Primary Health Care, 1979-81. Investigator or project director of more than a dozen studies on hypertension. Host of daily television program "Health Care U.S.A.," WATL, Atlanta, 1976; host of medical humor shorts, Cable News Network, 1981. Chairman, Georgia 2000 (citizens' health and environmental group), 1977-80; member of board of directors and chairman, Village Writers Group, 1978-84, and Windward Bound, Inc., 1978—; member of board of directors, American Minor Emergency Enterprises, 1980—, and LaRosh Productions, Inc., 1985; member of consumer advisory board, Georgia Power Co., 1979-82. Consultant, Inner City Community Health Center, 1980. Co-founder of Heart to Heart Program.

MEMBER: American Heart Association.

AWARDS, HONORS: National Voluntary Action Award from American Heart Association-Georgia affiliate, 1975, for health education in the young; Bronze Medallion for Meritorious Service from American Heart Association-Georgia affiliate, 1976; Inner City Award of Recognition, 1981, for assisting with the development of the Atlanta Inner City Community Health Center; Georgia State Legislature Recognition, 1983, for community work in the control of high blood pressure in Georgia; chairman emeritus, Village Writers Group, 1985.

WRITINGS:

NONFICTION

(With B. Corns and S. Heymsfield) *Up and Down: All about Blood Pressure,* Emory University (Atlanta), 1973.

(Editor with W. Dallas Hall and Elijah Saunders, and contributor) *Hypertension in Blacks: Epidemiology, Pathophysiology and Treatment,* Year Book Medical Publishers (Chicago), 1985.

(With Hall and Saunders) *High Blood Pressure,* Macmillan (New York City), 1987, revised edition, Dell (New York City), 1993.

(With Letitia Sweitzer) *Better Health Care for Less,* Hippocrene (New York City), 1993.

(With Sweitzer) *Understanding Growth Hormone: New Discoveries to Help Very Short Children,* Hippocrene, 1993.

(With James Reed and Charlene Shucker) *The Black Man's Guide to Good Health: Essential Advice for the Special Concerns of African-American Men,* Berkley (New York City), 1994.

The Key to Medical Literacy, Harcourt (San Diego), 1995.

FICTION

Finally . . . I'm a Doctor, Scribner (New York City), 1976.

What? Dead Again?, Legacy Publishing (Baton Rouge, LA), 1979.

The Backyard Tribe, St. Martin's (New York City), 1994.

(With Sibley Fleming) *What's in a Doctor's Bag?* (children's book), Rx Humor (Atlanta), 1994.

(With Fleming) *Under the Backyard Sky* (children's book), Peachtree Publishers (Atlanta), 1995.

Also author of *Second Wind.* Contributor to medical journals, including *American Journal of Public Health, Journal of Clinical Hypertension, Journal of the American Medical Association, American Journal of Epidemiology,* and *Journal of Community Health.* Member of editorial board, *Forum* (publication of American College of Physicians), 1979-80, and *Emory Magazine,* 1981-83. Coeditor and publisher, *Health Access News, Rx Humor Newsletter* and *Grey Hair Tours.*

ADAPTATIONS: What? Dead Again? was filmed as *Doc Hollywood* in 1991 and became the top-grossing movie of that year. Shulman served as associate producer.

BIOGRAPHICAL/CRITICAL SOURCES:

PERIODICALS

Atlanta, June, 1976.

Atlanta Journal and Constitution, September 9, 1976.

Chicago Tribune, August 16, 1976.

Philadelphia Inquirer, August 23, 1976.

*   *   *

SIDDONS, (Sybil) Anne Rivers   1936-

PERSONAL: Born January 9, 1936, in Atlanta, GA; daughter of Marvin (an attorney) and Katherine (a secretary; maiden name, Kitchens) Rivers; married Heyward L. Siddons (a business partner and creative director), 1966; children: (stepsons) Lee, Kemble, Rick, David. *Education:* Auburn University, B.A.A., 1958; attended Atlanta School of Art, c. 1958. *Avocational interests:* Swimming, cooking, reading, cats.

ADDRESSES: Home—3767 Vermont Rd. N.E., Atlanta, GA 30319; and (summer) Osprey Cottage, Brooklin, ME 04616.

CAREER: Worked in advertising with Retail Credit Co., c. 1959, Citizens & Southern National Bank, 1961-63, Burke-Dowling Adams, 1967-69, and Burton Campbell Advertising, 1969-74; full-time writer, 1974—. Member of governing board, Woodward Academy; member of publications board and arts and sciences honorary council, Auburn University, 1978-83.

MEMBER: Chevy Chase Club, Every Saturday Club, Ansley Golf Club.

AWARDS, HONORS: Alumna achievement award in arts and humanities, Auburn University, 1985; Honorary Doctorate in Humanities, Oglethorpe University, 1991.

WRITINGS:

NOVELS

Heartbreak Hotel, Simon & Schuster (New York City), 1976.

The House Next Door (horror), Simon & Schuster, 1978.

Fox's Earth, Simon & Schuster, 1980.

Homeplace, Harper (New York City), 1987.

Peachtree Road, Harper, 1988.

King's Oak, HarperCollins (New York City), 1990.

Outer Banks, HarperCollins, 1991.
Colony, HarperCollins, 1992.
Hill Towns, HarperCollins, 1993.
Downtown, HarperCollins, 1994.
Fault Lines, HarperCollins, 1995.

OTHER

John Chancellor Makes Me Cry (essays), Doubleday, 1975.
Go Straight on Peachtree (nonfiction guide book), Dolphin Books (New York City), 1978.

Contributor to *Gentleman's Quarterly, Georgia, House Beautiful, Lear's, Reader's Digest, Redbook,* and *Southern Living.* Senior editor, *Atlanta,* 1964-67.

ADAPTATIONS: Heartbreak Hotel was adapted as the film *Heart of Dixie,* Orion Pictures, 1989.

SIDELIGHTS: Novelist Anne Rivers Siddons identifies herself as an author of the South—an author of Atlanta in particular. "Everything I know and do is of here, of the South," she says in an interview in *Southern Living.* Her novels are most often concerned with the lives of Southern women; later books have occasionally seen these characters transplanted to other locales. Reviewer Michael Skube has called Siddons "Atlanta's best known writer."

Siddons's first book, *John Chancellor Makes Me Cry,* chronicles one year of her life in Atlanta, humorously reflecting on the frustrations and joys of life—serving jury duty, hosting parties, and taking care of a husband suffering with the flu. The author's style in *John Chancellor Makes Me Cry* has been favorably compared to that of Erma Bombeck, whose own review of the book praises Siddons: "She is unique. She's an original in her essays that combine humor, intimacy and insight into a marriage." Bombeck finds the most "poignant and very real" chapter to be the one describing "the month [Siddons's] husband lost his job, her Grandmother died, a Siamese cat they were keeping for a friend was hit by a car, their house was burgled and their Persian cat contracted a $50-a-week disease."

Siddons turned to fiction with her first novel, *Heartbreak Hotel* the story of a young Southern woman who must choose between her two suitors and the very different lifestyles they represent. Katha Pollitt asserts: "The author dissects the 1950's, Southern style, with a precision that is anything but nostalgic;

and yet somehow the very wealth of detail she provides makes *Heartbreak Hotel* a good-natured rather than an angry look backward. . . . This is a marvelously detailed record of a South as gone with the wind as Scarlett O'Hara's."

The House Next Door, Siddons's tale of an affluent couple whose lives are changed by the mysterious evils occurring in a neighboring house, was praised by Stephen King. In his critique on the horror genre, *Stephen King's Danse Macabre,* King devoted an entire chapter to an analysis of *The House Next Door,* comparing it to Shirley Jackson's *Haunting of Hill House.* Siddons, in an interview in *Publishers Weekly,* calls the book "something of a lark. It's different from anything I've ever written, or probably ever will. But I like to read occult, supernatural stories. Some of the world's great writers have written them, and I guess I wanted to see what I could do with the genre."

Later novels, such as *Homeplace* and *Peachtree Road,* won greater favor with critics and became best-sellers. Notes Bob Summers in *Publishers Weekly, Homeplace* "struck a national chord" with its account of an independent Southern-born woman returning home after more than twenty years. *Peachtree Road* is Siddons's "love letter to Atlanta," according to *Chicago Tribune* contributor Joyce Slater. "Siddons does an admirable job of tracing the city's rebirth after World War II without idealizing it." Slater concludes: *Peachtree Road* is Siddons's "most ambitious [book] to date."

Siddons's first novel set outside the South, *Colony,* is the saga of the family of a Carolinian woman who has been transplanted by marriage into the Brahmin milieu of a coastal Maine retreat. As a young bride, heroine Maude Gascoigne detests her new summer home and its people, but with the passing decades she grows to love it enough to fight hard to pass it on to her granddaughter. Joan Mooney, writing in the *New York Times Book Review,* calls Maude "a match for anything that's thrown her way—and plenty is." Others have also praised Siddons's development of character in *Colony:* a reviewer for *Publishers Weekly* describes the novel as "a page-turner by virtue of realistic characters who engage the reader's affection and concern," though *Booklist's* Denise Blank observes that "although her verbal artistry cannot be denied, Siddons never quite captures the feel of a place or a person—one is left with the impression of a very pretty painting that looks much like other very pretty paintings."

In her next novel, *Hill Towns,* Siddons again sends a Southern woman into new territory, this time even farther afield. Cat Gaillard suffers from what *Chicago Tribune* reviewer Joyce R. Slater terms "reverse acrophobia": she is only comfortable at heights that allow her to see for miles around her. She is also agoraphobic and is finally lured from an hermetic existence in her Appalachian lookout by an invitation to a wedding in Italy. Rome, Venice, and Tuscany have the expected loosening effect on Cat, though she and her husband "will not be corrupted by decadent Europeans, but by their fellow countrymen altered by extended sojourns abroad," according to Elaine Kendall in the *Los Angeles Times.* Among these are a famous expatriate painter and his wife, who work their separate wiles on Cat and her husband, Joe. Yet Cat pulls back from the brink: in the words of Slater, "Italy and the charismatic painter, Sam Forrest, are nearly Cat's undoing. Nearly."

Many reviewers identify Siddons's greatest strength in this book as her creation of character. Writing for the *Washington Post,* Natalie Danford says that the author's "portrayals of people, . . . are often stunning." Slater too praises Siddons in this regard, writing that she "sensitively describes the confusion of a woman who opts to travel from an existence of academic, almost Elysian perfection to one of the steamiest, most chaotic cities in the world."

Downtown, Siddons's 1994 novel set in the mid-sixties, is admittedly autobiographical. The circumstances that surround its main character, Smoky O'Donnell, a 26-year-old ingenue with the dream and drive to succeed as a writer for Atlanta's trendiest magazine, mirror those of Siddons's own past. As a writer for *Downtown* magazine, Smoky sees the up and down sides of Atlanta life at a time when "promises . . . hung in the bronze air like fruit on the eve of ripeness." For Smoky some of these promises are kept, but others, such as the promise that brightens within her growing awareness of the civil rights movement, are shot down as the decade approaches its close.

Critical reaction to *Downtown* has been mixed. The reviewer for *Publishers Weekly* writes of being "disappointed in [Siddons's] uninspired and often pretentious story line," and Jean Hanff Korelitz complains in the *Washington Post Book World* that Smoky's "responses are so predictable and her path to adulthood so well-worn that we can't escape feeling that we have already read this novel, that only the names and locations have been changed." Both reviewers

nevertheless write favorably of Siddons's evocation of the ambience of Atlanta in the 1960s.

In a 1994 interview for the *Atlanta Journal & Constitution,* Siddons hints that she was finished writing about Atlanta, although she toyed with the possibility of setting a future book in the nearby affluent enclave of Cobb County. But though she may take her novels out of the South, she doesn't believe she will ever take the South out of her novels. In *Southern Living* Siddons comments: "I have found I can move anywhere in my fiction. If I take it from the point of view of a Southerner traveling there, it's still an honest point of view."

BIOGRAPHICAL/CRITICAL SOURCES:

BOOKS

King, Stephen, *Stephen King's Danse Macabre,* Everest House, 1981.

PERIODICALS

Atlanta Journal & Constitution, October 9, 1988; July 14, 1991, p. N8; June 26, 1992, p. P1; June 28, 1992, p. N9; June 5, 1994, p. M1, p. N10.

Booklist, May 1, 1987, p. 948; July, 1988, p. 1755; August, 1990, p. 2123; June 1, 1991, p. 1843; November 15, 1991, p. 638; April 15, 1992, p. 1643; March 15, 1993, p. 1369; May 1, 1993, p. 1548; February 15, 1994, p. 1100; May 15, 1994, p. 1645.

Bookwatch, October, 1991, p. 6; August, 1992, p. 6.

Book World, July 28, 1991, p. 1; June 12, 1994, p. 8.

Chicago Tribune, June 14, 1987; November 11, 1988; July 25, 1993, p. 6.

Chicago Tribune Book World, June 28, 1981.

Christian Science Monitor, July 1, 1994, p. 10.

Kirkus Reviews, April 1, 1987, p. 510; August 1, 1988, p. 1093; August 1, 1990, p. 1038; June 1, 1991, p. 692; May 1, 1992, p. 564; April 15, 1993, p. 484; May 1, 1994, p. 587.

Kliatt, spring, 1985, p. 18; July, 1994, p. 89; January, 1995, p. 52; March, 1995, p. 53.

Library Journal, June 15, 1975; April 1, 1987, p. 165; August, 1990, p. 145; October 1, 1991, p. 159; September 15, 1992, p. 108; August, 1993, p. 178; October 15, 1993, p. 110; June 15, 1994, p. 97; November 15, 1994, p. 106.

Locus, January, 1990, p. 52.

Los Angeles Times, September 3, 1993, p. E6.

Los Angeles Times Book Review, September 18, 1988, p. 10; September 16, 1990, p. 8; August 4, 1991, p. 3; October 3, 1993, p. 8; July 10, 1994, p. 14.

New York Times, September 16, 1989.

New York Times Book Review, April 13, 1975; September 12, 1976; October 23, 1977; December 10, 1978; August 30, 1987, p. 20; August 14, 1988, p. 26; January 1, 1989, p. 14; November 4, 1990, p. 33; August 2, 1992, p. 20.

Publishers Weekly, May 1, 1987, p. 55; August 5, 1988, p. 72; November 18, 1988; November 3, 1989, p. 88; February 2, 1990, p. 50; August 3, 1990, p. 62; May 31, 1991, p. 61; March 30, 1992, pp. 21-26; May 18, 1992, p. 57; May 25, 1992, p. 51; May 24, 1993, p. 67; May 23, 1994, pp. 76-77.

Reader's Digest, January, 1987, pp. 53-55.

Southern Living, October, 1987, p. 96; March, 1991, p. 118; December, 1991, p. 83; September, 1994, p. 100.

Tribune Books (Chicago), June 14, 1987, p. 7; November 25, 1990, p. 4; July 25, 1993, p. 6.

USA Today, July 17, 1991, p. D5; August 1, 1991, p. D1.

Washington Post, August 3, 1987; July 28, 1991, p. July 13, 1993, p. E2.

Washington Post Book World, July 28, 1991, p. 1; June 12, 1994, p. 8.

Woman's Journal, February, 1995, p. 13.

* * *

SIMMONS, Dan 1948-

PERSONAL: Born 1948 in Peoria, IL; married; wife's name, Karen; children: Jane.

ADDRESSES: Home—Longmont, CO. *Office*—c/o Putnam, 200 Madison Ave., New York, NY 10016.

CAREER: Writer. Worked as an elementary school teacher.

AWARDS, HONORS: Fulbright scholarship, 1977; award from *Twilight Zone* for short story "The River Styx Runs Upstream," 1982; World Fantasy Award for best first novel, 1985, for *Song of Kali;* Hugo Award for best novel, 1989, for *Hyperion; Locus* Award for best science fiction novel, 1989, for *Hyperion,* 1990, for *The Fall of Hyperion,* and for best horror/dark fantasy novel, 1991, for *Summer of Night; Science Fiction Chronicle* award for best novel, 1990, for *The Fall of Hyperion;* Bram Stoker Award for best horror novel, 1990, for *Carrion Comfort,* and for best horror collection, 1991, for *Prayers to Broken Stones: A Collection.*

WRITINGS:

NOVELS

Song of Kali, Tor Books (New York City), 1985.

Hyperion (also see below), Doubleday (New York City), 1989.

Phases of Gravity, Bantam (New York City), 1989.

Carrion Comfort, Dark Harvest (Arlington Heights, IL), 1989.

The Fall of Hyperion (also see below), Doubleday, 1990.

The Hyperion Cantos (contains *Hyperion* and *The Fall of Hyperion*), Guild America Books (New York City), 1990.

Summer of Night, Putnam (New York City), 1991.

Children of the Night, Putnam, 1992.

The Hollow Man, Bantam, 1992.

Pele's Fire, Putnam, 1994.

Fires of Eden, Putnam, 1994.

Endymion, Bantam, 1996.

The Crook Factory, AvoNova, 1997.

SHORT STORIES

Banished Dreams (published in limited edition), Roadkill Press (Arvada, CO), 1990.

Entropy's Bed at Midnight (chapbook; published in limited edition), Lord John Press (Northridge, CA), 1990.

Prayers to Broken Stones: A Collection (includes "Vanni Fucci Is Alive and Well and Living in Hell" and "The Death of the Centaur"), Dark Harvest, 1990.

Lovedeath, Warner Books (New York City), 1993.

OTHER

Going After the Rubber Chicken (non-fiction collection), Roadkill Press, 1991.

Also author of *Endymion, Summer Sketches* and *Eyes I Dare Not Meet in Dreams.* Work represented in anthologies, including *Night Visions V,* edited by Stephen King, Dark Harvest, 1988. Contributor to periodicals, including *Galaxy, Omni,* and *Twilight Zone.*

WORK IN PROGRESS: Adapting *The Hyperion Cantos* for CD-ROM for Microsoft.

SIDELIGHTS: Dan Simmons has earned recognition as the author of various award-winning works of horror and science fiction. His first short story, "The River Styx Runs Upstream," appeared in Rod Serling's *Twilight Zone* magazine in 1982. Encouraged in the early 1980s by science fiction writers Harlan Ellison and Edward Bryant, Simmons's stories and novellas soon began appearing in major science fiction magazines such as *Twilight Zone, Omni,* and *Galaxy.* "The River Styx Runs Upstream" also brought Simmons a *Twilight Zone* award for best short story, the first of many writing awards he has received.

Simmons's first book, the novel *Song of Kali,* won one of the most prestigious of these awards, the World Fantasy Award, in 1985. It relates the gruesome action that ensues when the daughter of an American journalist is kidnapped in Calcutta, India, by deranged, bloodthirsty worshippers of the Hindu goddess Kali. According to Simmons, the germ of the novel began in 1977, when he was travelling through India on a Fulbright scholarship: "I've lived in cities before, and wasn't afraid of them, but Calcutta was different. The cultural chaos and poverty there make it hard to be objective." The protagonist depicts the city as a place of absolute, malignant evil. "Simmons's vision of Calcutta is stunningly realistic," declares *Fantasy Review* critic Bob Collins, "yet horrifyingly suggestive of a world rendered catatonic through brutalization, where the 'unthinkable' has become routine." Edward Bryant, who as a friend and mentor to Simmons was instrumental in encouraging him in the early years of his career, describes *Song of Kali* as "gripping" in his review of the novel for *Mile High Futures.* The book, writes Bryant, "is a suspense novel of terror in which the monster is a city: Calcutta. Simmons presents this Indian metropolis as a teeming, festering, purely evil hellhole." Faren Miller, writing in *Locus,* describes *Song of Kali* as "harrowing and ghoulish," adding that it "makes the stuff of nightmare very real indeed."

Critics of the first novel find its use of gruesome scenes of death and mutilation to be cutting-edge in the genre, along the lines of horror fiction pioneered by the likes of Stephen King and Clive Barker. But in Simmons' case the use of shocking and grisly story elements have a serious intention: a strong message of non-violence. According to Simmons,

that commitment to delivering a serious message put a lot of publishers off: "Several editors wanted a shoot-em-up, get-revenge ending, which I refused to do. I was trying to show a way for [the journalist hero] to *break* the cycle of violence, without making the ending of the novel anticlimactic."

Collins describes the experience of reading *Song of Kali* as being akin to "spending an evening in the rotting heart of a human compost heap." Bryant declares in his review that he couldn't put the book down and read it in one sitting. Miller observes that its tale of an American family's involvement with a cult of the dreaded bloodthirsty goddess could easily descend to a lower literary level, but Simmons elevates it "with fine characterization, prose that rarely escapes control, and—above all—a keen moral sense." Kali's evil, Miller concludes, is a reflection of the present day, immediate and current. A writer for *Science Fiction Chronicle* adds to the chorus of praise, observing that "there is no question that the novel is a powerful experience, and frequently a repulsive one. Simmons is an author to watch."

A hallmark of Simmons's writing is complexity of theme. *Carrion Comfort,* which earned Simmons the Bram Stoker Award for horror fiction in 1990, tells of a band of socially prominent vampires, including business executives and film moguls, who are capable of dominating others through mind control. Led by a survivor of the Holocaust of World War II, victims of these predatory vampires mount an opposition that results in gory conflicts. As he had done in *Song of Kali,* Simmons again used an exploration of morality to weave the subtle underpinnings of his tale. The vampire-like creatures of *Carrion Comfort* lose control of their reality when they become addicted to pain and death.

Much of Simmons's work shows a spirit of experimentation that serves serious themes. In *Summer of Night,* something is devouring children in a small midwestern town. The novel is set in 1960 and features giant lamprey eels, several evil adults, and a heroic boy who is determined to become a writer. *Phases of Gravity,* published in 1989, is another departure from the genre. With *Phases,* which narrates the tale of the psychic rejuvenation of a grounded astronaut, Simmons may have become the first science fiction writer of his generation to write an historical novel about the space program.

Hyperion and its sequel *The Fall of Hyperion* together constitute a lengthy chronicle of the Hegemony, a galactic civilization of humans who have promised their souls to the machine-based Technocore in exchange for advanced cosmological knowledge. Redemption for the Hegemony seems likely only on the planet Hyperion, an organic world—similar to Earth—with ties to the inscrutable, fearful Shrike. The two books, published together as the *Hyperion Cantos,* constitute a single, powerful tale set in a future time when a black hole has destroyed the planet Earth. The *Cantos* is classically rich, complex, space-opera science fiction that explores many themes, including time travel, religious quests, cyberspace, ecology, and bioengineering.

Appropriating the structure of Geoffrey Chaucer's medieval classic, *The Canterbury Tales,* Simmons's two-part saga concerns seven Hegemony pilgrims who journey to Hyperion hoping to realize salvation by confronting the Shrike. During the course of their journey, each pilgrim recounts the story of his or her life, revealing significant experiences that define who they are and how they came to be on this quest for transcendence. The form of the novel gave Simmons the opportunity to showcase his short story writing talents. Indeed, one of the pilgrim's tales, "Remembering Siri," was first published separately in 1983 as a short story. The form also gives Simmons the opportunity to use different science fiction idioms for each tale—to play with forms within the genre. The effect is a growing mosaic of styles and disparate tales that together form a cohesive whole. Gerald Jones, in his assessment for the *New York Times Book Review,* notes that *Hyperion* and *The Fall of Hyperion* are "generously conceived and stylistically sure-handed books." The reviewer adds that each of the pilgrims' stories "would make a superb novella on its own."

In addition to Chaucer, Simmons also took inspiration from the poet John Keats. Each of the two volumes that comprise the *Cantos* take the titles of Keats's long but never completed poems about the displacement of the old gods and the victory of a new pantheon. This theme is intricately woven into the futuristic, space-opera world of the *Cantos,* for the pilgrims are travelling to Hyperion to secure a transcendence (possibly of Time itself) that will save the war-torn, apocalypse-threatened Galaxy. Critics overall find that the intellectual brilliance of the conception of the twin novels made them a possibly definitive example of the devices and impulses of 1980s science fiction. But, regardless of their place in the history of the genre, the two novels affirmed

a trend in Simmons's work toward highly literate yet highly entertaining science fiction.

The Hollow Man is another example of Simmons's mixing of literary motifs into science fiction (the title is taken from a T. S. Eliot poem). It tells the story of Jeremy Bremen, a psychic who, following the death of his wife, liquidates his assets and sets off on a random journey that soon becomes a nightmare. Bremen's hollowness leaves him incapable or unwilling to use his power to read minds to help either himself or others, and the result is a downward spiral into violence and near-madness. Originally published by *Omni* magazine as a short story entitled "Eyes I Dare Not Meet in Dreams," the much-expanded novel is pure science fiction in rationale—structured to resemble a metaphysical journey into hell, along the lines of Dante's *Inferno,* and containing numerous references to Eliot's "The Hollow Man." In addition to tributes to Dante and Eliot, Simmons takes the opportunity in *The Hollow Man* to use quantum physics and Chaos-theory mathematics as a means of explaining and making real the possibility of ESP. Though *Washington Post Book World* contributor Gregory Feeley finds the novel ultimately "unsatisfying and ersatz," a reviewer for *Voice of Youth Advocates* cites the work as one that "should take its place next to other masterpieces of horror in older young adult collections."

In *Children of the Night* Simmons turned to classic vampire tales of Romania to construct a novel about AIDS. A major character in the novel, a priest named O'Brien, had appeared as a child in *Summer of Night.* In *Children of the Night,* Father O'Brien helps an American doctor to adopt a baby in Romania. When Kate Neuman, an American CDC research hematologist, adopts the Romanian orphan, she discovers that the boy has a unique ability to absorb transfused blood—and she becomes convinced that her adopted son's genetic mutation holds the key to a cure for AIDS. Someone tries to fake the murder of Kate's son and events lead her to follow a trail back to Romania, where with Father O'Brien's help she discovers that her son is about to be consecrated as successor to Count Dracula of Transylvania. Mary K. Chelton, reviewing the novel for *Voice of Youth Advocates* magazine, finds that the story's "progress from the initial scientific plausibility of the baby's rare blood disorder to a wonderfully melodramatic but equally plausible denouement is nonstop, well-written horror fantasy entertainment by a master of the genre." A *Publishers Weekly* critic describes the book as a "mesmerizing revival" of the classic Dracula tale.

With *Lovedeath,* Simmons returned to the familiar starting point of his career: the short story or novella. The 1993 collection, according to *Booklist* reviewer Elliott Swanson, "demonstrates the full range of one of the most gifted writers in the psychological horror field." Among the stories included in the collection are "Entropy's Bed at Midnight," which contrasts the loss of a child with the impersonal nature of actuarial tables, "The Man Who Slept with Teeth Women," which uses the voice of a Native American to recount a coming-of-age tale that involves humor, magic and horror, and "The Great Lover," which recreates the experiences of a World War I poet-soldier. "Simmons is one of the few authors associated with genre fiction who commands significant respect among literati," writes Swanson. Barbara Conaty, writing a review of the collection for the *Library Journal,* adds: "These fine novellas mark the newest epiphany in a career that spans some dozen books." The collection illustrates Simmons's abiding obsession with themes of love, death and loss.

Other notable story collections that Simmons has published include *Prayers to Broken Stones: A Collection,* which contains "Vanni Fucci Is Alive and Well and Living in Hell," a story about religious hypocrites, and "The Death of the Centaur," which explores the lives of children in a flawed education system. Edward Bryant, in a review for *Locus* magazine, describes the collection as "a marvelous range of intellectual concerns, passionate commitments, keenly honed artistic blades—and stretching exercises. . . . This book is an architectural plan for the construction of a major literary career."

Among Simmons's more recent novels is *Fires of Eden,* a 1994 novel that explodes with the author's trademark imagination and intellectual style. Described by *Publishers Weekly* as a "fractured horror novel," *Fires of Eden* features among other things a talking hog with a bad attitude, a hunchback with a shark's mouth protruding from his hump, the 19th-century author Mark Twain, and Byron Trumbo, a Donald Trump-like tycoon who has recently offended the Hawaiian volcano gods. The novel makes use of a double narrative, one a third-person chronicle of the volcano gods' revenge on a Hawaiian resort, and the other the first-person, 19th-century, diary-style account of similar difficulties undergone by a young

woman travelling the country with a young Mark Twain. This post-modern style science fiction tale, like so many of Simmons's prior works, assembles disparate but fascinating elements. Though the *Publisher's Weekly* critic thought the novel would have been better off focusing on the 19th-century Twain story (rather than the modern-day revenge of the volcano gods), A. M. B. Amantia's review for the *Library Journal* finds the book to be "as rich in Hawaiian mythology as it is in suspense."

Although they may differ in their opinions of the relative success of his efforts, critics recognize both Simmons's contributions to science fiction and his success in developing and expanding the genre. Most of all, however, they recognize his greatest strengths: the ability to tell a story that commands the reader's full and undivided attention, and to explore the darkest passions and terrors of the soul. "Come with Dan Simmons," urges Sister Mary Veronica in a review of *The Hollow Man* published in the *Voice of Youth Advocates,* "into the uncharted depths of tortured human minds."

BIOGRAPHICAL/CRITICAL SOURCES:

BOOKS

Contemporary Literary Criticism, Volume 44, Gale (Detroit), 1987.

PERIODICALS

Analog Science Fiction/Science Fact, December 15, 1989, pp. 179-80.
Bloomsbury Review, July-August, 1996, pp. 5, 10.
Booklist, October 15, 1993, p. 419.
Fantasy Review, October, 1986, pp. 13-14.
Library Journal, October 15, 1993, p. 92; October 15, 1994, pp. 88-89.
Locus, February, 1986, p. 13; October, 1990, pp. 23-24.
Mile High Futures, December, 1985, pp. 19-20.
New York Times Book Review, March 25, 1990, p. 30.
Publishers Weekly, December 14, 1990; April 26, 1993, p. 71; August 29, 1994, p. 60.
Science Fiction Chronicle, July, 1986, p. 40.
Voice of Youth Advocates, December, 1992, pp. 295-96; April, 1993, p. 46.
Washington Post Book World, September 27, 1992, p. 11.*

SIMON, John Y.   1933-

PERSONAL: Born June 25, 1933, in Highland Park, IL; son of Jay (a banker) and Jane (Younker) Simon; married Harriet Furst, July 22, 1956; children: Philip (deceased), Ellen. *Education:* Swarthmore College, B.A., 1955; Harvard University, M.A., 1956, Ph.D., 1961.

ADDRESSES: Home—805 Glenview Dr., Carbondale, IL 62901. *Office*—Ulysses S. Grant Association, Morris Library, Southern Illinois University, Carbondale, IL 62901.

CAREER: Ohio State University, Columbus, instructor in history, 1960-62, on leave, 1962-64; Southern Illinois University, Carbondale, executive director and managing editor, Ulysses S. Grant Association, 1962—, associate professor, 1964-71, professor of history, 1971—; faculty member, Institute for the Editing of Historical Documents, 1975, 1978-79; member of historians' advisory committee, Illinois Sesquicentennial Commission, 1965-68; chair of Founders Award committee, Museum of the Confederacy, 1973-75. Member, Illinois State Historical Records Advisory Board, 1976-79, and Governor of Illinois Advisory Task Force on Historic Preservation, 1985; panel member and consultant, National Endowment for the Humanities, 1979; historical consultant to *Ohio Has Saved the Union,* WOSU-TV, 1965; consultant to Illinois Humanities Council, 1975-76, and Chicago Historical Society, 1987.

MEMBER: American Historical Association, Organization of American Historians, Association for Documentary Editing (chair of steering committee, 1978; president, 1978-83; chair of constitution and bylaws committee, 1983-85; chair of documentary heritage trust steering committee, 1986-89; placement officer, 1987—), Illinois Association for the Advancement of History (member of steering committee, 1981-83; president, 1983-84; director, 1984-87; member of nominating committee, 1984-85), Illinois State Historical Society (vice president 1966-67, 1980-83; director, 1967-70), Abraham Lincoln Association (director, 1984-96, member of executive committee, 1986-95), Lincoln Group of Boston (associate member), Lincoln Fellowship of Wisconsin (honorary member).

AWARDS, HONORS: Illinois State Historical Society award of merit, 1970; Harry S. Truman Award, Kansas City Civil War Round Table, 1972; Fletcher Pratt Award, Civil War Round Table of New York, 1973; Delta Award, Friends of Morris Library, 1976; Moncado Prize Award, American Military Institute, 1982; Founders Award, Confederate Memorial Literary Society, 1983; Distinguished Service Award, Association for Documentary Editing, 1983; D.H.L., Lincoln College, 1983; Nevins-Freeman Award, Chicago Civil War Round Table, 1985.

WRITINGS:

Ulysses S. Grant Chronology, Ohio Historical Society for Ulysses S. Grant Association and Ohio Civil War Centennial Commission, 1963.

(Editor) *General Grant by Matthew Arnold with a Rejoinder by Mark Twain,* Southern Illinois University Press (Carbondale), 1966, Kent State University Press (Kent, OH), 1995.

(Editor) *The Papers of Ulysses S. Grant,* Southern Illinois University Press, Volume 1: *1837-1861,* 1967, Volume 2: *April-September, 1861,* 1969, Volume 3: *October 1, 1861-January 7, 1862,* 1970, Volume 4: *January 8-March 31, 1862,* 1972, Volume 5: *April 1-August 31, 1862,* 1973, Volume 6: *September 1-December 8, 1862,* 1977, Volume 7: *December 9, 1862-March 31, 1863,* 1979, Volume 8: *April 1-July 6 , 1863,* 1979, Volume 9: *July 7-December 31, 1863,* 1982, Volume 10: *January 1-May 31, 1864,* 1982, Volume 11: *June 1-August 15, 1864,* 1984, Volume 12: *August 16-November 15, 1864,* 1984, Volume 13: *November 16, 1864-February 20, 1865,* 1985, Volume 14: *February 21-April 30, 1865,* 1985, Volume 15: *May 1-December 31, 1865,* 1988, Volume 16: *1866,* 1988, Volume 17: *January 1-September 30, 1867,* 1991, Volume 18: *October 1, 1867-June 30, 1868,* 1991, Volume 19: *July 1, 1868-October 31, 1869,* 1995, Volume 20: *November 1, 1869-October 31, 1870,* 1995.

(Author of introduction) Rachel Sherman Thorndike, editor, *The Sherman Letters: Correspondence between General and Senator Sherman from 1837 to 1891,* Da Capo Press (New York City), 1969.

(Author of foreword) Thomas M. Pitkin, *The Captain Departs: Ulysses S. Grant's Last Campaign,* Southern Illinois University Press, 1973.

(Editor) *The Personal Memoirs of Julia Dent Grant,* Putnam (New York City), 1975, Southern Illinois University Press, 1988.

(Author of foreword) William M. Anderson, *They Died to Make Men Free: A History of the 19th Michigan Infantry in the Civil War,* Hardscrabble (Berrien Springs, MI), 1980.

(Editor and contributor with David L. Wilson)
Ulysses S. Grant: Essays and Documents, Southern Illinois University Press, 1981.

House Divided: Lincoln and His Father, Louis A. Warren Lincoln Library and Museum (Fort Wayne, IN), 1987.

(Author of foreword) Charles G. Ellington, *The Trial of U. S. Grant: The Pacific Coast Years 1852-1854,* Arthur Clark (Glendale, CA), 1987.

(Author of introduction) Arthur Charles Cole, *The Era of the Civil War 1848-1870,* University of Illinois Press (Champaign), 1987.

(Editor with Barbara Hughett and contributor) *The Continuing Civil War: Essays in Honor of the Civil War Round Table of Chicago,* Morningside, 1992.

(Author of chapter) Gabor S. Boritt, editor, *Lincoln's Generals,* Oxford University Press (New York City), 1994.

Contributor to the *Encyclopedia of Southern History,* Louisiana State University Press (Baton Rouge), 1979; *Illinois: Its History and Legacy,* edited by Roger D. Bridges and Rodney O. Davis, River City Publishers (St. Louis, MO), 1984; *Competing Belief Systems,* edited by Gunnar Boalt, Almqvist & Wiksell International (Stockholm), 1984; *The Presidents: A Reference History,* edited by Henry F. Groff, Scribner (New York City), 1984; and *U. S. Grant: The Man and the Image* (National Portrait Gallery exhibition catalogue), Southern Illinois University Press, 1985.

Also contributor of articles on Ulysses S. Grant to *Encyclopaedia Britannica,* 1970, and *World Book Encyclopedia,* 1971. Contributor of articles and reviews to numerous journals, including *Journal of the Illinois State Historical Society, Civil War History, Journal of American History, Military Affairs,* and *Ohio History.* Civil War editor, *Manuscripts,* 1967-72; editor of Ulysses S. Grant Association's *Newsletter,* 1963-73. Member of advisory committee, *Papers of Daniel Chester French,* 1975—; member of editorial board, *The Papers of Jefferson Davis,* Louisiana State University Press, 1980—, *Documentary History of the First Federal Elections,* University of Wisconsin Press, 1980—, *Charles Sumner Correspondence,* 1986-91, *Hayes Historical Journal,* 1991-93, Thaddeus Stevens Papers, 1992—; member of academic advisory committee, *The Lincoln-Douglas Debates,* C-SPAN, 1994.

SIDELIGHTS: Considered one of America's foremost experts on Ulysses S. Grant, John Y. Simon has devoted more than twenty years to editing the multivolume *The Papers of Ulysses S. Grant,* in which he presents the life of the military leader and eighteenth president of the United States through an estimated 30,000 documents. Praised by the *New York Times*'s Herbert Mitgang for his "immaculate editorship," Simon gathers such documents as Grant's personal correspondence with his family and friends as well as his official and military correspondence with members of his staff and commanders.

"This collection, when complete, will be definitive," writes R. J. Hayli in *Library Journal,* "and will help to assure General Grant his proper place in history as an extraordinary man who had his share of human failings, but had an inner strength." *The Papers of Ulysses S. Grant* "is an enterprise of archival importance, of course, but . . . it will have a more lively interest," according to a *New Yorker* reviewer, who adds that more than 100 of the letters are those to Grant's longtime fiancee Julia Dent Grant: "Through them we perceive a rather different person from the taciturn and colorless figure of many histories, for here, speaking for himself, is a man of quick feelings and perceptions." As a *Choice* contributor comments, "The personal letters to wife, father, and father-in-law are the most interesting because they reveal the intimate Grant."

BIOGRAPHICAL/CRITICAL SOURCES:

PERIODICALS

Annals of the American Academy of Political and Social Science, March, 1970.
Choice, February, 1970.
Library Journal, September 15, 1967.
New Yorker, August 26, 1967.
New York Times, December 1, 1982; July 13, 1985.
Times Literary Supplement, September 28, 1967.

*   *   *

SLIDE, Anthony   1944-
   (Anna Kate Sterling, Lennox Sanderson, Jr., Tony Clifford)

PERSONAL: Born November 7, 1944, in Birmingham, England; son of Clifford Frederick and Mary (Eaton) Slide. *Education:* Attended grammar school in Birmingham, England. *Politics:* None. *Religion:* None.

ADDRESSES: Office—4118 Rhodes Ave., Studio City, CA 91604.

CAREER: Silent Picture (quarterly devoted to the art and history of silent film), London, England, founder and editor, 1968-74; American Film Institute, Washington, DC, associate archivist, 1972-75; Academy of Motion Picture Arts and Sciences, Beverly Hills, CA, resident film historian, 1975-80; freelance writer and researcher, 1980—. Co-owner, Producers Library Service, 1986-90. Organizer of first silent film festival ever held in Europe, 1970. Research associate, American Film Institute, 1971-72. Lecturer, Museum of Modern Art, Pacific Film Archive, Columbia University, and Library of Congress. Consultant on silent film programming, National Film Theatre, London.

AWARDS, HONORS: Honorary Doctorate of Letters, Bowling Green University, 1990.

WRITINGS:

Sir Michael Balcon (monograph), British Film Institute (London), 1969.

Lillian Gish (monograph), British Film Institute, 1969.

(With Paul O'Dell) *Griffith and the Rise of Hollywood,* A. S. Barnes (San Diego, CA), 1970.

(With O'Dell) *Early American Cinema,* A. S. Barnes, 1971, revised edition, Scarecrow (Metuchen, NJ), 1994.

The Griffith Actresses, A. S. Barnes, 1973.

(With Edward Wagenknecht) *The Films of D. W. Griffith,* Crown (New York City), 1975.

The Idols of Silence, A. S. Barnes, 1976.

The Big V: A History of the Vitagraph Company, Scarecrow, 1976, revised edition, 1988.

Early Women Directors, A. S. Barnes, 1977, revised edition, Da Capo Press (New York City), 1984.

Aspects of American Film History Prior to 1920, Scarecrow, 1978.

Films on Film History, Scarecrow, 1979.

The Films of Will Rogers (monograph), Academy of Motion Picture Arts and Sciences (Beverly Hills, CA), 1979.

The Kindergarten of the Movies: A History of the Fine Arts Studio, Scarecrow, 1980.

(With Wagenknecht) *Fifty Great American Silent Films: 1912-1920,* Dover (New York City), 1980.

The Vaudevillians, Arlington House (New York City), 1981.

Great Radio Personalities in Historic Photographs, Dover, 1982, revised edition, Vestal (Vestal, NY), 1988.

A Collector's Guide to Movie Memorabilia, Wallace-Homestead (Des Moines, IA), 1983.

(Editor) *International Film, Radio and Television Journals,* Greenwood Press (Westport, CT), 1984.

Fifty Classic British Films: 1932-1982, Dover, 1985.

A Collector's Guide to TV Memorabilia, Wallace-Homestead, 1985.

The American Film Industry: A Historical Dictionary, Greenwood Press 1986.

The Great Pretenders, Wallace-Homestead, 1986.

(Editor) *Filmfront,* Scarecrow, 1986.

(With Judith Katten) *Movie Posters: The Paintings of Batiste Madalena,* Abrams (New York City), 1986.

(Editor) *The Memoirs of Alice Guy Blache,* Scarecrow, 1986.

Fifty Classic French Films: 1912-1982, Dover, 1987.

(Editor) *Selected Radio and Television Criticism,* Scarecrow, 1987.

The Cinema and Ireland, McFarland & Co. (Jefferson, NC), 1988.

(Editor) *Selected Vaudeville Criticism,* Scarecrow, 1988.

(Editor) *Picture Dancing on a Screen,* Vestal, 1988.

One Hundred Rare Books from the Margaret Herrick Library (monograph), Academy of Motion Picture Arts and Sciences, 1988.

(With Patricia King Hanson and Stephen L. Hanson) *Sourcebook for the Performing Arts,* Greenwood Press, 1988.

The International Film Industry: A Historical Dictionary, Greenwood Press, 1989.

Silent Portraits, Vestal, 1990.

The Television Industry: A Historical Dictionary, Greenwood Press, 1991.

Nitrate Won't Wait: A History of Film Preservation in the United States, McFarland & Co., 1992.

(Editor) *They Also Wrote for the Fan Magazines: Film Articles by Literary Giants from E. E. Cummings to Eleanor Roosevelt, 1920-1939,* McFarland & Co., 1992.

The Slide Area: Film Book Reviews, 1989-1991, Scarecrow, 1992.

Before Video: A History of the Non-Theatrical Film, Greenwood Press, 1992.

Gay and Lesbian Themes and Characters in Mystery Novels, McFarland & Co., 1993.

(Editor) *Robert Goldstein and the Spirit of '76,* Scarecrow, 1993.

The Encyclopedia of Vaudeville, Greenwood Press, 1994.

The Hollywood Novel, McFarland & Co., 1995.

Some Joe Don't Know: An American Biographical Guide to 100 British Television Personalities, Greenwood Press, 1996.

Lois Weber: The Director Who Lost Her Way in History, Greenwood Press, 1996.

The Silent Feminists: America's First Women Directors, Scarecrow, 1996.

EDITOR OF "SELECTED FILM CRITICISM" SERIES

Selected Film Criticism: 1896-1911, Scarecrow, 1982.

Selected Film Criticism: 1912-1920, Scarecrow, 1982.

Selected Film Criticism: 1921-1930, Scarecrow, 1982.

Selected Film Criticism: 1931-1940, Scarecrow, 1982.

Selected Film Criticism: 1941-1950, Scarecrow, 1983.

Selected Film Criticism: Foreign Films, 1930-1950, Scarecrow, 1984.

Selected Film Criticism: 1951-1960, Scarecrow, 1985.

EDITOR OF "SELECTED THEATRE CRITICISM" SERIES

Selected Theatre Criticism: 1900-1919, Scarecrow, 1985.

Selected Theater Criticism: 1920-1930, Scarecrow, 1985.

Selected Theater Criticism: 1931-1950, Scarecrow, 1986.

EDITOR; UNDER NAME ANNA KATE STERLING

The Best of Shadowland, Scarecrow, 1987.

Cinematographers on the Art and Craft of Cinematography, Scarecrow, 1987.

Celebrity Articles from The Screen Guild Magazine, Scarecrow, 1987.

OTHER

Also editor of "Filmmakers" series for Scarecrow. Contributor to several books on cinema, including *The International Dictionary of Films and Filmmakers, Film Review Annual,* and *Magill's Survey of Cinema.* Contributor of articles and reviews under names Lennox Sanderson, Jr. and Tony Clifford to numerous periodicals. Member of editorial board, *Film History.* Book review editor, *Classic Image,* 1989—.

SMALL, Bertrice   1937-

PERSONAL: Born December 9, 1937, in New York, NY; daughter of David R. (a broadcaster) and Doris S. (a broadcaster) Williams; married George S. Small (a photographer and designer), October 5, 1963; children: Thomas David. *Education:* Attended Western College for Women, 1955-58, and Katharine Gibbs Secretarial School, 1958-59. *Politics:* "I vote for candidates, not parties." *Religion:* Anglican.

ADDRESSES: P.O. Box 765, Southold, NY 11971.

CAREER: Secretary in New York City, 1959-61; Edward Petry & Co., New York City, sales assistant, 1961-63; freelance writer, 1969—.

MEMBER: Authors Guild, Novelist, Inc., Romance Writers of America/PAN.

AWARDS, HONORS: Honorable mention, Porgie Awards from *West Coast Review of Books,* 1979; Historical Romance Novelist of the Year Award, 1983, Best Historical Series Author Award, 1986, and Career Achievement Historical Fantasy Award, 1991, all from *Romantic Times;* Silver Pen Award, 1988.

WRITINGS:

HISTORICAL ROMANCES

The Kadin, Avon (New York City), 1978.
Love Wild and Fair, Avon, 1978.
Adora, Ballantine (New York City), 1980.
Skye O'Malley, Ballantine, 1980.
Unconquered, Ballantine, 1982.
Beloved, Ballantine, 1983.
All the Sweet Tomorrows, Ballantine, 1984.
This Heart of Mine, New American Library (New York City), 1985.
A Love for All Time, New American Library, 1986.
Enchantress Mine, New American Library, 1987.
Blaze Wyndham, New American Library, 1988.
Lost Love Found, Ballantine, 1989.
The Spitfire, Ballantine, 1990.
A Moment in Time, Ballantine, 1991.
Wild Jasmine, Ballantine, 1992.
To Love Again, Ballantine, 1993.
Love, Remember Me, Ballantine, 1994.
The Love Slave, Ballantine, 1995.
Hellion, Ballantine, 1996.

WORK IN PROGRESS: Darling Jasmine for Zebra Books, 1997, and several other novels.

SIDELIGHTS: Bertrice Small writes *CA:* "I consider myself one of the most fortunate people alive to be able to earn my living doing something that I love doing—writing historical fiction. My career has put me in contact with other authors, which is a great blessing for me, since novelists, like whooping cranes, are a very endangered species and enjoy congregating together occasionally with their own kind. It's nice to be with people who don't think you're strange because you earn your living doing something everyone always told you you couldn't possibly do and be successful. I hope to go on this way until I die!

"The greatest blessing of this rather odd lifestyle of mine, however, is that I have come in contact with the readers. I am amazed by the variety of people who read historical romance: men and women of all ages, educational backgrounds, and socioeconomic groupings. I have gained a great respect for the readers, and I only wish the publishers knew them as well as I do. My mail comes in from all over the world, including South Africa, where, I understand, I am no longer banned. My books are translated into French, Spanish, Italian, Dutch, German, Norwegian, Russian, Czech, Hungarian, Romanian, Latvian, Swedish, Danish, and Japanese."

* * *

SOMMERS, Lawrence M(elvin) 1919-

PERSONAL: Born April 17, 1919, in Clinton, WI; son of Emil L. (a farmer) and Inga (a homemaker; maiden name, Anderson) Sommers; married Marjorie Smith (a geographer), April 26, 1948; children: Laurie Kay. *Education:* University of Wisconsin, B.S., 1942, Ph.M., 1946; Northwestern University, Ph.D., 1950. *Avocational interests:* The geography of Norway, travel, gardening, bulb growing.

ADDRESSES: Home—4292 Tacoma Blvd., Okemos, MI 48864. *Office*—Department of Geography, Michigan State University, East Lansing, MI 48824; fax 517-432-1671.

CAREER: Michigan State University, East Lansing, began as instructor, became associate professor,

1949-55, professor of geography, 1955—, chair of department, 1955-79, assistant dean of International Programs, 1983-85, acting assistant provost, 1987-88, assistant provost, 1988-89, emeritus professor, 1989—. Chair of steering committee, Michigan State University Academic Council, 1981-84; member of Michigan State University Graduate council. Editor, Denoyer Geppert Company, Chicago, IL, 1960-85, and Modern Educational Systems, Inc., Goshen, IN, 1968—. *Military service:* U.S. Army, 1942-45.

MEMBER: American Geographical Society, Association of American Geographers (executive council, 1967-70; chair, consulting service, 1970-77), National Council for Geographic Education (executive board, 1967-70), American Scandinavian Foundation, American Association for the Advancement of Science, American Polar Society, Society for the Advancement of Scandinavian Studies, Explorers Club, Phi Kappa Phi (president, Michigan State University chapter, 1980-82, vice-president, north-central region, 1986-89, national president, 1992-95), Phi Delta Beta, Sigma Xi (president, Michigan State University chapter, 1959-60).

AWARDS, HONORS: Grants for research in Norway form Social Science Research Council and American-Scandinavian Foundation, 1948, in Denmark from Office of Naval Research, 1953, and in Sweden from Office of Naval Research, 1960; National Science Foundation grant, 1975-78; Sea Grants from University of Michigan and Michigan State University, 1978-79 and 1979-82; Outstanding Service Award, East Lakes Region of Association of American Geographers, 1987.

WRITINGS:

(Editor with Fred E. Dohrs and Donald R. Petterson) *Outside Readings in Geography,* T. Y. Crowell (New York City), 1955.

(Editor with Dohrs) *Introduction to Geography,* T. Y. Crowell, 1967.

(Compiler with Dohrs) *Physical Geography,* T. Y. Crowell, 1967.

(Compiler with Dohrs) *Cultural Geography,* T. Y. Crowell, 1967.

(Compiler with Dohrs) *Economic Geography,* T. Y. Crowell, 1970.

(With Dohrs) *World Regional Geography: A Problem Approach,* West Publishing (St. Paul, Minnesota), 1976.

(Editor) *Atlas of Michigan,* Michigan State University Press (East Lansing, MI), 1977.

(Editor with H. E. Koenig) *Energy and the Adaptation of Human Settlements,* Michigan State University Press, 1980.

(Editor with John F. Lounsbury and Edward A Fernald) *Land Use: A Spatial Approach,* Kendall/Hunt (Dubuque, IA), 1981.

Michigan: A Geography, Westview (Boulder, CO), 1984.

(Editor and author with Ole Gade and Vincent P. Miller) *Planning Issues in Marginal Areas,* Volume 3: *Occasional Papers in Geography and Planning,* Appalachian State University (Boone, NC), 1991.

Also author, with others, of *Border Towns in Nevada,* 1991, and *Patterns of Microgeographic Marginality in Michigan,* 1992-95. Contributor of articles and reviews to journals and books, including *Journal of Geography, The Scientific Monthly, Geographical Review, World Encyclopedia, Compton's Encyclopedia,* and *Cities of the World,* edited by Brunn and Williams, Harper, 1983. Associate editor of *Social Science Journal,* 1978-85.

WORK IN PROGRESS: Regional Development Issues in Norway; Spatial Impacts of Norwegian Oil and Gas Exploitation; Marginality in Michigan; "Indian Gaming in the United States" for *Focus,* 1997; *Norway* (Around the World Series) for American Geographical Society, 1997.

SIDELIGHTS: Lawrence M. Sommers told *CA:* "My writing is based on the conviction that there is a great need to eliminate geographical ignorance among young people in the United States. This nation and its people must be able to compete in an increasingly interdependent world."

*   *   *

SOUSTER, (Holmes) Raymond 1921-
(John Holmes, Raymond Holmes)

PERSONAL: Born January 15, 1921, in Toronto, Ontario, Canada; son of Austin Holmes and Norma (Baker) Souster; married Rosalia Lena Geralde (a bank clerk), June 24, 1947. *Education:* Attended University of Toronto, 1932-37, and Humberside Collegiate Institute, 1938-39. *Politics:* New Democratic Party. *Religion:* United Church of Canada.

ADDRESSES: Home—39 Baby Point Rd., Toronto, Ontario, Canada M6S 2G2.

CAREER: Poet and editor. Canadian Imperial Bank of Commerce, Toronto, Ontario, accountant, 1939-84. *Military service:* Royal Canadian Air Force, 1941-45; leading aircraftsman.

MEMBER: League of Canadian Poets (founding and life member; first chair, 1968-72).

AWARDS, HONORS: Canada's Governor-General Award, 1964, for *The Colour of the Times;* President's Medal, University of Western Ontario, 1967; Centennial Medal, 1967; Canadian Silver Jubilee Medal, 1977; City of Toronto Book Award, 1979; Officer of the Order of Canada, 1995.

WRITINGS:

(Contributor) *Unit of Five,* edited by Ronald Hambleton, Ryerson (Canada), 1944.

When We Are Young (poetry), First Statement Press, 1946.

Go to Sleep, World (poetry), Ryerson, 1947.

City Hall Street (poetry), Ryerson, 1951.

(Compiler) *Poets Fifty-six: Ten Younger English-Canadians,* Contact Press, 1956.

Selected Poems, Contact Press, 1956.

Crepe-hanger's Carnival: Selected Poems, 1955-58, Contact Press, 1958.

Place of Meeting: Poems, 1958-60, Gallery Editions, 1962.

A Local Pride: Poems, Contact Press, 1962.

The Colour of the Times: The Collected Poems, Ryerson, 1964.

Twelve New Poems, Goosetree Press, 1964.

Ten Elephants on Yonge Street (poetry), Ryerson, 1965.

As Is (poetry), Oxford University Press (Oxford), 1967.

(Editor with John Robert Colombo) *Shapes and Sounds: Poems of W. W. E. Ross,* Longmans, Green, 1968.

Lost & Found: Uncollected Poems by Raymond Souster, Clarke, Irwin, 1968.

So Far So Good: Poems, 1938-1968, Oberon, 1969.

(Editor) *Made in Canada,* Oberon, 1970.

(Editor) *New Wave Canada,* Contact Press, 1970.

(Editor with Richard Woollatt) *Generation Now* (poetry anthology), Longmans, Green, 1970.

The Years (poetry), Oberon, 1971.

Selected Poems, Oberon, 1972.

(Under pseudonym John Holmes) *On Target* (novel), Village Book Store Press, 1973.

(Editor with Woollatt) *Sight and Sounds* (poetry anthology), Macmillan (Toronto), 1973.

Change-Up (poetry), Oberon, 1974.

(Editor with Douglas Lochhead) *100 Poems of Nineteenth Century Canada* (poetry anthology), Macmillan (Toronto), 1974.

(Editor with Woollatt) *These Loved, These Hated Lands* (poetry anthology), Doubleday (Toronto), 1975.

Double-Header (poetry), Oberon, 1975.

Rain-Check (poetry), Oberon, 1975.

Extra Innings (poetry), Oberon, 1977.

(Compiler and author of introduction) *Vapour and Blue: Souster Selects Campbell* (selected poetry of William Wilfred Campbell), Paget Press, 1978.

(With Douglas Alcorn) *From Hell to Breakfast* (war memoirs), Intruder Press, 1978.

(Editor) *Comfort of the Fields* (selected poetry of Archibald Lampman), Paget Press, 1979.

Hanging In (poetry), Oberon, 1979.

(Editor with Woollatt) *Poems of a Snow-Eyed Country* (poetry anthology), Academic Press of Canada, 1980.

Collected Poems of Raymond Souster, Oberon, Volume 1: *1940-1955,* 1980, Volume 2: *1955-1962,* 1981, Volume 3: *1962-1974,* 1982, Volume 4: *1974-1977,* 1983, Volume 5: *1977-1983,* 1984, Volume 6: *1984-1986,* 1988, Volume 7: *1987-88,* 1992.

Going the Distance (poetry), Oberon, 1983.

(Editor with Lochhead) *Powassan's Drum: Selected Poems of Duncan Cambell Scott,* 1983.

Jubilee of Death: The Raid on Dieppe, Oberon Press, 1984.

(With Bill Brooks) *Queen City* (poetry), Oberon, 1984.

The Flight of the Roller Coaster (juvenile), Oberon, 1985.

It Takes All Kinds (poetry), Oberon, 1985.

(Editor with Lochhead) *Windflower: The Selected Poems of Bliss Carman,* 1986.

The Eyes of Love (poetry), Oberon, 1987.

Asking for More (poetry), Oberon, 1988.

Running out the Clock (poetry), Oberon, 1990.

Old Bank Notes (poetry), Oberon, 1993.

Riding the Long Black Horse (poetry), Oberon, 1993.

No Sad Songs Wanted Here (poetry), Oberon, 1995.

Close to Home (poetry), Oberon, in press.

Also author, under pseudonym Raymond Holmes, of the novel *The Winter of Time,* 1949.

SIDELIGHTS: Raymond Souster "is the most Torontocentric of Canadian poets," writes Robert Fulford in *Saturday Night.* What Souster has "been doing, all these years," Fulford declares, "is writing hymns of praise to the Toronto he loves and the professionals he admires." According to *Canadian Forum* reviewer David Jackel, "Souster's greatest strength is his ability to go on finding, in his own life and in the ordinary life around him, materials for poetry." *Canadian Literature* critic Mike Doyle comments that "singing small seems to be Raymond Souster's way of being a poet in the world," taking for his subject matter "the face of the ragged postcard seller on Yonge Street, the movement of cats ... [and] of small birds, the shapes and colours of old buildings, the small immediate actions of people." "Souster's Toronto is not so much vivid as it is simply, palpably there," points out *Tamarack Review* critic Hayden Carruth, "the great northern city, bare, cold, ugly, windswept, yet full of life, indispensable to that life. And this is the freshness that Souster brings to so much of his writing."

Souster commented in his collection *Ten Elephants on Yonge Street:* "Whoever I write to, I want the substance of the poem so immediate, so real, so clear, that the reader feels the same exhilaration—be it fear or joy—that I derived from the experience, object or mood that triggered the poem in the first place.

"I like to think I'm 'talking out' my poems rather than consciously dressing them up in the trappings of the academic tradition. For many years I held to the theory that all poetry must be written out of a sudden spontaneous impulse in which the poet is unbearably moved to write down the words of that vision. I am now more inclined to echo the view of [Italian poet] Giuseppe Ungaretti when he says: 'Between one flower gathered and the other given / the inexpressible Null.'

"I suppose I am truly an unrepentant regionalist. As [French author] Emile Zola put it to [French critic, poet, and novelist] Paul Bourget: 'Why should we be everlastingly wanting to escape to lands of romance? Our streets are full of tragedy and full of beauty; they should be enough for any poet.' All the experiences one is likely to encounter in Paris can be found in this city. Toronto has a flavor all its own. But beyond everything else is the fact that I was born here, my mother and father were born here, my maternal grandmother arrived from Ireland in 1889, and my paternal grandfather came here from a small Ontario town. My roots are here: this is the place that tugs at my heart when I leave it and fills me with quiet relief when I return to it."

BIOGRAPHICAL/CRITICAL SOURCES:

BOOKS

Contemporary Literary Criticism, Gale (Detroit), Volume 5, 1976, Volume 14, 1980.
Davey, Frank, *From Here to There: Our Nature, Our Voices 1,* Press Porcepic (Canada), 1974.
Davey, *Louis Dudek and Raymond Souster,* Douglas & McIntyre, 1980.
Profiles in Canadian Literature, Dundurn Press (Canada), 1982.
Souster, Raymond, *Ten Elephants on Yonge Street,* Ryerson, 1965.
Whitman, Bruce, *Collected Poems of Raymond Souster: A Descriptive Bibliography,* Oberon, 1984.

PERIODICALS

Canadian Forum, December, 1968; February, 1969; June, 1975; August, 1977.
Canadian Literature, fall, 1964; fall, 1972; winter, 1974.
Globe and Mail (Toronto), October 13, 1984.
Saturday Night, December, 1971; July, 1977.
Tamarack Review, winter, 1965.

*   *   *

STERLING, Anna Kate
   See SLIDE, Anthony

*   *   *

STINE, Jovial Bob
   See STINE, R(obert) L(awrence)

STINE, R(obert) L(awrence)   1943-
   (Jovial Bob Stine; pseudonyms: Eric Affabee, Zachary Blue)

PERSONAL: Born October 8, 1943, in Columbus, OH; son of Lewis (a shipping manager) and Anne (Feinstein) Stine; married Jane Waldhorn (owner/ managing director of Parachute Press), June 22, 1969; children: Matthew Daniel. *Education:* Ohio State University, B.A., 1965; graduate study at New York University, 1966-67. *Religion:* Jewish. *Avocational interests:* Swimming, watching old movie classics from the 1930s and 1940s, reading (especially P. G. Wodehouse novels).

ADDRESSES: Home—New York, NY. *Office*—c/o Parachute Press, 156 5th Avenue, New York, NY 10010.

CAREER: Writer. Social Studies teacher at junior high schools in Columbus, Ohio, 1967-68; *Junior Scholastic* (magazine), New York City, associate editor, 1969-71; *Search* (magazine), New York City, editor, 1972-75; *Bananas* (magazine), New York City, editor, 1972-83; *Maniac* (magazine), New York City, editor, 1984-85. Head writer for *Eureeka's Castle,* Nickelodeon cable television network.

MEMBER: Mystery Writers of America.

AWARDS, HONORS: Childrens' Choice Award, American Library Association, for several novels.

WRITINGS:

JUVENILES

The Time Raider, illustrations by David Febland, Scholastic Inc. (New York City), 1982.
The Golden Sword of Dragonwalk, illustrations by Febland, Scholastic Inc., 1983.
Horrors of the Haunted Museum, Scholastic Inc., 1984.
Instant Millionaire, illustrations by Jowill Woodman, Scholastic Inc., 1984.
Through the Forest of Twisted Dreams, Avon (New York City), 1984.
Indiana Jones and the Curse of Horror Island, Ballantine (New York City), 1984.
Indiana Jones and the Giants of the Silver Tower, Ballantine, 1984.
Indiana Jones and the Cult of the Mummy's Crypt, Ballantine, 1985.

The Badlands of Hark, illustrations by Bob Roper, Scholastic Inc., 1985.

The Invaders of Hark, Scholastic Inc., 1985.

Demons of the Deep, illustrations by Fred Carrillo, Golden Books, 1985.

Challenge of the Wolf Knight ("Wizards, Warriors and You" series), Avon, 1985.

James Bond in Win, Place, or Die, Ballantine, 1985.

Conquest of the Time Master, Avon, 1985.

Cavern of the Phantoms, Avon, 1986.

Operation: Deadly Decoy ("G.I. Joe" series), Ballantine, 1986.

Mystery of the Imposter, Avon, 1986.

Operation: Mindbender ("G.I. Joe" series), Ballantine, 1986.

Golden Girl and the Vanishing Unicorn ("Golden Girl" series), Ballantine, 1986.

Serpentor and the Mummy Warrior ("G.I. Joe" series), 1987.

Indiana Jones and the Ape Slaves of Howling Island, Ballantine, 1987.

Jungle Raid ("G.I. Joe" series), Ballantine, 1988.

Siege of Serpentor ("G.I. Joe" series), Ballantine, 1988.

The Beast, Minstrel, 1994.

I Saw You That Night!, Scholastic Inc., 1994.

The Beast 2, Minstrel, 1995.

R. L. Stine's the Ghosts of Fear Street: Hide & Shriek, Minstrel, 1995.

JUVENILES; UNDER NAME JOVIAL BOB STINE

The Absurdly Silly Encyclopedia and Flyswatter, illustrations by Bob Taylor, Scholastic Inc., 1978.

How To Be Funny: An Extremely Silly Guidebook, illustrations by Carol Nicklaus, Dutton (New York City), 1978.

The Complete Book of Nerds, illustrations by Sam Viviano, Scholastic Inc., 1979.

The Dynamite Do-It-Yourself Pen Pal Kit, illustrations by Jared Lee, Scholastic Inc., 1980.

Dynamite's Funny Book of the Sad Facts of Life, illustrations by Lee, Scholastic Inc., 1980.

Going Out! Going Steady! Going Bananas!, photographs by Dan Nelken, Scholastic Inc., 1980.

The Pigs' Book of World Records, illustrations by Peter Lippman, Random House (New York City), 1980.

(With wife, Jane Stine) *The Sick of Being Sick Book,* edited by Ann Durrell, illustrations by Nicklaus, Dutton, 1980.

Bananas Looks at TV, Scholastic Inc., 1981.

The Beast Handbook, illustrations by Taylor, Scholastic Inc., 1981.

(With Jane Stine) *The Cool Kids' Guide to Summer Camp,* illustrations by Jerry Zimmerman, Scholastic Inc., 1981.

Gnasty Gnomes, illustrations by Lippman, Random House, 1981.

Don't Stand in the Soup, illustrations by Nicklaus, Bantam (New York City), 1982.

(With Jane Stine) *Bored with Being Bored!: How to Beat the Boredom Blahs,* illustrations by Zimmerman, Four Winds (New York City), 1982.

Blips!: The First Book of Video Game Funnies, illustrations by Bryan Hendrix, Scholastic Inc., 1983.

(With Jane Stine) *Everything You Need to Survive: Brothers and Sisters,* illustrated by Sal Murdocca, Random House, 1983.

(With Jane Stine) *Everything You Need to Survive: First Dates,* illustrated by Murdocca, Random House, 1983.

(With Jane Stine) *Everything You Need to Survive: Homework,* illustrated by Murdocca, Random House, 1983.

(With Jane Stine) *Everything You Need to Survive: Money Problems,* illustrated by Murdocca, Random House, 1983.

Jovial Bob's Computer Joke Book, Scholastic Inc., 1985.

Miami Mice, illustrations by Eric Gurney, Scholastic Inc., 1986.

One Hundred and One Silly Monster Jokes, Scholastic Inc., 1986.

The Doggone Dog Joke Book, Parachute Press, 1986.

Spaceballs: The Book, Scholastic Inc., 1987.

Pork & Beans: Play Date, illustrations by Jose Aruego and Ariane Dewey, Scholastic Inc., 1989.

My Secret Identity: A Novelization, Scholastic Inc., 1989.

Ghostbusters 2 Storybook, Scholastic Inc., 1989.

One Hundred and One Vacation Jokes, illustrated by Rick Majica, Scholastic Inc., 1990.

The Amazing Adventures of Me, Myself, and I, Bantam, 1991.

JUVENILES; UNDER PSEUDONYM ERIC AFFABEE

The Siege of the Dragonriders ("Wizards, Warriors and You" series), Avon, 1984.

G.I. Joe and the Everglades Swamp Terror ("G.I. Joe" Series), Ballantine, 1986.

Attack on the King, Avon, 1986.

G.I. Joe-Operation: Star Raider ("G.I. Joe" series), Ballantine, 1986.

The Dragon Queen's Revenge ("Wizards, Warriors and You" series), Avon, 1986.

JUVENILES; UNDER PSEUDONYM ZACHARY BLUE

The Protectors: The Petrova Twist, Scholastic Inc., 1987.
The Jet Fighter Trap, Scholastic Inc., 1987.

YOUNG ADULT NOVELS

Blind Date, Scholastic Inc., 1986.
Twisted, Scholastic Inc., 1986.
Broken Date ("Crosswinds" series), Simon & Schuster (New York City), 1988.
The Baby-Sitter, Scholastic Inc., 1989.
Phone Calls, Archway (New York City), 1990.
Curtains, Archway, 1990.
The Boyfriend, Scholastic Inc., 1990.
Beach Party ("Point Horror" series), Scholastic Inc., 1990.
How I Broke up with Ernie, Archway, 1990.
Snowman, Scholastic Inc., 1991.
The Girlfriend, Scholastic Inc., 1991.
Baby-Sitter 2, Scholastic Inc., 1991.
Beach House, Scholastic Inc., 1992.
Hit and Run, Scholastic Inc., 1992.
Hitchhiker, Scholastic Inc., 1993.
Baby-Sitter 3, Scholastic Inc., 1993.
The Dead Girlfriend, Scholastic Inc., 1993.
Halloween Night, Scholastic Inc., 1993.
Call Waiting, Scholastic Inc., 1994.
Halloween Night 2, Scholastic Inc., 1994.

"FEAR STREET" SERIES; PUBLISHED BY ARCHWAY

The New Girl, 1989.
The Surprise Party, 1990.
The Stepsister, 1990.
Missing, 1990.
Halloween Party, 1990.
The Wrong Number, 1990.
The Sleepwalker, 1991.
Ski Weekend, 1991.
Silent Night, 1991.
The Secret Bedroom, 1991.
The Overnight, 1991.
Lights Out, 1991.
Haunted, 1991.
The Fire Game, 1991.
The Knife, 1992.
Prom Queen, 1992.
First Date, 1992.
The Best Friend, 1992.

Sunburn, 1993.
The Cheater, 1993.
The New Boy, 1994.
Bad Dreams, 1994.
The Dare, 1994.
Double Date, 1994.
The First Horror, 1994.
The Mind Reader, 1994.
One Evil Summer, 1994.
The Second Horror, 1994.
The Third Horror, 1994.
The Thrill Club, 1994.
College Weekend, 1995.
Final Grade, 1995.
The Stepsister 2, 1995.
Switched, 1995.
Truth or Dare, 1995.
Wrong Number 2, 1995.

"FEAR STREET: SUPER CHILLER" SERIES; PUBLISHED BY ARCHWAY

Party Summer, 1992.
Goodnight Kiss, 1992.
Silent Night 2, 1993.
Broken Hearts, 1993.
The Dead Lifeguard, 1994.
Bad Moonlight, 1995.
Dead End, 1995.

"FEAR STREET: CHEERLEADERS" SERIES; PUBLISHED BY ARCHWAY

The First Evil, 1992.
The Second Evil, 1992.
The Third Evil, 1992.
The New Evil, 1994.

"FEAR STREET SAGA" SERIES; PUBLISHED BY ARCHWAY

The Betrayal, 1993.
The Secret, 1993.
The Burning, 1993.

"GOOSEBUMPS" SERIES; PUBLISHED BY SCHOLASTIC INC.

Welcome to Dead House, 1992.
Stay Out of the Basement, 1992.
Monster Blood, 1992.
Say Cheese and Die, 1992.
The Curse of the Mummy's Tomb, 1993.
Let's Get Invisible, 1993.
Night of the Living Dummy, 1993.
The Girl Who Cried Monster, 1993.

Welcome to Camp Nightmare, 1993.
The Ghost Next Door, 1993.
The Haunted Mask, 1993.
Be Careful What You Wish For, 1993.
Piano Lessons Can Be Murder, 1993.
The Werewolf of Fever Swamp, 1993.
You Can't Scare Me, 1994.
One Day at Horrorland, 1994.
Why I'm Afraid of Bees, 1994.
Monster Blood 2, 1994.
Deep Trouble, 1994.
The Scarecrow Walks at Midnight, 1994.
Go Eat Worms!, 1994.
Ghost Beach, 1994.
Return of the Mummy, 1994.
Phantom of the Auditorium, 1994.
Attack of the Mutant, 1994.
My Hairiest Adventure, 1994.
A Night in Terror Tower, 1995.
The Cuckoo Clock of Doom, 1995.
Monster Blood 3, 1995.
It Came from Beneath the Sink, 1995.
The Night of the Living Dummy 2, 1995.
The Barking Ghost, 1995.
The Horror at Camp Jellyjam, 1995.
Revenge of the Lawn Gnomes, 1995.
A Shocker on Shock Street, 1995.
The Haunted Mask 2, 1995.
The Headless Ghost, 1995.
The Abominable Snowman of Pasadena, 1995.
How I Got My Shrunken Head, 1996.
Night of the Living Dummy 3, 1996.
Bad Hare Day, 1996.
Egg Monsters from Mars, 1996.
The Beast from the East, 1996.
Say Cheese and Die—Again!, 1996.
Ghost Camp, 1996.
How to Kill a Monster, 1996.

Author of *Tales to Give You Goosebumps,* and *More Tales to Give You Goosebumps.* Also author of "Give Yourself Goosebumps" series, including *Escape from the Carnival of Horrors, Tick Tock, You're Dead, Trapped in Bat Wing Hall, The Deadly Experiments of Dr. Eeek, Night in Werewolf Woods, Beware the Purple Peanut Butter, Under the Magician's Spell,* and *The Curse of the Creeping Coffin.*

"SPACE CADETS" SERIES; PUBLISHED BY SCHOLASTIC INC.

Jerks-in-Training, 1991.
Losers in Space, 1991.
Bozos on Patrol, 1992.

ADULT NOVEL

Superstitious (horror), Warner Books (New York City), 1995.

ADAPTATIONS: The "Goosebumps" series was produced by Scholastic Inc. as a live-action television series for the Fox Television Network beginning in 1995.

SIDELIGHTS: R. L. Stine has sold more than 90 million books, yet his name is unfamiliar to many adult readers. This best-selling author's success is based on his popularity among children and teens, who purchase the titles in his "Fear Street" and "Goosebumps" horror series at a rate of more than 1 million copies each month. A new book in each series is released every month, making Stine one of the most prolific authors of all time. To keep up with the demand for his frightening tales, Stine must turn out some twenty pages of manuscript six days a week. The result has not pleased all critics, some of whom dismiss his work as insignificant. But teachers, librarians, and parents report that many youngsters who were previously uninterested in books turned into avid readers after becoming hooked on Stine. The author himself once told *CA:* "I believe that kids as well as adults are entitled to books of no socially redeeming value."

Stine never wanted to be anything but a writer, and by the age of nine he was creating his own magazines filled with short stories and jokes. In college, he was editor of the campus humor magazine for three years. After graduation, he taught junior high school for one year, then set out for New York City in search of a job in magazine publishing. He paid his dues working for movie and fan magazines, and for a trade publication called *Soft Drink Industry,* then began a sixteen-year stint as an editor for Scholastic Inc., which publishes many classroom magazines and children's books. Stine worked on several titles before finally becoming editor of *Bananas,* a humor magazine for children aged twelve and older. He was thirty-two at the time and felt that he had achieved his life's ambition.

But greater success than he had ever dreamed of was still in store for him. For all his work in publishing, Stine had never published a book. His work on *Bananas* impressed an editor at Dutton, who asked him to create a humor book for children. *How To Be Funny: An Extremely Silly Guidebook* was published in 1978 and led to a long string of funny books, many of which were published under the name "Jovial Bob Stine." When financial difficulties led to Stine being fired from Scholastic in 1985, he stepped up his career as a book author, turning out action-adventure and "twist-a-plot" stories (which allowed the readers to direct the action) in addition to his humorous story and joke books. In 1986, the editorial director at Scholastic asked him to try writing a horror novel for young adults. Stine obliged with *Blind Date,* and was pleasantly surprised at the book's success.

Young-adult horror was a fast-growing genre, and Stine proved he could duplicate the appeal of *Blind Date* with two subsequent scary tales, *Twisted* and *The Baby-Sitter.* Stine's wife Jane, who is also involved in the publishing industry, suggested that he try to come up with an idea for a series. Thus "Fear Street," a horror series designed for readers aged nine to fourteen, was born. Fear Street is a place where terrible things happen and where "your worst nightmares live," according to copy on the covers of the early titles. The main characters change from one book to the next, but all attend Shadyside High—a fictional school with an appalling frequency of murder. After "Fear Street" came the idea for "Goosebumps," a less gory but still spooky series for 8-to 11-year-old readers. Both "Fear Street" and "Goosebumps" rely on cliff-hanger endings in each chapter to keep readers turning the pages. Stine also works hard to make his fictional characters speak and act like real, modern kids, and he freely admits to using "cheap thrills" and "disgusting, gross things" to pump up the appeal of his stories, as he was quoted as saying in a *Time* article by Paul Gray.

In 1995, Stine took another big step in his career: publishing his first novel for adults, a horror story called *Superstitious.* Contrasting the book with Stine's young-adult offerings, a *Publishers Weekly* reviewer comments that in *Superstitious,* "several characters . . . curse, enjoy X-rated sex and die gruesomely detailed deaths." Characterizing Stine's writing as "crude yet functional," the reviewer concedes that "even those with minimal attention spans will keep turning pages," and concludes that the book is "about as sophisticated, though as effective, as jumping out from a dark corner and yelling 'boo!'"

BIOGRAPHICAL/CRITICAL SOURCES:

PERIODICALS

Chicago Tribune, July 12, 1994, section 7, p. 1; December 6, 1994, section 7, p. 6.
English Journal, March, 1988, p. 86; April, 1989, p. 88.
Magazine of Fantasy and Science Fiction, August, 1995, p. 5.
New York Times, May 8, 1995, p. D8.
Publishers Weekly, August 22, 1986, p. 102; July 10, 1987, p. 71; June 9, 1989, p. 68; June 8, 1990, p. 56; September 19, 1994, p. 26; June 19, 1995, p. 47; July 17, 1995, pp. 208-209.
School Library Journal, November, 1986, pp. 108-109.
Time, August 2, 1993, p. 54.
USA Today, December 2, 1993, p. D6; October 27, 1994, p. D8; April 6, 1995, p. D4.
Voice of Youth Advocates, April, 1987, pp. 33, 34; December, 1987, p. 238; October, 1990, p. 220; February, 1991, p. 368; April, 1991, p. 9; June, 1991, p. 114; April, 1992, p. 36; August, 1992, p. 180; October, 1992, p. 232; December, 1992, p. 296; February, 1993, p. 360; April, 1993, pp. 20, 30, 47; June, 1993, p. 105; April, 1994, pp. 40, 41; August, 1994, p. 150; December, 1994, p. 290.
Washington Post, August 7, 1994, pp. B1, B4.*

* * *

STOWE, Leland   1899-1994

PERSONAL: Born November 10, 1899, in Southbury, CT; died January 16, 1994, in Ann Arbor, MI; son of Frank Philip (in lumber business) and Eva Sarah (Noe) Stowe; married Ruth F. Bernot, September 27, 1924 (marriage ended); married Theodora F. Calauz, June 17, 1952; children: (first marriage) Bruce B., Alan A. *Education:* Wesleyan University, A.B., 1921. *Politics:* Independent. *Religion:* Protestant.

CAREER: Worcester Telegram, Worcester, MA, reporter, 1921-22; *New York Herald,* New York City, staff reporter, 1923-24; news editor for *Pathe News,* 1924-26; *New York Herald Tribune,* New York City, staff reporter, 1924, 1926, Paris correspondent, 1926-35, political correspondent in North and South America, 1936-39; *Chicago Daily News,* Chicago,

IL, war correspondent in England, Finland, Norway, Hungary, Yugoslavia, Bulgaria, Romania, Turkey, Albania, and Greece, 1939-40, and in China, Burma, India, Thailand, Malaya, Indo-China, Iran, the Soviet Union, and Libya, 1941-43; American Broadcasting Co., New York City, radio commentator, 1944-46; lecturer and freelance writer, beginning 1947; University of Michigan, Ann Arbor, professor of journalism, 1956-69. Freelance war correspondent in France, Belgium, and Germany, 1944, and Italy and Greece, 1945; radio commentator for Mutual Broadcasting System, 1945-46; director of news and information service of Radio Free Europe, 1952-54.

AWARDS, HONORS: Pulitzer Prize for foreign correspondence, 1930, for coverage of events in Paris in 1929; Legion of Honor (France), 1931; M.A. from Wesleyan University, 1936, and Harvard University, 1945; distinguished service awards from Sigma Delta Chi, Overseas Press Club of America, and University of Missouri's School of Journalism, all 1941, for war reporting from Finland and Norway; LL.D. from Wesleyan University, 1944, and Hobart College, 1946; Military Cross (Greece), 1945; James L. McConaughty Award, Wesleyan University, 1963.

WRITINGS:

Nazi Germany Means War, Faber (London), 1933, published as *Nazi Means War,* Whittlesey House (New York City), 1934.
No Other Road to Freedom, Knopf (New York City), 1941.
They Shall Not Sleep, Knopf, 1943.
While Time Remains, Knopf, 1946.
Target: You, Random House (New York City), 1949.
Conquest by Terror: The Story of Satellite Europe, Random House, 1951.
Crusoe of Lonesome Lake, Random House, 1959.
The Last Great Frontiersman: The Remarkable Adventures of Tom Lamb, Stoddart (Toronto), 1982.

Contributor of nearly one hundred articles to national magazines, including *Harper's, Life, Look, Nation,* and *New Republic.* Foreign editor of *Reporter,* 1949-50; roving editor of *Reader's Digest,* 1955-76.

Stowe's works are collected at the Mass Communications History Center, Madison, Wisconsin.

SIDELIGHTS: Pulitzer Prize-winning journalist Leland Stowe's noteworthy career was built around his coverage of the war years of the early twentieth century for such newspapers as the *New York Herald-Tribune* and the *Chicago Daily News.* An educator later in life, Stowe was also the author of several books, including *Nazi Germany Means War, Target: You,* and *Crusoe of Lonesome Lake.*

Stowe's journalistic career began after he graduated from Wesleyan University in 1921. While aspiring to become a novelist, the young Stowe got a job as a reporter at the *Worcester* (Massachusetts) *Telegram* to help him broaden his understanding of people and life in general. "To my good fortune, the *Telegram* of 1921-23 was an exceptional training ground for cub reporters," Stowe would later write; indeed, the experience he received there gained him entry to the prestigious *New York Herald* (later the *New York Herald- Tribune*), where he signed on as a reporter in 1922. By 1926 he was stationed in Paris, first as assistant to ace World War I correspondent Wilbur Forrest, and then promoted to bureau chief in 1927.

Stowe's term in Paris was highlighted by his Pulitzer Prize-winning stories on the Reparations Conference held there following World War I, as well as the creation of the Young Plan and the Bank for International Settlements, all designed to convey financial restitution from Germany to various war-torn sites throughout Europe. Compiled over four months of interviews and intricate maneuverings and consisting of almost twenty-four exclusive stories on the unfolding of this international diplomatic action, Stowe's coverage of the events between February to June 1929 was cited by the Pulitzer Prize committee as "the best example of correspondence during the year, the test being cleanness and terseness of style; judicious, well-balanced and well-informed interpretative writing, which shall make clear the significance of the subject covered in the correspondence or which shall promote international understanding and appreciation."

Stowe returned to the United States in 1935, working as a roving foreign correspondent throughout the Western hemisphere. Convinced that Hitler's Nazi movement was a threat to the newfound peace in Europe, Stowe published *Nazi Germany Means War* in 1933; ironically, the book drew little interest and his warnings went unheeded. After the outbreak of renewed German aggressions he served as a war correspondent, covering the early developments of World War II in Europe for the *Chicago Daily News.* Stowe would do two seventeen-month tours through Europe, travel with seven different armies, and report from forty-four countries over four continents before it was all over. His excellent work during World War II made Stowe one of the most esteemed journalists of his generation—the last of the pre-television war correspondents.

Stowe's later articles on the war, for both newspapers and radio, focused on events in Asia. Among the major stories during this phase of his career was his discovery that the Chinese government was stockpiling U.S. lend-lease weapons for use against Communist insurgents rather than implementing them against their Japanese war enemy. In the late 1940s and early 1950s he served as foreign editor of *Reporter* magazine and as the news director of Radio Free Europe. From 1956 to 1969 Stowe was a professor of journalism at the University of Michigan. During and after his academic career he acted as a roving editor and writer for *Reader's Digest* magazine.

Throughout Stowe's life he published a number of books, his final work being the 1982 biography *The Last Great Frontiersman: The Remarkable Adventures of Tom Lamb.* He once explained to *Contemporary Authors* that his chief motivation was "to inform the public in the United States and other countries of important political and social developments directly affecting their lives." His writings and lectures—totaling over three hundred in the United States—included major forewarnings of the coming of World War II (1933-39), the assured ultimate victory of Britain and her allies over Nazi Germany (1941-43), the spread of Communist regimes and controls in Europe and China as a result of World War II (1941-45), and the inevitable Soviet nuclear menace to the United States (1946-57), which was the focus of his 1952 work *Conquest by Terror: The Story of Satellite Europe.*

"I am certain that the Soviet-American proliferation of nuclear missiles and other related weapons, still uncurbed, constitutes the greatest, almost inestimable peril not only to our people but to most of mankind," Stowe prophetically noted in his later years. "Next to this the energy crisis . . . threatens to undermine, if not destroy, democratic governments, including our own and much or most of free enterprise systems as we now know them."

BIOGRAPHICAL/CRITICAL SOURCES:

BOOKS

Dictionary of Literary Biography, Volume 29: *American Newspaper Journalists, 1926-1950,* Gale (Detroit), 1984.

Hohenberg, John, *Foreign Correspondence,* Columbia University Press (New York City), 1964.
Knightley, Philip, *The First Casualty,* Harcourt (New York City), 1975.
Mathews, Joseph J., *Reporting the Wars,* University of Minnesota Press (Minneapolis), 1957.

OBITUARIES:

PERIODICALS

Chicago Tribune, January 17, 1994, section 4, p. 9; January 23, 1994, section 2, p. 6.
New York Times, January 18, 1994, pp. B10, D23.
Washington Post, January 18, 1994, p. D8.*

*   *   *

STREETEN, Paul Patrick   1917-

PERSONAL: Born July 18, 1917, in Vienna, Austria; married Ann Higgins, June 9, 1951; children: Patricia Doria, Judith Andrea; stepchildren: Jay D. Palmer. *Education:* University of Aberdeen, M.A., 1940; Balliol College, Oxford, B.A. (with first class honors), 1947, M.A., 1952; attended Nuffield College, Oxford, 1947-48.

ADDRESSES: Home—Box 92, Spencertown, NY 12165.

CAREER: Oxford University, Oxford, England, fellow of Balliol College, 1948-66 and 1968-78, university lecturer and associate of Institute of Economics and Statistics, 1960-64, director of Institute of Commonwealth Studies and warden of Queen Elizabeth House, 1968-78; Ministry of Overseas Development, London, England, deputy director-general of economic planning staff, 1964-66; University of Sussex, Institute of Development Studies, Stanmer, Brighton, England, professor of economics, acting director, and fellow, 1966-68, member and vice-chairman of governing body; Boston University, Boston, MA, professor of economics, 1980-93, director, Center for Asian Development, 1980-94, director, World Development Institute, 1984-89, professor emeritus, 1993—. Visiting professor, Stanford University, 1956; visiting professor, University of Buenos Aires, 1963; visiting professor, Economic Development Institute of the World Bank, 1972; Jean Monet Professor, European University Institute, Florence, Italy, 1991; visiting lecturer at many universities throughout Europe. Research fellow, Johns Hopkins University, 1955-56; fellow, Center for Advanced Studies, Wesleyan University, 1962. Member of council, Walloon Institute of Economic Development; member of provisional council, University of Mauritius, 1965; UNESCO, member of United Kingdom National Commission, 1966, and vice-chairman of Advisory Committee on Social Sciences; member of the board, Commonwealth Development Corp., 1967-72; member of council, Dominion Students Trust, London; member of Africa Publications Trust. Member of Royal Commission of Environmental Pollution, 1974-76. Special advisor to the World Bank, 1976-80. Consultant to the United Nations Development Program on human development, 1990-96. Member of the board of trustees, Foundation for International Studies, University of Malta; member of advisory committee, Arab Planning Institute, Kuwait. *Military service:* British Army and Royal Marine Commandos, Hampshire Regiment, 1941-43; became sergeant; wounded in Sicily.

MEMBER: Society for International Development (part president of United Kingdom chapter), Royal Economic Society, American Economic Association, United Oxford and Cambridge Club.

AWARDS, HONORS: Rockefeller fellow in United States, 1950-51; LL.D., University of Aberdeen, 1980; honorary fellow, Institute of Development Studies, University of Sussex; honorary fellow, Balliol College, Oxford; Development Prize, Justus Liebib University, Gissen, Germany, 1987; D. Litt., University of Malta, 1992,

WRITINGS:

(Translator) Gunnar Myrdal, *The Political Element in the Development of Economic Theory,* Routledge & Kegan Paul (England), 1953.
Economic Integration: Aspects and Problems, Sijthoff (Rockville, MD), 1962, 2nd edition, 1964.
(With Diane Elson) *Diversification and Development: The Case of Coffee,* Praeger (New York City), 1971.
Aid to Africa, Praeger, 1972.
The Frontiers of Development Studies, Macmillan (New York City), 1972.
Trade Strategies for Development, Macmillan, 1973.
The Limits of Development Research, Pergamon (Elmsford, NY), 1974.
(With Santaya Lall) *Foreign Investment, Trans-nationals and the Developing Countries,* Macmillan, 1977.
Development Perspectives, Macmillan, 1981.
First Things First, Oxford University Press, 1981.

What Price Food? Agricultural Policies in Developing Countries, Macmillan, 1987.
Mobilizing Human Potential, UNDP, 1989.
Paul Streeten in South Africa: Reflections on a Journey, Development Society of South Africa (Innesdale, South Africa), 1992.
Strategies for Human Development, Handelshotskilens Forlag (Copenhagen, Denmark), 1994.
Thinking about Development, Cambridge University Press (New York City), 1995.

Also contributor to *UNESCO Dictionary of Political and Social Terms* and *Collier's Encyclopedia;* contributor of about 100 articles to journals in England, Germany, France, Belgium, Italy, Canada, and India. Contributor to books, including *Economic Growth in Great Britain,* edited by P. D. Henderson, Weidenfeld & Nicolson, 1966; *The Multinational Enterprise,* edited by John Harry Dunning, Praeger, 1972; *Pioneers in Development,* edited by Gerald M. Meier and Dudley Seers, Oxford University Press, 1985; and *A World Fit for People,* edited by Uner Kirdar and Leonard Silk, New York University Press, 1994. Former secretary and member of editorial board, "Oxford Economic Papers."

EDITOR

(Author of foreword) Grunnar Myrdal, *Value in Social Theory,* Routledge & Kegan Paul, 1958.
(With M. Lipton) *The Crisis of Indian Planning,* Oxford University Press, 1968.
Unfashionable Economics: Essays in Honor of Lord Balogh, Weidenfeld & Nicolson (England), 1970.
(With Hugh Corbet, and contributor) *Commonwealth Policy in a Global Context,* Cass, 1971.
(With Richard Jolly) *Recent Issues in World Development,* Pergamon, 1982.
Beyond Adjustment: The Asian Experience, International Monetary Fund (Washington, DC), 1988.
(With others) *The United Nations and the Bretton Woods Institutions: New Challenges for the 21st Century,* Macmillan, 1995.

Also editor of *World Development* and Oxford University Institute of Economics and Statistics *Bulletin,* 1961-64.

WORK IN PROGRESS: Research on global issues and on human development and basic needs.

SIDELIGHTS: Paul Patrick Streeten told *CA:* "Writing for me is as essential as breathing, or rather as refreshing and invigorating as breathing good, bracing, mountain air. When I write I feel more fully alive. It serves as occupational therapy when I am depressed, and as additional mood enhancer when cheerful, and when writing I am happier than in almost any other activity. But, though much of my writing is policy-oriented and aims at changing the world, I am not deeply worried if my advice is not accepted. In fact, I am always surprised when somebody tells me he or she has actually read one of my pieces. And a favorable review (that understands what I have written) makes the sun shine.

"Having a grasshopper mind that never likes dwelling for long on any one subject, I find it refreshing to graze on new pastures, including those outside economics. This was useful when I was a tutorial fellow at Balliol College, Oxford (1948-66), who had to teach a wide range of subjects in the School of Philosophy, Politics and Economics. This was before the present days, when economists have become ever more specialized, cultivating no longer fields or areas but confining themselves to patches.

"I always wished I had learned more mathematics. Without this grounding, one feels nowadays like a handloom weaver in the days after the introduction of the power loom. But the thought is made bearable by the fact that most of the power loom weavers seem to be weaving the Emperor's clothes. The rigor achieved by mathematical modeling is all too often the *rigormortis*. The fuzziness occurs when mathematical symbols are identified with real entities, such as individuals, households, firms, or farms. And the models, shapely and elegant though they may be, too often lack the vital parts."

BIOGRAPHICAL/CRITICAL SOURCES:

BOOKS

Lall, Sanjaya and Frances Stewart, *Theory and Reality in Development: Essays in Honour of Paul Streeten,* Macmillan, 1986.

*   *   *

SUCHLICKI, Jaime   1939-

PERSONAL: Born December 8, 1939, in Havana, Cuba; U.S. citizen; son of Salomon (in business) and Ana (Greinstein) Suchlicki; married Carol Meyer, January 26, 1964; children: Michael Ian, Kevin Donald, Joy Michelle. *Education:* Attended University of Havana, 1959-60; University of Miami, A.B. (cum laude), 1964, M.A., 1965; Texas Christian University, Ph.D., 1967.

ADDRESSES: Office—Graduate School of International Studies, University of Miami, 1531 Brescia Ave., Miami, FL 33124.

CAREER: University of Miami, Coral Gables, FL, assistant professor, 1967-71, associate professor, 1971-75, professor of history, 1975—; Center for Advanced International Studies, research associate, 1967-70, associate director, 1979-80; Institute of Interamerican Studies, associate director, 1970-71, director, 1971-73, 1982-92; North-South Center, executive director, 1992-94.

MEMBER: Conference on Latin American History, ADL (B'nai B'rith), Phi Alpha Theta.

WRITINGS:

The Cuban Revolution: A Documentary Bibliography, 1952-1968, Center for Advanced International Studies, University of Miami, 1968.
University Students and Revolution in Cuba, 1920-1968, University of Miami Press, 1969.
(Editor and author of introduction) *Cuba, Castro and Revolution,* University of Miami Press, 1972.
(With Irving B. Reed and Dodd L. Harvey) *The Latin American Scene of the Seventies: A Basic Fact Book,* Center for Advanced International Studies, University of Miami, 1972.
Cuba: From Columbus to Castro, Scribner (New York City), 1974, 2nd edition, Pergamon (Elmsford, NY), 1986.
(With staff of Cuban Studies Conference) *Cuba: Continuity and Change,* Institute of Interamerican Studies, University of Miami, 1985.
Historical Dictionary of Cuba, Scarecrow (Metuchen, NJ), 1988.
Mexico: From Montezuma to NAFTA, Brossey, 1996.

Contributor to *Latin American Panorama,* edited by Robert E. McNicoll, Putnam (New York City), 1968, and *Students and Politics in Developing Nations,* edited by Donald K. Emmerson, Praeger (New York City), 1968. Also contributor to encyclopedias and professional journals; editor, *Journal of Interamerican Studies and World Affairs,* 1982—.

SUTPHEN, Dick
  See SUTPHEN, Richard Charles

* * *

SUTPHEN, Richard Charles   1937-
  (Dick Sutphen; Todd Richards, a pseudonym)

PERSONAL: Surname pronounced "Sut-fen"; born April 3, 1937, in Omaha, NE; son of Earle Charles (a salesperson) and Jennie E. (a secretary; maiden name, Roberts) Sutphen; married second wife, Judith Ann, July 5, 1969 (divorced); married Trenna Laraine (divorced); married Nancy Tara, March 2, 1984; children: (from first three marriages) Scott, Todd, Steven, Jessi, Travis; (from fourth marriage) Hunter, Cheyenne. *Education:* Attended Art Center School, Los Angeles, CA, 1956-57. *Politics:* Democrat. *Religion:* "Metaphysics." *Avocational interests:* Zen, Eastern philosophy, martial arts, running, tennis.

ADDRESSES: Home—P.O. Box 38, Malibu, CA 90265.

CAREER: Art director for advertising firms in Omaha, NE, 1955, 1958-59; *Better Homes and Gardens,* Des Moines, IA, designer, 1959-60; Knox Reeves Advertising, Minneapolis, MN, art director, 1964-65; Dick Sutphen Studios, Inc., Minneapolis, and Scottsdale, AZ, operator of advertising design and illustration services and publisher of books for the advertising market, 1965-76; Sutphen Corp./Valley of the Sun Publishing, Malibu, CA, owner, 1976—. Conductor of Sutphen Seminars, 1976—. Designer of contemporary (studio) cards for Hallmark, and creator of a line of Arizona-oriented studio cards and framed prints. Publisher of *Master of Life* (a New Age quarterly periodical/catalogue). Has appeared on numerous nationally-syndicated radio and television shows.

AWARDS, HONORS: Nomination for Bram Stoker Award, Horror Writers of America, 1991, for *Sexpunks and Savage Sagas.*

WRITINGS:

(Under pseudonym Todd Richards) *Your Voice Makes My Knees Tickle!* (verse), Valley of the Sun (Malibu, CA), 1972.

UNDER NAME DICK SUTPHEN

(Editor) *Old Engravings and Illustrations,* Dick Sutphen Studios (Minneapolis, MN, and Scottsdale, AZ), two volumes, 1965.
(Editor) *Uncensored Situations,* Dick Sutphen Studios, 1966.
(Editor) *The Wildest Old Engravings and Illustrations,* Dick Sutphen Studios, 1966.
(Editor) *Designy Devices,* Dick Sutphen Studios, 1967.
Antiques, Filigree and Rococo, Dick Sutphen Studios, 1967.
The Mad Old Ads, McGraw (New York City), 1967.
Studio Cards, Famous American Studios, 1968.
The Encyclopedia of Small Spot Engravings, Valley of the Sun, 1969.
Sometimes the Words of Love Have No Words, Valley of the Sun, 1969.
A Deep Breath of Yesterday, Valley of the Sun, 1970.
I Love to Have You Touch Me, Valley of the Sun, 1971.
Sex, Liquor, Tobacco, and Candy Are Bad for You, Valley of the Sun, 1972.
Know Thy Higher Self, Valley of the Sun, 1972.
Burying Pompeii, Valley of the Sun, 1973.
Open Hand Love (poems), Valley of the Sun, 1975.
You Were Born Again to Be Together, Pocket Books (New York City), 1976.
The Pen and Ink and Cross Hatch Styles of the Early Illustrators, Art Direction Book (New York City), 1976.
Attention-Getting Old Engravings, Art Direction Book, 1976.
Past Life Hypnotic Regression Course, Valley of the Sun, 1977.
The Dick Sutphen Assertiveness Training Course, Valley of the Sun, 1978.
Past Lives, Future Loves, Pocket Books, 1978.
Unseen Influences, Pocket Books, 1980.
(With Trenna Sutphen) *The Master of Life Manual,* Valley of the Sun, 1980.
(With T. Sutphen) *Bushido SST Graduate Manual,* Valley of the Sun, 1981.
(With Lauren Leigh Taylor) *Past-Life Therapy in Action,* Valley of the Sun, 1983.
Rattlesnake Karma, Valley of the Sun, 1984.
Poet: 1970-1985, Valley of the Sun, 1985.
Enlightenment Transcripts, Valley of the Sun, 1986.
Sedona: Psychic Energy Vortexes, Valley of the Sun, 1986.
Lighting the Light Within, Valley of the Sun, 1987.
Predestined Love, Pocket Books, 1988.

Finding Your Answers Within, Pocket Books, 1989.
Earthly Purpose, Pocket Books, 1990.
The Oracle Within, Pocket Books, 1991.
Heart Magic (short stories), Valley of the Sun, 1992.
The Spiritual Path Guidebook, Valley of the Sun, 1992.
Sexpunks and Savage Sagas (anthology; horror fiction), Spine-Tingling Press, 1992.
Reinventing Yourself, Valley of the Sun, 1993.
Radical Spirituality, Valley of the Sun, 1995.

Also creator/producer of over three hundred hypnosis and self-help audio-and videotape programs for Valley of the Sun.

BIOGRAPHICAL/CRITICAL SOURCES:

BOOKS

Weisman, Alan, *We, Immortals,* Pocket Books, 1979.

PERIODICALS

American Artist, June, 1967.

T-V

TARRANT, Wilma
See SHERMAN, Jory (Tecumseh)

*   *   *

THIELE, Colin (Milton)   1920-

PERSONAL: Surname is pronounced Tee-lee; born November 16, 1920, in Eudunda, South Australia; son of Carl Wilhelm (a farmer) and Anna (Wittwer) Thiele; married Rhonda Gill (a teacher and artist), March 17, 1945; children: Janne Louise (Mrs. Jeffrey Minge), Sandra Gwenyth (Mrs. Ron Paterson). *Education:* University of Adelaide, B.A., 1941, Diploma of Education, 1947; Adelaide Teachers College, Diploma of Teaching, 1942.

ADDRESSES: Home—Endeavour Ln., Dayboro, Queensland 4521, Australia.

CAREER: Writer. South Australian Education Department, English teacher and senior master at high school in Port Lincoln, 1946-55, senior master at high school in Brighton, 1956; Wattle Park Teachers College, Wattle Park, South Australia, lecturer, 1957-61, senior lecturer in English, 1962-63, vice-principal, 1964, principal, 1965-72; director, Murray Park College of Advanced Education, 1973; Wattle Park Teachers Centre, Wattle Park, principal, 1973-80. Commonwealth Literary Fund lecturer on Australian literature; speaker at conferences on literature and education in Australia and the United States. *Military service:* Royal Australian Air Force, 1942-45.

MEMBER: Australian College of Education (fellow), Australian Society of Authors (council member, 1965—; president, 1987-90), English Teachers Association (president, 1957), South Australian Fellowship of Writers (president, 1961).

AWARDS, HONORS: W. J. Miles Poetry Prize, 1944, for *Progress to Denial;* Commonwealth Jubilee Literary Competitions, first prize in radio play section, for "Edge of Ice," and first prize in radio feature section, both 1951; South Australian winner in World Short Story Quest, 1952; Fulbright scholar in United States and Canada, 1959-60; Grace Leven Poetry Prize, 1961, for *Man in a Landscape;* Commonwealth Literary Fund fellowship, 1967-68; *Blue Fin* was placed on the Honours List, Hans Anderson Award, 1972; Visual Arts Board award, 1975, for *Magpie Island;* Austrian State Prize for Childrens Books, 1979, for *The SKNUKS,* and 1986, for *Pinquo;* Book of the Year Award, Childrens Book Council of Australia, 1982, for *The Valley Between;* Mystery Writers of America citation for *The Fire in the Stone;* numerous commendations in Australian Childrens Book Council awards.

WRITINGS:

Progress to Denial (poems), Jindyworobak, 1945.
Splinters and Shards (poems), Jindyworobak, 1945.
The Golden Lightning (poems), Jindyworobak, 1951.
(Editor) *Jindyworobak Anthology* (verse), Jindyworobak, 1953.
Man in a Landscape (poems), Rigby (Australia), 1960.
(Editor with Ian Mudie) *Australian Poets Speak,* Rigby, 1961.

(Editor) *Favourite Australian Stories,* Rigby, 1963.

(Editor, and author of commentary and notes) *Handbook to Favourite Australian Stories,* Rigby, 1964.

In Charcoal and Conte (poems), Rigby, 1966.

Heysen of Hahndorf (biography), Rigby, 1968, Tri-Ocean, 1969.

Barossa Valley Sketchbook, illustrations by Jeanette McLeod, Tri-Ocean, 1968.

Labourers in the Vineyard (novel), Rigby, 1970.

Selected Verse (1940-1970), Rigby, 1970.

Coorong, photographs by Mike McKelvey, Rigby, 1972.

Range without Man: The North Flinders, Rigby, 1974.

The Little Desert, photographs by Jocelyn Burt, Rigby, 1975.

Grains of Mustard Seed, South Australia Education Department, 1975.

Heysen's Early Hahndorf, Rigby, 1976.

The Bight, photographs by McKelvey, Rigby, 1976.

Lincoln's Place, illustrations by Robert Ingpen, Rigby, 1978.

Maneater Man, Rigby, 1979.

The Seeds Inheritance, Lutheran Publishing House, 1986.

South Australia Revisited, illustrations by Charlotte Balfour, Rigby, 1986.

Something to Crow About, illustrations by Rex Milstead, Commonwealth Bank, 1986.

Coorong, illustrations by Barbara Leslie, Wakefield Press, 1986.

A Welcome to Water, photographs by David Simpson and Ted James, Wakefield Press, 1986.

Ranger's Territory, Angus & Robertson (London), 1987.

CHILDREN'S BOOKS AND SCHOOL TEXTS

The State of Our State, Rigby, 1952.

(Editor and annotator) *Looking at Poetry,* Longmans, Green, 1960.

The Sun on the Stubble (childrens novel), Rigby, 1961.

Gloop the Gloomy Bunyip (childrens story in verse; also see below), illustrations by John Baily, Jacaranda, 1962.

(Editor with Greg Branson) *One-Act Plays for Secondary Schools,* Rigby, Books 1-2, 1962, one-volume edition of Books 1-2, 1963, Book 3, 1964, revised edition of Book 1 published as *Setting the Stage,* 1969, revised edition of Book 2 published as *The Living Stage,* 1970.

Storm Boy, illustrations by Baily, Rigby, 1963, Rand McNally (Chicago), 1966, new edition with illustrations by Ingpen, Rigby, 1974, film edition with photographs by David Kynoch, Rigby, 1976, original edition reprinted by Harper (New York City), 1978.

(Editor with Branson) *Beginners, Please* (anthology), Rigby, 1964.

February Dragon (childrens novel), Rigby, 1965, Harper, 1976.

The Rim of the Morning (short stories), Rigby, 1966.

Mrs. Munch and Puffing Billy, illustrations by Nyorie Bungey, Rigby, 1967, Tri-Ocean, 1968.

Yellow-Jacket Jock, illustrations by Clifton Pugh, F. W. Cheshire (Australia), 1969.

Blue Fin (childrens novel), illustrations by Roger Haldane, Rigby, 1969, Harper, 1974.

Flash Flood, illustrations by Jean Elder, Rigby, 1970.

Flip Flop and Tiger Snake, illustrations by Elder, Rigby, 1970.

Gloop the Bunyip (children's story in verse; contains material from *Gloop the Gloomy Bunyip*), illustrations by Helen Sallis, Rigby, 1970.

(Editor with Branson) *Plays for Young Players* (for primary schools), Rigby, 1970.

The Fire in the Stone, Rigby, 1973, Harper, 1974, film edition, Puffin Books (New York City), 1983.

Albatross Two, Rigby, 1974, published as *Fight against Albatross Two,* Harper, 1976.

Uncle Gustav's Ghosts, Rigby, 1974.

Magpie Island, illustrations by Haldane, Rigby, 1974, Puffin Books, 1981.

The Hammerhead Light, Rigby, 1976, Harper, 1977.

Storm Boy Picture Book, photographs by Kynoch, Rigby, 1976.

The Shadow on the Hills, Rigby, 1977, Harper, 1978.

The SKNUKS, illustrations by Mary Milton, Rigby, 1977.

River Murray Mary, illustrations by Ingpen, Rigby, 1979.

Ballander Boy, photographs by David Simpson, Rigby, 1979.

Chadwick's Chimney, illustrations by Ingpen, Methuen (Australia), 1980.

The Best of Colin Thiele, Rigby, 1980.

Tanya and Trixie, photographs by Simpson, Rigby, 1980.

Thiele Tales, Rigby, 1980.

The Valley Between, Rigby, 1981.

Little Tom Little, photographs by Simpson, Rigby, 1981.

Songs for My Thongs, Rigby, 1982.

The Undercover Secret, Rigby, 1982.

Pinquo, Rigby, 1983.

Coorong Captive, Rigby, 1985.

Seashores and Shadows, Walter McVitty Books, 1985, published as *Shadow Shark,* Harper, 1988.

Farmer Schulz's Ducks, Walter McVitty Books, 1986.

Shatterbelt, Walter McVitty Books, 1987.

Klontarf, Weldon (Australia), 1988.

The Ab-Diver, Horwitz, Grahame, 1988.

Jodies Journey, Walter McVitty Books, 1988.

Shatterbelt, Walter McVitty Books, 1989.

Stories Short and Tall, Weldon, 1989.

Poems in My Luggage, Omnibus Books, 1989.

Danny's Egg, Angus & Robertson, 1989, published in the United States as *Rotten Egg Paterson to the Rescue,* 1991.

Farmer Pelz's Pumpkins, illustrated by Lucinda Hunnam, Walter McVitty Books, 1990.

Emma Keppler, Walter McVitty Books, 1991.

Speedy, Omnibus Books, 1991.

The Australian ABC, illustrated by Wendy DePaauw, Weldon Kids, 1992.

The Australian Mother Goose, illustrated by DePaauw, Weldon Kids, 1992.

Aftershock, Walter McVitty Books, 1992.

Charlie Vet's Pet, illustrated by Michael Wright, Macmillan Australia, 1992.

Timmy, Walter McVitty Books, 1993.

Martin's Mountain, Lutheran Publishing House, 1993.

The March of Mother Duck, Walter McVitty Books, 1993.

Gemma's Christmas Eve, Open Book Publishers, 1994.

Reckless Rhymes, Walter McVitty Books, 1994.

(With Max Fatchen and Craig Smith) *Tea for Three,* Moondrake, 1994.

Maneater Man, Lansdowne (Australia), 1995.

Brahminy, Walter McVitty Books, 1995.

THE "PITCH, POTCH AND PATCH" STORIES SERIES

Patch Comes Home, Reading Rigby, 1982.

Potch Goes Down the Drain, Reading Rigby, 1984.

Pitch the Pony, Reading Rigby, 1984.

PLAYS

"Burke and Wills" (verse; first performed at Adelaide Radio Drama Festival, 1949), published in full in *On the Air,* edited by P. R. Smith, Angus & Robertson, 1959.

"Edge of Ice" (verse), first performed on radio, 1952.

"The Shark Fishers" (prose), first performed, 1954.

"Edward John Eyre" (verse), first performed at Adelaide Radio Drama Festival, 1962.

Author of other verse plays for radio, and radio and television features, documentaries, children's serials, and schools broadcast programs.

OTHER

National book reviewer for Australian Broadcasting Commission. Thiele's poetry and short stories have appeared in many anthologies and journals; also contributor of articles and reviews to periodicals.

ADAPTATIONS: Storm Boy and *Blue Fin* were made into feature films by the South Australian Film Corporation in 1976 and 1978, respectively; *The Fire in the Stone* was made into a television feature by the South Australian Film Corporation in 1983; *Danny's Egg* was made into a television feature by TCN 9 Sydney. *The Sun on the Stubble, The Shadow on the Hills, The Valley Between,* and *Uncle Gustav's Ghosts* were used to make a television mini-series of twelve half-hour episodes by an Australian-German consortium in 1996.

WORK IN PROGRESS: High Valley and *The Black Pyramid,* both children's books; *With Dew on My Boots,* an autobiographical account of the author's early life.

SIDELIGHTS: Colin Thiele told *CA:* "One of the tasks of the writer is indeed to 'hold the mirror up to Nature, to reveal humanity to humanity, to comment on the variousness of the human condition.' And although society and the environment in which people live have changed beyond recognition, and will continue to do so, human beings are still human beings. They still show human strengths and human weaknesses—kindness, cruelty, love, malice, wisdom, stupidity, and all the rest. They still suffer loneliness and rejection, still respond to love and compassion, still rise to heights of altruism and nobility, still stoop to depths of pettiness, perfidy, and meanness. In exploring these themes, it doesn't much matter whether the writer uses settings in Sleepy Hollow or at the Crossroads of the World—wherever they are. The universal verities of life can be revealed anywhere because they reside in the hearts of human beings, not in facades of city streets or ephemeral houses. It is to reflect these convictions that I hold up my particular mirror—unpolished and inadequate as it may be."

Thiele's children's books have been translated into numerous languages, including German, Russian, French, Italian, Chinese, Japanese, Spanish, Afrikaans, Swedish, Finnish, Greek, Danish, Dutch, and Czechoslovakian.

BIOGRAPHICAL/CRITICAL SOURCES:

BOOKS

Children's Literature Review, Volume 27, Gale (Detroit), 1992.
Contemporary Literary Criticism, Volume 17, Gale, 1981.
McVitty, Walter, *Innocence and Experience,* Nelson, 1981.
Something about the Author Autobiography Series, Gale, Volume 2, 1986.

PERIODICALS

Australian Book Review, Children's Supplement, 1964, 1967, 1969.
Books and Bookmen, July, 1968.
Bulletin of the Center for Children's Books, November, 1966.
Childhood Education, December, 1966, April, 1967.
Kirkus Reviews, January 1, 1966.
New York Times Book Review, May 1, 1966, February 23, 1975.
Young Readers Review, September, 1966.

* * *

TODD, H(erbert) E(atton) 1908-1988

PERSONAL: Born February 22, 1908, in London, England; died February 25, 1988; son of Henry Graves (a headmaster) and Minnie Elizabeth Todd; married Bertha Joyce Hughes, 1936 (died, 1968); children: Jonathan (died, 1964), Mark, Stephen. *Education:* Attended Christ's Hospital, Horsham, Sussex, England, 1919-25. *Religion:* Church of England.

CAREER: Houlder Brothers Ltd., London, shipping clerk, 1925-27; British Foreign and Colonial Corp., London, investment clerk, 1927-29; Bourne & Hollingsworth Ltd., London, hosiery underbuyer,

1929-31; F. G. Wigley & Co. Ltd., London, salesperson, 1931-47, director and sales manager, 1947-69. Children's Book Week storyteller in libraries and schools, beginning in 1953; broadcaster of Bobby Brewster stories on radio and television; broadcaster of children's musical programs. Performer in local operatic productions, 1945-62. *Military service:* Royal Air Force, 1940-45; became squadron leader.

MEMBER: Berkhamsted Amateur Operatic and Dramatic Society (choir master, 1948-52; chair, 1956-60; president, beginning 1961).

AWARDS, HONORS: White Rose Award, 1971, for *Bobby Brewster and the Ghost.*

WRITINGS:

JUVENILES

Bobby Brewster and the Winkers' Club, illustrated by Bryan Ward, Ward (London), 1949.
Bobby Brewster, illustrated by Lilian Buchanan, Brockhampton Press (Leicester, England), 1954.
Bobby Brewster—Bus Conductor, illustrated by Buchanan, Brockhampton Press, 1954.
Bobby Brewster's Shadow, illustrated by Buchanan, Brockhampton Press, 1956.
Bobby Brewster's Bicycle, illustrated by Buchanan, Brockhampton Press, 1957.
Bobby Brewster's Camera, illustrated by Buchanan, Brockhampton Press, 1959.
Bobby Brewster's Wallpaper, illustrated by Buchanan, Brockhampton Press, 1961.
Bobby Brewster's Conker, illustrated by Buchanan, Brockhampton Press, 1963.
Bobby Brewster—Detective, illustrated by Buchanan, Brockhampton Press, 1964.
Bobby Brewster's Potato, illustrated by Buchanan, Brockhampton Press, 1964.
Bobby Brewster and the Ghost, illustrated by Buchanan, Brockhampton Press, 1966.
Bobby Brewster's Kite, illustrated by Buchanan, Brockhampton Press, 1967.
Bobby Brewster's Scarecrow, illustrated by Buchanan, Brockhampton Press, 1968.
Bobby Brewster's Torch, illustrated by Buchanan, Brockhampton Press, 1969.
Bobby Brewster's Balloon Race, illustrated by Buchanan, Brockhampton Press, 1970.
Bobby Brewster's First Magic, illustrated by Buchanan, Brockhampton Press, 1970.
Bobby Brewster's Typewriter, illustrated by Buchanan, Brockhampton Press, 1971.

Bobby Brewster's Bee, illustrated by Buchanan, Brockhampton Press, 1972.

Bobby Brewster's Wishbone, illustrated by Buchanan, Brockhampton Press, 1974.

Bobby Brewster's First Fun, illustrated by Buchanan, Brockhampton Press, 1974.

The Sick Cow, illustrated by Val Biro, Brockhampton Press, 1974, Children's Press (Chicago), 1976.

Bobby Brewster's Bookmark, illustrated by Buchanan, Hodder & Stoughton (London), 1975.

George the Fire Engine, illustrated by Biro, Hodder & Stoughton, 1976, Children's Press, 1978.

Changing of the Guard, illustrated by Biro, Hodder & Stoughton, 1978.

The Roundabout Horse, illustrated by Biro, Hodder & Stoughton, 1978.

The Very, Very Long Dog, illustrated by Biro, Carousel, 1978.

Bobby Brewster's Tea-Leaves, illustrated by David Barnett, Hodder & Stoughton, 1979.

Here Comes Wordman!, illustrated by Biro, Carousel, 1979.

King of Beasts, illustrated by Biro, Hodder & Stoughton, 1979.

Santa's Big Sneeze, illustrated by Biro, Hodder & Stoughton, 1980.

The Crawly Crawly Caterpillar, illustrated by Biro, Carousel, 1981.

The Dial-a-Story Book, illustrated by Biro, Penguin, 1981.

Jungle Silver, illustrated by Biro, Hodder & Stoughton, 1981.

Bobby Brewster's Lamp Post, illustrated by Buchanan, Hodder & Stoughton, 1982.

Changing of the Guard; Wallpaper Holiday, illustrated by Buchanan, Penguin, 1982.

The Tiny, Tiny Tadpole, illustrated by Biro, Carousel, 1982.

The Scruffy Scruffy Dog, illustrated by Biro, Hodder & Stoughton, 1983.

The Tiger Who Couldn't Be Bothered, illustrated by Biro, Hodder & Stoughton, 1984.

The Clever Clever Cats, illustrated by Biro, Hodder & Stoughton, 1985.

Bobby Brewster's Hiccups, illustrated by Buchanan, Hodder & Stoughton, 1985.

Bobby Brewster's Old Van, illustrated by Barnett, Hodder & Stoughton, 1986.

The Silly Silly Ghost, illustrated by Biro, Hodder & Stoughton, 1987.

Bobby Brewster and the Magic Handyman, illustrated by Barnett, Hodder & Stoughton, 1987.

Bobby Brewster's Jigsaw Puzzle, illustrated by Biro, Hodder & Stoughton, 1988.

The Sleeping Policeman, illustrated by Biro, Hodder & Stoughton, 1988.

Also author of musical works, including *The Circus King, Blackbird Pie* (children's play) 1956, both with Capel Annand, and adult musical revues and children's musical programs produced by the British Broadcasting Corp., 1949-57.

Todd's manuscripts are housed in the de Grummond Collection, University of Southern Mississippi, Hattiesburg.

ADAPTATIONS: A total of seven "Bobby Brewster" stories by Todd and "Gumdrop" stories by Biro were adapted into the videocassette *Tales of Bobby Brewster and More Adventures of Gumdrop,* Nutland Video Ltd., 1982.

SIDELIGHTS: H. E. Todd turned from storyteller into author because his stories were so well liked by his listeners that he was convinced to write them down. Over the course of his prolific career, Todd told thousands of stories to both children and adults at schools, libraries, and universities, as well as through the mediums of radio and television. These stories often revolved around the character of Bobby Brewster, an ordinary boy who encountered amazing and wondrous things. Antony Kamm, in an essay for *Twentieth-Century Children's Writers,* explained the appeal of Todd's Bobby Brewster tales: "What is so good about the stories is that they are founded on everyday situations and everyday things. . . . Many of the situations are really funny. The stories have witty touches of detail, and they are told in public with the professional expertise, timing, and verve of many years' practice."

Todd once described Bobby Brewster as "a small boy, nine years old, who was three and a half [in 1942] when I started telling stories about him to my own sons. He is an ordinary boy who has the most extraordinary adventures with ordinary things. He has a round face, blue eyes, and a nose like a button—and he is part of me, part of my sons, and now part of the hundreds of thousands of children (girls as well as boys) who I meet every year."

The most common theme in the Bobby Brewster stories is the magical powers that inanimate objects possess whenever Bobby is around. In *The Roundabout Horse,* for example, Bobby is able to make a wooden carousel horse's dream come true when he rides him in a horse race. The power of communicating with zoo animals is granted to Bobby in *King of Beasts* when a monkey winks at him and he winks back. *Bobby Brewster's Lamp Post* features a lamp post that can actually talk and a Christmas card with bells that really ring. And in *Bobby Brewster and the Magic Handyman,* a strange handyman shows up at the Brewster household one day, offering his unique services to the family for an entire year. During the course of this year, garden tools magically dig on their own, different kinds of juices run out of the water taps, and ordinary brown paper thrown on the walls turns to patterned wallpaper. "The linked episodes run quickly and cheerfully for the delectation of young connoisseurs of practical nonsense," explained Margery Fisher in her *Growing Point* review of *Bobby Brewster and the Magic Handyman.* Fisher similarly praised Todd's use of magical elements in her review of *Bobby Brewster's Lamp Post* by stating that the "everyday veracity and amusing fancy is as expert as ever."

When not writing about Bobby Brewster and his fabulous adventures, Todd often wrote of animal characters. Among these is Libby, a well-educated cat who takes offense at the term "cat-burglar," which is being used to describe a neighborhood thief in *The Clever Clever Cats.* Determined to protest the use of this term, Libby, along with several other cats, starts a neighborhood surveillance to flush out the thief and drive him into the arms of the local constable. Nigel Thomas asserted in *Books for Your Children* that *The Clever Clever Cats* is "an amusing tale" in which "the cats are delightfully characterised."

Another humorous animal tale, *The Tiger Who Couldn't Be Bothered,* concerns an animal of the jungle who is failing to live up to the expectations of the other animals because he is too lazy. This tiger could never frighten even the gentlest of creatures, and he is so dirty that his stripes are not even visible. One day, though, he accidentally falls in the river and restores his appearance just in time to have his picture taken by passing photographers. When this photograph appears in an advertisement, the tiger is transformed into a glorious jungle beast. Jill Bennet maintained in her *Books for Keeps* review that "Todd and [his illustrator] Biro are a well-established partnership" and that *The Tiger Who Couldn't Be Bothered* is a "neatly constructed and drolly illustrated story."

Todd once commented, as quoted in *Twentieth-Century Children's Writers:* "I do not claim to write

stories of great literary merit, or to teach a lesson or point a moral. I write and tell stories simply for fun. And my stories are written in exactly the same language as I tell them, for *telling* stories was my first joy and I was only persuaded to write them because people seemed to enjoy hearing them."

BIOGRAPHICAL/CRITICAL SOURCES:

BOOKS

Twentieth-Century Children's Writers, 4th edition, St. James Press (Detroit), 1995.

PERIODICALS

Booklist, July 1, 1976, p. 1529.
Books for Keeps, June, 1987, p. 14.
Books for Your Children, autumn, 1985, p. 16.
Emergency Librarian, November, 1981, p. 35.
Growing Point, September, 1978, p. 3396; March, 1980, p. 3665; May, 1982, pp. 3905-3906; September, 1982, p. 3966; November, 1985, pp. 4516-4517; May, 1987, p. 4797.
Junior Bookshelf, February, 1975, p. 27; April, 1979, p. 98; February, 1980, p. 23; April, 1981, p. 67; June, 1985, p. 124.
School Librarian, September, 1980, p. 271; September, 1982, p. 230; December, 1982, p. 347.
School Library Journal, September, 1980, p. 64.
Times Literary Supplement, February 26, 1982, p. 26; July 23, 1982, p. 796.*

*   *   *

TODD, Janet M(argaret) 1942-

PERSONAL: Born September 10, 1942, in Wales; daughter of George and Elizabeth (Jones) Dakin; married Aaron R. Todd (a professor of mathematics), December 21, 1966; children: Julian, Clara. *Education:* Cambridge University, B.A., 1964; University of Leeds, diploma, 1968; University of Florida, Ph.D., 1971.

ADDRESSES: Office—School of English and American Studies, University of East Anglia, Norwich NR3 1ES, England.

CAREER: School teacher in Cape Coast, Ghana, 1964-65; University College of Cape Coast, Cape Coast, lecturer in English, 1965-66; English teacher in Bawku, Ghana, 1966-67; University of Puerto Rico, Mayaguez, assistant professor of English, 1972-74; Rutgers University, Douglass College, New Brunswick, NJ, assistant professor, 1974-78, associate professor, 1978-81, professor of English, 1981-83; Sidney Sussex College, Cambridge, England, fellow in English, 1983-89; University of East Anglia, Norwich, England, professor of English literature, 1989—. Visiting professor, University of Southampton, 1982-83, and Jawarharlal Nehru University, New Delhi, and University of Rajasthan, 1988; fellow at Huntington Library, 1993, and at Folger Shakespeare Library, 1994 and 1995.

MEMBER: British Society of Eighteenth Century Studies, Jane Austen Society.

AWARDS, HONORS: ACLS Award, 1978-79; Guggenheim fellowship, 1981-82; Leverhulme Award, 1991-93; Huntington Library fellowship, 1993; Folger Shakespeare Library fellowship, 1994-95.

WRITINGS:

In Adam's Garden: A Study of John Clare's Pre-Asylum Poetry, University of Florida Press (Gainsville), 1973.
Mary Wollstonecraft: An Annotated Bibliography, Garland Publishing (New York City), 1976.
(Editor) *A Wollstonecraft Anthology,* Indiana University Press (Bloomington), 1977.
Women's Friendship in Literature, Columbia University Press (New York City), 1980.
(Editor) *Gender and Literary Voice,* Holmes & Meier (New York City), 1980.
(Editor) *Jane Austen: New Perspectives,* Holmes & Meier, 1983.
(Coauthor) *English Congregational Hymns in the Eighteenth Century,* University Press of Kentucky (Lexington), 1983.
(Editor) *A Dictionary of British and American Women Writers 1660-1800,* Methuen (London), 1986.
Feminist Literary History, Polity Press (Oxford) and Routledge & Kegan Paul (London), 1988.
The Sign of Angellica: Women, Writing and Fiction, 1660-1800, Virago Press (London), 1989.
(Editor) *British Women Writers,* Ungar (New York City), 1989.
(Coeditor) *Mary Wollstonecraft: The Complete Works,* New York University Press (New York City), 1989.

(Editor) *Works of Aphre Behn,* Ohio State University Press (Columbus), 1992-96.
Gender, Art, and Death, Ungar, 1993.
(Editor) *Mary Wollstonecraft: Political Writings,* Oxford University Press (Oxford), 1993.
The Secret Life of Aphre Behn, Deutsch (London), 1996.

SIDELIGHTS: Much of Janet M. Todd's scholarly writing concerns literature by and about women. About *Feminist Literary History,* Barbara Hardy writes in the *Times Literary Supplement,* "Janet Todd's lucid, commonsensical and tolerant study of feminism is markedly attentive to history, in a defence of the American socio-historical tradition, and in her own emphasis on historicism." Finding that the book "takes in more than its central subject," Hardy adds, "Admirable, too, is her political reminder of that feminism which lies outside the theory and practice of literary criticism."

Todd once told *CA:* "I am concerned with bringing women writers into the mainstream of English literary history and of reevaluating established literature according to a feminist perspective. I am especially interested in the period from the late seventeenth to the late eighteenth century because so many of our cultural attitudes were then being formed."

BIOGRAPHICAL/CRITICAL SOURCES:

PERIODICALS

Times Literary Supplement, June 20, 1980; July 26, 1985; February 27, 1987; June 3, 1988.

*   *   *

TREMAINE, Jennie
See CHESNEY, Marion

*   *   *

TULLY, John (Kimberley)   1923-

PERSONAL: Born July 7, 1923, in Sutton Coldfield, England; son of John (an actor) and Ruby (an actress; maiden name, Kimberly) Tully; married Margaret Else; children: Richard, David, Katharine, Diana. *Education:* Attended schools in North Wales.

ADDRESSES: Home—209 Jersey Rd., Isleworth, Middlesex TW7 4RE, England.

CAREER: Writer. *Military service:* Royal Air Force, 1940-45; became flight sergeant.

MEMBER: Writers Guild of Great Britain (vice-chairman, 1976-77; joint chairman, 1977-78).

WRITINGS:

Woman Alive (play), Evans Brothers (London), 1958.
The Crocodile (juvenile; also see below), BBC Publications (London), 1972.
The Raven and the Cross (juvenile; also see below), BBC Publications, 1974.
The Glass Knife (juvenile), Methuen (New York City), 1974.
The White Cat (juvenile), Methuen, 1975.
The Man from Nowhere (film script), Children's Film Foundation, 1976.
One Hour to Zero (film script), Children's Film Foundation, 1976.
Johnny Goodlooks (juvenile), Methuen, 1977.
Inspector Holt and the Fur Van, Collins (London), 1977.
Inspector Holt Gets His Man, Collins, 1977.
Muhammad Ali: King of the Ring, Collins, 1978.
Where Is Bill Ojo?, Collins, 1978.
Johnny and the Yank (juvenile), Methuen, 1978.
The Bridge, Collins, 1979.
Cats in the Dark, Collins, 1980.
Natfact 7 (young adult), Methuen, 1984.
Inspector Holt and the Chinese Necklace, Collins, 1984.
Slade (novel), Methuen, 1985.
The Man with Three Fingers, Collins, 1987.
The Winning Team (film script), Addison-Wesley Longman (Reading, MA), 1995.
Out of the Blue (film script), Addison-Wesley Longman, 1995.
Operation Diam's, Bayard Editions (Paris), 1995.
The Merger (film script), Addison-Wesley Longman, 1996.

"STARPOL" SERIES; JUVENILES

Hunter 5, Ginn (London), Books 1-4, 1984, Books 5-8, 1985.
Hunter 3, Books 1-6, Ginn, 1987.
Hunter 4, Books 1-6, Ginn, 1988.
Day of Darkness, Ginn, 1990.
Killer on Ka, Ginn, 1990.

Land of the Kels, Ginn, 1990.
Death of a Lizard, Ginn, 1990.

OTHER

Author of television serials, including *The Viaduct,* 1972, *Thursday's Child,* 1973, *Tom's Midnight Garden,* 1974, *Kizzy,* 1976, *The Phoenix and the Carpet,* 1977, *Countdown, Maths Counts,* and *Mathspy;* also author of documentary films for Shell Oil Co., British Gas Council, Midland Bank, Mobil Oil Corp., Amoco Oil Co., British Electricity Council, British Central Electricity Generating Board, British Aerospace, and Services Sound & Vision Corp. Writer of television plays, including *The Crocodile, The Raven and the Cross, The King of Argos, A Choice of Friends, The Jo-Jo Tree,* and *The Silver Fish.* Also contributor to television series, including *Going to Work, Exploring Science,* and *Merry-Go-Round.* Tully's books have been published in Germany, Sweden, Demark, South Africa, Holland, and France.

WORK IN PROGRESS: Stage play, *Getting Rid of Roddy.*

SIDELIGHTS: John Tully told *CA:* "The BBC commissioned me to dramatise a children's novel. Broadcasting dates were fixed. The studio facilities were lined up. All that was lacking was a suitable book to dramatise. There are many good novels written for children but few fit the precise demands of time, budget, scope, and aims of a particular TV series. Everyone in the department was reading books furiously, to no avail. At last the producer, in desperation, suggested to me, 'Why don't you write an original television play, and then write the novel to go with it?' I snapped up the idea and wrote *The Crocodile.* While the play was in production I started writing the book, with a traumatic realisation that if children were being advised to read it, this had better be good! Not just a 'book of the film,' but something worth reading in its own right. I hope I succeeded. By the time I completed a second, similar exercise, *The Raven and the Cross,* I had caught the book-writing bug. What tales I could tell if I were not restricted by the mechanics of television! So why not write a book for its own sake, with no holds barred? The result was *The Glass Knife.*

"Drama was and is, I suppose, my first love because I was brought up in the theatre, both sides of the family being up to their hairlines in grease paint. My grandmother was writing popular melodramas and touring them around England before I was born. My childhood memories are of plays, revues, variety bills, and backstreet digs.

"I have written for a number of adult TV series as well as many children's programmes and I have learned a curious fact, that popular 'adult material' is often the most 'childish.' It's the kids who want to know the truth about the world in terms more thoughtful and sincere."

*   *   *

TYLER, Anne   1941-

PERSONAL: Born October 25, 1941, in Minneapolis, MN; daughter of Lloyd Parry (a chemist) and Phyllis (Mahon) Tyler; married Taghi Modarressi (a psychiatrist and writer), May 3, 1963; children: Tezh, Mitra. *Education:* Duke University, B.A., 1961; graduate study at Columbia University, 1961-62. *Religion:* Quaker.

ADDRESSES: Home—222 Tunbridge Rd., Baltimore, MD 21212. *Agent*—Russell & Volkening, 50 West 29th St., New York, NY 10001.

CAREER: Writer. Duke University Library, Durham, NC, Russian bibliographer, 1962-63; McGill University Law Library, Montreal, Quebec, Canada, assistant to the librarian, 1964-65.

MEMBER: PEN, American Academy and Institute of Arts and Letters, Authors Guild, Phi Beta Kappa.

AWARDS, HONORS: Mademoiselle award for writing, 1966; Award for Literature, American Academy and Institute of Arts and Letters, 1977; National Book Critics Circle fiction award nomination, 1980, Janet Heidinger Kafka prize, 1981, and American Book Award nomination in paperback fiction, 1982, all for *Morgan's Passing;* National Book Critics Circle fiction award nomination, 1982, and American Book Award nomination in fiction, PEN/Faulkner Award for fiction, and Pulitzer Prize nomination for fiction, all 1983, all for *Dinner at the Homesick Restaurant;* National Book Critics Circle fiction award and Pulitzer Prize nomination for fiction, both 1985, both for *The Accidental Tourist;* Pulitzer Prize, 1988, for *Breathing Lessons.*

WRITINGS:

NOVELS

If Morning Ever Comes, Knopf (New York City), 1964.
The Tin Can Tree, Knopf, 1965.
A Slipping-Down Life, Knopf, 1970.
The Clock Winder, Knopf, 1972.
Celestial Navigation, Knopf, 1974.
Searching for Caleb, Knopf, 1976.
Earthly Possessions, Knopf, 1977.
Morgan's Passing, Knopf, 1980.
Dinner at the Homesick Restaurant, Knopf, 1982.
The Accidental Tourist, Knopf, 1985.
Breathing Lessons (also see below), Knopf, 1988.
Saint Maybe, Knopf, 1991.
Ladder of Years, Knopf, 1995.

OTHER

(Editor with Shannon Ravenel, and author of introduction) *Best American Short Stories 1983,* Houghton (Boston, MA), 1983.
Anne Tyler: Four Complete Novels (omnibus volume; contains *Dinner at the Homesick Restaurant, Morgan's Passing, The Tin Can Tree,* and *If Morning Ever Comes*), Avenel Books (New York City), 1990.
Anne Tyler: A New Collection (omnibus volume; contains *The Accidental Tourist, Breathing Lessons,* and *Searching for Caleb*), Wings Books (New York City), 1991.
Tumble Tower, illustrated by daughter Mitra Modarressi, Orchard Books (New York City), 1993.
(With Robert W. Lenski) *Breathing Lessons* (screenplay based on her novel), Republic Pictures, 1994.

Contributor of short stories to *Saturday Evening Post, New Yorker, Seventeen, Critic, Antioch Review,* and *Southern Review.*

ADAPTATIONS: The Accidental Tourist, starring Kathleen Turner and William Hurt, was released by Warner Brothers in 1988. It was also recorded as a book on tape by Recorded Books in 1991.

SIDELIGHTS: Despite her status as a best-selling novelist, Anne Tyler remains a private person who rarely lets public demands interfere with her family life. She shuns most interviewers, avoids talk show appearances, and prefers Baltimore, Maryland—

where she lives with her husband and two daughters—to New York City. Nonetheless she is a well-established writer, having earned what former *Detroit News* reporter Bruce Cook calls "a solid *literary* reputation . . . that is based solely on the quality of her books."

Tyler's work has always been critically well received, but reviews of her early novels were generally relegated to the back pages of the book sections. Not until the publication of *Celestial Navigation* (1974), when she captured the attention of novelist Gail Godwin, and *Searching for Caleb* (1976), when John Updike recommended her to readers, did she gain widespread acclaim. "Now," says Cook, "her books are reviewed in the front of the literary journals and that means she is somebody to reckon with. No longer one of America's best unknown writers, she is now recognized as one of America's best writers. Period."

Born in Minnesota, Tyler lived in various Quaker communes throughout the Midwest and South before settling in the mountains of North Carolina for five years. She attended high school in Raleigh and at sixteen entered Duke University, where she fell under the influence of Reynolds Price, then a promising young novelist who had attended her high school. It was Price who encouraged the young Russian major to pursue her writing, and she did—but it remained a secondary pursuit until 1967, the year she and her husband settled in Baltimore.

In an interview with Bruce Cook, published in the *Saturday Review,* Tyler describes the city as "wonderful territory for a writer—so many different things to poke around in." And the longer she stays there, the more prominently Baltimore figures in her books, lending them an ambience both citified and southern and leading Reynolds Price to proclaim her "the nearest thing we have to an urban Southern novelist." Writing in the *New Yorker,* John Updike compares her to Flannery O'Connor, Carson McCullers, and Eudora Welty, noting: "Anne Tyler, in her gifts both of dreaming and of realizing, evokes comparison with these writers, and in her tone and subject matter seems deliberately to seek association with the Southern ambience that, in less cosmopolitan times, they naturally and inevitably breathed. Even their aura of regional isolation is imitated by Miss Tyler as she holds fast, in her imagination and in her person, to a Baltimore with only Southern exits; her characters when they flee, never flee north. Yet she is a citizen of the world, born in Minneapolis, a

graduate student of Russian at Columbia, and now married to a psychiatrist from Iran. The brand names, the fads, the bastardized vistas of our great homogenized nation glint out at us from her fiction with a cheerful authority."

Other reviewers, such as Katha Pollitt, find Tyler's novels more difficult to classify. "They are Southern in their sure sense of family and place," she writes in the *New York Times Book Review,* "but [they] lack the taste for violence and the Gothic that often characterizes self-consciously Southern literature. They are modern in their fictional techniques, yet utterly unconcerned with the contemporary moment as a subject, so that, with only minor dislocations, her stories could just as well have taken place in the twenties or thirties. The current school of feminist-influenced novels seems to have passed her by completely: her women are strong, often stronger than the men in their lives, but solidly grounded in traditional roles."

The key to Tyler's writing may well lie in the homage she pays to Eudora Welty, her favorite writer and one to whom she is repeatedly compared. "Reading her taught me there were stories to be written about the mundane life around me," she told Cook. Or as Tyler phrased it to Marguerite Michaels in the *New York Times Book Review,* "Reading Eudora Welty when I was growing up showed me that very small things are often really larger than the large things." Thomas M. Disch is one of several critics who believes that Tyler's insight into the lives of ordinary people is her special gift. Writing in the *Washington Post Book World,* he calls it an "uncommon accomplishment that she can make such characters interesting and amusing without violating their limitations." Despite their resemblances to people we meet in real life, Tyler's characters are totally fictitious. "None of the people I write about are people I know," she told Michaels. "That would be no fun. And it would be very boring to write about me. Even if I led an exciting life, why live it again on paper? I want to live other lives. I've never quite believed that one chance is all I get. Writing is my way of making other chances." She perceives the real heroes of her books to be those "who manage to endure" and those "who are somehow able to grant other people the privacy of the space around them and yet still produce some warmth."

Her major theme, according to Mary Ellen Brooks in the *Dictionary of Literary Biography,* "is the obstinate endurance of the human spirit, reflected in every character's acceptance or rejection of his fate and in how that attitude affects his day to day life. She uses the family unit as a vehicle for portraying 'how people manage to endure together—how they grate against each other, adjust, intrude and protect themselves from intrusions, give up, and start all over again in the morning.'" Frequently her characters respond to stress by running away, but their flight, Brooks explains, "proves to be only a temporary and ineffectual means of dealing with reality."

Because the action of her novels is so often circular—ending exactly where it begins—Tyler's fiction has been criticized for lack of development. This is especially true of her early novels where the narratives are straightforward and the pacing slow. In fact, what impressed reviewers most about Tyler's first book, *If Morning Ever Comes,* was not the story itself but the promise it seemed to hold for future works of fiction. "The trouble with this competently put-together book is that the hero is hardly better defined at the end than he is at the beginning," observes Julian Gloag in the *Saturday Review.* "Writing about a dull and totally humorless character, Miss Tyler has inevitably produced a totally humorless and mainly dull novel. Anne Tyler is only twenty-two, and in the light of this her refusal to take risks is a bit puzzling. I'd like to see what she could do if she stopped narrowing her own eyes and let herself go. It might be very good." The *Times Literary Supplement* reviewer echoes these sentiments: "It will be surprising if a writer so young does not outgrow her hesitant efforts to produce big answers to emotional muddles and her sometimes over-literary sentences, and let her considerable gift for dialogue and comedy produce a very good novel indeed."

For her part, Tyler reportedly now dislikes her first book as well as her second, which received similar criticism. Written largely to pass the time while she was looking for a job, *The Tin Can Tree* concerns the inhabitants of a three-family house on the edge of a North Carolina tobacco field and their reactions to the accidental death of the six-year-old girl who lives there. Though the family is initially devastated by the tragedy, their emotional balance is restored in the end, and, for this reason, some critics find the novel static. Millicent Bell, for example, writes in the *New York Times Book Review:* "Life, this young writer seems to be saying, achieves its once-and-for-all shape and then the camera clicks. This view, which brings her characters back on the last page to where they started, does not make for that sense of development which is the true novel's motive force. Be-

cause of it, I think, her book remains a sketch, a description, a snapshot. But as such, it still has a certain dry clarity. And the hand that has clicked its shutter has selected a moment of truth."

Perhaps the most salient feature of Tyler's next novel, *A Slipping-Down Life* (which was misclassified as young adult literature and thus not widely reviewed), is its genesis. In discussing her craft with Michaels, Tyler said: "Sometimes a book will start with a picture that pops into my mind and I ask myself questions about it and if I put all the answers together, I've got a novel. A real picture would be the old newspaper clipping about the Texas girl who slashed 'Elvis' in her forehead." In the novel, this incident is transformed into an episode in the life of Evie Decker, a fictive teenager grappling for her identity. "I believe this is the best thing I've ever done," Evie says of her self-mutilation. "Something out of character. Definite." In the *Dictionary of Literary Biography,* Brooks describes the novel as "an accurate description of loneliness, failure to communicate, and regrets over decisions that are irreversible—problems with which any age group can identify. Tyler, who describes *A Slipping-Down Life* as one of her most bizarre works, believes that the novel 'is flawed, but represents, for me, a certain brave stepping forth.'"

So, too, does Tyler's fifth novel, *Celestial Navigation,* a book that the author wrote while "fighting the urge to remain in retreat even though the children had started school." In the character of Jeremy Paulding, an agoraphobic artist who is afraid to leave his Baltimore block, Tyler sees much of herself. While her characters are not usually autobiographical, Tyler told Brooks that creating Jeremy was a way of investigating her own "tendency to turn more and more inward." The story opens with the death of Jeremy's mother and moves quickly to an exploration of the relationship he establishes with the woman who will take her place—a self-sufficient boarder named Mary Tell. Attracted by her sunny self-confidence, Jeremy proposes marriage and soon Mary has stepped in as Jeremy's intermediary to the outside world. As years pass, he comes to feel dwarfed by Mary's competence—she does not even alert him when she leaves for the hospital to have his fifth child because she knows he dreads the trip. Suffocated by her over-protectiveness, the disoriented artist withdraws even further into the private world of his studio where he fashions collages from scraps of other people's lives. Eventually Mary and the children abandon him, and Jeremy does venture out to find them. But the price he pays for conquering his fear is that he loses them for good. At the novel's end, Mary and Jeremy each remain in a separate existence, each still dominated by what Brooks calls "his innate driving characteristic. Jeremy returns to his life as a reclusive artist in a crumbling dark house while Mary prepares for winter in a rundown shack, knowing that another man will eventually provide for her."

Told from the viewpoints of six different characters, *Celestial Navigation* is far more intricate than Tyler's earlier novels, and most critics consider it a breakthrough. Katha Pollitt finds the work "extraordinarily moving and beautiful," while Doris Grumbach proclaims Tyler's "ability to enmesh the reader in what is a simple, uneventful story a notable achievement." In her *New York Times Book Review* article, Gail Godwin explains how "Tyler is especially gifted at the art of freeing her characters and then keeping track of them as they move in their unique and often solitary orbits. Her fiction is filled with displaced persons who persist stubbornly in their own destinies. They are 'oddballs,' visionaries, lonely souls, but she has a way of transcribing their peculiarities with such loving wholeness that when we examine them we keep finding more and more pieces of ourselves."

In her eighth novel, *Morgan's Passing,* Tyler turns from an exploration of the "oddball" as introvert to the "oddball" as extrovert in the creation of Morgan Gower—a 42-year-old hardware store manager with a knack for assuming other roles. Simply put, Morgan is an imposter, a man who changes identities every time he changes clothes. "You're walking down the street with him and this total stranger asks him when the International Brotherhood of Magicians is meeting next," his wife Bonny explains. "You're listening to a politician's speech and suddenly you notice Morgan on the platform, sitting beside a senator's wife with a carnation in his buttonhole. You're waiting for your crabs at Lexington Market and who's behind the counter but Morgan in a rubber apron, telling the other customers where he caught such fine oysters." These fantasies contrast sharply with the dullness of Morgan's actual life. At home, in the brick colonial house acquired with his wife's money, he feels overwhelmed by the clutter of his wife, their seven daughters, his adult sister, and his feeble-minded mother.

The novel opens with one of Morgan's escapades. During the performance of a puppet show, the pup-

peteer, Leon Meredith, emerges from behind the curtains to request a doctor's assistance: his wife Emily has gone into labor. Morgan steps forward and, posing as a doctor, delivers the baby in the back seat of his car. In the process he becomes fascinated by what he perceives to be the simple existence of the Merediths. Emily, in particular, becomes "an emblem for Morgan of that spartan order he longs to bring to his over-furnished life," says Thomas M. Disch in the *Washington Post Book World.* But neither Emily nor Leon are as blithe as they seem, and by juxtaposing the reality of these characters with Morgan's fantasies of them, Tyler creates her drama, critics say.

Though *Morgan's Passing* was nominated for a National Book Critics Circle Award in hardback and an American Book Award in paperback fiction, critics are sharply divided in their assessment of the work. Those who like it praise Tyler's handling of character and her artful mingling of comedy and seriousness. "Though she allows her tale to veer toward farce, Tyler always checks it in time with the tug of an emotion, a twitch of regret," writes *Time*'s Paul Gray. He concludes: "*Morgan's Passing* is not another novel about a mid-life crisis, it is a buoyant story about a struggle unto death." Tyler acknowledged in her *Detroit News* interview with Bruce Cook that her "big worry in doing the book was that people would be morally offended by [Morgan]." But critic Marilyn Murray Willison sings his praises. "In spite of his inability to restore order to his life, his nicotine-stained hands and teeth, his silly wardrobe, his refusal to accept reality, Morgan emerges from Tyler's book a true hero," she writes in the *Los Angeles Times Book Review.*

Other critics, however, dislike the character and consider the book a disappointment. "For all its many felicities of observation and incident, *Morgan's Passing* does not come up to the high standard of Anne Tyler's other recent work. There is a self-indulgence in the portraiture of Morgan himself, whose numerous identity assumptions became for me merely tiresome," Paul Binding writes in the *New Statesman.* And *New York Review of Books* contributing critic James Wolcott dismisses *Morgan's Passing* as "a book of small compass, pent-up energy. Long before Morgan and Emily link arms, the reader has connected the dots separating them, so there's no suspense, no surprise. Instead, the book is stuffed with accounts of weddings, crowded dinners, cute squabbles, and symbolic-as-all-get-out puppet shows. Sentence by sentence, the book is engaging, but there's nothing beneath the jokes and tussles to propel the reader through these cluttered lives. It's a book with an idle motor." Writing in the *New Yorker,* John Updike explains his disappointment: "Anne Tyler continues to look close, and to fabricate, out of the cardboard and Magic Markers available to the festive imagination, images of the illusory lives we lead. More than that it would be unkind to ask, did we not imagine, for the scope of the gift displayed, that something of that gift is still being withheld."

With *Dinner at the Homesick Restaurant,* her ninth and, some say, finest novel, Tyler redeems herself in many critics' eyes. Updike, for instance, maintains that this book achieves "a new level of power and gives us a lucid and delightful yet complex and sombre improvisation on her favorite theme, family life." Writing in the *Chicago Tribune Book World,* Larry McMurtry echoes these sentiments: "She recognizes and conveys beautifully the alternations of tragedy and farce in family life, and never more beautifully than in *Dinner at the Homesick Restaurant.*" Benjamin Demott is even more impressed. "Funny, heart-hammering, wise, [the novel] edges deep into truth that's simultaneously (and interdependently) psychological, moral and formal—deeper than many living novelists of serious reputation have penetrated, deeper than Miss Tyler herself has gone before. It is a border crossing," he writes in the *New York Times Book Review.*

The story's plot is a simple one—"deceptively simple," Sarah English notes in the *Dictionary of Literary Biography Yearbook.* Eighty-five-year-old Pearl Tull—who married late in life and bore three children before her traveling salesman husband deserted her—recalls her past from her deathbed. She reconstructs the moment, thirty-five years before, when Beck Tull announced he was leaving, the years of struggle that ensued as she singlehandedly (and sometimes heartlessly) raised her children, and the scars which Cody, Jenny, and Ezra still bear. "Something," Pearl thought, "was wrong with all her children. They were so frustrating—attractive, likeable people, the three of them, but closed off from her in some perverse way. She wondered if her children blamed her for something. Sitting close at family gatherings they tended to recall only poverty and loneliness. [They] referred continually to Pearl's short temper, displaying it against a background of stunned, childish faces so sad and bewildered that Pearl herself hardly recognized them. Honestly, she

thought, wasn't there some statute of limitations here?"

In this darkest of Tyler's novels, the answer is no. "None of the three Tull children manages to cut loose from the family past," explains Demott. "Each is, to a degree, stunted; each turns for help to Pearl Tull in an hour of desperate adult need; and Pearl's conviction that something is wrong with each of them never recedes from the reader's consciousness." Larry McMurtry believes that the book "amply demonstrates the tenacity of familial involvement," while *Los Angeles Times* reporter Carolyn See says Tyler shows how a family "is alive with needs of its own; it never relaxes its hold. Even when you are far away (especially when you're far away), it immobilizes you in its grip, which can—in another way—be looked at as a caress."

The novel unfolds in a series of self-contained chapters, each, in Updike's words, "rounded like a short story," and each reflecting a different family member's point of view. This narrative technique, as Sarah English notes, "allows [Tyler] to juxtapose past and present and thus to convey the vision—that she has always had—of the past not as a continuum but as layers of still, vivid memories. The wealth of points of view also allows Tyler to show more fully than ever the essential subjectivity of the past. Cody and Jenny remember Pearl as a witch; Ezra remembers her as a source of strength and security. Every character's vision of the past is different."

This portrait of family entanglements is too somber for some critics' tastes, including Cynthia Propper Seton's. "What may be the trouble with *Dinner at the Homesick Restaurant,*" she writes in the *Washington Post Book World,* "is that the Tull family is not marginal enough, its members are too grave a proposition for a mind so full of mischief as Anne Tyler's. They depressed her." In her *Detroit News* review, however, Cynthia King maintains that "despite the joyless atmosphere, the author's humor bubbles through in Pearl's tackiness, in Jenny's self-protective flippancy. And more than a few times—awful as Pearl is, warped and doomed as her children are—what keeps us turning pages is the suspicion that there may be a bit of each of them in each of us." "What one wants to do on finishing such a work as *Dinner at the Homesick Restaurant,*" concludes Benjamin Demott, "is maintain balance, keep things intact for a stretch, stay under the spell as long as possible. The before and after are immaterial; nothing counts except the knowledge, solid and serene, that's all at once breathing in the room. We're speaking obviously, about an extremely beautiful book."

The Accidental Tourist, Tyler's tenth novel, again combines the author's subtle, understated probing into human nature and her eye for comic detail. The title serves both as a reference to the protagonist's occupation and as a metaphor for his life. Macon Leary writes travel guides for people who dislike traveling and who would prefer to stay in the comfort and familiarity of their own homes. The guide books—the series is titled *The Accidental Tourist*—advise reluctant travelers on how to visit foreign places without experiencing the annoyances and jarring peculiarities that each new city offers. Thus, Macon counsels his readers on where they can find American-style hamburgers in Amsterdam, for instance, or on the type of reading material to carry on the plane so as to ward off chatty passengers.

Macon's suggestions are indicative of his own nature. Insular and wary of anything foreign or unexpected, Macon surrounds himself with rituals in an attempt to make his life ordered and safe. When his twelve-year-old son is murdered in a restaurant, he retreats even further into his cocoon, driving away his wife in the process. His son's dog, Edward, though, does not respond well to the changes in his environment. As Macon fills his life with more elaborate rituals, Edward develops a mean streak and begins to terrorize Macon's friends and relatives. Eventually, Edward requires a trainer, and it is this trainer that shocks Macon into reassessing his life. Muriel Pritchett is everything that Macon is not: impetuous, carefree, and disordered. Macon becomes attracted to Muriel and her odd lifestyle, seeing in it all the vitality and passion that his life lacks. When his wife changes her mind and asks Macon to resume their marriage, Macon is forced to choose between the two women. He opts for Muriel, recognizing the exuberance for life that she has awakened in him.

As with her previous novels, reviewers praised the gently ironic humor and sympathetic, likable characters that Tyler creates in *The Accidental Tourist.* Richard Eder of the *Los Angeles Times Book Review* notes that the character of Macon Leary "is an oddity of the first water, and yet we grow so close to him that there is not the slightest warp in the lucid, touching and very funny story of an inhibited man moving out into life." Other critics observe that in this book Tyler fuses the mix of tragedy and comedy that appears in most of her previous books. McMurtry, writing in the *New York Times Book*

Review about "the mingling of misery and contentment in the daily lives of her families" that Tyler constructs, comments that "these themes, some of which she has been sifting for more than twenty years, cohere with high definition in the muted . . . personality of Macon Leary." Some reviewers criticize Tyler for her tendency to draw sympathetic characters and to infuse humor into so many of her scenes. *Chicago Tribune Book World* critic John Blades wonders whether "Tyler, with her sedative resolutions to life's most grievous and perplexing problems, can be taken seriously as a writer." Most reviewers, though, praise the book and its author. As Eder notes, "I don't know if there is a better American writer going."

In her Pulitzer Prize-winning eleventh novel, *Breathing Lessons,* Tyler examines the themes of marriage, love, and regret. The story concerns Maggie and Ira Moran, married for twenty-eight years, and a journey they make to the funeral of an old friend. During the trip they both reflect on their years together—some happy, some sad. Maggie is gregarious and curious, while Ira is practical and withdrawn. Both at times regret their decision to marry, but they also recognize the strength of the bond between them. Critics still remark on Tyler's ability to evoke sympathy for her characters and her talent for constructing humorous scenes. Eder, again writing in the *Los Angeles Times Book Review,* sums up critical reaction by noting that "there are moments when the struggle among Maggie, Ira, and the melancholy of time passing forms a fiery triangle more powerful and moving . . . than anything she has done."

"Tyler's twelfth novel, *Saint Maybe,*" writes *Dictionary of Literary Biography* contributor Caren J. Town, "addresses most directly another important Tyler concern: religion." The protagonist of *Saint Maybe* is Ian Bedloe, a well-adjusted teenager. Ian's family life changes drastically when his older brother Danny marries a divorcee named Lucy, who has two children of her own. Danny commits suicide after the birth of his daughter Daphne and Lucy dies of an overdose of sleeping pills soon after. Ian is overcome with guilt; he seeks guidance from a fundamentalist sect known as the Church of the Second Chance, led by the charismatic Brother Emmett. Emmett charges Ian to care for his brother's children as a penance for his connection with Danny's death. "Tyler has a well-known skepticism about the premise of most religions," declares Town: "'It's not that I have anything against ministers,' she . . . [said] in a discussion about *Earthly Possessions,* 'but that I'm particularly concerned with how much right anyone has to change someone, and ministers are people who feel they have that right.'" "*Saint Maybe,*" remarks Brad Leithauser in the *New York Review of Books,* "winds up being something of a curious creation: a secular tale of holy redemption."

The novel continues Ian's life through the following two decades into middle age, when "he concludes that dramatic events, personal or religious—happiness, tragedy, sin, atonement, salvation—are really part of the fabric of life," states Town. "Ian knows that the children have completely changed his life, but 'people changed other people's lives every day of the year. There was no call to make such a fuss about it.'" Tyler uses her characters in *Saint Maybe* to examine the role of modern American family life. "Is the family an anchor in the storm?" asks Marilyn Gardner in the *Christian Science Monitor.* "Or is it a shackle? Do duty and devotion hold together the members who make up a family as well as the family itself? Or do families become, not support systems, but burdens of guilt, leading to damaging sacrifices of personal freedom?" "In many ways," writes *New York Times Book Review* contributor Jay Parini, "it is Anne Tyler's most sophisticated work, a realistic chronicle that celebrates family life without erasing the pain and boredom that families almost necessarily inflict upon their members."

Tyler moved in quite a different direction with her next book, *Tumble Tower*—which features illustrations by her daughter Mitra Modarressi—"a kid-pleasing story about Princess Molly the Messy and her royal family of neatnicks," according to *Christian Science Monitor* contributor and children's literature specialist Karen Williams. Unlike her obsessed parents and siblings, including Prince Thomas the Tidy, Molly lives a comfortably unkempt life. "The moral of Tyler's tale," declares Suzanne Curley in the *Los Angeles Times Book Review,* "is that a princess unfazed by half-eaten candy bars left under her chair cushions, kittens nesting among fluffy slippers on the closet floor or a bed 'all lumpy and knobby with half-finished books' probably has her priorities straight, and may have much to teach about the way clutter often goes hand-in-hand with coziness."

"In *Ladder of Years,* Ms. Tyler's 13th novel," states *New York Times Book Review* contributor Cathleen Schine, "the story that appears to unfold of its own accord is a fairy tale of sorts, a fairy tale with echoes of both the tragedy of *King Lear* and the absurdity of

the modern romance novel." "*Ladder of Years,*" writes Suzanne L. MacLachlan in the *Christian Science Monitor,* ". . . is written from the viewpoint of a woman approaching middle age who feels she is losing her family." One day Delia Grinstead simply walks out on her obnoxious husband and her uncaring teenaged children and starts a new life in a Maryland town some miles away. She becomes self-supporting, taking a job as a lawyer's secretary. "Just as she subverts the domestic with fantasy—her situations are earthbound until you notice that they are gliding along two inches above the earth—she subverts fantasy with the domestic," explains a *Los Angeles Times Book Review* contributor. Delia's old patterns of behavior begin to reassert themselves and she returns home for her oldest daughter's wedding. "Her eventual journey back to her home and family are, in many ways," MacLachlan states, "the universal search for self. She finds, in the end, that the people she has left behind have traveled further than she." "As always," declares *New York Times* reviewer Christopher Lehmann-Haupt, "Ms. Tyler writes with a clarity that makes the commonplace seem fresh and the pathetic touching."

BIOGRAPHICAL/CRITICAL SOURCES:

BOOKS

Bestsellers 89, Issue 1, Gale (Detroit, MI), 1989.

Contemporary Literary Criticism, Gale, Volume 7, 1977, Volume 11, 1979, Volume 18, 1981, Volume 28, 1984, Volume 44, 1987.

Croft, Robert William, *Anne Tyler: A Bio-bibliography,* Greenwood Press (Westport, CT), 1995.

Dictionary of Literary Biography, Gale, Volume 6: *American Novelists since World War II, Second Series,* 1980, Volume 143: *American Novelists since World War II, Third Series,* 1994.

Dictionary of Literary Biography Yearbook: 1982, Gale, 1983.

Evans, Elizabeth, *Anne Tyler,* Twayne (New York City), 1993.

Petry, Alice Hall, *Understanding Anne Tyler,* University of South Carolina Press (Columbia, SC), 1990.

Petry, Alice Hall, editor, *Critical Essays on Anne Tyler,* Hall (New York City), 1992.

Quiello, Rose, *Breakdowns and Breakthoughts: The Figure of the Hysteric in Contemporary Novels by Women,* Peter Lang (New York City), 1993.

Salwak, Dale, editor, *Anne Tyler as Novelist,* University of Iowa Press (Iowa City, IA), 1994.

Stephens, C. Ralph, editor, *The Fiction of Anne Tyler,* University Press of Mississippi (Jackson), 1990.

PERIODICALS

Atlantic Monthly, March, 1976.
Chicago Tribune Book World, March 23, 1980; March 21, 1982; July 20, 1986.
Christian Science Monitor, September 25, 1991, p. 13; December 17, 1993, p. 12; May 18, 1995, p. 13.
Commonweal, November 8, 1991, pp. 656-58; June 16, 1995, pp. 21-22.
Detroit News, April 6, 1980; April 18, 1982.
Globe and Mail (Toronto), September 21, 1985; October 8, 1988.
Kirkus Reviews, February 15, 1995, p. 180.
Library Journal, April 1, 1995, p. 127.
London Review of Books, March 12, 1992, pp. 23-24.
Los Angeles Times, March 30, 1982; September 14, 1983.
Los Angeles Times Book Review, March 30, 1980; September 15, 1985; September 11, 1988; September 5, 1993, p. 9; May 7, 1995, p. 3.
Ms., August, 1977.
National Observer, May 30, 1977.
National Review, June 26, 1995, pp. 59-60.
New Republic, May 13, 1972; May 28, 1977; March 22, 1980.
New Statesman, April 4, 1975; December 5, 1980.
Newsweek, April 5, 1982; September 9, 1985.
New Yorker, March 29, 1976; June 6, 1977; June 23, 1980; April 5, 1982; May 8, 1995, pp. 89-90.
New York Review of Books, April 3, 1980; January 16, 1992, pp. 53-55.
New York Times, May 3, 1977; March 17, 1980; March 22, 1982; September 30, 1983; September 3, 1988; April 27, 1995, p. B2.
New York Times Book Review, November 22, 1964; November 21, 1965; March 15, 1970; May 21, 1972; April 28, 1974; January 18, 1976; May 8, 1977; March 14, 1982; September 8, 1985; August 25, 1991, pp. 1, 26; May 7, 1995, p. 12.
Saturday Review, December 26, 1964; November 20, 1965; June 17, 1972; March 6, 1976; September 4, 1976; March 15, 1980.
School Library Journal, December, 1991, pp. 149-50.
Time, May 9, 1977; March 17, 1980; April 5, 1982; September 16, 1985.
Times (London), January 12, 1989.

Times Literary Supplement, July 15, 1965; May 23, 1975; December 9, 1977; October 31, 1980; October 29, 1982; October 4, 1985; January 20, 1989.
Tribune Books (Chicago), August 28, 1988.
Washington Post Book World, March 16, 1980; April 4, 1982; September 4, 1988.*

* * *

TYLER, Ron(nie) C(urtis) 1941-

PERSONAL: Born December 29, 1941, in Temple, TX; son of Jasper J. and Melba Curtis (James) Tyler; married Paula Eyrich, August 24, 1974. *Education:* Temple Junior College, A.A., 1962; Abilene Christian College (now University), B.S.E., 1964; Texas Christian University, M.A., 1966, Ph.D., 1968.

ADDRESSES: Home—4400 Balcones Dr., Austin, TX 78731. *Office*—Texas State Historical Association, 2/306 Richardson Hall, University Station, Austin, TX 78712.

CAREER: Austin College, Sherman, TX, instructor, 1967-68, assistant professor of history, 1968-69; Amon Carter Museum of Western Art, Fort Worth, TX, curator of history, 1969-82, director of publications, 1974-82, assistant director for history and publications, 1982-84, assistant director for collections and programs, 1984-86; Texas Christian University, Fort Worth, adjutant professor of history, 1971-72; University of Texas at Austin, professor of history, 1986—, director of Texas State Historical Association and Center for Studies in Texas History, 1986—. Chair, visiting committee for department of history, Abilene Christian University, 1985-95, committee to implement the research and educational agreement between the states of Texas and Coahuila and the University of Texas at Austin and the Universidad de Coahuila, University of Texas at Austin, 1988-92, and acquisitions advisory committee for the capitol, Texas State Preservation Board, 1988-95. Fellow, Texas Christian University.

MEMBER: American Antiquarian Society, Western History Association, Texas State Historical Association (fellow; president; vice president; council member), Texas Institute of Letters, Texas Folklore Society, Texas Association of Museums (chair of publications committee; council member), Tarrant County Historical Society (president, 1975-77; vice president; board member), Book Club of Texas, Phi Beta Kappa.

AWARDS, HONORS: American Philosophical Society grant, 1970-71; H. Bailey Carroll Award, Texas State Historical Association, 1973, for best article in *Southwestern Historical Quarterly;* Coral Horton Tullis Memorial Prize, Texas State Historical Association, 1975, for *The Big Bend: The Last Texas Frontier;* Outstanding Book Award, American Historical Print Collectors Society, 1995, for *Prints of the West.*

WRITINGS:

Joseph Wade Hampton, Editor and Individualist, Texas Western Press (El Paso), 1969.
Vision, Destiny—War!: Manifest Destiny and the Mexican War, Steck, 1970.
(Editor with Lawrence R. Murphy) *The Slave Narratives of Texas,* Encino Press (Austin, TX), 1971.
(With Leonard Sanders) *How Fort Worth Became the Texasmost City,* Texas Christian University Press (Fort Worth, TX), 1973.
Santiago Vidaurri and the Confederacy, Texas State Historical Association (Austin), 1973.
The Mexican War: A Lithographic Record, Texas State Historical Association, 1973.
The Cowboy, Ridge Press, 1975.
The Big Bend: The Last Texas Frontier, National Park Service, 1975.
The Image of America in Caricature and Cartoon, Amon Carter Museum of Western Art (Fort Worth), 1975, revised edition, 1976.
The Rodeo Photographs of John Addison Stryker, Encino Press, 1977.
(Picture editor) *Texas: The Land and Its People,* Hendrick-Long (Dallas), second edition, 1978, third edition, 1986.
(Editor) *Posadas Mexico,* Library of Congress (Washington, DC), 1979.
(With Gary Winogrand) *Stock Photographs: The Fort Worth Fat Stock Show and Rodeo,* University of Texas Press (Austin), 1980.
(Author of introduction) Mary Austin Holley, *Texas,* Overland Press, 1981.
(Editor) *Alfred Jacob Miller: Artist on the Oregon Trail,* Amon Carter Museum of Western Art, 1982.
Visions of America: Pioneer Artists in a New Land (Book-of-the-Month Club alternate selection), Thames & Hudson (New York City), 1983.
(Author of introduction) *Pecos to Rio Grande: Interpretations of Far West Texas by Eighteen Artists,* Texas A & M University Press (College Station), 1983.
(Editor with wife, Paula Eyrich Tyler) *Texas Museums: A Guidebook,* University of Texas Press, 1983.
(Editor with others, and contributor) *American Frontier Life: Early Western Painting and Prints,* Abbeville Press (New York City), 1987.
Views of Texas: The Watercolors of Sarah Ann Hardinge, 1852-1856, Amon Carter Museum of Western Art, 1988.
Audubon's Great National Work: The Royal Octavo Edition of "The Birds of America," University of Texas Press, 1993.
Prints of the West, Fulcrum, 1994.

Contributor to books, including *Observations and Reflections on Texas Folklore,* edited by Francis Edward Abernethy, Encino Press, 1972; *Encyclopedia of Southern History,* Louisiana State University Press (Baton Rouge), 1979; *American Paintings: Selections from the Amon Carter Museum,* edited by Linda Ayres and others, Oxmoor (Birmingham, AL), 1986; and *The May Family Collection of American Paintings,* Huntsville Museum of Art, 1988. Editor, *Prints of the American West: Papers Presented at the Ninth Annual North American Print Conference,* Amon Carter Museum of Western Art, 1983; editor, *Southwestern Historical Quarterly,* 1986—; editor-in-chief, *The New Handbook of Texas,* six volumes, 1996—. Also contributor to numerous history journals, including *Americas, American History Illustrated, Southwestern Historical Quarterly, American West, Journal of Negro History, Southwestern Latin Americanist,* and *Arizona and the West.*

*   *   *

URMUZ
  See CODRESCU, Andrei

*   *   *

VO-DINH, Mai   1933-

PERSONAL: Born November 14, 1933, in Hue, Vietnam; immigrated to United States, 1960, naturalized citizen, 1976; son of Thang (a civil servant) and Do-

Thi (Hanh) Vo-Dinh; married Helen Countant Webb (a teacher), August 17, 1964 (divorced June, 1986); married Laihong Tran, July 26, 1995; children: (first marriage) Katherine, Hannah; (second marriage) Quang Minh. *Education:* Attended Faculte des Lettres, Sorbonne, Paris, 1956, Academie de la Grande Chaumiere, Paris, 1957, and Ecole Nationale Superieure des Beaux Arts, Paris, 1959.

ADDRESSES: Home and office—c/o Mai Studio, P.O. Box 73, Brunswick, MD 21716.

CAREER: Artist, writer, and translator. Painting instructor, Hood College, Frederick, MD, summers, 1985 and 1986. Artist-in-residence, Synechia Arts Center, 1974, Middletown High School, 1985, and Brunswick Middle School, 1986. Work exhibited at Mars Hill College, 1981, Arsenal Gallery, 1982, Touchstone Gallery, 1983, Master Eagle Gallery, 1983, George Mason University, 1987, and Les Jardins du Boise, Montreal, Canada, 1992.

AWARDS, HONORS: Christopher Foundation Award, 1975; National Endowment for the Arts fellowship, 1984-85.

WRITINGS:

SELF-ILLUSTRATED

Wind Play: The Kite, UNICEF (New York City), 1964.
The Crimson Silk Portfolio, VDM Editions (PA), 1968.
The Jade Song, Chelsea House (New York City), 1970.
The Toad Is the Emperor's Uncle, Doubleday (New York City), 1970.
(With others) *Aspects of Vietnamese Culture,* Southern Illinois University (Carbondale, IL), 1972.
Vo Dinh, Suzuki and Feiden Galleries (New York City), 1972.
The Woodcuts of Vo Dinh, Hoa Binh Press (New York City), 1974.
Xu Sam Set, La Boi Press (Paris, France), 1980, Van Nghe House (CA), 1987.
Yoga Can Ban (title means "Basic Yoga"), Van Nghe House, 1989.
Doa Sen va Nu Cuoi (title means "The Lotus and The Smile"), Van Nghe House, 1990.
Sao Co Tieng Song (essays), Van Nghe House, 1991.
Lam Xep (stories), Van Nghe House, 1996.

TRANSLATOR AND ILLUSTRATOR

Doan-Quoc-Sy, *The Stranded Fish,* Sang-Tao Press (Saigon), 1971, Lang Van (Toronto, Canada), 1988.
Nhat Hanh, *The Path of Return Continues the Journey,* Hoa Binh Press, 1972.
Hanh, *Zen Poems of Nhat Hanh,* Unicorn Press (Chapel Hill, NC), 1976.
Fragrance of Zen, Buddhist Cultural Center (Los Angeles, CA), 1981.
Tuyet Dau Mua, LaBoi Press, 1981.
(Translator with Helen Coutant) *A Flower for You,* Nam-Tuyen Temple (VA), 1983.
(Translator with others) *Landscape and Exile,* Rowan Tree (Boston, MA), 1985.
The Moon Bamboo, Parallax Press (Berkeley, CA), 1989.
The Pine Gate, White Pine Press (New York City), 1989.
(Translator with others) *War and Exile* Vietnamese PEN (U.S.A.), 1989.
Literature of South Vietnam, 1954-1975, Vietnamese Language & Cultural Publications (Melbourne, Australia), 1992.
The Stone Boy, Parallax Press, 1995.

ILLUSTRATOR

Birds, Frogs, and Moonlight, translation by Sylvia Dassedy and Kunihiro Suetake, Doubleday, 1967.
Hanh, *The Cry of Vietnam,* Unicorn Press (Santa Barbara, CA), 1968.
All Year Long (calligraphy), Unicorn Press, 1969.
James Kirkup, *The Magic Drum,* Knopf (New York City), 1973.
H. Coutant, *First Snow,* Knopf, 1974.
Daniel Berrigan and Hanh, *The Raft Is Not the Shore,* Beacon Press (Boston, MA), 1976.
Hanh, *The Miracle of Mindfulness,* Beacon Press, 1976.
Ron Roy, *One Thousand Pails of Water,* Knopf, 1978.
The Way of Everyday Life (calligraphy), Shobogenzo Genjokoan Zen Center of Los Angeles (Los Angeles, CA), 1978.
The Brocaded Slipper, Addison-Wesley (Reading, MA), 1982.
The Land I Lost, Harper & Row (New York City), 1982.
The Happy Funeral, Harper & Row, 1982.
A Flash of Lightning, International Zen Institute of America (Los Angeles, CA), 1983.

Angel Child, Dragon Child, Carnival Press (Minneapolis, MN), 1983.

The Gift, Knopf, 1983.

The Miracle of Mindfulness, Beacon Press, 1988.

A Mother's Lullaby, Tu sach Canh Nam (VA), 1989.

TET, The New Year, Children's Museum (Boston, MA), 1991.

Sky Legends of Vietnam, HarperCollins (New York City), 1993.

PORTFOLIOS

Unicorn Broadsheet #4, Unicorn Press, 1969.

Let's Stand Beside Each Other, Fellowship Publications, 1969.

Recent Works by Vo-Dinh, Suzuki Graphics, 1972.

The Woodcuts of Vo-Dinh, Hoa-Binh Press, 1974.

OTHER

Views of a Vietnam Artist (lecture), Southern Illinois University Press, 1972.

(Translator) *A Day to Dispose Of,* Rowan Tree, 1985.

Contributor to English language publications, including *Unicorn Journal, Vietnam Forum, Vietnam Review,* and *Webster Review,* and to Vietnamese language publications, including *Dat Moi, Diendan Tudo, Hop Luu, Ngay Nay,* and *Van Hoc.*

WORK IN PROGRESS: Writing a collection of short stories in English.

SIDELIGHTS: Mai Vo-Dinh told *CA:* "Naturally, the war in Vietnam affected me, an artist, profoundly as it did, in other ways, all Vietnamese. An entire generation grew up, lived, and died with it. Yet, my work cannot, except for occasional flarings of outrage and sorrow, be called violent or pessimistic If anything, the war between Vietnamese and between Vietnamese and Americans has reinforced my faith in the miracle of life. It is a faith beyond hope or despair.

"Surprisingly enough, the contemporary paintings that I, born and bred in Vietnam, am most fond of are by two Britishers, Francis Bacon and Graham Sutherland. I also like Georgia O'Keefe, a great American lady, very much. I greatly admire Isaac Bashevis Singer.

"My opinion of modern art? I hope it counts! Modern art is but a reflection of modern life. Do you know the story from that Buddhist scripture?; 'A man gallops by on his horse. Someone shouts at him: "Where are you going?" The man hollers back: "Don't know! Ask the horse!"'"

W-Z

WALKER, Edward Joseph 1934-
(Ted Walker)

PERSONAL: Born November 28, 1934, in Lancing, England; son of Edward Joseph (a carpenter) and Winifred (Schofield) Walker; married Lorna Benfell, August 11, 1956 (died, April 1, 1987); married Audrey Joan Hicks, July 8, 1988; children: (first marriage) Edward, Susan, Margaret, William. *Education:* St. John's College, Cambridge, B.A. (with honors), 1956, M.A., 1977. *Politics:* "Leftish." *Religion:* "Apprehensive agnostic."

ADDRESSES: Home—Argyll House, The Square, Eastergate, Chichester PO20 6UP, West Sussex, England.

CAREER: Poet. High School for Boys, Chichester, Sussex, schoolmaster and teacher of French and Spanish, 1953-67; full-time author and broadcaster, 1967-71; New England College, Arundel, Sussex, poet-in-residence and professor of creative writing, 1971-92, emeritus professor, 1992—.

MEMBER: Royal Society of Literature (fellow).

AWARDS, HONORS: Society of Authors, Eric Gregory Award, 1964, Cholmondeley Award for Poets, 1966, for *The Solitaries;* Alice Hunt Bartlett Prize, Poetry Society, 1967, for *The Solitaries;* Major Arts Council of Great Britain award, 1978; J. R. Ackerley Prize, English Centre of International PEN, 1982, for *The High Path;* D.Litt., Southampton University, 1995.

WRITINGS:

POETRY; UNDER NAME TED WALKER

Those Other Growths, Northern House (Leeds, England), 1964.
Fox on a Barn Door, J. Cape (London), 1965, Braziller (New York), 1966.
The Solitaries, Braziller, 1967.
The Night Bathers: Poems, 1966-1968, J. Cape, 1970.
Gloves to the Hangman: Poems, 1969-1972, J. Cape, 1973.
Burning the Ivy: Poems, 1973-1977, J. Cape, 1978.
(With Alan Aldridge) *The Lions Cavalcade,* J. Cape, 1980.
Hands at a Live Fire, Secker & Warburg (London), 1987.

OTHER; UNDER NAME TED WALKER

The High Path (autobiography), Routledge & Kegan Paul (London), 1982.
You've Never Heard Me Sing (short stories), Heinemann (London), 1985.
In Spain (nonfiction), Secker & Warburg, 1987.
The Last of England (autobiography), J. Cape, 1992.
Granddad's Seagulls (children's poems), Blackie & Son (Glasgow), 1994.
Wind in the Willows (screenplay), Carlton TV, 1995.

Contributor of poems and short stories to various periodicals, including the *New Yorker.* Founding editor, with John Cotton, of *Priapus.*

SIDELIGHTS: A British writer, editor, radio and television dramatist, and translator, Ted Walker is best known for his carefully crafted poems, many of which follow the tradition of English nature poetry. In his precise observation of animals, fish, and birds, Walker detects a natural harmony that is missing in civilized life. He describes his works as "in the main a poetry of fear and loss which looks for the beauty that remains among the ruins of lost faith, lost innocence and lost animal strength," according to the *Library Journal.*

"His best poems are the ones in which he dramatizes segments of being that have been crushed or suppressed by the conditions of civilized life, 'wants kept caged on roofs/ of the mind's tenements," writes Laurence Lieberman in the *Yale Review.* "In weaker poems, the shifts from description to message—statement of human analogy—are abrupt and unaccountable, and jar in the reader's ear. In the best poems, these two movements are carried on simultaneously, joined and jointed, seamlessly, in the poem's drama."

Though Walker turned to prose for his autobiography *The High Path,* this work exhibits many of the qualities of his poems. There is the same respect for language—reflecting what *Times Literary Supplement* reviewer Edward Blishen calls "the poet's habit of not allowing words to report for duty half-asleep." Blishen commends Walker's powers of observation and his ability to make "sense of the brimming nonsense of a life," adding that the poet's father "had a term for anything beautifully done: *umpity poo.* There seems no better term for *The High Path.*"

Since the appearance of his autobiography in 1982, Walker has published more prose than poetry. He has written a book about his travels in Spain and a collection of short stories entitled *You've Never Heard Me Sing. In Spain* is a "labor of love," says Xan Fielding in the *Times Literary Supplement,* in which Walker tells how he submersed himself in Spanish culture, living in the country's small villages as a typical rural Spaniard would. *You've Never Heard Me Sing* is a collection of his previously-published stories from the *New Yorker* and other magazines. *Times Literary Supplement* reviewer Tim Dooley calls this work a "very satisfying, quietly moving book." The "growing recognition of [Walker's] achievement as a prose writer," Dooley asserts, "will be strengthened by the publication of this collection of his short fiction."

BIOGRAPHICAL/CRITICAL SOURCES:

BOOKS

Contemporary Literary Criticism, Volume 13, Gale (Detroit), 1980.
Dictionary of Literary Biography, Volume 40: *Poets of Great Britain and Ireland since 1960,* Gale, 1985.
Walker, Ted, *The High Path* (autobiography), Routledge & Kegan Paul, 1982.
Walker, *The Last of England* (autobiography), Blackie & Son, 1994.

PERIODICALS

Books and Bookmen, May, 1967.
Kenyon Review, January, 1967.
Library Journal, July, 1966.
New Statesman, May 12, 1967.
New York Times Book Review, November 20, 1966.
Observer (London), March 26, 1967.
Poetry, March, 1967; May, 1967.
Times Literary Supplement, June 18, 1970; June 8, 1973; January 14, 1983; November 15, 1985; November 17, 1987; May 20, 1988.
Yale Review, winter, 1968.

* * *

WALKER, Lou Ann 1952-

PERSONAL: Born December 9, 1952, in Hartford City, IN; daughter of Gale Freeman (a printer) and Doris Jean (a film librarian; maiden name, Wells) Walker; married Speed Vogel (a writer), September 8, 1986; children: Katherine Walker. *Education:* Attended Ball State University, 1971-73; Universite de Besancon, degree in French language and literature, 1975; Harvard University, B.A., 1976.

ADDRESSES: Home—New York, NY, and Sag Harbor, NY; fax 516-725-4788. *Agent*—Darhansoff & Verrill, 179 Franklin St., New York, NY 10013.

CAREER: Indianapolis News, Indianapolis, IN, reporter, 1976; *New York* (magazine), New York City, assistant to executive editor, 1976-77; *Esquire,* New York City, associate editor, 1977-79; *Cosmopolitan,* New York City, assistant to executive editor, 1979-80; *Diversion* (magazine), New York City, associate editor, 1980-81; *Direct* (magazine), New York City, editor, 1981-82. Sign language interpreter for New York Society for the Deaf. Consultant on special project for handicapped people for Museum of Modern Art, 1980-85. Consultant to Broadway's Theater Development Fund and sign language advisor on many Broadway shows, 1984—.

MEMBER: Authors Guild.

AWARDS, HONORS: Rockefeller Foundation humanities fellowship, 1982-83; Christopher Award, 1987, for *A Loss for Words: The Story of Deafness in a Family;* National Endowment for the Arts creative writing grant, 1988; Notable Book of the Year in the field of social studies, NCSS-CBC, 1986, for *Amy: The Story of a Deaf Child; Hand, Heart, and Mind* named one of the best children's books of 1994 by the New York Public Library.

WRITINGS:

Amy: The Story of a Deaf Child, photographs by Michael Abramson, Lodestar (New York City), 1985.
A Loss for Words: The Story of Deafness in a Family (autobiography), Harper (New York City), 1986.
(Author of introduction) Helen Keller, *The Story of My Life,* Penguin (New York City), 1989.
Roy Lichtenstein: The Artist at Work, Penguin, 1994.
Hand, Heart, and Mind, Dial (New York City), 1994.

Contributor of articles to *American Health, Harvard Magazine, Ladies' Home Journal, New York Times, Chicago Sun-Times, Parade, People, Encyclopedia Britannica,* and *Redbook.* Contributing editor, *New York Woman,* 1990-92.

WORK IN PROGRESS: A novel, *Jenny Jo.*

SIDELIGHTS: The oldest hearing child of profoundly deaf parents, Lou Ann Walker became the family's intermediary with the hearing world at an early age, dealing directly with doctors, teachers, and merchants while her parents were frequently dismissed as unintelligent and incapable. Marked by public embarrassment and isolation, it was a life that "seemed extraordinarily fragile" on the outside, as *Washington Post*'s Carol Eron quotes from Walker's autobiography. The family home, however, was warm and loving, with a devoted mother and jocular father who expressed their own brand of independence and joy in living. After college and career relocation, Walker

was still troubled by the years of trying to shield her parents from the ignorance of outsiders, caught between their silent world and her world of hearing people. "There were unbreakable bonds between us," she wrote, according to Ursula Vils of the *Los Angeles Times.* "Yet there was also an unbroachable chasm."

In *A Loss for Words: The Story of Deafness in a Family,* Walker recounts her singular past in an attempt to understand it. Taking nearly four years to complete, the book served as a kind of emotional catharsis for an existence that at times left her feeling like "a robot of words and sounds for people." Like her parents before her, the author eventually learns that there are two ways to address the unalterable: to be bitter, or to proceed and enjoy life. Hoping that this story of "lovely people, spunky daughter" can "do some good" for others, Hugh Kenner writes in the *New York Times Book Review:* "So profoundly other, then, is the unhearing culture that moving it into a language we learn by hearing took both gifts and a nearly savage determination." Pointing out the absence of self-pity "in this delicate, carefully drawn memoir," Eron reflects: "The effect of parental deafness on hearing children is a largely neglected subject."

Walker told *CA:* "Nothing is harder than writing a memoir. I can only hope that from here on, my work will be emotionally intense—but less wrenching for me.

"My husband, Speed, and I bike and run every day, and we spend the summers with friends in Europe. I'm fluent in French, and, although I have enough Italian to understand a greengrocer's recipes, I'm struggling with that language. I continue to discover the beauties of American Sign Language."

BIOGRAPHICAL/CRITICAL SOURCES:

BOOKS

Walker, Lou Ann, *A Loss for Words: The Story of Deafness in a Family,* Harper, 1986.

PERIODICALS

Los Angeles Times, March 30, 1987.
New York Times Book Review, October 5, 1986.
People, December 15, 1986.
Washington Post, November 7, 1986.

WALKER, Ted
  See WALKER, Edward Joseph

*   *   *

WALZER, Norman   1943-

PERSONAL: Born March 17, 1943, in Mendota, IL; son of Elmer and Anna (Johnson) Walzer; married Dona Lee Maurer, August 21, 1970; children: Steve, Mark. *Education:* Illinois State University, B.S., 1966; University of Illinois, M.A., 1969, Ph.D., 1970.

ADDRESSES: Home—727 Auburn Dr., Macomb, IL 61455. *Office*—Illinois Institute of Rural Affairs, 520 Stipes Hall, Western Illinois University, Macomb, IL 61455. *E-mail*—WalzerN@ccmail.wivedu.

CAREER: Western Illinois University, Macomb, assistant professor, 1970-74, associate professor, 1974-78, professor of economics, 1978—, director of Public Policy Research Institute, 1974—, chair of department, 1980-89, director of Illinois Institute for Rural Affairs, 1988—, interim dean of college of business and technology, 1993-95. Visiting professor at University of Illinois, 1977-78, 1979-80; research director of Illinois General Assembly's Illinois Cities and Villages Municipal Problems Commission, 1974-83.

MEMBER: American Economic Association, National Tax Association-Tax Institute of America, Community Development Society (member of editorial board, 1994—), Mid-Continent Section of Regional Science Association (past president), Midwest Economic Association, Illinois Development Council, Illinois Economic Association (president, 1979-80), Phi Kappa Phi (past president).

AWARDS, HONORS: Grants from Illinois Municipal League, 1971—, Southwestern Illinois Law Enforcement Commission, 1972, Western Illinois Crime Commission, 1972, Illinois Division of Vocational and Technical Education, 1972, 1973, 1974, U.S. Army Corp of Engineers, 1974, Municipal Problems Commission, 1974, 1975, U.S. Department of Labor, 1979, State of Illinois, 1980, 1981, and Community Information and Education Service, 1983; college of business award for professional excellence, 1973, presidential merit awards, 1977, 1978-79, senior faculty research award, 1990, faculty lecturer, 1993, administrative recognition award, 1995, all from Western Illinois University; recognition for outstanding achievements in community economic development awarded by State of Illinois, Rural Partners, 1993.

WRITINGS:

(With Glenn W. Fisher) *Cities, Suburbs, and Property Taxes,* Oelgeschlager, Gunn & Hain (Cambridge, MA), 1981.
(With David L. Chicoine) *Governmental Structure and Local Public Finance,* Oelgeschlager, Gunn & Hain, 1984.

Author of numerous monographs and reports. Contributor of chapters to approximately fifteen books. Contributor of over 150 articles and reviews to various professional journals. Editor of *Papers and Proceedings of the Illinois Economic Association,* 1981-83.

EDITOR

(With Chicoine) *Financing State and Local Governments in the 1980s,* Oelgeschlager, Gunn & Hain, 1981.
(With Chicoine) *Financing Local Infrastructure in Nonmetropolitan Areas,* Praeger (New York City), 1986.
(With Chicoine) *Local Economic Development Finance: Issues and Trends,* Praeger, 1986.
(With LaVonne A. Straub) *Financing Rural Health Care,* Praeger, 1988.
Rural Community Economic Development, Praeger, 1991.
(With Straub) *Rural Health Care: Innovations in a Changing Environment,* Praeger, 1992.
Local Economic Development: Incentives and International Trends, Westview Press (Boulder, CO), 1995.
Community Visioning Programs: Principles and Practices, Greenwood Press (Westport, CT), in press.

*   *   *

WARD, Charlotte
  See CHESNEY, Marion

WASSERSTEIN, Wendy   1950-

PERSONAL: Born October 18, 1950, in Brooklyn, NY; daughter of Morris W. (a textile manufacturer) and Lola (a dancer; maiden name, Schleifer) Wasserstein. *Education:* Mount Holyoke College, B.A., 1971; City College of the City University of New York, M.A., 1973; Yale University, M.F.A., 1976.

ADDRESSES: Home—New York, NY. *Agent*—Royce Carlton Inc., 866 United Nations Plaza, Suite 4030, New York, NY 10017.

CAREER: Dramatist and screenwriter. Teacher at Columbia University and New York University, New York City. Actress in plays, including *The Hotel Play,* 1981. Member of artistic board of Playwrights Horizons.

MEMBER: Dramatists Guild (member of steering committee and women's committee), British American Arts Association (board member), Dramatists Guild for Young Playwrights; WNET (board member), McDowell Colony (board member).

AWARDS, HONORS: Joseph Jefferson Award, Dramalogue Award, and Inner Boston Critics Award, all for *Uncommon Women and Others;* grant for playwriting from Playwrights Commissioning Program of Phoenix Theater, c. 1970s; Hale Mathews Foundation Award; Guggenheim fellowship, 1983; grant for writing and for studying theater in England from British-American Arts Association; grant for playwriting from American Playwrights Project, 1988; Pulitzer Prize for drama, Antoinette Perry Award (Tony) for best play from League of American Theatres and Producers, Drama Desk Award, Outer Critics Circle Award, Susan Smith Blackburn Prize, and award for best new play from New York Drama Critics' Circle, all 1989, all for *The Heidi Chronicles.*

WRITINGS:

PLAYS

Any Woman Can't, produced Off Broadway at Playwrights Horizons, 1973.

Happy Birthday, Montpelier Pizz-zazz, produced in New Haven, CT, 1974.

(With Christopher Durang) *When Dinah Shore Ruled the Earth,* first produced in New Haven, CT, at Yale Cabaret Theater, 1975.

Uncommon Women and Others (also see below; first produced as a one-act in New Haven, CT, 1975; revised and enlarged two-act version produced Off Broadway by Phoenix Theater at Marymount Manhattan Theater, November 21, 1977), Avon (New York City), 1978.

Isn't It Romantic (also see below; first produced Off Broadway by Phoenix Theater at Marymount Manhattan Theater, June 13, 1981; revised version first produced Off Broadway at Playwrights Horizons, December 15, 1983), Nelson Doubleday, 1984.

Tender Offer (one-act), first produced Off-Off Broadway at Ensemble Studio Theatre, 1983.

The Man in a Case (one-act; adapted from the short story of the same title by Anton Chekhov), written as part of *Orchards* (anthology of seven one-act plays, all adapted from short stories by Chekhov; produced Off Broadway by the Acting Company at Lucille Lortel Theater, April 22, 1986), Knopf (New York City), 1986.

Miami (musical), first produced Off Broadway at Playwrights Horizons, January, 1986.

The Heidi Chronicles (also see below; produced Off Broadway at Playwrights Horizons, December 11, 1988, produced on Broadway at Plymouth Theatre, March 9, 1989), Dramatists Play Service (New York City), 1990.

The Heidi Chronicles and Other Plays (contains *Uncommon Women and Others, Isn't It Romanic,* and *The Heidi Chronicles*), Harcourt (San Diego), 1990.

The Sisters Rosensweig (produced at Mitzi E. Newhouse Theater, Lincoln Center, October 22, 1992), Harcourt (New York City), 1993.

SCREENPLAYS; FOR TELEVISION

Uncommon Women and Others (adapted from Wasserstein's play of the same title; also see above), Public Broadcasting Service (PBS), 1978.

The Sorrows of Gin (adapted from the short story of the same title by John Cheever), PBS, 1979.

Also author of *'Drive,' She Said,* PBS, and of sketches for the series *Comedy Zone,* CBS-TV, 1984.

OTHER

Bachelor Girls (comic essays), Knopf, 1990.

Pamela's First Musical (children's picture book), Hyperion (New York City), 1996.

Author of unproduced film scripts, including (with Christopher Durang) "House of Husbands," adapted from the short story "Husbands"; and a script adapted from the novel *The Object of My Affection* by Stephen McCauley. Contributor of articles to periodicals, including *Esquire* and the *New York Times.* Contributing editor, *New York Woman.*

SIDELIGHTS: "Serious issues and serious people can be quite funny," said dramatist Wendy Wasserstein in the *New York Times.* In her best-known plays—*Uncommon Women and Others, Isn't It Romantic,* and *The Heidi Chronicles*—Wasserstein spotlights college-educated women of the postwar baby boom, who came of age in the late 1960s as feminism was redefining American society. Such women, she suggests, have been torn between a newfound spirit of independence and the traditional values of marriage and motherhood that they were taught as children. While portraying the struggles of her characters with deep sympathy, Wasserstein imbues her plays with a comic tone. "On some level, I'm terribly earnest," she told Sylvie Drake of the *Los Angeles Times.* "I almost have to look at problems with a sense of humor." Wasserstein has held the attention of theater critics since the late 1970s, when *Uncommon Women* opened to favorable reviews in New York City; a few years later, according to the *New York Times*'s Michiko Kakutani, she had "won recognition as one of this country's most talented young playwrights." In 1989, Wasserstein received the Pulitzer Prize in drama for *The Heidi Chronicles.*

Born into a New York City family in 1950, Wasserstein attended a series of young women's schools, including the elite Mount Holyoke College, that were marked by social conservatism. She rebelled against the schools' traditions of propriety, preferring to cultivate a lively sense of humor—"I always thought in terms of getting by on being funny," she said in the *New York Times.* She did graduate work at New York's City University, studying creative writing under playwright Israel Horovitz and novelist Joseph Heller before gaining a master's degree in 1973. That year saw Wasserstein's first professional production: *Any Woman Can't,* a bitter farce about a woman's efforts to dance her way to success in a male-dominated environment. The show was presented by a small experimental theater group, Playwrights Horizons, that would later prosper and play a major role in Wasserstein's career.

When Wasserstein graduated from City University, she was unsure of her future. The emergent women's movement brought the prospect of a career in law or business, but Wasserstein was not enthusiastic about these professions. She was drawn to a career as a playwright, a tenuous life made ever more so by the growing popularity of television and film. She applied to two prestigious graduate programs—Columbia Business School and Yale Drama School—was accepted by both, and opted for Yale. The leader of Yale's drama program was Robert Brustein, renowned in the American theater community as an advocate of professional discipline and artistic creativity. Under his auspices, according to *Horizon*'s Steve Lawson, Yale became "the foremost theatrical training ground in the country." Brustein "felt that theater was as important as law or medicine," Wasserstein later told the *New York Times.* "It gave you high standards to maintain." Her classmates at Yale included Christopher Durang and Albert Innaurato, later to become award-winning playwrights, and Meryl Streep, an actress who later earned acclaim in films.

With Durang's encouragement, Wasserstein became interested in the plays of Anton Chekhov, an acclaimed Russian writer of the late nineteenth century. Chekhov "got to do it all," Wasserstein later wrote in a *New York Times* tribute, noting that the writer could make his characters simultaneously tragic and comic. As Wasserstein suggested, Chekhov had the objectivity to mock his characters' flaws and delusions; but at the same time, he had the sympathy to portray their hopes and sorrows. The Russian playwright became an enduring role model for Wasserstein. "There is no better reason to write," she declared, "than to attempt to barely touch where he succeeded."

But as Wasserstein studied the works of famous playwrights, she perceived the same flaw noted by many feminists of the 1970s: such dramatists, predominantly male, had failed to reflect the full range of women's experiences. Female characters, Wasserstein realized, often seemed to be stereotypes such as prostitutes or uncaring mothers. Rarely did they resemble her own women peers, who were striving for professional and emotional fulfillment in a complex and frustrating world. So Wasserstein joined a wave of new women dramatists in America who were determined to bring a broader range of women characters to the stage. "I am not trying to write didactic theater," she said in the *Washington Post.* "It's not about two girls in lumber jackets on a tractor. . . . I want to do it subtly."

Accordingly, Wasserstein's work at Yale evolved from broad mockery to more subtle portrayals of character. Of her student plays, two are forthright satires: *Happy Birthday, Montpelier Pizz-zazz* shows the social maneuvers at a college party, and *When Dinah Shore Ruled the Earth,* written with Durang, mocks a beauty pageant. But in *Uncommon Women and Others*—which Wasserstein began as her Yale master's thesis—the characters are more complex; and the humor, more low-keyed, is underlain with tension.

Uncommon Women is about a fictional group of Mount Holyoke students who trade quips about men and sex while wondering about their own futures with a mixture of hope and apprehension. As the play makes clear, when feminism reached college campuses in the late 1960s it expanded women's horizons but filled them with uncertainty. The character Rita dominates the play as an outspoken aspiring novelist. As a student she tells her friends that "when we're thirty we're going to be pretty amazing," but she eventually hopes for a "Leonard Woolf" who will, like Virginia Woolf's husband, support her while she perfects her writing. Holly, dubbed "imaginative" and "witty" by *Nation*'s Harold Clurman, makes a pathetic effort to find a husband on the eve of graduation by phoning a young doctor she once met. He has since married and has forgotten all about her. Surrounding the central characters, each of whom struggles to define herself, are other young women whose self-assurance seems vaguely unsettling by contrast. Leilah, self-contained and inscrutable, makes a cold peace with the world, deciding to become an anthropologist and marry a man from the Middle East. Susie is a booster for outmoded college traditions; Carter, a stereotypical genius who seems guaranteed of success. The play's opening and closing scenes show the central characters at a reunion luncheon a few years after college. Most seem confused and unfulfilled. Rita now asserts that by the age of forty-five they will all be "amazing." Chekhov, Wasserstein later revealed, inspired Rita's funny-sad refrain.

Uncommon Women was first presented at Yale in 1975 as a one-act play. Then Wasserstein rewrote the play in a two-act version and prepared it for the professional stage, receiving encouragement along the way from both Playwrights Horizons and the Eugene O'Neill Playwrights Conference. The finished work received widespread attention from reviewers when it premiered in 1977 under the auspices of Phoenix Theater, a troupe that spotlighted new American plays. While *Time*'s T. E. Kalem found Wasserstein's characters "stereotypical," Richard Eder of the *New York Times* wrote that "if the characters . . . represent familiar alternatives and contradictions, Miss Wasserstein has made each of them most real." *New Yorker*'s Edith Oliver said the work was "a collage of small scenes" rather than a "play." Nonetheless, she found the result a "wonderful, original comedy" in which "every moment is theatrical," adding that "for all [the characters'] funny talk and behavior, they are sympathetically drawn." In conclusion, Oliver declared Wasserstein "an uncommon young woman if ever there was one." *Uncommon Women* soon reached national television as part of the Public Broadcasting Service's *Theatre in America* series.

Wasserstein began her next major work, *Isn't It Romantic,* as she approached the age of thirty in the late 1970s. Observing that many women her own age were suddenly planning to marry, she pondered the reasons for such a choice, including the possibility that women might marry simply because it was expected of them. "Biological time bombs were going off all over Manhattan," she told the *Washington Post.* "It was like, it's not wild and passionate, but it's *time.*" *Isn't It Romantic,* observed *Nation*'s Elliott Sirkin, "has the kind of heroine the whole world thinks of as a New Yorker: Janie [Blumberg], a bright, plump, emotionally agitated young Jewish woman, who insults herself with sophisticated quips" while resisting the entreaties of an earnest but boring young doctor. Janie's mother, outgoing and energetic, urges her daughter to get married. In contrast to the Blumbergs are Janie's best friend Harriet—an emotionally restrained Anglo-Saxon, more attractive and successful than Janie—and Harriet's mother, cooler and more successful yet. The play consists of many short scenes, abundant with comic one-liners, that explore how and why women choose a husband, a career, or a way of life. As the play ends, Janie, shocked to realize that Harriet is about to marry a man she does not love, pointedly refuses to move in with her own boyfriend.

When the original version of *Romantic* was premiered by the Phoenix Theater in 1981, a number of reviewers found that the play's episodic structure and Wasserstein's flair for jokes distracted from the issues that had inspired the work. Wasserstein is "better at parts than at wholes, more gag-than goal-oriented," wrote *New York*'s John Simon. He suggested that the first draft was encumbered by "Yale Drama School or Christopher Durang humor, which consists of scrumptious, scattershot bitchiness that . . . refus[es] to solidify into shapeliness." However, he concluded, Wasserstein "has a lovely forte: the comic-wistful line. . . . This could be a vein of gold, and needs only proper engineering to be efficiently mined."

Wasserstein apparently took such criticisms to heart, for she decided to thoroughly rewrite the play, removing excess one-liners and tightening the focus of the narrative. "The story of how the play was reborn," wrote Kakutani, "is the story both of an artist's maturation and of the painstaking work involved in reinventing a work." The financially troubled Phoenix Theater had become inactive in 1982, and Wasserstein turned instead to Playwrights Horizons and stage director Gerald Gutierrez. With his cooperation Wasserstein wrote seven successive new drafts of the play, revising even as rehearsals were in progress. Ultimately the new version was forty-five minutes shorter than the original. Several reviewers who were familiar with both versions of the play praised Wasserstein's efforts. The play has gained "momentum and a sense of purpose," wrote New Yorker's Edith Oliver, who noted that "the troubling emotions that were an undercurrent the first time around have now been brought to the surface, and without any loss of humor." Kakutani believed the revised play more clearly depicted Janie's "emotional growth." "It is clear now why [Janie] decides not to marry her hapless boyfriend," the reviewer explained. "Unlike Harriet, she is not willing to settle for someone or something that falls short of her romantic ideals—even if that means being alone." Time's Richard Corliss likened the play's "breadth and depth" to The Big Chill, a critically acclaimed and popular 1983 film in which several former college classmates from the 1960s face the realities of the 1980s.

As Wasserstein established her theater career, she became clearly identified with Playwrights Horizons, which also attracted Durang, Innaurato, and several other well-educated writers of about the same age. Under the growing influence of Andre Bishop, who joined as an administrator in 1975, Playwrights became "the most critically acclaimed Off Off Broadway group since Joseph Papp's Public Theater began in 1967," according to John Lombardi in the New York Times. "What [the dramatists at Playwrights Horizons] really have in common," Bishop told Lombardi, "is that they are all extremely literate and extremely intelligent, two qualities that don't neces-

sarily go together." He continued: "They come at the world from a humorous angle that is rooted in an angry desire for truth." Bishop wanted the organization and its writers to have lasting professional ties, and it developed such a relationship with Wasserstein. After producing the revised Romantic, Playwrights Horizons commissioned Wasserstein's next full-length work, Miami, a musical comedy about a teenage boy on vacation with his family in the late 1950s. The show received a limited run at the group's theater in early 1986. More successful was Wasserstein's subsequent full-length play, The Heidi Chronicles, which received its New York debut at Playwrights in late 1988.

The Heidi Chronicles was inspired by a single image in Wasserstein's mind: a woman speaking to an assembly of other women, confessing her growing sense of unhappiness. The speaker evolved into Dr. Heidi Holland, an art history professor who finds that her successful, independent life has left her alienated from men and women alike. Most of the play consists of flashbacks that capture Heidi's increasing disillusionment. Starting as a high-school girl, she experiences in turn the student activism of the late 1960s, feminist consciousness-raising of the early 1970s, and the tough-minded careerism of the 1980s. Friends disappoint her: a feminist activist becomes an entertainment promoter, valuing the women's audience for its market potential; a boyfriend becomes a manipulative and selfish magazine editor; a gay male friend tells her that in the 1980s, when gays are dying of AIDS, her unhappiness is a mere luxury. Heidi remains subdued until the play's climactic scene, when she addresses fellow alumnae from a private school for girls. "We're all concerned, intelligent, good women," she tells her old classmates, as quoted in the New York Times. "It's just that I feel stranded. And I thought the whole point was that we wouldn't feel stranded. I thought the point was we were all in this together." At the end of the play Heidi adopts a baby and poses happily with the child in front of an exhibition of works by Georgia O'Keefe, an acclaimed woman artist. "Heidi's search for self is both mirthful and touching," wrote Mel Gussow of the New York Times. Noting Wasserstein's enduring interest in comedy, he observed that "she has been exceedingly watchful about not settling for easy laughter, and the result is a more penetrating play." Other critics expressed similar praise. Newsday's Linda Winer, quoted in the Los Angeles Times, recalled that many authors had approached the themes of The Heidi Chronicles and announced: "Somebody finally got it right."

Reviewers debated how well the play reflected the reality of Heidi's, and Wasserstein's, generation. In *Village Voice,* Alisa Solomon suggested that the playwright lacked sympathy with the aspirations of feminism. *New York*'s John Simon felt the characters were oversimplified, averring that "Heidi's problem as stated—that she is too intellectual, witty, and successful for a mere hausfrau—just won't wash." Mimi Kramer, however, told readers of *New Yorker* that "Wasserstein's portrait of womanhood always remains complex." The reviewer found "generosity in the writing," contending that no character in the play "is made to seem ludicrous or dismissible." Praising Wasserstein's skill as a dramatist, Kramer declared that the playwright "never states anything that can be inferred. . . . She condemns these young men and women simply by capturing them in all their charm and complexity, without rhetoric or exaggeration." *The Heidi Chronicles* soon became Wasserstein's first show to move to a Broadway theater; soon afterwards, the play brought its author the Pulitzer Prize.

In 1990, Wasserstein published *Bachelor Girls,* a collection of humorous essays from *New York Woman* magazine. *Booklist* reviewer Ilene Cooper compared Wasserstein to Fran Lebowitz, whose humor also turns on the trials of being a single, Jewish woman in New York City. According to Cooper, the great difference is that Wasserstein's "wit is gently filtered rather than raw and rough." She noted, however, that "that doesn't mean she pulls her punches." *Time* contributor Margaret Carlson was less generous in her assessment of *Bachelor Girls,* stating that "the territory Wasserstein covers has been strip-mined by those who preceded her. . . . A piece about the split between women who shave their legs and those who don't would have to come up with some dazzling insights to merit another look." Carlson believed that Wasserstein's best work is most evident in the last piece in the book, a one-act play. A *Publishers Weekly* reviewer was also lukewarm, terming the collection only "semi-humorous," but a *Los Angeles Times Book Review* writer deemed it a "very funny blend of self-deprecation, pride and bemusement."

In her next play, Wasserstein again demonstrated humor underlaid with seriousness. *The Sisters Rosensweig* "looks at the lives of women who are weighing priorities and deciding which doors to open and deciding which gently to close," reported Linda Simon in the *Atlanta Journal-Constitution.* The play is set in London, where fifty-four-year-old Sara is celebrating her birthday with her two younger sisters. Twice divorced and having long abandoned any hope of real romance in life, she is surprised when love suddenly seems possible after all. "With her focus on the hidden yearnings and emotional resistance of the women, . . . [Wasserstein's] obvious debt is to Noel Coward. . . . *The Sisters Rosensweig* is very much a drawing room comedy." Mel Gussow, theater reviewer for the *New York Times,* found echoes of Chekhov in Wasserstein's work: "Overlooking the play is the symbolic figure of Anton Chekhov, smiling. Although the characters do not directly parallel those in *The Three Sisters,* the comparison is intentional. . . . Ms. Wasserstein does not overstate the connection but uses it like background music while diverting her attention to other cultural matters." Gussow concluded: "As the characters in Ms. Wasserstein's plays have become older, moving on from college to New York careers to the international setting of the current work, the author has remained keenly aware of the changes in her society and of the new roles that women play. In her writing, she continues to be reflexively in touch with her times."

In earlier plays, Wasserstein frequently presented remarkable women who, despite their gifts, felt their options closing down with the passing of the years. In *The Sisters Rosensweig,* the playwright presented images of strong, intelligent, middle-aged women whose lives are still full of possibilities. Several reviewers characterized it as Wasserstein's most hopeful play. Discussing the process of aging with Claire Carter for *Parade,* Wasserstein noted that she found turning forty to be a liberating experience. "Before turning 40, I got very depressed," she mused. "I kept making lists of things I had to do before 40. I drove myself crazy. Then after I turned 40, I thought, 'I don't have to do these things.' I was much happier after that."

BIOGRAPHICAL/CRITICAL SOURCES:

BOOKS

Contemporary Literary Criticism, Gale (Detroit), Volume 32, 1985, Volume 59, 1990.
Wasserstein, Wendy, *Uncommon Women and Others,* Avon, 1978.

PERIODICALS

American Book Review, November-December, 1989, p. 4.
Atlanta Journal-Constitution, May 23, 1993, p. N10.

Booklist, March 15, 1990, p. 1413.

Boston Globe, February 1, 1990, p. 69; March 3, 1991, p. B1; March 8, 1991, p. 25; March 22, 1991, p. 78; April 1, 1993, p. 61; January 27, 1994, p. 45; October 9, 1994, section 13, p. 7.

Chicago Tribune, October 12, 1985; November 10, 1985; April 24, 1990, section 5, p. 3; October 21, 1990, section 6, p. 1; March 15, 1992, section 13, p. 22; November 30, 1992, section 5, p. 1; October 9, 1994, section 13, p. 7.

Christian Science Monitor, April 30, 1986; April 30, 1991, p. 12; November 5, 1992, p. 13; November 15, 1994, p. 14.

Daily News (New York City), December 16, 1983; April 23, 1986.

Georgia Review, fall, 1989, pp. 573-85.

Horizon, February, 1978.

Los Angeles Times, January 31, 1984; October 28, 1984; October 30, 1984; December 17, 1988; October 15, 1990, p. F1; September 20, 1991, p. F20; July 31, 1994, section CAL, p. 45; December 29, 1994, p. F1.

Los Angeles Times Book Review, August 25, 1991, p. 10; May 30, 1993, p. 6.

Nation, December 17, 1977; February 18, 1984; May 1, 1989, pp. 605-06.

New Leader, December 7, 1994, p. 22.

New Republic, April 17, 1989, pp. 32-34.

Newsweek, March 20, 1989, pp. 76-77.

New York, June 29, 1981; January 2, 1989, pp. 48-49; March 27, 1989, pp. 66, 68; June 13, 1994, p. 72; November 7, 1994, p. 102.

New Yorker, December 5, 1977; June 22, 1981; June 13, 1983; December 26, 1983; December 26, 1988, pp. 81-82; November 14, 1994, p. 130; March 6, 1995, p. 132.

New York Post, November 22, 1977; December 16, 1983; April 23, 1986; December 12, 1988.

New York Times, November 22, 1977; May 24, 1978; June 23, 1978; December 27, 1978; June 8, 1979; February 15, 1981; May 24, 1981; June 15, 1981; June 28, 1981; July 17, 1983; December 16, 1983; January 1, 1984; January 3, 1984; February 26, 1984; June 13, 1984; January 3, 1986; March 28, 1986; April 23, 1986; January 11, 1987; August 30, 1987; January 24, 1988; June 8, 1988; December 11, 1988; December 12, 1988, p. C13; February 19, 1989; March 12, 1989; October 9, 1989, pp. C13, 16; January 24, 1991, p. C15; October 18, 1992, section 2, pp. 1, 24; October 23, 1992, p. C3; November 1, 1992, section 2, p. 5; December 6, 1992, section 9, p. 12; February 13, 1994, section 2, p. 5; May 23, 1994, p. C14; October 16, 1994, section 2, p. 5; October 27, 1994, p. C15; May 2, 1995, section 1, p. 37.

New York Woman, April, 1988.

Parade, September 5, 1993, p. 24.

People, March 26, 1984.

Publishers Weekly, March 2, 1990, p. 68.

Time, December 5, 1977; December 26, 1983; March 27, 1989, pp. 90-92; April 16, 1990, p. 83.

Variety, June 17, 1981.

Village Voice, December 20, 1988.

Wall Street Journal, December 16, 1988.

Washington Post, May 3, 1985; May 6, 1985; March 22, 1991, p. F3; November 12, 1991, p. D4; March 13, 1994, pp. G1, 6-7.

Women's Wear Daily, December 16, 1983; April 23, 1986.

*   *   *

WEART, Spencer R(ichard)   1942-

PERSONAL: Surname rhymes with "Burt"; born March 8, 1942, in Detroit, MI; son of Spencer A. and Janet (Streng) Weart; married Carole Ege, 1971; children: Lara Kimi, Spencer Gen. *Education:* Cornell University, B.A., 1963; University of Colorado, Ph.D., 1968; University of California, Berkeley, postdoctoral study, 1971-73. *Politics:* Independent. *Avocational interests:* Hiking, skiing.

ADDRESSES: Home—12 Buena Vista Dr., Hastings, NY 10706; fax 301-209-0882. *Office*—American Institute of Physics, One College Ellipse, College Park, MD 20740. *E-mail*—sweart@aip.org.

CAREER: Mount Wilson and Palomar Observatories, Pasadena, CA, research fellow, 1968-70; University of California, Berkeley, research assistant in history department, 1971-74; American Institute of Physics, New York City, later, College Park, MD, director of Center for History of Physics, 1974—.

MEMBER: American Astronomical Society, American Geophysical Union, History of Science Society, Society for Social Studies of Science.

WRITINGS:

Light: A Key to the Universe (juvenile), illustrated by Mark Binn, Coward (New York City), 1968.

(Self-illustrated) *How to Build a Sun* (juvenile), Coward, 1970.

Scientists in Power, Harvard University Press (Cambridge, MA), 1979.

Nuclear Fear: A History of Images, Harvard University Press, 1988.

EDITOR

Selected Papers of Great American Physicists: The Bicentennial Commemorative Volume of the American Physical Society, 1976, American Institute of Physics, 1976.

(With Gertrud Weiss Szilard) *Leo Szilard: His Version of the Facts-Selected Recollections and Correspondence,* MIT Press (Cambridge, MA), 1978.

(With Melba Phillips) *History of Physics: Readings from "Physics Today,"* American Institute of Physics, 1985.

(With William Hedeson and others, and contributor) *Out of the Crystal Maze: Chapters from the History of Solid State Physics,* Oxford University Press (New York City), 1992.

WORK IN PROGRESS: Never at War: Why Democracies Don't Fight Each Other, submitted to publishers, 1996; a history of the Greenhouse Effect.

SIDELIGHTS: In *Nuclear Fear: A History of Images,* Spencer R. Weart argues that humanity's fear of nuclear energy originated years before the first atomic explosion at Hiroshima. According to Alfred Kazin in the *New York Times Book Review,* "Weart . . . has gone beyond anyone else in collecting what I have called 'evidences' and he calls 'images.' 'Nuclear Fear: A History of Images' is a prodigious demonstration, item after item, of how Americans have responded to the new world of nuclear energy and its militarization. The new consciousness is revealed to be, under pressure, a very old, primitive, long-buried world of archaic images. Mr. Weart has been tireless in searching out even old movies, comic strips, forgotten best sellers, equally perishable military and official governmental pronouncements." In terms of archaic images, Weart points to the commonly held visions of total earthly destruction by mad scientists, the appearance of mutant monsters due to radiation exposure, and Garden of Eden-type utopias. Although fears and misconceptions concerning atomic energy are prevalent among nonscientists, Weart indicates that many of these images were actually fostered by scientists themselves. British chemist Frederick Soddy, for instance, predicted in a 1908

book that if man had the ability to transmute matter "such a race could transform a desert continent, thaw the frozen poles and make the whole world one smiling Garden of Eden," Weart records. Overall, Weart's purpose is to reveal the flaws in some of these recurring but misleading images. "Doomsday thinking is so common," writes Kazin, " . . . that a valuable feature of this book is Mr. Weart's effort to correct 'images' that do not correspond to the facts."

Critical response to Weart's study varies. Reviewer Peter Gorner for the *Chicago Tribune* expresses that "a few works have 'important' written all over them, and this is one. . . . [Weart] has spent 15 years indefatigably compiling countless 'images,' or symbolic associations, that have led to the thinking of our times. . . . If Weart has an axe to grind, it is that all of us, pro-and antinuclear proponents alike, have been conned by imagemakers." In turn, *Los Angeles Times Book Review* contributor Alex Raksin believes Weart's main argument—that much of humanity's fear of atomic energy is based on false images—will surely "provoke the ire" of anti-nuclear activists. Additionally, Raksin finds Weart's emphasis on the safety of nuclear power plants unrealistic: "Weart . . . is too quick to discount disasters such as Chernobyl. . . . Power plants are not always designed and operated perfectly. . . . To dismiss this book for its underestimation of nuclear dangers, however, would be to miss its extraordinary value as a detailed probing study of American hopes, dreams and insecurities in the 20th Century."

One additional complaint expressed by Kazin in the *New York Times Book Review* and John Gross in the *New York Times* is that Weart's history of atomic fear emphasizes psychological factors at the expense of socio-political factors. As Gross maintains, there is a "limit . . . to what you can usefully say if you push politics and policies so firmly into the background. . . . While Mr. Weart doesn't altogether ignore hard political considerations, the reasons he advances are mainly psychological: habituation, strategies of denial and so forth. . . . 'Nuclear Fear' certainly deserves to be read: it is never less than intelligent and absorbing. But it still leaves you feeling that although imagery is an important aspect of history, it is only an aspect." In a like manner, Kazin finds Weart's use of psychological factors over social and economic factors misleading at times. As an example Kazin points to Weart's suggestion that the lack of "early maternal support" connects divergent "'apocalyptic' thinkers" like Mary Shelley, Jack London, and Dr. Helen Caldicott to the turmoil of the atomic age. Kazin believes Weart could have covered other factors such as the use of the Star Wars image by defense contractors more thoroughly. Nevertheless, Kazin concludes that Weart's study is "a true history of our age—a cutting, indispensable, deeply troubling book. I trust it will trouble you."

BIOGRAPHICAL/CRITICAL SOURCES:

BOOKS

Weart, Spencer R., *Nuclear Fear: A History of Images,* Harvard University Press, 1988.

PERIODICALS

Bulletin of the Atomic Scientists, August, 1985.
Chicago Tribune, May 4, 1988.
Los Angeles Times Book Review, May 15, 1988.
New York Times, April 29, 1988.
New York Times Book Review, May 1, 1988.

*   *   *

WEST, Paul   1930-

PERSONAL: Born February 23, 1930, in Eckington, Derbyshire, England; son of Alfred Massick and Mildred (Noden) West; children: Amanda Klare. *Education:* University of Birmingham, B.A., 1950; Oxford University, graduate study, 1950-53; Columbia University, M.A., 1953. *Avocational interests:* Music, swimming, travel, and astronomy.

ADDRESSES: Office—c/o Elaine Markson, 44 Grenwich Avenue, New York, NY 10011.

CAREER: Memorial University of Newfoundland, St. John's, Newfoundland, began as assistant professor, associate professor of English, 1957-62; Pennsylvania State University, University Park, associate professor, 1963-69, professor of English and comparative literature, 1969-95, senior fellow of Institute for Arts and Humanistic Studies, 1969-95, professor emeritus, 1995—. Visiting professor, University of Wisconsin, 1956-66; Crawshaw Professor of English, Colgate University, 1972; Virginia Woolf Lecturer, University of Tulsa, 1972; Melvin Hill Distinguished Visiting Professor of Humanities, Hobart and William Smith Colleges, 1974; distinguished writer in residence, Wichita State University, 1982;

writer in residence, University of Arizona, 1984; visiting professor of English, Cornell University, 1987—; visiting professor and novelist in residence, Brown University, 1992. Judge, CAPS fiction panel, 1975, Heinz fiction prize, 1980 and 1986, National Book Award, 1990. *Military service:* Royal Air Force, 1954-57; became flight lieutenant.

MEMBER: Authors League of America, Authors Guild.

AWARDS, HONORS: Canada Council senior fellowship, 1959; Guggenheim fellowship, 1962-63; listed in "Books of the Year" by *New York Times,* 1969, for *Words for a Deaf Daughter,* 1970, for *I'm Expecting to Live Quite Soon,* 1971, for *Caliban's Filibuster,* and 1986, for *Rat Man of Paris; Words for a Deaf Daughter* included in "Best Books of the Year" list by *Time,* 1969; *Paris Review* Aga Khan Prize for fiction, 1974; National Endowment for the Humanities fellowship, 1975; National Endowment for the Arts fellowship, 1980, 1985; Governor of Pennsylvania's award for excellence in the arts, 1981; American Academy and Institute of Arts and Letters award in literature, 1985, 1986; Pushcart Prize, 1987; named Literary Lion by New York Public Library, 1987; nominated for Medicis, Femina, and Meilleur Livre prizes, and Grand Prix Halperine-Kaminsky (France), 1993; Lannan Prize for Fiction, 1993, for *Love's Mansion;* Distinguished Teaching Award, Graduate Schools of the Northeast, 1995; National Book Critics Circle Award nomination for fiction, 1996, for *The Tent of Orange Mist.*

WRITINGS:

A Quality of Mercy, Chatto & Windus (London), 1961.
Tenement of Clay, Hutchinson (London), 1965, McPherson & Co. (Kingston, NY), 1993.
Alley Jaggers (first novel in trilogy), Harper (New York City), 1966.
I'm Expecting to Live Quite Soon (second novel in trilogy), Harper, 1970.
Caliban's Filibuster, Doubleday (New York City), 1971.
Bela Lugosi's White Christmas (third novel in trilogy), Harper, 1972.
Colonel Mint, Dutton (New York City), 1973.
Gala (see also below), Harper, 1976.
The Very Rich Hours of Count von Stauffenberg (historical novel), Harper, 1980.
Rat Man of Paris, Doubleday, 1986.

The Place in Flowers Where Pollen Rests, Doubleday, 1988.

Lord Byron's Doctor (biographical novel), Doubleday, 1989.

The Women of Whitechapel and Jack the Ripper (historical novel), Random House (New York City), 1991.

Love's Mansion, Random House, 1992.

The Tent of Orange Mist, Scribner (New York City), 1995.

Sporting with Amaryllis, Overlook (New York City), 1997.

OTHER

The Fantasy Poets: Number Seven, Fantasy Press, 1952.

The Growth of the Novel, Canadian Broadcasting Corp., 1959.

The Spellbound Horses (poems), Ryerson, 1960.

Byron and the Spoiler's Art, St. Martin's (New York City), 1960.

I, Said the Sparrow (memoirs), Hutchinson, 1963.

(Editor) *Byron: A Collection of Critical Essays,* Prentice-Hall (Englewood Cliffs, NJ), 1963.

The Modern Novel (two volumes), Hillary, 1963, 2nd edition, 1965.

Robert Penn Warren, University of Minnesota Press (Minneapolis), 1964.

The Snow Leopard (poems), Hutchinson, 1964, Harcourt, 1965.

The Wine of Absurdity: Essays on Literature and Consolation, Pennsylvania State University Press (University Park), 1966.

Words for a Deaf Daughter (biography), Harper, 1969, expanded edition with new preface by West published as *Words for a Deaf Daughter* [and] *Gala,* Dalkey Archive (Normal, IL), 1993.

Out of My Depths: A Swimmer in the Universe (nonfiction), Anchor Press, 1983.

Sheer Fiction (essays), McPherson, 1987, Volume 2, 1991, Volume 3, 1994.

The Universe, and Other Fictions (short fiction), Overlook Press (Woodstock, NY), 1988.

Portable People (character sketches), drawings by Joe Servello, British American Publishers (Latham, NY), 1990.

A Stroke of Genius: Illness and Self-Discovery (autobiographical memoir), Viking, 1995.

My Mother's Music (memoir), Viking, 1996.

Regular contributor to *Washington Post Book World, Boston Phoenix,* and *New York Times Book Review.*

Also contributor of essays, poems, and reviews to periodicals, including *TriQuarterly, Iowa Review, Parnassus, Conjunctions, Quimera* (Barcelona), *Nation, Kenyon Review, Sinn und Form, Partisan Review, New Directions Literary Anthology, Paris Review, Yale Review, Chelsea,* and *Harper's.* Fiction critic, *New Statesman,* 1959-60.

SIDELIGHTS: Paul West's writings span the genres of poetry, essay, criticism, biography, and the novel. Although his work in each genre has received critical praise, West favors the novel form for expression and experimentation. As *Dictionary of Literary Biography* contributor Brian McLaughlin notes, "It is as a fiction writer that he seems most happy, for there he can demonstrate at one and the same time the strength of the critic and the grace of the poet." *Book World* contributor Diane Johnson likewise comments that one of the most positive aspects of West's work "is his faith in the novel as an art form, as a dignified production of the human mind, capable of rendering, in its infinite variety, social comment, philosophic statement, comedy, pain, all of which West can do—impressively." Within West's novels, the author takes the guise of a variety of characters, including Jack the Ripper, the Rat Man of Paris, and his deaf daughter. West even reflects upon his parents' courtship and love life before he was born.

A native of England, West made America his permanent home after coming to the United States twice, first as a student at Columbia University and later on a Guggenheim fellowship. His move to America was due in part to the warm reception his books were given by American publishers, and also to his love of America's "violent vitality," as he tells *Publishers Weekly* interviewer Amanda Smith. Despite the encouragement of American publishers and his affinity for the American way of life, West does not link himself with North American writers. He explains to Smith: "In moving to North America, I perhaps made a compass error and should have gone south. Latin American fiction takes risks. Imagination to them is a primal force, and they ride it like a breaker—it's like surfing. I feel very much in sympathy with that—this is the way my head works." McLaughlin also notes this similarity. He writes: "In his concern with the nature of fiction and the need to experiment, West carries on the investigations pioneered in the first half of this century and joins company with contemporary experimentalists such as Juan Goytisolo, Gabriel Garcia Marquez, and William Gass."

West's work is united by a single theme, which he describes to Rebecca Pepper Sinkler in the *New York Times Book Review* as the "trauma of being alive, existing, in light of the fact that we're determined by givens out of our control." West's protagonists do not passively accept their destiny, however. As *Nation* contributor Walton Beacham observes: "In all his imaginative books . . . West establishes a world in which the competition between structure and disorder drives man deeper into himself, so that if he ever emerges, it is as a creature who is frantic to control those forces larger than himself. He cries against the cosmos in defiance of his subservience, and struggles to establish order over the chaos as proof of his autonomy."

In his historical novel *The Very Rich Hours of Count von Stauffenberg,* for example, West portrays Count von Stauffenberg, a key figure in the anti-Nazi movement who orchestrated an unsuccessful plot to bomb Hitler's office in 1944. Von Stauffenberg was executed, and many of his conspirators were tortured and killed. "On these bones," writes Frederick Busch in the *New York Times Book Review,* "Mr. West lays a flesh of living words: Dead dreams—of self, love, nobility, military service—are the stuff of his narrative." Written as a fictional memoir, the novel reveals the various facets of von Stauffenberg's character and chronicles his transformation from a moderate supporter of Hitler to an activist against him. In a preface to the novel, West explains the genesis of *The Very Rich Hours of Count von Stauffenberg:* "I was devouring books about the bomb plot against Hitler, some grand, some shoddy, many of them giving details the others omitted, and almost all of them contradicting one another until I felt that some of what I was reading was fiction already and that a fictional attempt of my own—say an historical impersonation—might go."

The novel was indeed a critical success. *Partisan Review* contributor Ronald Christ comments: "Having resisted the temptation to write an account, or indictment, Paul West has written instead a novel . . . that never forgets language and the sensibility it issues from as the real protagonist. The richness of West's prose is the real wealth here, and it is, like Stauffenberg's hours, loaded with all the treasures of a 'truant mind.'" *Washington Post Book World* contributor Joe David Bellamy similarly observes, "There is little attention to conventional plotting and suspense, to the aspects that could have made the novel 'a thriller.' But a rich, textured style and metaphorical inventiveness are the dividends."

West's novel *Rat Man of Paris,* like *The Very Rich Hours of Count von Stauffenberg,* is based on a historical figure. Inspired by stories of a man who haunted the boulevards of Paris at the end of World War II, flashing a rat at passersby, West began to "[fill] in the blanks" of Rat Man's life, as he explains to Smith. West's Rat Man is Etienne Poulsifer, and he carries a fox stole, not a rat. The stole is one of the few belongings Rat Man was able to take with him after his family and their entire village were burned alive by Nazis. This event, reminiscent of the actual German extermination of the French village Oradour, has shaped Rat Man's existence. Observes *New York Times Book Review* contributor Lore Segal: "[*Rat Man of Paris*] addresses the large question of our time: How does one live one's daily life in the span between past atrocity and atrocity to come? What happens to the wound that does not heal, that will not scar over?" Despite Rat Man's various eccentricities—he also bathes with his clothes on and hangs his soiled sheets out his window in the hope that the police will, according to *Los Angeles Times* critic Richard Eder, "arrest and launder them"—Rat Man attracts a lonely high school teacher, Sharli, who views him as "another of her pupils: bigger, heavier, and more of a liability, to be sure, yet a fount of promise so long as he is able to take his time." West describes Rat Man in *Publishers Weekly* as "a parallel man, a man of distance who has a very uncertain relationship with civilization. He doesn't quite know what it is and where he belongs in it, and he's amazed that people think he *does* belong in it."

When Rat Man discovers that a Nazi war criminal has been extradited to France, he wrongly assumes that the convict is responsible for murdering the villagers. As an attempt at vengeance, Rat Man outfits himself like a Nazi and walks the streets of Paris carrying a sign with the Nazi's picture on it and wheeling the "rat" about in a pram. Rat Man becomes, like his real-life counterpart, a local celebrity, but his renown ends when he is injured by a sniper's bullet. Eder writes: "Up until the shooting, West's fable is compassionate and chilling. His Poulsifer, victim and avenger, has a questioning and original humanity. And then it all fogs over." Expressing a similar opinion, *Newsweek* reviewer Peter S. Prescott argues that "*Rat Man of Paris* achieves its quite dazzling effects early on and then settles down to work variations on them. The effect isn't one of motion or of answers obtained, but of a faint glow." *Washington Post Book World* contributor Howard Frank Mosher describes *Rat Man of Paris* as a novel of ideas and cautions that it is difficult to read. He maintains, however, that the novel is worth the effort. "Complex and magical strikes me as exactly the right way to describe Paul West's latest novel," writes Mosher. "In its beautiful language (both purple, and plain), its inventive plot, and its unsentimental revelation of the private life of a legendary fixture of a great city, *Rat Man of Paris* is a memorable and moving work of fiction."

West's 1988 novel, *The Place in Flowers Where Pollen Rests,* is set in a Hopi settlement in northeastern Arizona, and is told in various narrative voices, including those of George, Oswald, their deceased relatives, and Sotuqnangu, a mythical Hopi spirit. George The Place In Flowers Where Pollen Rests is a doll carver; his nephew Oswald Beautiful Badger Going Over The Hill wants to be a Hollywood actor. When Oswald leaves the community, he ends up as a pornographic movie star, and enlists for a tour of duty in Vietnam. Oswald, as Thomas R. Edwards reveals in a *New York Times Book Review* article on *The Place in Flowers,* "tries to live up to his name by deserting his birthplace" and his people in favor of the White occidental world. But for Oswald, the "Anglo world . . . both attracts and nauseates," and he returns to his Hopi people when "the horrors of White America come closer to destroying him."

Much critical attention focused on the textual complexity of *The Place in Flowers.* For John Calvin Batchelor, writing in the *Washington Post Book World,* West is "a writer's writer who aggressively goes too far, thinks too much, turns too many metaphors and explores too much strangeness for the casual reader." Steven Moore agrees that the novel is challenging, but finds that the textual intricacy conveys "not only the Hopi culture but its linguistic structure as well." In his review of the novel in the *Review of Contemporary Fiction,* Moore argues that the novel requires careful, slow reading, in order that "the reader can better appreciate the detailed, visceral texture of the places West describes." Edwards finds *The Place in Flowers* a "strong and moving novel," with "wholly credible imaging of desire, violence, and cultural bewilderment." The critic goes on to offer an answer to the criticism that West's novel is excessively difficult: "Serious fiction is not . . . obligated to be very reader-friendly, and it is scarcely a defect in a novelist that he writes inventively and thinks subtly about what art does." A *Publishers Weekly* reviewer claims West reveals a "Joycean genius in [his] exuberant play of language," and calls the novel "astonishing."

In the 1989 biographical novel *Lord Byron's Doctor,* West focuses on the small group of people who spent the summer of 1816 with the exiled George Gordon, Lord Byron, focusing specifically on John William Polidori. Polidori, the least famous member of the group which included Mary Wollstonecraft Godwin, Percy Bysshe Shelley and, Byron's mistress and Mary Godwin's step-sister, Claire Clairmont, was a "young physician traveling as the club-footed Byron's secretary and medical adviser. He also had a 500 commission from a London publisher to report on the poet's adventures," notes R. Z. Sheppard in a *Time* review of the novel. *Lord Byron's Doctor* is West's version of the events written about in Polidori's diary, including the love/hate relationship between the doctor and Byron, the sexual exploits of Byron and Shelley, and Polidori's suicide. Noting that the author is himself a Byron scholar, Steven Moore in the *Review of Contemporary Fiction* explains that West has fleshed out "Polidori's skeletal diary in a robust early-nineteenth-century style . . . [creating] a penetrating psychological portrait of Lord Byron's Doctor." Merle Rubin in the *Los Angeles Times Book Review* argues that "the accomplished, amazingly versatile writer Paul West is not out to 'prove' that the brilliant, rather unstable, young physician was actually a neglected man of genius." Rather, the critic declares, what interests West about Polidori "is precisely his secondariness: his resentment at snubs and slights; the love-hatred he feels for Byron and the displaced hatred he feels toward Shelley for being Byron's friend and equal; and his nonetheless unshakable conviction that this experience marks the high point of his life."

"Through Polidori, West compiles a lurid case history on the cruelty of genius," finds Sheppard, who sees the author as "one of the most vigorous and inviting literary talents still punching away in semiobscurity." Moore concludes that *Lord Byron's Doctor* is a "stylistic tour de force of nineteenth-century eloquence, slang and technical jargon; and a wholly successful recreation of that crucial year in literary history when Romantic yearnings confronted the darker recesses of the unconscious, wreaking havoc in the personal lives of their creators, but also giving birth to poetry and monsters that haunt us still."

West chose another infamous historical figure for the focus of his 1991 novel. In *The Women of Whitechapel and Jack the Ripper,* West revisits the fall of 1888 to explain the murders of five London prostitutes. The story begins some years prior, when

Queen Victoria's grandson, Prince Eddy, and the painter and Prince Eddy's chaperon, Walter Richard Sickert, are spending much of their time at London brothels. Sickert introduces Prince Eddy to the poor, young Annie Crook, the two fall in love, and soon after, Annie becomes pregnant. The pregnancy becomes the precipitating event to a savage conspiracy involving the royal family.

When the Queen learns of the affair, she and the Prime Minister, Lord Salisbury, arrange to have Annie kidnapped and taken to the royal family's personal physician, Sir William Gull, who lobotomizes and permanently hospitalizes her. One of Annie's friends, Marie Kelly, and a few of her fellow prostitutes at Whitechapel, sends a blackmail letter to the Queen, demanding Annie's release and a sum of money to keep the matter quiet. The Queen then sets Gull loose to hunt the prostitutes down and silence them, and Sickert is taken along to identify the women who signed the letter. Gull is eventually held in a private psychiatric hospital, and Sickert, who became increasingly entranced by the murders, takes into his own care Alice Margaret, the daughter of Prince Eddy and Annie.

The Women of Whitechapel is "superbly written and intricately choreographed, a work both sensational and serious," writes Sven Birkerts in a review of the novel in the *New Republic.* "But what finally remains vivid, long after the novel has shrunk down to its afterimage in the mind, is the feverish abandon of Gull and the descriptions of his myriad mutilations," continues Birkerts. "The passages are raw and uninhibited; they transmit perfectly Sickert's fascinated repulsion. The visual precision is a triumph of artistic detachment, even as it horrifies." West's "prose glistens with bright ideas and boldly inventive turns of phrase," comments Dan Cryer in *Newsday.* Josh Rubins in the *New York Times Book Review* concurs, finding that West's "specialty is filling in the missing details—psychological and otherwise—through verbally exquisite interior monologues or provocatively vivid evocations of unfamiliar milieus." Vance Bourjaily, in *Chicago Tribune Books,* calls West "possibly our finest living stylist in English."

In the Lannan prize winning *Love's Mansion,* West's 1992 semi-autobiographical novel, the author explores the life of his own parents before his conception. Albert Mobilio argues in the *Village Voice Literary Supplement* that only an author like West, who "dotes on the minds of assassins, madmen, and murderers . . . might be . . . adequately girded to

peer under the sheets on his parents' wedding night. In *Love's Mansion . . .* he does just that, pulling back the covers on both how he came to be, and how memory comes to life." *Love's Mansion* is the story of Clive Moxon, a novelist in his mid-fifties who asks his 94-year-old Mother Hilly about her relationship with his father. The novel recounts Clive's father Harry's adventure in World War I, from which he returns blind. Despite this handicap, upon his return, he and Hilly get married. Joseph Coates notes in *Chicago Tribune Books:* "Both of them know it's a misalliance, each having 'made a new demand on life' that excludes the other without having the resources to enforce it. Harry is an existentialist before his time, wanting nothing better than a life of continental vagrancy and sensuality; Hilly wanting a life in art." Over time, as Jonathan Yardley comments in the *Washington Post Book World,* their "marriage seems 'an enormous barrier to what used to be their affection.'" Yardley summarizes: "Hilly, determined over Harry's objections to have a child, at last becomes pregnant with Clive and then with a daughter, Kotch. However improbable a family they may be, a family is what they are: a small mansion with four rooms, but a mansion all the same."

Despite finding that the subject of West's *Love's Mansion* "may well have been too close to the author," with the result that West "overcompensate[s] by verbal acrobatics that lower the emotional temperature" of the work, Gary Davenport of the *Sewanee Review* nonetheless concludes: "Paul West at the top of his form is a talented writer who demonstrates the continuing possibilities for the historical novel and deserves a wide audience—more so I think than the [E. L.] Doctorows and other better known practitioners of the genre." Coates finds that "West the author . . . constantly impresses us with his gravely cheerful acceptance of mortality [and] seems to have gratefully tracked his talent to its source in this fully imagined valentine to his tumultuously romantic, disappointed but somehow fulfilled mother." Though finding that the narrator Clive's self-consciousness about dreaming and inventing "becomes the subject of the book" and hinders the narrative flow, Richard Eder in a *Los Angeles Times Book Review* piece on *Love's Mansion* admires West's "dream-memoir": "West invents beautifully, and his writing lives up to his invention."

With *The Tent of Orange Mist,* notes a *Publishers Weekly* reviewer, West's "versatility and imagination are again evident." Scald Ibis, a 16-year-old, becomes the property of Colonel Hayashi as her home is turned into a brothel for Japanese soldiers during the assault and occupation of Nanking, China. West's story of severe and unspeakable violence becoming commonplace, which was nominated for the National Book Critics Circle fiction award, comes highly recommended by Robert E. Brown, who calls the work in a *Library Journal* review, "both moving and intriguing. . . . An affecting novel." Commenting that West explores and "illuminates the consciousness of each of his . . . characters—especially Scald Ibis' struggle to come to terms with her pillaged youth," Donna Seaman in a *Booklist* review lauds West's "scorching insights into the consequences of evil." John David Morley in the *New York Times Book Review,* however, disagrees. Despite calling *Orange Mist* a "most arresting thesis," and West a "gifted writer," Morley faults the novel on credibility: " . . . that Scald Ibis should become reconciled to her fate with such savvy and bounce—is so far removed from experience that it is impossible to participate in the book's jollity. Victims of rape under the threat of imminent murder simply do not behave like this." Though arguing that West's narrative does wear "thin in spots," Seaman nonetheless concludes that West writes with "mind-stopping clarity and power." Richard Eder, in the *Los Angeles Times Book Review,* calls the novel "a small masterpiece," and argues that "West has never written anything so risky and triumphant."

One of West's most eloquently written and widely read books is *Words for a Deaf Daughter,* a biography of his daughter Mandy, born deaf and suffering from a brain dysfunction. Like the characters in some of West's novels, Mandy is an outsider. People turn away from her in the street because, according to West, "they don't like a universe that's absurd," relates Claire Tomalin in the *New Statesman.* Mandy is destructive yet obsessed with order and symmetry. She will fly into a rage because of a missing button or crooked barrette, for example, yet she will happily paint her face green, chew cigarettes, and cut her hair at random. The Wests' hope that Mandy will, with encouragement, develop fully, and the book is written in anticipation that she will one day be able to read about the early years of her life.

Novelist Chaim Potok observes in the *New York Times Book Review:* "Trapped, by whatever it is that traps people, into a potential horror and hell, West converted the trap into a doorway to a world filled with the strange fruit of nonverbal communication and creative silence." *Time* critic R. Z. Sheppard argues that "West writes joyfully for a can-be

Mandy, but obviously adores Mandy as is. . . . A lifelong slave of words and reasons, [West] envies the intensity with which Mandy perceives the world nonverbally through her four acute senses." *Commentary* contributor Johanna Kaplan, however, finds West's optimistic, celebratory portrait of Mandy disturbing. She disputes West's description of Mandy's handicaps as a special gift. "For whom is it a gift?" she asks. "Not Mandy, clearly, for so cut off is she from the ordinary and essential means of human interchange that to try to understand the function of everyday objects, to give them some kind of place in what is for her an especially confusing world, she must 'smell at a pencil newly sharpened, inhaling from the beechwood its own sour-soot bouquet, or trace with addicted fingers the corrugations on the flat of a halved cabbage before eating it raw.'"

Other reviewers maintain that *Words for a Deaf Daughter* realistically describes Mandy's handicaps and her parents' attempts to understand them. The *Times Literary Supplement* reviewer states that even though West describes Mandy as exceptional rather than handicapped, "this did not mean denying the handicap, but, so far as was possible, sharing it, searching for the motive behind the compulsive or seemingly irrational behaviour and for the compensating gifts and faculties that might—should—must be possessed by a child who was lacking in hearing (and so speech) and conventional intellect." Robert A. Gross notes in *Newsweek* that West is acutely aware of the possible futility of his efforts to communicate with Mandy. Gross writes: "He confronts the painful question of whether his words capture the reality of her experiences at all. . . . Even if he is wrong and his words deceive, West still draws comfort from the extraordinary reverence for life that Mandy has given him."

Words for a Deaf Daughter was reprinted with a new introduction by West in 1993. West comments to Amanda Smith in *Publishers Weekly:* "*Words for a Deaf Daughter* was written a long time ago, and it's a sort of hard and fast and settled book. Maybe the sense of the outsider, the dispossessed prince or princess, the pariah, the person who is shunned or spurned for whatever unjust reason—maybe this is a gathering pattern in one's work over twenty years. I'm sure one could make a good case, but I don't think in those terms. If I did, I wouldn't be able to write."

West's autobiographical work, *A Stroke of Genius: Illness and Self-Discovery,* explores the author's experience with several diseases, including migraine headaches, heart disease and diabetes, and his stroke, which forced him to accept a pacemaker implant to regulate his heartbeat. D. T. Max in the *Los Angeles Times Book Review* comments: "[West] must have been, without doubt, a nightmarish patient. As feckless as any autodidact, he reads and rereads the diagnostic manual with a fervor born of terror." Max praises *Stroke of Genius* despite finding that West buries disease itself under an "avalanche of prose." In West's book, the reader is allowed closer to the trauma of disease than in other memoirs of a similar nature, "not because West is braver—he is a complete chicken—but because he is franker," concludes Max. Dwight Garner notes in a *Nation* review that West focuses on his "generation's ingrained existentialism," which argues against passivity and leads "happily" to "a simple dignity in being a 'critic, fighter, and perfectionist to the end.'" Alexander Theroux, in a *Chicago Tribune* review of *Stroke of Genius,* quotes West's explanation for his preoccupation with his illness: "I ponder such matters in much the same spirit as I memorize the names of all the actors when a movie's final credits roll—not because I care who they are, but because I want to show myself I am still competent."

West told *CA:* "I started writing short stories—I'm sure very poor ones—when I was about twelve, I think. God knows what they were—hero-worship short stories about adventurers, pilots, people at the poles, and so on. They've all vanished; I don't know where they are. I did that for three or four years. Then, when I became an undergraduate, I started writing poems and did that pretty solidly. As I recall, my first three books were poetry. Then I wanted elbow room, and I started writing weekly essays. I did this for a long time, essays on every damn thing going, which was part of the educational system anyway. I wrote essays for fun for a long time, and I still do. Then I got fiction fever and into the novel. I was in my middle twenties when I thought, Well, maybe the novel is what I want to do. I haven't really turned away from it since.

"[When] I was . . . given an Academy prize for the body of my work . . . I felt for a while as if my career was over. I felt from it untimely ripped. Howard Nemerov consoled me on the stairs, and I cheered up. There are books—I'm not going to tell you which—I should never have allowed to see the light of day. Two I wish I had forgotten about. And I have my favorites. I think it's fairly easy, now that I've published thirty-odd books, when people say,

'What are your favorite books?' I think I know. But I don't read them again; I don't go back to them at all. I just look at the externals, the jackets, and say, 'That one was OK, and that one was not.' There's no law compelling you to get it right. You work with what's available at the time."

BIOGRAPHICAL/CRITICAL SOURCES:

BOOKS

Birkerts, Sven, *American Energies,* Morrow, 1992.
Contemporary Authors Autobiography Series, Volume 7, Gale (Detroit), 1988.
Contemporary Literary Criticism, Gale, Volume 7, 1977, Volume 14, 1980.
Dictionary of Literary Biography, Volume 14: *British Novelists since 1960,* Gale, 1983.
Madden, David W., *Understanding Paul West,* University of South Carolina Press (Columbia), 1993.

PERIODICALS

Booklist, August, 1994, p. 2017; August, 1995, p. 1929.
Book World, May 28, 1972.
Chicago Tribune Books, April 14, 1991, p. 1; October 18, 1992, p. 5; February 19, 1995, p. 13.
Commentary, January, 1971.
Commonweal, September 30, 1966; December 9, 1977.
Harper's, October, 1970.
Kirkus Reviews, December 15, 1992, p. 1534.
Library Journal, September 15, 1988, p. 95; May 1, 1993, p. 119; August, 1995, p. 121.
Los Angeles Times, March 21, 1983; February 12, 1986.
Los Angeles Times Book Review, October 9, 1988, p. 2; September 10, 1989, p. 3; September 6, 1992, p. 3; May 7, 1995, p. 1; September 10, 1995, p. 3.
Nation, January 8, 1977; March 20, 1995, pp. 391-394.
New Republic, August 19, 1972; May 6, 1991, p. 37. *Newsday,* April 21, 1991.
New Statesman, August 29, 1969.
Newsweek, August 31, 1970; March 10, 1986.
New Yorker, October 24, 1970; August 25, 1980.
New York Times Book Review, May 3, 1970; September 27, 1970; September 10, 1972; July 3, 1977; November 9, 1980; February 16, 1986; September 11, 1988, p. 7; May 12, 1991, p. 11; Octo-

ber 18, 1992; July 11, 1993, p. 20; September 20, 1993, p. 16; September 3, 1995, p. 17.
Partisan Review, summer, 1982.
Publishers Weekly, February 28, 1986; July 29, 1988, p. 219; July 21, 1989, p. 50; January 18, 1993, p. 464; July 11, 1994, p. 72; July 3, 1995, p. 48.
Review of Contemporary Fiction, fall, 1988, p. 156; fall, 1989, p. 215; spring, 1991 (special Paul West issue).
Sewanee Review, spring, 1993, p. 300.
Southern Review, winter, 1979.
Time, September 7, 1970; September 11, 1989, p. 82.
Times Literary Supplement, January 21, 1965; October 16, 1969; April 23, 1971; January 28, 1972; June 8, 1973; February 6, 1981; November 8, 1991, p. 31.
Voice Literary Supplement, September, 1992, p. 15.
Washington Post Book World, April 26, 1970; August 23, 1970; January 2, 1977; August 3, 1980; February 2, 1986; September 18, 1988, p. 3; September 27, 1992, p. 3.

*   *   *

WHITTEN, Leslie H(unter), Jr. 1928-

PERSONAL: Born February 21, 1928, in Jacksonville, FL; son of Leslie Hunter (an electrical engineer) and Linnora (Harvey) Whitten; married Phyllis Webber, November 11, 1951; children: Leslie Hunter III, Andrew Cassisus, Daniel Lee, Deborah Wilson Gordon. *Education:* Lehigh University, B.A. (magna cum laude), 1950.

ADDRESSES: Home—114 Eastmoor Dr., Silver Spring, MD 20901. *Agent*—David Henden, P.O. Box 990, Nyack, NJ 10960.

CAREER: Radio Free Europe, news editor in Munich, Germany, 1952-55, news chief in New York City, 1955-57; International News Service, desk editor, Washington, DC, 1957-58; United Press International, Columbia, SC, newsman, 1958; *Washington Post,* Washington, DC, reporter, 1958-62; Hearst Newspapers, Washington, DC, reporter, 1963-66, assistant bureau chief, 1966-69, columnist with Jack Anderson, 1969-92. Visiting associate professor, Lehigh University, 1968-70; adjunct professor, Southern Illinois University, 1984. *Military service:* U.S. Army, 1946-48; became staff sergeant.

MEMBER: American Civil Liberties Union, Washington Independent Writers.

AWARDS, HONORS: Honorable mention, Washington Newspaper Guild Public Service Award, 1963; California Hospital Association News Award, 1965; Edgerton Award from American Civil Liberties Union, 1974; in 1983, Lehigh University instituted a scholarship program in Whitten's name; awarded honorary doctorate of human letters from Lehigh University, 1989.

WRITINGS:

MYSTERY NOVELS

Progeny of the Adder, Doubleday (New York City), 1965.
Moon of the Wolf, Doubleday, 1967.
A Day without Sunshine, Atheneum, 1985.
Fangs of Morning, Leisure Books (New York City), 1994.

NOVELS

The Alchemist, Charterhouse Books, 1973.
Conflict of Interest, Doubleday, 1976.
Sometimes a Hero, Doubleday, 1979.
A Killing Pace, Atheneum, 1983.
The Lost Disciple (historical), Atheneum, 1989.

OTHER

Pinion, the Golden Eagle (juvenile), Van Nostrand (New York City), 1968.
(Translator) Charles Baudelaire, *"The Abyss",* The Smith (New York City), 1970.
F. Lee Bailey (biography), Avon (New York City), 1971.
Washington Cycle (poems), Horizon/The Smith, 1980.

Also author of numerous poems, articles, short stories, reviews, and translations of poems (French to English).

WORK IN PROGRESS: A novel; more poems; more translations from Baudelaire, Verlaine, and other French poets.

SIDELIGHTS: Leslie H. Whitten, Jr. has traveled in the United States, Latin America, Europe, Asia, the Middle East, and elsewhere as a newsman.

BIOGRAPHICAL/CRITICAL SOURCES:

BOOKS

Anderson, Jack, *The Anderson Papers,* Random House, 1973.

Downie, Leonard, *The New Muckrakers,* New Republic Book Co., 1976.

Dygent, James, *The Investigative Journalist,* Prentice-Hall, 1976.

Hume, Brit, *Inside Story,* Doubleday, 1974.

Kurzman, Dan, *Revolt of the Damned,* Putnam, 1965.

PERIODICALS

Chicago Tribune Book World, June 26, 1983.

New York Times, July 16, 1986.

Washington Post Book World, June 24, 1979, June 3, 1983, August 18, 1985.

*   *   *

WIEMER, Rudolf Otto   1905-
(Frank Hauser)

PERSONAL: Born March 24, 1905, in Friedrichroda, Germany; son of Fritz (a teacher) and Elisabeth (Kretzschmar) Wiemer; married Elisabeth Peinemann, October 12, 1932; children: Wolfgang, Reinhart, Uta. *Education:*Attended teacher's training college in Gotha, Germany, 1923-24. *Religion:* Evangelical Lutheran.

ADDRESSES: Home—Nussanger 73, 34 Goettingen, Germany.

CAREER: Teacher in Czechoslovakia, 1924-25, and then successively in Sondershausen, Hachelbich, Frankenhausen, Othfresen, Salzgitter, and Goettingen, Germany, 1925-67. *Military service:* German Army, 1940-45.

MEMBER: PEN.

AWARDS, HONORS: Sud-Verlag Konstanz Lyric Prize, 1948; Burgschreiber zu Plesse, 1976; Novel-Prize, Evang. Buechereien, 1980; Kuenstler-Stipendium, Niedersachsen, 1981; Ehrenmedaille, Stadt Goettingen, 1985; Ehrenring, Kogge, 1985; Ehrenhinger Friedrichroda, 1994.

WRITINGS:

Die Gitter singen, J. G. Oncken, 1952.

Der Mann am Feuer, J. G. Oncken, 1953, new edition, 1986.

Strasse, die du wandern musst, Deutscher Laienspielverlag, 1955.

Die Nacht der Tiere, Burckhardthaus, 1957.

Der Ort zu unseren Fussen, Steinkopf, 1958.

Das Kleine Rasenstuck, Steinkopf, 1959.

Pit und die Krippenmanner (juvenile), Steinkopf, 1960, translation published as *Pete and the Manager Men,* Muhlenberg Press, 1962.

Der Verlorene Sohn (juvenile), Mohn, 1960.

Machet die Tore weit, Guetersloher Verlagsanstalt Gerd Mohn, 1960.

Jona und der Grosse Fisch, Mohn, 1960.

Nicht Stunde noch Tag (novel), Steinkopf, 1961.

Fremde Zimmer (novel), Steinkopf, 1962.

Ernstfall (poems), Steinkopf, 1963.

Nele geht nach Bethlehem (juvenile), Steinkopf, 1963.

Stier und Taube (novel), Steinkopf, 1964.

Kalle Schneemann (juvenile), Steinkopf, 1964.

Joseph und seine Brueder (juvenile), Mohn, 1964, translation by Paul T. Martinsen published as *Joseph and His Brothers,* Augsburg, 1967.

Die Weisen aus dem Abendland (novel), Steinkopf, 1965.

Liebes altes Lesebuch, Anfstieg, 1966.

Der Gute Rauber Willibald (juvenile), Steinkopf, 1966, reprinted, Loewe, 1981, translation by Barbara Kowal Gollob published as *The Good Robber Willibald,* Atheneum (New York City), 1968.

Wir Tiere in dem Stalle, Steinkopf, 1966, translation published as *Animals at the Manger,* Augsburg, 1969.

Helldunkel, Steinkopf, 1967.

Come unto Me (originally published in German), translation by Martinsen, Augsburg, 1968.

Das Pferd, das in die Schule kam (juvenile), Steinkopf, 1970.

Unsereiner (novel), Steinkopf, 1971.

Beispiele zur deutschen grammatik (poems), Fietkau, 1971.

Geschichten aus dem Raeuberhut, Schwann, 1972.

Der Kaiser und Der Kleine Mann (juvenile), Steinkopf, 1972, reprinted, Boje Verlag, 1987.

Wortwechsel (poems), Fietkau, 1973.

Ein Weihnachtsbaum fuer Ludmilla Winzig (juvenile), Arena, 1974.

Selten wie Sommerschnee (juvenile), Schaffstein, 1974.

Bundes deutsch, Peter Hammer, 1974.

Wo wir Menschen sind, Schwann, 1974.

Zwischenfaelle (novel), Steinkopf, 1975.

Micha moechte gern (juvenile), Bitter, 1975.

Die Angst vor dem: Ofensetzer oder Glorreiche Zeiten (novel), Steinkopf, 1975.

Der Engel bei Bolt an der Ecke, Guetersloher Verlagshaus Gerd Mohn, 1976.

Die Schlagzeile (novel), Braun, 1977.

Er schrieb auf die Erde: Begegnungen mit dem Mann aus Nazareth, Herder, 1979.

Reizklima (novel), Braun, 1979.

Auf und davon und zurueck (juvenile), Arena, 1979.

Bethlehem ist ueberall, Guetersloher Verlagshaus, 1979.

Mahnke: Die Geschichte eines Lueckenbuessers (novel), Kerle, 1979.

Chance der Baerenraupe (poems), Kerle, 1980.

Lob der kleinen Schritte (novel), Reinhardt, 1980.

Schnee faellt auf die Arche (novel), Kerle, 1981.

Meine Kinderschuhe (poems), Schwabenverlag, 1984.

Sehnsucht der Krokodile (poems), Druckhaus Goettingen, 1985.

Jesusgeschichten (juvenile), Guetersloher Verlagshaus, 1985.

Haeuser, aus denen ich kam (novel), Quell Verlag, 1985.

Stimmen zu R. O. Wiemers 80. Geburtstag, Graphikum, 1985.

Wolke und Schnee (poems), Graphicum, 1985.

Fingerhut und Hexenkraut (poems), Lahn Verlag, 1986.

Ausflug ins Gruene (novel), Quell Verlag, 1986.

Es muessen nicht Maenner mit Fluegeln sein (novel and poems for Christmas), Quell Verlag, 1986.

Warum der Baer sich wecken lieb (juvenile), Patmos Verlag, 1986.

Schilfwasser (poems), Quell Verlag, 1986.

Der dreifaeltige Baum. Waldgeschichten (novel), Quell Verlag, 1987.

Ungewaschene Gebete (poems), Patmos Verlag, 1987.

Thomas und die Taube (juvenile), Patmos Verlag, 1987.

Die Erzbahn (novel), Quell Verlag, 1988.

Weil keiner nicht sicht, Quell Verlag, 1988.

Das am manden Orten senkicht (poems), Quell Verlag, 1990.

Breuu Feinerchen, breuu doch (novel), Quell Verlag, 1992.

Die Reise est dem Gropvaler (novel), Gritenloher Vrolapaustell, 1993.

Ein voller Gestaenduis (novel), Heinkopf, 1994.

Also author, under pseudonym Frank Hauser, of *Zweimal dreizehu zinken* (poems), 1968.

*   *   *

WIENER, Allen J. 1943-

PERSONAL: Born August 14, 1943, in Newark, NJ; son of Harry (a tavern owner) and Helen (an insurance claims officer; maiden name, Roth) Wiener; married Katherine Ann Zantal (a special education consultant), June 22, 1974; children: Amanda Lee. *Education:* Fairleigh Dickinson University, B.A., 1968; Rutgers University, M.A., 1971, additional graduate study, 1971-73. *Politics:* "I always manage to vote for the loser." *Avocational interests:* Gymnasium aerobics, weight lifting, swimming, gardening, reading (especially mysteries), film and record collecting.

ADDRESSES: Home—Potomac, MD. *Office*—Washington, DC. *Agent*—Carol Mann Agency, 55 Fifth Ave., New York, NY 10003.

CAREER: Morris County Daily Record, Morristown, NJ, news reporter and feature writer, 1968-69; Creative Communications, Inc., Newark, NJ, public relations writer and account executive, 1969-70; Federal Aviation Administration, Washington, DC, budget analyst, 1973-74; Federal Railroad Administration, Washington, DC, administrative assistant, 1974-75; U.S. Department of Transportation, Washington, DC, international transportation specialist in Policy Office, 1976—, policy analyst in Maritime and Surface Division of Office of International Transportation and Trade, 1986—. Professional actor on stage and in films, as well as in television and radio commercials; radio narrator. Member of board of directors of Georgetown Workshop Theater and Touring Company, 1976-77. *Military service:* U.S. Air Force, education and training specialist, 1961-65.

MEMBER: American Federation of Television and Radio Artists, Screen Actors Guild.

AWARDS, HONORS: Achievement Award, Federal Aviation Administration, 1973; Bronze Medal Award for Achievement, U.S. Department of Transportation, 1990.

WRITINGS:

The Beatles: A Recording History, McFarland & Co. (Jefferson, NC), 1986.
The Beatles: The Ultimate Recording Guide, Facts on File (New York City), 1992, revised edition, Bob Adams (Brighton, MA), 1994.

Contributor of articles and reviews to periodicals, including *Washington Post, People, Musician, American History, Goldmine,* and *Fi.*

WORK IN PROGRESS: A book about William Boyd and the Hopalong Cassidy films; various music articles and reviews; articles on film history and biographies.

SIDELIGHTS: Allen J. Wiener told *CA* that the research for his book, *The Beatles: The Ultimate Recording Guide* "and the chronological presentation of its results, takes in all known events (involving the Beatles) that exist in recorded form, including unreleased material, much of which is found on bootleg records. This emphasis on *recordings,* rather than commercially released *records,* may seem a fine distinction, but it is quite significant. Many collectors seek discs, accumulating the same recorded material in all its many physical forms of release (different label variations, cover art, country of origin, and reissues), but I have addressed the collector of *recorded* material, or events in the Beatles' careers that were recorded, including, but not limited to, their released studio work. Collectors focusing on my material do not necessarily care if they obtain every variation of the material's release, once they have at least one copy of the recording. My book catalogs all of these Beatles recordings and then directs the reader to records on which the material can be found.

"Writing is a discipline; it is seldom 'fun' in the strictest sense. You have to sit down and work until you get something started and it begins to take shape. Similarly, you must develop a network of magazine and book editors and a feel for what kinds of material they are looking for and the writing style they prefer. This is becoming increasingly difficult for freelancers as more publications cut their operating budgets, downsize, and buy fewer freelance pieces.

"The hardest part is getting started on any project. Just getting words on paper is the key, regardless of what type of writing you are doing or what subject matter you are treating. Once the first draft is done you have something to work with, edit, revise, or reconsider. Outside opinion and editing suggestions are essential—try to find how others see the results of your work and what they think should be added, deleted, or enlarged. When you do reference works, your aim is to make the book as complete and accurate as possible. In the case of recordings, this involves the expense and time of obtaining and listening to the recordings, which can take months or years. You also want to organize and design the book so that it is easy to use and allows readers to quickly find the information they need. The key here is a thorough, accurate index."

Wiener adds that "in writing more popular material, particularly for mainstream magazines, it is important to drop a lot of minor detail and confine yourself to major points, which appeals to a less-specialized mass audience."

BIOGRAPHICAL/CRITICAL SOURCES:

PERIODICALS

American Reference Books Annual, Volume 25, 1994, p. 565.
Asbury Park Press, February 1, 1987.
Washington Post, June 4, 1987.

*   *   *

WIER, Dara   1949-

PERSONAL: Born December 30, 1949, in New Orleans, LA; daughter of Arthur Joseph (a director of vocational rehabilitation services) and Grace (a teacher; maiden name, Barrois) Dixon; children: Emily Caitlin Pettit, Guy Gerard Pettit. *Education:* Attended Louisiana State University, 1967-70; Longwood College, B.S., 1971; Bowling Green State University, M.F.A., 1974.

ADDRESSES: Home—504 Montague Rd., Amherst, MA 01002. *Office*—Department of English, University of Massachusetts, Amherst, MA 01003.

CAREER: University of Pittsburgh, Pittsburgh, PA, instructor in English, 1974-75; Hollins College, Hollins, VA, instructor, 1975-76, assistant professor of English, 1977-80; University of Alabama, Tuscaloosa, associate professor, 1980-85, director of graduate studies, 1980-82, director of creative writing program, 1984-85; University of Massachusetts, Amherst, associate professor, 1985-87, professor, 1988—. Visiting professor, Emory University, summer, 1979, University of Utah, fall, 1979, Baylor University, summer, 1980, Bennington College, summer, 1982, University of Texas, spring, 1983, University of Idaho, 1985; Richard Hugo Memorial Chair, University of Montana, spring, 1993. Panelist, judge, and referee for numerous writing award and fellowship programs; lecturer and speaker at workshops, symposia, conferences, and meetings.

MEMBER: Authors Guild, Authors League of America, PEN, Poetry Society of America, Associated Writing Programs (member of board of directors, 1979-82; member of directors' council, 1986-88, 1992-95; vice-president, 1979-80; president, 1980-81).

AWARDS, HONORS: National Endowment for the Arts fellowship, 1980; University of Alabama research grant, 1984; Richard Hugo Memorial Award, 1991; Guggenheim fellowship, 1992-93.

WRITINGS:

POETRY

Blood, Hook, & Eye, University of Texas Press (Austin), 1977.
The 8-Step Grapevine, Carnegie-Mellon University Press (Pittsburgh, PA), 1981.
All You Have in Common, Carnegie-Mellon University Press, 1984.
The Book of Knowledge, Carnegie-Mellon University Press, 1989.
Blue for the Plough, Carnegie-Mellon University Press, 1992.
Our Master Plan, Carnegie-Mellon University Press, 1997.

OTHER

Contributor to anthologies, including *Intro Six,* edited by George Garrett, Anchor Books (New York City), 1974; *Tangled Vines,* edited by Lyn Lifshin, Beacon Press (Boston), 1978; *The Morrow Anthology of Younger American Poets,* edited by Dave Smith and David Bottoms, Morrow (New York City), 1985; *The Hampden-Sydney Poetry Review Anthology,* edited by Tom O'Grady, Hampden-Sydney College and Virginia Commission for the Arts, 1990; and *The Carnegie-Mellon Anthology of Poetry,* edited by Gerald Costanzo and Jim Daniels, Carnegie-

Mellon University Press, 1993. Editor, University of Alabama Press Poetry Series, 1980-86. Contributor of numerous poems, stories, essays, and reviews to periodicals, including *Southern Review, New Republic, North American Review, Iowa Review, American Poetry Review, New England Review,* and *Harvard Review.*

WORK IN PROGRESS: Short stories; a collection of craft essays.

BIOGRAPHICAL/CRITICAL SOURCES:

BOOKS

Jackson, Richard, editor, *Acts of Mind: Conversations with Contemporary Poets,* University of Alabama Press (Tuscaloosa), 1983.

*   *   *

WILSON, Gina   1943-

PERSONAL: Born April 1, 1943, in Abergele, North Wales; daughter of Arthur Gordon (a businessman) and Marion (a teacher; maiden name, Herbert) Jones; married Edward Wilson (a university teacher), July 22, 1972; children: Marion, Lewis, Harriet. *Education:* University of Edinburgh, M.A. (English, with honors), 1965; attended Mount Holyoke College, 1965-66.

ADDRESSES: Agent—Gina Pollinger, 222 Old Brompton Rd., London SW5 0BZ, England.

CAREER: Writer.

AWARDS, HONORS: Children's Book Award runner-up, Federation of Children's Book Groups, 1980, for *Cora Ravenwing;* shortlisted for Carnegie Medal, 1984, for *All Ends Up;* shortlisted for Kurt Maschler Award, 1994, for *Prowlpuss.*

WRITINGS:

YOUNG ADULT NOVELS

Cora Ravenwing, Atheneum (New York City), 1980.
A Friendship of Equals, Faber (London), 1981.
The Whisper, Faber, 1982.
All Ends Up, Faber, 1984.
Family Feeling, Faber, 1988.

Just Us, Faber, 1988.
Riding the Great White, Bodley Head (London), 1992.

PICTURE BOOKS

I Hope You Know . . . , illustrated by Alison Catley, Hutchinson (London), 1989.
Polly Pipes Up, illustrated by Jacqui Thomas, Heinemann (London), 1989.
Wompus Galumpus: King of the Deep, illustrated by Clive Scruton, Walker (New York City), 1989.
Prowlpuss, illustrated by David Parkins, Walker/Candlewick, 1994.

OTHER

Jim-Jam Pyjamas (poetry), illustrated by Sally Anne Lambert, J. Cape (London), 1989.

Contributor to *Times Literary Supplement* and to numerous anthologies. Assistant editor, *Scottish National Dictionary* and *Dictionary of the Older Scottish Tongue.*

SIDELIGHTS: Gina Wilson is the author of realistic novels about young adults facing major transitions, but her poetry and picture books have been equally well-received. As Dennis Hamley notes in *Twentieth-Century Children's Writers,* "Wilson's achievement and range are impressive. She stands as a vivid and accurate portrayer of adolescent understanding." Writing in *Growing Point,* Margery Fisher adds that "in all her books [Wilson] has taken care to balance the preoccupations of the young person chosen as the focal point with proper attention to the concerns of everyone else, adult or young."

Wilson once explained: "My childhood and teenage memories are very vivid and I like to write about children who are at the point of discovering the extent of their autonomy and isolation. They find themselves unexpectedly at variance with parents or friends. People seem to them to be behaving oddly or even quite wrongly. They feel alarmed and confused, often with good reason. It is this crucial and absorbing period which I delineate in my fiction."

Wilson's first book, *Cora Ravenwing,* is set during the 1950s. The teenaged narrator, Rebecca, has recently moved into an English village, and she soon becomes torn between her desire to be friends with a group of popular girls and her fascination with a mysterious outsider, Cora. "The circumstances of the outcast girl's childhood, and the gossip that circulates about her give a sinister element to the tale," Wilson once explained to *CA.* Hamley describes the outcome of the novel: "The cost of keeping in with the peer group and maintaining friendship with the outcast is too great: Rebecca loses both. But, in a process crucial to Wilson's novels, she gains self-knowledge, grows through the experience, and takes on valuable insights for life."

Similar themes run through Wilson's next novel, *A Friendship of Equals,* the story of the relationship between Stella, a physically handicapped girl from a wealthy background, and Louise, the daughter of the village shopkeeper. "Despite opposition from all sides, and personal problems of their own, they refuse to give up their friendship," Wilson told *CA.* *The Whisper,* published in 1982, also deals with the relationship between two young girls. Thirteen-year-old Lily feels threatened when her fourteen-year-old cousin, Marie, comes to live with her family. Marie is a talented musician and seems to fit in easily at school and at church. Lily's jealousy drives her to spread vicious rumors about Marie, and by the time the girls begin to draw closer to one another, it may be too late. In a review for *Books for Keeps,* Val Randall calls *The Whisper* "a thoughtful and absorbing read," while Judith Elkin comments in the *Times Literary Supplement* that "the story says a great deal about the complexities of genuine lasting friendship and family loyalty."

Wilson's next young adult novel, *All Ends Up,* focuses on Claudia, who harbors great bitterness toward her mother because of the fact that Claudia is an illegitimate child. These feelings also affect her relationships with her friends and her mother's boyfriend, though she finds refuge in a close friendship with her great-aunt Belle. A reviewer for *Junior Bookshelf* calls *All Ends Up* "a most sensitive story," noting that "it is high praise to say the style is so natural to be unnoticeable, and one meets the very pertinent moral only on subsequent reflection." A *Bulletin of the Center for Children's Books* critic finds that "the problems and concerns that are involved are universal."

Hamley calls Wilson's novel *Family Feeling* "a book of rare power dealing confidently and honestly with urgent adolescent themes," and remarks that "the clash between the generations is overt and powerful." The novel focuses on thirteen-year-old Alice and the difficult transition she faces when her widowed mother marries a man with two children. When Alice tentatively begins a romantic relationship with her quiet new stepbrother, fifteen-year-old Edwin, their parents are shocked and debate how to handle the situation. Fisher calls *Family Feeling* "a notably direct, expertly directed domestic novel," and comments that "moments of humour both in dialogue and in behaviour lighten a powerful exploration of the clashes of need and loyalty in a family."

In *Riding the Great White,* Wilson describes the reactions of a gang of teenagers, the Thakers, to the arrival of a mysterious stranger, Gav. The narrator, Gin, quickly enters into a relationship with Gav, which causes jealousy and disapproval among the other Thakers. Hamley calls *Riding the Great White* "a complex, subtle, fascinating novel," and explains that "the title refers to a roller coaster ride which serves as an appropriate image for Gin's experiences."

In addition to her novels for young adults, Wilson has also written a book of poetry and several picture books for younger readers. *Jim-Jam Pyjamas* contains twenty-seven poems about animals which use "an interesting range of approaches," according to Audrey Lasky in *School Librarian.* Some of the poems are intended to be funny, some scary, and some subtle and introspective. In her 1989 picture book, *Polly Pipes Up,* Wilson follows the excitement and disappointment of young Polly, who is unable to play a much-anticipated musical solo at her school's Christmas concert because of an injured finger. A *Junior Bookshelf* reviewer states that the book "describes feelings many children will have experienced." *Wompus Galumpus: King of the Deep,* published the same year, involves a sea creature who ventures into town one day, only to dry and shrivel in the sun. Writing in the London *Times,* Susan Hill comments that Wilson's "use of language . . . is of a quality rarely found" in picture book texts. Wilson's 1994 work *Prowlpuss* uses rhymed, rhythmic text to describe a shrewd tom cat's night. "An outstanding picture book—*Prowlpuss* is a star," *Guardian* critic Joanna Carey concludes.

BIOGRAPHICAL/CRITICAL SOURCES:

BOOKS

Twentieth-Century Children's Writers, 4th edition, St. James Press (Detroit), 1995.

PERIODICALS

Books for Keeps, July, 1991, p. 12; November, 1992.
Bulletin of the Center for Children's Books, June, 1984; November, 1984.
Growing Point, November, 1991, pp. 5594-5597.
Guardian, June 22, 1984; October 8, 1988; December 2, 1994, p. 12.
Junior Bookshelf, August, 1980; October, 1981, p. 220; October, 1984, p. 222; April, 1986, pp. 82-83; December, 1988, p. 316; April, 1990, p. 93; February, 1991, p. 28; August, 1993, p. 164.
Kirkus Reviews, May 1, 1980.
Observer, April 6, 1980.
School Librarian, August, 1990, p. 116.
School Library Journal, November, 1984, p. 140.
Times (London), September 30, 1990.
Times Literary Supplement, March 28, 1980; July 24, 1981; February 25, 1983; June 15, 1984, p. 677; May 9, 1986, p. 514.

*   *   *

WIRTHS, Claudine (Turner) G(ibson) 1926-

PERSONAL: Born May 9, 1926, in Covington, GA; daughter of Count Dillon (a professor of geology) and Julia (Thompson) Gibson; married Theodore Wirths (a National Science Foundation executive), December 28, 1945; children: William, David. *Education:* University of Kentucky, A.B. (cum laude), 1946, M.A., 1948; American University, M.Ed., 1980; doctoral study at University of North Carolina at Chapel Hill. *Religion:* Episcopal. *Avocational interests:* Wild flowers, vegetable gardening, camping.

ADDRESSES: Home—P.O. Box 335, Braddock Heights, MD 21714. *E-mail*—claudinew@AOL.com.

CAREER: Yale University, New Haven, CT, secretary and research assistant for departments of psychology and anthropology, 1946-47; North Carolina League for Crippled Children and Adults, Chapel Hill, program director, 1948-49; research psychologist with Savannah River Studies, Aiken, SC, for University of North Carolina, 1950-52; City Police Department, Aiken, police psychologist, 1952-56; Kirk School, Aiken, Head teacher in special education, 1956-58; homemaker, Aiken, 1958-62; social science consultant in Rockville, MD, 1962-77; Green

Acres School, Rockville, elementary schoolteacher, 1977-78; special education intern at high school in Springfield, VA, 1978-79; Gaithersburg High School, Gaithersburg, MD, special education teacher, 1979-81, coordinator of Learning Center, 1981-84; writer, 1984—; Frederick Community College, Frederick, MD, member of adjunct faculty, 1987—. Member of U.S. Department of Defense Advisory Committee on Women in the Services, 1960-63, Girl Guard Board of Salvation Army, 1961-62, board of directors of Montgomery County Mental Health Association, 1967-71, and advisory board of Maryland Department of Natural Resources, 1975-78.

MEMBER: Phi Beta Kappa.

AWARDS, HONORS: Conservation Award from Maryland Environment Trust, 1973; award from Maryland-Delaware Press Association, 1979, for feature story writing; American Library Association listed *I Hate School: How to Hang In and When to Drop Out* as a best book of 1986.

WRITINGS:

WITH MARY BOWMAN-KRUHM; JUVENILES

I Hate School: How to Hang In and When to Drop Out, Harper (New York City), 1987.
I Need a Job, J. Weston Walch, 1988.
Where's My Other Sock?: How to Get Organized and Drive Your Parents and Teachers Crazy, Harper, 1989.
Are You My Type?: Why Aren't You More Like Me?, Consulting Psychologists Press (Palo Alto, CA), 1992.
Time to Be a Teen, 21st Century Press (Tolland, CT), 1993.
I Need to Get Organized, J. Weston Walch, 1993.
How to Get Up When Homework Gets You Down, David Cook (Elgin, IL), 1993.
Upgrade—High Tech Road School Success, Consulting Psychologists Press, 1994.
I Need to Get Along on the Job, J. Weston Walch, 1995.
(With Wendie Old) *Busy Toes* (picture book), Whispering Coyote Press, in press.

OTHER

(With Richard H. Williams) *Lives Through the Years: A Study of Successful Aging,* Atherton, 1965.

Careers in Law Enforcement, Rosen Publishing (New York City), in press.

Also author of a three-book series, *Your New School, Your Circle of Friends,* and *Your Power with Words,* for Henry Holt. Work represented in anthologies, including *Humpty Dumpty's Bedtime Stories,* Parents Magazine Press, 1971. Contributor to magazines and newspapers, including *Law and Order, Maryland, Christian Ministry, Journal of Learning Disabilities, Parks and Recreation,* and *Cat Fancy.*

SIDELIGHTS: Claudine G. Wirths told *CA:* "I began writing almost as soon as I could read because of my good fortune at having the author of some of my favorite first books, Madge A. Bigham, living near me on St. Simons Island, Georgia. When I expressed my great fondness for her books, she urged me to write my own. My first work at age seven, 'The Tall Cat' (I'm six feet tall), was not published, but was highly satisfying to me, and I continued writing.

"First published with a brief article to the *Atlanta Journal* when I was fifteen, I had my first short story for children published in *Humpty Dumpty* some twenty years later. From my teens on there was the usual avalanche of rejection slips (which continues to this day), but I kept on writing. My first major children's book was put in my hands the day I turned sixty. Success takes a little longer for some of us!

"My interest in dropout students began in graduate school in 1948 when I learned about dyslexia. I was intrigued at the puzzle of how a bright child might fail to learn to read. I was soon to encounter many such children when I entered police work. Far too often, the child in trouble was learning disabled and a potential dropout. The frustration set up by the handicap of dyslexia turns school days into days of despair, and, unless the child receives special help (and sometimes even when they do), school becomes a permanent nightmare for the child and their parents.

"I was unable to give my full effort to this problem until I went back to graduate school a few years ago and took a degree in special education. Following this, I changed professions and have spent all my time since then writing, studying, teaching, and lecturing on learning disabilities. Currently retired from public school teaching, I write full-time with a close friend and colleague, Dr. Mary Bowman-Kruhm, who is a reading specialist with over twenty-five years of work with special-need students. We share compassion for the student who has school problems and we hope to help them understand how they can best help themselves. Our books do not talk down to readers but they do use simple language and clear ideas.

"Writing as a twosome has solved many of the problems that kept me from writing success in the past. I now keep to writing schedules, have a built-in editor, and, best of all, have someone to talk to who is as passionately concerned about writing and about problems of the learning disabled as I am. We each have a Macintosh computer and have worked out a joint writing system that works for us. We split profits and problems right down the middle."

* * *

WOOD, Michael 1936-

PERSONAL: Born August 19, 1936, in Lincolnshire, England; son of George William (a cashier) and Winifred (Horsefield) Wood; married Elena Uribe (an anthropologist), September 23, 1967; children: Gabriela, Patrick, Antony. *Education:* Cambridge University, B.A., 1957, M.A. and Ph.D., 1961. *Avocational interests:* Travel.

ADDRESSES: Home—26 Alexander St., Princeton, NJ 08540. *Office*—Department of English, Princeton University, Princeton, NJ 08544.

CAREER: Cambridge University, St. John's College, Cambridge, England, fellow in French literature, 1961-64; Columbia University, New York City, instructor, 1964-66, assistant professor, 1968-71, associate professor, 1971-74, professor of comparative literature, 1974-82; Exeter University, Exeter, England, professor of English, 1982-94; Princeton University, Princeton, NJ, visiting fellow, 1993, Charles Barnwell Straut Professor of English, 1995—

MEMBER: Royal Society of Literature (fellow).

AWARDS, HONORS: Guggenheim fellow, 1973-74; National Endowment for the Humanities fellow, 1978-79.

WRITINGS:

Stendhal, Cornell University Press (Ithaca, NY), 1971.

America in the Movies; or, "Santa Maria, It Had Slipped My Mind," Basic Books (New York City), 1975, with a new preface, Columbia University Press (New York City), 1989.

Gabriel Garcia Marquez: One Hundred Years of Solitude, Cambridge University Press (Cambridge), 1990.

The Magician's Doubts: Nabokov and the Risks of Fiction, Princeton University Press (Princeton, NJ), 1995.

Coauthor of screenplays: *Scene Nun, Take One,* 1966, and *Praise Marx and Pass the Ammunition,* 1968. Editor of the textbook *Literature: Fiction, Poetry, Drama,* 1977. Author of a regular column in *New Society.* Contributor to periodicals and newspapers, including *New Statesman, New York Review of Books,* and *Observer.*

SIDELIGHTS: Michael Wood has written about film and literature from an academic perspective and as the author of two screenplays. His *America in the Movies; or, "Santa Maria, It Had Slipped My Mind"* examines America's self-image as presented in American-made films. In *The Magician's Doubts: Nabokov and the Risks of Fiction,* Wood studies the differences between Nabokov's public personae and that found in his fiction.

In *America in the Movies* Wood focuses his analysis on the movies he believes helped to shape his own outlook on the world when he was young, including not only established film classics but personal favorites as well. Wood, writes Tom Shales in the *Washington Post Book World,* argues that movies of the 1930s through the 1950s established "the parameters of an illusory world and then faithfully [remained] within that world, not violating its strictures or what might be called its principles." Writing in the *New York Times Book Review,* David Bromwich states that Wood's study "has an almost unheard-of combination of virtues for a movie book—lucid, well-informed, and obviously written in high spirits." Shales concludes that *America in the Movies* "helps fill a void in film and social comment that lies somewhere between the intelligent movie review . . . and the overly inferential sociological tract."

The Magician's Doubts: Nabokov and the Risks of Fiction, Wood's study of novelist Vladimir Nabokov, is "a fine example of an endangered species: the full-length book of literary criticism dedicated to the appreciation and interpretation of a single author, addressed to the general reader," argues David Lodge in the *New York Times Book Review.* Wood's study focuses on the author's literary persona, a persona that Wood believes was at odds with Nabokov's public image. As Robert Taylor states in the *Boston Globe,* Wood asserts that Nabokov "presented a stoic mandarin mask to the world, but on occasion let the mask slip to reveal another, more humane and vulnerable face." "Wood's outstandingly brilliant new book is in part a corrective to the public persona adopted by his subject," writes John Lanchester in the *London Review of Books.* Other critics see a further goal behind Wood's study. "Wood's book," writes Gabriel Josipovici in the *Times Literary Supplement,* "is an invitation to dialogue . . . not a set of dogmatic assertions. . . . What this book does, finally, is to bring back the notion of criticism as conversation." "All the book pretends to be," Lodge explains, "is an attentive, thoughtful and readable commentary on some key works by a modern master of prose fiction."

BIOGRAPHICAL/CRITICAL SOURCES:

PERIODICALS

Books and Bookmen, April, 1972, p. 66.
Boston Globe, August 30, 1995, p. 65.
Christian Science Monitor, August 20, 1975, p. 23.
Guardian Weekly, November 13, 1994, p. 28.
London Review of Books, October 6, 1994, pp. 6-7.
Nation, June 5, 1976, p. 696.
National Review, September 12, 1975, p. 1002.
New Statesman, February 13, 1976, p. 200.
New York Review of Books, April 15, 1976, p. 33.
New York Times Book Review, August 3, 1975, pp. 4-5; October 29, 1995.
Observer, February 6, 1972, p. 32; December 14, 1975, p. 24.
Spectator, January 15, 1972, p. 80; November 22, 1975, p. 670.
Times Literary Supplement, May 21, 1976, p. 604; July 27, 1990, p. 801; August 26, 1994, p. 22.
Washington Post Book World, August 10, 1975.

*   *   *

YORK, Simon
  See HEINLEIN, Robert A(nson)

ZIRING, Lawrence   1928-

PERSONAL: Born December 11, 1928, in Brooklyn, NY; son of Israel and Anna (Berg) Ziring; married Raye Marlene Ralph, August 10, 1962; children: Leona, Sarah. *Education:* Columbia University, B.S., 1955, M.I.A., 1957, Ph.D., 1962.

ADDRESSES: Home—5139 Greenhill, Portage, MI 49081. *Office*—Department of Political Science, Western Michigan University, Kalamazoo, MI 49008. *E-mail*—lawrence.ziring@WMICH.edu.

CAREER: University of Dacca, Dacca, East Pakistan (now Bangladesh), lecturer in political science, 1959-60; Columbia University, New York City, lecturer in political science, 1960-61; Lafayette College, Easton, PA, assistant professor of political science, 1961-64; Syracuse University, Syracuse, NY, assistant professor of political science, 1964-67; Western Michigan University, Kalamazoo, associate professor, 1967-73, professor of political science, 1973—, director of Institute of Government and Politics, 1979-94, director of development administration programs, 1995—. U.S. Information Agency lecturer in Pakistan, 1959-60, 1974-75, 1976, 1981, 1983, 1985, India, 1981, and Nepal, 1983; lecturer at Defense Intelligence School, 1964, Foreign Service Institute, 1967, 1983-84, 1986, and Canadian Defense College, 1968. Adviser to Pakistan Administrative Staff College, 1964-66; external examiner, Karachi University, 1973—, University of Toronto, 1974, and Quaid-i-Azam University, 1988-96; member of board of trustees, American Institute of Pakistan Studies, 1973-95. Consultant to U.S. Department of State. *Military service:* U.S. Army, 1951-53.

MEMBER: Association for Asian Studies (chairman of Pakistan Studies Development Committee, 1972-77).

AWARDS, HONORS: Jones Superior Teaching Award, Lafayette College, 1963-64; Institute of Oriental Studies fellow, Soviet Union Academy of Sciences, 1974, 1981, and 1983; American Council of Learned Societies fellow, 1974-75; Distinguished Scholar award, Western Michigan University, 1982; American University research affiliate 1983-84; Oxford University fellow, 1984, 1989.

WRITINGS:

The Ayub Khan Era: Politics in Pakistan, 1958-1969, Syracuse University Press (Syracuse, NY), 1971.

(Editor with Ralph Braibanti and Howard Wriggins, and contributor) *Pakistan: The Long View,* Duke University Press (Durham, NC), 1977.

(With C. I. Eugene Kim) *An Introduction to Asian Politics,* Prentice-Hall (Englewood Cliffs, NJ), 1977.

(Editor and contributor) *The Subcontinent in World Politics: India, Its Neighbors, and the Great Powers,* Praeger (New York City), 1978, 2nd edition, 1982.

Pakistan: The Enigma of Political Development, Dawson, 1980.

Iran, Turkey, and Afghanistan: A Political Chronology, Praeger, 1981.

The Middle East Political Dictionary, American Bibliographical Center-Clio Press (Santa Barbara, CA), 1983.

(With Kim) *The Asian Political Dictionary,* American Bibliographical Center-Clio Press, 1985.

(Editor with Kim, and contributor) *Changing Asia,* Asian Studies Program, Western Michigan University (Kalamazoo, MI), 1987.

(Editor and contributor) *Asian Security Issues: National Systems and International Relations,* Institute of Government and Politics, Western Michigan University, 1988.

(With Burke) *Pakistan's Foreign Policy,* Oxford University Press (New York City), 1990.

Bangladesh: From Mujib to Ershad, an Interpretive Study, Oxford University Press, 1992.

The Middle East: A Political Dictionary, American Bibliographical Center-Clio Press, 1992.

(Editor) *The New Europe and the World,* New Issues Press (Kalamazoo, MI), 1993.

(With Jack Plano and Roy Olton) *International Relations: A Political Dictionary,* American Bibliographical Center-Clio, 1995.

Also coauthor of *Pakistan: A Country Study,* edited by Richard Nyrop 1984. Contributor to *Funk and Wagnalls Encyclopedia Yearbook,* 1984, and *Collier's Encyclopedia,* 1984. Contributor of more than one hundred articles and reviews to periodicals.

WORK IN PROGRESS: Pakistan in the Twentieth Century: A Political History, for Oxford University Press, anticipated publication in 1997.

SIDELIGHTS: Lawrence Ziring told *CA* that his "several volumes and numerous articles on Pakistan represent a comprehensive analysis of that country's political history. Students and researchers interested in identifying the character and patterns of political life in Pakistan will find useful information and insight. I have devoted more than thirty years to this study and I believe my findings and projections will stand the test of time.

"As for my other work, I continue to be involved in the examination of South Asian and Middle East politics and am attempting to assemble data useful in forecasting national political behavior and how it impacts on foreign policy decision-making.

"My reference books, notably the 1995 release, *International Relations: A Political Dictionary,* are an effort at defining the field, and hopefully they are useful to students as well as the reading public."